PROCESS MASTERY WITH LEAN SIX SIGMA

2nd EDITION (UPDATED)

2023.02

A Practical Guide to the Effective Application of Modern Day Lean and Six Sigma Methodologies

Written by

George Lee Sye

With additional tips and commentary by

Harry Sinko

A Soarent Publishing Publication

First edition published July 2004

Republished February 2009, Updated and First Published via Amazon in January 2023

Published by Soarent Publishing

PO Box 267,

Ravenshoe, Queensland

AUSTRALIA, 4888

Web: www.georgeleesye.com

Web: www.9skillsfactory.com

This Version - 2023.02

National Library of Australia Cataloguing-in-Publication entry

Author:	Lee Sye, George, 1959
Title:	Process Mastery with Lean Six Sigma : a complete body of knowledge for lean six sigma practitioners. / George Lee Sye.
Edition:	2nd ed.
ISBN:	978-0-6457182-0-1 (paperback)
	978-0-9872326-3-2 (hardback)
Notes:	Bibliography.
Subjects:	Lean Manufacturing.
	Six Sigma (Quality control standard)
	Production Management.
	Quality control.
	Statistical methods.
	Quantitative decision making.
Dewey Number:	658.4

Printed and bound by Amazon

Cover Design by Soarent Publishing

Table of Contents

The Author

George Lee Sye lives in Australia. He is the founder of Soarent Vision Pty Ltd, Soarent Publishing, and his professional development training and coaching platform known as 9 Skills Factory.

George's philosophies on life and progressive change have helped shape the lives of thousands of people who have had the good fortune to come into contact with him. His simple strategies for life are based on more than 30 years of studying human behaviour and built on a foundation of extensive knowledge of practical human psychology as it applies today.

He has had a remarkable life with an incredible range of working experiences that began in 1975. From rescuing hostages in high risk police operations in Australia to reducing cases of malaria in a remote area of Papua New Guinea, from developing plans to protect the President of the United States to locating lost aircraft and recovering victims in inhospitable terrain, from turning around an improvement initiative in a billion dollar company to coaching executives in leading sustainable change; George has been tremendously successful in integrating the 'scientific elements of continual improvement' with a profound understanding of 'human behaviour'

The end result is a depth and breadth of knowledge that he has been able to apply to great effect in making progressive change in virtually any environment or situation, with any individual or group of people.

Inspired to put pen to paper he has written and published multiple books in the areas of business improvement, leadership and personal development. He has consistently demonstrated the 'science of personal achievement' to great effect throughout his own life and is now devoted to passing on his knowledge of the subject and helping people the level of health, wealth and prosperity they desire. Helping individuals also means helping companies achieve the levels of performance they are potentially capable of.

His ability to simplify what are often considered to be complex topics is remarkable. As a result he has been able to create tremendous value for companies he has worked with in the area of business improvement and his popularity as a corporate educator has grown consistently.

For more information about George and his work, visit his web site.

www.georgeleesye.com

Introduction

It's not that long ago when employees only needed to come to work, do their job to the best of their ability, and then return home knowing their job was complete. There was little need for employees to change the way they worked, probably because there was little competition. No one else was changing the way they worked and the industries they worked in.

As we all know, that world no longer exists. The world is highly competitive, and companies are continually on the lookout for opportunities to create or enter markets. There is a such a high degree of competition within industries today, organisations must continually improve their business strategies and the way they repetitively do things to survive and prosper. Every single person in a company today *must* now accept a second job, and that is the job of continual improvement.

Continual Improvement is a concept that has been around forever; we only have to think about our past for a moment to realise it. We've gone from living in caves in the Stone Age to living in homes that can create environmental conditions to match our personal preferences, not just with the temperature but also with the music and a myriad of other aesthetic elements - perusing the list of features in Bill Gates home gives you an idea of what is available if you have the money. Think for a moment about the changes that have occurred in your lifetime, how about the changes that have taken place as recently as the past few years. Without continual improvement we would never have experienced microwave cooking, electricity, air travel, space travel, DVD's, and all of those things we now take for granted. We wouldn't have an iPod with capacity for 10 million songs, or whatever they hold. I'd still be handwriting letters to my my daughter while she does her student exchange in France and you'd be spending the weekend polishing your penny-farthing pushbike.

While the concept of improvement continues to be a fundamental part of our personal lives, it is a vital element in the survival of every company pursuing profit. Organisations that continually seek to improve will remain relevant in a rapidly changing world. Organisations that do not continue to improve will not. Employees that don't take on this additional role will also lose relevance in this dynamic world.

So how do you do this additional job?

Obviously you need a skill set relevant to the role. I guess the problem is deciding which skill set to pursue. There are many process improvement strategies that exist in the world today, none more significant than the two methodologies of Lean and Six Sigma, thus my decision to focus on these methodologies in this book.

What I have found during my years of involvement in business improvement is that this type of change requires more than the ability to define a problem or analyse numbers statistically or identify solutions. When we talk about improvement we must also include the 'people' element. There are many books out there that deal with the subject of change or emotional issues, and many dealing with the more technical aspects of process improvement. There are very few that I have found that address both topics well.

Let's think for a moment about the skill set that a process improvement project team leader requires today.

An organisation is really a product of the interaction of three elements:

- Its people,
- Its core business processes, and

- Its strategy.

With this understanding I believe a team leader needs four major skill sets.

Skill 1. Rapport Building and Connectivity

The people in an organisation give it life; they are the engines that move an organisation towards its desired outcomes. To make change to business processes requires the engagement of people, without which the change will simply not take place. To engage people so that they 'buy in' to change requires the ability to develop rapport. In fact, the ability to build rapport is essential for our survival in this world; we cannot exist in isolation and expect to be successful. If this is true, a process improvement project leader must be able to build rapport and connect with people from all parts of an organisation affected by an improvement project.

Skill 2. Team Productivity

In addition to this ability to connect individually to people, the team leader must also be able to bring a group of people together and manage the dynamics of how they interact for the purpose of maximising productivity. The power of a team is far greater than that of an individual, if and when they work as a team.

Skill 3. New Levels of Thinking

Project teams are most commonly comprised of people from within the organisation; people who work with the process being improved or interact with the process at the beginning or the end in some way. These people are brought together because of their knowledge of the process and its input and output components. This knowledge can be both an asset and a liability. Their level of knowledge will be a foundation for analysing what is happening in a process. They will have a strong sense about what cause and effect relationships exist in the process, and be able to provide valuable input at all stages of a project. On the other hand, this level of knowledge is that which created and supports the current level of performance. A nice way of saying the thinking that created the existing problem. The challenge for a team leader will be to take the team beyond the level of process knowledge that created the current state, to a level that can identify ways of raising the performance bar. As Albert Einstein eluded, the level of thinking that created the problem will not solve it.

Skill 4. Getting Change to Happen

The final and perhaps most important skill for a project leader to develop is that of change leadership. As we already know, change is all around us, we experience it everyday in our lives. The sad fact is, this is an area where many leaders are challenged. In the absence of formal authority, change will only occur when the *thinking, emotional, behavioural and contextual* aspects associated with a specific change are effectively addressed.

So think about this now. To lead a project team, you only need to learn four things:

- How to build **relationships** through establishing rapport and connection;
- How to manage **team dynamics** and build an effective / productive team;
- How to **generate new thinking** in order to identify and treat the critical few variables that cause process results to be the way they are; and
- How to **accelerate change** in a way that the new state is sustainable over the long term.

Undoubtedly, to learn these skills takes time. To learn them well, perhaps to the point of mastery, requires that you decide and commit to doing certain things. Over a period of more than 20 years of coaching and developing people, I've found that high achievement is a discipline, not an art; a choice, not an accident. If you do certain things, you cannot help but succeed. Whilst this subject is not the focus of the book, I can tell you that if you do these things you are well on the way to mastering this subject.

Read everything of relevance that you can get your hands on. You can accelerate the learning process by reading in a relatively short period of time what has taken authors years to learn. By reading you will increase the number of distinctions you're able to make about a particular topic. That's all knowledge really is; the ability to make distinctions. Let me give you an example of what I mean. Suppose a person could make the following distinctions when describing a golf club. 'The club is a forged steel 5 iron made by Taylor Made. It has a perimeter weighted design head that has no offset. It is 1 degree flatter than standard and has approximately 24 degrees of loft.' That person is more knowledgeable than the person who can only say it's a golf club or it's a 5 iron. The more distinctions you're able to make about your work in process improvement, the more knowledgeable you'll ultimately be.

Read this book from cover to cover. Not because I wrote it, but because you should. Research has shown that less than 10 percent of people actually read beyond the first chapter of a book. Imagine the distinctions they may have learned but missed out on. Which percentage do you belong to?

Try new tools and new ways of doing things. To grow you **must** step outside your comfort zone. When you step outside this zone, you step into the zone of unlimited possibilities. That's where you grow as an individual. Try some or all of the ideas from this book and if you get a result less than expected; remember there is no such thing as failure, only feedback and an opportunity to learn. Every time you try something, you'll be able to make more distinctions, thus become more knowledgeable and skillful. If you give up on a new way of doing things, you will never know how close you were to mastering it!

Be open and responsive to feedback. Feedback is essential to personal development. You should encourage feedback so that you learn at every opportunity. If you continue to think the way you do today, there is no doubt you will be left behind by others. There's no such thing as the status quo for you; only the perception of a status quo. When your thinking stops developing, people around you continue to develop, so relatively you drift backwards. In reality, the status quo only exists when we develop at the same rate as everyone else. Interesting paradox; to remain stationary we must continue to change! Very few people are able to challenge their own thinking, so they need these challenges to come from people around them.

Model successful behaviour. Find someone who's achieving the results you desire in your own life, whether it be business improvement work or something more personal. Find out what they're doing and model their process. The clues to success are everywhere around us, we just need to look for them and adapt them to our own situation.

Having said all of that, I want to take the time to answer 2 questions - Why did I originally write this book, and why did I produce this second edition.

The Original Publication

I wrote the original book, which by the way is the foundation for this second edition, for two reasons. My initial drive came from my dissatisfaction with the extent of information available in text form. It seemed to me that authors were holding things back, and no single text provided the depth of information that I desired while learning to be a Black Belt. If that was how I felt, then I'm sure other people feel that way also.

The second reason was based on my fundamental belief that the more you give, the more you get. I have a strong desire to document and share what I have learned, and provide new and interesting distinctions to people I come into contact with, knowing that they will share their distinctions with me as a result.

The Second Edition

This second edition was produced for a very simple reason. Continual improvement methodologies remain relevant when they are a product of their own principle - continual improvement! Since writing the first edition in 2003 we have continued to improve the way we implement and employ improvement methodologies in our own coaching work. We were at the point where the original version was way out of date and doing what we preach meant writing the book again.

The second edition was a more up to date reference to the modern day approach to improvement using the DMAIC process, so commonly known in Six Sigma circles. As you will see, I have integrated both Lean and Six Sigma with the belief that you choose whichever tools are most appropriate to the objectives of your project. Some projects, such as those that are dealing with process variation, are more suitable to traditional Six Sigma, while other projects, such as those with the goal of reducing cycle time or inventory, are more effectively addressed with Lean tools and processes. Some may even combine a mixture of tools; the bottom line is it doesn't matter, as long as you make the improvement happen.

I acknowledge that implementing specific tools in a carefully designed sequence, as in the pyramid building strategy that I so frequently see, can create a Lean workplace. However, that is not the focus of this book, rather I have focused on the 'lean project' approach to improvement using the DMAIC sequence.

I updated the second edition to this version in late 2022, early 2023. I did that firstly to align it with what we had learned over the two decades since we first wrote it. And secondly, to incorporate the latest guidelines and images associated with statistical analysis software (Excel, SigmaXL and Minitab) all of which had evolved quite a lot.

It's Not a Bible!

My primary goal was to write this book in a way that the concepts discussed can be easily understood, adapted and applied. As with the first edition, many of the underpinning theories are not discussed, particularly when covering statistical analysis methods. I firmly believe application and interpretation is far more useful to the practitioner. Underpinning theory is often a 'nice to know', and is far easier to understand *after* you learn to apply the concept.

Whilst it may be comprehensive in providing instructions for certain tools, this book was never meant to be a Bible for Lean or Six Sigma professionals. The components of statistical analysis cannot possibly be fully encapsulated in a single text of reasonable size. This text should instead be a simple reference for you in applying the basic concepts of team leadership, Lean and Six Sigma, and complimentary to other text dealing with similar subjects. As I said earlier, to make more distinctions, you must read widely and get the perspectives of multiple authors, not just my perspective.

Book Layout

For ease of reference, I have presented the book in a four-part format.

Part 1 - Lean and Six Sigma Foundations

The first part of the book discusses a range of topics I consider to be foundational knowledge from which we can move into more detail about the application of the Lean and Six Sigma methodologies.

We explore the ideas behind these approaches and also get into the nuts and bolts of the sequence you might follow when leading an improvement project.

One of the most important pieces, one we received many positive comments about from the original version, is the table of tools found at the end of Part 1. Of course this table has been enhanced and extended and I know it will be invaluable to you as a reference for many years to come.

Part 2 - Project Team Leadership

Part 2 addresses the subject of team leadership. I believe this is really about leadership. In fact, retired General Electric CEO, Jack Welch once described Six Sigma training as one of the most important and effective leadership development programs in that company.

In this part we discuss various ideas around challenges in leading teams and tools and tips for making it an area of growth for you. Most importantly, the basics for running team meetings is extensively covered.

Part 3 – Lean and Six Sigma Project Focus

This is where we really start to see how the second edition differs from the original. Part 3 of the book discusses the application of both Six Sigma and Lean Thinking in a project context.

When I originally designed this edition, I was going to write about Lean before the Six Sigma piece for one simple reason. *Most* companies will realise *most* benefit in the early phases of their initiative through the application of Lean Thinking. However, in my humble opinion, most want efficiencies and think Six Sigma is the answer. Sadly they realise how much more challenging it has been without the benefit of a much broader and more appropriate toolkit, but I guess that's a story I should save for another time.

Once I get into writing this edition, I found it easier to blend the two together and introduce relevant pieces from Lean and Six Sigma as I moved through the 20 step DMAIC roadmap.

One thing I will point out to you is this. The whole Lean package is still employed within Six Sigma's DMAIC framework when you are approaching this from a project perspective.

In Part 3, we get into the real nuts and bolts of Lean Six Sigma. With such a comprehensive array of tools and processes, I have addressed the fives phases of Lean Six Sigma project work (DMAIC) in separate chapters.

As you will see, each phase has its own specific outcomes, and is an integral part of the process improvement model.

Each of the five DMAIC model chapters is followed by two support chapters. One chapter will have instructions for the application of the tools for the respective phase, and the other will present tollgate questions and process checklists relevant to the phase. I know you will find these invaluable.

Part 4 - Appendices

As with the original edition, appendices contain a range of information to either support some of the technical pieces presented earlier, or to provide additional information that might serve you in your application of Lean Six Sigma. A comprehensive bibliography is presented at the end of the book.

In closing ...

I would like to wish you good fortune with your learning the way to master the continual improvement of business processes. Remember to keep things simple and you will make considerable progress. I hope that this book offers as much value for you in your work as it did for me during the writing of it.

Acknowledgments

The production of a book like this is really a team effort, particularly one of such epic proportions. I cannot close without acknowledging the contribution of some very important people who have either directly or indirectly made the original book and this second edition possible.

To the ladies who formed the original editing team, Chris Cornwell, Marie Low and Carissa Matthews, I'm sure you know how much I appreciate your tireless commitment to reading this material from cover to cover and offering your open and honest feedback.

I've heard it said that luck is really what happens when preparation meets opportunity. Well I have spent a lifetime preparing, and opportunity has definitely followed. To Richard Johns, Mike Anglin, Colleen Kindler, Pamela Dennis, Bob Miller, Roger Higgins and David Hannegan; thank you for the opportunities you gave me with 'Lean Six Sigma'. Your faith and friendship is and will always be appreciated.

To all of the fantastic people I have worked with, coached and been coached by over the years. In particular Stephanie Redman, Adam Raffe, Sheena Livesey, Pete Gough, Lynne Fitzpatrick, Dr. Morgan Jones, Bob Waters, Andy Morrow, Bruce Grey, Ivan (Magpie) Brodie, Commissioner Bob Atkinson, Bob Watson, Glen (Hammer) Damro, Kerrie Danes, John Rolfe, Don McKay, Tim Young, Graeme Gully, Adrian Manger, Mona Draper, Neal Kenny, Jose Campos, Frony Ward, Alicia Hare, Simon Wandke, Liz Keim, Aled Roberts, Harry Sinko, Mark Simmons, Gary Warden, John McDowall, Jeff Stitt, Derek Pangbourne, Richard Tatnall, Craig Hurkett and Francisco Melero. Your willingness to share your friendship and experience has been a foundation for my own personal growth. Thank you.

To the fantastic people who have supported me in my business endeavours and the incredible professionals I have worked with who continue to contribute to my education - without your influence I would never have gotten as far as I have.

Dedication

A special mention to Vicki, without whose years of support and friendship I could never have originally completed this work; thank you for the tireless work you did in proof reading this material on so many occasions. To my fantastic children, Nicky and Matt for your endless support and commitment to the completion of this project along with many others; thank you for being incredible people. I dedicate this book to you.

George Lee Sye

Ravenshoe, Australia, January 2023

'Simplicity is one of the keys to progress. Complexity results in procrastination, paralysis, and unnecessary delay, so keep it simple and make progress while others sit and ponder.'

PART 1 - SIX SIGMA & LEAN THINKING FOUNDATIONS

CHAPTER 1: QUALITY ASSURANCE VERSUS QUALITY IMPROVEMENT

To get us started on the right foot, I think it's important to have an up front discussion about Quality Assurance and Quality Improvement.

Two terms that are often referred to, and in many cases confused with one another, are 'Quality Assurance' and 'Quality Improvement'. Both 'Quality Improvement' and 'Quality Assurance' are approaches that contribute positively to business success if implemented effectively. They are however, not one and the same. Let's make the necessary distinctions between the two, so that we have a clearer understanding of what role they each play in quality management.

QUALITY

The common element of both approaches is 'quality'. It would be remiss of me to try and distinguish between the two terms without first describing the common element.

There are many ways we can look at quality, and this is reflected in the many definitions of the term that exist in the world today. The difference in definitions stems from the existence of five major approaches to defining quality. These approaches can be described as:

- **Transcendental** – quality is something that we can recognise and understand but cannot define, a higher plane approach to the issue you might say
- **Product based** – quality is a measurable variable that can be obtained at a higher price
- **Manufacturing based** – quality is conformance to design or specifications at the supplier end of the spectrum
- **User based** – quality is inextricably linked with customer satisfaction with the assumption that customer's needs and wants differ
- **Value based** – quality is conformance or performance at an acceptable price or cost

According to Feigenbaum[1] (1990), "... quality is, in its essence, a way of managing. Total-quality-control's organisation-wide impact involves the managerial and technical implementation of customer-oriented quality activities as a prime responsibility of general management, and of the mainline operations of marketing, engineering, production, industrial relations, finance, and service as well as the quality-control function itself at the most economical levels which provide customer satisfaction".

There is no doubt that quality means different things to different people. Ultimately, to be successful in business we need to recognise that quality must be a value of the consumer of a process, service or product, and as such must change with trends, tastes and preferences. Perhaps the statement by the Australian Quality Council[2] (1999), "quality is determined by the customer" best defines quality.

However, Improvement of Quality and Assurance of Quality are different dimensions of quality management.

QUALITY IMPROVEMENT

The focus of quality improvement is significantly different from quality control in that it is on creating new standards of quality and not just remaining within existing standards. This approach is the cornerstone of Total Quality Management and a continuous improvement culture within an organisation. It is an approach to management of an organisation that focuses on quality as the key to success.

One thing is quite clear: quality improvement cannot be successful without the involvement of all stakeholders. Managers do not do the work that allows quality to be realised; the workforce does the work. Quality improvement must therefore be a journey whereby everyone is focused on continuous improvement in quality directed towards customer (internal and external) satisfaction.

Quality improvement requires a management style that is flexible, not averse to change, stakeholder focused, and participative in response to the need for employee 'buy-in'. It is management's job to lead the way and demonstrate commitment to the principles of quality improvement.

Whilst management may lead the way and establish the framework within which Quality can be improved, ultimately the control of quality will rest with all employees at all levels of an organisation, working in a coordinated and collaborative environment.

Why would an organisation want to implement Quality Improvement? In his 40 steps to Quality Improvement, Feigenbaum[3] (1990) provides a sound business case for quality improvement.

"... quality is explicitly structured to contribute to business profitability and positive cash flow. Total-quality-control programs are highly cost-effective because of their results in improved levels of customer satisfaction, reduced operating costs, reduced operating losses and field service costs, and improved utilisation of resources".

Deming's Chain[4], demonstrates that by improving quality, costs decrease, productivity improves, additional market share is able to be captured with better quality and lower price products, and the company is able to remain in business and provide jobs for the workforce.

What is not mentioned by Feigenbaum or Deming is the opportunity for increased employee satisfaction.

---

[1] "Feigenbaum's 40 Steps to Quality Improvement" http://mijuno.larc.nasa.gov/dfc/key/feig40.html, 2 December 2000

[2] "Australian Business Excellence Framework - 1999", Australian Quality Council, Sydney

[3] "Feigenbaum's 40 Steps to Quality Improvement" http://mijuno.larc.nasa.gov/dfc/key/feig40.html, 2 December 2000

[4] MNG0916 Topic 8 "Total Quality Management", Southern Cross University, pp.8-15

Quality improvement is not a project with a limited life. In a successful organisation, quality improvement will be continuous and institutionalised as a part of day-to-day operations. It must ultimately be a shared value within the organisational culture.

Through necessity, quality improvement will bring with it an administrative framework. Just controlling quality requires administration including process designs, work instructions, plans, designs and specifications, and standard operating procedures etc. For the improvement to be continuous there will also be a need to plot and record consumer trends, and preferences.

The success of any quality improvement initiative may ultimately be measured by one dimension, market share. However it is more likely that indicators of success will stem from the organisation's motives for implementing the program in the first place. These would include:

- Additional market share
- Customer satisfaction
- Employee satisfaction
- Reduced costs associated with re-work, failures or complaints
- Keeping pace with or exceeding customer needs
- Improved bottom line results

The Australian Quality Council believes that an organisation's performance in this regard must be interpreted in a broad sense that is beyond financial performance. Trends and comparisons with targets, competitors or best in class organisations can be used as indicators of success and might also include stakeholder objectives and shared values. The Council also promotes the evaluation of sustainability.

Quality isn't just an internal issue; it is a social issue. A company successful in quality improvement must be in touch with society so that it can both understand and anticipate changing tastes and preferences.

So how does an organisation engender customer confidence that it is committed to quality? It does so through Quality Assurance.

QUALITY ASSURANCE (QA)

The focus of quality assurance is on establishing customer confidence in the quality systems of an organisation. It takes the TQM approach further than just meeting or improving quality standards. It is about guaranteeing that an organisation has a quality management system in place and is conforming to system standards. Michailidis[5] (1995) provides a definition for QA that helps distinguish it from Quality Improvement. "*Simply put, QA is nothing more (and nothing less) than a management system, in compliance with a standard, that gives the customer confidence that what they want is what they'll get (and perhaps a little more)*".

QA is a less philosophical approach than Quality Improvement, and is more standards driven. It does not improve quality, but rather establishes a framework that allows us to monitor the extent to which quality will and is being controlled. An interesting observation by Beckman[6] (1998) is that a Quality Management System under the framework of ISO 9000 could be developed and implemented without any improvement in quality whatsoever. This supports the suggestion that QA does not improve quality.

[5] Michailidis, L. (1995), "What is the value of QA Certification", The Quality Magazine, April, p.50

[6] Beckman, J. (1998), "Quality: A Critical Introduction", Routledge, London, p.240

Why would an organisation implement QA? As customers have limited capacity to directly observe how a company operates, satisfaction with quality of a product does not necessarily mean that they are confident about a firm's commitment to quality or its quality systems. In Australia, companies apply AS3900 standards on a voluntary basis. Companies are not compelled to do so, except when entering into contractual agreements with governments or regulatory authorities.

Beyond contractual requirements, some of the more common reasons for implementing QA include (a) protection against prosecution and civil claims, (b) it's good business practice, (c) it may be necessary for survival as other firms achieve QA, and (d) for marketing advantage.

According to Bernath and Francis[7] (1994), *"... a quality assurance system can provide a basis for improving the productivity, efficiency, and hence profitability of an organisation"*.

QA's impact on society will stem from the value that customers place on Certification to relevant QA standards. As suppliers compete for market share, they continually offer higher quality products or services for consumption by society. As customers continue to expect greater quality and value for money in products, so might the demand for QA increase. It certainly becomes a means of differentiation by organisations. As more and more organisations achieve QA Certification, social awareness of quality will increase as will consumer expectations.

The management style required for successful QA does not differ from that required for Quality Improvement. However management must be committed to the administrative requirements of a QA system, and will need to possess well-developed change management skills to be able to establish coalition and commitment from the workforce. Without workforce 'buy-in', the QA system will not be established to a certifiable standard.

QA requires an administrative structure that can be audited. QA needs to be built into the process in the form of quality and procedural manuals, work instructions, records, forms, documented plans and specifications, and other auditable mechanisms that have a role in guaranteeing a standard of quality. Ideally, those people who actually carry out the tasks should develop the documentation and procedures, thus there is a significant need for workforce 'buy-in' and commitment.

Is QA a passing fad you might ask? The life of QA depends entirely on the business and social environment. Whilst some contracts continue to require QA Certification, larger firms will continue to pursue QA, if only for economical reasons. This need for organisations to be competitive with other firms that already have a QA Certification will extend further and further beyond the contract issue as society's expectation of quality increases. This last factor may ultimately drive the case for longevity of QA in any organisation.

A firm's commitment to quality is evaluated through a process of audit. The international standards for quality are identified in the ISO 9000 series. In Australia, the AS3900 series of standards provide the basis for QA. A firm that meets all the requirements of the relevant standard will have its QA Certified for that particular standard. A proponent of Certification, Cooke[8] (1995), says that certification is essential, and brings with it a number of benefits including:

- Management commitment to quality
- A disciplined system
- Regular checking by an external organisation
- A base upon which to build more sophisticated quality improvement

[7] Whitford, B., Andrew, R. (1994) "The Pursuit of Quality", Prentice Hall, Sydney, p.26

[8] Cooke, C. (1995), "Certification: Essential step on the quality journey", The Quality Magazine, April, p.63

The audience of this certification will ultimately be both the customers and the workforce.

So how do we know when a firm is successful with QA? We could simply say that success is indicated by recognition through certification or registration to a particular AS or ISO standard. Michailidis[9] (1995) says that "... *QA is only of true value when it is understood and used properly, by both the supplier and the purchaser, for the ultimate aim of achieving real and lasting quality in the products and/or services provided. Anything short of this makes QA certification a farce, and is not value adding to our economy*". If we believe this, then perhaps the true indicator of success lies in the measurement of real and lasting quality in a firm's outputs.

Conclusion

In conclusion, the two terms are not synonymous with one another. Both can exist in an organisation without the other.

Quality Improvement takes quality control to a higher level, with a focus on continuously improving quality to meet the ever-changing tastes and preferences of consumers.

QA provides the framework for giving customers confidence that an organisation has a quality management system in place, and is adhering to quality standards.

Perhaps the most significant difference is identifiable in the following statements.

- Quality Improvement provides a foundation for product or service differentiation.
- Quality Assurance provides a basis for differentiation of the organisation itself from its competitors.

While they each involve the documentation of processes, neither Lean Thinking nor Six Sigma has a direct association with QA. Both Lean and Six Sigma are focused on continued and sustainable improvement, thus the emphasis of this book is on Quality Improvement.

[9] Michailidis, op.cit., p.51

CHAPTER 2: SIX SIGMA & LEAN

WHAT IS SIX SIGMA?

Six Sigma can be described as a methodology used by an organisation to make sure its core business processes are as effective as they can possibly be. In achieving that goal, product defects and work mistakes are minimised or eliminated.

In even more simple terms, Six Sigma is a consistently successful means for reducing variation or eliminating problems in the repetitive processes of an organisation – another way of saying process performance improvement or quality improvement. The goal of this methodology is defect elimination (where defects are defined by the customer).

The most common process improvement sequence followed by organisations implementing Six Sigma is known by the acronym DMAIC. (Often pronounced as DA-MAY-ICK)

How does Six Sigma work?

Think for a moment about a holiday trip you may have taken in the past. To get to your destination, you (a) identified where you were, (b) you selected the best way to get from your present location to your desired destination using logical reasoning, and (c) you then took appropriate action to make that happen. The sequence of DMAIC is much like that.

Project teams identify where they are now, identify what the desired state needs to be and then using sound logic choose the best path to follow for achieving that desired outcome. Six Sigma's DMAIC process (explained in more detail later) provides a framework for the acceleration of this process and the ability to continually improve the process even though ways to do so may no longer be obvious.

A major strength of the process of DMAIC is that all decisions are based on facts and not 'gut feel'. As many proponents have found out, Lean Six Sigma is not rocket science; it is just a logical sequence of steps complimented by a package of traditional quality tools that have continued to evolve over the years.

In essence, both Lean and Six Sigma are products of their own primary principle - *continual* improvement.

THE SIMPLICITY OF SIX SIGMA - 2 PRINCIPLES

The First Principle of Six Sigma

'Continual Improvement is an ongoing process of change followed by consolidation.'

Every process has a performance curve that might be represented by a diagram as shown in the figure below.

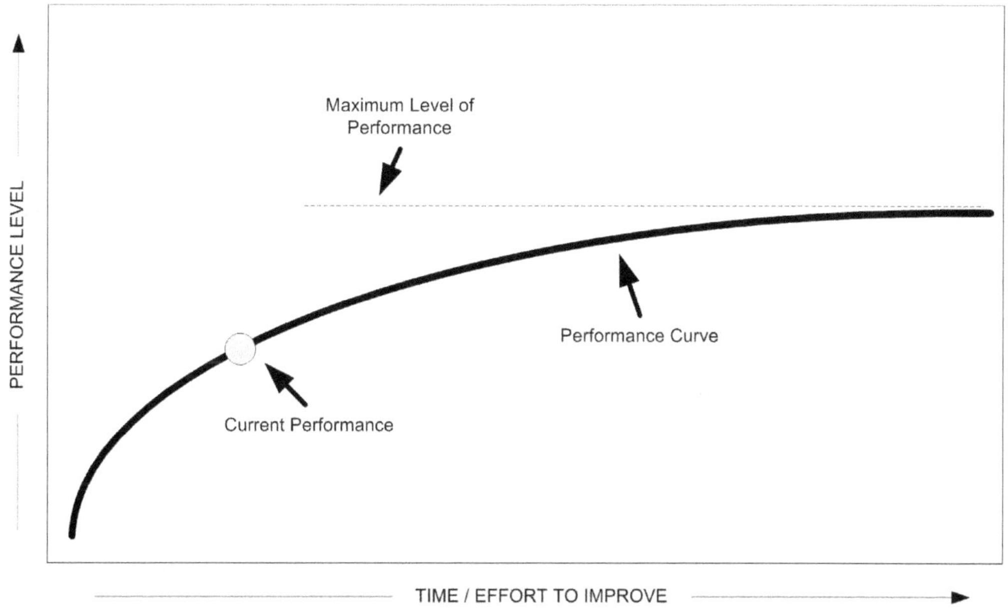

Figure 1: A Theoretical Performance Curve

The fundamental error many managers make is to set out to achieve 'one step' maximum improvement. For example, suppose the current level of performance was as shown in the diagram. If a manager were to initiate a project to solve all of the process performance problems or take the performance of a process to its maximum level in one step, that manager is going to be disappointed.

That project would drag on and seem to take forever. It would be like trying to solve world hunger in one hit. In reality there are simply too many variables to work with to be able to maintain adequate focus.

And, no improvement methodology or tool is able to identify every single variable that needs to be controlled or fixed to achieve that level of 'one step' improvement.

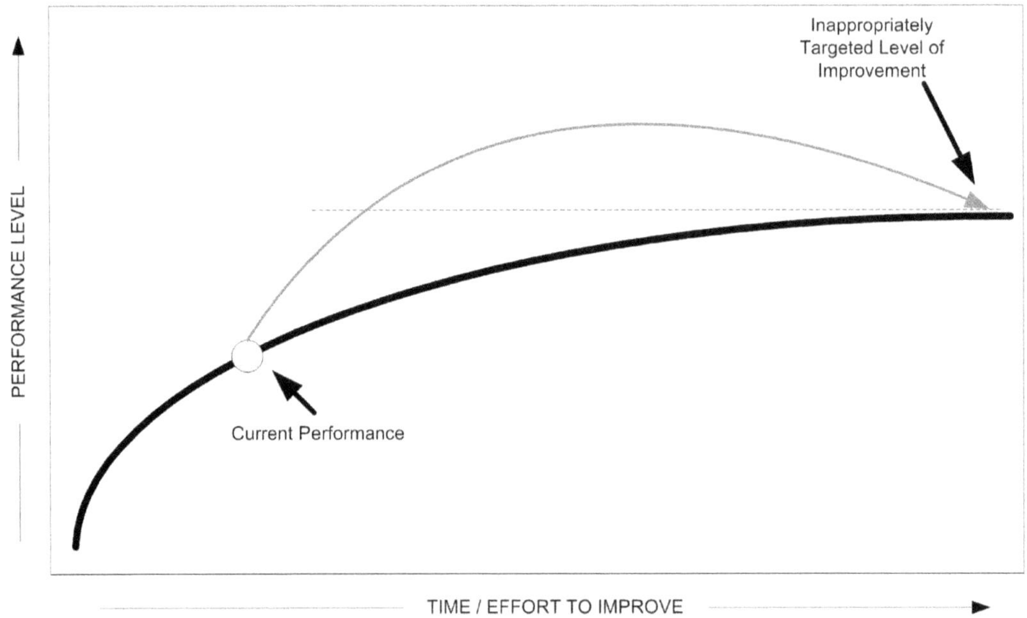

Figure 2: Unrealistic Expectations

The reason why the concept is called *continual* improvement is because it works well when managers recognise that massive momentum can be generated when a small improvement is made and then locked in. A consolidation period allows the process to become stable with the most recent improvements becoming sustainable.

This period of consolidation is then followed by another improvement to the process, which is again locked in during a period of consolidation. And so the process is repeated.

The benefits of the *continual* improvement approach are four fold:

- Gains or wins are experienced much sooner than would otherwise be realised.
- Gains are more easily locked in and sustained over time.
- The workforce gets comfortable with continual improvement because of the wins being experienced.
- The culture of an organisation can shift to one of continually pursuing improvement.

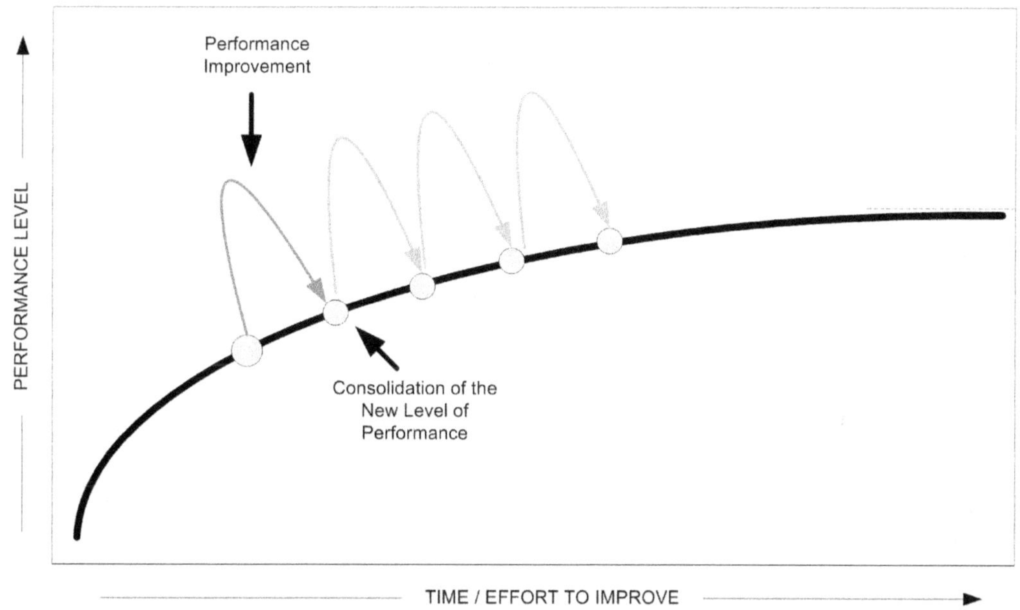

Figure 3: Continual Improvement in Action

'We've all heard the term 'success breeds success'. In essence that is what a continual improvement approach establishes – the opportunity for employees to repeatedly improve processes which ultimately improves their work, the customer's experience and the organisation's growth.'

Harry Sinko

The Second Principle of Six Sigma

'Y is a function of multiple x's, rapid improvement occurs when you focus on the key x's.'

$$y=fx$$

This is the mathematical way of saying that the output of a process (an output is represented by the term y), is a function of its input and process variables (a variable is represented by the term x). What this means is that variation or changes in y are a direct result of variation or changes in relevant x's.

This concept can also be represented visually in the format shown in the diagram.

The output variable y is a function of changes that occur with variables x_1, x_2, and x_3.

In its purest form, the way Six Sigma works is quite simple. The project team is charged with reducing the variation in a specific variable (y), for example material hardness or tensile strength or useful life cycle of a product.

Using their experience and knowledge of the process the team generates ideas about what it is that causes variation in the y.

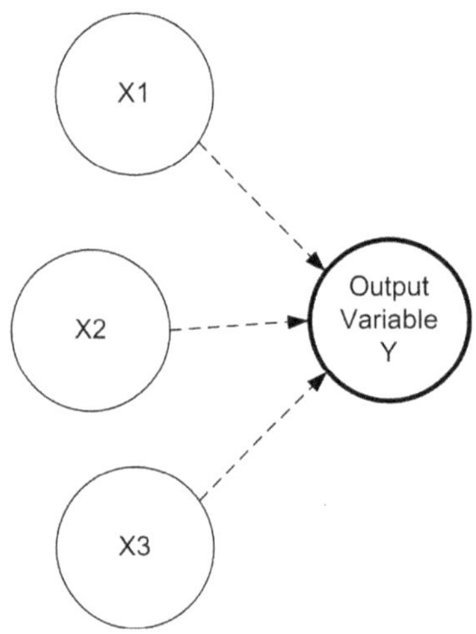

Figure 4: Variation in y is Caused by Variation in x's

Their 'hypothesis' extends beyond the first level of causes to lower level variables with the intent of finding *the most significant causes* of variation.

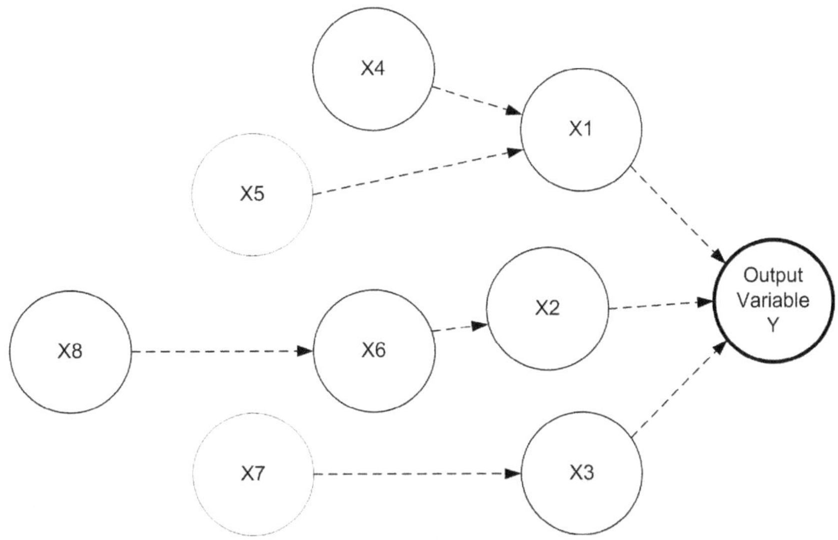

Figure 5: Hypothesised Causes of Variation

In the diagram you can see that the team in this case has hypothesised that up to eight variables cause variation in the *y*. We know that not all of these variables would have the same degree of impact on the *y*. Improving *y* begins with finding the 'critical few' *x*'s that really do cause *y* to be as it is, and that's where the strength of Six Sigma comes to the fore.

Using various tools and methods, the project team moves beyond hypothesis by validating which of these variables have the greatest impact on variation in *y*.

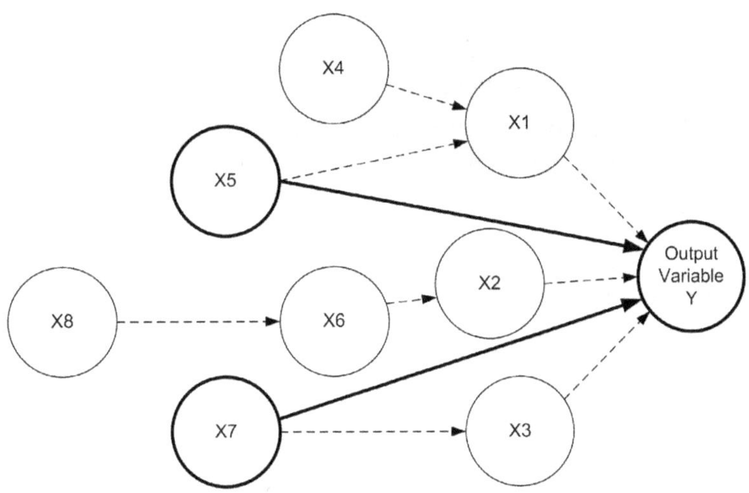

Figure 6: Validated Major Causes of Variation

Once these relationships are validated, solutions are generated to treat those variables in such a way that the output metric of the process (output variable *y*) is what you want it to be. Six Sigma's DMAIC model provides the framework and tools for finding and controlling those critical few *x*'s.

WHAT IS LEAN?

The term 'lean' comes from the concept of using half the manufacturing space, half the human effort, half the tools and half the time to develop a new product. While a mass producer would traditionally have a 'good enough' view of production and believe that to get better would cost more than it was worth, lean producers have an entirely different belief and continue to pursue perfection.

Lean thinking recognises that few processes are created to deliver customer defined value in the most *efficient* way. In most cases, processes are created to maximise the quality of a product. How many larger organisations, particularly those that have products passing through a production line or documents passing through a process of approval or even customers moving through a queue, focused on making sure their processes produced high quality outputs with little thought to maximising flow and minimising waste? In working with literally hundreds of companies, my experience has been there are many opportunities to enhance performance by including these concepts in the scope of their continual improvement endeavour.

Studies have found as little as 10 to 15 percent of steps in a process are involved in adding value for a customer, and this can be as little as 5 percent of overall cycle time. As much as 95 percent of time is engaged in non-value adding activities, in other words *waste.*

Six Sigma

As we have already discussed, in its purest form Six Sigma focuses on **reducing variation and increasing process capability and yield** through the application of statistically oriented tools. In a nutshell, Six Sigma is the study and control of process variables, an effort in maximising process *effectiveness.*

Lean

Lean on the other hand is primarily concerned with **eliminating waste and improving flow through a process** via the application of Lean principles.

We can define waste as anything that is not necessary in the process of producing the product or service. For example a loan application with four levels of approval contains waste. Lean clears the path of waste and is primarily focused on maximising business *efficiency.*

When integrated with Six Sigma, an organisation can undertake improvements in quality and variation as well as improving flow through the process and removing unnecessary time.

Clearly Defining Waste

Let's make sure we're all clear on what waste is. Even if you believe you *have to* engage in any of these, all of the seven following activities or outcomes are considered waste.

- Defects
- Inventory
- Motion
- Transportation
- Over Production
- Waiting
- Non Value Added Processing

A useful acronym once told to me for remembering these seven forms of waste is this.

D - I - M - T - O - W - N

Defects – Any product or service that does not conform to customer specifications or expectations, and results in dissatisfaction is a defective product or service. The hidden costs associated with defects include unnecessary labour and wasted materials. The costs that are hard to quantify are those associated with lost business in the future because of poor quality.

Inventory – This is waste. Goods, regardless of what they are, sitting in a store ties up capital. Hewlett Packard reported a $1 million saving in reduced inventory due to improved flow. That is cold hard cash directly in their pocket.

Inventory includes excess raw materials, work in progress, completed or finished goods as well as repair parts and supplies. Inventories not only tie up capital, they require a company to locate and allocate space and use time to handle whatever it is in the inventory.

'An interesting observation is that inventory tends to exist where there is a change in process ownership. It seems as though there is a trust or confidence issue that drives its accumulation. As well, non-aligned performance metrics along a value chain impact significantly on inventory.'

Harry Sinko

Motion – This term refers to unnecessary steps or movement undertaken by workers or equipment involved in core business processes to accommodate inefficient layout or anything that does not add value to the process such as defects, reworking, reprocessing and storage. Suppose an employee's job was to service a piece of mobile machinery, and his toolbox was in such a location that every time he needed a new tool, he had to walk five metres to the toolbox and back again. How much of the total time to service this vehicle would be involved in that movement to and from the toolbox. Most people would say the time is of little consequence. How much time would that amount to over the course of a full year? I think you'd agree that the total accumulated time would probably be equal to the time it would take to service a number of vehicles. The point is this, motion adds time to a process, just like transport, and is ultimately wasted time. Seen once, it seems like a nothing, but it accumulates and offers a great opportunity to increase throughput for no more effort.

Transportation – This is unnecessary movement of materials such as the movement of partially completed units from one operation to another. Transportation results in (a) additional non value adding time to a process, and (b) increased risk of damaged units.

Over Production – Over production is the continued production of units resulting in excess quantities that must be stored. In effect, over production is the creation of products before the customer actually needs them and results in the creation of inventory.

Waiting – We can also refer to waiting as queueing. In this context, waiting is a period of inactivity in a downstream process that is the result of an upstream process not delivering on time.

Non-Value Added Processing – This term refers to *additional* or *extra* activities such as reworking, re-handling, reprocessing and storage. These are usually the result of over production, excess inventory and defects.

D - I - M - T - O - W - N

Figure 7: The 7 Wastes of Processes

Some companies use a slightly different sequence for labelling waste. Though essentially the same as the DIMTOWN list, it ends up having a different acronym.

- Transportation
- Inventory
- Motion
- Waiting
- Over Processing (aka Non Value Added Processing)
- Over Production
- Defects

The acronym for remember the seven forms of process waste in this sequence is this.

T - I - M - W - O - O - D

THE FOCUS OF LEAN - 5 PRINCIPLES

Just like Six Sigma, Lean comprises a range of tools, all of which are aligned to a number of core principles. The 5 Lean principles are these.

- Zero **Waiting**
- Zero **Inventory**
- Customer **Pull** (as opposed to operational push)
- Maximum **Flow**
- Minimum **Time** (referring to lead times and process cycle times)

Since these are self explanatory, I haven't expanded on the principles. For further reading on this topic, refer to my 2007 publication titled *'Process Alchemy - 2nd Edition'*.

FOUR TECHNICAL APPROACHES TO IMPROVEMENT

In dealing with different scenarios, practitioners will usually take an approach that fits one of these four strategies. The purpose of this section is to define those four scenarios in order that you have a greater understanding of the fit of Six Sigma, Lean Thinking and various other approaches to process improvement.

1. Problem Solving

Problem Solving **addresses variation in a process that is not by chance**, but assignable to a specific cause. For example, suppose a mine site had 3 shovels operating in an open pit. The daily tonnages moved by each of these shovels could be plotted on a run chart, and this would represent the performance of the shovelling process over a period of time. If a failure occurred in a component of one of the shovels and it was unable to move material for a period of 24 hours, this would appear as a significant 'blip' on the record of daily tonnages. This is a problem that is not a part of the normal behaviour of the process, something that we call 'special cause variation'. This variation is temporary and unpredictable, and is often related to specific events. This type of 'blip' must be eliminated from the process before moving onto reducing overall variation. A problem solving approach is employed to resolve this 'problem'.

A multitude of approaches exist for 'solving event based problems' including:

- SPS (Soarent Vision's Systematic Problem Solving method);
- KT (Kepner Tregoe's Problem and Solution Analysis method);

- Apollo Root Cause (Cause Effect analysis developed by Dean Gano); and even
- Tap Root (a system the author observed at one time).

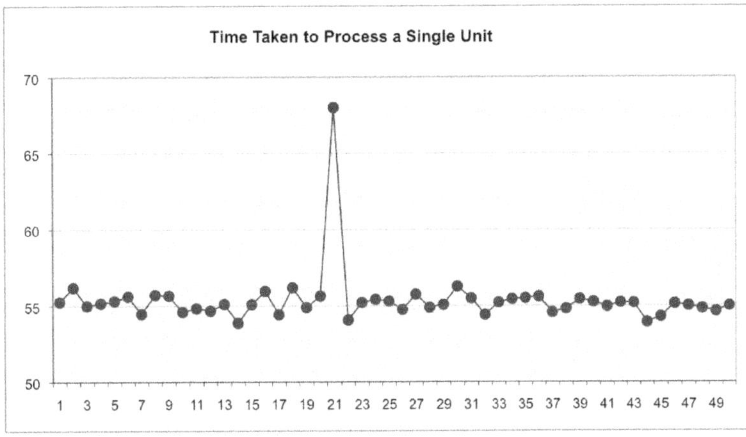

Figure 8: A One-off Special Cause Event

2. Process Improvement

By contrast, process improvement **addresses variation that you would expect** to see in a process, something we refer to as 'common cause variation'. This variation is always present in a process. In the process improvement approach, the goal is to reduce variation and eliminate results outside customer specifications, results we call 'defects'.

In most cases, process improvement requires a greater degree of statistical thinking than problem solving does.

Approaches for making improvements through adjusting common cause variation include:

- Six Sigma (the DMAIC model); and
- Shewhart-Deming's PDCA strategy.

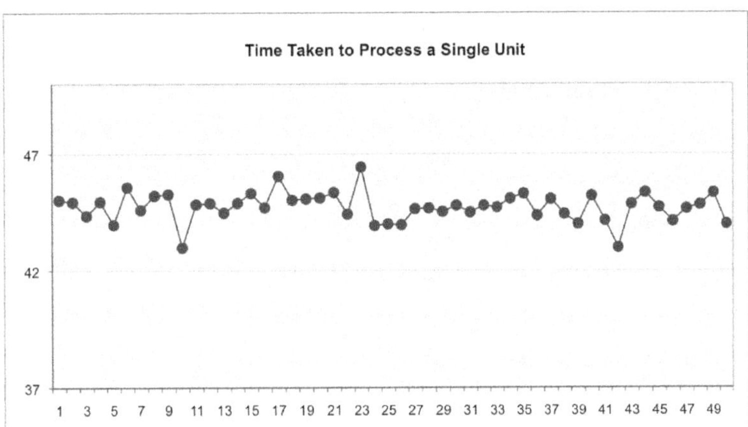

Figure 9: Normal or Expected Variation

3. Waste Elimination

Waste elimination is quite a broad term, though waste has been cleverly defined in the world of process improvement. All of the seven following outcomes are considered waste in a business: (a) Defects, (b) Inventory, (c) Motion, (d) Transportation, (e) Over Production, (f) Waiting, and (g) Non Value Added Processing. For more information on these, read *Process Alchemy - 2nd Edition* (2007).

The most common methods for eliminating waste, particularly anything that relates to time and inventory, include:

- Lean Thinking (or lean manufacturing);
- Theory of Constraints (TOC); and
- Just in Time Manufacturing (JIT).

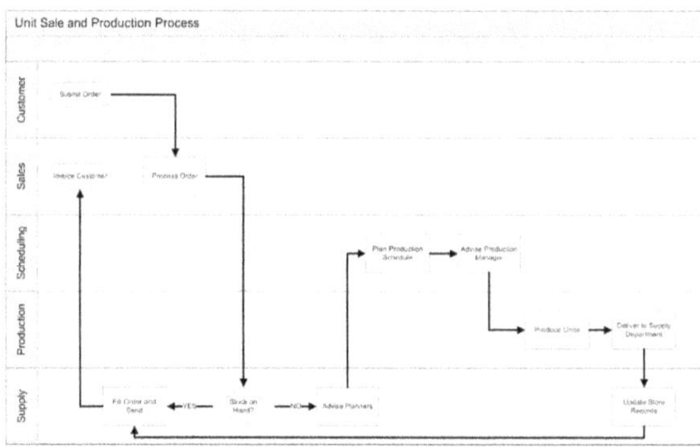

Figure 10: Processing Handoffs Adding Time to the Process

4. Process Design

Continual improvement also encompasses the creation of new processes. Six Sigma's Design for Six Sigma (with it's DMADV sequence) is one of the most effective and well known approaches to process design.

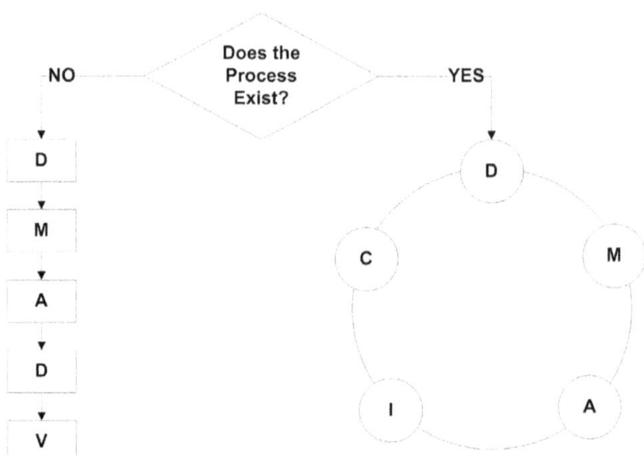

Figure 11: Design for Six Sigma Approach

The DMAIC Model – A High Level View

DMAIC is the acronym for Define, Measure, Analyse, Improve and Control. These are the chronological steps that categorise the actions taken and tools used by Lean Six Sigma project teams. Each selected Lean Six Sigma project must go through these five phases in chronological order. When I teach Lean Six Sigma, I like to explain to participants that to employ the DMAIC process for Six Sigma specific work, they simply have to do fifteen things – three activities within each of the major steps.

Not all of these activities are undertaken in a Lean specific project.

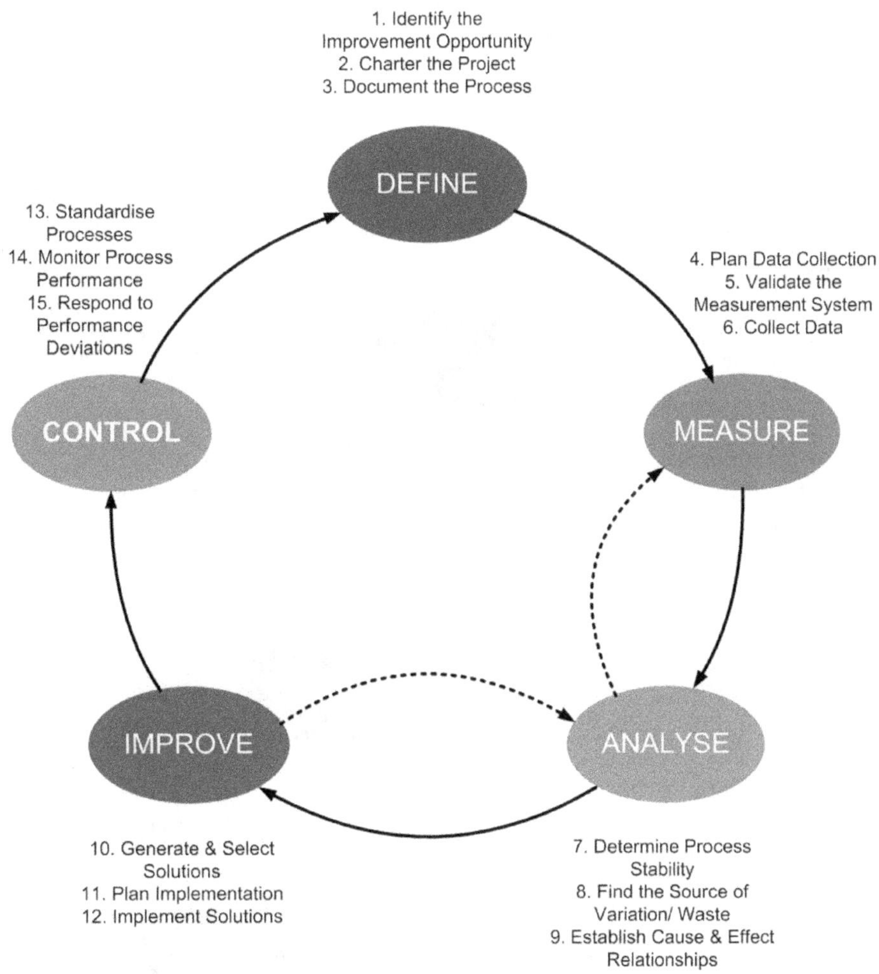

Figure 12: The Phases of the DMAIC Process

DMAIC Sequence Outcomes

The problem / opportunity is defined and summarised with other key elements in a project charter. The team is brought together and the process is documented in a way that is relevant to the work being undertaken.

The appropriate measure/s are identified as a pre-requisite to data collection. Preliminary data is collected for analysis from either a variation perspective, or a process efficiency perspective. Measurement systems may be analysed to ensure that data collected is reliable. The opportunity exists to determine baseline process capability during this phase.

Collected data is analysed to identify what's happening and where it's happening. The process is analysed to identify opportunities to eliminate non-value adding work and simplify the process so that the chance of defects occurring is minimised. A root cause analysis may be undertaken to identify potential causes of the problem or the observed variation. These are then validated using evidentiary methods often involving statistical tools.

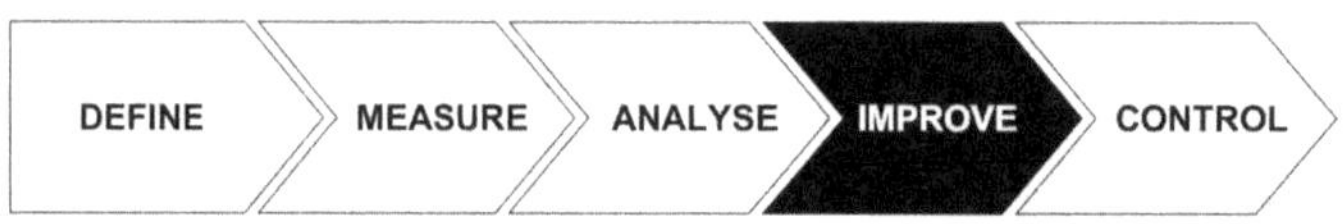

Ideas for treating the root causes of the problem or the variation are generated, with the most appropriate ideas being selected and implemented. Specific tools from the Lean toolkit may be used to rapidly improve process efficiencies.

Once the improvements are implemented, a system of monitoring and responding is established to ensure that the improvements are sustained. Processes are standardised to ensure defects are minimised or eliminated, and success is celebrated.

THE DMAIC ROADMAP IN DETAIL

To successfully employ the DMAIC approach, a Black Belt must be familiar with more than just the tools of process improvement. They must be familiar with the steps to take within each of the 'phases' of the Lean Six Sigma process improvement methodology.

Before discussing a 'roadmap', let me discuss the philosophy behind our approach to Lean Six Sigma. This philosophy is based on (a) my experience and observations of projects that have generated returns totalling 100s of millions of dollars and (b) the belief that the only constant in process improvement work is the start and end point – there are many ways to get to the desired outcome.

- **There is no one-way to do Lean or Six Sigma.** There are many effective ways to get from the start point to the desired end point. Much like a traveller finding her way to a new destination, the Black Belt is able to design his or her path through the steps of DMAIC according to their particular circumstances.
- **There are some elements that must be completed for every project.** These include (a) define the problem up front, (b) collect reliable data with relevant stratification variables, (c) find the source of most variation, (d) find and validate root causes of that variation, (e) generate and select solutions that treat root causes and fit criteria important to the customer and the business, (f) implement solutions using project management skills, (g) standardise the process and control its performance, and finally, (h) celebrate at the end of the project.
- **Whilst appearing linear, any 'roadmap' is iterative in that it is often necessary to go back at some point or move forward at other points in the process.** There will be occasions when easy wins or 'just do it' solutions are implemented while the analysis phase continues, in effect working in two parts of the DMAIC process at the one time. The only constant across Lean Six Sigma projects is the start and end point. The project starts with the identification of a performance gap, and the final destination is the closing of that gap. There is no one path between the two points.
- **Black Belts are given an extensive toolbox, but not every tool needs to be used.** Much like a motor mechanic working on different cars, they draw tools from that toolbox when they are needed for a specific purpose. Each tool helps generate answers to specific questions, and when the questions arise, that is the time for the tool or tools to be used.
- **Special cause variation must be eliminated before working on common cause variation.**

So when using this roadmap, or any other, I would suggest keeping in mind that it is a starting point on your journey to mastering Lean Six Sigma.

Over time you will find yourself creating your own general guidelines. Be cautious to ensure that any roadmap does not become prescriptive and kills the innovation and adaptability of your Lean Six Sigma work.

20 STEPS TO SUSTAINABLE PROCESS IMPROVEMENT

The 20-step process shown in the roadmap on the following page has proven successful in guiding many Black Belts and Green Belts in the effective employment of the DMAIC approach. It may prove useful in helping you start your journey to mastery of Lean Six Sigma through improvement project work.

Define Phase

1. Identify the improvement opportunity
2. Allocate the project to a team leader
3. Develop the project charter (an activity that involves the participation of team leader, process owner and project sponsor)
4. Start up the project team
5. Document the key elements of the process being worked on

Measure Phase

6. Plan the collection of data
7. Validate the measurement system used to collect data
8. Collect the data
9. Measure baseline performance (process capability or process efficiency)

Analyse Phase

10. Evaluate process stability
11. Eliminate special cause variation if you need to OR go straight on to identifying the source of variation or waste
12. Analyse cause & effect relationships where you need to

Improve Phase

13. Generate and select solutions
14. Mitigate potential errors or consequences
15. Develop the implementation plan
16. Implement solutions

Control Phase

17. Standardise processes
18. Develop monitoring and response plans
19. Monitor performance
20. Respond to deviations from plan

Tollgates / Stakeholder Check-ins

While each company might develop its own approach to these components, tollgates and stakeholder check-ins are vital to (a) the learning process and (b) engaging people impacted by any change resulting from the project work.

These steps are shown in diagrammatic form on the following page.

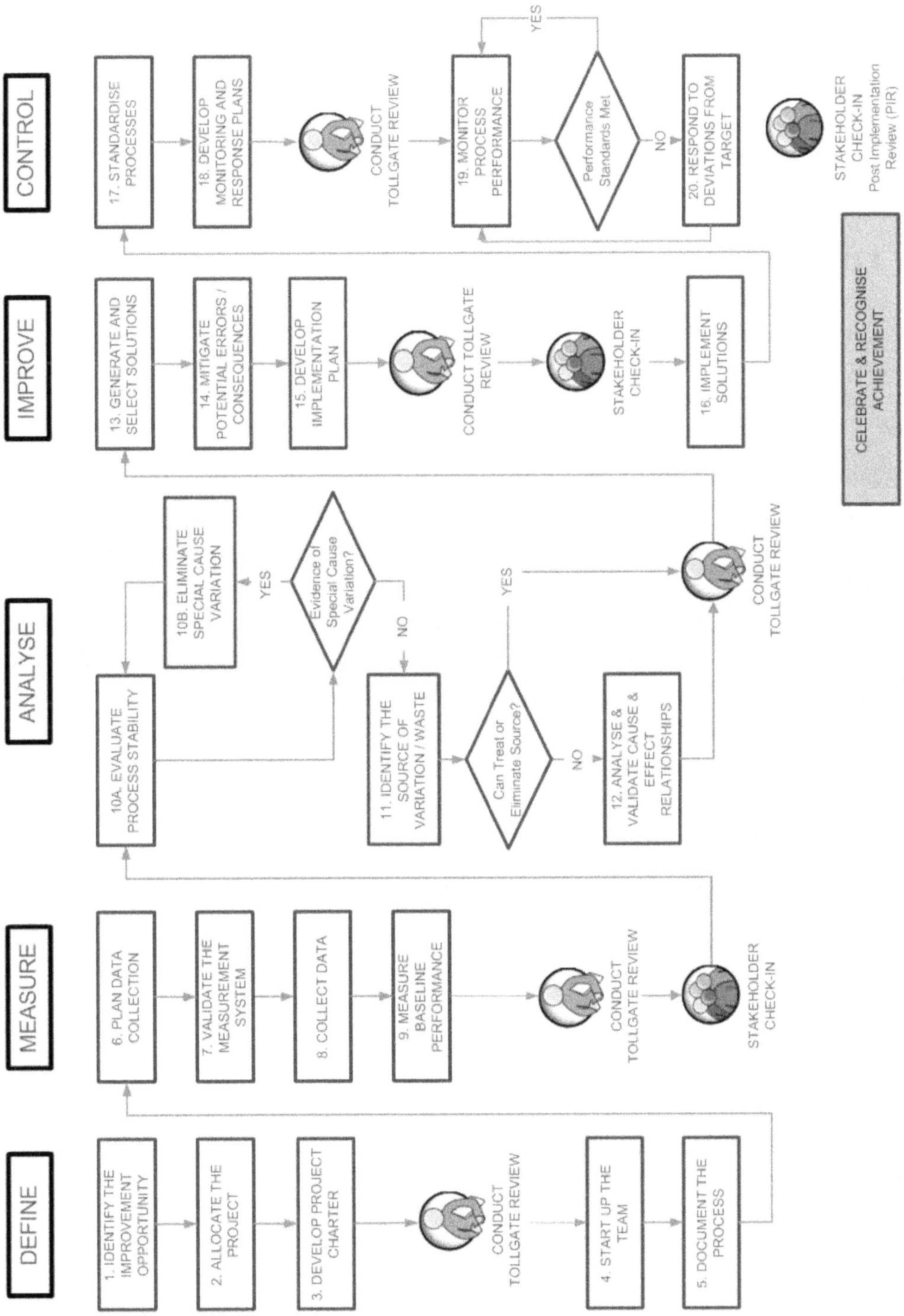

Figure 13: DMAIC Roadmap - 20 Steps to Success

DMAIC AND TRADITIONAL PROJECT MANAGEMENT

I'm often asked about the relationship between Six Sigma and traditional Project Management. I like to answer the question in this way.

Traditional Project Management

Traditional project management (such as that taught in technical colleges) is a framework for facilitating the planning, scheduling and controlling of all activities necessary for achieving specified project objectives.

DMAIC as a Project Management Process

Interestingly enough, the DMAIC sequence can be defined in a similar way, though its application was intended to be in the context of process improvement. With the need for certain principles and tools to be applied in a defined sequence to realise genuine and value-adding improvements, DMAIC has proven to be both efficient and effective in the right context as it is easily repeated and provides the right guidance to the project leader.

2 Projects in One

What's interesting is there are really two projects within the DMAIC sequence. The first project, for which DMAIC is extremely effective, is the *solution identification project*. The second project is the *solution implementation project*.

Traditional project management gets a guernsey within the DMAIC model as a framework and set of tools for managing the implementation of solutions *after* they've been chosen by the team - the second project in this case. The traditional framework and tools are used extensively in steps 15 and 16 as defined in our 20 step roadmap shown on previous pages.

Note:

1. More detail on project management is provided in the Lean Six Sigma Project Improve Phase chapter of this book.
2. Read the next section, particularly the notes on 'project phases'.

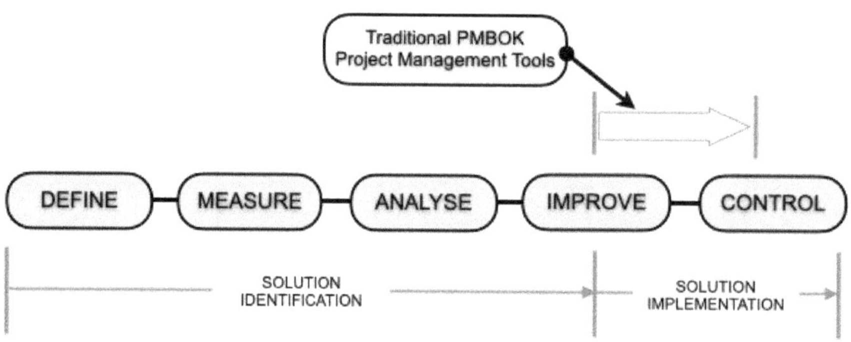

Figure 14: DMAIC Project Management & Traditional Project Management

THE IMPROVEMENT PROJECT COMPONENT MATRIX

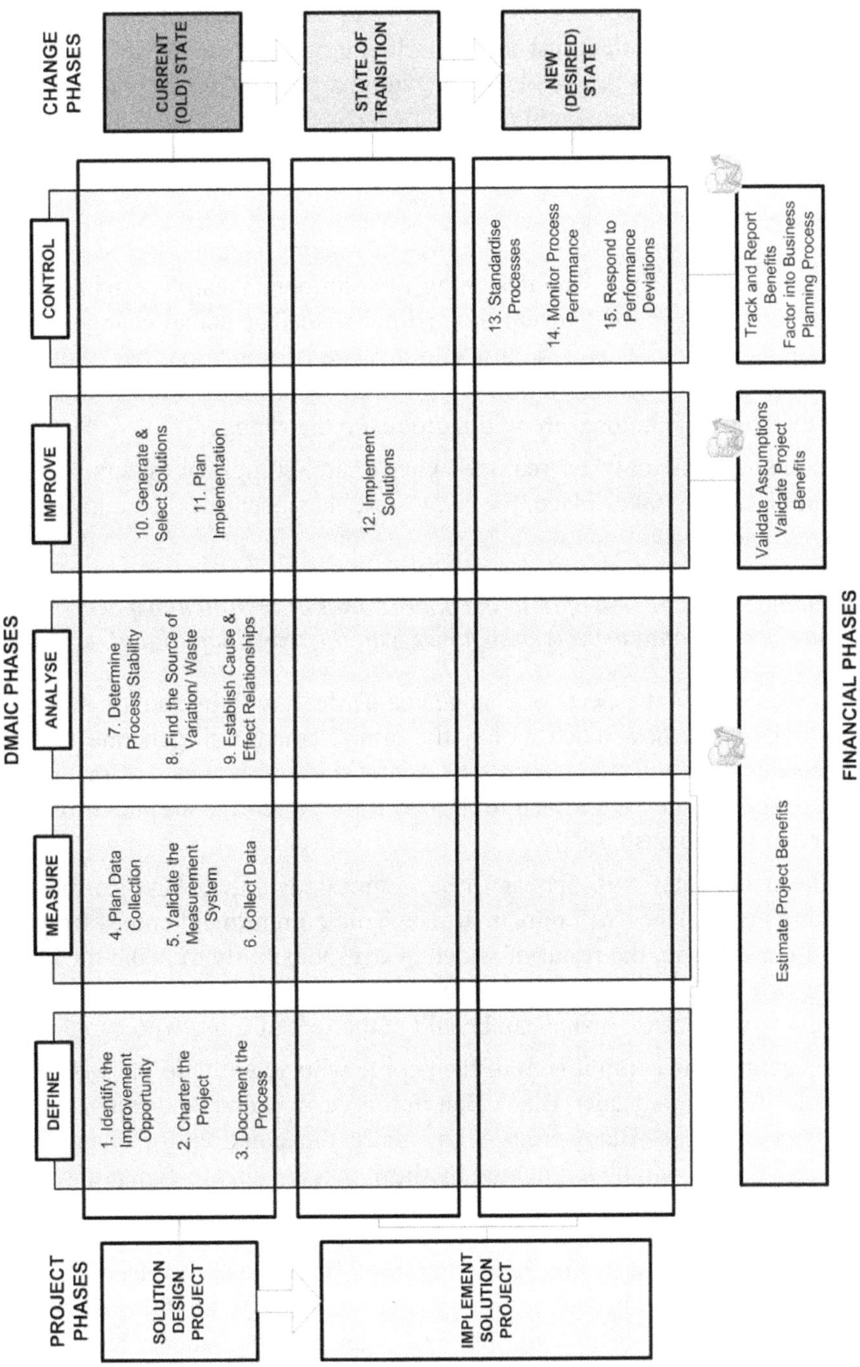

Figure 15: Improvement Project Component Matrix

Project Components

Virtually all text I have ever read on the subject of Six Sigma makes continual reference to the DMAIC component of Lean Six Sigma project work. Whilst this is an integral part of the overall initiative, in reality there is much more to the initiative than just the DMAIC pieces. In reality, DMAIC is the major part of a group of interlocking pieces at the project level. In summary, DMAIC interlocks with the elements of Change Leadership, Financial Management and Project Management as shown in the figure on the previous page.

Change Phases

An improvement project is undertaken for the purpose of making change, hence the need to consider the phases associated with leading change. The designing of solutions takes place while the old way of doing things exists, in effect remaining in the 'current or existing' state. The actual change takes place when steps are taken to implement a solution. This is a shift into a 'state of transition' between the old state and the intended new state. Strategies for dealing with the emotional aspects of change must be employed by the Black Belt to ensure that key stakeholders are willing to make the change.

Sustainability of the change will only be realised when that willingness occurs. Once the solutions are implemented and commissioning takes place, the 'new state' has been reached and focus shifts to ensuring the new way stays over time.

*'Effective change is a function of both the **operational or technical aspects** of the desired state, and the **emotional aspects** associated with the transition to that desired state.'*

I've heard it said that the emotional aspects of change can be dealt with by showing the financial benefits of the new state. By demonstrating how much money the improvement will generate will be sufficient to get people on board. Consider this: will those people be committed on the basis of (a) the work will generate money for the business and (b) they have been told to do it by those who are measured on the basis of how much money is generated for the business?

My experience has been that they will appear to be committed if they have to, however the long-term sustainability of process performance will remain at risk. True commitment comes from having participated in the development of the solution, the result of which is a responsibility to make the change actually work. When a solution is thrown at people on the basis of how much money it will generate, there is no emotional connection to making it work because blame can be laid at the feet of those who came up with the idea.

Unless a Black Belt generates the commitment of the people who actually do the work with the process, the project is at risk of failure. The true leader, Black Belt in this case, is one who can get people to change their behaviour willingly, not by force. Black Belts who ignore the emotions of change and rely on formal authority and money as a driver, will be left behind by those that are able to generate willing commitment.

Financial Phases

One of the driving forces for any Lean Six Sigma initiative is the desire to grow the value of a business. Let's be realistic about this, most businesses in the world today, with the exception of not-for-profit organisations, exist for the purpose of making money for its owners. Without the connection to financial benefit, the leaders of the organisation will not give the initiative the focus that it requires and deserves. Their energies will be directed to those initiatives that do grow the value of the business.

Black Belts will ultimately progress through three financial phases. I want to acknowledge at this time that some projects will deliver benefits other than financial, for example some projects will result in the reduction of risk. These types of benefits can be treated in much the same way as financial benefits with respect to the three phases.

In phase one the Black Belt will be required to estimate the benefits that the project will deliver. Estimates will be based on the size of the performance gap that has been identified, and the corresponding cost (or missed opportunity) that this gap brings to the organisation. At this time however, there may not be enough information at hand to accurately estimate that cost, and even less to finalise improvement goals which ultimately determine the benefits that the team will generate. In phase two, these benefits and associated assumptions are validated as greater knowledge of the process and the context of the project is generated. The projected benefits at this time are a more accurate indicator of the projects worth. In phase three benefits are tracked and reported, and gains are factored into future forecasts (business plans).

It is worthy of mention here that the highest risk for Lean Six Sigma in a business is associated with the accuracy of claimed financial benefits. The credibility, hence the long-term viability of Lean Six Sigma, may well rest on how accurate claimed benefits are. The true benefits are those that are captured and locked into the financial management system of the business. Unless claimed benefits *actually reach the bottom line*, and ultimately earnings per share, they are not benefits at all. Regardless of whether or not they were inaccurately calculated in the first place or diverted elsewhere, those that determine how much a business is worth will only be interested in the bottom line figures.

Project Phases

Now while all of these things are happening, the Black Belt must not lose sight of the fact that they are in fact managing a number of sequential projects. The first project, with the goal of designing a solution has its own life cycle and a team with the content knowledge to get to the solution. The team's work passes through the 'DMA' and most of the 'I' phases of DMAIC.

The second project phase takes place when the solution is actually implemented and the 'I' part of DMAIC is completed. This phase may even involve a different team of people to finalise. In all cases, this phase requires the development of a project plan with its own life cycle. This phase takes the process into a state of transition and the components of change leadership are an integral part of the implementation plan.

The final component of this phase takes place when the solutions have been implemented, and the focus shifts to sustaining performance over the long term. During this period the 'C' component of DMAIC is completed.

I have discussed these interlocking pieces very briefly. However, the intent of this book at this time is to focus on the DMAIC component of Lean Six Sigma. This is not to suggest that those other pieces are not important. Some of the tools of change leadership have been included in the material, it is important however to recognise that the strategy of how to accelerate sustainable change is not covered.

CHAPTER 3: ORGANISING FOR LEAN SIX SIGMA PROJECT WORK

ROLES AND RESPONSIBILITIES

Project Sponsor

Whether or not a steering committee exists, one of the most critical roles in Lean Six Sigma is that of project sponsor. Without the backing of an effective sponsor, even the best team leaders will find it difficult to function. In some organisations, this role is referred to as 'project leader'.

A project sponsor is usually a high level manager or business leader who has a clear understanding of CI and Lean Six Sigma concepts, and whose behaviour demonstrates total commitment to continually improving the business.

The sponsor is ultimately responsible for the project work, and hence functions include:

- Selecting improvement opportunities that add real value to stakeholders
- Chartering projects
- Allocating resources to the project
- Setting project goals (in conjunction with the team leader and process owner)
- Defining and approving the project scope (in conjunction with the team leader and process owner)
- Holding regular project reviews with the team leader and process owner
- Represent the project team and present periodic progress reports to the business leader or steering committee
- Remove barriers to project progress
- Collaborate with process owners to ensure support for the work and a smooth handover at completion of the project

A sponsor who is both proactive and highly supportive can significantly influence the success of any improvement project. A common challenge for team leaders in the initial stages of their project work is scoping the project effectively. There is often hesitancy for team leaders to deal with this issue for fear of disappointing project sponsors, or to avoid what they perceive might be conflict. A very important role of the project sponsor is to help the team leader to narrow the scope of the project so that the team can focus and make rapid progress.

Process Owner

Suppose you were responsible for a process in your organisation, perhaps the process of managing stock inventories. If you wanted to reduce the number of inventory accuracy errors in your process, you might 'sponsor' a black belt or green belt to undertake a Lean or Six Sigma project if you did not have the time or the resources to do it yourself. Thus, a project sponsor is an individual within the company responsible for a core business process, who 'sponsors' the project team leader in undertaking improvement work with that process.

The process owner is responsible for:

- Allocating resources to the project (such as team members, work space, materials etc);
- Setting project goals in conjunction with the team leader and sponsor;
- Supporting the team leader in accelerating the project through the DMAIC phases – the faster the project can be completed, the sooner benefits are realised;
- Providing process knowledgeable input to the project work;
- Taking responsibility for seeing that solutions are implemented and sustained during the 'Improve' and 'Control' phases of the project; and
- Taking responsibility for controlling and tracking any benefits once solutions are implemented (team leaders should develop monitoring and response plans during the 'improve' phase, and support the sponsor in this work).

These responsibilities vary from organisation to organisation, however one common theme emerges in successful organisations, and that is the assumption of responsibility for the process once the project cycle is completed. It is good practice to free the team leader so they can commence another value adding project.

Master Black Belt

Master Black Belts are responsible for mentoring Black Belts (and Green Belts) throughout the life of a project. Their role is to ensure the project stays on track, and that project team leaders are able to follow the Lean Six Sigma process from a technical perspective and give appropriate focus to the change requirements of their work. The Master Black Belt is an expert in the application of the tools of Lean and Six Sigma, including advanced statistical analysis. They should also be an expert in the concepts of change leadership and application of Lean Six Sigma in a business sense. In reality, good Master Black Belts are a rare commodity, highly sought after and able to make a tremendous contribution to any business. Specific functions of a Master Black Belt include:

- Resolving conflict within project teams where the team is unable to do so themselves;
- Providing statistical support to project team leaders;
- Validating reported financial benefits in conjunction with the Finance Representative;
- Mentoring project sponsors and process owners;
- Mentoring business leaders;
- Facilitating change acceleration activities;
- Facilitate project selection activities in support of line managers; and
- Leading training for Sponsors, Process Owners, Black Belts and Green Belts.

In many organisations they play the role of organisation change agents, promoting the use of Lean Six Sigma processes and tools. They can assist the steering group with value stream analysis and project selection.

Project Team Leader

The project team leader role is likely the most critical role in any CI strategy implementation. Team leaders are responsible for using the tools and processes of your improvement methodology, which should include 'change leadership' and 'statistics'. The period of training (for a Lean Six Sigma practitioner receiving competency based training) can vary between three and six weeks spread over the course of three to six months. During this time it's ideal that participants work on an actual project and apply a week's worth of tools between training sessions. It's really a strategy of 'Just in Time' training.

For simple CI initiatives, my experience is that quality training can range from two days of basic tools to nine days of training in both the technical and people side of improvement and problem solving.

The most effective team leaders demonstrate qualities such as these:

- High levels of energy;
- Drive and leadership; and
- Competency in the application of tools of a statistical nature, as well as change leadership and team facilitation.

Team Leaders are usually employees with high potential for promotion, and (if full time) ideally serve a period of 18 to 24 months in this role. Functions of this role include:

- Developing the project charter in conjunction with the project sponsor and process owner;
- Selecting the project team in conjunction with the project sponsor and process owner;
- Preparing and maintaining a project schedule, and progressing the project according to the agreed schedule;
- Planning and facilitating team meetings;
- Follow the 'improvement process' and apply appropriate tools from the 'improvement tool-box';
- Maintaining a record of the project work, and communicating progress;
- Transfer knowledge to team members on the use of the tools of Lean Six Sigma;
- Facilitating the creation of a detailed implementation plan for solutions;
- Reporting realised financial benefits for an agreed period of time, post-solution implementation;
- Monitoring implementation progress, post-handover to the process owner; and
- Ensuring team successes are recognised and celebrated.

Project team leaders are most commonly referred to as black belts or green belts in a Lean Six Sigma strategy, although the functions may differ in some ways from organisation to organisation. Black belts are trained to a higher standard (advanced statistical analysis tools) and are appointed to a full-time position working on larger scale cross-divisional projects. Green belts are part-time team leaders who work on more localised projects. They do not receive the same level of training as a black belt, so are supported by those people with respect to managing change and analysing data using advanced statistical analysis tools.

It's not uncommon to have Black Belts as mentors to Green Belts.

Project Team Member

In recognising that one of the most effective ways to improve a process is to ask the people who work with it, the reportable improvement efforts of a company implementing CI will come from the work of project teams. Team members provide the content input for the project, as well as helping spread the word about CI. They are primarily drawn from the group of people who are knowledgeable about the process being worked on. The team may also include customers, suppliers, ad hoc experts, and individuals with specific qualities you need at different stages of the project.

In most cases, project teams are part time, and meet with the black belts or green belts on a regular basis.

Financial Analyst

The financial analyst's role is critical to the credibility of Lean Six Sigma, and the claimed impact the initiative has on the bottom line performance of the organisation. Usually a representative of the organisation's finance group, the finance analyst's tasks include:

- **Benefit Estimates** - to assist project team leaders, process owners and sponsors in estimating benefits from CI project work.
- **Signing Off** - for claimed financial benefits.
- **Tracking Results** - of all projects and providing regular reports as required by the organisation.
- **Identifying and Documenting New Assumptions** – for business planning cycles. Benefits will never be long term unless any improvements in specific metrics (for example tyre life before replacement, production rates, consumption rates per unit for some material, etc) that are used to build business plans, are actually applied during the next planning cycle. It's not uncommon to realise a benefit against a specific variable that adds bottom line value, but the saving is spent elsewhere and nothing really changes where it matters most.

Typically, financial benefit estimates are made during project selection, the define stage of the project, and just before implementation of any solutions or changes to the process. Actual benefits are then recorded and reported post-implementation.

The financial analyst should be trained to the level of green belt as a minimum to ensure they have a clear understanding of the technical aspects of Lean and Six Sigma methodologies.

PROJECT REPORTING STRUCTURE

The way in which project structures are defined is determined by the availability of resources, and the maturity of the organisation in question.

The figure below depicts the structure for Lean Six Sigma or CI projects that reflects the principles of leading practices I've observed.

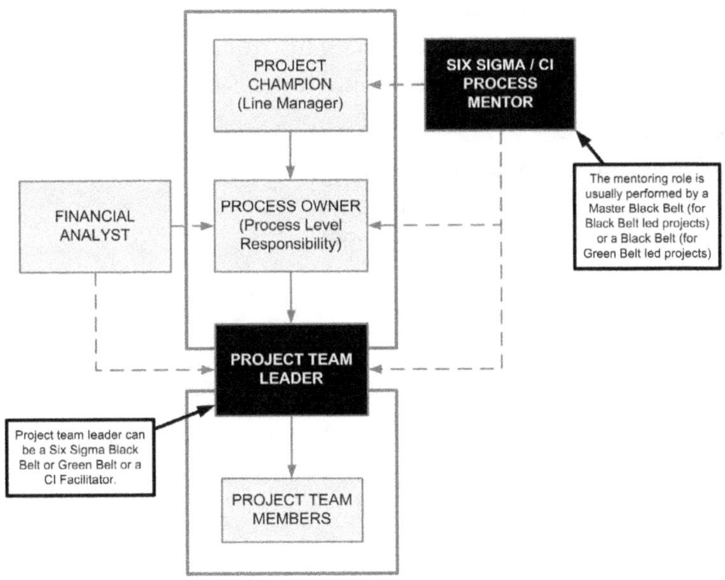

Figure 16: Project Organising Structure

Why This Structure Works

The principles behind the success of a structure such as this one include these.

- Line Managers are actively engaged and play a role in progressing projects that add value to their area of accountability – they don't just hand it over to the team to look after;
- Project Team Leaders receive mentoring and coaching, a vital element in building capability and maximising results; and
- Reported financial benefits are more likely to withstand scrutiny when someone with relevant financial expertise supports process owners and project team leaders.

REPORTING PROJECT PROGRESS

Project progress reviews are absolutely vital to the success of the formal project approach. Why - because of the behaviours the review strategy consistently drives.

- When a Business Leaders are aware of the value a project will bring to their area of responsibility, they are more likely to give leverage to its progress;
- Sponsors must actively interact with project team leaders and process owners if they have to report project progress and its value to a business leader; and
- Sponsors take on more accountability for project progress due to the level of accountability placed on them by the business leader.

Frequency of Review

How often should progress reports be delivered? Let me offer you these suggestions as a guideline.

Project Team Leader TO Project Sponsor and Process Owner

Weekly report on progress over the past week, any benefits to date, progress planned for the next month, changes to the proposed value the project will deliver and timings etc.

Project Sponsor TO Business Leader

Monthly on a formal basis, no team leader to help, present project status, actual progress, plans for the future, actual and estimated benefits to the business, and any relevant time frames etc.

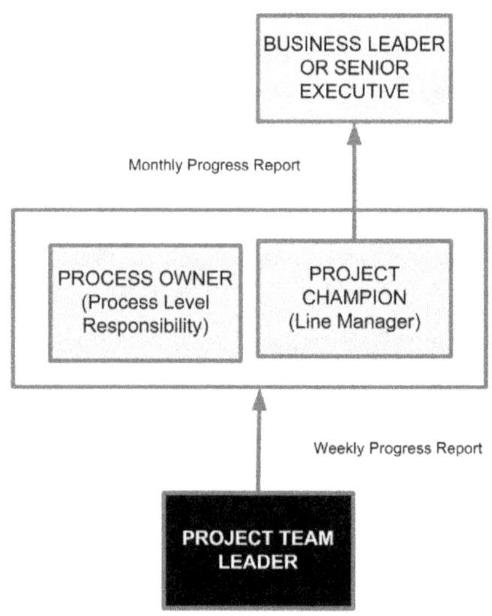

Figure 17: Reporting Structure and Frequency

KEY LEARNING POINTS

- QA and QI are not synonymous with one another. Both can exist in an organisation without the other.
- Quality Improvement takes quality control to a higher level, with a focus on continuously improving quality to meet the ever-changing tastes and preferences of consumers.
- QA provides the framework for giving customers confidence that an organisation has a quality management system in place, and is adhering to quality standards.
- Six Sigma focuses on **reducing variation and increasing process capability and yield** through the application of statistically oriented tools. Six Sigma is the study and control of process variables, an effort in maximising process *effectiveness*.
- Lean is primarily concerned with **eliminating waste and improving flow through a process** via the application of Lean principles.
- When Lean and Six Sigma are integrated, an organisation can undertake improvements in quality and variation as well as improving flow through the process and removing unnecessary time.
- Project team leaders must be aware that there is more to leading an improvement project than just the tools and pieces of DMAIC.
- The DMAIC strategy interlocks with elements of change leadership, project management and financial management.
- Improvement project team leaders must develop project management and change leadership skills as well as the technical skills of improvement methodologies such as Six Sigma.
- Line Managers must be actively engaged and play a role in progressing projects that add value to their area of accountability – they cannot just hand it over to the team to look after.
- Project progress reviews are absolutely vital to the success of the formal project approach.

CHAPTER 4: IMPROVEMENT TOOLS

THE SIX SIGMA TOOLKIT

The table below provides a summary of the most common tools associated with traditional Six Sigma and the DMAIC sequence.

STEP	COMMON SIX SIGMA TOOLS	
DEFINE	Quality Function Deployment (QFD) Customer Comments Worksheet Customer Priority Worksheet Surveys, interview, focus groups etc. CTQ Tree Diagram	Kano Analysis SIPOC / IPO Mapping Project Stakeholder Worksheet Project Charter Process Mapping
MEASURE	XY Worksheet Data Collection Plan Sampling Stratification Plan Rolled Throughput Yield	Gage Accuracy Analysis Gage R&R (Reproducibility & Repeatability) Process Capability Indices Process Sigma
ANALYSE	Control Charts, Run Charts Histograms Graphical Analysis Tools Hypothesis Testing, ANOM Charts Analysis of Variance (ANOVA) Failure Mode & Effect Analysis (FMEA)	Cause & Effect Relationship Diagrams / Tools Scatter Plots / Matrix Plots Correlation & Linear Regression Logistic Regression Multi Vari Analysis Experimental Design (DOE, RSM, Taguchi)
IMPROVE	Regression Models Benchmarking Idea Generation and Decision Making Tools Process Design / Re-design Pilot Studies Implementation Planning Work Breakdown Structure (WBS) Critical Path Method (CPM)	Network Diagrams Program Evaluation & Review Technique (PERT) Schedule Bar Charts (Gantt Charts) Failure Mode & Effect Analysis (FMEA) Project Risk Management Communications Plan Project Management Tools and Techniques
CONTROL	Standard Operating Procedures Training Plan SIPOC CE Tree Diagram	CE Matrix Process Performance Monitoring Plan Statistical Process Control Plan, Control Charts Visual Controls

INTEGRATING LEAN THINKING WITH TRADITIONAL SIX SIGMA

How does Six Sigma's DMAIC model relate to Lean?

I think it is worth highlighting a very important fact: the DMAIC process is a sequence of logic for starting with a performance gap and ending with long term solutions for closing that gap.

Is that the purpose of Lean?

Of course it is. Just like Six Sigma the intent is to implement solutions for improving the efficiencies and effectiveness of processes. The only difference is the focus of the work.

One focuses primarily on reducing variation as a performance measure while the other focuses on minimising processing time and maximising flow.

Different tools are used to achieve these complementary goals, however the logic of (a) defining the performance gap and the process up front, (b) collecting data, (c) undertaking analysis so you understand what you have to treat, (d) identifying and implementing solutions; and (e) making sure new performance levels are controlled and locked in for long term improvement is still the same.

So if that's true, Lean can work within the DMAIC framework, albeit with slightly different tools.

The following diagram offers one perspective of how the technical elements of Lean can be integrated with Six Sigma and the DMAIC approach to improvement project management.

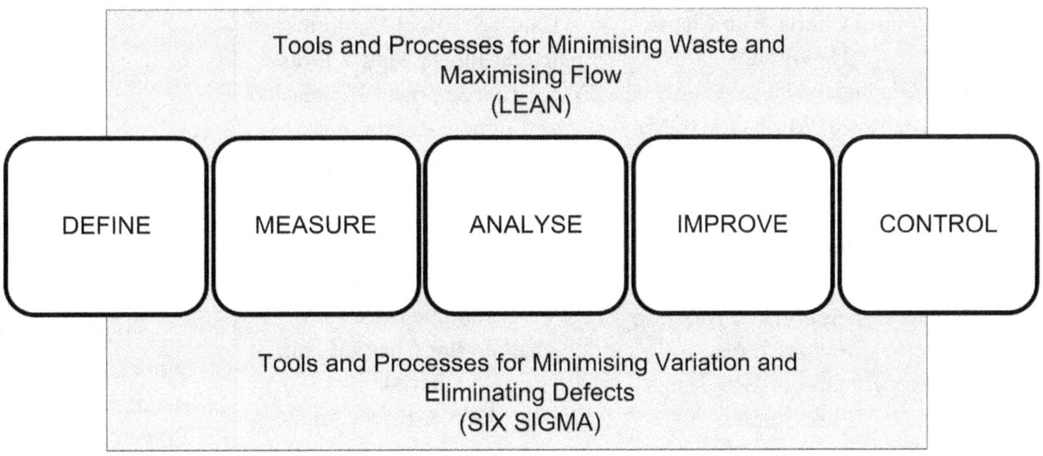

Figure 18: DMAIC with Lean Thinking and Six Sigma

THE LEAN & SIX SIGMA TOOLKIT

The table below provides a summary of the most common tools associated with traditional Six Sigma **and Lean Thinking** as they relate to the full DMAIC sequence.

(NOTE: While this appears similar to the previous table, this one includes Lean tools.)

STEP	COMMON SIX SIGMA TOOLS		LEAN TOOLS
DEFINE	Quality Function Deployment Customer Comments Worksheet Customer Priority Worksheet Surveys, interview, focus groups etc.	CTQ Tree Diagram Kano Analysis SIPOC / IPO Mapping Project Stakeholder Worksheet Project Charter Process Mapping	Value Stream Analysis (Work Flow, Materials Flow, Information Flow) Activity Flowcharting
MEASURE	XY Worksheet Data Collection Plan Sampling Stratification Plan Rolled Throughput Yield	Gage Accuracy Analysis Gage R&R (Reproducibility & Repeatability) Capability Indices Process Sigma	Process Efficiency Metrics (PCE, Total Lead Time, Little's Law) Time Value Analysis
ANALYSE	Control Charts, Run Charts, Histograms Graphical Analysis Tools Analysis of Means (ANOM) Hypothesis Testing Analysis of Variance (ANOVA)	Cause & Effect Diagrams Scatter Plots / Matrix Plots Correlation & Linear Regression Logistic Regression Experimental Design (DOE, RSM, Taguchi)	Takt Time Charts Spaghetti Diagrams Cross Functional Flowchart
IMPROVE	Regression Models Benchmarking Idea Generation and Decision Making Tools Process Design / Re-design Pilot Studies Implementation Planning Work Breakdown Structure (WBS) Critical Path Method (CPM)	Network Diagrams Program Evaluation and Review Technique (PERT) Schedule Bar Charts (Gantt Charts) Failure Mode & Effect Analysis (FMEA) Project Risk Management Communications Plan Project Management Tools	5S / 6S Process Balancing Pull Systems Work Cell Optimisation Mistake Proofing & Mistake Prevention (Poka Yoke) Single Minute Exchange Die (SMED) / QCO Total Productive Maintenance
CONTROL	Standard Operating Procedures Training Plan SIPOC CE Tree Diagram CE Matrix	Performance Monitoring Plan Process Control Plan Control Charts Visual Controls Production Boards	Visual Controls Lean Production Boards

TOOL SUMMARY TABLE 1 – IN DMAIC SEQUENCE

Arranged by DMAIC Step

The following is a list of the most common tools used for process improvement with modern Lean Six Sigma. These are arranged according to the phase of the DMAIC strategy where the tool is commonly used.

The number associated with the sub headings, for example 'Voice of the Customer (Step 1)', refers to the step on the DMAIC roadmap to which this piece applies.

TOOL	REF PAGES	D	M	A	I	C
VOICE OF THE CUSTOMER (STEP 1)						
Voice of the Customer Concepts (VOC)	117, 738	◉				◉
Critical-to-quality (CTQ) Tree Diagram	750, 784	◉				◉
Customer Comments Worksheet	751, 785	◉				◉
Kano Analysis	755	◉				◉
Customer Priorities Worksheet	753, 786	◉				◉
OPPORTUNITY GENERATION (STEP 1)						
Project Idea Generation Tools (various)	115	◉				
SIPOC	118, 733, 782	◉				
Value Stream Analysis	120, 142	◉				
Project Prioritisation Matrix	—	◉				
Quality Function Deployment	126, 146	◉				
CLARIFYING THE PROBLEM / OPPORTUNITY (STEP 3)						
Project Charter	138, 152, 169, 174	◉				
Project Plan	140, 170, 177	◉				
Problem Statement	153	◉				
Goal Statement	157	◉				
Project Constraints and Limitations	158	◉				
Project Scoping	160	◉				
Cost Benefit Forecasting	163	◉				
Project Participant Worksheet	167	◉				
START UP THE PROJECT (STEP 4)						

TOOL	REF PAGES	D	M	A	I	C
Operating Agreement	182	◉				
Meeting Agenda	80, 184, 201	◉	◉	◉	◉	◉
Meeting Tools	68	◉	◉	◉	◉	◉
Communications Planning	185, 200	◉			◉	
Elevator Speech	186	◉	◉	◉	◉	◉
PROCESS DOCUMENTATION (STEP 5)						
Activity Flowcharting	188, 199, 134	◉			◉	◉
IPO Worksheet	191, 198, 237	◉				
KEY PROCESS VARIABLES (STEP 6)						
Descriptive Statistics	212		◉			
Confidence Intervals / Interval Estimation	223		◉			
Data Types / Types of Variables	227		◉			
Frequency Distributions	229		◉	◉		
PLANNING DATA COLLECTION (STEP 6)						
Data Collection Plan	235, 245		◉			
XY Worksheet	240, 344		◉			
Stratification Plan	245		◉			
Operational Definition	243, 346		◉			
Sampling Concepts	247		◉			
Sample Size Calculations	250, 347, 348		◉			
COLLECTING DATA (STEPS 7 & 8)						
MSA Concepts	261		◉			
Gage Bias	264		◉			
Gage Linearity	264		◉			
Gage Stability	265		◉			
Gage Discrimination	265		◉			

TOOL	REF PAGES	D	M	A	I	C
Gage R&R (Variables)	266		◉			
Gage R&R (Attribute)	—		◉			
Data Collection / Data Worksheet	278		◉			
BASELINE PERFORMANCE (STEP 9)						
Probability Distributions	280		◉	◉		
Normality Testing	300		◉			
Project Sigma (DPMO Method)	308, 348		◉			
Process Sigma (Z Score Method)	313, 350		◉			
Short-term / Long-term Variation	315		◉			
Capability Indices	319		◉			
Final Yield	331		◉			
Rolled Throughput Yield	331		◉			
Time Value Analysis	334, 351, 353		◉			
Total Lead Time (Little's Law)	341, 351		◉			
Process Cycle Efficiency (PCE)	342, 351		◉			
PROCESS STABILITY (STEP 10)						
Statistical Process Control Concepts	360, 369			◉		
Run Charts	363			◉		
Control Charts (Attributes)	379, 558			◉		
Control Charts (Variables)	384, 559			◉		
FINDING THE SOURCE OF VARIATION (STEP 11)						
Graphical Data Analysis	395, 560			◉		
Stratification	400			◉		
ANOM Charts	404			◉		
Pivot Charts	405			◉		
Central Limit Theorem	410			◉		

TOOL	REF PAGES	D	M	A	I	C
Hypothesis Testing	416, 562			◉		
2 Way Analysis of Variance (ANOVA)	521			◉		
FINDING THE SOURCE OF WASTE (STEP 11)						
Takt Time Chart	462, 563			◉		
Spaghetti Diagram	465, 564			◉		
Cross Functional Flowchart	467			◉		
STUDYING CAUSE & EFFECT RELATIONSHIPS (STEP 12)						
Cause and Effect Analysis	468			◉		
Cause Effect Diagram	471, 565			◉		
Cause Effect Chain (5 Whats)	473, 566			◉		
Cause Effect Structure Tree	474, 567			◉		
Comparative Cause Effect Analysis	—			◉		
VALIDATING CAUSE & EFFECT RELATIONSHIPS (STEP 12)						
Scatter Plot	480			◉		
Matrix Plot / Scatter Matrix	497			◉		
Pearsons Correlation	482, 500, 568			◉		
Linear Regression	482, 504, 568			◉	◉	
Logistics Regression	517			◉		
Design of Experiments	519, 535, 573			◉	◉	
IDENTIFYING SOLUTIONS - Clues from Others (STEP 13)						
Benchmarking	582				◉	
IDENTIFYING SOLUTIONS - Treating Causes (STEP 13)						
Linear Regression (response optimization)	482, 504, 568				◉	
Design of Experiments (response optimization)	519, 535, 573			◉	◉	
Brainstorming	684				◉	
Channel Brainstorming	684				◉	

TOOL	REF PAGES	D	M	A	I	C
Nominal Group Technique	685				◉	
Solution Thought Mapping	687				◉	
IDENTIFYING SOLUTIONS - Innovation (STEP 13)						
Creativity Principles and Concepts	588				◉	
Anti Solution Brainstorming	685				◉	
Process Analogy Brainstorming	689				◉	
Moments of Truth	743				◉	
IDENTIFYING SOLUTIONS - Organising Ideas (STEP 13)						
Advocacy	692				◉	
Affinity Grouping	692				◉	
Multi Voting	691				◉	
Multi Voting (weighted)	691				◉	
IDENTIFYING SOLUTIONS - Deciding (STEP 13)						
Solution Packaging	599				◉	
Payoff Analysis	695				◉	
Potential Failure Analysis	696					
Absolute Criteria Screening	694				◉	
Weighted Criteria Rating	697				◉	
Paired Ranking	700				◉	
Payback Period	603				◉	
Return on Investment (ROI)	605				◉	
Net Present Value (NPV)	606				◉	
Internal Rate of Return (IRR)	609				◉	
IDENTIFYING SOLUTIONS - Lean Principles (STEP 13)						
5S / 6S	610				◉	
Process Balancing	614, 702				◉	

TOOL	REF PAGES	D	M	A	I	C
Pull Systems	617, 703				◉	
SMED / QCO	619, 704				◉	
Work Cell Optimisation	622, 706				◉	
Total Productive Maintenance	623, 707				◉	
FAILURE / CONSEQUENCE MITIGATION (STEP 14)						
Potential Consequence Analysis	626				◉	
Failure Mode and Effect Analysis (FMEA)	627, 709				◉	
Mistake Prevention & Mistake Proofing	642, 708				◉	
IMPLEMENTATION PLANNING (STEP 15)						
Project Management	643				◉	
Work Scheduling (Gantt / Schedule Bar Charts)	647, 710				◉	
Work Breakdown Structure	647, 711				◉	
Network Diagram	650, 712				◉	
PERT	651, 713				◉	
Critical Path Method (CPM)	653, 714				◉	
Responsibility Matrix	715				◉	
Project Risk Management Planning	659, 721				◉	
Stakeholder Commitment Evaluation	671, 716				◉	
Stakeholder Engagement Planning	673, 717				◉	
Communication Planning	674, 719				◉	
Force Field Analysis	675, 720				◉	
Solution Piloting	676, 723				◉	
Stakeholder Check-In	682					
STANDARDISE PROCESSES (STEP 17)						
Process Documentation	730					◉
Training Plan	731, 781					◉

TOOL	REF PAGES	D	M	A	I	C
PERFORMANCE MONITORING PLANNING (STEP 18)						
Voice of the Customer Concepts (VOC)	738	◉				◉
Critical-to-quality (CTQ) Tree Diagram	750, 784	◉				◉
Customer Comments Worksheet	751, 785	◉				◉
Kano Analysis	755	◉				◉
Customer Priorities Worksheet	753, 786	◉				◉
SIPOC	733, 782	◉				◉
Cause Effect Tree Diagram	761, 787	◉				◉
Cause Effect Matrix	764, 788	◉				◉
Process Performance Monitoring Plan	767, 790	◉				◉
PROCESS PERFORMANCE CONTROL PLANNING (STEP 18)						
Visual Controls	771					◉
Takt Boards	772					◉
Production Boards	773					◉
Performance Dashboards	773					◉
Process Performance Control Plan	777, 791					◉
MISCELLANEOUS						
Accelerated Improvement Projects / Kaizen	815	◉	◉	◉	◉	◉

PART 2 - IMPROVEMENT PROJECT LEADERSHIP

CHAPTER 5: PROJECT LEADERSHIP

SHIFTING PARADIGMS

Many participants in Lean Six Sigma training experience a significant paradigm shift. Let's just think about our education for a moment.

All of us studied hard to be where we are today. Most of us undertook training to learn how to find solutions to problems, how to provide the answer to specific questions within your area of study. We then entered the workforce and found ourselves providing answers to questions. Over years of work we continue this approach, moving into management roles where we not only continue to provide solutions, but are also *expected* in most cases to provide solutions.

Is that how it should work? Have you ever experienced resistance when you try to roll out a solution that you came up with? Would resistance change if the workforce actually came up with the ideas themselves?

Lean Six Sigma is focused on the concept of 'empowerment' or 'workforce collaboration'. This empowerment or collaboration occurs when leaders recognise that solutions are provided upward, and the role of the leader is that of vehicle or conduit through which workers are able to generate and implement solutions.

The paradigm shift for Black Belts occurs when they realise their role shifts according to the table below.

THE OLD PARADIGM		THE NEW PARADIGM
Giving the Answers	➽	Extracting the Answers
Focus on Content or Subject Matter	➽	Focus on the Process
Focus on Technical Elements of Change	➽	A Balanced Focus on both Technical and Emotional Elements of Change
Come up with Ideas through Creative Thinking	➽	Promote and Facilitate Creative Thinking and Innovation

What are the implications of this shift in mental models? Well quite simply, the Black Belt role is that of a leader. The Black Belt has to 'lead' a team to a new way of thinking, and this role does not come without its challenges.

THE CHALLENGE OF LEADING TEAMS

Team leadership can provide all types of wonderful challenges for a Black Belt. To be able to do so effectively, taking the team and the project to a successful conclusion is both a rewarding and growing experience.

At appropriate times throughout the book, you will see tips from Black Belts who have experienced the challenges of leading project teams.

Over the next few pages, you will see various processes and tools to help you facilitate your project to a successful conclusion. This type of result can be consistently achieved if you give these tools a try, and adapt them to your particular facilitative style.

WORKING WITH THE TEAM

> *'In an effective team, team spirit has to be created so that the members work for the benefit of the group. To achieve its task the group needs each member, and so it is in the interests of the group to develop the skills of each member ... Good individuals do not automatically make a good team until they learn to operate as one.'*
>
> ***David Trethowan (Teamwork)***

Teamwork is an essential element of Lean Six Sigma project success. Some of the benefits associated with Lean Six Sigma project work in teams include:

- Capitalising on the synergy created through the depth and diversity of knowledge that exists within a team.
- Improvements can be accelerated and sustained due to the level of ownership that can be generated.
- The methodologies of Lean and Six Sigma will permeate day to day work and over the long term create a shift in thinking (with respect to problem solving and process improvement).

Regardless of whether it's on the field for sports, or in the workplace, it takes time for a team to come together. There is a natural development process or maturing process every team progresses through. Psychologist B.W. Tuckman describes the four stages of team development as:

1. FORMING – the phase during which a team is getting to know one another and the roles each will perform in the team structure.
2. STORMING – conflicts are brought to the surface and resolved.
3. NORMING – members settle into their team roles and a sense of team membership begins to develop.
4. PERFORMING – the team unites in working towards common goals.

Teams can cycle through these stages relatively easily or they can get stuck in a stage. Teams in the past have disbanded because it was never able to progress beyond the storming stage. A team that has progressed to the point of norming can get thrown back to the storming stage with the inclusion of new people in the team.

Let's take a closer look at each of these stages.

Forming

Think about your first days at school. I remember that on my first day everyone was very polite, uncertain about what to expect, and probably more cautious about what they did and said than at any other time. The forming stage for a team is much like that. Team members are getting to know one another, trying to get comfortable with the new relationships that are forming. They will be trying to understand their role and the role of others in the group, and may be unsure, nervous and even suspicious of one another. This stage will be defined by certain behaviours including:

- Trying to define the task at hand and who is responsible for what;
- Telling team members about their achievements and who they are outside the team;
- Conceptual discussions at the macro level; and even
- Pairing off.

The team leader should schedule time and activities to let team members get to know one another. The purpose of the team, roles and expectations should be defined up front.

Storming

As the team enters the storming stage, politeness will wear off and dissension may occur over who is responsible for what things, the process being used, and whose ideas are going to progress. This stage is the most difficult one, albeit a necessary one for healthy team development. When team members build enough trust to be able to air their differences or speak the 'unspeakable', it's a signal that the team is ready to work things out for themselves and become a team.

This stage will be defined by certain characteristics including:

- Team members showing their true nature;
- Impatience with one another;
- Impatience over any lack of progress;
- Competition for roles of perceived importance; and
- General disagreement over process and content issues.

This stage must not be ignored. Recognise that it is a natural and necessary step in the process of team development and surfacing and addressing conflicts within the team. Ground rules will prove invaluable, as will reflection on the desired outcome of the team. By focusing them on the goal, commitment to team progress will be greater.

Norming

When differences have been recognised and settled, the team moves into the norming stage. This is the stage when they see ideas as those of the team, progress as a result of the team's work and decisions as team decisions. The energy that was being absorbed in working out differences and emotional conflicts now gets spent on progressing towards the team's desired outcome.

This stage will be defined by certain characteristics:

- Ground rules will be taken more seriously;
- Behavioural norms will become obvious;
- The team will want to discuss items more openly;
- All team members will participate in activities;
- Subgroups may be formed to progress work; and

- Any conflicts that arise are quickly addressed and easily resolved.

During this stage, the team leader should not lose focus on process. Ground rules should be revisited at the start of each meeting. Effective behaviour should be recognised and positively reinforced.

Performing

Performing is the final stage of team development. Performing teams are highly effective and can solve content and process problems quickly and efficiently.

The performing stage will be defined by certain characteristics including:

- The team will accomplish tasks on time and look for more to do;
- The team will demonstrate initiative, not waiting for direction to take useful action;
- Members will show loyalty for one another and the team; and
- Dissension and disagreement will be addressed in a manner that shows respect for different perspectives.

In the performing stage, the team will be self-directing. The role of the team leader will be to ensure that the direction taken by the team is one that leads to achievement of the desired outcome, not some other outcome. A team can easily get caught up in content and lose sight of the goal.

The Role of Project Team Leader

A project team leader's role is to ensure that a performing team is developed as quickly as possible. One of the most serious mistakes a team leader can make is to focus the first team meeting agenda on content items. The first team meeting is critical in starting the process of team building and time must be scheduled for that purpose. Some of the most useful agenda items will be those drawn from the following section that discusses the elements of team performance.

ELEMENTS OF TEAM PERFORMANCE

A performing team is one that demonstrates certain characteristics. The key characteristics of an effective team include those that fall into the categories of focus, leverage, understanding and motion.

FOCUS	LEVERAGE
UNDERSTANDING	MOTION

Figure 19: Four Characteristics of an Effective Team

Focus

A team that is focused has power, and by power I mean 'the ability to act'. By focus I mean that all heads are turned in the same direction, work is specific to the desired outcomes of the team, and the work of the team is not a means to an end in itself but rather work that is value adding to the team's customers. A focused team knows:

- What their ultimate purpose is – their mission;
- What they must specifically achieve - specific goals;

- Who their customers are – primary and tertiary;
- What the needs and expectations of their customers are; and
- The scope of their work and constraints they have to work under.

Focus can be generated by (a) defining the mission or reason why the team has been brought together, (b) discussing the specific goals to be achieved, (c) having the team identify the customers of their work, (d) documenting expectations the customers have of the team's work – these may be beyond the 'specific goals' of the team, and (e) identifying the scope of the team's work and the constraints under which the team has to work and make decisions.

Leverage

Leverage is created when there is a reason for doing something.

Reasons come before action, and when compelling enough, are driving forces for action. The team is leveraged when team members share:

- Compelling reasons to do the work.

Leveraged teams demonstrate commitment to the mission of the team because they know why it's important to achieve. To leverage a team, have them document (a) why the work is important to do in terms of the benefits that will be gained by doing it, and (b) the consequences of not doing anything.

Understanding

Part of the challenge with working in teams, is associated with the dynamics that result from the diversity that exists amongst people. A functional team can be created when all team members have a clear understanding of:

- Team roles and responsibilities;
- Expectations for working together;
- The values that the team must share to drive the right individual and team behaviour; and
- What it is that each person brings to the team.

Understanding can be achieved by (a) defining roles and responsibilities up front, (b) establishing ground rules, (c) listing the behaviours that are necessary for success, and the values that would underpin those behaviours, and (d) documenting and recognising the skills and knowledge that each person brings to the team.

Motion

A team in motion is one that is working effectively towards the desired outcome, a state I like to refer to as 'directed motion'. The characteristics of a team in directed motion are:

- Actions are planned;
- Individual tasks are completed on time; and
- Expected results are being achieved.

This type of motion is achieved through (a) the development and execution of action plans that are results focused and purpose driven [sound action plans will describe the results to be achieved, who does what, when that action is to be completed, and why the result is important to achieve], and (b) progress against action plans is monitored and reviewed to ensure 'directed motion' is maintained.

MEETING ROLES

One of the key elements of team success is the definition of roles. The most common roles in meetings include these.

1. Project team leader;
2. Facilitator;
3. Time keeper;
4. Scribe;
5. Recorder; and
6. Team member.

The responsibilities associated with the last four of these roles are listed below. The role of project team leader as facilitator is discussed in the next section.

Time Keeper

The timekeeper role is not necessary when the facilitator takes responsibility for his or her own time keeping. One limitation associated with that approach however, is that ownership and accountability for managing time is retained at the facilitator level. By appointing a timekeeper, the accountability for time shifts to the team with positive effect. When times get tight, it's not the facilitator putting pressure on the team but a peer.

Some of the tasks of a timekeeper include:

- Ensure a clock or watch is available for the meeting
- Participate as a team member
- Ask facilitators how they want to be notified about time (5 minutes before deadline etc)
- Monitor meeting timings
- Notify facilitators as the deadline approaches for each agenda item according to your agreement with them

Scribe

The scribe is the person who captures information on a flip-chart or whiteboard in full view of the meeting participants.

Some of the tasks of a scribe include:

- Participate as a team member
- Write on boards or flip-charts according to the instructions given by the facilitator
- Record the words of the speaker where possible

Recorder

The recorder is responsible for capturing key items from the meeting that are taken away for follow up.

Some of the tasks of a recorder include:

- Participate as a team member
- Record action items (who, what, by when)
- Record key meeting items
- Prepare meeting minutes in association with the project team leader

Team Member

Team members are extremely important to the success of any project. The team member role extends beyond the duration of the meeting and includes:

Preparation for the Meeting

- Check that any necessary tasks are completed
- Bring any item as requested
- Confirm your attendance
- Preview the agenda
- Prepare to contribute to the meeting
- Prepare to bring an open mind to the meeting

Follow Up After the Meeting

- Complete allocated tasks by the agreed time / date

During the Meeting

- Actively participate
- Share experience and knowledge
- Help the team leader with keeping the meeting on track, i.e., help with the meeting process
- Provide honest and constructive feedback
- Volunteer for action items
- Schedule the next meeting in your calendar
- Provide meeting feedback at its conclusion

By defining and building agreement around these roles at the start of a team's work together, the probability of success is substantially greater.

'In a Quality Improvement environment, meetings are a mechanism where opportunities are identified and resolved. They are also learning environments. This requires that we tap into the diverse knowledge that individuals possess. In order to best achieve this, meetings need to stimulate and engage team members. This requires meetings to be interactive both physically and mentally as physical activity promotes greater mental activity. We only need to think about meetings we've attended where we passively sit at a table with a notebook in front of us. How creative is that type of meeting? Is it the best learning environment where people can contribute? The challenge in most organisations is to break these traditional paradigms.'

Harry Sinko

MEETING TOOLS AND TECHNIQUES

Some of the most common and effective yet simple tools used by meeting facilitators include:

- Ground Rules
- 'I' Time
- The Parking Lot
- Brainstorming
- Multi Voting
- Meeting Feedback

Meeting Ground Rules

Why do you suppose a game of soccer has rules that the players have to abide by? Imagine a game of soccer without rules; it would be chaos. And so it is with meetings. Rules are necessary for ensuring behaviours that allow a team to achieve the results they are supposed to achieve.

Rules for meetings are usually referred to as ground rules. Ground rules help a team leader manage the dynamics of a team during a meeting and are the basis for behavioural norms. They describe what will and won't happen during a meeting and are generated by asking the team questions like 'What rules do we need to establish for our meetings, to ensure we achieve our desired outcomes in the most effective way?'

Here is an example of a set of meeting ground rules.

Ground Rules

- Meetings to start on time
- Punctual return from breaks
- Turn off mobile phones
- Ask questions
- One person speaking

Figure 20: Example Ground Rules for a Team Meeting

Individual (I) Time

'I' time is defined as time for the individual. 'I' time is established to allow individuals to think and reflect on questions or ideas. Recognising that we each process information and 'incubate' ideas at our own rate, 'I' time allows individual team members to think without feeling pressured to come up with answers at the same rate as other members of the team. The desired outcome is the generation of quality input from all team members.

To use this process, the facilitator should establish a specific time limit (e.g. five minutes) for members to sit quietly and concentrate on the question or idea under discussion. It is often useful to allow team members to find a location that best suits them.

Parking Lot

Parking lots are temporary holding areas for suggestions, ideas or topics that are not directly related to the purpose of the meeting. When ideas outside the boundaries of the meeting purpose come up, they can potentially take the team meeting off track, result in lost time and ultimately prevent the team achieving what they set out to achieve. If these ideas are 'parked' temporarily while the meeting progresses, ideas are not lost while the desired outcomes of the meeting are still achieved.

Facilitators should post a separate flip-chart labeled 'Parking Lot' so that it is visible to all team members.

If an idea or suggestion comes under discussion and the team agrees that it is one worth keeping but not one associated with this meeting, the idea should be written down in the parking lot for later discussion.

It's important to remember to review parking lot items at the end of a meeting.

If items are resolved, they can be removed, otherwise these might form items for the next team meeting agenda.

Brainstorming

Brainstorming is the fundamental procedure used by teams to generate data.

Formally developed in 1941 by A.F. Osborne, the process involves a team generating as many responses as they can to a question, usually in a limited time frame. Quantity, not quality, is the goal.

A scribe captures ideas directly onto a flip chart, or alternatively they can be individually written on 'Post It Notes' by the originators of the idea and then posted on a board. When ideas are thrown up randomly from the group, this is sometimes referred to as the 'Popcorn' method of brainstorming.

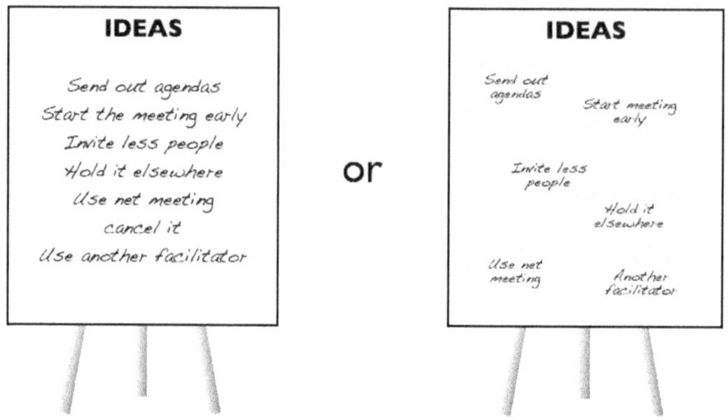

The rules of brainstorming are:

- All ideas are recorded, verbatim. Use the words of the person who made the suggestion.
- Avoid any discussion of ideas during the session – discussion will immediately channel team members' thoughts away from the goal of idea generation.
- Do not criticise ideas, regardless of how crazy you perceive them to be.
- Listen to all team members' ideas and look for connections or ideas that can be built upon.
- Encourage a low risk creative environment. Do not censor ideas.
- When using Post It Notes, have team members state their idea verbally as they write it down.

Brainstorming variations can be used to provide variety for a team, as well as work through any dynamics that has the potential to stifle the creativity of the team. Variations are wide and varied and include the following (Some of these are discussed in more detail in Chapters 18 and 19):

- Round Robin Brainstorming – Each person takes turn to generate ideas. Nominal Group Technique (NGT) is a variant of this approach.
- Channel Brainstorming – A problem or subject is segmented into parts or different ideas that become the categories for channeling the thoughts of participants. Brainstorming is then undertaken within each category.
- Anti Solution Brainstorming – Members brainstorm ideas to achieve a goal that is ulterior to the real goal. For example, if a team wants ideas for reducing time, they start by brainstorming ideas for extending time. The underlying principles are identified before ideas are then generated for achieving the original goal.
- Anonymous Alternatives Brainstorming – Members record their ideas on cards. These are collected and posted in such a way that the originator remains anonymous. The originator has the option of clarifying or remaining anonymous during discussion.

- Association Brainstorming – Ideas are generated from the association made with an analogy, a word or even a picture.

Multi Voting

With so many ideas generated through brainstorming, how does a team reduce the list?

Multi voting is one approach that draws upon the content expertise of the team, driving them towards choosing those ideas that are more likely to be the best ideas for achieving the desired outcome. It is referred to as a group aggregation tool where a facilitator can 'aggregate' the collective bias of a knowledgable team.

Multi voting involves each person indicating their preferences by choosing 1/3 of the ideas that they believe best answer the question or address the problem at hand.

They can indicate by placing a tick against 1/3 of the ideas, or a sticky dot, or silently recording an alphabetical reference for each idea they choose.

When tagging ideas for reference, facilitators should use alphabetical references as opposed to numbers that might indicate priority.

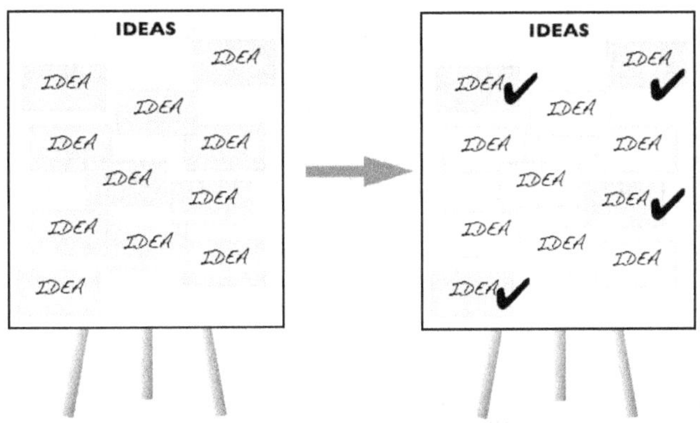

Multi voting is usually used when the team has a good knowledge of the content being discussed. In the absence of that knowledge, the choices made are less likely to be the most appropriate for achieving the desired outcome.

Meeting Feedback

One of the best ways to improve performance is to get feedback. Meetings are no different, and facilitators should seek to be continually improving their meeting processes, particularly when they involve a series of meetings with the same team.

Feedback should involve identifying (a) those things that worked well for the team and they want to see continued or repeated, and (b) the changes that the team would like to see and [most importantly] a suggestion for doing that.

Numerous approaches can be undertaken to capture these ideas including:

- Place a flip chart near the exit and have team members write their ideas on Post It Notes and place them on the flip chart as they exit.
- Discuss as a group and capture ideas on the flip chart as they come up.

Meeting feedback is sometimes referred to as Plus Deltas (Delta or △ is Greek for change) or Pluses and Minuses, taken from the headings used on the flip chart.

DECISION MAKING IN A TEAM

The decision making style employed in a team environment may well be one of the most important decisions a team leader makes; deciding how to decide. Decision-making styles range from autocratic at one end of the continuum, to total agreement at the other end. In true 'situational leadership' form, the style employed by the team leader will be determined by the context and circumstances of the decision being made. The situation will be the driving force behind the style used.

AUTOCRATIC ←→ CONSULTATIVE ←→ DEMOCRATIC ←→ CONSENSUS ←→ TOTAL AGREEMENT

Figure 21: Decision Making Continuum

Autocratic

Autocratic decision-making is where one person decides alone. Whilst the team may have been formed in response to an autocratic decision, it is unlikely that this type of decision-making will be employed formally in the team's work.

Advantages:	Disadvantages:	Used When:
Decision making is fast as it doesn't require consultation	Risk of no buy in by stakeholders In a team environment, can lead to distrust and low morale	Time is critical such as in a crisis The decision maker is totally accountable for the outcome Matter is insignificant or full support of the team is not necessary

Consultative

The decision is made only after consultation with others. Whilst one person still makes the final decision, the thought processes of those impacted, those with an interest in the outcome, subject matter experts or any person who can offer input, are solicited. This style of decision-making is used widely in business at the leadership level.

Advantages:	Disadvantages:	Used When:

Information from a range of sources helps make a better decision People like being consulted about their opinions or knowledge	Raised expectations of those consulted that the decision will follow their way of thinking	The decision maker does not have all the information at hand The decision maker is totally accountable for the outcome Matter is insignificant or full support of the team is not necessary

Democratic

The process of choosing our political representatives is based on a democratic style of decision-making. In this case the majority rule, with the majority being as small as fifty one percent of the vote. Fifty one percent on board may not be enough to move ahead successfully; hence this is not always the best method in a team environment.

Advantages:	Disadvantages:	Used When:
It's a fair method with equal input from everyone	Creates a win / lose scenario – can lead to insufficient support for a decision to work Critical mass may not be achieved to make a decision work	Want to know the general opinion of the team – a quick check in or 'straw poll' if you like The impact of the decision is not critical The full support of the team is not necessary

Consensus

Consensus is achieved when all members agree to support the decision when they leave the meeting, regardless of whether or not they believe it is the best decision. Consensus can only be achieved when (a) members believe they have had the opportunity to share their views in open dialogue, (b) they have heard and understand all of the issues and are willing to share their views in an open dialogue. It's important to remember that consensus is not agreement, only a willingness and commitment to support the decision. In process improvement work there are usually many ways to treat a problem, so what is more important is the commitment by the team to making a solution work. Hence this is probably the most common decision making style used by a project team.

Advantages:	Disadvantages:	Used When:
High degree of buy in from participants	Slower process as generating consensus requires discussion and facilitation May not be the best decision - technically speaking	The team is accountable for the outcome Buy in is critical The team has the knowledge and information to make a good decision

Total Agreement

Agreement is defined by the Australian Oxford Dictionary as *"an act or state of agreeing; holding of the same opinion"*. Total agreement is the basis for decision-making in our judicial system, where a jury of twelve must all agree on a decision of guilt.

Advantages:	Disadvantages:	Used When:
Total buy in by participants	Time to make a decision is lengthy due to the need for lengthy discussion and facilitation	The team is totally accountable for the outcome Buy in is absolutely critical The team has the knowledge and information to make a good decision The consequences of a bad decision are high

'It is also important to recognise that within each of the decision making styles there are ranges. For instance a Consultative decision making style can be presented with support reasoning and reference to the input of others, or it can be silent on that input. The key to decision making in teams is to respect and acknowledge the input of team members.'

Harry Sinko

Deciding how to decide

One of the more recent additions to the contingency approach to leadership is the **leader-participation model** proposed by Victor Vroom and Phillip Yetton[10]." It relates leadership behaviour and leader participation to decision making. Recognising that task structures have varying demands for routine or non-routine activities, these researchers suggest that leader behaviour must adjust to reflect the task structure. The following considerations for deciding how to decide have been adapted from that model.

- **Decision Urgency** – What is the level of urgency for the decision?
- **Quality Requirement** – How important is the technical quality of the decision?
- **Commitment Requirement** – How important is the commitment of team members to the decision?
- **Leader's Information** – Does the leader have sufficient information to make a quality decision alone?
- **Problem Structure** – Is the problem well structured or complex?
- **Commitment Probability** – How likely is team member commitment to the decision if the leader makes it?
- **Goal Congruence** – Do team members share the goals to be attained in solving this problem?
- **Team Member Information** – Do team members have sufficient information to make a quality decision?

[10] Stephen P Robbins, Terry Waters-Marsh, Ron Cacioppe, Bruce Millett (1994), *"Organisational Behaviour - Concepts, Controversies and Applications"*, Prentice Hall, Sydney, pp. 491-492

The Most Common Style Used in Business Improvement

Each style has it own particular pros and cons and has application under certain conditions. The most common form of decision-making in process improvement work is that of *Consensus*.

THE PROJECT TEAM LEADER AS FACILITATOR

The word 'facilitation' has been mentioned in this text already. What is facilitation? Justice and Jamieson (1999)[11] define facilitation as:

> **Facilitation:** *'The design and management of structures and processes that help a group do its work and minimise the common problems people have working together.'*

Justice and Jamieson continue their description of facilitation as a neutral process that focuses on:

- What needs to be accomplished;
- Who needs to be involved;
- Design, flow and sequence of tasks;
- Communication patterns, effectiveness and completeness;
- Appropriate levels of participation and the use of resources;
- Group energy, momentum and capability; and
- The physical and psychological environment.

Process Focus

It's important to note that no mention is made of meeting content. However, this is not always practical in the case of Lean Six Sigma project work. In many cases the team leader is also a content expert. When this is the case, the facilitator must never lose focus on the process of the meeting, a challenge that can only be met through self-awareness.

One strategy that has served many content knowledgeable facilitators well is to appoint a process checker who has the responsibility for formally monitoring the meeting process as well as being a team member.

The Role of Facilitator

The role of a facilitator comprises tasks across three phases:

1. Preparation for the meeting;
2. Conduct of the meeting; and
3. Follow up after the meeting.

<u>Meeting Preparation</u>

- Prepare the detailed meeting agenda in consultation with key stakeholders
- Contact meeting participants
- Contact agenda item facilitators
- Publish and circulate the meeting agenda
- Arrange the meeting venue
- Prepare meeting resources (markers, paper, note taking materials etc)

---

[11] Justice, T., Jamieson, D.W. Phd., (1999), *'The Facilitators Fieldbook'*, AMACOM, New York, p. 5

Meeting Conduct

- Introductions
- Overview the agenda
- Establish meeting ground rules
- Make relevant appointments (time keeper, recorder etc)
- Manage processes associated with data generation
- Manage processes associated with decision-making
- Monitor group dynamics
- Intervene when necessary
- Evaluate group process (meeting quality)
- Wrap up meetings with a summary of agreed actions
- Seek agreement on next meeting time, date and location

Meeting Follow Up

- Evaluate and summarise meeting feedback (meeting quality evaluations)
- Prepare and circulate meeting minutes
- Communicate with team members, post meeting (where relevant)
- Monitor action plan completion

MEETING MANAGEMENT

Have you ever watched any of the John Cleese training videos?

In one of the scenes in his video on meetings, he is sitting in bed with his brief case on his lap doing some paperwork. His wife rolls over and asks him what he's doing. He says he's doing his work because at work all he does is attend meetings. Does that sound a little familiar to you?

Let me ask you this - How many meetings per week do you regularly attend? What proportion of these meetings would be effective in your view? By that, I mean effective in achieving desired outcomes in the most efficient way possible.

Choose your answers from the following table.

# Meetings Per Week	Percent Effective
< 3	> 75%
4 - 6	50 - 75%
7 - 9	25 - 50%
> 9	< 25%

Effectiveness of Meetings

When I undertake this activity with students in change leadership seminars, it is not unusual to find that many people attend more than 9 meetings per week. At the time of writing this book, approximately 52% of the people I have spoken to indicated that only 25 to 50% of these meetings were effective.

When people perceive meetings as being 'not effective', what associations do they develop with the term 'meeting'. When someone says come to a meeting, how do you immediately feel? What emotions do you associate with the thought of going to another meeting?

I have asked this question of many people and the responses I get often include these terms:

- Anxiety
- Trepidation
- Just don't want to go

Have you ever felt that way about a meeting you have to attend?

So let's think about meetings that you run for a moment. How do people feel about your meetings? What would you like people to say when you invite them to one of your meetings?

I'm sure you would like people to want to come to your meetings and be the ones they look forward to most of all. One of the most significant deficiencies in meetings I have observed is the lack of control for the process of the meeting. Without a process, it is highly unlikely that any meeting will achieve its desired outcomes.

The first step towards ensuring a successful meeting is to plan the meeting through the development of an agenda.

Planning the Meeting

How much time should be spent planning a meeting? A rule of thumb is the time spent planning is the same as the time spent in the meeting itself. When I say this, people often respond by saying "I don't have the time to spend planning".

Think about this for a moment. We never have time to do it right the first time, but we are always able to find the time to do it again.

Think about the space shuttle Challenger disaster in 1986. There was no way the flight could be delayed according to the decision makers, it just had to go ahead in spite of what the makers of the solid fuel rocket boosters had to say about o-rings. After 72 seconds of flight, all of a sudden there was the time and funding to undertake extensive investigation and implement significant improvements to the shuttle program. Ironic isn't it.

Isn't that the case at work? There's never time to do it right the first time, but always time to do it again.

One of the most useful ways to plan a meeting is to do so in 'chunks'. That is to break the meeting into a number of its most obvious pieces and plan within each piece. One way to 'chunk' your meeting is to ask yourself some good questions.

STEP 1 Ask: *'What are the specific outcomes we want at the end of this meeting?'*

This is a statement of what it is that the meeting is ultimately going to achieve. When this is achieved then the meeting can be considered a success. Desired outcomes can be both content oriented (to establish agreement about ...) and learning oriented (to practice the use of ...).

STEP 2 Ask: *'Why are these outcomes important to us?'*

The answer to this question provides a reason for having the meeting in the first place. When you have purpose, your actions become far more important and you have drive. You don't just have any old meeting, you have an outcome focused, purpose driven meeting. A little different don't you think?

STEP 3 Ask: *'What specific results do we need to get in order to achieve our outcomes?'*

Results are the specific pieces that when completed ensure that the desired outcome is achieved. These are the 'chunks' of your meeting, and the key to ensuring effectiveness.

STEP 4 Ask: *'What must we do to achieve each of these results?'*

At this point you need to think about the process you will use. The process can be described in terms of the tools you will use and the specific approach or activity you will undertake.

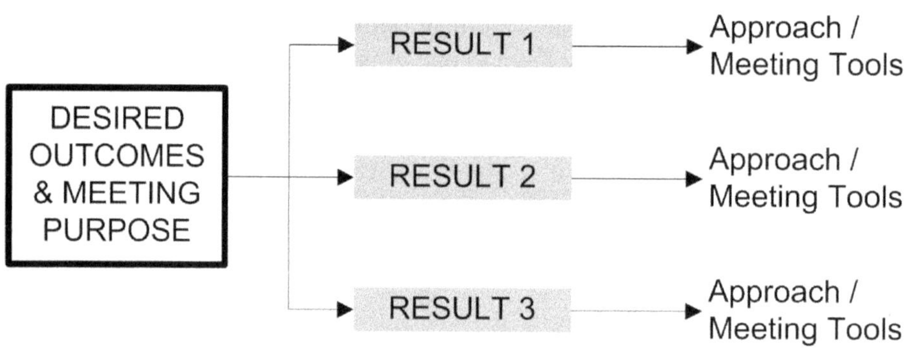

Figure 22: The Core Elements of a Meeting Agenda

Meeting Agenda Elements

A meeting agenda is a commonly used format for summarising the entire meeting. So in recapping some of the items identified in the steps above, an agenda is comprised of the following elements as a minimum:

1. Desired Outcomes

A statement of what it is that you ultimately want to achieve at the end of the meeting.

2. Purpose

These are the reasons why these outcomes are important, the real drive for holding the meeting.

3. Results

These are the chunks of the meeting that when all completed contribute to the achievement of the desired outcomes.

Results can be tangible items such as lists, action plans or documented 'things' that can be physically taken away from the meeting.

They can also be intangibles such as an understanding, awareness, agreement or a decision.

4. Action Plan

A description of the approach, the tools and the actions you will take in getting the results you have targeted for each part of the meeting.

5. Responsibilities

A statement of who will facilitate each particular piece of the meeting.

6. Timings

Usually stated in the form of a fixed interval of time (07:30 am to 08:00 am) as opposed to a period in minutes (30 min), this is a guide to the facilitator as to the time period that has been allocated to the particular piece.

By stating the specific time, your meeting has a far better chance of staying on time. When you only state time in minutes, if there are overruns these accumulate to push the entire meeting over time.

<table>
<tr><td>Outcomes</td><td colspan="4">(indicate the overall outcomes you want to achieve by the end of this meeting – this is the basis for how you will judge whether or not your meeting was successful)</td></tr>
<tr><td>Purpose</td><td colspan="4">(indicate why these outcomes are important to the group involved)</td></tr>
<tr><th>ITEM</th><th>RESULTS</th><th>ACTION PLAN</th><th>WHO</th><th>TIMINGS</th></tr>
<tr><td>(name the item or the topic)</td><td>(indicate the result you want to get for this piece of the agenda – can be a soft result such as an agreement, or a hard result such as a list or a document)</td><td>(describe the process you will follow and tools you will use to achieve the result indicated)</td><td>(who will facilitate this piece)</td><td>(indicate planned timings by the clock)</td></tr>
</table>

Meeting Agenda Format

Meeting management is a fundamental skill of a Black Belt, and one of the most effective ways to ensure meetings are results focused and purpose driven, is to create an effective agenda.

The benefits of having an agenda are:

- The team has clear focus for the duration of the meeting
- A plan can be followed and timings can be kept
- The team leader has a framework to drive focus on the process and not the content

SAMPLE PROJECT TEAM MEETING AGENDA

DESIRED OUTCOMES:

- Develop a simple communication tool to describe the project
- Agree on the plan for collecting data relevant to potential variables of interest

PURPOSE:

- Have everything we need to complete the data analysis prior to the second meeting

TOPIC	RESULTS	ACTION PLAN	WHO	TIMINGS
Opening	Start up the team meeting	Review Agenda Ground Rules, Operating Agreement	Gerry	1250-1300
Project Startup	Build the foundations for momentum and process measurement	Present and discuss project charter (15) CB Analysis (15) Create Elevator Speech (30) Develop project SIPOC (90)	Gerry	1300-1530
Data Collection	Understand non value added time and prepare for data collection	Cycle Time / Time value analysis (30) Create Data Collection Plan (30) Develop survey questions (15)	Gerry	1530-1715
Close	Agree on meeting outcomes	Summarise the meeting + / Δ	Gerry	1715-1720

Sample Meeting Agenda

RATING MEETING QUALITY

A simple tool for checking the quality of your meeting is based on rating how well the meeting process was managed across six dimensions. These six dimensions are drawn from process characteristics that are important for meeting success.

- Listening
- Participation
- Focus
- Energy
- Time Management
- Outcomes

The meeting quality rating form or template shown on the following page may be completed at the end of a meeting with input from all members. Ideas for improving the meeting according to performance for different elements are captured before leaving the meeting.

Meeting Quality Rating Template

ELEMENT	LOWER END RESULTS	1	2	3	4	5	6	7	UPPER END RESULTS
		RATING SCALE							
LISTENING	Members did not practice active listening.	☐	☐	☐	☐	☐	☐	☐	Team members showed an interest in what each member had to say and made obvious use of good listening skills.
PARTICIPATION	There was an imbalance of participation with a few members dominating while some remain quiet throughout the meeting.	☐	☐	☐	☐	☐	☐	☐	All team members actively contributed ideas and participated constructively in decision-making processes.
FOCUS	The meeting was not focused on any particular outcome, and wandered from one topic to another without direction.	☐	☐	☐	☐	☐	☐	☐	The meeting remained focused on the desired outcomes, and followed a clearly defined agenda.
GROUP ENERGY	Energy and levels of enthusiasm for the meeting was low.	☐	☐	☐	☐	☐	☐	☐	A high degree of enthusiasm and energy was evident throughout the meeting.
TIME MANAGEMENT	Time was poorly managed with too much time spent on some agenda items while insufficient time was spent on others.	☐	☐	☐	☐	☐	☐	☐	Time was managed well with time spent on agenda items being proportionate to the importance of the item and the needs of the team.
OUTCOMES	The desired outcomes of the meeting were not achieved.	☐	☐	☐	☐	☐	☐	☐	The desired outcomes of the meeting were clearly achieved.
To improve the quality of our meetings, we must do the following:									

Meeting Quality Rating Template

TEAM MEMBER PERSONALITIES

Anyone who has ever led teams will have found that the personalities of individual members differ greatly. It is this diversity of personalities that make team work both challenging and rewarding. As a team leader, a Black Belt must be able to deal with the different behaviours that will be driven primarily by the different personalities of each individual. Some of the most common behaviours that are detrimental to effective teamwork are listed below, with some tips on how to deal with them.

The Mis-matcher:

Every discussion with this person results in some form of conflict, they are always finding fault.

Pros: - The Mis-matcher is a good devil's advocate.

Cons: Contributes to conflict.

Tips for dealing with the 'Mis-matcher':

- Provide time for them to explain their thinking
- Allow time for other members to advocate for ideas
- Ask for solutions
- Use process tools to build consensus
- Refer to the desired outcome

The Veteran:

The veteran has already done it before.

Pros: - The Veteran has experience.

Cons: Often rigid and not open to change.

Tips for dealing with the 'Veteran':

- Acknowledge the veteran's experience
- Tap into their experience to add value to the group's work
- Summarise their comments and then seek the comments of other team members
- Help them find a new way, avoid imposing your own way on them

The Perfectionist:

Everything has to be perfect before work can proceed.

Pros: - Dots the I's and crosses the T's.

Cons: Slows down the rate of progress.

Tips for dealing with the 'Perfectionist':

- Establish agreed deadlines
- Establish agreement on important criteria for decision-making up front
- Refer to the desired outcome
- Use process tools to build consensus

The Lawyer:

Lives by the rules.

Pros: - The Lawyer is focused on process and procedures.

Cons: Sometimes inflexible if the rules are challenged.

Tips for dealing with the 'Lawyer':

- Use their experience to check procedures
- Ask questions that promote alternative thought – "What would happen if we didn't follow that rule?"
- Provide direct feedback

The Boss:

The boss wants to take over the meeting.

Pros: The Boss is focused on meeting outcomes.

Cons: The Boss may also be focused on himself or herself

Tips for dealing with the 'Boss':

- Be cautious about giving them the pen
- Use a process to generate ideas in silence (NGT / Brain Writing)
- Recognise the team
- Rotate roles within the team
- Provide direct feedback

The Talker:

Non-stop input / talking during the meeting.

Pros: The Talker is an active participant.

Cons: Can be a significant disruption to the team.

Tips for dealing with the 'Talker':

- Make use of them to keep meeting momentum
- Invite others to speak by referring to them directly
- Check in with ground rules at the beginning of every meeting; let the team manage any disruption

There are many other types of behaviours that a team leader will be confronted with, and ways to deal with all of these will only be learnt through application and experience.

COMMUNICATING TO DIFFERENT PEOPLE

'Nothing in life is more important than the ability to communicate effectively.'

US President Gerald Ford

One of the best ways to experience the astonishing diversity of people is to talk to a group. You can say the same thing to everyone, and the reactions you get will invariably differ across your audience. Have you ever wondered why you can tell a joke to a group of people and some of them laugh while some seem totally unaffected. What about when you tell an inspirational story, some of the group is totally transfixed while a few are bored beyond belief. Why is that the case? It's like they were listening to another set of words entirely.

Why is it that a group of people can get the same message from the same source, yet some feel energised and motivated, while others react totally differently? To be a master communicator, to be an individual who can persuade while others seem incapable of doing it, you must find the key to communicating in terms that everyone hears.

The following paragraph was sent to me some years ago by a friend, take a moment to read it.

> Aoccdrnig to a rscheearch at an Elingsh uinervtisy, it deosn't mttaer in what order the ltteers in a word are, the only iprmoetnt thing is that frist and lsat ltteer is at the rghit pclae. The rset can be a total mses and you can still raed it wouthit a porbelm. Tihs is bcuseae we do not raed ervey lteter by itslef but the word

It's obviously a mess yet you can still read it. Why is that? Quite simply we have the ability to get meaning from the combination of letters as opposed to individual letters. Their proximity to other words and general sound allows us to make sense of what could otherwise be considered a pile of garbage.

Take a moment to quickly read this statement.

What's wrong with it? You may not have noticed, but the word 'the' appears two times in succession. Did you miss it?In most cases people don't see it because they only see what comes through the filters they apply to the communication. The second 'the' is filtered out of the message.

Let me ask you another question - What do you see?

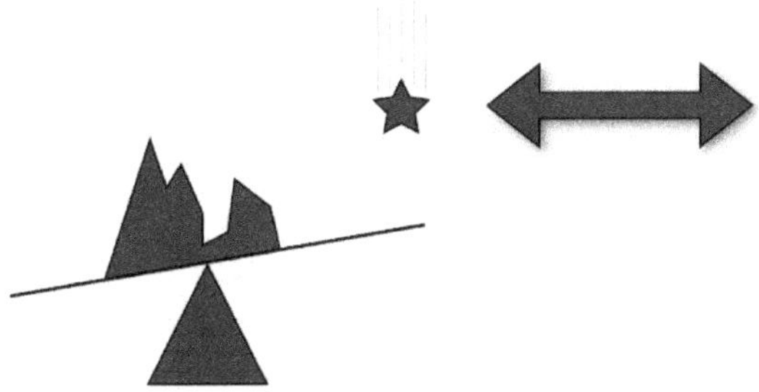

Well, what did you see?

You had to interpret what I meant by that question didn't you? Did I mean what do you see in the picture above, or did I mean what do you see on this page, or was it what do you see in your surrounding environment?

In most instances, people interpret the question to mean 'describe what you see in the picture on the page below'. Regardless of what I meant, you had to interpret it before you could respond to it.

Interpretation is affected by context, proximity, experience, feelings and a myriad of variables, most of which are invisible to us.

Chunking, Filtering and Interpretation

The point I'm really trying to make here is that we are all chunking, filtering and interpretation machines. We do it because we have to. We receive so many pieces of information that our brains filter, sort, delete, distort, generalise and interpret information constantly. This is necessary because our brains can only process so many pieces of information at any given time.

If you quickly look outside your window and then look away, what do you remember? Probably the big things that were most obvious, things like buildings, plants, and dominant colours. There is no way you can take in all of the detail of the lawn across the road, or the leaves that make up a tree unless you focused your attention on those things.

It's interesting to me that people behave in exactly the same way in communication with one another. They process information according to patterns they have developed through constant repetition over long periods of time until they were embedded at a neurological level.

By recognising these patterns in both yourself and other people, you have a foundation for communicating in ways that causes all people to sit up and take notice, not just a few.

Much of this chapter will help you deal with these issues when, not if, they arise.

COMMUNICATION AND MEANING

If I stood in front of a class of grade 5 students and said "Good morning boys and girls", I would probably receive a friendly greeting in return. If I said exactly the same words with the same voice cues and use of body language to a group of men and women in an improvement project team that I had never met before, what would their response be?

The meaning they attach to my words could be completely different to the meaning the grade 5 students gave. They might perceive my communication to be demeaning, when in fact it was my way of having a little light-hearted fun to break the ice.

The Meaning is in the Response

My message here is quite simple: information and meaning are not the same thing. The meaning of any communication is determined by the response it gets. Whether or not I intended to have some light-hearted fun is irrelevant. If the receivers perceive the message to mean I think I am better than they are and this is my way of demeaning them, then this is what the message means.

Responsibility for Meaning

So, who must take responsibility for the meaning given to a piece of information in any communication? As difficult as it may be to accept for some people, responsibility rests with the sender, not the receiver. As a Lean Six Sigma project team leader, application of this principle is vital if you are to effectively lead people who make up your team, and create change in the workplace as a result of your project work.

Four Steps to Effective Communication

There are four simple steps to communicating effectively.

- Know what the **intended meaning** of your communication is;
- Communicate in a way that maximises the probability that the receiver will **understand** the message **as you intended**;
- Be **sensitive to feedback** so that you know if the message was understood as intended; and
- When the message is misunderstood, **change your approach** until the message is understood as intended.

COMMUNICATING TO BUILD RAPPORT & CONNECTION

'Rapport is the cornerstone of all mutually effective relationships. It needs constant vigilance and nurturing to keep it alive and effective.'

Richard Storey – *The Influencing Pocketbook*

How important is rapport in leading change? What do you think? Before I discuss the answers, let's define the term rapport. According to the Australian Oxford Dictionary, rapport is defined as follows.

Rapport (*n*): *harmonious and understanding relationship between people; feeling of being in harmony (with something)*

Building Rapport

Rapport is harmonious connectivity between people, and it can be built through various means including:

- Face to face communication;
- Email or electronic communication;
- Over the phone;
- Through letters; and even
- In your own mind.

Rapport building goes beyond the use of words. Rapport is generated through the use of all of the resources you have at your disposal, including:

- How you use your physiology;
- How you present yourself;

- Your use of language and how you deliver it;
- The content of your verbal communication;
- The way you present information in digital form (ie; presentation); and
- How you listen.

So let me ask you again, how important do you think rapport building is in leading change? Dictatorial leadership, command and control styles of leadership will not progress for long in the business world of today. Do they work in getting change to occur? Of course they do but they rely on formal authority. If that is your only style of leadership, you'll probably only be successful in making change under certain conditions.

- You're the boss in a formal structure.
- You maintain control (the moment you turn your back you cannot guarantee change remains).
- People don't choose to leave.

Autocratic styles of leadership are necessary in certain circumstances, no doubt about it. But if that's the approach you choose as a general rule you won't be able to get people to change their behaviour in many day-to-day circumstances.

Not only do you need rapport to *consistently* lead effective change in any organisation, you need it to succeed in life.

In a nutshell, how effectively we connect with people is essentially driven by how we communicate with people. Studies have shown that in face-to-face communication, the words you use have only a small impact on how people react and respond to the communication, in proportion to your voice cues and physiology. Imagine Eddie Murphy standing in front of you swearing and calling you names. It would probably send most people into fits of laughter. If I did the same thing, I'd probably get punched in the nose, even if the words were the same. The difference lies in the voice cues and physiology that accompany the words.

Mehrabian Studies

During an extensive study on trust and respect between people, Albert Mehrabian (a professor of psychology) came to the conclusion in 1971 that when verbal and non-verbal behaviour were congruent, the person was trusted and perceived as being genuine. When verbal and non-verbal behaviour were not congruent (for example, a positive statement made in a monotone voice while frowning), the person was distrusted and not well regarded. In addition to that, when verbal and non-verbal behaviours did not match, people responded to the message contained in the non-verbal part.

Mehrabian's research revealed that *93 percent of all communication is non-verbal.* The way we use our physiology (body language) constitutes 55 percent of the message, voice cues contribute 38 percent, and the words themselves only convey 7 percent of the message.

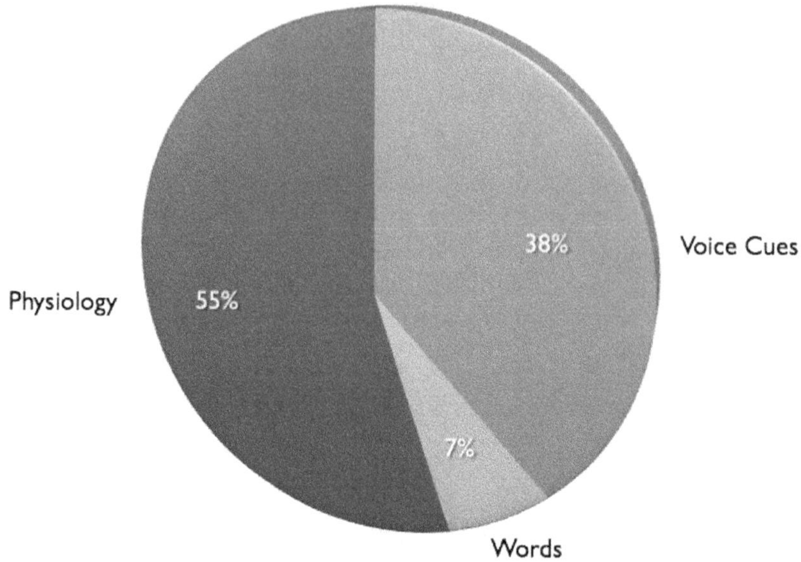

Figure 23: Resources in Communication

Looking for the Clues

One thing I continually reinforce with people I coach is this: the clues to success are all around us and obvious in our own lives if we look for them. This applies to the concept of successfully building rapport. Let's think about rapport in your own life for a moment.

I want you to think of someone you definitely do not have rapport with, do not seem to have connection with. If you can't think of anyone in your existing network, think about someone from your past that you just didn't connect with. Now write down all of the things that you perceived to be a cause for disconnect.

What are the characteristics or traits they have that give you cause for disconnect?

....

....

....

....

....

Now think of someone you have total rapport with. They can be a friend or relative, or even your partner.

What is it about them that you connect with? Write down your answers as they come to mind.

....

....

....

....

....

....

When I do this with seminar participants, most answers fall within these types of categories in both cases.

- How they move - mannerisms
- How they talk – pace, voice cues, volume, words and phrases they use
- The types of conversations they have – subject matter
- What they laugh at – jokes, humorous situations
- Physiology – body type, how they sit, how they position their legs and arms
- Personal space – how close they stand to you when they talk
- The symbols they use – motor vehicle owned, how they dress, use of letters after their names

The bottom line is this, when there is a perceived difference in any of these elements, rapport may not exist. When you and another person are not like one another, rapport does not occur naturally, connection is difficult to make.

So when rapport doesn't naturally occur, or there is a perceived difference, how can you build rapport? Like I said, the clues to success are already in front of you. If you model what you do when you have rapport, you will be able to build rapport with anyone! And, by the way, it doesn't matter what nationality people are, the principles hold true across international and cultural boundaries.

This Section

My intention in this section is to give you an overview of some key concepts that will positively impact your ability to lead, influence, motivate and teach the people you come into contact with, whether it be in a project team environment, whether it be on a personal level away from work, or whether it be in your role as a leader of a multi national company.

The details provided are based on certain strategies that are guaranteed to help you build rapport or connection with virtually anyone. The strategies are these:

1. Show respect for the fundamental beliefs and values of individuals.
2. Listen effectively.
3. Reduce perceived difference by:
    a. Matching their physiology;
    b. Verbally communicating in their preferred style; and
    c. Using language (words, phrases etc) that they use and relate to.
4. Use effective language to build on differences in opinions or beliefs.

Let me provide you with some information about a few of these.

LISTENING - A TOTAL BODY RAPPORT BUILDING BEHAVIOUR

The traditional model of communication, at least this is how it was explained to me so many years ago, describes the sequence in this way.

In the first instance, the sender transmits a message to the receiver. The sender receives feedback, which contains information about whether or not the meaning of the message was received as intended.

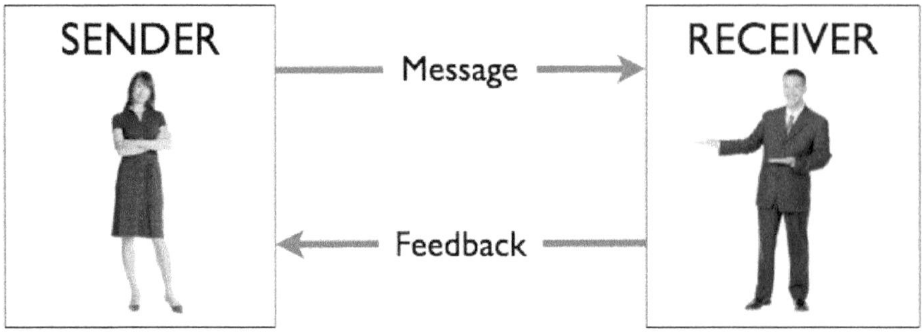

Figure 24: Standard Communication Model

This model tends to focus us on the role of the sender, which in my humble opinion is only half of the equation.

While some models place onus fairly and squarely on the shoulders of the sender to get the message right, and continue to adjust their communication until it gets across, the best communicators are also aware of the role that a receiver can play in the process of communication.

Selection and Interpretation

We are all prone to select, filter, distort and interpret the data we expose our senses to. So much is going on, it would be impossible to take in everything *and* interpret it accurately every time, so we take short cuts.

The factors that influence what we select and how we interpret include our values, beliefs, experience, what's happening at the time, emotions, whether or not we like the person, whether or not rapport exists and so on.

This is not limited to any single party in a communication, it is the practice of all parties; senders and receivers alike. This is a major factor in how well we receive any communication, whether it be the original message or the feedback from the recipient that follows, so as a leader we must be aware of this.

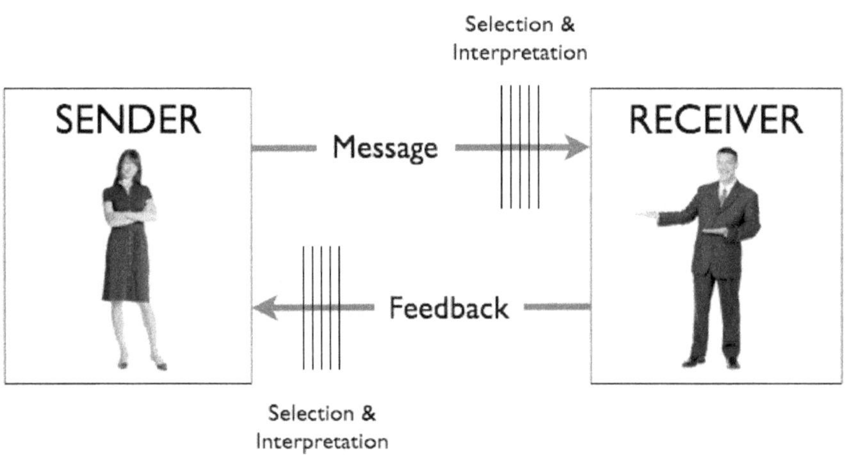

Figure 25: Selection and Interpretation in Communication

So what do we do about it? As leaders, it's not only our responsibility to carefully construct the messages we send, but to listen effectively as a recipient of any message.

'Listening is the highest form of courtesy.'

Tom Peters

Influencers are Listeners

A leader who listens with skill and genuine care will generate respect and be able to significantly influence others. Effective listening is a critical element in the process of building rapport.

Through effective listening you will not only understand the intent of their communication, but also get an insight into what people are thinking and how they are feeling. To be an effective listener, you must learn how to use all of the resources you have to listen. In reality, listening is a total body experience.

When I teach 'effective listening' to participants in our leadership programs, I have them undertake a short activity to help them understand the need for total body listening. I start the activity by having them pair off, and then sending one person outside. The remaining people are asked to think of something they are passionate about that they can tell their partner about. The people outside the room are briefed to be as disinterested as possible in the story their partner is going to tell them.

They are then brought together where a passionate communicator tells the story to a totally disinterested listener.

In the debrief that follows, it becomes very clear that the listeners do not hear or remember much, if anything, about the story. The communicators almost always express dissatisfaction and funnily enough, disconnect with the listener.

I will never forget a young man in South Africa who got so genuinely upset at the listener that he verbally chastised him. He had no idea that the listener had been briefed to be disinterested and he perceived his actions as a sign of disrespect.

We then repeat the activity, this time the listeners take total interest in what the communicator has to say. The results are obviously much different. The listeners know and remember much more about what the communicator said. Both parties experience a feeling of connection, and the emotional experience is positive for all involved.

The differences in behaviour that we identify in these two scenarios commonly include these on the part of the receiver.

Not Listening (Disinterested)	Effectively Listening
Internally focused on own thoughts and dialogue Distractions are allowed to interrupt the process Body posture is away from the communicator Physiology is mismatched Disinterest shows on the face of the receiver Uses words like "I" and "Me"	Mental focus on the communicator Curious about the content Sometimes words or phrases are repeated Body posture is towards the communicator Physiology is often matching Uses words like "You" and "We" Prompts are used to encourage talk Distractions are ignored

'Give every man thy ear, but few thy voice.'

William Shakespeare

A Total Body Listening Strategy

Total body listening is an extremely effective way of (a) ensuring understanding, and (b) building rapport.

Total Body Listening Utilises the Power of Four Elements

The Power of Focus: Focus can be achieved by:

- Focusing your physiology towards the communicator;
- Eliminating distractions – turn them off, defer them or ignore them; and
- Paying attention to what is being said – treating every communication as an opportunity to learn something useful will generate a mindset of attention.

The Power of Personal Space: An effective listener, intent on rapport, will work in the personal space that the communicator is most comfortable with.

The Power of Curiosity: By staying curious about what the communicator is saying, you will draw out more information; hence learn more about what is being said. A curious listener will use:

- Prompts to encourage talking on the part of the communicator. These include nods and gestures, sounds like 'uh-huh', and words like 'okay' and 'I see'. The use of prompts demonstrates that you are interested.
- Open questions to generate informative answers. Questions that begin with how, what, when, where and who, encourage sentenced answers. Questions that begin with 'did you', 'would you', 'could you', 'should you' etc, encourage answers of yes or no and are considered closed questions. Questions that begin with 'why' can be perceived as challenging.
- Reflective questions to guide the speaker to delve deeper into the subject matter and reflect. Questions like: 'How is this like ......?' or 'When has this occurred in the past?' or even 'What learnings were taken away from this?', cause the speaker to reflect and provide a great deal more information.

The Power of Paraphrasing: Paraphrasing is the process of restating what the communicator said in your own words. This process has two benefits; (a) you must listen, and (b) understanding can be confirmed.

PHYSIOLOGICAL RAPPORT

'Birds of a Feather Flock Together'

The next time you go to a party or some social event where people get the opportunity to relax and mingle, take a close look at what's happening. Watch people who are in a state of high rapport, people who are very relaxed and comfortable in each other's company. You'll see a lot of active listening – prompting, nodding and focus on each other. You'll also see a matching of physiology. They'll be closely aligned in the way they use their body. For example, if they're sitting down, you might see both with their legs crossed in the same way, or they might both be leaning forward with arms on the table in a matching way. If they're standing, they might both have their arms crossed or hands in their pockets, or they'll both be holding a drink in one hand with the other hand in their pocket.

What you are seeing is the result of an unconscious process.

The concept of 'birds of a feather flock together' is very real. Just think about people in the world for a moment. Like people congregate.

What do you notice about a biker gang, or a group of skinheads or hippies? They all look the same to most people. They dress the same, they wear similar clothing and they mark or paint their bodies in similar ways to each other. People even congregate by occupation or the industry in which they work.

Police and soldiers have a tendency to hang out together, accountants and lawyers seem to be an inseparable group. Nurses and doctors spend much of their personal time socialising with their work peers.

What about undercover police – how do they get to be accepted by a group into which they wish to infiltrate? They must be like them – walk, talk, dress and act in the same way – a sure way to accelerate the building of rapport.

Mirroring and Matching

It's possible to accelerate the process of rapport building during any communication, whether it is with an individual or with a group of people.

With an individual, all you need to do is consciously match or mirror his or her physiology.

Matching: Suppose I was talking to a person and they were standing with their left hand in their pocket and right hand holding a drink. If I wanted to match them, I would adopt a similar physiology with my left hand in my pocket and my right hand holding my drink.

Mirroring: However, if I were to mirror his or her physiology, I would adopt a stance that appears as a mirror image to that person. In other words as I face them my right hand would be in my pocket and my left hand would be holding the drink.

By doing this, the person on the other side of the exchange experiences a sense of connection or rapport. They won't know why, but the absence of obvious difference leads to rapport. This whole process is known as matching and mirroring.

I've used this process literally thousands of times and have found that mirroring is more effective than matching.

Pacing and Leading

To maintain the connection in the early stages of building rapport, you have to stay pace with them as they change their physiology. I don't mean that as they make a move you do as well. What I mean is when they adopt a new stance, after a short while you also adopt a similar stance. This is referred to as 'pacing'.

Now what's really interesting is this, the connection can become so strong that you can actually start leading the way the other person uses *their* physiology. Surprisingly this is called 'leading'. To test this, simply change your physiology to an obvious new position such as folding your arms, and see how they respond.

Working with groups of people

You can also apply these principles to groups of people you may be required to address. To do this requires that you're comfortable with the content of your communication, because you have to be able to take notice of what is happening in the room while you talk.

The way I use it is to take notice of how people are sitting in the room. I then adopt pieces of how people sit as I focus in their direction or even address them personally. For example, someone might have their arms folded, another person might be sitting with their hands under their chin while another person is sitting back with their hands in their pockets and feet crossed. As I look at and talk to the people with arms folded and hands under their chin, I might put my right arm across my body and underneath my left upper arm, while I hold my left hand to my chin.

In this way I'm taking on pieces of the physiology of two or more different people. If I turn to the third person I might then cross my feet and put my hands in my pockets. Crazy as this might sound, it works.

I've been ignoring the so called 'rules' for how I should dress, stand and use my body as a presenter for a long time now and the results have absolutely convinced me that connection and rapport is a far more powerful ingredient in getting people to change than fitting a particular image. The skill is to be able to focus on the process of communication as well as the content.

Key Points

- By matching the physiology of people, you put yourself in a good position to influence, motivate, help learning and build rapport.
- The matching of physiology does not have to be exact, only close enough that mismatching does not exist. Caution should be exercised to avoid being seen by the other person as copying them.
- Mirroring involves adopting the same physiology as though the other person was looking into a mirror. For example, if they cross their left leg over the right leg, to mirror them you would cross your right leg over your left when facing the other person.
- You can learn the skill of matching physiology; it takes constant practice to master it.
- Mismatched physiology will contribute to conflict where it exists. Rapport will be difficult to establish, and conflict will be slower to resolve.

SYMBOLIC RAPPORT

One element of communication that is hardly ever mentioned is that of symbolic communication. The way you groom yourself, adorn your body and dress, projects to other people who you are. If you ever go to Melbourne, take a look at the way people appear. Business executives wear their own uniform, as do members of many different organisations. Personal possessions are also a means of communication. A new Harley owner is immediately accepted as a part of a group, as are owners of motor vehicles such as BMWs and Ferraris.

At the project leadership level, the ability to establish rapport with a team can be helped or hindered by the way the team leader dresses and how they symbolically present themselves. A team leader wearing a suit and tie will have considerable difficulty building true rapport when the team is made up of operators dressed in overalls. Conversely, a team leader dressed in jeans and polo shirt may have difficulty building rapport with a team of IT people in Melbourne dressed in suit and tie.

One business leader who has had an enormous impact on the success of Six Sigma in a business was David Moffatt who was a senior executive of Telstra Corporation at the time of writing the first edition of this book. I had the opportunity to observe David open Six Sigma courses at Telstra on numerous occasions. Every time his commitment and enthusiasm was clear and his energy for the initiative obvious. It was his ability to build rapport, however, that serves as a good example here. One thing he would do during these talks was dress down. He would come into the room dressed in a business suit. But when he began his talk he would remove his jacket. He was able to build rapport very quickly through reducing the level of perceived difference, evidenced by the feedback from every participant I questioned about it.

Another example of this type of connection is that of a gentleman that I had the pleasure of working with over a number of years. Mike Anglin, who at that time was Vice President for Operating Excellence globally for the mining giant BHP Billiton, never allowed his dress to become a source of perceived difference. On the many occasions he spoke to seminar participants that I had been working with, he appeared to be just like them. He was able to build rapport very quickly as a foundation for successfully communicating the message he was intent on giving.

Remember this: rapport is built on *perceived* similarity or *perceived* likeness between the two parties concerned. Where difference is perceived, rapport will be difficult to sustain or even build in the first place.

Key Points

- By matching the dress of people in your team, you are in a good position to influence, motivate, help learning and build rapport.
- The matching of symbols does not have to be exact, only close enough that mismatching does not exist.
- When introducing yourself to a team, avoid mismatching the level of education and qualifications you have with those of the team. Your enthusiasm for telling them about your Bachelor Degree and MBA may very well be a source of perceived difference when they do not have professional qualifications.
- Be conscious of the words that you use in your communication. Big words used with the intention of impressing, may very well be a source of perceived difference and ultimately disconnect with the people you wanted the relationship with.
- If you choose to look different from the people you want to influence, be aware that rapport will be difficult to establish. The relationship you need to create will be a challenge to build and conflict will be slower to resolve.

MATCHING INTERNAL REPRESENTATION SYSTEMS

All of us gather and process information through our five senses – sight (visual), hearing (auditory), touch or feeling (kinaesthetic), smell (olfactory), and taste (gustatory). In an ideal world we would all be able to process information equally well with all five of these senses or modes as I will refer to them, but that's not the case.

Here I want to delve deeper into this subject through discussing how these modes and our preferences affect the way we think and process information.

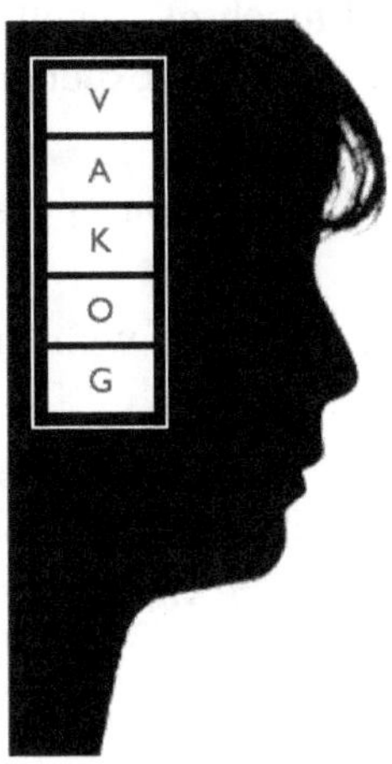

Each of us uses these modes to create and store inner representations of our experiences. An internal representation is nothing more than a mental *re*-presentation of something that we've experienced in the past.

These *re*-presentations are mostly in visual, auditory and kinaesthetic forms.

They are our mechanisms for storing experiences for later recall, and are referred to as *representation systems* or *modalities*.

Whilst the five senses include smell (olfactory) and taste (gustatory), our focus is on the first three. Interestingly enough, we each have an individual preference for which of these senses we use primarily.

Visual

People who are much more comfortable using pictures and images than they are with sounds and feelings, like to recall experiences through pictures. Ideas or memories are internally represented as mental images.

A visual perspective predominantly influences them, particularly one that is big, bright and colourful. They may consistently use visual type words or phrases such as 'see', 'its clear to me', 'looks about right'.

Highly visual people have a tendency to talk fast, trying to keep up with the pictures in their mind that appear at a much faster rate than they can speak.

They usually have a higher pitch voice and tend to point a lot and gesture upwards with their hands. As they talk you might see them creating the picture of what they're talking about with their hands.

Visual people are less effective with auditory and kinaesthetic people whose tendency is to talk too much or too slow for their liking. About 70 percent of people you come into contact with will have a natural preference for the visual modality.

Auditory

Some people are more comfortable with dialogue and sounds. When recalling ideas or memories they use internal dialogue or sounds as their internal representation. If you ask them about an experience, they'll probably talk through it in their minds as a part of the process of recall.

They like to sound out their ideas. They have a tendency to use words or phrases like 'listen', 'sounds okay to me', 'I hear you'.

They like engaging in conversation and respond well to changes in voice pitch and intensity.

Auditory people are less effective with visual and kinaesthetic people if they communicate with words only. Visual people want to convert words into models and pictures.

They can very quickly start to lose interest in the content if the information in a presentation is in words only. About 20 percent of people you come into contact with will have a preference for the auditory modality.

Kinaesthetic

By contrast, some people are more comfortable using feelings than they are with pictures and sounds. These feelings can be either emotions (proprioception or visceral sensations) or the physical touch of something (somesthesis or tactile sensations). When you are highly kinaesthetic, you really have to experience something to learn it.

Kinaesthetic people like to 'get in touch' with their thoughts, work hard on 'grasping' a new concept, and use words and phrases to indicate these preferences. They tend to rely on intuition.

Kinaesthetic people often speak more slowly with a deeper tone of voice. When they gesture with their hands, it is often downwards to the left or right.

Kinaesthetic people may be less effective with visual and auditory people if they don't adjust their communication style. If they talk too slowly during a presentation, highly visual people will become impatient. The information is delivered far too slow for the way they process it. About 10 percent of people you come into contact with will be predominantly kinaesthetic.

Impact on Communication

What impact does this have on communication?

During my son's last year of school, I had the opportunity to listen to a conversation he was having with his mother (my wife at the time) after dinner one night. Matt was explaining to her the concepts of an interesting activity he had seen on a web site.

The activity was called 'The Flash Mind Reader'[12] and involved the visitor calculating a number and then choosing the corresponding symbol for that number from a table of choices. The user would then click on the eye in the centre of the web page that would, to the amazement of the user, tell them the symbol that they had chosen. As we unconsciously do, he was communicating in such a way that it directly reflected his preferred way of internally representing his knowledge of the subject.

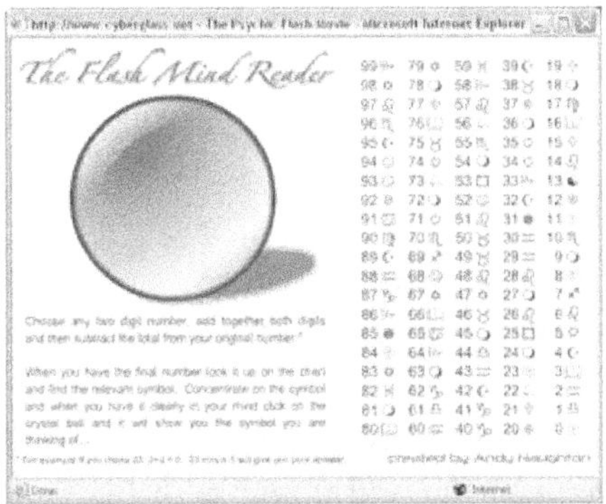

Being a highly visual person, Matt was using phrases and terms to create visual images for his mother. He would hold his hands up to reproduce the picture he was seeing in his own mind, and at the same time describing the picture he was trying to physically represent:

"In the centre of the page here is this big eye, and down the left side here is a table with a series of numbers and symbols."

Vicki's continual response was "I don't get what you're saying."

Matt became increasingly frustrated, as did Vicki, who just happens to have a strong preference for the kinaesthetic mode.

She would ask a question about how she would actually do what he was telling her and he would respond by giving the description in visual terms. Of course his message was never communicated so that she understood it. They may as well have been talking two different languages.

This is an example of what happens when two people communicate in their preferred mode and the other's preferred mode is different from theirs. There is disconnect, and effective communication cannot take place until the right connections are made, until both are talking the same language.

The bottom line is this; you cannot have effective communications unless you have rapport. Without some connection, then the likelihood of you teaching, influencing or persuading another person is low. Poor communication creates a scenario where there is a 'perceived difference'. The concepts of 'rapport' and 'difference' are in conflict.

One way of making this connection is to determine which of the modalities the other party is using at any particular point in time, or find out their preferred mode, and communicate in that mode.

---

12 This was originally viewed at http://www.flashpsychic.com/ but is no longer viewable.

In the example discussed, Matt would have been better getting Vicki to draw the numbers and symbols on paper and then showing her how the web site was so accurate in selecting the relevant symbol. She needed to experience the process to understand it.

Saving Memories for Later Representation

During 2003 I had the opportunity to demonstrate an interesting concept to a group of seminar participants. On the afternoon of the second day of what was a week long seminar, participants were offered time to give a presentation of their project work to their peers. During the session a participant gave a presentation during which she displayed a poster comprised of eight pictorial slides. During the presentation she made continual reference to the models and charts shown on these slides. She completed the presentation and answered all questions in about 10 minutes.

Her presentation was followed by one in which the gentleman gave a 10 minute talk without any aids. The presentation was followed by a long question and answer session, taking the entire presentation to around 17 minutes.

On the following day, I asked each participant to write down as much about the second presentation as they could remember in one minute. I then asked them to do the same with regard to the first presentation. What do you suppose the results showed?

The things consistently remembered from the second presentation included one particular item about a piece of machinery, what the presenter was wearing and doing with his hands, and where he stood. The things consistently remembered about the first presentation were associated with the charts and diagrams, the sequence of her talk, and a higher level of detail than was the case with the second presentation.

Now why did this occur?

If we have a preference for visually *re*-presenting memories, then we must first save these memories in visual form. Much like a PC cannot create a picture file from a saved word document, it's a challenge for us to create an accurate visual representation when the input was never delivered or converted into that format.

The second presentation was delivered in an auditory format. People remembered the bit about a piece of machinery because when it was delivered, they were able to create a visual representation of the words as they were said; hence they were able to save the memory in their preferred modality. (Almost the entire group was highly visual in this case.) They struggled with trying to recall much of what was said around that, however, were able to recall other pictures associated with what the presenter was wearing and where he was standing.

The first presentation by contrast, was delivered with visual aids. When asked to recall, most people were able to recreate these visual representations and give a far more detailed account of what was delivered. The visual records were a stimulus to the auditory component of the presentation. In effect the stories were anchored to pictures.

Learning and Motivation

Because these modalities are the basis for how we internally represent the external world and our experiences, they have a large impact on how we learn and the degree to which we experience a sense of motivation as the result of some external stimulus.

Learning

Visual people often learn best when they're able to translate the information into models, diagrams or process maps.

When they are able to link pieces together into a picture or map, they are in effect creating a visual representation of what it looks like.

I often make use of different types of mind maps when teaching or working with individuals or groups of people.

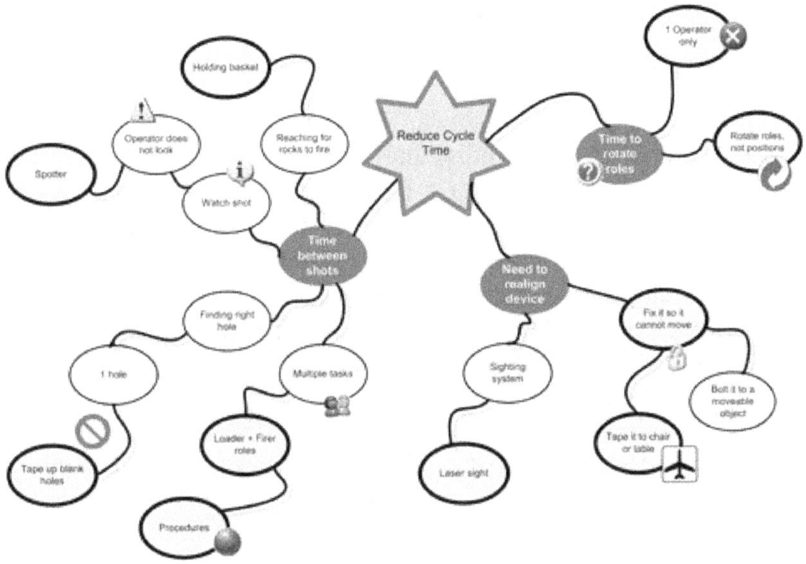

Visual people tend to have good short-term memory for numbers if they chunk them into about three groups. Ask a visual person to spell a word or recite a phone number backwards for you and they will often turn the word or number into a picture and then read it back to you. Visual people are often able to learn a skill by observing someone else doing it. They are able to play back the movie and reproduce the skill with considerable accuracy. If you tell them in words how to do something, they will have difficulty doing it unless they are able to convert it into pictures.

During my studies of law when training to become a police officer in Australia, I discovered something that proved to be an effective way of retaining information. During one of the classroom sessions, our instructor said that there would be a question during our upcoming practice exam that would come from Chapter V of the law book dealing with criminal responsibility. In total, there were 15 sections of law text. Over the next week I went over the entire set of pages enough times that I was able to turn the pages into pictures. Much to my surprise, and delight, the question asked during the exam was "Outline your knowledge of sections 22 to 36 of the Criminal Code." I simply wrote out the entire 15 sections recalling the exact words as I read the pictures of the pages in my mind. Not surprisingly, the instructor asked me about this after he marked the exam. This was when I started to realise the differences that existed in the way people learned and recalled information.

Auditory people are often able to remember names when they are said during introductions at a party. When they hear a description of how a task is done they will have considerable success in carrying out that task. They're more inclined to read the directions in operating a new piece of equipment, as opposed to visual people who will go directly to the pictures or flowchart diagram.

Kinaesthetic people must ultimately feel it or do it to learn it. When they experience the sensation or emotion they are more likely to be able to reproduce the skill. If they only ever see it done, it's highly unlikely that they will be able to do it. They're more inclined to learn if they are walked through the process.

Motivation

Some of the most effective sales people in the world are fully aware of the power of communicating in the preferred modalities of potential customers. Think about a significant purchase that you recently made. It might be a car, or a watch or some item of clothing. What was it about that item that first caught your attention and had you thinking about buying it? Was it the shape, colour, appearance or some other visual stimulus? Was it the description given to you by the sales person, the sound that it made, or was it the comments that you imagined people giving you if you owned the item? Or was it the weight, texture or feel of the item that attracted you to it.

The answers to these questions will tell you much about the process by which you can learn and be motivated. The motivational strategies of an individual can be determined through questioning. By asking specific questions about what motivated them at a particular time, the primary modality, as well as the motivational strategy can be identified. Skilled sales people use this knowledge in motivating customers to buy. They know that if they can get someone to look at the product (see the highly polished motor vehicle in the showroom), hear all about it (the sound of the engine running, its engine and performance specifications), and finally touch and feel the product (sit in it and take it for a drive), they have a much higher potential for making the sale to any person.

Making Presentations

When presenting information to a group of people, many, if not most people fall into the trap of crowding presentation slides with words. When the words are all the *same font* and the *one colour*, they are in effect auditory stimulus. The detail is input by reading it and converting it into internal dialogue. When this is accompanied by a presenter's dialogue, much of what is intended to be passed on is lost to the audience who are not primarily auditory.

So how can we change this? There are a number of ways the presentation can be made more effective.

Stimulate All Senses

My preference is to use pictures and models as the visual stimulus, accompanied by dialogue in the form of stories or analogies that help convey the meaning of the pictures. The pictures can be of virtually anything that's relevant to the subject. In many cases when I'm coaching a group, the picture is incomplete and requires the final part to be drawn on a flip-chart. As I draw it they listen to what I'm saying, watch what I'm doing and draw it in their journals.

By taking these approaches I stimulate all of the senses and the key points are more easily stored by the entire group; irrespective of an individual's sensory preference.

What else could we do?

Use Highlights

We could colour key words with big, bright and bold colours and increase their size so the top 2 or 3 items are clearly identified and can be stored as mental images.

When getting people to remember a number of key points I might get them to hold their hands up and work through the fingers as I highlight the elements or even get them to make a specific physical gesture with each point. This is one way of engaging the kinaesthetic mode in remembering information.

The point to remember is this, if you are going to present to a group, your goal is to connect with as many people as possible. You can only do that when you stimulate all of the three main senses we use for processing, storing and retrieving our experiences.

DEALING WITH CONFLICT

In this piece, I have taken a different approach to all other parts of the book. I have included a number of short activities for the purpose of helping you learn and develop empowering associations. I would encourage you to do the activities proposed, as I am sure you will benefit. All you will need is a pen or pencil.

What is Conflict?

I want you to reflect for a moment and take one minute to write as many responses as you can to this question.

Q1: When you hear the word conflict, what words immediately come to mind?

....

....

....

....

What do you notice about the words you've written? What qualities or attributes do they have? I would be quite confident in assuming that most of the words you have written reflect conflict as a negative thing.

My experience with people across many different industries has shown that this belief is conditioned from an early age and generally becomes a part of the culture of an organisation. That is not to suggest that every person views conflict the same way. For example, members of gangs go out looking for conflict, many individuals trained in the martial arts or pugilism are more than happy to engage in conflict. Different people view conflict in different ways.

So how is the word formally defined?

Conflict Defined

The definitions relevant to the concept from the dictionary and thesaurus are these.

- **Verb** - At war with, to clash, to be at odds, to be inconsistent with, to differ;
- **Noun** - A violent clashing, a trial of strength, a strong disagreement;
- **Thesaurus** - Fight, battle, struggle, dispute, controversy, squabble.

Just as I thought, even these books define conflict in negative terms. The word conjures up pictures of battle, war, disagreement and loss. Anne Fox (2002) suggests that conflict is somewhere between harmony and war.

Conflict is a powerful driver in invoking a whole range of different emotions in people. When it exists in a positive context such as in a sporting event or anywhere where competition is sought, the emotions experienced are positive. However, conflict also exists in contexts that are not positive, and the emotions experienced can be less than desirable. Now while the words used to define conflict give it a negative connotation, conflict is not all bad.

Think about a body builder, how do they develop the muscles they have? By pushing against massive resistance. As they get stronger they are able to push greater resistance. When they stop pushing weights, they start to lose the muscles they have gained. Such is the way we develop our emotional muscles. We develop emotional strength by pushing against resistance through experiencing and confronting challenges, and conflict is one of those recognisable challenges that managers and leaders will be confronted with. Challenges are the implements of the great big gymnasium of life. So let's think about the value that conflict might bring to a team environment.

Over the next **two minutes**, write down as many answers as you can to this question.

Q2: What value can conflict bring to a team?

....

....

....

....

You may have found yourself thinking that conflict can in fact add value to a team. Some of the ways that it does add value might include:

- Encouraging creativity
- Inspiring new ideas
- Overcoming stagnation
- Preventing apathy

As a facilitator, you will have team members from any and every part of an organisation or society in general, depending on the context of your work. In any case, when you bring together a whole bunch of people from all walks of life, conflict is inevitable. You will have to deal with different personality types, personal agendas, individual and group norms, and this means that you have to be able to deal with conflict in an intelligent manner if you are to consistently achieve your desired outcomes.

Conflict may very well cater to one of our basic needs, the need for variety or uncertainty. I know some people look forward to conflict; in fact they seem to be at the heart of conflict as instigators. People like that can be a challenge to work with.

Reactions to Conflict

Conflict can appear in various forms, from a muted disagreement to an event of raised voices, to the extreme where actual violence takes place. These differing forms of conflict are associated with different levels of emotion, and emotions often drive conflict. Once conflict exists, the emotions that are usually generated in a team may be destructive if left unchecked. The bottom line for facilitators is that conflict cannot be ignored.

Reactions

Your values and belief system drives the way you think, and the way you think determines how you behave in different circumstances. Your values and beliefs about conflict will affect how you react to conflict. This reaction will have a great influence over how you deal with conflict. If we want to influence our natural response to conflict, then we need to change the way in which we view conflict.

What you believe is true, and what you think you can create. If you think that conflict is hard to deal with, difficult to resolve then it probably will be. If you believe that conflict is a challenge to be tackled intelligently and opportunity for personal growth, then you're right as well.

For the next minute, write down as many answers as you can to this question.

Q3: As a facilitator, what value can you and the team extract from dealing with conflict?

....

....

....

Now write down as many answers as you can to this question.

Q4: As a facilitator, if you do not deal with conflict, what could be the consequences of that?

....

....

....

If you only thought of conflict in negative terms before reading the text, what do you think of conflict now? I hope you have some positive connotations with the word as a result of this discussion.

Attitudes

Let me add to the conversation by discussing how you can affect the final outcome without even intending to. Your values and beliefs are a foundation for your attitudes. Your attitudes and the way you think will drive how you behave. How you behave is represented by language, voice cues and use of physiology. Think about this for a moment. If you go into a situation with the belief that conflict is inevitable, then this belief will drive your behaviours. You will communicate using your physiology and voice cues in such a way that this conveys conflict as the theme. Your 'self fulfilling prophecy' will be the activation of conflict.

Have you ever experienced that? A simple strategy for preventing this is based around these words. 'Seek and ye shall find' – to find gold you must first look for gold. If you go looking for dirt, then you will find dirt. If you enter a situation looking for evidence of conflict, then you will probably find it. Look for evidence of teamwork, look for areas of agreement and use these as levers to develop the team into a cohesive unit.

Conflict and Team Development

As I mentioned earlier, teams go through a number of development stages. Team behaviours and emotions change as the group moves through these stages. You will notice that I have included the additional stage of adjourning, a stage relevant to project teams that comes together for defined periods.

Phase of Development	Behaviours, Signs
Forming	Exploring behaviours, Boundary testing, Emotions in check
Storming	Familiarity, Express disagreement, Flexing muscles, Out to impress, Defend beliefs, Fragmentation, Pecking orders
Norming	Avoid conflict, Maintain harmony, Ground rules, Cohesion, Confiding, Positive conflict
Performing	Achieve desired outcomes, Accept others thinking and beliefs, Seek to succeed, Constructive, Harmony, Inward looking focus
Adjourning	Disbanding, Fear of change, Upset dynamics, Loyalty, References to the past

Team Development Stages

The phase in which conflict is most likely to be experienced is during the storming phase. One of the strategies of successful team leaders is to accelerate through this phase by using various team-building activities. During the first team meeting, it is important to not jump right into the project content, but to spend time on building the team.

Signs of Involvement in Conflict

Just because someone perceives conflict, does not mean that they feel conflict. Perceived conflict exists when one or more people are aware that conditions of conflict exist. On the other hand, someone who feels conflict is emotionally involved and may feel anxiety, tenseness, frustration or even hostility.

An individual feeling that they are in conflict may exhibit any number of signs. The most common include flushed complexion, shallow breathing, sweating, staring, clenching of fists, talking quickly, and even incoherent speech.

Whilst many people will exhibit these types of signs, people ultimately respond differently to each other. The change may not involve the outward signs mentioned, however any shift from normal behaviour to a state of withdrawal or quietness, could very well be an indicator of conflict of some kind.

Inferences and Conflict

'Peace is easily maintained; trouble easily overcome before it starts. Deal with it before it happens. Set things in order before there is confusion.'

Lao-Tzu (Chinese Philosopher – 6th Century BC)

One of the easiest ways to prevent conflict is to understand the implications of the inference ladder. Let me give you a scenario to start the conversation. I'm facilitating a meeting one morning and a team member arrives 20 minutes late. He comes into the meeting and excuses himself. As the facilitator I experience some emotion, possibly annoyance, maybe even anger. I respond to his late entry with a clear message about how I feel. "Good afternoon" I say as he looks sheepishly towards me and then around the room. Now, have you ever done that I wonder?

Let's break down what occurred into its components.

I observed the team member enter the meeting room 20 minutes after the scheduled start time, and he excused himself. He was dressed in a certain way and he took his place at the table. This was basically the extent of the observed data.

From that data I unconsciously chose to focus on his arriving 20 minutes after the scheduled start time, as this was most important to me. Now one of my values is punctuality, so on the basis of this, I added a personal meaning that this was wrong.

My assumption now was that he arrived late when in fact he could have arrived on time if he had wanted to. This assumption led to the conclusion that he did not care enough about the meeting, nor was he disciplined enough to get there at the right time.

My belief was that he was undisciplined, so on the basis of this, my response was to get a message across that I disapprove of his behaviour by saying; 'good afternoon' and wrapping it in a package of sarcasm.

Climbing the Ladder of Inference

We all do this, not the sarcastic response; I mean we all filter our observations and take action based on a perception. Many times the action taken is totally inappropriate.

So we really understand the concept, as it is key to the success we experience in any relationship, let me describe the process this way.

- We **observe and take in data** from our experiences through our senses.

- We **select certain pieces** of that data (or we could say filter out certain pieces) based on many aspects of our character, natural tendencies, the way we are conditioned to think and so on.
- We **give meaning** to our observations (which are filtered observations by the way), and our values, beliefs and experiences are the determining factors in what that meaning is.
- We then **take action based on the meaning** we've given the experience.

Obviously if the meaning we give to an experience is incorrect, i.e.; my friend actually arrived late because his wife had to be taken to hospital, the action we take is probably going to be inappropriate.

Metaphorically speaking, this is the concept of the **ladder of inference** discussed by Peter Senge in his book the *'Fifth Discipline Fieldbook'*. Senge suggests that we build our own inference ladders about our experiences. The truth is that if we never reflect on the observations that start the sequence, we build the ladder on very shaky foundations.

The diagram below[13] provides a visual representation of the sequence described.

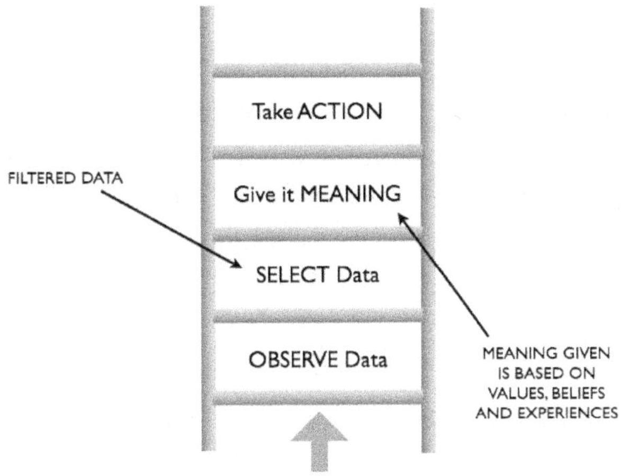

Figure 26: Climbing the Ladder of Inference

Climb Back Down the Ladder

Senge suggests using certain questions to challenge where we are on our ladder of inference, and question our own thinking and reasoning before taking action. The following questions may be useful in preventing conflict between yourself and a team member. Some of these work best when asked of yourself.

- *'What is the observable data here?'*
- *'What data have I excluded that should be considered?'*
- *'When you said (insert quotation), did you mean (insert your inference)'?*
- *'I noticed that you (insert what was observed), help me understand more about that behaviour?'*

When helping resolve conflict between other people, the following questions will be useful.

- *'What is the observable evidence that supports what you're saying?'*
- *'What else could this mean?'*
- *'When has this occurred previously and not meant what you think it means?'*

---

13 Adapted from Peter Senge's ladder of inference described in *'The Fifth Discipline Fieldbook'*.

'Seek first to understand, then to be understood.'

Dr. Stephen Covey

Conflict Management Tips

This text is not intended to be a complete guide to conflict management, but rather provide Black Belts with some useful thoughts on how conflict can be useful, and how to avoid creating unnecessary conflict in a project context.

The following are some common sense tips for resolving conflict.

<u>What You Should Do</u>

- Establish rules for dealing with conflict during the start up meeting with the team
- Bring conflict out into the open when it is safe to do so – i.e.; when a solution will be able to be generated
- Do not take sides – remain impartial
- Take responsibility for building rapport *with* conflict participants
- Interrupt any pattern of behaviour that is not conducive to progress
- Help the participants identify the desired outcome early – that is to successfully resolve the conflict – this creates a common goal, hence common interest that is not content related
- Allow the team or conflict participants to own the solutions
- Focus on interests and not positions. Work to a collaborative solution; i.e. where the interests of both parties are satisfied
- Approach conflict with an open mind, looking for the value it can offer the team
- Have participants focus on the problem, not on other participants to the point where it becomes personalised

<u>What You Should NOT Do</u>

- Emphasise the negative aspects of conflict in the team when it occurs – focus on the positives instead
- Allow conflict to fester by avoiding it – deal with it
- Allow conflict to become personalised – focus on the problem, not the people
- Downplay the importance of the issue – it may well be the most important issue there is for participants

TOO MUCH AGREEMENT & TOO LITTLE AGREEMENT

We all know there can often be too little agreement in a team environment. Terms synonymous with this situation include conflict, disagreement, non-alignment, discord, dispute, difference of opinion, contention, division, dissent, disparity, divergence, clash, contrast, non-conformity etc.

Let me suggest there can also be too much agreement in a team. Terms synonymous with this situation include channelled thinking, acquiescence, like-mindedness, submissive behaviour, dominant behaviour,

What causes too much or too little agreement?

TOO MUCH AGREEMENT	←→	TOO LITTLE AGREEMENT
• Fear to Challenge • High Power Authority • Dominant People • High Relationship Values		• Low Teamwork • Storming • Personal Goals Dominate • Low Relationship Values

Here are a number of easy ways to address these two contrasting situations.

Dealing with TOO MUCH agreement:

- Speak up, state observations
- Ground rules
- Use process tools
- Appoint 'Devils Advocate'

Dealing with TOO LITTLE agreement:

- Speak up, state observations
- Refer to desired outcomes
- Change the process
- Focus on areas of agreement
- Use process tools

THE TEAM LEADER AS COACH

'Regardless of our position in society, every one of us needs a coach or mentor. Without one, our existing paradigms may never be challenged, and the beliefs we currently hold that won't move us beyond today may never be altered.'

The most common role of coach that we think about is that of a sporting coach. In fact the Australian Oxford Dictionary refers to coach in the context of sport. A sporting coach's role is to take the team or individual from where they are to their full potential. In effect, closing the gap between the existing level of achievement to the desired level.

The same applies to coaching in the context of Lean Six Sigma project team leadership. The team leader can and should be a coach to the team. Why would they want to do that? In the first instance, the purpose of coaching is to help people improve their performance. As people around you increase their skill level, they will perform better, and finally they are able to take on more and more responsibility.

A Lean Six Sigma project team leader who acts as coach to the team will experience a number of benefits:

- **Reduced workload** and supervision time, hence more time to devote to project leadership and results.
- **Project acceleration** through increased productivity and follow through. When people own something, they are more likely to see it to its conclusion.
- **Greater recognition**, respect and loyalty from those around you.
- The attraction of others towards you. People are drawn to quality leaders.
- **The multiplication of influence**. By coaching others effectively, you are developing leaders. A leader who willingly develops other leaders, experiences a multiplication of personal influence.
- A **greater sense of fulfilment** as a person
- **Encouragement** in return – encouragement in the growth of others makes them want to encourage you in return.

George Elton Mayo's Hawthorne Experiments

Harvard Business School professor George Elton Mayo conducted a series of studies at the Western Electric Company Hawthorne Works in Chicago (USA) to understand the variables that affected productivity.

These studies, which ran from 1927 to 1932, grew out of preliminary experiments at the plant from 1924 to 1927 in which time he studied the effects of lighting on productivity.

The preliminary experiments consisted of turning up the level of illumination on the factory floor, at the same time measuring productivity. Just as Mayo had hypothesised, production went up with the increased illumination.

To validate his experiment, Mayo reduced the amount of illumination and again measured productivity. To his surprise, production stayed up. He found that no matter what he did with the lighting, production stayed up. During his discussions with the workers involved, Mayo found out that the interest shown by his team of researchers in the performance of the workers had made them feel valued. The increase in morale experienced had led to the increased levels of production.

Mayo subsequently studied numerous other variables and their affect on productivity, resulting in his description of an effect known widely as the 'Hawthorne Effect'.

The 'Hawthorne Effect' can be reproduced in a project team if the team leader is one who values each individual team member, and satisfied their intrinsic need to grow as a person.

The Western Electric Hawthorne Works in Chicago (USA), the site of George Elton Mayo's 1927 to 1932 experiments on productivity.

BEING A SUCCESSFUL COACH TO POTENTIAL LEADERS

Coaching is a commitment to the growth and development of the people around you. A successful coach is one that supports individuals and team members to grow in order that they achieve their true potential. To do that requires the coach to develop a broad range of knowledge and skill. To be a successful coach, you must:

Master The Art of Questioning

To get good answers, all you have to do is ask good questions. By asking more questions and giving fewer answers, you promote an environment of thought, discussion and ultimately learning. Teaching people how to find answers, is much more valuable to them than giving them the answers all of the time. *'Give a man a fish and you feed him for a day, teach a man to fish and you feed him for a lifetime.'*

Interrupt Limiting Patterns

The barriers and limitations to our true potential are the patterns of thinking and behaviour that we have conditioned over time. A successful coach is able to recognise and interrupt these patterns consistently until they no longer exist. Pattern interruptions include:

- Humour;
- Sudden or fast movement;
- Major physiological shifts; and
- Good questions.

Turn Every Experience Into a Learning Experience

In the words of poet Archibald MacLeish: *"There is only one thing more painful than learning from experience, and that is not learning from experience."*

High achievers know there is no such thing as failure, only results. Results are feedback from which we can learn, and successful coaches reinforce this principle through effectively questioning people. Questions such as 'What did you learn from that', or 'What must you do differently to make it work', or 'What can you use from that to make the next time better', all change the way a person perceives a particular experience.

"Sometimes we win, sometimes we learn."

Empower Team Members

According to John Maxwell (1995), empowerment is fundamental to developing the people around you. One of the most effective ways to empower a team is to teach them the skills of Lean Six Sigma during project work.

Instead of facilitating everything yourself, try the strategy of teaching the process to the team using a non project related subject, and then coaching them through the process of facilitating the process using the project content. Empowerment occurs when you provide people with three things:

- Opportunity to do things they have never done before;
- Freedom to do it their own way; and
- Security in knowing that you will stand by them if the result is not as expected.

Model The Behaviour You Desire

"Your actions speak so loudly that I cannot hear what you are saying."

The bottom line to leadership is this – people will do as you do, they will model what they see modelled, thus congruence between what you say and do is of the utmost importance.

Albert Schweitzer was absolutely correct when he said *"Example is not the main thing in influencing others ..... it is the only thing."*

Participate in Two Way Feedback

Tell people what they need to hear to take them to the next level. Encourage people to tell you what you need to hear in order for you to take yourself to the next level.

Developing Coaching Skills

If you want to develop your skills as a coach, I would encourage you to do this simple exercise.

1. Find someone that you would like to coach, who has a personal challenge they would like help with
2. Effectively listen as they tell you about their challenge
    a. Build rapport
    b. Ask open questions
3. Confirm understanding
    a. Paraphrase what they are saying
    b. Summarise what they said at the end
4. Put yourself in their shoes
    a. Imagine you are that person or those people
    b. Think about what you would do if you were them
5. Ask good questions to facilitate a solution
    a. Discuss the potential causes of the current situation
    b. Help them generate as many ways to resolve the situation as possible
    c. Help them choose a way of resolving the situation
6. Learn from feedback
    a. Identify what worked and what might be done differently next time

THE GIFT OF FEEDBACK

Feedback is a Constant

Feedback is a constant in our lives. As people drive to work in their motor vehicles each day and constantly watch the dashboard of dials and gauges, they are constantly using feedback to make decisions. That feedback is used to inform the observer about the current state, and allow them to quickly make decisions about what course of action must be taken to either sustain or change the current state. If the feedback says the speed is too slow, the driver then makes a decision to accelerate to the desired speed.

Feedback in the context of Lean Six Sigma project leadership work is a powerful tool for rapidly enhancing the performance of you, the team and its individuals. My experience over the years is that people who manage meetings, underutilise the power of feedback, in fact some people I have worked with never use feedback as a formal tool for improvement in the way they manage teams.

Why is that? Think about this for a moment. When you receive feedback about your performance, do you have a propensity for defending when the feedback is perceived to be negative? Many people do.

Over years of repetition, most people I have worked with have conditioned a negative association with feedback that doesn't tell them how wonderful they are. In fact the association is so strong in some cases, people in supervisory positions cannot give feedback about less than expected performance.

In essence, what you believe about feedback, and the associations you have conditioned with feedback will determine how you give and receive feedback.

Empowering Beliefs About Feedback

Let me offer you some empowering beliefs to hold about feedback:

- There is no failure, only results – the only meaning these results have is the meaning we give them.
- Feedback is fundamental to learning. It is a gift from which we can grow as people.
- When people give feedback, they are telling you what they truly believe. Their perception is their reality. Defence of your perception is a pointless exercise.
- What we feedback to others is a reflection of what we accept or don't accept of ourselves.

Receiving Feedback

Giving feedback is only half of the equation. We must also receive feedback and this is often the most challenging half of the equation. To become better at giving feedback, we must first master the receipt of feedback. The following tips will serve to turn feedback into the gift that it is.

- Remind yourself of the beliefs you should have about feedback;
- Seek to fully understand at the behavioural level;
- Take full responsibility for building and maintaining rapport with the person giving feedback;
- Ask how to do it differently, what behaviour would change that person's perception;
- Do not defend your perception or behaviour;
- Effectively listen; and finally
- Be an example of how you want people to respond when you give them feedback.

Giving Feedback

I will always remember the first 'Australian Idol' television show series shown during 2003, for one particular incident. One of the panel judges, Ian (Dicko) Dickson, gave a female singer who was in the final top five, feedback about her appearance. She had worn a gold dress that was not really suited to her build (this was the opinion of many who watched the show according to media over the next few days). He said: "You should change what you wear or shed a few pounds." Well as you can imagine, the uproar that resulted was enormous. Over the next 24 hours the comment was played repeatedly on general radio, talk back shows and current affair programs. In the harsh world of music, the feedback was honest and sincerely intended. In our culture of never mentioning the unmentionables, emotions run riot.

We're all experts at giving feedback, when it's positive of course. The challenge is to give feedback that may be perceived as negative, in such a way that it is constructive. The following tips will serve to turn your feedback into the gift that it is:

- Take full responsibility for building rapport;
- Describe behaviours and observations;
- Provide examples or evidence of the behaviours;
- Offer a suggestion for how to do it differently; and
- If understanding is not evident, change the way you communicate the message until understanding is confirmed.

Remember, feedback is a gift. Feedback serves to help every one of us grow, and as Lean Six Sigma practitioners we must seek feedback at every opportunity. Specific opportunities include (a) at the end of a meeting, (b) at the end of the project, and (c) any time you are engaged in a face-to-face discussion.

PART 3 – LEAN SIX SIGMA PROJECT FOCUS

CHAPTER 6: A LEAN MENTALITY

LEAN - SIMPLY A WAY OF THINKING

The term 'lean' comes from the concept of using half the manufacturing space, half the human effort, half the tools and half the time to develop a new product. While a mass producer would traditionally have a 'good enough' view of production and believe that to get better would cost more than it was worth, lean producers have an entirely different belief and continue to pursue perfection.

Lean thinking recognises that few processes are created to deliver customer defined value in the most *efficient* way possible. In reality, most production processes are created to *maximise the quality* of a product.

Let me give you an example. My company used to produce Audio CDs for personal development. The process involved a *one time only* activity of making the recording, and then the ongoing activities of burning, printing, packaging and shipping. The focus of our work in designing the process was on the quality of the product.

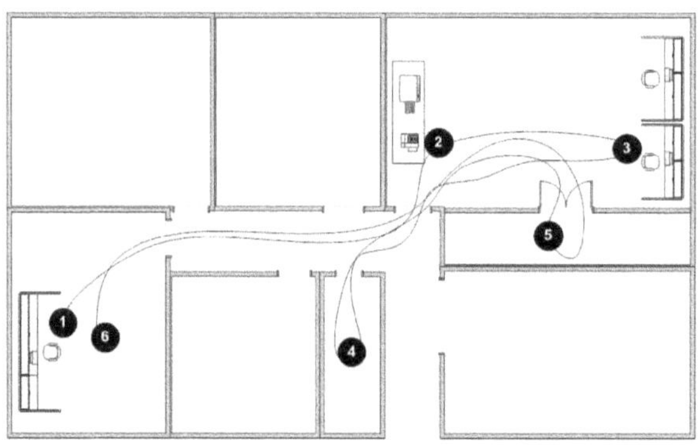

Figure 27: Example of an Inefficient Workplace Layout

The concept of flow through the process never even entered our minds. The CD cases were stored wherever space permitted with no thought to how much movement we would have to undertake to fill orders, a large number of disks were stored for future supply and sometimes these would be moved around as we cleaned or rearranged the office.

The diagram shown on the previous page is a plan of the office with a line representing the movement undertaken by a person when responding to an order for CDs. Notice how far a person had to walk to complete the task. Now while time and flow were never considered, we got away with it due to the size and nature of our organisation. However, that does not mean it's efficient!

How many larger organisations, particularly those that have products passing through a production line or documents passing through a process of approval or even customers moving through a queue, focused on making sure their processes produced high quality outputs with little thought to maximising flow and minimising waste? My experience has been there are many opportunities to enhance performance in every company by including Lean Thinking concepts in the scope of their continual improvement endeavour[14].

DIFFERENT APPROACHES TO LEAN

The Lean Workplace / Lean Pyramid

Many consulting firms and outside agencies try to replicate the success Toyota had in the development of their 'Toyota Way', by implementing specific tools, one at a time, in a pyramid building approach.

What's important to recognise is that one of the keys to Toyota's success lies in the fact that employees were totally committed to the objectives they were trying to achieve and 'the Toyota Way' was developed with their participation.

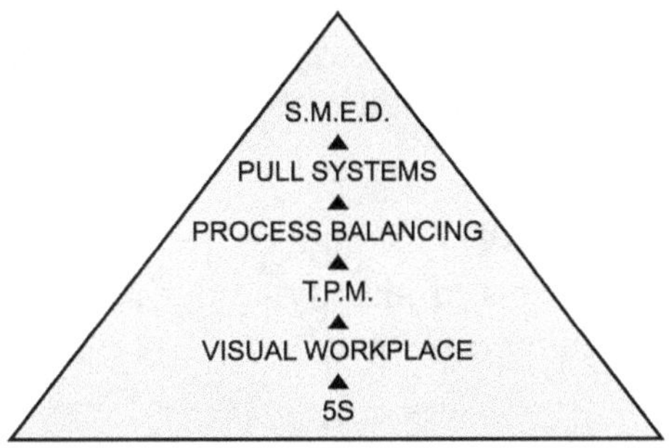

Figure 28: Example Lean Pyramid

There is always risk in trying to achieve the same level of success by trying to sequentially roll out specific lean tools as a 'management initiative'. I am no longer surprised by the fact that many people think Lean is actually 5S. And most of the people who think that, tell me about the bad experiences they've had with roll outs of these tools.

Lean Projects

Lean projects on the other hand differ in that the work follows the traditional DMAIC process.

While the DMAIC sequence is more commonly referred to in a Six Sigma context, it is totally relevant to projects focused on reducing time, inventory or any form of waste that is best treated using Lean specific tools.

This textbook focuses on this project / problem solving approach to the application of Lean.

[14] For more information on this topic, read the author's 2007 publication - *'Process Alchemy - 2nd Edition'*

CHAPTER 7: 'DEFINE' PHASE FOR SPONSORS AND PROCESS OWNERS

THE MOST IMPORTANT ACTIVITY OF BUSINESS IMPROVEMENT

Identification of the improvement opportunity is probably one of the most important activities business leaders / managers can undertake, yet in my opinion it is possibly the most undervalued and poorly performed task. I don't believe this is due to any fault on the part of those leaders or managers involved; rather, it is a fault of the system and lack of proper education in that organisation.

Whose job is it to identify the opportunities that Lean Six Sigma Green and Black Belts work on?

It is a role of business leaders and managers to choose relevant improvement projects for any formal improvement initiative such as Lean Six Sigma. While every employee must participate in improvement, it is these big-ticket projects that will add the most value to the organisation, and get the most focus from the leaders involved.

In this part of the book I will present a number of ways you might approach this task for one very good reason. It is highly likely that you, as a Green Belt or Black Belt, will have to facilitate or help with the process.

Approaches to Project Identification

Three major tools we can use in the process of identifying our most significant improvement projects are drawn from Six Sigma, Lean and Design for Six Sigma.

- SIPOC
- Value Stream Analysis
- Quality Function Deployment

Before I expand on these tools, I think it makes sense to first have a conversation on the topic of business processes.

CORE BUSINESS PROCESSES

Michael Porter (as presented by Mintzberg and Quinn[15] - 1996) describes business processes as being of two types - Primary Processes and Secondary Processes. Let me start with a discussion of the latter.

Secondary Processes

These are the processes involved in supporting primary processes. Through the provision of inputs, technology, human resources, and various other organisation wide functions, secondary processes support or *enable the creation of value*.

Secondary processes most commonly include those that are associated with:

[15] Mintzberg, H., Quinn, J., *'The Strategy Process – Concepts, Contexts, Cases'*, Porter's Generic Strategies, New Jersey, Prentice Hall Inc. (1996)

Primary Processes

By contrast, primary processes are those involved in the actual or physical creation of the products or services, their sale and transfer to customers, and after sales service.

Primary processes are those that actually create value for the business, and usually include these major elements:

- Inbound logistics
- Operations
- Outbound logistics
- Marketing and sales
- Service

The diagram below shows how the two relate to one another. Primary processes are represented across the top as the major steps that create the outputs the company passes on to customers. Secondary processes are shown supporting these from the bottom of the diagram.

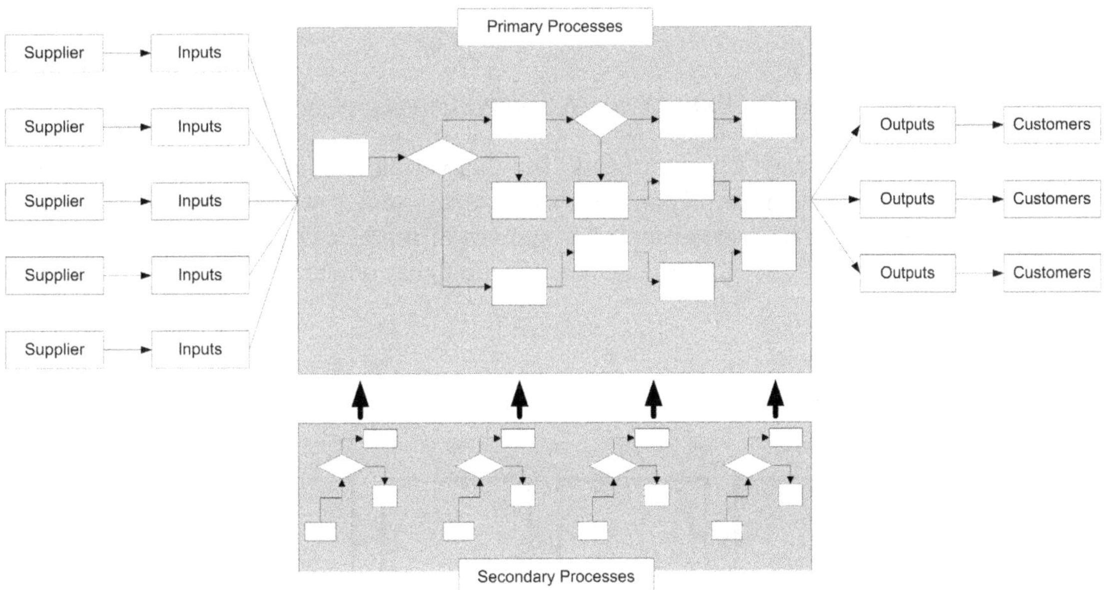

Figure 29: Primary and Secondary Business Processes

So that's an overview of business processes. Let's explore the value stream concept.

THE IDEA OF A VALUE STREAM

We might define a Value Stream in this way:

Value Stream (*n*): *The consolidated sequence and flow of all of the activities or operations required for the design, ordering, production and delivery of products or services to a customer.*

So when we talk about value streams, we are really discussing the major process components in their linear sequence from the most upstream point of design to the end point of delivery to the customer. In other words, a reference to the primary process of a business.

Single or Multiple Value Streams

Depending on the organisation, the company's value stream can consist of a single series of processes or multiple series of processes.

For example, a company that has a single sequence of macro processes in its value stream would be a commodity producer such as a coal mine. Core business processes can be represented by a single chain as shown in the figure below, thus it would have one value stream.

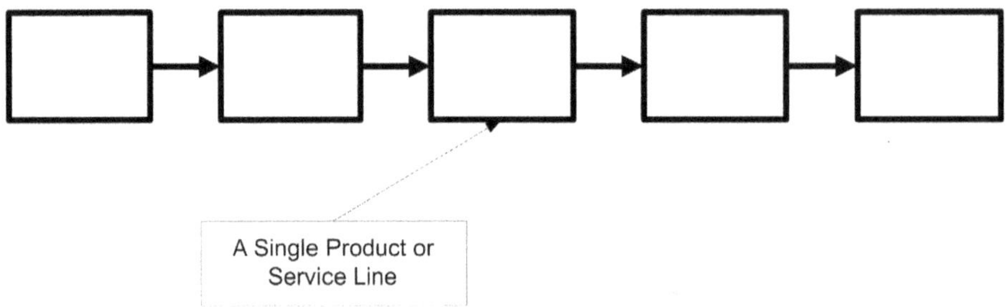

Figure 30: Value Stream for Single Product or Service

A company that has numerous value streams for delivering goods and services would be a telecommunications company such as Telstra, which provides a range of products and services. Core or primary business processes can be represented by a number of product or service streams that transgress across the individual functions of the business as shown in the figure on the next page.

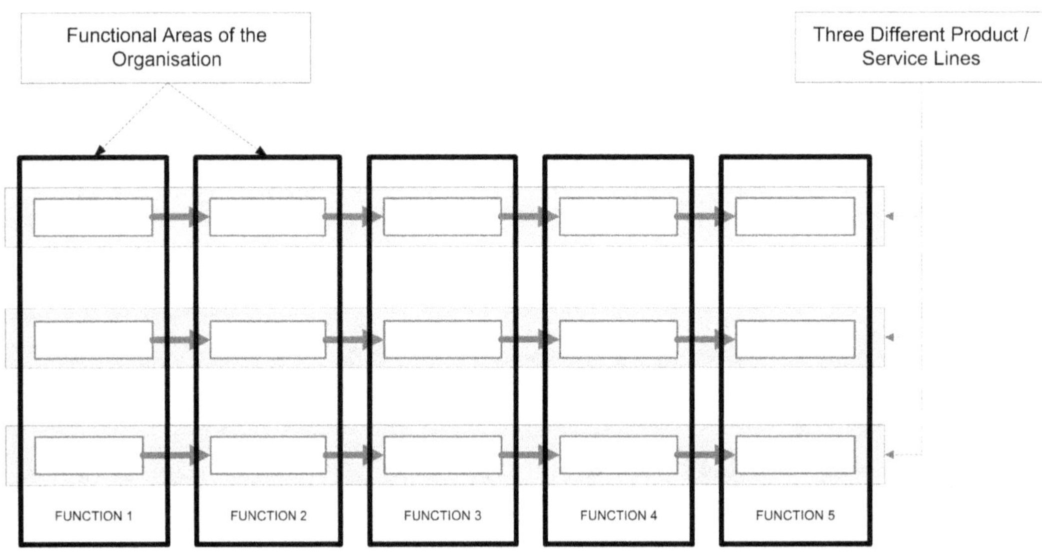

Figure 31: Value Streams for Multiple Products or Services

LISTENING TO VOICES

In the world of psychology, Sigmund Freud may have referred to you as someone in need of closer scrutiny if you had told him you were listening to voices. However, in the world of business improvement, if you aren't listening to voices, you're probably way off the mark when it comes to sustainable success.

The four voices we must continually listen to in order to maintain direction and progress are these.

- **The Voice of the Customer:** Represented by customer needs or requirements - where gaps exist in meeting customer needs (internal and external), opportunities arise to be more effective in our work.
- **The Voice of the Business:** Represented by business needs or requirements - where gaps exist in meeting business goals or achieving specific internal performance targets (ideally linked to strategy and business plans), opportunities arise to be more efficient *and* effective in our day-to-day activities.
- **The Voice of the Process:** Represented by process data, either plotted collectively in relevant charts or viewed as the result of some equation - where undesirable variation and unnecessary waste is observed, opportunities exist to take greater control of the efficiency *and* effectiveness of a process.
- **The Voice of Stakeholders:** Represented by the concerns and ideas of all stakeholders - where improvements can be made in general that result in increased morale, greater satisfaction, enhanced safety of key stakeholders and stakeholder groups (such as employees, staff, owners etc), opportunities exist to become a much better organisation to work for, to supply to, to invest in and to buy from.

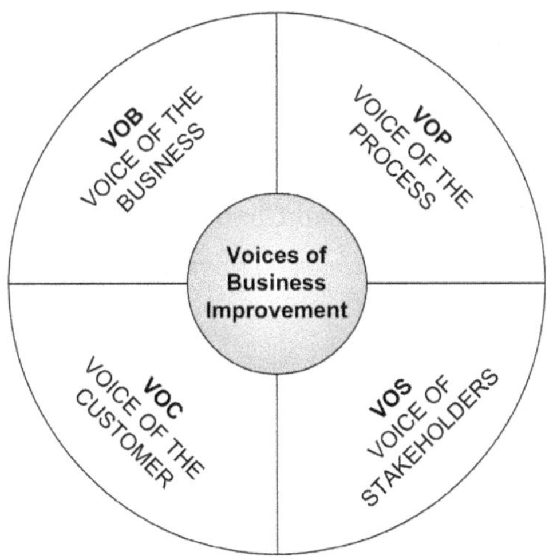

Figure 32: Voices of Business Improvement

Documenting the Voices and Recording Performance

All businesses that have experienced success with Lean and Six Sigma, are great at clarifying and documenting the voice of customers and the business (their needs or requirements), and collecting and displaying performance data linked to those requirements (the voice of the process).

The tools that follow provide process owners with a process for doing that remarkably well.

- **S.I.P.O.C.** provides a framework for recording customer and business requirements.
- **Value Stream Analysis (VSA)** on the other hand, provides a framework for understanding actual performance against those specified *efficiency* and *effectiveness* needs.

- **Quality Function Deployment (QFD)** links the business directly with the customer through a thorough analysis of customer requirements for any product or service.

Keep these voices in mind as you work through the remainder of the material, for they are the only voices that really matter.

IDENTIFYING OPPORTUNITIES WITH S.I.P.O.C.

This tool is one of the most widely known tools from Six Sigma. It's quite simply a framework for documenting a core business process and its associated input and output components. It is usually referred to by the SIPOC acronym, the letters of which are drawn from the headings of the main columns of the tool that you will see below. The tool is sometimes referred to as a SIPOCR or SIPOC+R as customers' 'requirements' also form an integral part of the tool.

Misunderstanding of SIPOC

In my opinion, SIPOC is one of the tools that has slowly, but surely, drifted away from its original intent. It is often taught to Six Sigma Green Belts and Black Belts as a 'must do' for each and every project at the start of the process.

The SIPOC was originally developed to help a process owner determine what a customer wanted from a process, and where the greatest opportunity was to reduce the production of defective products. If a process owner uses this tool to achieve these outcomes (i.e. know what to measure and where to focus improvement efforts), a Six Sigma project team leader does not need to prepare a SIPOC at the beginning of a project.

Assuming the project team already knows what key process metric the project is supposed to be improving, the tool most appropriate to their needs at the beginning of a project is one that helps them identify relevant variables as pre-work to any data collection. For reasons explained in the 'control' phase of this textbook, the SIPOC certainly becomes relevant to a team at the end of the project.

(For more information, refer to the Define phase and Control phase notes in this textbook.)

SIPOC is a tool that should be used by every process owner, not just as a part of opportunity identification, but as a part of process performance management.

SIPOC Format

The SIPOC is comprised of eight elements that we layout in the following format.

<table>
<tr><th>Suppliers</th><th>Inputs</th><th>Process</th><th>Outputs</th><th>Customers</th></tr>
<tr><td>(who supplies the inputs)</td><td>(the inputs required to be able to produce the outputs of the process)</td><td>(a high level macro process map)</td><td>(the tangible products or services provided to the customer)</td><td>(the recipient/s of the outputs defined)</td></tr>
<tr><th colspan="2">Input Requirements</th><th>Business Requirements</th><th colspan="2">Customer Requirements</th></tr>
<tr><td colspan="2">(the requirements that must be met by suppliers for relevant inputs)</td><td>(the requirements the business places on the process - these relate to specific business needs)</td><td colspan="2">(the requirements the customer has of the outputs provided - must be met to prevent a 'defect' being experienced)</td></tr>
</table>

Figure 33: SIPOC Format

The SIPOC shown on the following page was developed for the process associated with the deployment of new PC's at a remote business site.

The example shows a simple process with a small number of 'macro level' steps. In reality this simplicity can be carried over to the core processes of any business. For example, the creation of a Boeing aircraft could be documented in six or seven high level steps.

Example SIPOC

Suppliers	Inputs	Process	Outputs	Customers
Compaq IS Dept. Customer Customer IS Dept. IS Dept. Microsoft IS Dept.	**Materials** New PC Cables **Information** PC Order User Details IP Address **Resources** Software SOE Disks LAN	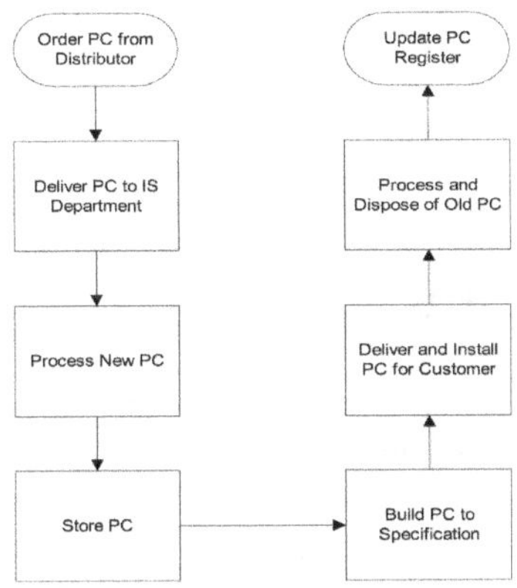	Installed PC	End Users

Input Requirements	Business Requirements	Customer Requirements
• PC matches order (accuracy) • PC delivered within 14 days - undamaged • Customer order specifies extra software requirements • Functional Network	• Single PC supplier (contracted) • All PC purchases within supplier contract specifications • Old PCs disposed of within 120 day cycle • Comply with HSE legislation, policies and procedures • Breakdown PC replacements available same day	• New PC • PC matches order (accuracy) • SOE installed • Specified software installed • Functional Network - email etc • Connected to peripherals • Delivered and installed within 45 days

Figure 34: SIPOC Example

This tool provides a solid foundation for process owners and managers to understand the entire process from its inputs through to its outputs, as well as the requirements the customer has of these outputs and the service provided.

Some businesses use this tool as the framework for their standard operating procedures. When it is used as a foundation for understanding the following, a SIPOC can be an invaluable aid in effectively managing and improving core business process performance.

- The requirements your customers have of you,
- The requirements you have of your suppliers, and
- Any business related performance requirements.

SIPOC IN IMPROVEMENT PROJECT IDENTIFICATION

Having laid the information out in this format, the process owner is in a much better position to understand what to measure and then where to focus attention to add greater value to the end customer and the business itself.

Through:

1. Knowing *what* the needs of the business, customer and the process are;
2. Collecting data; and
3. Clarifying actual performance with respect to those needs;

projects can be chosen that target improvement where these needs are not being effectively met and the greatest opportunity to add value exists. While a SIPOC doesn't give you this information specifically, it does tell you what you need to measure performance against.

For more information about creating a SIPOC, refer to the Control Phase chapter of this text.

IDENTIFYING OPPORTUNITIES WITH VALUE STREAM ANALYSIS

'The value chain focused organisation is one that focuses on multiple processes from an end-to-end perspective. An organisation with this approach moves away from the traditional hierarchical structure to a structure based on a horizontal process flow. Primary relationships are customer - supplier based, and the style of leadership shifts from authoritarian to participative. Business leaders and managers aim to establish a seamless link between processes through optimising exchanges and interfaces. The interface between processes and customers will be the driving force for decision-making and behaviour.'

Value Stream Analysis

Value Stream Analysis (VSA) is a process for:

a. **Documenting** the flow of information, materials and activities through each of the product or service value streams used by a company to generate profits; and
b. **Analysing** the *actual performance* of that process with respect to the needs of the customer and the business as well as other efficiency metrics.

It can most effectively be used following the development of a SIPOC.

Why would we do VSA?

The desired outcome is to distinguish value adding from non-value adding activities and to understand the existence of waste as a product goes through a process.

It differs from typical process mapping used in traditional Six Sigma in a number of ways.

- A value stream map usually represents a process at a much higher level than a process map or flowchart. It usually covers the process from receiving raw materials through to delivery of finished products.
- It displays a broader range of information by representing a combination of information, material and production flow as units pass through the process.
- A value stream map helps to make waste in a process more obvious.

The Value Stream Map

VSA involves the use of simple graphics and icons that are assembled in such a way that the 'value stream' for a particular product or service can be understood.

This assembly of icons is referred to as a 'value stream map' as shown in the following example.

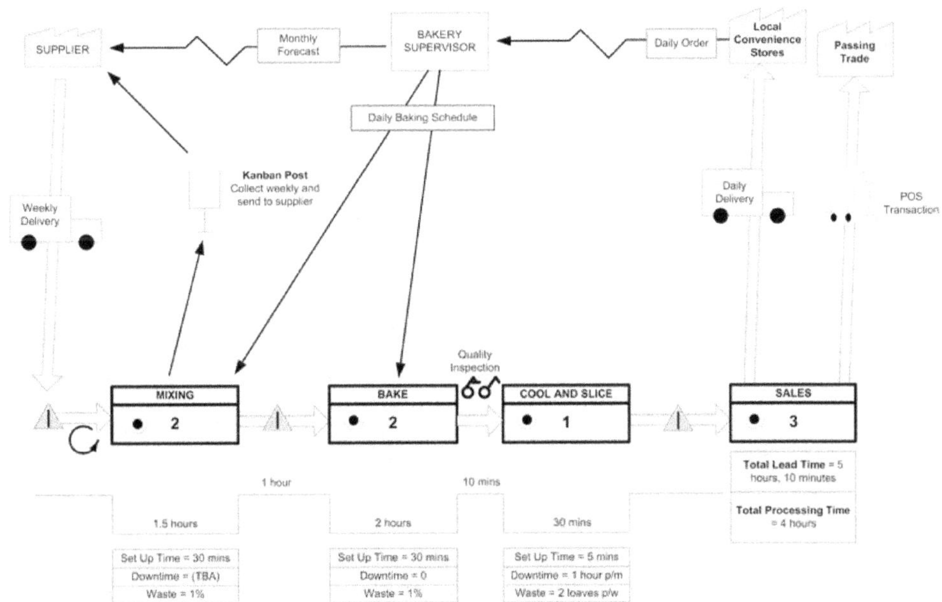

Figure 35: Value Stream Map Example

You will notice in this particular example, boxes represent the process and the sequence from 'mixing' to 'sales' is laid out at a macro level.

The flow of information is indicated in various ways, and a series of measurements are captured at the lower part of the map.

Value Stream Map Icons

To understand a value stream map, you must first understand the standard icons and notations used in the map. The following diagram depicts some of the most commonly used icons.

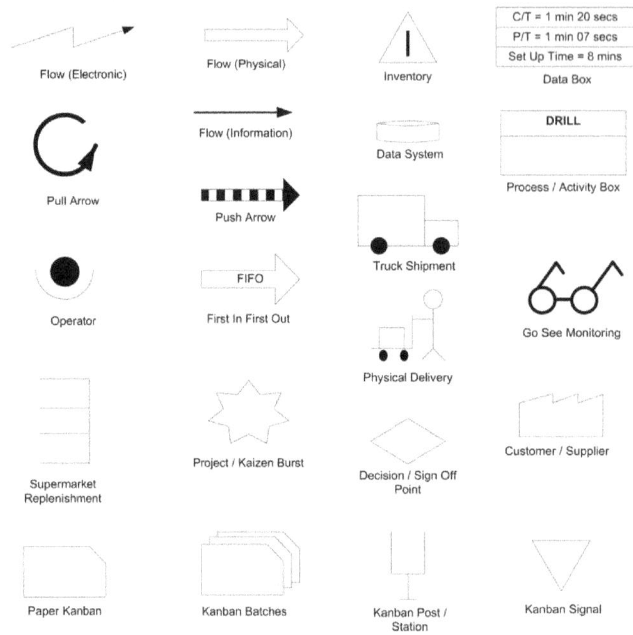

Figure 36: VSM Icons

DIMENSIONS OF VALUE STREAM MEASUREMENT

There are three principal dimensions for measuring the performance of value streams:

- **Horizontally through** the value stream as customer needs are interpreted
- **Vertically down** into the value stream as the business needs are interpreted
- In the **space between process steps** where the factory of waste conceals itself

1. Horizontally Through the Value Stream

This dimension relates to how effective one is in meeting the needs of the *customer*. The measure has application across the business as a whole and for each of the functional areas within the business who all have internal customers. Effectiveness measures can also be linked to the requirements that suppliers must meet in order for you to meet your customer's requirements.

Key Horizontal Metrics

As you will find, a number of metrics from the Six Sigma toolkit are designed to help you understand and identify major effectiveness issues.

These include:

- **Cycle Time:** The time that passes between the start and completion of a process or process step (eg: leave processing, Software Loading etc).
- **Yield:** A measure for determining process performance based on the proportion of units that are defect free.

- **Final Yield:** A measure for determining the proportion of units produced that are defect free at the end of the process.
- **Rolled Throughput Yield:** A measure for determining the performance of the process as a whole, taking into consideration yield at each step along the way.
- **Process Sigma Quality Level:** A measure for determining the performance of a process based on the number of Defects Per Million Opportunities (DPMO) produced and how this number relates to variation.

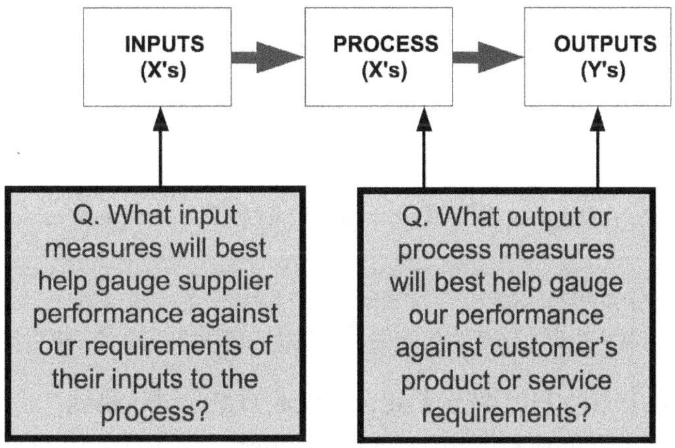

Figure 37: Questions to Identify Effectiveness Measures

2. Vertically Down into the Value Stream

This relates to how efficient one is in the use of resources, linked to the needs of the *business*. Efficiency measures mostly focus on use of time, money and physical resources.

Key Vertical Metrics

These include:

- **Cost Per Unit:** The actual cost of producing one unit of a product. Units can be defined by weight (e.g. one tonne of product) or any other product relevant metric.
- **Units Per Hour Worked:** This metric takes into consideration total hours worked by employees and units produced per worked hour (whereas units per hour or cycle time to produce one unit do not).
- **Productivity Measures:** In economics, productivity refers to actual output from production processes per unit of input. For example, labor productivity may be typically measured as a ratio of units (the output) per labor-hour (the input).

A vitally important point to remember is this:

'In the absence of effectiveness measures (customer focused), efficiency measures will drive a silo mentality and ultimately result in lost efficiency across the company'.

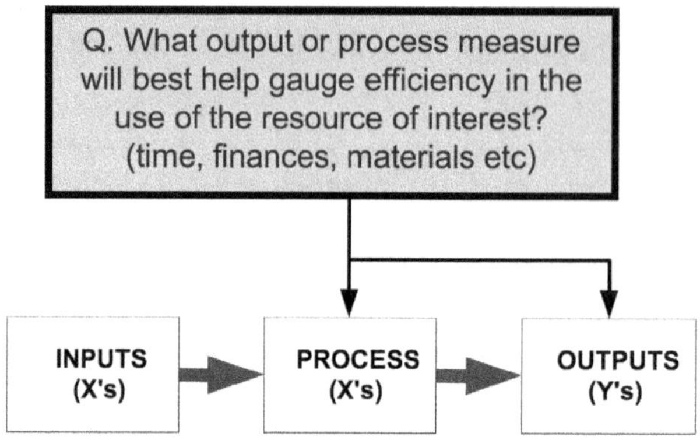

Figure 38: Questions to Identify Efficiency Measures

3. In the Process Where the Hidden Factory of Waste Exists

As you will find, a number of metrics from the Lean toolkit are perfectly designed to help you identify major efficiency issues, predominantly those associated with speed and flow. These are often missed by standard productivity measures mentioned previously.

Key Efficiency Metrics

These include:

- **Processing Time:** The time taken to complete one cycle of a designated activity or operation in a work process.
- **Process Cycle Efficiency:** PCE is a measure of overall process health and is calculated as a percentage by dividing value added time by total lead time (refer to Little's Law). A PCE of 25 percent is considered to be world class, although it will vary according to different applications.

$$\text{PCE} = \frac{\text{Value Added Time}}{\text{Total Lead Time}}$$

- Sometimes referred to as the 'law of velocity', Little's Law is the equation used to calculate total lead time. It simply involves dividing total work in progress by the average completion rate. Reducing total lead time involves increasing capacity or average completion rate, or reducing work in progress.

$$\text{Total Lead Time} = \frac{\text{Work In Progress (WIP)}}{\text{Average Completion Rate}}$$

- **VA/NVA Ratio:** This is a ratio that is calculated by comparing the amount of value added (VA) time to non value added (NVA) time in a work process.
- **Set Up Time:** Time taken to actually set up for production of a particular unit. This becomes particularly relevant when changing dies in a production line that produces multiple types of

products.

- **Inventory Turns:** The number of times inventory is consumed in a specific period of time.
- **Inventory:** A measurement of parts, products or material that sit for a period of time in a production line, store or stockpile. Inventory includes raw materials, work in progress as well as finished or final products.
- **Queueing Time:** The length of time a unit waits in line before work commences on it. Also referred to as wait time.

USING VALUE STREAM ANALYSIS IN PROJECT IDENTIFICATION

A process owner can create a framework for selecting excellent projects using Value Stream Analysis in this way:

- Develop a **SIPOC** of the process so there is a clear understanding of the requirements placed on the process by the customer and the business as well as the requirements placed on suppliers by the process itself – these provide clues as to some of the key measures to include in your Value Stream Map
- Develop the **Value Stream Map** and obtain performance data for key measures of effectiveness and efficiency
- Select and prioritise **projects** based on the greatest opportunities for value growth according to how well the process is performing against these measures

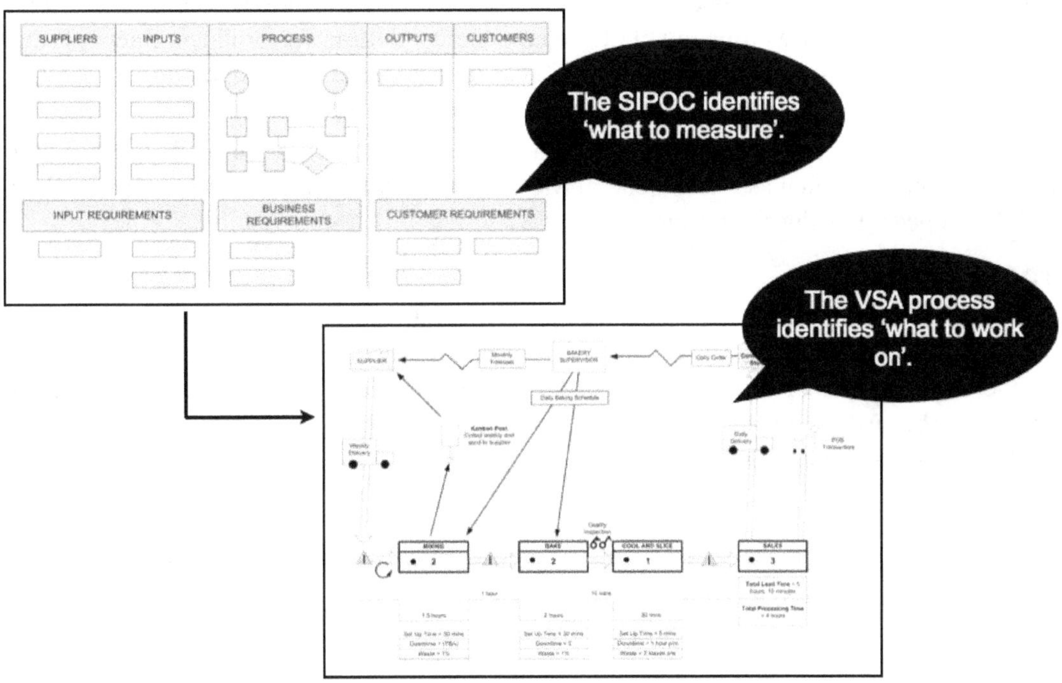

Figure 39: Project Selection with VSA

IDENTIFYING OPPORTUNITIES WITH QFD

'No matter how effectively a company meets the initial needs of its customers, it must remain constantly alert and responsive to its customers' continuing wants and needs. If the company is not responsive to these changing needs, the passage of time will erode its early advantages.'

Ronald G. Day (Author of Quality Function Deployment – Linking a Company with Its Customers)

Quality Function Deployment

Quality Function Deployment (QFD) is a process that directly links the voice of the customer to internal processes. It is used extensively in designing processes to produce products (or services) that meet or exceed the changing expectations of customers, and is well known to practitioners of Design For Six Sigma (DFSS).

It has design application in a variety of industries or business functions including manufacturing, service delivery and technology development.

Before we discuss its application in opportunity identification, let's explore its history first.

History of QFD

Yoyi Akao and associates reportedly first used QFD at Mitsubishi's Kobe shipyard in Japan during the early 1970's. Its use soon spread into the Japanese quality movement, and examples from the motor vehicle industry show how invaluable this process has been to some large organisations. Besterfield (1999) cites the example of Honda and Toyota who were able to reduce the cycle time for producing new products to less than three years through use of QFD. At that time, US car manufacturers were operating on a five-year cycle time, leaving the Japanese manufacturers with a considerable market advantage.

QFD proved so successful that its use extended to process improvement work in the United States during the mid 1980's. Companies such as Ford, General Motors, Hewlett Packard, Xerox, Jaguar and AT&T have adopted and developed QFD since that time.

The Purpose of QFD

The *primary* purpose of QFD is to translate customer needs into design features or technical requirements related to the specific product or service being developed. Its use creates a situation where people fully understand the requirements of a product or service being offered by their company. Used correctly, it organises voice of the customer data in such a way, that the relationship between design features and those needs and expectations are understood.

The House of Quality

The tool used in QFD is comprised of a number of matrices, and when these matrices are assembled they resemble the structure of a house, hence its name 'house of quality'.

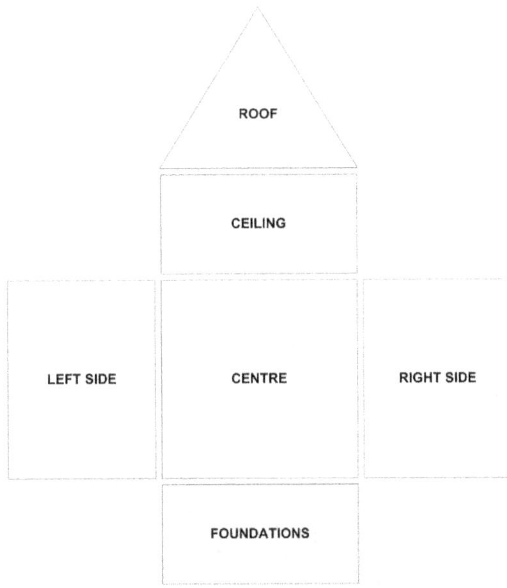

Figure 40: House of Quality Format

House of Quality Components

The house of quality consists of two main components, each of these distinguished by the plane on which they sit.

The **horizontal plane** focuses entirely on the customer. It defines what the customer actually wants from a product or service, how important these expectations are, and how well competitors are meeting their expectations.

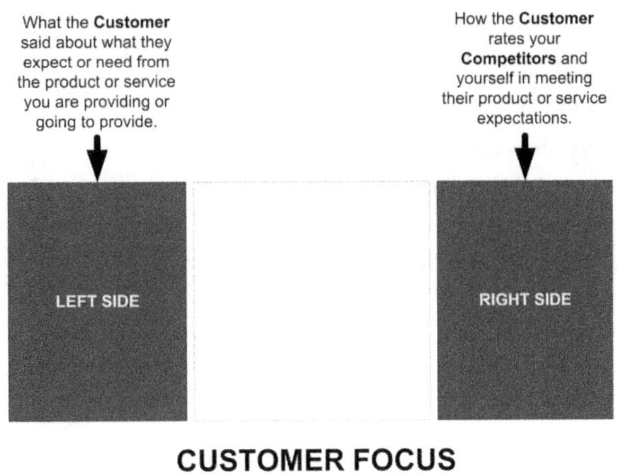

Figure 41: Horizontal Plane of the House of Quality

The **vertical plane** of the house of quality focuses on the technical aspects of the product or service. It translates customer expectations into design features, defines those features that are critical and establishes the targeted values that must be met for the business to be competitive in the market.

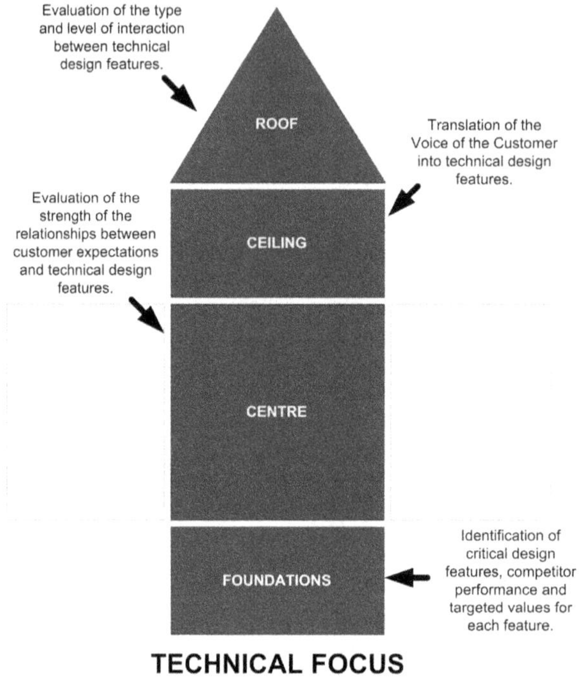

Figure 42: Vertical Plane of the House of Quality

These two planes are integrated to form the full house of quality as shown in the shown diagram.

Developing this 'house of quality' has the effect of focusing design and development work on producing a product or service that is highly likely to generate greater customer satisfaction than that experienced with competitors' products or services.

Figure 43: House of Quality Components

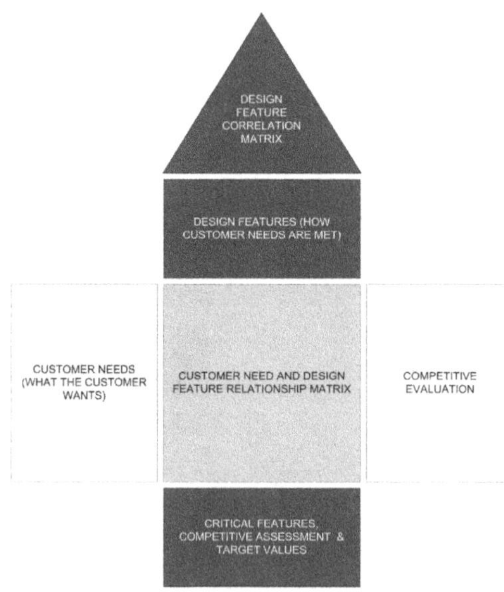

THE APPLICATION OF QFD

QFD is a Process

While it may be a principle 'Design for Six Sigma' tool, let's be very clear about one thing; QFD does not redesign processes! It simply supports the business by getting you to understand tolerances and process design requirements. It does not lay the process out for you. It gets you to really understand market requirements, process requirements and the competitive situation so you end up with a process that produces the right product in the leanest way possible.

It makes more sense to refer to QFD as a process, not a tool per se, so let's do that.

QFD is a process for planning and producing products and services, in response to the changing needs of the customer.

Its application requires the development of a series of matrices. The simplest form of QFD is undertaken through developing the first house of quality in the sequence described in the following pages.

QFD Sequence (Primary House of Quality)

1. Understand what your customers want
2. Understand your competitive position
3. Translate customer expectations into design features
4. Determine critical design features
5. Evaluate the interaction of design features
6. Determine where to focus and establish target values

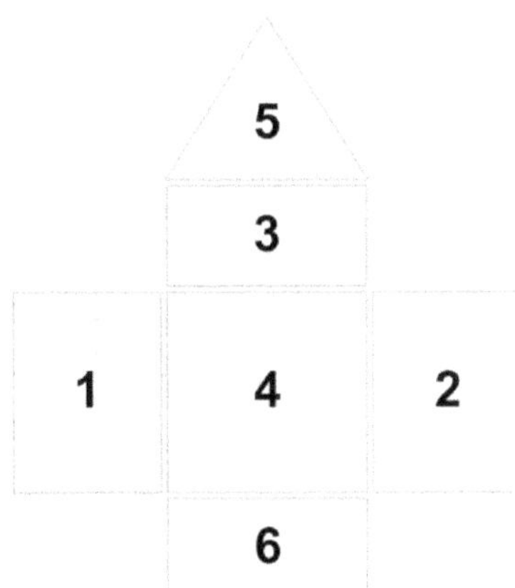

1. Understand What Your Customers Want

The starting point for QFD is the needs or wants of the customer.

Customer needs (can be referred to as expectations) are collected through various means including surveys, focus groups, interviews and trade-shows, and recorded in the left side of the house. These needs are rated on a scale of 1 to 10 according to their relative importance to the customer, and then prioritised.

You might choose to use a different scale, and if you take notice of our discussion about Likert Scales, you will be more likely to use a scale of 1 to 7 or even 1 to 5.

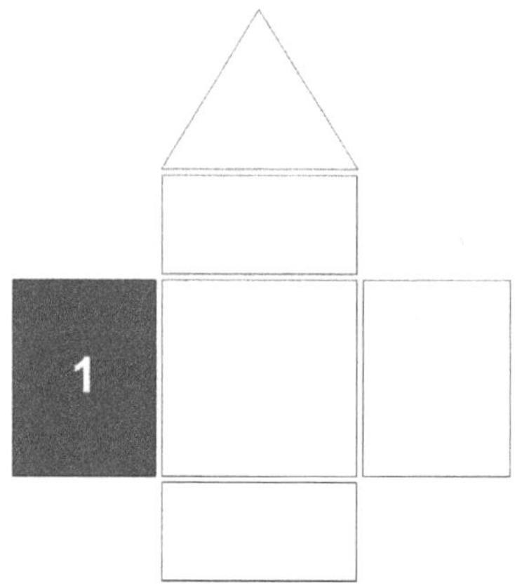

At this point in time, the team knows exactly what the customer wants and how important those requirements are to that customer.

2. Understand Your Competitive Position

A competitive evaluation is undertaken, and the results documented on the right side of the house. The team uses information gathered from competitors to quantify how well they are fulfilling the needs of customers.

Competitor performance can be rated according to a 1 to 5 scale, with 1 for lowest performance, and 5 for highest performance.

Once completed, the team quantifies and documents how well *their* existing product or service is fulfilling the needs of the customer, again using the same scale.

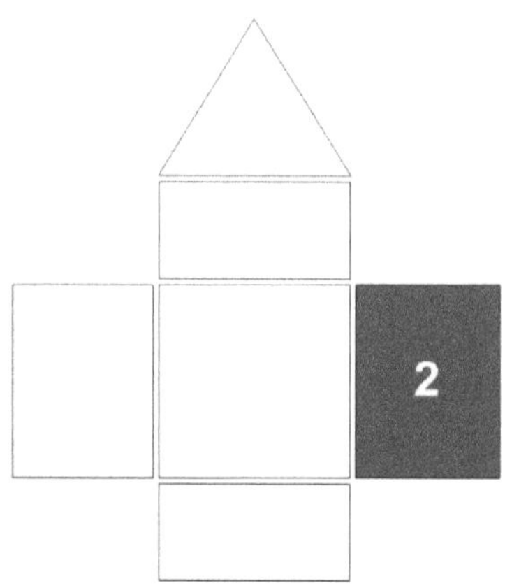

An alternative way of documenting competitor evaluation is to simply indicate whether or not the existing product of the organisation is better, same as or worse than competitors.

It might be appropriate at this time for you to identify any obvious actions you might take to close any gaps between yourself and your competitors.

3. Translate Customer Expectations into Design Features

Product or service features (design features or technical requirements) are documented as columns. The features or requirements that are likely to affect one or more of the customer needs are identified and become the ceiling of the house. These are identified through a process of translation.

By translation, I mean converting a customer need (what they want) into technical requirements (how that need will be met). A well-worded feature or design requirement is one that describes a measurable feature that can be met in many different ways.

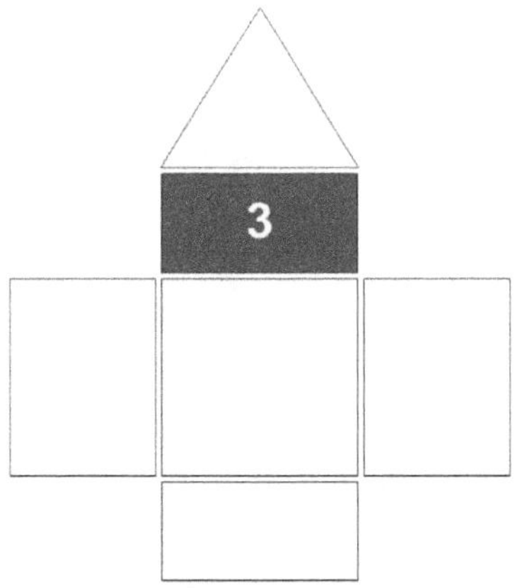

For example, a *customer's need* of a motor vehicle might be 'high performance'. A suitable *technical requirement*, that is not prescriptive, might be 'power to weight ratio'.

The direction of maximum satisfaction for each feature or requirement is identified and documented beneath each of these features or requirements to finish off the ceiling of the house. When I say direction of maximum satisfaction, I mean whether or not the design feature or technical requirement should be maximised, minimised or exactly met.

Various approaches can be used to indicate direction including arrows or negative and positive symbols as shown below.

- ↑ or + meaning the larger the value of the variable measured for this requirement, the greater the level of customer satisfaction.
- ↓ or - meaning the smaller the value of the variable measured for this requirement, the greater the level of customer satisfaction.
- = or ◉ or T meaning meeting or hitting the target value of the variable measured for this requirement, offers the best level of customer satisfaction.

4. Determine Critical Design Features

The relationship between customer requirements and product or service features is indicated in the cell where the respective columns and rows intersect. These cells form the centre of the house.

The relationship can be quantified in any number of ways. One way suggested by Creveling, Slutsky and Antis (2003) is to use an exponential scale within the range of 0 to 9.

- 9 = A strong relationship between need and requirement or feature
- 3 = A moderate relationship between need and requirement or feature
- 1 = A weak relationship between need and requirement or feature
- 0 = No relationship between need and requirement or feature

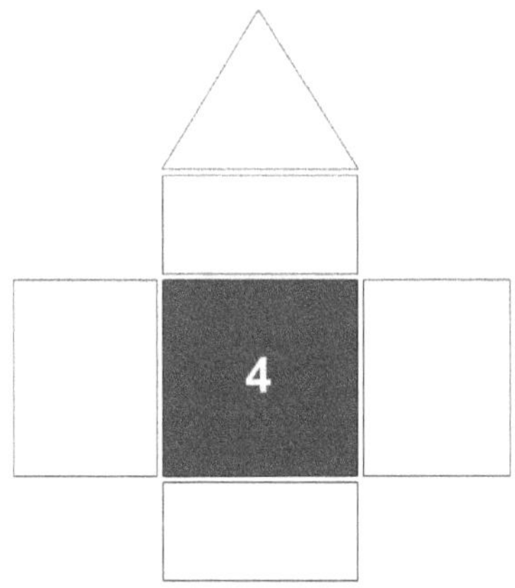

The sum-product of each of these ratings for each design feature or technical requirement is then recorded at the bottom of the matrix. The resulting values help the team establish which of the design features or technical requirements are critical to meeting customer needs. Features or requirements that are particularly difficult to fulfil but critical to generating customer satisfaction must be the focal point of the team and resource allocation.

5. Evaluate the Interaction of Design Features

The relationship between each of the product or service features or design requirements is quantified and documented to form the roof of the house. Both positive (supportive relationships) and negative interactions (unsupportive relationships) are identified to help the team understand where conflicts can occur.

Once again, the relationship can be quantified using the 0 to 9 scale.

- +/- 9 meaning a strong (+/-) relationship between requirements or features
- +/- 3 meaning a moderate (+/-) relationship between requirements or features
- +/- 1 meaning a weak (+/-) relationship between requirements or features
- 0 meaning no relationship between requirements or features

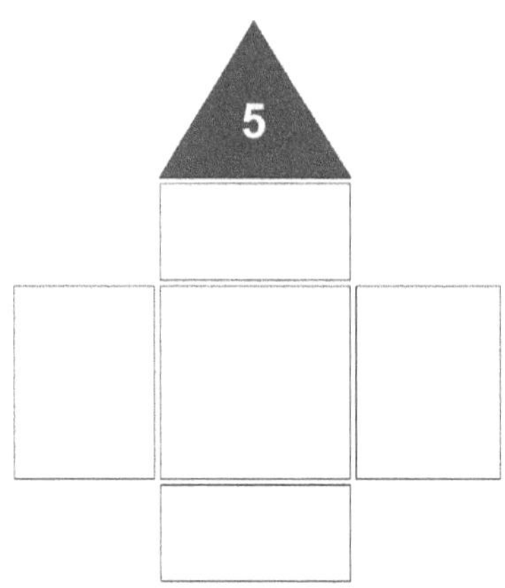

Conflicts between requirements or features are referred to as *anti-synergistic interactions*. It's important for the team to identify these conflicts, as they are usually unintentionally created during the design phase. These conflicting relationships are addressed at the requirement level so that designs are developed to create synergies, not anti-synergies. Once these relationships are identified, the team can work on creating synergies between features or requirements.

6. Determine Where to Focus and Establish Target Values

A second competitive evaluation is undertaken, this time in relation to how well customers are performing in respect of the technical aspects of the product or service.

Using a rating scale of 1 to 5 (1 = lowest performance and 5 = highest performance), we establish how competitors compare to one another, and how we compare to competitors for each of the specified design features. The results are documented at the lower end of the house.

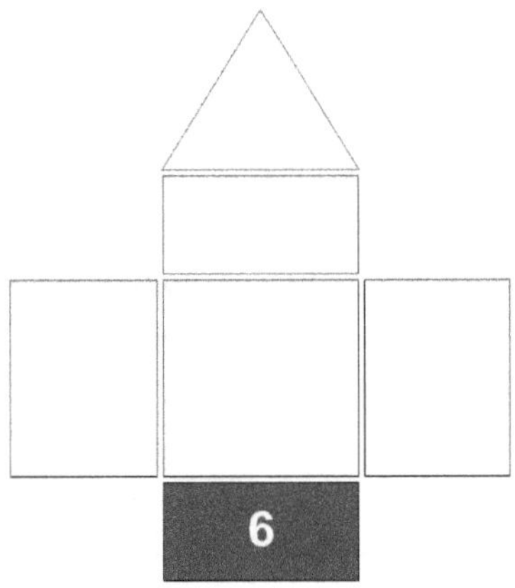

As an alternative, you could simply indicate whether or not the existing product of the organisation is better, same as or worse than competitors. Regardless of the method undertaken, at the end of this step you should start to get a sense of where you might have to focus your energies.

Target values should now be determined for features or design requirements. These can be identified through various means including the following:

- Internal benchmarking
- Competitor benchmarking
- Review of relevant standards

These values become the foundations for the house. To complete this work, the team must (a) define the unit of measure, and (b) establish target value associated with that unit of measure.

The finished house of quality provides a simple graphical format that describes customer needs, product or service characteristics and a competitive analysis. Time spent completing the house properly is well spent, as this is the foundation for the QFD process, and any work completed here will be transferred into the final products or services you deliver.

An example of a completed QFD Matrix for an existing product is shown on the following page.

Challenges and Traps with QFD

During my conversations with various industry professionals, including good friend Morgan Jones, it became clearly evident to me that many challenges confront users of QFD. Users can also fall into some simple traps that make the process more difficult to use. I want to point out some of those as they have been identified to me.

- Inadvertently **including requirements of the business** in the left side of the house of quality (e.g. profit margin, cost per unit etc). Leave these out of the process as QFD is only relevant to customer requirements.
- Users often **miss or assume the latent or basic requirements of the customer**. These are the unspoken requirements that we so often take for granted. For example, if you bought a boat, one of your expectations would be that it floats. Include all requirements, even those unspoken[16].
- Undertaking **competitive analysis without getting the real story** about what customers are doing and how they are performing. If you limit your research to people in sales, marketing or production, it does not mean you understand the customer.
- When undertaking **technical analysis** around target values, **failing to involve the right people** may lead to erroneous target values. For example, if you were working on a beer making process and discussing bubbles, it would make sense to involve BOC who actually make the gas for creating the bubbles.
- Addressing **multiple market sectors** in a single QFD. The process is designed for use with a single market sector. For example, you would study engines for farmers separately from a study of engines for boat constructors.
- As you probably already know, **defining the questions to ask** is often the most challenging task. You must ask the right questions to get the most appropriate answers for completing the house of quality.
- Inadvertently **designing for the intermediate customer, not the end user customer**. When Honda designs cars, they are designed for the person who drives the car. They don't design the car for the Honda dealer, who incidentally is the next in line customer to the car manufacturer.

Dealing with Complexity

The house of quality can get quite complex, depending on the level of analysis you are undertaking. An example provided to me by my friend Morgan Jones was based on the study of an entire machine, not just the engine or a single component. The process produced a house of quality with a centre matrix that was some 1,100 rows high (customer requirements) by 950 columns wide (design features). As he said; 'this wasn't a house, it was a housing estate'.

He solved the complexity problem by breaking it down into sub element houses of quality; i.e., one QFD for the engine system, one QFD for the telescopic arm and so on.

[16] Refer to notes in this text on the subject of Kano Analysis

Example QFD Matrix for T Shirt Range

INTERACTIONS
++ Strong Positive
+ Positive
- Negative
-- Strong Negative

RELATIONSHIP RATING
9 - Strong Relationship
3 - Moderate Relationship
1 - Weak Relationship
0 - No Relationship

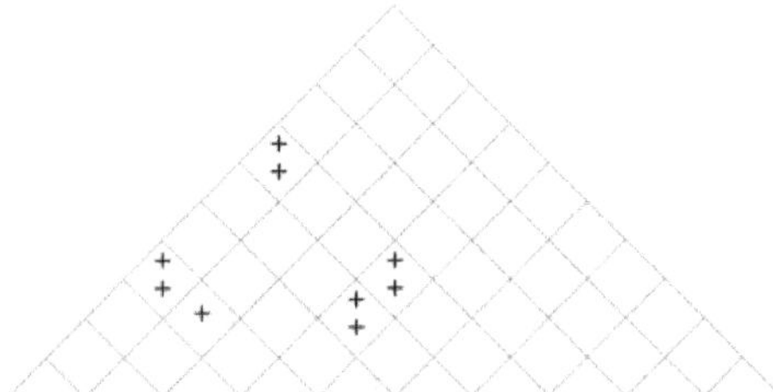

DESIGN FEATURES		Sweat Absorption	Stitched Seams	Size Labelling	Cost	Branding	Colour Options	Fire Retardation							
		1	2	3	4	5	6	7							
DIRECTION FROM TARGET VALUE		T	T	T	–	T	+	+							
CUSTOMER NEEDS												OUR EXISTING PRODUCT	Competitor A	Competitor B	**ACTIONS**
Value for Money	10	3	3	0	9	3	1	3				3	4	2	Benchmark Competitor A
Durable	7	9	9	0	9	0	0	9				3	2	3	
Appealing	8	9	3	0	0	9	9	3				4	2	3	
Fit	9	3	1	3	0	0	0	0				3	3	4	Benchmark Competitor B
Colour Fast	10	3	0	0	1	0	9	3				2	2	3	
Absolute Values		27	16	3	19	12	19	18							
Weighted Values		222	126	27	163	102	172	147							
Critical Design Features		X			X		X	X							

COMPETITIVE TECHNICAL ASSESSMENT	1	2	3	4	5	6	7				
	2	3	1	4	1	3	2				Competitor A
	4	3	3	2	4	4	3				Competitor B
	2	1	4	2	1	3	2				OUR EXISTING PRODUCT
TARGET VALUES	60% Cotton	Double Stitching	Metric Sizes Labeled	$20	Worn by a Celebrity	5 Colour Options	Comply with ASNZ Stds.				

Figure 44: QFD Example for a Range of T Shirts

SUBSYSTEM LEVEL HOUSES OF QUALITY

Before I leave this section, it would be remiss of me to not complete the conversation in regard to QFD in its traditional form. While the intent of this book is not *Design for Six Sigma*, I must point out that we have only discussed the first level house of quality.

The 'Macabe' approach to QFD application involves multi level houses of quality that sequentially take the design team's conversation from customer needs through to production planning.

According to King (1987) this approach consists of developing four matrices that are sequentially related.

- Product planning matrix (the one we've already discussed)
- Part deployment matrix
- Process planning matrix
- Production planning matrix

These matrices are simply subsystem level houses of quality. The design features or technical requirements of the first level house become the customer needs of the next level house, and so on throughout the sequence.

The following diagram provides a clue for how this works.

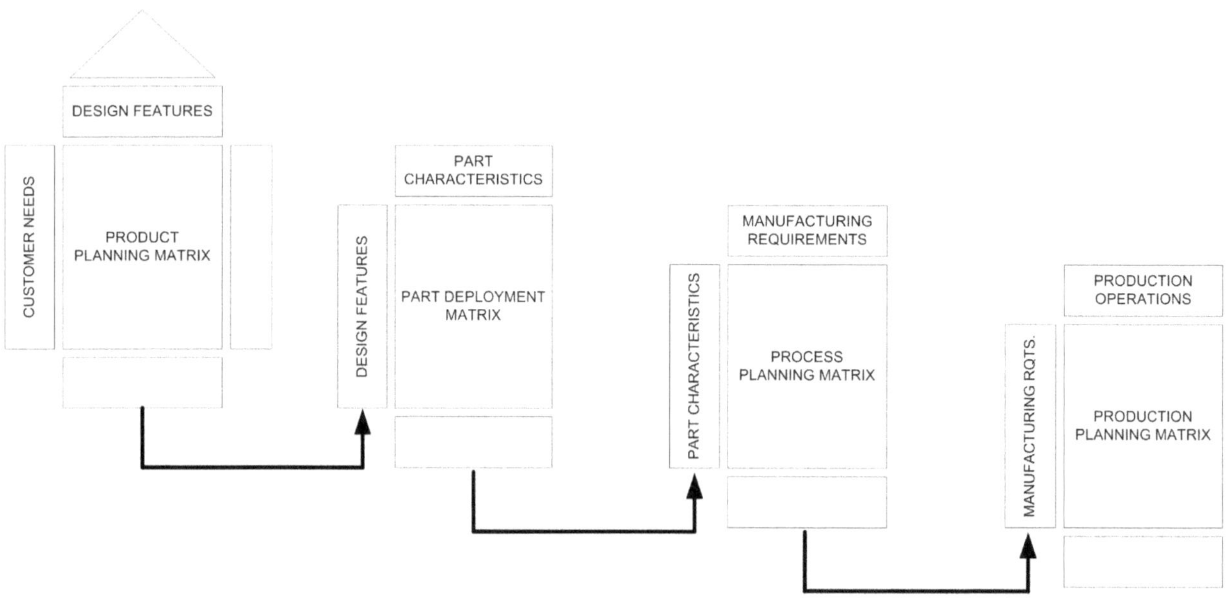

Figure 45: Sub-system Level Houses of Quality

Further Reading

For more detailed information about the application of QFD in design work, I recommend you read the following textbook.

Day, Ronald G., *'Quality Function Deployment – Linking a Company with Its Customers'*, ASQ Quality Press (1993).

CHARACTERISTICS OF GOOD LEAN & SIX SIGMA PROJECTS

Irrespective of the method you choose to use, good project selection is vital to the success of any improvement initiative.

While all projects may offer value of some nature to those doing the work, only those projects that meet certain criteria should be allocated to scarce resources such as a company's Green Belts or Black Belts.

Characteristics of projects can be categorised as either must have or should have characteristics.

Must haves are those characteristics for which you assess whether or not the project has them – a yes or no answer.

On the other hand, should haves are those characteristics that are desirable, and the more the characteristic is satisfied, the better.

These are the Must Haves (Yes or No)

1. The process actually **exists** (if it does not, process design is the more appropriate approach)
2. The process is **repetitive** (i.e. we recommend that it has at least one full cycle per week in order that you can actually obtain sufficient quantitative data to analyse)
3. The metric you are working to improve is **a process performance metric** generated directly from process data (e.g. cycle time, defect rates, inventory levels, down time, throughput or production etc), not an emotionally driven metric with a strong connection to opinions (e.g. satisfaction, retention and the like)
4. The project would return a **quantifiable benefit** against relevant business performance measures (i.e. revenue, cost, capital, risk, inventory etc)
5. The process will **continue to be used** for some period of time after improvement takes place (no point working on a process that is probably going to be replaced, a problem that arises in technology focused industries)
6. A **project team** can be formed with employees who **work in the process**

These are the Should Haves (More is Better)

1. Quality **data** is available and accessible
2. Returns can be measured in economic terms (i.e. a **financial return**)
3. Relatively easy to **implement change**
4. Can be completed in a **reasonable time frame**
5. Contributes to the achievement of **business objectives** relevant to the existing business environment and the department concerned

If you consistently apply these characteristics as criteria for project selection, the projects you select may well set you up to generate real value for your company and yourself.

CHARTERING THE PROJECT

The Project Charter

A Charter is defined[17] as: *'A document issued by a sovereignty, legislature, or other authority, creating a public or private corporation, such as a city, college, or bank, and defining its privileges and purposes.'*

Purpose of the Charter

In the context of process improvement projects, the charter is a contract between the organisation's leadership and the project team, the purpose of which is to:

- **Transfer** the project from the sponsor to the team
- **Clarify** what is expected of the team and eliminate any confusion
- Provide a basis for setting obtainable and sustainable **goals**
- **Focus** the team's work through defining boundaries
- Establish clear **understanding** around limitations, constraints and assumptions under which the team must operate

Charter Format

The major portion of a Lean Six Sigma project charter is comprised of 9 core components.

- **Project Details** – title etc
- **Team Details** – who leads and participates in the project
- **Problem Statement** – an expression of what has been occurring
- **Primary Metric** – information about specification limits, baseline and targeted performance levels
- **Project Goals** – the desired outcomes of doing the project work
- **Constraints** – limitations that will impact the team and their decision making
- **Scope** – boundaries of the project, what the team will and won't work on
- **Business Case** – a projection of financial value offered by the project
- **Primary Metric Chart** – a graphical display of performance over time

<table>
<tr><td colspan="2">Project Details</td></tr>
<tr><td colspan="2">Team</td></tr>
<tr><td>Problem Statement</td><td>Primary Metric</td></tr>
<tr><td>Project Goals</td><td>Constraints</td></tr>
<tr><td>Project Scope</td><td>Business Case</td></tr>
<tr><td colspan="2">Primary Metric Chart</td></tr>
</table>

Who develops the Project Charter?

Charters can be developed according to a number of different approaches.

- Developed by **project sponsors** and given to an appointed Green Belt or Black Belt

17 Source: The American Heritage® Dictionary of the English Language, Fourth Edition

- Developed by the **Green Belt or Black Belt** and presented to the management group
- Developed by the Green Belt or Black Belt in association with project sponsors and process owners

In the absence of a formal operating system, the last of these options is the most common. Regardless of the approach used, endorsement by the management group is essential in ensuring support and commitment. Where the management group drafts the charter, it can only partially be completed. The project team leader must complete the work after being allocated the project.

Project Charter Format - Part 1

Part 1 of the charter provides all relevant details to guide the work of the team.

TEAM			
Team Leader: Susan Carter	Members:		
Sponsor: Mike Jeffrey	Peter Jones	Mark Smith	Clare Jones
Process Owner: Steve Davis	Steve Racknel	Lynda Everest	

PROBLEM / OPPORTUNITY STATEMENT
For at least the past 12 months, new PC deployment cycle time has exceeded customer expectations on 75% of occasions. The result has been that departments have bypassed the internal ordering system to purchase their own PCs, costing us $XX in missed discounts.

PRIMARY METRIC			
Metric	Spec. Limits	Base KPI	Target KPI
PC Deployment Cycle Time	Max 45 working days	75% longer than 45 days	< 25% longer than 45 days

DESIRED OUTCOMES / GOALS
(1) > 75% of new PCs take less than 45 days to deploy
(2) Capture discounts for 100% of PCs purchased

DECISION CONSTRAINTS / LIMITATIONS
Any capital expenditure must exceed the ROI rate of 20%.
No negative impact on risk exposure.
Solutions implemented by 30-08-01.

PROJECT SCOPE
The boundaries of the process are:
START: PC is ordered by the customer
END: PC is installed and running on the customer's desk
What is in and out of 'Scope'
IN: Process for ordering, policy and procedures, support processes, software installation
OUT: Supplier contracts, PC make and brand

BENEFIT TYPE	Cost Reduction (EBIT)	
Forecast One Off Costs / Benefits		
	Initial Forecast	Revised Forecast
OPEX	(13,000)	
CAPEX		
REVENUE		
Forecast Annualised Costs / Benefits		
COST SAVINGS	125,000	
REVENUE		

PRIMARY METRIC CHART			
[INSERT CHART HERE]			
Baseline Period:	January – July 2001 (6 months)	Source of Data:	IT Group Deliver Records

Project Charter Format - Part 2 (The Plan)

Part 2 of the charter is a framework for managing the project, and is developed and maintained by the project team leader. Obviously other project management tools could be used instead.

Lean Oriented Projects

When the project is more oriented towards the use of *lean methodology*, the plan might look like this.

Phases	Project Activities	Planned Completion	% Completed	Date Completed
PROJECT SET UP (DEFINE & MEASURE)	Project Charter developed with Sponsor	27-6-2021	100	26-6-2021
	Pre-measure / observe and collect basic data	14-7-2021	100	12-7-2021
	Analyse process stability & measure baseline performance	15-7-2021	100	12-7-2021
	Plan the project from beginning to end	17-7-2021	50	
	Stakeholder analysis / develop engagement plan	"	0	
	Establish Operating agreement with Sponsor	18-7-2021	0	
	Lock in meetings with team members	"	0	
	Conduct TOLLGATE REVIEW (Tollgates #1 and #2)	20-7-2021	0	
DEFINE, MEASURE & ANALYSE	Start up the project team (first meeting)	22-7-2021	0	
	Document the process as a Cross Functional Flowchart	"	0	
	Undertake Time Value Analysis	"	0	
	Develop Takt Chart/s	"	0	
	Confirm where waste needs to be removed to improve process	"	0	
	Conduct TOLLGATE REVIEW (Tollgates #2 and #3)	24-7-2021	0	
IMPROVE	Develop / select solutions that treat waste and solve the problem	27-7-2021	0	
	Error proof solutions / conduct FMEA	"	0	
	Develop solution implementation plan	"	0	
	Analyse Stakeholders / develop engagement plan	"	0	
	Develop implementation project risk management plan	"	0	
	Develop Project Storyboard / Poster	28-7-2021	0	
	Conduct STAKEHOLDER CHECK-IN	"	0	
	Adjust the implementation plan as required	"	0	
	Conduct TOLLGATE REVIEW (Tollgate #4)	29-7-2021	0	
CONTROL	Standardise the new process	3-8-2021	0	
	Document the new process in SIPOC format	"	0	
	Develop monitoring / response plans	"	0	
	Update Project Storyboard / Poster	"	0	
	Conduct TOLLGATE REVIEW (Tollgate #5)	4-8-2021	0	
	Implement monitoring / response plans	8-8-2021	0	
	Develop a mechanism for reporting benefits	"	0	
	Recognise the team and celebrate project completion	TBA	0	
	Conduct POST IMPLEMENTATION REVIEW	TBA	0	
	Formally Close the Project	TBA	0	

Six Sigma Oriented Projects

When the project is more oriented towards the use of *six sigma methodology*, the plan might look like this.

Phases	Project Steps	Planned Completion	% Completed	Date Completed
PROJECT SET UP (DEFINE & MEASURE)	Project Charter developed with Sponsor Pre-measure / observe and collect basic data Analyse process stability Measure baseline performance Plan the project from beginning to end Stakeholder analysis / develop engagement plan Establish Operating agreement with Sponsor Lock in meetings with team members Conduct TOLLGATE REVIEW (Tollgate #1 and #2)			
DEFINE, MEASURE & ANALYSE	Start up the project team (first meeting) Document the process as an Activity Flowchart Plan data collection Validate the measurement system Collect data Analyse data for Xs that impact the Y and record findings Conduct STAKEHOLDER CHECK-IN Conduct TOLLGATE REVIEW (Tollgate #2 and #3)			
IMPROVE	Conduct cause & effect analysis as required & validate causes Develop and select solutions that treat validated causes Error proof solutions / conduct FMEA Develop solution implementation plan Stakeholder analysis / develop engagement plan Develop implementation project risk management plan Develop Project Storyboard / Poster Conduct STAKEHOLDER CHECK-IN Adjust the implementation plan as required Conduct TOLLGATE REVIEW (Tollgate #4)			
CONTROL	Standardise the new process Document the new process in SIPOC format Develop monitoring / response plans Conduct TOLLGATE REVIEW (Tollgate #5) Update Project Storyboard / Poster Implement monitoring / response plans Develop a mechanism for reporting benefits Recognise the team and celebrate project completion Conduct POST IMPLEMENTATION REVIEW Formally Close the Project			

CHAPTER 8: TOOLKIT FOR SPONSORS & PROCESS OWNERS

S.I.P.O.C.

Refer to the 'Control Phase Toolkit' chapter in this textbook for instructions.

VALUE STREAM ANALYSIS

What is it?

Value Stream Analysis (VSA) is a process for:

a. **Documenting** the flow of information, materials and activities through product or service value streams; and

b. **Analysing** the *actual performance* of that process.

It can most effectively be used following the development of a SIPOC.

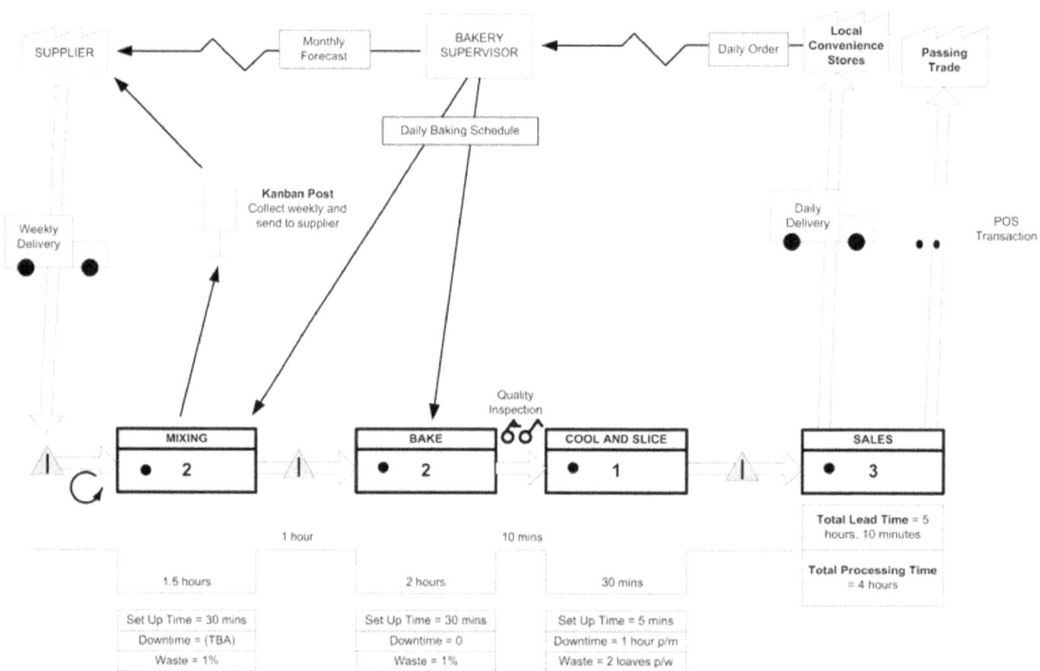

VSA is used to distinguish value adding from non-value adding activities, understand where waste is created as a product goes through a process, and identify the greatest areas of opportunity for improvement that will positively impact the business.

Value Stream Icons and Symbols

When we develop a Value Stream Map (VSM), we use the following generic icons and symbols to represent specific things:

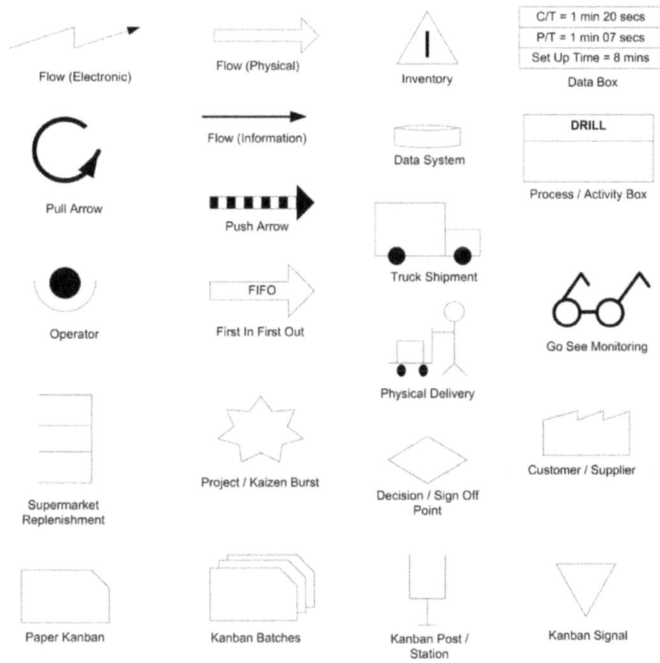

Instructions

Value stream analysis requires the creation of a Value Stream Map (VSM). The VSM is created in the following sequence.

1. Define the Product or Service
2. Establish Process Flow
3. Establish Materials Flow
4. Establish Information Flow
5. Add Time Data
6. Add Process Data
7. Validate the VSM

These steps are explained in detail over the following pages.

Step 1: Product or Service

Identify the product or service process you want to analyse. Ideally your process will meet all of the following criteria.

- A highly repetitive, high volume process
- Core to the strategic objectives of the business
- Has major impact on the company's customer or chosen customer segment

In the example shown over the following pages, we have chosen the baking process for a medium sized bakery in a prominent suburban community of an Australian capital city.

Step 2: Process Flow

Draw the flow of the process or sequence of macro service delivery or product development steps.

- Starting at the customer end, work backwards through the process
- Indicate major activities or process steps
- Place these activities in their sequence
- Use relevant mapping icons

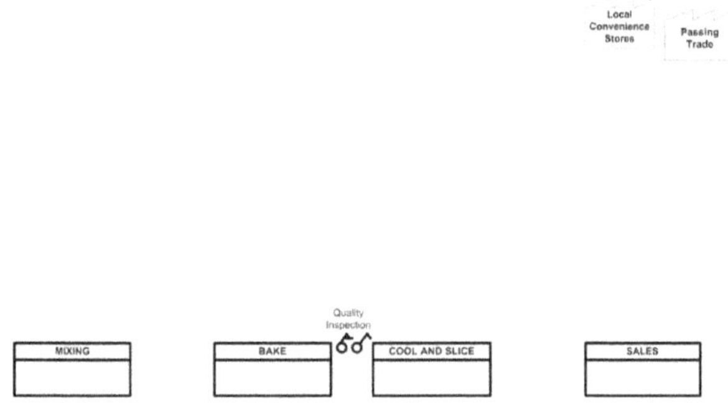

Step 3: Materials Flow

Add in the flow of materials.

- Indicate movement of material (transportation method, inventory, flow to different process steps, inspection etc)
- Material with the same flow is grouped together
- Add in supplier
- Use relevant mapping icons

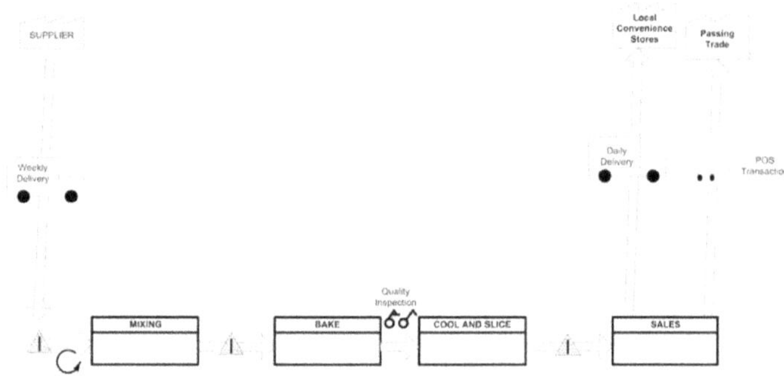

Step 4: Information Flow

Add in the flow of information.

- Indicate communication flow between the process and customers, how the communication occurs (electronic, hard copy or face to face) and frequency
- Indicate communication flow between the process and suppliers, how the communication occurs (electronic, hard copy or face to face) and frequency

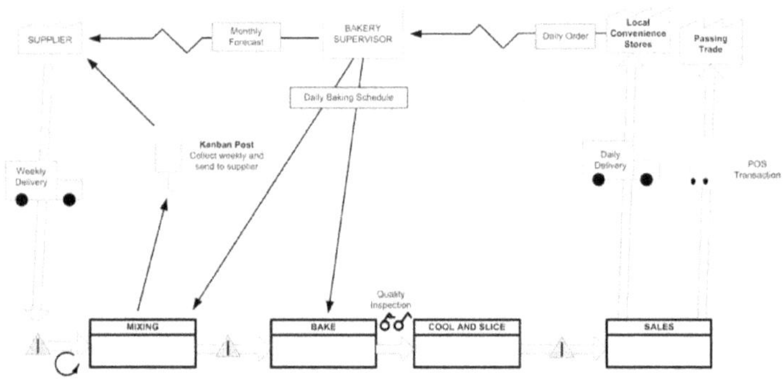

- Indicate flow and how production or service delivery requirements are communicated to the process and frequency
- Use relevant mapping icons

Step 5: Time Data

Add any relevant lead-time data and processing time data.

NOTE - This is normally only relevant for manufacturing types of industries or any value stream where you can follow individual units through the flow.

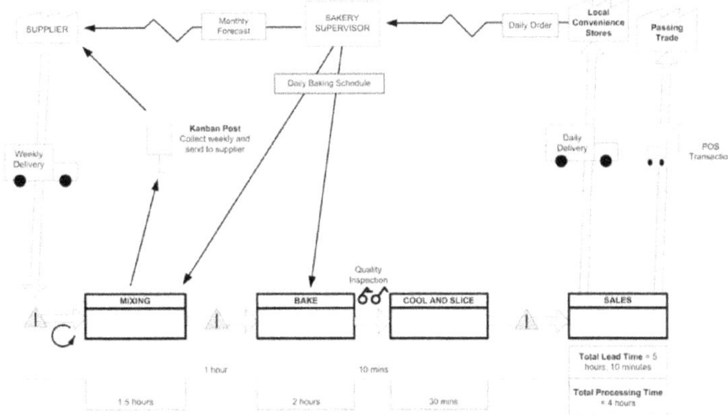

Step 6: Process Data

Collect and add in process data. This may include, but is not limited to the following types of data:

- Defect rate / waste information
- Plant or machinery availability
- Production or processing volumes (per hour, per day, per month etc)
- Cost per unit produced (or other financial data of relevance)

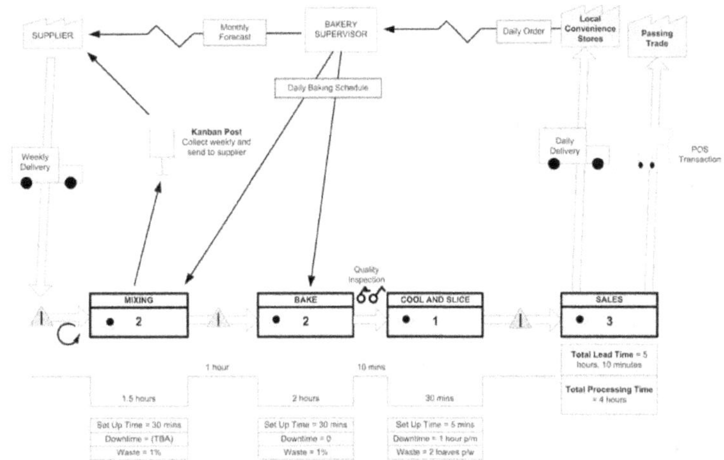

Refer to the discussion in the previous chapter on relevant metrics for a Value Stream Analysis.

Note: Where a VSA is preceded by development of a SIPOC, relevant customer and business metrics can also be included.

Step 7: Validate the Value Stream Map

Check-in with users of the process who are not on the team to make sure the value stream map is a true reflection of what occurs. If you are unsure you should check-in with customers and suppliers.

Make any necessary changes before producing your final value stream map.

QUALITY FUNCTIONAL DEPLOYMENT

What is it?

QFD is a process for identifying customer expectations and linking them directly to a company's core business processes.

Instructions:

1. Identify customers and their requirements or expectations
2. Undertake a competitive evaluation
3. Identify product or service features relevant to meeting those expectations
4. Establish the relationship between requirements and features and identify critical design features
5. Establish the level of interaction between all features (as they impact one another)
6. Determine where to focus and relevant target values for design features

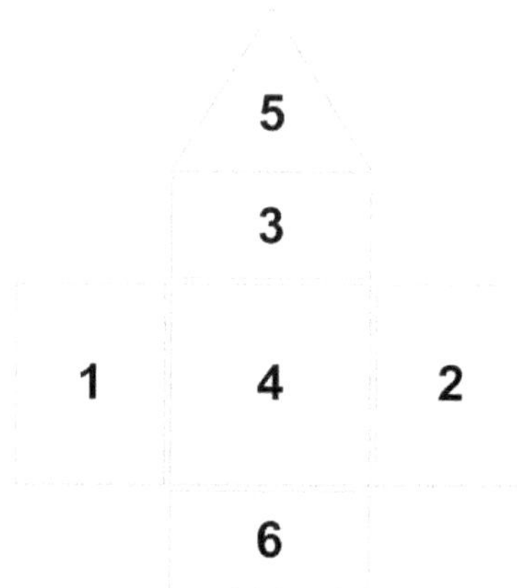

These steps are explained in detail over the following pages.

Step 1: Identify Customers and Requirements (Expectations)

The sequence is as follows:

- Define customer expectations
- Establish a scale of importance (1 to 5, 1 to 7 or 1 to 10)
- Rate customer needs according to relative importance

CUSTOMER NEEDS

Value for Money	10
Durable	7
Appealing	8
Fit	9
Colour Fast	10

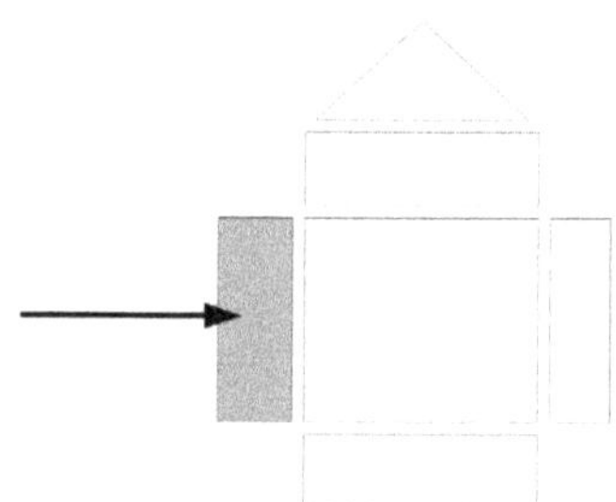

Step 2: Undertake a Competitive Evaluation

The sequence is as follows:

- Identify relevant competitors
- Establish how well competitors are meeting customer expectations on a 1 to 5 scale
- 1 (lowest level of satisfaction)
- 5 (highest level of satisfaction)
- Using the same scale, determine how well you are meeting customer expectations (if this relates to an existing product or service)

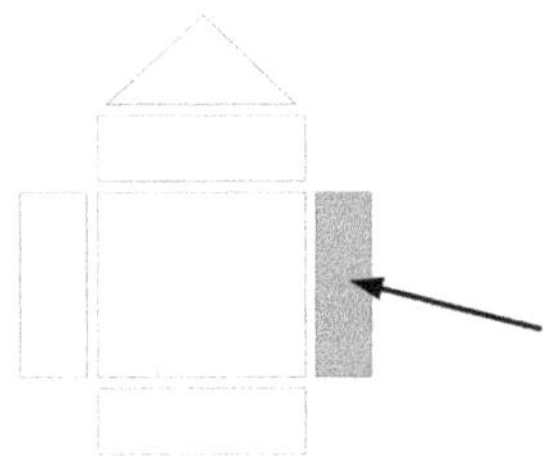

Our Existing Product	Competitor A	Competitor B	ACTIONS
3	4	2	Benchmark Competitor A
3	2	3	
4	2	3	
3	3	4	Benchmark Competitor B
2	2	3	

- Highlight where opportunities exist to improve your market performance
- Determine any actions that will help you identify how to close competitive gaps

Step 3: Identify Product or Service Features Necessary for Meeting Customer Expectations

The sequence is as follows:

- Translate customer expectations (what they want – e.g. high performance) into technical requirements (how it will be met – e.g. power to weight ratio)
- Identify the direction of maximum satisfaction for each requirement using symbols such as those below
- ↑ or + (the larger the value of the variable measured for this requirement, the greater the level of customer satisfaction)
- ↓ or – (the smaller the value of the variable measured for this requirement, the greater the level of customer satisfaction)

DESIGN FEATURES	Sweat Absorption	Stitched Seams	Size Labelling	Cost	Branding	Colour Options	Fire Retardation			
	1	2	3	4	5	6	7			
DIRECTION FROM TARGET VALUE	T	T	T	–	T	+	+			

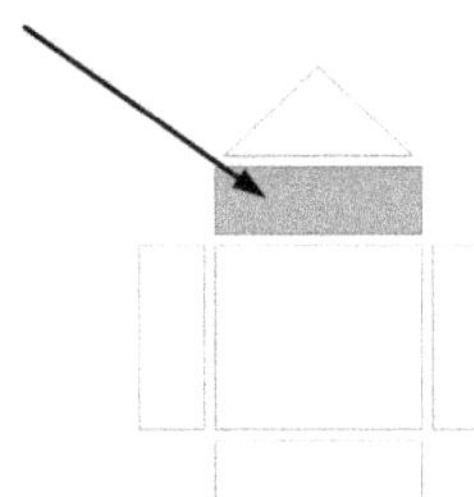

- = or ● or T (meeting or hitting the target value of the variable measured for this requirement, offers the best level of customer satisfaction)

Step 4: Establish Relationship between All Requirements and Features

DESIGN FEATURES		Sweat Absorption	Stitched Seams	Size Labelling	Cost	Branding	Colour Options	Fire Retardation			
		1	2	3	4	5	6	7			
DIRECTION FROM TARGET VALUE		T	T	T	_	T	+	+			
CUSTOMER NEEDS											
Value for Money	10	3	3	0	9	3	1	3			
Durable	7	9	9	0	9	0	0	9			
Appealing	8	9	3	0	0	9	9	3			
Fit	9	3	1	3	0	0	0	0			
Colour Fast	10	3	0	0	1	0	9	3			
Absolute Values		27	16	3	19	12	19	18			
Weighted Values		222	126	27	163	102	172	147			
Critical Design Features		X			X		X	X			

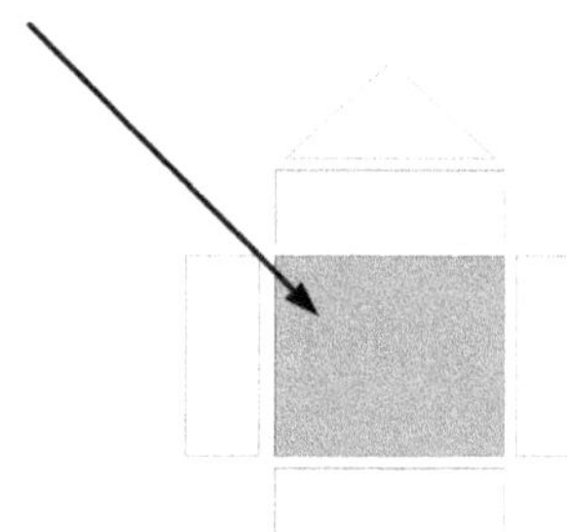

Use the cells that form the centre of the house of quality.

- Define the scale you will use – we use and recommend the following:
- 9 = A strong relationship between need and requirement or feature
- 3 = A moderate relationship between need and requirement or feature
- 1 = A weak relationship between need and requirement or feature
- 0 = No relationship between need and requirement or feature
- Allocate a relationship strength value to every possible pairing of an expectation and a design feature
- Record the sum-product of each of these at the bottom of the matrix beneath the relevant design feature (these are the weighted values shown in the diagram)
- Indicate those features that are most important (critical design features)

Step 5: Identify the Level of Interaction between Design Features

The sequence is as follows:

- Define the scale you will use, we recommend the following:
- +/- 9 (a strong (+/-) relationship between requirements or features)
- +/- 3 (a moderate (+/-) relationship between requirements or features)
- +/- 1 (a weak (+/-) relationship between requirements or features)
- 0 (no relationship between requirements or features)

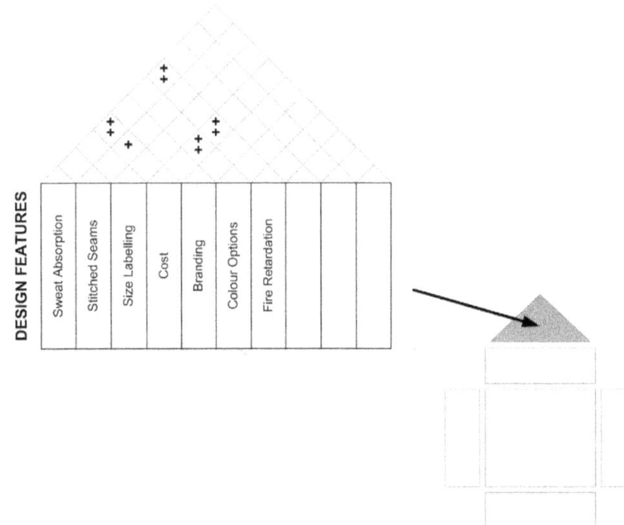

- Identify any conflicts (or anti-synergistic interactions) whereby a change in one feature moves another feature in an undesirable direction

Step 6: Determine Target Values for Design Features

The sequence is as follows:

- Establish how well competitors perform with regard to design features on a 1 to 5 scale
- Using the same scale, establish your own level of performance
- Highlight any obvious competitive gaps – these are where your opportunities lay
- Determine the relevant metrics for design features
- Determine target values for those metrics

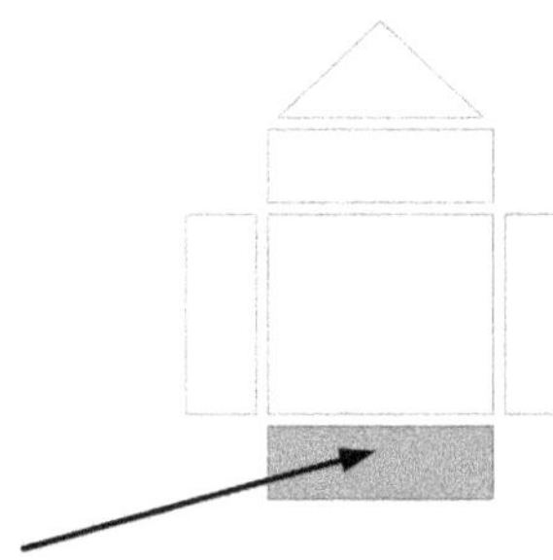

COMPETITIVE TECHNICAL ASSESSMENT	2	3	1	4	1	3	2				Competitor A
	4	3	3	2	4	4	3				Competitor B
	2	1	4	2	1	3	2				OUR EXISTING PRODUCT
TARGET VALUES	60% Cotton	Double Stitching	Metric Sizes Labeled	$20	Worn by a Celebrity	5 Colour Options	Comply with ASNZ Stds.				

Note: You can utilise various methods to determine metrics and target values including internal and external benchmarking.

Step 7: Use the House of Quality

With the fully assembled house of quality (refer to the following diagram), the key is to use it now to make improvements.

- Treat anti-synergies or conflicts identified in Step 5
- Work on those features that offer the greatest opportunity to improve market performance

INTERACTIONS
++ Strong Positive
+ Positive
- Negative
-- Strong Negative

RELATIONSHIP RATING
9 - Strong Relationship
3 - Moderate Relationship
1 - Weak Relationship
0 - No Relationship

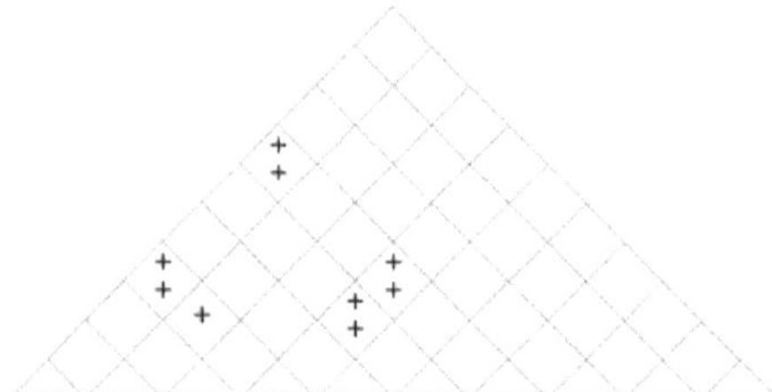

DESIGN FEATURES		Sweat Absorption	Stitched Seams	Size Labelling	Cost	Branding	Colour Options	Fire Retardation				OUR EXISTING PRODUCT	Competitor A	Competitor B	
		1	2	3	4	5	6	7							
DIRECTION FROM TARGET VALUE		T	T	T	_	T	+	+							
CUSTOMER NEEDS															**ACTIONS**
Value for Money	10	3	3	0	9	3	1	3				3	4	2	Benchmark Competitor A
Durable	7	9	9	0	9	0	0	9				3	2	3	
Appealing	8	9	3	0	0	9	9	3				4	2	3	
Fit	9	3	1	3	0	0	0	0				3	3	4	Benchmark Competitor B
Colour Fast	10	3	0	0	1	0	9	3				2	2	3	
Absolute Values		27	16	3	19	12	19	18							
Weighted Values		222	126	27	163	102	172	147							
Critical Design Features		X			X		X	X							

COMPETITIVE TECHNICAL ASSESSMENT	1	2	3	4	5	6	7				
	2	3	1	4	1	3	2				Competitor A
	4	3	3	2	4	4	3				Competitor B
	2	1	4	2	1	3	2				OUR EXISTING PRODUCT

TARGET VALUES	60% Cotton	Double Stitching	Metric Sizes Labeled	$20	Worn by a Celebrity	5 Colour Options	Comply with ASNZ Stds.			

Figure 46: Completed House of Quality

Final QFD Tips

Tip #1: You can't really separate QFD from the concepts presented in the Kano Model[18]. Customer requirements can be identified in the very first step of QFD using the categories of Dissatisfiers, Satisfiers and Delighters as starting points.

This 'channelling' approach will ensure that (a) the latent or unspoken expectations of customers are not missed (the dissatisfiers), and (b) the thoughts of the team go beyond the known expectations of the customer (the delighters) when in fact the customer may not even know what could be available.

This is particularly true of technology products. As you are already aware, with some of the functions of technology you see today, we don't even know about them until they are placed in front of us.

Tip #2: If you are using QFD to design processes, then you must design the process for the future, not for today. While this may be contrary to some thinking, we also have to be futurists.

You can use the process to add delighters to the equation. Your primary question is obviously; *'what expectations would you need to meet now?'* Your secondary question should be; *'what expectations might you need to meet in the future?'*

If you were working for a company like Caterpillar, you might find you end up offering different engine sizes in your machinery to match future scenarios your customers may be exposed to.

Tip#3: When undertaking competitive analysis, consider getting people from sales, marketing and production to undertake the work. Be cautious of customers undertaking competitive analysis.

Tip #4: If you are working with multiple market sectors, you may find the most effective way to do it is to create the first level house for each sector and then merge these into one house.

Alternatively, you could just choose a single market to work with. Your choice will be affected by your answers to two primary questions.

- What is the biggest market now?
- Which market is likely to grow most in the future?

[18] Refer to notes in this text on Kano Analysis

PROJECT CHARTER

What is it?

A project charter is primarily a form of contract between the organisation's leaders and the project team.

The charter is created for the purpose of:

- Transferring the project from the process owner to the team;
- Clarifying what is expected of the team and eliminating any confusion;
- Providing a basis for setting obtainable and sustainable goals;
- Focusing the team's work through defining boundaries; and
- Establishing clear understanding around limitations, constraints and assumptions under which the team must work.

Instructions

The charter is created at the start of the project work. It is introduced to the team and finalised when they have their first project meeting. As a *living document*, it can be reviewed at any time during the project as more is learnt about the process.

The project charter is created in the following sequence.

Step 1: Develop the problem statement

Step 2: Identify the primary metric for the project

Step 3: State the desired outcomes or project goals

Step 4: Identify constraints or limitations that the team must operate under

Step 5: Define the project scope, primarily deciding upon the start and end points of the process, and what is to be included in the scope of the project and what is not

Step 6: Understand the type of benefit the project will generate

Step 7: Forecast any once-off or ongoing costs or benefits

Step 8: Identify those individuals who will make up the team

Step 9: Develop a primary metric chart of data over a selected baseline period

Step 10: Plan the phases of the project by identifying the planned completion date for each activity (this portion is the responsibility of the project team leader)

<table>
<tr><td colspan="2">Project Details</td></tr>
<tr><td colspan="2">Team</td></tr>
<tr><td>Problem Statement</td><td>Primary Metric</td></tr>
<tr><td>Project Goals</td><td>Constraints</td></tr>
<tr><td>Project Scope</td><td>Business Case</td></tr>
<tr><td colspan="2">Primary Metric Chart</td></tr>
</table>

STEP 1 – DEVELOP THE PROBLEM STATEMENT

While I prefer to speak in terms of opportunities in my day-to-day language, I will use the term 'problem statement' in this textbook.

Describing the problem begins with a simple statement of what has been observed or experienced. The most effective way to think of a problem statement is to think about the gap in performance you are observing. They simply describe the difference between the current level of performance and a targeted level of performance. This targeted level of performance may be an existing target that is not being met or a newly identified target level of performance. I've provided some example in the following table.

Example 1 20% of calls are being placed on hold for 3 minutes or longer	**Example 2** Time between order and installation is taking up to 7 days, which is 3 days longer than the targeted maximum of 4 days
Example 3 Throughput is averaging 210,000 tonnes per day, 30,000 tonnes short of the targeted 240,000 tonnes per day	**Example 4** 23% of applications have insufficient details to process payment without contacting the customer

To demonstrate the link to the business case, the statement includes a description of the impact of the problem, or alternatively, the benefits that could be gained by doing the work (if the wording is to reflect an opportunity).

Let me continue with the examples already provided.

Example 1 20% of calls are being placed on hold for 3 minutes or longer ….. **which has resulted in a 50% increase in the number of complaints from customers**	**Example 2** Time between order and installation is taking up to 7 days, which is 3 days longer than the targeted maximum of 4 days …. **costing the business 12 additional sales per month valued at $56,000**
Example 3 Throughput is averaging 210,000 tonnes per day, 30,000 tonnes short of the targeted 240,000 tonnes per day ….. **resulting in missed revenue opportunities of at least $25,000 per day**	**Example 4** 23% of applications have insufficient details to process payment without contacting the customer **…. which results in an average of 12 hours per month spent following up on applications, and lost sales to the value of $22,000 per month**

Three Elements of a Problem Statement

A Problem Statement should:

- Be a clear and concise statement of **what is happening** – what is being observed
- Indicate **how long** the situation has existed, or been known to exist
- Describe its impact on the business or the potential gain from improving

You will notice in the examples provided, quantitative terms are used in each of the elements of the problem statements. By using quantitative terms, you can:

- Be clear about the level of improvement you have achieved post solution deployment

- Identify the benefits to the business in terms understood by the business leaders
- Identify goals for the project work

Detail Is Not Known

Often the exact detail might not be known at this point in time. I recommend that you insert a symbol such as 'X' where you don't know the value. As you learn more about the process you can come back and amend the charter.

Problem Statement Worksheet

The following table presents a simple tool for preparing a problem statement and some examples of well-worded statements. To use the process, simply ask the three questions shown at the top.

Q1. What is the problem?	Q2. How long has it been a problem?	Q3. What is its impact on the business?
Gold recoveries are averaging 64%, which is less than the expected recovery level of 70%.	This has been happening for at least the past 2 years …	… and is costing the business $22 million per annum.
22% of customers are experiencing a delivery time of greater than the agreed 10 days for product 'X'.	This has been happening for the past 12 months …	… and is resulting in a 15% drop in follow up sales which equates to $XX.XX per annum.
On average, 8% of our sheet metal cabinets are folded incorrectly resulting in asymmetrical shaped products that have to be discarded.	This has been occurring for at least the past 3 months …	… and is costing us $XX.XX per month in waste and resulting in delays of up to 7 days in delivering products to our customers.
New PC deployment cycle time has exceeded customer expectations on 75% of occasions ...	… for at least the past 12 months …	… departments have bypassed internal ordering system to purchase their own PCs, costing us $XX in missed discounts.

Getting Stuck

Having trouble getting to the actual problem?

One question that may help break the pattern of thinking when you get stuck is this.

- Ask 'How do you know you have a problem?'

This will take the discussion towards the problem from a different angle and hopefully break any 'stuck' pattern.

Problem Statement Review

All problem statements can be evaluated by determining whether or not they possess these characteristics.

- Is a **clear and concise statement** of what it is that is being observed - accelerated action will come from focus.
- Does not state **opinions** - we are entitled to an opinion but you want facts.
- Comprised of **3 elements** – (a) what the problem is, (b) how long it's been a problem and (c) what its impact is on the business.

- Contains **quantitative** terms. (i.e.; percentages, number of days or months etc)
- Does not describe a **cause** - this assumes the cause and may lead to an erroneous solution.
- Does not allude to a **solution** - the solution may well not solve the problem and the team wants openness and opportunity to explore as many options as possible.
- Does not **assign blame** to any person or work group for the problem - a sure way to start conflict with people who may well be those you need to solve the problem.

You can review the quality of your work by using the review questions shown below.

Problem Statement Review Questions (Part A)	**Response**	
Q1. Is my problem statement a clear and concise statement of what is happening, of what is being observed?	□ Yes	□ No
Q2. Does it indicate how long the situation has existed or been known to exist?	□ Yes	□ No
Q3. Does it describe its impact on the business or the potential gain from improving in quantitative terms?	□ Yes	□ No

If you answered yes to all of these questions you have all three components essential for a good problem statement. If you answered NO *to any of these questions*, you should review your problem statement before moving on. Continue the review by asking the following questions.

Problem Statement Review Questions (Part B)	**Response**	
Q4. Is the statement somewhat vague about what the problem actually is? e.g. Things are not going well with our online service.	□ Yes	□ No
Q5. Does it state opinions as opposed to stating what can be observed? e.g. Load time takes too long.	□ Yes	□ No
Q6. Does it assign blame or responsibility to some person or some work group? e.g. Supply people are not getting parts to us on time.	□ Yes	□ No
Q7. Does it describe a cause? e.g. Re-fuelling time takes too long because the pump size is too small.	□ Yes	□ No
Q8. Does it allude to a solution? e.g. We need more staff to complete the tasks on time.	□ Yes	□ No
Q9. Are multiple problems consolidated into one in this statement? e.g. Service time is taking 4 hours longer than necessary and most jobs miss all service	□ Yes	□ No

If you answered NO to all of these questions, you have a well-written problem statement and should continue with the charter development. If you answered YES to *any of these questions*, you should review your problem statement before moving on.

STEP 2 – IDENTIFY THE PRIMARY METRIC

The primary metric is the variable of most interest for the duration of the project.

It is the *variable* the team wishes to improve, hence the requirement to define it up front. When documenting the metric on the charter, the specification limits, baseline KPI (current level of performance) and targeted KPI (from the goal) are also stated.

Instructions

The primary metric component of the charter is developed in the following steps.

- Step 1 – Confirm the primary metric (the primary variable)
- Step 2 – Identify any existing specification for that metric (customer or business driven) – this is your 'Specification Limit'
- Step 3 – Define the current level of performance – this is your 'Base KPI'
- Step 4 – Determine the 'Target KPI'

Your completed work might look like this.

PRIMARY METRIC			
Metric	**Spec Limits**	**Base KPI**	**Target KPI**
PC Deployment Cycle Time	Max. 45 working days	75% longer than 45 days	< 25% longer than 45 days

Primary Metric Review

Review the quality of your work by asking the following questions.

Primary Metric Review Questions	Response	
Q1. Is the primary metric a direct reflection of the measure we wish to improve in this project?	☐ Yes	☐ No
Q2. Is it written as something you can measure? (eg; percentage availability, number of defects, standard deviation of length, cycle time for one unit produced etc)	☐ Yes	☐ No
Q3. Have you defined any relevant customer or business requirements for the primary metric?	☐ Yes	☐ No
Q4. Is the performance level currently being achieved with this measure reflected as your 'Base KPI'?	☐ Yes	☐ No
Q5. Does the targeted level of performance for this measure, written as the 'Targeted KPI', reflect the target in your goal statement?	☐ Yes	☐ No

If you answered yes to all of these questions you have completed this step.

If you answered NO to *any of these questions*, you should review work before moving on.

If you have not completed the Base KPI or Targeted KPI component, these should be completed at some point before the project starts. If you are having trouble determining the Base KPI, you should discuss whether or not this project is really a Lean or a Six Sigma project.

STEP 3 – STATE THE PROJECT'S DESIRED OUTCOMES OR GOALS

Goal setting is extremely important in managing the progress and performance of the team. Without the existence of clear goals, it would be very difficult to accurately measure success, and to motivate a team to complete their work with maximum efficiency. Success in anything is based on knowing what the desired outcome is in the first place. This is a basis for focused action and has the effect of creating dissatisfaction with the current state. By stating the goal up front, the team is able to focus their actions towards its achievement. It is also a source of reflection at any time the project work feels like it may be wandering from the intended path.

Effective project goals would be those that meet the following criteria remembered by the acronym SMARTA:

- **Specific** – only one goal is contained within the statement, not a combination of goals. The goals are precise, and are not ambiguous.
- **Measurable** – with quantitative terms the determination as to whether the goal was met is relatively simple. I sometimes refer to this requirement as 'sensory rich' in that it must be observable with one of the senses. If it is observable then it is measurable.
- **Attainable** – must be a goal that is within the control of the team. A goal that the 'team' believes is attainable.
- **Relevant** - to the problem being worked on.
- **Time bound** – a clear deadline is stated so that the work does not go on forever.
- **Agreed to** - by the key stakeholders of the project

Goal Statement Worksheet

A tool called a goal statement worksheet helps focus the discussion around specific questions that must be answered to write an effective goal statement. To use the tool, simply ask the three questions shown at the top.

Q1. What is our desired outcome in broad terms?	Q2. What is the specific measure we want to improve?	Q3. What is our specific goal or objective?
Increase gold recoveries	Percentage yield	Increase average yield by 2% to 65.28% by 2nd of February 2003
Reduce the number of deliveries taking greater than the agreed 10 days.	Percentage defects	Increase defect free rate to ≥ 90% by 22nd November 2002.
Increase the number of defect free products.	Percentage defects	Increase the non defect rate by 5% from 92% to 97% by 1st June 2005.
Reduce the number of new PCs taking excessively long to deploy	Percentage of PCs deployed on time	More than 75% of new PCs being deployed take less than 45 days after 30th of August, 2001

Goal Statement Review

Review the quality of your work by asking the following questions.

Goal Statement Review Questions	Response	
Q1. Is my goal statement specific about exactly what we want to achieve?	□ Yes	□ No
Q2. Is my goal statement linked directly to the problem and associated performance measure?	□ Yes	□ No
Q3. Does my goal statement define a specific date for achieving the goal?	□ Yes	□ No
Q4. Do I believe this goal is actually achievable?	□ Yes	□ No

If you answered yes to all of these questions you have a well-written goal statement. If you answered NO to *any of these questions*, you should review your goal statement before moving on.

STEP 4 – IDENTIFY PROJECT CONSTRAINTS & LIMITATIONS

What would be some of the most common constraints or limitations (in broad terms) that would affect project work of this nature in your business?

....

....

....

....

....

These are some of the general constraints that affect decision-making in your organisation today. It is highly likely they will have an impact on your project and your choice of solutions so it makes sense to think about these when you start your project.

Common Constraints

The most common constraints or limitations I've observed include those listed below.

- MONEY - Money value, budgets, return on investment, payback period etc (e.g.: any solution investment must payback within 90 days)
- LEGAL - Regulatory, compliance issues, legal requirements (e.g.: solutions must comply with all health regulations as defined in …….)
- POLICIES - Company policies or values (e.g.: solutions must comply with our policy of …..)
- PEOPLE - Human resource issues including safety (e.g.: there is to be no negative impact on safety risk)
- CUSTOMERS - Impact on the ability to meet customer requirements (e.g.: our ability to meet customers' requirements must not be negatively impacted)
- TIME - Times, deadlines (e.g.: the project work must be completed by June 1st)
- PRIORITIES - Workloads and priorities (e.g.: team members cannot contribute more than six hours per week on the work of the team)
- AUTHORITY - Decision-making authority (e.g.: the team can implement decisions to a certain $ value, provided all other constraints or limitations are met)
- SCOPE - What's in or out (e.g.: the team will not do any work on a particular aspect of the process)

Perceived Constraint Versus Actual Constraint

I often see limitations or constraints on charters that inhibit the generation of good ideas to some degree. One way to avoid this is look deeper within each stated limitation, as it may be the case that the true limitation is something else.

For example; suppose we were told that a limitation to our project was this - no capital expenditure. The question I would ask is this.

- 'What criteria, if met, would remove this limitation or constraint?'

In this case, it might be something like this; If we were able to generate a return on investment of 20 percent or greater, then we can spend capital. This is the true or actual constraint, not the original perceived constraint. (Note: I am not suggesting that capital cannot be constrained.)

Refer to the examples in the following table

<table>
<tr><th>PERCEIVED LIMITATION / CONSTRAINT</th><th>➔</th><th>ACTUAL LIMITATION / CONSTRAINT</th></tr>
<tr><td>No capital expenditure</td><td rowspan="6">ASK
What criteria, if met, would remove this limitation?
What would it take to overcome this limitation?
Is this criteria realistic?</td><td>Payback within X days
IRR / ROI of => 20%</td></tr>
<tr><td>No operating expenditure to be incurred</td><td>Neutral or Positive impact on margins</td></tr>
<tr><td>No new staff</td><td>Neutral or Positive impact on margins</td></tr>
<tr><td>No negative impact on safety</td><td>AS PERCEIVED</td></tr>
<tr><td>No organisation restructuring</td><td>Stakeholder approval must be given for any restructuring</td></tr>
<tr><td>Must comply with legislation</td><td>AS PERCEIVED</td></tr>
</table>

My goal in introducing this approach is to help organisations avoid introducing constraints or limitations that impede the potential of the work undertaken by the team. The belief that you cannot spend capital has a significantly different effect on your thought processes than the belief that you must return a minimum of 20 percent for any capital expenditure.

Sourcing Project Constraints

Where do we get these constraints? Who determines these? The most common constraints listed above give the clues as to where these come from. They can be sourced from:

- Legislation;
- Company policies;
- Business Leaders / Managers / Supervisors; and
- Customers.

STEP 5 – SCOPE THE PROJECT

What do we mean when we say project scope? I hear this question repeatedly and I find that many project leaders, if not most, struggle with the concept of 'scoping'.

Scoping your project is one of the most important parts of your work, as a well-scoped project allows a team to move forward quickly with focus and clarity. I would say that at least 90% of the projects that I have worked with over the past decade have all been scoped *too large* at the commencement of work. These projects often suffer from 'scope creep' when an enthusiastic, and often ill informed sponsor adds to the scope of the team's work. The effect on the team, and particularly the team leader, is loss of focus, confusion, and frustration over where to start tackling this monster.

Once the scoping issue is resolved, the project will steam ahead. The team benefits from having a clear focal point, and they are no longer caught up in a world of confusion and frustration. Always remember one thing, focus is power, and power means 'the ability to act'.

Project scoping is completed in two parts.

- Part A - Bound the process.
- Part B - Determine what is in scope and what is out of scope.

Part A - Process Bounding

Bounding is the process of determining the start and end point of the process the team will focus on.

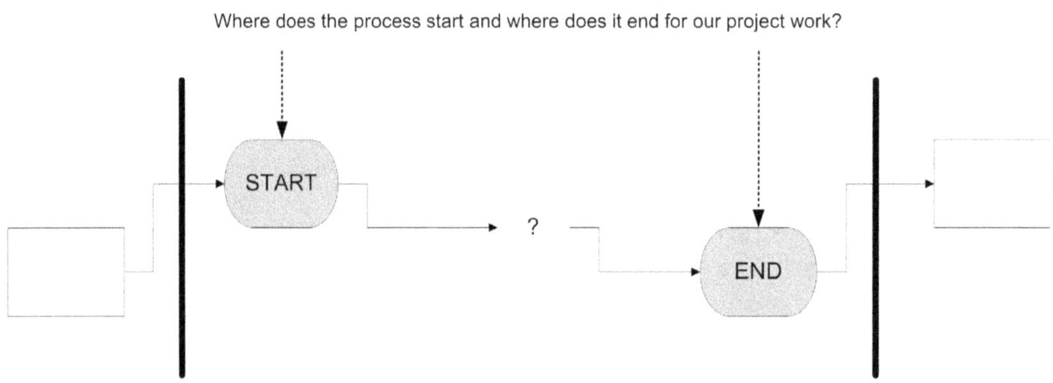

Instructions

Process bounding is completed in the following sequence.

- Step 1 – Brainstorm the high level sequence of steps in the process.
- Step 2 – Determine the activities that fall within the scope of the project.
- Step 3 - Define the start point (first activities within the scope of work) and the end point (the final activity within the scope of work).

Useful Facilitation Questions

The following questions will assist you in completing this process.

- What is the macro sequence of steps for this process?
- What steps are within the scope of our work or scope of our focus?

Part B - Scoping Lens

The scoping lens is a framework for having a focused discussion around the scope of the project. It is a visual thinking tool that helps us separate the elements designated to be within the scope of the project, and those that are not, and is used during the startup phase of a project. At the conclusion of this work, the outputs are captured in the project charter.

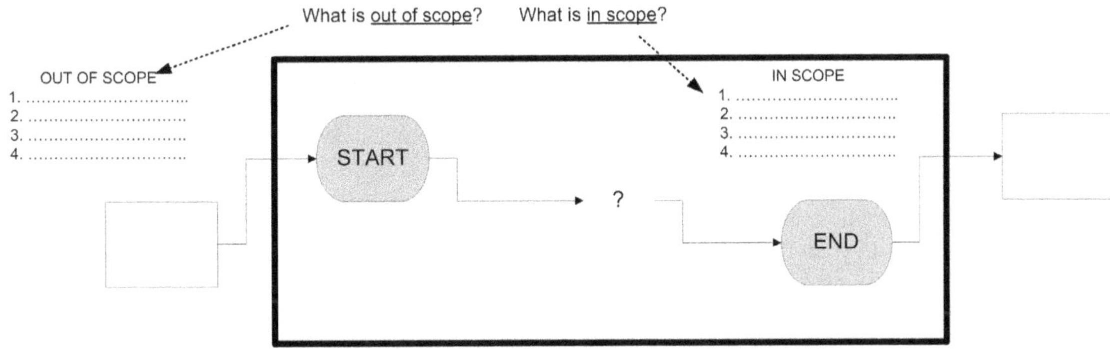

Instructions

Work with the scoping lens is completed in the following sequence.

- Step 1 – Draw a rectangle on a flip chart or whiteboard that represents the viewfinder for your work.
- Step 2 – Brainstorm everything that could potentially be improved or changed by the project work.
- Step 3 - Put everything that is 'in scope' inside the viewfinder, leave everything else out. Where you are not sure, place the idea on the border of the rectangle to indicate you are not sure if it's 'in' or 'out'.

Useful Facilitation Questions

The following questions will assist you in completing this process.

- What is involved in the process we are working on? OR
- What could potentially be changed as a result of our work?
- What is not in our scope?
- What do we need to focus on? (keep these inside, move others outside or on to the border of the rectangle)

The outcome of your work in this step may look like this.

PROJECT SCOPE
The boundaries of the process are: START: PC is ordered by the customer END: PC is installed and running on the customer's desk What is in and out of Scope? IN: Process for ordering, policy and procedures, supporting processes OUT: Supplier contracts, PC make and brand

Project Scope Review

Review the quality of your work by asking the following questions.

Project Scope Review Questions	Response	
Q1. Does the scope clearly define the boundaries of the process to be worked on? (it has a defined start and end point)	□ Yes	□ No
Q2. Are necessary exclusions stated as 'out of scope' items?	□ Yes	□ No
Q3. By looking at this information, is it likely that the team leader will understand where they are to focus their attention and what they are not to focus on?	□ Yes	□ No

If you answered YES to all of these questions you have a well-defined scope.

If you answered NO to *any of these questions*, you should review the project scope before moving on.

Re-Scoping

The project can be re-scoped at any time. It is not uncommon for re-scoping to occur during the 'analysis' phase of DMAIC when the source of variation, or the source of the problem is located.

STEP 6 – UNDERSTAND BUSINESS BENEFITS

To generate a compelling business case, you must be able to talk the language of those who make the decisions about allocation of resources. The language of those people is more often than not associated with benefits to the business in the form of risk and / or returns in economic terms.

Classifying Business Benefits

Business benefits are usually classified as one of the following.

- Earnings Before Interest and Tax (EBIT) – these are benefits that impact on operating cost or revenue (reflected in the company's Profit and Loss Statement)
- Shareholder Value – whilst EBIT type benefits contribute here, the intent is to identify those that fall outside EBIT such as reductions in the cost of capital, reduced working capital and even increased value to the business by extending its life or share price (some of these may be reflected in a company's Balance Sheet)
- Risk Reduction – these are benefits that ensure that downside risk can be better managed in the event of something occurring, or ensuring that the risk of missing opportunities is reduced or eliminated (may be reflected in a company's risk profile)

Business Benefit Identification

To identify the business case for doing this project, we simply ask a series of questions. The business benefit worksheet shown is designed to guide you in this process.

The worksheet shown provides examples of different answers from a range of projects and is completed in the following sequence.

- Step 1 – Identify the improvement that will be seen once the project is completed.
- Step 2 – Identify the impact on the business from this improvement focusing on issues such as working capital, revenue, cost, production, risk etc.
- Step 3 – Nominate the category of this impact, choosing from - (Shareholder impact beyond EBIT, Earnings before Interest and Tax (EBIT) or Risk Reduction)

Q1. What potential improvements will be experienced?	Q2. What would be the impact on key business measures if these improvements were experienced?	Q3. What type of benefit would this constitute? (Benefit Category)
Reduce inventory levels	Reduced working capital	Shareholder Value
Increase availability	Increase revenue through increased	EBIT
Reduce number of stoppages	Increase revenue through increased	EBIT
Speed up cycle time	Increase revenue through increased	EBIT
Prevent safety incidents	Reduce risk to safety	Risk Reduction (Threat based)
Improve product quality	Increased revenue through increased sales Reduced cost through less defects	EBIT
Less PCs purchased from non-contracted suppliers, more from contracted suppliers.	Capture contracted purchase discounts.	Cost reduction (EBIT)

Business Case Review

Review the quality of your work by asking the following questions.

Business Case Review Questions	Response	
Q1. Are you now in a position to be able to communicate the type of improvement you expect to get?	☐ Yes	☐ No
Q2. Could you explain how this improvement converts into some business benefit?	☐ Yes	☐ No

If you answered YES to all of these questions you are in a position to show a benefit to your organisation.

If you answered NO to *any of these questions*, you should review your work before moving on.

STEP 7 – FORECAST COSTS AND FINANCIAL BENEFITS

Bottom line impacts (benefits or costs) are able to be defined when the team knows what it will cost to implement solutions as a once only expense (e.g.; operating or capital expenses for purchase of equipment), what once only revenues will be realised (e.g.; reduction in working capital such as stockpiles or work in progress), what one off cost reductions will be captured (e.g.; reduction in supply inventories), and what will be the benefit to the business in terms of cost reduction or increasing revenues.

Example 1: The following example shows the cost benefit forecasts for a Lean Six Sigma project associated with the reduction in unscheduled downtime for a conveyor system.

The table is drawn straight from the project charter template.

BENEFIT TYPE		Increased Revenue (EBIT)
Forecast Once Off Costs / Benefits (AUD)		
	Initial Forecast	**Revised Forecast**
OPERATING EXPENSES	(30,000)	(30,000)
CAPITAL EXPENDITURE	(90,000)	(95,000)
REVENUE	0	0
Forecast Annualised Costs / Benefits (AUD)		
COST SAVINGS	(25,000)	(25,000)
REVENUE	150,000	245,000
NOTE: Costs are represented in brackets, benefits are represented in positive values.		

There is an initial outlay from both operating expenses and capital to implement solutions, however the payoff forecast is by way of increased revenues. The difference shows both a positive impact on EBIT and an acceptable return on investment (ROI).

Example 2: The following example shows the cost benefit forecasts for a Lean Six Sigma project associated with decreasing supply group inventory errors.

BENEFIT TYPE		Reduced Costs (EBIT)
Forecast Once Off Costs / Benefits (AUD)		
	Initial Forecast	**Revised Forecast**
OPERATING EXPENSES	25,000	30,000
CAPITAL EXPENDITURE	0	0
REVENUE	0	0
Forecast Annualised Costs / Benefits (AUD)		
COST SAVINGS	30,000	25,000
REVENUE	0	0
NOTE: Costs are represented in brackets, benefits are represented in positive values.		

Through process enhancements, the enhanced accuracy in inventory records resulted in the group being able to reduce inventory levels. The effect was reduced working capital resulting in a once off reduction in operating costs until new inventory levels settled, and an ongoing reduction in freight costs associated with returned goods and urgent deliveries.

One Time Cost / Benefits

Once off cost / benefits are usually associated with the initial implementation of solutions. Costs incurred through the expenditure of capital (CAPEX) or operating expenses (OPEX) are separately identified according to the organisation's relevant financial policies.

Activities such as reducing inventories may not result in ongoing revenue increases to the business, however a boost in revenue to the value of the inventory drop will be realised. These values are identified in the 'one off cost / benefits' portion of the charter.

Ongoing Cost / Benefits

Ongoing cost / benefits refers to those values that are going to be realised over time. Increasing costs (that should be offset by increasing revenues) are represented as an outflow in brackets.

Non Financial Benefits

Projects that target safety related risk reduction may not have a foreseeable financial impact on the business.

For example, a project team working on reducing dust levels in a workplace area will have a positive effect on the safety of employees. This is a worthwhile project to do. However, unless there is a resulting increase in production or reduced costs, the bottom line of the business will not be impacted.

I have participated in many discussions on this subject and I am always surprised by the variety of approaches taken. My view of this is based on the view that will be taken by the owners of the business. Unless financial margins are positively impacted, there is no financial impact on the business, and financial improvements cannot be reported. A business cannot report a $1M saving to owners when this was the value of the forecast costs that *will be avoided* by virtue of a Lean Six Sigma project. A $500K saving cannot be reported if this is the potential cost of a litigation claim avoided by virtue of a Lean Six Sigma project.

Let me offer some key points to consider with regard to completing the charter:

- Risk reduction projects fall in the benefit type category of **Reduced Risk.**
- Unless reflected on the bottom line, there is no Cost / Benefit to the business.
- Where a project results in 'cost avoidance', include the projected value in the problem / opportunity statement.
- Where a project results in 'cost avoidance', use the benefit type category of **Reduced Risk** as this is reducing the likelihood of the expenditure occurring in the future.

Exercise caution when forecasting benefits that relate to (a) working hours if the employee position remains in the company, (b) risk avoidance unless it's a reduction in insurance costs, and (c) deferment of capital expenditure.

- My recommendation is always this – GET ADVICE!

Financial Projections and Lean Six Sigma Accreditation

Some organisations have a requirement on team leaders to demonstrate competencies associated with financial analysis as an element of their Black Belt / Green Belt accreditation process. Where this is the case, financial calculations and projections should be documented for the purposes of that accreditation.

Cost Benefit Forecast Review

Review the quality of your work by asking the following questions.

Cost Benefit Review Questions	Response	
Q1. Have you identified the potential one off costs associated with project completion?	□ Yes	□ No
Q2. Have you indicated your estimate of the one off financial benefit that this project will bring to the business?	□ Yes	□ No
Q3. Have you identified the potential ongoing costs associated with solution implementation?	□ Yes	□ No
Q4. Have you indicated your estimate of the ongoing financial benefits that this project will bring to the business?	□ Yes	□ No

If you answered YES to all of these questions you have a sound platform for understanding the benefits that this project will bring to the business.

If you answered NO to *any of these questions*, you:

- Are working on a project that brings about a **reduction in risk** and no real cost or revenue benefit can be quantified; or
- You are working on a project that is **difficult to quantify** any benefit from and should consider another project; or
- You are **unable to estimate benefits at this time** and should have your respective team leader complete this step as more information becomes available.

STEP 8 – SELECT PROJECT PARTICIPANTS

The work of your team will affect and be affected by people and groups of people both inside and outside your organisation; these are your stakeholders. Knowing who these people are and involving them along the way will help you to:

- Understand important elements (through the eyes of the stakeholder) of your work;
- Identify better solutions to problems;
- Establish commitment to selected solutions;
- Identify limitations and pitfalls; and
- Identify where to get information at each phase of the project.

Who To Consider

So who do you put on the project team? When making this decision, you must not only consider *knowledge* of the subject matter but also the *need to involve certain stakeholders* for the purpose of accelerating changes to the process in a way that is sustainable. Consider looking at people from the following groups as a part of your team selection process.

- **Process Owners / Managers** – the people who are responsible for business processes and ultimately ensure performance of these processes beyond the project work, have a vested interest in making the project work successful.
- **Operators** – those who actually use the process you are working on probably know more about how to improve the process than most people.
- **Content experts** – people from outside the organisation that can assist with input.

- **Customers** – as the requirements of the customer are critical, their input in the development of solutions is important.
- **Suppliers** – problems may not only be experienced in the process, but with inputs as well.
- **Trade unions or industrial groups** – when thinking about change that will affect the workforce, union participation (where relevant) early in the project may prove useful.
- **Finance** – support may be required up front to establish a base line case against which financial gains can be calculated. You may also require support in putting together a case to support a submission for operating or capital expenditure.

Project Participant Worksheet

The project participant worksheet (shown below) provides a framework for having a discussion about who the key stakeholders are, what their relationship with the project is, and the extent of their participation in each phase of the project.

	PROJECT RELATIONSHIP					**PARTICIPATION BY PHASE**				
STAKEHOLDERS	Impacted	Can Impact the Project	Subject Matter Expert	Provide Resources	Decision Authority	D	M	A	I	C
Peter Jones	MOD	HIGH	✔			M	M	M	M	M
Steve Racknel	HIGH	MOD	✔			M	M	M	M	M
Michelle Irwin	MOD	NIL				I			I	I
Clare Jones	NIL	HIGH	✔			M	M	M	M	M
Mark Smith	HIGH	MOD	✔			M	M	M	M	M
Jack Black	NIL	MOD				I		I	I	I/R
Lynda Everest	HIGH	LOW	✔			M	M	M	M	M
Isaac Melrose	NIL	LOW						R		R
Mike Jeffrey	LOW	HIGH			✔	I			I/A	I
Steve Davis	HIGH	HIGH	✔	✔		I			I	M

Impact Rating	Participation
HIGH – Major impact by or on the project **MOD** – Moderate level of impact **LOW** – Low level of impact **NIL** – No impact ✔ – High level of contribution in this category	**M** – Team member **A** – Authority is required **R** – Ad hoc resource to the team **I** – Interested party - should be kept informed

Instructions

The worksheet is completed in the following sequence of steps.

STEP 1 Identify the people who you believe are the key stakeholders and list them in the left hand column of the worksheet.

STEP 2 Identify their respective relationships with the project and indicate in the middle set of columns.

STEP 3 Identify the extent of participation each stakeholder will have with the project and indicate in the right hand set of columns using: M = Member of the team, A = Authority Required, R = Resource on an ad hoc basis and I = Interested party that must be kept informed.

STEP 4 Identify any subject matter experts and professional resources that you might consider and repeat steps 2 to 3 for each one.

NOTE: This work is to be finalised in conjunction with your respective project team leader and process owner. Not all stakeholders need to be team members.

Project Participant Review

Review the quality of your work by asking the following questions.

Project Participant Review Questions	**Response**	
Q1. Does your team consist of members who are representatives of those who do the work with the process?	□ Yes	□ No
Q2. Do you know who should be kept informed throughout the duration of the project?	□ Yes	□ No
Q3. Do you know who has to give authority for any expenditure decisions at any stage of the project?	□ Yes	□ No
Q4. Do you believe that the team you have chosen is likely to complete the work in a timely and effective manner?	□ Yes	□ No

If you answered YES to all of these questions you have completed your work in identifying team members and other project participants.

If you answered NO to *any of these questions*, you should review work before moving on.

CONSOLIDATE YOUR WORK INTO PAGE 1 OF THE CHARTER

Your work to this point in time can be consolidated to look something like the example shown. It is finished when you are able to display your baseline data in some form of chart.

<table>
<tr><th colspan="4">PROJECT CHARTER</th></tr>
<tr><td rowspan="2">Project Title:
PC DEPLOYMENT</td><td colspan="3">Date Issued: 2nd of August 2001</td></tr>
<tr><td>Date Revised:</td><td>Revision No:
1</td><td>File No:
BI2001.18</td></tr>
</table>

<table>
<tr><th colspan="4">TEAM</th></tr>
<tr><td>Team Leader: Susan Carter</td><td colspan="3">Members:</td></tr>
<tr><td>Sponsor: Mike Jeffrey
Process Owner: Steve Davis</td><td>Peter Jones
Steve Racknel</td><td>Mark Smith
Lynda Everest</td><td>Clare Jones</td></tr>
</table>

<table>
<tr><th>PROBLEM / OPPORTUNITY STATEMENT</th><th colspan="4">PRIMARY METRIC</th></tr>
<tr><td rowspan="2">For at least the past 12 months, new PC deployment cycle time has exceeded customer expectations on 75% of occasions. The result has been that departments have bypassed the internal ordering system to purchase their own PCs, costing us $XX inmissed discounts.</td><td>Metric</td><td>Spec. Limits</td><td>Base KPI</td><td>Target KPI</td></tr>
<tr><td>PC Deployment Cycle Time</td><td>Max 45 working days</td><td>75% longer than 45 days</td><td>< 25% longer than 45 days</td></tr>
<tr><th>DESIRED OUTCOMES / GOALS</th><th colspan="4">DECISION CONSTRAINTS / LIMITATIONS</th></tr>
<tr><td>(1) More than 75% of new PCs take less than 45 days to deploy after 30-08-01.
(2) To capture discounts for 100% of PCs purchased after 30-08-01.</td><td colspan="4">Any capital expenditure must exceed the ROI hurdle rate of 20%.
No negative impact on risk exposure.
Solutions implemented by 30-08-01.</td></tr>
</table>

<table>
<tr><th rowspan="11">PROJECT SCOPE

The boundaries of the process are:
START: PC is ordered by the customer
END: PC is installed and running on the customer's desk

What is in and out of 'Scope'
IN: Process for ordering, policy and procedures, support processes, software installation
OUT: Supplier contracts, PC make and brand</th><th>BENEFIT TYPE</th><td colspan="2">Cost Reduction (EBIT)</td></tr>
<tr><th colspan="3">Forecast One Off Costs / Benefits</th></tr>
<tr><td></td><td>Initial Forecast</td><td>Revised Forecast</td></tr>
<tr><td>OPEX</td><td>(13,000)</td><td></td></tr>
<tr><td>CAPEX</td><td></td><td></td></tr>
<tr><td>REVENUE</td><td></td><td></td></tr>
<tr><th colspan="3">Forecast Annualised Costs / Benefits</th></tr>
<tr><td>COST SAVINGS</td><td>125,000</td><td></td></tr>
<tr><td>REVENUE</td><td></td><td></td></tr>
</table>

<table>
<tr><th colspan="4">PRIMARY METRIC CHART</th></tr>
<tr><td>Baseline Period:</td><td>January – July 2001 (6 months)</td><td>Source of Data:</td><td>IT Group Deliver Records</td></tr>
</table>

Figure 47: Completed Project Charter (Page 1)

Project Charter - Part 2

The following are planning guides to help you assemble the contents of your project plan.

Lean Oriented Project Planning Guide

Phases	Project Activities	Tick if Relevant
PROJECT SET UP (DEFINE & MEASURE)	Project Charter developed with Sponsor	
	Pre-measure / observe and collect basic data	
	Analyse process stability	
	Measure baseline performance	
	Plan the project from beginning to end	
	Stakeholder analysis / develop engagement plan	
	Establish Operating agreement with Sponsor	
	Lock in meetings with team members	
	Conduct TOLLGATE REVIEW (Tollgates #1 and #2)	
DEFINE, MEASURE & ANALYSE	Start up the project team (first meeting)	
	Document the process as a Cross Functional Flowchart	
	Undertake Time Value Analysis	
	Develop Takt Chart/s	
	Confirm where waste needs to be removed to improve process	
	Conduct TOLLGATE REVIEW (Tollgates #2 and #3)	
IMPROVE	Develop / select solutions that treat waste and solve the problem	
	Error proof solutions / conduct FMEA	
	Develop solution implementation plan	
	Analyse Stakeholders / develop engagement plan	
	Develop implementation project risk management plan	
	Develop Project Storyboard / Poster	
	Conduct STAKEHOLDER CHECK-IN	
	Adjust the implementation plan as required	
	Conduct TOLLGATE REVIEW (Tollgate #4)	
CONTROL	Standardise the new process	
	Document the new process in SIPOC format	
	Develop monitoring / response plans	
	Update Project Storyboard / Poster	
	Conduct TOLLGATE REVIEW (Tollgate #5)	
	Implement monitoring / response plans	
	Develop a mechanism for reporting benefits	
	Recognise the team and celebrate project completion	
	Conduct POST IMPLEMENTATION REVIEW	
	Formally Close the Project	

Six Sigma Oriented Project Planning Guide

Phases	Project Steps	Tick if Relevant
PROJECT SET UP (DEFINE & MEASURE)	Project Charter developed with Sponsor	
	Pre-measure / observe and collect basic data	
	Analyse process stability	
	Measure baseline performance	
	Plan the project from beginning to end	
	Stakeholder analysis / develop engagement plan	
	Establish Operating agreement with Sponsor	
	Lock in meetings with team members	
	Conduct TOLLGATE REVIEW (Tollgate #1 and #2)	
DEFINE, MEASURE & ANALYSE	Start up the project team (first meeting)	
	Document the process as an Activity Flowchart	
	Plan data collection	
	Validate the measurement system	
	Collect data	
	Analyse data for Xs that impact the Y and record findings	
	Conduct STAKEHOLDER CHECK-IN	
	Conduct TOLLGATE REVIEW (Tollgate #2 and #3)	
IMPROVE	Conduct cause & effect analysis as required & validate causes	
	Develop and select solutions that treat validated causes	
	Error proof solutions / conduct FMEA	
	Develop solution implementation plan	
	Stakeholder analysis / develop engagement plan	
	Develop implementation project risk management plan	
	Develop Project Storyboard / Poster	
	Conduct STAKEHOLDER CHECK-IN	
	Adjust the implementation plan as required	
	Conduct TOLLGATE REVIEW (Tollgate #4)	
CONTROL	Standardise the new process	
	Document the new process in SIPOC format	
	Develop monitoring / response plans	
	Conduct TOLLGATE REVIEW (Tollgate #5)	
	Update Project Storyboard / Poster	
	Implement monitoring / response plans	
	Develop a mechanism for reporting benefits	
	Recognise the team and celebrate project completion	
	Conduct POST IMPLEMENTATION REVIEW	
	Formally Close the Project	

CHAPTER 9: PROJECT 'DEFINE' PHASE

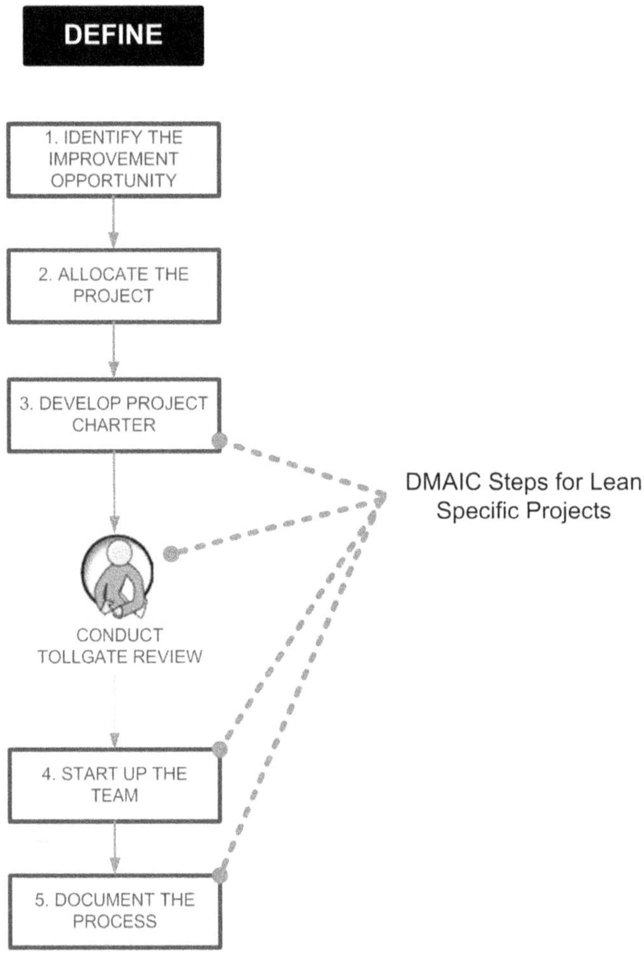

THE DEFINE PHASE AS A PROCESS

Define is the first phase of a team's work with the Lean Six Sigma process improvement strategy. The purpose of the define phase is to answer the following questions:

- What is the problem / opportunity we are working on?
- Who is going to work on this project?
- What is the agreed level of improvement we are targeting and how will we measure that?
- What is the sequence of activities in the process?
- What are the input and output variables in this process?

The first three steps of our 20-step roadmap are there to guide Project sponsors and Process Owners.

The DEFINE Phase as a Process

Let's assume that the project has been identified and allocated to a team leader and a project charter has been prepared. The following table represents our view of the 'define' phase as a process at this point in the project.

INPUTS	PROCESS	OUTPUTS
An improvement project that adds value to the business (meets the designated selection criteria)	1. Develop the Project Management Plan 2. Start up the team 3. Document the Process	A Project Charter A Project Management Plan A team that is committed to the project work, and who understands the goal and reasons why the achievement of that goal is important An IPO Worksheet or Flowchart that consolidates the sequence of process activities and associated elements A communications plan (which may include an elevator speech)

The process elements can be expanded further in the following way.

Develop the Project Management Plan

The team leader's role is to manage the project as it progresses through the DMAIC model. Thus, project management is a fundamental component.

As far as our 20-step roadmap is concerned, this is really an element of Step 3 – Develop the Project Charter. It is primarily the responsibility of the project team leader.

Starting up the Team

As a part of the start up process, the team must have a clear understanding of the goal, and the reasons why that goal is important to the team and the organisation.

One leading practice to undertake before moving on is to develop a short statement of (a) what the project is about, (b) what the goal is, (c) the reasons why the project is important, and (d) some indication as to how people can help.

Starting up the team really means getting the team motivated to do the project work and committed to the achievement of project goals.

Documenting the Process

The sequence of activities is laid out in flow chart format.

For projects focused on improving some output related variable, the tangible product or service outputs of the process are defined and the inputs necessary for producing those outputs are also defined.

COMMON DEFINE PHASE TOOLS

Two Sets of Tools and Processes

I must point out that there are really two sets of tools used by a project team leader. Those that are fundamentally technical in nature and address the *content* of the project, and those that are people oriented and address the process and *change* side of the equation.

For your reference, I've presented both sets of commonly used tools at the beginning of each chapter that describes processes and tools within the phases of the DMAIC model.

TECHNICAL TOOLS / PROCESSES	PEOPLE TOOLS / PROCESSES
Project Charter Project Management Plan or Schedule Gantt Chart Resource Plan Value Stream Analysis / Mapping Process Mapping / Flowcharting IPO Worksheet	Facilitation Processes and Tools Meeting Tools (Agenda, Parking Lot, Meeting Feedback) Team Building Processes Consequence Benefit Analysis Visioning Tools / Behaviour Alignment Operating Agreements Elevator Speech Communications Plan

DEVELOPING THE PROJECT CHARTER (STEP 3)

Project Charter

Before a project team is brought together to undertake project work, some work associated with getting the project off the ground must be completed. The questions that specifically need answering at this time include:

- What is the problem or opportunity the team is going to be working on?
- Who will comprise the team?
- What is the scope of the work and specifically, what is the process the team will be working on?
- What are the constraints or limitations that will affect the team's work and decision-making?
- How does this work contribute to the objectives of the business?
- What is the targeted level of improvement?

These questions should have been addressed through the development of a project charter; a task usually the responsibility of the project sponsor and / or process owner.

Getting Buy-in

Whilst the responsibility for the charter rests with the project sponsor, the sponsor should not be the sole owner of the content of the charter.

When the content is *dictated* to the team leader, and subsequently the team, there is always risk of a lower level of commitment by that team. A team leader that does not agree or believe that the project goals are achievable within the constraints, or a team leader who does not believe that the project can be completed in the stipulated time frame, given certain goals and resources, is unlikely to be truly committed to the project.

I had an experience back around 2003 working with a Black Belt who had been avoiding project start up for almost 2 weeks. The Black Belt, who worked in the information technology industry, had been told by his project sponsor what the scope of the project was and the time frame to have it completed. The Black Belt did not believe for one minute that it was achievable, thus his focus was on all the reasons why the project should not start.

This is a recipe for disaster and something that can be avoided through discussion and working towards consensus.

The project plan (part two of the project charter) is the responsibility of the project team leader. Time frames for completion of a Lean Six Sigma project are typically a function of the resources (staff and money) that are provided, the scope of the project, and the level of performance targeted.

This concept is discussed in detail in the 'Improve' phase of this text.

Charter Meeting with Sponsor and Process Owner

Before any project work with the team commences, the project team leader must meet with the Project sponsor and Process Owner to finalise (a) details of the project charter, and (b) how they will work together for the duration of the project.

Operating Agreements for Working Together

One of the most important aspects of starting a project is establishing agreements around how people will operate, and how the project will function. These are called Operating Agreements. By not forming agreements at the start, there is a high risk of conflict, indecision and hesitation down the track as the project progresses.

Operating agreements can be established at different levels:

- Between the Black Belt and Project sponsor and Process Owner
- Between the Black Belt and the Project Team
- Between the Black Belt and the Master Black Belt

The following guide provides a checklist for establishing an operating agreement with your project sponsor and process owner. An operating agreement between the Black Belt, Project sponsor and Process Owner is established before starting up the team, and is created in the following sequence.

- Step 1 – Choose relevant topics
- Step 2 – Draft 'operating agreements'
- Step 3 – Establish agreement between both parties

Rules for Establishing Operating Agreements

Some rules must apply if these agreements are to work as intended.

- The operating agreements are generated in an open and transparent environment.
- The agreements are two way (not just the team leader agreeing to do as the Project sponsor wants)

- Agreements are freely entered into – NO is an option.

Operating Agreement Content

Some of the most relevant topics might include.

- How often the Project sponsor and or Process Owner will meet with the team leader
- Where these meetings will take place
- Decision making authority for the team (i.e.; up to $X)
- Documentation requirements (i.e.; cost benefit analysis, etc)
- The process for implementing scope changes
- How to keep each other informed
- Supporting activities the Black Belt requires of the sponsor

Charter Meeting Checklist

When all boxes can be checked, the project is ready to progress to the first team meeting.

PROJECT CHARTER	
A problem statement describing what the problem is, how long it has existed and its impact has been defined	☐
Project goals that meet the requirements of 'SMARTA Goals' have been defined	☐
Project constraints have been discussed and documented	☐
The scope of the project describes the start and end points of the process under review, and what is in and what is out of scope	☐
Team members have been chosen on the basis of some logical reasoning using the Project Stakeholder	☐
The primary metric and base KPI of the project has been defined, and the target KPI has been agreed to in principle	☐
Project benefits have been estimated, OR agreement about time frames for completing benefit estimates has been established	☐
OPERATING AGREEMENT	
How often each will formally meet	☐
Where meetings will take place	☐
How to keep each other informed of changes	☐
The level of decision making the team has	☐
Documentation requirements	☐
Action to take if team members are withdrawn or resources are not forthcoming	☐
Process for implementing scope changes	☐
Support activities the team leader needs of the Sponsor and / or Process Owner	☐

FINISHING THE PROJECT CHARTER

With the first page of the project charter developed, only one question remains.

- What is the schedule of activities for completing this project?

The task of answering this question rests with the project team leader who has responsibility for project management.

Project Management

The guide to the project management body of knowledge (PMBOK 1996) developed by the 'Project Management Institute defines a project as:

> *'..... a temporary endeavour undertaken to create a unique product or service. Temporary means that every project has a definite end. Unique means that the product or service is different in some distinguishing way from all similar products or services.'*

Work with Lean Six Sigma projects is consistent with this definition, hence the need for team leaders to learn the skills and tools associated with 'project management'.

The second page of the charter, a portion of which is shown below, provides a framework for a Black Belt or Green Belt to plan and track the completion of relevant activities throughout the DMAIC process.

Project Management Plan – Charter Page 2

The project team leader's role is to plan and coordinate the project activities; thus the second piece of the project charter is a project management plan. A maintained project management plan might look something like this.

Phases	Project Activities	Planned Completion	% Completed	Date Completed
PROJECT SET UP	Project Charter developed with Sponsor	27-6-2021	100	26-6-2021
	Pre-measure / observe and collect basic data	14-7-2021	100	12-7-2021
(DEFINE & MEASURE)	Analyse process stability & measure baseline performance	15-7-2021	100	12-7-2021
	Plan the project from beginning to end	17-7-2021	50	
	Stakeholder analysis / develop engagement plan	"	0	
	Establish Operating agreement with Sponsor	18-7-2021	0	
	Lock in meetings with team members	"	0	
	Conduct TOLLGATE REVIEW (Tollgates #1 and #2)	20-7-2021	0	

Refer to Chapter 8 to view the full project management plan.

Project Management Plan Format

1. **Phases** – The five phases of DMAIC are listed in the left hand column.
2. **Activities** – A list of outcomes for the team as they work through the phases of DMAIC are listed in the second column from the left. Refer to the 20-step roadmap to develop your activities list.
3. **Planned Completion** – The date initially proposed for completing the activity is listed in the centre column.
4. **% Completed** – The percentage that each step is completed is regularly updated.
5. **Date Completed** – The actual date that the activity is completed and recorded for later reference.

Note: The project team leader, not the sponsor, prepares this portion of the charter.

Tools that might assist in the development and / or presentation of this plan include those discussed over the next few pages.

Schedule Bar Chart

One tool that may be used to present the project schedule at this phase of the work is the **Schedule Bar chart**. It was originally designed before the First World War by Henry Gantt to help with planning and controlling shipbuilding projects. In acknowledgement of his contribution, schedule bar charts often bear his name. The bar chart displays activities (scope of work) as they occur in respect to time. Each activity has a horizontal bar associated with it that indicates the start and stop point of that specific activity, in other words, the schedule of that activity. The length of that line is proportionate to its estimated duration. Consider the following activity data for a Lean Six Sigma project.

ACTIVITY	DURATION	COMMENCE	END
Set Up Phase	1 week	2 June	8 June
Define and Measure	3 weeks	9 June	29 June
Measure and Analyse	2 weeks	30 June	13 July
Improve the Process	4 weeks	14 July	10 August
Control Phase	2 weeks	11 August	24 August

This project activity data can be presented in bar chart format. The following is a schedule bar chart in its simplest form.

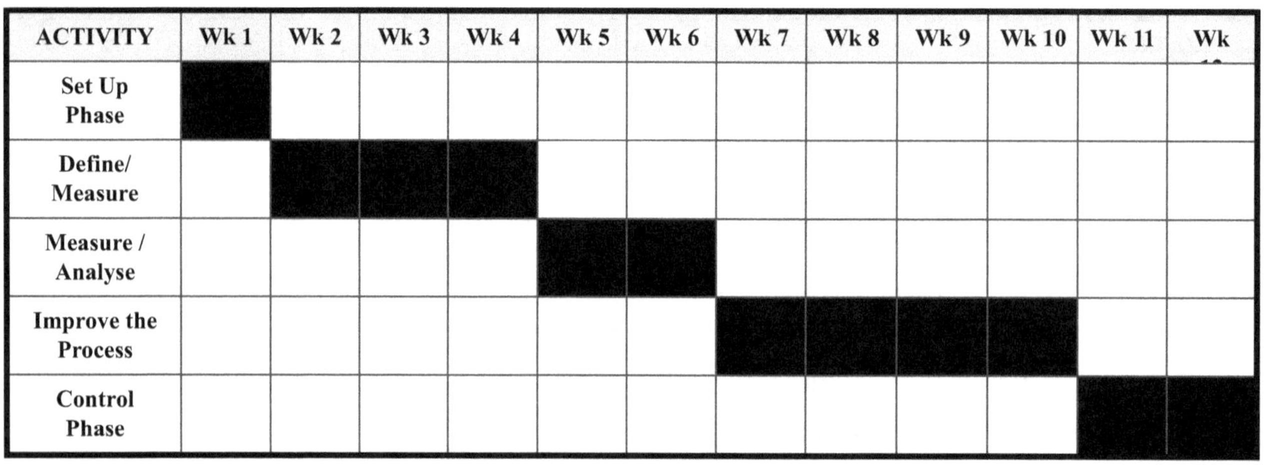

Gantt Chart with MS Project

Whilst not absolutely necessary for simple projects, tools such as Gantt Charts become important when the project activities are more complex. Tools of this nature, and software packages such as MS Project are used extensively at the 'Improve' phase of the project.

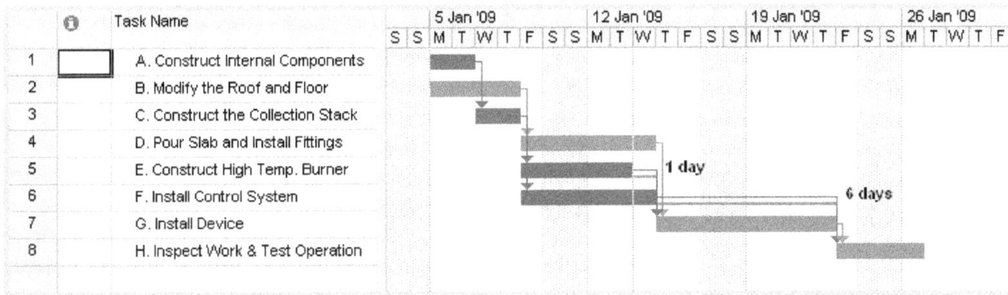

Additional Project Management Tools

Project management tools that will help a project team leader create a project management plan and control work associated with the project include these[19]:

- WBS - Work Breakdown Structure
- PERT – Program Evaluation and Review Technique
- CPM – Critical Path Method

Refer to the 'Improve Phase' of this textbook for more information about these tools.

PROJECT DURATION

Industry Realities

When delivering Lean Six Sigma training, it's very easy to lose sight of the effect of industry realities on managing projects. The effects of isolation, decentralisation, shift work, culture and business focus at any point in time are almost always felt at the project level.

In large technology companies that I have worked with, decentralisation has a tendency to impact on the ability of the team leader to bring people together in a face-to-face scenario. In the mining industry, shift work makes it very difficult to bring people together at the same time without disrupting production.

Don't let any of these be barriers. There are many ways to overcome these constraints and limitations including split meetings, virtual meetings, online workshops, teleconferences, overtime and even contractor supplementation. The suggestions I most commonly give to Black Belts in these situations are not solutions but ways to come up with solutions: You could try:

- Bringing a team together and letting them brainstorm solutions. Solutions they select are more likely to be successful.
- Discussing these challenges with responsible business leaders. Again, commitment is more likely to be forthcoming if they come up with the ideas.
- Benchmarking other Black Belts, finding out what they are doing because these problems have all been solved before.

The bottom line is this, don't focus on the problem; take action to come up with ways that help progress your project.

[19] Project Management Tools are explained in detail in the 'Improve Phase' chapter of this textbook.

'From a team perspective, a project is simply a set of meetings and execution activities that a team completes. In applying Lean principles of eliminating waste (non-value added activity) a project plan can help minimise the amount of time team members need to come together.'

Harry Sinko

PLAN THE PROJECT FROM START TO END

The project execution plan shown on the following page is an example only, but it is a reflection of how we guide our lean six sigma coaching candidates in the execution of their project work.

It closely reflects how I think about completing a project in the most effect way possible, and is built on a number of assumptions.

- The team leader is full time and the team is part time.
- Piloting of solutions is not necessary.
- Solution implementation time frames are dependent on the type of solution being implemented.
- Not every tool has to be used – only use those that add value to the project.

Obviously where piloting is required, time frames will be affected accordingly.

A project following this example would have the following characteristics:

- A cycle time of 3 to 4 weeks.
- Approximately 2 to 3 team meetings of no less than 4 hours duration.
- Data analysis being completed by the team leader with results reported to the team.

Benefits of Planning an Entire Project

The benefits of planning a project in its entirety include these:

- The entire schedule can be visualised, presented and managed
- Resource requirements can be planned with advance notice given to stakeholders impacted
- The team leader is forced to take a holistic look at the entire project

Project Execution Plan Example

This closely reflects how I think about completing a project in the most effect way possible. This is how we have been planning and leading improvement project work for the past 15 years with major customers.

PHASES	ACTIVITIES / OUTCOMES	PLANNED COMPLETION
SET UP PHASE	Charter the project with the Sponsor Pre-measure / observe the process Develop full project plan Establish an operating agreement with the Sponsor Engage with stakeholders	Week 1 " " " "
ANALYSIS PHASE	Bring the team together Map the process Locate the source of variation / find potential causes	Week 2 " "
	Collect data / validate causes as required	Week 3
SOLUTIONS PHASE	Continue the analysis if required Develop solutions Develop a broad implementation plan Engage with stakeholders, get buy-in Develop full implementation plan	Week 4 " " " "
EXECUTION	Implement solutions Develop and implement controls Formally close the project and handover to process owner Celebrate	As required

STARTING THE PROJECT (STEP 4)

OPERATING AGREEMENT WITH THE TEAM

Establishing an Operating Agreement

An operating agreement in this context is a contract between the project team leader and the team that describes the expectations for how they will work together. Expectations can be stated in relation to any of the following.

Roles and Responsibilities

- Who does what role
- Who is responsible for what
- Rotation of roles

The Project

- Level of authority (decision making)
- Information sharing

Meetings

- Locations
- Frequency
- Attendance
- Ground rules
- Decision making
- Confidentiality
- Giving feedback

The Rules for Creating an Operating Agreement

When you create your operating agreement, make sure you apply these rules:

- **Freely Entered** - It must be a freely entered agreement on the part of both parties, coercion is unnecessary and in any case will lose its affect beyond the meeting.
- **In Person** – The meeting is held in a face to face situation where full communication can take place as opposed to phone or email.
- **Specific Expectations** – Make sure there is no ambiguity and expectations cannot be misinterpreted by either party.
- **Relationship Symmetry** – It is a 50/50 agreement where both parties get to express their expectations of the other.

PREPARING FOR THE FIRST TEAM MEETING

The first team meeting may well be the most important you undertake with the team. The opportunity exists to start off on a good footing or a bad footing; the choice is yours. A good foundation for any project work is to focus on team development up front and not make the mistake of getting into the content too early. Spend time developing the team at the start; it will be time well spent and in the overall scheme of things will result in the project progressing at a greater rate than for a team that is highly content focused but not functional.

Thinking About The Questions To Be Answered

Each activity for effectively starting up a project team can be viewed in terms of what answers the activity provides for participants. So ultimately the start up meeting activities can be viewed as a series of questions that are being answered.

THE QUESTION TO BE ANSWERED	ACTIVITY	RESOURCES
1. What do we want to achieve today, and how will we make sure we achieve it?	Review Agenda Create Ground Rules	Agenda Flipcharts
2. Why have we been brought together as a team?	Review the problem Show a graph of problem data Discuss the goal	Project Charter Graph of data
3. What does each member bring to the team?	Create a Group Resume	Flipcharts
4. What is the urgency to do this work?	CB Analysis	Flipcharts
5. What is the vision and what behaviours must we engage in to make that become reality?	Revisit the Goal Visualise the Desired Outcome Commitment to Key Behaviours (musts for the team)	Project Charter
6. How will we achieve this?	DMAIC awareness session	Some form of DMAIC awareness training (eg; presentation or hands on with a catapult)
7. Who will do what?	Team Roles	
8. How will we work together?	Operating Agreement	
9. How will we communicate to people outside this team about this project in a way that is engaging?	Elevator Speech	Flipcharts

This information is reproduced in an agenda format as shown in the following example.

Sample First Team Meeting Agenda

(Note: This is planned as a full half-day meeting.)

Desired Outcomes:	To start up the project team in such a way that they are motivated to come to the project meetings
Why Outcomes are Important:	Make sure once we start, we maintain momentum throughout Get the best out of the team

Item	Result	Action Plan	Who	Timing
Opening	Agreement on agenda, establish ground rules	Presentation / Review Agenda. Q&A Brainstorm ground rules, Test for consensus	Team Leader	0800 - 0810 10 min
Overview	Establish awareness of what the project is about	Review project charter Seek consensus re project goals	"	0810 - 0825 15 min
Icebreaker	Build awareness of the experience of other team members	Break group into two teams Develop a group resume Consolidate and present	"	0825 – 0845 20 min
Urgency to do the project	Generate a sense of urgency to undertake the change	Consequence Benefit Analysis Teams feedback to each other Discuss biggest drivers for the project	"	0845 - 0920 35 min
Focus	Generate focus of the team on the desired outcome	Visioning session (current state to new state discussion) Vision to Behaviour (musts for the team)	"	0920 - 0950 30 min
Morning Tea	Refresh	Take a break		0950 – 1000
DMAIC	Establish awareness of the process to be followed	DMAIC Coaching Session with Catapult or Simulation Activity Q&A	"	1000 - 1115 75 min
Team Roles	Establish agreement on team roles	Presentation, Q&A Test for consensus	"	1115 - 1135 20 min
Operating Agreement	Build operating agreement between the team and BB	Discuss topics Generate ideas, Short list and test for consensus	"	1135 - 1155 20 min
Project Communication	Develop a Project Elevator Speech	Present concept Breakout activity – Elevator speech development Consolidate work, Test for consensus	"	1155 – 1215 20 min
Wrap Up	Close the meeting	Summarise actions Next meeting (date and time – will do process documentation and data collection planning) Feedback	"	1215 - 1230 15 min

'It should be noted that the Tuckman team development stages can be accelerated by ensuring that there is sufficient focus on team development. On many occasions I have found the need to have a contingency plan in the agenda to deal with issues. Frank and open discussion is critical, as are activities and physical movement. This is where the topics discussed in Chapter 5 become important to understand and apply.'

Harry Sinko

COMMUNICATION PLANNING

My experience has been that communication is often overlooked during the early phases of a Lean Six Sigma project. When I mention this to Black Belts, I often hear comments based on incorrect beliefs about project communications:

- "No change is taking place so there is no reason to communicate yet."
- "Team members will keep people informed."
- "I'll keep them informed as we progress."

Whilst no actual change in the process might be occurring at the present time, it is not unusual to make changes during the project as 'just do it' solutions are identified and actioned. Keeping people informed throughout the project's progress helps the implementation of these early wins. Keeping the leadership team informed of progress helps keep project work on their horizon, and may prove invaluable when your project reaches the 'Improve' phase and solutions are chosen.

As you probably already know, if you fail to plan it, it is unlikely that it will eventuate in any meaningful way. Without planning, communication can be disjointed, incomplete, inappropriate and even misleading. In most cases, without planning, communication is often non-existent, and those key stakeholders on your list who are interested parties will probably not be kept well informed. If you choose to not formally plan any communications at this time, you do so at your own peril.

Communication Plan

Project: PC DEPLOYMENT	Date Issued:	Page:	1 of 1
	Date Revised:	Revision No:	File No:

AUDIENCE	**CONTENT**	**TIMING**	**MEDIUM**	**RESPONSIBILITY**
Workgroup Supervisors	Project progress update summary	Fortnightly	Email	BB
Project sponsor	Project progress update summary Key challenges Project Plan	Friday – weekly	Face to face	BB
General Manager	Project progress update summary Forecast project plan	Fortnightly	Face to face	Sponsor

When planning communication, the team must answer these questions.

- Who must be communicated to?
- What do they need to know?
- When and how often do they need to know it?
- How can it be communicated so that we can be sure the communication is received?
- Who is responsible for the communication?

When planning communication, it will prove useful to involve the process owner and project sponsor, as they too can play a role.

Elevator Speech

One of the most useful approaches to communication during project work is the 'elevator speech'. Referred to in various ways, including elevator pitch, car park speech or car park pitch, the elevator speech evolved from the concept of how to communicate to a stranger (perhaps a company executive) in the time it took to travel from the ground floor to the top floor in a corporate office, during which time you had their total attention and wanted to have a positive impact on them. Studies have shown that 16 seconds is the average time spent with a stranger in an elevator. It's also all the time needed to make a favourable impression.

In our project context, an elevator speech is comprised of four parts that answer four simple questions.

- What – *What are you working on?*
- Why – *Why is this important to the business?*
- Where – *Where do you intend to be or what do you intend to achieve at the end of this work?*
- How – *How can I help?*

Elevator speeches can be created by the team in either full sentence form or alternatively in point form (individuals add their own sentences around the key points).

<u>Example 1</u>

> We are currently working on a restructure of our supply department.
>
> The reason this is important is because the current framework is resulting in an order accuracy level of only 65%, which is costing the company $xx.xx in returned goods.
>
> At the conclusion of this work, we will have a framework for providing a more efficient and effective customer service.
>
> You can help by taking the time to complete our customer satisfaction survey.

<u>Example 2</u>

> We are working on improving the cycle time and quality of deployment of new PC's.
>
> This project is important because the deployment of PC's has been a source of continual customer complaint. Employees expect a new PC to be 100% functional and a vast improvement over their existing computer, and problematic computers have the potential to disrupt employee's working days making them inefficient. Ultimately this costs the company money through lost productivity.
>
> By doing this project we would like to be able to provide end users with an installation in 50% of the time it currently takes, and reduce the number of reworks by 75%.
>
> You can help by letting us know how your PC is performing, and being specific when you report problems.

Using Elevator Speeches

Elevator speeches can be used in multiple ways.

- As a means for consistent communication from the team about the work being undertaken.
- As a lead-in to a survey.
- As part of your presentation to the leadership team, supported by one or two key graphs.
- An interesting point to remember is that elevator speeches can also be developed for the purpose of marketing anything including you.

EXPANDING YOUR LEVEL OF THINKING

One thing that I always mention to participants in our Lean Six Sigma training is the concept of increasing their level of thinking. To move to a new level of performance you must think at a different level. Let me give you an example of what I mean.

A golfer who plays 'C' grade thinks according to her existing capability. In essence she thinks like a 'C' grader, she certainly does not think like a professional golfer. The professional's focus on the course is different; the thought patterns that are the basis for their game is different.

Now if the 'C' grader wants to become a professional golfer, not only must she improve the technical aspects of her game, she must also change her patterns of thinking.

The same applies to process improvement or problem solving work.

If you continue to look at the process or problem in the same way you always have, you may not get beyond the current level of performance. If you do change your level of thinking, you may well achieve results beyond agreed targets.

So to change your level and patterns of thinking, you can employ a number of different strategies, all relevant to the topic of concern.

- Read as much as you can about the content you are working on, and the processes you employ to resolve problems and/or improve performance
- Participate in formal study
- Participate in formal training

Inquisitiveness Leads to New Thinking

I recall a story of an engineer working at an Iron Ore plant in Western Australia. The company had been experiencing a nagging problem with a particular type of valve in some tanks used during the processing of the ore. This problem had been around for quite some time.

One of the engineers quite remarkably solved the problem one day when he adapted and installed a completely different type of valve. As it turned out, he had been reading about a similar type of process in another industry in which they described the use of this other type of valve. He became inquisitive and subsequently ordered a number of these to see if he could do something with them. As a result, he was able to fully resolve the problem with the valves.

This was the result of expanding his knowledge and changing the level of thinking with which he had been trying to solve the problem over previous months.

DOCUMENTING THE PROCESS (STEP 5)

Our desired outcome for our Six Sigma specific project now is to create a model that represents the relationship of all key elements associated with the process including:

- The **Process**,
- The **Output** or Outputs of the process, and
- The **Inputs** to the process.

The purpose is to start setting ourselves up to understand key process variables that contribute to process variation.

We refer to this particular model as an IPO Worksheet (the acronym for Inputs, Process and Outputs). Other companies may not use this approach, preferring instead to teach and use a tool most commonly referred to as a SIPOC[20] (an acronym for Suppliers, Inputs, Process, Outputs and Customers).

Note for Practitioners Regarding Use of SIPOC

Many practitioners are taught to document a process and its key elements in SIPOC format as I was. We stopped doing this long ago for this reason. If you study the intent of the SIPOC (which is discussed in length in the Control Phase in this text as well as in Chapter 6), you will find it was designed to help users understand a defined process and the upstream and downstream elements core to the performance of that process. Those elements include:

- Its outputs;
- The recipients of those outputs, i.e.: the customers;
- The requirements of those customers;
- The inputs necessary for producing those outputs; and
- The suppliers of those inputs.

This is vital information in the process of *identifying what to work on* (choosing the project) as Motorola discovered so many years ago. By understanding customer requirements, data can be collected to determine which of these requirements can be more effectively met and the number of defects reduced or eliminated.

In all of the years I have worked with Lean and Six Sigma, I have *never* seen a project allocated to a team where the specific process variable was not already identified!

The SIPOC is an important tool for a Process Owner in this phase of the DMAIC sequence. Through its use Process Owners can build the platform for understanding performance against specific requirements, and then choose value-adding projects to allocate to the relevant people to work on.

If this were a textbook for Process Owners, the SIPOC would appear at this point. However, this text is intended for Green Belts and Black Belts, thus it appears at the relevant point for a project team leader.

The point in the project where the *other* customer related variables (those linked to their other requirements) become important to the team is when they start to create their monitoring plan. You can read more in the monitoring planning section in the Control Phase of this text.

PROCESS FLOWCHARTING

Before we discuss the specific tools of Six Sigma, it's important we properly understand the concept of process flowcharting. Process flowcharting (or process mapping) is nothing more than the practice of

[20] Refer to Chapter 7 for notes relating to the S.I.P.O.C.

visually laying out the sequence of activities that take place in order to produce some product or deliver a service. Sub-process flowcharting or mapping refers to the activity of taking one or more of the steps of a higher level macro process, and breaking them down into the more detailed steps.

The benefits of flowcharting include:

- Being able to see unexpected complexity
- Visualise non value adding steps including rework loops
- Increase understanding and make opportunities for improvement obvious

The flowcharts most commonly used include these.

- High Level (Macro) Flowchart
- Activity Flowchart
- Cross Functional Flowchart

Activity Flowchart

An activity flowchart details the action steps and decision steps within a process.

The following is an example.

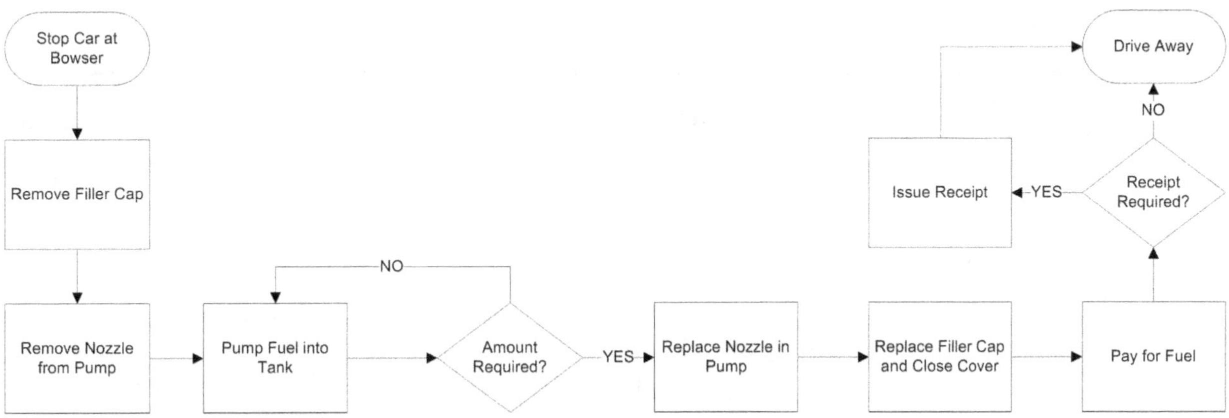

Figure 48: Activity Flowchart Example

Flowchart Symbols / Shapes

The main symbols used in this process flowchart are these:

Oval: Sometimes referred to as a 'terminator', the oval represents a start or end point in the process. These can be used inside the process as well as the obvious beginning and end.

Rectangle: Used to indicate an actions step. Wording inside the rectangle should be framed around a verb.

Diamond: The diamond represents a decision point where the process goes one way or the other, depending on the answer given. The question should be formed so that it drives a yes or no answer.

Connecting Line: Use to identify the sequence of steps and direct one takes going through the process.

Which Flowchart to Use

High Level (Macro) Flowchart	**Activity Flowchart**	**Cross Functional Flowchart**
• Identifying only the major steps of the process	• Identifying complexity within the process • Identifying all major decision and action steps • Identify rework loops • Seperate value adding from non value	• Identifying hand-off points between people or functions • Clarification of individual roles and interdependencies
↑ Commonly used by process owners for documenting processes in SIPOC form It answers the question -	↑ ↑ Commonly used by project teams during the define, measure and analyse phases of the project These should answer the question - How do we do that?	

Level of Detail

The level of detail in a process flowchart can vary quite significantly. My tip for you is that you should map detail that is useful or adds value to your work.

For example one of the steps in checking in a macro level process for coffee selling will be 'make the coffee'. That tells us 'what' we do which is make the coffee.

This could be broken down or sub-process mapped into a series of steps such as those shown below, which shows us 'how' we make the coffee.

Understanding the distinction between 'what do we do' and 'how do we do that' can be very useful to you as a process mapping facilitator.

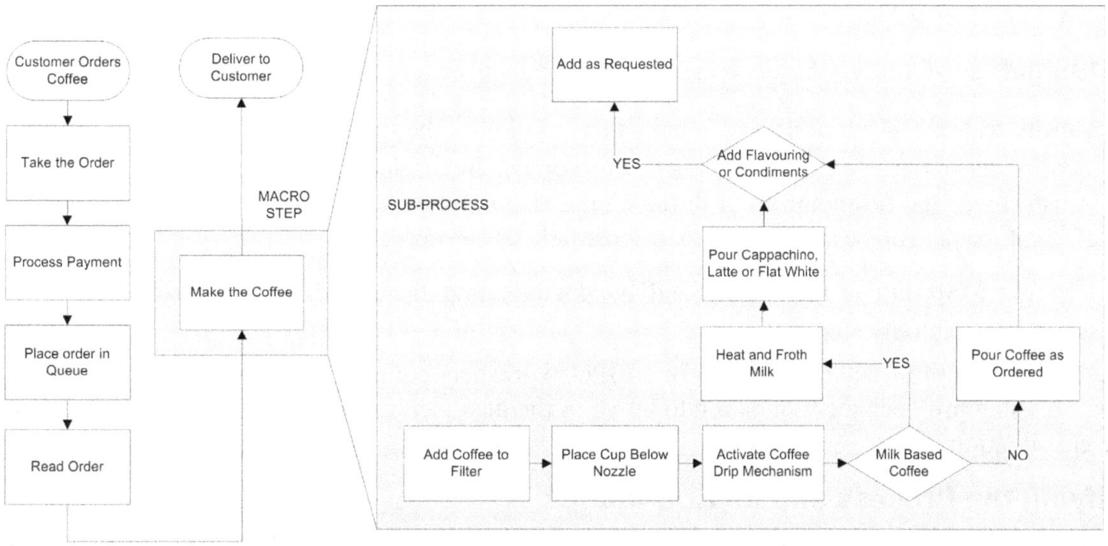

Figure 49: Example Macro Step with Detailed Equivalent

If it makes sense to record this higher level of detail, you should go ahead and do that. If it does not assist beyond providing information and a lot of detail about the process, these steps should be consolidated into the higher-level step.

DOCUMENTING THE PROCESS FOR SIX SIGMA PROJECTS

IPO Worksheet

The tool we use to document the process at the start of a project is referred to as an IPO Worksheet.

INPUTS	PROCESS	OUTPUT/S
Materials (the consumables you require to produce the output) **Data / Information** (the information or data that you need to produce the output) **Resources** (the fixed resources you require to produce the output)	(the activity flowchart that visually shows the sequence of activities)	(a statement describing the process output or outputs)

The IPO Worksheet is created in the following sequence:

1. **Process Boundaries** are established – by doing this we ensure that the team is focused on what they should be focused on.
2. **Outputs** are defined – these are the tangible products or services provided by the process.
3. **Inputs** to the process are listed – now that you know the process and its outputs, you are able to identify the inputs you need to create the outputs. Inputs include **materials** that are consumed or transformed, and **information** or **data**. Whilst also inputs, fixed **resources** enable the transformation of inputs to take place and are grouped separately as 'resources'.
4. **Process Mapping** is then completed by documenting the process in a chronologically arranged sequence of activity steps.

The documentation of these key elements in an IPO Worksheet concludes the **define phase** of the DMAIC process. This step provides the foundation to move to the next step in the process - measuring and analysing the current situation.

Identifying the Process and its Boundaries

The first step of this work is to identify the process boundaries so that we have a clear understanding of what is in and out of the process when we discuss it. It is not necessary to map the entire process at this time.

The process boundaries are the start and stop points of the process, and should have been identified during the scoping work when the project was first chartered.

Identifying Process Outputs

The outputs are the tangible ***products or services*** that are produced by the process. Some processes produce products as the result of transformation of inputs, whilst other processes are service oriented only. For example, a plastic toy manufacturing process transforms all of the materials and components into a single toy, hence this is a transformational process. A call centre on the other hand is service oriented.

I have found that where multiple outputs to a process have been identified during a project, it is useful to have a discussion to determine if one of the following has occurred:

- The team is working on multiple processes; or
- The process has multiple customers; or
- Some of the ideas may not be outputs as per the definition – (a mistake often made is to include (a) waste such as tailings, scrap or bi-products, or (b) benefits of the process such as profit, sales, money etc).

Identifying Inputs

We now focus our efforts on the upstream aspects of the process. As we know, the process takes inputs and through the process of adding value, turns them into outputs. I'm reminded of the old saying here, garbage in garbage out.

So what are inputs? These can be defined as the vital components required by the process to produce outputs.

- (a) Materials, (b) Resources and (c) Information

These inputs may well be the outputs of another process, and as customers of that process, we can define our requirements of those outputs (our inputs).

It's important to remember that we include all the inputs needed by the process, not just those needed at the first step to get the process started.

Completing the Process Flowchart

To map the process we will use what are known as flowcharts. Flowcharts are graphical representations of the steps in a process.

What is the purpose of flowcharting? By graphically representing the steps in a process, a team will be able to achieve the following:

- Clarify the steps or sequence of events.
- Generate common understanding within the team.
- Make it much easier to separate value adding tasks from non value adding tasks.
- Identify improvement opportunities such as complexities, delays, reworks, bottlenecks and waste.
- Make problems in the process more obvious.
- Reveal to the team how the process *really* works.

Mapping the 'AS IS' Process

We are now ready to finish the work in the define stage of the improvement process. At this time we need to complete the activity flowchart we are working on.

I am often asked why we complete the activity flowchart as the last step in preparation of an IPO Worksheet (or SIPOC for that matter). One thing worth considering is that this is the step where time can vary considerably, if only due to differences in opinions on what the process actually looks like. Individuals will have a different view of the process, based on their level of interaction with it. I have found it useful to save this, the most challenging piece of work until all of the other work for completing the worksheet is finalised.

Process mapping can be performed in a number of different ways, depending very much on the process being mapped, and the thought processes of the group. I have found the closer to the work the team members are, the more detailed the team tends to be in terms of the steps they describe in the process.

- **Sequential** – The facilitator asks the group to identify the first step in the sequence, then the next step and so on until all steps are identified. This is useful when the group is able to think at the macro process level.
- **Brainstormed Steps** – The facilitator asks the group to identify all of the steps as they come to mind, these steps are then arranged in chronological order.
- **Storyboarding** – The steps are brainstormed, these are then grouped into categories, the categories are given titles (as action steps), and then arranged chronologically. These titles form the steps at the macro level. This is particularly useful when the group generates a large number of micro level steps.

It may be obvious there are many more steps within each of the steps shown. However, there is no need to identify any more than a reasonable number of major steps at this point in time. These individual 'almost macro' level steps can be broken down further into sub-processes if required later when we understand more about where to focus our efforts.

Processes That People Do Not Follow Every Time

Problems often occur when people do not follow the designated process. So what is happening in the process? Quite simply, a decision making step has been introduced by those using the process.

I worked with a mining business in Western Australia where staff were on most occasions, failing to forward the first part of a safety incident report to relevant supervisors. Whilst the desired process was clear in the requirement, users had introduced a decision making step – 'do I forward part 1 of the form'. If the answer was yes, the form was forwarded, if the answer was no, then the form was not forwarded.

When mapping a process where multiple courses of action are taking place, you will need to have a discussion around where the additional decision making steps have been introduced.

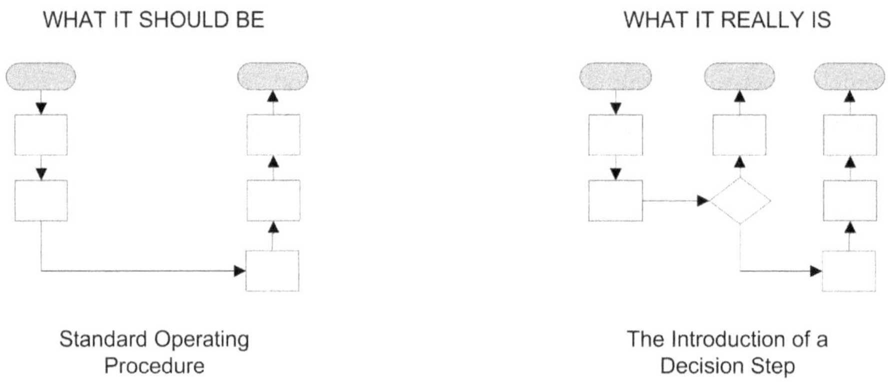

Figure 50: Unplanned Decision Steps in Processes

Processes That Include 'Wait' or 'Queueing' Time

Process mapping on the first pass may miss wait or queueing steps. This becomes obvious when you start to undertake value analysis in the process analysis stage.

You options are to (a) identify another step or (b) simply include this step and its time frame in the original step. The benefit of identifying a separate step is that you can focus on eliminating the step or making it as efficient as possible at a later stage if you know it's there.

Four Levels of Process

There are basically four levels of process as shown in the table below.

What We Think It Is This is our first pass process map developed by the team.	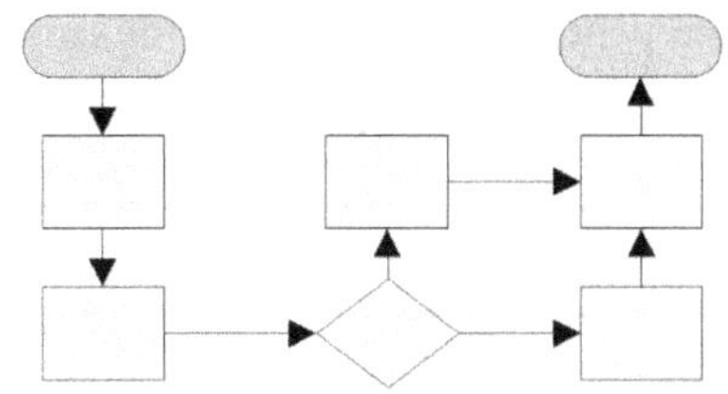
What It Actually Is This is the 'as is' process map refined through (a) validation with the people who work in or with the process, or (b) by actually following the steps in the process itself.	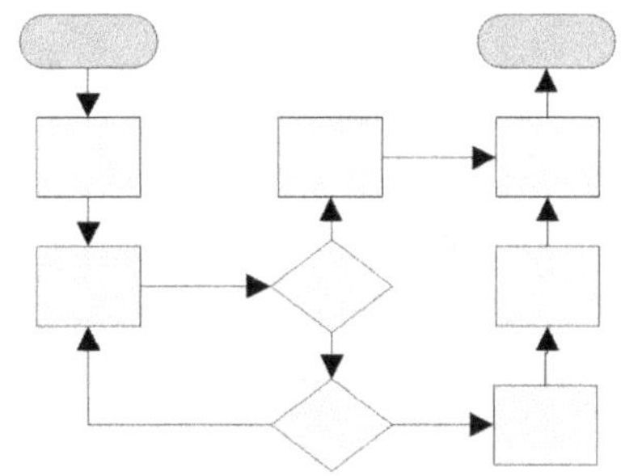
What It Should Be This is the new process created during the 'improve' phase of our project.	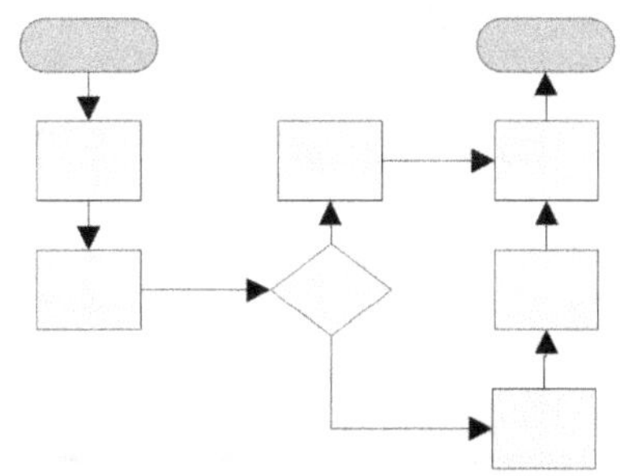
What It Could Be This is a process developed through the use of 'Process Design' tools (not covered in this book).	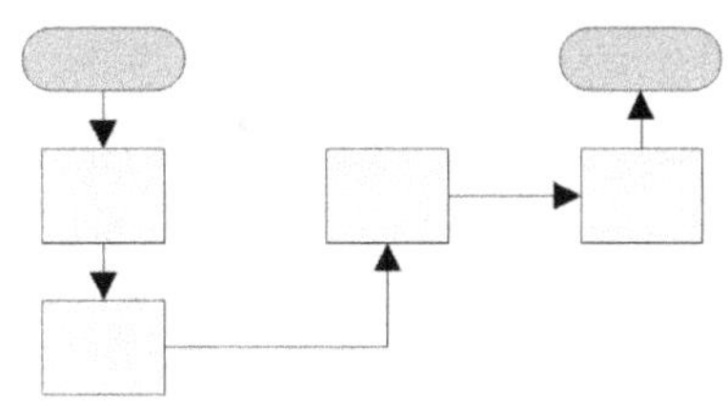

Table 2: Four Levels of Process

A common mistake teams tend to make is to map a process as they think it 'should be'.

It is essential that the team identifies the **'AS IS'** process, hence the need to validate after the initial mapping session.

Case Study - The Coffee Shop

To help demonstrate the tools we intend introducing in this book, we will study the work of a project team tasked with reducing the number of returned and wasted coffees at a café because of temperature issues.

The process is the 'coffee making' process and the output is simply a cup of coffee.

The final product for our coffee-making example looks like the IPO Worksheet shown below.

INPUTS	PROCESS	OUTPUT/S
Materials Water Milk Coffee Beans Condiments Foam cups Flavouring **Data / Information** Customer order Recipe Menu **Resources** Coffee Machine Staff Ceramic Cups Utensils Temperature Probe	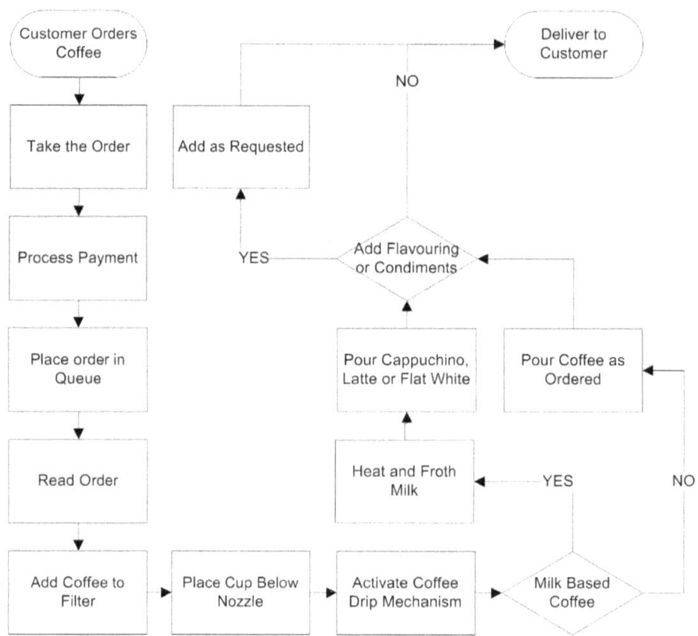	Cup of Coffee

Figure 51: Case Study – IPO Worksheet

DOCUMENTING THE PROCESS FOR A LEAN PROJECT

Lean is refined to the point where it has a range of very specific tools for analysing a process in order to reduce or eliminate waste. As such, it is not usually necessary to understand inputs and outputs for Lean specific projects such as those targeted with removing time from a process.

That activity is more useful for Six Sigma methodology oriented projects where the study of variables that cause variation in some output metric is necessary.

Let's use a second case study for looking at the tools associated with a lean project.

Case Study - Document Tube Factory

The activity flowchart below shows the entire process for the sale and manufacture of a product we will refer to as a 'document tube'.

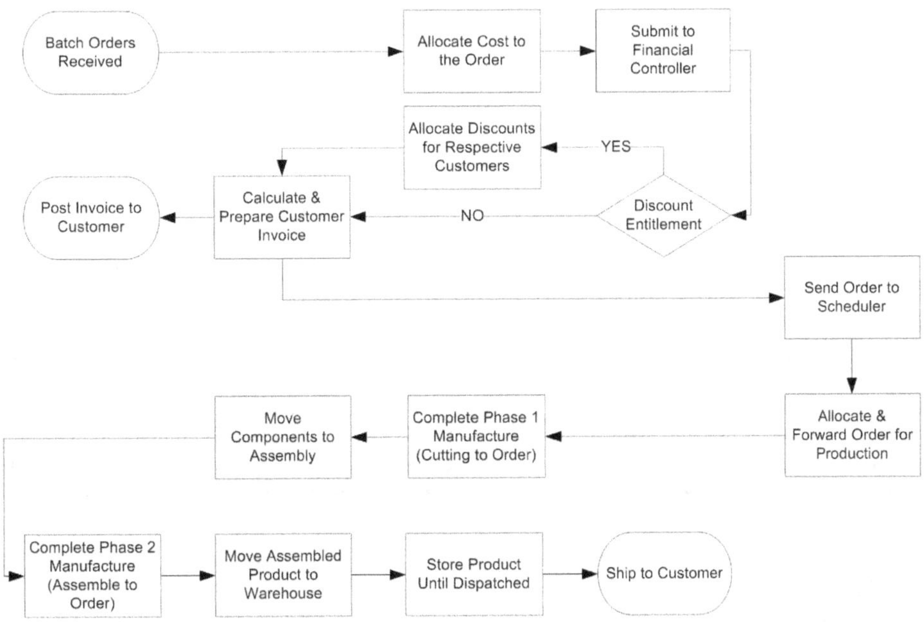

Figure 52: Activity Flowchart of Document Tube Sale and Production Process

We will continue to use this process in our Lean specific examples that continue in the next chapter.

DO'S AND DON'TS OF THE DEFINE PHASE

What you should do

- Identify all material, resource and data inputs required of the process if the project is focused on improving the quality of an output
- Document your process at the 'activity' level
- Use the affinity storyboard to get to the high level process when your team identifies too

What you should NOT do

- Start the project without establishing an 'operating agreement' with your sponsor and process owner
- Create a full S.I.P.O.C. unless you absolutely have to
- Push forward to the 'should be' process map

CHAPTER 10: THE DEFINE PHASE TOOLKIT

IPO WORKSHEET (SIX SIGMA ORIENTED PROJECTS)

What is it?

This tool is called an IPO Worksheet, which is the acronym for Inputs, Process and Outputs.

The purpose of this tool is to consolidate the activity level process and all of the relevant elements associated with it (including inputs and outputs) that assist with the later identification of key variables to study.

INPUTS	PROCESS	OUTPUT/S
Materials (list the consumables you require to make the output) **Data / Information** (insert information or data that you need) **Resources** (list the fixed resources you require)	(insert activity flowchart)	(insert output or outputs)

Instructions:

1. **Process Boundaries** are established – by doing this we ensure that the team is focused on what they should be focused on.
2. **Outputs** are defined – these are the tangible products or services provided by the process. For example, a cup of coffee is the output of the coffee making process.
3. **Inputs** to the process are listed – now that you know the process and its outputs, you are able to identify the inputs you need to create the outputs. Inputs include **materials** that are consumed or transformed, and **information** or **data**. Whilst also inputs, fixed **resources** enable the transformation of inputs to take place and are grouped separately as 'resources'.
4. **Process Mapping** is completed by documenting the flow of process activities in chronological order.

PROCESS FLOWCHARTS (LEAN PROJECTS)

What is it?

Process flowcharting or mapping refers to the activity of breaking down a process into a series of steps between a defined start and end point. These steps are represented in the form of flowcharts.

The flowcharts most commonly used are:

- High Level (Macro) Flowchart
- Activity Flowchart
- Cross Functional Flowchart

High Level (Macro) Flowchart	Activity Flowchart	Cross Functional Flowchart
• Identifying only the major steps of the process	• Identifying complexity within the process • Identifying all major decision and action steps • Identify rework loops • Separate VA from NVA tasks	• Identifying hand-off points between people or functions • Clarification of individual roles and interdependencies
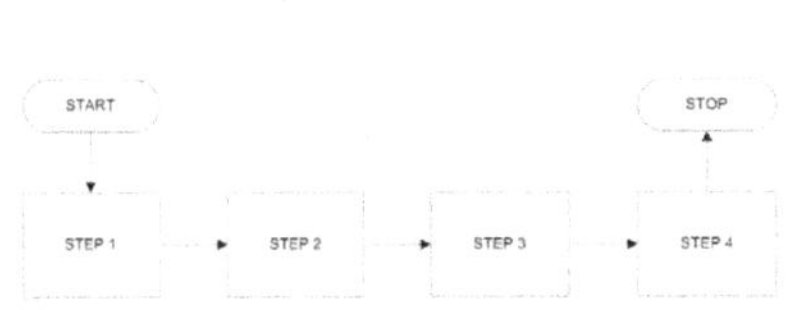	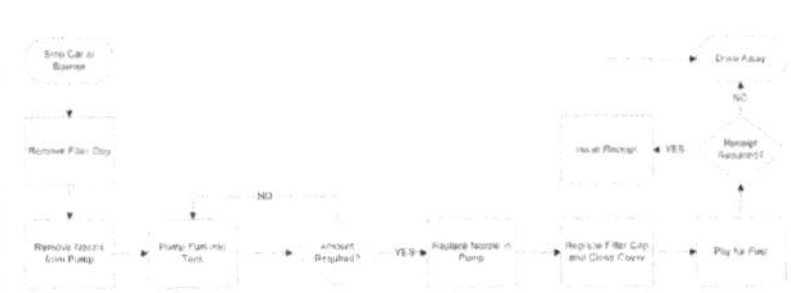	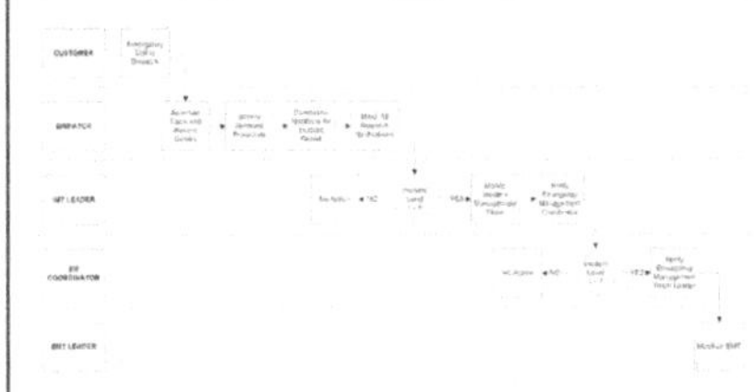
↑ Commonly used by process owners for documenting processes in SIPOC form Answers the question - What do we do?	↑ ↑ Commonly used by project teams during the define, measure and analyse phases of the project Answers the question - How do we do that?	

Instructions (Basic Activity Flowchart)

STEP 1 Define boundaries (start and end point)

STEP 2 Identify actions taken and decisions made in chronological sequence

STEP 3 Draw arrows to indicate flow through the process

STEP 4 Validate the flowchart. The key to validation is determining if the process is the one that is currently being used – the **as is** process.

The team may find value in mapping the ideal process and comparing it to the as is process, as opportunities for improvement may become obvious quickly.

COMMUNICATIONS PLAN

What is it?

The communications plan is a worksheet for defining and documenting the key elements associated with an effective communication strategy.

he worksheet is used during the planning phase for any change, usually at the beginning of a Lean Six Sigma project and during the work associated with solution implementation planning.

<table>
<tr><th colspan="5">Communication Plan</th></tr>
<tr><td colspan="2" rowspan="2">Project:</td><td>Date Issued:</td><td>Page:</td><td></td></tr>
<tr><td>Date Revised:</td><td>Revision No:</td><td>File No:</td></tr>
<tr><th>AUDIENCE</th><th>CONTENT</th><th>TIMING</th><th>MEDIUM</th><th>RESPONSIBILITY</th></tr>
<tr><td></td><td></td><td></td><td></td><td></td></tr>
<tr><td></td><td></td><td></td><td></td><td></td></tr>
<tr><td></td><td></td><td></td><td></td><td></td></tr>
<tr><td></td><td></td><td></td><td></td><td></td></tr>
</table>

Instructions

STEP 1 Determine who the audience is by asking: ‘Who needs to be informed for this project to be successful?’ Document in the ‘Audience’ column of the worksheet.

STEP 2 Determine what information each needs to know about the proposed change for the purpose to be achieved. Document in the ‘Content’ column of the worksheet.

STEP 3 Decide when and how often they need to receive information. Document in the ‘Timing’ column of the worksheet.

STEP 4 Determine the medium most appropriate for ensuring effective communication. Choices are numerous and might include

(a) newsletter,

(b) tool box talks,

(c) shift change over briefings,

(d) radio talk back,

(e) face-to-face discussion,

(f) formal presentation and

(g) phone call.

Document these in the column of the worksheet titled ‘medium’.

STEP 5 Determine who is responsible for taking action and document in the ‘Responsibility’ column of the worksheet.

MEETING AGENDA

What is it?

A meeting agenda is a description of a meeting and its specific components.

Its purpose is to summarise the entire meeting, and describe the specific components that ensure the meeting achieves its desired outcome in the most effective and efficient way possible.

Outcomes:	• (insert outcomes)			
Purpose:	• (insert reason why outcomes are important)			
Item	**Result**	**Action Plan**	**Responsibility**	**Timing**

Instructions:

Creating an agenda involves asking a series of good questions and documenting your answers in the format provided.

1. **Outcomes** - '*What are the specific outcomes we want at the end of this meeting*?'
2. **Purpose** - '*Why are these outcomes important to us?*'
3. **Results** - '*What specific results do we need to get in order to achieve our outcomes?*'
4. **Action Plan** - '*What must we do to achieve each of these results?*'
5. **Responsibility** - '*Who will facilitate this piece?*'
6. **Timing** - '*How long will it take to complete these actions?*' *and* '*When should it start and when should it end?*'

CHAPTER 11: DEFINE PHASE TOLLGATE & CHECKLISTS

A tollgate review is essentially a process for ensuring that the project is progressing, will continue to progress, is going to add value to the organisation and the Black Belt is effectively employing the tools and processes of the continual improvement methodology being used, in this case Lean and Six Sigma.

TOLLGATE QUESTIONS

One of the key skills of any manager or leader is the art of questioning. Good questions promote thought, focus and learning. The following questions are the kind that may be asked by your Master Black Belt or Lean Six Sigma Project sponsor during a 'Define Phase Tollgate Review' which is indicated as the point between step three and step four on our 20-step roadmap.

	Lean	Six Sigma
CHARTER • What is the problem / opportunity? • Why is this project worth doing? • How do you know that? • What is the scope of this project? • How did you decide that was the scope? • What key business performance measures will be affected by this project? • How will it affect those measures? • How will you know if this project is successful? • Has a similar project been undertaken elsewhere? • How can we learn from that work? • What are your project milestones? • What communications have you planned to undertake with key	✓	✓

	Lean	Six Sigma
TEAM • Who is on the team? • How and why did you select those members? • What level of commitment do you expect to get from your team? • How do you propose to deal with that? (if relevant) • What agreements have you established with your project sponsor and process owner for how you will work together? • What level of commitment do you expect to get from the process owner? • How do you propose to deal with that? (if relevant)	✓	✓

	Lean	Six
CUSTOMER PARTICIPATION • Who are the customers of the process? • What involvement have you planned for customers?		✓

	Lean	Six
GENERAL • What challenges do you anticipate you will have with this project? • What risks could affect project progress? • How are you going to deal with those risks? • What is your plan from here? • How can I assist?	✓	✓

PROJECT CHARTER CHECKLIST

Lean and Six Sigma Specific Projects

If you have responded appropriately to each of the following statements, then you are ready to move forward in the 'Define' phase of your project.		YES	NO	NA
1	You can confirm that the project is important to undertake now by explaining the relationship between the project and business goals.			
2	The leadership team of the business supports the project.			
3	The project is a problem or opportunity that is based on an existing and repetitive business process. (Fits the DMAIC methodology)			
4	Team membership and roles are defined.			
5	Have agreed upon the definition of the problem in a clear statement of what is happening, how long it has been occurring and what its impact to the business is.			
6	The primary metric has been defined, along with the baseline KPI.			
7	A preliminary target KPI has been defined and agreed to by the team.			
8	The improvement goal/s for the team have been agreed upon by team members and the project sponsor, and stated in measurable terms that are linked to the problem. No solutions are proposed in the goal statements.			
9	Limitations or constraints that may impact project work or potential solution selection have been identified and discussed with the Sponsor and Sponsor.			
10	The scope of the project is clearly defined to ensure focus.			
11	The benefit type for this project has been defined.			
12	Initial 'one off' and 'annualised' cost benefits have been estimated.			
13	Performance to date over a relevant baseline period has been graphically represented and is available for presentation if required.			
14	A preliminary plan or schedule for the project work is prepared.			

DEFINE PHASE CHECKLIST

Lean and Six Sigma Specific Projects

If you have responded appropriately to each of the following statements, then you are ready to move to the 'Measure' phase of your project.		YES	NO	NA
1	A project charter has been developed and agreed to by the Sponsor, Process Owner and Project Team Leader.			
2	The schedule and associated deliverables for each phase of the project has been stated.			
3	Operating agreements have been established with the Sponsor, the Process Owner, the Team, and the Master Black Belt (where applicable).			
4	The team shares a common vision of where the project will take them and the desired outcome or goal is captured in words.			
5	The team has identified the short and long term consequences of not doing the project work.			
6	The team has identified the short and long term benefits of doing the project work.			
7	The tangible products and / or services (the output of the process) are defined.			
8	The material and data inputs to the process have been identified.			
9	The resources that enable the process to turn inputs into outputs have been identified.			
10	The process as it occurs today has been mapped using an Activity Flowchart.			
11	All work has been summarised in the form of an IPO worksheet.			
12	Project storyboard or poster has been commenced.			
13	A strategy for communicating to key stakeholders and relevant parties has been agreed to by all team members.			
14	Team members have developed an 'Elevator Speech' for the purpose of consistently communicating the key elements of the project.			

CHAPTER 12: PROJECT 'MEASURE' PHASE

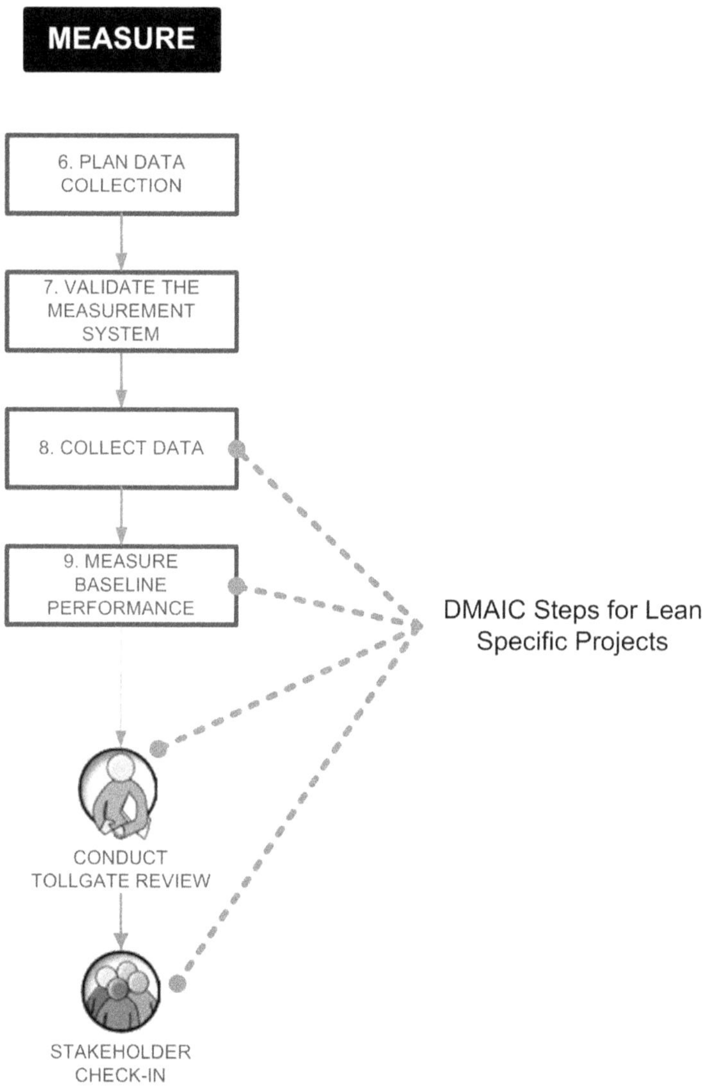

PREPARING FOR ANALYSIS

An understanding of the current state, in any context, is fundamental to *consciously* and effectively making a successful shift or transition to some pre-determined new state. This also applies to process improvement work in that it's necessary for a team to understand the state of the process before they can deliberately make and sustain improvements *and* achieve the desired level of performance. This understanding (in a Lean Six Sigma project context) is only achieved through undertaking some form of measurement, and studying and listening to the messages that come from process data.

The purpose of the 'measure' phase is to create the foundation for the 'Analyse' phase through the collection of data.

The type of data collected is determined by the context of the project. A project that is targeting improvement for a specific performance requirement, whether stipulated by the customer or the business, will require the collection of performance data relevant to that particular requirement. A project that does not have a goal targeting improvement for a specific metric (albeit highly unusual today) might well involve the collection of performance data across the entire range of customer or business requirements.

Different Data for Different Contexts

In a **Six Sigma context**, data is collected through undertaking measurement within each of the three main categories of measures (input, process and output).

In a **Lean context**, data is collected for specific efficiency characteristics.

THE MEASURE PHASE AS A PROCESS

Measure is the second phase of a team's work with the Lean Six Sigma process improvement strategy. In this phase the focus of the team shifts from *qualitative* to *quantitative* components of the Lean Six Sigma methodology.

The purpose of the measure phase is to answer the following questions:

- What data should the team collect in order to accelerate progress towards solutions?
- How reliable is the measurement system in producing valid and reliable process data?
- What is the level of performance we are going to compare progress against as a baseline?

The Effect of Measuring

The act of 'measuring' and its effect is a very interesting topic. A phenomenon recognised by performance management practitioners is this - if you measure something that's important, it tends to get managed. Think about people who undertake weight loss. They usually identify some key measures they will monitor continuously such as weight, body fat, and calorie intake. Measuring these variables results in an individual focusing on what is important to them.

If you remember, we have already spoken about the 'Hawthorn Effect'. Let me just remind you of the story. It was during the period of 1924 to 1927 when Professor Elton Mayo undertook a number of experiments involving changing the level of lighting in production areas at the Western Electric Hawthorne Works in Chicago to see if it had an effect on production output. The experimenters collected data on production and then increased the level of lighting. They found that the level of production went up. What a wonderful discovery.

To validate their assumptions, they reduced the level of lighting to its original level, and to their amazement the production output continued to increase. What was happening?

As it turned out, the increase in production had nothing to do with the level of light; it had resulted from the fact that the workers' performance was being measured.

As Dr. W. Edwards Deming said: 'What gets measured gets done.' Keep this in mind as you start your work on the measure phase of the project.

The MEASURE Phase as a Process

The following diagram represents our view of the 'measure' phase as a process.

INPUTS	PROCESS	OUTPUTS
A Project Charter A Project Management Plan A team that is committed to the project work, and who understands the goal and reasons why the achievement of that goal is important An IPO Worksheet that consolidates the sequence of process activities and associated elements (or just the flowchart as might be the case with a Lean focused project) A Communications Plan (which may include an elevator speech)	**Six Sigma Specific Project** 1. Plan the collection of data 2. Analyse measurement system variation 3. Treat measurement system variation where it is excessive 4. Collect data as per the plan 5. Establish a 'process capability' baseline **Lean Specific Project** 1. Collect process efficiency data 2. Establish a 'process efficiency' baseline	A collection of valid process data (relevant to the type of project you are undertaking) A baseline measure of process performance (either capability or efficiency) for post-improvement comparison

COMMON MEASURE PHASE TOOLS

TECHNICAL TOOLS / PROCESSES	PEOPLE TOOLS / PROCESSES
XY Worksheet Data Collection Plan Sampling Stratification Planning Measurement System Analysis Tools Rolled Throughput Yield / First Pass Yield Process Sigma Quality Level Process Capability Indices Time Value Analysis (Lean) Process Efficiency Metrics (Lean)	Facilitation Processes and Tools Meeting Tools (Agenda, Parking Lot, Meeting Feedback) Elevator Speech

The Importance of Planning and Data Collection

As you read through this chapter, I want you to bear in mind that the quality of your data collection planning (particularly for Six Sigma specific projects) and data collection will determine the speed and quality of your work in later phases.

For this reason I have put quite a lot of effort into explaining (a) how to create your data collection plan and (b) how to assemble collected data into a worksheet format for statistical analysis. This is the area where we have observed the greatest levels of improvement over the past decade and my goal is to share these learnings with you in order that your project work is that much more effective.

MEASURE PHASE FOUNDATIONS

Before we move our discussion into the measure phase proper, it's necessary for us to discuss the concepts of variation and descriptive statistics. These are foundation concepts for data collection planning, thus they must be addressed at this point in the book.

Let's start that discussion by thinking about data and information.

Data Versus Information

As we tell our Lean Six Sigma practitioners, it's very difficult to make a great deal of sense from raw data. The most effective way to analyse the data is to present it in such a way that it is informative. This processing of raw data is how we convert it into information.

Information is not the end point, however many organisations find it difficult to move beyond this point. If you take a look around in large organisations you'll find there is a ton of data and information out there, but what do they do with it? Its usefulness can only be realised when you are able to turn this information into knowledge that can be used to determine what action to take.

Let me give you a non-work related example. We collect a sample of data comprising 30 golf scores. This is raw data, and in its current form is not useful. The average of these scores is 83. This is information that tells us something about the scores. However, this is not a basis for taking any action.

If we found out there was a direct relationship between the number of putts made and the resulting score, we would be able to make more distinctions. This would be knowledge that provides a basis for us to take some action to positively impact the scores we are able to achieve.

This wall between information and knowledge is common. The strength of Lean Six Sigma lies in its drive towards turning raw data into useful knowledge about the process that we can act upon.

In essence, the focused approach of Lean Six Sigma on statistical thinking takes us beyond the information wall and allows us to make more distinctions about a process and how it performs.

The Wall Between Information and Knowledge

Space Shuttle Challenger

I'm sure many of you will remember the events of January 1986 when NASA launched the space shuttle 'Challenger'. Let me tell you a little about that story which highlights the need to make decisions on the basis of fact, and that statistical thinking is a mechanism for dealing with 'gut feel' risk in that process.

In January 1986, NASA was planning to launch the 'Challenger' space ship from Florida with a seven person crew including one school teacher, the first non- specialist astronaut.

Engineers from the rocket manufacturers, Morton Thiokol, had some doubts about launching in January especially since the weather forecast for the launch date predicted sub- freezing temperatures. The engineers were focusing on the problem of blow-by around the sets of O-rings, each about 10 metres in diameter, which were installed to accommodate the relative movement of the joining pieces of the solid rocket motor casings.

They phoned NASA some 48 hours ahead of the launch to express their concern and NASA's response, quite justifiably, was to ask for evidence to support their concerns. The engineers used their professional experience to influence NASA but were unable to produce any convincing evidence for the NASA personnel. The engineers complained that they had asked for test work to be done on the effects of temperature on the O-rings but no report was apparently issued.

The MT engineers worked hard to produce a chart that detailed all previous 24 flights, in chronological order. The chart displayed drawings of 48 rockets (2 per flight) with the location of the blow-by and the extent of the O-ring damage drawn on relevant rocket motors.

Temperature at the time of launch was also recorded. Despite receiving these charts, NASA was adamant that there was insufficient evidence to delay the launch.

Their bosses took over the pleading but they eventually backed down when the NASA officials explained that the launch date was important since President Reagan wanted to talk to the astronauts during his 'State of the Union' message in front of congress and a large nationwide TV audience. Did Morton Thiokol want to tell the President? was the rhetorical question.

As we know the space shuttle Challenger took off as scheduled. Seventy-two seconds into the launch the space shuttle blew up.

Temperature	Damage Index
53	11
57	4
58	4
63	2
66	0
67	0
67	0
67	0
68	0
69	0
70	4
70	0
70	4
70	0
72	0
73	0
75	0
75	4
76	0
76	0
78	0
79	0
81	0

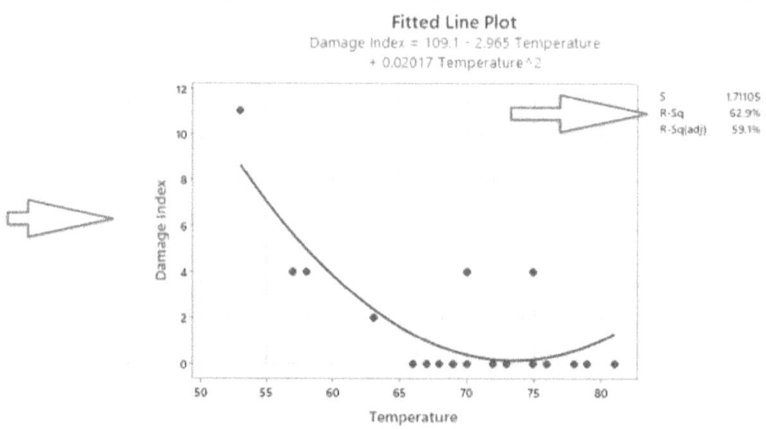

Figure 53A: Fitted Line Plot Using The Quadratic Function

The Presidential Commission included physicist Richard Feynman who had worked on the Manhattan project and later won the Noble Prize for Physics.

He took the Morton Thiokol data and displayed only two parameters on a single graph; launch temperatures on the X- axis, and O-ring damage on the Y-axis. [Refer to the image above]

The following image shows that data displayed as a scatter plot.

In presenting the data, I have applied a quadratic function to represent the relationship. As a result we can see that in this case some 62.9 percent (the R-Square value) of the variation in the damage index (the vertical axis), is explained by variation in temperature (the horizontal axis).

The graph is self-explanatory, yet it contains less data than the charts put together by the Morton Thiokol engineers.

The previous lowest launch temperature was 53°F when the most O-ring damage was incurred. While the data was sparse, the trend was dangerous enough to have warned people of some unpredictable risks if they were to launch at even colder temperatures.

Unfortunately, the launch temperature for Challenger was 29°F, which converts to -1.6 degrees celsius.

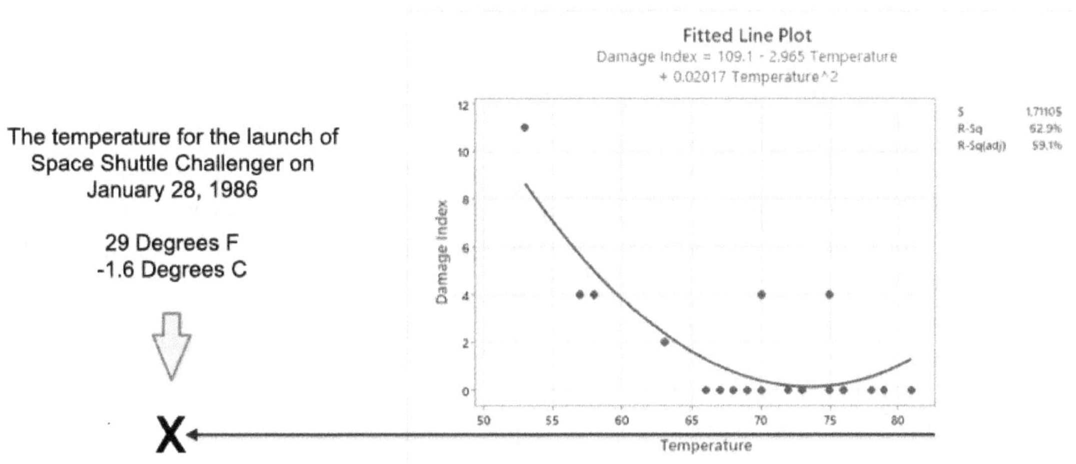

Figure 53B: The Temperature at The Time of Challenger's Launch

So what does that mean for us?

Statistical thinking is a foundation for taking us beyond information to the point of being able to take action on the basis of knowledge or facts.

As my good friend Tony Eltringham used to say to me: *'Everyone is entitled to their own opinions, but not their own facts.'*

DESCRIPTIVE STATISTICS

'Statistical thinking will one day be as necessary for efficient citizenship as the ability to read and write.'

H. G. Wells

Types of Statistics

Numerous types of statistics exist, they include:

- Descriptive Statistics
- Inferential Statistics
- Mathematical Statistics
- Exact Statistics

The two main forms we are concerned with as a Lean Six Sigma practitioner are Descriptive Statistics and Inferential Statistics.

Descriptive Statistics

Descriptive statistics describe, summarise and display the characteristics of data (typically a sample of data from a population). Descriptive statistics encompass both quantitative and graphical techniques and help us understand the following.

- Central tendency of the data
- Spread of the data
- Symmetry of the data
- Distribution of proportions
- We will discuss descriptive statistics at length in this chapter.

Inferential Statistics

Inferential statistics model patterns in data in such a way that uncertainty and randomness are accounted for and relatively accurate inferences can be made about a specific process or population.

Inferential statistics utilise various advanced methods to help us understand the following.

- Whether or not samples come from different populations (e.g. hypothesis testing)
- Whether or not one or more variables are associated with variation in one or more other variables (e.g. correlation)
- Models for estimating outcomes for a specific dependant variable when other independent variables are altered (e.g. regression)
- The accuracy of estimates of population characteristics (e.g. interval estimation)
- We will discuss inferential statistics at length in chapters associated with the Analyse and Improve Phases.

Definitions

To undertake descriptive statistics effectively, you must understand the following terms.

Parameter	A parameter is a numerical measure that describes a characteristic of a *population.* • The average operating cost per month across our entire business is \$5.75m • 30 percent of all university students in 2002 made application for HECS fees
Statistic	A statistic is a numerical measure that describes a characteristic of a *sample* of data taken from a population. For example: • The average height of the 50 students we sampled is 173.5 cm • The range of heights for the 50 students we sampled was 163cm to 191cm • 25 percent of the products we sampled last week were oversize
Continuous Numerical Variables	Data generated through measuring characteristics using an infinitely divisible scale. The result depends on the accuracy of the instrument being used to measure. (e.g.: time, weight, length, width, height, thickness, strength etc)
Discrete Numerical Variables	Data generated through counting attributes. The results are whole units that are technically not divisible. (e.g.: number of defects, number of males, number of players, number of complaints, shots on a golf course etc)
Discrete Attributes	Data generated through observing categorical variables (or characteristics). The results are qualitative in the information provided and yield values that can only be placed into categories or classes. (e.g.: pass or fail, causes of failure, defective or non defective, male or female, low, medium or high etc)

Since data can refer to either the whole population in a study or to just some sample selected from that population, it is important to distinguish between measures that describe a population or a sample.

MEASURES OF CENTRAL TENDENCY

There are three measures of central tendency; they are the mean, median and mode.

Mean

The mean (μ) is the average of a set of numbers or values. The mean of a population is calculated using this equation.

$$\mu = \frac{\sum_{i=1}^{N} x_i}{N} = \frac{x_1 + x_2 + x_3 + \ldots + x_N}{N}$$

Where:

N = Number of data points in the population

$\sum_{i=1}^{N} x_i$ = Sum of all values from first to last

The mean of a sample ($\overline{X}$) is calculated in the same way using all data points in the sample.

$$\text{Example: Average number of defects} = \frac{1+3+5+7+9}{5} = 5$$

Median

The median is the centre of a series of sorted data. 50% of the data is above the median, and 50% is below. Where there is an even number of data points, the median is the average of the two middle numbers.

Example:

- The median of odd numbered data set: 1 2 4 5 6 6 7 = 5,
- The median of even numbered data set: 1 2 4 4 5 6 6 7 = 4.5.

Mode

The mode is the most frequently occurring value or values in a set of data.

Example: The mode of data set: 1 2 4 5 6 6 7 = 6.

MEASURES OF SPREAD OR DISPERSION

Range

The range is the difference between the largest and smallest numbers in the data set.

Range = maximum value observed – minimum value observed

Example: The range of data set 1 3 5 5 6 7 9 is equal to 9 – 1 = 8

Deviation

The deviation is the distance between any data point and the mean; in other words how much a data point *deviates* from the mean.

Deviation = ($X - \mu$)

Example: The mean of data set 1 3 5 5 6 7 9 = 36 ÷ 7 = 5.14, therefore the deviation of data point 9 = 9 – 5.14 = 3.86.

Variance – Population Data

The variance of a population (σ^2) is the average squared deviation about the mean. This is calculated by taking the average squared deviation of each individual data point from the mean using the following equation.

$$\sigma^2 = \frac{\sum_{i=1}^{N}(x_i - \mu)^2}{N}$$

Where:

N = Number of data points in the *population*

σ^2 = Variance of the *population*

Variance – Sample Data

The variance of a sample (s^2) is calculated using a slightly different equation that gives the best estimate of the population standard deviation.

$$s^2 = \frac{\sum_{i=1}^{n}(x_i - \bar{x})^2}{n-1}$$

Where:

n = Number of data points in the *sample*

$s^2 = \hat{\sigma}^2$ (Estimate of the population variance)

Standard Deviation – Population Data

The standard deviation (σ) of a population is the square root of the average squared deviation about the mean (i.e.: the square root of the variance). This is the most commonly used measurement to describe variation. The equation for calculating standard deviation of a population is:

$$\sigma = \sqrt{\frac{\sum_{i=1}^{N}(x_i - \mu)^2}{N}}$$

Where:

N = Number of data points in the *population*

σ = Standard Deviation of the *population*

Standard Deviation – Sample Data

The standard deviation (s) of a sample is calculated using the following equation:

$$s = \sqrt{\frac{\sum_{i=1}^{n}(x_i - \bar{x})^2}{n-1}}$$

Where:

n = Number of data points in the *sample*

$s = \hat{\sigma}$ (Estimate of the population standard deviation)

<u>EXAMPLE</u>

The sample variance and sample standard deviation for data set 1 2 2 3 3 3 4 4 5 is calculated in the following table.

Observation	x	$x-\bar{x}$	$(x-\bar{x})^2$
1	1	-2	4
2	2	-1	1
3	2	-1	1
4	3	0	0
5	3	0	0
6	3	0	0
7	4	1	1
8	4	1	1
9	5	2	4
Sum	**27**		**12**

Number (n)	=	9	$n-1$	=	8
Mean ($\bar{X}$)	=	3	s^2	=	1.5
			s	=	1.22

$$s^2 = \frac{\sum_{i=1}^{n}\left(x_i - \bar{x}\right)^2}{n-1}$$

$$s = \sqrt{\frac{\sum_{i=1}^{n}\left(x_i - \bar{x}\right)^2}{n-1}}$$

Why n-1 for Sample Variance and Standard Deviation

Why do we use n-1 for calculating sample variance and sample standard deviation?

This is a question often asked, and I like to answer it this way. Both population and sample standard deviations are the square root of the variance.

Unlike **population** variance, the **sample** variance is calculated by dividing the sum of the deviations by n-1 (the number of data points less 1).

The term n-1 gives a better estimate of the true variance of the population. Remember the purpose of calculating any statistic is to make some inference about a population parameter.

As n-1 is smaller than n, we obtain a larger variance value with small sample sizes than we would if we just used n.

According to Levine, Ramsey and Smidt (2001), as n approaches 120, the effect of subtracting 1 is negligible, which is appropriate, as large sample sizes more closely resemble the population than small sample sizes.

SKEWNESS AND KURTOSIS

Two additional measures that describe the shape of a distribution are Skewness and Kurtosis. Both of these measures describe the manner in which data are distributed about the mean.

Skewness

Skewness is a measure of *asymmetry* (lack of symmetry).

A distribution with a skewness value of zero is perfectly symmetrical. Both normal and uniform distributions have skewness values of zero.

A positive skewness value indicates that the distribution is skewed to the right – the tail is stretched to the side above the mean.

A negative skewness value indicates that the distribution is skewed to the left – the tail is stretched to the side below the mean.

Skewness of a distribution, symbolised by the notation *k*, is determined by this equation.

$$K = \frac{\frac{\sum_{i=1}^{n} x_i^3}{n} - \frac{3\bar{x}\sum_{i=1}^{n} s_i^2}{n} + 2\bar{x}^3}{s^3}$$

The following table compares different distributions with a range of skewness values.

K < Zero	*K* = Zero	*K* > Zero

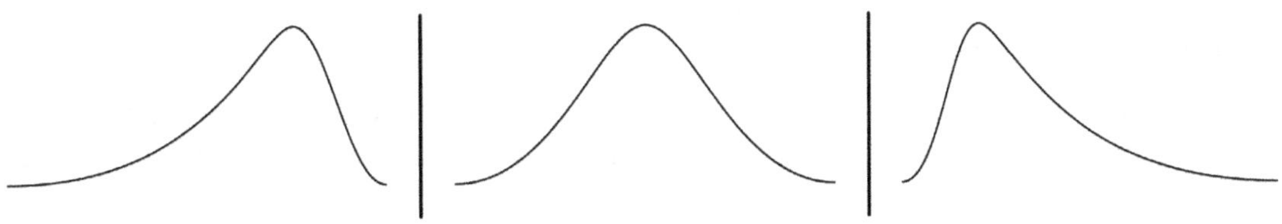

Skewness Values and Respective Distribution Shapes

Kurtosis

Kurtosis is a value that describes the relative concentration of values in the centre of the distribution as compared to the tails. In effect, it is a measure of peakedness; i.e. the higher the kurtosis value, the more peaked the distribution is.

Kurtosis, symbolised by the notation β_2, can be determined by this equation.

$$\beta_2 = \frac{\frac{\sum_{i=1}^{n} x_i^4}{n} - 4\bar{x}\frac{\sum_{i=1}^{n} x_i^3}{n} + 6\bar{x}^2\frac{\sum_{i=1}^{n} x_i^2}{n} - 3\bar{x}^4}{s^4}$$

Levine, Ramsey and Smidt (2001) describe three different distribution shapes as shown below.

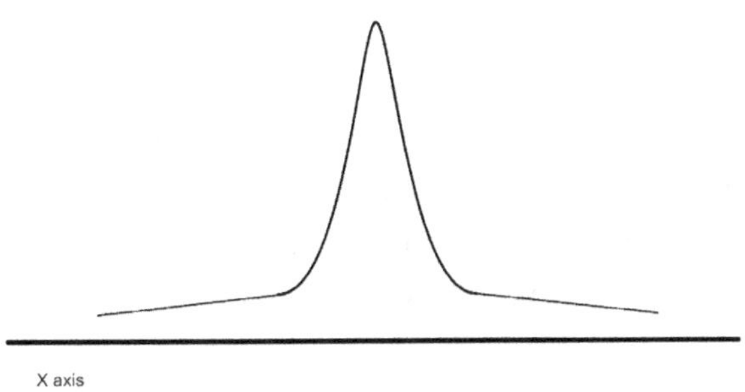

Leptokurtic – A distribution with a prominent peak and a relatively large proportion of values located in the tails.

$\beta_2 = 5.0$

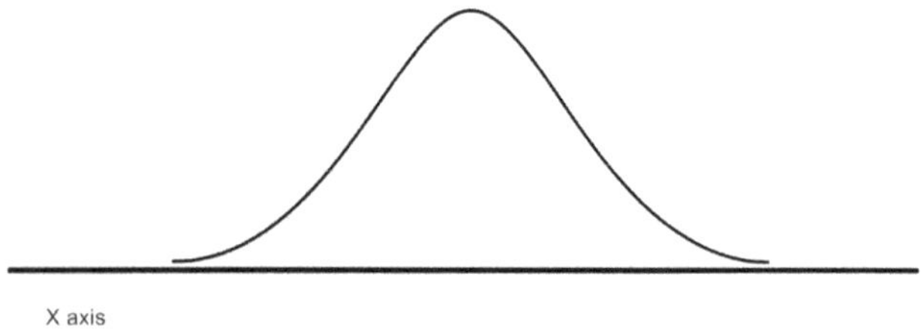

Mesokurtic – Most of the values are located in the centre of the distribution, with relatively few values located in the tails. A good example of a Mesokurtic distribution is the normal distribution.

$\beta_2 = 3.0$

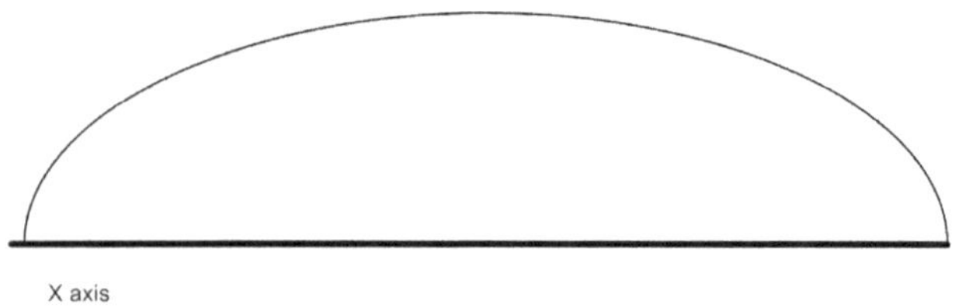

Platykurtic – The data are spread out through the range of the distribution resulting in a flat peak and few values in the tails.

$\beta_2 = 1.0$

Different Distribution Shapes

SUMMARY OF NOTATIONS

The table below shows the notations associated with the most commonly used characteristics of either samples or populations. Greek letters denote most parameters, while Roman letters denote most statistics.

CHARACTERISTIC	POPULATION (Parameter)	SAMPLE (Statistic)
Mean	μ (mu)	$\bar{X}$ (x bar)
Standard Deviation	σ (sigma)	S
Variance	σ^2 (sigma squared)	S^2
Median	ũ (mu tilde)	(x tilde)

Refer to appendices for a full description of a range of mathematical and statistical notations.

DESCRIPTIVE STATISTICS WITH EXCEL, SIGMAXL & MINITAB

Numerous software programs are available for shortcutting the calculation of descriptive statistics (a package of summary statistics from a data set). Microsoft Excel is the one most usually accessible by most PC users, though in the world of Six Sigma, statistical analysis packages offer more functionality and the opportunity.

- MS Excel is limited in its application in statistical analysis. Although many of the functions you need are available, they are more difficult to use and interpret than other dedicated statistical packages. Note - you will need the *Analysis Toolpak Add-In* to be activated in order to use these functions in MS Excel.
- SigmaXL® statistical analysis software is a brilliant Excel Add-in package that is now gaining prominence with practitioners around the world. It is simple to use with commands and menus functioning just like MS Excel.

- MINITAB® software is widely recognised as the ultimate statistical analysis tool for the serious six sigma practitioner. The package is now very user friendly and its functionality is second to none.

Descriptive Statistics with MS Excel

Microsoft Excel is capable of producing a descriptive statistics table. The dialogue box for Descriptive Statistics is activated by clicking on Data > Data Analysis and then choosing the item you want.

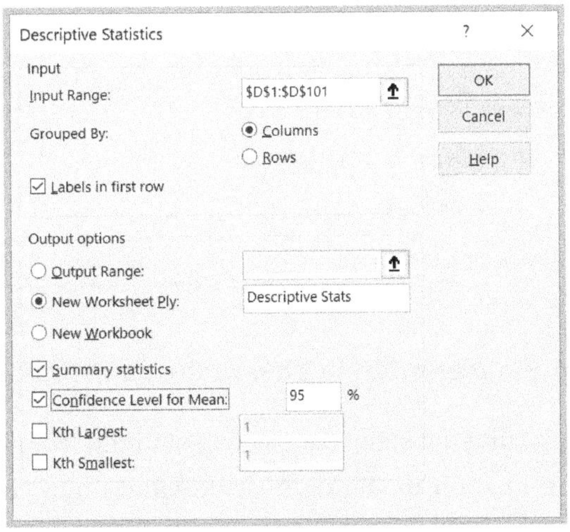

Figure 54: Dialogue Box for Descriptive Statistics - MS Excel

Note that Excel and SigmaXL (on following pages) automatically calculate Skewness and Kurtosis values.

For more information about *Standard Error*, refer to 'central limit theorem' and the discussion on the *standard deviation of the distribution of sample means* for they are the same thing.

The standard error is used to determine confidence intervals for the true mean of a population.

	A	B	C
1	*Avg No. of orders per mo*		
2			
3	Mean	34.054	
4	Standard Error	1.019431828	
5	Median	33.75	
6	Mode	32.4	
7	Standard Deviation	10.19431828	
8	Sample Variance	103.9241253	
9	Kurtosis	0.291962221	
10	Skewness	0.278522365	
11	Range	54.8	
12	Minimum	7.1	
13	Maximum	61.9	
14	Sum	3405.4	
15	Count	100	
16	Confidence Level(95.0%)	2.022773915	
17			
18			
19			
20			
21			
22			
23			
24			

Descriptive Stats | DATA

Figure 55 : Descriptive Statistics Output - MS Excel

Descriptive Statistics with SigmaXL

The dialogue box for generating descriptive statistics in SigmaXL is activated by clicking on SigmaXL > Statistical Tools > Descriptive Statistics.

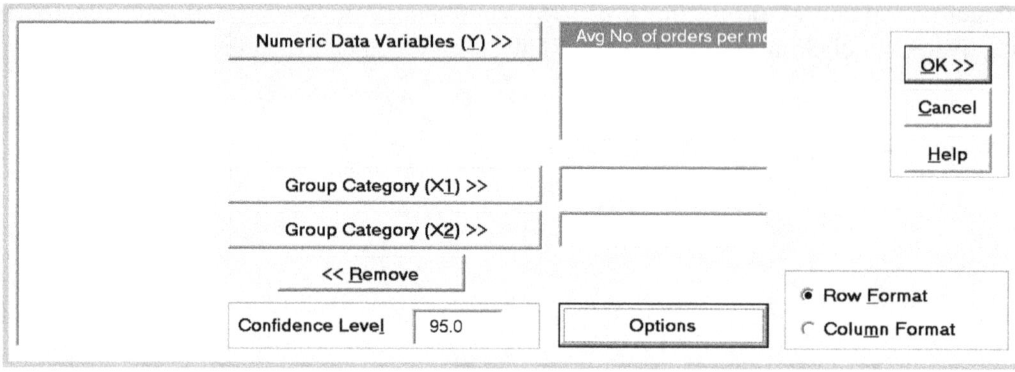

Figure 56: Dialogue Box for Descriptive Statistics – SigmaXL

The results shown were generated using the same data as the example from Excel.

SigmaXL provides additional information including quartile values and confidence intervals for the mean and standard deviation.

25th Percentile (Q1) – This is the maximum value of data containing the lower 25 percent (quarter) of all values.

50th Percentile (Median) - This is the maximum value of data containing the lower 50 percent (half) of all values. In other words, this is the value of the median.

75th Percentile (Q3) - This is the maximum value of data containing the lower 75 percent (three quarters) of all values.

95.0 CI (Mean and Sigma) – You can be 95 percent confident that the mean and standard deviation of the population are contained in the intervals presented.

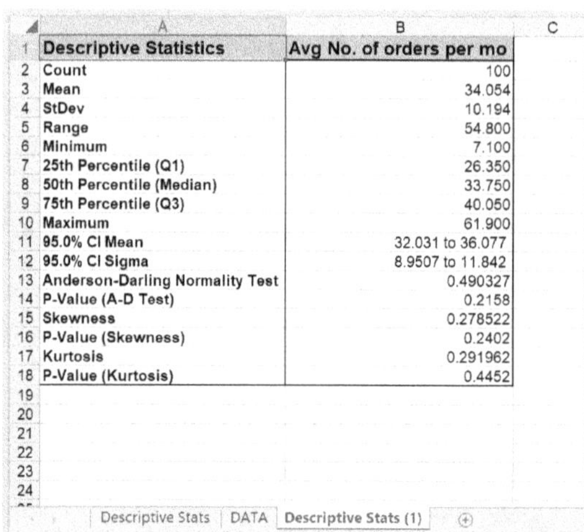

Descriptive Statistics	Avg No. of orders per mo
Count	100
Mean	34.054
StDev	10.194
Range	54.800
Minimum	7.100
25th Percentile (Q1)	26.350
50th Percentile (Median)	33.750
75th Percentile (Q3)	40.050
Maximum	61.900
95.0% CI Mean	32.031 to 36.077
95.0% CI Sigma	8.9507 to 11.842
Anderson-Darling Normality Test	0.490327
P-Value (A-D Test)	0.2158
Skewness	0.278522
P-Value (Skewness)	0.2402
Kurtosis	0.291962
P-Value (Kurtosis)	0.4452

Descriptive Stats | DATA | Descriptive Stats (1)

Figure 57: Descriptive Statistics Output - SigmaXL

Descriptive Statistics with Minitab

The dialogue box for generating descriptive statistics in Minitab is activated by clicking on Stat > Basic Statistics > Display Descriptive Statistics.

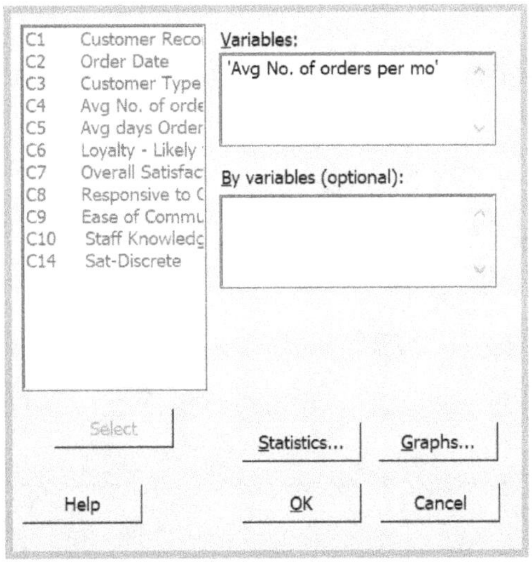

Figure 58: Dialogue Box for Descriptive Statistics – Minitab

MINITAB output can be tailor made to provide additional information by selecting 'statistics' in the main dialogue box.

Q1 – This is the maximum value of data containing the lower 25 percent (quarter) of all values.

Median - This is the maximum value of data containing the lower 50 percent (half) of all values. In other words, this is the value of the median.

Q3 - This is the maximum value of data containing the lower 75 percent (three quarters) of all values.

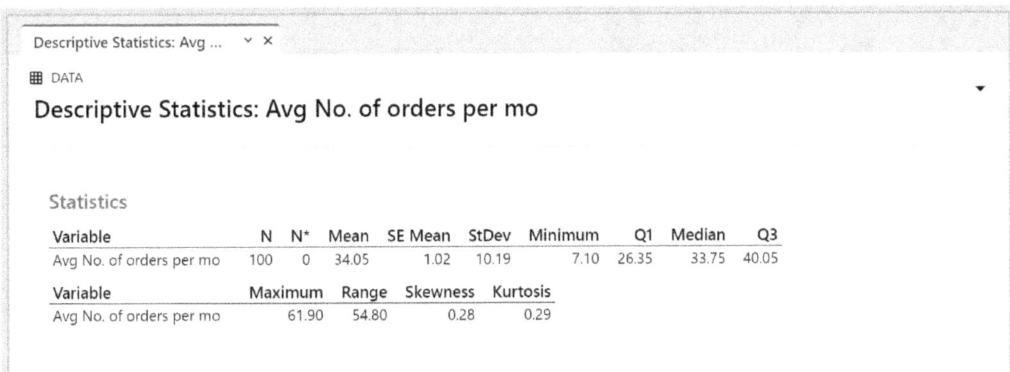

Descriptive Statistics: Avg ...

DATA

Descriptive Statistics: Avg No. of orders per mo

Statistics

Variable	N	N*	Mean	SE Mean	StDev	Minimum	Q1	Median	Q3
Avg No. of orders per mo	100	0	34.05	1.02	10.19	7.10	26.35	33.75	40.05

Variable	Maximum	Range	Skewness	Kurtosis
Avg No. of orders per mo	61.90	54.80	0.28	0.29

Figure 59: Descriptive Statistics Output - Minitab

NOTE: The range between Q1 and Q3 contains the middle 50 percent of data values and is referred to as the 'Inter Quartile Range (IQR). This range is represented by the box in the centre of charts known as 'Box Plots' (presented later in this text book).

Graphical Summary with Minitab

Minitab is capable of providing a graphical summary of descriptive statistics. The dialogue box for generating a graphical summary is activated activated by clicking on Stat > Basic Statistics > Graphical Summary.

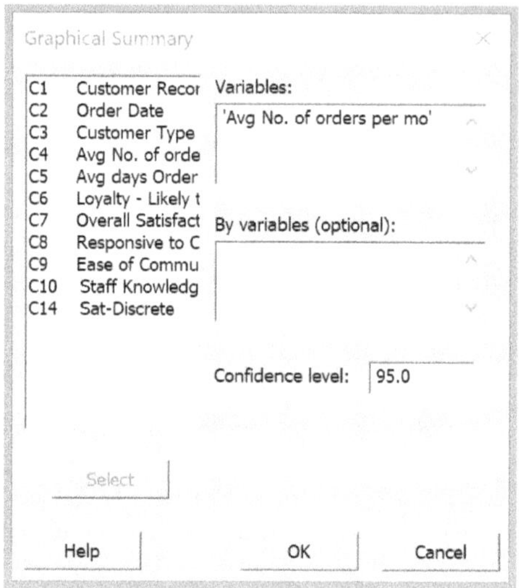

Figure 60: Dialogue Box for Graphical Summary - Minitab

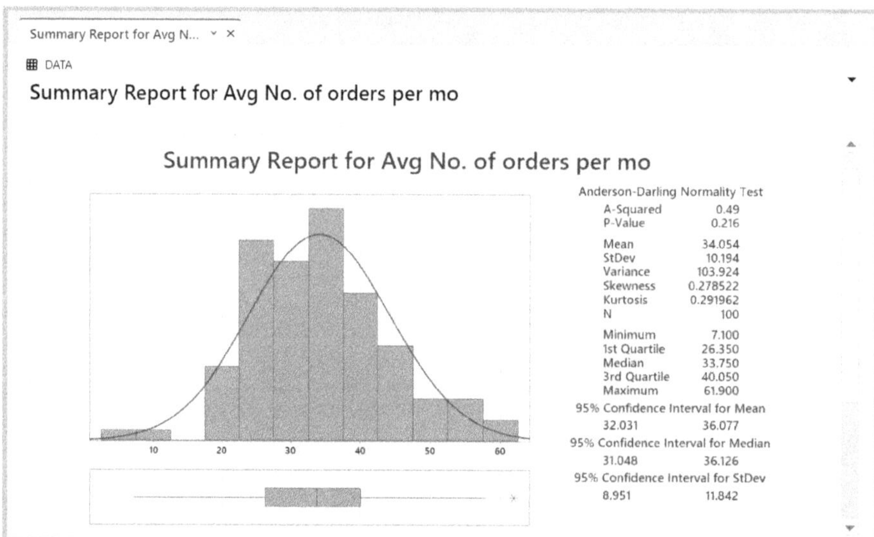

Figure 61: Graphical Summary Output - Minitab

The graphical summary provides useful information, some of which is not presented in either Excel of SigmaXL.

- It provides the results of the Anderson-Darling Normality Test to help determine whether or not the data is normally distributed (refer to Normality Testing)
- It shows the 95 percent confidence interval for the Mean and Median of the population

- It describes the 95 percent confidence intervals for the Mean, Standard Deviation and Median of the population
- It shows the 'Box Plot' of the raw data and describes the various reference points including Q1, median and Q3.

INTERVAL ESTIMATION

Point Estimates

The discussion with descriptive statistics so far has included reference to specific values such as sample mean, sample standard deviation and sample variance.

As single values used to represent population parameters, they are referred to as *point estimates*.

- **Point Estimate** – a single value determined from sample data, used as an estimate of the value of an unknown population parameter.

Interval Estimation

Project team leaders also need to understand the concept of *interval estimation*, which is the construction of an interval around statistics that has a pre-determined probability of containing the true population parameter.

For example, if the sample has a mean of 22, can we infer that the population mean is also 22?

We cannot be sure, so we construct an interval around that value that will give us some stated probability of it containing the true population mean.

For example, we can construct an interval around the mean of 22 that will allow us to state that we are 95 percent confident that the true population mean is somewhere between 20 and 24.

Remember, statistics involve working with probability, not truth. Statisticians are involved in the process of making inferences about populations from samples, on the basis of probability.

- **Interval Estimate** – two values that define or bound, at some specified probability level, a range of values that will enclose the unknown population parameter.

Confidence Intervals

The interval described by this estimate is referred to as the confidence interval. The confidence interval comprises a lower confidence limit and an upper confidence limit, and is referred to by its confidence coefficient.

- **Confidence Coefficient** – the level of confidence, stated as a probability that an interval will contain the true value of the unknown population parameter. It is usually expressed as a decimal and denoted by ($1 - \alpha$) one minus alpha where α is the level of risk you have stipulated. (i.e.: If you want to be 95 percent confident, α would be equal to 5 percent or 0.05 – the three levels of risk commonly used are 0.10, 0.05 and 0.01[21])
- **Lower Confidence Limit** – is the lower end of the range of reasonable values for the unknown population parameter.
- **Upper Confidence Limit** – is the upper end of the range of reasonable values for the unknown population parameter.

[21] Refer to section describing levels of risk and confidence levels in Hypothesis Testing

Interval Estimates for the MEAN (Large Sample Sizes)

The sampling distribution of $\overline{X}$ has a mean $\mu_{\bar{x}}$ and a standard deviation $\sigma_{\bar{x}}$ determined by $\sigma_{\bar{x}} = \frac{\sigma_x}{\sqrt{n}}$. By virtue of the Central Limit Theorem[22] we know that for large samples ($n \geq 30$), the sampling distribution of $\overline{X}$ is approximately normal, and normal tables[23] can be used to find the probability that the sample mean will be within a given interval.

For example, 95 percent of values from a sample will be within $+/- 1.96 \times \sigma_x$ of the sample mean[24]. We also know that for the distribution of sample means, 95 percent of values for the mean will be within $+/- 1.96 \times \frac{\sigma_x}{\sqrt{n}}$ of $\mu_{\bar{x}}$.

This interval is referred to as the 95 percent confidence interval for the estimation of μ_x, and can be shown by the following notation:

$$\bar{x} - 1.96 \times \frac{\sigma_x}{\sqrt{n}} < \mu < \bar{x} + 1.96 \times \frac{\sigma_x}{\sqrt{n}}$$

The value, 1.96, is the Z value obtained from the Z table shown in appendices. Since the normal distribution is symmetrical, 2.5 percent of values lie above the Z value of 1.96, and 2.5 percent of values lie below the Z value of –1.96.

By convention, the notation commonly used to denote Z values for the construction of confidence intervals is $Z_{\alpha/2}$, where $\alpha/2$ represents the 2.5 percent below or above respective Z values just mentioned.

For example, suppose we wanted 95 percent confidence in our interval estimation, we know that $\alpha = 0.05$, hence $(1 - \alpha) \times 100$ percent = 95 percent, and $Z_{0.05/2} = 1.96$.

The table below shows $Z_{\alpha/2}$ values for some of the most common confidence coefficients.

Confidence Coefficient (1 - α)	α	**Zα**	**α/2**	**Zα/2**
0.80	0.20	0.84	0.10	1.28
0.90	0.10	1.28	0.05	1.645
0.95	0.05	1.645	0.025	1.96
0.98	0.02	2.05	0.01	2.33
0.99	0.01	2.33	0.005	2.58

Table of Common Confidence Coefficients

22 Refer to notes on the Central Limit Theorem

23 Refer to Z Tables in Appendices

24 For more information, refer to notes on Continuous Probability Distributions

Worked Example – Large Sample Sizes (n ≥ 30)

Suppose we determine that the standard deviation of a population is 2. If we collected a sample of $n = 36$, and found that the sample mean $\overline{X} = 22$, using the equation described, we can calculate the 95 percent confidence interval for the population mean μ.

$$22 - 1.96 \times \frac{2}{\sqrt{36}} < \mu < 22 + 1.96 \times \frac{2}{\sqrt{36}}$$

$$22 - 1.96 \times \frac{2}{6} < \mu < 22 + 1.96 \times \frac{2}{6}$$

$$22 - 0.6533 < \mu < 22 + 0.6533$$

$$21.3647 < \mu < 22.6533$$

Based on the data analysed, we now have *95 percent confidence* that the true population mean is *contained in the interval* between 21.3467 and 22.6533.

Interval Estimation With MS Excel

Microsoft Excel has the capability of estimating confidence intervals for large sample sizes (n ≥ 30).

In the example shown on the following page, the value returned by MS Excel's 'confidence' function is 0.65332133. To determine the lower confidence limit, subtract this value from the mean. To find the upper confidence limit simply add this value to the mean.

- Mean = 7.54
- Lower Confidence Limit = 7.54 – 0.65332133 = 6.88667867
- Upper Confidence Limit = 7.54 + 0.65332133 = 8.19332133

In this example, we can be 95 percent confident that the true population is somewhere in the range bounded by the upper and lower confidence limits shown.

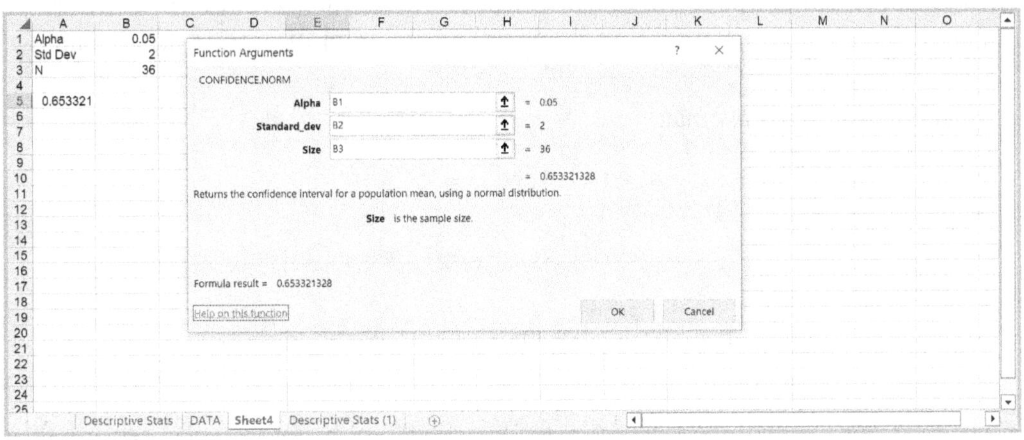

Figure 62: Confidence Interval Estimation - MS Excel

Interval Estimates for the Mean (Small Sample Sizes)

Due to the work of a gentleman by the name of William S. Gosset in the very early part of the 1900's (refer to notes on Student's *t* distribution), we know that for small sample sizes ($n < 30$), the variability exhibited by the sample is not a good estimate of variability in the population. Therefore when working with small samples to estimate confidence intervals for the population mean, we replace the Z value with a *t* value obtained from tables for the Student's *t* distribution. Hence $Z_{\alpha/2}$ is now $t_{\alpha/2}$.The *t* values are obtained from the *t* value tables shown in appendices.

Worked Example – Small Sample Sizes (*N* < 30)

Suppose we calculated the standard deviation of a sample as 2. If we collected a sample of $n = 20$, and found that the sample mean $\overline{X} = 22$, replacing the Z value for a *t* value in the equation above, we can calculate the 95% confidence interval for the population mean μ.

$$22 - 2.093 \times \frac{2}{\sqrt{36}} < \mu < 22 + 2.093 \times \frac{2}{\sqrt{36}}$$
$$22 - 2.093 \times \frac{2}{6} < \mu < 22 + 2.093 \times \frac{2}{6}$$
$$22 - 0.69766 < \mu < 22 + 0.69766$$
$$21.30234 < \mu < 22.69766$$

Based on the data analysed, we now have 95 percent confidence that the true population mean is contained in the interval between 21.30234 and 22.69766.

The interval is clearly wider than the one previously calculated from a large sample size due to the greater variability that exists in a small sample size. When working with means, degrees of freedom *df* is calculated by $n - 1$. In this case, $df = 19$, hence $t_{\alpha/2} = 2.093$.

Degrees of Freedom

A term I have just mentioned, and one that will come up more in discussion about distributions, is *degrees of freedom*. I am often asked what 'degrees of freedom' actually means. Let me explain it this way.

Suppose we had 10 data values with a mean of 15. If we knew the value of one of these points, suppose it was 6, are we able to determine what the absolute values of the remainder will be? Obviously we couldn't. How many of these values would we need to know before we could determine the absolute value of the remainder?

From the information given we know that:

$$n = 10 \text{ and } \overline{X} = 15$$

and:

$$\sum_{i=1}^{n} X_i = 150 \qquad \text{because} \qquad \sum_{i=1}^{n} X_i \div n = \overline{X}$$

At the point when we know *nine* of the values, the tenth one will not be *free to vary*, because the sum of the ten values must equal 150.

For example if we knew nine of the values and they added up to a total of 127, the tenth value could only be 23. If we knew eight values and they added up to 120, the remaining two can still have a range of values (e.g.: 10 and 20, or 16 and 14), as long as the sum total adds up to 150.

Therefore, there are *n*-1 degrees of freedom in this case (10 – 1 = 9 degrees of freedom).

In a nutshell, the term *degrees of freedom* means freedom to vary.

DATA TYPES

"Any opinion not supported by data, is still just an opinion."

Data essentially falls into either one of two categories – Qualitative Data or Quantitative Data. These categories are often described in reference materials in numerous other ways such as Hard or Soft Data, or Numerical or Categorical.

In this book I will make reference to the latter of these terms.

Let me give you an example of where we use different types of data in our every day lives.

Those of you with children will be familiar with this. When a child is sick, what is the first thing you usually do? Often the action you take is to place your hand on the head of the child and make a determination as to whether or not the child has a high temperature.

What you get is qualitative data that can be expressed in words – the child has a high temperature or the child does not have a high temperature. This type of data makes reference to discrete attributes – 'hot' or 'not hot'.

If the child does have a high temperature, this doesn't give a whole lot of useful information, so you would most likely take the child's temperature with a thermometer to obtain data that is expressed in numbers.

This data is quantitative, and is much more informative than qualitative in this case.

Let's take a closer look at the different types of data.

Categorical Data

Categorical data (also referred to as **discrete attribute** data) is generated through *observation* of categorical variables and is *qualitative* in the information it provides. These variables yield values that can only be placed into categories or classes.

Some good examples include describing the type of cars owned by people, causes of unscheduled downtime, and countries represented at the soccer world cup. In many textbooks, this type of data is simply referred to as 'discrete' data.

This data remains purely 'categorical' whilst it exists in a word or language format. At the point where we start to count or measure the size of each of these categorical variables, we generate quantitative data through the introduction of numerical variables.

For example, if I asked you how many players represented each of the countries in the last soccer world cup, you would give an answer expressed in quantitative terms.

Numerical Data

Numerical data is generated from numerical variables. These variables are one of two types – discrete [numerical] variables or continuous [numerical] variables.

Continuous Numerical Variables are those that are obtained through *measurement*, and come from an infinitely divisible measurement scale. The accuracy of the variable will usually depend on the degree of precision the measurement device is capable of producing. A micrometer will obviously produce a more precise measurement than a ruler. Examples of continuous variables include temperature, length, weight, height etc. Data obtained using continuous variables is called 'Continuous Data'.

Discrete Numerical Variables are those that are obtained through *counting* and comprise whole units. Discrete data usually answers the question 'How many?' Examples of discrete variables include number of trucks in a fleet, number of clubs in a bag, golf score etc. Data obtained using discrete variables is called 'Discrete Data'.

Discrete data is often easier to collect than continuous data, however the latter is far more informative. The table below shows Categorical and Numerical data equivalents.

Continuous Numerical Variable	Discrete Numerical Variable	Discrete Attribute
Time to fill a fuel tank	Number of times filling took > 8 minutes	> 8 minutes or < 8 minutes
Width of steel shafts	Number of shafts out of specification	In spec or Out of spec
Uptime for a web site	Number of times a web site goes down per month	Online or Not Online
Delivery cycle time	Number of units delivered too late	On time or Not on time

Categorical and Numerical Data Equivalents

Confusion often occurs when discrete data is observed in what might appear to be a continuous form. This is most common when it is represented as a percentage.

For example, if an organisation had 38 women employees and 49 men employees, we see that women make up 43.67 percent of employees and men make up 56.32 percent. Whilst you have decimals in the data, you are still counting the number of people with a shared attribute; therefore the data is still discrete.

Distinguishing Variable Data Types

The objective is to determine the type of data that will be generated so that relevant tools can be used to display and analyse the data.

As explained, data falls within either one of two categories:

- Categorical (Discrete Attributes) or
- Numerical (Discrete Numerical Variables or Continuous Numerical Variables).

Understanding the difference between the two is important, as the type of data you wish to collect will influence how you define it, collect it and what information you will be able to extract from it.

The significance of differentiating between the two types becomes very evident when we start using control charts and advanced statistical analysis tools.

THE POINT 5 TEST

A test you can apply to determine the type of *variable data* you are dealing with is the 'Point 5 Test'. Ask yourself, would point 5 of what we are measuring make sense?

For example, would point 5 of a kilogram make sense? In this case the answer is yes. As the unit of measure is divisible, it must be continuous variable data. Would point 5 of a defect make sense? The answer is no so it is discrete variable data as the unit of measure must remain whole.

The table presented expands on this concept with some examples. It would not make sense to apply a point 5 multiple to any of the *discrete variables* shown in the table.

	Type of Data	Examples
Numerical	Continuous Variable (measuring)	**Service:** Cycle time to deliver a product **Product:** Length or diameter of a part, production rates according to weight
	Discrete Variable (counting occurrences)	**Service:** Number of - times the cycle time exceeded x hours, late shipments, late notifications **Product:** Number of - parts out of specification, times production rates were less than expected, defects, damaged items
	Discrete Proportion (counting occurrences and non-occurrences)	**Service:** Proportion of – items delivered late, late shipments **Product:** Proportion of – parts out of specification, defective items, damaged components
Categorical	Discrete Attribute (observation)	**Service:** Type of order, type of error, method used **Product:** Type of defect, type of product supplied

Different Data Type Examples

FREQUENCY DISTRIBUTIONS

A frequency distribution is quite simply a table into which data is arranged into relative numerically ordered classes or categories. When data is condensed into a frequency distribution table, the representation provides a more useful and informative framework for analysing and interpreting the characteristics of the data set.

Frequency distributions are relevant to both categorical and numerical data, as you will see.

Frequency Distributions for Categorical Data

Frequency distributions for categorical data show the categories into which data is partitioned, and the number of units that fall into each category. For example, the number of students enrolled at a college is displayed in the following frequency distribution.

Frequency Distribution for students enrolled at ABC College by classification.

	(Frequency)	(Relative Frequency)	(Proportion)
Pre School	248	6.96%	0.0696
Junior School	1,655	46.42%	0.4642
Middle School	582	16.33%	0.1633
Senior School	1,080	30.29%	0.3029
TOTALS	**3,565**	**100.00%**	**1.0000**

Frequency Distribution for Categorical Data

The number of categories does not have to be calculated for obvious reasons – the categories are already determined by the nature of the data.

Graphical Representation

One of the most expedient ways to convert data into useful information is to represent data in the form of charts. The most common charts used with displaying *categorical frequency distributions* are bar charts and pie charts.

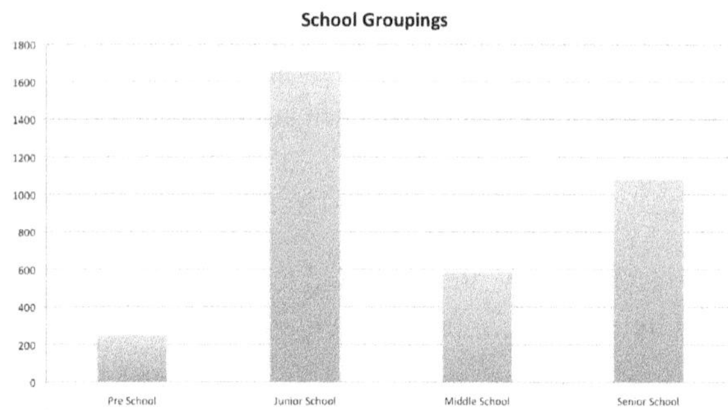

Column Chart

A column chart displays the relative size (in this case frequency) of each category in no particular order. Whilst column charts typically display counts for each category, it can also display the measured size of each category.

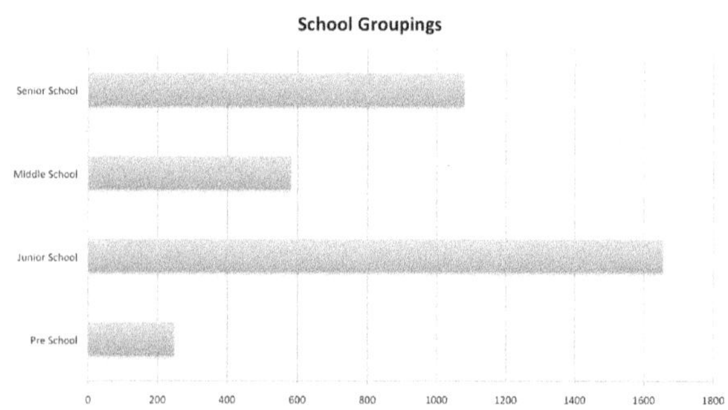

Bar Chart

A bar chart is like a column chart though it displays data in a horizontal format.

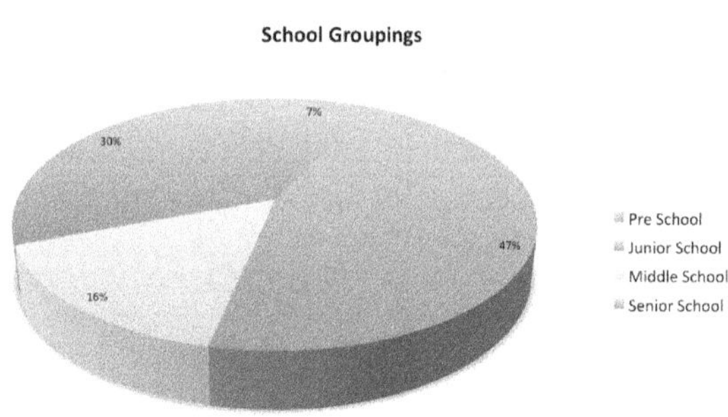

Pie Chart

By contrast, a pie chart displays data as proportions (or percentages) of the whole, rather than count or measurement.

Frequency Distributions for Numerical Data

Frequency distributions for numerical data show the classes or bins into which data is partitioned, and the number of units that fall into each of these bins. For example, the time taken to deliver pizza for home delivery can be displayed as follows.

Time taken in minutes to deliver pizza for home delivery.

19.5	13.5	12.5	17	20
19	12.5	17	18.5	22.5
15	14	16	20	18
22	17	14	15	18.5
17.5	16.5	21	15.5	17
20	19	17.5	18	14.5
12.5	15	16.5	16	15.5
17	16	15.5	17	16.6

The steps for creating a frequency distribution are as follows:

Step 1 - Number of Bins: Identify the number of bins of data (non overlapping) required for the amount of data being placed in the table.

One method suggested by Louise Clark (1991) for identifying the number of bins is to (a) count the number of data points being tabulated, and (b) identify the first power of 2 that is *equal to or greater* than this number. This value is the number of bins you will require for tabulating your data.

$2^1 = 2$	$2^4 = 16$
$2^2 = 4$	$2^5 = 32$
$2^3 = 8$	$2^6 = 64$

In this particular case we have 40 data points, therefore we would choose 6 bins (because $2^6 = 64$) within which we place values and then identify frequency of occurrence.

Step 2 - Bin Size: Identify the size of each bin of data by first calculating the range of our data, i.e.: the difference between the maximum value and minimum value 22.5 – 12.5 = 10

Step 3 - Bin Values: Determine the highest and lowest values for each bin of data by dividing the range by the number of bins. 10 ÷ 6 = 1.6

Step 4 - Bin Tallies: Tally the frequency for values falling into each of the defined bins

The completed frequency distribution table is shown in the following table.

Frequency Distribution for Pizza Delivery Times

Bins	Tally	(Frequency)	(Relative Frequency)
12.5 – 14.1	111111	6	15.0
14.2 – 15.8	1111111	7	17.5
15.9 – 17.5	11111111111111	14	35
17.6 – 19.2	111111	6	15
19.3 – 20.9	1111	4	10
20.9 – 22.5	111	3	7.5
TOTALS		**40**	**100.0%**

Frequency Distribution Table for Numerical Data

Graphical Representation

The most common chart used to display *frequency distributions* for numerical data is the Histogram. It is sometimes called a 'Frequency Plot'.

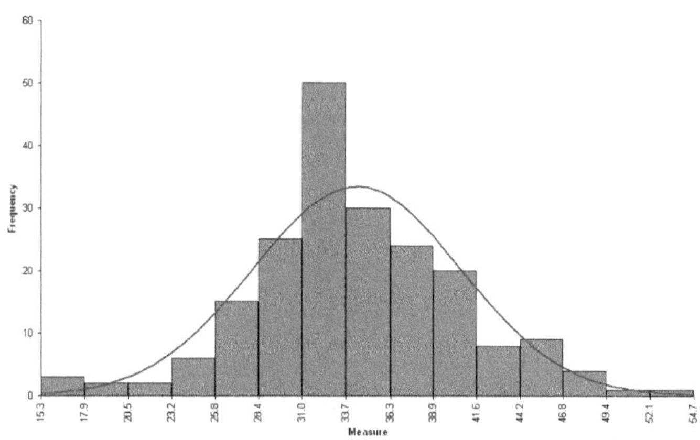

Histogram

A **Histogram** is a graphical method for displaying the distribution of frequencies of values of a data set in bar form. The values displayed in a histogram can be discrete or continuous numerical variables.

To effectively show a distribution, a large enough sample (usually > 50 data points) is required.

The shape of the histogram can be used to assess:

- Central tendency of the data
- Variation
- The shape or underlying distribution of the data
- Information that helps answer the question: 'Is my process capable of meeting customer requirements?'

Common Histogram Shapes

Some of the most common shapes are those shown and explained in the following table.

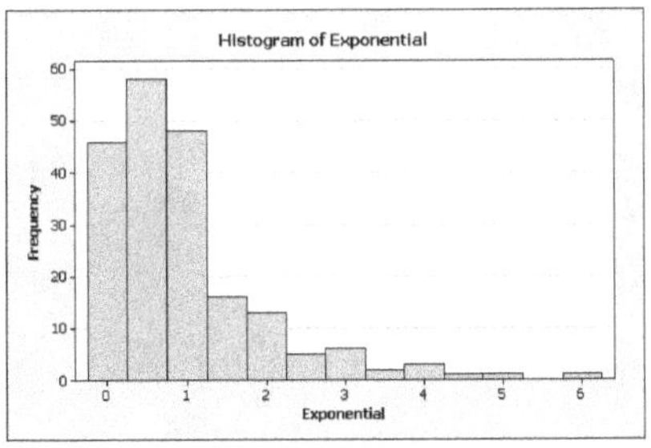

Skewed Distribution (positively skewed)

The figure represents a positively skewed distribution. The long tail of the distribution points in the direction of positive values of *x*.

The median will be located between the mode and the mean. A skewed distribution of this nature is often referred to as 'exponential'. Data that exhibits this type of shape is often bounded by a minimum value of zero, such as cycle time for delivery, home prices, or wait time in queues.

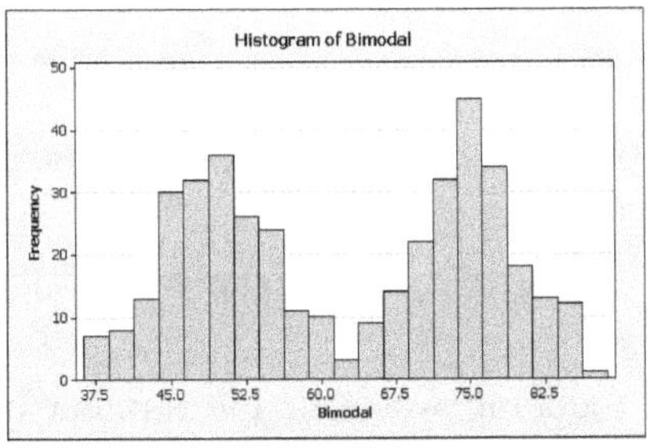

Bimodal Distribution

A bimodal distribution is one with two modes. The existence of two modes is an indication that two processes are probably included in the data set.

The first course of action in this case is to stratify the data set to separate the two processes from one another.

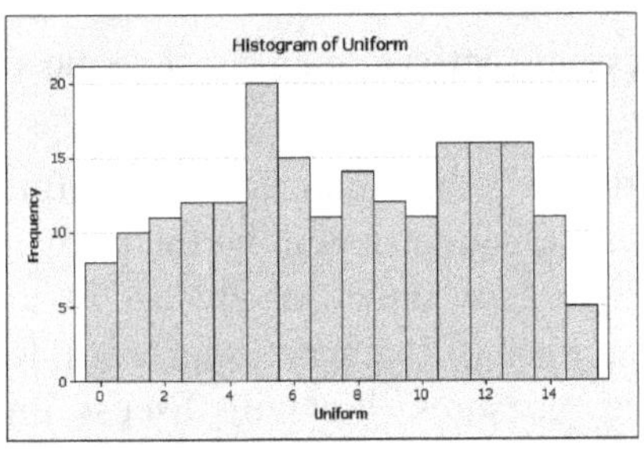

Uniform Distribution

A uniform distribution is one where the frequency of data values across the range remains consistent.

<u>Histogram Tips for Black Belts</u>

- Some processes are naturally skewed so do not expect every distribution to follow the shape of the normal distribution.
- When multiple modes are observed, stratify data to separate these processes from one another and prepare separate histograms.

PLANNING DATA COLLECTION (STEP 6)

'I often say that when you can measure what you are speaking about and express it in numbers, you know something about it, but when you cannot measure it, when you cannot express it in numbers, your knowledge is of a meagre and unsatisfactory kind. It may be the beginning of knowledge, but you have scarcely, in your thoughts, advanced to the stage of science.'

Lord William Thomson Kelvin

DATA COLLECTION FUNDAMENTALS

Types of Measures

Determining what to measure is a decision influenced by the context of your project. Different projects have different purposes. For example, projects may be initiated for the purpose of:

- Improving performance relevant to a specific product or service **quality requirement** of the customer, or
- Improving **efficiency** in terms of the use of resources such as reducing waste or the number of defects - in this case the business itself is the customer, or
- Improving results or outcomes with respect to specific **business objectives** such as revenue or production volumes.

It is highly unlikely that a project will be initiated without some specified focal point such as waste or time reduction, or performance improvement for a specific customer requirement. One metric will be the primary driver of the project. The material presented in this book assumes this is the case with your project. When you do not know your focal point, such as when you are just creating some form of 'balanced scorecard' for process performance, you will collect data on *all* relevant performance measures. We will discuss this further during the 'Control' phase of this book.

So, thinking in the context of improvement project work, projects with different goals will have different measuring requirements with respect to performance.

Performance Measure Type
Measures of Effectiveness
Measures of Efficiency
Measures of Outcomes

Performance Measure Types

Effectiveness Measures

Measures of **effectiveness** are those that indicate how well a process is meeting the critical-to-quality product or service requirements of the customer. These are more the focus of a Six Sigma project.

Efficiency Measures

Measures of **efficiency** on the other hand, give an indication of how efficient the process is in the use of resources such as materials, time, labour etc, and are connected to the efficiency requirements of the business itself. These are more the focus of a Lean project.

Outcome Measures

Measures of **outcomes** are those that give an indication of how well the business is performing against strategic goals. These are not usually the primary metrics for a project, but rather secondary metrics.

The table below provides some examples of measures for each category.

	INPUTS	PROCESS	OUTPUTS	OUTCOMES
Effectiveness Measures 1 How effective is our process in meeting customers' requirements?		Timeliness Accuracy	Quality Process Sigma	
Effectiveness Measures 2 How effective are our suppliers' processes in meeting our requirements?	Quality Timeliness Accuracy Process Sigma			
Efficiency Measures How efficient is the process in the use of resources?		Cost per unit Cycle Time Waste / Scrap / Yield / Reworks Availability / Utilisation		
Outcome Measures How well is the process performing against business performance goals?				Margin Production Volumes Profit / Loss Share Price

Examples of Measures Across Inputs, Process and Outputs

PLANNING DATA COLLECTION

Collecting data requires effective planning. The old military saying - 'time spent on reconnaissance is never wasted' - has relevance here. The intent of these words is that the preparation stage is of the utmost importance if you are to maximise your chances of achieving what you want.

I have seen many different formats for data collection plans. I never consider them to be wrong or right, only different from each other. No matter what the case, the best type of plan is one that through its development focuses the team's discussion around what they need to know in order to (a) effectively undertake data collection, and (b) set themselves up to come up with answers during the analyse phase with an absolute minimum of re-measurement.

Defining the Purpose of Data Collection

The purpose of data collection at this point in time (relative to a Six Sigma specific project) is to provide sufficient quality data to be able to:

- *Understand variation* that exists in the process;
- Find any potential *source* and / or *cause of variation*; and
- Locate any obvious improvements.

Thus, any data collection plan you develop must assist you in achieving that.

The Data Collection Plan

The following table shows the format of the data collection plan we have designed around the purpose stated above.

PRIMARY METRIC (Y)			CATEGORICAL Xs	
The Metric (Y)	**What It Is**	**How To Collect It**	**Categorical**	**Sampling Plan**
What is the variable we are fixing	What exactly is that variable (in plain simple terms)	How exactly do we collect / measure that so we all get the same results	What categorical variables potentially impact the primary metric	How many data points will be collected / how long will we collect data, and what is our sampling approach

NUMERICAL Xs		
Numerical Variable	**What It Is**	**How To Collect It**
What numerical variables potentially have a relationship with variation in the primary metric	What exactly is that variable (in plain simple terms)	How exactly do we collect / measure that so we all get the same results

Figure 63: Data Collection Plan Format

The Data Collection Planning Sequence

The creation of a data collection plan is undertaken in 3 steps.

Step 1 – Document the process and it's inputs and outputs

Step 2 – Identify the potentially significant variables that impact the Y

Step 3 – Develop your data collection plan which includes:

- Operationally defining the *primary metric* by describing what it is and how to measure it.
- Inserting the *categorical variables* that will guide you in *stratifying* (slicing and dicing) primary metric data when you analyse it
- Inserting and then operationally defining each of the *numerical variables* by describing what it is and how to measure it
- Deciding on a *sample size and method* of sampling
- Decide how you will collect the data

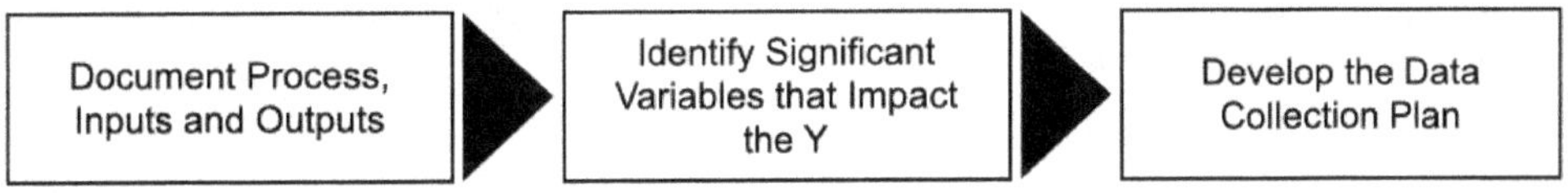

Figure 64: Data Collection Planning Sequence

Separating Sources of Variation from Causes of Variation

In my years of working specifically with Six Sigma concepts, the most enlightening discovery for me was this simple principle.

'First find the source of variation and then either eliminate it or find the cause of variation within that source.'

Let me give you an example of what I mean.

Suppose we worked for an airline company and our project target was to reduce baggage unload times.

We would collect data for unload times and analyse it for the purpose of finding the source of the longest unload times, or most variation in unload times.

We would do this by slicing and dicing the data (a process called stratifying) until we found the source of most variation, in other words **where** most variation exists. This could be at a particular airport, or for a particular plane type, or even for a particular day of the week.

Once the source is found, we can then either *eliminate the source* or find out the root cause of **why** it is different from the other sources in order to treat it.

I would summarise the key points in this way.

The source of variation refers to the specific *location* of the problem or most variation.

The cause explains *why* the variation observed exists.

The most common tools for finding the source is Pareto analysis, something we will discuss during the Analyse phase.

If you create your data collection plan in the format discussed, this principle is maintained. And as a result your post data collection analysis will be that much easier and faster to undertake.

The diagram below shows how the data collection plan relates to this principle.

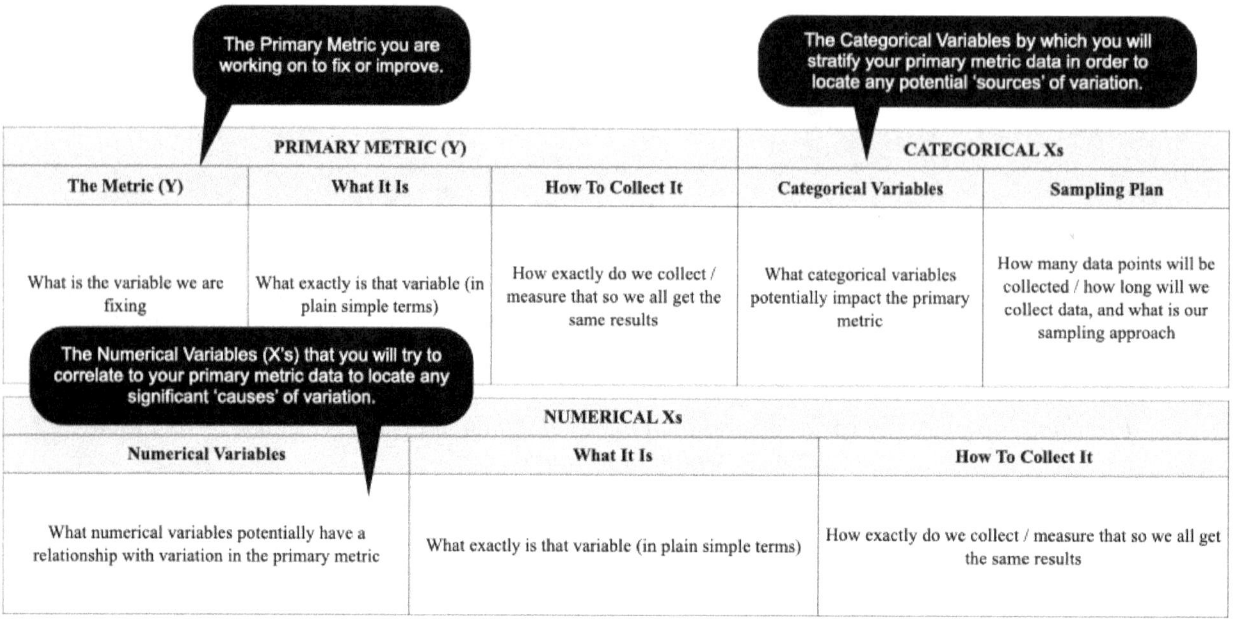

PRIMARY METRIC (Y)			CATEGORICAL Xs	
The Metric (Y)	**What It Is**	**How To Collect It**	**Categorical Variables**	**Sampling Plan**
What is the variable we are fixing	What exactly is that variable (in plain simple terms)	How exactly do we collect / measure that so we all get the same results	What categorical variables potentially impact the primary metric	How many data points will be collected / how long will we collect data, and what is our sampling approach

NUMERICAL Xs		
Numerical Variables	**What It Is**	**How To Collect It**
What numerical variables potentially have a relationship with variation in the primary metric	What exactly is that variable (in plain simple terms)	How exactly do we collect / measure that so we all get the same results

Figure 65: Key Variables of the Data Collection Plan

STEP 1 - DOCUMENT THE PROCESS, ITS INPUTS AND OUTPUTS

We've already spoken about this in the 'Define' phase discussion where we introduced you to the IPO Worksheet. When I assemble a data collection plan, this is my go to tool for establishing understanding of how the process works and all of the potential variables associated with it.

INPUTS	PROCESS	OUTPUT/S
Materials (the consumables you require to produce the output) **Data / Information** (the information or data that you need to produce the output) **Resources** (the fixed resources you require to produce the output)	(the activity flowchart that visually shows the sequence of activities)	(a statement describing the process output or outputs)

This is now an input into step 2.

STEP 2 - IDENTIFY SIGNIFICANT VARIABLES THAT IMPACT THE 'Y'

The ability to determine what to measure requires an understanding of one important concept that I mentioned at the beginning of this book. The performance of any process (which we refer to as the *y*) is a function of all of the variables that influence it (which we refer to as the *x*'s).

Mathematically this statement is represented by the equation:

$$y = f(x_1, x_2, x_3, \ldots . x_n)$$

When we start measuring for our project, we do so with an understanding that our desired outcome is to understand what is happening with respect to process performance (*y*), and which of the variables (*x*) have the greatest influence over that performance.

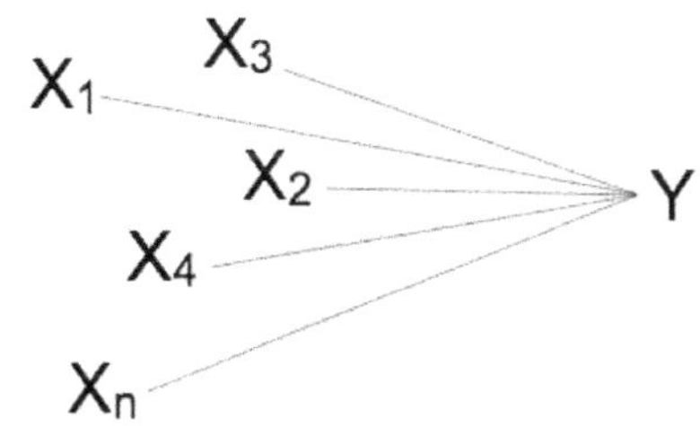

These *x*'s will be the sources or causes of variation in *y* and the point of focus for your improvement work. To change the *y*, you simply change the most significant *x*'s.

Using the Principles of Cause Effect Diagrams to Identify Variables

While I am going to discuss using a process or tool we call an XY Worksheet (discussed next) to identify key variables, it will serve you to understand the format of a Cause Effect Diagram.

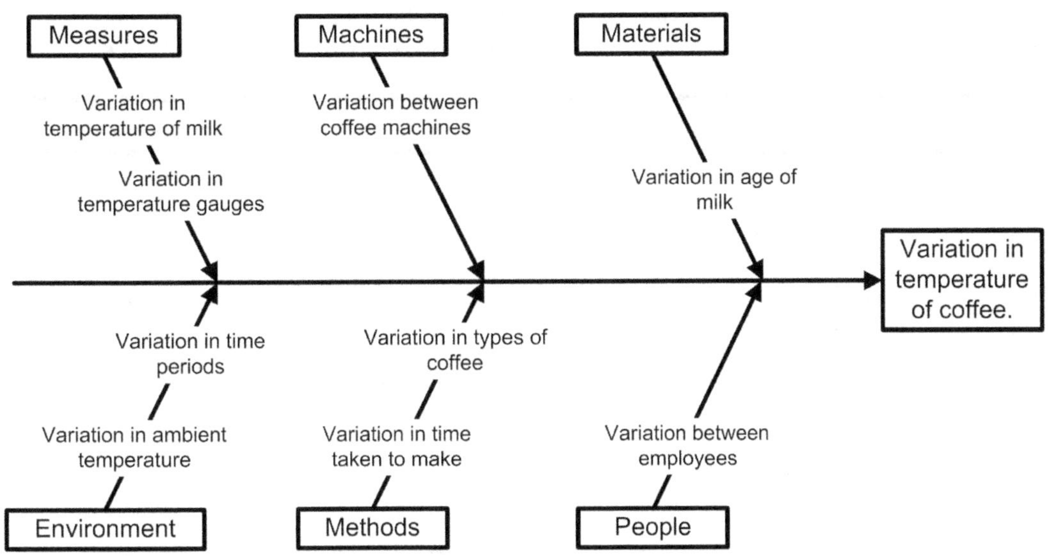

Figure 66: Identifying Variables Using A Cause Effect Diagram

The Cause Effect Diagram is a process used to identify *potential causes* of some defined outcome. The process is created from the idea that most causes can be identified from within six standard categories, thus the process of identifying variables starts by channelling thoughts through these categories.

We are going to apply this principle to our work in this step.

For more information on using a Cause Effect Diagram, refer to the Analyse Phase where 'Cause and Effect Analysis' is discussed at length.

Identifying Key Variables with the XY Worksheet

The method I recommend you use for identifying potential x's that have an impact on the variable y is to use an XY Worksheet. It is simply a process of asking a sequence of three questions.

- **Q1.** What variables (the x's in this case) potentially have an impact on variability in the primary metric (y) we are studying? We are going to look in two places for a sense of what those variables are - (a) the IPO worksheet which lists all of the process inputs, and (b) within the six standard categories defined in the Cause Effect Diagram.
    - Materials
    - Machines
    - Measures
    - Methods
    - Environment
    - People
- **Q2.** If we recorded values for this variable, what type of data would it generate? (It would be either Categorical or Numerical.)
- **Q3.** If we vary this x (ask for every x) within its normal operating range, how much effect would it have on variation in the primary metric (y)? (We rate the effect on a scale of 0 to 5 that is explained in the Define Phase toolkit in more detail.)

These questions focus the discussion on finding what the team believes to be the most significant x's in this model. The conversation is framed by following the format laid out in the XY Worksheet shown below.

Primary Metric Y	Potential X's that have an impact on Primary Metric Y	Data Type	Impact on Y
SERVICE CYCLE TIME	Truck type	C	1
	Staff member doing the work	C	4
	Work location	C	1
	Time since last service	N	2
	Day of the week	C	3
	Service type	C	3
	Cycle time of actual work	N	5
	Time between drop off and job start (parked time)	N	3

Figure 67: Identifying Key Variables with XY Worksheet

In the example shown, the team has agreed that the time it takes to service a vehicle (service cycle time) is potentially affected by variation in the x's listed.

Set Up For Success

This process works extremely well in identifying key project variables under the following circumstances.

- The team is comprised of people *who work in and have experience with* the process in question.
- The completed *IPO Worksheet is available* as a reference for identifying variables.
- You don't try and make the rating scale *perfect*.
- Only make a judgment about effect on *y* based on the *realistic or actual operating range* of the variable in question.

Now we know what the key variables might be for our process, we create the portion of the data collection plan relevant to the primary metric.

STEP 3 - DEVELOP THE DATA COLLECTION PLAN

FOCUSING FIRST ON THE PRIMARY METRIC

I've stated earlier that there are different types of projects you can be allocated; one to improve performance against customer requirements, or one to improve performance against business requirements. Your approach to identifying what you will measure for each of these types may differ slightly, however both focus on a *single or primary metric*.

PRIMARY METRIC (Y)			CATEGORICAL Xs	
The Metric (Y)	**What It Is**	**How To Collect It**	**Categorical**	**Sampling Plan**
What is the variable we are fixing	What exactly is that variable (in plain simple terms)	How exactly do we collect / measure that so we all get the same results	What categorical variables potentially impact the primary metric	How many data points will be collected / how long will we collect data, and what is our sampling approach

Figure 68: Focusing on the Primary Metric (y)

Identifying the Primary Metric - The Line Manager / Sponsor's Role

Let me just go back to our earlier discussion about who does what. It's not the job of the Black Belt or the project team to work out what the primary metric is. In an ideal world that is a business decision made by those involved in line management. We refer to these people as project sponsors and process owners.

However, just in case you are confronted with the question of what primary metric to work on, let me recap what we have discussed in an earlier chapter.

The start point for identifying what to work on is the SIPOC. A properly developed SIPOC presents a range of information with respect to output measures and the variables that potentially impact these.

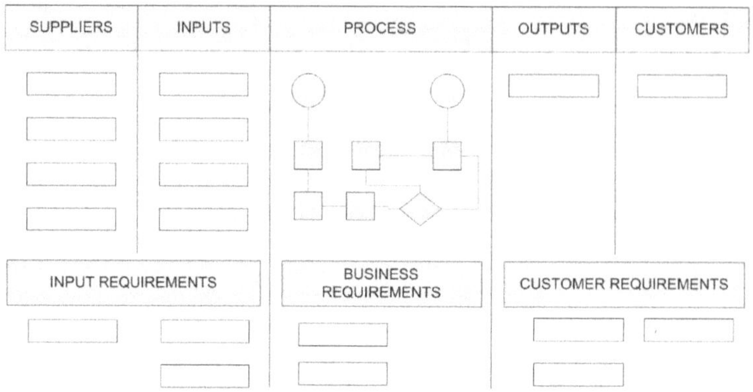

Figure 69: Identifying 'What to Measure' from the SIPOC

<u>What Is the Performance Measure of Interest?</u>

What a SIPOC doesn't tell you is the actual performance of the process in regard to those measures. One of the most effective ways to find out what the performance measure of interest should be is to understand actual performance; that's where *value stream analysis* comes into play.

(Refer to Chapter 7 for more information about the process of Value Stream Analysis.)

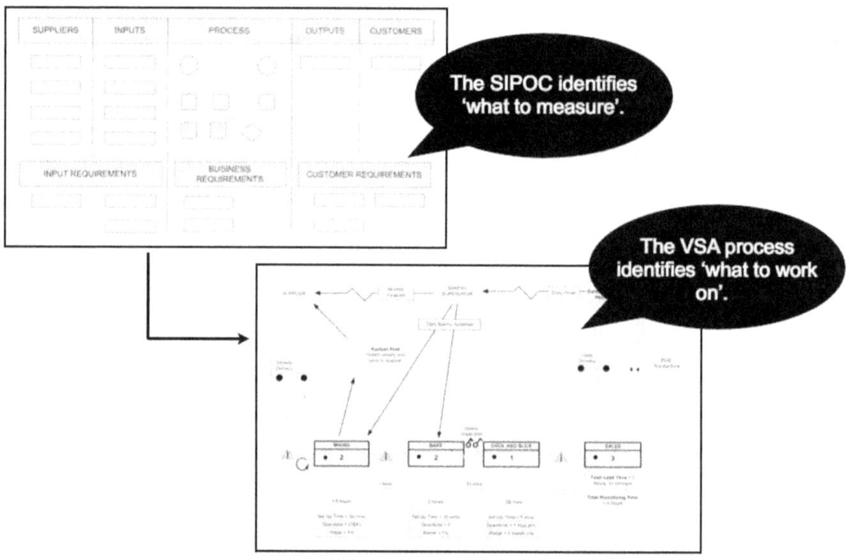

Figure 70: Identifying 'What to Work On' with VSA

Should You Measure Other Performance Metrics?

Where you are targeting improvement for a specific customer requirement, you should be measuring performance specifically against that requirement. While it may prove useful to measure performance against other product or service requirements as well, my experience is that it is not essential at this point in a project.

Example: A project targeting a reduction in variation of the width of a machined component is concerned with unit width. Whilst important, it may not serve any purpose to measure customer service requirements such as order accuracy or delivery cycle time whilst working on this project.

However, we do recognise that those measures do contribute to the overall management of process performance outside of the work of the project. These types of measures will be *brought back into focus* during the control phase of our work. If you suspect that there could be a negative impact on any of these variables as a result of the project work, it might be worthwhile monitoring those variables.

The Primary Metric for Data Collection Planning

Let me assume the business improvement system you are operating in has leaders and process owners playing their role as we've described in this textbook.

In this case, you simply refer to the project charter to locate the primary metric.

Since we know our primary metric; our objective now is to define *what to collect* and *how to collect it* in order to guarantee consistency of the data we actually collect for analysis.

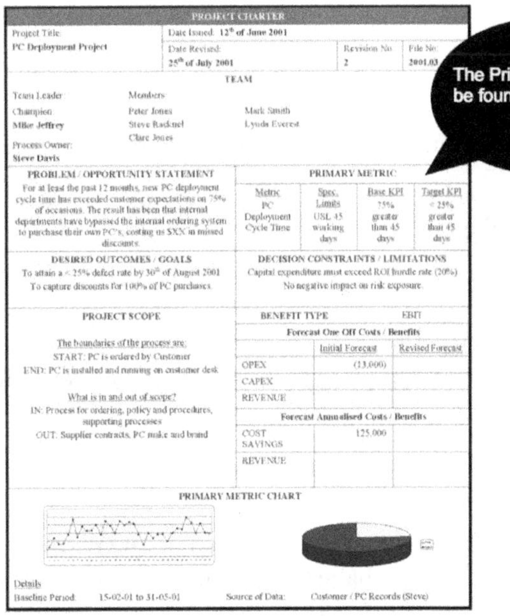

OPERATIONAL DEFINITION

Interpretation and Ambiguous Meaning

When teaching Lean Six Sigma, I have students participate in a simple activity that reinforces the need for operational definitions. I give each person a sheet of A4 paper. I then ask them to close their eyes and fold the paper in half. I ask them to fold it in half again and then to tear off the right hand corner. When I ask them to open their eyes and hold up their unfolded piece of paper, it's amazing to see the variety of shapes that are produced.

The reason for that is quite simple. People interpret information in different ways on the basis of their beliefs, values and how they individually filter incoming data.

When information given to any person allows room for ambiguity and interpretation, then the likelihood of that person giving that information some different meaning than what was intended is high.

If I asked a number of people to state what 'on time departure' for an airline flight meant to them, I am sure they would come up with different versions. Someone would say when the plane became airborne whilst someone else would say when the aircraft pulled away from the terminal.

Unless the variation in interpretation is eliminated, there is a high probability that additional variation will be introduced into the data that is collected. For example if we sent two people out to measure the difference between scheduled departure and actual departure for 20 flights each, then the data would not be useful if they both gave different meanings to the term 'on time departure'.

The purpose of defining our measures up front is to ensure that anyone who participates in measuring or interpreting data; measures and interprets the same thing consistently and with minimal variation.

EXAMPLE OF TERMS OPEN TO AMBIGUOUS MEANING	
• Length of a working day	Does it include breaks or not? Does it start when you leave home or when you arrive?
• Fuel tank filling time	Does the time include removing the cap or does it only start when fuel starts pumping?
• Delay time for airline departure	Does delay time end when the aircraft leaves the terminal or when its wheels leave the ground on takeoff?
• Baggage wait time	Does time start when the passenger exits the plane or when she arrives at the baggage carousel?

Operational Definition

To prepare operational definitions, we will make reference to four elements.

- **The measure** – A statement of what you are going to measure.
- **Definition of what to measure** – A definition of exactly WHAT the measure is that is clear and easy to understand by any person.
- **How to measure it** – A clear description of HOW the measurement is made. When you write this you should imagine that you have to tell someone how to go about measuring what you want measured.
- **Feasibility** – Can it actually be collected / can it be collected within a reasonable time frame and at an acceptable cost?

A sample of how this process works is shown in the worksheet below.

Measure	WHAT the Measure is	HOW to Measure	Feasible
Cycle time	Time in minutes between start and finish of the cycle	Measure the time taken in minutes between activation of the 'Start' button and when the conveyor automatically shuts down.	Yes
Cost per unit	The cost in Australian Dollars for producing one unit.	Divide the total operating cost for the business by the total number of units produced in the same period.	Yes
Weekly throughput	The total number of whole units produced by the process each week.	Count the number of whole units produced between 12:00 am Monday and 12:00 pm Sunday.	Yes
Span of delivery	The time taken to deliver and install an ordered unit to a customer.	Measure the time elapsed in hours between submission of the order and when the machine is switched on and functioning.	Yes

Now that we have defined the primary metric, we are going to identify the potentially significant categorical variables that we will use to *stratify* the primary metric data when we analyse it. Stratification is simply the process of slicing and dicing data.

IDENTIFYING STRATIFICATION VARIABLES (CATEGORICAL VARIABLES)

When you stratify data, you simply break the data up into specified categories. The objective of stratification is to identify any *source* of variation (i.e.: where most variation exists or where the problem lies).

Let me explain how this works with some simple examples.

- Suppose we collected data on the cycle time for delivering pizza to homes. We could group or stratify this cycle time data into data from each driver (driver A, driver B and so on). When we do this we might find that most of the excess delivery time relates to driver A.
- Suppose we measured the height of students at a school, we could stratify this data into groups according to gender (male or female). We could also stratify this same data into groups according to country of origin (Australian, Asian, European, American etc). We might find that both gender and country of origin has an impact on this data, thus are sources of height variation.

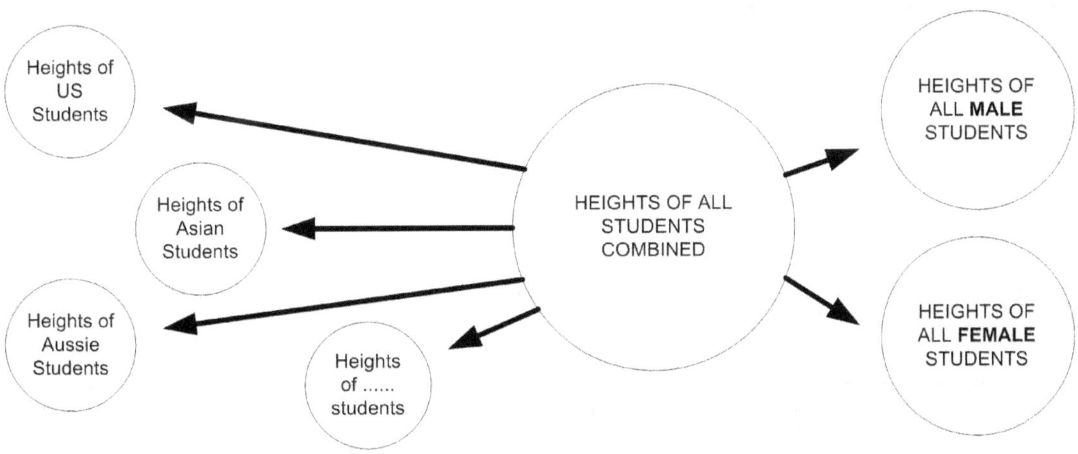

Figure 71: Stratifying Height Data

Example Stratification Variables

The table below shows examples of stratification variables based on some common factors: who, what, when and where.

FACTOR	EXAMPLE	FACTOR	EXAMPLE
Who	Employee Department Work Location Customer Group	**When**	Day of the week Shift (day / night) Month Period (am / pm, quarter)
What	Defect type Complaint type Reason Product type	**Where**	Work Location City State Location of the Product

Stratification Variable Examples

Referencing the XY Worksheet

Let me reinforce this most important point: the purpose of stratification is to help the team identify the source of a problem or the source of most variation.

In this space of the data collection plan or worksheet, you simply list the *categorical variables* from your XY Worksheet that you identified as potentially having the greatest impact on the primary metric (y).

As you can see in the example shown below, the *arrows* indicate all of the categorical variables that potentially have an impact on the primary metric.

The *circles* indicate which of these the team believes have the biggest impact on the primary metric. It's these that get included in the data collection plan.

Primary Metric Y	Potential X's that have an impact on Primary Metric Y	Data Type	Impact on Y
SERVICE CYCLE TIME	Truck type	C	1
	Staff member doing the work	C	4
	Work location	C	1
	Time since last service	N	2
	Day of the week	C	3
	Service type	C	3
	Cycle time of actual work	N	5
	Time between drop off and job start (parked time)	N	3

Figure 72: Selecting Stratification Variables From The XY Worksheet

Now we know how we will break up or stratify the data when we analyse it, we need to determine *what method* will be used to sample data and *how much data* to collect.

DETERMINING YOUR SAMPLING PLAN

What is sampling?

Sampling is the process of collecting a portion of data from all of the data that is available (which we refer to as the population). Using this sample data, we hope to be able to make an accurate inference about the population from which the data was collected.

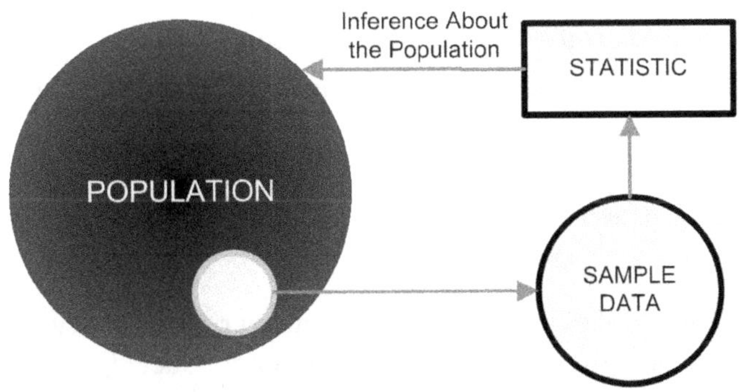

Figure 73: The Process of Sampling

Circumstances Leading to Sampling

There are many circumstances under which you might choose to conduct sampling including:

- When it is simply impractical to collect all of the data from the population for reasons associated with:
    - Cost
    - Time
    - Access Limitations
    - Production Impacts
- When the sampling process is destructive
- When sound inferences can *actually* be made about the population from a sample

Sampling Error

When a sample is selected from a population, we expect to see some difference between the results provided by the sample, and the results we would have been provided had we used the full population. This difference is known as **sampling error**, and this error will vary from sample to sample.

Jim and Matt

Let me tell you about Jim and Matt, high school graduates from Brisbane city in Australia. They decided they wanted to make a living capturing and relocating crocodiles. To do this they needed resources including a cage for transporting crocodiles from the point of capture to their new destination. What Jim and Matt didn't know was how big to make this cage. Their plan was simple; capture a crocodile, measure it, then build the cage to suit. So they did this, capturing a 1.5 metre crocodile in a river system north of Brisbane.

My question is this – is this sufficient enough data to build a cage to hold an average size crocodile? Of course not! The obvious question is: Why not? When I ask this question during training, the response I get usually includes: 'This is not sufficient data to make a judgment about the size of all crocodiles.' This is the concept of sampling error - the difference between the length of this crocodile and the average length of all crocodiles.

Sampling Error Is a Function of Three Factors

- The **size** of the sample taken;
- The **dispersion or variation** that exists within the population, and consequently the sample itself; and
- The amount of **bias introduced** by the sampling approach taken.

So how many crocodiles would Jim and Matt have to measure to be confident that they are close to the mark when they make their cage?

To be able to confidently make some inference about a population, we must collect sample data that is **representative** (i.e.: the sample data has characteristics similar to that of the population).

1932 US Presidential Election

I sometimes tell the story about the US presidential elections during 1932. Two gentlemen by the names of Hoover and Roosevelt were standing for election. A newspaper conducted a phone survey for the purpose of predicting who would win the election. They asked the survey participants which way they would cast their vote and the result indicated that the Republican Party (Hoover) was going to win with an overwhelming majority. As we know, the Democrat Party went on to win with Roosevelt becoming the President.

Now why did the survey indicate otherwise? Quite simply the sample collected was not representative of the population. At that particular time, only wealthy people owned phones, most of which supported the Republican Party. In essence, the newspaper had collected a sample that was **biased**, thus the inference was incorrect. The actual population they had sampled consisted of people who owned phones. A more correct inference would have been this: If only people who owned phones voted in the Presidential election, Hoover would have won with an overwhelming majority.

To maximise the potential for sample data to be representative, it must be collected in such a way as to minimise sampling error.

- The method of collection does not introduce unintentional or intentional bias; and
- Sufficient data is collected so that statistical inferences can be made about the population with some degree of confidence.

Methods of Sampling

Different sampling methods that reduce the likelihood of sampling bias include these.

Random sampling – collecting population data at random so that every item has an equal chance of being selected.

It is often a challenge to select data randomly as unconscious bias can be introduced.

Bias can be avoided by using random numbers generated by computer software (e.g.: MS Excel) to select data.

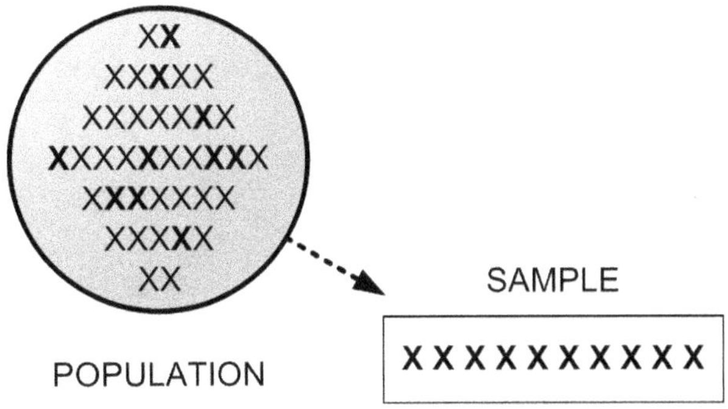

Figure 74: Random Sampling

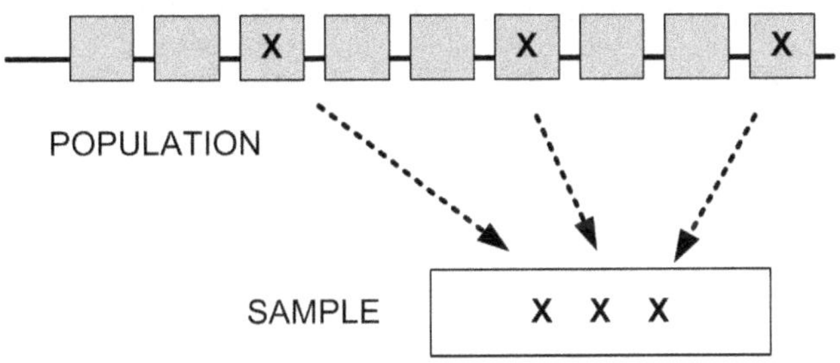

Figure 75: Systematic Sampling

Systematic sampling – taking sample data from a process at predetermined intervals (e.g.: every hour, once a day, every 10th item etc).

Be aware that bias can be introduced by virtue of the system used. For example in our golf practice, if we collected data on every fifth shot which just happened to be a 5 iron, this would not be representative of our entire game of golf.

Stratified sampling – this involves dividing the population into different groupings or sub-groups, and then taking sample data at random from these different groupings. If we were to collect sample data, at random, from each golf club grouping (i.e.: woods, long irons, middle irons, short irons etc), this would tell us something about each of those groups without bias towards any particular one.

This makes sense when data can be grouped, and the cause of a problem might come from a particular group.

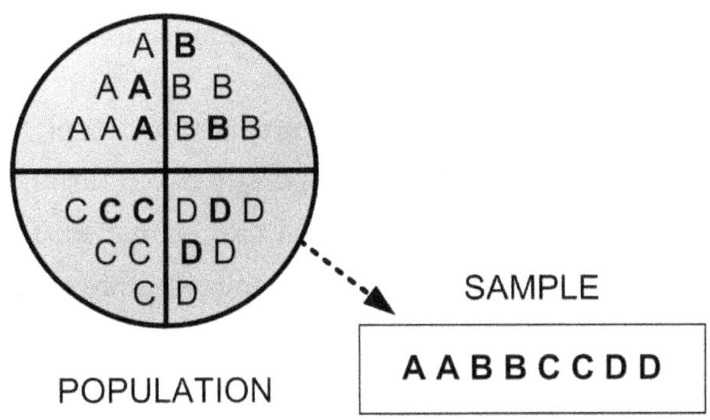

Figure 76: Stratified Sampling

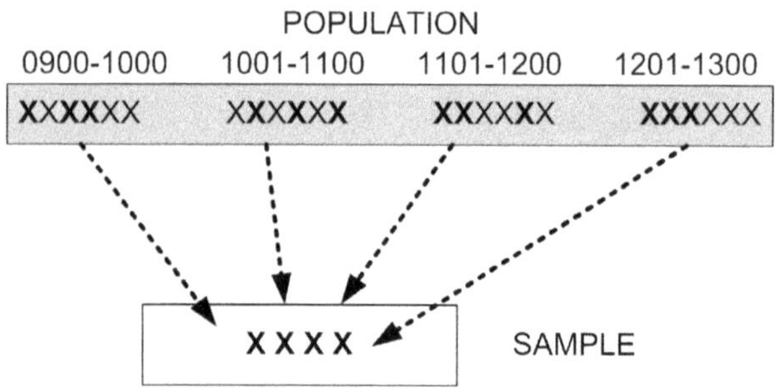

Figure 77: Subgroup Sampling

Subgroup sampling – this approach involves sampling a number of units within every sub group from a process, and then calculating and recording the mean for every subgroup.

The types of sampling shown can be mixed to produce a variety of sampling approaches.

Sample Size - A General Discussion

How much data is enough? This is a common question asked by project teams and data analysts alike, and should be one of your first considerations when undertaking sampling activities.

Whilst this book focuses on the statistical requirements for calculating sample size, business factors must also be taken into consideration.

These might include factors such as:

- Time frame
- Cost
- Impact on the business through data collection
- Risk, etc

There are a number of different approaches you can take in determining sample sizes. Two common approaches are detailed below with supporting worksheets shown in the chapter dedicated to the Measure Phase toolkit.

<u>Sample Size for Estimating a Mean</u>

One of the most common reasons for collecting samples is to calculate an average that we use as an estimate of the average of the entire population. To ensure we minimise sample error, we calculate our sample size on the basis of three elements:

- The degree of error we are prepared to accept;
- The level of confidence we desire of our result; and
- The degree of dispersion or variation that exists within the population, and consequently our sample.

The equation for determining sample size for estimating the mean is:

$$n = \left(\frac{Z\sigma}{E}\right)^2$$

Where:

n = The sample size

Z = The standard normal score based on the degree of confidence you desire (obtained from the Table of Areas Under the Standard Normal Curve)

σ = The population standard deviation (sigma)

E = The degree of precision that you desire (plus or minus some value)

Where you do not know the standard deviation of the population, then a useful starting point is to collect a sample of 30 data points and calculate the standard deviation to insert into the equation.

Worked Example

A project team wishes to estimate the average cycle time for delivery of PCs to customers over the past year. The team leader wishes the estimate to be made with 95 percent confidence, and within an error factor of +/- 2 days. A sample of 30 cycle times is recorded and this shows a standard deviation of 5 days.

The values for our equation are:

- $\sigma = 5$ days
- E = 2 days
- Z = 1.96 (obtained from the Table of Areas Under the Standard Normal Curve)

So we substitute the values into the equation to calculate our sample size.

$$n = \left(\frac{Z\sigma}{E}\right)^2 = \left(\frac{1.96 \times 5}{2}\right)^2 = (4.9)^2 = 24.01$$

In rounding up the fractional value, we know that to be 95 percent confident we have estimated the true mean delivery time within +/- 2 days, we must sample the delivery time for at least 25 PCs.

Sample Size for Estimating a Proportion

Another common reason for collecting samples is to calculate a proportion that we use as an estimate of the proportion of the entire population with the characteristic of interest. To ensure we minimise sample error, we calculate our sample size on the basis of three elements:

- The degree of error we are prepared to accept;
- The level of confidence we desire of our result; and
- The estimated proportion of the population with the characteristic of interest.

The equation is:

$$n = \frac{Z^2 \times \pi \times (1-\pi)}{E^2}$$

Where:

n = The sample size

Z = The standard normal score based on the degree of confidence you desire (obtained from the Table of Areas Under the Standard Normal Curve)

π = The proportion of the population having the characteristic of interest (Pi)

E = The degree of precision that you desire (plus or minus some value)

Where the population proportion is not known, then a useful start point is to sample until you find 5 items with the attribute you are concerned with and then calculate the proportion of that sample that has the attribute. This value can be inserted into the equation.

Worked Example

A project team wishes to estimate the proportion of services that are completed on time to be 95 percent confident of being within +/- 0.05 of the true proportion. Based on the experience of workers, they expect the proportion to be around 75 percent. The values for our equation are:

- $\pi = 0.75$
- E = 0.05
- Z = 1.96 (obtained from the Table of Areas Under the Standard Normal Curve)

So we substitute the values into the equation to calculate our sample size.

$$n = \frac{Z^2 \times \pi \times (1-\pi)}{E^2} = \frac{1.96^2 \times 0.75 \times (1-0.75)}{0.05^2} = \frac{0.7203}{0.0025} = 288.12$$

In rounding up the fractional value, we know that to be 95 percent confident that we have estimated the true proportion of on time services within +/- 5 percent, we must obtain a sample size of at least 289 data points.

Why Worry About Determining a Sample Size?

Why should you worry about taking the time to determine a particular sample size? It's a great question that I'm sure goes through the mind of everyone undertaking their first Six Sigma project.

Let's think about why we use statistics. We use it to infer certain things about a population and make decisions based on those inferences.

If we get those decisions wrong, and there is no real consequence, then perhaps we don't really have a problem. If we get it right by chance then we get away with it.

If we get the decision wrong on the other hand, and it costs the business a lot of wasted money or time, or the problem is not solved, then we could very well be challenged about our decision making process. The true test of your decision making process is to be able to withstand a challenge.

Black Belts have said to me that other Black Belts do not do the equations. My response is that you can do anything if the results turn out okay and you are never challenged on the process. This does not mean that it is good practice. You can drive all day at 160 kilometres per hour on the highway if you do not crash or are not challenged. However, this does not make it okay to do.

The collection of a sample size that is based on some statistical calculation provides the foundation for the statistician to state the degree of confidence that can be placed in the statistics calculated.

For example, if you took a sample to estimate the population mean, and used the equation for a 95 percent confidence interval, you could make the following statement. *'I am ninety five percent confident that I have calculated the true population mean to within plus or minus (insert whatever your chosen error range was).'*

Confidence Levels

The Z value in each equation denotes the level of confidence associated with the sample size. Obviously increasing the sample size would increase the probability of getting results that represent the population, hence an increased level of confidence, and vice versa. The equations show the number '1.96', which is the default confidence level of 95 percent. You can alter your confidence levels simply by changing the Z value you use according to the table below. In most cases a confidence level of 95 percent is quite okay. And it is far more practical in terms of data collection than would be a 99 percent level of confidence.

Confidence Level	Z Value
90%	1.645
95%	1.96
99%	2.58

Z Values for Confidence Levels

Sample Size - For Data Collection Planning in a Six Sigma Project

You might have noticed in the previous section, we spoke about sample size calculations for single point estimates (i.e. means and proportions).

That didn't answer the question, how many rows of data should I collect for all of these variables in my data collection plan?

I want to give you a guideline for working out a minimum sample size that I have been using for the past 20 plus years of business improvement work.

Later in the book where we discuss hypothesis testing, there is a section that describes a concept called the Central Limit Theorem (CLT). That theorem makes reference to what we might refer to as the 'magic number' of 30.

Without explaining why at this point in time, all I do in determining how many data points / rows of data I need to collect as a minimum is this:

(a) I first identify the categorical variable in my plan with the most chunks in it - e.g. day of the week is a categorical variable with seven chunks, cup sizes might be small medium and large hence has three chunks

(b) I then make sure my minimum sample size is based on comparing those chunks with at least 30 data points in each chunk - e.g. if day of the week is the variable with the most chunks, then I want to collect at least 30 data points from each day which means I end up with a minimum sample size of 210 rows of data

This has been the simplest way for me to quickly calculate a sample size based on some logic. I'll let you find out why when you get to the central limit theorem section.

Process Sampling vs. Population Sampling

Population Sampling

This is the process of taking a sample from a population of data that already exists. For example, population sampling occurs when a survey of a designated number of people is undertaken to determine the level of support for political party leaders.

Process Sampling

This is the process of taking samples from a process as units are produced or work is undertaken. For example, process sampling occurs when samples of parts are measured as they come off the production line, or when the delivery time for pizzas is measured as the deliveries occur.

The table below will guide you in undertaking sampling for either processes or populations.

	Process Sampling	**Population Sampling**
The Purpose	Monitor variation over time Predict future process behaviour Determine sources / causes of process variation	Estimate population characteristics (means, proportions or std. deviations) Make inferences about populations (hypothesis testing)
Sample Size Calculations (Point Estimates)	**Stable Process** Use equations shown for population data. **Unstable Process** Continue to plot data in time order until it is stable.	Means (Numerical Data) $n = \left(\frac{Z\sigma}{E}\right)^2$ Proportions (Categorical Data) $n = \frac{Z^2 \times \pi \times (1-\pi)}{E^2}$
Sample Size Calculations (Six Sigma Oriented Cause / Effect Analysis)	**General Rule of Thumb** At least 30 data points for each categorical chunk	**General Rule of Thumb** At least 30 data points for each categorical chunk
Sampling Method	100 Percent Sampling until .. Systematic Sampling Sub Group Sampling	Random Sampling Stratified Sampling
Graphical Representation	**Categorical Data** Pie Chart, Bar Chart, Pareto Chart **Numerical Data** Run Chart, Control Chart, Histogram	**Categorical Data** Pie Chart, Bar Chart, Pareto Chart **Numerical Data** Histogram

Process vs. Population Sampling Guide

Now we have finalised the plan around the primary metric and stratification variables, we can complete the process by developing the data collection plan for secondary measures.

FOCUSING ON THE NUMERICAL VARIABLES AS POTENTIAL CAUSES

We refer to these secondary numerical variables as *cause* variables because we are going to attempt to establish how strong they *correlate* with variation observed in the primary metric. Simply stated that means we are going to determine how strong the relationship is between variation in these measures (x's) and variation in the primary metric (y).

As a *numerical* variable, each one of them needs to be operationally defined to ensure that data is collected consistently so we can undertake valid data analysis.

NUMERICAL Xs		
Numerical Variable	**What It Is**	**How To Collect It**
What numerical variables potentially have a relationship with variation in the primary metric	What exactly is that variable (in plain simple terms)	How exactly do we collect / measure that so we all get the same results

Figure 78: Focusing on Secondary Numerical Variables (x's)

Measures Associated with Cause

The key behind successful process improvement work is the identification of the critical few variables (x's) that cause the output (y) to be the way it is. Once these are identified they can be treated to produce the result you want. One way of introducing efficiency in the work of the project team is to identify likely causes of variation before process performance data is actually collected and include these in the data collection plan.

The advantages of doing this include:

- **Paired data** is collected during the first phase of data collection, which might accelerate the validation of root causes of variation.
- The team is focused on **cause and effect early** in the project.
- **Additional data collection** (post root cause analysis) might be avoided.

These variables would explain *why* the variation occurs. It would be difficult to stratify your data using these variables, as any data collected would be associated with some numerical scale as opposed to categories. The variables identified as 'stratification variables' are attribute or categorical type data. As such would be *sources* of variation, not *causes*. (i.e.; they help explain *where* the variation occurs, not *why* it occurs)

Referencing the XY Worksheet

Having completed the process of developing an XY Worksheet, it is simply a matter of transferring the information into the data collection plan.

As you can see in the example shown below, the *arrows* indicate all of the numerical variables that potentially have an impact on the primary metric. The *circles* indicate which of these the team believes have the biggest impact on the primary metric. It's these that get included in the data collection plan as your secondary measures.

Primary Metric Y	Potential X's that have an impact on Primary Metric Y	Data Type	Impact on Y
SERVICE CYCLE TIME	Truck type	C	1
	Staff member doing the work	C	4
	Work location	C	1
	Time since last service	N	2
	Day of the week	C	3
	Service type	C	3
	Cycle time of actual work	N	5
	Time between drop off and job start (parked time)	N	3

Figure 79: Selecting Numerical Variables From The XY Worksheet

THE COMPLETED DATA COLLECTION PLAN

A completed data collection plan for a project working on reducing 'Service Cycle Time' might look something like this.

Project Title: Service Cycle Time Reduction

PRIMARY METRIC (Y)			CATEGORICAL Xs	
The Metric	**What It Is**	**How to Collect It**	**Categorical Variables**	**Sampling Plan**
Cycle time for truck servicing	Time in minutes between start and finish of the service (as perceived by customer)	Service cycle time is determined by measuring the time taken in minutes between (a) the time logged for vehicle drop off and (b) the time logged for work completion.	1. Staff member doing work 2. Day of the week 3. Service type	A minimum sample size of 44 units. Collect all data points until the minimum sample size is satisfied.

NUMERICAL Xs		
Numerical Variable	**What It Is**	**How To Collect It**
Cycle time of actual work	Time taken in minutes to complete truck service work	Calculate the time in minutes between the logged start of work and the logged completion of work time
Parked time	Time in minutes between drop off at the service centre and starting the work	Calculate the time in minutes between (a) the logged drop off time and (b) the logged time for start of work

CASE STUDY – THE COFFEE SHOP

A project team working on reducing the number of defects associated with cold coffee.

Step 1 – Document the Process, Inputs and Outputs

<u>Referencing the IPO Worksheet</u>

The IPO Worksheet developed in the define phase of the project becomes an input to the discussion. It describes the sequence of activities and lists a range of inputs that give clues to the variables that might impact the primary metric.

<table>
<tr><th>INPUTS</th><th>PROCESS</th><th>OUTPUT/S</th></tr>
<tr><td>Materials
Water, Milk, Coffee Beans, Condiments, Foam cups, Flavouring
Data / Information
Customer order, Recipe, Menu
Resources
Coffee Machine, Staff, Ceramic Cups, Utensils, Temperature Probe</td><td>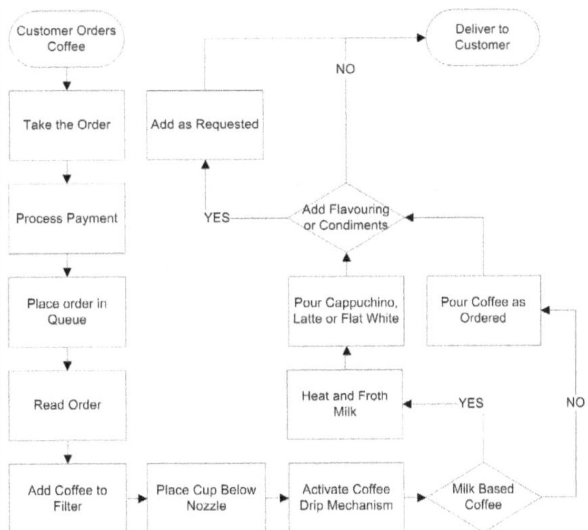
</td><td>Cup of Coffee</td></tr>
</table>

Figure 80: IPO Worksheet

Step 2 – Identify Significant Variables that Impact the Y

<u>XY Worksheet</u>

To complete the XY worksheet, we simply ask a series of questions.

Q1. What variables (the x's in this case) potentially have an impact on variability in the primary metric (y) we are studying? To answer the question we have chosen to refer to the following categories and have generated a list of variables as shown in the table below.

Materials	Machines	Measures	Methods	Environment	People
Cup Type (foam or ceramic).	Temperature probes.	Size of the coffee (small, regular, large).	Coffee type (milk or water based). Cycle time for making the coffee.	Ambient Temp. # Customers in the store. Time period in the day (am/pm). Day of the week.	Staff member making the coffee.

The results are simply recorded in the XY Worksheet and the final two questions are asked of each variable.

Q2. If we recorded values for this variable, what type of data would it generate? (It would be either categorical or numerical.)

Q3. If we vary this *x* (ask for every *x*) within its normal operating range, how much effect would it have on variation in the primary metric (*y*)? (You can rate the effect on a scale of 0 to 5.)

The end result of this process might produce an XY Worksheet that looks like this.

Primary Metric Y	Potential X's that have an impact on Primary Metric Y	Data Type	Impact on Y
COFFEE TEMPERATURE	Cup type (foam or ceramic)	C	4
	Temperature probes (1 in each jug)	C	1
	Size of coffee (small, regular, large)	C	2
	Coffee type (milk based or water based)	C	5
	Cycle time for making the coffee	N	3
	Ambient temperature	N	4
	# Customers in the store	N	4
	Time period (am or pm)	C	3
	Day of the week	C	2
	Employee who makes the coffee	C	5

XY Worksheet

Step 3 – Develop The Data Collection Plan

The Primary Metric

Going back to the project charter, the team identified the performance measure of concern or primary metric in this project as being *coffee temperature.*

Operational Definition

The team then defined that measure by stating what it was and how it would need to be measured.

Measure	WHAT is it?	HOW do we measure it?	Feasible
Coffee Temperature	The temperature of the coffee in Degrees Celsius at the time of delivery to the customer.	Place a digital temperature probe in the coffee down to the bottom centre of the cup. Hold in place for at least 10 seconds and then record the temperature value in Degrees Celsius to the nearest 0.1.	Yes

Operational Definition for Primary Metric

Categorical Variables

The first step in determining stratification variables (or sources of variation) was to make reference to the completed XY Worksheet.

The categorical variables identified as potentially having the biggest impact on the primary metric were (a) Cup type, (b) Coffee type, (c) Employee who makes the coffee and (d) Time period.

Sampling Plan – A Practical Approach

While practitioners sometimes want to apply statistical methods to calculate sample sizes, there is a simple rule I apply that sets me up for the analysis phase. The rule is this:

'Collect at least 30 data points for each of the major categorical chunks.'

For example, when I record a value for 'Cup Type' it will be small, medium or large. I know in this case there are three categorical chunks. So I would make sure I record coffee temperature for at least 30 small cups, 30 medium cups and at least 30 large cups of coffee.

Why do I do this? The reasons will become clear when we explain Hypothesis Testing and the Central Limit Theorem. For the moment, just use this principle if you want to be able to maximise the results from any later statistical analysis.

For this project, the team leader has decided to state the sampling plan as this.

- Collect the temperature value for all coffees over a full 7-day period.

This should ensure the data set includes:

- At least 30 from each Barista
- At least 30 from the morning and 30 from the afternoon
- At least 30 for milk based coffee and 30 for water based coffee
- At least 30 for each of the cup types (small, medium and large)

Let's take a look at a more quantitative method.

Sampling Plan – Statistical Method for :Point Estimates

We are going to consider both point estimate sample size equations (mean and proportions) to see which of these is larger. The intent is to consider collecting the larger of the two in order to meet requirements for both mean and proportion inferences about the population.

Population Mean (Average Temperature)

The team found that over the previous week that the average temperature of served coffee (based on a sample of 20 units) was 68 degrees with a standard deviation of 3 degrees. Using the equation shown below, to be 95 percent confident of estimating the true average temperature to within plus or minus 1 degree, they would need to sample a minimum of 35 cups of coffee.

$$n = \left(\frac{Z\sigma}{E}\right)^2 = \left(\frac{1.96 \times 3}{1}\right)^2 = 34.57$$

If the team wanted to estimate the mean using a confidence level of 99 percent to within plus or minus 1 degree, they would need to sample a minimum of 60 cups of coffee.

$$n = \left(\frac{Z\sigma}{E}\right)^2 = \left(\frac{2.58 \times 3}{1}\right)^2 = 59.9$$

Population Proportion (Proportion Defective or Outside Desired Temperature Range)

Of the 20 units sampled, 2 were outside the designated temperature range for coffee. Using the equation below, to be 90 percent confident of estimating the true proportion of coffees that are outside the correct temperature range to within plus or minus 5 percent, they would need to sample at least 98 cups of coffee.

$$n = \frac{Z^2 \times \pi \times (1-\pi)}{E^2} = \frac{1.645^2 \times 0.1 \times (1-0.1)}{0.05^2} = \frac{0.2435}{0.0025} = 97.4$$

If the team wanted to determine the proportion of defective cups of coffee within a 95 percent confidence interval, according to the calculation shown below they would need to sample at least 139 cups of coffee.

$$n = \frac{Z^2 \times \pi \times (1-\pi)}{E^2} = \frac{1.96^2 \times 0.1 \times (1-0.1)}{0.05^2} = \frac{0.3457}{0.0025} = 138.29$$

Numerical Variables (Xs)

Secondary numerical variables were identified from the XY Worksheet by locating those numerical variables the team considered to be most significant. In this case ambient temperature and the number of customers in the store were chosen and then defined.

Measure	WHAT is it?	HOW do we measure it?	Feasible
Ambient Temperature	Room temperature in Degrees Celsius.	Record the temperature shown on digital thermometer [mounted on the wall] at the time the temperature is recorded for each sample.	YES
# Customers in the Store	How many customers are standing in line for service at the time of making the coffee.	When the temperature of the coffee is taken, count and record the number of customers who are standing in line waiting to be served or being served.	YES

Operational Definition for Secondary Measures

Completing the Data Collection Plan

Having answered all of the necessary questions, the team then consolidated their work into a single data collection plan.

PRIMARY METRIC (Y)			CATEGORICAL Xs	
The Metric (Y)	**What It Is**	**How To Collect It**	**Categorical Variables**	**Sampling Plan**
Coffee Temperature	The temperature of the coffee in Degrees Celsius at the time of delivery to the customer.	Place a digital temperature probe in into the coffee down to the bottom centre of the cup. Hold for no less than 10 seconds and record the temperature value in Degrees Celsius to the nearest 0.1 of a degree.	1. Cup type 2. Coffee type 3. Employee 4. Time period	100% sampling for a period of 7 full days or until at least 30 data points for each Barista is collected (whichever occurs first)

NUMERICAL Xs		
Numerical Variable	**What It Is**	**How To Collect It**
Ambient Temperature	Room temperature in degrees Celsius.	Record the temperature shown on digital thermometer at the time the temperature is recorded for each sample.
# Customers in the store	How many customers are standing in line for service at the time of making the coffee.	When the temperature of the coffee is taken, count and record the number of customers who are standing in line waiting to be served or being served.

Completed Data Collection Plan for Coffee Temperature Project

ANALYSE THE MEASUREMENT SYSTEM (STEP 7)

Suppose the situation existed where data used in your project was created and input into a system by more than one person.

Also suppose these people all had their own particular way of measuring and the results produced by one person would be different from the results another person would produce if they measured exactly the same thing. What would be the effect of that on your project?

This is measurement system variation.

When a measurement system is a source of variation, the organisation concerned may well be calling a good unit a defect, and a defective unit a good unit. In the context of a Six Sigma process improvement project, the team will make certain inferences about the population of units on the basis of data collected.

Additional variation introduced by the measurement system itself, can result in inferences that are incorrect and misleading.

Measurement System Analysis (MSA) is a series of specific tests that help a team determine whether or not the system of measurement is reliable and not contributing to the variation being observed in the collected data.

While it is not required for every project, it should at least be considered for every project.

Sources of Variation

Let's look at the components of a measurement system for variable data. They include:

- Units being measured
- The gauge used to do the measurement
- The operator who does the measuring
- The methods being employed to measure

Sources of variation within the system are shown in the figure below.

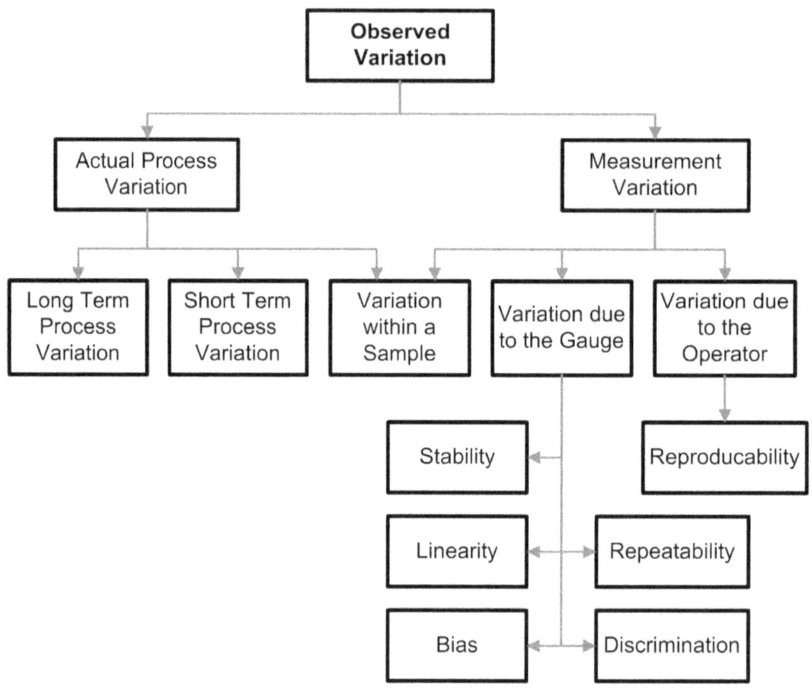

Figure 81: Sources of Variation

MEASUREMENT SYSTEM VARIATION

Measurement system variation (or measurement system error) can be broken down into two categories: accuracy and precision.

- **Accuracy** refers to the difference between the measured characteristic of a part and its actual value. Accuracy of a measurement system is determined through analysing bias, linearity, stability, and discrimination.
- **Precision** refers to the variation that exists in results when you measure the same characteristic of the same unit repeatedly with the same measurement device (or gauge). Precision of a measurement system is determined through analysing both *repeatability* (same operator can get the same result each time) and *reproducibility* (different operators can produce the same results).

These concepts are visually represented in the following diagram. It depicts the four different results a shooter might produce when firing a number of shots (in this case eight shots) at a single target. These potential results are described in terms of accuracy and precision.

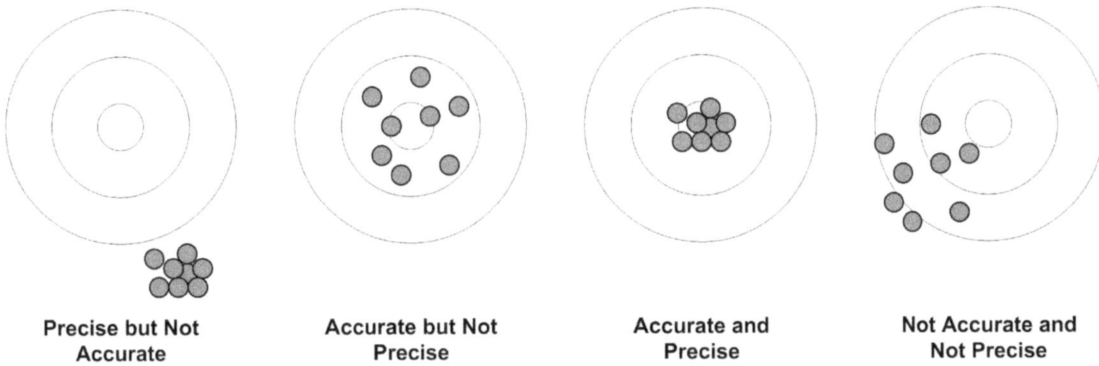

Figure 82: Precision versus Accuracy

Accuracy

Bias is the difference between the observed value (or measured value) and the actual true value. When an operator takes a measure of a part that has a known value (e.g.: a 1 kilogram calibrating weight), bias exists when the observed value is different from the standard.

For example, when technicians calibrate gauges, they simply perform this type of analysis and adjust the gauge to eliminate bias or inaccuracy.

Linearity studies determine how the size of the *part being measured* affects the accuracy of the measurement system. Linearity is the difference between the observed or measured accuracy values through the expected range of measurements.

For example, suppose a manufacturing company had an overhead crane with a working range between 1 tonne and 10 tonne. If the bias or inaccuracy between the actual weight lifted and observed weight at the operator's console increased as loads got larger, than linearity would exist. If the inaccuracy remained the same throughout the working range (e.g.: 100 kilograms too heavy at every point), the measurement system has a bias problem, not a linearity issue.

Stability of a measurement system refers to how accurately the measurement system performs *over time*. It is the total variation obtained with a particular gauge when measuring the same characteristic of the same part over time. It brings into play variables associated with time such as temperature or operator tiredness.

Discrimination (or resolution) of any measurement system refers to the ability of the system to *detect small changes or variation* in the characteristic of the parts being measured.

Precision

Repeatability refers to the ability of the measurement system to return the same value when *one operator* measures the *same characteristic* of the *same part* repeatedly.

Reproducibility determines the degree of consistency between *multiple operators* when they measure the *same characteristics* of the *same unit.*

Now you have an understanding of what they are, let's look at how we study these various forms of variation through measurement system analysis.

ACCURACY STUDIES FOR VARIABLE DATA

Bias

The objective of a 'bias' study is to determine whether or not inaccuracy exists within a measurement system.

- **Step 1** – Obtain a known standard that is a representation of a value within the normal operating range of the unit.
- **Step 2** – One operator measures the standard a minimum of 10 times using the same gauge.
- **Step 3** – Record all measures and calculate the mean.
- **Step 4** – Compare the mean to the known standard.

If the mean is above or below the standard, calibrate the gauge accordingly.

Remember to use the **same operator,** the **same gauge**, and the **same standard** throughout the analysis.

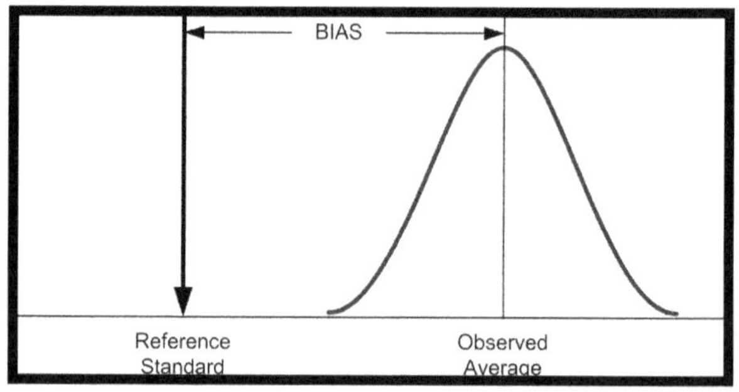

Linearity

The objective of a 'linearity' study is to determine whether or not bias exists over the operating range of the gauge. (Refer to notes on correlation presented in later chapters.)

- **Step 1** – Define four or more standard reference units that span the range over which the gauge is likely to be used.
- **Step 2** – Determine bias for the gauge when measuring each standard reference unit.
- **Step 3** – Create a scatter plot with bias plotted on the Y axis and the standard reference unit on the X axis.
- **Step 4** – Determine the 'goodness of fit' using R^2 value (coefficient of determination)

Linearity is determined by the slope of the fitted line – The higher the slope the worse the linearity. Conversely, the lower or flatter the slope the less linearity exists.

When undertaking linearity testing, it is essential that the same operator conduct the measurements across the range in order to minimise the introduction of additional variation.

Remember to use the **same operator** and the **same gauge** throughout the analysis.

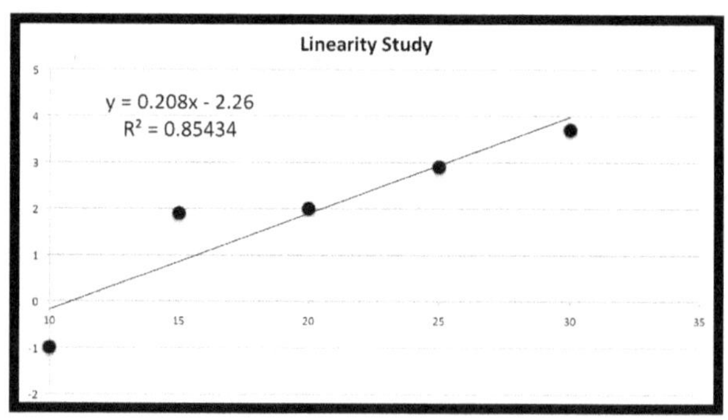

Stability

The object of studying 'stability' is to determine whether or not bias changes or drifts over time.

- **Step 1** – Obtain a standard reference unit
- **Step 2** – Measure 3 to 5 times at regular time intervals
- **Step 3** – Plot results on an X-bar R chart.
- **Step 4** – Take corrective action when the measurement system does not demonstrate good stability over time.

Both the X bar and the R chart are used to determine stability over time (refer to Control Charts for more information).

The range chart (R chart) shows variation *within* sub-groups over time.

The mean bar chart (X bar chart) shows variation *between* sub-groups of data over time.

Remember to use the **same operator** and the **same gauge** throughout the analysis.

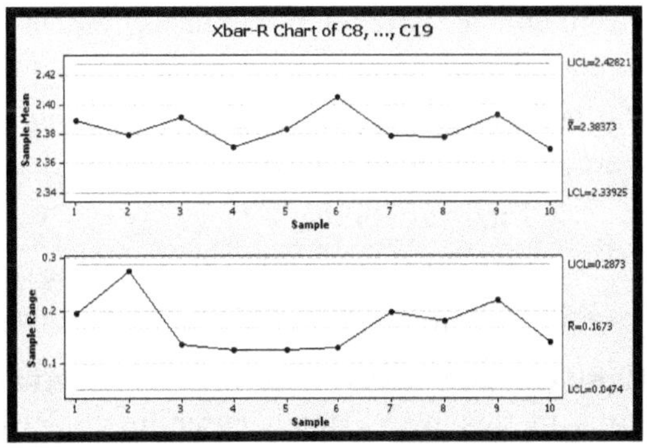

Discrimination

If we were to measure the length of a marker pen to the nearest centimetre, we would find that all marker pens of the same brand and type were exactly the same length. There is a lack of discrimination or resolution due to the *rounding off* effect.

It is widely recognised as a general rule that the measurement system should be able to discriminate to *one tenth of the customer's specified tolerance* (Between the Upper Spec Limit and the Lower Spec Limit).

For example, if the customer's requirement is for parts with a length between 130 and 140 cm, then the measurement system should be able to measure to at least the nearest centimetre (which is one tenth of the gap between lower and upper specifications). If the requirement was for a part with a length between 130 and 131 cm, then the measurement system should be able to measure to at least the nearest millimetre (which is one tenth of the gap between lower and upper specifications).

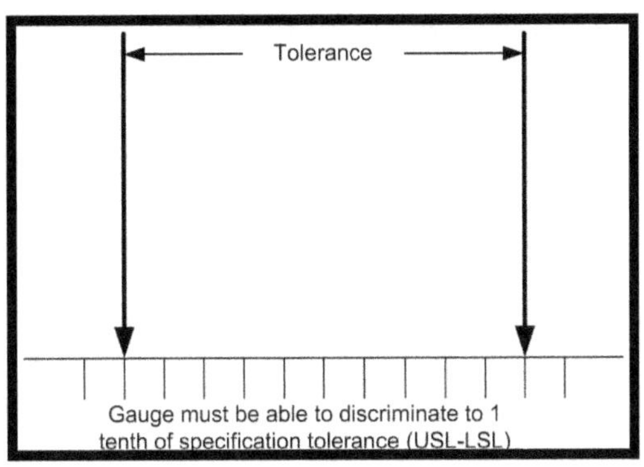

Figure 83: Discrimination to 1/10 of Customer Tolerance

PRECISION STUDIES FOR VARIABLE DATA - GAGE R&R

Components of Variation for Measurement System Analysis

Anytime you measure a part, you not only capture the variability of the part being measured, but also any variability that may exist because of poor repeatability of the gauge and poor reproducibility of the operators and the methods of measuring that they employ. A test known as Gage Repeatability and Reproducibility (or Gage R&R) can be performed to determine whether or not excessive variation exists within the measurement system.

A Gage R&R study will help you answer the question: 'How much of the variation we are seeing is attributable to variation in the measurement system?' Where this variation is excessive, we must take action to minimise it.

The test is such that the sources of variation within the measurement system can be partitioned. These sources will include:

- Total variability (TV)
- Part to part variability (product variation)
- Measurement system variability – also known as measurement system error or precision (P)

These components are shown in the diagram on the following page and can be explained in mathematical terms in this way - total variability = Part-to-part variability + Measurement system variability; or in mathematical form .,

$$\hat{\sigma}^2 \text{ Total} = \hat{\sigma}^2 \text{ Part - to - part} + \hat{\sigma}^2 \text{ MS}$$

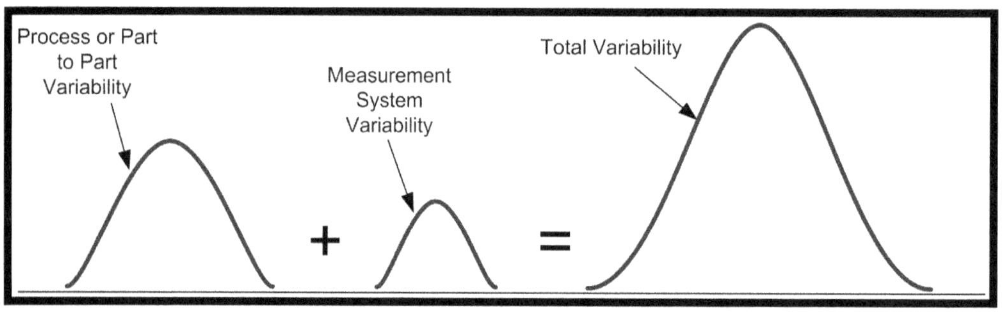

Figure 84: Components of Variation for MSA

Components of Measurement System Variability

Measurement system variability can be further divided into two components.

MS Repeatability

The ability of *one operator* to measure the same characteristic of the same part multiple times with little variation

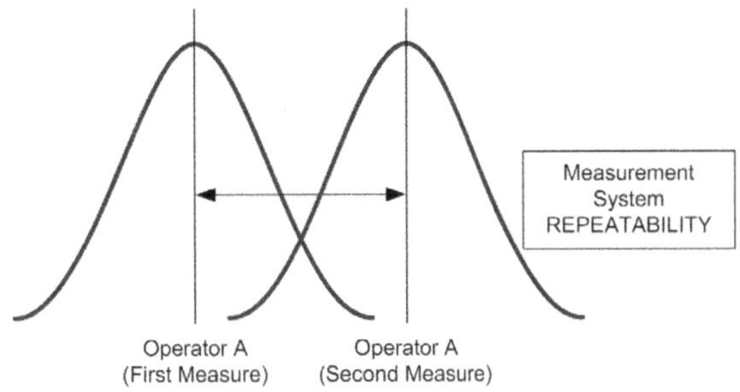

MS Reproducibility

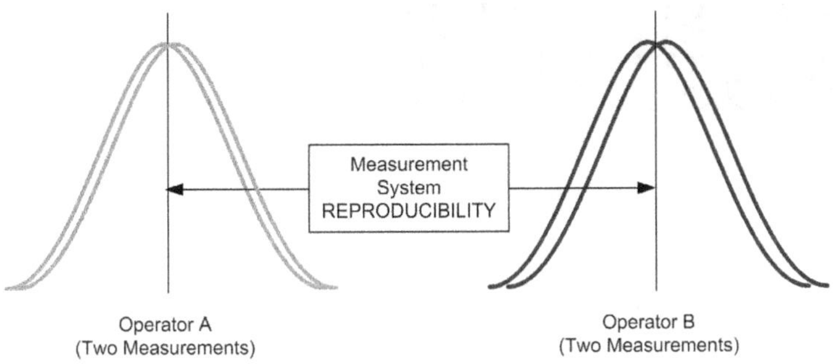

The ability of *two operators* to measure the same characteristic of the same parts and return similar average measurements with little variation in those averaged values.

How Gage R&R Works

Take a moment to look at the following table. It shows the result of a measurement activity with the following characteristics.

- Two operators
- Each measured the same ten parts – twice
- The same gauge was used every time
- Parts were measured at random

(**Note:** If undertaking measurement system analysis with SigmaXL or Minitab software, do not lay your data out in this format, this layout is shown for discussion purposes.)

Part	Operator A		Range	Mean
A	10	10	0	10.0
B	11	11	0	11.0
C	13	14	1	13.5
D	12	11	1	11.5
E	14	13	1	13.5
F	11	12	1	11.5
G	10	10	0	10.0
H	11	11	0	11.0
I	12	13	1	12.5
J	13	12	1	12.5
Averages			0.6	11.7

Part	Operator B		Range	Mean
A	10	11	1	10.5
B	12	12	0	12.0
C	12	12	0	12.0
D	11	12	1	11.5
E	13	12	1	12.5
F	10	11	1	10.5
G	11	11	0	11.0
H	12	12	0	12.0
I	11	11	0	11.0
J	13	12	1	12.5
Averages			0.5	11.55

If average ranges were close to 0, it would indicate an operator could REPEAT the measurement and get the same results both times.

Figure 85: Determining Repeatability

Determining Repeatability

If *one operator* gets a very similar result for their first and second measurement of each part, this means the process is repeatable. Thus, the range between first and second measurement of each part is important. If the average range is close to zero, the measurement is repeatable.

Determining Reproducibility

Reproducibility exists when *two operators* can get similar results measuring the same parts with the same gauge. Thus, the average of mean measurements becomes important.

This is obviously a simplistic example for discussion purposes. Gage R&R offers much more information and can be undertaken by hand. But in the modern world, it is far easier and more effective to undertake the process using relevant software such as Minitab or SigmaXL.

Part	Operator A		Range	Mean
A	10	10	0	10.0
B	11	11	0	11.0
C	13	14	1	13.5
D	12	11	1	11.5
E	14	13	1	13.5
F	11	12	1	11.5
G	10	10	0	10.0
H	11	11	0	11.0
I	12	13	1	12.5
J	13	12	1	12.5
Averages			0.6	11.7

Part	Operator B		Range	Mean
A	10	11	1	10.5
B	12	12	0	12.0
C	12	12	0	12.0
D	11	12	1	11.5
E	13	12	1	12.5
F	10	11	1	10.5
G	11	11	0	11.0
H	12	12	0	12.0
I	11	11	0	11.0
J	13	12	1	12.5
				11.55

If average means were similar, it would indicate each operator can REPRODUCE similar results as the other.

Figure 86: Determining Reproducibility

Acceptance Criteria (for Gage R&R)

The issue for us is not that there is variation in the measurement system. The issue is whether or not the variation that exists is excessive. To determine whether or not the measurement system repeatability and reproducibility are acceptable, we make reference to a number of statistics. These are:

- Percent contribution of Gage R&R variance to total variance (indicated by the notation **% Contribution**)
- Percent of the total variation (measured as standard deviation) contributed by measurement system standard deviation (indicated by the notation **% P/TV**)
- The ratio of the spread of 99 percent of measurement system variation to customer tolerances (indicated by the notation **% P/T**)

The table on the following page provides a guide to levels of acceptance for each of these statistics.

Take notice that % Contribution is calculated with variance while the others are calculated with standard deviation.

	% Contribution	**% P/TV**	**% P/T**
	$\frac{\hat{\sigma}^2 \text{ MS}}{\hat{\sigma}^2 \text{ Total}} \times 100$	$\frac{\hat{\sigma} \text{ MS}}{\hat{\sigma} \text{ Total}} \times 100$	$\frac{5.15 \times \hat{\sigma} \text{ MS}}{\text{Tolerance}} \times 100$
Marginally Acceptable	< 9%	< 30%	< 30%
Good	< 4%	< 20%	< 20%
Excellent	< 1%	< 10%	< 10%

Legend

MS - Measurement System **P** – Precision **TV** - Total Variation **T** - Tolerance

Percent Contribution is the measure most commonly used by Six Sigma practitioners. It is a ratio of variances that give an indication of how much of the total variation is attributed to variation within the measurement system. Obviously, the smaller this value the better.

Precision to Total Variation (P/TV) is the ratio of measurement system standard deviation to the standard deviation observed in the sample data.

Precision to Tolerance (P/T) is the ratio of 5.15 times the measurement system standard deviation to the tolerance (USL – LSL). The value 5.15 refers to the number of standard deviations that contain 99 percent of the variation within a normal distribution. This measure is used to determine if the organisation can appropriately accept or reject their product using this measurement system.

Undertaking Gage R&R Studies (for Variable Data)

The purpose of any Gage R&R study is to determine whether or not the measurement system has an acceptable level of repeatability and reproducibility. The process for completing a Gage R&R comprises five steps.

- **Step 1** – Identify the characteristics of the part to be measured, the gauge and the operators.
- **Step 2** – Define the number of parts that span the range of long-term variation (typically ten units).
- **Step 3** – Plan the study.
- **Step 4** – Conduct the Gage R&R in the environment where the measurement usually takes place.
- **Step 5** – Analyse the Gage R&R to determine repeatability and reproducibility.

Terms

Two terms you have to be familiar with.

- **Crossed** – A crossed study is undertaken when all operators measure parts from the same batch, in other words *the batch is repeatedly measured.*
- **Nested** – A nested study is undertaken when all operators measure different parts such as with destructive testing, in other words *each batch is only measured once.*

Example Gage R&R with MINITAB (Crossed)

A project team leader decides to test the measurement system for repeatability and reproducibility before collecting data for analysis. To do this, *three operators* measure *10 parts* twice using the *same gage*.

The 10 parts measured are kept the same for each operator.

Note:

The data is laid out in a worksheet as shown in the format on the right.

The full worksheet consists of 60 data points (3 operators x 10 parts x 2 measures each).

↓	C1	C2	C3
	Part	Operator	Response
1	1	1	0.65
2	1	1	0.60
3	2	1	1.00
4	2	1	1.00
5	3	1	0.85
6	3	1	0.80
7	4	1	0.85
8	4	1	0.90

Interpreting Statistical Results (Minitab)

%Contribution (of VarComp): The results indicate that the measurement system is unacceptable. We can see from the results that 10.67 percent of the total variation is attributable t Gage R&R, less than 9 percent is marginally acceptable while results less than 1 percent are considered to be excellent (refer to Gage R&R acceptance criteria).

The majority of variation in the measurement system is attributed to reproducibility (7.56 percent). This is further broken down into its components of operator (2.19 percent) and operator-by-part interaction (5.37 percent). The interaction result gives an indication that some operators measure some parts differently than others, a question that would need answering to treat variation.

%Study Var (%SV): The value of 32.66 percent shows the same outcome. Being > 30 percent, it indicates MS variation is excessive.

```
Gage R&R

                                %Contribution
Source               VarComp     (of VarComp)
Total Gage R&R      0.023474            10.67
  Repeatability     0.006833             3.10
  Reproducibility   0.016641             7.56
    Operator        0.004825             2.19
    Operator*Part   0.011817             5.37
Part-To-Part        0.196599            89.33
Total Variation     0.220074           100.00


                                  Study Var  %Study Var
Source              StdDev (SD)    (6 * SD)       (%SV)
Total Gage R&R         0.153213     0.91928       32.66
  Repeatability        0.082661     0.49597       17.62
  Reproducibility      0.129002     0.77401       27.50
    Operator           0.069460     0.41676       14.81
    Operator*Part      0.108705     0.65223       23.17
Part-To-Part           0.443395     2.66037       94.52
Total Variation        0.469120     2.81472      100.00


Number of Distinct Categories = 4
```

Figure 87: Gage R&R (Crossed) Statistical Output – Minitab

Interpreting Graphical Results (Minitab)

The graphical output of a Gage R&R study looks like the following diagram. Minitab produces these in a single chart format.

Components of Variation (Top Left Chart): This is the graphical representation of two parts of the Minitab session window output. The left-side bars in each pair represent the **% Contribution** of the measurement system (the Gage R&R), each component of the measurement system (repeatability and reproducibility) and part-to-part variation (variation in the process itself). The values for part-to-part and Gage R&R add up to 100 percent.

The right-side bars in each pair represent **% Study Variation** of the same components. This value for Gage R&R is the same as the statistic we referred to earlier - % P/TV. Note that values for part-to-part and Gage R&R do not add up to 100 percent.

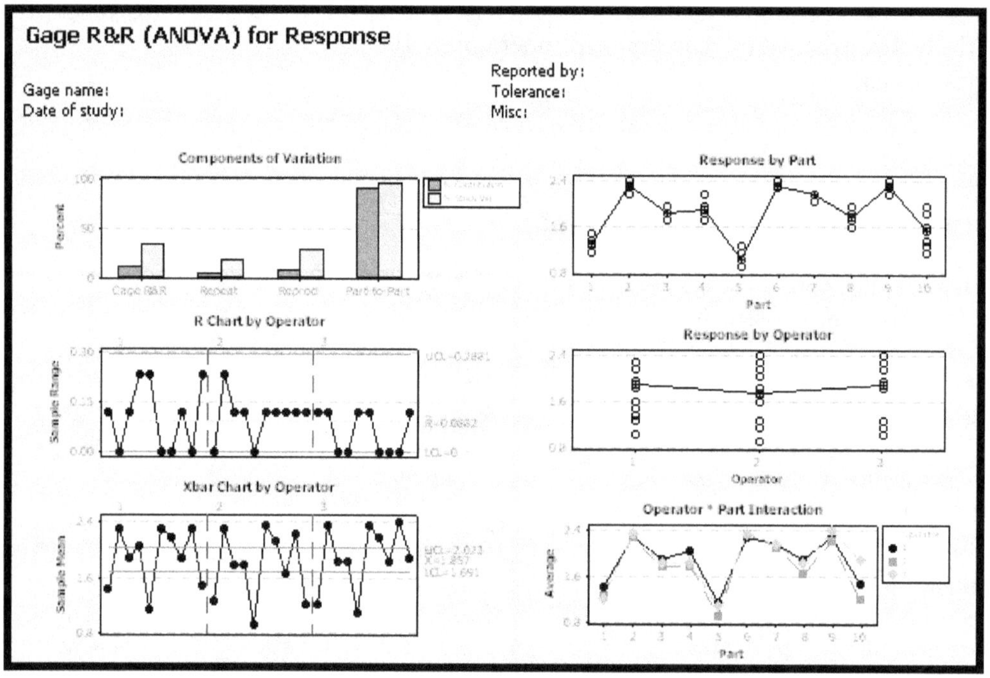

Figure 88: Gage R&R (Crossed) Graphical Output - Minitab

R Chart by Operator (Centre Left Chart): The range chart by operator displays variation in measurements by each operator. This chart gives an indication if special causes are operating. Where special causes exist, the causes should be treated and the analysis undertaken again. In this case, the range chart shows that the system is stable.

The range chart also gives an indication of 'discrimination'. A guideline offered is to ensure that there are at least five levels of possible values. In this case, there are only three, hence evidence of a lack of 'discrimination' or 'resolution.'

When interpreting results of the study, it is always important to study the R chart for stability first.

X-bar Chart by Operator (Lower Left Chart): Whilst the R chart displays variation that exists within each part, X-bar charts display variation that exists between parts by operator. The X-bar chart displays actual mean measurement values by operator for each part in relation to the overall mean (represented by the data points).

Control limits do not relate to variation between parts; rather they represent variation within the measurements of each part (repeatability). Low variation in the results obtained for each part means the process is repeatable and we have tighter control limits. So a good result would be variation that exists between parts (part-to-part component of variance) is much greater than variation that exists in the measurement system (within part variance). That means the chart shows an *out-of-control state*, exactly what we desire in this unique instance.

The chart shows 66 percent of values outside control limits indicating an out of control state. This is ideal and suggests that the measurement system is adequate.

Response By Part (Top Right Chart): The *'by part'* chart displays the mean measurement for each part. When the measurements are replicated many times, box plots may be used to represent data values.

Response By Operator (Centre Right Chart): The *'by operator'* chart displays the mean measurement for each operator. Once again, when the measurements are replicated many times, box plots may be used to represent data values.

Operator*Part Interaction (Lower Right Chart): The *'operator*part interaction'* chart shows an overlay of the average chart details for each operator. Where lines cross, this suggests that there is an operator-by-part interaction – not all operators are measuring parts in the same way. This chart is only displayed when undertaking crossed studies.

Interpreting Statistical Results (SigmaXL)

The following diagram is the results of a Gage R&R study (for variables data) using SigmaXL.

Analysis of Variance with Part * Operator Interaction:

Source	DF	SS	MS	F	P
Part:	9	88.362	9.818	492.29	0.0000
Operator:	2	3.167	1.584	79.406	0.0000
Part * Operator:	18	0.358982	0.019943457	0.433721	0.9741
Repeatability:	60	2.759	0.045982222		
Total:	89	94.647	1.063450699		

Analysis of Variance without Part * Operator Interaction (P for Interaction >= 0.1):

Source	DF	SS	MS	F	P
Part:	9	88.362	9.818	245.61	0.0000
Operator:	2	3.167	1.584	39.617	0.0000
Repeatability:	78	3.118	0.039973276		
Total:	89	94.64711222	1.063450699		

Gage R&R Metrics	StDev	StDev Lower 90% CI	StDev Upper 90% CI	6 * StDev	% Total Variation (TV)	% TV Lower 90% CI	% TV Upper 90% CI
Gage R&R:	0.302372	0.235108	1.033372445	1.814	27.86	15.46	70.93
Operator (AV Appraiser Variation):	0.226838	0.127545	1.013789066	1.361	20.90		
Part * Operator (INT Interaction):	0	0	0	0	0.00		
Reproducibility (SQRT(AV^2 + INT^2)):	0.226838	0.127545	1.013789066	1.361	20.90		
Repeatability (EV Equipment Variation):	0.199933	0.176915	0.230560	1.200	18.42		
Part Variation (PV):	1.042327494	0.758821	1.717	6.254	96.04		
Total Variation (TV):	1.085299563	0.816099	1.811	6.512	100.00		

Gage R&R Metrics	Variance Component	Variance Component
Gage R&R:	0.091428538	7.76
Operator:	0.051455261	4.37
Part * Operator:	0	0.00
Reproducibility:	0.051455261	4.37
Repeatability:	0.039973276	3.39
Part Variation:	1.086446604	92.24
Total Variation:	1.178	100.00

Gage R&R Metrics	NDC	NDC Lower 90% CI	NDC Upper 90% CI
Number of Distinct Categories (Signal-to-Noise Ratio: 1.41 * PV/R&R):	4.9	1.4	9.0

Figure 89: Gage R&R (Variables) Statistical Output - SigmaXL

The top two tables in the diagram are referred to as Anova (Analysis of Variance) tables. We are not going to discuss those in this text, instead we will simplify the process and simply focus on the Gage R&R metrics shown in the bottom three tables, after all these tell us what we want to know.

% Total Variation (TV): Also known as %R&R and %Tolerance, this is the ratio of measurement system standard deviation to the standard deviation observed in the sample data. A value of < 10 percent indicates an excellent measurement system; a value of > 30 percent indicates an unacceptable measurement system. In this particular example the value is 27.86 percent.

Variance Component (Percent Contribution): This is a ratio of variances that give an indication of how much of the total variation is attributed to variation within the measurement system; obviously the smaller the value the better. A value of < 1 percent indicates a good measurement system; a value of > 9 percent indicates an unacceptable measurement system. In this example the value is 7.76 percent.

The Number of Distinct Categories (NDC) should be at least 5. A value of less than 5 indicates that discrimination in the measurement system may be insufficient. (In many cases, NDC is represented as an integer value, but SigmaXL is more informative in that it reports to one decimal place). The value in this example is 4.9.

SigmaXL also reports the **confidence intervals** for the Gage R&R metrics. Note that when the confidence intervals are taken into account, it is possible that this measurement system is totally inadequate. This strongly suggests that the measurement system needs to be improved but it also points out the weakness of the traditional Gage R&R study with 10 Parts, 3 Operators, and 3 Replicates. These sample sizes will typically yield wide confidence intervals.

Interpreting Graphical Results (SigmaXL)

Multi-Vari Chart

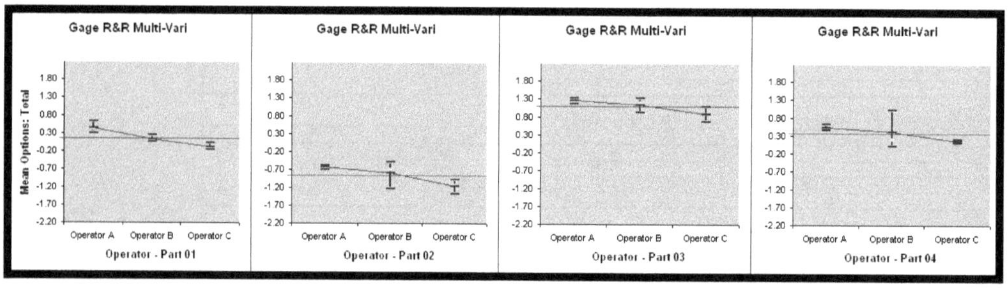

Figure 90: Gage R&R Multi-Vari Chart - SigmaXL

The Multi-Vari chart shows the measurement results of each part as a separate graph. Each Operator's response readings are denoted as a vertical line with the top tick corresponding to the maximum value, bottom tick is the minimum, and the middle tick is the mean. The horizontal line across each is the overall average for each part.

X-Bar Chart and Range Chart by Operator

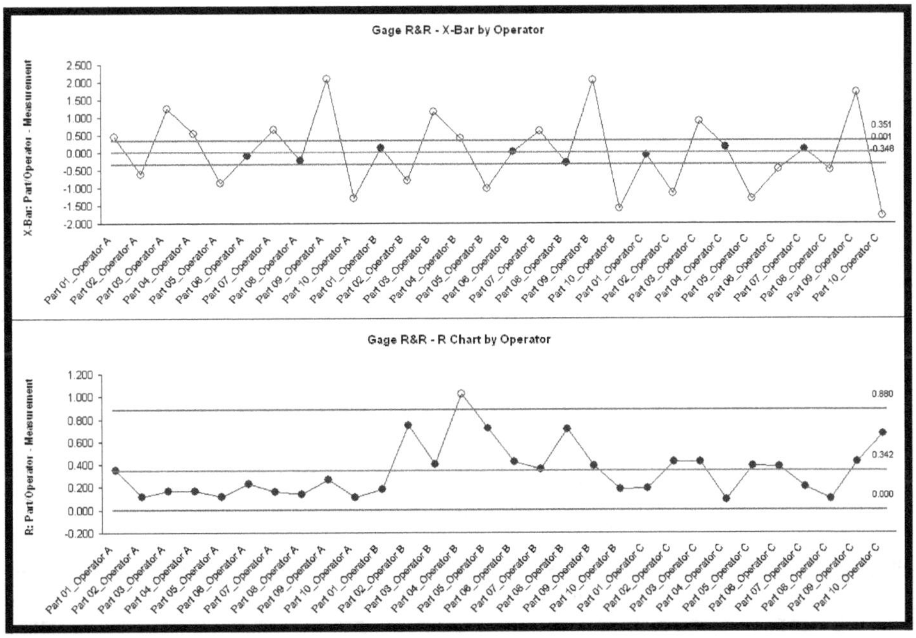

Figure 91: Range (R) Chart by Operator - SigmaXL

When interpreting the X-bar and R chart for a Gage R&R study, it is desirable that the X-bar chart shows an *out-of-control state*, and the Range chart shows an *in-control state.*

Confused?

Let me tell you, you certainly aren't the first, nor will you be the last.

Whilst the R chart displays variation that exists within each part, X-bar charts display variation that exists between parts by operator. The X-bar chart displays actual mean measurement values by operator for each part in relation to the overall mean (represented by the data points). Control limits do not relate to variation between parts, rather they represent variation within the measurements of each part (repeatability). Low variation in the results obtained for each part means the process is repeatable and we have tighter control limits. So a good result would be that variation that exists between parts (part-to-part component of variance) is much greater than variation that exists in the measurement system (within part variance). This means the chart shows an *out-of-control state*, exactly what we desire in this unique instance.

The range chart by operator displays variation in measurements by each operator. This chart gives an indication if special causes are operating. Where special causes exist, the causes should be treated and the analysis undertaken again. In this case, the range chart shows an outlier, indicating Operator B's measurements of one of the parts were very different. In fact we can see Operator B is very inconsistent in the results obtained, thus repeatability is brought into question.

The range chart also gives an indication of 'discrimination'. A guideline offered is to ensure that there are at least five levels of possible values. In this case it appears there is sufficient 'discrimination' or 'resolution' in the level of measurement being undertaken.

When interpreting results of the study, it is always important to study the R chart for stability first.

DESIRED MSA RESULTS

The results you would like to see in your measurement system are indicated in the table below.

	Desired Result	Characteristics
Accuracy	No Bias	The average value for repeatedly measuring a known standard with the one gauge is the same as the standard itself.
	Low Linearity	Bias (the difference between the known standard and the average result) remains the same across the operating range of the gauge.
	High Stability	The average value for measuring a known standard with the one gauge remains the same over time.
	Adequate Discrimination	The gauge can measure to at least 1 tenth of the customer specified tolerance.
Precision	Repeatability	The same operator, using the same gauge, obtains the same value when measuring the same parts multiple times.
	Reproducibility	Different operators, using the same gauge, obtain the same value as each other when measuring the same parts.

DEALING WITH EXCESSIVE VARIATION

When excessive variation exists in the measurement system, the team must first understand the cause before trying to treat the problem. A key point I make in all seminars I facilitate is this: the philosophy of Six Sigma must continue to be applied. That means *validating* any potential causes before you try to find solutions. So let's apply that principle here.

The process for reducing MS variations consists of three steps.

- **Step 1** – Identify potential causes of MS variation
- **Step 2** – Validate causes of MS variation
- **Step 3** – Take action to treat causes of variation

Cause Effect Analysis

A most useful tool for identifying causes is the Cause Effect Diagram shown in the following diagram.

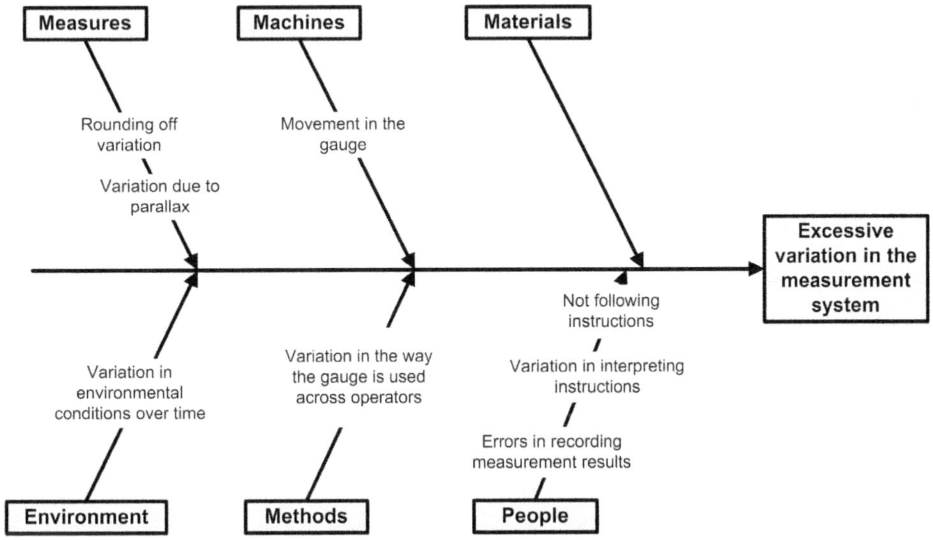

Figure 92: Analysing for Root Causes of Measurement System Variation

Validating Causes

Any potential causes identified can be validated through investigating the process of measuring. Your investigation may look something like the example shown in the following table.

Key Questions to Answer	Source	Recommended Approach
Did operators employ different methods? Was variation introduced due to the parallax effect or refraction effect? Was rounding off a contributing factor? Did operators follow instructions?	Operators	Have each operator demonstrate the way they measured. Have each operator show the way they determined the measurement value. Compare actual method used against instructions for measuring.
Were errors made in documenting measurement results?	Study Leader	Discuss possibility. Look for significant outliers in measurement results.
Does movement exist in the gage?	The Gauge	Undertake a 'bias' study.
Did environmental conditions change over time?	Operators	Ask questions about environmental conditions. Discuss the possibility that the method of measuring introduced instability.

Investigating Measurement System Variation

Note: Just in case you haven't heard the word, the meaning of the term *Parallax* is this.

Parallax (*n*): *the effect whereby the position or direction of an object appears to differ when viewed from different positions, e.g., through the viewfinder and the lens of a camera, or through water from different angles, or from a measurement device from different angles.*

Key Learning Points

1. Accuracy refers to the centering or positioning of measurement results, while precision refers to the amount of variation that exists in measurement results.
2. Accuracy is determined through studying
    a. bias,
    b. stability,
    c. linearity, and
    d. discrimination.
3. Precision is determined through studying
    a. repeatability, and
    b. reproducibility.
4. Total observed variation in a set of data is the sum of actual process variation and measurement system variation.
5. When studying Gage R&R, variation in the measurement system is acceptable if it is less than 9 percent of total variation (if using % Contribution values). When it is not less than that value, observed variation is probably distorted.
6. MSA answers the question – 'How much of the variation we're seeing is made up of variation in the measurement system?' MSA does not provide the answer to these questions; that's your role.
    a. What is the cost or impact of measurement system variation to the business or the project?
    b. Is it actually viable to treat this measurement system variation?

COLLECT THE DATA (STEP 8)

Method of Collection

There are many different tools or methods for collecting data. Some of the most common include these.

- Tally sheets
- Log sheets
- Data Compilation Sheet (Excel Spreadsheets and Minitab Worksheets)

Tools may already exist to help you collect the data, or they may have to be designed and constructed. In any case the project team must define the specific method of collection.

Developing Collection Tools

Where no tool exists for collecting data, a tool needs to be developed. These can be either manual tools or tools that generate the data automatically through extraction from databases that already exist.

A well-designed data collection tool has characteristics that include the following.

- Simple - easy to understand
- Easy to use - well labeled with sufficient space for data entry
- Relevant – only includes space for relevant and not superfluous data

Where data is collected using multiple forms, these need to be consolidated in some consistent way. Often called **compilation sheets**, a spreadsheet prepared in MS Excel or a worksheet prepared in Minitab are the most common forms of consolidation that help the user analyse collected data.

Everything we do in an improvement project is driven by the nature of cause and effect. So in order to undertake this most effectively we must continually remind ourselves of the key principle. The performance of any process (which we refer to as the *y*) is a function of all of the variables that influence it (which we refer to as the *x*'s). This is mathematically represented by the equation:

$$y = f(x_1, x_2, x_3, \ldots.. x_n)$$

So it stands to reason that we should collect and compile data in such a way that these *x* - *y* relationships can be quantified, wouldn't you agree?

Case Study – The Coffee Shop

Having selected categorical variables for stratifying our primary metric data as well as some numerical variables that are likely causes of variation, we are going to collect the data in a way that allows us to connect all of these variables together for analysis.

Let's look at our coffee temperature example. The data compilation sheet (or worksheet) is going to have column headings like this.

Coffee Temp	Coffee Type	Size (S/M/L)	Time Period (AM/PM)	Barista	Cycle Time	Temp of Milk	Ambient Temp		

As we are also interested in defect rate and the types of defects, we've added an additional columns that convert primary metric data in additional data we can use for later analysis.

Coffee Temp	Coffee Type	Size (S/M/L)	Time Period (AM/PM)	Barista	Cycle Time	Temp of Milk	Ambient Temp	Defect Status	Defect Type

By laying out your data in this format, the ability to link source and cause variables to the primary metric is maintained. Analysis to find the source and even validate some of the potential causes will be significantly simplified.

The diagram below shows the connection between these dependent and independent variables, and terms used in the data collection plan.

Primary Metric	Categorical Xs				Numerical Xs				
Coffee Temp	**Coffee Type**	**Size (S/M/L)**	**Time Period (AM/PM)**	**Barista**	**Cycle Time**	**Temp of Milk**	**Ambient Temp**	**Defect Status**	**Defect Type**
63	Latte	S	Am	Mick	1.25	64	24	DEFECT	COLD
65	Flat white	M	Am	Mick	1.5	65	24	GOOD	NA
63	Flat white	M	Am	Michelle	1.1	64	24	DEFECT	COLD
60	Latte	S	Am	Sue	2.1	63	25	DEFECT	COLD
66	Latte	L	Pm	Michelle	0.55	67	25	GOOD	NA
↑	↑	↑	↑	↑	↑	↑	↑		
Y	X^1	X^2	X^3	X^4	X^5	X^6	X^7		

If you want to set yourself up to be able to do a solid piece of work in analysing the relationship between variables and the primary metric, this is exactly how you do it.

Collection period

How long do you collect data for?

This is always a valid question, and one that must be discussed by the team. I've undertaken data collection for periods as little as half a day, and for as long as 4 months. It depends very much on the circumstances and type of project you are undertaking. In any case a decision needs to be made that allows collection of sufficient data to make logical assessments, yet not so much that you end up in a situation of 'paralysis by analysis'.

In your sampling plan, you should have identified how much data you need to collect, and you should stick to this fairly rigidly unless business constraints impede or you find there is a reason to change your plan.

Remember, this is a point in time analysis and a mechanism for identifying root causes as well as establishing baselines for future comparison. There is no need to continue sampling beyond what you need for analysis unless this is going to form part of the ongoing monitoring and control process.

ESTABLISH BASELINE PROCESS CAPABILITY (STEP 9)

To be able to determine process capability, it's vital we have a full understanding of probability distributions.

PROBABILITY DISTRIBUTIONS

One of the key concepts that you need to understand is that of a **random variable**. The term is a description of the assignment of numerical values to the outcomes that could occur within a specific experiment. For example, if an experiment involved pizza delivery, the random variable could be the delivery cycle time. If the experiment involved rolling a dice, the random variable could be the number of times '6' was rolled. The terms in this concept have the following meanings:

- **Random** – the outcome or result cannot be predicted with absolute certainty; and
- **Variable** – observed outcomes may vary.

All random variables can be characterised by probability distributions. The two types of probability distributions of concern to us that we will discuss in this book are these:

- Discrete Probability Distributions
- Continuous Probability Distributions

DISCRETE PROBABILITY DISTRIBUTIONS

Discrete random variables are those that are collected through *counting*.

When a random variable can only have specific values within a nominated range of numerical values, it is still referred to as discrete. However, this particular type of variable is the basis for what we refer to as discrete probability distributions. Examples include the number of hearts in 12 cards drawn from a deck of cards, number of heads that turned up in ten tosses of a coin.

A probability distribution for a discrete random variable is the full set of all possible outcomes and the associated probabilities of each outcome occurring. The sum of probabilities must equal 1.

The discrete probability distributions we will discuss are these.

- Binomial Distribution
- Poisson Distribution (pronounced pwah-san)
- Uniform Distribution

Binomial Probability Distribution

The binomial probability distribution has three important properties:

- Each trial has only *two possible outcomes* which are mutually exclusive and collectively exhaustive; for example: pass or fail, male or female, yes or no, defective or non defective, good or bad. This is known as the *Bernoulli Process*.
- The probability of each outcome (success or failure) remains constant from trial to trial.
- The outcome (success or failure) of a trial is independent of the outcome of any other trial.

The binomial probability distribution is characterised by two parameters:

- n – the number of trials
- p – the probability of obtaining a success, which remains constant from trial to trial

The following mathematical model represents the binomial probability distribution for obtaining a certain number of successes, given knowledge of the parameters n and p.

$$P(X = x \backslash n, p) = \frac{n!}{x!(n-x)!} p^x (1-p)^{n-x}$$

Where:

x = Some value of the random variable

n = Number of trials

p = Constant probability that the event will occur on each trial

! = Factorial: e.g., 6! = 6 x 5 x 4 x 3 x 2 x 1 = 720

Worked Example 1

A coin (one without bias) is tossed 4 times (or alternatively 4 coins could be tossed simultaneously). What is the probability that exactly 3 heads will turn up in 4 throws?

Using the equation provided, we find that the probability is 0.25 or in other words there is a 25 percent chance of getting 3 heads in 4 throws.

$$P(X = 3 \backslash n = 4, p = 0.5) = \frac{4!}{3!(4-3)!} 0.5^3 (1-0.5)^{4-3}$$

$$= 4(0.125)(0.5)$$

$$= 0.25$$

Binomial probability density function with MS Excel and Minitab Software:

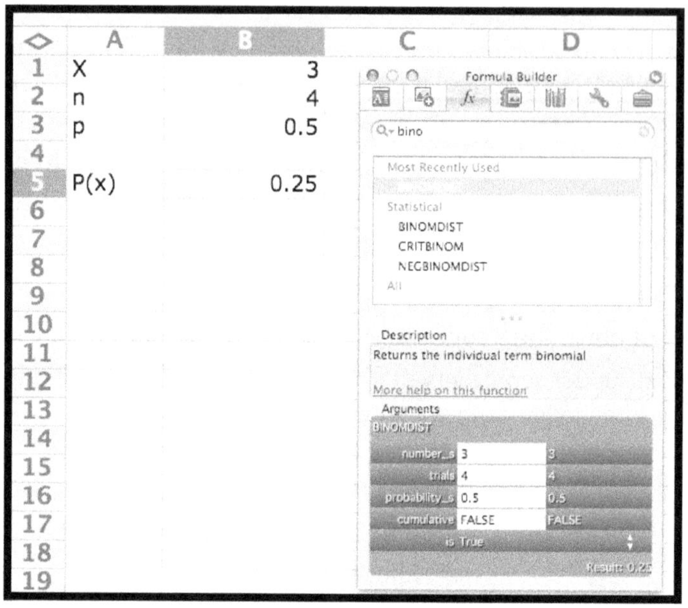

Figure 93: Binomial Probability Density Function - MS Excel

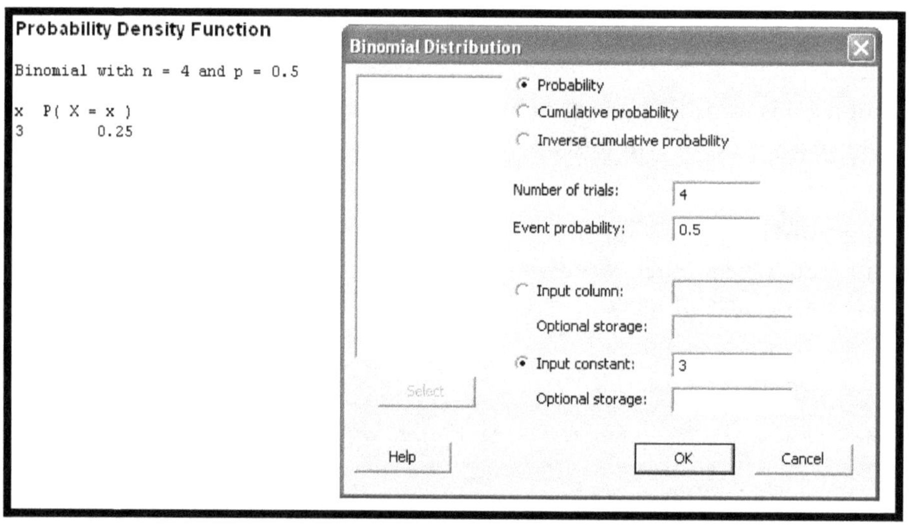

Figure 94: Binomial Probability Density Function - Minitab

<u>Worked Example 2</u>

We know that 10 percent of PCs delivered by the IT group do not have all of the necessary software loaded and are therefore considered defective.

If 10 items are selected at random on any given day, what is the probability only 1 will be found to be defective?

$$P(X=1 \setminus n=10, p=0.1) = \frac{10!}{1!(10-1)!}0.10^1(1-0.10)^{10-1}$$
$$= 0.3874$$

Binomial probability density function with MS Excel and Minitab Software:

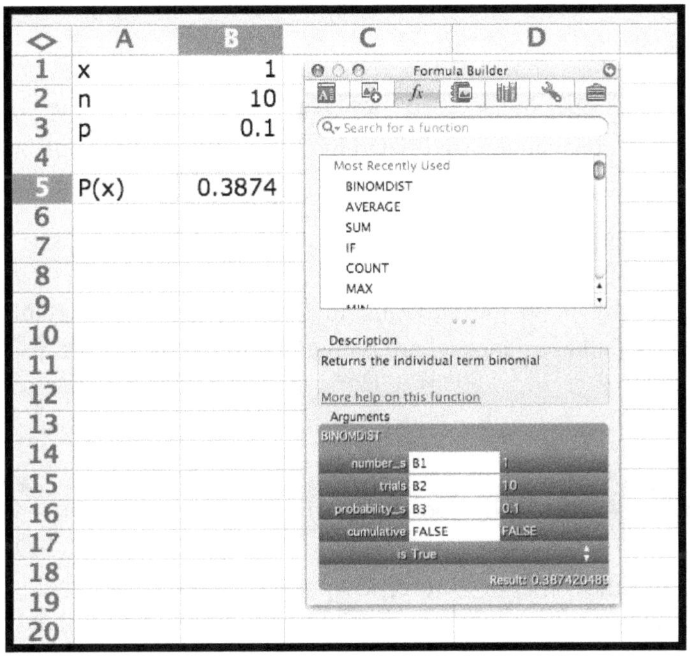

Figure 95: Binomial Probability Density Function - MS Excel

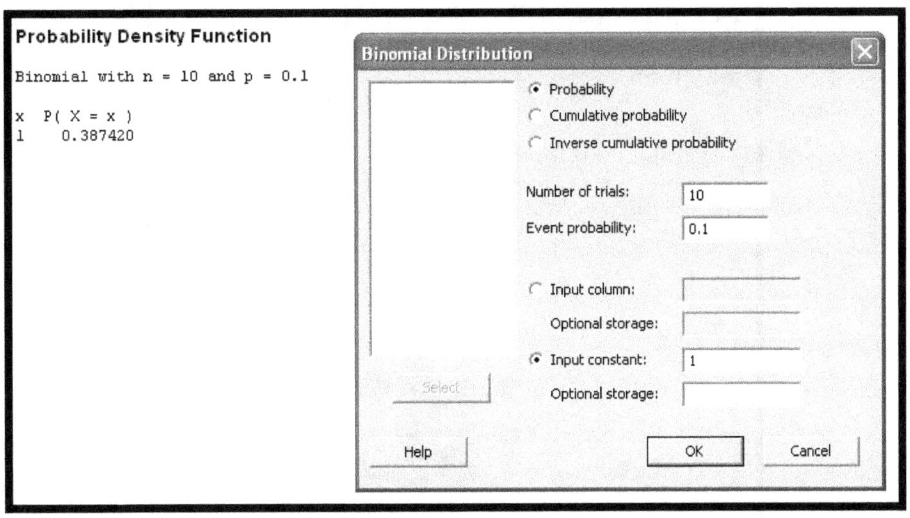

Figure 96: Binomial Probability Density Function - Minitab

Poisson Probability Distribution

The Poisson probability distribution is used to determine the probability of an occurrence within an area of opportunity (i.e. designated time interval, space, area or volume). For example, the probability of getting 5 customers in one hour, or the probability of getting only 1 unit with a defect.

The following mathematical model represents the Poisson probability distribution for obtaining a given number of occurrences when the average number of occurrences per time period or space is known.

$$P(X = x) = \frac{\lambda^x e^{-\lambda}}{x!}$$

Where:

x = Number of successes per area of opportunity in the sample

e = A constant approximated by 2.718281 – the base of the natural logarithm

λ = Expected number of successes per area of opportunity

! = Factorial: e.g. 6! = 6 x 5 x 4 x 3 x 2 x 1 = 720

You may see λ represented by μ in the equation in some text. An important property of the Poisson distribution is that the mean μ_x and variance σ^2 are both equal to the parameter λ.

Worked Example 1

A company web site experiences an average of 5 outages per month, what is the probability that it will experience only 3 outages in a month?

For more information about the value of e, refer to appendices for notes on Exponential Equations.

$$P(X = 3) = \frac{5^3(2.718281)^{-5}}{3!}$$

$$= \frac{125(0.006737957)}{6}$$

$$= 0.140374$$

Poisson probability density function with MS Excel and Minitab Software:

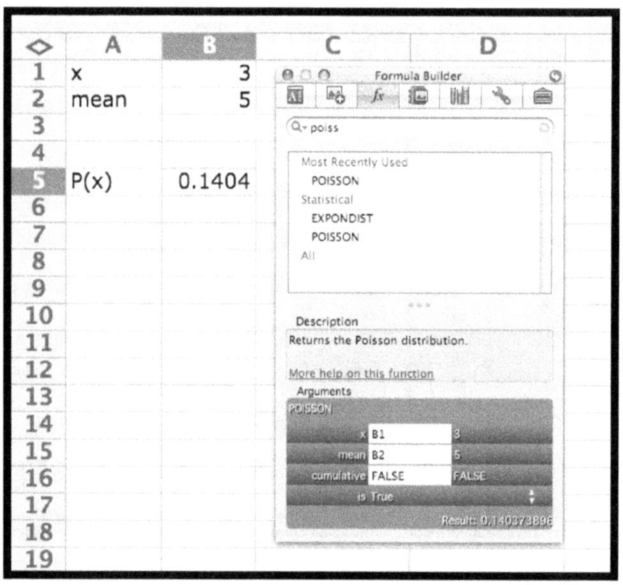

Figure 97: Poisson Probability Density Function - MS Excel

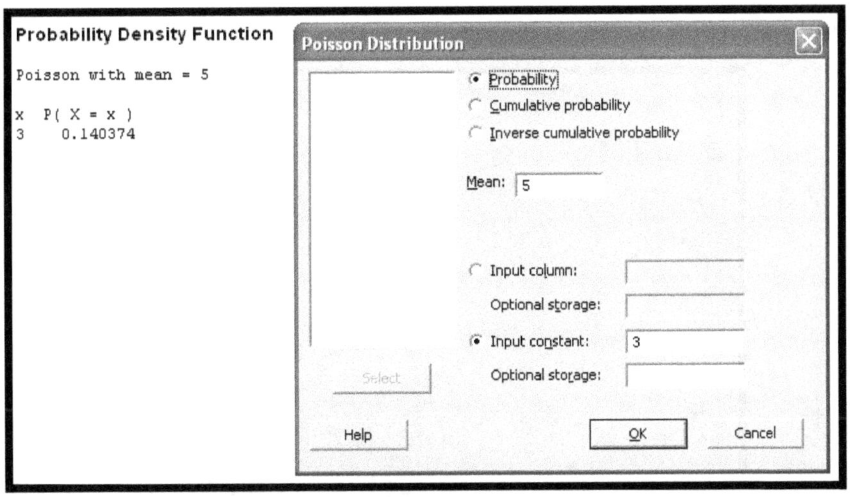

Figure 98: Poisson Probability Density Function - Minitab

Worked Example 2

A mine site dragline experiences an average of 16 hours downtime per month, what is the probability that it will experience only 8 hours downtime in a month?

$$P(X=8)=\frac{16^{8}(2.718281)^{-16}}{8!}$$
$$=\frac{4{,}294{,}967{,}296(0.000000112)}{40{,}320}$$
$$=0.0119875$$

Poisson probability density function with MS Excel and Minitab Software:

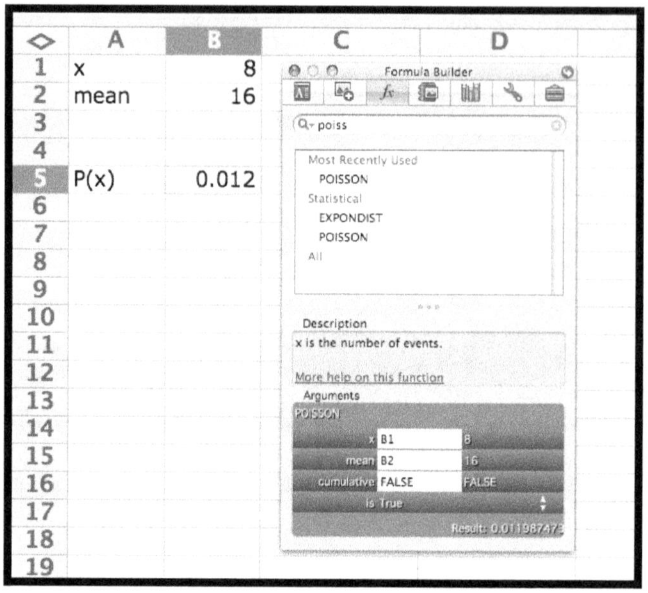

Figure 99: Poisson Probability Density Function - MS Excel

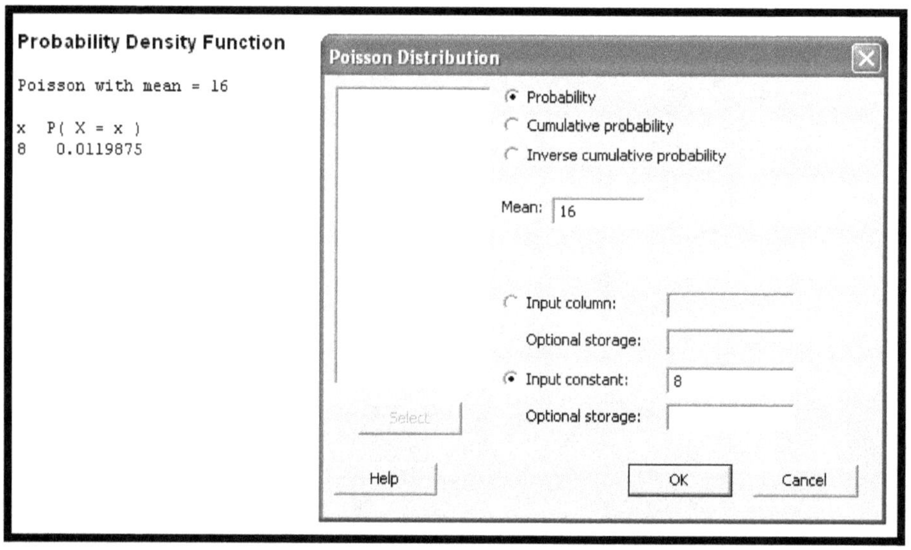

Figure 100: Poisson Probability Density Function - Minitab

Uniform Probability Distribution

A uniform distribution is one in which the probability of occurrence of each value of the random variable is the same.

Worked Example 1

If a single unbiased dice is rolled, the probability distribution associated with results is uniform – the probability of getting each value in a single roll is the same for each, 1/6th or 0.1666.

Worked Example 2

If an unbiased coin is thrown, the probability distribution associated with results is uniform – the probability of getting a HEAD is 0.5, and a TAIL is 0.5.

CONTINUOUS PROBABILITY DISTRIBUTIONS

When a random variable can take on any value within a specific range of values, it is referred to as a 'continuous random variable'. Examples would include values associated with height, weight, time, length etc.

Normal Probability Distribution

The most important of all continuous probability distributions is the **normal probability distribution**, as these are the basis for many inferential techniques used in Six Sigma.

The normal distribution is characterised by two parameters:

- Mean
- Standard Deviation

The figure below shows three different normal distribution curves. Each has the same mean (μ), however different standard deviations (σ).

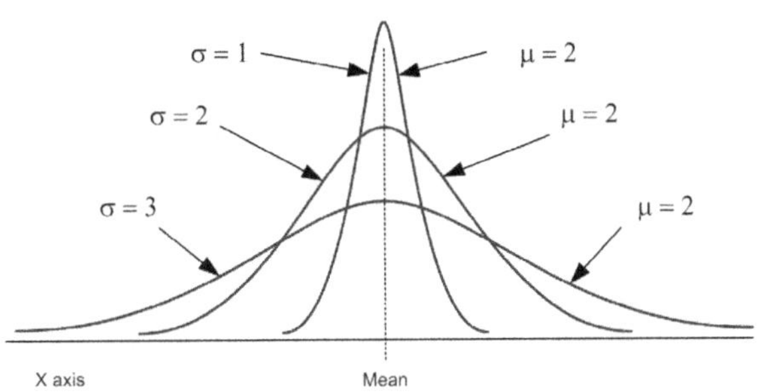

Figure 101: Normal Distribution Curves - Same Mean, Different Standard Deviations

The following figure shows three normal distribution curves once again.

This time they each have different means (μ), however the same standard deviation (σ).

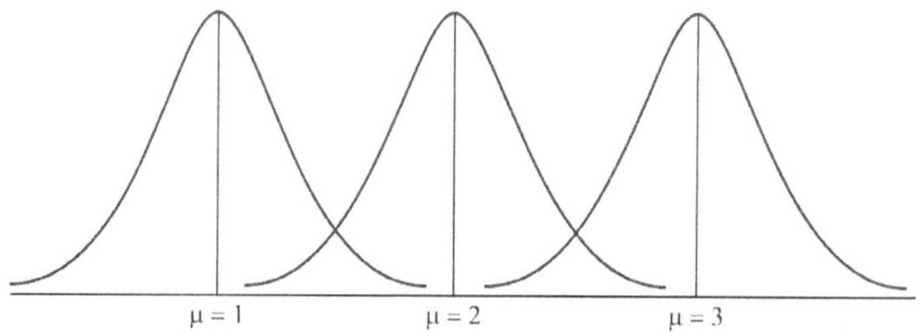

Figure 102: Normal Distribution Curves - Different Mean, Same Standard Deviation

We can see from the distribution curves above that changing the mean only changes the location of the curve. By contrast, the standard deviation controls the shape of the curve. As the standard deviation gets smaller, the thinner the curve becomes.

The properties of the normal distribution are these.

- **Symmetrical** – the mean is located in the centre with an equal amount of data on each side
- **Bell Shaped** – data is concentrated towards the centre, a result of greater relative frequencies near the mean and less towards the extremes
- **Asymptotic to the x-axis** – the curve associated with the distribution is infinite and theoretically extends indefinitely in both directions without touching the axis
- **Proportions of Data Within the Curve are Predictable** - this is often referred to as the empirical rule of probability, and it only applies to curves of this type. The proportions of data underneath the normal distribution curve are as follows.

Between +/- 1σ of the mean = 68.26 percent

Between +/- 2σ of the mean = 95.44 percent

Between +/- 3σ of the mean = 99.73 percent

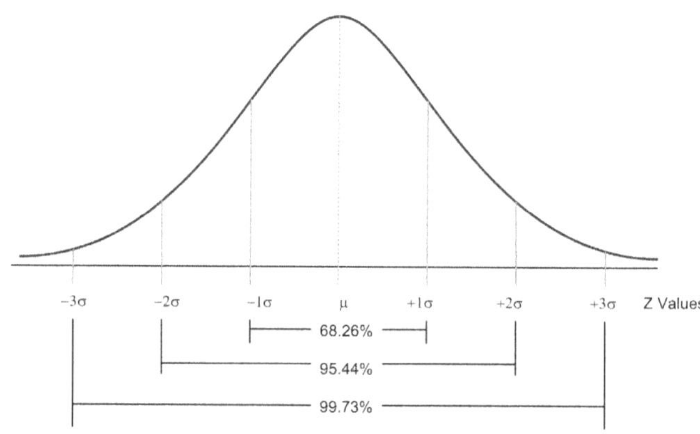

Figure 103: Proportion of Data Beneath The Normal Distribution Curve

'Standard' Normal Distribution

A data value that is *standardised* is one that has been converted to a value (called a standard normal score) that represents its relative position underneath the curve in the number of standard deviations from the mean.

For example, a data value of 24 will have a standard normal score of 2.5 if it is 2.5 standard deviations above the mean. A data point that is positioned 1.35 standard deviations below the mean will have a standard normal score of –1.35.

Data that follows any normal distribution can be standardised by using the following equation.

$$Z = \frac{x - \mu}{\sigma}$$

Where:

Z = Standard normal score

x = Value of the random variable

μ = Mean

σ = Standard deviation

When the distribution is standardised, the proportion of data underneath any part of the curve can be determined, as we already know how much data exists between standard deviations.

By referring to a table known as a Z table (shown in appendices) we can determine the proportion of data that exists between any two Z values of a standard normal distribution. Once we determine the proportion, we are able to determine the probability of getting a value within that range of data.

The standard normal distribution always has these characteristics: $\mu = 0$, and $\sigma = 1$.

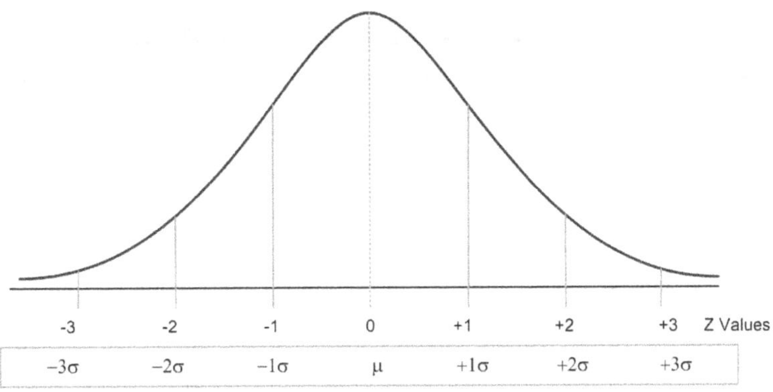

Figure 104: The Standard Normal Distribution

<u>Worked Example</u>

Suppose the cycle time for manufacturing a piece of equipment is normally distributed with $\mu = 26.75$ hours, and $\sigma = 1.5$ hours.

If an employee is selected at random, what is the probability that it will take the employee less than 24 hours to produce an item of equipment?

Step 1

Draw a hypothetical distribution with relevant data.

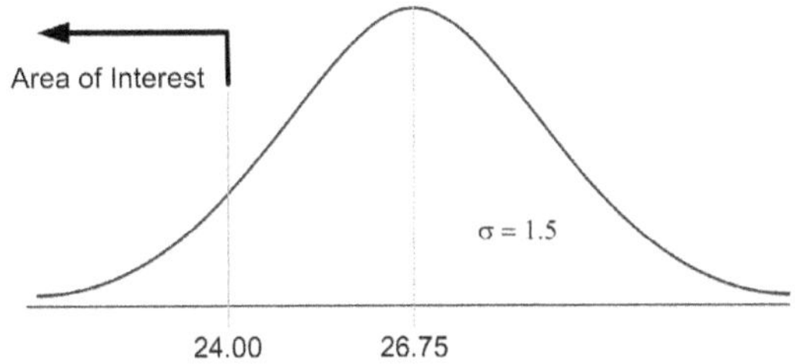

Step 2

Standardise the nominated value or values.

$$Z = \frac{x-\mu}{\sigma} = \frac{24-26.75}{1.5} = 1.83$$

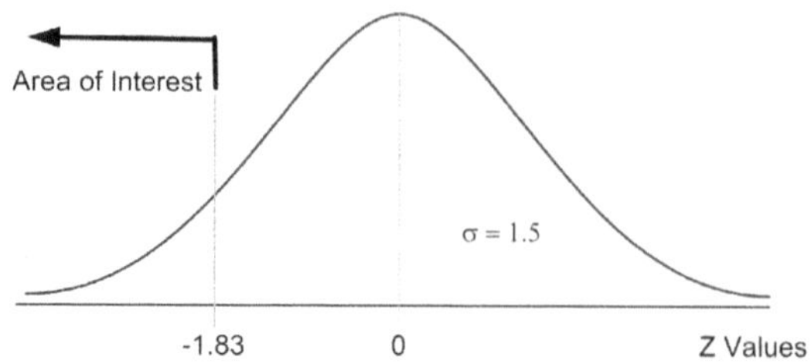

Step 3

Refer to Z Table (appendices) to determine the area of interest underneath the curve.

The area between Z Values of 0 and –1.83 = 0.4664

The area below Z value of –1.83 = 0.5 – 0.4664 = 0.0336

The probability of doing the task in less than 24 hours is 0.0336 or 3.36 percent.

Normal Probability Calculations with MS Excel and Minitab

As with many other distributions, Microsoft Excel and Minitab software have the capability to analyse normal probabilities.

<u>Worked Example</u>

Suppose that the breaking strength of a particular dimension rope is normally distributed with $\mu = 150.776$ kilograms and $\sigma = 2.175$ kilograms.

What proportion of ropes produced by this manufacturer will be less than the customers' specification of a minimum breaking strength of 147 kilograms?

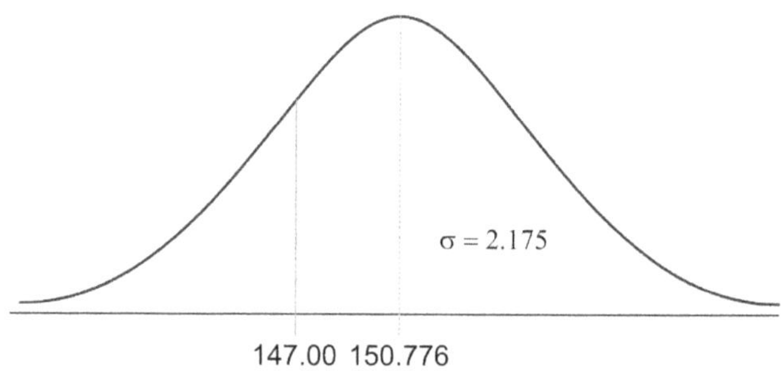

To solve the problem using MS Excel or Minitab, simply enter the values for *x*, the mean, and standard deviation to obtain the relevant cumulative probability.

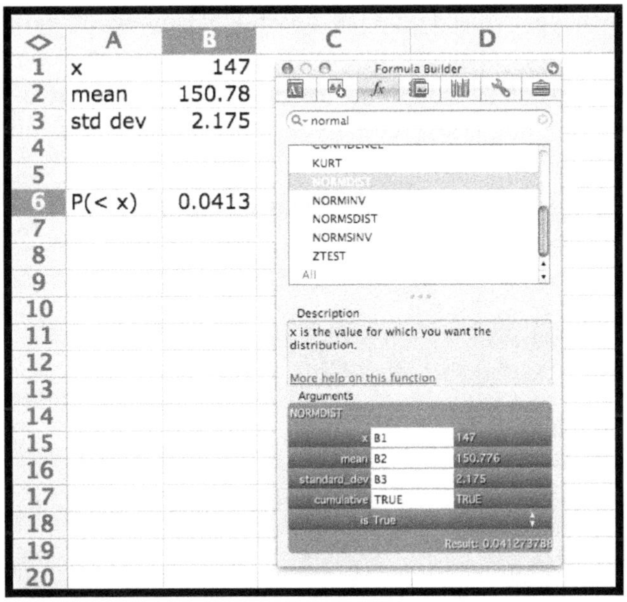

Figure 105: Normal Cumulative Distribution - MS Excel

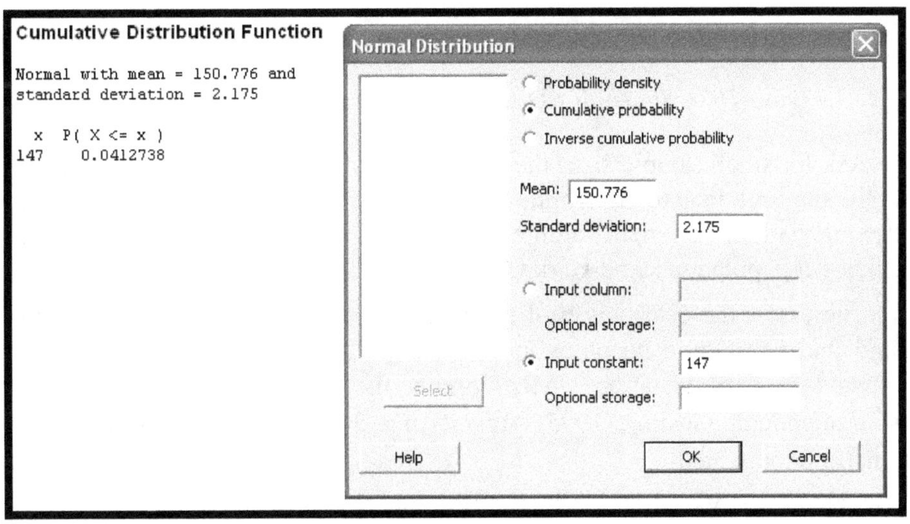

Figure 106: Normal Cumulative Distribution - Minitab

In both cases, we can see that the 0.041273 or 4.12 percent of ropes will have a breaking strength of less than 147 kg. Thus 4.12 percent of product will be defective.

Student's t Distribution

William Sealy Gosset, a brewery worker in the United Kingdom who applied statistical analysis to improve brewing processes, developed the *t* distribution. Gosset was continually frustrated with the application of the standard normal distribution when working with small sample sizes. He found that his data generally had more variation than that which was predicated by statistical theory.

The breakthrough came when he realised that an additional source of variation existed, and that was variation between the estimation of standard deviation s, and the true population standard deviation σ. Gosset was able to determine the exact sampling distribution of the variable, but due to the fact that the organisation he worked for did not allow employees to publish, he published his results under the pseudonym 'Student'.

The name stuck, and this distribution is often referred to as 'Student's t'.

The t distribution is similar in shape to the standard normal distribution, however it is generally flatter with greater area in the tails.

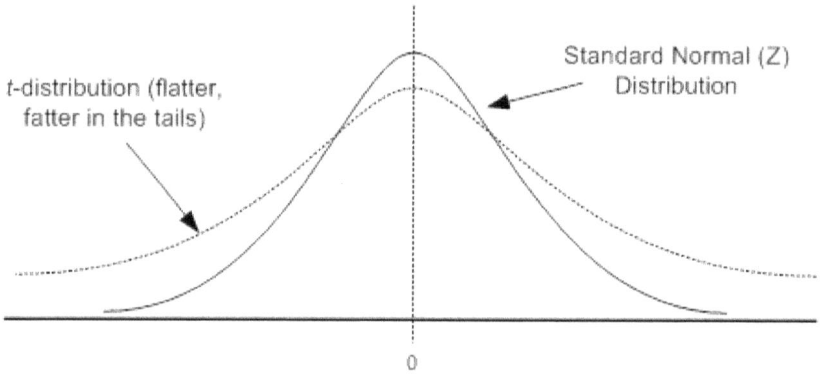

Figure 107 : Student's t Distribution versus Normal Distribution

As Gosset discovered, for small sample sizes the t statistic has greater variability than the z statistic. This is primarily driven by the fact that to determine both t and z statistics, we are required to estimate the population standard deviation. For small sample sizes, the sample standard deviation s, is not an accurate estimate of the unknown population standard deviation σ, as variation is greater with small samples.

As sample sizes n increases, the distribution of the t statistic shows decreasing variability. The area in the tails decreases and the distribution becomes more peaked. This is due to the fact that as sample sizes increase, the estimated standard deviation s, gets closer to the true population standard deviation σ. As the sample size gets large enough, Gosling (1995) suggests $n \geq 30$, the t distribution looks very similar to the standard normal distribution.

As you may have already worked out, the t distribution depends on sample size. This dependence is expressed as a quantity known as **degrees of freedom**. This is denoted by the Greek symbol, ν (nu). When we vary the sample size n, we vary the degrees of freedom, and also the shape of the distribution as shown in the diagram on the following page.

Gosset's need to quantify small experiments resulted in the development of the probability integral of the ratio previously referred to as the t statistic. This statistic is calculated by:

$$t = \frac{\overline{X} - \mu}{s/\sqrt{n}}$$

One of the most common applications of the Student's t test involves hypothesis about the means of samples. This is discussed at length in the section on Hypothesis testing.

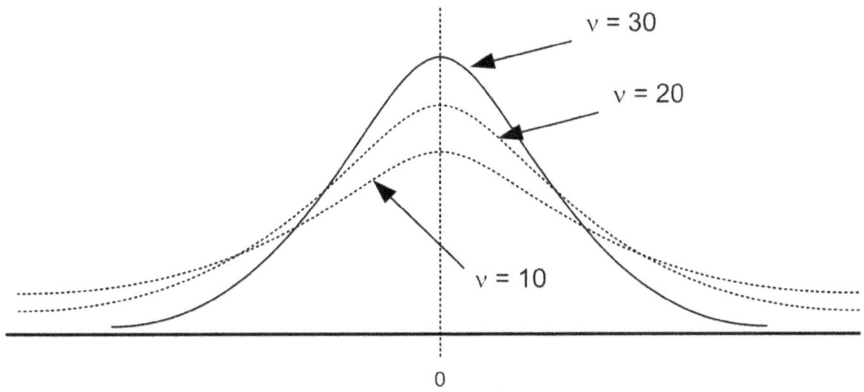

Figure 108: Distribution Curves with Varying Degrees of Freedom

Chi-square Distribution

In instances where data has the characteristics of a normal distribution, it can be mathematically shown that the distribution of sample variances follows a Chi-square distribution, symbolised as χ^2. The Chi-square distribution is skewed to the right and varies according to degrees of freedom, denoted by the Greek symbol ν (nu). Because the Chi-square distribution is formed from combinations of random variables, they are generally not used to model physical phenomena like you do with the exponential distribution. They are used to construct confidence intervals and make decisions.

The probability density function for the Chi-square distribution is given by:

$$f(\chi^2) = \frac{e^{-\chi^2/2}(\chi^2)^{(\nu-2)/2}}{2^{\nu/2}\left(\frac{\nu-2}{2}\right)}$$

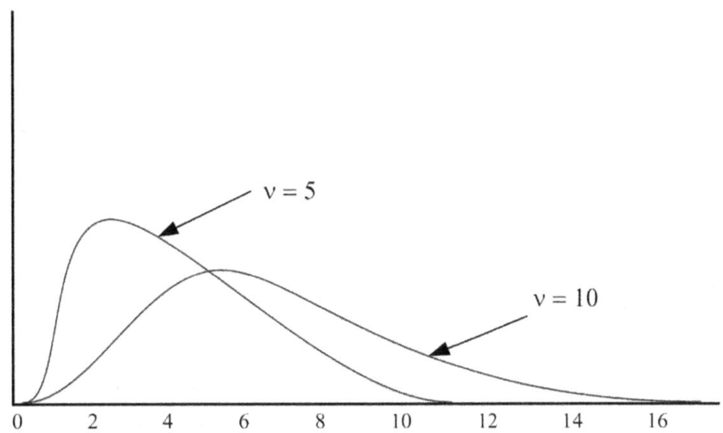

Figure 109: Chi-square Distribution

As you will see later in the section dealing with Hypothesis testing, Chi-square distributions can also be used to test for differences in two proportions using the χ^2 statistic, given by:

$$\chi^2 = \sum \frac{(fo - fe)^2}{fe}$$

Where:

fo = observed frequency

fe = theoretical or expected frequency

F Distribution

When two samples are drawn independently from a population [irrespective of sample size], the ratio of the two measures of variability divided by their respective degrees of freedom follows a distribution known as the F distribution. Similar in shape to the Chi-square distribution, in that starting at zero it is skewed to the right and varies according to degrees of freedom.

In the case of the F distribution, the exact shape of the distribution is determined by two degrees of freedom; one for the numerator of the ratio, v_1, and one for the denominator of the ratio, v_2.

The F statistic is given by the equation:

$$F = \frac{s_1^2}{s_2^2}$$

One of the most common applications of the F test involves studying the equality of population means using the analysis of variance procedure. This is discussed at length in the section on Hypothesis testing.

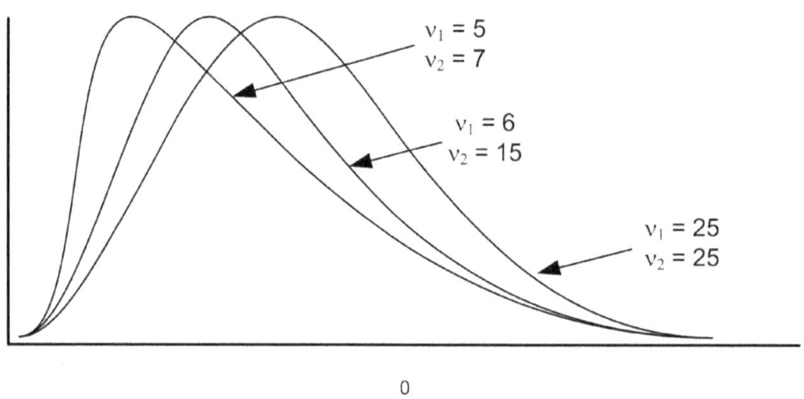

Figure 110: F Distribution

The Exponential Distribution

The exponential distribution is widely used in queueing theory. In this type of application it is used to model the length of time between arrivals at any service facility. Examples include time between arrivals at checkout counters, toll ways on highways, ATM machines and the emergency room in a hospital. The distribution is also used in the study of reliability of plant. The distribution can be used to model time between failures. The distribution is defined by one parameter, λ. (Lambda)

The mathematical model shown represents the probability density function for the length of time between arrivals or failures.

$$f(x) = \lambda e^{-\lambda x} \text{ for } x > 0$$

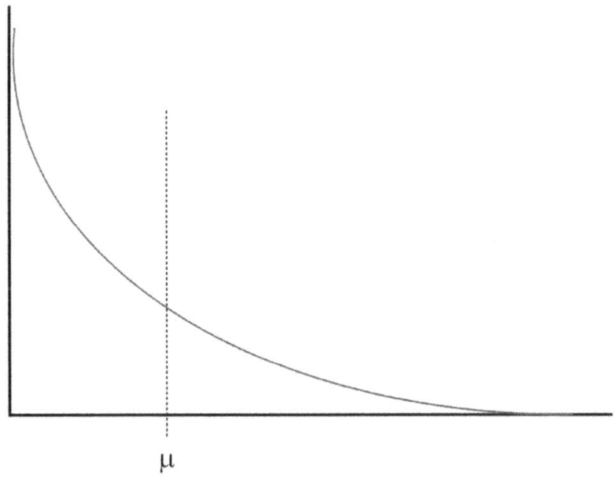

Figure 111: Exponential Distribution

The exponential distribution is highly skewed with most of the area underneath the curve falling below the mean. In fact more than 60 percent of the area underneath the curve falls below the mean.

In most cases, the user is interested in the probability associated with the length of time between arrivals or failures. The cumulative distribution for the probability associated with the length of time before the next arrival or failure being less than a nominated value (x), is given by:

$$P(X \leq x) = 1 - e^{-\lambda x}$$

Where:

x = Some value of the random variable

e = A constant 2.718281 – the base of the natural logarithm (refer to appendices)

λ = The average number of events (arrivals/failures) per unit of time

Probabilities can be determined directly from the equation as it is a closed form cumulative density function. Therefore, unlike the normal distribution, no table of areas underneath the curve is necessary.

Worked Example 1

Suppose a company web site experiences an average of 5 outages per month (60 per year / 365 days). What is the probability the next outage will occur in 4 weeks (28 days)?

For this example:

$x = 28$

e = a constant 2.718281 – the base of the natural logarithm (refer to appendices)

$\lambda = 0.164$ (average number of failures per day)

$$P(X \le 28) = 1 - e^{-0.164(28)}$$
$$= 1 - 2.718281^{-4.592}$$
$$= 1 - 0.010132587$$
$$= 0.989867413$$
$$= 98.98\%$$

Exponential cumulative distribution function with MS Excel:

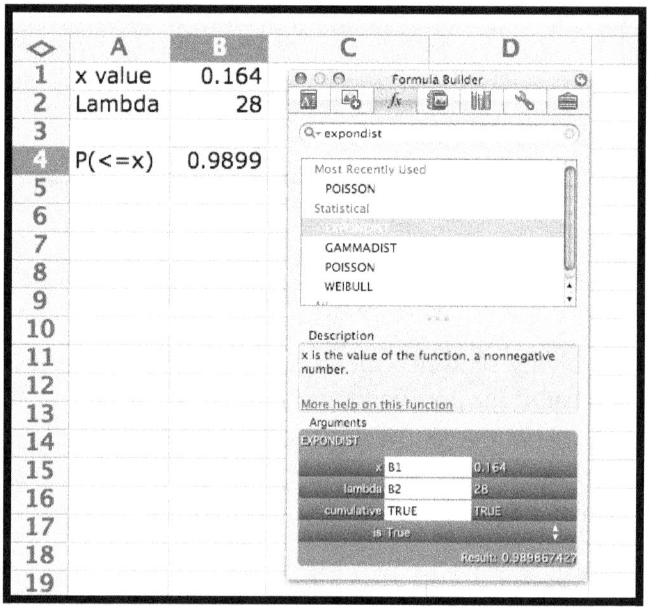

Figure 112: Exponential Cumulative Distribution Function - MS Excel

<u>Worked Example 2</u>

Suppose a piece of machinery breaks down an average of 3 times per month (36 times per year or 8760 hours).

If we have just repaired the machine today and it's Friday, what is the probability that the on call service team will be called out this weekend? (between 5pm Friday and 6am Monday)?

For this example:

$x = 61$ hours (time the team will be on call over the weekend)

e = a constant 2.718281 – the base of the natural logarithm (refer to appendices)

$\lambda = 0.004109589$ (average number of failures per hour)

$$P(Time \le 61) = 1 - e^{-0.004109589(61)}$$
$$= 1 - 2.718281^{-0.250684929}$$
$$= 1 - 0.778267601$$
$$= 0.221732399$$

Exponential cumulative density function with MS Excel:

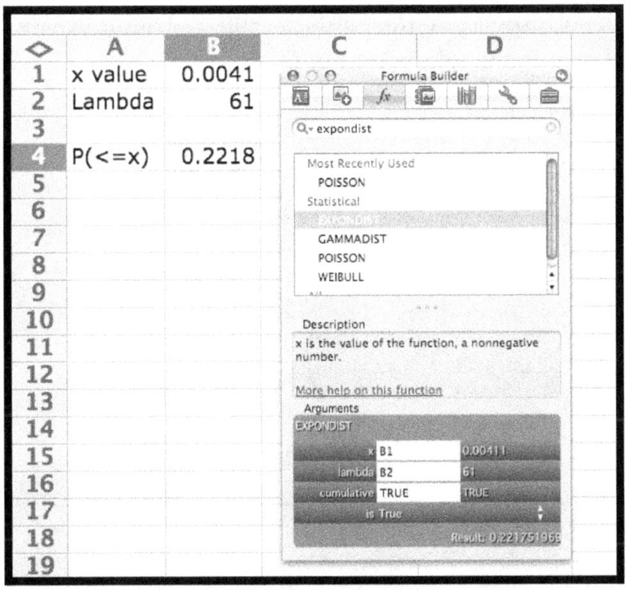

Figure 113: Exponential Cumulative Density Function - MS Excel

The Weibull Distribution

The Weibull distribution can be used to study and model many phenomena including time until failure, time to repair and strength of material. The distribution is defined by two parameters; α (alpha) and β (beta).

The α value represents a parameter for the shape of the distribution. The β value represents a parameter for the scale or size of the units in which X is measured. The *shape* parameter gives the Weibull distribution considerable flexibility. By changing the shape parameter, the distribution can model a wide variety of distributions.

The exponential distribution, discussed in the previous pages, is a special case of the Weibull distribution in which $\alpha = 1$, and $\beta = 1/\lambda$. If $\alpha = 2$, the Weibull distribution is identical to the Rayleigh distribution.

The Weibull distribution will approximate the normal distribution when $\alpha = 3$ to 4.

The effects of changing the shape parameter α are shown in the following figure.

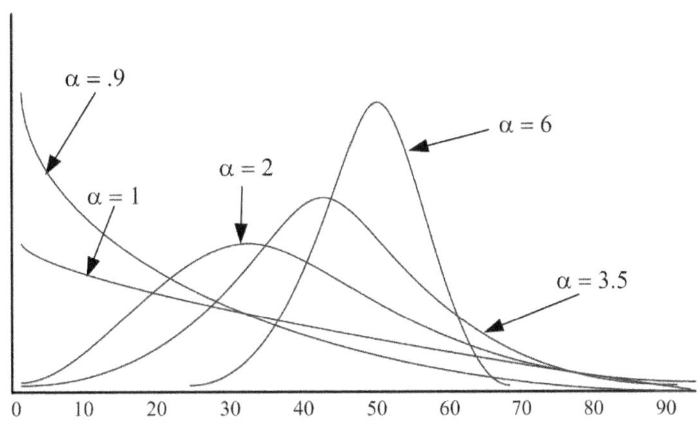

Figure 114: Weibull Distribution - Shape Parameter Changes

The *scale* parameter β, which corresponds to the 63rd percentile, determines the range of the distribution. Its effect on the distribution is shown in the following figure.

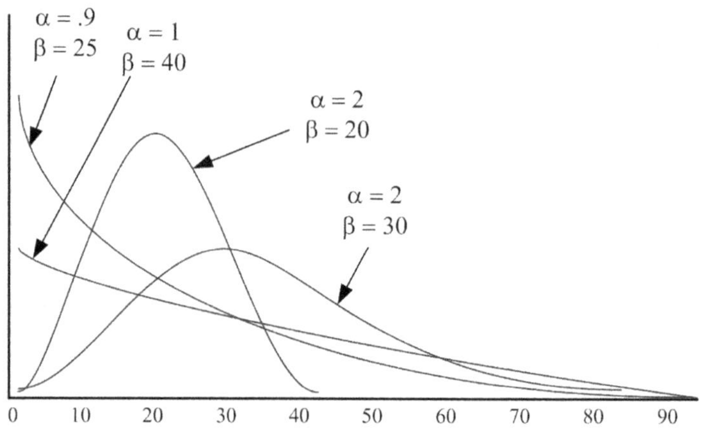

Figure 115 : Weibull Distribution - Scale Parameter Impact on The Distribution

The probability density function for the variable X, that follows a Weibull distribution is given by:

$$f(X)=\frac{\alpha}{\beta^{\alpha}}X^{\alpha-1}e^{-(x/\beta)^{\alpha}} \text{ for } X\geq 0$$

The cumulative distribution function for the probability associated with the length of time being studied being less than a nominated value (x), is given by:

$$P(X\leq x)=1-e^{-(x/\beta)^{\alpha}}$$

Where:

x = Some value of the random variable

α = A shape parameter for the distribution

β = A parameter for the size of the units being measured

e = A constant 2.718281 – the base of the natural logarithm

Worked Example 1

Suppose once again a company web site experiences an average of 5 outages per month (60 outages per year / 365 days). What is the probability that the next outage will occur in 4 weeks (28 days)? We know that x in this case follows an exponential distribution.

For this example:

$x = 28$

e = a constant 2.718281 – the base of the natural logarithm (refer to appendices)

$\alpha = 1$

$\lambda = 0.164$ (average number of failures per day)

$\beta = 6.09756$ (we know that $\beta = 1/\lambda$)

$$P(X \leq 28) = 1 - 2.718281^{-(28/6.09756)^{1}}$$
$$= 1 - 2.718281^{-4.592}$$
$$= 1 - 0.010132587$$
$$= 0.989867413$$

Note the result is exactly the same as with the exponential cumulative probability function.

Weibull cumulative probability function with MS Excel and Minitab:

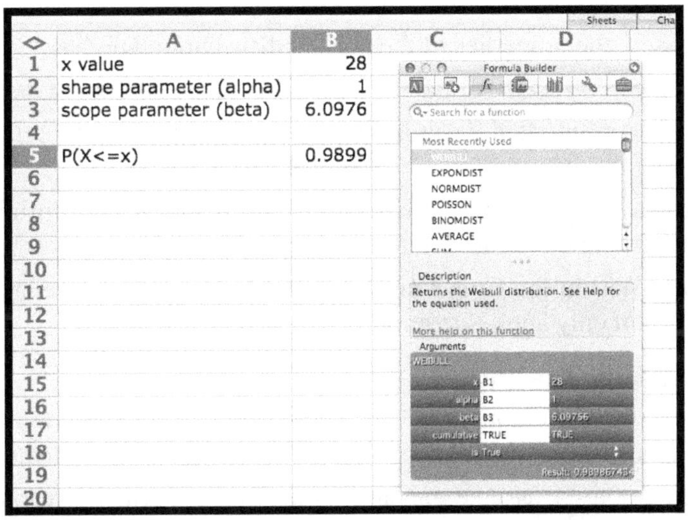

Figure 116: Weibull Cumulative Probability Function – MS Excel

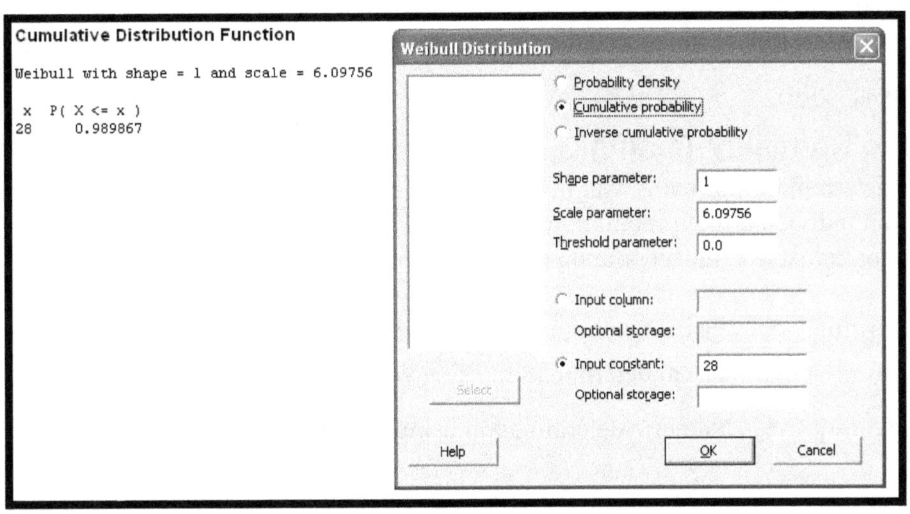

Figure 117: Weibull Cumulative Probability Function – Minitab

Key Learning Points

- *Probability Distributions* fall within one of two categories – Discrete Probability Distributions or Continuous Probability Distributions
- The most important of all continuous probability distributions is the *normal distribution*
- Values in a normal distribution can be *standardised* by determining how many standard deviations a value is away from the mean
- Probability can be *estimated for various distributions* using equations and functions offered in software packages such as MS Excel and Minitab

TESTING FOR NORMALITY

When we test a data set for normality, the intent is not to determine whether or not the data is normal, but rather if the data has the *same properties* as a normal distribution.

As we have already discussed, the properties of the normal distribution are these.

- **Symmetrical** – the mean is located in the centre with an equal amount of data on each side
- **Bell Shaped** – data is concentrated towards the centre, a result of greater relative frequencies near the mean and less towards the extremes
- **Asymptotic to the x-axis** – the curve associated with the distribution is infinite and theoretically extends indefinitely in both directions without touching the axis
- **Proportions of Data Within the Curve are Predictable** - this is often referred to as the empirical rule of probability and it only applies to curves of this type.

Why Undertake Normality Testing

Why would we want to undertake normality testing? Many statistical analysis tools or tests assume that the data under analysis follows a specific distribution. These methods are referred to as 'parametric tests'.

A number of these 'parametric tests' assume the data comes from a normal distribution, thus there is a need to determine if a sample of data is normal or comes from a normally distributed population. Some of the tools or tests that fall into this category include:

- T Tests and Z Tests
- Analysis of Variance
- Process Capability

Approaches to Normality Testing

Approaches for determining normality can be either *subjective* or *objective* in their assessment. Subjective approaches rely on individual interpretation, whilst objective approaches rely on statistical methods to make decisions about normality. The most common approaches include:

Subjective Testing	• Visual determination using Histograms • Visual determination using Normal Probability Plots
Objective Testing	• Numeric determination using Normality Tests

Subjective Method 1 - Histograms

With the histogram, determination as to whether or not the data set is approximately normal is made by visually observing to see if the data set has the properties of a normal distribution. The properties we can visualise are (a) symmetry and (b) shape.

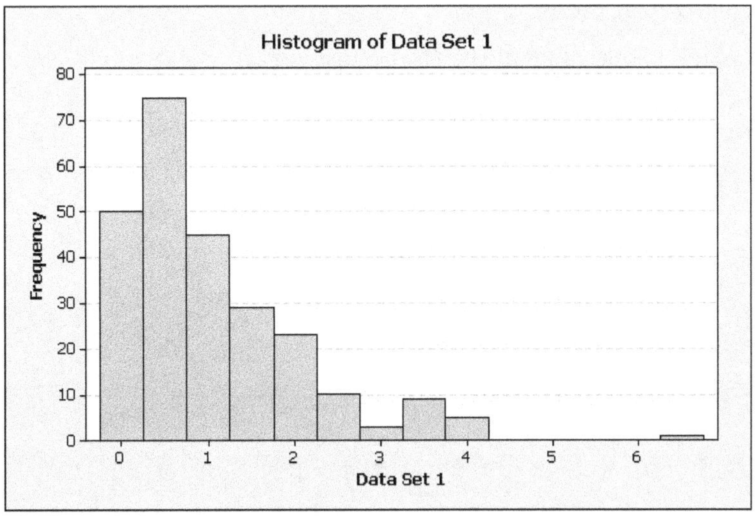

Figure 118: Histogram - Non Normal Data Set

In this particular case, we can see that the distribution is skewed; therefore its *lack of symmetry* is such that we would say that it is 'not normal'. In fact, this particular data set is in fact 'exponentially' distributed.

The following figure provides a good example of a distribution that does look 'approximately normal'. It shows both symmetry and a bell shape.

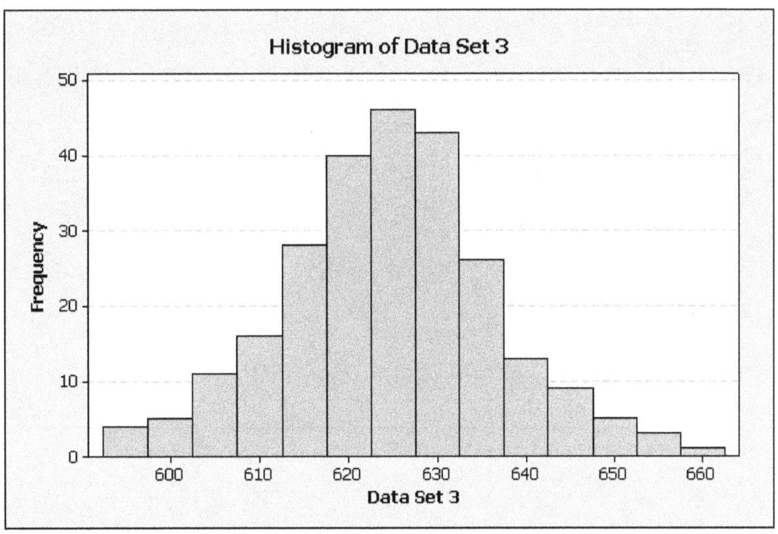

Figure 119: Histogram - Normal Data Set

Histograms are not the only way to visualise a distribution.

Subjective Method 2 - Normal Probability Plots

Normal probability plots are another graphical method of visually determining if a distribution is approximately normally distributed. This approach involves the transformation of the vertical scale of cumulative probabilities in a special way.

To explain this, let's revisit the areas underneath the normal curve.

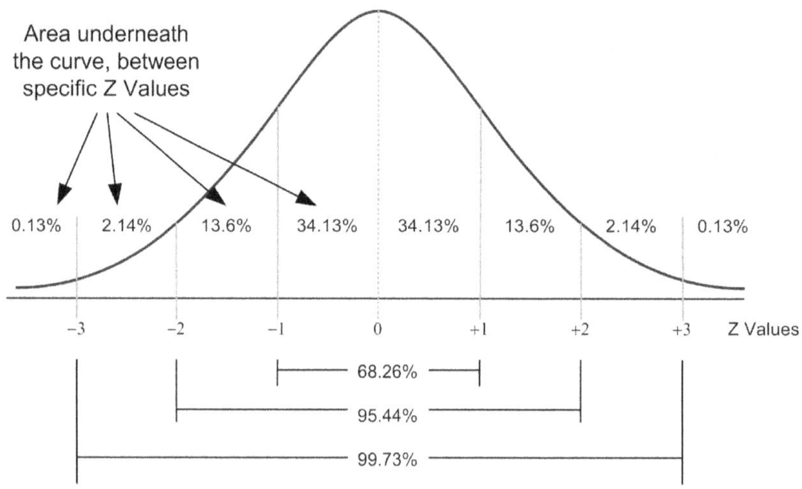

Figure 120: Proportions Beneath the Standard Normal Distribution Curve

In the previous diagram, we see how much of the distribution can be found between Z values (the number of standard deviations a specific value is from the mean). For example, 2.14 percent of the data is located between Z values of –2 and –3. Hence, the probability of getting a result between those two Z values is 0.0214 or 2.14 percent.

If we look at this from a cumulative perspective, from left to right, we get the following result.

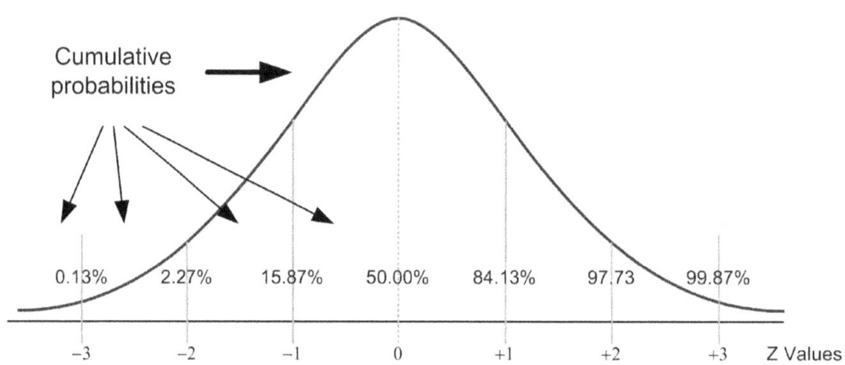

Figure 121: Cumulative Probabilities - Standard Normal Distribution

In this case, we can see that 15.87 percent of the distribution is located to the left of the Z value of –1. We can also see that 84.13 percent of the distribution is to the left of the Z value of +1.

If we plot these Z values against their corresponding cumulative percentages, we can create a 'cumulative probability polygon'.

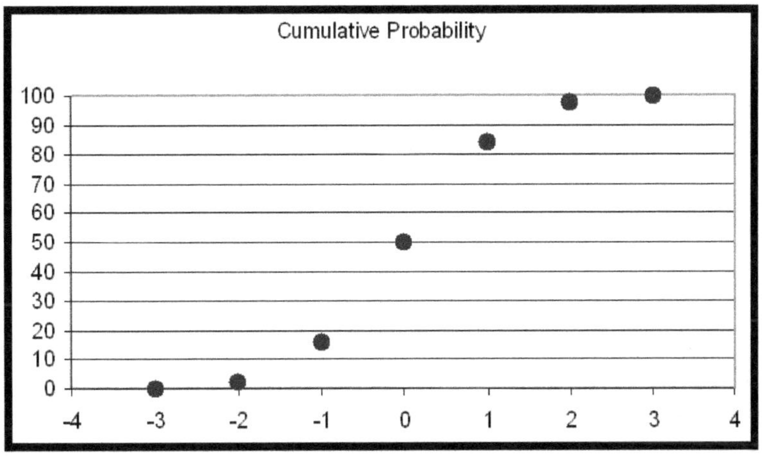

Figure 122: Cumulative Probability Polygon - Normal Distribution

The previous diagram shows the S-shaped cumulative probability polygon typical of a normal distribution. In creating a normal probability plot, the vertical Y-axis is transformed in such a way, that the data points of a normal distribution can be plotted approximately along a straight line.

When any data set is plotted on the same transformed Y-axis, if it approximately forms a straight line, the distribution of data will be approximately normally distributed. Let's continue with two examples.

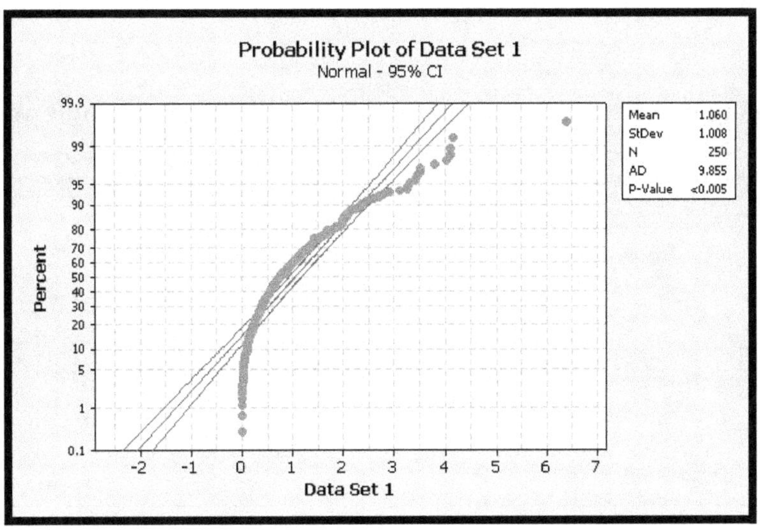

Figure 123: Probability Plot - Non Normal Data Set

Once the normal probability plot is created, the determination as to whether or not the data set is approximately normal is made by visually observing how closely the plotted values fit the straight line. If the data set has the properties of a normal distribution, the values will closely follow the straight line.

In this particular case, we know that the distribution is skewed [remember our histogram]. Notice that the plotted values do not closely fit the straight line, therefore we would conclude that it's 'not normal'.

The data set in the following plot provide a good example of a distribution that does look 'approximately normal'. The plotted values closely fit the straight line.

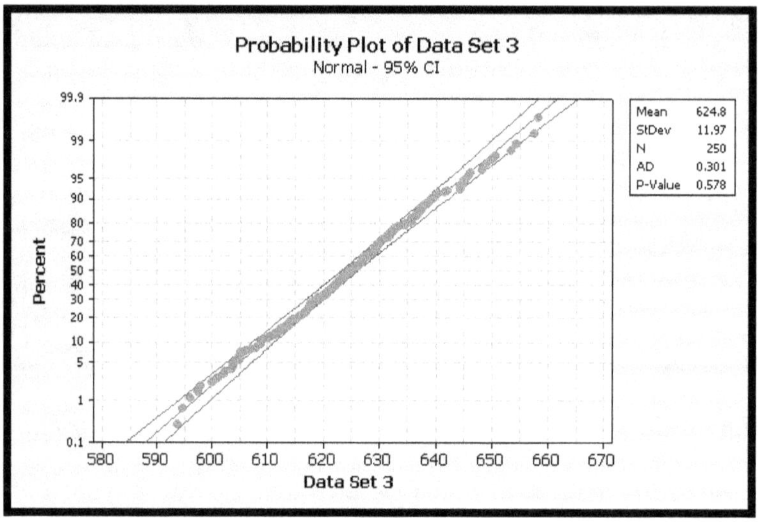

Figure 124: Probability Plot - Normal Data

Common Normal Probability Plot Patterns

The following table shows some of the common patterns that you will observe with particular distribution types.

Probability Plot Pattern	**Distribution Equivalent**
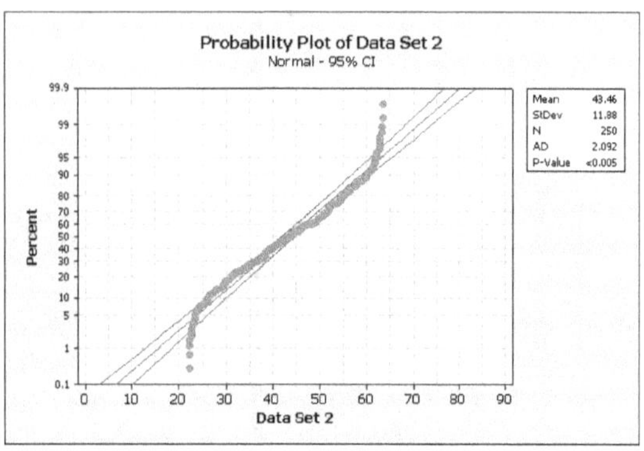	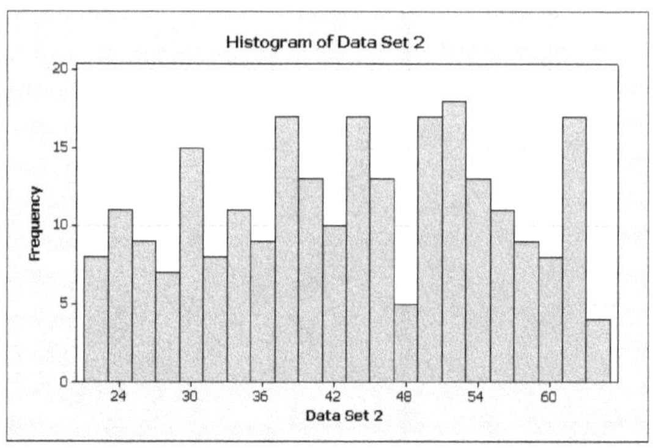

Probability Plot Pattern | **Distribution Equivalent**

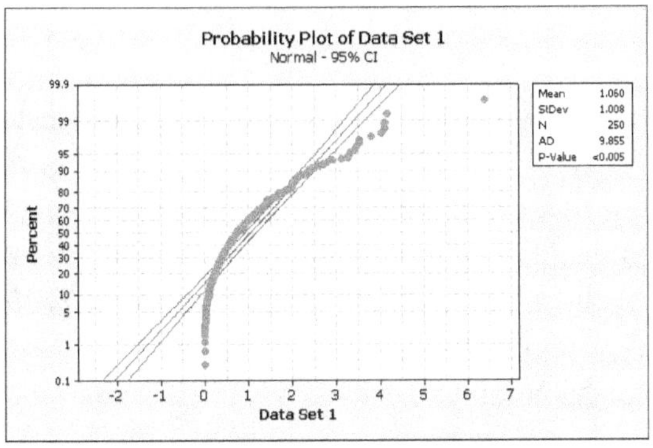

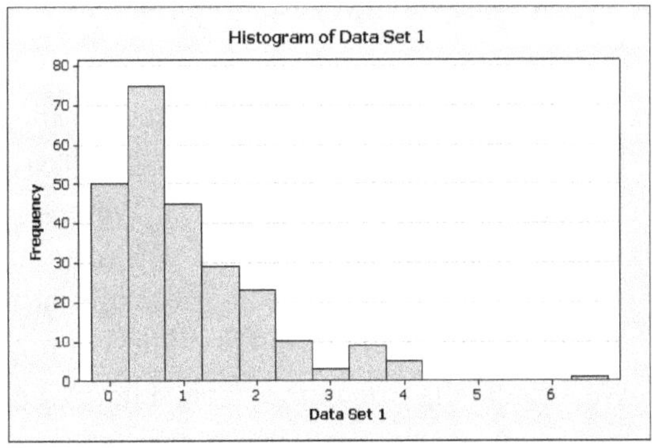

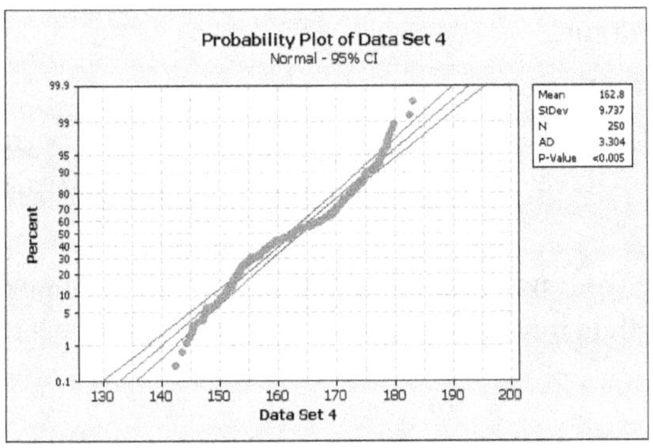

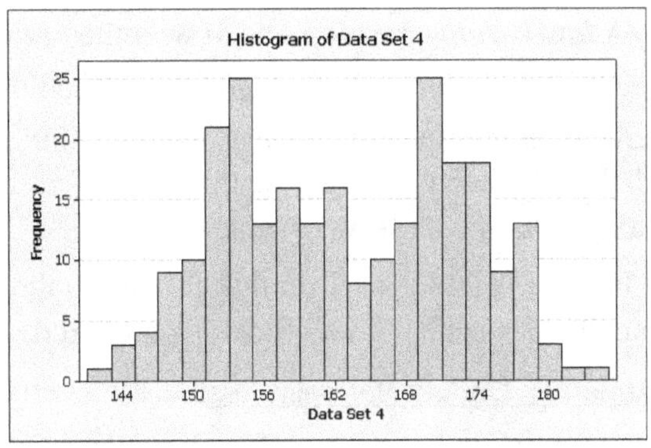

Limitations With Subjective Testing Methods

The limitation of using Histograms or Normal Probability Plots is that they rely on interpretation. At what point is the departure from the symmetrical bell shape, or fit with the straight line, sufficient to say that the data is not normally distributed?

One way to overcome these issues is to use statistical methods to make determinations about normality.

Objective Method 1 - Anderson Darling Normality Test

The Anderson-Darling normality test is a quantitative method that makes use of P-values.

Using P-Values

As this subject is covered in greater detail in the chapter dealing with Hypothesis Testing, let me just give you a quick explanation of how P-values are used.

P-values range between 0.00 and 1.00. We are always going to start the test by assuming the data comes from a normal distribution. Then we will use the P-value to decide if the departure from normality (as we will probably never see a perfectly normal distribution in reality) is significant enough to say it *probably* does not come from a normal distribution. Let me summarise what I just said in this way.

- We assume the data comes from a normal probability distribution
- We run the test and obtain a P-value for the test statistic
- A *low P-value* means a *low fit* with the normal distribution
- A *high P-value* means a *high fit* with the normal distribution

We have to use a specific number to determine the cut off point between low and high P-values. This is called the 'Alpha' value (α), sometimes referred to as the 'level of significance'. As a general rule for normality testing we use an α value of 0.10.

If the P-value is less than α (in this case 0.10) the departure from normality is statistically significant, so we assume the data set has a low fit with a normal distribution, thus it is not normal.

The Anderson Darling Normality Test

The output of the Anderson-Darling Normality Test in Minitab is a Normal Probability Plot. The determination as to whether or not the data set is approximately normal is made by taking note of the P-value associated with the A squared test statistic.

If the data set is approximately normal, the P-value will be greater than the level of significance we have chosen. As I said, for normality testing we will use an α value of 0.10.

In this particular case, we know that the distribution of Data Set 1 is skewed. As we would expect, the plotted values do not closely fit the straight line.

You will also notice that the P-value associated with the test statistic is less than α (0.10). Therefore we would conclude that the data set is 'not normal'.

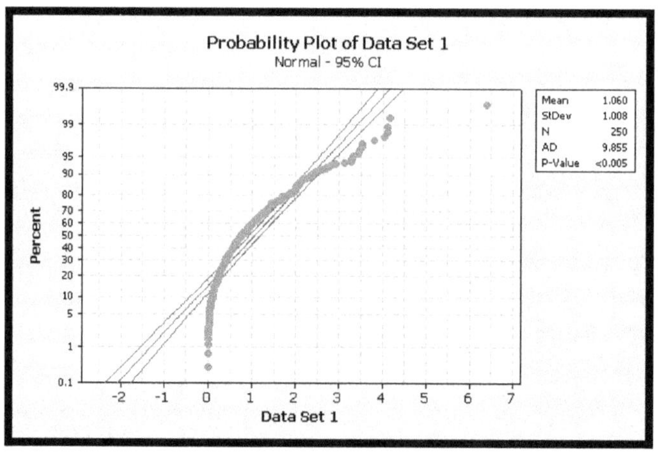

Figure 125:Anderson-Darling Normality Test - Non Normal Data

The data set shown provides a good example of a distribution that does look 'approximately normal'.

The plotted values closely fit the straight line, and the P-value of the test statistic is greater than α (0.10).

Our conclusion in this case is that the data is 'approximately normally distributed'.

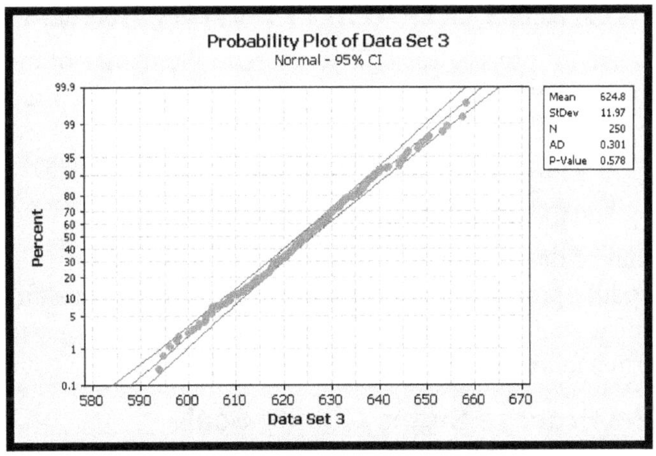

Figure 126: Anderson-Darling Normality Test - Normal Data

Descriptive Statistics with Minitab

Similar data is also available in the graphical summary associated with Minitab's descriptive statistics.

The 'Descriptive Statistics' dialogue box is activated from Minitab's 'Stat' menu under the sub-menu of 'Basic Statistics'. The graphical summary is generated from the 'Graphs' sub-dialogue box.

The graphical summary output includes not only descriptive statistics, but also the results of the Anderson-Darling Normality Test.

The output shown is the result obtained from Data Set 3 used in previous examples.

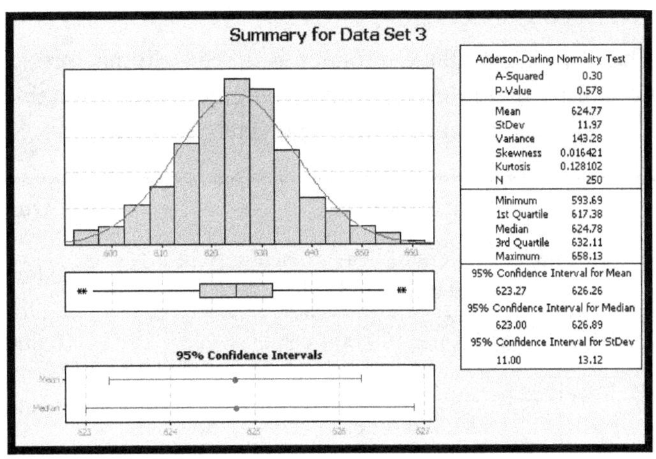

Figure 127: Graphical Summary Output for Normal Data Set

PROCESS CAPABILITY WITH SIGMA QUALITY LEVELS

The term 'process capability' refers to the ability of a process to consistently make a product or deliver a service that meets a customer specification range. Process capability can be evaluated using a number of approaches. These include:

- Process sigma calculations
- Capability indices

Both of these approaches provide a snapshot at a particular point in time of the capability of the process to produce products or services that meet or exceed customer expectations. These snapshots may or may not be indications of variation in the process over the longer term, hence the need to discuss the concept of short-term and long-term variation later in this chapter.

The Process Sigma Quality Scale

If someone said to you that 99 percent of their products were defect free, what would you think about quality? Sounds good doesn't it? What about 99.9 percent quality, now that's fantastic. What would be the effect of 99.9 percent quality on our lives? Consider the following examples of what 99.9 percent looks like.

- 291 pacemaker operations in the United States will be performed incorrectly this year
- 4.9 million articles would be mishandled each year by Australia Post
- 133,335 documents will be misplaced by the Australian Taxation Office each year
- 58,500 credit cards will fail to work when paying for goods
- Webster's dictionary will have 315 misspellings in it
- More than 4,000 parts will fail on every Boeing 747 aircraft

Would 99.9 percent be 'good enough' for you if you experienced an error in the scenarios above? More importantly, would 99 percent, or even 99.9 percent be good enough for your customers in respect of your products or services?

When we hear that a product is a 'Six Sigma' product we know that its quality is excellent and the probability that it has a defect is extremely low. The table below demonstrates this by showing a comparison between 90 percent quality, 99 percent quality and 'Six Sigma' quality.

Item Measured	90% Quality	99% Quality	Six Sigma Quality
Downtime for an item of heavy machinery in a 30 day month	72.0 hours	7.2 hours	0.14688 minutes
Defective vehicles per 100,000 vehicles sold	10,000	1,000	< 1
Received parts not matching orders per 250,000 orders	25,000	2,500	< 1
Period of unsafe drinking water each day	2.4 hours	14.4 minutes	0.004896 minutes
Period without electricity each week	16.8 hours	1.68 hours	0.034272 minutes

Quality Level Comparisons

There are many industries where a Six Sigma result would not be good enough – pharmaceutical, aviation, space aeronautics, medical and the like. Much higher results [measured in the parts per billion] must be sustained where the consequences of a defect are unacceptable.

One of the unique features of Six Sigma is its quality measurement scale. The designers of the scale recognised the resistance that is normally experienced in western culture when there is talk of zero defects. Tell your staff that you want zero defects and you are likely to get comments like – "It can't be done", "You've got to be kidding mate". The process sigma measurement scale acknowledges this likely resistance and helps to overcome it in four ways:

- It provides the foundation for setting and achieving improvement milestones, and helps create a culture of continual improvement
- It measures performance against customers' requirements
- It provides a basis for consistent performance comparison
- It forces the conversation around what actually constitutes a defect in the eyes of the customer

The process sigma level is calculated on the basis of Defects Per Million Opportunities (DPMO). When we talk about opportunities, we are referring to opportunities for a defect per unit produced. You will notice on the measurement scale, that as you achieve a higher process sigma, DPMO (Defects Per Million Opportunities) are reduced exponentially. You may also notice that process yield[25] improvements get smaller.

Process Sigma (Short Term)	**Process Yield (%)**	**Defects Per Million Opportunities (DPMO)**
6	99.99966	3.4
5	99.977	233
4	99.38	6,210
3	93.32	66,807
2	69.15	308,537
1	30.85	690,000

Process Sigma Scale

At the 'Six Sigma' quality level, a process would only produce 3.4 defects per million opportunities, which equates to a process yield of 99.99966 percent. Prior to starting a 'Six Sigma' quality initiative, many of an organisation's processes will operate at a quality level of between 1 and 3 sigma. It is often quite startling for process owners to find out that their process produces no less than 66,000 defects for every million opportunities. Whilst this level of performance may have served them well to this point in time, there are competing organisations out there working hard at reducing their level of defects.

25 Process Yield refers to the proportion of total units produced that are defect free.

Distributions

So what does a Six Sigma distribution look like? To demonstrate what Six Sigma Quality would look like as a frequency distribution let us use the example of a manufacturer of 'steel rods'. The customer who buys these 'steel rods' requires them to be no longer than 125 mm (upper specification limit) and no shorter than 123 mm (lower specification limit). These requirements are critical-to-quality, because a 'steel rod' outside of the required length cannot be used. The examples below assume that the data has been collected over a long period of time and represents the long-term variation of the process.

+/- 3 Standard Deviations

The standard deviation of the process is 0.3333 mm. The figure below shows that the distribution of the lengths of 'steel rods' produced has +/- 3 standard deviations within the customer's upper and lower specification limits. This means that 99.73 percent of 'steel rods' produced are within specification limits and therefore defect free. This equates to a long-term quality level of 3 Sigma.

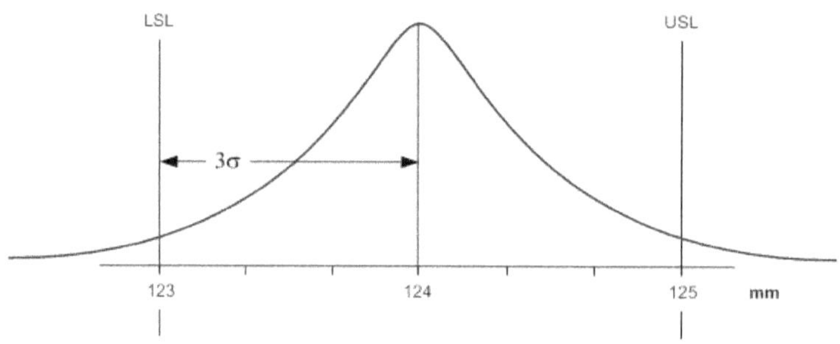

Figure 128: Process Performing at 3 Sigma Level (Long Term)

+/- 6 Standard Deviations

Now after a lot of work to improve the process, the degree of variation in the 'steel rods' producing process has been significantly reduced. The standard deviation of the process has now been reduced to 0.1666 mm.

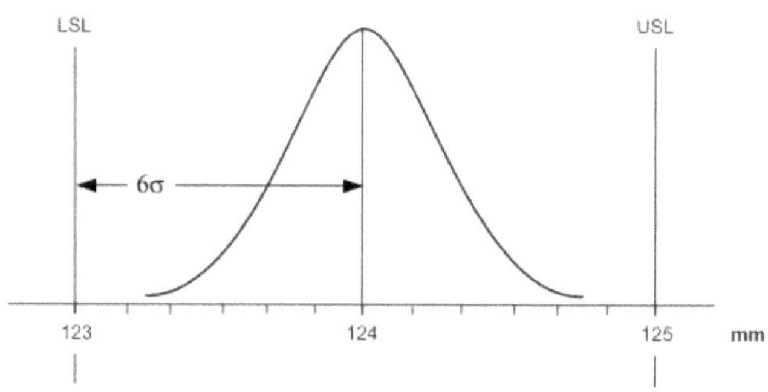

Figure 129: Process Performing at 6 Sigma Level (Long Term)

While the average length is still the same, the figure above shows that the distribution of the lengths of 'steel rods' produced now has +/- 6 standard deviations within the customer's upper and lower specification limits. This means that 99.9999998 percent of 'steel rods' produced are within specification limits and therefore defect free.

This equates to a long-term quality level of 6 Sigma or a 2 parts per billion defect rate.

Calculating Process Sigma using the DPMO Method

A very useful approach to assess performance against customer requirements is a method of calculating the process performance on the Sigma Quality Scale using discrete variables. This is the only method for calculating your sigma quality level when you have more than one critical-to-quality characteristic against which you wish to measure performance.

To calculate our sigma quality level, we first need to familiarise ourselves with the following terms:

- **A Unit** – this is the thing or item produced or processed, or the service provided (for example – trucks repaired, online web sites, orders from customers, flight seat booked, loan application, MP3 player, audio cd etc).
- **A Defect** – this is any critical-to-quality (CTQ) characteristic that does not meet customers' requirements. These must be mutually exclusive, and the key word here is critical to quality in the eyes of the customer. These are those things that if they occur, would most likely cause the customer to consider the product or service to be defective. Defects can be specified in respect of the product itself (for example - torn upholstery, outside the specified width, web site not available etc), or in respect of their interaction with the process (for example - time to deliver longer than specified time, repair time exceeding 24 hours, order details taken incorrectly the first time, incorrect ticket destination etc).
- **A Defect Opportunity** – this is any opportunity for a unit to not meet the CTQ requirements of the customer. This answers the question – 'How many opportunities would there be for a customer to be dissatisfied with our product or service, and consider it to be defective? It is essentially the number of defects that can appear for each unit produced.

Process Example	**A Unit**	**A Defect**	**Defect Opportunities Per unit**
Leave application	A leave application	• Not returned to originator within 14 days	1
Motel check-in	Check in	• No room available • Takes longer than 10 minutes	2
Vehicle Service	A Delivery Truck	• Oil leak • Incomplete Service • Cycle time longer than quoted	3

Examples of Process Sigma Terms

We can use either one of two equations to start the process of identifying our Sigma quality level. DPMO (defects per million opportunities) or Process Yield, both take into account **multiple requirements** associated with an output, and will produce the same Sigma Quality level result.

In both cases, once you have made the calculation (DPMO or Process Yield), you then convert the result to a 'Short Term Sigma' value using the conversion chart shown at the end of this book.

Equations are shown in the following table.

DPMO	PROCESS YIELD
$1{,}000{,}000 \times \frac{D}{N \times O}$ Where: D = Number of defects N = Number of units counted O = Number of opportunities per unit	$\left(1 - \frac{D}{N \times O}\right) \times 100$ Where: D = Number of defects N = Number of units counted O = Number of opportunities per unit

Some keys points to remember:

- The number of defect opportunities must stay constant before and after improvement if the comparison of results is to be useful – remember that any convention, even if flawed, is useful if used consistently
- Where many defects might be listed, these may be categorised into one major defect heading (i.e., for a motor vehicle manufacturer, CTQ defects associated with the engine, gear box and differential could be categorised under the main heading of 'Drive Train Failure')

Case Study – The Coffee Shop

The worksheet shown in the following example can be used to approximate 'Process Sigma' for any process. We have calculated both DPMO and Process Yield for the example, though one will suffice as both generate the same Sigma quality level result.

1. What is the process?	Coffee Making
2. What is the unit produced by this process?	A cup of coffee
3. In the eyes of the customer, what would constitute a defect in a unit produced by this process? (Refer to customer requirements)	A defect is: • Product delivered does not match order • Dirty cup • Liquid content not within 2mm of top of the cup • Order to delivery takes longer than 2 minutes
4. Calculate the defect opportunities per unit (O) by adding the total number of defects you identified in step 3.	Every time a customer buys a cup of coffee, any one of the 4 listed defects can occur. O = 4
5. How many units (N) were processed?	N = 340
6. From the units processed in step 5, how many defects (D) of the type described in step 3 did you observe?	D = 27

7. Calculate DPMO using the equation: $1{,}000{,}000 \times \frac{D}{N \times O}$ Where: D = Number of defects N = Number of units counted O = Number of opportunities per unit **OR**	$1{,}000{,}000 \times \frac{27}{340 \times 4} = 19{,}853$
8. Calculate Process Yield using the equation: $\left(1 - \frac{D}{N \times O}\right) \times 100$ Where: D = Number of defects N = Number of units counted O = Number of opportunities per unit	$\left(1 - \frac{27}{340 \times 4}\right) \times 100 = 98\%$
9. Convert DPMO OR Process Yield to a Short Term Process Sigma using the conversion table.	Process Sigma (short term) = 3.5

Process Sigma Worksheet (DPMO Method)

Calculating Process Sigma using Z Scores

As we already know, the area underneath the curve of a normal distribution can be determined because we know how much of the curve exists between certain points. We can expand on previous diagrams to include up to six standard deviations each side of the mean as shown in the diagram on the following page.

The proportion of values underneath the curve are:

Between +/- 1σ of the mean = 68.26%

Between +/- 2σ of the mean = 95.44%

Between +/- 3σ of the mean = 99.73%

Between +/- 4σ of the mean = 99.9937%

Between +/- 5σ of the mean = 99.99994%

Between +/- 6σ of the mean = 99.9999998%

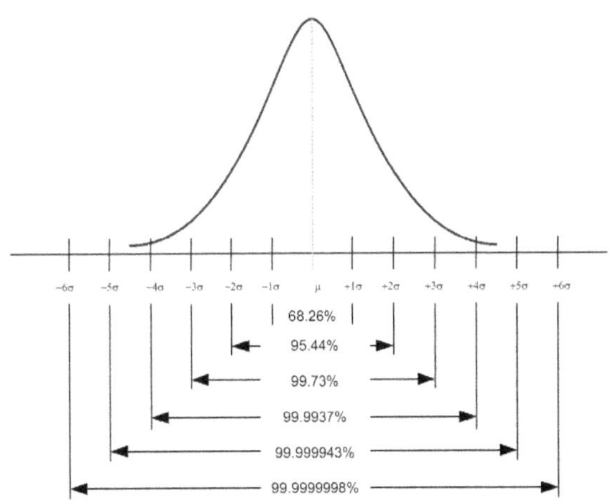

Figure 130: Distribution to +/- 6 Standard Deviations

When a data set is normally distributed, we can use the mean and standard deviation to determine the proportion of observations that fall within a designated range underneath the curve.

The steps for calculating process sigma are simply based around the concept of identifying the area underneath the curve that is between customer specification limits – in other words this is the defect free area or process yield – and converting it to a process sigma value.

This approach is relevant to a single variable that is measured in some way such as length, height, volume, strength or weight. It is applied when you have:

- Data that follows the *normal distribution*; and
- Customer *specification limits*.

The steps involved in this process are:

Step 1 – Draw the distribution with relevant data.

Step 2 – Standardise the values associated with customer specification limits.

Step 3 – Calculate the area underneath the curve that falls within customer specification limits using the Z Table (shown in appendices).

Step 4 – Convert process yield to a Process Sigma value using the conversion table.

<u>Worked Example</u>

Suppose data was obtained over the past 9 months and it was found that the cycle time for manufacturing and delivering a unit of machinery is normally distributed with $\mu = 85$ calendar days, and $\sigma = 3$ days. If customers specify a delivery cycle time of no earlier than 75 days and no later than 90 days after ordering, what process sigma level is this process operating at?

Step 1

Draw a hypothetical distribution with relevant data.

(Indicate the defect free area by shading in)

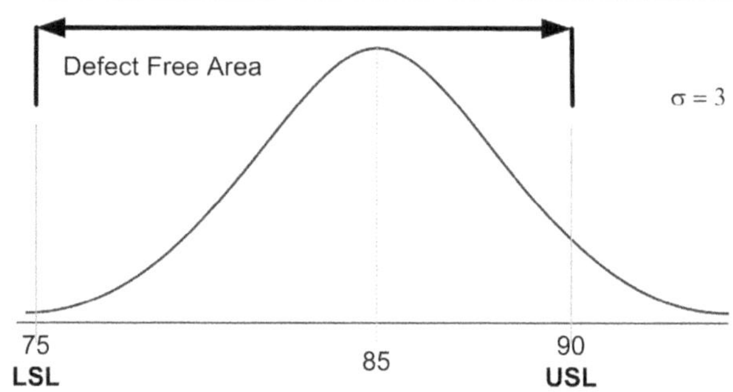

Step 2

Standardise the values associated with customer specification limits.
(Where there is only one spec limit, the other half of the distribution curve will be equal to 0.5)

$$(USL)Z = \frac{X-\mu}{\sigma} = \frac{90-85}{3} = 1.66$$

$$(LSL)Z = \frac{X-\mu}{\sigma} = \frac{75-85}{3} = -3.33$$

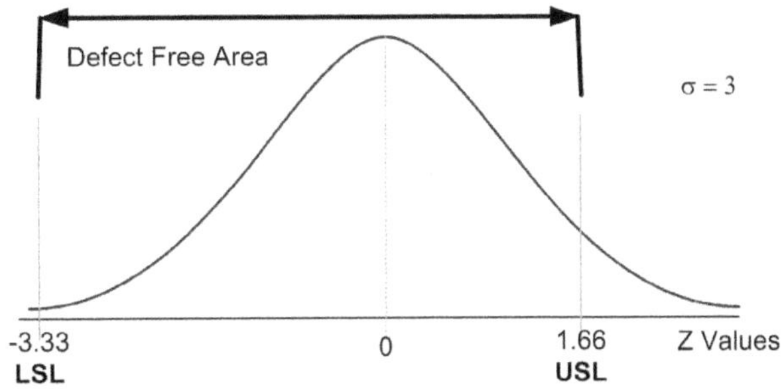

Step 3

Calculate the area underneath the curve that falls within customer specification limits using the Z Table.

USL - The area between Z Values of 0 and +1.66 = 0.4515
LSL - The area between Z Values of 0 and –3.33 = 0.49957
Total Area = 0.95107
Multiply x 100 to obtain a **Process Yield** = 95.107 percent

Step 4

Convert process yield to a short-term Process Sigma value using the conversion table.

Process Sigma (short-term) = between 3.1 and 3.2 sigma

Short Term versus Long Term Variation

Imagine the following scenario if you will. Two independent teams are studying the same process and measuring exactly the same characteristic of its output. One team (Team A) collects a sample of one data point each day for a month, while the other team (Team B) collects one sample of 30 data points in a single day.

Which of these data sets do you suppose would show more variation?

In most cases we would expect to see more variation in the sample taken by Team A over the period of the full month. Team A's sample is more likely to represent the full variation of the process and give the team an understanding of the 'long-term' variation it exhibits, while Team B's data does not give the full picture, only an understanding of variation in the 'short-term'.

Short Term Data

Short-term data is that which is collected from the process in sub-groups. Each sub-group is collected over a short period of time, and is a snapshot of the process at a particular point in time. Short-term data tends to focus on common cause variation, as it may not capture data from different sources of variation. Lets take the example of a process that operates 24 hours per day. Different shifts come and go to maintain that 24-hour capability. A short-term sample would be one taken from just one of the shifts.

Let me give you another example. A process receives and processes inputs that are received in batches from suppliers. Short-term data would be that which is taken from a sample of outputs produced from only one of those batches or a small number of those batches. Short-term data does not display variation across the full range of variables.

Long Term Data

Long-term data is that which is considered to contain both common cause and special cause variation that can be observed when all variables have varied over their full range. Long-term data would be the consolidation of multiple short-term data samples taken from all sources of variation, resulting in the full range of variation being observed. Long-term data provides the user with an understanding of what variation actually is over the long-term.

The previous figure provides a graphical representation of the difference between short-term and long-term variation. On six separate occasions, subgroup samples of data were collected. The smaller distributions reflect the variation exhibited in those six different samples. When all of the data collected over the six separate occasions is compiled, the long-term variation would look like that shown in the large distribution.

So the lesson for us is this - over the long-term, processes tend to exhibit more variation than in the short-term. To quantify long-term variation, you must take both short-term and long-term samples from the process.

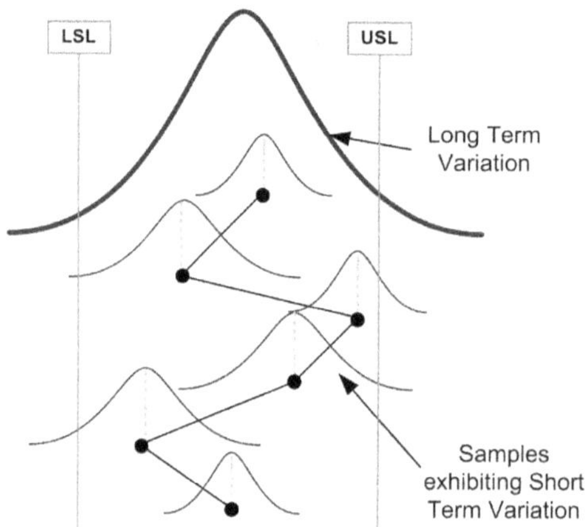

Figure 131: Short Term versus Long Term Variation

Sigma Capability and Short-Term Versus Long-Term Variation

Notice that we have drawn customer specification limits on the previous diagram of short and long term variation. What do you notice about performance with respect to those specification limits for each of the short-term samples, and how that compares to the long-term variation?

In the short-term, proportionately more of the data values will be inside specification limits. The process shows that it can drift from being close to the lower specification limit to being closer to the upper specification limit. In the short term, the capability of the process can appear to be much higher than what the *actual* long-term capability of the process really is.

Numerous Six Sigma authors, including Mikel Harry and Richard Schroeder[26], report that experience has shown short-term 'snapshots' of a process will shift or drift in one direction or the other by approximately 1.5σ. This shift and drift factor is accounted for in the process sigma conversion table referred to earlier in this chapter.

[26] Harry, M., Schroeder, R., (2000), *'Six Sigma – The Breakthrough Management Strategy'*, Doubleday, New York, pp. 141-145

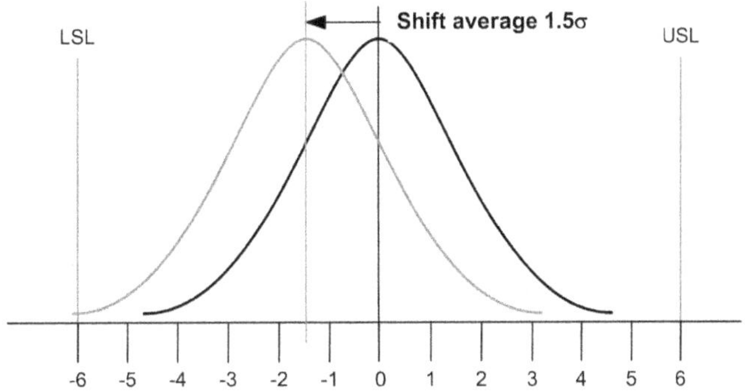

Figure 132: Process Shift and Drift

The short term process shown in the diagram above has +/- 6σ within customer tolerances, hence it would be a long-term six sigma process if there were no shifting or drifting of the process over time. It would have a yield of 99.9999998 percent, which equates to 0.002 defects per million opportunities or 2 parts-per-billion. We know, a process is dynamic like everything else in the world, and the mean shifts and drifts over time. As explained by Harry (1997)[27], the average shift in the process of 1.5σ leads us to adjust our long-term yield expectation to 99.99966 percent, which equates to 3.4 defects per million opportunities.

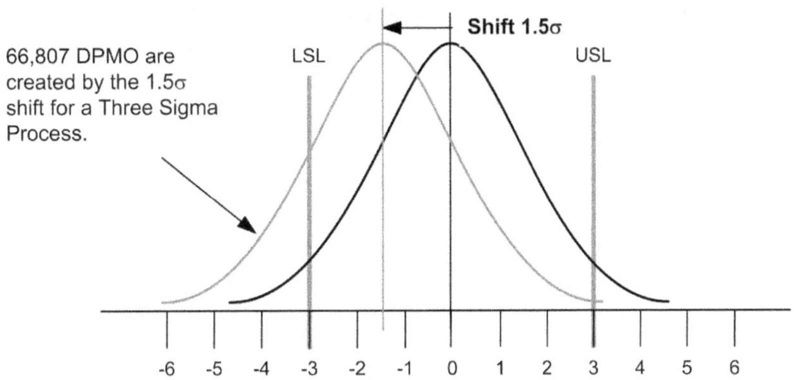

Figure 133: 1.5 Sigma Shift

This discussion leads us to two important concepts:

- **Short-term process capability** – the potential capability of the process if it was centered and there were no shift and drift in the process.
- **Long-term process capability** – the actual capability of the process, taking into account shift and drift.

[27] Harry, M.J., (1997), *'The Nature of Six Sigma Quality'*, Motorola University Press, pp. 10 - 11

As discussed earlier in this chapter, process capability can be represented by a 'process sigma' value. I will refer to this 'process sigma' value by the notation **Z**.

The diagram shown of the distribution of cycle time data sows the relationship between Z scores and the process sigma philosophy.

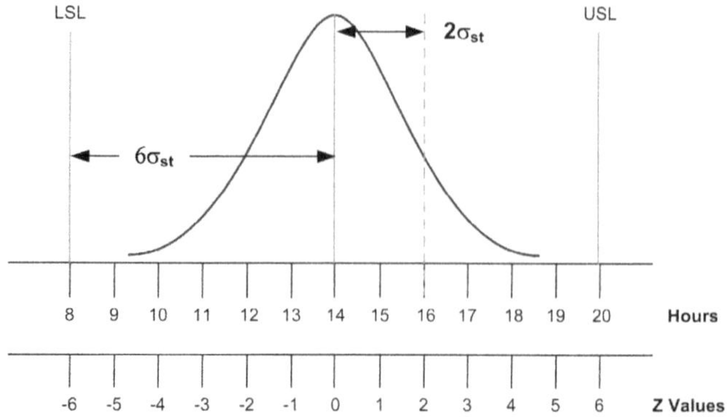

Figure 134: Process Sigma and Z Values

A process with +/- 6σ within tolerances has a short-term process sigma value or a $\mathbf{Z_{st}}$ of Six Sigma. As we know, short-term process means have a tendency to drift 1.5σ, therefore our long-term process sigma (Z_{lt}) equals the short-term process sigma (Z_{st}) less the shift and drift factor. We can represent this mathematically as: $\mathbf{Z_{lt} = Z_{st} - 1.5}$

Therefore the long-term capability for our example above is calculated as:

$$\mathbf{Z_{lt} = Z_{st} - 1.5 = 6 - 1.5 = 4.5}$$

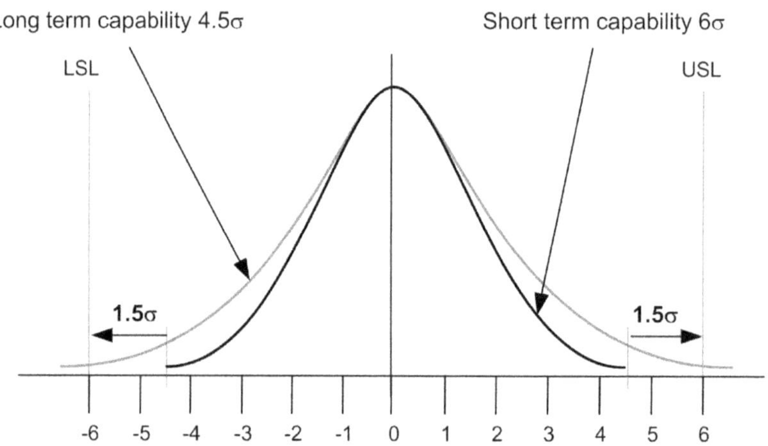

Figure 135: Short Term versus Long Term Capability

DPMO is directly related to Z_{st} and Z_{lt}. Accordingly, a table for converting DPMO to a Z_{st} value and vice versa is shown in appendices.

LONG-TERM PROCESS CAPABILITY INDICES

It's often necessary to study the amount of variation present in a 'stable' process. Specifically, this type of analysis helps determine whether the amount of normal variation is small enough that most customers will be satisfied with the product or service, or whether its so large there are too many dissatisfied customers and a process change is necessary.

Defining Process Capability

The term 'process capability' refers to the ability of a process to consistently make a product or deliver a service that meets a customer specification range. The long-term capability of a process to produce within this range can be predicted through the use of two capability indices.

- Long term capability index (referred to by the notation Pp)
- Long term capability index compared to some constant – k (referred to by the notation Ppk)

Purpose of Capability Indices

Capability indices help the team understand the relationship between process variation and customer specifications limits. Ultimately capability indices help answer the question – 'Is the process capable?'

A capable process is one where +/- 3σ is contained within customer specification limits.

Requirements for Use of Long-Term Capability Indices

- The process must be in a state of statistical control (i.e., a stable process)
- **Long-Term** Capability Indices <u>can only be used</u> when you are working with data that is *normally distributed* for the following reason – 'You will be working with actual data standard deviation, and the proportion of data between + and – 3 standard deviation limits (or control limits) is assumed to be consistent with the properties of a normal distribution' (if not normal, I recommend that you use Potential Capability Indices)

Instructions

The process for calculating capability indices comprises 5 steps:

- **Step 1** - Identify the Upper Specification Limit (USL) and Lower Specification Limit (LSL).
- **Step 2** - Calculate the standard deviation of the process.
- **Step 3** - Calculate the mean of the process.
- **Step 4** – Calculate capability index (Pp).
- **Step 5** – Calculate capability index compared to some constant k (Ppk).

Long-Term Capability Index (Pp) using Overall Standard Deviation

This is the ratio of customer specification tolerance to six standard deviations (+/- 3 standard deviations) of long-term process variation. The result is calculated without regard to the location of the process average within the customer specified tolerances. Pp is sometimes referred to as 'process potential'. Pp is calculated using the following equation.

$$Pp = \frac{USL - LSL}{6(\sigma)}$$

Where:
Pp = Capability Index
USL = Upper Specification Limit
LSL = Lower Specification Limit
σ = Standard Deviation

If the result of the equation were 1.0, this would indicate that the range between control limits and the range between specification limits are the same. A result less than 1.0 indicates that the range of the process data (6σ) is greater than the customer specifications (USL-LSL), a bad result. The ideal scenario is a Pp of 1.0 or greater, a result that indicates the spec limits are wider than the distribution.

Long Term Capability Index (Ppk) using Overall Standard Deviation

Ppk is the ratio of the distance between the process mean and the *closest* specification limit to three standard deviations of **long-term process variation**. Unlike Pp, Ppk takes into account the actual alignment of the process with customers' specifications.

The diagram below shows the side of the distribution with more of its area outside specification limits (i.e., the left side of the mean shows more values below the lower specification limit), is where most of the problem lies. If it were a capable process, by definition 3 standard deviations of data on either side of the mean would fit within specification limits. If it is not capable, as is the case with this particular example, at least one end has its 3σ reference point outside the specification limit.

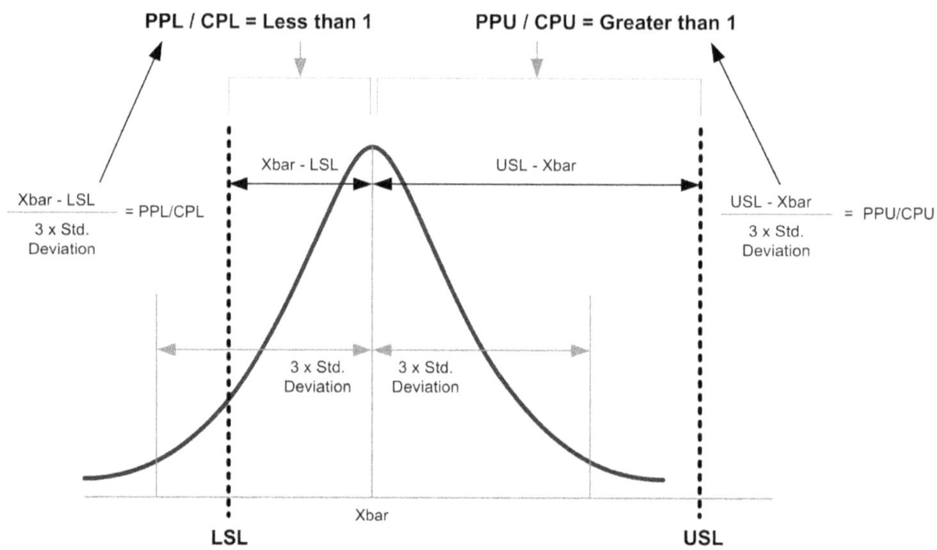

Ppk is determined by comparing two ratios and determining which of them is the smaller. The smaller ratio indicates whether or not the side of the distribution where the mean is closest to a specification limit, sits outside that limit. The ratios are calculated according to these equations.

$$Ppk = \text{min. of PPU and PPL}$$

$$PPU = \frac{USL - \overline{X}}{3(\sigma)}$$

$$PPL = \frac{\overline{X} - LSL}{3(\sigma)}$$

Where:

Ppk = Capability Index compared to some constant (k)
PPU = Pp Upper
PPL = Pp Lower
USL = Upper Specification Limit
LSL = Lower Specification Limit
X-bar = Mean
σ = Standard Deviation

We choose the smaller of the two results, as this is an indication of which specification the mean is closer to. A result of 1 would again indicate that the distance from our mean to the specification limit is the same as the distance from the mean to +/- 3 standard deviations. A result less than 1.0 indicates that the point at +/- 3 standard deviations is outside the specification limits, and therefore the process is not capable of producing consistently to customer specifications.

Pp / Ppk => 1.0 = Capable

Pp / Ppk < 1.0 = Not Capable

Conclusions about capability shown in the following table are based on the assessment of long-term process capability.

Process is NOT Capable	**Process IS Capable**	**Process IS Capable**

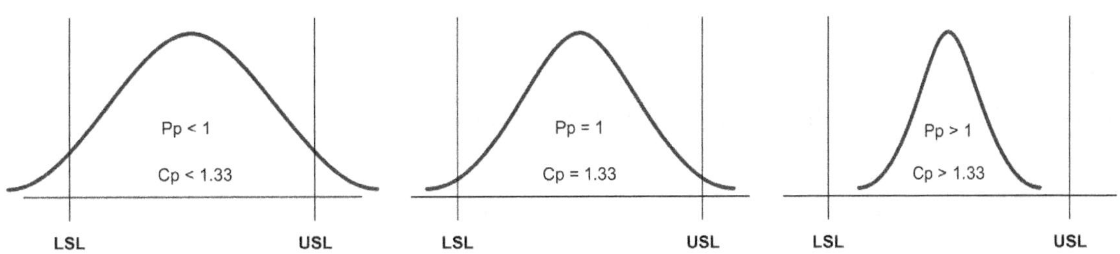

Regardless of whether or not this process is centered, the +/- 3σ limits fall outside customer tolerances; hence it is not capable.	If this process were centred, the +/- 3σ limits would align with customer specifications; hence it would be capable. It would produce a minimum of 0.27 percent defects.	If this process were centred, the +/- 3σ limits fall inside customer specifications; hence it would be considered a capable process.

POTENTIAL CAPABILITY INDICES

Defining Process Capability

The term 'process capability' refers to the ability of a process to consistently make a product or deliver a service that meets a customer specification range. The short-term or potential capability of a process to produce within this range can be predicted through the use of two capability indices.

- Capability index (referred to by the notation Cp)
- Capability index compared to some constant – k (referred to by the notation Cpk)

Difference Between Long-Term Capability and Potential Capability

Where Pp and Ppk use actual standard deviation of the data being analysed and provides an indication of actual capability, Cp and Cpk use an estimated standard deviation and provide an indication of potential capability.

Requirements for Use of Long-Term Capability Indices

- The process must be in a *state of statistical control* (i.e., a stable process)
- **Potential** Capability Indices can be used with *normal and non-normal data* as the same bias correction factors as used in control chart construction are applied

Instructions

The process for calculating potential capability indices consists of 5 steps:

- **Step 1** - Identify the Upper Specification Limit (USL) and Lower Specification Limit (LSL).
  NOTE: Where only an upper or lower specification limit is stipulated, identify that.
- **Step 2** - Calculate the within standard deviation of the process. (this is an estimate of population std. deviation, not the standard deviation of the sample being analysed)
- **Step 3** - Calculate the mean of the process.
- **Step 4** – Calculate capability index (Cp).
- **Step 5** – Calculate capability index compared to some constant k (Cpk).

Different Types of Data

When undertaking capability studies, data can be collected and analysed in two different formats.

Subgroup Data

Data is collected in groups and then consolidated to make up the sample. e.g. every hour five items are sampled to form a subgroup of data that comprises 5 values. After ten hours, the sample size would be 50 values comprised of 10 subgroups each made up of 5 values.

Individuals Data

Data is collected individually to make up the sample. Every hour for 24 hours, one value is collected to make up a sample of 24 values.

Potential Capability Index (Cp) using Within Standard Deviation

This is the ratio of customer specification tolerance to 6 standard deviations (+/- 3 standard deviations) of process variation. The result is calculated without regard to the location of the process average within the customer specified tolerances. Cp is sometimes referred to as 'process potential'. Cp is calculated using the following equation.

Working With Individuals

$$Cp = \frac{USL - LSL}{6\left(\frac{\overline{MR}}{d_2}\right)}$$

Where:

Cp = Potential Capability Index (using within StDev)

USL = Upper Specification Limit

LSL = Lower Specification Limit

$\overline{MR}$ = Average Moving Range

d_2 = Bias Correction Factor

$\frac{\overline{MR}}{d_2}$ = Estimate of Population Standard Deviation

Working With Subgroup Data

$$Cp = \frac{USL - LSL}{6\left(\frac{\overline{R}}{d_2}\right)}$$

Where:

Cp = Potential Capability Index (using within StDev)

USL = Upper Specification Limit

LSL = Lower Specification Limit

$\overline{R}$ = Average Range of Subgroups

d_2 = Bias Correction Factor (refer to appendices)

$\frac{\overline{R}}{d_2}$ = Estimate of Population Standard Deviation

If the result of the equation were 1.0, this would indicate that the range between control limits and the range between specification limits are the same. A result less than 1.0 indicates that the range of the process data (6σ) is greater than the customer specifications (USL-LSL), a bad result. The ideal scenario is a Cp of 1.0 or greater.

$Cp \geq 1.0$ = Capable (if centred)

$Cp < 1.0$ = Not Capable

Potential Capability Index (Cpk) using Within Standard Deviation

Cpk is the ratio of the distance between the process mean and the closest specification limit to three standard deviations of process variation. Unlike Cp, Cpk takes into account the alignment of the process with customers' specifications.

Working With Individuals Data

$$Cpk = \text{min. of CPU and CPL}$$

$$CPU = \frac{USL - \overline{X}}{3\left(\frac{\overline{MR}}{d_2}\right)}$$

$$CPL = \frac{\overline{X} - LSL}{3\left(\frac{\overline{MR}}{d_2}\right)}$$

Where:

Cpk = Capability Index compared to some constant (k)

CPU = Cp Upper

CPL = Cp Lower

USL = Upper Specification Limit

LSL = Lower Specification Limit

X-bar = Mean

$\overline{MR}$ = Average Moving Range

d_2 = Bias Correction Factor

$\frac{\overline{MR}}{d_2}$ = Estimate of Population Standard Deviation

Working With Subgroup Data

$$Cpk = \text{min. of CPU and CPL}$$

$$CPU = \frac{USL - \overline{\overline{X}}}{3\left(\frac{\overline{R}}{d_2}\right)}$$

$$CPL = \frac{\overline{\overline{X}} - LSL}{3\left(\frac{\overline{R}}{d_2}\right)}$$

Where:

Cpk = Capability Index compared to some constant (k)

CPU = Cp Upper

CPL = Cp Lower

USL = Upper Specification Limit

LSL = Lower Specification Limit

X-double bar = Average Subgroup Mean

$\overline{R}$ = Average Range of Subgroups

d_2 = Bias Correction Factor

$\frac{\overline{R}}{d_2}$ = Estimate of Population Standard Deviation

We choose the smaller of the two results, as this is an indication of which customer specification limit the mean outcome is actually closer to. A result of 1 would again indicate that the distance from our mean to the specification limit is the same as the distance from the mean to +/- 3 standard deviations. A result less than 1.0 indicates that the point at +/- 3 standard deviations is outside the specification limits, and therefore the process is not capable of producing consistently to customer specifications.

Cpk ≥ 1.0 = Capable

Cpk < 1.0 = Not Capable

WHAT ARE GOOD CP / PP VALUES?

If the result of either of the equations were 1.0, this would indicate that the range between control limits and the range between specification limits are the same. A result less than 1.0 indicates that the range of the process data (6σ) is greater than the customer specifications (USL-LSL), a bad result.

Assuming the data is normally distributed and the process was centered, the ideal scenario is a long-term ratio of 1.0 or greater. Pp uses long-term variation to calculate the ratio therefore a value of 1.0 or greater is desirable. By contrast, Cp uses short-term variation; therefore a value of 1.0 is only the potential capability of the process, not actual capability.

Process Capability and 6 Sigma Processes

You may have noticed by now that process capability, which has been around for many years, is focused on +/- 3 standard deviations.

As such, this is only a 3 Sigma process on the process sigma quality scale. Maybe this is a little out of touch with the competitive expectations of your customers.

Numerous Six Sigma professionals including Thomas Pyzdek (2003)[28] suggest that the generally accepted minimum value for Cp is 1.33.

Cp	Pp	Conclusion
≥ 1.33	≥ 1.0	Capable in the long-term (if the distribution of values is centered)
< 1.33 1.0 – 1.33	< 1.0	Not Capable in the long-term Capable in the short-term (if the distribution of values is centred)
< 1.0		Not Capable

Capability Study Conclusions with Cp and Pp

Shortcomings with Cp and Pp

Cp and Pp have two shortcomings:

- Cannot be used unless both upper and lower specifications exist
- They do not take process centering into consideration – if the process is not exactly centered, CP and Pp will give misleading results

Let's take a look at how you study process capability with SigmaXL and Minitab.

[28] Pyzdek, T., (2003), *'The Six Sigma Handbook'*, McGraw-Hill, New York, pp. 473 - 474

PROCESS CAPABILITY ANALYSIS WITH MINITAB

Minitab software provides functionality for studying process capability for both normally distributed and non-normally distributed data. Approaches to process capability analysis with Minitab include capability analysis with transformation, and capability analysis for Weibull, Exponential and Poisson distributions.

Process Capability Analysis (Normal Distribution)

Minitab software provides the opportunity to take capability studies to a new level. Capability analysis for normal distributions is found within the 'Quality Tools' selection of the 'Stat' menu.

The result of a Capability Analysis for a sample of 100 data points is shown in the figure below.

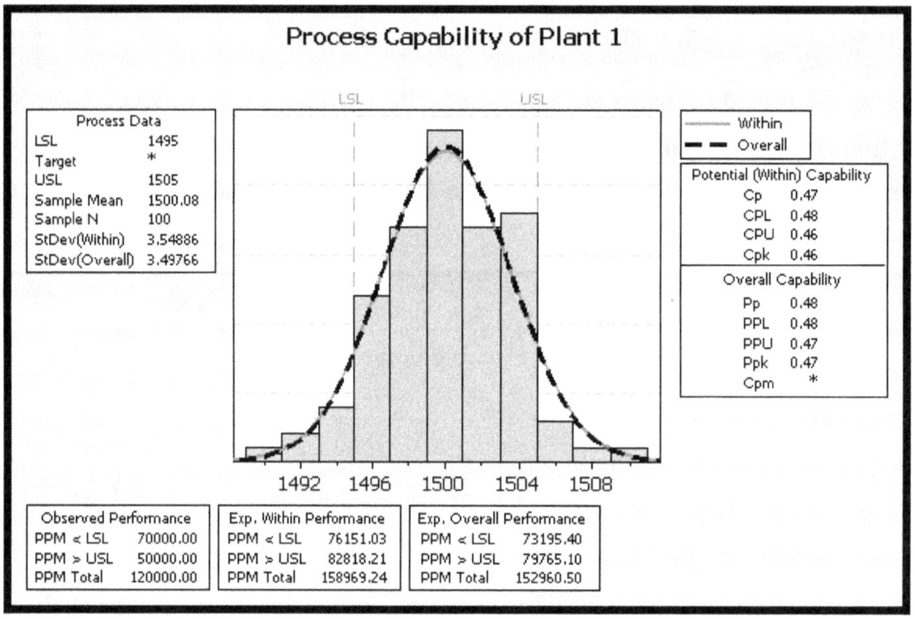

Figure 136: Capability Study (Normal Distribution) Output - Minitab

Potential (Within) Capability – Cp, CPU, CPL and Cpk are values that represent the *potential* capability of the process – that is what the process would be capable of if *shifts and drifts were not experienced in the subgroup means*. In calculating these values, MINITAB estimates σ_{within}, taking into account the variation within the subgroups but not the variation between subgroups.

Overall Capability – Pp, PPU, PPL, and Ppk are values that depict how the process is *actually* performing relative to the specification limits. Any significant difference between Overall and Within variation may indicate that the process is out of control, or there are sources of variation not estimated by the within capability.

Exp. Within Performance – The numbers shown in this small table at the centre of the three at the lower edge of the chart indicate the parts-per-million defect rate. In this case a total of 158,969 defects per million opportunities is being experienced based on the data analysed. You can convert this number to a 'process sigma' value using the relevant conversion table.

Process Capability Sixpack

An additional option is to study process capability using what Minitab refers to as a 'sixpack'. Capability analysis sixpack for normal distributions is also found within the 'Quality Tools' selection of the 'Stat' menu.

The result of a Capability Analysis Sixpack for the same sample of 100 data points is shown below.

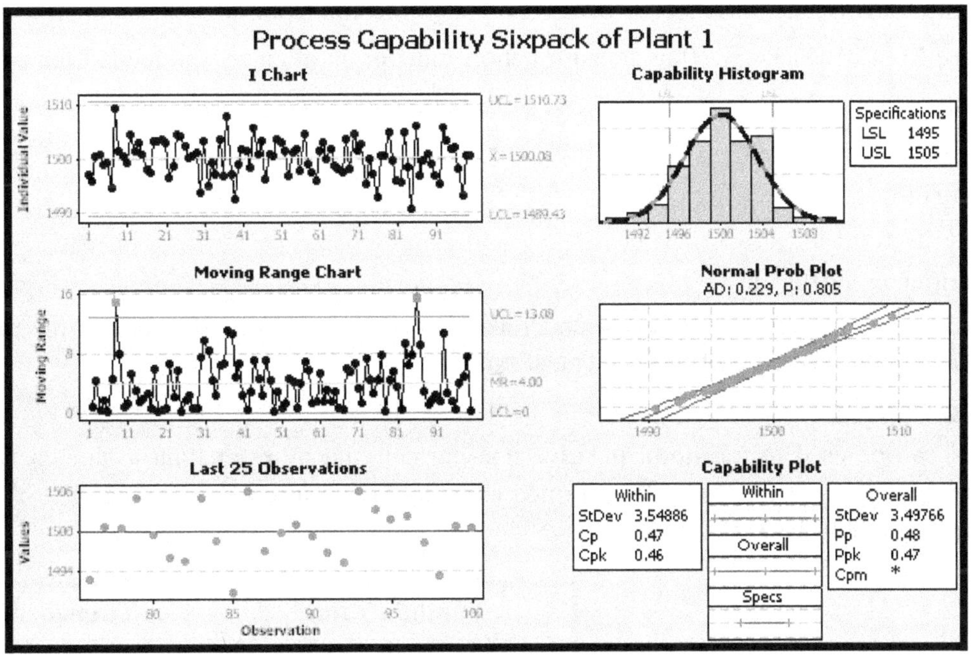

Figure 137: Capability Sixpack (Normal Distribution) Output - Minitab

Individual and MR Chart – Random distribution of values between control limits implies a stable process. The outlier on the Moving Range chart indicates a large range between 2 successive values in this case, and the respective values would need to be investigated.

Capability Histogram / Normal Probability Plot – This particular study assumes that the data is normally distributed. The capability histogram and normal probability plot give an indication as to the normality of the data being studied.

Capability Plot – The capability plot shows the +/- 3σ range of within and overall variation against customer tolerances. In this case the process is not capable, supported by Cp (0.47) and Pp (0.48) values.

Data Transformation

One approach to studying the capability of a process when the distribution of data is non-normal is to undertake a transformation of the data. While I don't believe we actually need to apply transformation methods in process capability analysis, (preferring instead to use the 'potential process capability' method) I'll still explain it.

Transformation in this context refers to the 're-expression of non-normal data as normal data'. The process of transformation involves three generic steps:

- Test data for normality
- Utilise a transformation function to transform the data

- Re-test data for normality

Transformation Approaches

It is often a challenge to select the right function to use for data transformation. This is often undertaken by using the standard transformation functions shown below, in an iterative process of trial and error. For each transformation undertaken, the data set is tested for normality using the Anderson-Darling Normality Test.

Standard transformation functions that can be used alone or in conjunction with one another include these:

- Square Root of Data: $\sqrt{X}$ (this transformation function is often recommended for count data that follows a Poisson distribution)
- Reciprocal of Data: 1/x
- Square of Data: x^2
- Data Offset: x + a
- Logarithmic: log10x etc.

Some software programs offer the ability to undertake data transformation using one of the most common approaches to transformation: the 'Box Cox Transformation'

Box Cox Transformation

The Box Cox can be used to transform **positive** non-normal data by estimating a lambda value (λ) that minimises the standard deviation of the transformed variable. The resulting transformation is Y^{λ} when $\lambda \neq 0$, and the natural log InY when $\lambda = 0$.

The most common transformation functions of the Box Cox Transformation are those listed in the table.

The notation Y' is a reference to the transformed value of Y.

Lambda Value	Transformation
$\lambda = 2$	$Y' = Y^2$
$\lambda = 0.5$	$Y' = \sqrt{Y}$
$\lambda = 0$	$Y' = lnY(Log_e Y)$
$\lambda = -0.5$	$Y' = 1/(\sqrt{Y})$
$\lambda = -1$	$Y' = 1/Y$

Common Transformations

Box Cox Transformation Using Minitab

The 'Box Cox Transformation' dialogue box is activated from within the 'Control Chart' section of the 'Stat' menu.

The output of the Box Cox Transformation is a graph that displays three specific elements.

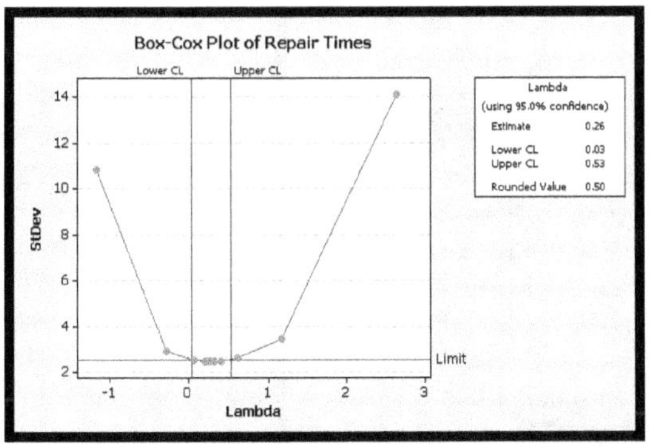

- The best estimate of lambda to be used for the transformation, in this case 0.261
- Two closely competing values for the estimate of lambda shown as the 'lower' and 'upper' values, and
- A 95 percent confidence interval for the true value of lambda

Figure 138: Box Cox Transformation Output - Minitab

Where the 95 percent confidence interval contains the value of 1, very little would be gained by undertaking any transformation, as the transformed value of Y would be almost the same as Y.

Process Capability Analysis (With Transformation)

MINITAB software provides the opportunity to study process capability for non-normal data by transforming it as a part of the process. Customer specification limits are transformed at the same time. Before undertaking this approach, the optimal lambda value for the transformation must be identified. The capability analysis is then undertaken using the normal capability analysis approach described earlier in this section, with the additional step of transforming both the data and customer specification limits. Transformation details are inserted into the 'Box Cox' sub-dialogue box as shown below.

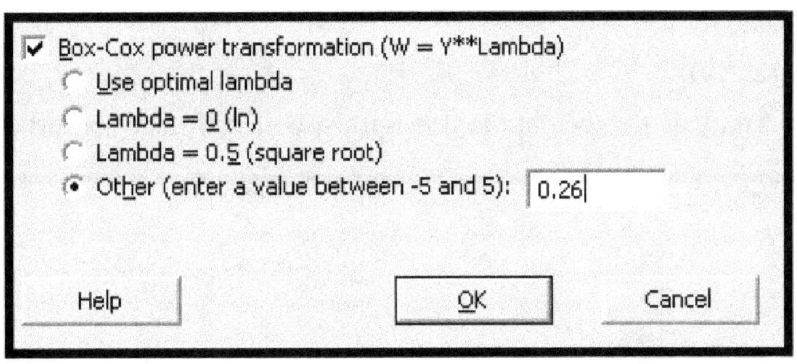

Figure 139: Sub-Dialogue Box for Capability Study with Transformation – Minitab

The result of a Capability Analysis includes a chart of the pre-transformed distribution as well as the details of the capability analysis for the transformed data.

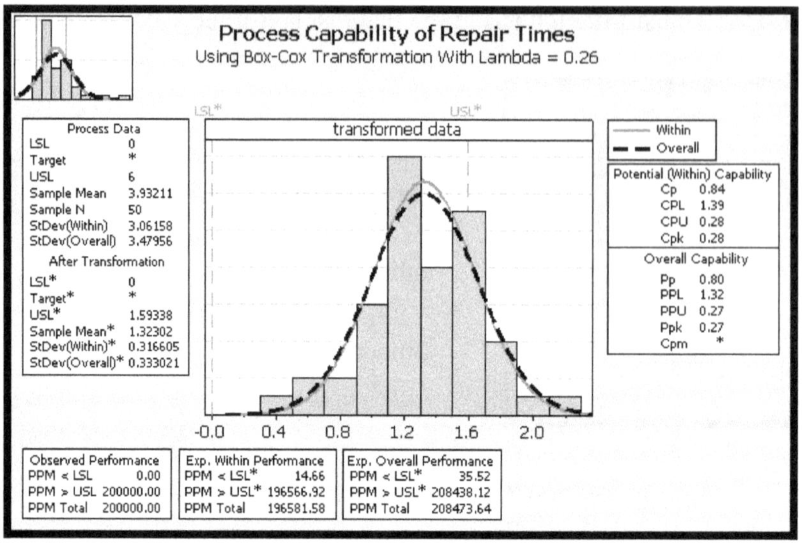

Figure 140: Capability Study (Normal Distribution) with Transformation - Minitab

PROCESS CAPABILITY WITH SIGMAXL

Process Capability Analysis (Normal Distribution)

SigmaXL software provides the functionality to study process capability for normal data. Capability analysis is found within the 'Process Capability' selection of the 'SigmaXL' menu.

Suppose we were analysing data for hotel breakfast delivery times. Deviation Time is the deviation around targeted delivery time in minutes. The Critical Customer Requirements (CCRs) are:

- USL = 10 minutes (late)
- LSL = -10 minutes (early).

The result of a Capability Analysis for the data is this with specifications overlaid on the histogram.

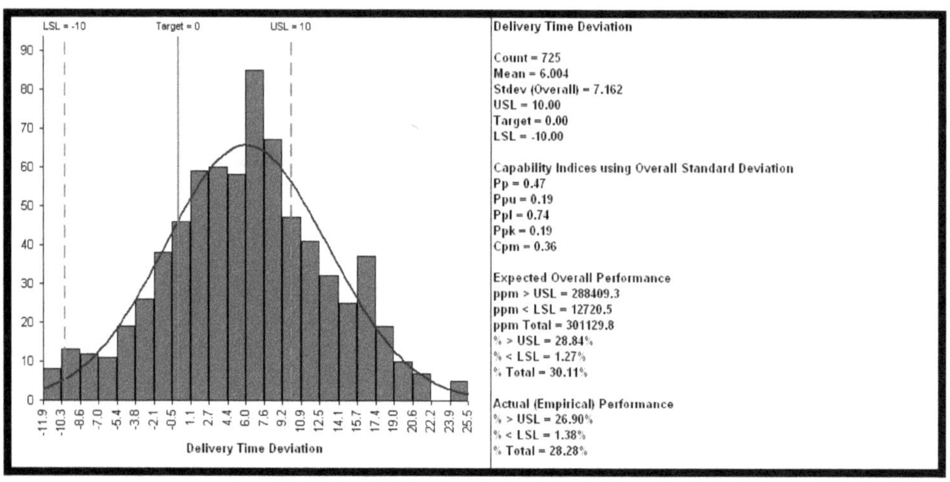

Figure 141: Process Capability with SigmaXL

Capability Indices using Overall Standard Deviation – Pp, Ppu, Ppl, and Ppk are values that represent the overall capability of the process and depicts how the process is *actually* performing in the long term.

Where Cp and Cpk use an estimated standard deviation and provide an indication of potential capability, Pp and Ppk use *actual* standard deviation of the data being analysed (assuming it is population standard deviation) and provides an indication of actual capability of the data being analysed.

A reminder

- The process must be in a state of statistical control (i.e. a stable process).
- Long Term Capability Indices can only be used when you are working with data that is normally distributed (refer to earlier discussion about long-term process capability).

Process Capability Analysis (Non-Normal Distribution)

SigmaXL does have the functionality to undertake process capability analysis with transformation. The method is more complex than that shown with Minitab. Thus, I have left it out of this material. For more information, refer to the SigmaXL Handbook available from our website.

PROCESS YIELD CALCULATIONS

Across many industries, yield is often calculated to help management understand the performance of a process. In manufacturing however, yield at the end of a process (Final Yield) may not tell the full story of what is happening in the process. The two measures I will introduce here are:

- Final Yield
- Rolled Throughput Yield

Final Yield

Yield is simply determined by calculating the proportion of units that are defect free. Final Yield is a measure for determining the proportion of units produced that are defect free at the end of the process. For example, the final yield of the production line for motor vehicles is the proportion of vehicles at the end of the process that are defect free. If the production line produces 100 cars and 2 of these are defective, the final yield of the process is 98 percent.

An equation for calculating final yield (expressed as %) is:

$$\left(1-\frac{\text{Defective Units}}{\text{Total Units}}\right)\times 100$$

To demonstrate this, we can work through the following example.

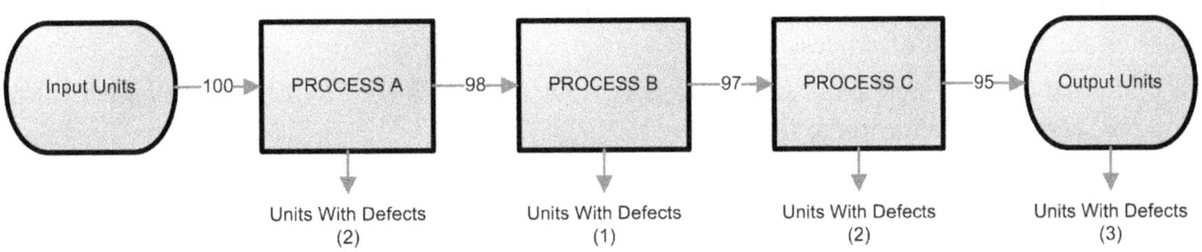

In the example above, 95 units are produced at the end of the process, with 3 of these being defective.

The final yield of the process shown is calculated as follows:

$$\left(1-\frac{3}{95}\right)\times 100 = (1-0.03157)\times 100 = 96.84\%)$$

Final yield calculations do not take into consideration the performance of the process before the final step. Whilst often used as a measure of performance in business today, the true story is hidden in the final figure produced.

An alternative method more suitable to quality improvement is rolled throughput yield.

Rolled Throughput Yield

Rolled Throughput Yield (RTY) is a measure for determining the performance of the process as a whole, taking into consideration yield at each step along the way. Many process owners are lulled into complacency by high Final Yield values, or even average process yields. Confusion occurs when they realise that despite high values, the ratio of end of the process output to start of the process input tells another story. RTY helps process owners recognise what really is happening in their process.

The equation for calculating Rolled Throughput Yield (expressed as %) is:

(Yield Process A) x (Yield Process B) x (Yield Process C) x (Final Yield) = RTY

Using the same example, we can demonstrate the difference between Final Yield and RTY.

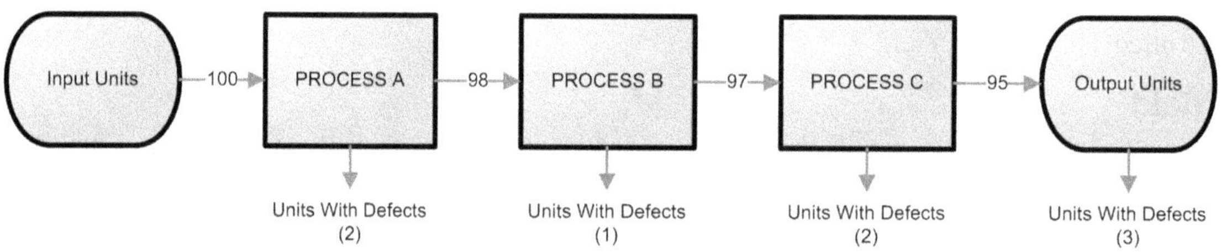

As you can see, each of the steps in this manufacturing process produces defects. These are hidden inside the process when the determination for performance is based on Final Yield. RTY on the other hand will provide a different picture. The RTY of the process shown is calculated as follows:

(98/100) x (97/98) x (95/97) x (92/95) x 100

= 0.98 x 0.9898 x 0.9794 x 0.9684 x 100 = 92.00%

Notice that the Rolled Throughput Yield (92 percent) is less than the worst yield value of any process step (96.84 percent for the output of process C).

Where a particular process step shows a significantly low yield, this step will be a relevant focal point for improving process performance in the first instance.

KEY LEARNING POINTS

- Remember the purpose of data collection planning and use a planning format that best serves that purpose.
- The best type of team to identify key variables is one that predominantly consists of people who work with and in the process.

- The process described in most cases is not necessary for a Lean specific project, the team can simply consider operationally defining the efficiency metric/s to be collected and then go collect the data.

ESTABLISH BASELINE PROCESS EFFICIENCY (STEP 9)

Process Analysis Versus Data Analysis

In the process of identifying the greatest causes of variation in the quality of an end product or service, Six Sigma focuses on data analysis. The variables that have the largest impact are located with the use of statistical methods. Solution generation methods are then used to treat those variables in a way that has the desired impact on the measurable variable of concern.

Lean on the other hand tends to focus more on *process analysis* than *data analysis*. The goal is ultimately to identify the greatest opportunities for minimising or even eliminating waste from the process itself.

Process efficiency (as a measure) is used to establish a baseline from which to begin your project. The process described in this section also sets you up for some later work in identifying where the sources of waste are, thus where you should focus your energies for the greatest improvement.

PROCESS EFFICIENCY METRICS

Establishing the process efficiency baseline can be undertaken in five steps. The first step should have been completed in the 'define' phase of the project.

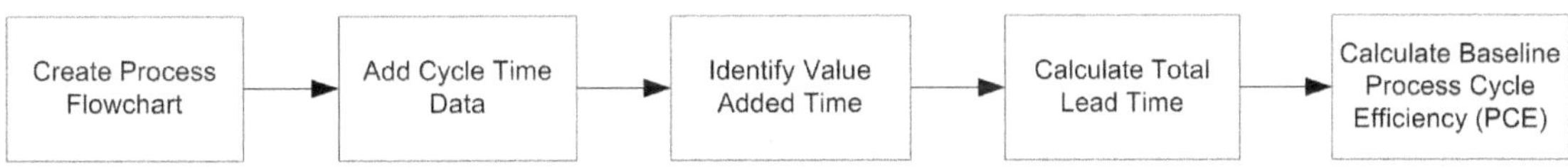

Identify Cycle Time Data For Process Steps

By eliminating time in a process, delivery of outputs can occur in a shorter time span. In manufacturing or supply of inventoried items, lead times are reduced, hence the reduction in the size of inventories held. This is the type of value a customer is demanding.

- Less work in progress
- Shorter lead times
- Time freed up to do other activities
- The trail is warmer for root cause analysis

So in working towards that goal, let's add *average* cycle time data to the process flowchart we've already documented (for our Lean case study).

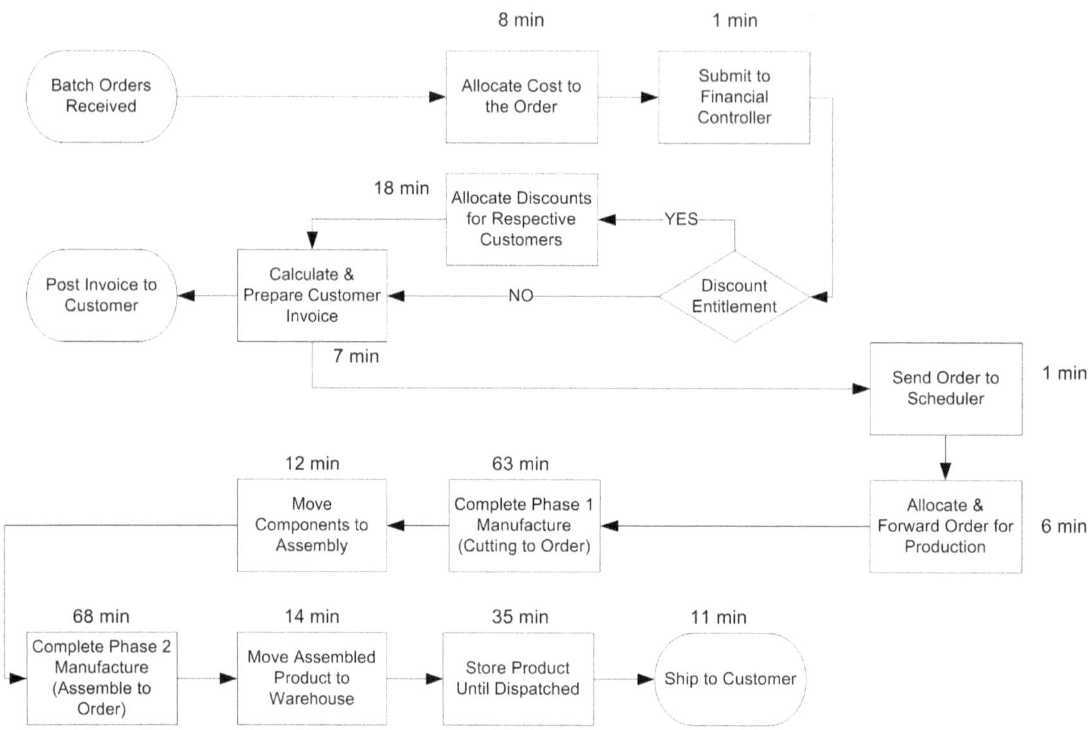

Figure 142: Process Flowchart with Average Time Included

Identify Value Added Steps

Take a look around you at work. Most people are very busy working hard. Think about your own working day - Are you busy? The question to ask is 'how much of this working time is actually spent adding value to respective customers?' Studies have found as little as 10 to 15 percent of steps in a process are involved in adding value for a customer and this can be as little as 1 percent of overall cycle time.

Time value analysis is the activity of analysing a process to understand how much time adds value and how much time does not add value. This work re-emphasises the requirement to look at a process through the eyes of the customer. In this analysis, each process step is placed into one of three categories (a) value adding, (b) value enabling and (c) non-value adding.

Value adding time is associated with any activity essential for delivering a product or service to the customer that meets their requirements.

Some Examples:

- Steps that add form or feature to a product or service
- Steps performed for the purpose of meeting customer requirements
- Steps that the customer would be willing to pay for if they knew about it

Not sure about value add, try asking 'what would the customer think or feel if we did not do this step?' If they complain then it's probably value-adding time.

Every step can be justified otherwise the steps would never have existed in the first place. Even a re-work step can be justified, but justification does not mean the step adds value to the customer. A re-work step is only necessary because of the poor performance of the process in the first place.

To determine if a process step is actually value adding, we can simply assess it against the following criteria.

- **The Customer Cares About It** - Some useful questions to ask include: 'Would the customer be prepared to pay for this step to occur if they knew about it?', OR 'Would the customer recognise this as being important?' If the answer is yes, then they probably care about it.
- **Some Change Takes Place** - When the service or product in question is being changed, the activity is contributing to the final result and this is something that the customer cares about. Sometimes there are challenges in determining whether or not this is happening when it is not a manufacturing environment.
- **This is the First and Only Time This is Performed** - When work is done right the first time, there is no need to have any rework loops in the process. A rework loop forms a 'hidden factory' that consumes resources and does not add value to the customer in any way.

Value Enabling time is associated with any activity required to do the value adding work, but do not add real value from a customer perspective. For example, the servicing of plant or equipment may not be something the customer considers value adding. However, this work is essential as the equipment enables the creation of the final product or service.

To determine if a non-value adding process step is actually value enabling, we can simply assess it against the following criteria.

- **Ensures Compliance with Legislation** – It is necessary for making sure the process and the company comply with existing legislation.
- **Provides Information Necessary for Process Function** – Vital for providing data without which the process would not be able to function properly.
- **Enables Internal Customers** – Necessary in order for some internal customers to be able to perform value-adding or value-enabling work of some type.

Caution should be exercised to ensure everything that does not fit the value-adding category is automatically labelled as value enabling.

Non-Value Adding time is that which does not meet value adding or value enabling criteria. Let me quickly remind you of the seven wastes of business process discussed earlier in the book. You should remember now all of the following are waste:

- DEFECTS
- INVENTORY
- MOTION
- TRANSPORT
- OVERPRODUCTION
- WAITING
- NON VALUE ADDED PROCESSING

Non-value adding time includes any activities that fit within this framework. The table below lists examples of non-value added activities related to these, all of which can be summarised into the seven categories listed in the right side column.

Example Non-Value Added Activities	Summarised Category
Reworking a part Returning a report to originator for correction	**Defect - Internal**
Processing a Warranty Claim Replacing or swapping a defective product Returning to do the work again	**Defect - External**
Moving inventory from the plant to a warehouse Doubling handling stockpiles Physical movement between any two locations Walking to the toolkit to obtain a tool	**Move / Shift / Transfer**
Passing a customer order from one person to another person, or from one department to another Passing the product from work group (a) to work group (b) as a part of the manufacturing process	**Handoff**
Measuring for the purpose of quality control Testing after repair work	**Inspection / Quality Control**
Changing dies in an item of manufacturing equipment Setting up a machine to do a task Re-setting a machine as product type changes Re-calibrating equipment Warming up a vehicle	**Set Up**
A document waiting for approval A part sitting in storage between receipt and issue A finished product sitting in the warehouse waiting to be dispatched to the customer	**Delay / Wait**

So let's look at two options for using this knowledge to determine value added time in the process.

- Time Value Analysis Detailed (with non-value added detail)
- Time Value Analysis Simplified (simplified model focusing on value add only)

Time Value Analysis (Detailed Option)

The Time Value Analysis Worksheet shown on the following page helps a team to separate value adding, value enabling and non-value adding *steps* in a process. If we know the average time for each of these steps, we can also separate value adding, value enabling and non-value adding *time* in that process.

This option provides detail about the type of non-value adding behaviour as a guide to help you determine what you need to do to reduce or eliminate it from the process.

I have continued to use our 'document tube' case study for the example.

				Non Value Adding						
PROCESS STEP	**Time**	**VA**	**VE**	**Defect (Int)**	**Defect (Ex)**	**Move**	**Hand Off**	**Inspec**	**Set Up**	**Wait / Delay**
Batch orders recd.										
Allocate cost to order	8								√	
Send to financial controller	1					√				
Allocate discounts	18	√								
Prepare invoice	7								√	
Post invoice	1					√				
Send order to scheduler	1					√				
Allocate for production	6								√	
Component preparation	63	√								
Send to assembly	12					√				
Assemble	68	√								
Move to warehouse	14					√				
Store product	35									√
Ship to customer	11					√				
TOTAL TIME	245	149				40			21	35
% OF TIME	100	61				16			8	15

Figure 143: Time Value Analysis Worksheet – Option 1

In the example, we can see that of total time, 61 percent is value adding. There is an opportunity to eliminate as much as 20 percent of existing time from the process simply through eliminating unnecessary waiting time and transfers.

Time Value Analysis (Simplified Option)

An alternative method of studying the value of time in a process differs from the previous in two ways.

First it is simplified by dropping the analysis of the 'non-value adding' time. Secondly, the process is described as though you were the unit passing through it. In the example this time you will notice 'wait' time has been included as steps in the process (refer to steps marked **).

PROCESS STEP	TIME (Minutes)	VALUE ADDING (✓)	VALUE ADDING TIME
Batch orders recd.			
** Wait in Tray	3		
Allocate cost to order	5		
Send to financial controller	1		
** Wait in Tray	5		
Allocate discounts	13	√	13
Prepare invoice	7		
Post invoice	1		
Send order to scheduler	1		
Allocate for production	6		
** Wait in Tray	12		
Component preparation	51	√	51
Send to assembly	12		
** Wait in Queue	14		
Assemble	54	√	54
Move to warehouse	14		
Store product	35		
Ship to customer	11		
TOTAL TIME	**245**		**118**
% OF TIME	**100%**		**48.16%**

Figure 144: Time Value Analysis Example – Option 2

In this case we can see only 48 percent of the total time taken to process document tube sales actually adds value. The rest of the time is not value adding and the team should work on either eliminating the time where it can be or where it is value enabling make it as efficient as possible.

Combined Process Mapping & Time Value Analysis

An interesting approach I observed whilst working with a Black Belt during 2003 was the combining of the process map and time value analysis. This activity involved mapping the process using standard symbols, indicating the value of each step by colour coding and marking each step with the estimated time taken. The approach is worth sharing, as I believe it delivers a number of benefits.

- Value adding and non-value adding steps can be *visually* observed
- A process devoid of non-value adding steps can *visually* observed
- It is very effective for conveying information during stakeholder presentations

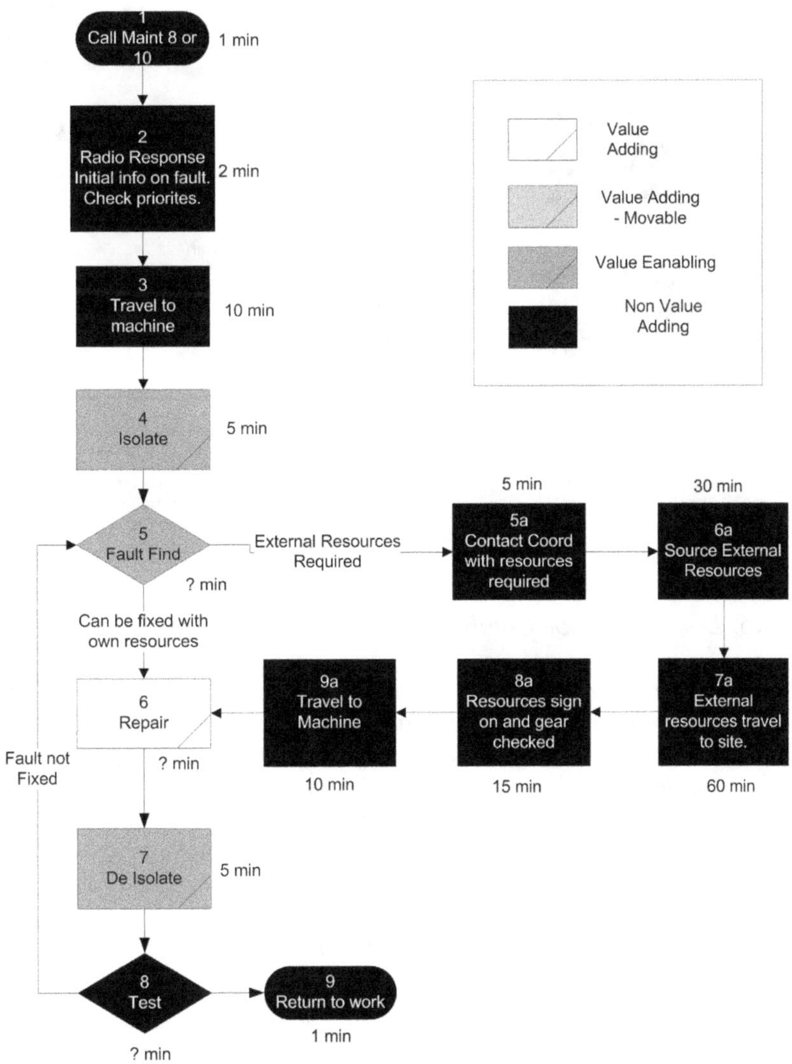

Figure 145: ***Source****: Scott McGeachie, Anglo Coal (2003), Reproduced with Permission.*

Taking our cue from this work, my preference is now to simplify the process by using a similar visual method as shown in the following diagram.

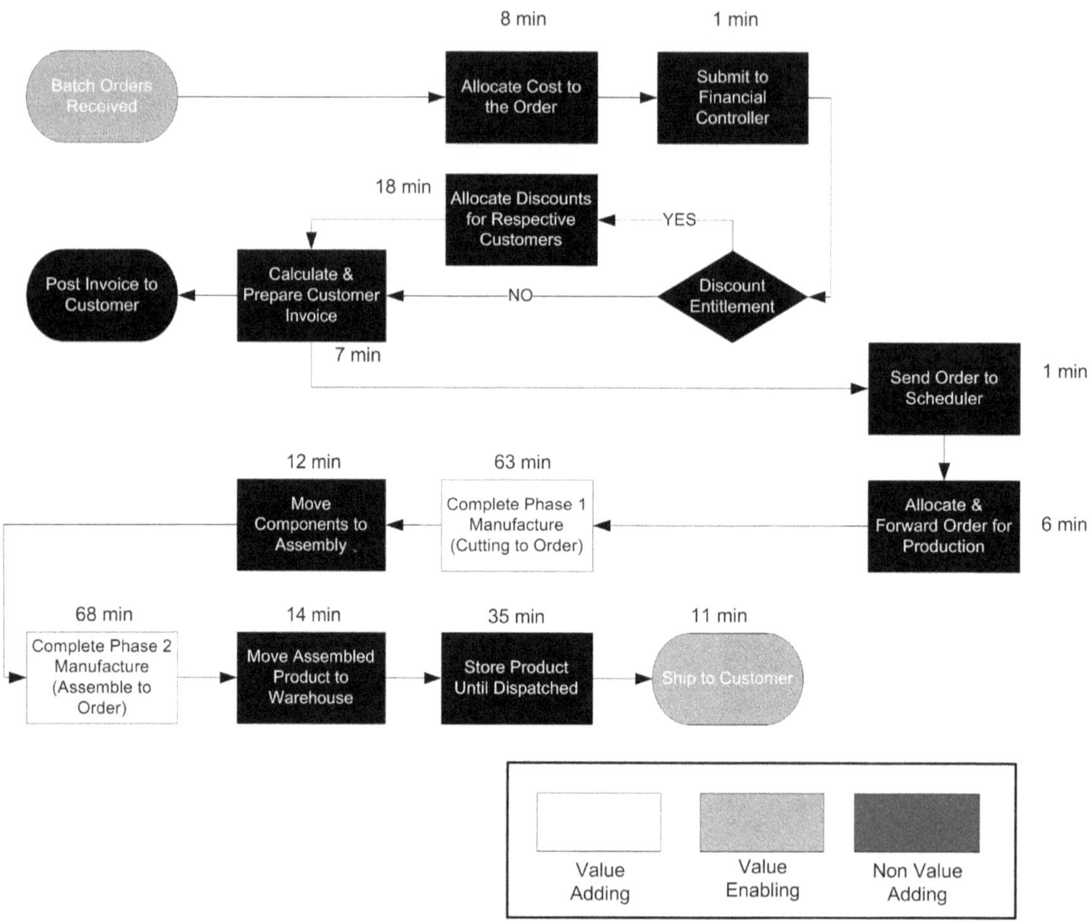

Figure 146: Document Tube Combined Process Flowchart & Time Value Analysis

'Conducting a Time Value Analysis or categorising activities can cause some level of concern for people involved in the process. In particular where a number of their activities fall into the non-value adding category. It is important to remember that this category assists in focusing the effort of the team in areas that will provide the greatest benefit. In many cases a level of non-value added activity will continue to exist. The goal is to reduce this to a minimum so that the overall lead time is the shortest it can be, with available time being transferred to other activities.'

Harry Sinko

Calculate Total Lead Time

Process efficiency formula presented here requires an understanding of how to calculate total lead-time. The formula used is known as 'Little's Law'.

Little's Law

In queueing theory, Little's Theorem (Little's Law) states that:

> *'The long-term average number of customers in a stable system (represented by N), is equal to the long-term average arrival rate (represented by λ), multiplied by the long-term average time a customer spends in the system (represented by T).'*

Mathematically this can be presented as a formula:

$$N = \lambda T$$

This simple equation implies that this behaviour is entirely independent of any of the detailed probability distributions involved and requires no assumptions about the schedule according to which customers arrive or are provided service.

The theorem, first proved by John Little of Case Western University (1961), applies to any system. It can even be applied to systems within systems. For example, the line up and service of customers at one of our banks is a system. The customer line itself could be treated as one subsystem. Each of the tellers could be treated as additional subsystems. We could apply Little's Theorem to each of the individual subsystems or we could apply it to the entire system.

Requirements for Application of Little's Law

The only requirements are these:

- The system is stable
- The system is not in an initial startup or shutdown phase

Since we know this equation is also true, we can use it to determine lead-time required for units passing through a system or process.

$$T = N \div \lambda$$

Calculating Total Lead Time With Little's Law

Total Lead Time is the total time it will take to meet a customer's request or demand as defined by the supplier.

Sometimes referred to as the 'law of velocity', Little's Law is the equation used to calculate total lead-time. It simply involves dividing total work in progress by the average completion rate or exit rate.

Total Lead Time = Work in Progress (WIP) ÷ Average Completion Rate

As a worked example, suppose one of our core business processes was to assess and approve loan applications.

If there were usually about 14 applications in the system at any one time and we were completing application evaluations at a rate of about 2 per day, we would calculate total lead-time as follows.

Total LT = 14 units / 2 per day
= 7 days (or 56 hours @ 8 hour working day)

If we wanted to reduce the lead-time, we would simply approach it in this way.

- Increase capacity or average completion rate, or
- Reduce work in progress (WIP).

Calculate Process Cycle Efficiency (PCE)

PCE is a measure of overall process health and is calculated as a *percentage* by dividing **value added time** (customers) by **total lead-time**.

PCE = Value Added Time (Customers) ÷ Total Lead Time (TLT or LT)

A PCE of 25 percent would be considered to be world class for continuous flow manufacturing processes. Target values will vary according to different industry applications, for example transactional business processes can achieve a standard of 50 percent and continuous one-piece flow processes can achieve a level of up to 75 percent.

Determining a Baseline PCE

Suppose we found that our loan application evaluation process used in the previous example had a total of 13 hours of value added time from a total processing time of 56 hours (7 days to process @ 8 hours per day).

We would be able to determine that our process is operating at about 23 percent efficiency using the figures provided and inserting them in the equation shown.

PCE = 13 ÷ 56
= 0.2321
= 23 percent

For a service industry the result is not really good enough. Though it would not be that unusual to find this and lower values where units spend long periods of time sitting in trays or being passed from person to person.

Case Study – Document Tube Factory

Total Lead Time

The team identified an average of 48 orders in the system at any one time, with orders being finalised at a rate of about 8 per day.

Total LT = 48 units ÷ 8 per day
= 6 days or 54 hours (9 hours per day)

Process Cycle Efficiency

With a total lead time of 54 hours (3,240 minutes), and value added time of 2 hours 11 minutes (131 minutes) per cycle, the team determined the baseline PCE of this process.

PCE = 131 ÷ 3,240
= 0.040
= 4.0 percent

You might have realised by now that it will require the collection of relevant timing data *after* you have laid out the process in flowchart form. After all, you have to know what steps you are going to actually go out and measure cycle time for.

Sequence

The sequence of work in completing this step may flow something like that shown on the following page.

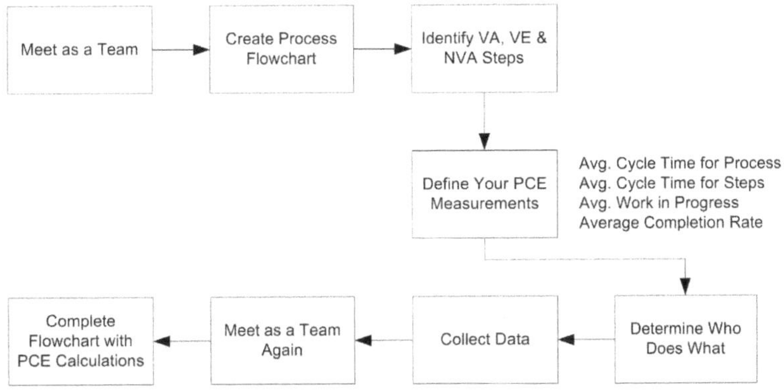

All of work discussed in this step of the DMAIC roadmap can be consolidated into a single diagram as shown in the example.

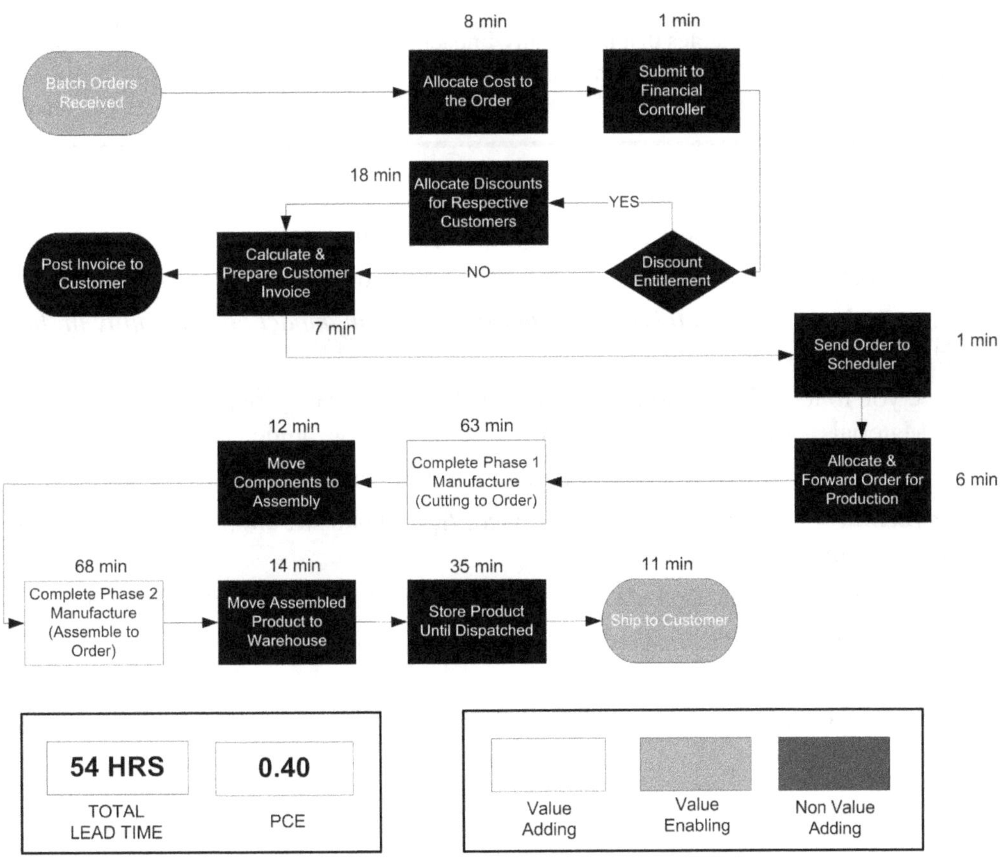

Figure 147: Baseline Process with Cycle Efficiency Metrics

CHAPTER 13: THE MEASURE PHASE TOOLKIT

XY WORKSHEET

What is it?

An XY Worksheet is simply a framework for identifying variables that potentially have high impact on primary metric variation and should be studied during the analyse phase of the project.

Primary Metric Y	Potential X's that have an impact on Primary Metric Y	Data Type	Impact on Y
(the primary metric of interest – the y)	(a list of variables that potentially impact the primary metric)	(the data type as either a C for categorical or N for numerical)	(the perceived level of impact on the primary metric y on a 0 to 5 scale)

Instructions

Step 1 - Insert the project's primary metric as the *y* you are focusing on.

Step 2 - Identify 'variables that impact the *y*' by asking a simple question.

- Ask: *What variables (the x's in this case) potentially have an impact on variability in the primary metric (y) we are studying?*
- It will serve you to look for variables within the six standard categories defined in the Cause Effect Diagram (Materials – Machines – Measures – Methods – Environment – People)

Step 3 - Separate categorical variables from numerical variables and indicate with letters.

- Ask: *If we recorded a value for this variable, what type of data would it generate?* (It would be either C for categorical or N for numerical.)

Step 4 - Rate the effect variation in each *x* has on the *y* by asking another simple question.

- *Ask: If we vary this x within its normal operating range, how much effect would it have on variation in the primary metric (y)?*
- Ratings should be on a scale of 0 to 5 where (0 = none, 1 = low, 2 = minor, 3 = moderate, 4 = major, 5 = significant).

DATA COLLECTION PLAN

What is it?

The data collection plan is a template designed to help you plan how you will collect sufficient quality data to analyse the process effectively.

PRIMARY METRIC (Y)			CATEGORICAL Xs	
Primary Metric	**What It Is**	**How To Collect It**	**Categorical Variables (Xs)**	**Sampling Plan**
What is the variable we are working to fix	How do we define the primary metric actually is so everyone understands	Exactly how do we collect it so we all do it the same way	What categorical variables do we think cause variation in the Y	How will we approach the sampling, and how many or how long will we collect in this sample

NUMERICAL Xs		
Numerical Variables	**What It Is**	**How To Collect It**
What numerical variables do we think cause variation in the Y	How do we define those numerical variables so everyone understands what they are	Exactly how do we collect these so we all do it the same way

Instructions

Process	Supporting Tools
Step 1 - Document the Process and its Inputs and Outputs • Understand the flow of work, and all potential variables for	IPO Worksheet
Step 2 – Identify the potentially significant variables that impact the Y • The most significant 'variables' will be inputs to the DC plan	XY Worksheet RCA Tools
Step 3 – Develop your Data Collection Plan • Operationally defining the primary metric by describing what it is and how to measure it. • Inserting the categorical variables that will guide you in stratifying (slicing and dicing) primary metric data when you analyse it • Inserting and then operationally defining each of the numerical variables by describing what it is and how to measure it • Deciding on a sample size and method of sampling • Decide how you will collect the data	Data types Sampling Methods Sample size calculations Operational Definition

OPERATIONAL DEFINITION

What is it?

People interpret information in different ways on the basis of their beliefs, values and experiences. When information given to any person allows room for ambiguity and interpretation, then the likelihood of that person giving that information some different meaning than what was intended is high.

The purpose of defining our measures at the start is to ensure that anyone who participates in measuring or interpreting data actually measures and interprets the same thing consistently and with minimal variation.

The process here must be used in defining numerical variables of any kind. But the tool itself (shown below) is entirely optional and not something that 'must' be created in the process of data collection planning.

The Metric	What It Is	How To Measure It	Feasible

Instructions

Step 1 – Identify the Metric - This is the performance measure under scrutiny, normally a numerical variable.

Step 2 – Describe What The Metric Is - This is a definition of the metric in a clear and easy to understand description that informs the data collector exactly 'what the measure is', and everyone can understand it.

Step 3 – Describe How to Measure It - This is a clear instruction for making the measurement and recording the data correctly. Imagine you had to tell someone how to go about measuring, this is how you should write up the instruction for how to measure this variable.

Step 4 – Determine the Feasibility of taking the measurement. A feasible measure is one that meets the following criteria.

- Is able to be collected
- Can be collected within a reasonable time frame
- Can be collected at an acceptable cost

Those that do not meet the criteria are probably not going to be collected.

ESTIMATING PROPORTIONS OF A POPULATION

Identify Data Profile: Q. What characteristic is being counted?	A Unit =
Q. What proportion (π) of the population do you believe has this characteristic? (express this as a decimal point e.g.: 0.15 – this is the same as 15%) NOTE: Sample until you find >5 units to estimate π	π = ____________________
Q. What degree of precision (***E***) do you wish to obtain? (express this as a decimal point +/- .05 is the same as +/- 5%)	***E*** = ____________________
Calculate the Minimum Sample Size: The equation to calculate the minimum sample size (*n*) for 95% confidence is: $n = \frac{1.96^2 \times \pi \times (1-\pi)}{E^2}$	(substitute your values below) $n = \frac{1.96^2 \times \quad \times (1- \quad)}{\quad^2} =$

Confidence Levels

Confidence Level	Z Value
90%	1.645
95%	1.96
99%	2.58

ESTIMATING THE MEAN OF A POPULATION

Identify Data Profile: Q. What is the measure? Q. What is being measured?	Measure ________________ A Unit = ________________
Q. What do you estimate the standard deviation of the population to be? (express this using the relevant unit of measure, e.g.: 6.5 hours, 8.27 kilograms etc) NOTE: Sample 30 units to estimate σ	$\sigma =$ ________________
Q. What degree of precision (*E*) do you wish to obtain? (express this using the relevant unit of measure, e.g.: +/- 0.5 hours, +/- 1 kilogram etc)	***E*** = ________________
Calculate the Minimum Sample Size: The equation to calculate the minimum sample size (*n*) for 95% confidence is: $n = \left(\frac{1.96\sigma}{E}\right)^2$	(substitute your values below) $n = \left(\frac{1.96 \times}{\qquad}\right)^2 =$

Confidence Levels

Confidence Level	Z Value
90%	1.645
95%	1.96
99%	2.58

PROCESS SIGMA - DPMO METHOD

1. What is the process?	
2. What is the unit produced by this process?	
3. In the eyes of the customer, what would constitute a defect in a unit produced by this process? (Refer to customer requirements)	A defect is: • ________ • ________ • ________ • ________ • ________
4. Calculate the defect opportunities per unit (O) by adding the total number of defects you identified in step 3.	O =
5. How many units (N) were processed?	N =
6. From the units processed in step 5, how many defects (D) of the type described in step 3 did you observe?	D =
7. Calculate DPMO using the equation: $1{,}000{,}000 \times \frac{D}{N \times O}$ Where: $D =$ Number of defects $N =$ Number of units counted $O =$ Number of opportunities per unit **OR**	
8. Calculate Process Yield using the equation: $\left(1 - \frac{D}{N \times O}\right) \times 100$ Where: $D =$ Number of defects $N =$ Number of units counted $O =$ Number of opportunities per unit	
9. Convert DPMO or Process Yield to a Short Term Process Sigma using the conversion table. (see appendices)	Process Sigma (short term) =

PROCESS SIGMA - Z SCORE METHOD

Step 1 Draw the distribution with relevant data. (Indicate the defect free area by shading in)	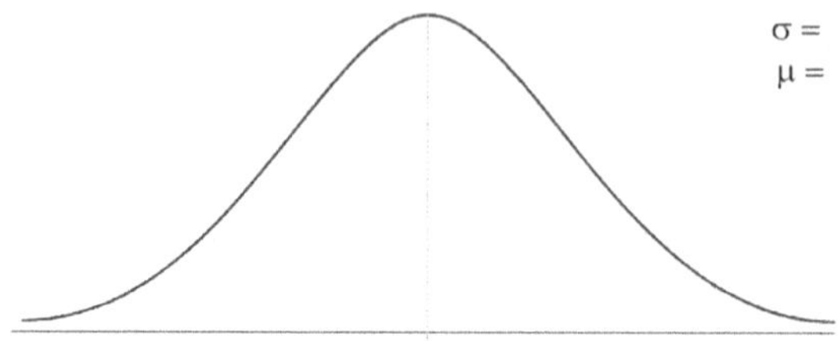
Step 2 Standardise the values associated with customer specification limits. (When only one limit is specified, disregard the other)	$(USL)Z = \frac{X-\mu}{\sigma} =$ ________ = ________ $(LSL)Z = \frac{X-\mu}{\sigma} =$ ________ = ________ 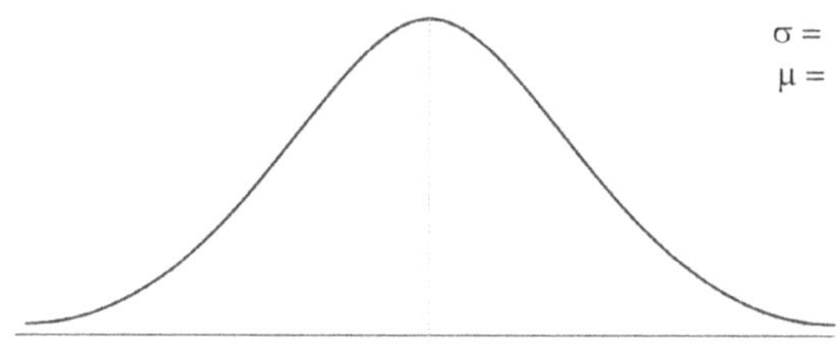
Step 3 Calculate the area underneath the curve that falls within customer specification limits using the Z Table. (Where there is only one spec limit, the other half of the distribution curve will be equal to 0.5 in any case)	**USL** -The area between Z Values of 0 and ________ = ________ **LSL** -The area between Z Values of 0 and ________ = ________ **Total Area** = ____________________ Multiply x 100 to obtain a **Process Yield** = ________________
Step 4 Convert process yield to a Process Sigma value using the conversion table. (see appendices)	**Process Sigma** = ______________ sigma.

PROCESS CYCLE EFFICIENCY METRICS

What is it?

Process Cycle Efficiency (PCE) is a measure of overall process health and is calculated as a *percentage* by dividing **value added time** (as it relates to customers) by **total lead time**.

$$\text{PCE} = \frac{\text{Value Added Time (Customers)}}{\text{Total Lead Time}}$$

Instructions

Step 1 – Identify average cycle time data for each step of the process

Step 2 – Identify value added time / steps in the process

Step 3 – Calculate Total Lead Time using Little's Law

Step 4 – Calculate PCE

Little's Law

Total Lead Time is the total time it will take to meet a customer's request or demand as defined by the supplier. It is calculated using an equation drawn from Little's Law (or theorem). It simply involves dividing total work in progress by the average completion rate or exit rate.

$$\text{Total Lead Time} = \frac{\text{Work in Progress (WIP)}}{\text{Average Completion Rate}}$$

The output of this equation is used as an input to the PCE equation.

TIME VALUE ANALYSIS (DETAILED OPTION)

What is it?

A process used to help understand value adding, value enabling and non-value adding steps in a process. Non-value adding steps are those that are associated with (a) internal failures, (b) external failures, (c) shifts or transfers, (d) handoffs, (e) set up or preparation or (f) delays.

				Non Value Adding						
PROCESS STEP	**Time**	**VA**	**VE**	**Defect - Internal**	**Defect - External**	**Move / Shift / Transfer**	**Handoff**	**Quality Control /**	**Set Up**	**Wait / Delay**
Step 1	5	✓								
Step 2	10	✓								
Step 3	25		✓							
Step 4	5					✓				
Step 5	20									✓
Step 6	12	✓								
Step 7	5						✓			
Step 8	5							✓		
TOTAL TIME	87	27	25			5	5	5		20
% OF TIME	**100%**	31%	16%			6%	6%	6%		22%

Instructions

- **Step 1** – Plot the steps in the process from the products' perspective, i.e. as though you were the product going through the process.
- **Step 2** – Identify all value adding steps on the basis of their fit with the three criteria listed earlier. The following is a summary.
    - The Customer Cares About It
    - Some Change Actually Takes Place
    - This is the First and Only Time This is Performed
- **Step 3** – Identify all value enabling steps on the basis of their fit with the three criteria listed earlier. The following is a summary.
    - Ensure Compliance with Legislation
    - Provides Information Necessary for Process Function
    - Enables Internal Customers
- **Step 4** – Identify the category of activity that best fits all remaining non-value enabling steps.

TIME VALUE ANALYSIS (SIMPLIFIED OPTION)

What is it?

Time value analysis is a simple process used to help understand value adding time in a process.

PROCESS STEP	TIME	VALUE ADDING (✓)	VALUE ADDING TIME
Step 1	0.50	√	0.50
Step 2	3.00		
Step 3	24.00		
Step 4	0.25	√	0.25
Step 5	2.00		
Step 6	1.00	√	1.00
Step 7	36.00		
Step 8	0.50	√	0.50
TOTAL TIME	**67.25**		**2.25**
% OF TIME	**100%**		**3.34%**

Instructions

- **Step 1** – Plot the steps in the process from the products' perspective. i.e. as though you were the product going through the process.
- **Step 2** – Identify all value adding steps on the basis of their fit with the three criteria listed earlier. The following is a summary.
    - The Customer Cares About It
    - Some Change Actually Takes Place
    - This is the First and Only Time This is Performed

CHAPTER 14: MEASURE PHASE TOLLGATE & CHECKLISTS

TOLLGATE QUESTIONS

The following questions are the kind that may be asked by your Master Black Belt or Lean Six Sigma Project sponsor during a 'Measure Phase Tollgate Review' which is indicated as the point between step nine and step ten on our 20-step roadmap.

	Lean	Six Sigma
CHARTER / SCOPE • What revisions need to be or have been made to the charter? • How has the scope of the project changed? • What changes need to be made to the project time line?	✓	✓
PROCESS DOCUMENTATION • How did you document the process? • Who was involved? • How do you know this is the actual process used today?	✓	✓
DATA COLLECTION • What variables did you collect data on? • How did you choose those variables? • How did you collect the data? • How do you know the data is valid and reliable? • How do you / will you know the system for measuring performance is reliable and not affecting the result? • How much data did you collect? • How did you choose your sample size? • How do you know it is a representative sample? • What time period is covered by the data you collected? • How do you know that time period is not too long or too short to be valid?		✓

	Lean	Six Sigma
BASELINE PERFORMANCE (CAPABILITY) • Did you analyse process capability? • What were the results? • Did you calculate a baseline process sigma? • What is the baseline process sigma calculation for the process? • How did you define defects, a unit and opportunities?		✓
BASELINE PERFORMANCE (EFFICIENCY) • Did you analyse process cycle efficiency? • What were the results? • How do you know the cycle time data you used is valid and reliable?	✓	
THE TEAM • Who has been involved as a team member to date? • What is the attendance rate of team members? • What level of commitment are you experiencing with your team? • What level of commitment do you perceive from the process owner? • What do you plan to do to positively impact the level of commitment demonstrated by ___? • What does the team understand of the desired outcome? • What involvement have customers had with this project to date?	✓	✓
COMMUNICATIONS • What communications have you planned to undertake with key stakeholders?	✓	✓
GENERAL • What challenges are you experiencing that I can assist with? • What is your plan from here?	✓	✓

MEASURE PHASE CHECKLIST

Six Sigma Specific Project

If you have responded appropriately to each of the following statements, then you are ready to move to the 'Analyse' phase of your project.		YES	NO	NA
1	The measure or measures relevant to performance of concern have been identified.			
2	Potential sources of variation (stratification variables) have been defined and captured on the data collection plan.			
3	Each measure has been operationally defined to ensure consistency in the method of collection.			
4	Operational definitions have been tested to ensure consistent interpretation.			
5	A data collection plan has been prepared in which the most likely 'cause' variables have been identified.			
6	Measurement system variation has been analysed to ensure that its contribution to total variation is acceptable, OR alternatively the team has confidence in the measurement system used to collect data and has made the decision not to study measurement system variation.			
7	Sample sizes have been calculated to provide designated confidence levels for relevant statistics (mean and or proportions).			
8	Data has been collected in such a way as to link stratification variables and likely cause variables to performance measures.			
9	A baseline Process Sigma has been calculated.			
10	The capability of the process to produce outputs within customer tolerances has been studied and Capability Index values have been calculated.			

Lean Specific Project

If you have responded appropriately to each of the following statements, then you are ready to move to the 'Analyse' phase of your project.		YES	NO	NA
1	Average cycle time data for each step of the process has been collected.			
2	Value adding process steps (and corresponding time) have been identified.			
3	Baseline Process Cycle Efficiency (PCE) has been calculated.			

CHAPTER 15: PROJECT 'ANALYSE' PHASE

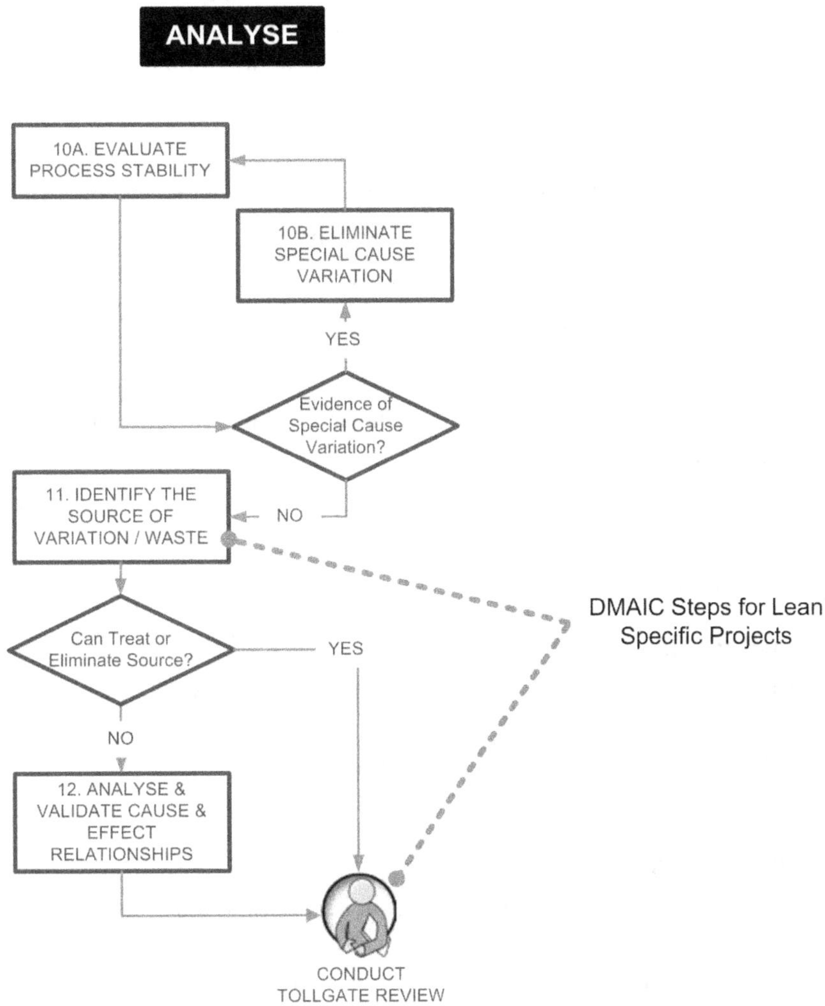

FORMS OF ANALYSIS

If any of the phases of DMAIC could be more important than the others, it's probably this phase. During the 'Analyse' phase, the work focuses on identifying what it is that can be treated to generate the desired level of improvement, irrespective of whether it's a more Six Sigma oriented project or a Lean focused project. It's at this point that you have to utilise your investigative skills and analyse the clues that are right there in front of you. These clues will be found in two locations – the performance data that you have collected and the process that you have documented.

You will probably have a sense now that much of the work you engaged in during the Define and Measure phases was either preparing you for analysis (data collection) or it actually involved some form of analysis (process capability and efficiency). In essence, analysis can take on any one of the forms discussed below.

Product or Service Analysis

This is the process of analysing a collection of data for the purpose of identifying baselines, trends, patterns and relationships that will generate and reject or support hypothesis about cause and effect relationships.

- Establishing a performance baseline for later comparison
- Evaluating process stability
- Locating the source of most variation

Process Analysis

This is the process of identifying opportunities to reduce waste, particularly that are associated with time.

- Understanding lead time
- Evaluating value adding time in the process
- Analysing process cycle efficiency
- Locating sources of waste

Cause and Effect Analysis

This is the process of identifying the variables (x's) that have the greatest impact on process performance variation (y's).

- Generating hypothesis about major causes of variation
- Validating cause and effect relationships

Relevance to Lean and Six Sigma

In the traditional Six Sigma project context, a team will take the data analysis route through to cause and effect analysis using a variety of quantitative and qualitative tools.

In the Lean focused project, the process analysis approach is primary. What's interesting is the analysis tools of Lean make the relationship between cause and effect quite evident.

THE ANALYSE PHASE AS A PROCESS

Analyse is the third phase of a team's work with the Lean Six Sigma process improvement strategy. The purpose of the analyse phase is to answer the following questions:

- Is this process stable?
- Is there a discernible source of most variation and where is it?
- If we cannot eliminate the source of variation, what is the cause that we can treat?
- Is there a discernible source of most waste and where is it? (lean orientation)

The ANALYSE Phase as a Process

The following table represents our view of the 'analyse' phase as a process at this point in the project.

INPUTS	PROCESS	OUTPUTS
A collection of valid process data (relevant to the type of project you are undertaking) A baseline measure of process performance (either capability or efficiency) for post-improvement comparison	**Six Sigma Specific Project** 1. Determine if the process is stable (treat if not) 2. Identify any sources of variation and eliminate if possible 3. Identify and validate causes of variation **Lean Specific Project** 1. Locate sources of most waste (involves the study of time, WIP etc)	**Six Sigma Specific Project** A list of validated causes **Lean Specific Project** Knowledge of what needs to be treated in order to minimise or eliminate waste from the process

Determining the State of Statistical Control

Through the use of run charts and control charts, the state of control of the process can be quickly determined. Where unexpected or special cause variation exists, the team must eliminate it before they can work effectively with expected or common cause variation.

Identifying the Source of Variation

The source of variation is identified through slicing and dicing the data using different statistical analysis tools including bar charts, Pareto charts and histograms. When the source of variation is located, the team's energy will be focused at the right level to accelerate improvement.

Identifying Causes of Variation

Any cause that has not had its relationship with the effect that is being observed validated, is only a potential cause. These are identified through the use of visual thinking tools such as cause effect trees and diagrams.

Root causes are confirmed in various ways that fall into the evidentiary categories of sensory specific, inferred or intuitive evidence. The most effective ways to confirm cause effect relationships is through the use of inferential statistical analysis tools.

Locating Sources of Waste

For Lean oriented projects, the source of waste is identified through using some very useful lean tools such as Takt Time charts, cross function flow charts and spaghetti diagrams.

Throughout this chapter, the tools associated with each of these steps are discussed in detail.

COMMON ANALYSE PHASE TOOLS

TECHNICAL TOOLS / PROCESSES	PEOPLE TOOLS / PROCESSES
Six Sigma Specific Project Control Charts / Run Charts Graphical Analysis Tools (Pareto Chart, Histogram, Multi-vari Chart, Box Plots, ANOM Charts, Scatter Plots etc) Pivot Charts, Stratification Cause Effect Relationship Analysis Tools (tree diagrams, Ishikawa diagram, five what's etc) Statistical Analysis Tools (Hypothesis Tests, Correlation Analysis, Design of Experiments etc) **Lean Specific Project** Takt Time and Takt Rate Charts Spaghetti Diagrams / Time and Motion Studies Cross Functional Flowcharts Constraint Analysis / Bottleneck Analysis	Facilitation Processes and Tools Meeting Tools (Agenda, Parking Lot, Meeting Feedback) Team Building Processes

EVALUATING PROCESS STABILITY (STEP 10)

Unless a process is stable, there is little point in trying to reduce normal variation. A process is stable when it is free of special cause variation, usually treated using some form of 'problem solving' approach. Once the process is stable then we would use a 'process improvement' approach to reduce variation.

STATISTICAL PROCESS CONTROL

Understanding Variation

Variation is not totally undesirable. Variation is the basis for satisfying our needs for new and exciting things that enrich our lives and stimulate our thinking. However, in areas where consistency and dependability are desirable, variation has a negative impact on quality and performance excellence.

Having said that, we must recognise that all processes have variation in the results they produce. No two things are exactly the same, even though they may appear to be the same. Differences will be distinguishable when we examine closely enough. To be able to improve the quality of processes, a Six Sigma Black Belt must have an understanding of the sources of variation and its effect on the results produced by the process.

We often refer to these results or outcomes as:

- The Effect
- The Response
- The *y*'s
- The dependent variables

The variables within these sources of variation that cause the results produced are often referred to as:

- The Causes or Sources
- The Factors
- The *x*'s
- The independent variables

Causes of variation can be broken into two main categories. Shewhart and Deming referred to these categories in slightly different ways.

Walter Shewhart	W. Edwards Deming
• Chance Causes • Assignable Causes	• Common Causes • Special Causes

Common Cause Variation

Common cause variation is variation we expect to see within a process. At any time, there are numerous factors that individually and in interaction with other factors cause detectable variation in a process and its outputs.

These factors operate in a random fashion, and are inherent or common to the process, hence the term '*common cause*' variation. Variation of this type is due to the system, responsibility for which rests with the organisation's Management.

To reduce variation, a project team will use a 'process improvement' approach.

Shewhart recognised that variation caused by chance causes is constantly present in a system, and the patterns of variation produced by chance causes are stable over time. If a set of data is analysed and found to show a pattern similar to the patterns produced by chance cause variation, we can assume that only chance or common cause variation is operating in the system.

In these circumstances, the process is said to be in a state of **statistical control** and therefore considered to be **stable**.

Stable Process: A process that is in a state of statistical control and has only common or chance causes of variation operating on it.

Special Cause Variation

Special cause or unexpected variation results from the undue or excessive influence of one or more causes of variation. Because the results are recognisable and able to be assigned or attributed to specific special circumstances or factors, these are referred to as *special causes* or *assignable causes.*

Examples of special or assignable causes include the following:

- **People** – differences between what people do can impact the process
- **Environment** – the effects of changes in the surroundings or natural environment in which the process operates
- **Machinery** – differences in tools, equipment and machines of all types
- **Materials** – differences or changes in the raw materials required of the process, these can include

information or data

- **Methods** – differences in the way the work is done - processes, operating procedures, job instructions etc
- **Measures** – differences in the way in which measures are taken

These headings describe the most common 'sources' of variation in a process, and form a basis for identifying root causes. Eckes (2002) refers to these as *Process Component Contributors*.

If a set of data is analysed and found to show a pattern that is not similar to the patterns produced by chance cause variation, we can assume that special cause variation is operating in the system.

In these circumstances, the process is said to be **out of statistical control**.

In these types of scenarios, the role of a project team is to eliminate the cause of unexpected variation. This is usually done through the use of a 'problem solving' approach.

Summary of Key Points

When a process is in a state of statistical control it is said to be a stable process. Only common cause variation is operating on the process – there is no undue influence by any of the sources of variation.

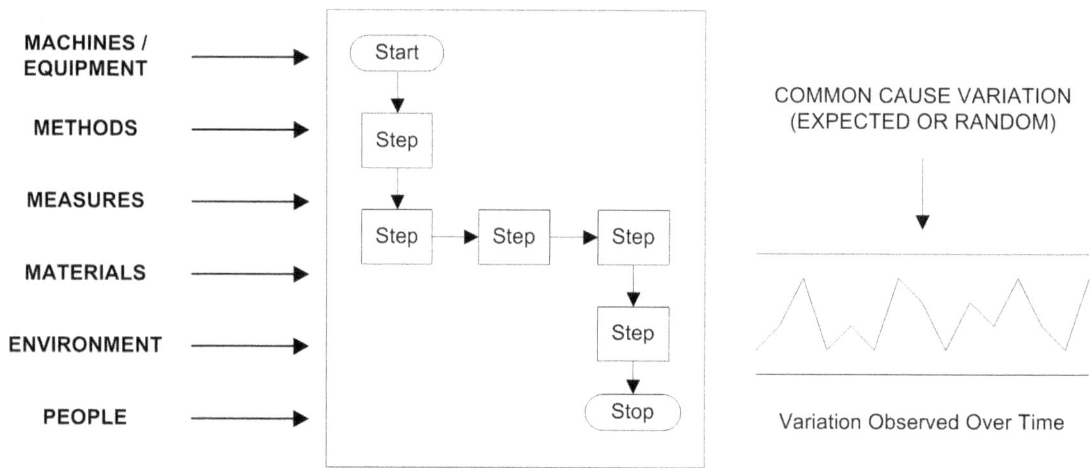

Figure 148: Common Cause Variation

When a process has special cause variation operating on it, it is said to be out of statistical control – there is undue influence by one or more of the sources of variation.

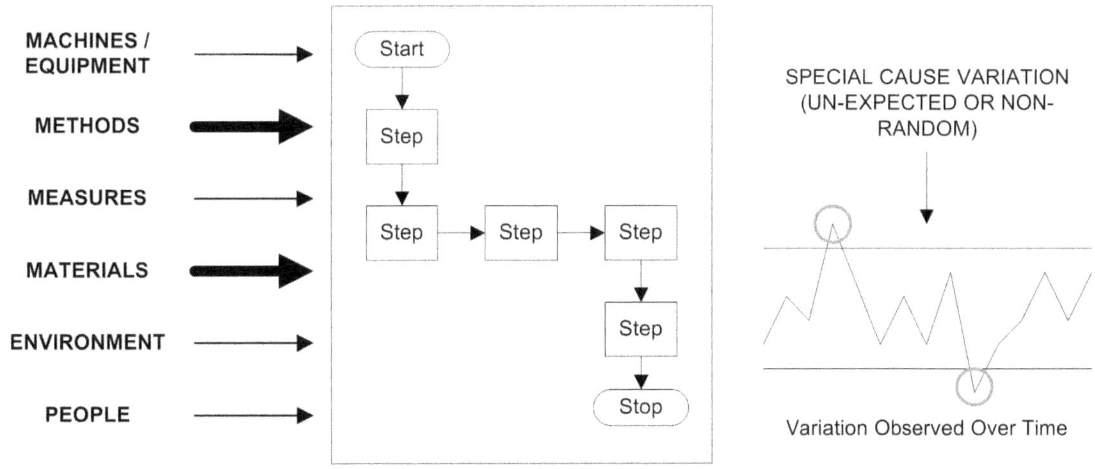

Figure 149: Special Cause Variation

In the previous diagram we see that special cause variation is being experienced because of the undue influence of variables associated with methods and materials.

The goal of teams undertaking quality improvement is quite simply to:

- Identify the causes of variation occurring within the 'sources of variation';
- Quantify the effects that these causes (x's) have on the response (y); and
- Eliminate or control the causes of variation.

RUN CHARTS

Run Charts are used to present data in what can be described as a 'movie' format. Other charts (e.g.. bar chart) can be likened to a 'snapshot' of the data at a particular point in time, however they give no indication of how the process acts in response to the dimension of time.

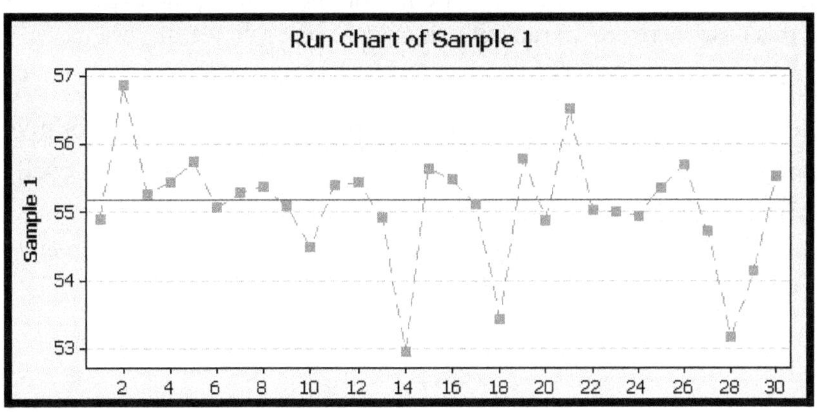

Run charts help the user identify any patterns that are starting to appear in the process by plotting data in chronological order around a centreline defined by the *median* value of the data.

Creating and Using Run Charts

A run chart is created and used in the following sequence.

- **Step 1** – Collect performance data, usually a minimum of 20 data points
- **Step 2** – Generate the run chart
- **Step 3** – Analyse 'runs about the median'
- **Step 4** – Analyse 'runs up and down'
- **Step 5** – Check for special causes

Runs About the Median

A single 'run about the median' is a series of values on the same side of the median. A series can be of any length however it does not include any values that are actually on the median.

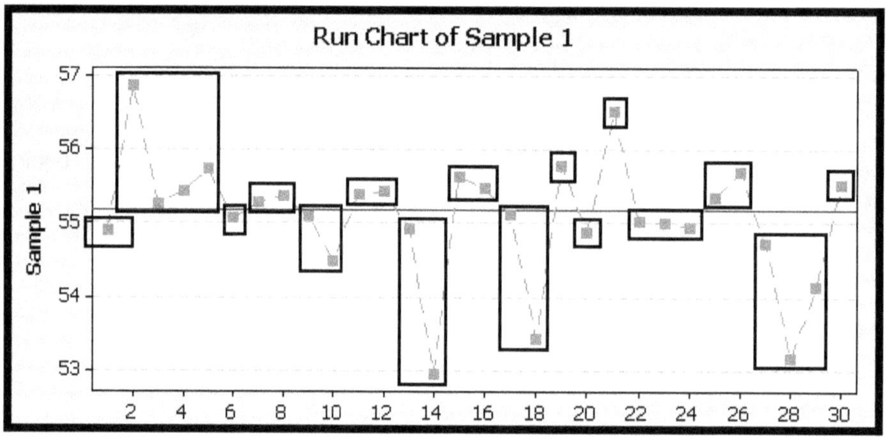

Figure 150: Runs About the Median

The diagram represents a run chart of 30 data points. By referring to the table on the following page, we can see that for a data set consisting of 30 values that are not on the median, the expected number of runs would be from 11 to 20. In this case there are 16 runs which is an acceptable result.

Expected Number of Runs About the Median

The table on the following page provides a guide to the expected number of runs for given circumstances.

- When we experience too many runs, process behaviour is moving towards a cyclic situation that is referred to by the term *mixtures*.
- When we experience too few runs, process behaviour is moving towards a *clustering* pattern where big groups of consecutive values are clustered along the time line.

Table of Expected Number of Runs About the Median

The number of runs you should expect when only common cause variation is acting on the process is in the range of values defined by the lower and upper limits in the table.

Data Points Not On Median	Lower Limit	Upper Limit	Data Points Not On Median	Lower Limit	Upper Limit
10	3	8	**34**	12	23
11	3	9	**35**	13	23
12	3	10	**36**	13	24
13	4	10	**37**	13	25
14	4	11	**38**	14	25
15	4	12	**39**	14	26
16	5	12	**40**	15	26
17	5	13	**41**	16	26
18	6	13	**42**	16	27
19	6	14	**43**	17	27
20	6	14	**44**	17	28
21	7	15	**45**	17	29
22	7	16	**46**	17	30
23	8	16	**47**	18	30
24	8	17	**48**	18	31
25	9	17	**49**	19	31
26	9	18	**50**	19	32
27	9	19	**60**	24	37
28	10	19	**70**	28	43
29	10	20	**80**	33	48
30	11	20	**90**	37	54
31	11	21	**100**	42	59
32	11	22	**110**	46	65
33	11	22	**120**	51	70

Runs Up and Down

A 'run up' is a series of values consecutively increasing in value. Conversely, a 'run down' is a series of values consecutively decreasing in value. A series (a run up or a run down) can be of any length without regard to their relationship with the centreline (median value).

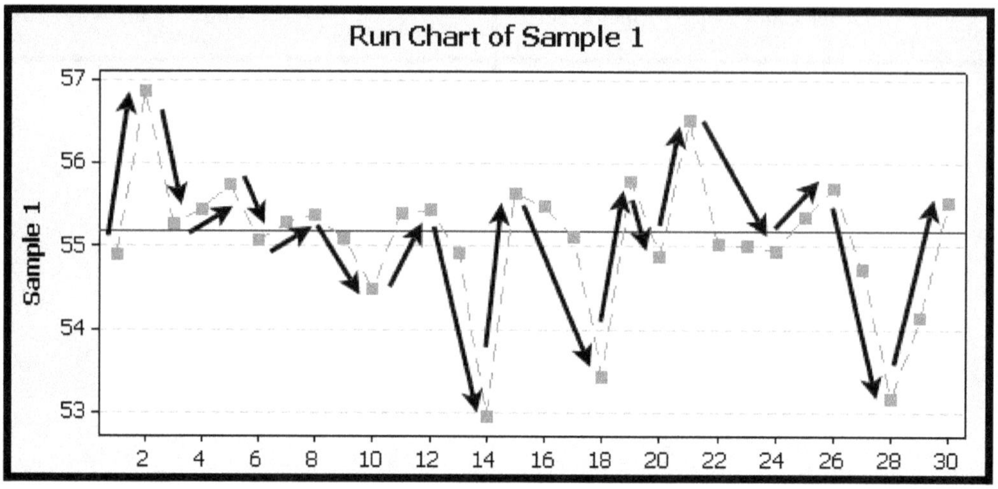

Figure 151: Runs Up and Down

The run chart of 30 data points shows a total of 17 runs up and down.

Expected Number of Runs Up and Down

Too many and too few runs up and down are signals that special causes exist.

- When we experience too many runs up and down, process behaviour is moving towards a cyclic situation that is referred to by the term *oscillation*.
- When we experience too few runs, process behaviour is moving towards a *trending* pattern.

Length of a Single Run Up or Down

The length of any single run up or run down is also an important factor in determining special causes that contribute to a trend (as we will discuss in the control chart section).

The following table provides a guideline for how many data points in a run up or down might indicate special cause variation.

Total Number of Data Points	**Number of Consecutive Data Points (Indicating Special Cause)**
5 to 8	4+
9 to 20	5+
21 to 100	6+
> 100	7+

Run Chart Patterns For Out of Control Situations

Run charts can be used to check a process for special causes. Where any of the following patterns are observed, this is an indication that special causes may be operating on the process.

- Too many runs about the median (Mixture Pattern)
- Too few runs about the median (Cluster Pattern)
- Too many runs up and down (Oscillation Pattern)
- Too few runs up and down (Trend Pattern)

Runs About the Median	Runs Up and Down
MIXTURE PATTERN 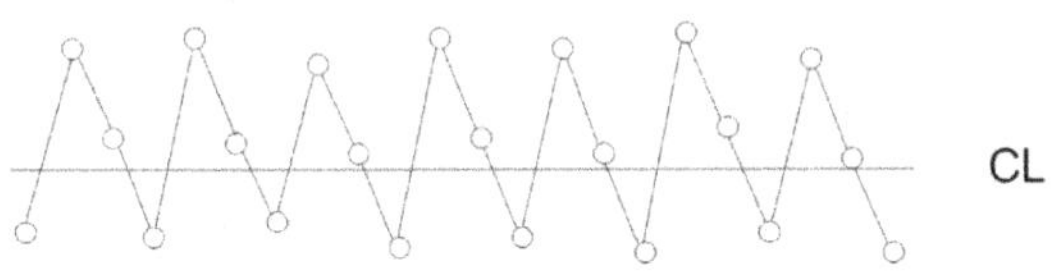 	**OSCILLATION PATTERN** 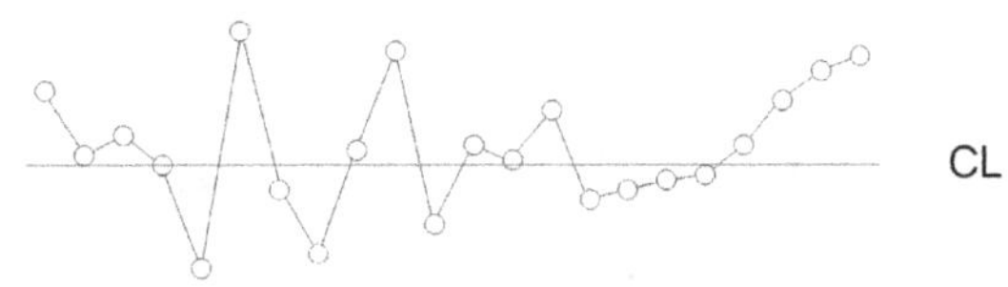
CLUSTER PATTERN 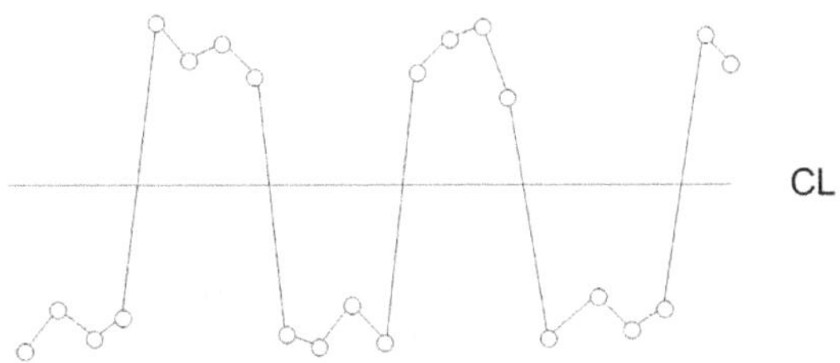 	**TREND PATTERN** 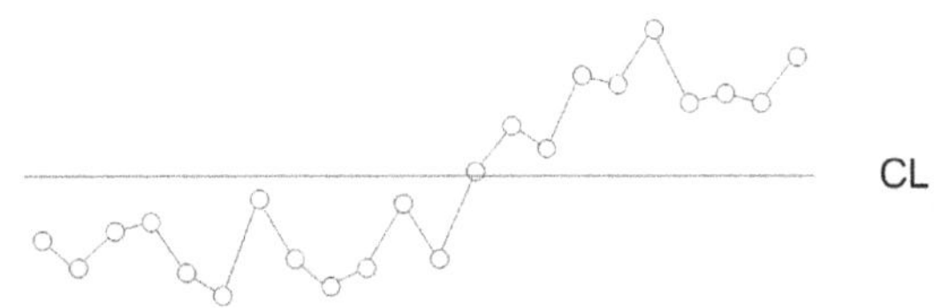

More information about these types of patterns is contained in the next section dealing with Control Charts.

Using P-values with Run Charts

While this subject is covered in much greater detail in the section on Hypothesis Testing, let me just give you a quick explanation of how P-values are used with Run Charts.

P-values range between 0.00 and 1.00. We will use the p-value to decide if the departure from what we would expect to see if only common cause variation existed is significant enough to say special causes are probably acting on the process.

We have to use a specific number to determine the cut off point between low and high P-values. This is called 'Alpha' (α) or the 'level of significance'. As a general rule for all statistical analysis other than normality testing, we use an α value of 0.05.

If the P-Value is less than α, the departure from what we expect to see is statistically significant, so we assume special causes.

Example Run Chart With P-Values

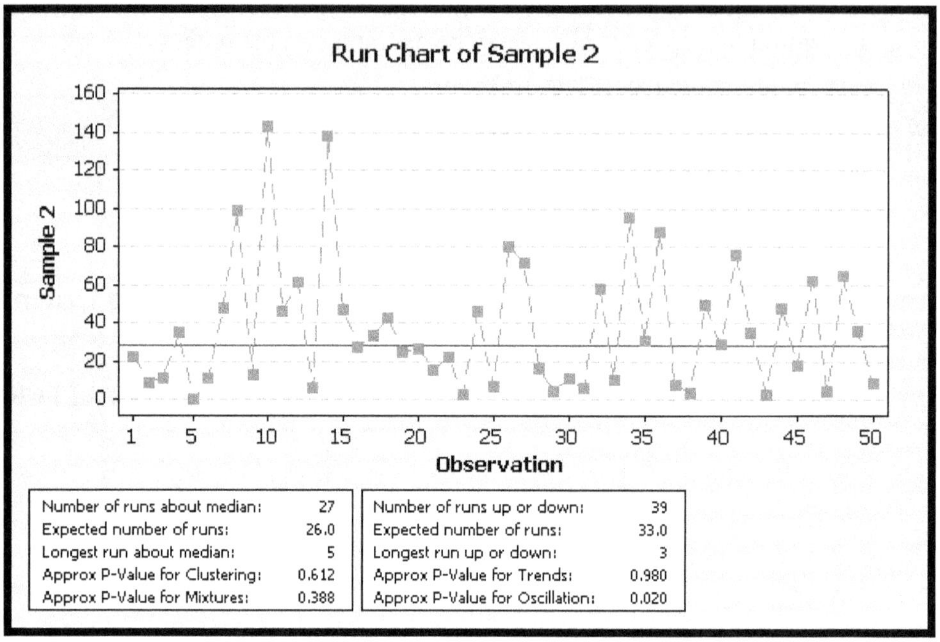

Figure 152: Run Chart with P-values for Patterns

Referring to the table below, P-values in our example run chart indicate (a) no clustering, (b) no mixtures, (c) no trends, but (d) the existence of an oscillation pattern.

We can observe a tendency for the process to oscillate up and down more frequently then should be the case in the absence of any special causes.

In this case, it could be that an operator adjusts the process in response to up and down results in an effort to control variation. In the process of doing this the operator creates a situation where results oscillate up and down.

Interpreting Run Chart P-Values

Runs About the Median	Runs Up and Down
Mixtures A *low P-value* = EXISTS A *high P-value* = DOES NOT EXIST **Clusters** A *low P-value* = EXISTS A *high P-value* = DOES NOT EXIST ——— NOTE: Only one of these situations can exist at any one time.	**Oscillation** A *low P-value* = EXISTS A *high P-value* = DOES NOT EXIST **Trends** A *low P-value* = EXISTS A *high P-value* = DOES NOT EXIST ——— NOTE: Only one of these situations can exist at any one time.

CONTROL CHARTS

Introduction

Control charts are one of the most revealing tools you will use in helping understand the process you are measuring. Walter Shewhart introduced control charts in 1924. They were created for the purpose of separating the variation you see in your process into two categories.

As discussed earlier, these categories are:

- COMMON CAUSE VARIATION: Variation that we would expect to see within the process, it is sometimes referred to as 'expected', 'normal' or 'random' variation. It is the natural variation of the process.
- SPECIAL CAUSE VARIATION: Variation due to the undue influence of one or more of the components in the process, it is sometimes referred to as 'unexpected', 'non-normal' or 'assignable' variation. It is the result of some event or action, or a series of events or actions.

It is not economically worthwhile to try and sort out why a particular value occurred, while the process is in a state of statistical control, as this result exists within the limits of expected variation. It is however, worthwhile looking for the cause of a value appearing outside the control limits, as this will be due to some undue, assignable or special cause.

Control charts provide a mechanism for identifying signals that special cause variation is operating on the system, against the background noise of common cause variation. Where special cause variation is detected, these can be treated to reduce overall variation. Where only common cause variation is operating, any attempts to adjust and respond to individual values will only have the effect of increasing variation, not reducing it. In this situation, it is management's responsibility to change the process in order to reduce common cause variation and improve quality.

Distribution of Data – Does It Need To Be Normal or Not?

There is often a perception that because the control limits are calculated on the basis of +/- 3σ, the data needs to be normally distributed.

According to Shewhart, this is not the case.

In fact Shewhart once stated: *"All attempts to find a unique functional form [distribution] for statistical control are blasted"*. Shewhart refers to these limits as economic limits and not probability limits, indicating that it is economically worthwhile looking at values outside these limits.

Therefore, we do not talk about the requirement of a normal distribution and its probability properties being relevant to statistical process control. You will see later that control charts are also developed for data that follow Poisson and Binomial Distributions.

(For those of you wanting more information, I would recommend text by statistician, Donald Wheeler.)

Purpose of a control chart

The purpose of a control chart is to:

- Focus attention on detecting and monitoring process variation over time.
- Separate common cause variation from special cause variation as a guide to management action.
- Monitor the mean and variation about the mean.
- Provide a foundation for common language for discussing process performance.

Basic Format of a Control Chart

Constructing a control chart requires estimating a measure of central tendency (the mean in this case) and a measure of variation (standard deviation or standard error of a statistic). Once determined, control limits and the centre line can be calculated and placed on the chart with the plotted values under analysis. Just as we do with run charts, these individual values are plotted from left to right in the relevant time order.

Let's look at this in more detail.

The figure shown represents the normal distribution.

We will refer to this distribution as it provides a simple basis from which to explain the principles of a control chart.

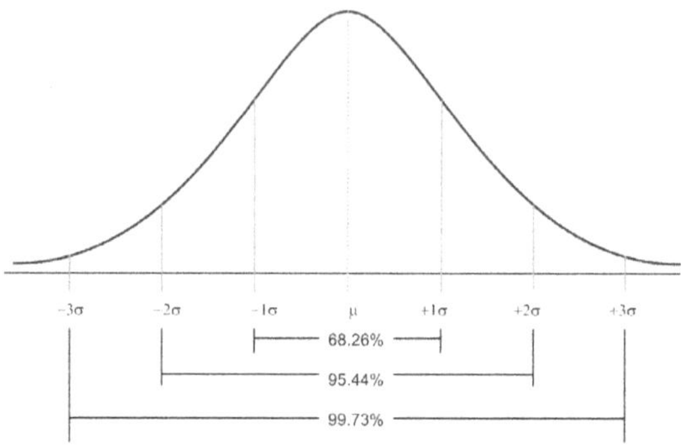

Figure 153: Normal Distribution

From our studies of normal distributions, we know that 99.73 percent of the area underneath the normal curve falls between +3 and –3 standard deviations from the mean.

Therefore, we also know that only 0.27 percent of the area falls outside these limits. If only common cause variation was operating on this process, we would expect 99.73 percent of individual values to fall within +/- 3 standard deviations from the mean. The likelihood or probability of getting a value outside these limits for a stable process is only 0.27 percent, small enough for us to suspect that special cause variation may be present in our process.

The following diagram, adapted from Levine, Ramsey and Smidt (2001), shows the relationship between a control chart and [in this case] a normal distribution.

The control chart has a **Centre Line (CL)** that corresponds to the distribution mean.

The **Lower Control Limit (LCL)** is placed at a position -3σ from the mean, and the **Upper Control Limit (UCL)** is placed at a position +3σ from the mean.

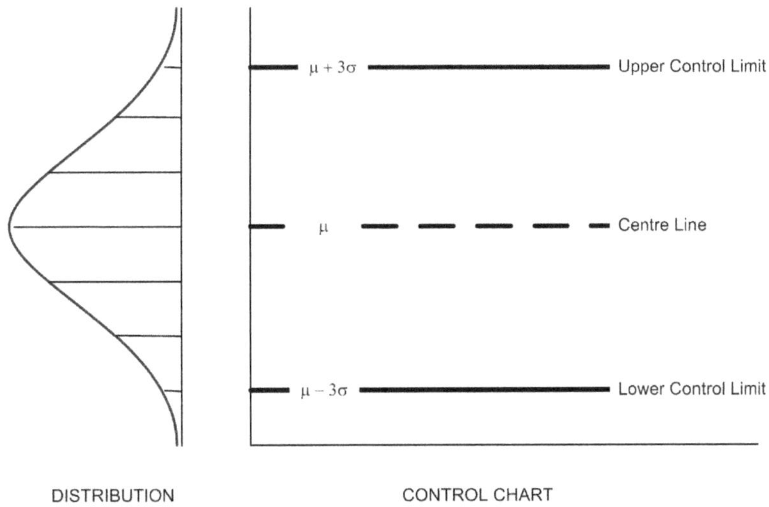

Figure 154: Control Limits and their Relationship To The Normal Distribution

The control limits help you make a decision about whether or not a value has departed from the norm to the point that it should be investigated. For example, when a value appears outside control limits, this is a signal to investigate the cause so that it can be resolved.

Why +/-3 Standard Deviations?

To answer this quite reasonable question, let's refer to the four diagrams shown.

Exhibit 1. Control limits are positioned quite close to the centre line, in fact they are so close that an out of control state is indicated, yet only common cause variation is acting on the process. Too close and we start reacting to erroneous signals.

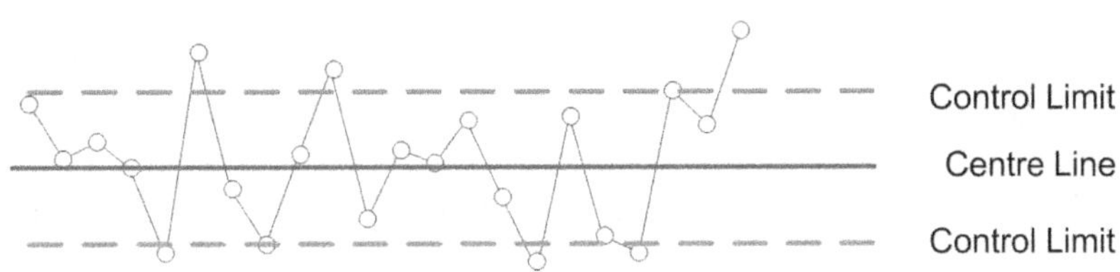

Figure 155: ***Exhibit 1*** *- Control Limits Set Too Close to the Centre Line*

Exhibit 2. Control limits are positioned well away from the centre line beyond 3 standard deviations. Special causes are acting on the process yet control limits are so wide that the chart indicates the process is in control. Too far apart and we don't get the signals so we don't respond when we should.

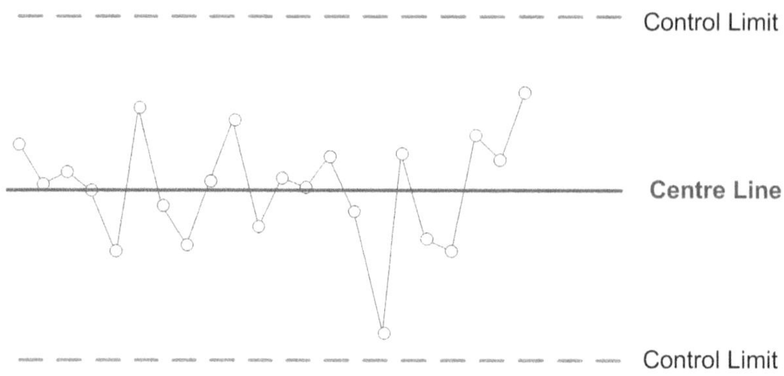

Figure 156: ***Exhibit 2*** *- Control Limits Set Too Far From the Centre Line*

Placing control limits at plus and minus 3 standard deviations provides the best balance between false signals and no signals.

Remember, the probability of a value falling above the upper control limit [at +3 standard deviations] when only common cause variation is operating is approximately 0.00135 or 0.135 percent. The same probability exists with respect to a value falling below the lower control limit [at -3 standard deviations] when only common cause variation is operating.

The following two diagrams present the same two situations with correctly placed control limits.

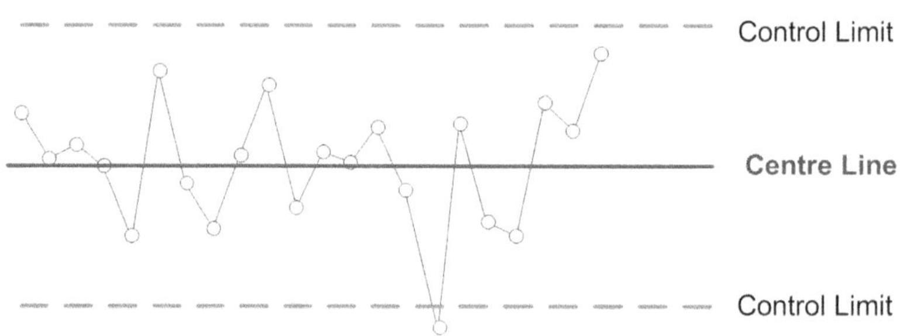

Figure 157: ***Exhibit 3*** *- Control Limits Set Correctly - Special Cause Variation is Present*

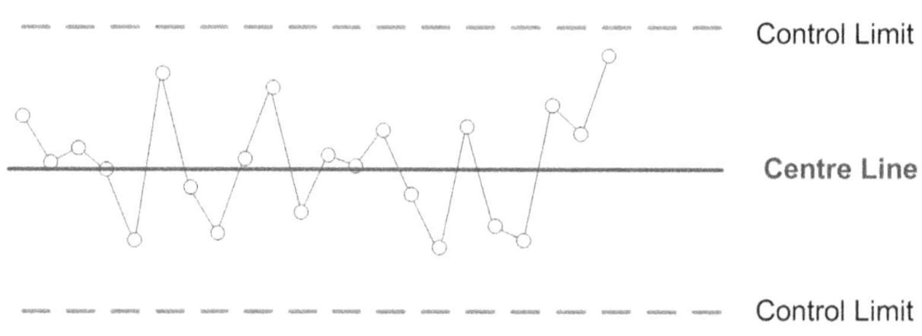

Figure 158: ***Exhibit 4*** *- Control Limits Set Correctly – Only Common Cause Variation Present*

Without the existence of control limits, we exist in a subjective world where I am sure we would end up chasing our tails trying to resolve variation that is normal or expected process variation.

Out of Control Signals and Patterns

I've mentioned the idea of a single value being undesirable if it's outside the control limits, however this is not the only signal that a process is not stable.

A process is said to be *out of statistical control* if it exhibits any of the following signals or patterns.

OUTLIER – Any value that falls outside the upper or lower control limits is considered to be an outlier. Pyzdek (2003) refers to these as "freaks" as they are the result of "freak causes".

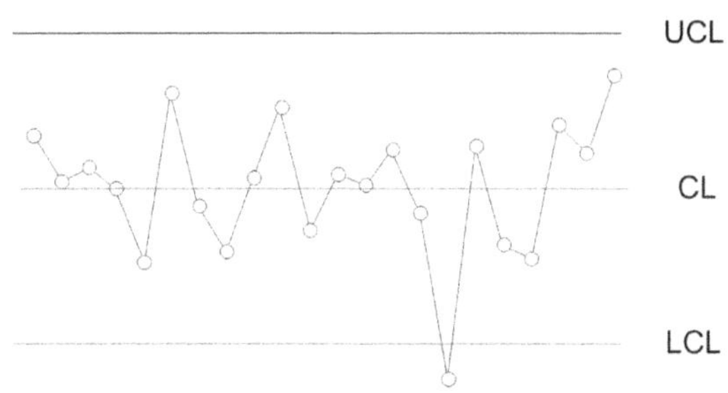

Figure 159: Outlier Patterns

When an outlier is identified, the cause should be identified. When the result can be explained, the decision can be made to remove the value from the analysis.

For example, suppose the value was the result of a planned shutdown of a piece of equipment, it would make no sense to leave the value in the analysis.

CYCLIC PATTERN – The cyclic pattern is characterised by a wave like pattern along which values increase for a period, then decrease for a period and then repeat these periods.

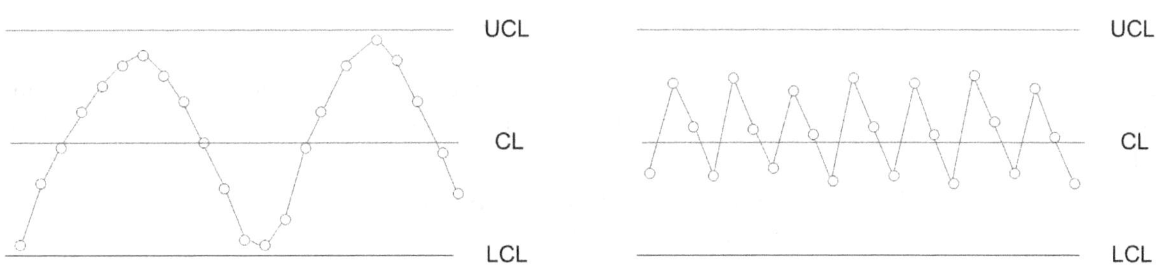

Figure 160: Cyclic Patterns

Similar to a mixture pattern, this pattern provides signs that the data can be broken down further as multiple processes exist. The pattern is the result of special causes such as systematic environmental changes over a period of time, e.g. seasons.

The pattern could also be the result of changes in materials, equipment or people. For example, performance levels across three shifts may differ significantly, however, within each shift the process is in control.

If this data was plotted in histogram format, it is likely that a multi modal distribution will be evident.

CLUSTER PATTERN – The cluster pattern is characterised by groupings of data at extremes of the chart. Very few values lie on or about the centre line.

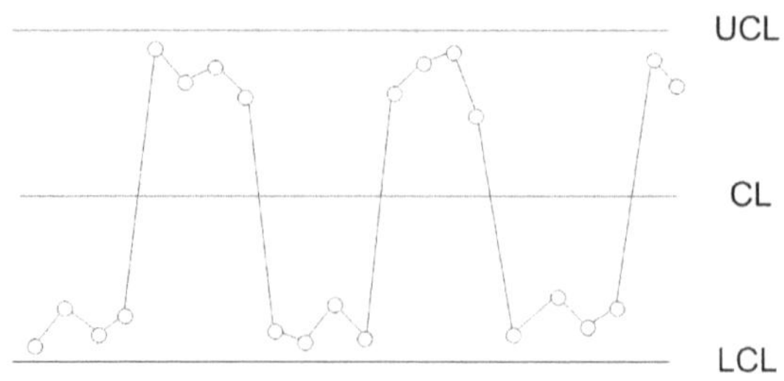

Figure 161: Cluster Pattern

A cluster pattern is an indication that the data is from multiple populations (e.g. day shift and night shift results) and it should be stratified to find the source of each cluster. If the data shown above were plotted in a histogram, the result would be a *bimodal* distribution.

TREND – A trend is characterised by the movement of values in one direction, either up or down.

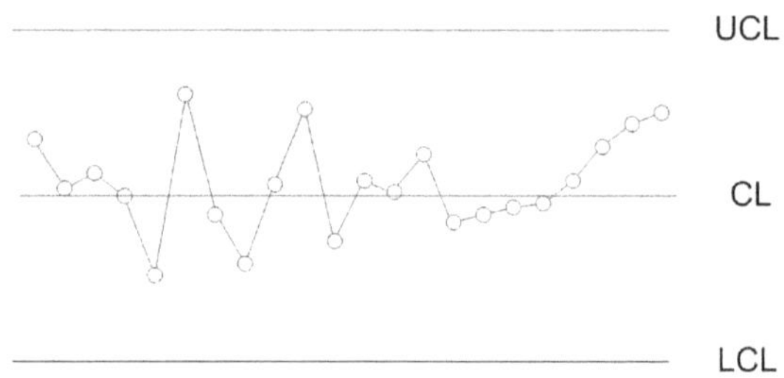

Figure 162: Trend Pattern

These may be signs of wear and tear or fatigue in people or equipment, or changing environmental conditions over time such as temperature or moisture conditions, build up of material or waste, or settling of materials.

On the upside, this may be an indication that performance is improving due to the learning process, or conditions are becoming more favourable in a systematic way.

PROCESS SHIFT – When the values move from a random pattern and fall on one side of the centre line, this indicates something in the process has changed.

This could be a change in personnel, materials, equipment or the like. In any case the process is no longer the same.

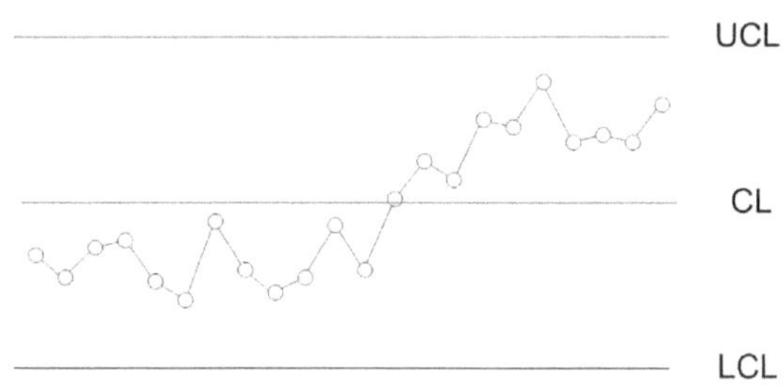

Figure 163: Process Shift

PROCESS DRIFT – Any pattern showing a process shift followed by a sudden shift back to the original values and then shifting again is a sign that the process is changing over time and then being brought back to original settings.

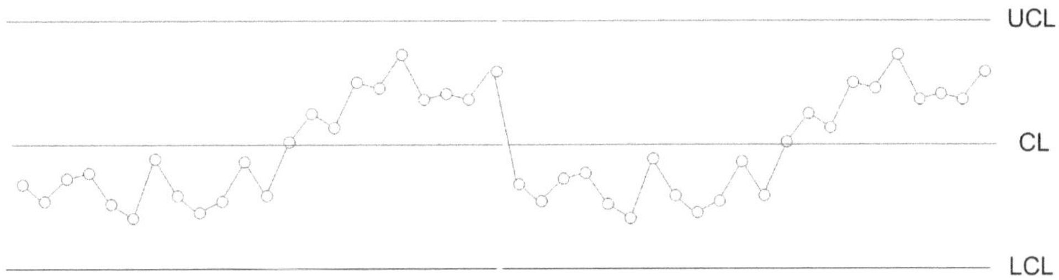

Figure 164: Process Drift

For example, a relatively old crusher located at one of the iron ore plants in Western Australia experienced continually changing settings. The crusher would be set to crush at a particular size and over the course of a week, this setting gradually got larger. It was weekly practice to reset the crusher settings manually before the ore size coming out of the crusher was too large for the processing plant. The control chart of ore size from that crusher showed a drift in the process on a weekly basis.

Conditional Probability

Almost all of the decision rules about what constitutes one of these patterns or signals are based on conditional probability.

Conditional probability refers to the probability of getting a specific result, given that a specific result has already occurred. For example,

- The probability of getting a head in the toss of a fair coin is 0.5.
- The probability of getting two heads in a row in two tosses of a fair coin is 0.5 x 0.5 = 0.25.
- The probability of getting 5 heads in a row in five tosses of a fair coin is 0.5 x 0.5 x 0.5 x 0.5 x0.5 = 0.03125.

The key point to remember is this: these probabilities are based on only common cause variation acting on the coin.

If the coin is biased towards one side (a special cause would exist), obviously probabilities would change. The same applies to process performance.

For example, the probability of getting 8 or more consecutive points in a row on one side of the centre line, if only common cause variation was acting on the process, is so low that it is more likely to be the result of special causes.

Decision Rules

The rules for deciding when a process is out of statistical control vary between textbooks. The table below provides a number of examples.

Pattern	Levine, Ramsey & Smidt (2001)	Minitab Defaults
CYCLE		14 points in a row alternating up and down.
OUTLIER	A point falls above the upper control limit or below the lower control limit.	1 point more than 3σ from the centre line.
SHIFT	8 or more consecutive points lie above or below the centre line.	9 points in a row on the same side of the centre line.
TREND	8 or more consecutive points move upward or downward in value.	6 points in a row, all increasing or decreasing.
"	2 out of 3 consecutive points fall outside either + 2σ or - 2σ limits.	2 out of 3 points more than 2σ from the centre line, on the same side.
"	4 out of 5 consecutive points fall outside either + 1σ or - 1σ limits.	4 out of 5 points more than 1σ from the centre line, on the same side.
"		15 points in a row less than 1σ from the centre line.

Out of Control Decision Rules

Using Control Charts

There are four steps to follow in using controls charts.

- **Step 1** - Identify your data type
- **Step 2** - Select the relevant control chart
- **Step 3** – Plot the data over time using the relevant control chart
- **Step 4** – Analyse the chart and take action for any out of control situations.

Identifying your data type

Control charts are used to plot two types of data:

Variables Data	Attribute Data
Any discrete or continuous numerical variables: • Number of golf strokes for 18 holes, • Width of a part, • Cycle time for a delivery etc.	Any counts of: (a) the number of defects in a sample, or (b) number of defective units in a sample.

Selecting the Appropriate Control Chart

The decision flowchart shown in the following diagram provides a simple method of choosing the most appropriate control chart for your data set.

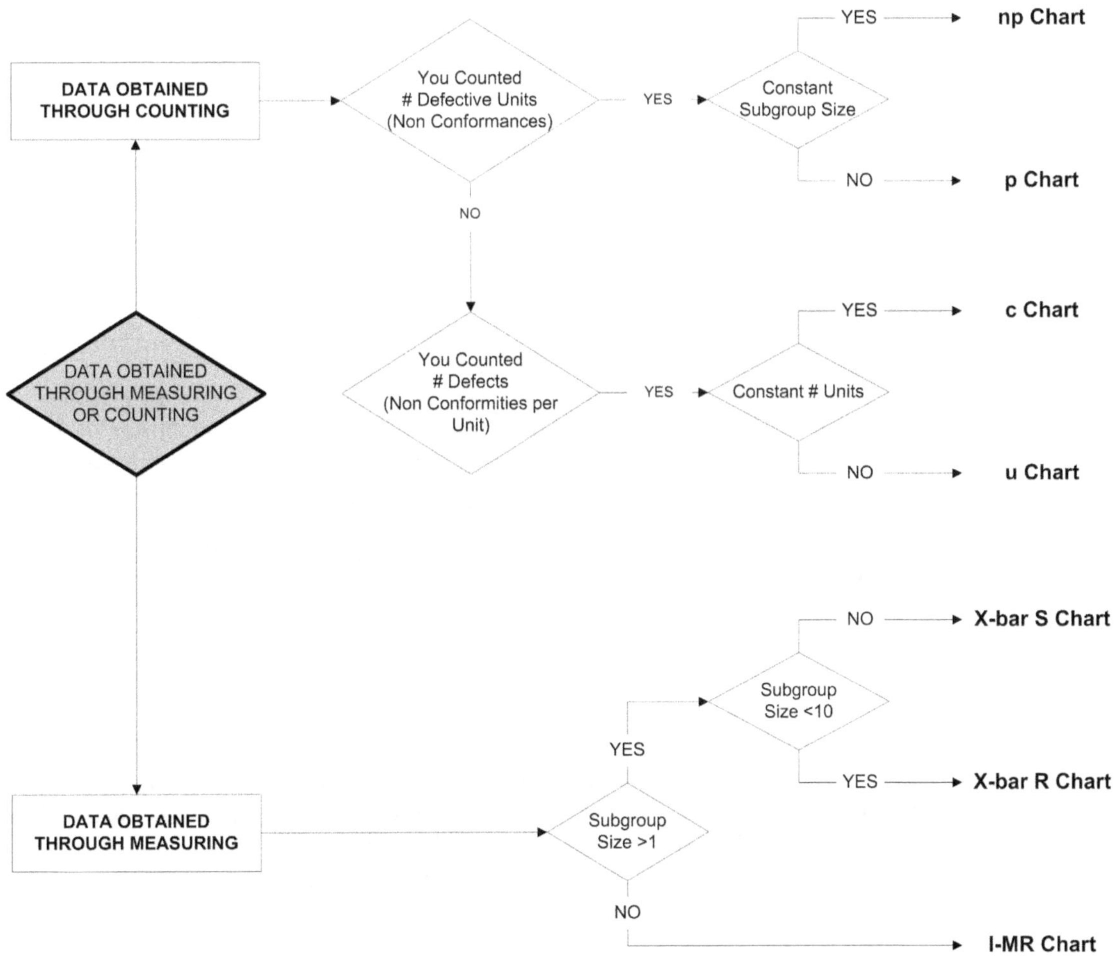

Figure 165: Decision Flowchart for Control Chart Selection

Common Control Charts

Control charts can effectively be arranged in two categories according to the type of data used to generate the control chart. The two categories are (a) **Attribute Control Charts**, and (b) **Variables Control Charts**.

A summary of the most common charts used and their application is shown in the following table.

Chart	Data Type	Sample Size	Application
Individual Chart	Variables	1	Plots **individual** values
Moving Range Chart	Variables	1	Plots the **moving range** (range from each value to the next)
X-bar Chart	Variables	>1	Plots the **mean** of a subgroup of values
R Chart	Variables	2 – 9	Plots the **range** of subgroups of values
S Chart	Variables	≥ 10	Plots the **standard deviation** of subgroups of values
NP Chart	Attributes (defective units)	Constant	Plots the **number** of items in a consistent sized sample or subgroup that are non-conforming (**defective**). For example, counting defective units each day from a consistent sample of 50 units per day. As the number of non-conforming items is expected to be the proportion (p) times the sample size (n), these are often called np charts. These charts are based on the Binomial Probability Distribution.
P Chart	Attributes (defective units)	Variable	Plots the **proportion** of units that are non-conforming (**defective**). They can be used with both equal and unequal sample or subgroup sizes. This chart is based on the Binomial Probability Distribution.
U Chart	Attributes (defects)	Variable	Plots the statistic '**u**', which is the ratio of number of **defects** counted to the size of the subgroup. Used when the size of the subgroup is not consistent. For example counting the number of defects through the production line each day when the number of units changes each day. This chart is based on the Poisson Probability Distribution.
C Chart	Attributes (defects)	Constant	Plots the relevant **count** of **defects** when the subgroup size remains constant. For example, counting vehicle defects in a consistent sample of 20 vehicles per day. This chart is based on the Poisson Probability Distribution.

Table of Commonly Used Control Charts

Attribute Control Charts

NP Charts

NP Charts are used to plot the **number** of items in a consistent sized sample or subgroup that are non-conforming (**defective**). As the number of non-conforming items is expected to be the proportion (p) times the sample size (n), these are often called *NP* charts. These charts are based on the Binomial Probability Distribution.

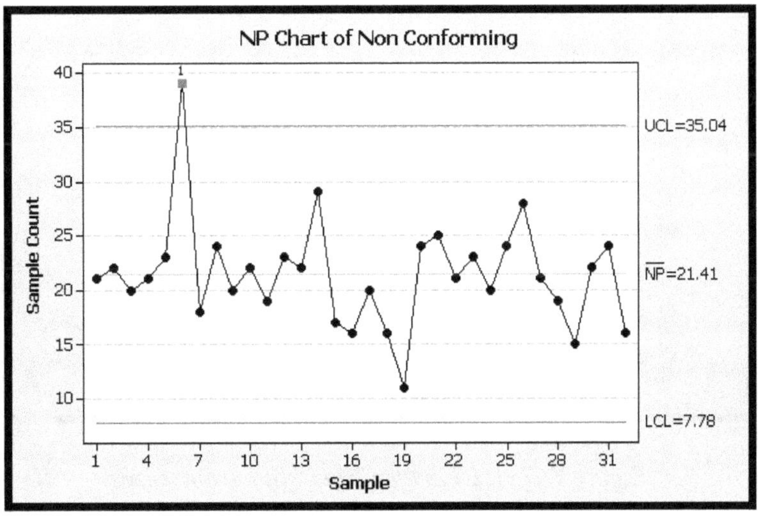

Figure 166: NP Chart

Centre Line

The centre line on a control chart represents the process mean. In this case, the process mean is the average of *np* where:

$$n\bar{p} = \frac{\text{Total number of non conforming items in all subgroups}}{\text{Number of sub groups}}$$

Control Limits

Control limits are placed at + and – 3 standard deviations from the centre line. To determine the location of control limits we need to estimate standard deviation σ. The standard deviation σ of a binomial distribution is determined by the equation:

$$\sigma = \sqrt{np(1-p)}$$

As sample data is used, the standard deviation σ is estimated by s using the following equation, where p is estimated by the average value of p:

$$s = \sqrt{n\bar{p}(1-\bar{p})}$$

The upper control limit (UCL) and lower control limit (LCL) are then calculated by the following equations.

$$UCL = n\bar{p} + 3\sqrt{n\bar{p}(1-\bar{p})} \qquad LCL = n\bar{p} - 3\sqrt{n\bar{p}(1-\bar{p})}$$

P Charts (for Equal Subgroup Sizes)

P Charts are used to plot the **proportion** of units that are non-conforming (**defective**). They can be used with both equal and unequal sample or subgroup sizes. This chart is based on the Binomial Probability Distribution.

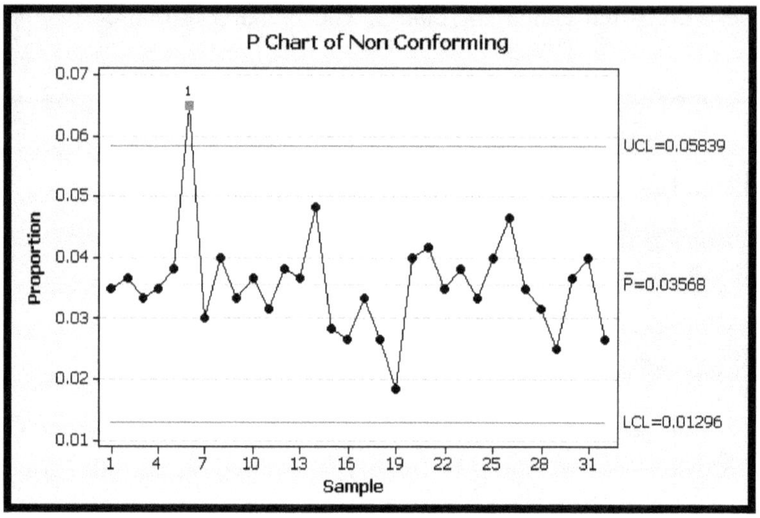

Figure 167: P Chart for Equal Subgroup Sizes

Centre Line

The centre line on a *p* chart is determined by the average value of *p* where:

$$\bar{p} = \frac{\text{Total number of non comforming items in all subgroups}}{\text{Total number of items in all sub groups}}$$

Control Limits

The upper and lower control limits are placed at + and – 3 standard deviations respectively from the centre line. To determine the location of control limits we need to estimate standard error σ_p of the proportion. The standard error σ_p is estimated by s_p where:

$$s_p = \sqrt{\frac{\bar{p}(1-\bar{p})}{n}}$$

The upper control limit (UCL) and lower control limit (LCL) are then calculated by the following equations.

$$UCL = \bar{p} + 3\sqrt{\frac{\bar{p}(1-\bar{p})}{n}} \qquad LCL = \bar{p} - 3\sqrt{\frac{\bar{p}(1-\bar{p})}{n}}$$

P Charts (for Unequal Subgroup Sizes)

Where samples per subgroups are unequal in size, the *np* chart is not appropriate, however the *p* chart can be used. As we saw in the previous section, the standard error s_p of the proportion of non conforming items is based on the subgroup size *n*. Therefore every time *n* varies, the control limits will vary.

Hence, the standard error of a proportion for each subgroup is:

$$s_{p_i} = \sqrt{\frac{\bar{p}(1-\bar{p})}{n_i}}$$

Where:

n_i = the number of observations in subgroup *i*

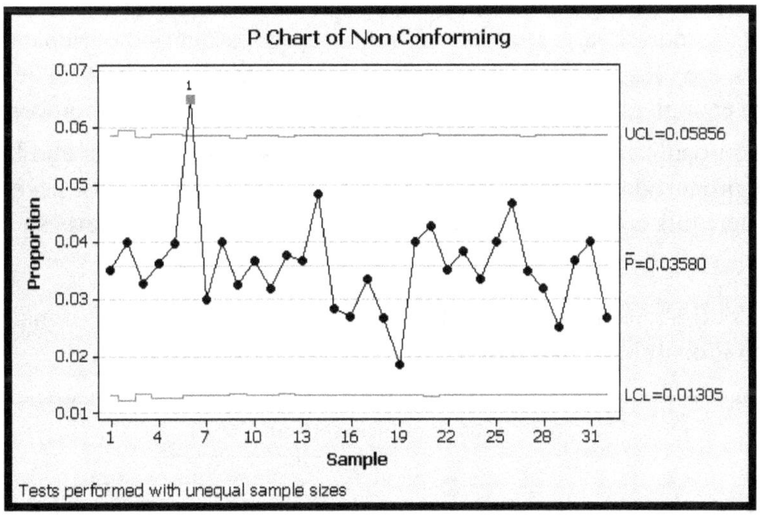

Figure 168: P Chart for Unequal Subgroup Sizes

There are two ways of dealing with this challenge.

- **Calculate UCL and LCL using the average value of n** – This is the simplest method and does not require calculation of limits for each subgroup. However, it is not as sensitive as the second method and can result in erroneous conclusions about process control. As a general rule, this method should not be used if samples are more than +/- 20 percent different from each other.
- **Calculate UCL and LCL for each subgroup** – This is a complex method to undertake manually, however more statistically sensitive than the average value method. Minitab and similar software packages use this approach.

Control Limits (Average Subgroup Size)

The average subgroup size is represented by the average value of *n* where:

$$\bar{n} = \frac{\text{Total number of items in all sub groups}}{\text{Total number of sub groups}}$$

The upper control limit (UCL) and lower control limit (LCL) are then calculated by the following equations.

$$UCL = \bar{p} + 3\sqrt{\frac{\bar{p}(1-\bar{p})}{\bar{n}}} \qquad LCL = \bar{p} - 3\sqrt{\frac{\bar{p}(1-\bar{p})}{\bar{n}}}$$

Control Limits (Different Limits for each Subgroup)

Due to the complex and tedious nature of this approach, statistical analysis software packages such as Minitab is used to generate these charts. You may notice UCL is not represented by a straight line. This is because control limits vary according to variation in subgroup sizes.

Sample Sizes for *NP* and *P* charts

Attribute charts generally require larger sample or subgroup sizes than do variables charts due to the fact that attribute measures are less sensitive than variables measures. Rice (1947) recommends that that a sample should be large enough to have a 90 percent chance of detecting a non-conforming unit.

As the proportion of non-conformances gets less and moves towards 0.0, larger and larger sample sizes will be required. When the proportion of non-conformances is close to 0.0, it may be necessary to undertake 100 percent inspection. Where this is the case, variable measures and associated charts should be used instead.

C Charts

C Charts are used to plot the relevant **count** of **defects** when the subgroup size remains constant. This chart is based on the Poisson Probability Distribution.

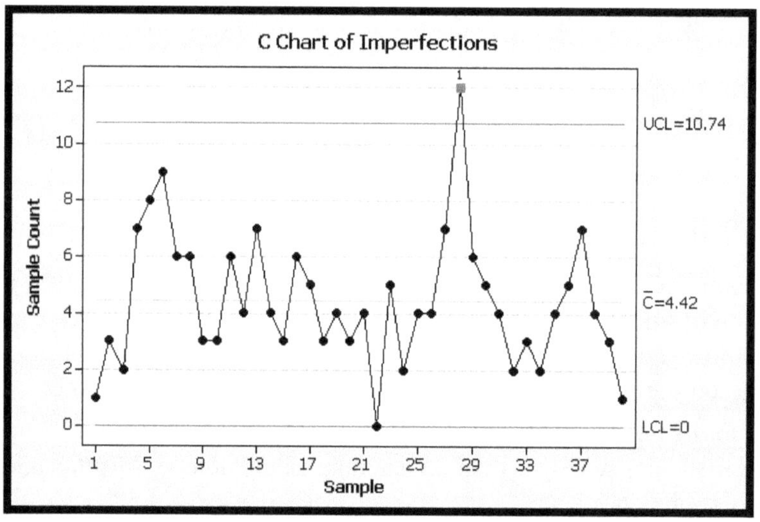

Figure 169: C Chart

Centre Line

The centre line on a control chart represents the process mean. In this case, the process mean is the average value of *c* where:

$$\bar{c} = \frac{\text{Total number of events of interest}}{\text{Number sub groups}}$$

Control Limits

Control limits are placed at + and – 3 standard deviations from the centre line. To determine the location of control limits we need to estimate standard deviation, and in the case of a Poisson distribution, its standard deviation $\sqrt{\lambda}$ can be estimated by $\sqrt{\bar{c}}$.

The upper control limit (UCL) and lower control limit (LCL) are then calculated by the following equations.

$$UCL = \bar{c} + 3\sqrt{\bar{c}} \qquad LCL = \bar{c} - 3\sqrt{\bar{c}}$$

A Poisson distribution is not symmetrical [it is skewed], the risk of observing false alarms [with respect to out of control patterns] is not evenly distributed above and below upper and lower control limits respectively. According to Levine, Ramsey and Smidt (2001), this is generally not a problem when the average c value is equal to or greater than 20. Where the result is less than 20, results should be cautiously interpreted. Rules associated with 1σ and 2σ limits for out of control signals should be disregarded.

U Charts

There will be scenarios where subgroup sizes vary. In these cases the *C* chart is inappropriate, however the *U* chart can be used.

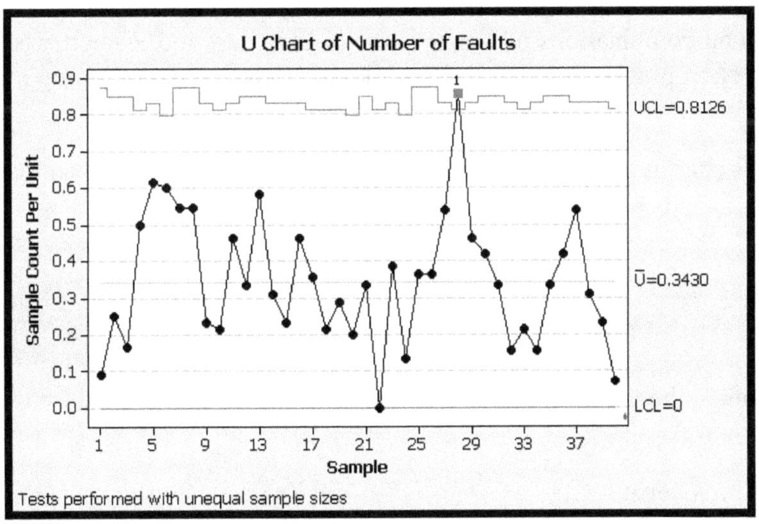

Figure 170: U Chart

U Charts are used to plot the statistic '***u***', which is the ratio of number of **defects** counted to the size of the subgroup. Used when the size of the subgroup is not consistent, this chart is based on the Poisson Probability Distribution.

Centre Line

The centre line on a u chart is determined by the average value of u where:

$$\bar{u} = \frac{\text{Total number of events of interest}}{\text{Total number of units in all sub groups}}$$

Control Limits

As was the case with P charts for unequal subgroup sizes, the control limits for U charts vary from subgroup to subgroup. In fact, the relationship between the size of subgroups and distance between control limits is an inverse one. Small subgroups have widely spaced limits, while large subgroups have narrower limits. The most desirable method for dealing with this is to calculate limits for each subgroup, and once again due to the complexity of this approach, the use of statistical analysis software packages such as Minitab and SigmaXL make it more feasible.

The upper and lower control limits are placed at + and – 3 standard deviations respectively from the centre line. To determine the location of control limits for unit i, we use the following equations:

$$UCL = \bar{u} + 3\sqrt{\frac{\bar{u}}{n_i}} \qquad LCL = \bar{u} - 3\sqrt{\frac{\bar{u}}{n_i}}$$

Variables Control Charts

Variable control charts are more statistically sensitive than attribute control charts, hence they are more effective in detecting out of control states for a process.

Range (R) Chart

One of the most common combinations of charts is the X-bar chart and R chart. Used in conjunction with one another, the X-bar chart plots subgroup means while the R chart plots subgroup ranges.

Centre Line

The centre line of the R chart represents the average range of subgroups calculated by:

$$\bar{R} = \frac{\text{The sum of sub group ranges}}{\text{Total number of sub groups}}$$

Control Limits

To calculate control limits, the variability of the sample ranges, σ_R is estimated by the standard error of the ranges, s_R.

$$s_R = \frac{d_3\bar{R}}{d_2}$$

Where:

d_2 = a factor that represents the relationship between range and standard deviation for varying subgroup sizes (refer to appendices)

d_3 = a factor that represents the relationship between standard deviation of the range, and standard deviation of the process for varying subgroup sizes (refer to appendices)

The upper and lower control limits are placed at + and – 3 standard deviations respectively from the centre line. To determine the location of control limits we use the following equations:

$$UCL = \bar{R} + 3\frac{d_3\bar{R}}{d_2} \quad \text{and} \quad LCL = \bar{R} - 3\frac{d_3\bar{R}}{d_2}$$

These two equations can be simplified by using tabled values of the equations:

$$1+3\frac{d_3}{d_4} \quad \text{and} \quad 1-3\frac{d_3}{d_4}$$

The equations are represented by the terms D_4, and D_3 respectively (refer to appendices). Thus we use the following equations to calculate control limits.

$$UCL = D_4\bar{R} \quad \text{and} \quad LCL = D_3\bar{R}$$

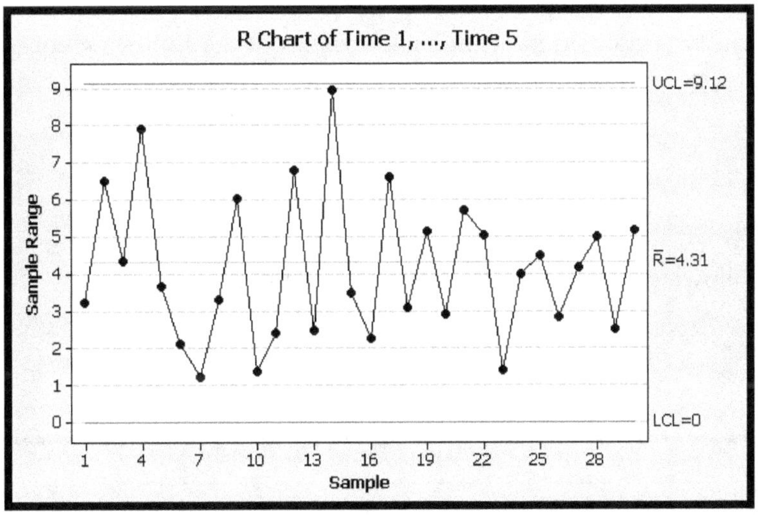

Figure 171: Range (R) Chart

X-Bar Chart With R Chart (XBar-R)

The X-bar chart is used to plot subgroup means, and as stated earlier, is most commonly used in conjunction with the R chart.

Centre Line

The centre line of an X-bar chart represents the average of subgroup means and is calculated by:

$$\bar{\bar{X}} = \frac{\text{The sum of sub group averages}}{\text{Total number of sub groups}}$$

Control Limits

To calculate control limits, the standard error of the mean must be estimated.

$$\sigma_{\bar{x}} = \frac{\sigma_x}{\sqrt{n}}$$

In this case, d_2 is a factor that represents the relationship between the range and the standard deviation.

As the standard deviation of the process is: $\sigma_x = \dfrac{\overline{R}}{d_2}$ ... the standard error of the means can be estimated by: $s_{\bar{x}} = \dfrac{\overline{R}}{d_2\sqrt{n}}$

The upper and lower control limits are placed at + and – 3 standard deviations respectively from the centre line, thus we use the following equations to estimate their location:

$$UCL = \overline{\overline{X}} + 3\frac{\overline{R}}{d_2\sqrt{n}} \quad \text{and} \quad LCL = \overline{\overline{X}} - 3\frac{\overline{R}}{d_2\sqrt{n}}$$

These two equations can be simplified by using tabled values of the following equation that is represented by the term A_2 (refer to appendices).

$$\frac{3}{d_2\sqrt{n}}$$

Thus, we can use the following equations to calculate control limits.

$$UCL = \overline{\overline{X}} + A_2\overline{R} \quad \text{and} \quad LCL = \overline{\overline{X}} - A_2\overline{R}$$

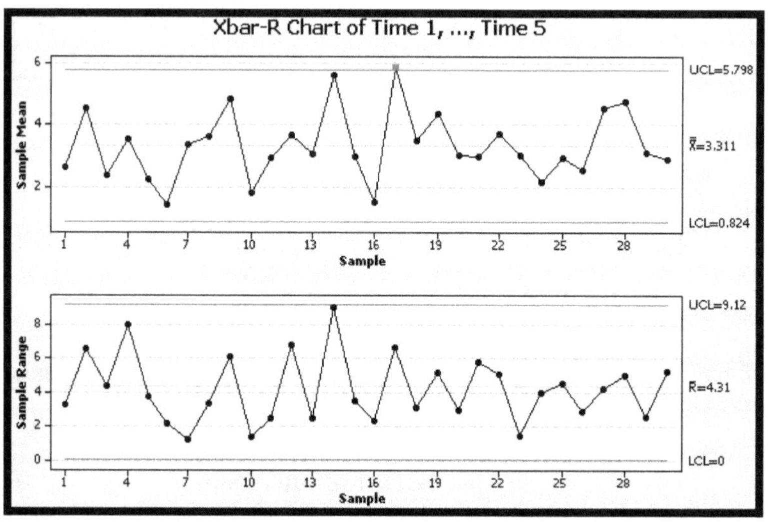

Figure 172: XBar-R Chart

S Chart

As sample sizes within subgroups increase, the range becomes less and less efficient as a measure of variability within a process. As the range ignores all values between the extremes, the amount of information being used gets proportionately smaller as the sample size gets larger.

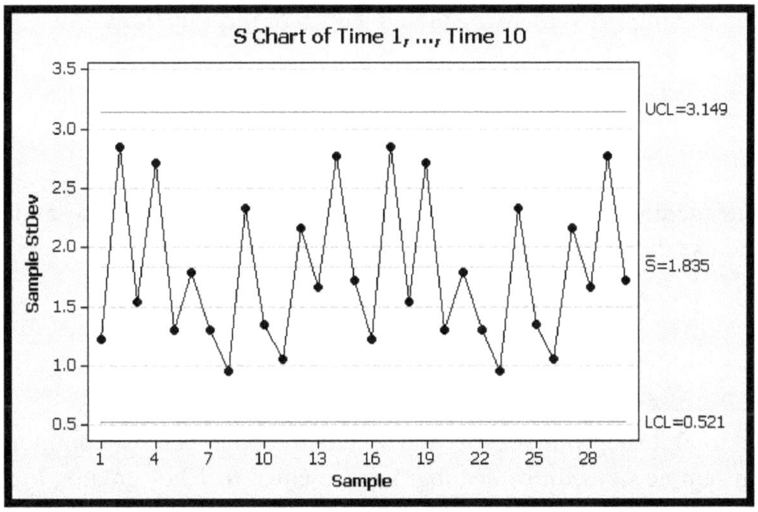

Figure 173: S Chart

For example, when n = 5, 40 percent of available information is being used by the range to measure variability. When n = 10, the range is only using 20 percent of available information.

In addition, the probability of observing an extreme value (outlier) increases, as the sample size *n* gets larger.

Thus, the standard deviation (*s*) of each subgroup is a better estimate of process variation than the range. As a general rule, for subgroup sizes < 10, X-bar R charts should be used. For subgroup sizes of 10 or larger, X-bar S charts should be used.

Centre Line

The centre line of the S chart represents the average standard deviation of subgroups calculated by:

$$\bar{s} = \frac{\text{The sum of sub group standard deviations}}{\text{Total number of sub groups}}$$

Control Limits

The upper and lower control limits are placed at + and – 3 standard deviations respectively from the centre line. For S charts, the average standard deviation is used as the value for the centre line, thus we use the following equations to determine the location of control limits:

$$UCL = \bar{s} + 3\bar{s}\frac{\sqrt{1 - C_4^2}}{C_4} \quad \text{and} \quad LCL = \bar{s} - 3\bar{s}\frac{\sqrt{1 - C_4^2}}{C_4}$$

In this case, C_4 is a factor that represents the relationship between the subgroup standard deviations and the process standard deviation for varying subgroup sizes. This factor is used to adjust for the discrepancy that the average standard deviation of subgroups does not equal the standard deviation of the population, σ.

These two equations can be simplified by using tabled values of the equations:

$$1+\frac{3\sqrt{1-C_4^2}}{C_4} \quad \text{and} \quad 1-\frac{3\sqrt{1-C_4^2}}{C_4}$$

These equations are represented by the terms B_4, and B_3 respectively (refer to appendices). Thus we can simplify the process and use the following equations to calculate control limits.

$$UCL = B_4\bar{s} \quad \text{and} \quad LCL = B_3\bar{s}$$

X-Bar Chart(With S Chart (XBar-S)

The X-bar chart is used to plot subgroup means, and as stated earlier, is most commonly used in conjunction with the R chart. When sample sizes for each subgroup are equal to 10 or greater, the X-bar chart should be used in conjunction with the S chart.

Centre Line

The centre line of an X-bar chart represents the average of subgroup means and is calculated by:

$$\bar{\bar{X}} = \frac{\text{The sum of sub group averages}}{\text{Total number of sub groups}}$$

Control Limits

The upper and lower control limits are placed at + and – 3 standard deviations respectively from the centre line. When used with S charts, we use the following equations to estimate their location:

$$UCL = \bar{\bar{X}} + 3\frac{\bar{s}}{C_4\sqrt{n}} \quad \text{and} \quad LCL = \bar{\bar{X}} - 3\frac{\bar{s}}{C_4\sqrt{n}}$$

These two equations can be simplified by using tabled values of the following equation.

$$\frac{3}{C_4\sqrt{n}}$$

The equation is represented by the term A_3 (refer to appendices), thus we can use the following equations to calculate control limits.

$$UCL = \bar{\bar{X}} + A_3\bar{s} \quad \text{and} \quad LCL = \bar{\bar{X}} - A_3\bar{s}$$

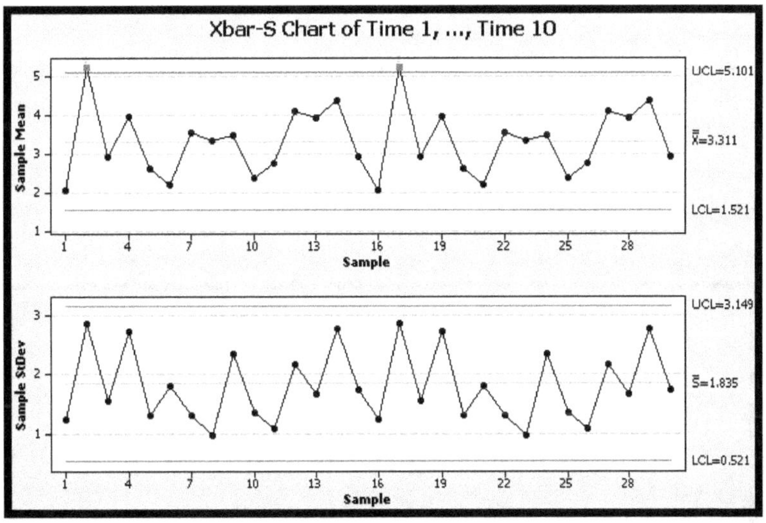

Figure 174: XBar-S Chart

Individual Values Chart With Moving Range (I-MR)

Moving Range (MR) Chart

Moving range refers to the difference between each pair of consecutive values. The moving range method estimates process variability by considering these differences, and is calculated by:

$$MR_i = | x_{i+1} - x_i |$$

Where:

MRi = Moving range for observation i

$| \quad |$ = The absolute value of

X_i = The value of observation i

X_{i+1} = The value of observation $i + 1$

Centre Line

The centre line of an MR chart represents the average of moving range values. As moving range is calculated from two consecutive values, any set of k observations will only have $k - 1$ moving range values. Thus the average moving range is determined by:

$$\overline{MR} = \frac{\sum_{i=1}^{k-1} MR_i}{k-1}$$

Where:

k = The number of moving range observations

As with the R chart, the average moving range is used as the centre line of the MR chart, and we can simplify the equation by:

$$\overline{MR} = \frac{\text{The sum of moving averages}}{\text{Total number of moving range values } (k-1)}$$

Control Limits

The upper and lower control limits are placed at + and – 3 standard deviations respectively from the centre line, in this case being the average moving range value. Using control chart factors D_4 and D_3 we calculate control limit locations with the following equations:

$$UCL(MR) = D_4\overline{MR} \quad \text{and} \quad LCL(MR) = D_3\overline{MR}$$

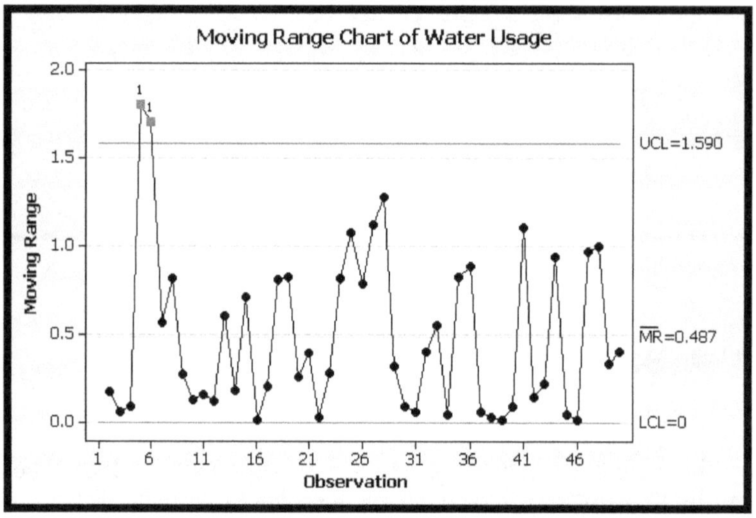

Figure 175: Moving Range (MR) Chart

Individual Values (I) Chart

Individual values charts (I or X charts) plot the individual values of each data point.

Centre Line

The centre line represents the process mean, μ, estimated by the sample mean calculated by:

$$\bar{x} = \frac{\sum_{i=1}^{k} x_i}{k}$$

Control Limits

The upper and lower control limits are placed at + and – 3 standard deviations respectively from the centre line, in this case being the sample mean. The sample standard deviation *s* is estimated by dividing the average moving range by the factor d_2. Thus control limit locations are calculated as:

$$UCL = \bar{X} + 3\frac{\overline{MR}}{d_2} \quad \text{and} \quad LCL = \bar{X} - 3\frac{\overline{MR}}{d_2}$$

These two equations can be simplified by using tabled values of the equation 3 divided by d_2. The equation is represented by the term E_2 (refer to appendices), thus we use the following equations to calculate control limits.

$$UCL(X) = \bar{x} + E_2\overline{MR} \quad \text{and} \quad LCL(X) = \bar{x} - E_2\overline{MR}$$

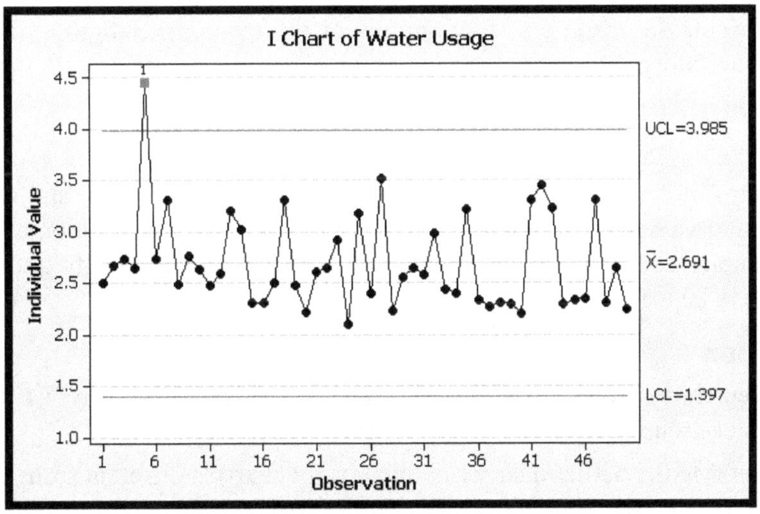

Figure 176: Individuals (I) Chart

Individuals and Moving Range Charts can be combined into I-MR Charts as shown in the following figure.

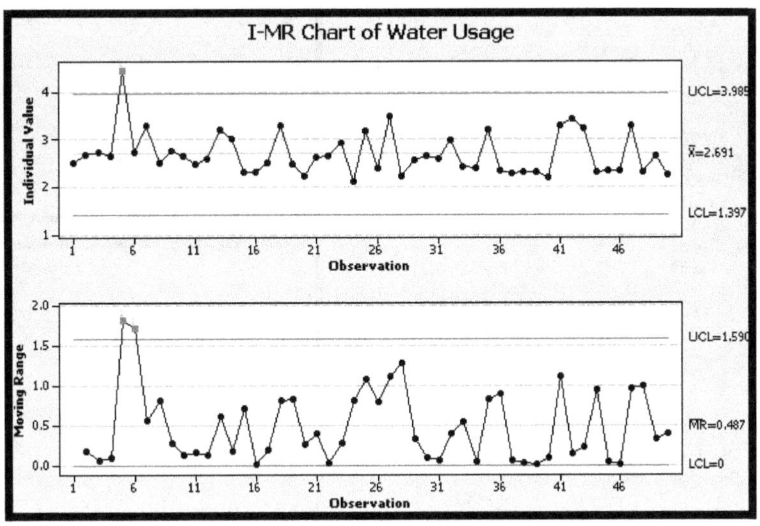

Figure 177: I-MR Chart

PRACTICAL SUBGROUPS VERSUS RATIONAL SUBGROUPS

The process of constructing variables charts begins with the selection of individual samples (I-MR Charts) or subgroups of samples (XBar-R Charts).

Subgroup data can be described as '*consistent sized groups of data collected at frequent intervals and combined to form a data set*'.

For example, three samples each hour or day form a subgroup of three data points. When these are combined they form a data set made up of subgroups of three values. Subgroup data allows the user to monitor two types of variability.

- Random variation in the process
- Random variation in process average

For subgroups, measures of central tendency are calculated, such as the mean, and measures of variability such as the range or standard deviation. These statistics are used in the construction of control limits. Before we even begin to sample, decisions about sample size and subgroup size, frequency of collection and sampling method have to be made.

Practical Subgroups

While it may be convenient to group items together, the example below shows that it is incorrect to group together different lines or groups that are effectively different processes.

The fact that Line 4 (refer to the outlier data set in upper right chart) is different from the others is concealed in the XBar-R Chart (refer to lower right chart).

	A	B	C	D
1	**Line 1**	**Line 2**	**Line 3**	**Line 4**
2	31.9448	30.9936	30.519	25.6303
3	33.401	31.2603	30.2786	23.6319
4	33.2989	30.782	33.1276	28.2034
5	32.0466	31.485	30.237	25.8308
6	37.0374	30.0453	32.4065	25.5324
7	29.8201	33.957	31.6085	23.7298
8	31.6702	33.0366	29.7215	25.2223
9	36.2174	32.311	35.4318	25.7661
10	34.8341	32.9576	33.187	24.9685
11	32.5107	31.8109	30.0531	24.2587
12	29.3246	30.6759	34.7344	30.7815
13	33.9878	35.3098	34.1982	24.0856
14	29.8002	30.8038	33.0265	23.6029
15	32.7132	27.0328	28.7602	22.4814
16	30.048	29.4864	26.8969	25.3085
17	28.4139	34.2633	35.7322	23.1455
18	32.5945	34.4257	35.3151	24.596
19	28.6301	31.524	32.821	22.2914
20	31.6624	32.5166	32.2616	24.2523
21	29.4777	26.245	32.4402	26.8836
22	30.3351	34.7259	32.0479	24.7859
23	29.4959	31.9334	35.2021	25.4455
24	32.8406	31.5264	32.6271	24.1749
25	29.8942	33.3598	31.6142	26.8147
26	29.5585	30.5848	32.0035	25.9304
27	30.457	29.1269	35.7425	27.6508
28	32.9963	33.283	32.2073	22.4007
29	33.4722	32.0373	32.5929	28.3093
30	30.8408	31.154	33.4564	23.7463
31	30.119	31.0461	35.362	25.2348

Source Data

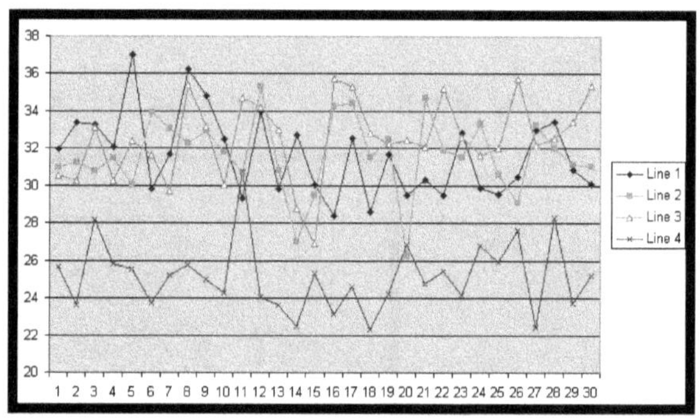

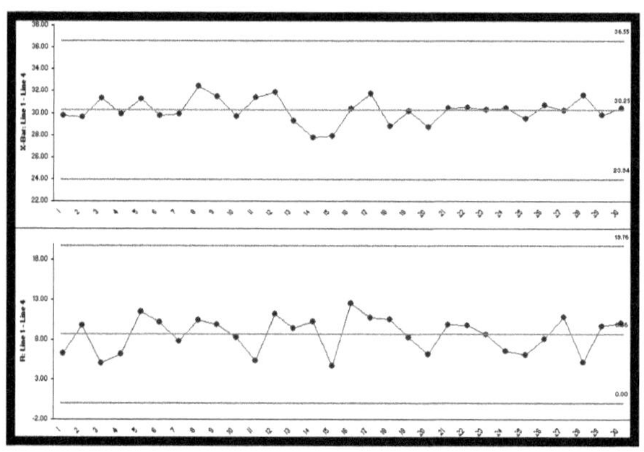

Rational Subgroups

Rational subgroups on the other hand are subgroups from a single process. (e.g. 5 units every hour from line 1)

Two basic strategies can be considered in the selection of subgroups.

- Select samples produced closely together in time: For example, if our intended subgroup size was 4, we might select four consecutive units every hour on the hour. Variation *within* the subgroups would be minimised with an increase in the likelihood of detecting variation *between* subgroups.
- Systematically select samples during a sampling interval: Instead of collecting four consecutive units, we might choose one unit each quarter of an hour with the sampling interval being one hour. Those four units would make up one subgroup. This method maximises variation *within* the subgroups and is not as effective when shifts in process average must be detected.

Since the invention of the control chart by Walter Shewhart, subgroup sizes of 4 to 5 have been most commonly used for XBar Charts.

Sample Size

As with all sampling; the larger the sample size the more accurate the results. Though as a general rule a sample size of 25 to 100 values is large enough to study process variation, but not so large that the control chart becomes unreadable like the following example which displays more than 700 data points in a single chart.

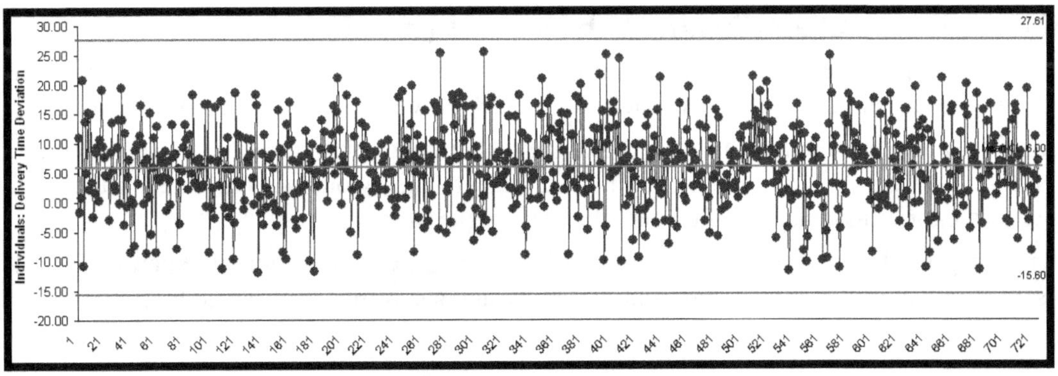

Figure 178: Control Chart with Excessive Number of Data Points Displayed

The designers of SigmaXL have recognised the challenges of working with large data sets. In response they have provided an innovative scrolling mechanism that allows the user to select a specific 'window width' and scroll through the entire data set.

The following diagram presents the same data set, this time viewing a 30 data point window.

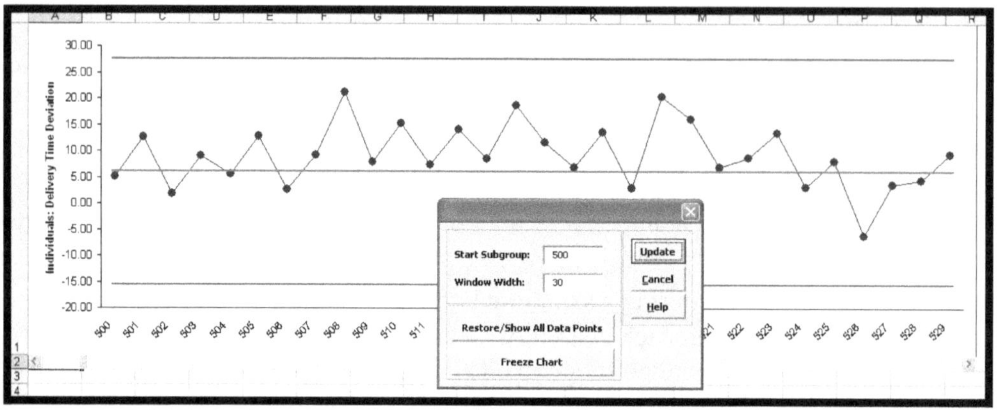

Figure 179: Control Chart 'Scrolling' with SigmaXL

Sampling Frequency

The ability of a control chart to detect the presence of special causes is directly related to the sampling frequency. The more frequently you sample, the more sensitive control charts are to process variation. The reality of industry is such that sample size and collection frequency has to be balanced against cost and production requirements.

LOCATING THE SOURCE OF VARIATION (STEP 11)

A friend of yours approaches you for help. She tells you that she is spending far too much of her weekly salary and wants your help to reduce how much she spends. How would you go about helping her?

When I ask this question of students in Lean Six Sigma seminars, they usually answer by telling me they would first find out where most of the money is being spent. They would do this by splitting up the weekly spending into categories associated with where they spend the money.

For example, they might spend their salary on mobile phones, fuel, food, school expenses etc. They would then focus on *where* most of the spending is taking place and see if they can reduce that.

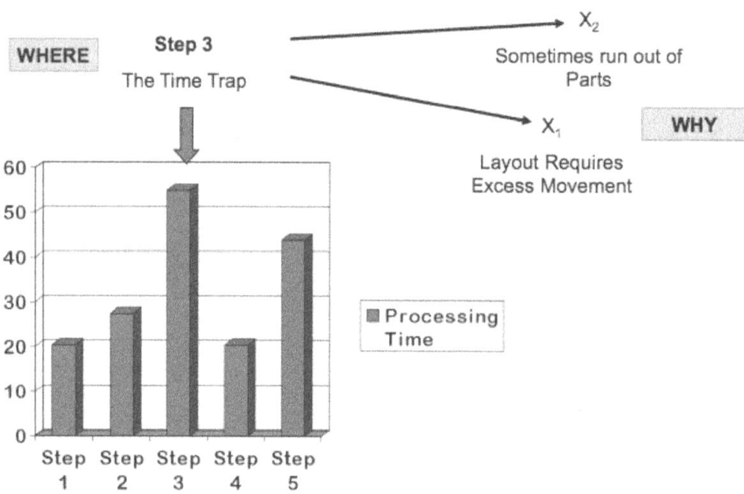

In the example shown above we see that most processing time is spent in step 3 of the process. This is *where* we spend most time (the source), running out of parts and excess movement in that step explains *why* time is excessive in that step (the cause).

I believe this is the most effective strategy to take in Lean Six Sigma project work. If we can find out where most of the variation or most of the waste is coming from, we can focus our energies in that area to have the biggest impact on process performance. We may not yet know *why*, at least we know *where* to focus.

The Power of Analysis

The analysis of data provides an opportunity to understand where performance variation exists within the process and generate information that might prove useful later when attempting to validate cause effect relationships.

So on the basis of that, our desired outcome is to find out as much as we can about process performance and drill down to the greatest source of variation. That will give us the focus we need when we undertake deeper level cause effect analysis and ultimately find solutions for process improvement.

Through effective analysis we can ultimately determine what we can do to minimise or even eliminate the influence of those process component contributors – people, environment, methods, materials, machines and measures.

Our analysis for projects dealing with a variation driven problem (Six Sigma oriented) will require the application of two different types of statistics:

- Descriptive Statistics – the use of graphical techniques to visually stratify and locate obvious sources of variation
- Inferential Statistics – the use of statistical methods to validate any differences observed

We commence our data analysis with the use of graphing techniques to break up and study the data using stratification variables identified on the data collection plan.

METHODS FOR GRAPHICALLY REPRESENTING DATA

Charts and graphs are used throughout most organisations and in essence they are a mechanism for helping to present data in a visual way during the analysis phase. This visualisation is far more meaningful than just looking at the numbers. It provides the basis for making discoveries about what is happening, that the numbers on their own would not reveal. Teams will present their data using more than one chart, as each one tells something different about the data.

Rotating the Data Package

As I often say to my students, treat your data as a package. Different charts allow you to turn the package around and view it from different angles. And incidentally, one of the most important questions about any single representation of data is this – What doesn't this tell me about the data or the process? Multiple representation forms helps you avoid missing unseen information.

Over the following pages I have tabled a comprehensive list of different graphical formats, only the most common of these will be discussed in detail in this text.

The charts shown in the following table can be generated with statistical analysis software packages. In this case all charts were developed with Minitab.

Chart & What it Displays	Its Use	Example
3D Scatter Plot Individual values across three dimensions defined by *x*, *y* and *z* variables	To assess the relationship between three variables	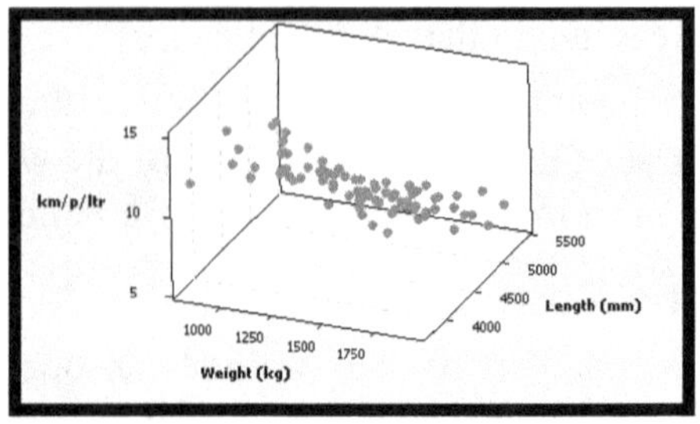
3D Surface Plot A surface or grid representing individual values across three dimensions defined by *x*, *y* and *z* variables	To assess the relationship between three variables	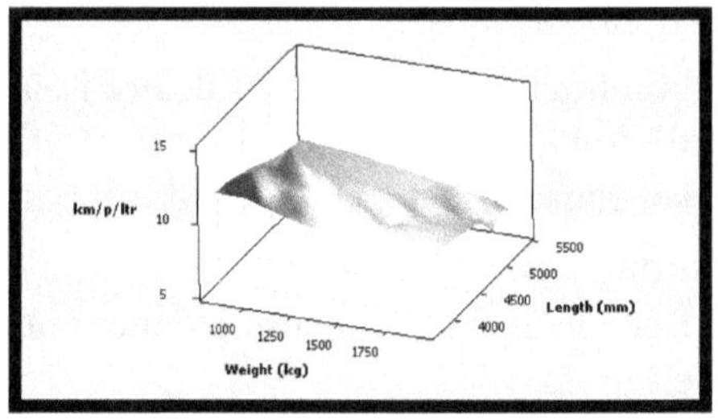
Bar Chart The relative size of each group or category OR The individual values of a variable by group	To assess the distribution of grouped values OR Compare a statistic (e.g., mean) across groups	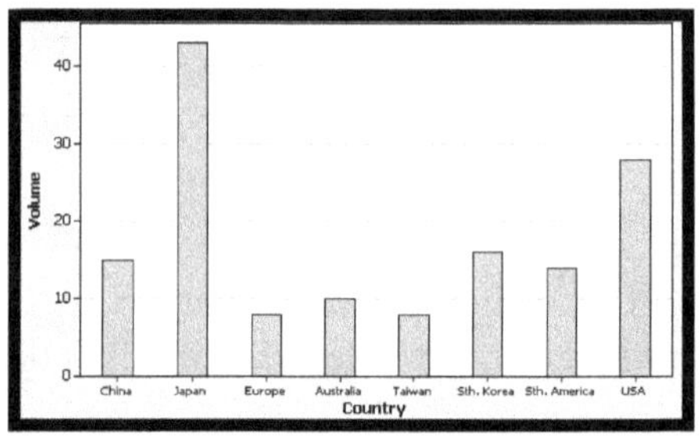
Box Plot The distribution of data across its range in quartiles.	To assess the distribution of data, including the relationship between the centre 50 percent and the quartiles at the extremities.	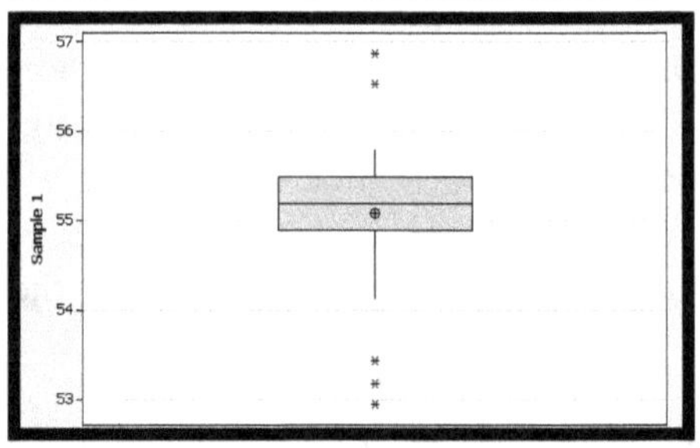
Contour Plot Measurement values as a function of two other variables	To assess the relationship between three variables	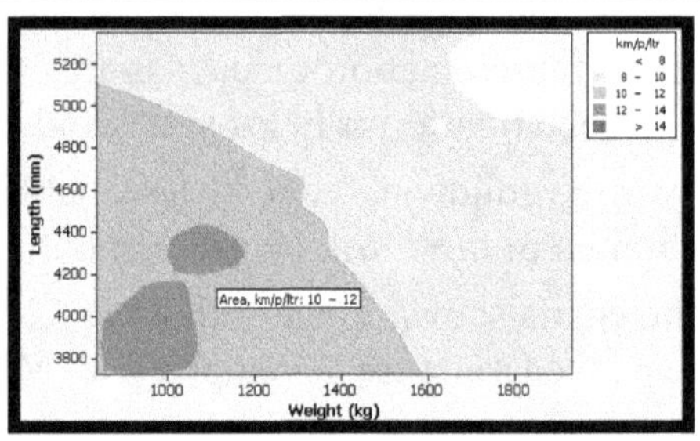

Chart & What it Displays	Its Use	Example
Dot Plot Similar to histograms (useful with small amounts of data)	To assess the shape and central tendency of a data set	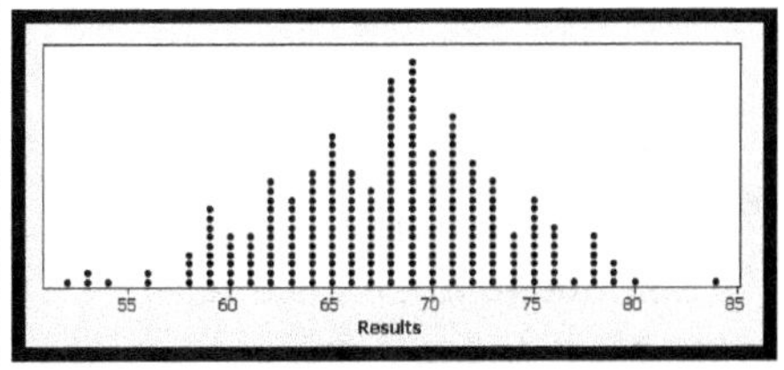
Histogram The relative frequency of each occurrence across a variable scale	To assess the shape and central tendency of a data set	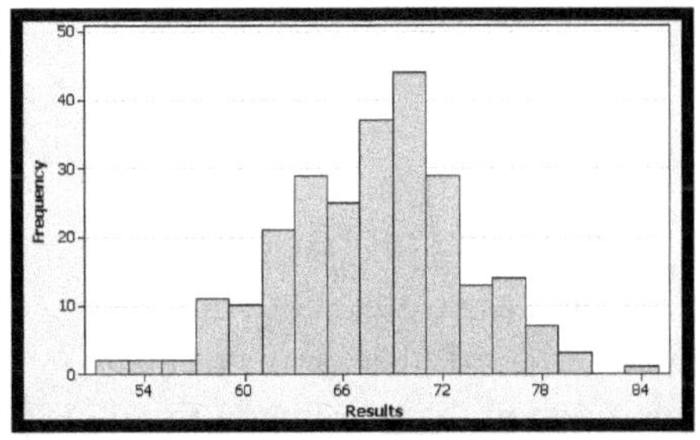
Individual Value Plot Individual values of a variable	To assess and compare individual values as a collective group	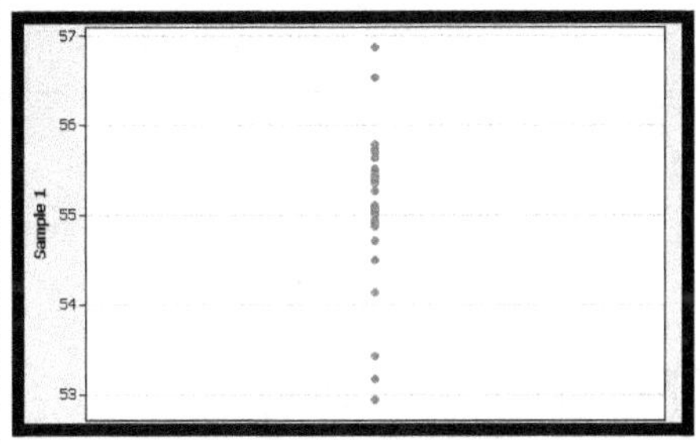
Interval Plot Means and confidence intervals	To assess or compare confidence intervals and respective means of individual or multiple data sets	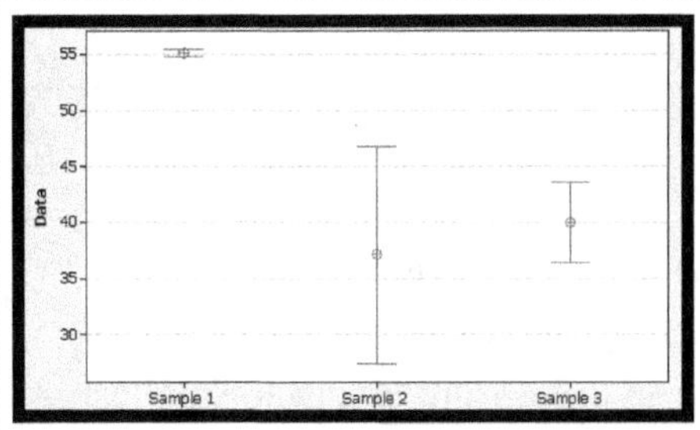
Marginal Plot (Box Plots) Same as scatter plot with the addition of box plots of each variable in the margins of the plot	To assess correlation (the strength of the relationship) between two variables	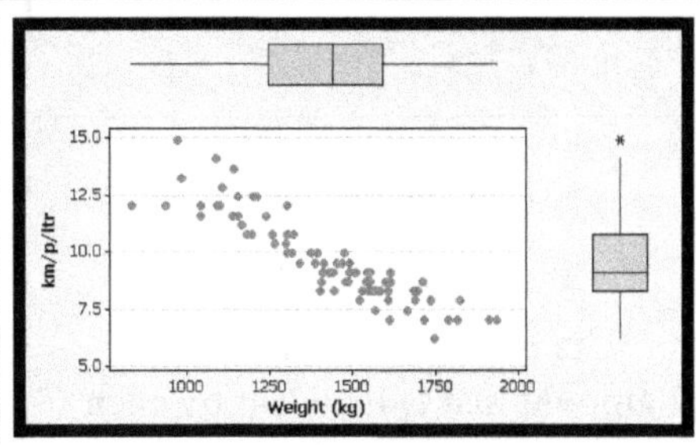

Chart & What it Displays	Its Use	Example
Marginal Plot (Dot Plots) Same as scatter plot with the addition of dot plots of each variable in the margins of the plot	To assess correlation (the strength of the relationship) between two variables	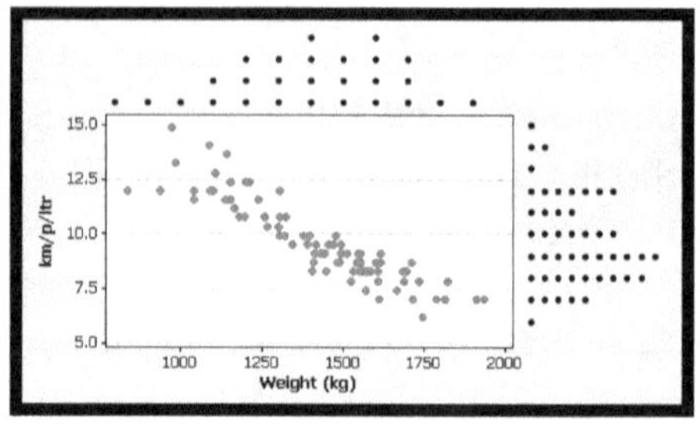
Marginal Plot (Histograms) Same as scatter plot with the addition of histograms of each variable in the margins of the plot	To assess correlation (the strength of the relationship) between two variables	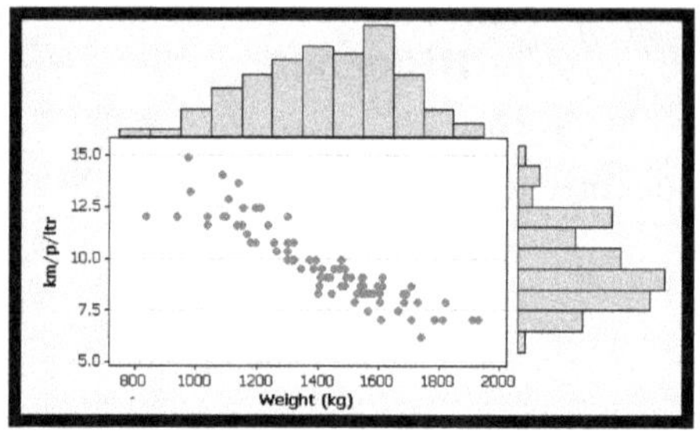
Matrix Plot The relationship between multiple pairs of variables on a single chart	To assess correlation (the strength of the relationship) between various paired combinations of variables	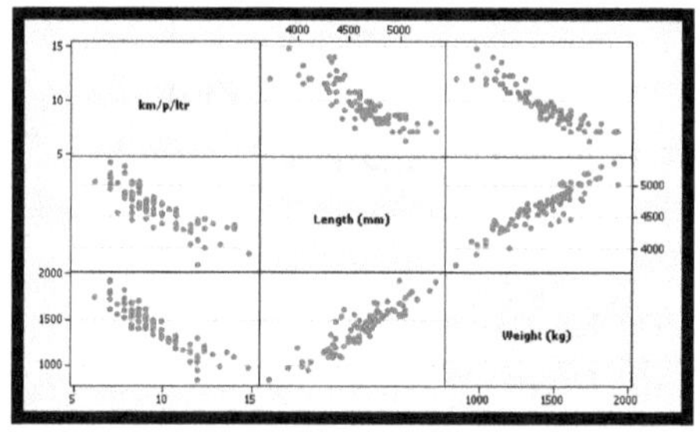
Pareto Chart The relative size of each category in order from largest to smallest	To assess the magnitude of each category, and identification of the largest categories	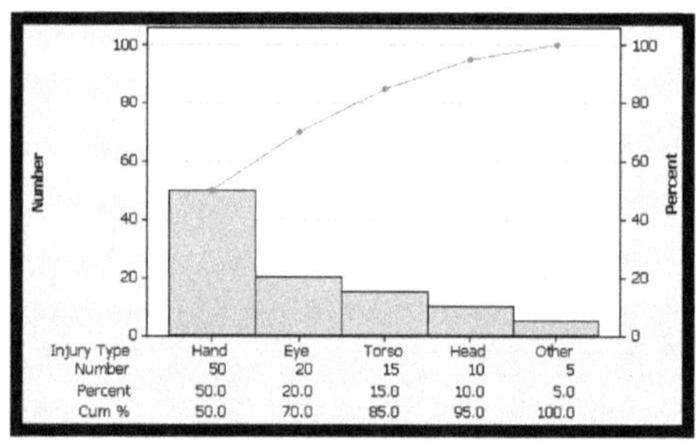
Pie Chart The proportion of the whole amount that is made up by each group or category	To assess the distribution of categorised values	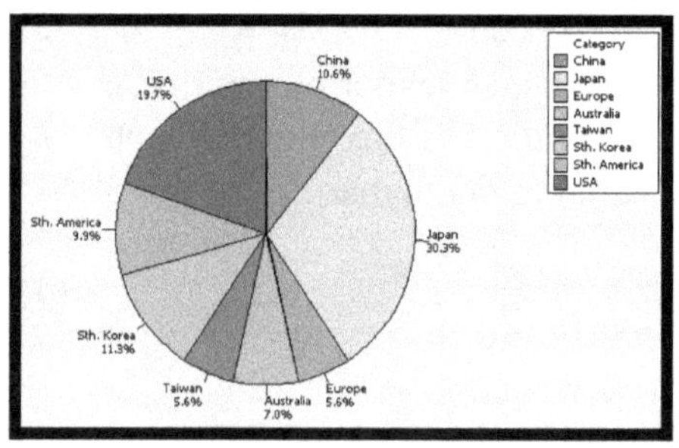

Chart & What it Displays	Its Use	Example
Probability Plot How well a data set follows a particular distribution	To assess whether or not a data set follows a particular distribution	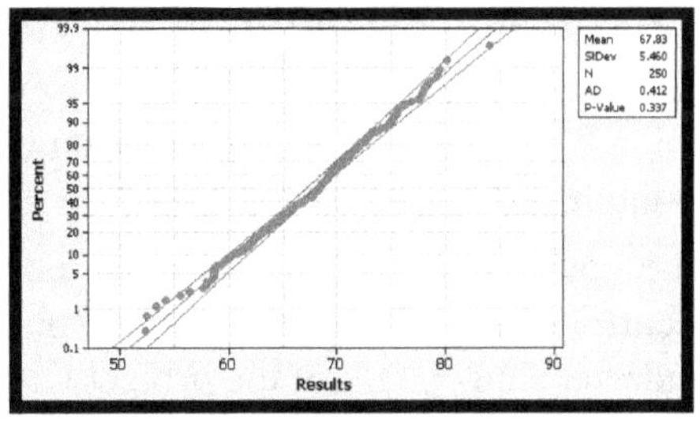
Run Chart Multiple data points over time	To assess variation over time with reference to the middle point (the median)	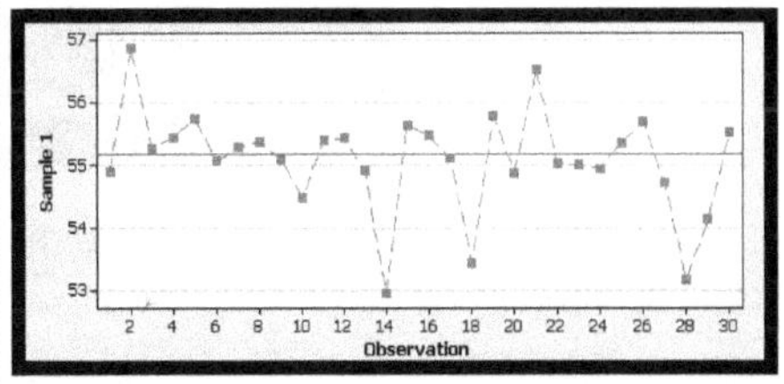
Scatter Plot The relationship between two variables by plotting single data points against two separate axis	To assess correlation (the strength of the relationship) between two variables	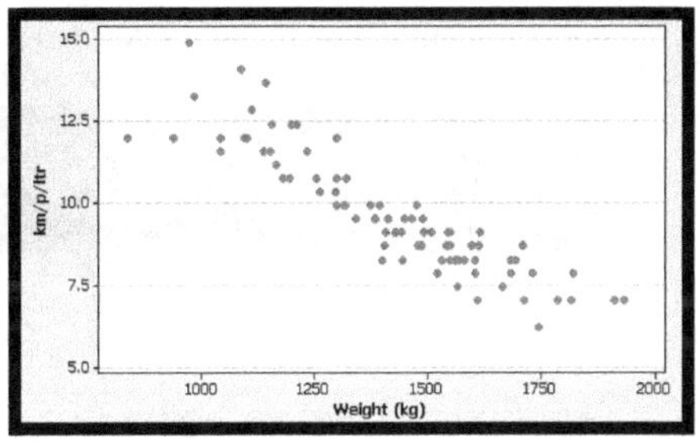
Stem and Leaf Plot Actual data values in a binned format (similar to Histograms)	To assess the shape and central tendency of a data set	3 5 223 5 5 45 9 5 6777 21 5 888888889999 35 6 00000011111111 61 6 22222222222222333333333333 90 6 44444444444444445555555555555 118 6 6666666666667777777777777777 (47) 6 88888888888888888888999999999999999999999999999 85 7 000000000000000000111111111111111 52 7 222222222222223333333 31 7 44444455555555555 14 7 6667777 7 7 88899 2 8 0 1 8 3
Time Series Plot Multiple data points over time (similar to Run Chart)	To assess variation over time	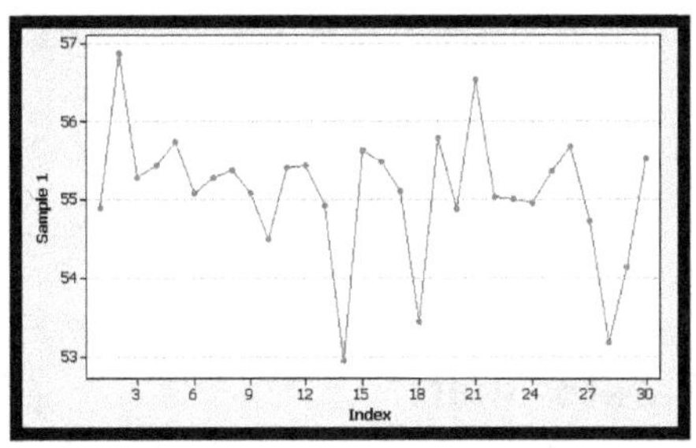

COMMON GRAPHICAL METHODS FOR STRATIFICATION

Categorical (Stratification) Variables

Before I quickly cover the most useful methods for stratifying data, let me remind you of one important point. The quality of the team's data collection plan and the quality of their actual data collection now come to the fore.

The sources of variation you are now attempting to confirm are primarily the categorical variables you identified in your data collection plan. A well-planned and well-executed data collection sets you up to undertake this phase of the project with ease and speed.

The Primary Metric you are working on to fix or improve.

The Categorical Variables by which you will stratify your primary metric data in order to locate any potential 'sources' of variation.

PRIMARY METRIC (Y)			CATEGORICAL Xs	
The Metric (Y)	**What It Is**	**How To Collect It**	**Categorical Variables**	**Sampling Plan**
What is the variable we are fixing	What exactly is that variable (in plain simple terms)	How exactly do we collect / measure that so we all get the same results	What categorical variables potentially impact the primary metric	How many data points will be collected / how long will we collect data, and what is our sampling approach

The Numerical Variables (X's) that you will try to correlate to your primary metric data to locate any significant 'causes' of variation.

NUMERICAL Xs		
Numerical Variables	**What It Is**	**How To Collect It**
What numerical variables potentially have a relationship with variation in the primary metric	What exactly is that variable (in plain simple terms)	How exactly do we collect / measure that so we all get the same results

Locating Sources of Variation Through Stratification with Categorical Variables

While a myriad of charts exist, the most useful I have found for stratification are these five.

Pareto Charts (counts)

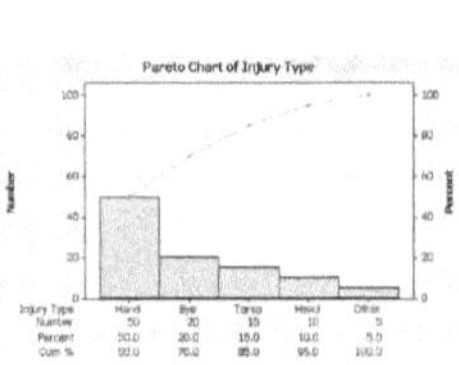

Box Plots (frequencies)

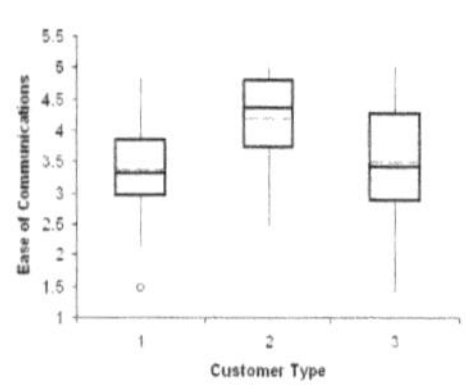

Multi-Vari Charts (means/range)

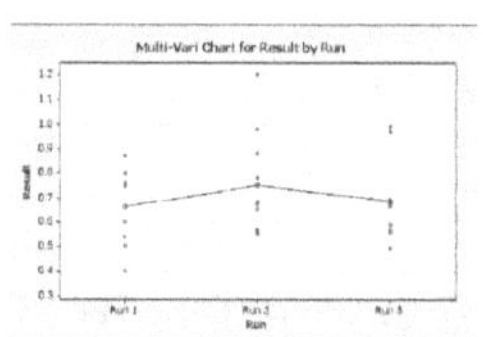

Pie Charts (proportions)

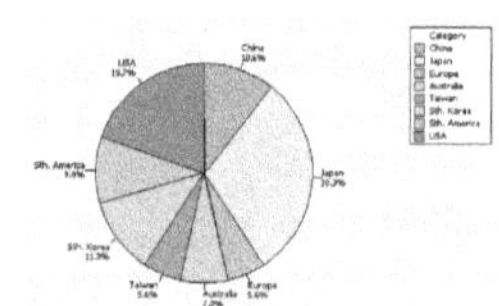

ANOM Charts (means/variances)

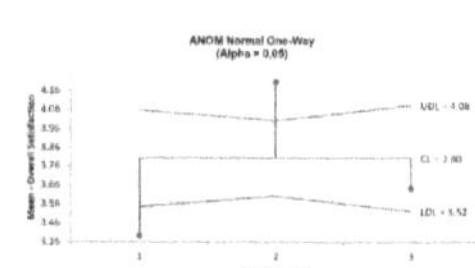

Pareto Chart

During the period between the two World Wars, an Italian economist by the name of Vilfredo Pareto conducted research on distribution of wealth. His research revealed that in Italy, 80 percent of the wealth was held by 20 percent of the population. He extended this study internationally, and he established the same ratio. This became the foundation for what he believed to be a universal law – 80 percent of anything can be attributed to 20 percent of its causes.

Some examples of this law include:

- 80 percent of absenteeism in an organisation can be attributed to 20 percent of the workforce;
- 80 percent of accidents on roads are attributed to 20 percent of the causes of road accidents; and finally
- 80 percent of emergency room patients attend as a result of 20 percent of the reasons for attendance.

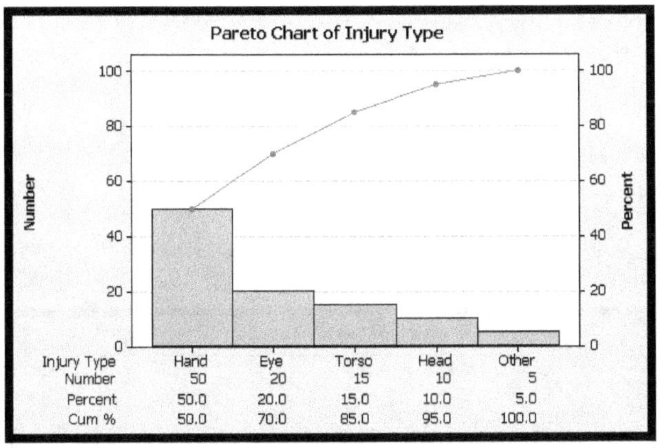

The **Pareto Chart** is a graphical display used to analyse a process from the perspective of the 'Pareto principle of unequal distribution'. The Pareto principle, named by Dr Joseph Juran in the late 1940s after its founder, implies that 80 percent of our problems are caused by 20 percent of the contributors.

The Pareto Chart visually expresses categorical data in a vertical bar chart format. The categories are arranged in descending order and provide the user with the opportunity to compare the length of each bar against a fixed scale. The bar chart is combined with a cumulative proportion polygon on the same scale.

It enables the user to separate the 'vital few' from the 'trivial many'. By looking at the data in this way, a team can determine which of the categories they should focus their attention on to make the biggest impact.

The Pareto Chart above demonstrates that most safety injuries (approximately 70 percent) are hand injuries. If a team wanted to make the biggest impact on safety injury frequencies, they should focus their attention on injuries to the hand. In effect, the 'source' of most injuries has been located.

Creating Pareto Charts

Pareto charts are created in the following sequence.

- **Step 1** – Determine the problem or opportunity that you want to study. (e.g. safety injuries)
- **Step 2** - Identify the characteristics or categorical variable that will be studied. (e.g. injuries to the hand, torso, head, eye and others)
- **Step 3** – Create a frequency distribution table for the relevant data. (refer to the example)
- **Step 4** – Create the Pareto Chart.

Creating Frequency Distributions

As discussed in the 'Measure' phase, a frequency distribution is quite simply a table into which data is arranged into relative numerically ordered classes or categories.

Frequency distributions for categorical data show the categories into which data is partitioned, and the number of units that fall into each category.

For example, the number of safety injuries by type is displayed in the following frequency distribution.

Frequency Distribution for Safety Injuries by Type.

	(Frequency)	(Relative Frequency)
Hand	50	68.5
Torso	13	17.8%
Head	7	9.6%
Eye	2	2.7%
Others	1	1.4%
TOTALS	73	100.00%

Stratifying Pareto Charts

The largest category can be analysed further using the Pareto principle by breaking it down (stratifying) into next level Pareto Charts. Our example depicts the number of safety injuries experienced at a work site, categorised by where on the body the injury was sustained. The chart showed most safety injuries suffered are to the hand.

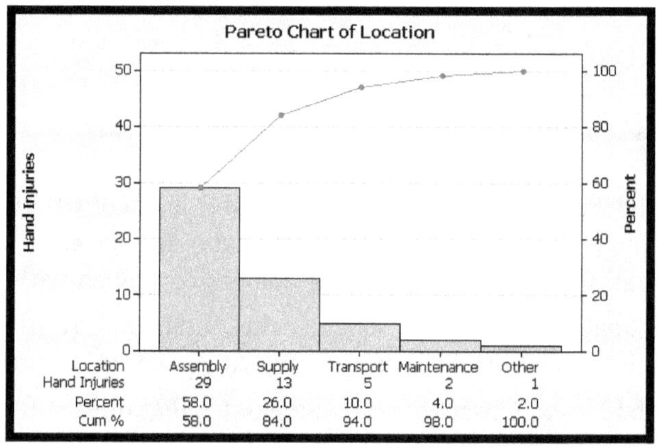

In the example, the hand injury data can be broken down further by work location using a second level Pareto Chart. This action will help us see if most of the hand injuries occur within a particular work group.

In the example we see that of the 50 hand injuries recorded, most occurred in assembly.

This type of analysis can lead a team closer to the source of the problem. If we wanted to make the biggest impact on reducing the number of injuries, we would focus our attention on treating the root cause of hand injuries within the assembly group.

What the Chart Does Not Tell You

Always remember to think carefully about what the chart is **not** telling you. In this case the chart tells us how many, but does not tell us the impact of all of the different types of injuries.

If our goal were to reduce sick time due to injuries, then we would also need to look at the number of day's sick time for each of the injury types.

Always ask - *What doesn't this chart tell us?*

Box Plots

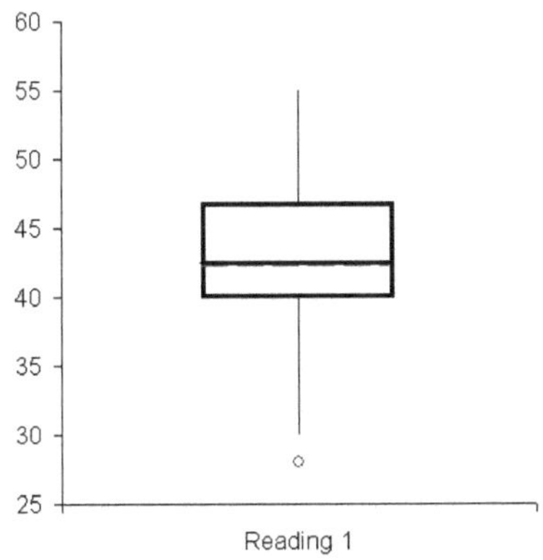

A **Box Plot** is useful in representing the distribution of a data set.

Through the use of quartiles, the box plot displays variation and centreing of a variable output (y) versus an attribute input (x) at one or more levels.

Quartiles rank-order the data through identifying the 25th, 50th and 75th percentiles.

The outline of the box represents the middle 50 percent of data. These are the middle two quartiles referred to as the 'Inter Quartile Range' (IQR).

The lines (or whiskers) are limited in length to no longer than *one and a half times the length* of the inter quartile range. Any values that fall beyond those limits are represented as asterisks. The line inside the box represents the median of the data set.

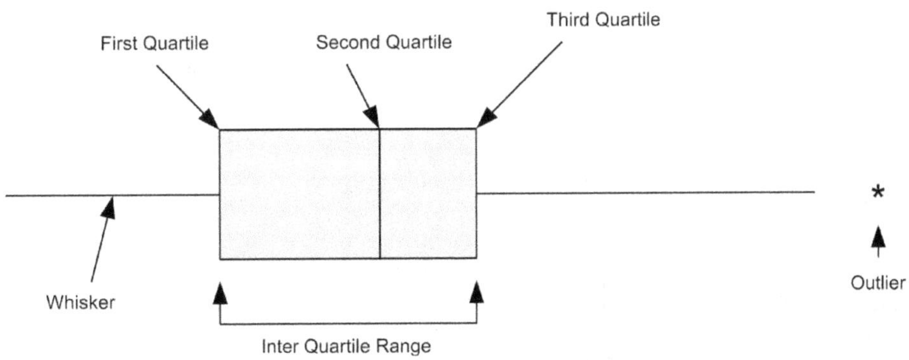

Figure 180: Box Plot Characteristics

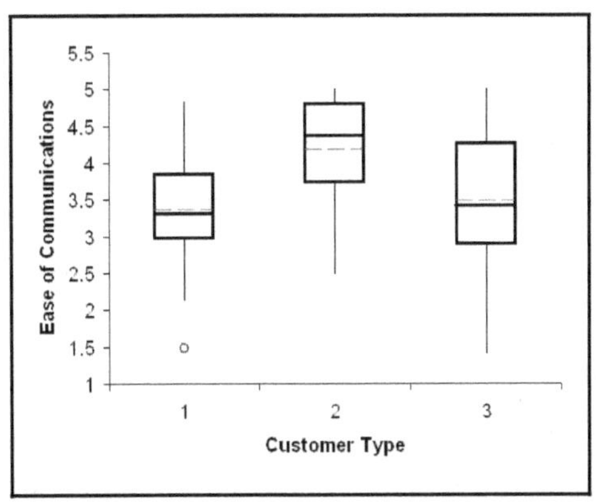

Stratification With Box Plots

Box plots can also be used to compare different data sets. In the example shown, the user has stratified the data by day of the week in order to compare the results of each day.

Multi-Vari Charts

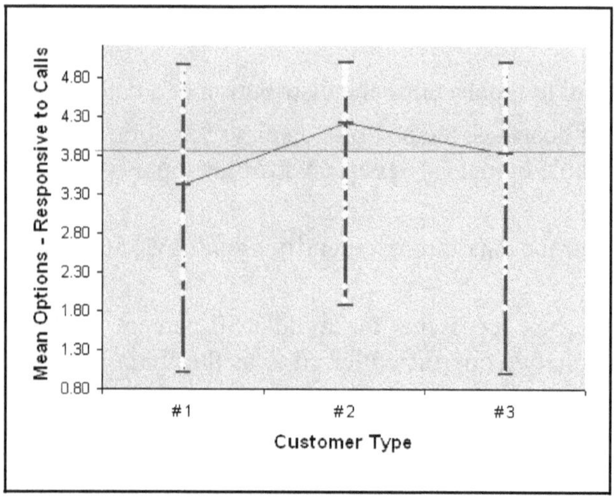

A **Multi-Vari Chart** is a stratification tool.

It's useful in presenting the distribution of a data set by displaying minimum and maximum and mean values for each individual category under analysis. It also displays the overall group mean.

The multi-vari chart allows the user to observe the variation 'within' each of the categories as well as how each element performs against the 'group means'.

As with all other stratification tools, this comparison makes potential sources of variation easy to locate.

ANOM Charts (Means and Variances)

The **analysis of means** (ANOM) is an alternative procedure (to ANOVA).

It can be used to compare means and variances and draw statistically sound conclusions about any observed differences.

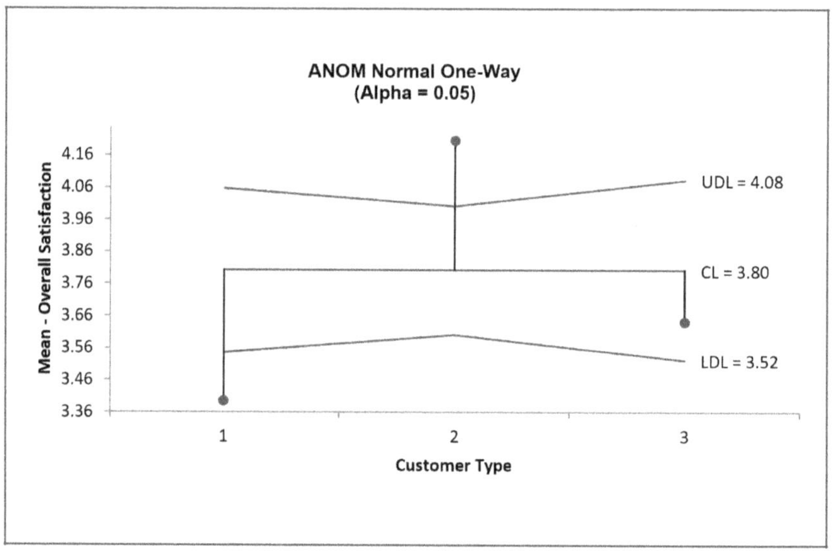

ANOM has the advantages of being much more intuitive and providing an easily understood graphical result. It also allows for easy assessment of practical as well as statistical significance.

You can see in the example, the ANOM Chart shows the mean result for each of the categories as they compare to the overall mean. Where all means are within the decision limits, you cannot say they are different.

When one or more of the results, indicated by the dots at the end of the vertical lines, is outside decision limits, you can then draw conclusions about there being a difference.

Varying decision limits (as shown in the image) will appear if your data has varying sample sizes for each category; smaller sample size gives wider limits in a manner similar to a control chart. If the data are balanced the decision limit lines will be constant.

PIVOT CHARTS

One of the most useful tools ever taught to me for finding sources of variation was Pivot Charts. I originally learnt how to use pivot tables with MS Excel and used to teach the same method to my students. A pivot table is an extremely powerful method for manipulating data and breaking it into pieces in order for you to answer specific questions about that data. My view of how to approach this process was altered forever when my good friend Craig Hurkett introduced me to pivot charts. A pivot chart does the same thing as a pivot table. However, it does so through user interaction with a highly visual interface. Whereas pivot tables focus entirely on numbers within tables, pivot charts suit the more common visual nature of people, thus I believe they are far more intuitive to use. Let me pass on the favour shown to me and introduce you to pivot charts.

- A **Pivot Table Report** is an interactive table that quickly combines and compares large amounts of data. You can rotate its rows and columns to see different summaries of the source data, and you can display the details of areas of interest.
- A **Pivot Chart Report** provides a graphical representation of the data in a Pivot Table report. You can change the layout and data displayed in a Pivot Chart report just as you can in a Pivot Table report.

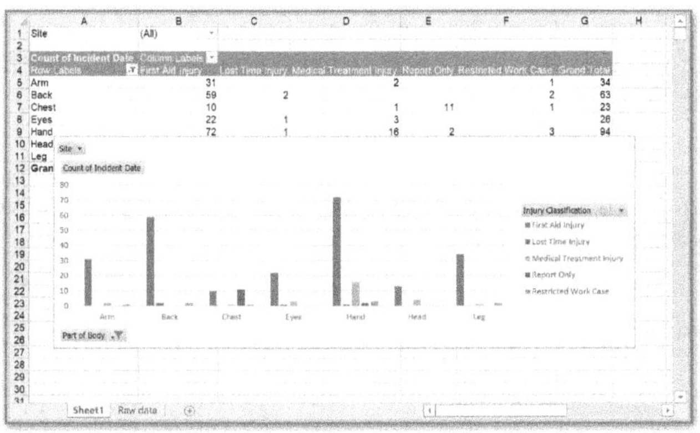

I should point out here that this text will not teach you how to use Pivot Charts, only introduce you to them and maybe help simplify how they work for those of you already familiar.

For more information you should seek out practical training similar to that which we deliver in our Lean Six Sigma programs.

The diagram is a screenshot of a Pivot Chart Report.

Pivot Chart Fields

Pivot Chart Reports are accessed by making a cell of your worksheet active, and then clicking on Insert > Pivot Table > From Table/Range.

Pivot Chart reports for later versions of Excel have specific terms you must be familiar with. Effectively they relate to the same functions, though different words are used.

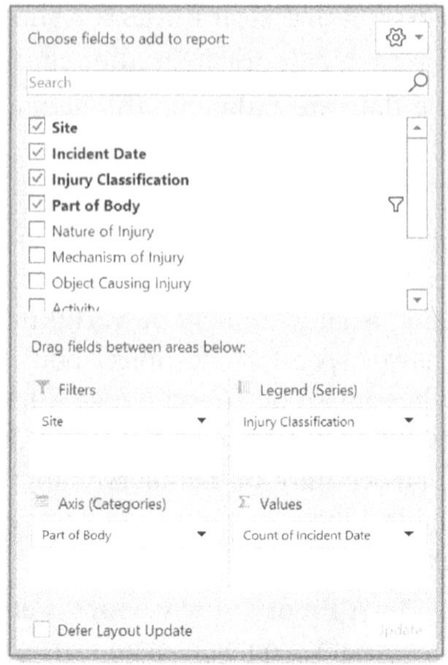

Figure 181: Pivot Chart Report Main Screen

Fields

A field is a collection of data from the source data. It is drawn from the data column headings and can comprise any type of data - categorical (e.g. part of the body injured), numerical (eg. number of days off work), dates etc.

To set up our Pivot Table and Pivot Chart, or to change what we are analysing, we simply drag these into the areas below. Where they go depends on what you want to look at.

Filters

A filter is a field that you use to filter data by specific items. In the example, the Site field allows you to view data for all sites together, or select one or more specific sites.

It dictates what the overall Pivot Chart shows.

Refer to the example Pivot Chart shown below where the chart shows results for all sites.

Rows / Axis (Categories)

This controls what is shown across a chart, for example when the field 'Part of the Body' is placed here, it dictates how the chart is stratified.

For example if we create a column chart as our Pivot Chart, this would dictate what the columns would refer to, in this case various parts of the body.

Refer to the example in the next image.

Columns / Legend (Series)

The items in the field dictate the individual data series. In the example, there are 5 different injury classifications, so if we were counting number of injuries and displaying these as a column chart showing the counts for various body parts, this field would stratify each of those columns and show counts by injury classification.

Refer to the Pivot Chart shown below.

Σ Value

This is a field from the underlying source data that provides values to compare or measure.

In the example, we've added the Incident Date field and set it up to Count events.

So the values being displayed in the Pivot Chart in this case will be a count of events for each element in the chart.

Depending on the source data you use for the report, you can change the summary function from the default setting of 'Count' to Average, Sum, Product, or some other calculation.

Set It Up, Then Drag and Drop

In setting up the chart (click on Pivot Table Analyse > Pivot Chart), you choose the type of chart you want. That chart will then be placed on to the Pivot Table worksheet which is based on how you set up your fields.

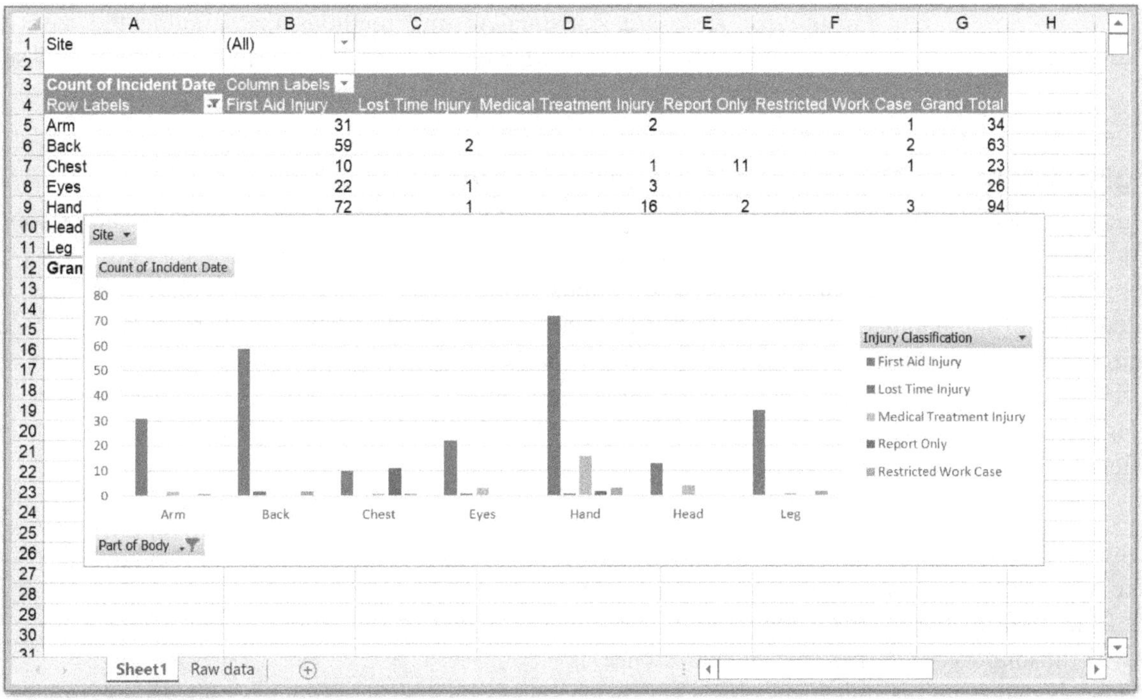

Site (All)

Count of Incident Date	Column Labels					
Row Labels	First Aid Injury	Lost Time Injury	Medical Treatment Injury	Report Only	Restricted Work Case	Grand Total
Arm	31		2		1	34
Back	59	2			2	63
Chest	10		1	11	1	23
Eyes	22	1	3			26
Hand	72	1	16	2	3	94
Head						
Leg						
Gran						

The chart above shows what one would see using the field choices shown in the image earlier where we discussed the various areas and terms of a Pivot Table.

An extremely powerful tool at this point of your project, and as I said earlier, it will be worth your while to learn about Pivot Chart Reports if you've never worked with them before.

INFERENTIAL STATISTICS

The term ***Inferential Statistics*** is used to describe the activities of collecting and analysing samples of data in order to make inferences about population parameters.

Definitions:

To undertake inferential statistics you need to understand the following terms.

Statistical Inference	***Statistical Inference*** is a prediction or decision about certain characteristics of a population based on information contained in a sample drawn from that population.
Parametric Tests	***Parametric Tests*** are statistical testing methods that assume the data being studied subscribes to a specific distribution i.e., normal, binomial, chi-square etc. Conversely, Non Parametric Tests make no such assumptions.

Bringing Graphical Techniques & Statistical Methods Together

Graphical methods such as Box Plots, Pareto Charts and Multi-Vari Charts help us to locate a source of variation by distinguishing results within different categories. However, they do rely entirely on visual interpretation. When results show clear distinctions within any category, provided our data set is representative of the population we can start to treat the source of variation. For example, if we observe in our Pareto Chart that 90 percent of all lost time relates to hand injuries, or we see in our stratified box plots that all coffee made on a Monday is outside the required temperature range while all other days are inside, we don't need some rocket scientist to come along and tell us whether or not any difference we observe is significant.

However, if the differences we observe between say coffee temperature results on the Monday and the rest of the week are quite overlapped and we cannot say with absolute confidence that the difference is not just because of sample variation, we bring inferential statistics into play.

Its role is to minimise the risk of us focusing on one variable when in fact it was never a source of variation in the first place. At this point we use inferential statistics to validate our hypothesis that a particular source of variation is in fact a source of variation we should treat.

The diagram to the right shows common graphical techniques as well as statistical methods used to locate and validate sources of variation.

Many of the most commonly used statistical tools are discussed in the following pages.

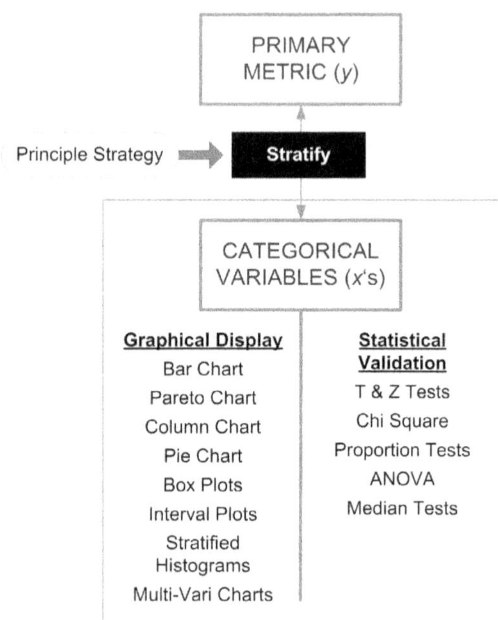

Selecting Statistical Analysis Techniques

Knowing the type of data you are working with will determine the type of analysis that can be performed. Independent variables are essentially input or process variables that cause outputs to be the way they are.

These are also known as:

- *x*'s
- Factors
- Sources
- Causes

Dependent variables are output variables which are also known as:

- *y*'s
- Responses
- Effects

As discussed in the 'measure' phase, these variables will consist of different data types. Knowing which data type is important in the process of determining which tool to use to analyse relationships. Let's revisit those data types.

Type	Explanation
Categorical Data (Discrete Attribute Data)	Data generated from **Categorical Variables** that is qualitative in the information it provides. These variables yield values that can only be placed into categories or classes. Some good examples include describing the type of cars owned by people, causes of unscheduled downtime and countries represented at the soccer world cup. In many textbooks, this type of data is simply referred to as 'Attribute Data'.
Numerical Data	Numerical data is generated from numerical variables. These variables are one of two types – discrete [numerical] variables or continuous [numerical] variables. **Continuous Numerical Variables** are those obtained through measurement and come from an infinitely divisible measurement scale. The accuracy of the variable will usually depend on the degree of precision the measurement device is capable of producing. A micrometer will obviously produce a more precise measurement than a ruler. Examples of continuous variables include temperature, length, weight, height etc. Data obtained using continuous variables is called 'Continuous Data'. **Discrete Numerical Variables** are those that are obtained through counting and comprise whole units. Discrete data usually answers the question 'How many?' Examples of discrete variables include number of trucks in a fleet, number of clubs in a bag, golf score etc. Data obtained using discrete variables is called 'Discrete Data'.

Key Learning Points

- To select tools for analysing relationships, Black Belts must know the types of data they are working with.
- Data under analysis can be categorical (discrete attributes) or numerical (discrete or continuous variables)

- A determination must be made as to whether a variable is an independent variable (x's) or a dependent variable (y's) in order to accurately understand relationships

Before we go any further into the different statistical methods, it's necessary for us to have a full understanding of the Central Limit Theorem.

CENTRAL LIMIT THEOREM

To understand CLT, you first need to understand the concept of:

- Distribution of the sample means
- Comparison of statistics from different samples

Let me give you an example to consider.

Suppose a project team was charged with reducing the cycle time for customers checking into a motel.

Using samples taken over a period of one month, the team found the average cycle time for each of the days of the week was as shown in the table to the right.

Does it take longer on average for customers to check-in on Fridays than Saturdays?

DAY OF THE WEEK	CYCLE TIME (MINS)
Monday	8.25
Tuesday	8.00
Wednesday	7.75
Thursday	8.15
Friday	11.25
Saturday	10.75
Sunday	6.75

The usual approach is to compare the absolute values and say that the average check-in cycle time is greatest on Fridays. Now for the following month a sample of cycle times shows that the average check-in cycle time for Fridays is 10.95, and Saturdays 11.05 minutes.

Which one takes longer on average now?

When we analyse samples, we do so for the purpose of understanding something about the *population*, not just the *sample* being analysed. For our example, the change in average cycle times is the result of variation in the process, and in reality there is probably no significant difference in the average cycle time for all (the population) check-ins on Fridays and Saturdays. If a team were making decisions on the basis of this type of absolute value comparison [from samples], and the consequences of a wrong decision was millions of dollars, then this approach would be considered un-sound.

Let's see if we can explain this further.

In analysing a sample of data, we find that it has a mean of 162. The next sample we take will probably have a different mean, as there is going to be variation in the values of the data we collect. To have no variation in these values would be by pure chance only.

The means for each of the samples of random variables taken will themselves form a distribution around their own mean. It is this distribution that we calculate and compare in statistics for the purposes of identifying if there is a statistically significant difference between samples of data. We call this the 'Distribution of the Sample Means'.

Distribution of Sample Means – A Practical Explanation

Let me explain further what a distribution of sample means is as simply as I can. Suppose I undertook the following actions.

- I took a sample of 20 data points at random from a population and recorded the mean of that sample
- I took another sample of 20 data points at random from the same population and recorded the mean of that second sample
- I continued to do the same thing another 18 times
- I then created a histogram of the 20 recorded means (taken from those 20 separate samples)

What I would have created is a distribution of sample means. The mean of that distribution would be called the *mean of the distribution of sample means*. The standard deviation of that distribution would be called the *standard deviation of the distribution of sample means* or what is referred to in some statistical methods as the *standard error*.

Now to compare the means of two different samples, such as comparing your current results to those results achieved three months ago, or the coffee temperature results from different days of the week, you can use statistical analysis methods such as Hypothesis testing. The standard requirement for this type of **parametric test** is that the distribution of the sample means is 'normal'.

So with that understanding, let me continue with my explanation of the CLT.

The Central Limit Theorem

The CLT essentially states:

Part 1	**Part 2**
If the population is normally distributed, then regardless of the size of the sample, the distribution of the 'sample means' is also normally distributed	If the population is not normally distributed, the distribution of the 'sample means' is normally distributed for large sample sizes only (large samples = 30 or more data points)

Samples Taken from Normal Population Distributions

When samples (x's) are taken from a population of data that is normally distributed, the **distribution of the sample means** is also **normally distributed**, irrespective of sample size.

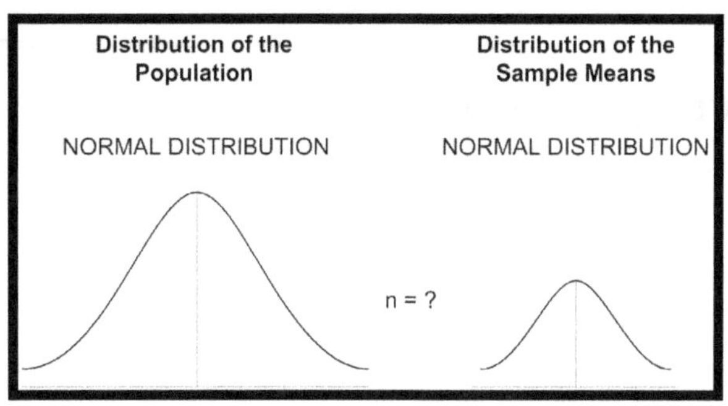

Given that such a population of size n with a continuous variable x, is normally distributed [with the mean μ and standard deviation σ_x], the distribution of the sample means formed by taking all possible samples of size n, irrespective of size, will also be normally distributed with:

This standard deviation of the distribution of sample means is also known as the **standard error** of the mean.

Samples taken from Non-Normal Population Distributions

Having said that, the **Central Limit Theorem** provides that:

Regardless of the shape of the distribution of the underlying population of the variable x, with a mean of μ_x and a standard deviation of σ_x, the distribution formed by plotting the mean of all possible samples of a given size n [taken from that underlying parent population], will more closely approximate a **normal distribution** as the sample size n increases.

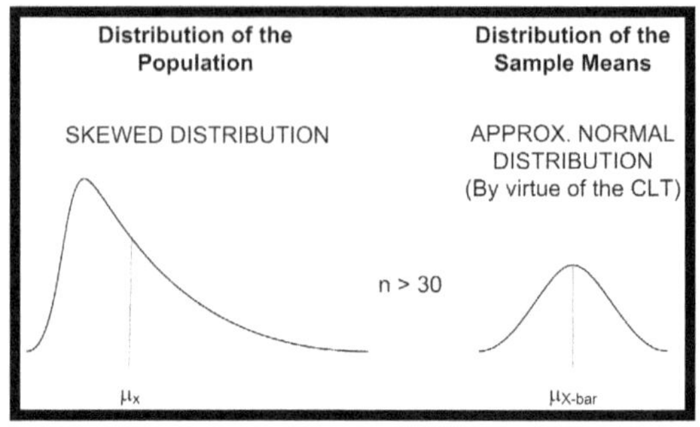

Furthermore, this normal distribution will exhibit the following properties:

- The **sample mean** will be the same as the mean of the parent distribution
- The **sample standard deviation** will be equal to the standard deviation of the parent population divided by the square root of the sample size.

For small sample sizes taken from non-normal populations, the distribution of sample means may or may not exhibit the characteristics of a normal distribution.

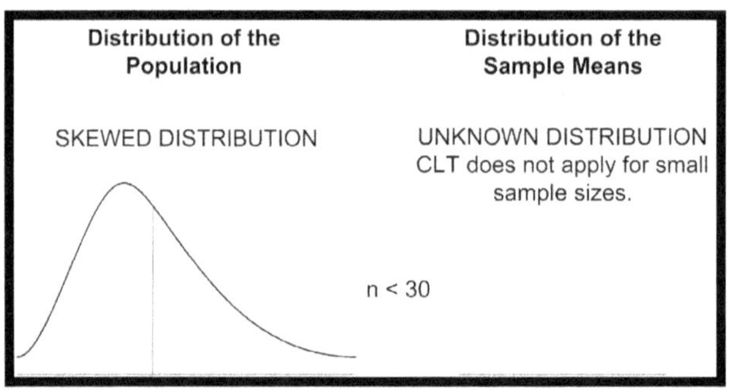

CLT Case Study

To illustrate the effect of the Central Limit Theorem, an experiment undertaken with non-normal data is reported in the following case study.

Exhibit a

The distribution below is obviously *non*-Normal, and in fact approximates a **uniform** distribution. This distribution has a population n of a continuous variable x. We will call it the parent distribution. (The normal curve has been superimposed for visual purposes only)

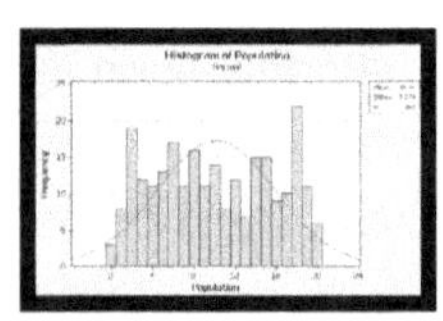

Though this distribution is not normal, we calculated the following parameters to

Exhibit B

A sample of **two** data points was drawn at random from the parent distribution and averaged to generate a value for X-bar. This process was repeated 199 times with the averages being plotted in the frequency distribution shown below.

The parameters of this distribution of sample means are:

Sample size $n = 2$

$\mu = 10.301$

$\sigma = 4.293$

Range = 17.874

The Anderson Darling normality test resulted in a p-value of 0.050, indicating that the distribution is *not normal.*

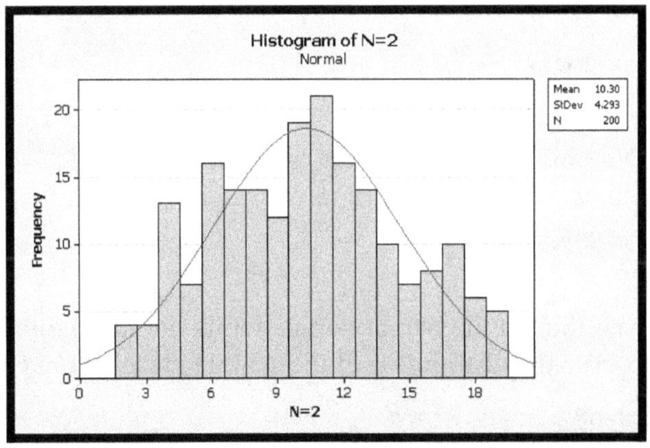

Exhibit C

Repeatedly taking a sample of **six** from the parent distribution, and computing the averages, produced the frequency distribution below.

The parameters of this distribution of sample means are:

Sample size $n = 6$

$\mu = 10.220$

$\sigma = 2.363$

Range = 14.697

Our normality test resulted in a p-value of 0.529, as this was greater than our alpha of 0.10, we concluded that the distribution in this case is *approximately normal.*

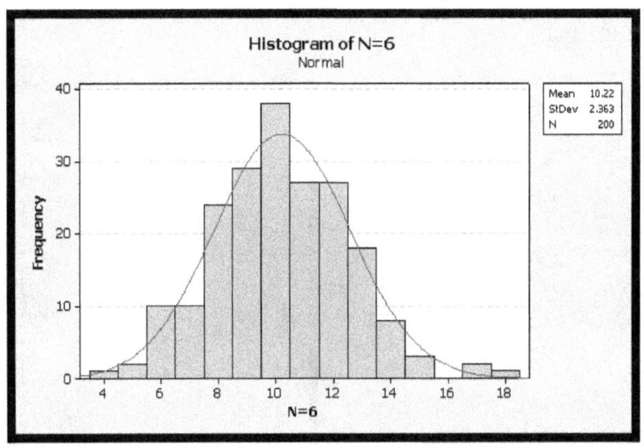

Exhibit D

Repeatedly taking samples of **thirty** from the parent distribution and plotting the averages produce the frequency distribution below. Notice when the sample size approaches thirty, the distribution of the average is considered normal, even though the parent distribution is not normal.

The parameters of this distribution of sample means are:

Sample size $n = 30$

$\mu = 10.172$

$\sigma = 1.039$

Range = 5.948

Our normality test resulted in a p-value of 0.431, indicating that the distribution is *approximately normal.*

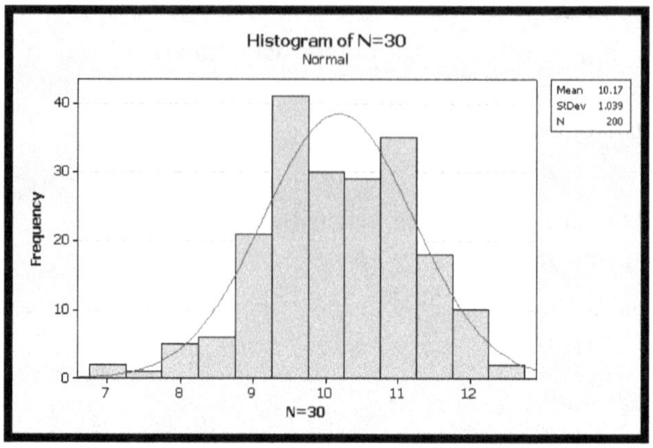

Even though the parent population is not normally distributed, as the size of the sample increases, we will observe the distribution of the sample means more closely approximating a normal distribution.

Exhibit E

We can also observe the means of all sampling means distributions are almost the same as the mean of the parent population. Interestingly enough the mean closest to that of the population value (10.152) is the mean of the sampling distribution created from samples of 30 data points (10.172).

Finally, as the size of the sample increases, the standard deviation of the sample means gets smaller, indicating less variation in the sample means. This reducing variation is demonstrated in the following diagram.

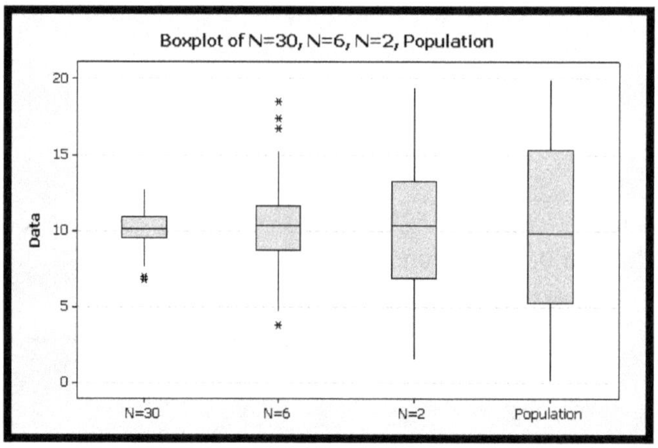

Figure 182: Boxplots of Sampling Distributions and the Population

Practical Application of the 'CLT'

The Central Limit Theorem is the foundation for many statistical procedures, including those that are used to test hypothesis about the means.

Hypothesis Testing

The comparison of the distribution of sample means is the foundation for hypothesis testing about the means of different populations. For example, a Black Belt may need to determine if the average cycle time of making a part on day shift was different from night shift. If the Black Belt only had sample data, he or she would use a test that compared the distribution of sample means to each other to make that determination.

Where the parent population is not normally distributed, provided the Black Belt has a sample of 30 or greater, by virtue of the CLT the Black Belt would know that:

- The mean of the sample data will be equal to the mean of the population; and
- The distribution of the sample means will be normally distributed, therefore its standard deviation (standard error of the mean) can be calculated using the equation:

$$\sigma_{\bar{x}} = \frac{\sigma_x}{\sqrt{n}}$$

So in procedures where the underlying requirement is that the distribution of sample means is normal (i.e. t and z tests), distributions can be compared without testing for normality and conclusions made about hypotheses with a relevant degree of confidence.

Summary of the CLT

By comparing the means of sample sizes of at least **30 data points**, you are able to assume that the normality requirements [of the distribution of sample means] are met by virtue of the CLT and undertake no further testing.

If your data is not normally distributed, and you have less than 30 data points, then you cannot undertake Hypothesis testing with the data on hand unless you use non-parametric procedures.

This *does not mean*:

- *You need to collect 30 data points each time you take a sample.* What you can do is consolidate the data you have into a sample size of at least 30 data points, and work with that. (i.e.: collect a sample of 5 each day, if you consolidate a weeks worth of data you now have a sample size of 35 data points to work with). This only applies when the data is collected from the same population of data.
- *The data itself is normally distributed.* For large sample sizes, only the distribution of sample means can be assumed to be normal. Where a test requires the data itself to be normal, it must be evaluated and the assumption met. (For example Analysis of Variance hypothesis testing.)

Key Learning Points

- The CLT applies to the 'Distribution of Sample Means' only.
- The CLT states that when samples sizes are large (≥ 30 data points), the distribution of sample means will be approximately normal regardless of the population distribution.

VALIDATING SOURCES OF VARIATION WITH HYPOTHESIS TESTS

'When we analyse samples, we do so for the purpose of understanding something about the population, not just the sample being analysed. If we only want to understand the sample, hypothesis testing methods are not required.'

Hypothesis Testing

The term 'Hypothesis is defined in the Pocket Macquarie Dictionary as:

> *'1. a proposition, idea, theory or other statement adopted as a starting point for discussion, investigation, study etc. 2. a statement accepted as basic in an argument. 3. a guess; assumption.'*

Hypothesis testing is used extensively in statistical analysis and can be used to help a Six Sigma Black Belt to:

- Determine whether or not there are *statistically significant differences* between two or more process outputs (outputs that have been categorised in some way)
- Determine whether or not making a change to categorical input or independent process variables (x's) significantly changes output or dependent variables (y's)

Whether or not it is caused by sampling variation or just variation in the process, it is highly unlikely that two samples will have the same characteristics – mean, standard deviation etc. These two samples may even come from the same population and yet have different characteristics. What we need to be concerned about is not whether there is any difference, but how significant any difference between the samples actually is. That's where Hypothesis Testing comes into play for a project. Hypothesis testing answers the question:

- Where there is a difference, is it statistically significant enough to say it is more than sampling variation?

Hypothesis testing can be used to analyse sample data so we can make inferences about population parameters such as means, medians, variance and proportions. It allows us to manage uncertainty, test assumptions and manage the risk of making decision errors.

Hypothesis testing is very useful when conclusions may be unpopular. When decisions or recommendations can be supported with statistical data, any decision to do other than that recommended must be a conscious decision to ignore *probability based logic*.

So in a nutshell, Hypothesis Testing enables us to make inference about a population parameter by analysing differences between the results we observe and the results we would expect to obtain if some underlying hypothesis were true.

Null and Alternative Hypothesis

Hypothesis testing begins with us making some assertion about a parameter of a population.

Example: The diameter of a titanium pin for the first 6 months of the year averaged 1.026 cm, with a standard deviation of 0.008 cm. In this case, our interest lies in determining whether or not the average has changed since that time. To do this, we would select a sample of pins and collect data on the diameter of each. For the purpose of our test, we start by identifying the **null hypothesis** (H_O), which is always a hypothesis of no difference. In this case our null hypothesis would be that the average diameter of pins is equal to the old average of 1.026 cm. The null hypothesis is stated as:

$$H_O: \mu = 1.026$$

We would be concerned if the average diameter was smaller or larger than 1.026 cm, so in this case the **alternate hypothesis** (H_A) is that the average diameter of pins is *not equal to* the old average of 1.026 cm. The alternative hypothesis is stated as:

$$H_A: \mu \neq 1.026$$

If a smaller diameter size was not a problem, we would only be concerned that the average diameter was larger, thus we would write our alternative hypothesis differently.

$$H_A: \mu > 1.026$$

All processes have variation, and for our study we have only taken a sample of the data from that process. As we only recorded the measurements of a few of the pins produced and not all of them, the likelihood that our sample data would provide an average value that was exactly the same as the average diameter of *all* pins ever made during the period of concern is low. However, as we would have sampled a specific number of pins on the basis of some equation, we have a degree of confidence that the true average diameter of all pins will be within some interval around our sample average.

'When it is not in our power to determine what is true, we ought to follow what is most probable.'

Descartes

Our alternative hypothesis represents the conclusion we would draw should we reject the null hypothesis. We would only reject the null hypothesis if there were sufficient evidence to indicate that it is unlikely to be true.

Failure to reject the null hypothesis however is not proof that it is true, just like a rejection of guilt in a court of law is not proof of innocence. We can only conclude that any difference is not significant enough to infer that the populations from which samples are drawn are different; hence there is insufficient evidence to warrant its rejection.

Let me summarise the key points of the null and alternative hypotheses.

Null Hypothesis	**Alternative Hypothesis**
• Writing the Null is very easy • Represented by the notation H_O • Always a hypothesis of 'no difference' • Always contains (=) • Is either *rejected* or *not rejected*, it is never accepted (similar to guilty or not guilty)	• Takes more thought to write Alternatives • Represented by the notation H_A • Always a hypothesis of 'difference' • Always contains (≠, <, or >) • Is *accepted* when the null is rejected

Example Hypotheses

Let me provide you with some written examples in layman terms with the relevant notations.

The Null Hypothesis		The Alternative Hypothesis	
The average head grade is the same for day & night shifts	$\mu_{night} = \mu_{day}$	The average head grade is not the same for day & night shifts	$\mu_{night} \neq \mu_{day}$
Variation in ore size is the same for each crusher	$\sigma^2_A = \sigma^2_B$	Crusher A has more variation than crusher B	$\sigma^2_A > \sigma^2_B$
Avg. temp at the end of the process is same as the start	$\mu_{end} = \mu_{start}$	Avg. temp at the end of the process is lower than the start	$\mu_{end} < \mu_{start}$
The proportion of scrap now equals 10 percent	$\pi = 0.10$	The proportion of scrap now is less than 10 percent	$\pi < 0.10$
The average temperature of coffee is the same every day	$\mu_{mon\text{-}fri} =$	The average temperature of coffee is not the same every day	$\mu_{mon\text{-}fri} \neq$

The Test Statistic as a foundation Concept

In hypothesis testing a **test statistic**, calculated from the sample data analysed, is used to assist in the decision making process. If the value of the test statistic is not what we would expect it to be if the null hypothesis were true, we simply reject the null hypothesis in favour of the alternative hypothesis.

A question that now comes to mind is how do we know which values of the test statistic imply that the null hypothesis should or should not be rejected? Remember one thing, the test statistic is a variable due to the fact the sample statistic is a variable. Hence, the test statistic has a distribution that provides the probability of all possible values that the test statistic can take, assuming the null hypothesis is true.

The possible values of the test statistic can be divided into two groups:

- **Unlikely to occur** – these are values of the test statistic that are *unlikely* to occur if the null hypothesis is true, forming the *rejection region* of the test statistic distribution.
- **Likely to occur** – these are values of the test statistic that are *likely* to occur if the null hypothesis is true forming the *non-rejection region* of the test statistic distribution.

If the computed value of the test statistic falls in the rejection region, the null hypothesis is rejected. P-values (discussed later in this section) are a method of determining whether or not the test statistic falls into the rejection region or the non-rejection region of the test statistic distribution.

The decision rules associated with the test statistics and rejection regions are shown in the diagrams on the following page.

Two tail test with the following hypothesis:

H$_O$: ? = ?

H$_A$: ? ≠ ?

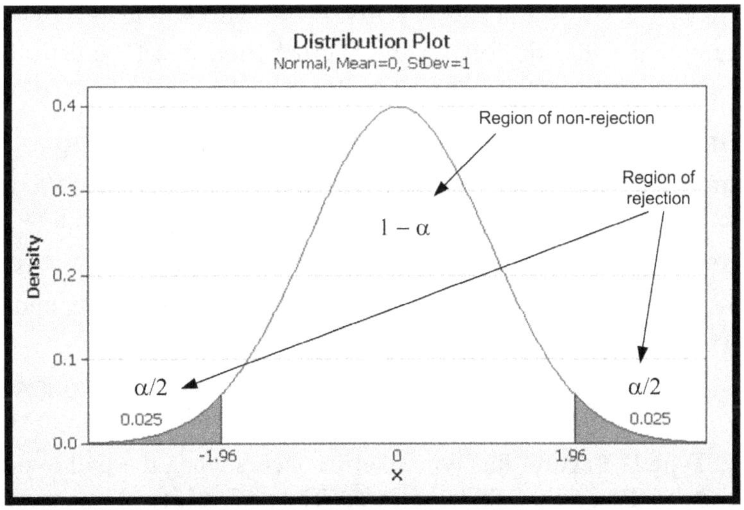

One tail test with the following hypothesis:

H$_O$: ? = ?

H$_A$: ? < ?

Note: the rejection region is in the tail the 'inequality' points towards in the alternative hypothesis, i.e. the < sign points towards the left.

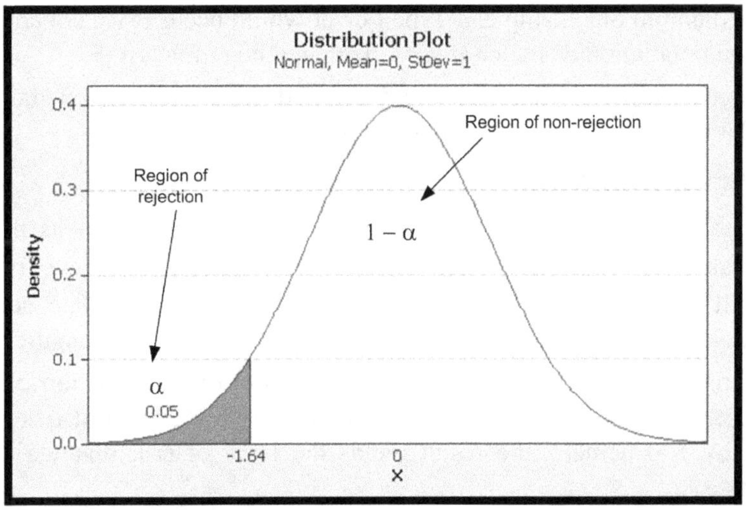

One tail test with the following hypothesis:

H$_O$: ? = ?

H$_A$: ? > ?

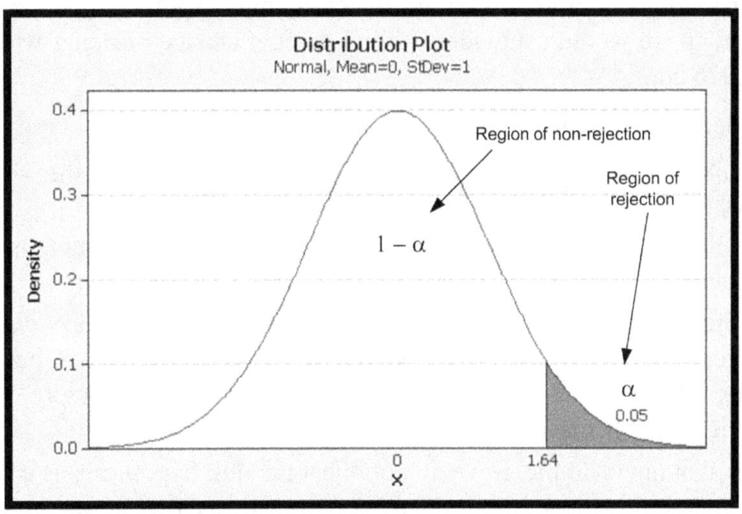

You will observe these test statistics are often referred to in accordance with the distribution they follow.

For example a *t* statistic follows the *t* distribution, the F statistic follows the F distribution, and the Chi-square statistic follows the Chi distribution.

Risk in Decision Making using Hypothesis Testing

Remember the purpose of working with samples. The purpose is to make some inference about a population parameter by studying some statistic taken from a sample of data.

When making such inferences, there is some risk that an incorrect conclusion (error) will be drawn.

In hypothesis testing, two different types of errors can be made, and these are referred to as Type I and Type II errors.

- **Type I Error** – this type of error occurs when the null hypothesis (H_O) is rejected, when in fact it is true and should not be rejected. The probability of this type of error occurring is α (alpha).
- **Type II Error** – this type of error occurs when the null hypothesis (H_O) is not rejected, when in fact it is false and should be rejected. The probability of this type of error occurring is β (beta).

In our titanium pin example, a Type I error would occur if we concluded on the basis of sample data that the average population diameter *is not* 1.026 cm when in fact it *is*.

Alternatively a Type II error would occur if we concluded on the basis of sample data that the average population diameter *is* 1.026 cm when in fact it *is not.*

Significance Level (A)

The probability of making a Type I error (α) is referred to as the **significance level** of the test being undertaken. We control the significance level by deciding the level of risk (α) we are prepared to accept that we will *reject the null hypothesis when in fact it is true*. The decision is made prior to the test being undertaken. Traditionally, researchers select values of 0.05 or smaller.

The most significant factor in deciding the level of risk is the consequence of making a Type I error. Where the risk is high in terms of cost or safety, then a lower level of risk may be appropriate. If we multiply this value by 100 percent, the result yields the level of risk that we are wrong when we do reject the null hypothesis.

In our titanium example, if we do reject the null hypothesis as a result of our test at the 0.05 significance level, then we would conclude with a 5 percent chance of being wrong that the average diameter of pins is not 1.026 cm.

Confidence Coefficient (1 - A)

The *confidence coefficient* (1 - α) is the compliment of the significance level. It is the conditional probability that the null hypothesis is not rejected when in fact it is true and *should not* be rejected. In other words the probability of making the correct inference about the population when you do not reject the null hypothesis.

If we multiply this value by 100, the result yields the level of *confidence* we can have that our decision to not reject the null hypothesis is the correct decision. Remember, because we are working with samples and making inferences about the population, we cannot be absolutely certain that the decision is correct, only that it is probably correct.

In our titanium example, if we do not reject the null hypothesis as a result of our test at the 0.05 significance level, we would conclude with 95 percent confidence that the average diameter of pins is actually 1.026 cm.

The B Risk

Sometimes referred to as the *consumers' risk* level, β represents the risk of making a Type II error. Where we can control the risk of a Type I error by selecting α, the probability of making a Type II error is highly dependent on the difference between the hypothesised value and the actual value of the population parameter. The probability of making a Type II error is likely to be small when the difference between hypothesised and actual values is large.

One way to reduce this risk is to increase the size of the samples taken.

The Power of the Test (1 - B)

The *power of the test* $(1 - \beta)$ is the complement of the probability of making a Type II error. It is the conditional probability that the null hypothesis is rejected when in fact it is false and *should be rejected.* In other words this is the probability of making the correct inference about the population when you reject the null hypothesis.

In the titanium pin example, the power of the test is the probability of concluding that the average diameter is not 1.026 cm when it is not in reality for the population.

The power of a test is increased as sample size is increased.

Balancing Decision Making Risks

The risks of making decisions with regard to the null can be summarised as follows.

	ACTUAL SITUATION	
DECISION MADE	**Null is True**	**Null is False**
Do Not Reject Null	Correct Decision (Confidence = $1 - \alpha$)	Type II Error (Probability = β)
Reject Null	Type I Error (Probability = α)	Correct Decision (Power = $1 - \beta$)

Decision Making Risks in Hypothesis Testing

One way of reducing the probability of making a Type II error is to increase the sample size. Larger sample sizes permit the detection of small differences between sample statistics and actual population parameters. Thus for a given α value, β can be decreased through increasing sample size, which in turn increases the power of the test $(1 - \beta)$ to determine the null hypothesis is false.

By contrast, when α is decreased, for example from 0.05 to 0.01, β is increased. So when we reduce the risk of a Type I error (rejecting the null hypothesis when it is in fact true) we increase the risk of a Type II error (not rejecting the null hypothesis when it is in fact false). An α of 0.05 provides a reasonable balance between making Type I and Type II errors.

The P-Value Approach

When undertaking hypothesis testing with statistical analysis software, P-values are generated to help us make a determination about whether or not to reject the null hypothesis. A P-value less than our chosen level of significance α, indicates the test statistic is in the rejection region of its distribution. Alternatively a P-value equal to or greater than the chosen level of significance indicates the test statistic is in the non-rejection region of its distribution.

Standard P-Value Decision Rules

The decision rule for using P-values is:

- If the P-value is greater than or equal to α, the null hypothesis is *not rejected.*
- If the P-value is less than α, the null hypothesis is *rejected.*

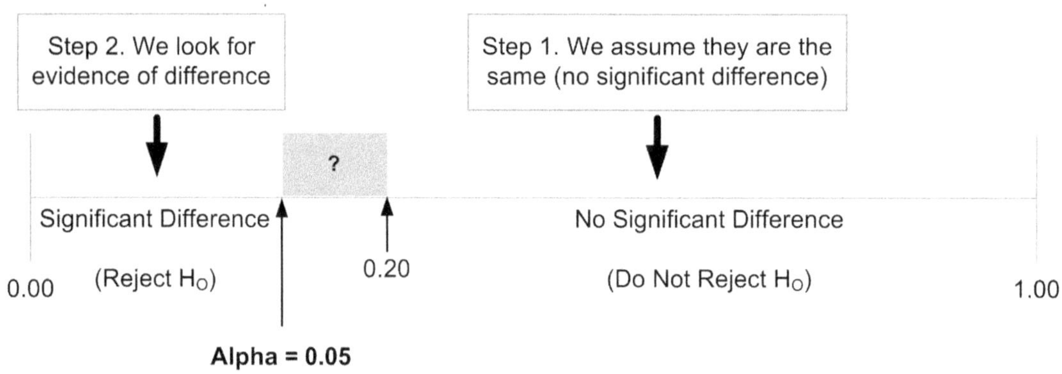

Figure 183: P-Value Decision Making Continuum

P-values Between 0.05 and 0.20

Many courses teach students 'power of the test' calculations (the subject is not covered in this text). However, a simple rule taught to me by my good friend Frony Ward has served me well over the years when it comes to Type II error situations is this.

When you generate a P-value in the range between 0.05 and 0.20, you really have insufficient data to make a clear distinction about whether or not any observed difference is actually significant. By increasing the size of your samples, the confidence intervals around the parameter of interest for each sample becomes tighter. Thus you reduce the risk of making a Type II error in that you are less likely to *not reject the null hypothesis* when in fact it is false.

New P-Value Decision Rules

The decision rules for using P-values for Six Sigma practitioners might well be extended to read as follows:

- If the P-value is **greater than 0.20**, the null hypothesis is *not rejected.*
- If the P-value is in the **range from α to 0.20**, increase your sample size and re-run the hypothesis test
- If the P-value is **less than α,** the null hypothesis is *rejected.*

As a practitioner intent on simplification, this is certainly how I approach hypothesis testing anyway.

Writing a Conclusion

In our titanium pin example, suppose for a moment we had tested our null hypothesis that the mean is *equal* to 1.026 cm, with the alternate hypothesis that the mean is *not equal* to 1.026 cm. Our conclusion will be comprised of three parts:

1. A reference to the P-value and α value;
2. A statement as to whether the null hypothesis is *rejected* or *not rejected*; and
3. A final concluding statement with reference to the parameter under analysis.

Example 1

Suppose our test resulted in a P-value of 0.53, and we decided α would be 0.05, our conclusion would be this.

> Since the P-value of 0.53 is greater than α (0.05), we do not reject the null hypothesis and conclude with 95 percent confidence the average pin dia. is 1.026 cm.

Example 2

Suppose our test results in a P-value of 0.042, our conclusion can be either one of these.

For what may be an obvious reason, my preference is to use the second version.

> Since the P-value of 0.042 is less than α (0.05), we reject the null hypothesis and with a 5 percent chance of being wrong and conclude the average pin dia. is not 1.026 cm.
>
> **OR**
>
> Since the P-value of 0.042 is less than α (0.05), we reject the null hypothesis at the 0.05 significance level and conclude the average pin dia. is not 1.026 cm.

Parametric versus Non–Parametric Tests

Some of the most commonly used hypothesis tests are detailed in the table below. All these can be placed into one of two categories.

- **Parametric Tests** – tests that assume the data subscribes to a particular distribution.
- **Non-Parametric Tests** – tests that do not assume any particular distribution.

	Hypothesis Test	**Underlying Distribution**	**Used for ...**
PARAMETRIC	1 Sample *t* Test	Normal	Comparing a sample mean to a historical or target mean
	2 Sample *t* Test	Normal	Comparing the means of two independent samples
	Paired *t* Test	Normal	Comparing the means of two dependent samples
	1 Way ANOVA	Normal	Comparing the means of two or more independent samples
	F-test (Bartlett's Test) for Equal Variances	Chi	Comparing the variances of two or more independent samples
	Chi Square	Chi	Compares the proportions of two or more samples
	1 Proportion Test	Binomial	Compares the proportion of a sample to a historical or target proportion
	2 Proportion Test	Binomial	Compares the proportions of two independent samples
NON	1 Sample Sign Test	Na	Compares a sample median to a historical or target median
	Mann Whitney Test	Na	Compares the medians of two independent samples
	Moods Median Test	Na	Compares the medians of two or more independent samples
	Levene's Test	Na	Comparing the variances of two or more independent samples

Table 33: Parametric versus Non Parametric Tests

NOTE: This table is not a complete list of tests, only those we mostly use in our work.

Non Parametric Methods

Non-parametric methods can be used as an alternative to parametric methods when the assumptions about distributions cannot be met.

The most commonly used include these.

PARAMETRIC TEST		NON PARAMETRIC ALTERNATIVE
Bartlett's Test / F Test	→	Levene's Test
1 Sample *t* Test	→	1 Sample Sign Test / 1 Sample Wilcoxon
2 Sample *t* Test	→	Mann Whitney Test
Paired *t* Test	→	1 Sample Sign Test **
1 Way ANOVA	→	Moods Median Test / Kruskal Wallis

** Can be applied to determine if the distribution of differences between paired variables is equal to zero.

9 Step Hypothesis Testing Method

Using statistical analysis software, hypothesis testing can be undertaken in the following steps.

1. Create a '**Visual Representation**' of the comparison you are making.
   a. This will involve presenting the categorised data in bar chart, Pareto chart, pie chart, box plot, stratified histogram form etc.
2. State the '**Null Hypothesis**' about the population – identified by the term HO
   a. Null hypothesis is always a statement of no difference. The null hypothesis will be there is no difference in proportions (π), means, (μ), or variances ($\sigma 2$) of populations, or the mean (μ) equals a specific number.
3. State the '**Alternative Hypothesis**' about the population – identified by the term HA
   a. A two-sided test is a statement that the parameters / values are not equal.
   b. A one-sided test is a statement that one parameter is less than or greater than the other parameter or value.
4. State the **significance level** 'alpha'
   a. The alpha value refers to the level of risk of concluding that the null hypothesis is false, when in fact it is true – a Type I error. Alpha values are typically 0.05.
5. Choose the **appropriate Hypothesis Test** (use the decision flowchart shown on the next page)
6. Test **assumptions** to see if they are met for the test chosen
   a. Some assumptions (e.g., assumptions of normality) are tested before the hypothesis test, whilst others such as normality of residuals (1 Way ANOVA) are tested last.
7. Compute the **test statistic and its P-value**
8. Compare P-values to 'alpha' and either **reject or not reject the null** (HO)
   a. Conclusions always contain reference to (a) P-values, and (b) the rejection or non-rejection of the null hypothesis.
9. Confirm your **conclusions** make sense (compare conclusions with the diagrams you prepared in step 1 – does the picture support the conclusion you've drawn?).

Choosing a Hypothesis Test

One of the challenges confronting Six Sigma Black Belts is the choice of which Hypothesis test is most appropriate. The following decision flowchart can assist in that regard.

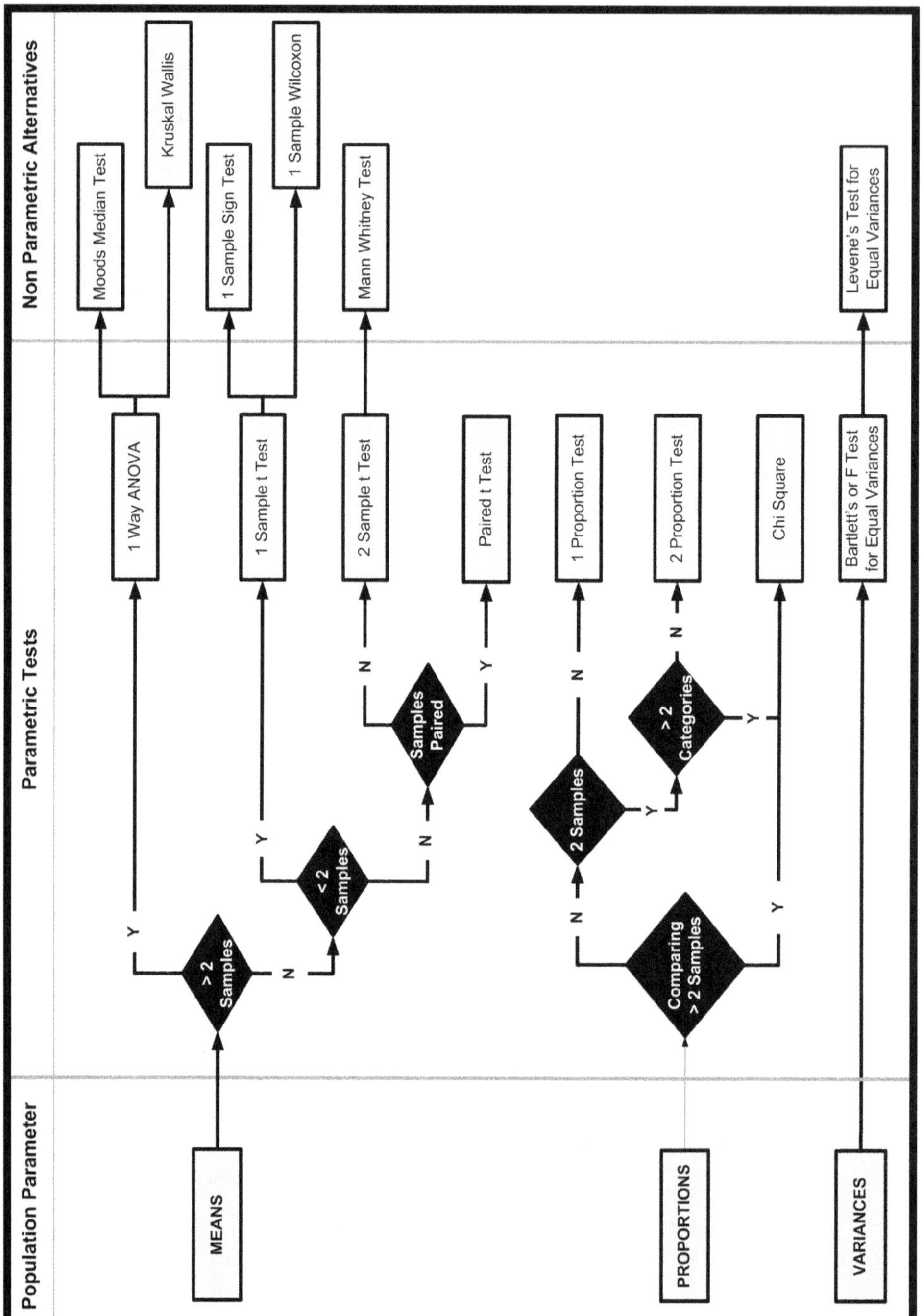

Figure 184: Decision Flowchart for Hypothesis Testing

Hypothesis Test Summary

The table below offers a summary of the most common tests and the assumptions relevant to those tests.

Test	Parameter of Interest	Used when looking for differences ...	Test Assumptions
Chi-Square	Proportions	In proportions between 2 or more populations.	Count data Counts in each cell ≥ 5
1 Proportion Test	Proportions	Between a single proportion of a population and a target proportion.	Binomial Proportions Independent sample
2 Proportion Test	Proportions	Between a single proportion of two independent populations.	Binomial Proportions Independent samples
1 Sample t Test	Means	Between mean of a population and target mean.	Normally distributed sample means
2 Sample t Test	Means	Between means of two independent populations.	Independent samples Normally distributed sample means Equal Variances (is desirable)
Paired t Test	Means	Between means of two paired populations.	Paired data (by some factor) Normally distributed sample means
1 Way ANOVA	Means	Between means of more than two independent populations.	Independent samples - Independence of Error (residuals) Normally Distributed data -Normality of Error (residuals) Equal Variances - Constant Error Variance (residuals)
Test for Equal Variances (F Test, Bartlett's Test, Levene's Test)	Variances	Among variances of two or more independent populations.	Independent samples Normally distributed data (for F Test / Bartlett's Test) Continuous probability distribution (for Levene's Test)
1 Sample Sign Test	Medians	Between median of a population and target median.	
Mann Whitney Test	Medians	Between medians of two independent populations.	Independent samples
Moods Median Test	Medians	Between medians of two or more independent populations.	Independent samples Populations have similar shaped distributions Equal Variances

BASIC HYPOTHESIS TESTING WITH SIGMAXL AND MINITAB

Focus on Practical Application

My goal in this section is to keep this as simple as possible as hypothesis testing is actually quite an easy concept to grasp and apply. It's made complex when we try to teach you how to be an expert in the underlying formulas and theory.

In order to achieve the simplicity goal, I want to teach you how to use hypothesis testing to answer questions and how to interpret the output from your statistical analysis software, that's it. The formulas do not matter to you as a practitioner.

My advice is you should get a solid grasp of its application first and then if you want to learn more about the theory and mathematics go for it, the understanding will be much greater as a result.

TEST FOR EQUAL VARIANCES

'Test for Equal Variances' is a parametric test used to compare and answer questions about differences in population variances. The types of questions that would lead to the use of this test are these:

- Is the variance in battery life for one type of battery the same as or different than the variance in battery life for another battery type?
- Is there greater variation in response times in the suburbs than in the city?
- Now that the process has improved, is the customer experiencing less variation in the product quality?
- Are variances in coffee temperature the same for each day of the week?

Some tests have an assumption of **homogeneity of variance;** that is the variances are the same. (Homogeneity means 'the same').

Not only is the tool used to answer questions about population variances, the test for equal variances is also used to validate assumptions of equal variance for other hypothesis tests such as the 2 Sample *t*-Test and Analysis of Variance.

Application	Assumptions	Hypothesis (H_O and H_A)
Comparing the variances of two or more independent populations.	Independent samples Normally distributed data (use F-Test or Bartlett's Test) Continuous probability distribution (use Levene's Test if data is not normal)	H_O: σ^2 are equal (variances are equal) H_A: σ^2 are not equal (variances are not equal)

Test for Equal Variances Using Minitab

<u>Setting It Up</u>

The Test for Equal Variances function is activated by clicking on Stat > Basic Statistics > Test for Equal Variances.

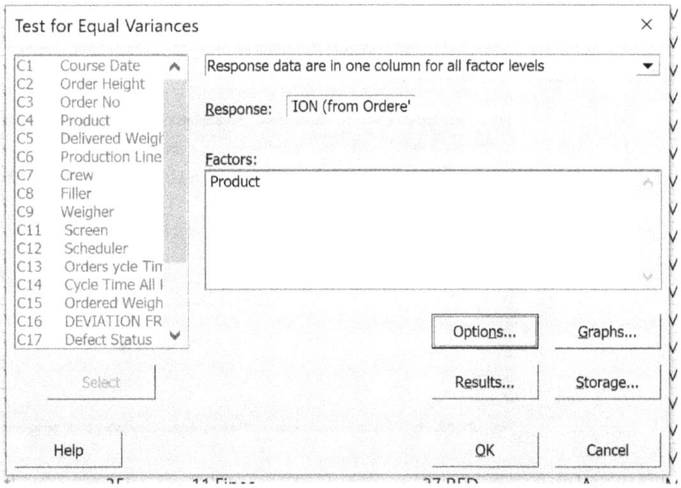

<u>Interpreting Results</u>

Minitab displays a test statistic and P-value for both an Bartlett's Test (referred to as Multiple Comparisons) and Levene's Test.

P-value - The P-value is used to make a decision as to whether or not the difference in variations between the variables under consideration is statistically significant.

When the P-value is less than α (usually 0.05), the difference is statistically significant.

In this case the P-value of 0.006 is less than 0.05, so we reject the null hypothesis and conclude there is a difference in variances across each of the factors.

If the sample data was not normally distributed, we would use Levene's Test results which would lead to the same conclusion in any case.

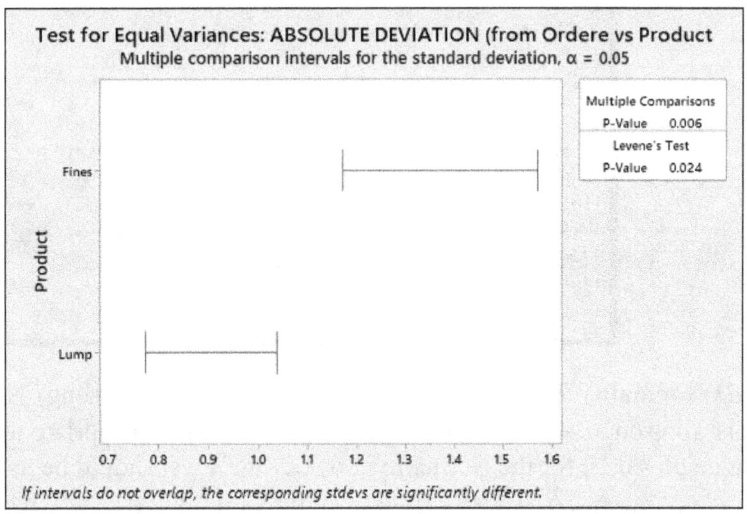

Bartlett's Test for Equal Variances Using SigmaXL

Setting It Up

The Bartlett's Test for Equal Variances function is activated by clicking on Statistical Tools > Equal Variance Tests > Bartlett.

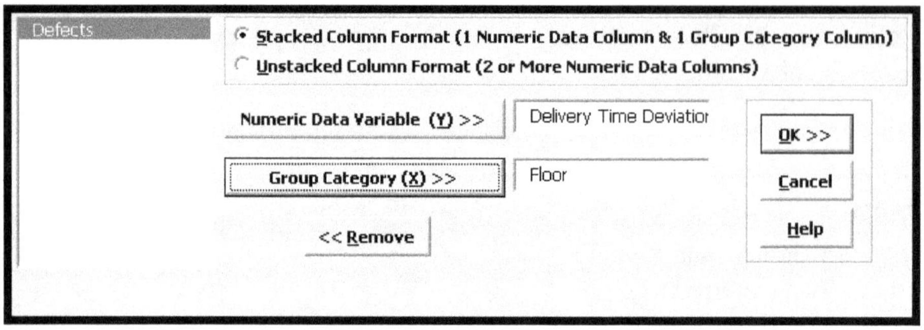

Interpreting Results

SigmaXL displays a test statistic and P-value that is used when data is normally distributed.

	A	B	C	D	E	F	G	H	I	J	K
1	Bartlett's Test For Equal Variance: Delivery Time Deviation										
2	(Use with normal data)										
3											
4	H0: Variance 1 = Variance 2 = ... = Variance k										
5	Ha: At least one pair Variance i ≠ Variance j										
6											
7	Floor	1	2	3	4	5	6	7	8	9	10
8	Count	73	73	73	73	73	72	72	72	72	72
9	Mean	4.989	6.064	6.242	5.581	6.250	8.004	6.647	3.649	6.539	6.084
10	Median	4.847	6.411	6.476	6.061	7.148	7.261	5.906	3.619	6.799	6.393
11	StDev	7.019	7.612	7.782	6.827	7.608	6.223	7.015	6.682	7.634	6.653
12	AD Normality Test P-value	0.8084	0.9515	0.4024	0.7642	0.0693	0.4844	0.1543	0.4230	0.4014	0.1475
13											
14	Bartlett's Test Statistic	7.073									
15	P-value	0.6295									
16											

AD Normality Test P-value - If all AD (Anderson-Darling) Normality Test P-values are ≥ 0.10, assume that all group data are normal and Bartlett's is the appropriate test to use. If any one of the groups has a P-value of < 0.10 for the Normality test, Levene's test should be used as an alternative.

P-value for Bartlett's Test Statistic - When the P-value is < 0.05, at least one pairwise set of variances are not equal. Therefore you reject the null hypothesis at the 0.05 significance level and conclude there is a difference in population variances.

In this case the P-value of 0.6295 is greater than 0.05, so we do not reject the null hypothesis and conclude with 95 percent confidence that variance is the same for all floors.

Levene's Test for Equal Variances Using SigmaXL

Setting It Up

The Levene's Test for Equal Variances function is activated by clicking on Statistical Tools > Equal Variance Tests > Levene.

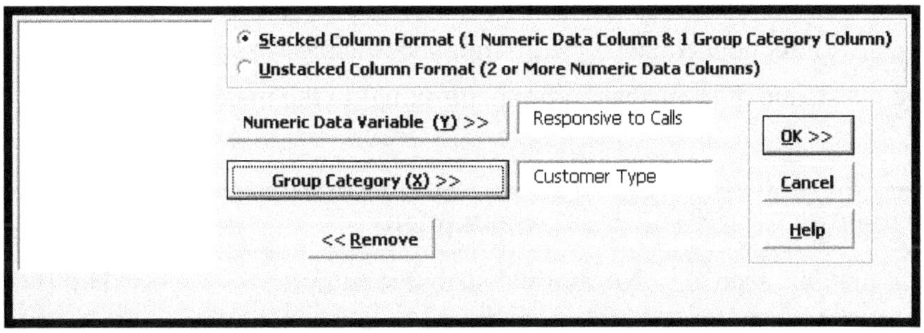

Interpreting Results

To test the null hypothesis against the alternative, SigmaXL computes a test statistic and its associated P-value.

P-value for Levene's Test Statistic - When the P-value is ≥ 0.05, we do not reject the null hypothesis and conclude with 95 percent confidence that population variances are the same.

In this case the P-value of 0.0144 is < 0.05, so we reject the null hypothesis at the 0.05 significance level and conclude there is a difference in variances.

Since Levene's Test is robust to the assumption of normality, it is the correct test for equal variances when normality assumptions cannot be met.

	A	B	C	D
1	Levene's Test For Equal Variance: Responsive to Calls			
2	(Use with non-normal data)			
3				
4	H0: Variance 1 = Variance 2 = ... = Variance k			
5	Ha: At least one pair Variance i ≠ Variance j			
6				
7	Customer Type	1	2	3
8	Count	31	42	27
9	Mean	3.412	4.226	3.821
10	Median	3.500	4.720	4.180
11	StDev	1.304	0.921232	1.091543381
12	AD Normality Test P-value	0.0021	0.0000	0.0190
13				
14	Levene's Test Statistic	4.433		
15	DF Num	2		
16	DF Den	97		
17	P-value	0.0144		
18				

1 SAMPLE *T* TEST

A One Sample *t* Test is a parametric test used to answer questions about the mean of a single population. The types of questions that would lead to the use of this test are these:

- Is the average head grade less than the targeted head grade of (a specified value)?
- On average is the cycle time now faster than the customer's specification of 5 minutes?
- Is the average thickness now equal to the 20 mm specification?
- Is the average resistance of electrical components equal to the manufacturer's specification of 0.33 ohms?

Application	Assumptions	Hypothesis (H_O and H_A)
Comparing the population mean to a historical or target mean.	Normally distributed sample means	H_O: μ = (a value) H_A: μ ($< \neq >$) (a value)

Normality and Non-normality of Sample Data

If sample data itself is not normally distributed, it does not imply the P-value for the One Sample t-test is incorrect. With sample sizes of ≥ 30, we can apply the Central Limit Theorem (ie; the distribution of averages tends to be normal for large sample sizes, even if the individual sample observations are non normal).

For sample size of ≥ 30, the t-test is fairly robust against skewed data.

1 Sample *t* Test Using Minitab

<u>Setting It Up</u>

The 1 Sample *t* Test function is activated by clicking on Stat > Basic Statistics > 1 Sample t.

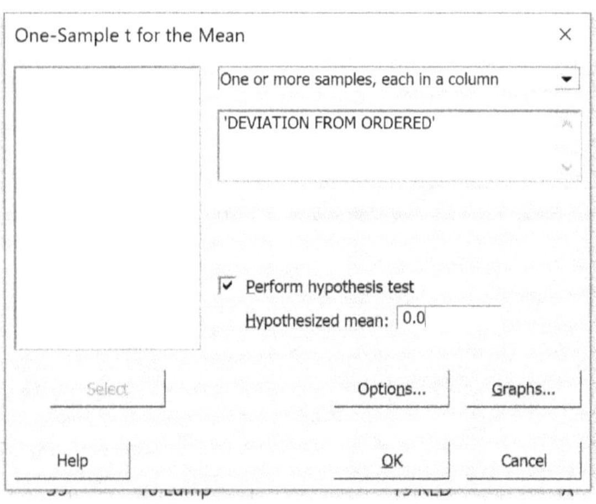

Users of Minitab will find they often must select the 'options' sub-dialogue box to input their 'alternative hypothesis' selection.

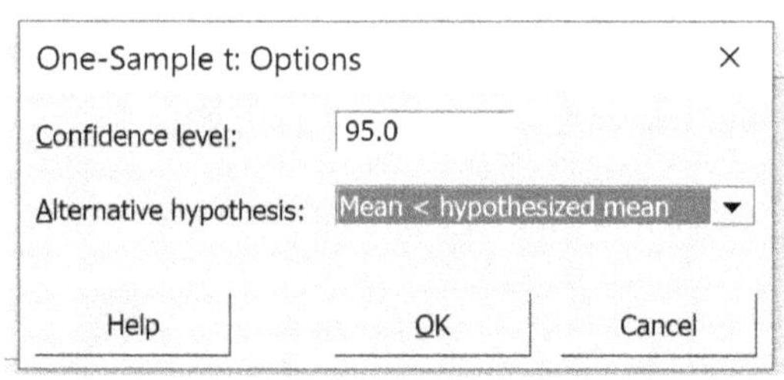

Interpreting Results

Test Statistic – To test the null hypothesis against the alternative, Minitab computes a *t*-statistic and its associated P-value.

Descriptive Statistics

N	Mean	StDev	SE Mean	95% Upper Bound for μ
240	0.1917	1.3244	0.0855	0.3328

μ: mean of DEVIATION FROM ORDERED

Test

Null hypothesis H_0: μ = 0
Alternative hypothesis H_1: μ < 0

T-Value	P-Value
2.24	0.987

95% Upper Bound (or Lower Bound) – The upper or lower bound represents the confidence interval within which we can be 95 percent confident the true mean of the population lies.

For one-tail tests (< or >), only one bound will be displayed. In this particular case we are 95 percent confident the true population mean lies somewhere below the upper bound of 52.19.

95% CI – For two tailed tests (≠), both bounds of the confidence interval will be displayed. This represents the interval that we can be 95 percent confident the true mean of the population lies within.

P-value - The P-value is used to make a decision as to whether or not any observed difference is statistically significant. When the P-value is < α (usually 0.05), we reject the null hypothesis at the 0.05 significance level and make a conclusion consistent with the alternative hypothesis (there is a difference).

In this case the P-value is > 0.05, so we do not reject the null and conclude with 95 percent confidence the true population mean deviation amount is equal to 0.

1 Sample *t* Test Using SigmaXL

Setting It Up

The 1 Sample *t* Test function is activated by clicking on:

Statistical Tools > 1 Sample t-Test & Confidence Intervals.

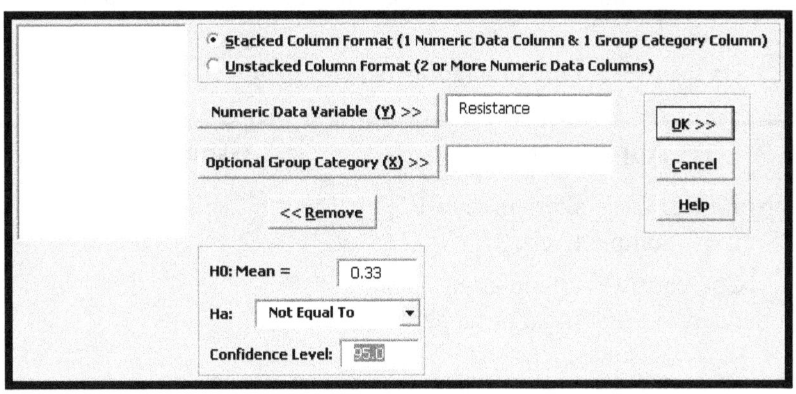

Interpreting Results

Test Statistic – To test the null hypothesis against the alternative, SigmaXL computes a *t*-statistic and its associated P-value.

	A	B
1	1 Sample t-test	
2		
3	H0: Mean (Mu) = 0.33	
4	Ha: Mean (Mu) Not Equal To 0.33	
5		
6		Resistance
7	Count	30
8	Mean	0.331267
9	StDev	0.01206572
10	SE Mean	0.002202889
11	t	0.575002
12	P-value (2-sided)	0.5697
13	UC (2-sided, 95%)	0.335772
14	LC (2-sided, 95%)	0.326761
15		
16		
17		

P-value - When the P-value is less than α (usually 0.05), the difference is statistically significant so we would reject the null hypothesis.

In this case the P-value of 0.5697 is > 0.05, so we do not reject the null hypothesis and conclude with 95 percent confidence the mean resistance is equal to the customer's specification of 0.33 ohms.

UC and LC Confidence Intervals - The values associated with UC and LC represents the 95 percent confidence interval for the true mean of the population. For example, we are 95 percent confident that the true mean of the population in this case (not the sample) is contained between the values of 0.326761 and 0.335772. The hypothesised mean value falls within this confidence interval, thus the P-value is greater than 0.05.

1 SAMPLE SIGN TEST

A One Sample Sign Test is a non-parametric test used as an alternative to the One Sample t Test to answer questions about the median of a single population. The types of questions that will lead to the use of this test are these:

- Is the median resistance of electrical components equal to the manufacturer's specification of 0.33 ohms?
- Is the median life of a laptop battery greater than 3.5 hours (210 minutes)?

Application	Assumptions	Hypothesis (H_O and H_A)
Non-parametric alternative to 1 Sample t Test. Comparing the population median to a historical or target mean.	nil	H_O: Median = (a value) H_A: Median (< ≠ >) (a value)

1 Sample Sign Test Using Minitab

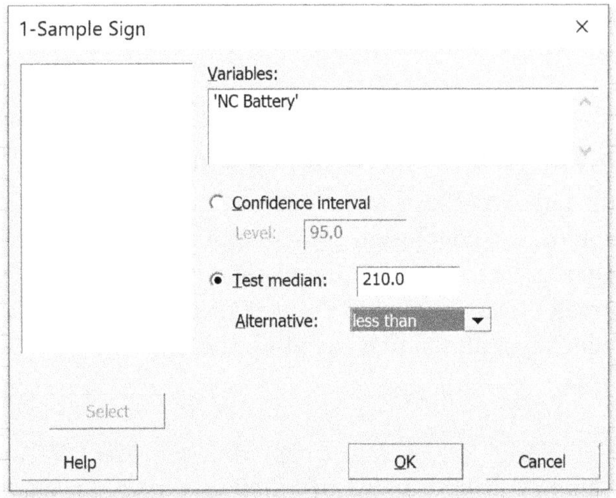

Setting It Up

The 1 Sample Sign Test function is activated by clicking on:

Stat > Nonparametrics > 1 Sample Sign

Interpreting Results

Test Statistic – To test the null hypothesis against the alternative, Minitab computes a test statistic and its associated P-value.

Test

Null hypothesis H_0: $\eta = 210$

Alternative hypothesis H_1: $\eta < 210$

Sample	Number < 210	Number = 210	Number > 210	P-Value
NC Battery	13	0	12	0.500

P-value - When the P-value is < 0.05, we reject the null hypothesis at the 0.05 significance level and draw a conclusion consistent with our alternative hypothesis (the population median is less than, greater than or equal to the hypothesised value, whichever alternative we nominated).

In this case the P-value of 0.50 is > 0.05, so we do not reject the null hypothesis and conclude with 95 percent confidence the median battery life is equal to 210 minutes.

1 Sample Sign Test Using SigmaXL

Setting It Up

The One Sample Sign function is activated by clicking on:

Statistical Tools > Non-Parametric Tests > 1 Sample Sign

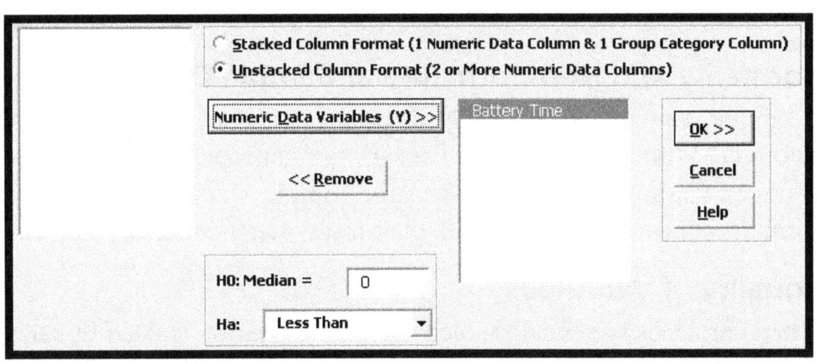

Interpreting Results

Test Statistic – To test the null hypothesis against the alternative, SigmaXL computes a P-value for the test statistic.

P-value - When the P-value is < 0.05, we reject the null hypothesis at the 0.05 significance level and draw a conclusion consistent with our alternative hypothesis (the median is less than, greater than or equal to the hypothesised value, whichever alternative we nominated).

	A	B	C	D	E
1	1 Sample Sign Test for Medians: Battery Time - Battery Time				
2					
3	H0: Median = 0				
4	Ha: Median Less Than 0				
5					
6		Battery Time			
7	Count (N)	25			
8	Median	207.63			
9	Points Below 0	0			
10	Points Equal To 0	0			
11	Points Above 0	25			
12	P-value (1-sided)	1.0000			
13					

In this case the P-value of 1.000 is > 0.05, so we do not reject the null hypothesis and conclude with 95 percent confidence the median battery life is equal to 210 minutes.

2 SAMPLE *T* TEST

A Two Sample *t* Test is a parametric test used to compare and answer questions about the means of two independent populations. The types of questions that would lead to the use of this test are these:

- Does the average cycle time of day shift differ from that of the night shift?
- Now that the process has been improved, has the average cycle time been reduced?
- Is the average output in minutes for one battery type the same or different to the average output in minutes for another battery type?

Application	Assumptions	Hypothesis (H_O and H_A)
Comparing the means of two independent populations.	Independent samples Normally distributed sample means Equal variances (desirable)	H_O: $\mu_1 = \mu_2$ H_A: μ_1 (< ≠ >) μ_2

Normality and Non-normality of Sample Data

If sample data are not normally distributed, it does not imply that the P-value for the 2 Sample t-test is incorrect. With sample sizes of ≥ 30, we can apply the Central Limit Theorem (ie; the distribution of averages tends to be normal for large sample sizes, even if the individual sample observations are non normal). For sample size of ≥ 30, the t-test is fairly robust against skewed data.

Equality of Variances

When variances are equal, pooled standard deviation is used in calculating the test statistic. Equal variances make this test more robust, though unequal variances do not preclude you from using the test.

2 Sample *t* Test Using Minitab

<u>Setting It Up</u>

Two Sample *t* Test function is activated by clicking on:

Stat > Basic Statistics > 2 Sample t

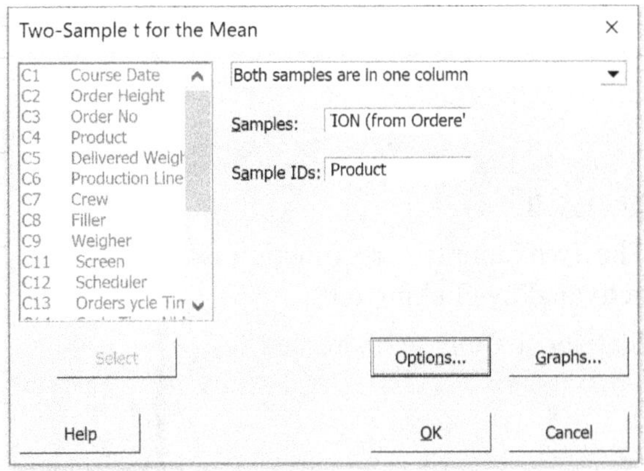

<u>Interpreting Results</u>

Test Statistic – To test the null hypothesis against the alternative, Minitab computes a *t*-statistic and its associated P-value.

Descriptive Statistics: ABSOLUTE DEVIATION (from Ordere

Product	N	Mean	StDev	SE Mean
Fines	120	0.85	1.35	0.12
Lump	120	0.517	0.889	0.081

Estimation for Difference

Difference	95% CI for Difference
0.333	(0.043, 0.623)

Test

Null hypothesis $H_0: \mu_1 - \mu_2 = 0$

Alternative hypothesis $H_1: \mu_1 - \mu_2 \neq 0$

T-Value	DF	P-Value
2.27	206	0.025

P-value - When the P-value is less than α (usually 0.05), the difference is statistically significant and we would reject the null hypothesis. In this case the P-value of 0.777 is > 0.05, so we do not reject the null hypothesis and conclude with 95 percent confidence there is no difference in customer satisfaction for different customer sizes.

Pooled StDev – When 'assume equal variances' is checked, the sample standard deviations are pooled to obtain a single estimate of σ. The test is more powerful with equal variances.

2 Sample *t* Test Using SigmaXL

Setting It Up

The Two Sample *t* test function is activated by clicking on:

Statistical Tools > 2 Sample t-test

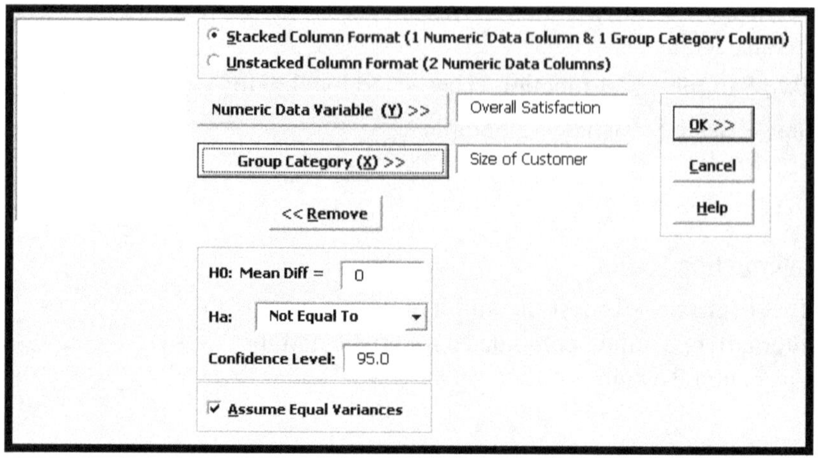

Interpreting Results

Test Statistic – To test the null hypothesis against the alternative, SigmaXL computes a t-statistic and its associated P-value.

P-value - When the P-value is < 0.05, we reject the null hypothesis at the 0.05 significance level and draw a conclusion consistent with our alternative hypothesis. (i.e., the mean of population 1 is less than, greater than or not equal to the mean of population 2, whichever alternative we nominated)

In this case the P-value of 0.7769 is > 0.05, so we do not reject the null hypothesis and conclude with 95 percent confidence the mean customer satisfaction level is the same for both small and large customers.

	A	B	C
1	2 Sample t-test: Overall Satisfaction		
2			
3	H0: Mean Difference = 0		
4	Ha: Mean Difference Not Equal To 0		
5	Assume Equal Variance		
6			
7	Size of Customer	Large	Small
8	Count	45	55
9	Mean	3.826	3.781
10	Standard Deviation	0.817706	0.759412
11			
12	Mean Difference	0.044909091	
13	Std Error Difference	0.158016	
14	DF	98	
15	t	0.284206	
16	P-value (2-sided)	0.7769	
17	UC (2-sided, 95%)	0.358487	
18	LC (2-sided, 95%)	-0.268668	
19			

NOTE: The order in which samples are input into the main dialogue box determines how the less than and greater than alternative is applied. For example, if you input Small Customer first and Large Customer second, a 'less than' alternative means that Small < Large.

Confidence Intervals (UC and LC) - The values associated with UC and LC represent the 95 percent confidence interval for the true mean difference between the 2 samples. For example, we are 95 percent confident that the true mean difference between the two populations in this case (not the samples themselves) is contained between the values of -0.268668 and 0.358487. The hypothesised mean difference of 0 falls inside this confidence interval, thus the P-value is greater than 0.05.

MANN WHITNEY TEST

A Mann Whitney Test is a non-parametric test used to compare and answer questions about the medians of two independent populations. The types of questions that would lead to the use of this test are these:

- Does the median cycle time of week day shifts differ from that of the weekend shifts?
- Is there a difference in the median throughput rate for the two lines?
- Is the median output in minutes for one battery type the same or different to the median output in minutes for another battery type?

Application	Assumptions	Hypothesis (H_O and H_A)
Alternative to 2 Sample t Test Comparing the medians of two independent populations	Independent Samples	H_O: $Median_A = Median_B$ H_A: $Median_A$ (< ≠ >) $Median_B$

Mann Whitney Test Using Minitab

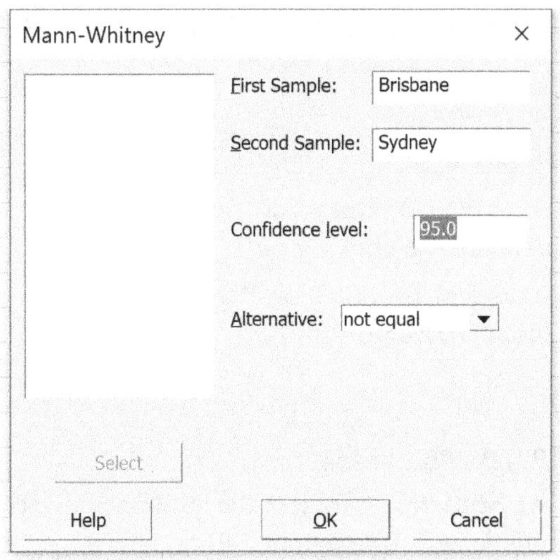

<u>Setting It Up</u>

The Mann Whitney Test function is activated by clicking on:

Stat > Nonparametrics > Mann-Whitney

<u>Interpreting Results</u>

Test Statistic – To test the null hypothesis against the alternative, Minitab computes a test statistic and its associated P-value.

P-value - When the P-value is ≥ 0.05, as it is in this case, we do not reject the null hypothesis and conclude with 95 percent confidence there is no difference between the population medians.

Descriptive Statistics

Sample	N	Median
Brisbane	20	1.540
Sydney	20	1.505

Estimation for Difference

Difference	CI for Difference	Achieved Confidence
0.235	(-0.6, 1)	95.01%

Test

Null hypothesis	H_0: $\eta_1 - \eta_2 = 0$
Alternative hypothesis	H_1: $\eta_1 - \eta_2 \neq 0$

Method	W-Value	P-Value
Not adjusted for ties	434.50	0.516
Adjusted for ties	434.50	0.516

Mann Whitney Test Using SigmaXL

Setting It Up

The Mann Whitney Test function is activated by clicking on:

Statistical Tools > Non-Parametric Tests > 2 Sample Mann Whitney

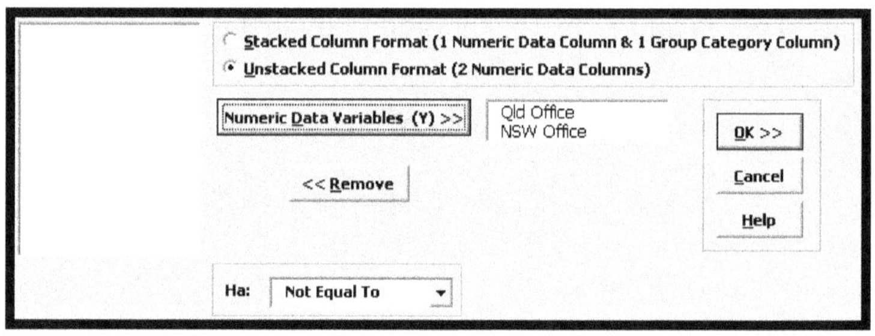

Interpreting Results

Test Statistic – To test the null hypothesis against the alternative, SigmaXL computes a Mann Whitney Statistic and its associated P-value.

P-value – In this case the P-value of 0.5161 is > 0.05, so we do not reject the null hypothesis and conclude with 95 percent confidence the median difference between the two populations is equal to the hypothesised value of zero.

In simple terms, the median response time for the two offices is the same.

	A	B	C
1	2 Sample Mann-Whitney		
2			
3	H0: Median Difference = 0		
4	Ha: Median Difference ≠ 0		
5			
6		Old Office	NSW Office
7	Count	20	20
8	Median	1.540	1.505
9			
10	Mann-Whitney Statistic	434.50	
11	P-value (2-sided, adjusted for ties)	0.5161	
12			

While this does not refer to the mean, at least we understand the central tendency of both populations is similar.

PAIRED *T* TEST

The parametric Paired *t* Test is used to compare and answer questions about the means of two populations in which values are paired by some factor. The types of situations and questions that will lead to the use of this test are these:

Scenario	**Question**
• 25 golfers each hit 2 different brand balls and the driving distance is recorded.	• Does the average driving distance differ across the two different golf ball brands?
• 2 different brands of fuel were tested for average mileage by running a full tank of each brand in 20 different trucks.	• Does the average mileage covered for a full tank of fuel differ between brands of fuel?
• A boat manufacturer pours resin into 20 separate moulds of the same boat component. The hardness of the components is tested at 2 days and at 5 days of curing.	• Does a 5 day curing time produce harder components than a 2 day curing time?

The dependency between two samples occurs when the data is **paired** or **matched** according to some characteristic, or because **repeated measurements** have been taken from the same set of items.

Application	Assumptions	Hypothesis (H_O and H_A)
Comparing the means of two dependent or paired populations.	Paired data (by some factor) Normally distributed sample means	H_O: $\pi_1 = \pi_2$ H_A: $\pi_1 \neq \pi_2$

Paired *t* Test Using Minitab

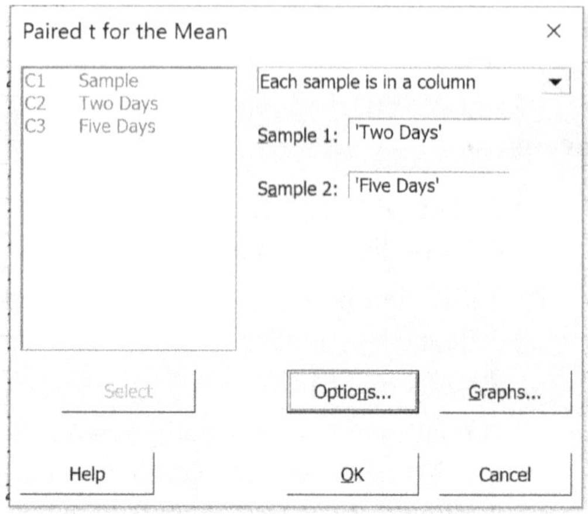

Setting It Up

The Paired t test function is activated by clicking on:

Stat > Basic Statistics > Paired t

Interpreting Results

Test Statistic – To test the null hypothesis against the alternative, Minitab computes a *t*-statistic and its associated P-value.

Descriptive Statistics

Sample	N	Mean	StDev	SE Mean
Two Days	40	1.4955	0.2480	0.0392
Five Days	40	1.7721	0.2518	0.0398

Estimation for Paired Difference

Mean	StDev	SE Mean	95% CI for μ_difference
-0.2766	0.1866	0.0295	(-0.3363, -0.2169)

μ_difference: mean of (Two Days - Five Days)

Test

Null hypothesis H_0: μ_difference = 0

Alternative hypothesis H_1: μ_difference ≠ 0

T-Value	P-Value
-9.37	0.000

P-value - When the P-value is *greater* than α (usually 0.05), any observed difference is *not* statistically significant and we would not reject the null hypothesis.

When the P-value is *less* than α (usually 0.05), any observed difference is statistically significant and we would reject the null hypothesis.

In this case the P-value of 0.000 is < 0.05, so we reject the null and conclude there is a difference in the mean strength for the two different curing times (two days of curing versus fives days of curing).

Paired t Test Using SigmaXL

<u>Setting It Up</u>

The Paired *t* Test function is activated by clicking on:

Statistical Tools > Paired t-test

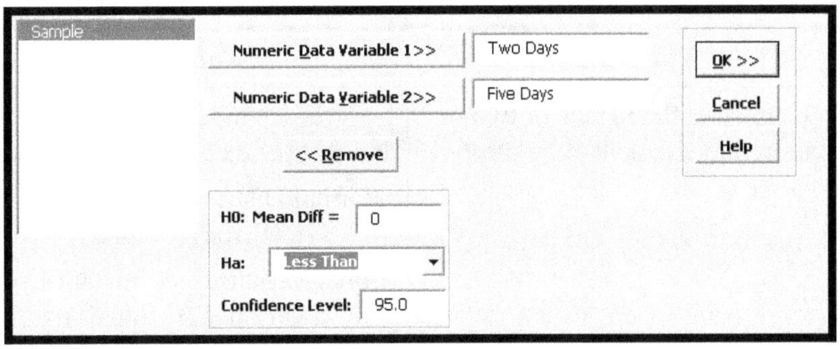

<u>Interpreting Results</u>

Test Statistic – To test the null hypothesis against the alternative, SigmaXL computes a *t*-statistic and its associated P-value.

P-value - When the P-value is ≥ 0.05, we do not reject the null hypothesis and conclude with 95 percent confidence that the mean difference between the populations is equal to the hypothesised value of zero (i.e., means are the same)

In this case the P-value of 0.00 is < 0.05, so we reject the null hypothesis at the 0.05 significance level and conclude that strength after 2 days of curing is less than strength after 5 days of curing.

	A	B	C
1	Paired t-test		
2			
3	H0: Mean (Mu) = 0		
4	Ha: Mean (Mu) Less Than 0		
5			
6		Two Days - Five Days	
7	Count	40	
8	Mean	-0.276563	
9	StDev	0.186632	
10	SE Mean	0.029509164	
11	t	-9.372	
12	P-value (1-sided)	0.0000	
13	UC (1-sided, 95%)	-0.226843	
14			

NOTE: The order in which samples were input into the main dialogue box determines how the less than and greater than alternative is applied.

For example, if you input 5 days first and 2 days second, a 'less than' alternative would actually mean 5 days < 2 days.

ONE WAY ANOVA

One Way ANOVA is a parametric test used to compare and answer questions about the means of two or more populations. The types of questions that would lead to the use of this test are these:

- Does the average distance travelled change with the type of material (4 different types) it is constructed by?
- Is the average temperature of the coffee the same for the three different cup sizes?
- Does the average cycle time differ between days of the week?
- Is there a difference in the level of sulphide emission from our 3 plants?

Whilst this is one of numerous hypothesis tests, I have extended the discussion for analysis variance due to the added level of complexity.

Application	**Assumptions**	**Hypothesis (H_O and H_A)**
Compares the means of two or more independent populations.	Independent samples - Independence of Error (residuals) Normal Distribution - Normality of Error (residuals) Equal Variances - Constant Error Variance (residuals)	H_O: μ's are equal H_A: μ's are not equal

Partitioning of Variation

The use of the term 'analysis of variance' may appear to be confusing to some, particularly since we are hypothesising about means. The basis for this approach is that through the analysis of variation among the sample groups and within the sample groups, certain conclusions about means can be drawn provided a number of assumptions are met. As variation is used to analyse the difference in means, One-Way ANOVA involves the partitioning of total variation in the experiment.

Total variation among all observations around the grand mean is represented by the sum of squares total (SST). Total variation (SST) is comprised of variation within the groups (SSW), and variation among the groups (SSA). Total variation (SST) is computed as follows.

$$SST = \sum_{j=1}^{c} \sum_{i=1}^{n_j} \left(x_{ij} - \bar{\bar{x}}\right)^2$$

Where:

x-double bar = The overall or grand mean

c = The number of groups or levels of the factor of interest

n_j = The total number of observations in group j

x_{ij} = The value of the ith observation for group or level j

Variation among groups is referred to as the *sum of squares among groups* (SSA). It represents the sum of squared differences between the sample mean of each group and the grand mean, weighted by the sample size *n*. Variation within groups is referred to as the *sum of squares within groups* (SSW). It represents the sum of squared differences between each value and the mean of its own group.

The diagram represents this partitioning of total variation.

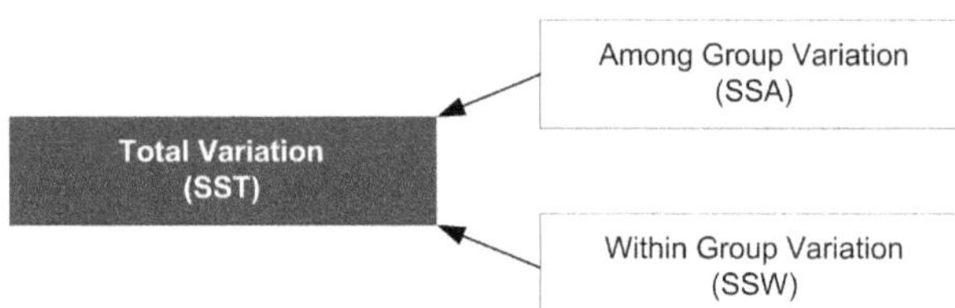

Figure 185: Partitioning of Total Variation - One Way ANOVA

Since we use statistical analysis software, we have no need to manually do these computations.

Analysis of Variance Table

When undertaking One-Way ANOVA studies with both SigmaXL and MINITAB, an analysis of variance table in the following format is generated.

Source	DF	SS	MS	F	P
Among Groups	c-1	SSA	MSA = SSA / (c-1)	F = MSA / MSW	P
Within Groups (error)	n-1	SSW	MSW = SSW / (n-1)		
Total	n-1	SST			

Where: DF = Degrees of freedom
SS = Sum of Squares
MS = Mean Sum of Squares
F = F statistic
P = P-value of the F statistic

The mean sum of squares for each of the sources of variation (MSA, MSW) is obtained by dividing the sum of squares by its associated degrees of freedom.

To test the hypothesis that there is no difference in population means, we calculate the F statistic with the equation:

$$F = \frac{MSA}{MSW}$$

Where the P-value associated with this F statistic is less than the significance level α, the null hypothesis is rejected.

ANOVA Assumptions

To know whether or not the One Way ANOVA was an appropriate test to analyse the sample data, it is necessary to determine whether or not certain assumptions have been met. The three major assumptions of the test are:

- Data is normally distributed - Normality of Error (residuals)
- Variances are Equal (or Homogeneity of Variance) - Constant Error Variance (residuals)
- Independent Samples - Independence of Error (residuals)

Normally Distributed Data – Provided distributions are not extremely different from the normal distribution, the level of significance of the F-test is usually not greatly affected, particularly when the sample sizes are large. When the departure from normality is significant, non-parametric alternatives should be considered.

Homogeneity of Variance – This states that the variance for all populations should be equal. This is necessary in order to pool the variances for each group into a single 'within-group' source of variation (SSW).

When samples sizes are the same for each group, inferences based on the F-test, which you should treat with caution, might not be seriously affected by unequal variances. However problems arise when you have unequal sample sizes and unequal variances.

Where possible, keep sample sizes the same. A modified Analysis of Variance called Welch's ANOVA can be used as an alternative in this situation.

Assumptions associated with **Normality of Error**, **Error Variance**, and **Independence of Error** are all tested through the analysis of residual plots shown on following pages.

One-Way ANOVA using Minitab

Setting It Up for Stacked Data

One-way ANOVA function is activated by clicking on:

Stat > ANOVA > One-Way

NOTE: SigmaXL can also be used for un-stacked data.

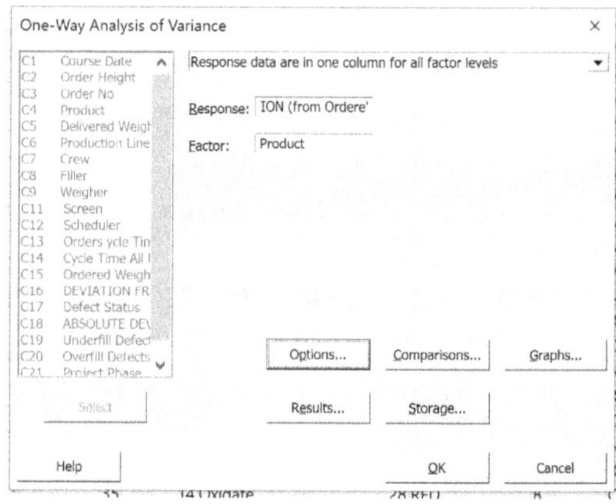

Interpreting Results

Test Statistic – The test statistic (F) is calculated as the ratio of two variances; MSA (estimate of variation among groups) to MSW (estimate of variation within groups).

This ratio follows an F distribution, hence the term F test statistic. Minitab calculates this test statistic using the ratio shown to the right.

$$F = \frac{MSA}{MSW}$$

If the null hypothesis were true, we would expect the F statistic to be approximately equal to 1.

P-value – When the P-value is less than α (usually 0.05), any difference is considered statistically significant.

In this case the P-value of 0.339 is > 0.05, so we do not reject the null hypothesis and conclude with 95 percent confidence there is no difference in the average deviation across the 3 product types.

Analysis of Variance

Source	DF	Adj SS	Adj MS	F-Value	P-Value
Product	2	157.9	78.96	1.08	0.339
Error	357	25999.9	72.83		
Total	359	26157.8			

Model Summary

S	R-sq	R-sq(adj)	R-sq(pred)
8.53398	0.60%	0.05%	0.00%

Means

Product	N	Mean	StDev	95% CI
Fines	120	0.850	1.345	(-0.682, 2.382)
Lump	120	0.5167	0.8886	(-1.0154, 2.0488)
Oxidate	120	2.06	14.69	(0.53, 3.59)

Pooled StDev = 8.53398

95% CIs For Mean – The confidence intervals for the mean of each of the variables under analysis is shown to provide a graphical representation that supports the analysis conclusions.

Interpreting Residual Plots

The following table provides a guide to the interpretation of Minitab generated residual plots in validating assumptions for analysis of variance experiments.

Refer to notes on linear regression for more explanation of the terms 'error' and 'residual'.

Normal Probability Plot

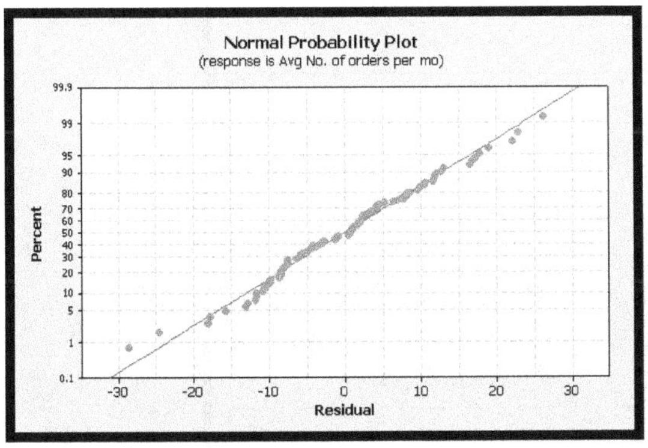

Normality of Error (Residuals)

The closer the sequence of data points represents a straight line, the more normal the distribution.

NOTE: Histograms are not as informative as normal probability plots for smaller numbers of data points, i.e. less than 30.

In this case, residuals appear to be approximately normally distributed and the assumption of 'Normality of Error' is met.

Residuals versus Fits

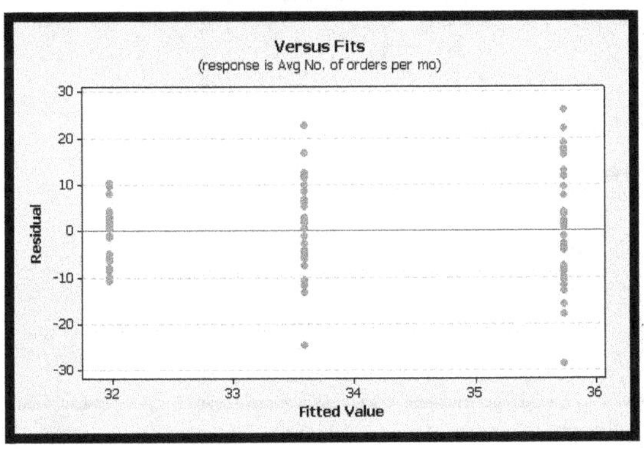

Constant Error (Residual) Variance

A random pattern of data points when residuals are plotted against fitted values indicates constant variance; i.e., variation remains constant across the range of fitted values. Fitted values in this case represent the mean of each sample.

Any pattern such as a fan shape would be an indication that the assumption of *homoscedasticity* has been violated.

In this case it appears that variance is fairly constant across the range of fitted values and the assumption of 'Constant Error Variance' is met.

Residuals versus Order

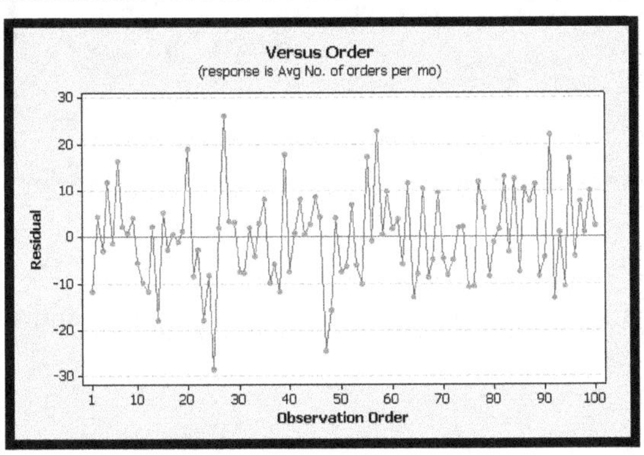

Independence of Error (Residuals)

As with 'constant variance', a random pattern of data points indicates residuals are independent of one another.

As this chart shows the chronological sequence of data collection, any pattern or trend (i.e., upwards, downwards, shift or drift pattern etc) would give cause for concern that the relationship between variables is affected by some factor related to time.

For example, when measuring the relationship between bounce height and drop height of tennis balls, the increasing ambient temperature from morning into full day could gradually change the bounce capability of a tennis ball. Any dependence amongst variables and time is readily apparent when residuals are plotted against the order of collection. A clear pattern will emerge.

In this case, the data is spread randomly across the plot indicating the assumption of independence is met.

<u>Four in One Residual Plots</u>

Minitab offers a function where all residual plots are consolidated into one chart. The example shown represents the same results discussed in the previous section on 'Interpreting Residual Plots'.

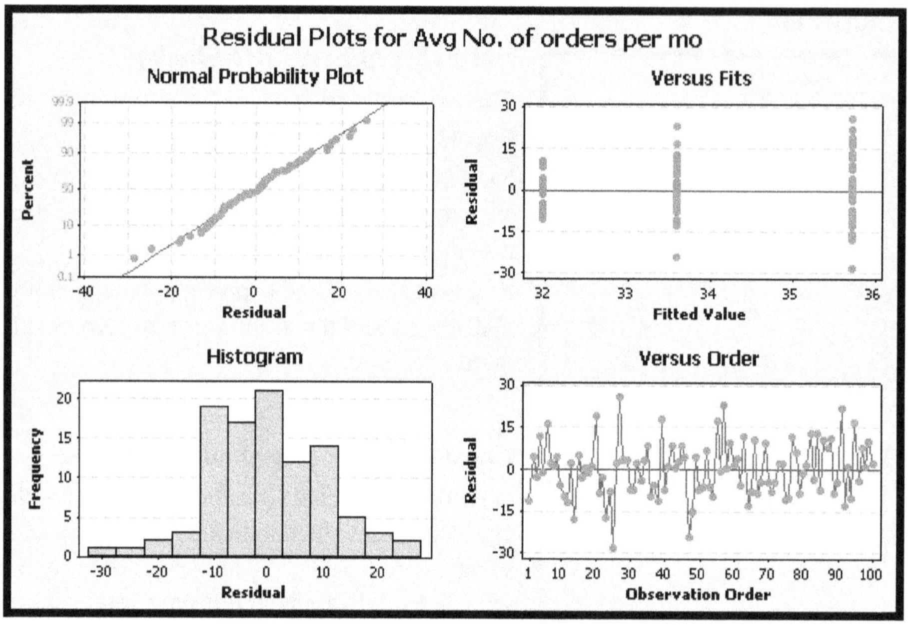

Figure 186: Minitab's Four in One Residual Plots

1 Way ANOVA Using SigmaXL

<u>Setting It Up (Un-stacked Data)</u>

One-way ANOVA function is activated by clicking on:

Statistical Tools > One-Way ANOVA & Means Matrix

NOTE: SigmaXL can also be used for stacked data.

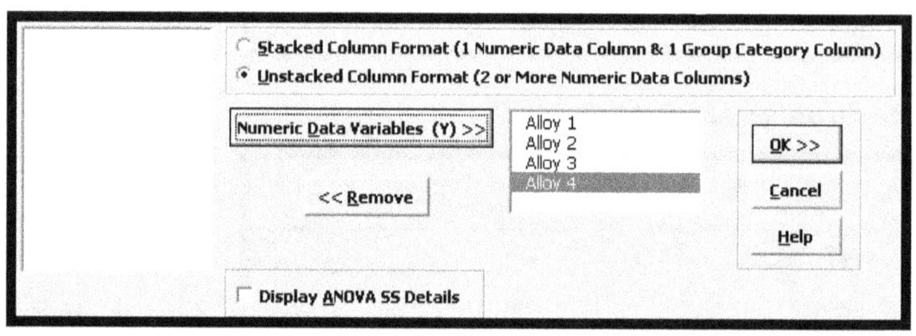

<u>Interpreting Results</u>

Test Statistic – To test the null hypothesis against the alternative, SigmaXL computes an F statistic and its associated P-value.

	A	B	C	D	E
1	One-Way ANOVA & Means Matrix:				
2					
3	H0: Mean 1 = Mean 2 = ... = Mean k				
4	Ha: At least one pair Mean i ≠ Mean j				
5					
6		Alloy 1	Alloy 2	Alloy 3	Alloy 4
7	Count	5	5	5	5
8	Mean	1000.6	1007.4	1005.4	1000.8
9	Standard Deviation	5.683	22.434	16.041	16.769
10	UC (2-sided, 95%, pooled)	1016.1	1022.9	1020.9	1016.3
11	LC (2-sided, 95%, pooled)	985.06	991.86	989.86	985.26
12					
13	ANOVA:				
14	Pooled Standard Deviation =	16.387		R-Sq =	3.86%
15	DF =	16		R-Sq adj. =	0.00%
16	F =	0.214195			
17	P-value =	0.8851			
18					
19					
20	Pairwise Mean Difference (row - column)	Alloy 1	Alloy 2	Alloy 3	Alloy 4
21	Alloy 1	0	-6.800	-4.800	-0.200000
22	Alloy 2		0	2	6.600
23	Alloy 3			0	4.600
24	Alloy 4				0
25					
26	Pairwise Probabilities	Alloy 1	Alloy 2	Alloy 3	Alloy 4
27	Alloy 1		0.5211	0.6495	0.9848
28	Alloy 2			0.8494	0.5332
29	Alloy 3				0.6631
30	Alloy 4				

P-value for the F Statistic - When the P-value is < 0.05, at least one pairwise set of means are not equal so we would reject the null hypothesis and draw a conclusion consistent with our alternative hypothesis. (i.e., there is a difference in means for the populations tested)

In this case the P-value is > 0.05, so we do not reject the null hypothesis and conclude with 95 percent confidence the mean value is the same for all alloy types. This conclusion should be consistent with what you observe in the graphical output.

R-Square (R-Sq) - The R-Square value indicates the proportion of variation observed in the *y* explained by variation in the *x*'s in the study.

For example, the **R-Sq** value of 3.86% indicates that variation in Customer type 'explains' approximately 4 percent of the variation in Overall Satisfaction. (for more information, refer to linear regression notes)

Pairwise Probabilities - P-values for differences in the means of pairwise samples are provided in matrix format. The means matrix P-values could easily trigger type I errors when the number of *x* levels gets large. You should only consider the results of the Means Matrix if the ANOVA P-value is < 0.05.

TWO WAY ANOVA

For information about 2 Way ANOVA, refer to designed experiments at the end of this chapter.

MOOD'S MEDIAN TEST

Mood's Median Test is a non-parametric test used to compare and answer questions about the medians of two or more independent populations. It is used as an alternative to One Way ANOVA and the types of questions that will lead to the use of this test are these:

- Does the median distance travelled change with the type of material (4 different types) it is constructed by?
- Is the median temperature of the coffee the same for the three different cup sizes?
- Does the median cycle time differ between days of the week?
- Is there a difference in the median level of sulphide emission from our 3 plants?

Application	Assumptions	Hypothesis (H_O and H_A)
Alternative to One Way ANOVA Test Compares the medians of two or more independent populations	Independent Samples Similar Distribution Shapes Equal Variances	H_O: Medians are equal H_A: Medians are not equal

Mood's Median Test Using Minitab

Setting It Up (Stacked Data)

Mood's Median Test function is activated by clicking on:

Stat > Nonparametrics > Mood's Median Test

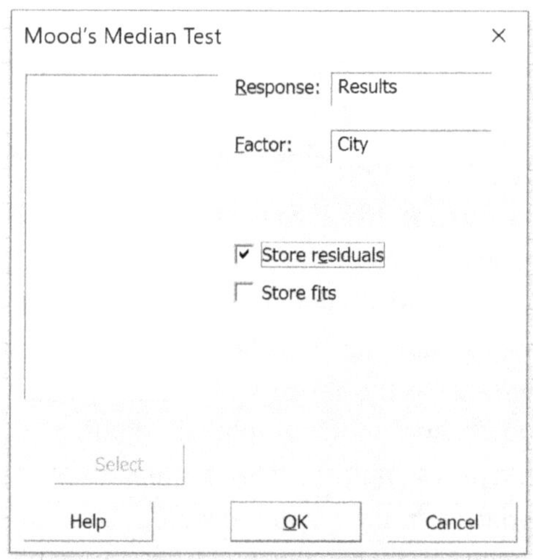

Interpreting Results

Test Statistic – To test the null hypothesis against the alternative, Minitab computes a Chi-Square statistic and its associated P-value.

P-value for Chi-Square Statistic - When the P-value is ≥ 0.05, we would not reject the null hypothesis and conclude with 95 percent confidence the medians of the populations are the same as each other.

Descriptive Statistics

City	Median	N <= Overall Median	N > Overall Median	Q3 – Q1	95% Median CI
Brisbane	557	18	12	165.00	(517.431, 647.937)
Melbourne	581	19	11	147.25	(561, 669.027)
Sydney	679	8	22	115.00	(620.915, 717)
Overall	605				

Test

Null hypothesis H_0: The population medians are all equal
Alternative hypothesis H_1: The population medians are not all equal

DF	Chi-Square	P-Value
2	9.87	0.007

In this case the P-value is < 0.05, so we reject the null hypothesis at the 0.05 significance level and conclude the median response times are not the same for the three offices. This conclusion is supported by what we can observe with Individual 95% CIs (confidence intervals).

Mood's Median Test Using SigmaXL

Setting It Up for Un-stacked Data

Mood's Median Test function is activated by clicking on:

Statistical Tools > Non-Parametric Tests > Mood's Median Test

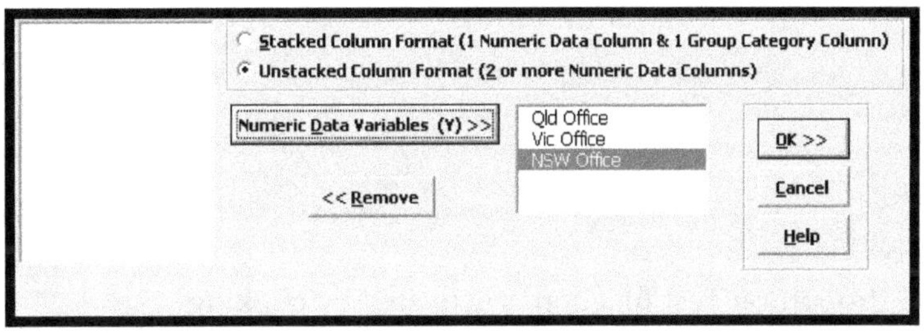

Interpreting Results

Test Statistic – To test the null hypothesis against the alternative, SigmaXL computes a Chi-Square statistic and its associated P-value.

P-value for Chi-Square Statistic - When the P-value is ≥ 0.05, you do not reject the null hypothesis and conclude with 95 percent confidence that the medians of the populations are the same as each other.

	A	B	C	D
1	Mood's Median Test			
2				
3	H0: Median 1 = Median 2 = ... = Median k			
4	Ha: At least one pair Median i ≠ Median j			
5				
6		Qld Office	Vic Office	NSW Office
7	Count (N <= Overall Median)	13	3	14
8	Count (N > Overall Median)	7	17	6
9	Median	1.540	2.860	1.505
10	UC Median (2-sided, 95%)	3.041	3.405	3.018
11	LC Median (2-sided, 95%)	0.981762	2.664	0.611762
12				
13	Overall Median	2.385		
14	Chi-Square	14.800		
15	DF	2		
16	P-value (2-sided)	0.0006		
17				

In this case the P-value of 0.0006 is < 0.05, so we reject the null hypothesis at the 0.05 significance level and conclude the median response times are not the same for all offices.

2 PROPORTION TEST

Two Proportion Test is a parametric test used to compare and answer questions about the proportions of two independent populations. The types of questions that would lead to the use of this test are these:

- Does Production Line 1 proportionately produce more or less defects than Production Line 2?
- Has the proportion of defects in product A dropped since we implemented those solutions?
- Proportionately do we experience more returned coffees in our take away containers than we do in our ceramic mugs?

Application	Assumptions	Hypothesis (H_O and H_A)
Compares proportions of two independent populations.	Nil	H_O: $\pi_1 = \pi_2$ H_A: π_1 ($<$ $\neq$ $>$) π_2

2 Proportion Test Using Minitab

Setting It Up

2 Proportion Test function is activated by clicking on:

Stat > Basic Statistics > 2 Proportion

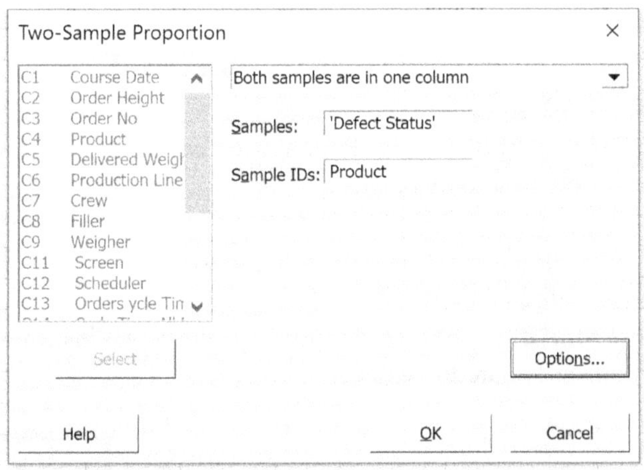

Interpreting Results

Test Statistic – To test the null hypothesis against the alternative, Minitab computes a z statistic and its associated P-value.

Descriptive Statistics: Defect Status

Product	N	Event	Sample p
Fines	120	102	0.850000
Lump	120	114	0.950000

Estimation for Difference

Difference	95% CI for Difference
-0.1	(-0.174847, -0.025153)

CI based on normal approximation

Test

Null hypothesis	H_0: $p_1 - p_2 = 0$
Alternative hypothesis	H_1: $p_1 - p_2 \neq 0$

Method	Z-Value	P-Value
Normal approximation	-2.62	0.009
Fisher's exact		0.016

P-value for Z Statistic - When the P-value is < 0.05, we would reject the null hypothesis and draw a conclusion consistent with our alternative hypothesis.

In this case the P-value is < 0.05, so we reject the null hypothesis and conclude the proportions of defects are not the same for both products.

2 Proportion Test Using SigmaXL

Setting It Up and Interpreting Results

The 2 Proportion Test function is activated by clicking on Templates & Calculators > Basic Statistical Templates > 2 Proportions Test and Fischer's Exact.

Once values are input, the test statistic and associated P-value is calculated in the main window.

Hypothesis Test for the Equality of Two Proportions

Sample Data (user inputs)		
Number of elements in sample #1 in category of interest:	x_1	78
Size of Sample #1:	n_1	120
Number of elements in sample #2 in category of interest:	x_2	68
Size of Sample #2:	n_2	115
Hypothesis Test Results:		
Proportion (sample #1)	$P_1 = x_1/n_1$	0.6500
Proportion (sample #2)	$P_2 = x_2/n_2$	0.5913
Z_0 Statistic		0.927
Normal approximation p-value (2-sided, Ha: $P_1 \neq P_2$)		0.354
Normal approximation p-value (1-sided, Ha: $P_1 < P_2$)		0.823
Normal approximation p-value (1-sided, Ha: $P_1 > P_2$)		0.177
Fisher's exact p-value (2-sided, Ha: $P_1 \neq P_2$)		0.420
Fisher's exact p-value (1-sided, Ha: $P_1 < P_2$)		0.856
Fisher's exact p-value (1-sided, Ha: $P_1 > P_2$)		0.214

P-value (2-sided) - When the P-value is < 0.05, we reject the null hypothesis at the 0.05 significance level and draw a conclusion consistent with our alternative hypothesis. (i.e. the proportions are not equal)

In this case the (2-sided) P-value of 0.420 is > 0.05, so we do not reject the null hypothesis and conclude with 95 percent confidence the proportions are the same across both populations.

NOTE: As a 2-tail test, the alternative hypothesis will always be 'not equal to'.

CHI-SQUARE TEST

Chi-Square Test (pronounced like 'pie square') is used to compare and answer questions about the proportions of specific characteristics across two or more populations. The types of questions that would lead to the use of this test are these:

- Does each site's conveyor system experience the same proportion of downtime events by specific causes (power, belt, blockage and rollers)?
- Does each shift (A, B, C and D) produce the same proportion of defectives and non-defectives as each other, or does one shift produce proportionately more defects?
- Now that the process has improved, can we confidently say the proportion of defects has been reduced?
- Does each business unit have the same proportion of safety incidents according to hand injuries, eye injuries, back injuries and other injuries?

Application	Assumptions	Hypothesis (H_O and H_A)
For comparing the proportions of multiple samples.	For accurate results to be achieved, the *observed* value in each cell should be equal to or greater than 5. NOTE: There is hesitation among statisticians to use the chi-square test when more than 20 percent of the cells have *expected* values of less than 5.	H_O: $\pi_1 = \pi_2$ H_A: $\pi_1 \neq \pi_2$

Preparing Data for Analysis

The method for undertaking a Chi-Square Test is quite simple. When two categorical (or discrete attribute) variables that have two or more levels each are studied, the frequency of occurrences at each level can be displayed in what is known as a **contingency table** or in **stacked format**. In the example shown below, the two categorical variables are Work Site (a, b, c & d) and Injury Type (hand, eye, other). The question we would seek to answer here is this - Is there a difference in the proportions of injuries for each type across the different sites?

Contingency Table Format

A contingency table is a summary of frequencies and is laid in matrix format as shown.

RESULTS	SITE A	SITE B	SITE C	SITE D	TOTALS
Hand Injuries	30	48	112	12	202
Eye Injuries	20	30	69	8	127
Other Injuries	15	20	42	6	83

Table 35: Contingency Table Example

Stacked Categorical Data Format

When data is not summarised in a contingency table, it will usually be laid out in 'stacked' format.

When 'stacked' in categorical form and not tabled, it appears as shown.

In this form, Chi-Square analysis within the 'Cross Tabulation' option of analysis software is necessary as the frequency of each category has to be determined before the test can be undertaken.

⇩	C1-T	C2-T
	Work Site	**Injury Type**
1	A	Head
2	A	Eye
3	B	Eye
4	C	Other
5	C	Head

Table 36: Stacked Format Example

Stacked Summary Table Format

When occurrences have been 'counted', a table of 'stacked' data can be created as shown.

This layout is relevant to users of SigmaXL software.

⇩	Work Site	Injury Type	Count
1	A	Head	20
2	A	Eye	21
3	B	Head	17
4	B	Eye	25
5	C	Head	12

Table 37: Stacked Summary Table Example

Chi-Square Test Using Minitab

Setting It Up

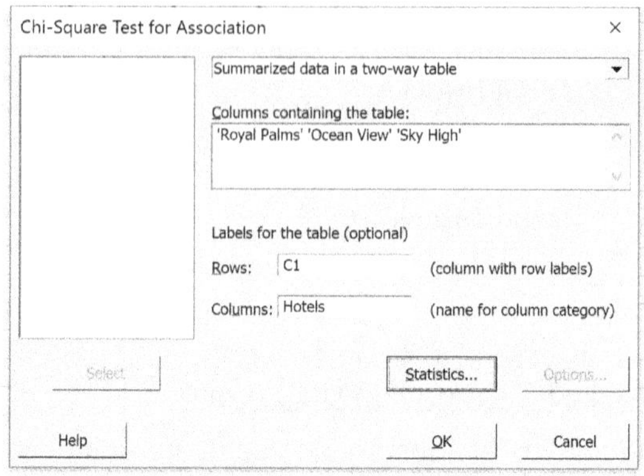

The Chi-Square test function is activated by clicking on:

Stat > Tables > Chi-Square Test for Association

This command is used when the data is laid out in a contingency table format.

Interpreting Results

Chi-Square - To test the null hypothesis against the alternative, Chi-Square test uses the observed and expected frequencies from the contingency table to compute the chi-square test statistic and its associated P-value.

$$\chi^2 = \sum_{\text{all cells}} \frac{(o-e)^2}{e}$$

Where:

o = The observed value in a specific cell

e = The expected value in a specific cell if the null hypothesis were true calculated using the following equation:

$$e = \frac{(\text{row total}) \times (\text{column total})}{(\text{total number of observations})}$$

TWO WAY TABLE

Chi-Square Test for Association: C1, Hotels

Rows: C1 Columns: Hotels

	Royal Palms	Ocean View	Sky High	All
Price	23 31.53	7 11.82	37 23.65	67
Location	39 28.24	13 10.59	8 21.18	60
Room	13 14.59	5 5.47	13 10.94	31
Other	13 13.65	8 5.12	8 10.24	29
All	88	33	66	187

Cell Contents
Count
Expected count

Chi-Square Test

	Chi-Square	DF	P-Value
Pearson	27.410	6	0.000
Likelihood Ratio	28.762	6	0.000

P-values - We use the 'Pearson P-Value' when all of the observed counts are > 5. If any of these are < 5 then we use 'Likelihood P-Value'.

With that in mind, when the P-value is less than α (usually 0.05), any observed difference is statistically significant.

In this case the P-value of 0.000 is < 0.05, so we reject the null hypothesis at the 0.05 significance level and conclude there is a difference in the proportionate distribution of reasons for leaving across the different hotel sites.

Chi-Square Test Using SigmaXL

Setting It Up

The Chi-Square Test function is activated in a number of ways, I choose:

Chi-Square Tests - Exact > Chi-Square Test Fisher's Exact

The example shown shows the approach when the data is laid out in a stacked summary table format.

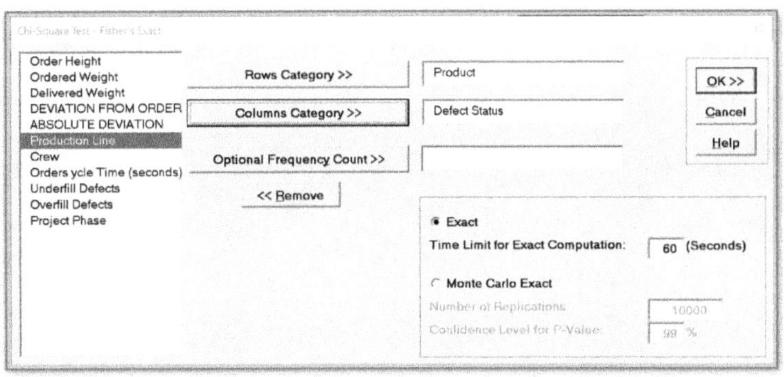

Interpreting Results

Chi-Square - To test the null hypothesis against the alternative, Chi-Square test uses the observed and expected frequencies from the contingency table to compute the chi-square test statistic and its associated P-value.

$$\chi^2 = \sum_{\text{all cells}} \frac{(o-e)^2}{e}$$

Where:

o = The observed value in a specific cell

e = The expected value in a specific cell if the null hypothesis were true calculated using the following equation:

$$e = \frac{(\text{row total}) \times (\text{column total})}{(\text{total number of observations})}$$

	A	B	C
1	**Chi-Square - Fisher's Exact**		
2	**Product - Defect Status**		
3	**Observed Counts**	**Defect**	**Good Product**
4	Fines	19	61
5	Lump	13	67
6	Oxidate	39	41
7			
8	**Expected Counts**	**Defect**	**Good Product**
9	Fines	23.667	56.333
10	Lump	23.667	56.333
11	Oxidate	23.667	56.333
12			
13	**Std. Residuals**	**Defect**	**Good Product**
14	Fines	-0.959264	0.621762
15	Lump	-2.193	1.421
16	Oxidate	3.152	-2.043
17			
18	**Chi-Square**	22.242	
19	**DF**	2	
20	**Chi-Square P-Value**	0.0000	
21	**Fisher's Exact P-Value**	0.0000	
22			
23			
24			

DATA | Chi-Square - Fisher's Exact (1)

P-values - We use the 'Chi-Square P-Value' when all of the observed counts are > 5. If any of these are < 5 then we use 'Fisher's Exact P-Value'.
With that in mind, when the P-value is less than α (usually 0.05), any observed difference is statistically significant.
In this case the P-value of 0.000 is < 0.05, so we reject the null hypothesis and conclude there is a difference in proportions of defects across the different product types.

Note - The observed counts table in the output shown can be plotted as a 100% Stacked Column chart for visual display purposes.

PRACTICAL HYPOTHESIS TESTING

General Examples

TOOL	APPLICATION EXAMPLE
Chi-Square	**Safety** - Comparing proportions of work injuries by type (hand, eye, body, other) with other mine sites – to determine if the proportion of hand injuries was the same or different. **Staffing** – Comparing the proportion of male and female employees between different organisations. **Competency** – Studying the proportion of defects in processing applications, for before and after training to make a determination about the value of the training being given. **Industrial** – To understand if a business has proportionately, more or less working days lost through industrial action than other businesses. **Proportion of Defects** – Comparing before and after scenarios to determine if the proportion of defects after improvement is less than it was before the improvement work

TOOL	APPLICATION EXAMPLE
1 Sample t-test	**Air Emissions** – The air emissions from a plant was compared to the maximum value stated in the license to operate to determine if they were conforming. **Production** – Testing to see if the average diameter of a manufactured part is the same as the customers' specification.
2 sample t-test	**Phone Repair Times** – Testing to see if the average time taken to repair phones with cameras took longer than time to repair phones without cameras. **Production Lines** – The mean yield (% recoveries) for each flotation circuit was compared to determine if there was a different between the two, it was suspected that one was performing less than the other **Shovel Output** – An Australian mining company compared the output of their shovels to the output of shovels operating at a similar mine in North America **Shift Output** – Testing to see if the day shift and night shift production outputs differ. **Before and After** – Comparing before and after scenarios to determine if averages after improvement are less than before improvement.
Paired t-test	**Tyres** – A mine ran a mileage test on two different tyre types, differences in results were confirmed by comparing the mean mileages of each – these were paired by truck (a tyre from each supplier was put on the front and rear of each test truck) **Golf Ball Distance** – A golfing company provides 25 golfers with two different types of balls to test driving distances, the mean distance of each brand golf ball was compared to the other – these were paired by golfer.

TOOL	APPLICATION EXAMPLE
Test for Equal Variances	**Production Lines** – A test was conducted between two flotation circuits to see if the variance of each was the same or different. It was suspected that one had greater variation than the other. **Tensile Strength** – A manufacturing plant tested to see if the variation in tensile strength for a manufactured part differed between seasons. It was suspected that during colder months, tensile strength varied to a greater level resulting in more breakages.
1 Way ANOVA	**Load Times** – The mean rail loading times for ore was compared for five different mine sites to determine if there was statistically significant difference between them. Once confirmed, the site with the best performance was benchmarked so that leading practices could be shared amongst the other four. **Seed Life** – The useful life of seeds was evaluated under 4 different temperature settings. The results obtained from all temperature settings were compared to determine if there was in fact a difference.

Six Sigma Project Examples

TOOL	APPLICATION EXAMPLE
Chi-Square	**Reduce lost working days** – To understand if a department has proportionately, more or less working days lost through injury than other departments. The team working on reducing leave due to injury can identify the source of greatest loss. **Reducing connection delays due to addressing faults** – A team compared the proportion of address faults by category amongst different geographical regions to find the area with the most defects associated with one specific category. **Coffee Shop Case Study** – Comparing proportions of returned coffees by barista to confirm or negate the hypothesis that 'who' makes the coffee is a contributing factor that must be treated to solve the problem.
1 Sample t-test	**Production** – Testing to see if the average diameter of a manufactured part is the same as the customers' specification.
2 sample t-test	**Reduce cycle time** – The average cycle time of week days and weekends were compared to find out if either was a source of excess cycle time and a point of focus. **Shift Output** – Testing to see if the day shift and night shift production outputs differ to see if either shift was to be a point of focus. **Reduce repair cycle time** – A comparison between average cycle time for repair of mobile phones before improvement and after was conducted to support the hypothesis that improvements had in fact been achieved. **Coffee Shop Case Study** – Comparing average coffee temperatures for AM and PM periods to confirm or negate the hypothesis that time period is a contributing factor.

TOOL	APPLICATION EXAMPLE
Paired t-test	**Resin Strength** – In testing a proposed solution, resin was poured into 20 different moulds at a boat manufacturing facility. The strength of the resin in each mould was measured after 2 days of curing and after 5 days of curing to study if shorter curing time reduced strength. Each 2 day and 5 day value is paired according to the mould they were
Test for Equal Variances	**Reduce cycle time variation** – A test was conducted to see if the variation in cycle time for delivering ordered parts each day of the week was the same. The day with the greatest variation was to become the point of focus for cause and effect analysis. **Reducing Breakages** – A team in a manufacturing plant tested to see if the variation in tensile strength for a manufactured part differed between materials supplied by different suppliers. It was suspected that tensile strength varied to a greater level from one supplier resulting in more breakages and the test was used to validate root cause analysis. **Coffee Shop Case Study** – Comparing coffee temperature variation by employee, cup type and coffee type to confirm or negate the hypothesis that these variables are major sources of variation. (3 separate tests)
1 Way ANOVA	**Reduce PC Deployment Time** – A team in an IT department of a major corporation compared the mean delivery times for deployment of different types of PC's (laptops, desktops, servers) to determine if there was a difference. The goal was to find the source of the most cycle time and focus energies in that area in the first project iteration. **Coffee Shop Case Study** – Comparing coffee temperature averages by employee, cup type and coffee type to confirm or negate the hypothesis that these variables are major sources of variation. (3 separate tests)

IDENTIFYING SOURCES OF WASTE (STEP 11A)

If you are working on a Lean specific project, it's highly likely you would have moved directly to this step after establishing your baseline process cycle efficiency in the measure phase. The statistical analysis tools discussed earlier in this chapter have no real relevance to your project as they are specifically focused towards studying sources of *variation*. As you will see, you already have much of the data you need to complete this step for a lean project, if in fact it is necessary for you.

Through the analysis of categorical data and application of various stratification methods, Six Sigma identifies the variables you should focus on to have the greatest impact on variation.

Lean on the other hand offers a range of specific tools for identifying waste in your process that is relevant to your primary metric.

Tools to Assist With Waste Identification

In addition to the tools discussed in this section, many of the tools already presented in earlier sections also help to identify waste.

- **Value Stream Analysis** (Work in Progress, Inventory, Defect Rates, Time etc)
- **Cross Functional Flowcharting** (Handoffs and Wasted Time)
- **Rolled Throughput Yield** (Defects)
- **Constraint Analysis** (Bottle Necks)

In this section I will discuss those tools most appropriate to this particular step, given where you would be in your project. They include:

- **Takt Time Chart** (Constraints and Time Traps)
- **Spaghetti Diagram** (Movement and Wasted Time)

Bear in mind these two points.

(1) All of these tools can be applied at all levels of process detail – at the macro level or at the detailed sub-process level.

(2) We could argue all day as to whether a tool belongs in the measure phase or the analysis phase. It's actually more important to decide which tool to use at the right time in your project.

So with those thoughts as a foundation, let's look at a couple of incredibly useful lean tools that will help you to identify where waste exists in your process.

TAKT TIME CHART

Understanding Takt Time & Takt Rate

Takt is the German term for the baton used by an orchestra conductor to regulate the beat or timing at which the musicians play.

In the context of manufacturing, Takt Time refers to the time it will take to produce units to meet customer demand (i.e., 1 every 8 minutes, 1 every 2 hours 15 minutes etc). For example, if customer demand at a supermarket checkout is 30 people per hour, Takt Time is equal to 2 minutes (i.e., a person must pass through every 2 minutes in order for demand to be met).

Takt Time is equal to the time required to produce one unit to meet customer supply requirements and is defined by the following equation.

$$\text{Takt Time} = \frac{\text{Net Operating Time Per Period}}{\text{Customer Demand Per Period}}$$

Net Operating Time = Total time available, less unproductive time such as lunch, morning tea, afternoon tea etc.

Takt Rate refers to the actual rate of production (e.g., 7 units per hour, 16 units per day etc) and is defined by the following equation.

$$\text{Takt Rate} = \frac{\text{Number of Units Processed or Produced}}{\text{Processing / Production Time Available}}$$

Takt Time Charts

A Takt Time Chart studies the cycle time of each resource in a production process to complete a cycle of work, and how the time taken by each resource relates to the rate of production necessary to meet customer demand.

The ideal situation is where each of the resources that operate linearly in a process spend equal amounts of time (similar to Takt Time) to complete a cycle of work.

A continuous flow manufacturing line must be engineered to operate at a certain pace. If it operates too slowly customer demand cannot be met (lost opportunity), and if it operates too fast customer demand is exceeded and surplus units must be held in inventory (increased capital).

How do I create and use a Takt Time Chart?

The process is quite simple.

First we determine how long each step in the process takes to complete. Since we have already determined cycle times for each of the process steps we simply use that data.

We then plot the results in vertical bar chart form to show the cycle time for each resource.

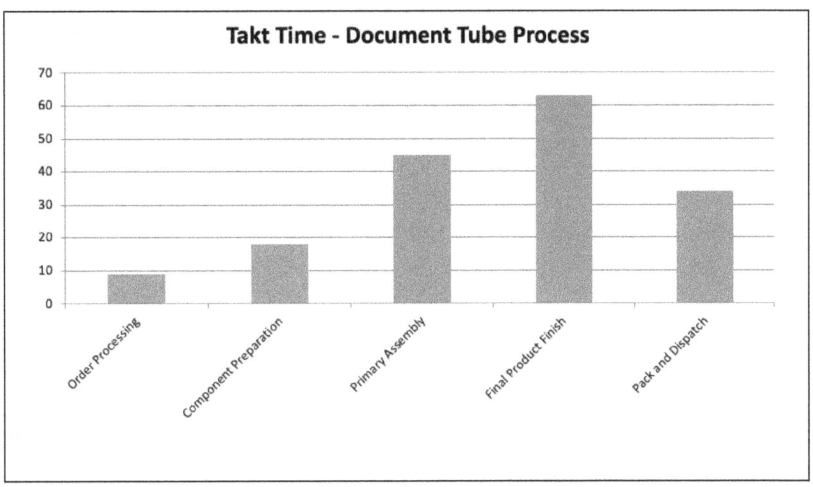

The next step is to calculate Takt Time, which we can do as shown in the following table.

ELEMENT	DESCRIPTION	TIME (min)
Net operating time available per day	1 shift per day, 540 minutes available per day (9 hrs)	540
	Breaks: 2 x 10 minutes	- 20
	Lunch: 1 x 40 minutes	- 40
	Net Operating Time	**480**
Customer requirements per day	Monthly units	240
	Working days per month	20
	Units Required Per Day	**12**

$$\text{Takt Time} = \frac{\text{Net Operating Time Per Period}}{\text{Customer Demand Per Period}} = \frac{480}{12} = 40 \text{ min}$$

The rate of production for this process is 40 minutes per unit produced. Slower production results in missed revenue, faster production results in unnecessary inventory.

The Takt Time line is then plotted on the bar chart and we end up with a finished product like the one shown below.

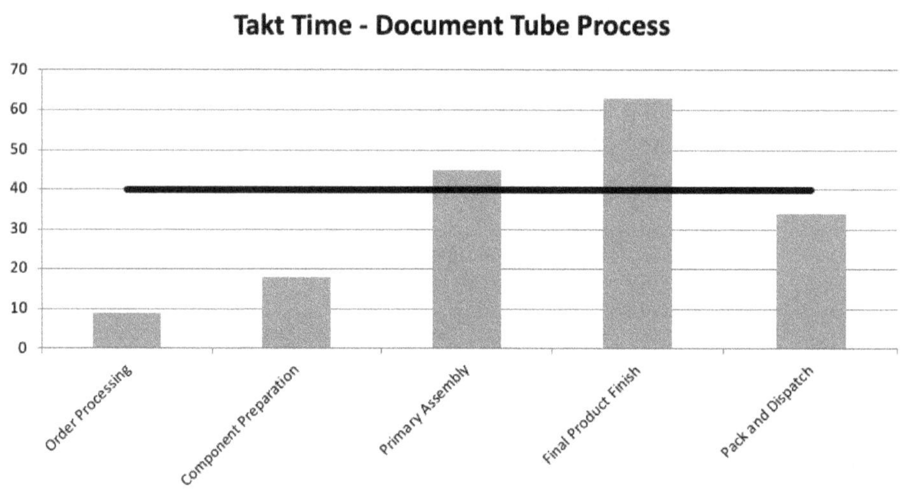

Constraints

Any process step that takes longer than Take Time constrains the process. In the diagram shown, both steps 5 and 7 are constraints in that they add time to how long it takes to produce units.

The rate of production is determined in this case by step 7 – one unit every 68 minutes. Remember, the rate of production required is 1 unit every 40 minutes to meet demand. With a demand of 12 units per day, this would equate to approximately 5.6 hours (12 x 28 extra minutes of production = 336 minutes) of overtime per day to ensure demand is met.

Through better processing, a considerable saving could be made.

Time Traps

A time trap is defined as the process step that takes the longest to complete. In the diagram shown, step 5 is the time trap. A time trap is only a constraint if it takes longer than Takt Time to complete.

Course of Action

Our course of action from here is to come up with ways for creating a balanced process. A balanced process is one where each step takes the equivalent of Takt Time to be completed. This means no steps add time to the process (time traps), nor is a situation of excess production (inventory) created.

For more information, refer to the improve phase where we discuss process balancing in detail.

SPAGHETTI DIAGRAMS

In this particular case study, let's assume that two factors emerge for the project team.

- They observe that time problems exist within the manufacturing phases; and
- They suspect a contributing factor might be time wasted through excess movement.

Therefore, it might be appropriate to take a look at how much movement takes place within the process by creating a spaghetti diagram.

Spaghetti diagrams provide a visual representation of the workplace layout and the flow of events in a process. Waste is often created through poor workshop or office design. When workstations or functions are laid out in a random or haphazard fashion, excess movement or 'motion' is often required to complete a sequence of steps in a process.

The purpose is to identify where improvements can be made to workplace design in order to minimise waste.

'Spaghetti Diagrams can be used at a high level or detailed level. They can be very effective in identifying waste when used to document flow and movement within each process step.'

Harry Sinko

How are they created?

Each of the steps in a process is numbered and the sequence is overlaid on the workplace layout by a continuous line that indicates where each of the steps occurs.

A pattern of crisscrossing lines like that in the diagram indicates that opportunities exist to improve process flow by simply modifying the layout of the workplace and arrangement of tools and resources.

Spaghetti diagrams can also be used to show the flow or movement of:

- Information
- Materials
- People
- Products in a process

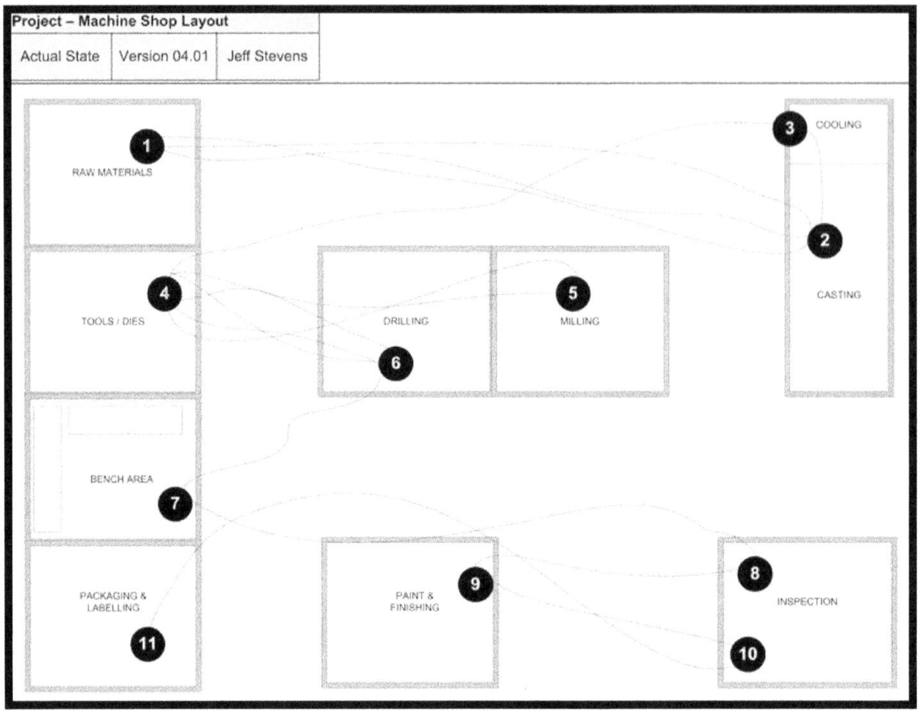

Figure 187: Spaghetti Diagram of Poorly Designed Workplace

In the diagram shown above you can see how inefficient movement is within the work area. For example, excess movement between (4) tools and dies and (5) drilling adds unnecessary time to the production process. Looking at the workplace with respect to steps 8, 9, 10 and 11 of the process, you might see the opportunities to re-design and reduce movement and time.

Improving the Workplace Layout

Improvements to workplace layout can be achieved by applying certain principles:

- Consider the process sequence when designing workplace layout
- Arrange work-cells for maximum efficiency (refer to the work-cell optimisation discussion in the Improve Phase)
- Organise tools, parts and materials so they are more accessible to where they will be needed most
- Establish a system of 6S housekeeping
- Involve those who work with the process

Through improving the layout of the workshop, unnecessary motion can be removed from the process and the affect should be:

- Increased productivity
- Reduction in lead-time
- Increased workplace morale

For instructions on the use of Spaghetti Diagrams, refer to the Analyse Phase Toolkit.

CROSS FUNCTIONAL FLOWCHART

A cross-functional flowchart (also referred to as a swim lane chart) details the action steps and decision steps within a process, much like an activity flowchart. However, each activity or decision step is assigned to the relevant person or group who is responsible for that step. Cross-functional flowcharts not only make complexity within the process obvious, but also provide information on the handoffs that occur across the process.

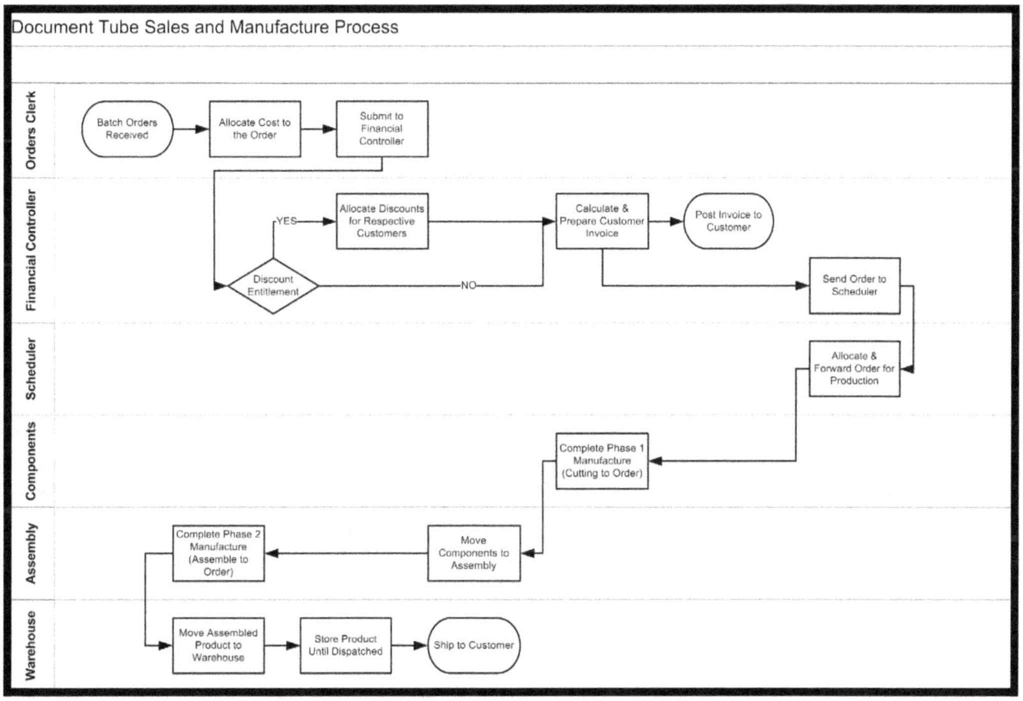

Figure 188: Cross Functional Flowchart for Document Tube Process

UTILISING OTHER LEAN TOOLS

It's important to point out that many other tools could be brought back into the process and used again at a new level to assist in solving the problem quickly. Let's look at our 'document tube' process as an example. We found that steps 5 and 7 (shown in our Takt Time Chart discussion) are obviously constraints. What could we do now? Here are some options.

- A **spaghetti diagram** might be created for each of these steps (5 to 7 as shown, or 5 and 7 separately) to identify where unnecessary time [lost through movement] can be taken out of those steps through workplace design.
- Detailed **sub-process mapping** could be undertaken and then **time value analysis** undertaken to see where non-value adding time exists within each step.
- A **Takt Time Chart** for each specific step could be developed to understand where the time trap and any constraints exist within that sub-process.

It's up to you to choose the tools that best help you make rapid improvements.

STUDYING CAUSE & EFFECT RELATIONSHIPS (STEP 12A)

I believe most of the tools used through the DMAIC sequence, irrespective of whether it's Six Sigma or Lean, are in some way involved in cause and effect analysis. They all contribute in some way to our understanding of where to focus our attention in order to change the effect.

In this section I now want to be more specific and focus on some of the tools that are more obviously developed for cause & effect analysis or root cause analysis.

As we go into this section, I want you to remember one thing: There are no single answers to these problems, as solutions can be found in an infinite set of causes along a cause effect chain.

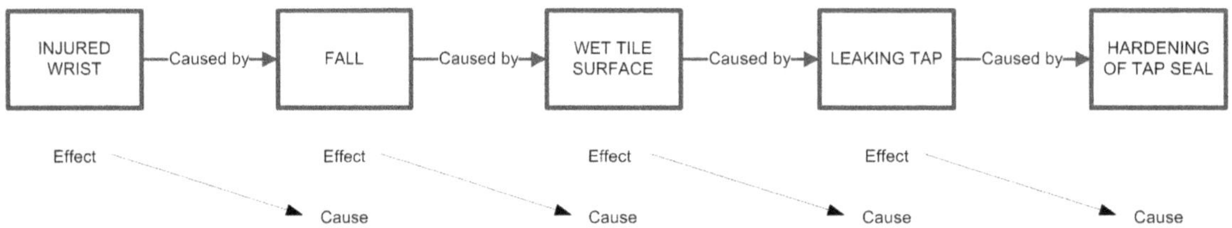

Figure 189: Cause Effect Chain

An effect is the consequence of a cause. When we ask 'Why?' of a cause it then becomes the effect, hence the term 'cause effect chain'. This cause effect chain is an infinite continuum and our perspective in a given circumstance determines our reference point or the primary effect we are concerned with. In the example shown, our primary effect is the injured wrist. It is the cause of the effect called 'pain', however in referring to the injured wrist as our starting point, it is now the effect caused by a fall. The fall in turn becomes the effect caused by the wet tile surface and so on, potentially into infinitum.

Our task in the first instance is to identify the probable causes of variation (x's) that we can actually do something about.

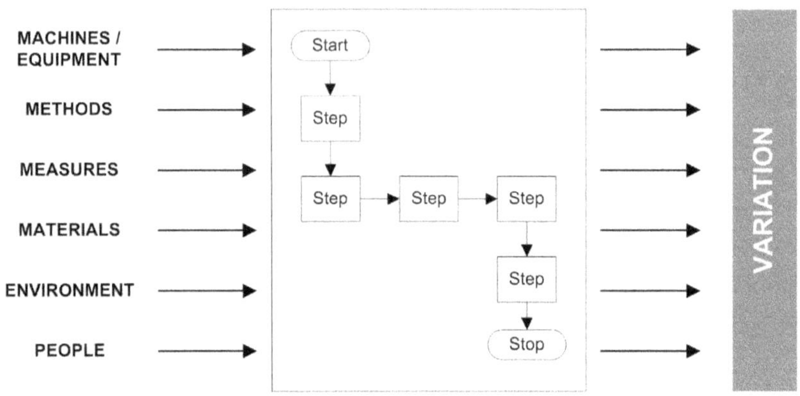

These are usually found within the six general 'sources of variation' shown in the diagram and discussed previously in the data collection planning section.

Figure 190: Sources of Variation

Rather than reproduce the same information in this book, I recommend that you read the problem solving book I first published in 2005, *'It's Still Not a Problem'*, for greater discussion about cause and effect.

Potential causes from within these sources of variation can be generated through the use of what we might refer to as visual thinking tools.

These include:

- Cause Effect Diagrams
- Cause Effect Chains
- Cause Effect Structure Trees
- Cause Effect Tree Diagrams

Once these potential causes are identified, our task then is to generate evidence to validate the hypothesised relationship between these causes (x's) and the effect or response (y). The most commonly used tools that allow us to quantify the relationship between cause & effect include:

Numerical Variables

- Correlation Studies
- Design of Experiments

Categorical Variables

- Hypothesis Testing
- Design of Experiments

THE ART OF QUESTIONING IN CAUSE EFFECT ANALYSIS

(**Source:** Much of this section has been drawn from the author's 2005 publication, *'It's Still Not a Problem'*.)

The skill of questioning is one of the most important skills to master in the process of problem solving. I live by the principle of 'ask and you shall receive'. As you will now become even more aware, this principle has great significance in the process of asking questions.

Good questions generate good answers, poor questions result in poor answers. What you ask for you will get. Many people struggle with this proposition, but once they see its power, they will recognise the quality of results that can be attained through effective questioning. I am always amazed that people generally know the answers already yet fail to recognise them. They just need the right questions asked to them to stimulate the appropriate thinking processes.

I make a living doing this. I often teach people new concepts without actually telling them anything new. All I do is tell stories about subjects they already know, ask questions about those stories to draw out the key points, and then get them to make links between those points and a new concept. They already know the answers; they just have not yet made the connections. If you really want to master this material, always remember this point:

'The quality of the questions you ask determines the quality of the answers you get. The most important skill of leadership may well be the skill of asking questions.'

Don't Ask Why

Many students of 'root cause' analysis training are taught to ask questions based on 'why'. I am convinced that this is not the best word to use in your questioning.

The limitation of the word 'why' in cause and effect analysis is that it can lead down the path of generating *reasons* for the outcome, not *causes* of the outcome. What do I mean by that? Let me distinguish between the two in this way.

Imagine yourself driving along the road in your motor vehicle. As the vehicle travels along it suddenly swerves to the left and runs off the road, totally out of control. This specific outcome or event can be described as unexpected or special cause variation in the path taken by the motor vehicle. To identify the cause of that outcome or event, suppose we asked this question.

- 'Why did the vehicle run off the road?'

This question is potentially misleading. For example, the following answers clearly follow on from this question that starts with the word 'why'.

- I wasn't strong enough to hold the wheel straight.
- The road is only two lanes wide.
- The left edge of the road is so close to the vehicle, the only place it had to go when it swerved was off the road.

Not one of these answers takes us down the root cause path. These are *reasons* why the car ran off the road, not *causes* that help us to solve the problem. Building bigger muscles so you can hold the wheel straight might help stop the vehicle running off the road, but it does not really treat the true cause of the problem. I realize these types of answers *may* not be thrown out, however, a much more effective question to ask would be one that specifically directs our minds toward seeking out *causes of that event* which will help us to eliminate the problem.

- 'What caused the vehicle to run off the road?'

Now in this case the answers will certainly be different than those generated for the first question. This time the answers might be:

- The steering gear failed.
- I went to sleep at the wheel.
- A tyre blowout made it uncontrollable.

A Better Range of Questions

<u>What Is the Cause of ..... ?</u>

Once again, imagine yourself driving along the road in your motor vehicle. If you plotted your course in detail, it would not be a straight line as there would be slight variations in the direction travelled, slight variations that you would be constantly monitoring and adjusting for. This would be expected, or in other words, *common cause* variation. If you wanted to reduce the amount of variation that you were experiencing, you would start by identifying and treating the most significant cause of that variation. The question to ask then should be one that seeks out *causes of variation*:

- '**What is the cause** of variation in the route travelled by the vehicle?'

This question causes participants to focus their thought processes around identifying what it is that causes the variation. We are concerned with variation so we ask a question specific to variation.

<u>..... Is Caused by What?</u>

Another option would be to ask questions starting with the effect, followed by the term 'Is caused by .....

- 'Variation in the route travelled by the vehicle **is caused by what .....**'

In essence, the questions we ask during root cause analysis should be determined by the context of our analysis. Where we are looking at an event driven problem (special cause variation), we ask questions about the event, understanding that events are caused by the interaction of specific conditions and specific actions. Where we are looking at a process variation driven problem (common cause variation), we ask questions about the variation.

The table below details some of the different forms of questions you might consider when undertaking root cause analysis.

Common Cause Variation	Special Cause Variation
Q. What causes variation in ____ Q. What causes ____ to occur Q. ____ is caused by ____	Q. What caused ____ to occur Q. ____ was caused by ____

Questions in Cause and Effect Analysis

CAUSE AND EFFECT DIAGRAM

Sometimes referred to as the Ishikawa or Fishbone Diagram, the cause effect diagram is a visual model that helps focus a team's discussion around identification of the potential root cause or causes of a specific condition or problem.

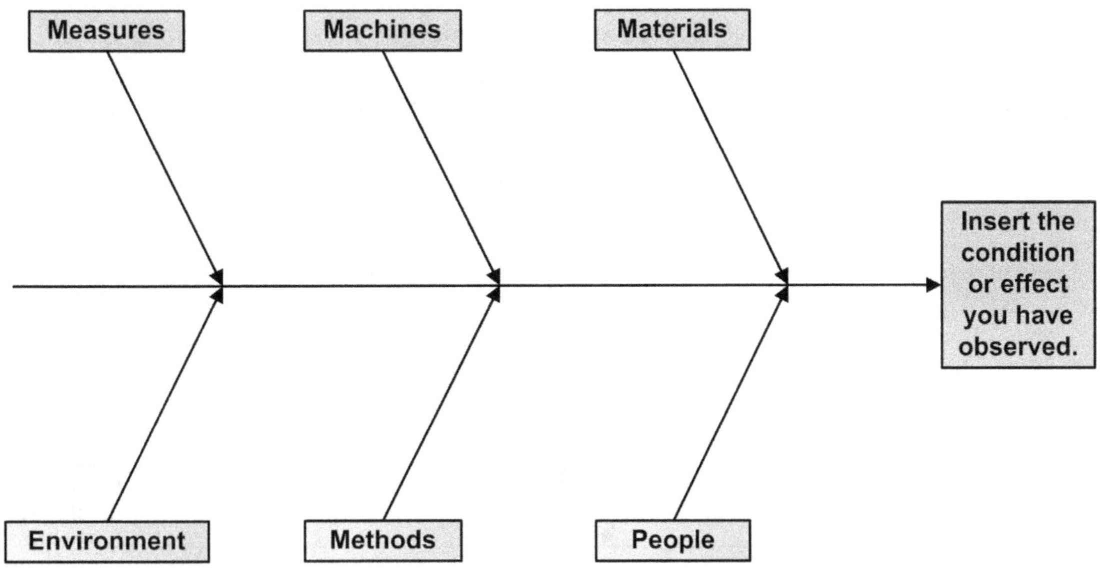

Figure 191: Cause Effect Diagram

Preparing the Diagram

The Cause Effect Diagram is another visual thinking tool, however this one is constructed in the form of a fish skeleton comprising of six bones. The condition or problem that you have observed is written at the head of the fish. The six bones of the fish represent the six categories of variables that influence (or are the source of) process variation. These categories are written at the end of each bone.

Fishbone Categories

I am often asked if these are the only categories that you can use in the analysis. You can use other categories, though if you take a good look, there may well not be anything that does not fall within one of these categories. One option is to split existing categories (e.g., electrical machines and hydraulic machines, specific steps within the method being used etc) or add new categories (e.g., policies, technology etc), however my bias is to *not remove* any of these primary categories. The removal of categories assumes that there will be no cause from within this group. However, a true professional does not assume anything. Another option is to add categories you think bring value to the process.

Generating Potential Causes

Causes are generated through a process of brainstorming. At the end of this brainstorming session, you will have generated a number of ideas that are potential causes of the variation being observed.

The brainstorming approaches you employ may change according to circumstances.

- *Open Brainstorm* – Potential causes are identified in an open format and then placed in relevant categories.
- *Channel Brainstorm* – Potential causes are identified within each category in sequence. For example you might ask: 'What environmental issues would cause this (the condition) to occur?' You capture all the ideas until exhausted, and then repeat for the next category until all are covered.

Drilling Down to Root Causes

You can drill down further in your analysis for root causes by using the dispersion method:

- *The dispersion method* – The potential causes identified by team members are placed within the relevant categories until all ideas are exhausted. You then ask: 'What causes this (the potential cause) to occur?' for each of the potential causes to generate a second level of analysis where possible. This can be repeated for additional levels where relevant. This approach is useful when a small number of first level causes are identified.

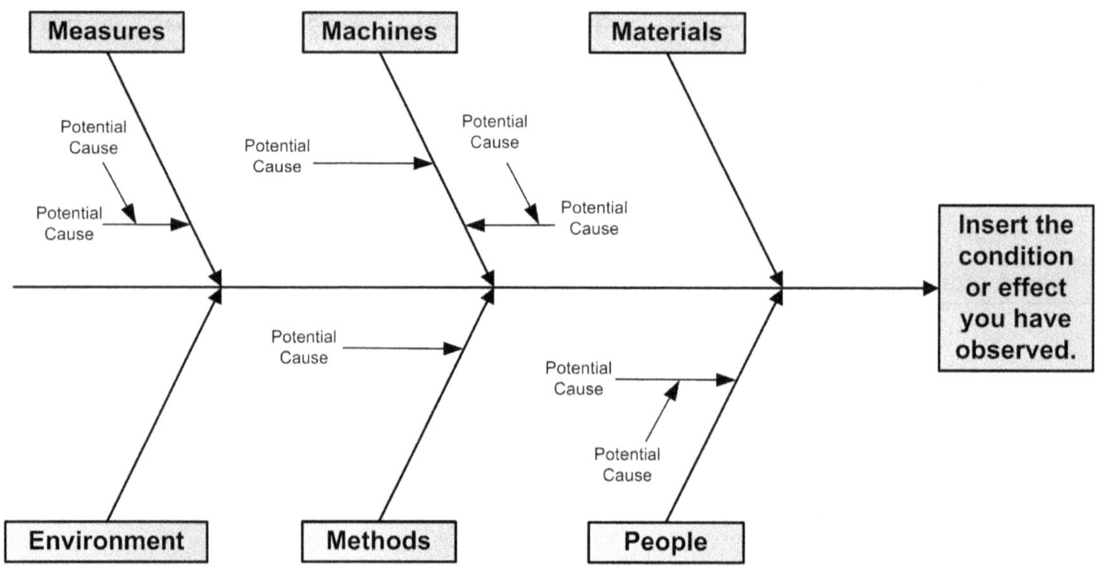

Figure 192: Dispersion Method of Root Cause Analysis

Another alternative is to use the Cause Effect Diagram in your first pass analysis, and then taking some of the potential causes and drilling down further using the Cause Effect Structure Tree.

For instructions on the use of the Cause Effect Diagram, refer to the Analyse Phase Toolkit in the next chapter.

When to Use the Ishikawa diagram

Use this tool when you have a broad high level problem. It is often a good starting point in project work led by a green belt or black belt.

5 WHAT CAUSE EFFECT CHAIN

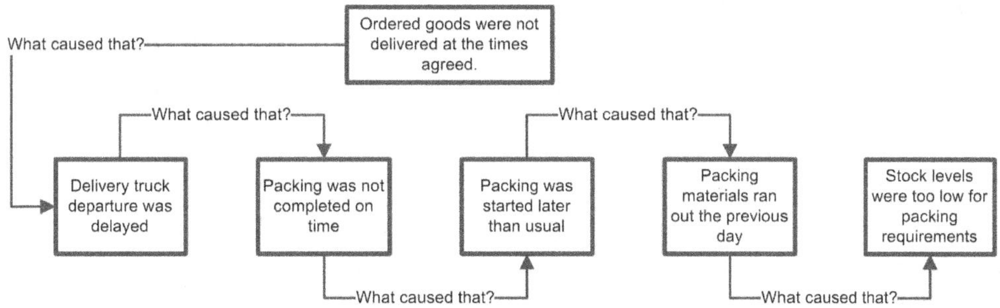

Figure 193: Five What CE Analysis

The 5 What Cause Effect (CE) Chain (adapted from the 5 Why's tool first developed by the Toyota Company) is a tool that helps the team to identify potential root causes for simple event based problems.

The tool allows participants to quickly drill down to the probable root cause of a specific effect, and is particularly useful when you have a simple variation or event based problem.

In the example shown, the event being analysed was associated with orders goods not being delivered at a time agreed.

The probable root cause of this event was found by continually asking the question: "What caused that?" of the effect, and each successive answer to that question.

The question was asked five times, with the analysis stopping at a point where the cause effect chain can be interrupted to prevent it happening again.

The basis of the tool is a questioning attitude, continually probing deeper to find the true cause.

The reason these types of approaches are called Five Why's or Five What's, is due to the fact that a treatable cause for *simple events* can usually be identified within that space.

As I've mentioned, the cause effect chain is an infinite continuum, and by imposing these boundaries useful work does not become pointless work.

When to Use 5 What CE Analysis

Use this tool when you have a very specific event or you want to drill down from a higher level cause. In most circumstances, this tool is not really relevant to the type of work a green belt or black belt would be involved in. They would be better using one of the more sophistical RCA tools like the one described next.

CAUSE EFFECT STRUCTURE TREE

The cause effect structure tree is a tool that helps the team to identify root causes at a much deeper level of analysis using the principles of the '5 What Cause Effect Chain'.

The tool is particularly useful when you are analysing a focused event or condition.

By that I mean the starting point for the tool is not just a broad event or condition that will result in a torrent of ideas for potential causes.

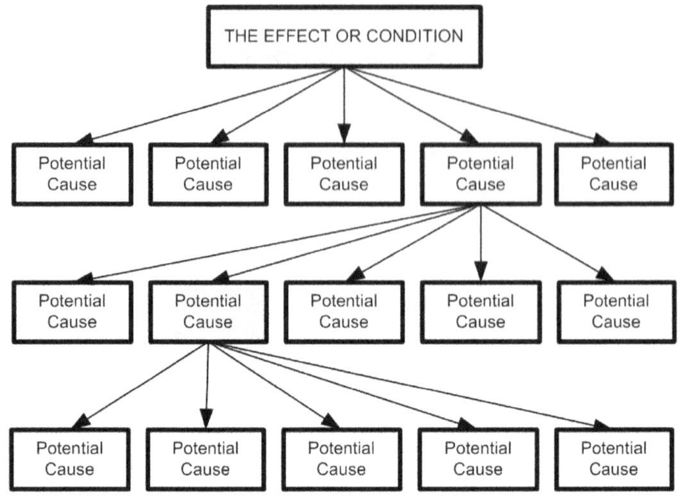

Figure 194: Cause Effect Structure Tree

It is often used as a follow up to the 'Cause Effect Diagram' when more specific causes have been identified, or for event based root cause analysis[29].

When to Use CE Structure Tree

Use this tool when you have a more complex problem or event or you want to drill down from a higher level cause you might have identified using the Ishikawa diagram. This tool is a more sophisticated form of the 5 Whats and more relevant for the type of work a Green Belt or Black Belt would be involved in.

Reducing the list of Potential Causes

The list of potential causes can be reduced effectively by following a simple two-step approach.

- Drop items that are definitely not causes; and
- Short-list the remainder using list reduction techniques.

Not a Cause. Ask 'Does evidence exist that would indicate that any of these is not a root cause?' If it does, then exclude the idea from the list.

Likely Causes. Short list to the top 1 or 2 potential causes using multi voting. With the right people involved, your team will naturally be biased towards the most probable causes because of process knowledge and experience.

Refer to the next chapter for instructions for using the Cause Effect Structure Tree.

When To Stop Analysing

One of the most challenging aspects of root cause analysis is to know when to stop drilling down. You must stop when you get to a cause that you cannot influence. For example, suppose we thought the potential cause of a 'frozen pipe' was 'extremely low temperatures' which in turn was caused by 'onset of winter'.

[29] Refer to the author's 2005 publication, *'It's Still Not a Problem – Systematic Problem Solving for Business'*.

Winter is outside our span of control so there would be no point focusing on it. However, if low ambient temperatures were inside our span of control, we would stop our analysis at that point.

The key is to stop at a point where you can treat the cause, if you pass that point, simply go back.

Get The Words 'Lack Of' Out Of The Process

There will be many situations where the words 'lack of' appear in the nominated causes of the condition or effect under analysis. Some of the most common include these.

- Lack of money
- Lack of resources
- Lack of procedures
- Lack of training
- Lack of time

My suggestion is this. Where possible, get those words out of the process. Here's why.

Suppose the words 'lack of training' were listed as a cause. What would be the solution to this cause? Obviously the solution in this case is to provide training, would you not agree? A cause preceded by the words 'lack of' forces a team into a single solution situation.

How? - Ask a Better Question

My approach is to ask a question like this when I see lack of.

- Q. How do you know there is a lack of (in this case training)?

Responses such as 'the person can't do the job properly' leads the team towards the real cause. In this case it might be something like 'skill level does not match task requirements'. Now, how many ways might you potentially go about treating this new cause? Potential solutions would include these.

- Automate the task
- Eliminate the task
- Provide education and mentoring
- Recruit a new employee with suitable skills
- Lower the standard of performance expected

I'm sure you get my point here.

CASE STUDY – THE COFFEE SHOP

Suppose the project team found through stratification that the source of the problem was really the milk based coffees which were being produced at a defect rate of around 48 percent. They could now attempt to determine causes through use of the *Cause Effect (CE) Diagram* as shown.

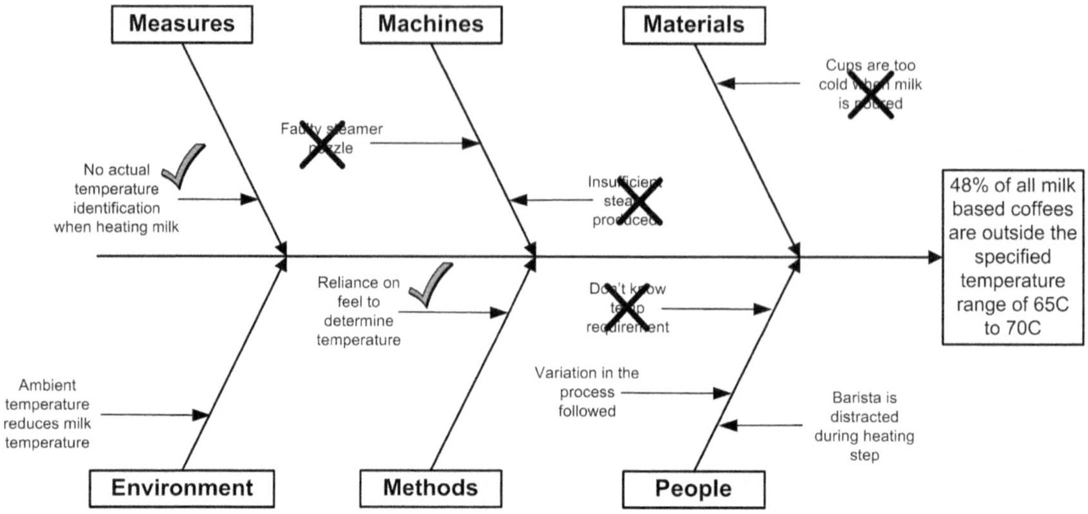

Figure 195: Case Study Cause Effect Diagram

NOTE: The CE Diagram is shown as an example only, in this case study only the CE Structure Tree would be used.

<u>Preference for Drilling Down</u>

Notice that we have ended up with only one level of causes and have not really 'drilled down' into the cause effect chain.

My personal preference is to use CE Diagrams when working on a high level or broad problem. The process helps determine some starting points for drilling down further. At the detailed level of this work (the case study), I've found the *Cause Effect (CE) Structure Tree* to be far more effective in determining potential causes through drilling down into a multitude of variables.

An example of this approach is also shown on the following page.

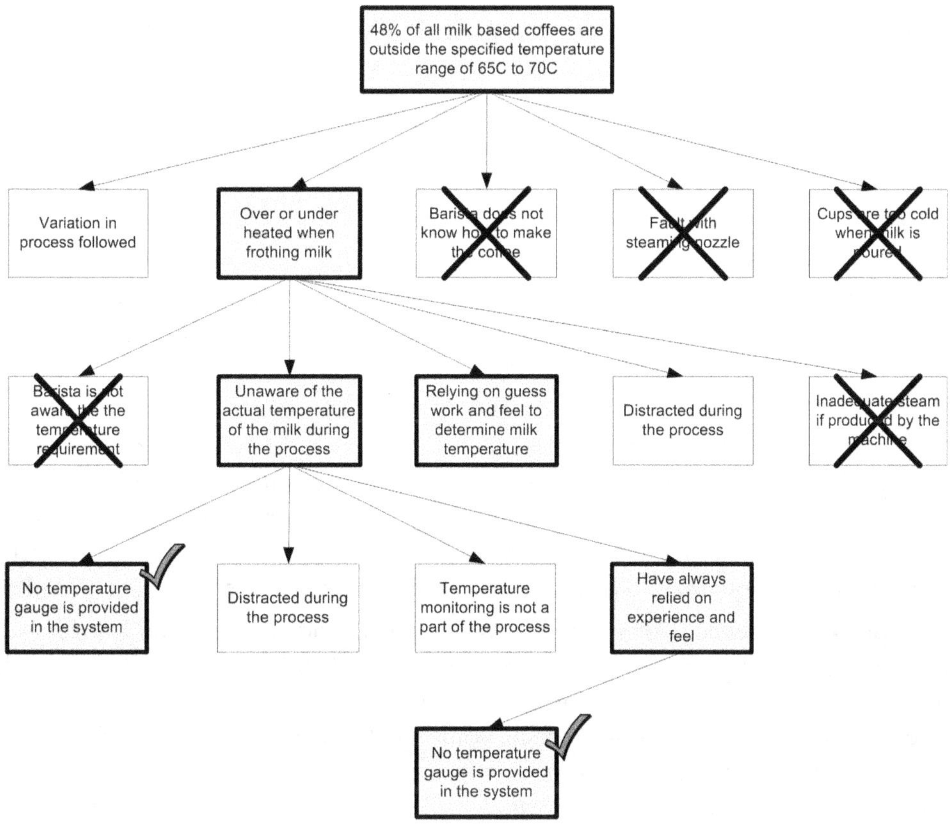

Figure 196: Case Study Cause Effect Structure Tree

VALIDATING CAUSE & EFFECT RELATIONSHIPS (STEP 12B)

At this point in time, the team has only hypothesised about potential root causes. They are not true root causes until validated. To validate a root cause, you simply need to prove the strength of the causal relationship between the variable and the condition or problem. This proof is established through the generation of evidence or data that supports any stated conclusion.

Evidence to validate hypothesised root causes varies in quality.

- **Intuitive evidence** – this is also a form of inferred evidence, however, is evidence based on feelings or emotions generated through awareness at the unconscious level. Words such as 'I just know it's right but I can't tell you how I know' are signs of intuition. Interestingly enough, there is a place for this level of evidence and decision-making. Just because someone cannot state why they know, doesn't mean they are not unconsciously aware of some important factors.
- **Inferred evidence** – this type of evidence is based on knowledge of repeated cause effect relationships. While we may not have observed it, we know that pressing the foot on the accelerator causes more fuel to enter the motor. While we may not be electricians, we can confidently say that moving the light switch to the ON position causes electricity to travel along the wiring to the light bulb. This evidence is qualitative in nature and based on the experience of the provider.
- **Sensory specific evidence** – this is the highest quality evidence that can be obtained, and is data that can be observed using the senses, i.e. see it, feel it, hear it, smell it or taste it. The use of quantitative analysis tools such as correlation and regression fits within this quality level as this evidence can be seen in the form of data. Some qualitative evidence also fits within this quality level; for example, where a potential root cause is the non existence of some control, such as a process or a guidebook, this can be validated by determining existence - the answer to which is yes it does or no it does not exist.

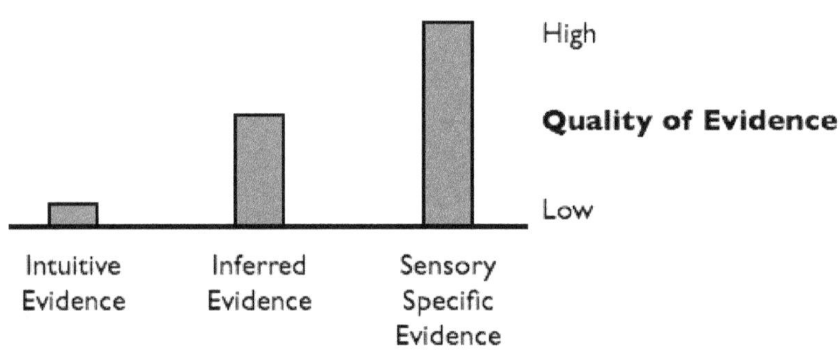

Figure 197: Three Levels of Evidence Quality

TOOLS FOR EXAMINING RELATIONSHIPS

Choice is Determined by Variable Type

There will be occasions when your cause effect hypothesis involves categorical data. For example we might hypothesise that variation in the linear strength of our product (a continuous numerical variable) is caused by variation or differences between suppliers (discrete categories) of raw materials.

To validate this hypothesis we need to be able to confirm that there is a difference in the quality according to different suppliers and this difference is actually significant enough to make inferences about the populations under scrutiny. The tools we would choose in this case would allow us to see and prove that there was or was not a difference.

By contrast, there will be cases when our cause effect hypothesis involves variable data. For example we might hypothesise that variation in the hardness or strength of a product (continuous numerical variable) is caused by variation in temperature or curing time (continuous numerical variables).

Our hypothesis might relate to discrete numerical variables, for example variation in the time to unload an aircraft (continuous numerical variable) is caused by variation in the number of bags unloaded (discrete numerical variable). Variation in our golf score (discrete numerical variable) is caused by variation in the number of putts (discrete numerical variable) we make.

In these different cases we would use different analysis tools to either validate or disprove our hypothesis.

The tables that follow provide guides as to which tool you might consider using for different data types according to whether they are:

- An independent or dependent variable variable; and
- A Categorical or Numerical variable

Visually Displaying Relationships Between Xs and Ys

		Dependent Variable / Effect / Response (*Y*)	
		Categorical Y	**Numerical Y**
Independent Variable / Cause / Factor (*X*)	**Categorical X**	Pie Chart, Bar Chart or Column Chart (using counts), Pareto Chart	Stratified Box Plots, Time Series Plots, Multi-Vari Chart, Stratified Histograms
	Numerical X	Stratified Histograms, Stratified Box Plots	Scatter Plot, Marginal Plots, Matrix Plot, Contour and Surface Plot

Tools for Visually Examining Cause Effect Relationships

Statistically Validating Relationships

		Dependent Variable / Effect / Response (*Y*)	
		Categorical Y	**Numerical Y**
Independent Variable / Cause / Factor (*X*)	**Categorical X**	Chi-Square, Logistic Regression, Proportion Tests	*t* Tests, *z* Tests, Analysis of Variance (ANOVA), Equal Variance Tests, Analysis of Means (ANOM), Median Tests, Design of Experiments (DOE)
	Numerical X	Logistic Regression	Pearson's Correlation, Linear Regression (for developing prediction models), Design of Experiments (DOE)

Tools for Validating Cause Effect Relationships

SCATTER PLOTS

One of the tools used to validate the relationship between potential causes and the effect is the scatter plot.

Scatter Plots are charts that visually demonstrate the relationship between two paired numerical variables in a process, so that we are able to determine if there is a relationship between the two. We refer to this type of data as 'bivariate' data. If the relationship or correlation appears to be strong, then this might give reason to suspect that variation in one causes variation in the other, however, care should always be exercised when making these types of inferences.

Scatter plots are used to:

- Discover if there is a relationship between two variables
- To test the idea of a cause effect relationship in a visual way (although finding a correlation does not always imply causation)

Creating and Using Scatter Plots

The process for using scatter plots is comprised of three steps:

- **Step 1** – Collect 'bivariate' data (i.e. when the output measure is taken, a paired measure is recorded at the same time, for example if we measured the time it took to deliver a pizza to a house, we would also record the distance from the shop to the house for that delivery if we wanted to imply distance variation creates variation in time)
- **Step 2** – Determine which of the variables is the response or dependent variable (Y-axis) and which is the potential predictor or independent variable (X-axis)
- **Step 3** – Create a scatter plot and interpret the observed pattern.

I will discuss the creation of scatter plots in the next section as a part of correlation analysis.

Interpreting Scatter Plots

The interpretation of scatter plots is simply the process of finding and interpreting patterns.

The tighter data points are clustered together, the stronger the relationship between the variables. A pattern that slopes upward towards the top right side of the plot indicates that as the variable on the X-axis increases, so does the variable on the Y-axis – a positive correlation.

Example: Scientists interested in determining whether or not they can predict tree height by measuring its diameter at a specified height have created a scatter plot of data.

We can see from the example that there appears to be a linear relationship between the diameter measurement and its aged height measurement.

So with a degree of confidence we might say that the larger the diameter of the tree at 1.5 metres tall, the taller that tree will eventually grow.

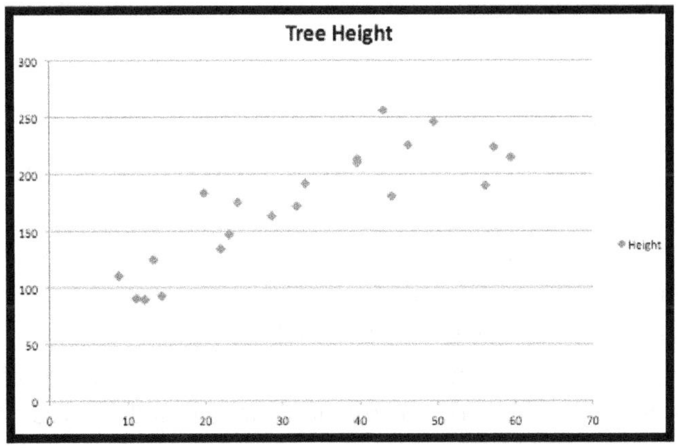

A pattern that slopes downward towards the bottom right side of the plot indicates that as the variable on the X-axis increases in value, the variable on the Y-axis decreases – a characteristic we would refer to as a negative correlation.

Correlation and Causation

While there may be a high degree of correlation between two variables, this does not imply causation.

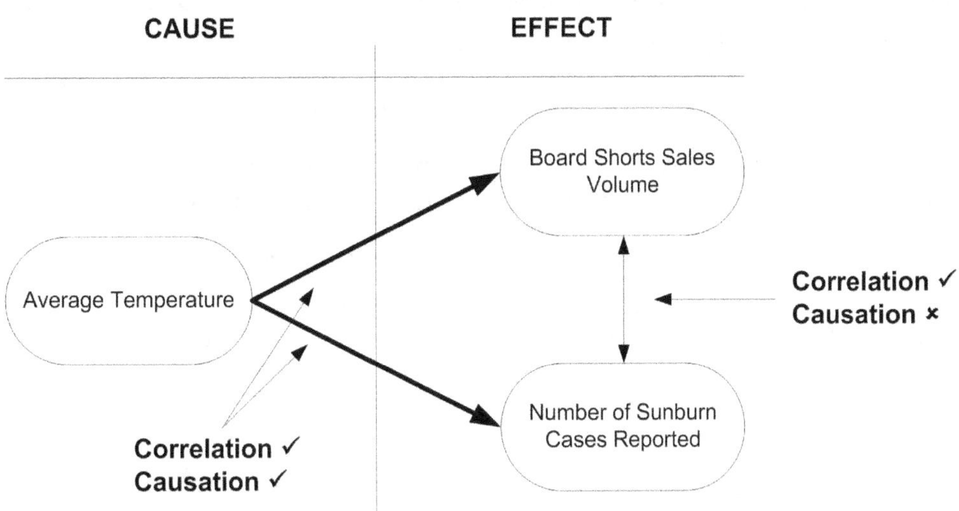

For example, there would be a high correlation between the numbers of sunburn cases in Australia each month and the volume of sales of board shorts. We know that buying shorts does not cause sunburn, however we do know that weather cycles, thus temperature, would have an impact on both.

This is referred to as a 'lurking variable.

On the other hand the lack of obvious correlation does not mean that a cause effect relationship does not exist. There may very well be a correlation over a wider range or a different portion of the range of data.

CORRELATION ANALYSIS AND LINEAR REGRESSION MODELLING

Correlation and Regression are terms often used together.

Correlation analysis is the process of making determinations about the **strength of relationships** between variables.

The relationship analysis can be about single or multiple independent variables (also called the predictor variables or regressors), and a dependent variable (also called a response or explanatory variable).

As such, correlation has direct application in the process of **validating the causal relationship** between your numerical *x*'s and the numerical *y*.

Regression analysis is used primarily for the purpose of **prediction**. The goal is to develop a statistical model that can be used to predict the values of a dependent or response variable from the value of one or multiple independent or predictor variable.

As such, regression models have great application in the improve phase. However, as you will see it makes sense to present both correlation analysis and regression analysis together.

When You Might Study Correlation and Regression

The occasions where you might consider using correlation and regression include:

- You want to validate the hypothesised cause effect relationship between a dependent or response variable, and an independent or explanatory variable (or variables).
- You want to be able to predict the response you will get for a given value of an independent variable

Types of Regression Modelling

There are various forms of regression that a statistician might use to analyse relationships between variables in a data set. The most common include:

Type	Description
Simple Linear Regression	This is the analysis of a single *x* to a single *y*. The model has a single predictor variable (*x*) and is linear with respect to coefficients of the equation. The equation looks like: $$y = \beta_0 + \beta_1 x + \varepsilon$$
Multiple Linear Regression	This is the analysis of multiple *x*'s to a single *y*. The model has multiple predictor variables (*x*'s) and is linear with respect to coefficients of the equation. The equation looks like: $$y = \beta_0 + \beta_1 x_1 + \beta_2 x_2 + \dots\dots\dots \beta_n x_n + \varepsilon$$

Type	Description
Logistic Regression	This is the analysis of a single x or multiple x's (categorical or variable) to a single y (categorical). The 'logit' equation looks like: $$P(x)=\frac{e^{\alpha+\beta_1 x_1+\beta_2 x_2+\dots\dots\dots\beta_n x_n}}{1+e^{\alpha+\beta_1 x_1+\beta_2 x_2+\dots\dots\dots\beta_n x_n}}$$ Approaches include Binary, Nominal and Ordinal Logistic Regression.

Simple Correlation and Linear Regression

Simple correlation and linear regression analysis can be used when you want to validate the hypothesised cause and effect relationship between a single response variable (y) and a single independent or predictor variable (x).

Both dependent and independent variables must be numerical variables, and as they are paired they are known as 'Bivariate' data. **Bivariate Data** are paired values obtained by measuring two different characteristics of an observed unit.

Correlation and linear regression can be undertaken in four steps.

- **Step 1** – Create and Analyse a Graphical Representation of Correlation Data
- **Step 2** – Evaluate Correlation
- **Step 3** – Create a Regression Model
- **Step 4** – Check Validity of the Regression Model

Case Study

An engineering firm was experiencing problems with the tensile strength of the 50mm diameter pins they produced for a major machinery maker – i.e. the pins were breaking and in most cases, experiencing a life cycle well short of customers expectations.

The tensile strength of broken pins was examined and found to be outside the specifications required to generate an acceptable working life for each pin. A project team was tasked with reducing the number of defects, and during their analysis of data found that the process was in control.

They could not find any significant source of variation, therefore focused their attention on all 50mm pins in general.

During their root cause analysis, the team proposed that variation in tensile strength (the effect or response variable) was caused by variation in Rockwell Hardness (the cause or predictor). In the absence of evidence this is only a hypothesis. The question is how does the team validate that hypothesis?

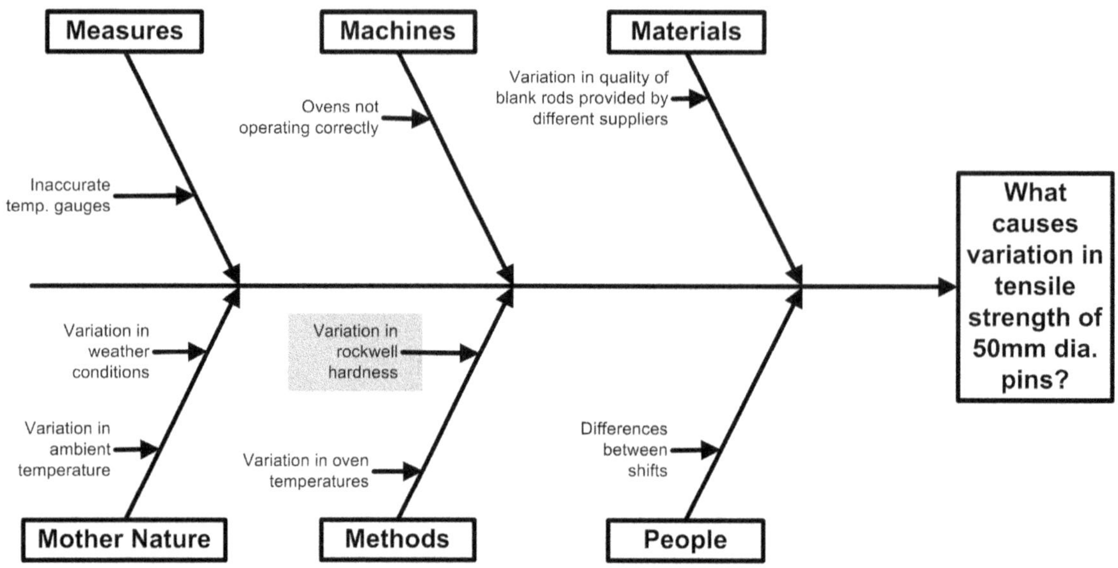

This case study will be used throughout our first discussion on Simple Linear Regression.

Create a Graphical Representation of Data

The most relevant way to present the relationship between paired data is with a scatter plot. Scatter plots can be quickly created in both Minitab and SigmaXL.

Creating a Scatter Plot Using Minitab

In Minitab scatter plots are accessed by clicking on Graph > Scatterplot.

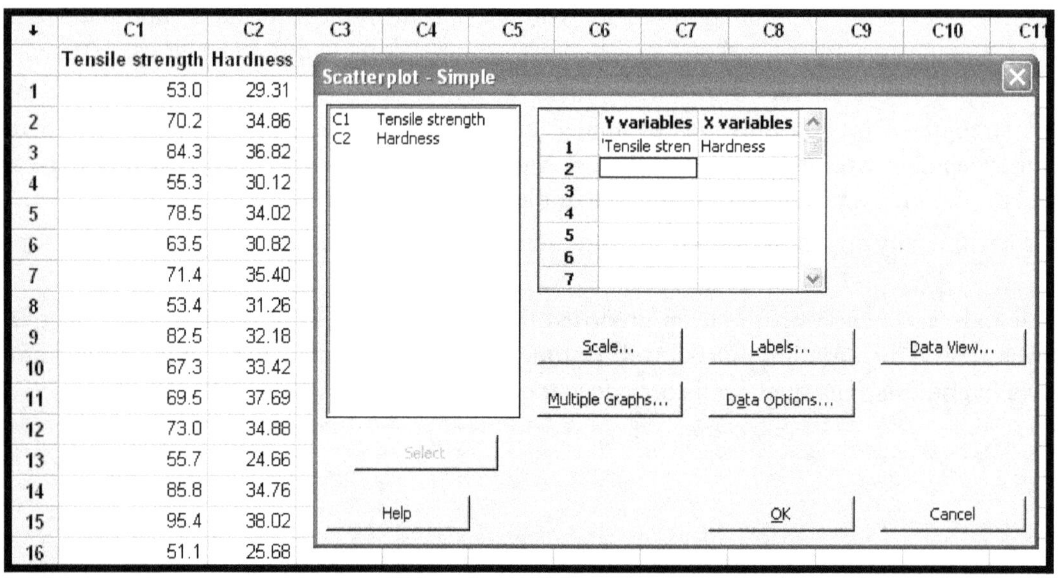

Figure 198: Dialogue Box for Scatter Plots - Minitab

Creating a Scatter Plot Using SigmaXL

In SigmaXL, they are accessed by clicking on Graphical Tools > Scatter Plots.

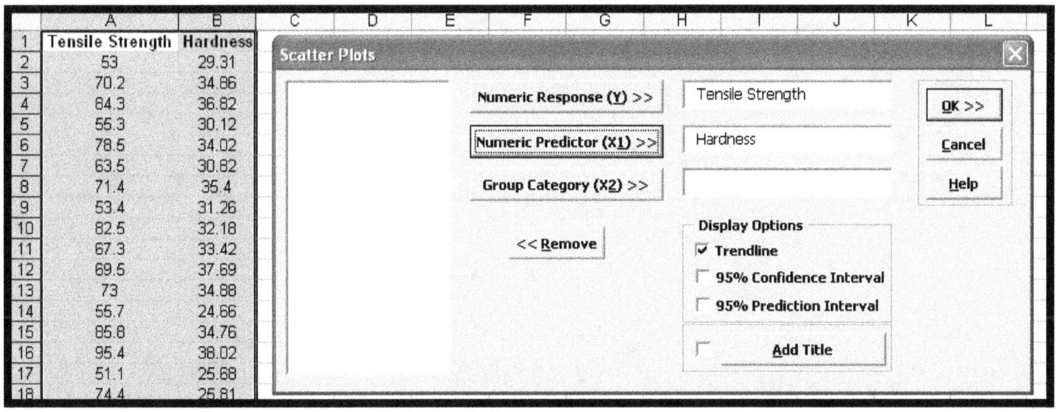

Figure 199: Dialogue Box for Scatter Plots – SigmaXL

Analysing Scatter Plots

In the example provided, we can see that as hardness increases, tensile strength appears to increase also.

Such a visual pattern may suggest a relationship between the two variables as hypothesized in the team's root cause analysis.

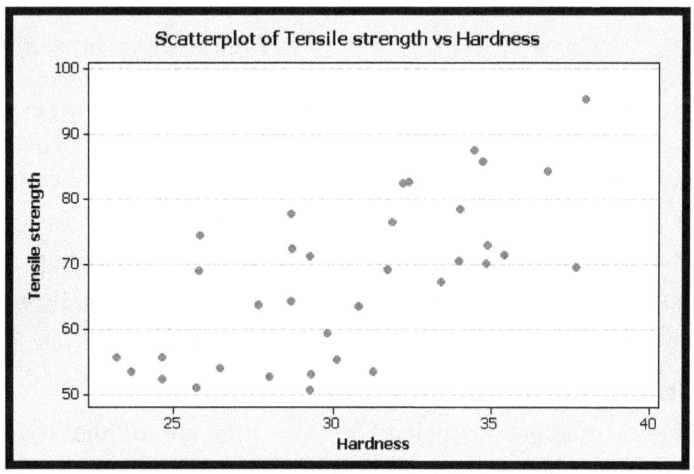

Scatter plots provide the opportunity to visualise the relationship between the *x* and *y* variables under analysis. Different patterns are generated for different types of relationships between variables as shown in the diagram below.

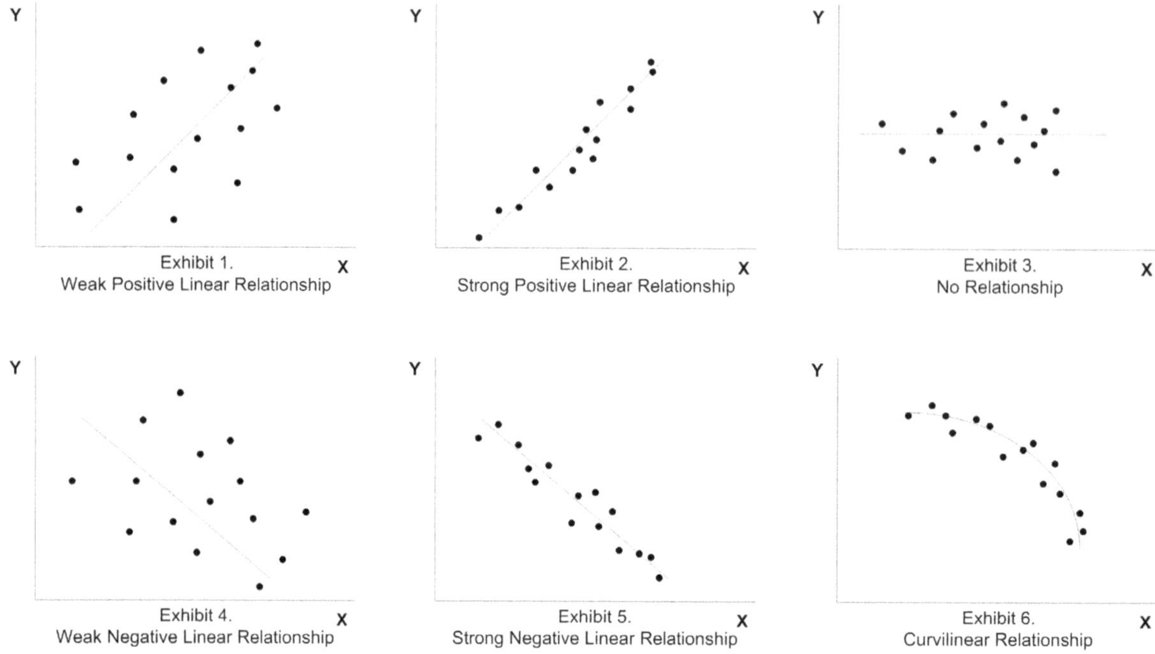

Figure 200: Correlation Patterns

In exhibits 1 and 2 we see that as the predictor variable (x) increases, the response variable (y) also increases linearly, which indicates a positive linear relationship. The time taken to drill a hole in the ground (y) would have a positive linear relationship with the depth to which the hole is to be drilled (x).

In exhibits 4 and 5 we observe that as the predictor variable (x) increases, the response variable (y) decreases linearly indicating a negative linear relationship.

Exhibit 3 shows a set of data in which there is virtually no relationship between the response variable (y) and the predictor variable (x). A curvilinear relationship is shown in exhibit 6.

Compute Correlation

The correlation coefficient (r) is a measure of the **strength of the linear relationship** between two variables. The r value is always in the range of -1 to $+1$. The stronger the correlation between the variables under analysis, the higher the absolute value of r.

This can be characterised in a scatter plot by a tighter distribution of pairs of data around the 'line of best fit'. Both the slope of the line and the closeness of the data to that line affect the correlation coefficient.

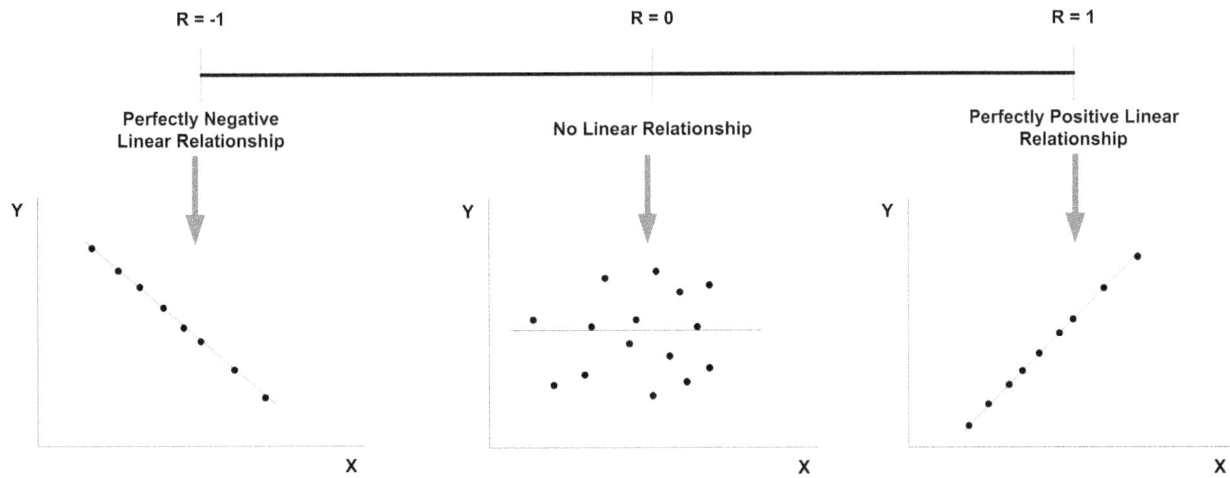

Figure 201: Correlation Coefficient (R)

A positive r indicates that as one variable increases, the other variable also increases. A negative r indicates that as one variable increases, the other variable decreases.

Correlation is measured by the Pearson's product moment 'correlation coefficient' (r). The sample correlation coefficient value is calculated using the following equation:

$$r_{xy} = \frac{\sum_{i=1}^{n}(x_i - \bar{x})(y_i - \bar{y})}{\sqrt{\sum_{i=1}^{n}(x_i - \bar{x})^2(y_i - \bar{y})^2}}$$

Simple Correlation with Minitab

With the advent of statistical analysis software packages such as Minitab, we do not need to do the computation manually.

Correlation function is activated by clicking on Stat > Basic Statistics > Correlation.

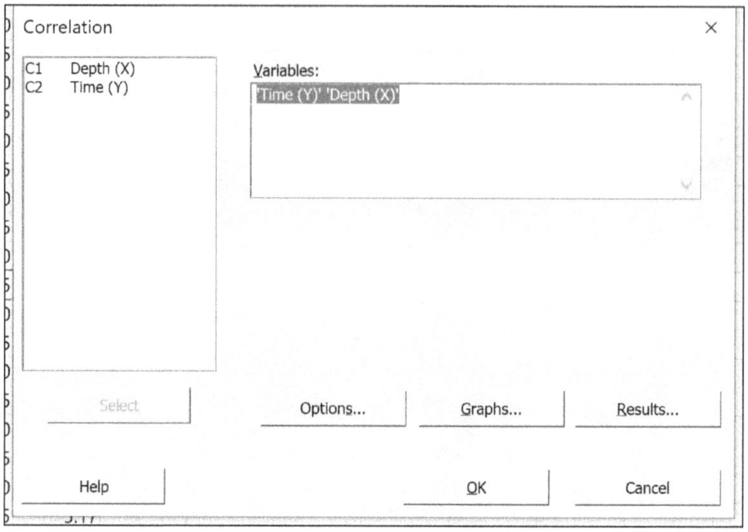

Figure 202: Dialogue Box for Correlation Analysis - Minitab

Interpreting Results

The output of the computation is shown in the session window and looks like the example below.

Method

Correlation type	Pearson
Number of rows used	50

ρ: pairwise Pearson correlation

Correlations

	Time (Y)
Depth (X)	0.452

Pairwise Pearson Correlations

Sample 1	Sample 2	N	Correlation	95% CI for ρ	P-Value
Depth (X)	Time (Y)	50	0.452	(0.199, 0.649)	0.001

Figure 203: Correlation Analysis Output - Minitab

Pearson Correlation - The correlation coefficient in this case is 0.452. This indicates there is a relatively strong positive correlation between the response and the independent variable.

Statistical analysis software calculates p values to help make a determination about the significance of this relationship.

P-Value - The P-Value in correlation analysis is used to make a decision as to whether or not the correlation coefficient (r) between the variables is statistically significant.

When the P-Value is less than α (refer to hypothesis testing), then we conclude the correlation coefficient is significant and a relationship of some significance exists.

In this particular case the p-value of 0.0000 is less than our chosen α of 0.05, thus we conclude that the relationship between tensile strength and hardness is significant.

Simple Correlation with SigmaXL

Let's look at a different data set with SigmaXL.

In this case we are studying the relationship between depth of drilling (as the predictor) and time to drill 1 metre into the earth (as the response variable).

We can see from the scatter plot shown to the right that there could be some correlation between the two variables.

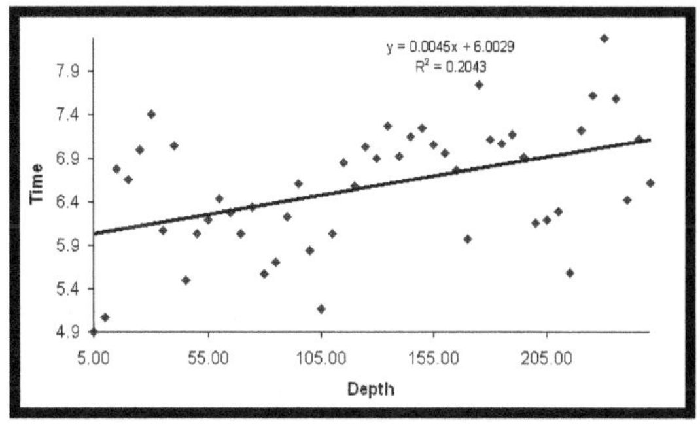

Correlation function is activated by clicking on Statistical Tools > Correlation Matrix.

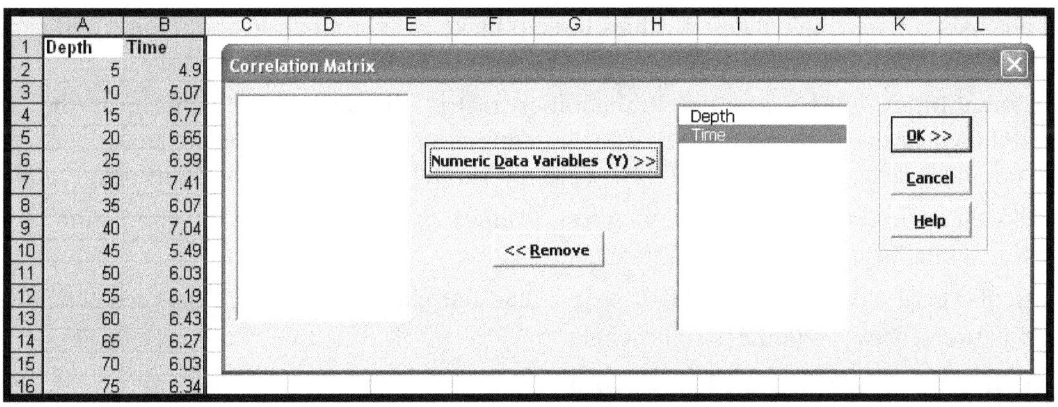

Figure 204: Dialogue Box for Correlation Analysis - SigmaXL

The output of the computation is shown in the session window, and looks like the example below.

	A	B	C
1	Pearson Correlations	Depth	Time
2	Depth	1.0000	0.4520
3	Time		1.0000
4			
5	Pearson Probabilities	Depth	Time
6	Depth		0.0010
7	Time		
8			
9	Spearman Rank Correlations	Depth	Time
10	Depth	1.0000	0.4279
11	Time		1.0000
12			
13	Spearman Rank Probabilities	Depth	Time
14	Depth		0.0019
15	Time		

Figure 205: Correlation Analysis Output - SigmaXL

Pearson Correlations - The correlation coefficient in this case is 0.4520. This indicates there is a weak positive correlation between the response (time) and the predictor variable (depth).

Statistical analysis software calculates P-values to help make a determination about the significance of this relationship.

Pearson Probabilities – The Pearson Probabilities matrix displays the p-values for the correlation coefficients shown in the upper matrix. P-Value in correlation analysis is used to make a decision as to whether or not the correlation coefficient (r) between the variables is statistically significant.

When the P-Value is less than α (refer to hypothesis testing), then we conclude the correlation coefficient is significant and a relationship of some significance exists.

In this particular case the p-value of 0.0010 is less than our chosen α of 0.05, thus we conclude that the relationship between depth and time is significant.

Developing a Simple Regression Model

Regression analysis produces a line that quantifies the relationship between x and y. The slope of the line can be determined by using the regression equation: $y = \beta_0 + \beta_1 + \varepsilon$.

- The y intercept (represented by the parameter β_0) is the point on the y-axis through which the 'line of best fit' passes.
- Sometimes referred to as the coefficient of the predictor variable x, the slope of the line (represented by the parameter β_1) is the amount of change in the value of y per unit increase in x.
- As the model is a probabilistic[30] model, it will contain error (refer to notes on residuals later in this section) which is represented by the term ε.

The **least squares method** gives a procedure for determining the values of the slope and y intercept in such a way that the resulting estimated regression line fits the data so that the total error around the line is as small as possible. Using the least squares method to find estimates of the parameters β_0 and β_1, leads us to the following estimated regression equation.

[30] Probabilistic Model – One where the value of Y can only be estimated and not determined exactly.

$$\hat{y} = b_0 + b_1 x$$

Where:

- y-hat is an estimate of the predicted value y
- b_0 is a sample estimate of the parameter β_0
- b_1 is a sample estimate of the parameter β_1

It's important to keep in mind that the pattern that emerges on any scatter plot should reflect the relationship between the two variables in the population.

Therefore the 'line of best fit' we draw on the scatter plot to summarise the relationship of the two variables should be a reasonable approximation of the true linear relationship between the two variables defined by the model $y = \beta_0 + \beta_1 x + \varepsilon$.

The estimated regression line defined by the model y (estimate) = $b_0 + b_1 x$, is quite simply that 'line of best fit'.

Computing the Regression Equation

The equations shown represent those that must be solved to obtain the components of the regression equation.

Computing the Slope, b_1

$$b_1 = \frac{SSXY}{SSX}$$

Where:

$$SSXY = \sum_{i=1}^{n}(x_i - \bar{x})(y_1 - \bar{y}) = \sum_{i=1}^{n} x_i y_i - \frac{\left(\sum_{i=1}^{n} x_i\right)\left(\sum_{i=1}^{n} y_i\right)}{n}$$

and

$$SSX = \sum_{i=1}^{n}(x_i - \bar{x})^2 = \sum_{i=1}^{n} x_i^{\,2} - \frac{\left(\sum_{i=1}^{n} x_i\right)^2}{n}$$

Computing the y intercept, b_0

$$b_0 = \hat{y} - b_1\bar{x}$$

Where:

$$\bar{y} = \frac{\sum_{i=1}^{n} y_i}{n}$$

and

$$\bar{x} = \frac{\sum_{i=1}^{n} x_i}{n}$$

With the development of statistical analysis software such as Minitab and SigmaXL, the process of calculating regression equations can be expedited.

Developing a Simple Regression Model with Minitab

Setting It Up

The Regression Model function is activated by clicking on Stat >Regression > Regression >Fit Regression Model.

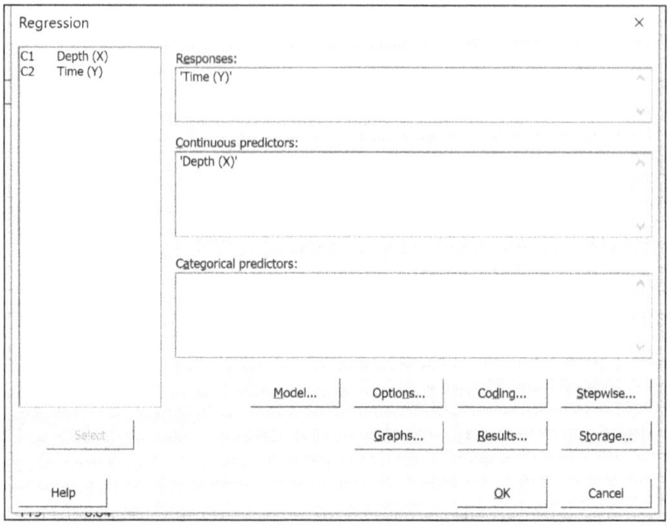

Figure 206: Dialogue Box for Regression Analysis - Minitab

Interpreting Results

The output of the regression analysis is generated in the Minitab session window and looks like that shown in the diagram.

The regression equation represents the model y (estimate) = $b_0 + b_1x$.

Regression Analysis: Time (Y) versus Depth (X)

Coefficients

Term	Coef	SE Coef	T-Value	P-Value	VIF
Constant	6.003	0.186	32.26	0.000	
Depth (X)	0.00446	0.00127	3.51	0.001	1.00

Model Summary

S	R-sq	R-sq(adj)	R-sq(pred)
0.647945	20.43%	18.78%	12.35%

Analysis of Variance

Source	DF	Adj SS	Adj MS	F-Value	P-Value
Regression	1	5.176	5.1756	12.33	0.001
Depth (X)	1	5.176	5.1756	12.33	0.001
Error	48	20.152	0.4198		
Total	49	25.328			

Figure 207: Regression Analysis Output - Minitab

Predictors and Coefficients: P-Values for the regression analysis are used to make determinations as to whether or not regression coefficients (the values that represent b_0 and b_1) are statistically significant.

- P-Values for the Constant – a value less than 0.05 indicates the constant (in this case 6.003 represents b_0) is significant in the regression model.
- P-Value for the Slope (depth) - a value less than 0.05 indicates that the slope of the predictor (in this case 0.00446 represents b_1) is significant in the regression model.

R-Sq: The coefficient of determination (r^2) allows us to describe how much of the variation in the response (y), can be attributed to its relationship with the independent variable (x).

It is the square of the correlation coefficient, and the closer it is to 1.0 (100 percent), the less the error in the equation. In this case 20.43 percent of the variation in drill time is explained by variation in depth.

R-Sq (adj): This is a modified measure of (r^2) that takes into consideration the number of terms and number of data points in the model.

As the number of terms increases in the model (multiple linear regression), this value will get smaller when these terms offer little value to the regression. It is primarily used for multiple regression models (i.e. multiple Xs).

Analysis of Variance Table (P-Value): P-Values for the Regression Model – a value less than 0.05 indicates that at least one regression coefficient is significant in the model.

Developing a Simple Regression Model with SigmaXL

Setting It Up

The Regression Model function is activated by clicking on Statistical Tools > Regression > Multiple Regression.

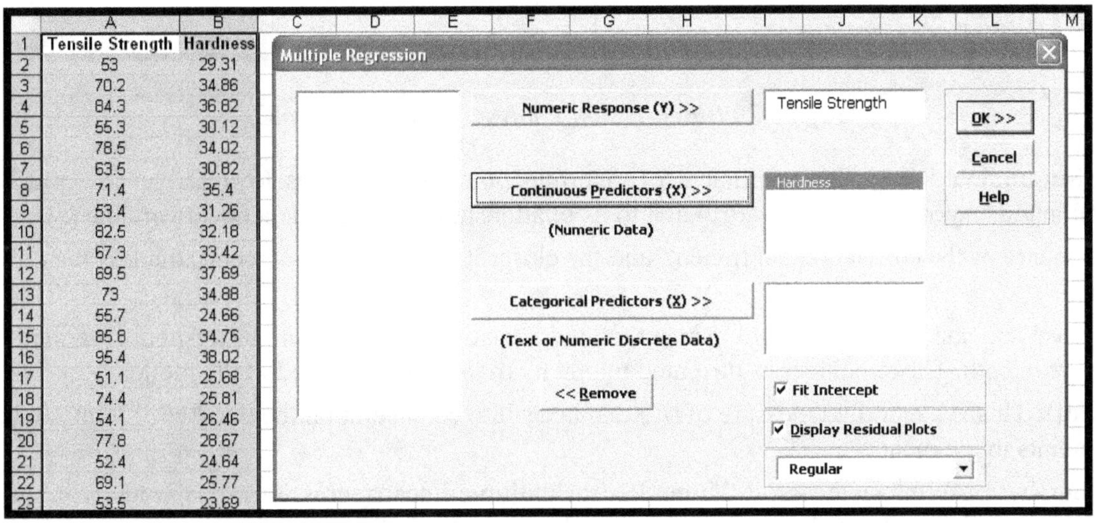

Figure 208: Dialogue Box for Regression Analysis - SigmaXL

The output of the regression analysis looks like that shown below. The regression equation represents the model y (estimate) = $b_0 + b_1x$.

Multiple Regression Model: Tensile Strength = (6.048) + (2.019) * Hardness

Model Summary:	
R-Square	46.13%
R-Square Adjusted	44.50%
S (Root Mean Square Error)	9.062

Parameter Estimates:

Predictor Term	Coefficient	SE Coefficient	T	P	VIF	Tolerance
Constant	6.048	11.689	0.517412	0.6083		
Hardness	2.019	0.379822	5.316	0.0000	1	1

Analysis of Variance for Model:

Source	DF	SS	MS	F	P
Model	1	2320.3	2320.3	28.258	0.0000
Error	33	2709.7	82.113		
Lack of Fit	32	2497.6	78.049	0.367842	0.8910
Pure Error	1	212.18	212.18		
Total (Model + Error)	34	5030.1	147.94		

Durbin-Watson Test for Autocorrelation in Residuals:

DW Statistic	2.617
P-Value Positive Autocorrelation	0.9676
P-Value Negative Autocorrelation	0.0263

Figure 209: Regression Analysis Output - SigmaXL

Model Summary: R-Sq: The coefficient of determination (r^2) allows us to describe how much of the variation in the response (y), can be attributed to its relationship with the independent variable (x).

It is the square of the correlation coefficient, and the closer it is to 1.0 (100 percent), the less the error in the equation.

In this case we can state that 46.13 percent of the variation observed in the response variable can be attributed to depth. The remainder is attributed to other variables not included in the model.

R-Sq (adj): This is a modified measure of (r^2) that takes into consideration the number of terms and number of data points in the model.

As the number of terms increases in the model (for multiple linear regression), this value will get smaller when these terms offer little value to the regression. Used primarily for multiple regression models.

P-Value for Predictor Terms (Parameter Estimates): P-Values for the regression analysis are used to make determinations as to whether or not regression coefficients (the values that represent b_0 and b_1) are statistically significant.

- P-Values for the Constant – a value less than 0.05 indicates the constant (in this case 6.048 represents b_0) is significant in the regression model. In this case the p-value of .6083 is > 0.05, thus it is insignificant enough that we could remove the constant from the regression model.
- P-value for the Slope (hardness) - a value less than 0.05 indicates that the slope of the predictor (in this case 2.019 represents b_1) is significant in the regression model.

Analysis of Variance for Model: P-values for the Regression Model – a value less than 0.05 indicates that at least one regression coefficient is significant in the model.

Using the Regression Equation for Prediction

Interpolation

A regression equation associated with a line that is a good fit with the data can be used to approximate values of y for values of x under certain conditions.

- Values of x should be within the range of x values used to generate the regression equation.

This type of estimation is called *interpolation*.

Extrapolation

Even if the line is a good fit, it is dangerous to estimate values for y using x values outside the range of values used to generate the equation. There is no guarantee that the pattern or trend outside these values will remain linear and the answers provided may be completely incorrect. This type of estimation is called *extrapolation*.

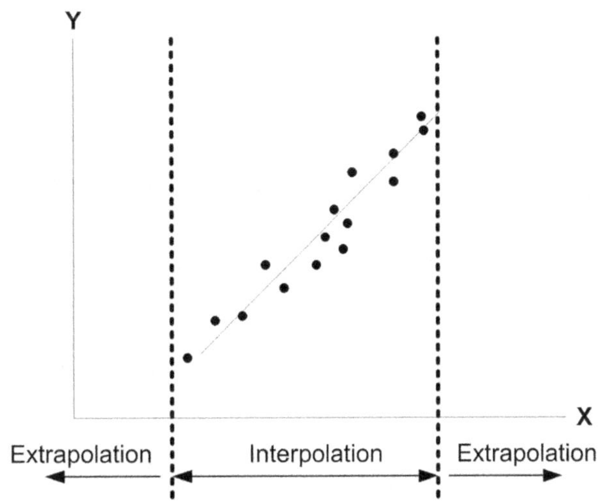

Croucher (1998)[31] provides a useful example to highlight the danger of extrapolation.

In a study of the relationship between height (x) and weight (y), a range of values for x between 156 cm and 169 cm were used to generate the regression equation for predicting weight based on a specified height.

$$y \text{ (estimate)} = -1.06 + 1.05x$$

If we substituted x (height) with a value of 100 cm, we get an approximated value for y (weight) of:

$$y \text{ (estimate)} = -106.0 + 1.05\ (100) = -106.0 + 105.0 = \mathbf{-1}$$

Through extrapolation we've determined that a child who is 100 cm tall weighs –1 kg.

31 Croucher, J.S., (1998), *'Introductory Mathematics & Statistics for Business'*, McGraw-Hill, New York, pp. 492 - 493

Summary of Simple Linear Regression results

The table below provides a summary of the key terms used in simple linear regression studies.

Item	Definition	Range of Values	What it means
R	Correlation Coefficient	-1 to +1	An indication of the strength of the linear relationship between the response (*y* values) and the predictor or explanatory variable (*x* values). A result close to zero indicates no relationship.
R^2 (R-sq)	Coefficient of Determination	0.00 to 1.00	This indicates the amount of variation in the response (*y* values) that is explained by its relationship with the independent or explanatory variable (*x* values). Multiply by 100 to explain the relationship in
P-value	The probability that the *y* intercept and the slope are significant in the regression model	0.00 to 1.00	If P-values are less than 0.05, (a) the constant is significant and (b) the slope of the fitted line is significant in the regression model.
Residual	The difference between observed value of *y* and the	No limit	Where common cause variation exists only, residuals will be normally distributed with a mean of zero.
S	Standard deviation of residuals	0 and higher	This gives an indication of how much the typical observed value differs from the predicted value.
Standardise d Residual	Equals the residual divided by the standard deviation	–3 to +3 (approx.)	A standardised residual with an absolute value of >3 is an unusual observation that should be investigated. Minitab reports those with values of >2.
Influential Observation	An observation with an *x* value that has a large influence on the values of coefficients.	No limit	Can be observed as an outlier. A decision is necessary as to whether they should be included in the regression analysis or removed.

Figure 210: Summary of Regression Terms

Estimating beyond the range of values of *x* used to generate the equation can result in impossible predictions, hence the statement of caution.

Multiple Correlation and Linear Regression

Multiple correlation and linear regression analysis can be used when a project team wishes to validate the hypothesised cause and effect relationship between a single response variable (*y*) and *multiple* independent or predictor variables (*x*'s). Both dependent and independent variables must be numerical variables.

A team might undertake multiple linear regression when:

- They want to validate the hypothesised cause and effect relationships between multiple *x*'s and a *y*
- They want to be able to predict the response you will get for given values of a number of independent variables

Case Study

A national limousine company was experiencing decreasing margins due to increases in running costs for its fleet of limousines. The company had tasked a project team with finding solutions for reducing the fuel consumption of their extensive fleet of vehicles in an effort to save costs.

During root cause analysis work, the team proposed that variation in fuel consumption (the effect) was caused by variation in length and weight of vehicles (the causes).

In the absence of evidence, this is only a hypothesis, hence the need for the team to validate the hypothesis.

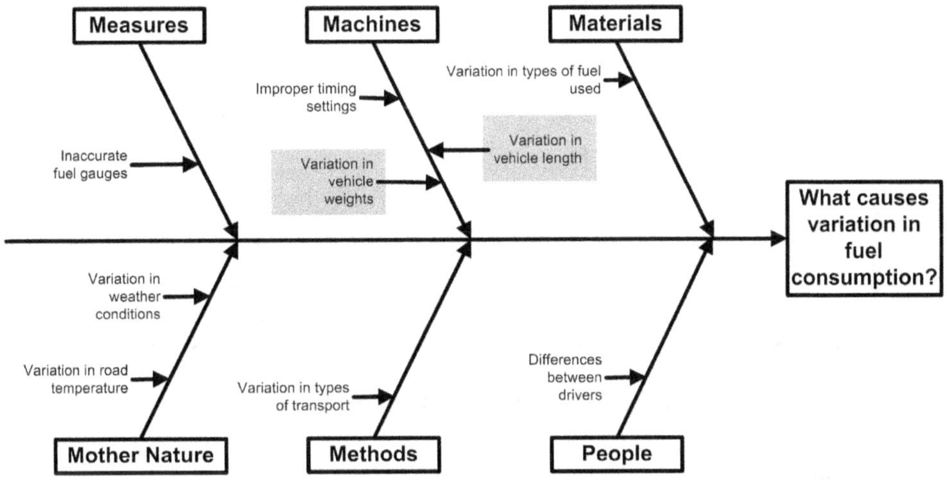

Graphical Representation of Multiple Correlation Data Using Minitab

Setting It Up

Minitab provides a method of graphically analysing correlation for all variables using scatter plots in one simple step. It does so through the generation of **Matrix Plots** which is accessed by clicking on Graph > Matrix Plot.

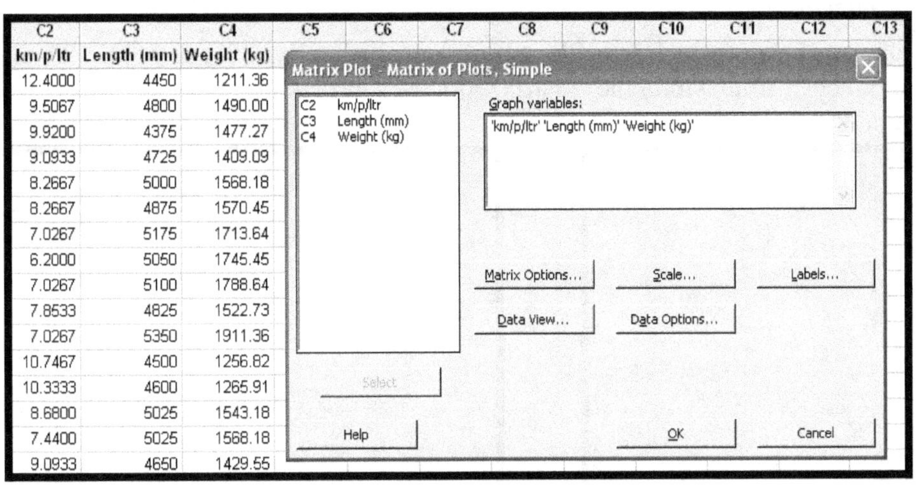

C2 km/p/ltr	C3 Length (mm)	C4 Weight (kg)
12.4000	4450	1211.36
9.5067	4800	1490.00
9.9200	4375	1477.27
9.0933	4725	1409.09
8.2667	5000	1568.18
8.2667	4875	1570.45
7.0267	5175	1713.64
6.2000	5050	1745.45
7.0267	5100	1788.64
7.8533	4825	1522.73
7.0267	5350	1911.36
10.7467	4500	1256.82
10.3333	4600	1265.91
8.6800	5025	1543.18
7.4400	5025	1568.18
9.0933	4650	1429.55

Figure 211: Dialogue Box for Matrix Plots - Minitab

Interpreting Results

Matrix plots are groupings of scatter plots on a single chart.

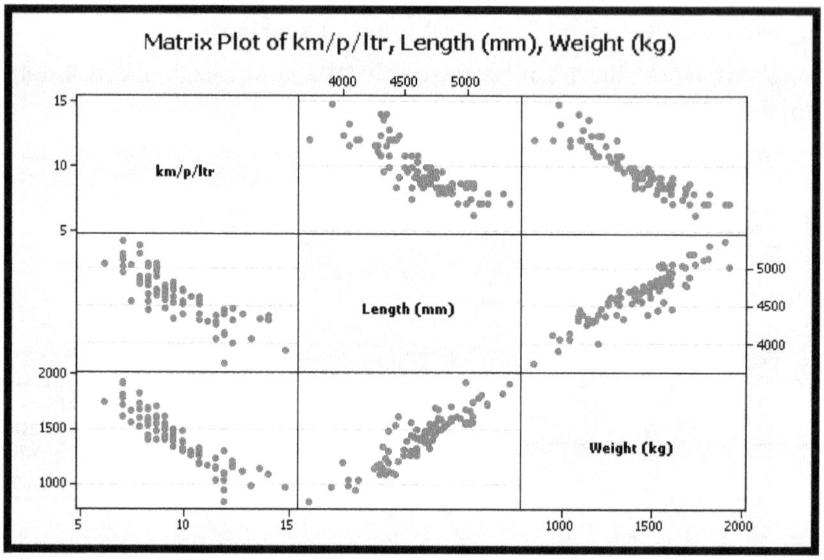

Figure 212: Matrix Plot - Minitab

The matrix plot shown graphically displays pairings of data in scatter plots.

All possible pairings are plotted: for example, the bottom left chart has plotted weight as the dependent variable and kilometres per litre as the predictor.

By contrast, the top right chart has plotted the same variables, however weight is the predictor and kilometres per litre is the dependent variable.

These plots show patterns consistent with strong linear relationships between variables, however in the absence of numerical data, we can only rely on subjective interpretation to make any comment about the strength of these relationships.

If you are not concerned about which variable appears on which axis of the plot, Minitab allows the user to drop parts of the full chart from within the 'Matrix Options' sub-dialogue box.

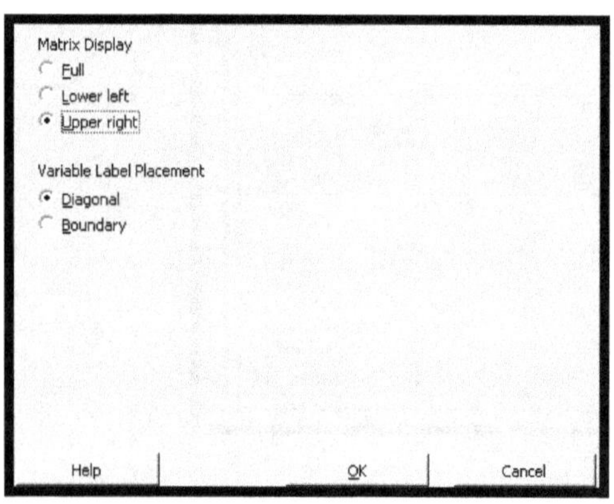

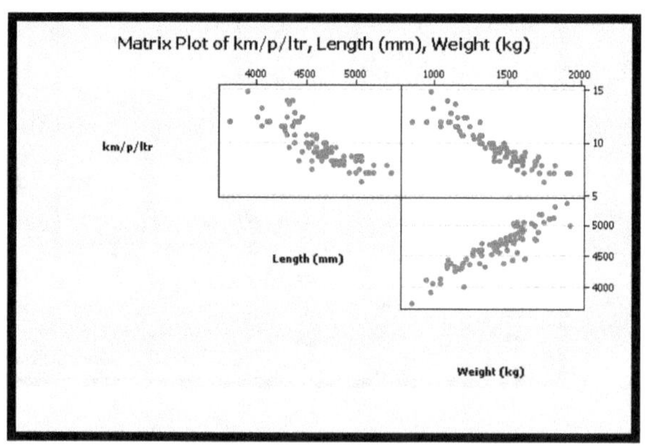

In the chart shown, only the upper right portion has been retained in order to view plots with km/p/ltr on the y-axis.

Graphical Representation of Multiple Correlation Data With SigmaXL

Setting It Up

SigmaXL provides a method of graphically analysing correlation for all variables using scatter plots in one simple step by generating a **Scatter Plot Matrix** which you can access by clicking on Graphical Tools > Scatter Plot Matrix.

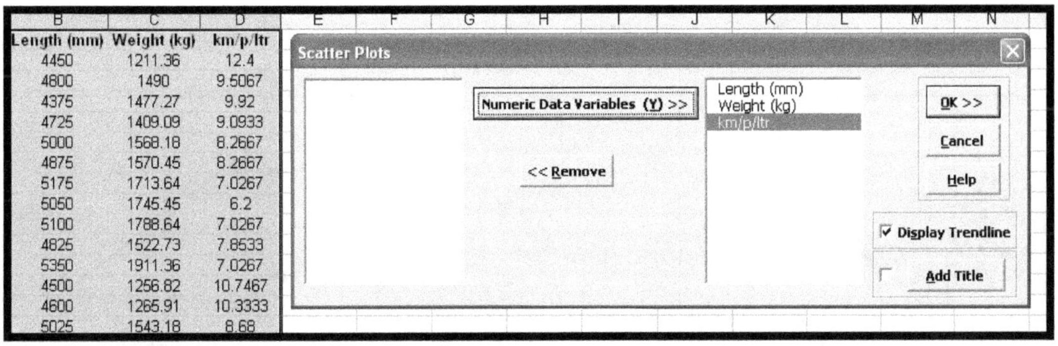

Figure 213: Dialogue Box for Scatter Plot Matrix – SigmaXL

Interpreting Results

A Scatter Plot Matrix is a grouping of scatter plots on a single chart.

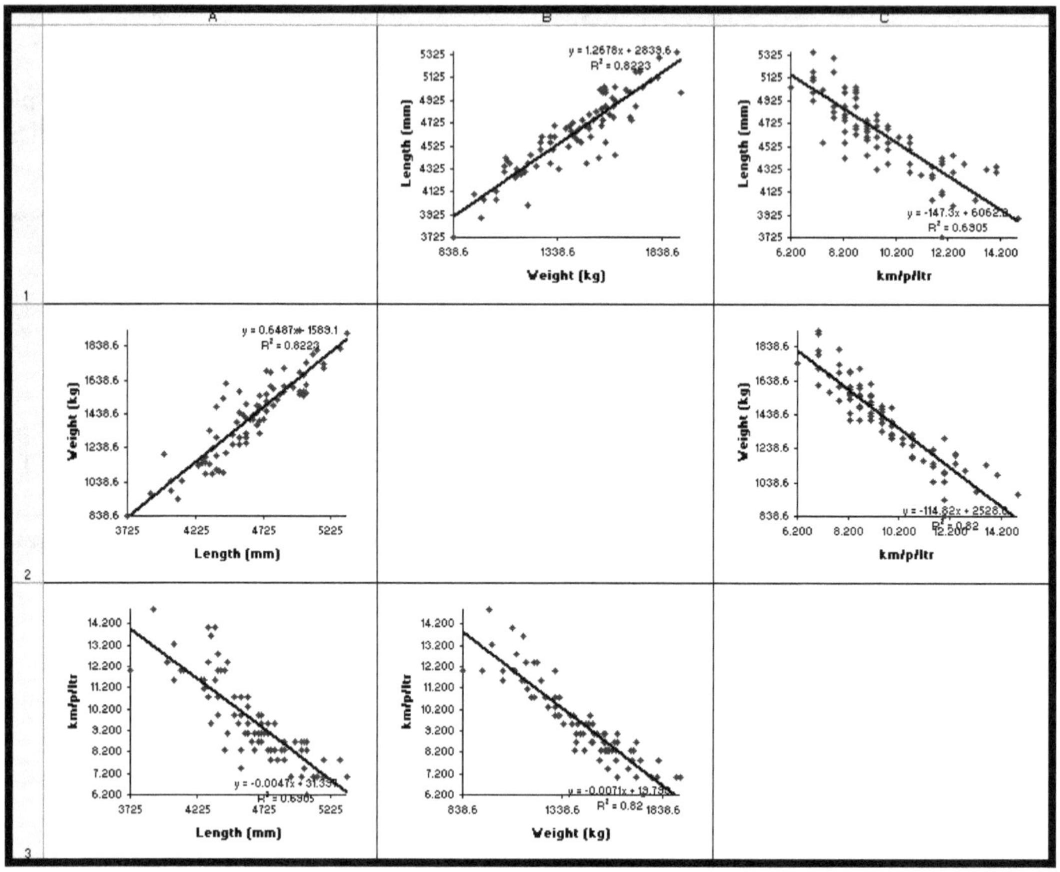

Figure 214: Scatter Plot Matrix – SigmaXL

The scatter plot matrix shown displays pairings of data in scatter plots. All possible pairings are plotted; for example, the bottom left chart has plotted overall satisfaction as the dependent variable (y-axis) and average number of orders per month (x-axis) as the predictor.

By contrast, the top right chart has plotted the same variables, however overall satisfaction is the predictor and average number of orders per month is the dependent variable.

You need to determine which of the charts are most relevant to you.

Compute Correlation using Minitab

Setting It Up

This step requires the analysis of correlation between *all* variables used in the study, and is generated in Minitab by clicking on Stat > Basic Statistics > Correlation.

In multiple regression studies, it is important to remember that correlation might not only exist between the x's and the y, but also between the x's themselves.

This is referred to as **collinearity**.

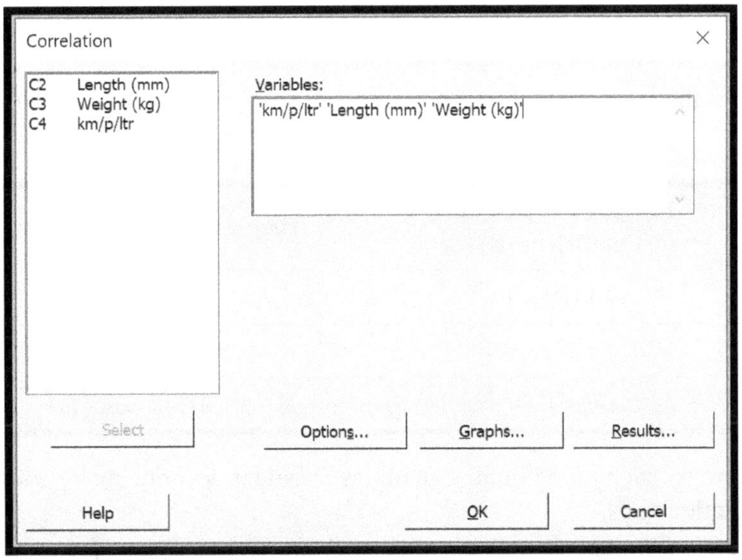

Figure 215: Dialogue Box for Correlation Analysis - Minitab

<u>Interpreting Results</u>

Minitab generates the correlation information in the session window as shown in the diagram.

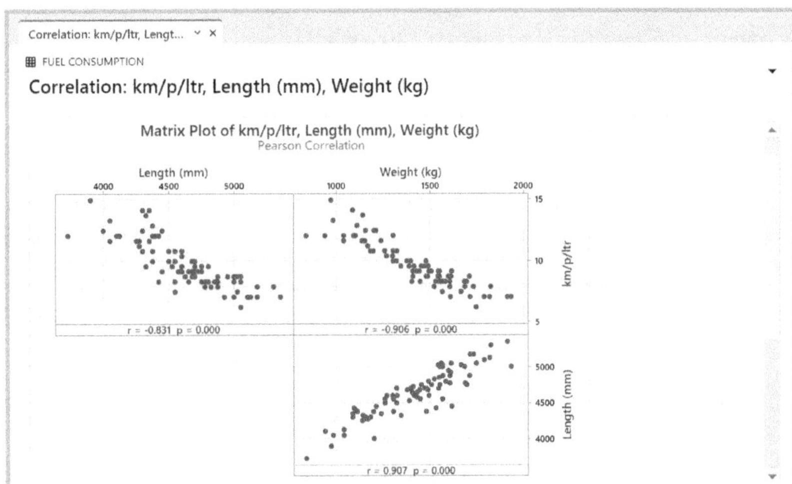

Figure 216: Correlation Analysis Output - Minitab

Pearson Correlation - The correlation coefficient (*r*) for each possible pair of variables (and the associated P-value) is shown at the bottom of each of the scatter plots in the matrix. For example, the correlation coefficient for length and km/p/ltr is – 0.831. This suggests a strong *negative* relationship between the two variables (i.e., as length increases the number of kilometres driven per litre decreases).

The correlation coefficient of 0.907 for weight and length suggests a strong *positive* relationship between the two variables (i.e., as length increases, weight also increases). As the project team has proposed that these two variables are the predictors, it seems that there might be a case of what is referred to as *collinearity*. I will discuss this a little later in this chapter.

The table below shows the approximate relationship between Pearson Correlation Statistic (r) and the degree of association.

Pearson Correlation Coefficient (R)	Degree of Association
0.90 ≤ (R) ≤ 1.00	Strong
0.70 ≤ (R) < 0.90	Moderate
(R) < 0.70	Weak

Statistical analysis software such as Minitab calculates P-values to help make a determination about the significance of these relationships.

P-values - The P-value in correlation computations is used to make a decision as to whether or not the correlation coefficient (R) between the variables is statistically significant.

When the P-value is less than α (refer to hypothesis testing), then the relationship is statistically significant.

In all cases shown, P-values are less than our chosen α of 0.05, hence our conclusion that the relationship between all variables is significant.

Compute Correlation with SigmaXL

<u>Setting It Up</u>

This step requires the analysis of correlation between *all* variables used in the study, and is generated in SigmaXL from within the 'Statistical Tools > Correlation Matrix' selection in the 'SigmaXL' menu. In multiple regression studies, it is important to remember that correlation might not only exist between the *x*'s and the *y*, but also between the *x*'s themselves. This is referred to as **collinearity**.

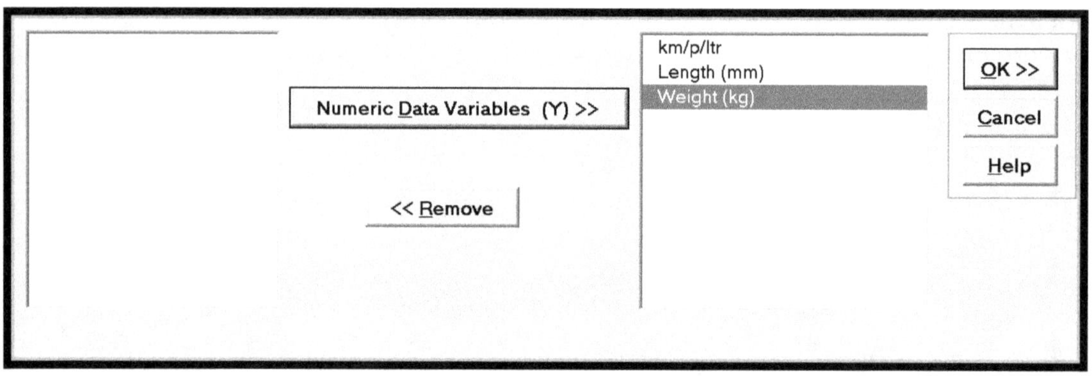

Figure 217: Dialogue Box for Correlation Analysis – SigmaXL

Interpreting Results

SigmaXL generates the correlation information in the session window as shown below.

Pearson Correlations	km/p/ltr	Length (mm)	Weight (kg)
km/p/ltr	1	-0.8309	-0.9055
Length (mm)		1	0.9068
Weight (kg)			1

Pearson Probabilities	km/p/ltr	Length (mm)	Weight (kg)
km/p/ltr		0.0000	0.0000
Length (mm)			0.0000
Weight (kg)			

Spearman Rank Correlations	km/p/ltr	Length (mm)	Weight (kg)
km/p/ltr	1	-0.8583	-0.9259
Length (mm)		1	0.8994
Weight (kg)			1

Spearman Rank Probabilities	km/p/ltr	Length (mm)	Weight (kg)
km/p/ltr		0.0000	0.0000
Length (mm)			0.0000
Weight (kg)			

Figure 218: Correlation Matrix - SigmaXL

Pearson Correlation - The correlation coefficient (*r*) for each possible pair of variables (including pairings with themselves) is shown in the matrix at the top. For example, the correlation coefficient for fuel consumption (km/p/ltr) and length is -0.8309. This suggests a strong *negative* relationship between the two variables.

The correlation coefficient of – 0.9055 for fuel consumption and weight suggests a strong *negative* relationship between the two variables.

The table below shows the approximate relationship between Pearson Correlation Statistic (r) and the degree of association.

Pearson Correlation Coefficient (R)	Degree of Association
0.90 ≤ (R) ≤ 1.00	Strong
0.70 ≤ (R) < 0.90	Moderate
(R) < 0.70	Weak

Statistical analysis software calculates P-values to help make a determination about the significance of these relationships.

Pearson Probabilities – This matrix displays the P-values associated with corresponding *r* values in the matrix above. The P-value in correlation computations is used to make a decision as to whether or not the correlation coefficient (*r*) between the variables is statistically significant.

When the P-value is less than α (refer to hypothesis testing), then the relationship is statistically significant.

In both cases, P-values of 0.00 are less than our chosen α of 0.05, thus our conclusion that the relationship between these variables is significant.

Spearman's Rank Correlation – Results complement Pearson's Correlation in that it provides a robust measure of association. Spearman's rank is based on correlated ranks that are not sensitive to outliers.

Develop The Multiple Linear Regression Model

Multiple linear regression involves the study of more than one predictor variable with a single response variable.

In our particular case study where we have two predictor variables (length and weight), a three dimensional graph can be generated, however, with the addition of more predictor variables this is not possible.

As you can imagine, the nature of a multiple regression study says that a single line can no longer represent the relationship between variables, particularly where we have more than 2 predictor variables in the study.

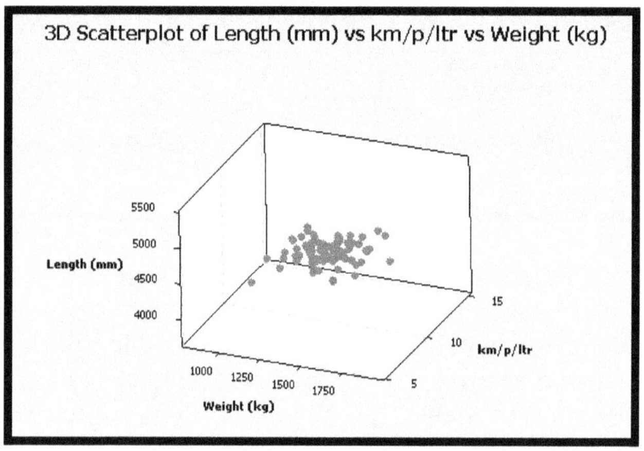

Figure 219: 3D Scatter Plot of Three Variables

In multiple linear regression the relationship between x's and the y is 'cubic polynomial' in nature and no single line represents the total relationship.

However, a linear relationship exists with respect to the coefficients as we assume a linear relationship between each of the predictor variables and the response y.

The multiple linear regression model is expressed by the equation: $y = \beta_0 + \beta_1 x_1 + \beta_2 x_2 + \beta_3 x_3 + \ldots + \beta_k x_k + \varepsilon$, where:

- β_0 = The y intercept
- β_1 = The slope of y with variable x_1, when variables $x_2, x_3, \ldots x_k$ are held constant
- β_2 = The slope of y with variable x_2, when variables $x_1, x_3, \ldots x_k$ are held constant
- β_3 = The slope of y with variable x_3, when variables $x_1, x_2, \ldots x_k$ are held constant
- ε = random error in y for each observation
- k represents the number of independent variables in the model

As is the case for simple linear regression, estimates of the parameters β_0 and $\beta_1, \ldots \beta_k$ lead us to the following estimated regression equation.

$$\hat{y} = b_0 + b_1 x_1 + b_k x_k$$

Where:

- y-hat is an estimate of the predicted value y
- b_0 is a sample estimate of the parameter β_0
- b_1 is a sample estimate of the parameter β_1
- b_k is a sample estimate of the parameter β_k
- k represents the number of variables in the model

Collinearity

A problem that can exist in the use of multiple regression analysis is collinearity.

A collinear situation exists when some of the predictor (or what might be referred to as explanatory) variables are highly correlated with one another. Where this exists, variables that are collinear do not provide additional information for the model.

In such cases the values of regression coefficients can fluctuate widely, hence are poorly estimated.

A method of measuring collinearity results in a value called the Variance Inflation Factor (VIF). The VIF equation for each explanatory variable is:

$$VIF_j = \frac{1}{1 - R_j^2}$$

When sets of variables are not correlated with one another, the value of VIF will be equal to 1. Where collinearity exists, VIF values can exceed 10. Marquardt (1980)[32] suggests that a VIF of greater than 10 gives cause for concern that excessive collinearity exists.

Other researchers such as Montgomery and Peck (1982)[33] suggest a VIF greater than 5 gives reason for employing alternative models.

Let me summarise it in this way. **Variance Inflation Factor** (VIF) is a measure of the degree of collinearity that exists between explanatory variables (x's).

VIF = 1	No correlation exists between the respective variable and any other explanatory variable.
VIF ≥ 5	Excessive correlation may exist between variables resulting in regression coefficients that are poorly estimated.

Course of action for high VIF values might include:

- Identify collinear variables – drop one or more from the model if an xy relationship is established
- Collect additional data
- Use different explanatory (predictor) variables

32 Marquardt, D.W., (1980), "You should standardise the predictor variables in your regression models", *'Journal of the American Statistical Association No. 75'*, pp. 87-91

33 Montgomery, D.C., Peck, E.A., (1982), *'Introduction to Linear Regression Analysis'*, John Wiley & Sons

- Use an alternative to the least squares method of studying regression

Develop A Multiple Linear Regression Model With Minitab

Setting It Up

Multiple regression models are generated in Minitab in the same way as simple regression studies - by clicking on Stat >Regression > Regression > Fit Regression Model.

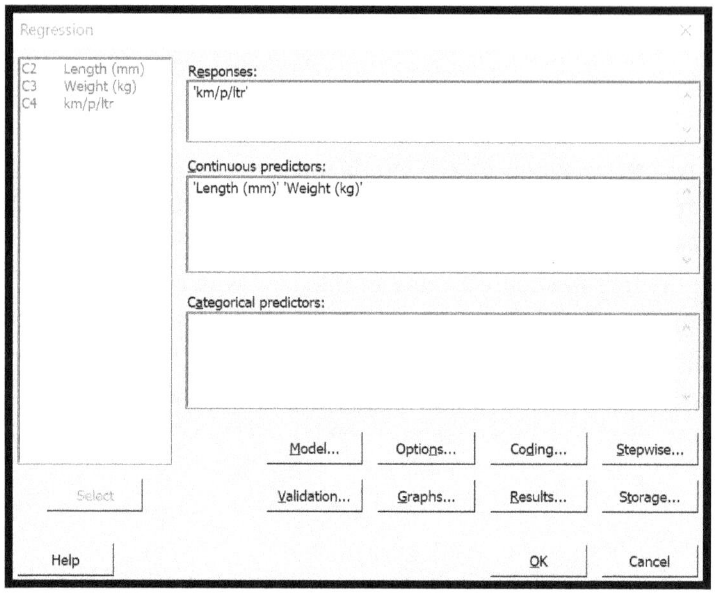

Figure 220: Dialogue Box for Multiple Regression Analysis - Minitab

Interpreting Results

Minitab generates the regression information in the session window shown in the diagram.

The regression equation fits the model where the estimate of y (estimate) = $b_0 + b_1x_1 + b_2x_2$.

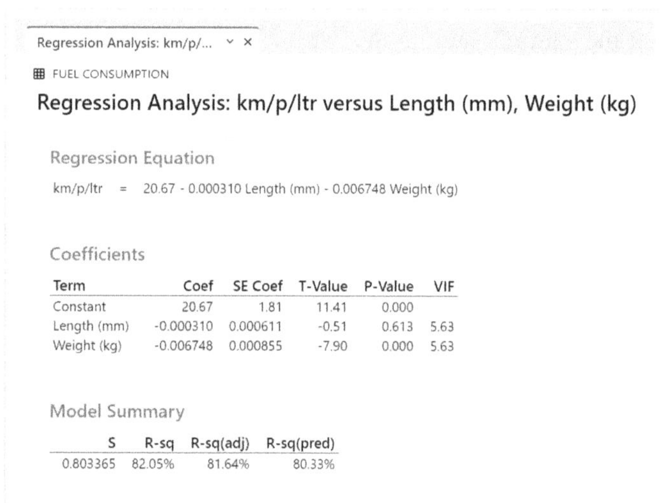

Regression Analysis: km/p/...

FUEL CONSUMPTION

Regression Analysis: km/p/ltr versus Length (mm), Weight (kg)

Regression Equation

km/p/ltr = 20.67 - 0.000310 Length (mm) - 0.006748 Weight (kg)

Coefficients

Term	Coef	SE Coef	T-Value	P-Value	VIF
Constant	20.67	1.81	11.41	0.000	
Length (mm)	-0.000310	0.000611	-0.51	0.613	5.63
Weight (kg)	-0.006748	0.000855	-7.90	0.000	5.63

Model Summary

S	R-sq	R-sq(adj)	R-sq(pred)
0.803365	82.05%	81.64%	80.33%

Figure 221: Multiple Regression Analysis Output - Minitab

The Regression Table

Coef – The upper table provides the estimated coefficients for the *y* intercept and slope and their standard errors.

P-values: P-values for the regression analysis are used to make determinations as to whether or not regression coefficients are statistically significant.

- $P \geq 0.05$ = Regression Coefficient is Not Significant (in this case length is considered insignificant and can be dropped from the prediction model even though it showed a strong correlation with fuel consumption, refer to VIF discussion)
- $P < 0.05$ = Regression Coefficient is Significant (in this case the constant or y-intercept and weight are both considered significant and should be kept in the prediction model)

VIF – The VIF values of 5.629 suggest the existence of collinearity. Knowing a little about the motor vehicles, we would expect to see a correlation between length (x_1) and weight (x_2).

Taking this to the next level, we could confidently say that the length of the vehicle has a direct impact on its weight, which in turn impacts on fuel economy. Thus, the relationship can be expressed as shown in the table below.

Hypothesised Relationship Model	**Actual Relationship Model**
Length and weight each affect fuel economy	Length affects weight which affects fuel economy
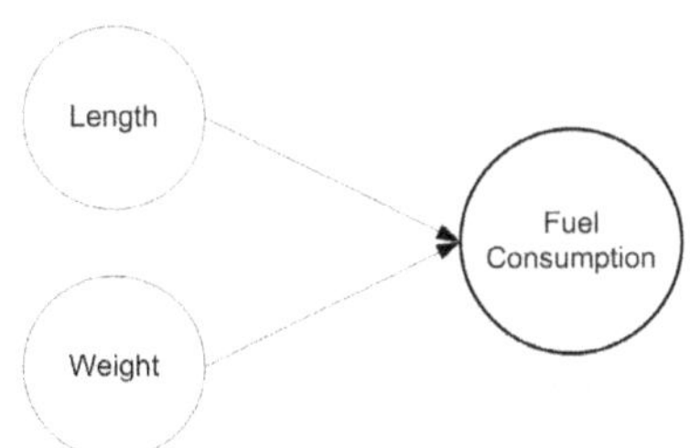	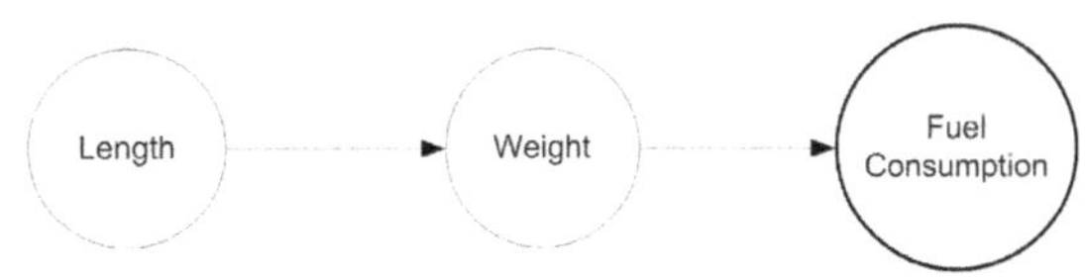

Figure 222: Hypothesised versus Actual Relationship

The course of action from here is to drop one of the explanatory variables from the model. The decision is made easy by simply referring to the P-values for regression coefficients in the regression table.

R-Sq: The coefficient of determination (R^2) allows us to describe how much of the variation in the response (y) can be attributed to its relationship with the independent variable (x).

The closer it is to 100 percent, the less the error in the equation.

R-Sq (adj): This is a modified measure of (R^2) that takes into consideration the number of terms and number of data points in the model.

As the number of terms increases in the model (multiple linear regression), this value will get smaller when these terms offer little value to the regression.

In this case we can state that 81.6 percent of the variation in kilometres per litre is explained by variation in length and weight.

The table shows the approximate relationship between Coefficient of Determination Value (R-Sq) and the degree of association.

R-Square Percentage Value (R-Sq%)	Degree of Association
(R-Sq) ≥ 80%	Strong
50% ≤ (R-Sq) ≤ 80%	Moderate
(R-Sq) < 50%	Weak

Analysis of Variable Table

The value in the F column represents the F test statistic for the hypothesis that regression coefficients are = 0. The P-value to the right of this represents the significance of any difference from 0.

- $P \geq 0.05$ = Regression Coefficients are Insignificant
- $P < 0.05$ = At Least 1 Regression Coefficient is Significant

Analysis of Variance

Source	DF	Adj SS	Adj MS	F-Value	P-Value
Regression	2	253.793	126.896	196.62	0.000
Length (mm)	1	0.166	0.166	0.26	0.613
Weight (kg)	1	40.231	40.231	62.34	0.000
Error	86	55.504	0.645		
Lack-of-Fit	79	54.735	0.693	6.31	0.008
Pure Error	7	0.769	0.110		
Total	88	309.297			

Develop A Multiple Linear Regression With SigmaXL

Setting It Up

Multiple regression models are generated in SigmaXL in the same way as simple linear regression studies - by clicking on Statistical Tools > Regression > Multiple Regression.

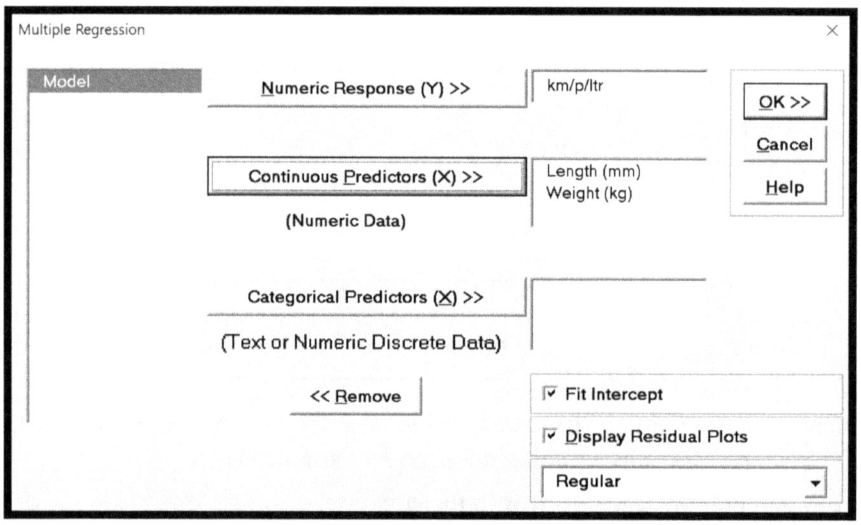

Figure 223: Dialogue Box for Multiple Regression Analysis - SigmaXL

Interpreting Results

SigmaXL generates the regression information in the session window shown in the following diagram.

The regression equation fits the model where the estimate of y (estimate) = $b_0 + b_1x_1 + b_2x_2$.

Multiple Regression Model: km/p/ltr = (20.674) + (-0.00031) * Length (mm) + (-0.00675) * Weight (kg)

Model Summary:

R-Square	82.05%
R-Square Adjusted	81.64%
S (Root Mean Square Error)	0.803365

Parameter Estimates:

Predictor Term	Coefficient	SE Coefficient	T	P	VIF	Tolerance
Constant	20.674	1.812	11.408	0.0000		
Length (mm)	-0.000310437	0.000611371	-0.507771	0.6129	5.629	0.177666
Weight (kg)	-0.006748144	0.000854703	-7.895	0.0000	5.629	0.177666

Analysis of Variance for Model:

Source	DF	SS	MS	F	P
Model	2	253.79	126.90	196.62	0.0000
Error	86	55.504	0.645395		
Lack of Fit	79	54.735	0.692851	6.308	0.0077
Pure Error	7	0.768800	0.109828571		
Total (Model + Error)	88	309.30	3.515		

Durbin-Watson Test for Autocorrelation in Residuals:

DW Statistic	1.892
P-Value Positive Autocorrelation	0.2919
P-Value Negative Autocorrelation	0.6840

... Correlation Matrix (1) | **Multiple Regression** | Mult Reg Residuals (1)

Figure 224: Multiple Regression Analysis Output – SigmaXL

Model Summary

R-Square or coefficient of determination (R^2) allows us to describe how much of the variation in the response (y) can be attributed to its relationship with the independent variable (x).

The closer it is to 100 percent, the less the error in the equation.

Adjusted R-Sq is a modified measure of (R^2) that takes into consideration the number of terms and number of data points in the model.

As the number of terms increases in the model (multiple linear regression), this value will get smaller when these terms offer little value to the regression.

In this case we can state that almost 82 percent of the variation in y is explained by variation in the x's in the model.

The table shows the approximate relationship between Coefficient of Determination Value (R-Sq) and the degree of association.

R-Square Percentage Value (R-Sq%)	Degree of Association
(R-Sq) ≥ 80%	Strong
50% ≤ (R-Sq) ≤ 80%	Moderate
(R-Sq) < 50%	Weak

Parameter Estimates: (Coefficients and P-values) - The Coefficient for the Constant refers to the Y intercept (b_0) in the regression model.

Additional Coefficients represent the slope values in the regression model for each of the predictor variables or x's (e.g., b_1 and b_2). (Refer to the equation shown at the top of the regression worksheet.)

P-values: P-values for the regression analysis are used to make determinations as to whether or not regression coefficients are statistically significant.

- $P \geq 0.05$ = Regression Coefficient is Not Significant (in this case length is considered insignificant and can be dropped from the prediction model even though it showed a strong correlation with fuel consumption, refer to VIF discussion)
- $P < 0.05$ = Regression Coefficient is Significant (in this case the constant or y-intercept and weight are both considered significant and should be kept in the prediction model)

Parameter Estimates: (VIF) – The VIF values of 5.629 suggest the existence of collinearity.

- VIF = 1 indicates the absence of any relationship among predictors and is highly desirable;
- VIF > 1 indicates that the predictors are correlated to some degree;
- VIF ≥ 5 indicates that the regression coefficients are strongly correlated and this will lead to poor estimates of the coefficients.

(Refer to VIF notes for Multiple Regression with Minitab.)

Analysis of Variance for Model: (F Statistic and P-values) - The top most value in the F column represents the F test statistic for the hypothesis that regression coefficients are = 0.

The P-value to the right of this represents the significance of any difference from 0.

- $P \geq 0.05$ = Regression Coefficients are Insignificant
- $P < 0.05$ = At Least 1 Regression Coefficient is Significant

Durban-Watson Test for Auto-Correlation is used to determine if the residuals are auto-correlated. If either P-value is < 0.05, there is significant auto-correlation.

This is likely due to an external bias factor affecting your process over time (e.g. warm-up effect, seasonality etc). This will also be evident in the plot of residuals versus observation order. Autocorrelation in the residuals is not a problem for this model.

CHECK VALIDITY OF THE REGRESSION MODEL

Validating the Regression Model

Regression studies are validated through the analysis of residuals. Residuals are the estimated error values, and are calculated by subtracting the estimated value for each y from the actual value for each y. Refer to appendices for an interesting example of the use of residuals in root cause analysis.

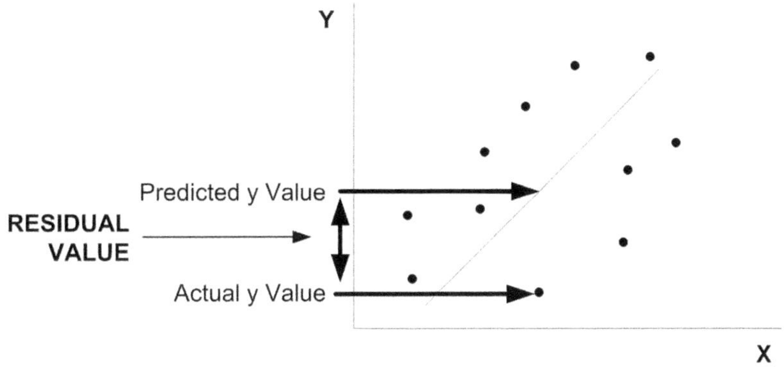

Figure 225: Residuals in Regression Studies

A number of assumptions are made in respect to residuals of the model. For the model to be valid, these assumptions must be tested and met.

Assumptions of a Valid Regression Model

The assumptions associated with the regression are similar to those in Analysis of Variance studies:

- **Normality of Error (Normal Probability Plots):**
  - The closer the sequence of data points represents a straight line in the normal probability plot, the more normal the distribution.
  - Histograms are not as informative as normal probability plots for smaller numbers of data points (i.e., less than 30).
- **Constant Error Variance (Residuals Versus Fitted Values):**
  - A random pattern of data points when residuals are plotted against fitted values indicates constant variance. (i.e. variation remains constant across the range of fitted values)
  - Any pattern such as a fan shape or wedge shape would be an indication that the assumption of *homoscedasticity* has been violated.
- **Independence of Error (Residuals Versus Order of Data):**
  - As with 'constant variance', a random pattern of data points indicates that residuals are independent.
  - The existence of patterns that indicate a trend would give cause for concern that the relationship between variables is affected by some factor related to time.
  - For example, when measuring the relationship between bounce height and drop height of tennis balls, the increasing ambient temperature from morning into full day could gradually change the bounce capability of a tennis ball.
  - Any dependence amongst variables and time is readily apparent when residuals are plotted against the order of collection. A clear pattern will emerge.

Generating Residual Plots in SigmaXL

SigmaXL generates residual plots in a similar form to Minitab's four-in-one residual plots.

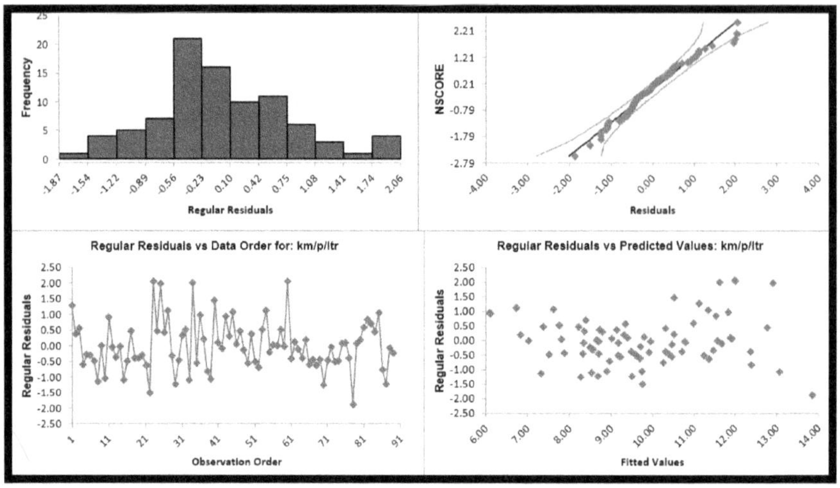

Figure 226: Residual Plots with SigmaXL

Generating Residual Plots in Minitab

Setting It Up

The sub-dialogue box for residual plots is opened from the main dialogue box via 'Graphs'.

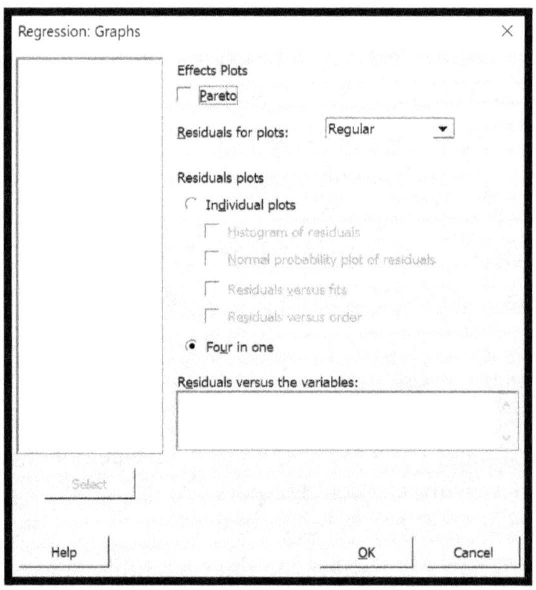

Figure 227: Sub-dialogue Box for Residual Plots - Minitab

Individual plots or a four in one plot can be generated according to the users preferences. Individual plots show each item individually, while the four in one plot is exactly that, all four plots consolidated into one graph.

Interpreting Residual Plots

The following details provide a guide to the interpretation of residual plots in validating assumptions. For more information on individual plots, refer to 'Interpreting Residual Plots' in the section describing One Way ANOVA.

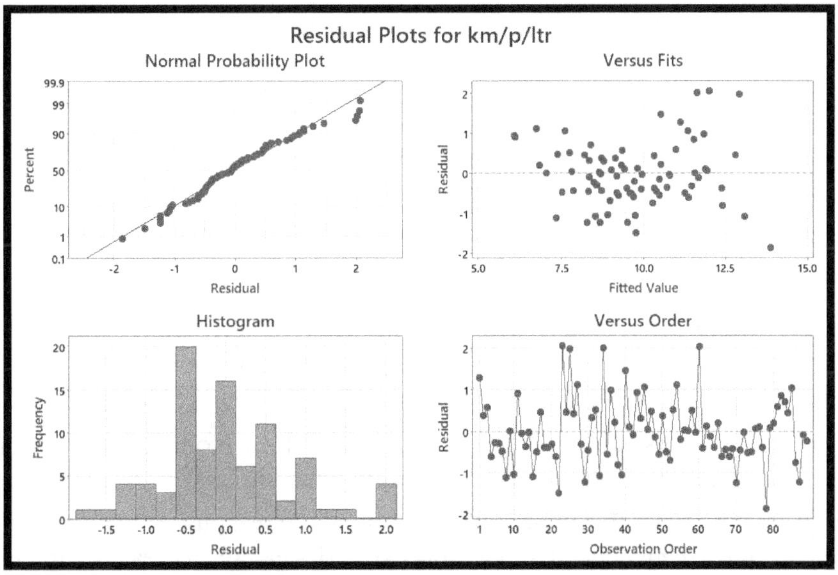

Figure 228: Four In One Residual Plot - Minitab

Residual Patterns

Residuals from valid regression models have three characteristics.

Residual Characteristic	How Assessed	Valid Pattern	Invalid Pattern
Residuals are approximately normal	Normal Probability Plot of Residuals Histogram of Residuals (useful for more than 30-50 data	Similar characteristics to normally distributed data.	Non-normal distribution
Residuals should have constant variance across the range of fitted values	Residuals versus Predicted Values	Constant variance across the range of fitted values from left to right.	Wedge shaped Diamond shaped Trend up or down Shifts Saw tooth shaped
Residuals, in the order of collection, should behave randomly over time	Residuals versus Data Order	Random pattern such as you would see in a control chart of data that has only common cause variation.	Trend up or down Shifts Saw tooth shaped

Regular versus Standardised Residuals

Minitab offers the choice of plotting standardised or regular residuals.

Type	Use	To Calculate
Regular	Used to examine residuals on the original scale of the data.	Response – fitted value
Standardised	Used for identifying observations that do not fit well with the model. i.e. a residual with a standardised value of > 2 is tabled as an 'unusual observation'.	Residual / standard deviation of residuals

Key Learning Points

Take note of the following key points when developing prediction models with multiple linear regression.

- The independent variables (x's) included in the regression study should be those that appear to be highly correlated with the response variable (y)
- When independent variables (x's) are highly correlated with each other, results must be interpreted with caution – may produce regression coefficients that are too large or have the wrong sign
- R^2 and R^2 (adjusted) measure the amount of variation in the response (y) values explained by the linear relationship with the independent variables (x's) (R^2 always increases with additional x, R^2 (adj) increases only if additional x is significant)

ANALYSING GRAPHS *AND* NUMBERS

Anscombe Study

A statistician by the name of Anscombe[34] provides a perfect example that gives reason for going beyond the basic analysis of numbers. Anscombe provides four different sets of data as shown in the table below.

Data Set A		Data Set B		Data Set C		Data Set D	
X1	**Y1**	**X2**	**Y2**	**X3**	**Y3**	**X4**	**Y4**
10	9.14	8	6.58	10	8.04	10	7.46
14	8.10	8	5.76	14	9.96	14	8.84
5	4.74	8	7.71	5	5.58	5	5.73
8	8.14	8	8.84	8	6.95	8	6.77
9	8.77	8	8.47	9	8.81	9	7.11
12	9.13	8	7.04	12	10.84	12	8.15
4	3.10	8	5.25	4	4.26	4	5.39
7	7.26	19	12.5	7	4.82	7	6.42
11	9.26	8	5.56	11	8.33	11	7.81
13	8.74	8	7.91	13	7.58	13	12.74
6	6.13	8	6.89	6	7.24	6	6.08

Table 40: Anscombe Study Data Set

Statistical Representation

The regression analysis showed that each of these data sets produces the same results.

N	11	**R**	0.82
Mean (x)	9.0	R^2 / R-Sqr (%)	0.67 (67%)
Mean (y)	7.5	SSR (row sum of squares)	27.50
Regression Equation	$y = 3.00 + 0.500(x)$	SSE (error sum of squares)	13.75
		SST (total sum of squares)	41.2

[34] Anscombe, F.J., 1973, *"Graphs in Statistical Analysis"*, American Statistician, Vol. 27, pp. 17-21

Graphical Representation

The value of supporting any numerical analysis with a study of the graphical displays (scatter plots) is shown when we take a look at each of these data sets graphically.

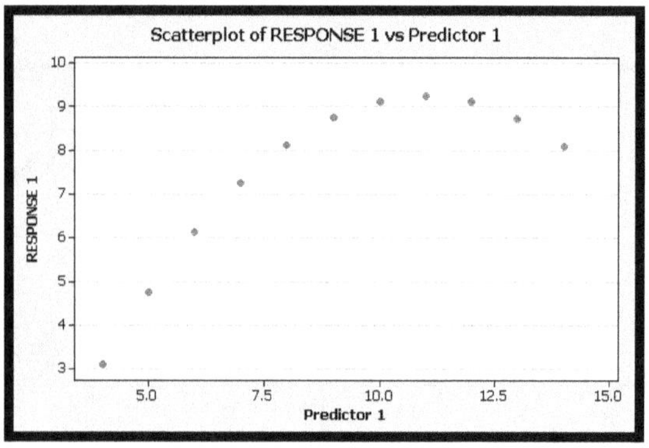

Data Set A

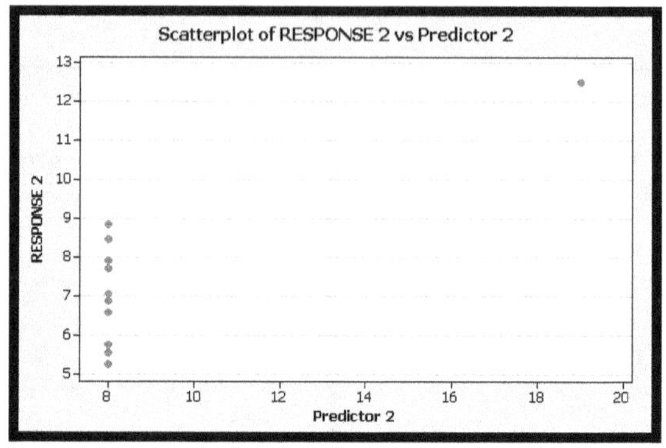

Data Set B

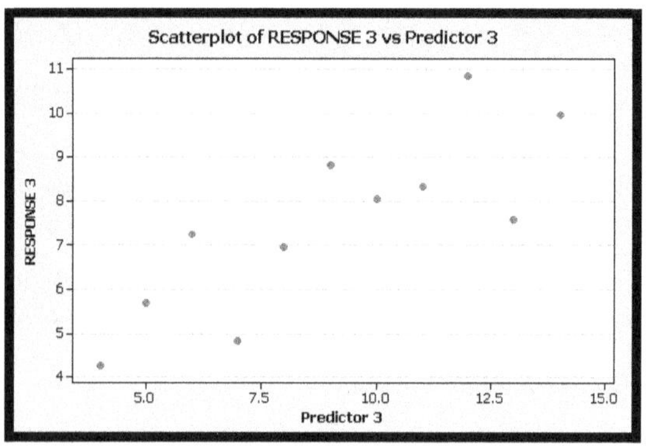

Data Set C

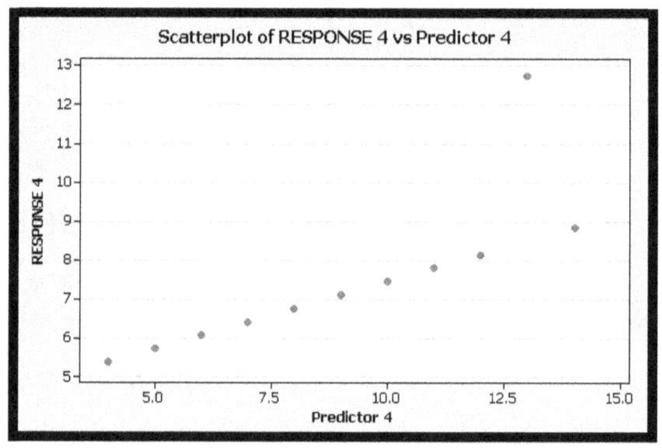

Data Set D

The four scatter plots shown represent each of the four data sets. From the scatter plots we can see how different each of these data sets is from the others.

Only one data set appears to show a linear relationship between the predictor and the response – data set C (X3 and Y3).

The key point being made here is that there is good reason to observe the relationships between variables in addition to the quantification of the relationship.

Avoiding the Pitfalls

Some of the most common pitfalls can be avoided by:

- Examining scatter plots up front so that you observe the relationships between *x*'s and *y*'s
- Checking assumptions of the regression before using the results of the regression model

LOGISTIC REGRESSION

Like the least squares method used for linear regression, logistic regression studies the relationship between predictor variables (one or more) and a response variable. The difference lies in the type of data being analysed.

Whilst linear regression studies response variables that are continuous data, logistic regression studies response variables (y's) that are categorical (attribute) data.

	Binary Logistic Regression	Ordinal Logistic Regression	Nominal Logistic Regression
Number of Response Categories	2 Categories	3 or more	3 or more
Characteristics of the Response	2 levels	Data has a natural order	Data does not have any natural order
Example Responses	Yes / No Pass / Fail Buy / Don't Buy Male / Female On / Off	Low / Medium / High Cool / Warm / Hot Unsatisfied / Moderately Satisfied / Highly Satisfied	French / Australian / Italian / British Holden / Ford / Mazda Blue / Brown / Green

Logistic Regression Analysis Approaches

General Principle

The principle of logistic regression is quite simple. The response variable (y) is categorical.

For example, the response might be whether or not a haul truck tyre achieves its targeted life cycle. The predictor variable (x) can be either categorical or variable.

For example, the predictor might be brand of tyre, rubber compound, and type of truck the tyre is fitted to. Logistic regression would produce an equation that can be used to predict the probability of a tyre reaching its targeted life cycle based on the brand, type of truck it is fitted to and the compound of the rubber.

A logistic regression model can have multiple predictor variables (x's) but only one response variable (y).

The Logit

The default equation for logistic regression used by most statistical analysis software is referred to as the 'Logit'. Whilst it may appear complex in the first instance, the logit closely resembles the equation used for linear regression.

Notice that e is raised to the power of the multiple linear regression model for the x's.

The main difference in equations is that whilst the linear regression equation models a straight-line relationship, the 'logit' can take on a wide variety of curve shapes as the estimate parameters vary.

$$P(x) = \frac{e^{\alpha+\beta_1 x_1+\beta_2 x_2+\dots\dots\dots\ \beta_n x_n}}{1+e^{\alpha+\beta_1 x_1+\beta_2 x_2+\dots\dots\dots\ \beta_n x_n}}$$

Odds Ratio

When the logit is used, logistic regression develops the ratio of the odds of some event of interest occurring against the odds of it not happening.

This is known as the 'odds ratio'.

It's appropriate to point out that odds and probability are similar but not the same. The odds of throwing a six in one roll of a dice are 6-to-1. The probability of throwing a six is 1-in-6.

Logistic regression uses the 'odds ratio' for its calculations.

Consider the following example. A Black Belt was trying to determine if the brand of haul truck tyres across the business was a contributing factor in the number of tyres not meeting their targeted life cycle of 5,000 hours minimum. A sample of 96 tyres across the entire business was taken at random to obtain the results shown in the table below.

	FAILED	MET TARGET
Brand A	22	31
Brand B	14	29

Let's take a look at the odds in this scenario:

- The odds of meeting the targeted life cycle with Brand A is 31/22 = 1.409
- The odds of meeting the targeted life cycle with Brand B is 29/14 = 2.07
- The odds ratio based on Brand B to Brand A is 2.07/1.409 = 1.469.

It seems that the odds of a tyre reaching its targeted life cycle with Brand B is 47% better than Brand A. Whilst this may appear to be significant on face value, this is only a sample from which we are going to make an inference about the population of tyres. Hence the need to use a statistical approach to determining if this difference is statistically significant.

In this case we can use logistic regression, or alternatively Chi-square analysis.

More Information

Given the significant changes in statistical software over the past 12 years, and the complexity in interpreting the outputs of a logistic regression study, more detail about the use of this tool will be provided in the 3rd edition of Process Mastery with Lean Six Sigma. (Note from George - 18 January 2023)

Key Learning Points

Take note of the following key points when using logistic regression.

- Logistic regression can be used when the response variable is categorical.
- Predictor variables can be categorical or variable data, and multiple x's can be included in the model.
- Binary Logistic Regression is used when there are 2 response categories.
- Ordinal Logistic Regression is used when there are greater than 2 response categories that have no particular order.
- Nominal Logistic Regression is used when there are greater than 2 response categories that do have a specific order.

DESIGN OF EXPERIMENTS

Many statistical analysis tools are useful for understanding and providing answers to a range of questions about:

- The performance of a process
- Cause and effect relationships between process and output variables
- Whether or not special cause variation exists within a process
- The relationship between variables from different populations

These statistical analysis and statistical process control mechanisms can be considered *passive interventions* to a process. The tools require historical data, so any actions taken are the result of signals generated by the process itself.

This could be referred to as a 'reactive' or 'lag' approach.

By contrast, the concept of experimentation with different combinations of process variables is a scientific approach for *actively intervening* for the purpose of process improvement.

We could refer to this as a 'proactive' or 'lead' approach.

Design of Experiments (DOE)

Design of Experiments is one of the key tools of the Six Sigma methodology. It is a method of exploring the cause and effect relationship between input and process variables (x's) and output variables (y's). By using DOE, a team is able to measure the effect that each of the x's has on the y variable and determine which of those are most significant in creating output variation.

There is a natural tendency for us to undertake a form of experiment called 'changing one factor at a time'. Think about a golfer for a moment. I have observed many golfers who change their grip to see if their results improve. If the results are no better, they return to the original grip and then change some other variable such as stance or ball position.

What the golfer does not understand is the effect the relationship these variables in combination with one another have on the results. For example, a changed grip with a changed ball position might produce a completely different result because of the interdependent relationship between these two factors.

DOE differs from 'one factor at a time' experimentation in that the various combinations of x's are changed so that the effect the interaction of variables has on the y variable can be understood as well. This cannot be measured when changing one factor at a time.

The History of DOE

DOE has been around for more than 70 years, having been developed by a statistician named R. A. Fisher who is also famous for his work with f distributions. Fisher's original work was for the purpose of improving agricultural experimentation at the Rothamsted experimental station in England.

His contribution to DOE was the development of several important principles. First and foremost Fisher developed an experimentation strategy whereby **multiple factors** of interest could be studied simultaneously. His strategy differed significantly from the 19th century approach (which is still practiced today in some quarters) of changing one factor at a time.

Secondly, he developed the concept of **randomisation** to help control the variation introduced by factors that cannot be seen or controlled.

Thirdly, to control the variation that could be introduced by factors that can be seen and controlled, he introduced the strategy of **blocking**.

DOE spread across Europe and the United States during the years following and was applied in the fields of agriculture, biology, medicine, pharmaceutical research, psychology and education. It wasn't until the early 1980's that an entire philosophy surrounding process improvement based on DOE principles developed by the Japanese engineer Genichi Taguchi became popular in Japan.

Even though the principles of DOE have been around for more than half a century, it wasn't until the 1990's that DOE became popular in the United States as a mechanism for process improvement.

Why Use DOE in Process Improvement Work?

DOE can help you to:

- Identify the causes of variation (x's)
- Quantify the effects that significant factors (x's) have on the response (y), as well as the interaction between x's
- Quantify the relationship between factors (x's) and the response (y) so that the equation $y = f(x_1, x_2, x_3 \ldots\ldots x_n)$ can be defined

When Would You Use DOE?

DOE can be tremendously useful under these circumstances.

- When you do not have data
- When you have data but have little faith in its validity or relevance
- You wish to validate the cause effect relationship between both categorical *and* numerical variables and a response variable
- You wish to optimise a number of response variables (y's) through adjusting a set of specific input variables (x's)

DOE is commonly used in the **analysis stage** of a Six Sigma project to validate cause effect relationships, but are also used in the **improve stage** to optimise process variables as part of the solution.

Types of Experiments

To this point I have only mentioned DOE. I should also point out that one form of Analysis of Variance (ANOVA) in most cases is actually a designed experiment.

The choice between ANOVA and the different types of DOE designs is based on various planning factors including cost and time limitations and your desired post-analysis outcomes. The most common experiments include those detailed in the following table.

Type of Design	Number of Factors	Used for Identifying ....
2 Way Analysis of Variance (2 Way ANOVA)	2	All main effects and interactions
Screening Design	> 5	Main effects
Fractional Factorial Design	3 to 10	Main effects and some interactions
Full Factorial Design	2 to 5	All main effects and interactions

Choosing an Experiment Design

My Approach To This Section

I should point out here that due to the complexity involved in experimentation, I have no intention of providing a 'how to' guide for conducting designed experiments.

My work here is intended for use in conjunction with some formal training program *and* as a post training reference on the key elements of experimentation.

With that thought in mind, we will start our conversation by looking at a simple experimentation process – Two Way ANOVA (Analysis of Variance).

TWO WAY ANALYSIS OF VARIANCE (ANOVA)

Two Way ANOVA experiments evaluate the effects of two factors (x's) on a single response variable (y) simultaneously. Two Way ANOVA uses the same approach as One Way ANOVA, in that the variance of groups of data are studied for the purpose of making a determination about the differences in the means of the groups.

The following matrices show a number of different examples for which Two Way ANOVA can be used to determine the effect of two factors on the response variable.

One factor (x) is represented across the top of the matrix with its different levels, and the second factor (x) is represented on the left side of the matrix also with its different levels.

Later, we will make reference to these as row factors and column factors.

The output result produced (y) for each of the different combinations is represented by the variable in the centre.

		Compound		
		S	M	H
Pressure (PSI)	25	TYRE LIFE (y)		
	30			
	35			

		Day or Night	
		D	N
Shift	A	THROUGHPUT (y)	
	B		
	C		

		Reagent		
		A	B	C
Ore Size (mm)	100	YIELD (y)		
	150			
	200			

		Temperature (c)			
		250	300	350	400
Time in Kiln	30	TENSILE STRENGTH (y)			
	35				
	40				
	45				

		Day of the Week						
		M	T	W	T	F	S	S
Department	A	NUMBER OF ERRORS (y)						
	B							
	C							
	D							

If we take our 'Tensile Strength' example above (lower left matrix), this might be an experiment that emerges from a project team hypothesising that variation in tensile strength (y) is caused by variation in time in the kiln (x_1) and temperature settings (x_2).

By undertaking a Two Way ANOVA experiment, the team would be able to make determinations about the differences that exist across tensile strength results for different time periods in the kiln and for different temperature settings.

Where differences exist, the team can confidently say that the factor is in fact a significant cause of variation in tensile strength.

Terms and Concepts

A number of terms must be understood before undertaking Two Way ANOVA.

Replication

Replication means to repeat all of the experiment combinations two or more times. Replication allows the experimenter to:

- Measure error: the amount of variation that occurs among runs performed under the same conditions (common cause variation)
- See clearly if a factor is or isn't significant: understanding whether or not the difference between responses is due to change in factor conditions (special cause) or due to common cause variation

By undertaking replication, residuals (referred to as error) are produced and can be analysed to validate the model.

Lurking Variable

A lurking variable is an uncontrolled or uncontrollable variable that has an important effect on the relationship among variables in an experiment or study. It is not included among the variables studied.

We might consider weather conditions, ambient temperature, staff skill level and quality of materials in some experiments.

Lurking variables in Two Way ANOVA are managed through randomising the collection of data from different combinations of variables.

Randomisation

The process of assigning the order in which different combinations will be conducted using a random method of selection. Where avoidable, it should not be a conveniently chosen order.

The purpose of randomisation is:

- To average the effect of 'lurking' variables across all factors in the experiment
- To minimise the chance of the effect of a 'lurking' variable being attributed wrongfully to another factor

Residuals

These are measures of error in a model. A prediction equation estimates the output of a process at various levels within the operating range of factors (inference space).

These values are referred to as *fits*. A residual is the difference between the actual response (y) and a fitted value (what we would expect it to be - the average of all replicates for a particular combination of factor settings).

Conducting Experiments with Two Way ANOVA

Designed experiments using Two Way ANOVA are normally conducted in these six simple steps.

1. STEP 1 – Determine the following:
    a. Response (y)
    b. Factors to be included in the experiment (x's)
    c. The levels within each factor (these are the settings that you will control)

2. STEP 2 – Design the experiment. (Your design will depend on (a) how many factor levels you are studying, (b) how much time and money you are prepared to spend on the study, and (c) how much information you want to get from the study.) You will need to complete the following.
    a. Determine the number of replicates for each combination
    b. Create the template for capturing data that suits the way your statistical software
    c. Randomise the sequence (if possible)
3. STEP 3 – Run the experiment and capture data.
    a. Run the experiment in the randomised order you planned
    b. Insert data directly into the worksheet
4. STEP 4 – Analyse the experiment.
    a. Main effects
    b. Interaction effects
5. STEP 5 – Summarise conclusions drawn from the analysis.
    a. Identify significant effects
6. STEP 6 - Confirm validity of the model
    a. Study diagnostic plots (residuals versus fits, residuals versus order, probability plot of residuals)

To help explain the process we are going to refer to a worked example.

Two Way ANOVA

A Six Sigma project team working on eliminating defects associated with the **tensile strength** of a component developed an hypothesis that the most significant causes of variation were the **treatment temperature** and the **material type** used to make the component.

An experiment was designed to study the effects of these *two factors* on the tensile strength of the metal component.

In running the experiment *without replication*, only one item was sampled from each combination of treatment temperature and material type with the tensile strength measured and recorded.

In this case, 'Two Way Analysis of Variance' test is used to answer two questions:

- Q1: 'Are the means for tensile strength for each level of treatment temperature the same or different?', and
- Q2: 'Are the means for tensile strength for each level of material type the same or different?'

Similar to One Way ANOVA, this experiment is really a hypothesis test.

Application	Assumptions	Hypothesis (H_O and H_A)
Compares the means of two or more independent populations (levels in each *x*) within two totally independent factors (*x*'s).	Independent samples - Independence of Error (residuals) Normal Distribution - Normality of Error (residuals) Equal Variances - Constant Error Variance (residuals)	**H_O:** Row μ's are equal / Column μ's are equal **H_A:** Row μ's are not equal / Column μ's are not equal

Understanding Experiment Variation

Because variation is used to analyse the difference in means, Two Way ANOVA involves the partitioning of total variation in the experiment.

Total variation among all observations around the grand mean is represented by the sum of squares total (SST). Total variation in the experiment (SST) comprises row factor variation (SSR), column factor variation (SSC), and random variation (SSE).

Total variation (SST) is computed with the following equation.

$$SST = \sum_{i=1}^{r} \sum_{j=1}^{c} \sum_{k=1}^{n} \left(x_{ijk} - \bar{\bar{x}}\right)^2$$

Where:

x double bar = the overall or grand mean

r = the number of levels of the row factor

c = the number of levels of the column factor

n' = the number of values (replications) for each cell

n = the total number of observations in the experiment (where n = rcn')

x_{ijk} = the value of the kth observation for level i of the row factor and level j of the column factor

The way variation is studied might be easier to understand if we refer to the matrix below in my explanation[35].

		Temperature (c)			
		250	300	350	400
Material Type	A	TENSILE STRENGTH (y)			
	B				
	C				
	D				

The difference between the various levels of the row factor (in this case material type) and the grand mean is represented by the *sum of squares for the row factor* (SSR).

The difference between the various levels of the column factor (in this case temperature setting) and the grand mean is represented by the *sum of squares for the column factor* (SSC).

The *sum of squares error* (SSE) represents the differences between the observations within each cell and the corresponding cell mean.

35 While reference is made of a matrix, this is not how you lay your worksheet out for statistical analysis. Examples of how to lay out data are shown on following pages.

The diagram to the right visually depicts the partitioning of total variation for Two Way ANOVA *without* Replicates.

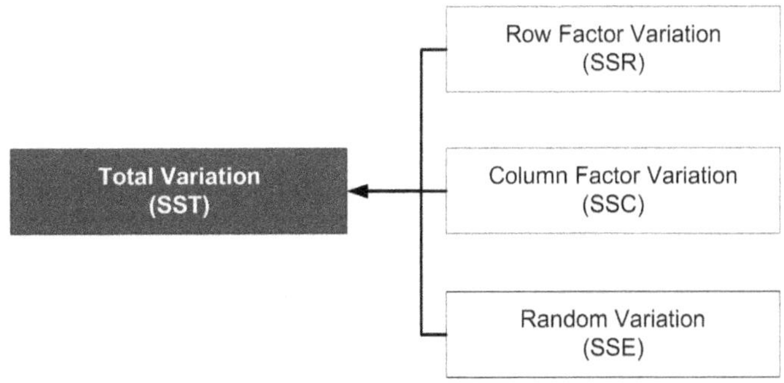

Figure 239: Partitioning Total Variation - Two Way ANOVA (Without Replicates)

Here's the good news - with the advent of statistical analysis software, these computations do not need to be done manually.

Analysis of Variance Table (Without Replicates)

When undertaking Two-Way ANOVA studies with both SigmaXL and Minitab, an analysis of variance table in the following format is generated.

Source	DF	SS	MS	F	P
(Row Factor)	r-1	SSR	MSR = SSR / (r-1)	F_R = MSR / MSE	P_R
(Column Factor)	c-1	SSC	MSC = SSC / (c-1)	F_C = MSC / MSE	P_C
Error	rc(n'-1)	SSE	MSE = SSE / rc(n'-1)		
Total	n-1	SST			

Where:
DF = Degrees of freedom
SS = Sum of Squares
MS = Mean Sum of Squares
F = F statistic
P = P-value of the F statistic

The mean sum of squares for each of the sources of variation (MSR, MSC, MSE) is obtained by dividing the sum of squares by its associated degrees of freedom.

To test the null hypothesis that there is no difference due to the row factor (HO: row μ's are equal), we calculate the F statistic with the equation:

$$F_R = \frac{MSR}{MSE}$$

To test the null hypothesis that there is no difference due to the column factor (HO: column μ's are equal), we calculate the F statistic with the equation:

$$F_C = \frac{MSC}{MSW}$$

Where the P-value associated with these F statistics is less than the significance level α, the null hypothesis is rejected.

Two-Way ANOVA (without Replication) using Minitab

The Two-Way ANOVA function is activated by clicking on Stat > ANOVA > Balanced ANOVA.

Minitab automatically identifies whether or not replication of runs occurs, hence no reference to replication in the dialogue box.

Data is best tabled in the format shown.

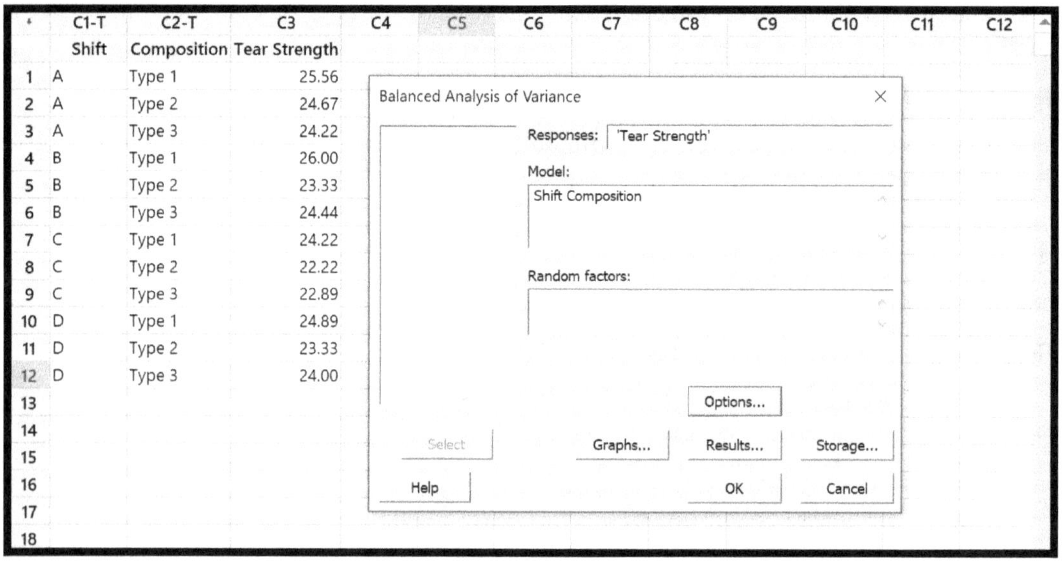

Figure 240: Dialogue Box for Two Way ANOVA - Minitab

The output of this work is an analysis of variance table like the one shown.

P-value – The P-value is used to make a decision as to whether or not any observed difference is statistically significant. When the P-value is less than α (usually 0.05), the difference is statistically significant.

In this case the P-values for shift and composition are < 0.05, hence our conclusion is we reject the null hypothesis, and conclude at the 0.05 significance level that shift and composition are significant factors in creating variation in tear strength.

Factor Information

Factor	Type	Levels	Values
Shift	Fixed	4	A, B, C, D
Composition	Fixed	3	Type 1, Type 2, Type 3

Analysis of Variance for Tear Strength

Source	DF	SS	MS	F	P
Shift	3	5.169	1.7229	9.59	0.010
Composition	2	6.724	3.3622	18.71	0.003
Error	6	1.078	0.1797		
Total	11	12.972			

Model Summary

S	R-sq	R-sq(adj)
0.423918	91.69%	84.76%

Figure 241: Analysis of Variance Table – Minitab

The Absence of Replication

Analysis of variance without replicates is limited in that the experiment will not tell the user anything about the interaction of factors.

For example, in this case, the user cannot determine if the combinations of different types of materials and temperatures has an interaction effect on the tensile strength of the final product. This can only be determined if the experiment is replicated.

Two-Way ANOVA (With Replicates)

Replication simply means that each combination of levels for each factor is run more than once. When an experiment is replicated, additional variation is introduced into the model that allows the user to understand the level of interaction between the two factors.

The diagram visually depicts the partitioning of total variation for Two Way ANOVA with Replication.

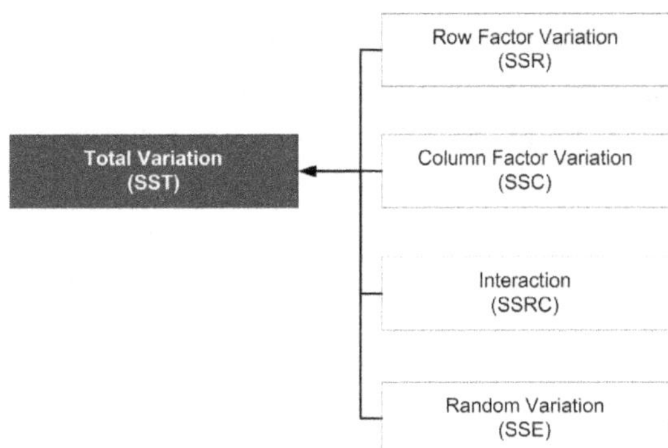

Figure 242: Partitioning Total Variation - Two Way ANOVA (With Replicates)

Understanding Interaction Effects

To analyse replicated experiments, you must understand the concept of 'interaction effects'.

If no interaction effect was present, the difference in the response variable between the levels of the row factor, would be the same for each level of the column factor.

The concept of interaction can be graphically illustrated by plotting the average result for each level of each factor.

<u>No Interaction Effect</u>

In the example provided, the amount of dirt removed from clothes when washed in varying water temperatures (hot and cold), with two different brands of detergent was assessed in a designed experiment.

We can see that the difference in dirt removed by Brand A from cold water to hot water, is similar to the difference in dirt removed from Brand B across the range of water temperatures.

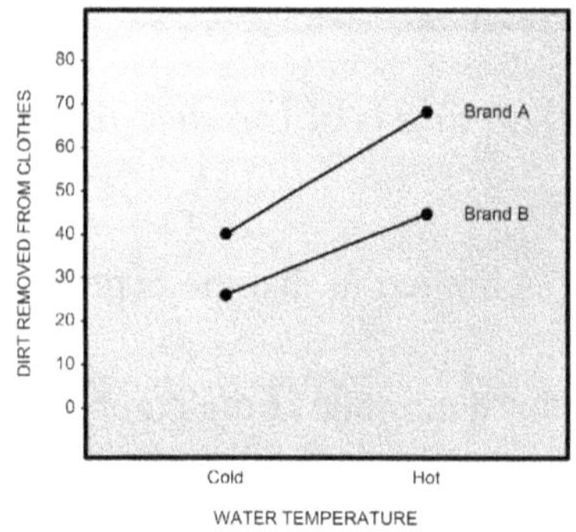

In this case, no interaction effect is present, indicated by the almost parallel lines. Regardless of the brand used, most dirt will be removed in hot water.

<u>Interaction Effect Present</u>

Unlike the previous example, the lines intersect indicating the presence of a strong interaction effect.

Any difference that exists between the two brands, changes as water temperature changes.

The example indicates that Brand A is better in cold water and Brand B is better in hot water. This means that if the brand was changed, then the water temperature would also have to be changed to maximise the amount of dirt removed.

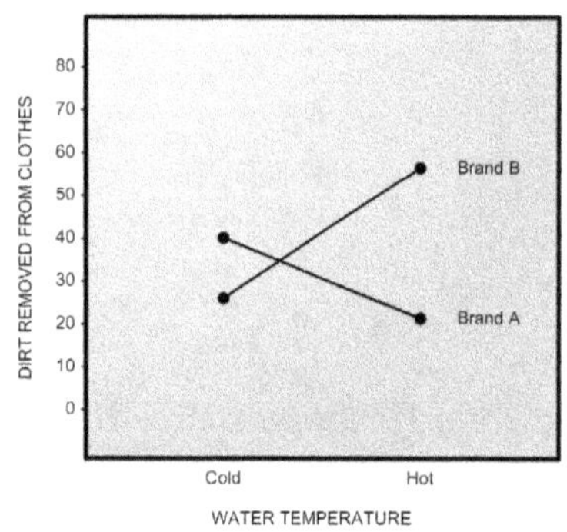

This knowledge is of particular importance when determining optimal settings at the **solution stage** of a project. In determining the best combination of variables to produce a desired response, an understanding of the impact each individual independent variable has on the response is not enough.

It is necessary to understand the interaction between variables so that when one variable setting is changed, the appropriate changes are made to interacting variables so that the desired response is achieved.

This concept has application in both Two Way ANOVA and Design of Experiments.

Analysis of Variance Table (With Replication)

The analysis of variance table will display an additional F statistic to allow the user to determine the significance of the interaction of the two factors.

Source	DF	SS	MS	F	P
(Row Factor)	r-1	SSR	MSR = SSR / (r-1)	F_R = MSR / MSE	P_R
(Column Factor)	c-1	SSC	MSC = SSC / (c-1)	F_C = MSC / MSE	P_C
Interaction	(r-1) (c-1)	SSRC	MSRC = SSRC / (r-1) (c-1)	F_{RC} = MSRC / MSE	P_{RC}
Error	rc(n'-1)	SSE	MSE = SSE / rc(n'-1)		
Total	n-1	SST			

Where:
DF = Degrees of freedom
SS = Sum of Squares
MS = Mean Sum of Squares
F = F statistic
P = P-value of the F statistic

The mean sum of squares for the interaction (MSRC) is obtained by dividing the sum of squares (SSRC) by its associated degrees of freedom.

Two-Way ANOVA (With Replication) using SigmaXL

The Two-Way ANOVA is activated by clicking on Statistical Tools > Two-Way ANOVA.

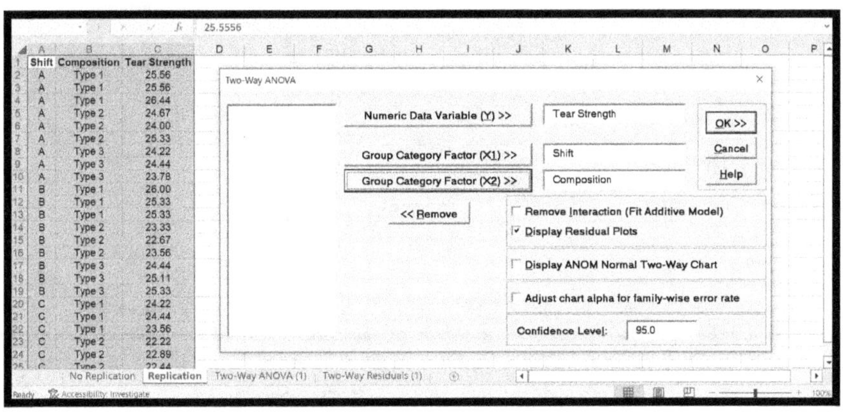

Figure 243: Dialogue Box for Two Way ANOVA (With Replicates) - SigmaXL

The output of this work is an analysis of variance table.

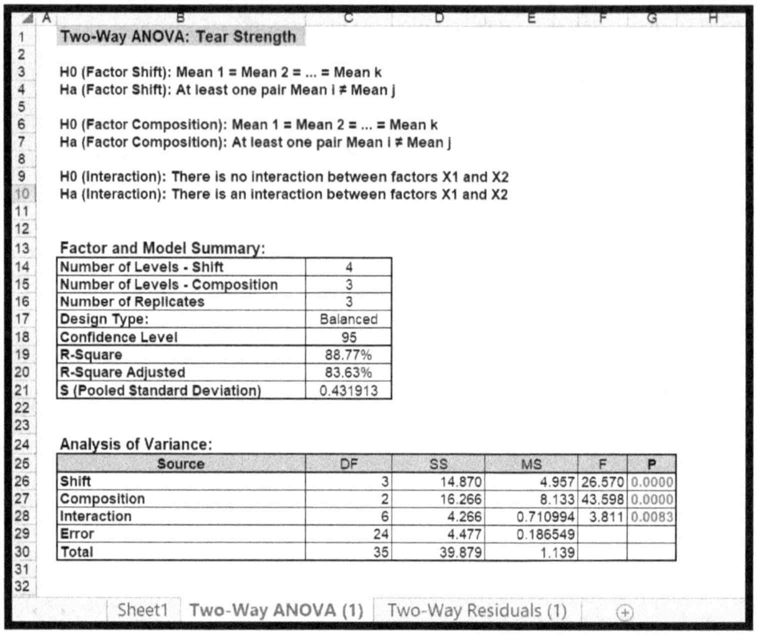

Two-Way ANOVA: Tear Strength

H0 (Factor Shift): Mean 1 = Mean 2 = ... = Mean k
Ha (Factor Shift): At least one pair Mean i ≠ Mean j

H0 (Factor Composition): Mean 1 = Mean 2 = ... = Mean k
Ha (Factor Composition): At least one pair Mean i ≠ Mean j

H0 (Interaction): There is no interaction between factors X1 and X2
Ha (Interaction): There is an interaction between factors X1 and X2

Factor and Model Summary:

Number of Levels - Shift	4
Number of Levels - Composition	3
Number of Replicates	3
Design Type:	Balanced
Confidence Level	95
R-Square	88.77%
R-Square Adjusted	83.63%
S (Pooled Standard Deviation)	0.431913

Analysis of Variance:

Source	DF	SS	MS	F	P
Shift	3	14.870	4.957	26.570	0.0000
Composition	2	16.266	8.133	43.598	0.0000
Interaction	6	4.266	0.710994	3.811	0.0083
Error	24	4.477	0.186549		
Total	35	39.879	1.139		

Sheet1 | Two-Way ANOVA (1) | Two-Way Residuals (1)

Figure 244: Analysis of Variance Table - SigmaXL

P-value – The P-value is used to make a decision as to whether or not any observed differences in levels for each factor is statistically significant. When the P-value is less than α (usually 0.05), the difference is statistically significant. In this case:

- P-values for both Temperature and Material is < 0.05, so we would reject null hypotheses at the 0.05 significance level and conclude (a) there is a difference in the tensile strength of components for different treatment temperatures and different material types.
- P-value for the interaction of variables is < 0.05, so we conclude that an interaction effect is present. This is supported by the crossing of lines shown in the generated interaction plots.

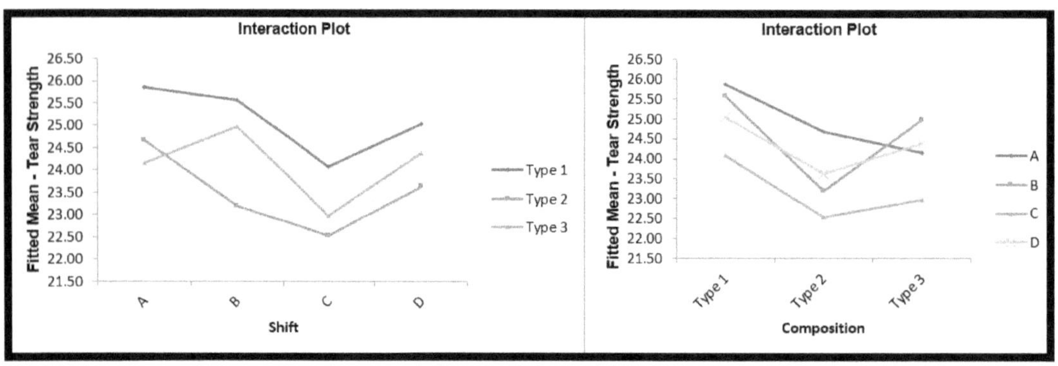

Figure 245: Interaction Plots - SigmaXL

Two-Way ANOVA (With Replicates) using Minitab

The Two-Way ANOVA function is activated by clicking on Stat > ANOVA > Balanced ANOVA. Minitab automatically identifies replication of runs, hence no reference to replication in the dialogue box.

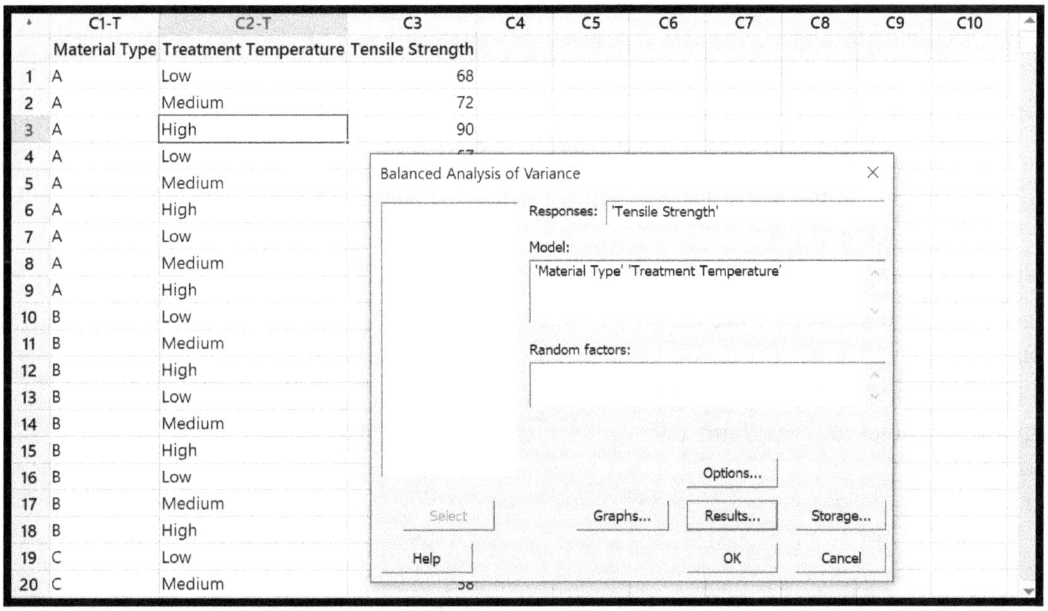

Figure 246: Dialogue Box for Two Way ANOVA (With Replicates) - Minitab

The output of this work is an analysis of variance table.

Factor Information

Factor	Type	Levels	Values
Material Type	Fixed	4	A, B, C, D
Treatment Temperature	Fixed	3	High, Low, Medium

Analysis of Variance for Tensile Strength

Source	DF	SS	MS	F	P
Material Type	3	2753.0	917.66	89.84	0.000
Treatment Temperature	2	4994.9	2497.44	244.49	0.000
Error	30	306.4	10.21		
Total	35	8054.3			

Model Summary

S	R-sq	R-sq(adj)
3.19606	96.20%	95.56%

Figure 247: Analysis of Variance Table – Minitab

P-value – The P-value is used to make a decision as to whether or not any observed difference is statistically significant.

When the P-value is less than α (usually 0.05), the difference is statistically significant.

In this case the P-values for both predictor variables (material 0.000 and temperature 0.047) are less than our chosen α of 0.05, so our conclusion is to reject the null hypothesis at the 0.05 significance level and conclude that there is a difference in the tensile strength of components for different material types and different treatment temperatures.

Interaction plots will display any interaction between the two factors in the analysis. We can generate these by clicking on:

Stat > ANOVA > Interaction Plot

We can see from these plots there are no interactions present.

For more information on interpretation, refer to earlier explanation notes and diagrams on 'interactions'.

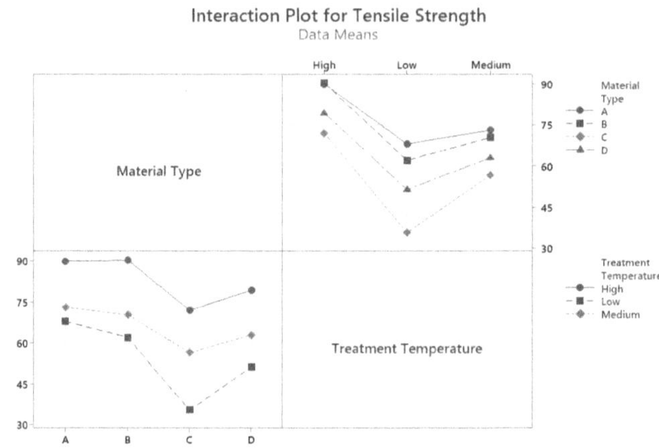

Figure 248: Interaction Plot - Minitab

Main Effects Plots can also be generated to display the results for the various settings of the two factors. These are access by clicking on Stat > ANOVA > Main Effects Plot.

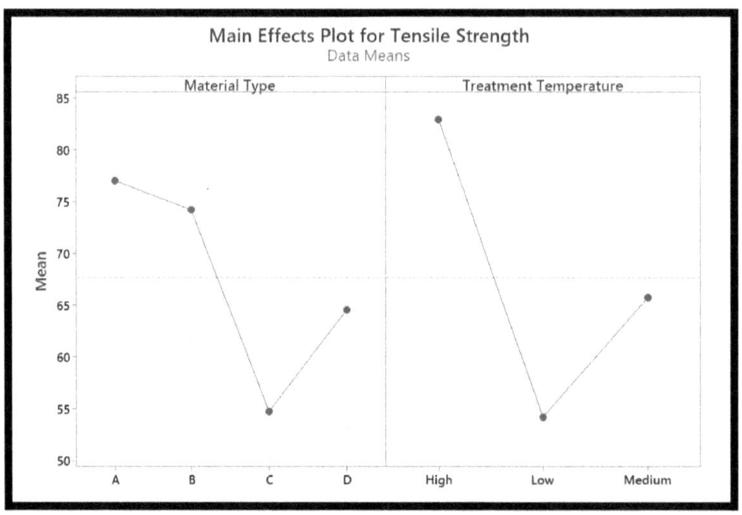

Figure 249:Main Effects Plot - Minitab

Assumptions of Two Way ANOVA

To know whether or not the Two Way ANOVA is able to produce valid results, it is necessary to determine whether or not certain assumptions have been met. The three major assumptions of the experiment are these.

- Sample Data for each factor is normally distributed - Normality of Error (residuals)
- Variances are Equal (or Homogeneity of Variance) - Constant Error Variance (residuals)
- Independent Samples - Independence of Error (residuals)

Normally Distributed Data (Normality of Error) – Provided distributions are not extremely different from the normal distribution, the level of significance of the F-test is usually not greatly affected, particularly when the sample sizes are large through multiple replications.

When the departure from normality is significant, a transformation can be applied (not discussed here) or alternative approaches should be considered.

Variances are Equal (Constant Error Variance) – Variation around the fitted values for each level must be constant. This is necessary in order to pool the variances for each group into a single 'within-group' source of variation.

Plotting residuals against fitted values assesses this assumption. When variance is constant, no patterns emerge along the range of fitted values.

Independent Samples (Independence of Error) – Error (residuals) should be independent for each value of x. When this is the case, samples are independent of one another.

Plotting residuals against the order or sequence in which the observed data were collected can assess the independence of error.

Assumptions associated with **Normality of Error**, **Error Variance**, and **Independence of Error** are all tested through the analysis of residual plots shown on following pages.

The 'Four in One' residual plots generated in Minitab can be used for assessing the validity of the model.

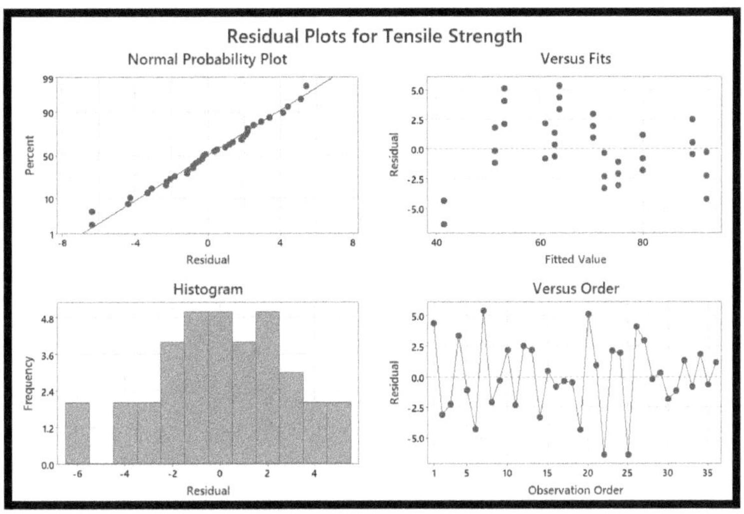

Figure 250: Two Way ANOVA 'Four in One' Residual Plots – Minitab

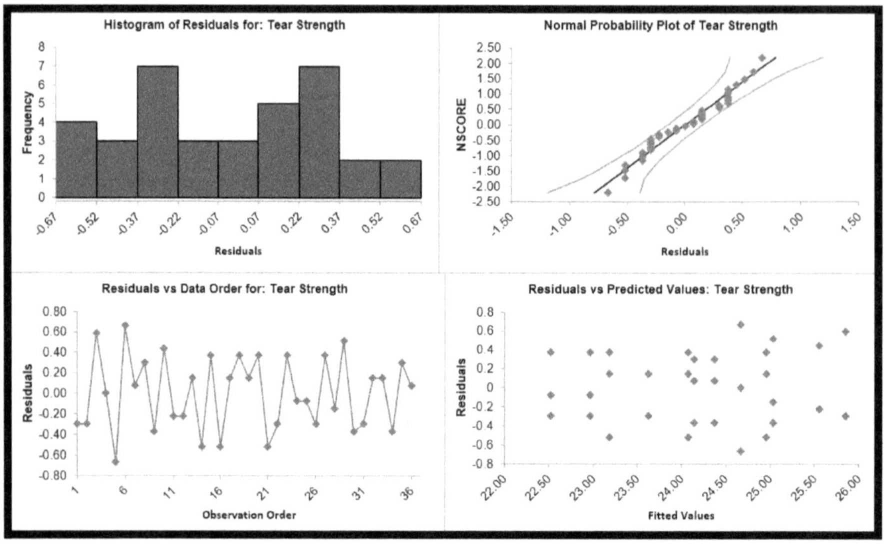

Figure 251: Two Way ANOVA Residual Plots – SigmaXL

DESIGN OF EXPERIMENTS (DOE)

The factorial approach to designed experiments can be simply explained in the following way:

- Allows us to change several factors simultaneously as opposed to 'one factor at a time'
- May test all combinations of factor conditions (full factorial), or alternatively a carefully selected fraction of the full set (fractional factorial)

The advantages of using factorial designs include:

- Uses common cause variation to determine which of the factors are important
- Relatively simple to analyse
- Makes use of various methods (randomisation and blocking) to address factors that are not controlled in the experiment so that conclusions remain valid

DOE Terms and Concepts

A number of terms must be understood before undertaking factorial designs.

Replication

To repeat all the experiment conditions two or more times. This allows the tester to:

- Measure error: the amount of variation that occurs among runs performed under the same conditions (common cause variation)
- See clearly if a factor is or isn't significant: understanding whether or not the difference between responses is due to change in factor conditions (special cause) or due to common cause variation

By undertaking replication, residuals (also referred to as error) are produced and can be analysed to validate the model.

Lurking Variable

This is an uncontrolled or uncontrollable variable that has an important effect on the relationship among variables in an experiment or study. It is not included among the variables studied.

The following might be considered lurking variables in an experiment – weather conditions, ambient temperature, staff skill level and quality of materials.

Lurking variables are managed through the use of randomisation and blocking.

Randomisation

The process of assigning the order in which runs will be conducted using a random method of selection. It is not the standard order, nor a conveniently chosen order. The purpose of randomisation is to:

- Average the effect of 'lurking' variables across all factors in the experiment
- Minimise the chance of the effect of a 'lurking' variable being attributed wrongfully to another factor

Blocking

It is not always possible to conduct all runs under identical experimental conditions. Using a blocked design can eliminate the effect of factors that can be a nuisance to the experiment.

For example, an experiment requires the collection of data in two different plants that have differences in temperature, humidity and employees doing the work. Variation may be introduced by virtue of the differences between the two plants and not the factors being tested in the experiment.

Observations to be collected in each of these different plants can be blocked so that the two blocks (one block of runs from one plant, and another block of runs from the second plant) can be compared to each other to see if there is a statistically significant difference between the two.

Blocking is the process of separating experimental runs according to some known factor outside the experimental design.

Aliasing or Confounding

This only occurs in 'fractional design' and is best described as confusion which occurs when we are not sure if the effect observed is due to a **single factor** or **interaction of factors** which mathematically produce the same result.

Some software packages such as Minitab display an 'alias' table to specify the confounding patterns that exists within a specific design. Because some effects are confounded, care should be taken in choosing any fractional design in order that you achieve meaningful results.

More information is provided later on this topic.

Resolution

Resolution refers to the degree and structure of aliasing (confounding) that will occur in an experimental design. Resolution values are shown as roman numerals.

Resolution	Confounding
III	• Main effects are confounded with two factor and higher interactions
IV	• Main effects are confounded with three factor and higher interactions • Two factor interactions are confounded with other two factor and higher interactions
V	• Main effects are confounded with four factor and higher interactions • Two factor interactions are confounded with three factor and higher interactions

Resolution and Associated Confounding

Resolution III designs have the most confounding. Resolution III and IV are commonly used designs in screening to determine which factors should be analysed in a full factorial design. A full factorial design has no confounding and is referred to as a 'Full Resolution' design.

Residuals

These are simple measures of error in a model. A prediction equation estimates the output of a process at various levels within the operating range of factors (inference space).

These values are referred to as *fits*. A residual is the difference between the actual response (y) and a fitted value (what we would expect it to be - the average of all replicates for a particular combination of factor settings).

Inference Space

This is the operating range of factors in the experiment. Predictions for factor settings outside the inference space (the range between minimum and maximum values) should not be made as this is outside the region that was analysed in the design – extrapolation.

A Balanced Design

This is one with an equal number of runs at each combination of the high and low settings for each factor.

Orthogonality

An orthogonal design is one where:

- The sum of the coded values for each factor column is equal to zero; and
- The correlation between factor columns is equal to zero.

When a design is orthogonal:

- Terms in the regression model are estimated independently; and
- Effects are independent of each other and any insignificant terms can be removed simultaneously to create a 'reduced model' without any adverse effects.

Assumptions of a Designed Experiment

The validity of any designed experiment is determined by a study of residuals. The assumptions associated with an experiment are:

- **Normality of Error** – residuals are normally distributed around the mean
- **Constant Error Variance** – variance is constant for all fitted values
- **Independence of Error** – residuals are independent for each value of *x*

Conducting the Designed Experiment

Designed experiments (DOE) using statistical analysis software, such as SigmaXL and Minitab can be conducted by following these steps.

1. STEP 1 Determine the following.
    a. Response (y)
    b. Factors to be included in the experiment (x's)
    c. Low level settings
    d. High level settings
    e. Center points
    f. Blocks
2. STEP 2 Design the experiment. Your design will depend on (a) how many factor levels you are studying, (b) how much time and money you are prepared to spend on the study, and (c) how much information you want to get from the study. You will need to complete the following.
    a. Select the design – (a) Full factorial - Full resolution, (b) Fractional factorial - Resolution IV and V, (c) Screening design - Resolution III
    b. Determine the number of replicates for each combination
    c. Generate the template for capturing data that suits the way your statistical software package inputs for analysis (these will be generated automatically in each software package)
3. STEP 3 Run the experiment and capture data.
    a. Run the experiment in the randomised order shown on the worksheet (if it is a software designed experiment)
    b. Insert data directly into the worksheet
4. STEP 4 Analyse the experiment.

   a. Session window output (effects, aliasing)
   b. Effects plots
   c. Factorial plots (main effects, interaction effects, cube plots)

5. STEP 5 Sequentially reduce the model until all insignificant interaction terms have been removed and the final model is produced.
6. STEP 6 Summarise conclusions drawn from the analysis.
   a. Identify significant effects
7. STEP 7 Confirm validity of the model.
   a. Study diagnostic plots (residuals versus fits, residuals versus order, probability plot of residuals)

Cost and Time Versus Information

The chart below visually shows the different designs and their respective positioning against cost / time versus information provided.

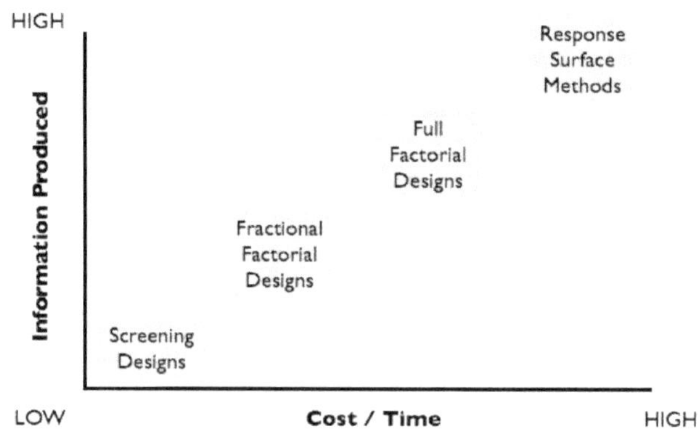

Figure 252: Experiment Cost and Time versus Experiment Information

Note: Response surface methods are not discussed in this text.

Full Factorial Design (DOE)

A full factorial is the most desirable design to run to allow a team to gather information on all main effects and two way and higher interactions. A full factorial is an experiment where all possible combinations of factors and levels are tested.

Choosing Factors and Levels

Thinking about where we are along the DMAIC sequence, factors chosen usually represent those we believe have the most significant effect on the response we are testing.

These factors would have been identified during our cause effect analysis work and we are simply going to use DOE to help validate the cause effect relationships that have been hypothesised.

During the design phase of an experiment, the team must choose the settings for each factor, commonly referred to as levels. These levels may be determined by:

- **Process Knowledge** – people who work with the process will have a good understanding of what might be the most appropriate settings.

- **Benchmarking** – finding out what settings are used elsewhere.
- **Manufacturer's Specifications** – limits may be described in manufacturer's documentation. Any settings outside these limits may well disqualify claims for warranty.

The choice of levels will be influenced by:

- **Cost** – cost may prohibit the setting of levels at some extremes.
- **Risk** – some extreme settings may pose risk to the safety of people and equipment.

The Experiment

Prior to running any experiment, a data collection sheet must be created. While software will actually do this work for you, it is worth you understanding how they are created and how high and low settings are coded for mathematical analysis.

The simplest way to create the sheet is using the 'Standard Order'. In the example below coding has been used to indicate levels for each factor. Coding is the representation of factor settings in a standardised format (1 for high settings and –1 for low settings).

To design the collection sheet, start by indicating all possible run combinations for the first factor.

For each factor this will be a combination of two runs indicated by the coded terms –1 and 1.

Factor A	Factor B
-1	-1
1	-1
-1	1
1	1

Factor	Level	
	Low	High
Factor A	-1	1
Factor B	-1	1

Adding another factor into the design simply requires that the design is doubled, and the next factors levels are alternated in pairs as shown in the two-factor diagram above.

Adding a third factor requires that the previous design is duplicated (in other words the row number doubles).

Then the next factor levels are alternated in groups of four as shown in the three-factor diagram shown …

(Factor A, Factor B and Factor C in the lower right table).

Factor A	Factor B
-1	-1
1	-1
-1	1
1	1

Factor	Level	
	Low	High
Factor A	-1	1
Factor B	-1	1
Factor C	-1	1

Adding another factor duplicates the design

Factor A	Factor B	Factor C
-1	-1	-1
1	-1	-1
-1	1	-1
1	1	-1
-1	-1	1
1	-1	1
-1	1	1
1	1	1

Fortunately with the advent of statistical analysis software such as SigmaXL and Minitab designing experiments is made very easy.

Creating the Design With Minitab

The 'Create Factorial Design' function is activated by clicking on Stat > DOE > Factorial > Create Factorial Design.

You then choose your design and insert details associated with centre points, blocks, replicates and factor settings.

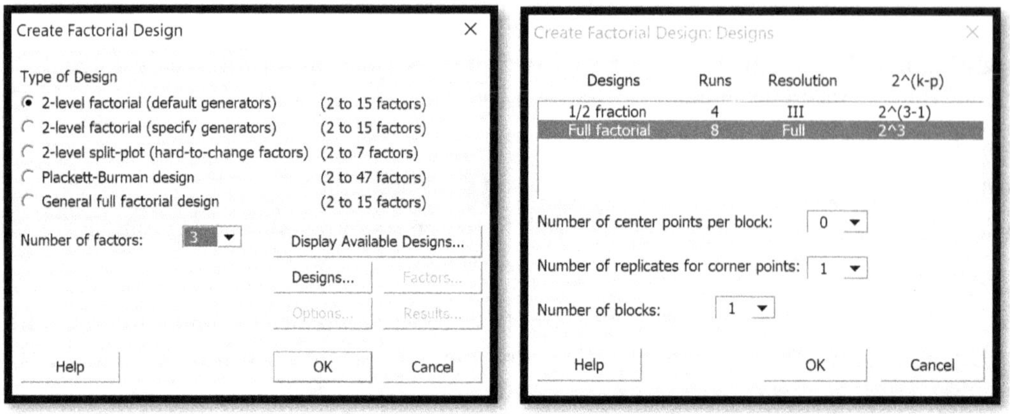

Figure 253A: Dialogue Boxes for Creating a Factorial Design in Minitab

The end result is a worksheet containing all of the key elements for running and analysing your DOE.

↓	C1	C2	C3	C4	C5	C6	C7	C8
	StdOrder	RunOrder	CenterPt	Blocks	Factor A	Factor B	Factor C	
1	8	1	1	1	1	1	1	
2	6	2	1	1	1	-1	1	
3	1	3	1	1	-1	-1	-1	
4	4	4	1	1	1	1	-1	
5	2	5	1	1	1	-1	-1	
6	3	6	1	1	-1	1	-1	
7	5	7	1	1	-1	-1	1	
8	7	8	1	1	-1	1	1	
9								

Figure 253B: DOE Worksheet Generated by Minitab

<u>Creating the Design With SigmaXL</u>

The DOE design function is activated by clicking on:

Design of Experiments > 2 Level Factorial / Screening > 2 Level Factorial / Screening Designs

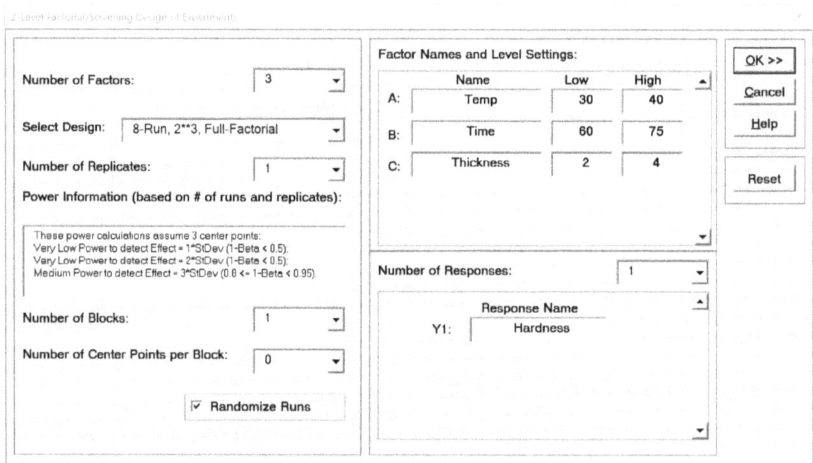

Figure 254A: Creating a Factorial Design in SigmaXL

Once you click OK, a worksheet containing all of the key elements for running and analysing your DOE is generated.

Title:	
Date:	
Name of Experimenter:	
Notes:	

Design Type:	3 Factor, 8-Run, 2**3, Full-Factorial
Number of Replicates:	1
Number of Blocks:	1
Number of Center Points per Block:	0
Number of Responses:	1

Run Order	Std. Order	Center Points	Blocks	A: Temp	B: Time	C: Thickness	Hardness
1	4	1	1	40	75	2	
2	2	1	1	40	60	2	
3	6	1	1	40	60	4	
4	5	1	1	30	60	4	
5	8	1	1	40	75	4	
6	1	1	1	30	60	2	
7	7	1	1	30	75	4	
8	3	1	1	30	75	2	

Do not add or delete rows or sort this worksheet.

Aliasing of Effects:
None (Full Factorial Design)

Figure 254B: The DOE Worksheet Generated by SigmaXL

Understanding Effects

Two types of effects can be observed when analysing an experiment – (a) main effects, and (b) interaction effects. Let's look at the terminology a little more.

Effects – The 'effect' for each factor and interaction, is the average change in response when the factor or interaction moves from a Low level (coded as -1) to a High level (coded as +1).

That value is calculated using the following equation.

Effect = (the avg. response values at the high level) – (the avg. response values at the low level)

Main Effects – While most factors will have some effect on the response variable, a main effect occurs when the average effect of a factor on the response is considered to be statistically *significant*.

Interaction Effects – To explain the idea of an interaction effect, let me describe an example.

A clinic supporting patients in the reduction of cholesterol offers a choice of two diets as well as an exercise program. It was found over time that both diets were equally effective in reducing cholesterol for patients that did not exercise.

It was also found that the exercise program on its own was effective in reducing cholesterol. Patients who followed diet 1 as well as the exercise program experienced the benefits of both (the effect of the diet plus the effect of the exercise).

However, patients who followed diet 2 and exercised as well received a bonus. They experienced the effect of the diet plus the effect of the exercise plus an interaction effect because diet 1 and exercise in combination produced much better results than they did in the absence of the other.

In the absence of any interaction, the difference in the response for both levels of one factor would be the same as the difference in the response for both levels of another factor.

When an interaction exists, the difference in response for each level is not the same for each factor.

(**NOTE:** For more information, refer to notes in the Two Way ANOVA section in this chapter.)

2nd Order or Higher Interaction – A 2nd order or higher interaction occurs when the interaction effect of 2 factors or higher on the response is considered to be significant. A 3rd order interaction is a significant interaction effect of 3 factors.

Analysing the Experiment in Minitab

The DOE analysis function is activated by clicking on Stat > DOE > Factorial > Analyse Factorial Design.

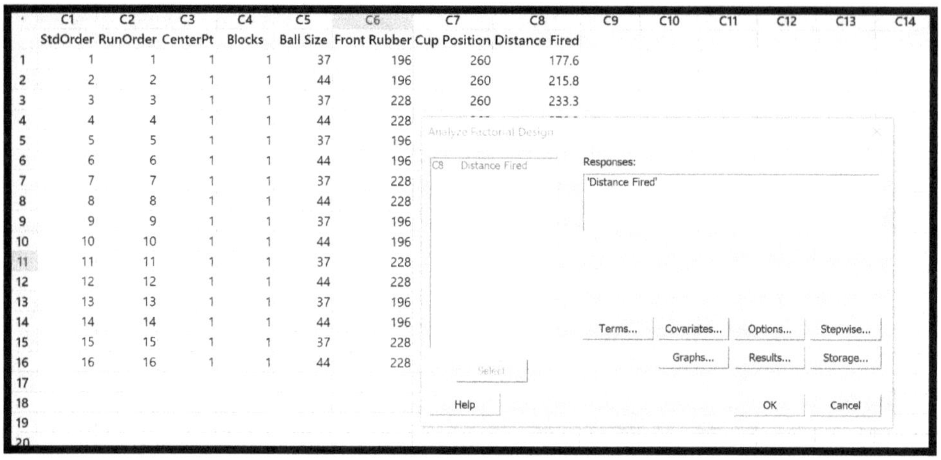

	C1 StdOrder	C2 RunOrder	C3 CenterPt	C4 Blocks	C5 Ball Size	C6 Front Rubber	C7 Cup Position	C8 Distance Fired
1	1	1	1	1	37	196	260	177.6
2	2	2	1	1	44	196	260	215.8
3	3	3	1	1	37	228	260	233.3
4	4	4	1	1	44	228		
5	5	5	1	1	37	196		
6	6	6	1	1	44	196		
7	7	7	1	1	37	228		
8	8	8	1	1	44	228		
9	9	9	1	1	37	196		
10	10	10	1	1	44	196		
11	11	11	1	1	37	228		
12	12	12	1	1	44	228		
13	13	13	1	1	37	196		
14	14	14	1	1	44	196		
15	15	15	1	1	37	228		
16	16	16	1	1	44	228		

Figure 255: Analysing Factorial Designs in Minitab

Interpreting Results with Minitab

Minitab produces a multiple regression table and analysis of variance table in the session window. Let's discuss the multiple regression table first.

Coded Coefficients

Term	Effect	Coef	SE Coef	T-Value	P-Value	VIF
Constant		270.37	2.27	118.88	0.000	
Ball Size	28.89	14.44	2.27	6.35	0.000	1.00
Front Rubber	56.44	28.22	2.27	12.41	0.000	1.00
Cup Position	72.24	36.12	2.27	15.88	0.000	1.00
Ball Size*Front Rubber	2.84	1.42	2.27	0.62	0.550	1.00
Ball Size*Cup Position	-12.26	-6.13	2.27	-2.70	0.027	1.00
Front Rubber*Cup Position	1.74	0.87	2.27	0.38	0.712	1.00
Ball Size*Front Rubber*Cup Position	2.69	1.34	2.27	0.59	0.571	1.00

Model Summary

S	R-sq	R-sq(adj)	R-sq(pred)
9.09687	98.27%	96.76%	93.08%

Figure 256: Multiple Regression Table for DOE - Minitab

Effect – The effect value for each factor and interaction of factors represents the average effect when the levels change from a low level setting to a high level setting.

P-value – The P-value is used to make a decision as to whether or not any observed effect is statistically significant. When the P-value is < α (usually 0.05), the effect is considered to be significant.

Analysis of Variance

Source	DF	Adj SS	Adj MS	F-Value	P-Value
Model	7	37626.4	5375.2	64.95	0.000
Linear	3	36951.7	12317.2	148.84	0.000
Ball Size	1	3338.0	3338.0	40.34	0.000
Front Rubber	1	12740.8	12740.8	153.96	0.000
Cup Position	1	20873.0	20873.0	252.23	0.000
2-Way Interactions	3	645.8	215.3	2.60	0.124
Ball Size*Front Rubber	1	32.2	32.2	0.39	0.550
Ball Size*Cup Position	1	601.5	601.5	7.27	0.027
Front Rubber*Cup Position	1	12.1	12.1	0.15	0.712
3-Way Interactions	1	28.9	28.9	0.35	0.571
Ball Size*Front Rubber*Cup Position	1	28.9	28.9	0.35	0.571
Error	8	662.0	82.8		
Total	15	38288.4			

Figure 257: Analysis of Variance Table for DOE – Minitab

The analysis of variance table provides a summary of main effects and interactions.

The P-values in the ANOVA table are used to determine which of the effects in the model are statistically significant. Typically you look at the interaction effects in the model first because a significant interaction will influence how you interpret the main effects.

- Where the P-value is < α (usually 0.05), you conclude that *at least one effect* of that order (main effects or 2-way interactions) is significant. In this case there are multiple main effects with P-values < 0.05.
- Where the P-value is equal to or greater than α (usually 0.05), you conclude that no effect of that order is significant. In this case there looks to be one 2-way interaction of significance with a P-value of 0.027 which is < 0.05.

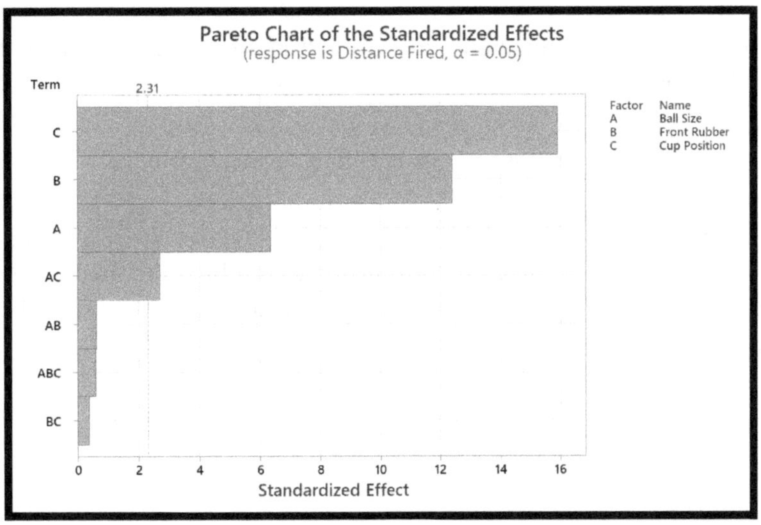

Figure 258: Pareto Chart of Effects for DOE - Minitab

Pareto Chart of the Effects: This chart displays the absolute value of the effects in decreasing order. It assists the user by drawing an alpha value line on the chart (note the vertical line with an indicated value of 2.31). Any effect that extends past the line to the right is considered significant.

In the absence of error terms an estimated line is drawn using an approach known as Lenth's method. When error terms exist (replicated experiments, designs with centre points and reduced models) it is far more accurate with the t-values being used to determine its location.

Normal Probability Plot of the Effects: This plot provides similar information to the Pareto chart. It compares the relative magnitude and the statistical significance of all effects.

The angled vertical line indicates where the points would be expected to fall if there were no effects.

Significant effects are larger and lie further from the line then do effects not considered to be significant.

Significant effects are indicated in this case by Minitab with a red square symbol.

This plot presents the same information as the Pareto Chart albeit in a different form.

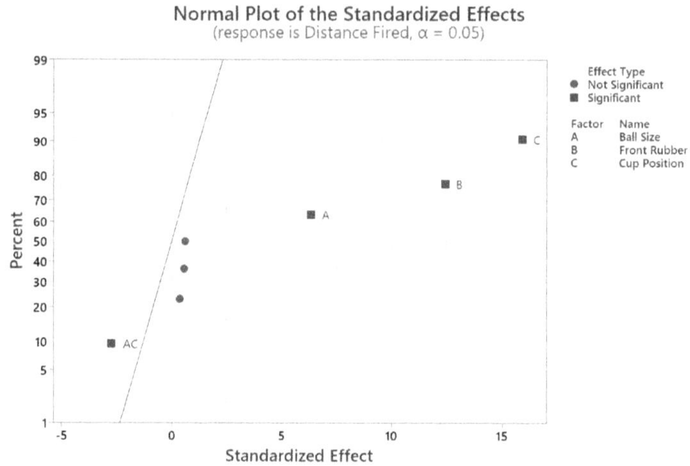

Figure 259: Normal Probability Plot of Effects for DOE - Minitab

Factorial Plots: These plots can be generated with Minitab in various forms including main effects plots, interaction plots and cube plots.

The **main effects plot** is a plot of the mean response at each level of all factors. Values for the average response at the low level and average response at the high level are plotted with a line joining these two values.

A main effect occurs when the average response changes across the levels of a factor, represented by a line that follows an upward or downward trend. The more vertical the line, the greater the average effect of the factor on the response variable. The average effect of the two factors represented in the two left hand plots is much greater than the average effect of the factor in the right hand plot.

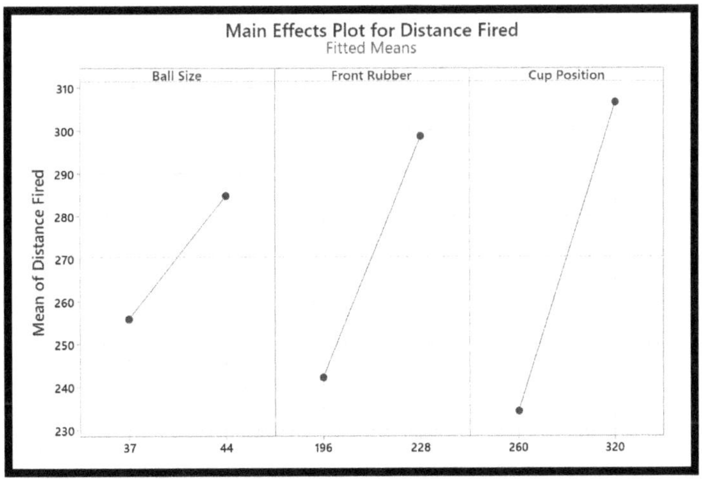

Figure 260: Main Effects Plot - Minitab

An **interaction plot** is a plot of the mean effects for each level of a factor with the level of a second factor held constant.

When the change in response from the low level to the high level for one factor is not the same as the change in response at the same two levels for a second factor, an interaction exists.

The interaction plot helps identify these interactions that will be visible by the relationship between the two lines in each plot.

When no interaction exists the lines in each plot will not intersect. When an interaction does exist the lines of the respective plot will intersect with one another.

The significance of the interaction can be determined from the results displayed in the ANOVA table. Such interactions are important when determining the optimal factor settings during the improve phase of the project.

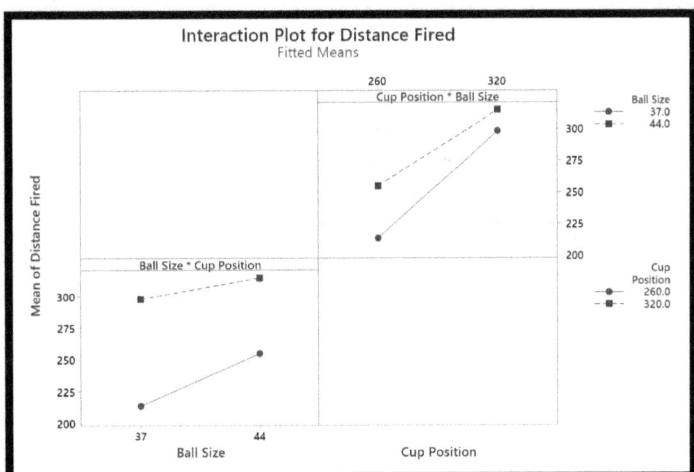

Figure 261: Interaction Plot – Minitab

Reducing the Regression Model

DOE can be used to (a) confirm cause and effect relationships, and (b) create a model for actually optimising process performance in the solution phase.

If your desire is to create that model, which incidentally is nothing more than a multiple regression model, you will need to understand the process of model reduction explained here.

Suppose our Pareto Chart of the Effects (standardised in this case) presented information like that shown.

The regression model made up of factors and interaction terms would be quite large and many of those terms are unnecessary in the model.

Our goal now is to drop unnecessary terms from that model.

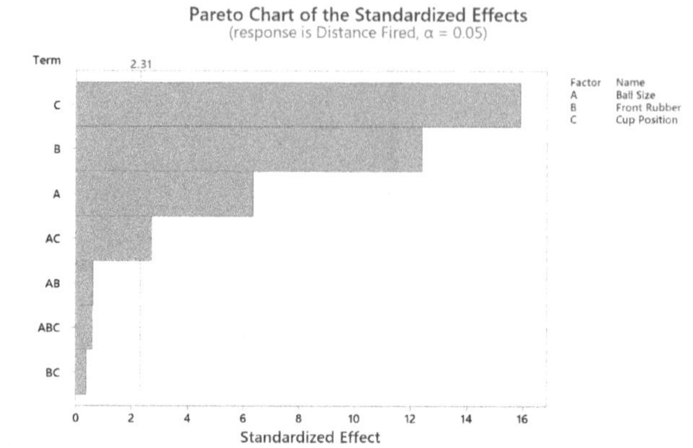

The process of reduction that I teach follows these principles.

- **Only drop terms from one order at a time** (e.g., we would only drop interaction terms from the 3rd order in a single reduction step before touching 2nd order terms).
- Start with the highest level order first (e.g., start with 3rd order terms, then 2nd order terms etc).
- **Leave all factors (*x*'s) in the model** unless the variable is actually removed from the process, regardless of the significance of its effect (indicated in the multiple regression table). In my experience the model has greater predictive accuracy if all active factors are included.
- **The final regression model** is comprised of all significant interaction terms and all factors.

Let me show you how I approach this by referring to an experiment with four factors.

Reducing the Model - Phase 1:

We drop the highest level insignificant terms first (in this case the 3-way interaction terms of ABC) from the model and then create a new Pareto Chart of the effects.

We can now see we have one 2-way interaction that looks to be significant (ball size and cup position).

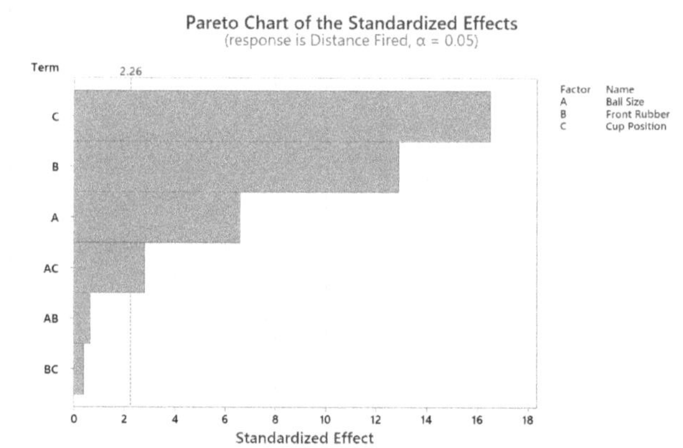

Reducing the Model - Phase 2

We now drop the next highest level insignificant terms (in this case the 2 way interactions of AB and BC) from the model and then create a new Pareto Chart of the effects.

This now would be our final model with three main effects, and one 2-way interaction (ball size and cup position).

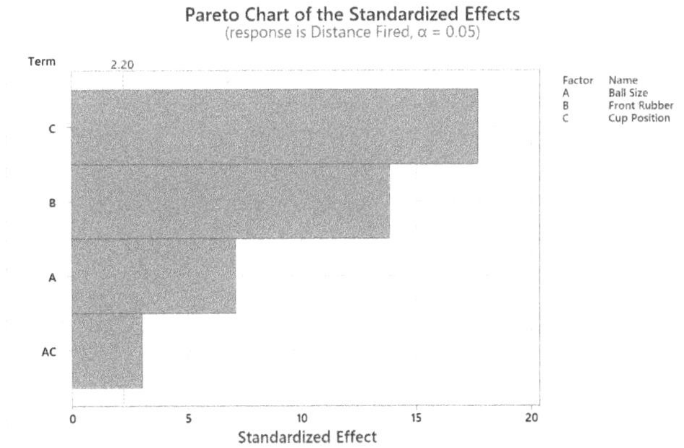

Generally speaking, we sequentially work through 3rd order interactions first, then 2nd order interactions next, before getting to our final regression model.

<u>Validating the Regression Model</u>

The assumptions of DOE analysis are validated through analysing residual plots.

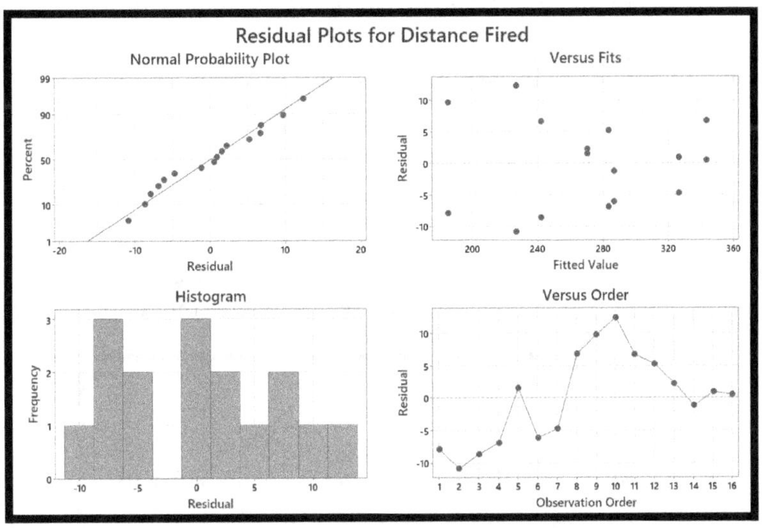

Figure 262: Four in One Residual Plots – Minitab

Residual Plots and Patterns

Residual Plots	Desirable Plot	Undesirable Plot	Actions
Residuals versus Order	No Pattern	Pattern Trending Up or Down	Any pattern means that some factor related to time, influences the response (y). Investigate to find that variable.
Residuals versus Fitted Value	No Pattern	Fan Shape (either direction)	A fan shape means that the variation increases (or decreases) as the average of each condition increases and is therefore not constant. Try a square root, log or inverse transformation on the response (y) and rerun the analysis.
Normal Probability Plot of Residuals	Close Fit With The Line	Non Normal	If residuals do not appear to be normal, try a transformation on the response (y) and re-run the analysis.

Figure 263: Guide to Analysing Residual Plots

FRACTIONAL FACTORIAL (DOE)

It is often impractical to run due to the number of runs that would be required. To run a full factorial DOE with 6 factors at 2 levels would require 64 runs, 7 factors at 2 levels would require 128 runs.

Fractional factorial designs are good alternatives to full factorial. We could test the 6 or 7 factors in as little as 8 runs with the loss of some information.

When you do not run all factor / level combinations (full factorial design), some of the effects will be confounded. As these effects cannot be estimated separately they are said to be *aliased.*

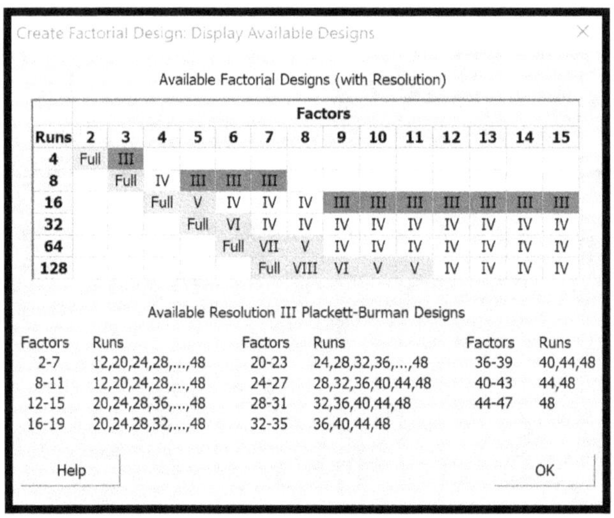

Figure 264: Available Designs with Resolution

Interpretation of this matrix is quite simply a matter of identifying the resolution level in the matrix that corresponds to the number of factors in your design and the number of runs you intend to undertake. For example, a designed experiment in which the team would test 8 combinations of 3 factors would be a 'Full' resolution design (full factorial design).

Resolution	Confounding
III	• Main effects are confounded with two factor and higher interactions
IV	• Main effects are confounded with three factor and higher interactions • Two factor interactions are confounded with other two factor and higher interactions
V	• Main effects are confounded with four factor and higher interactions • Two factor interactions are confounded with three factor and higher interactions
FULL	• No confounding exists

Resolution III designs are usually used for screening designs (screening for the most important factors to use in a full factorial design or a higher resolution fractional design).

Resolution IV and V designs provide quality information without the need to go to a full resolution design.

Interpreting Results from Fractional Factorial Designs

The confounding structure of fractional factorial designs often causes problems in interpreting results of an experiment. Three fundamental principles can be effectively utilised in the analysis to both interpret results and overcome any confounding problems are described as follows.

Principle	Explanation
EFFECT SPARSITY	This principle is aligned with the Pareto principle, and suggests that our attention should be focused on the critical few effects. The principle states that: • The numbers of relatively important effects in a factorial experiment are small
HIERARCHICAL ORDERING	The application of this principle is particularly effective when the experiment results in a large number of factorial effects. The principle states that: • Lower order effects are more likely to be important than higher order effects • Effects of the same order are equally likely to be important
EFFECT HEREDITY	Where the effect of an interaction is said to be significant, unless one of the factors in the interaction has a significant effect on the response by itself, the interaction is not significant. The principle states that: • At least one of its parent factors should be significant in order for an interaction to be significant

Principles for Analysing Designed Experiments

These principles can be useful in defining which confounding is of concern and cannot be de-aliased.

Focus on 2nd Order Interactions (2 Way Interactions)

A number of years ago I did my own research to find out more about interaction effects and how to deal with them in a fractional factorial design. It was enlightening to discuss this issue with a gentleman who had performed countless designed experiments with research organisations over many years.

His advice to me was to focus on 2nd Order Interactions and not worry about the rest. In his many years of experience he had never observed a 4th Order Interaction, and 3rd Order Interactions were extremely rare in reality.

Most of the problems in fractional factorial designs are mathematical in nature. The same effect value will be calculated for specified main effects and interactions, regardless of whether or not a real interaction exists.

Analysing The Fractional Factorial Design with Minitab

The analysis of a fractional factorial experiment is almost the same as the analysis for a full factorial design. Issues associated with confounding introduce additional complexity and this can be demonstrated by case study.

Let's say that we wish to run an experiment with 6 factors at 2 levels. To test all possible combinations would require a minimum of 64 runs (2^6). This is not practical so we choose to run a fractional factorial design with only eight runs (2^{6-3}). We acknowledge that whilst we will save time and money, we will not get the same degree of information we would get with a full factorial.

Having generated the design with Minitab, the session window displays the information shown in the figure below.

Design Summary

Factors:	6	Base Design:	6, 8	Resolution:	III
Runs:	8	Replicates:	1	Fraction:	1/8
Blocks:	1	Center pts (total):	0		

Figure 265: Design Details in Session Window – Minitab

This portion of the session window tells us that the design is based on a study of 6 factors with a total of 8 runs. Therefore it is 1/8 of a full factorial design. As a Resolution III design, we know that main effects are confounded with two-way and higher interactions.

The second portion of the session window tells us about the confounding that will occur in the design that has been generated.

* NOTE * Some main effects are confounded with two-way interactions.

Design Generators: D = AB, E = AC, F = BC

Alias Structure

I + ABD + ACE + BCF + DEF + ABEF + ACDF + BCDE
A + BD + CE + BEF + CDF + ABCF + ADEF + ABCDE
B + AD + CF + AEF + CDE + ABCE + BDEF + ABCDF
C + AE + BF + ADF + BDE + ABCD + CDEF + ABCEF
D + AB + EF + ACF + BCE + ACDE + BCDF + ABDEF
E + AC + DF + ABF + BCD + ABDE + BCEF + ACDEF
F + BC + DE + ABE + ACD + ABDF + ACEF + BCDEF
AF + BE + CD + ABC + ADE + BDF + CEF + ABCDEF

Figure 266: Alias Structure - Minitab

The alias structure displays ***all possible confounding*** that occurs in our resolution III design. We know that there are a total of 64 possible combinations of the different factors at different levels in our design. However, we have only chosen to run 8 of those.

To demonstrate the confounding that will occur in our particular design, let's take a look at the design generators and use these to demonstrate confounding. We can see that in our design Factor D is confounded with the two-way interaction of A*B, factor E is confounded with the two-way interaction of A*C, and factor F is confounded with the two-way interaction of B*C.

We can display our fractional factorial design as shown in the following table.

You might notice that coded units (+1's and –1's) are used in place of the un-coded high and low level descriptors for each factor.

This will help us understand the low and high levels for each of the interactions.

Run	A	B	C	D	E	F	D = AB	E = AC	F = BC
1	-1	-1	-1	1	1	1	1	1	1
2	1	-1	-1	-1	-1	1	-1	-1	1
3	-1	1	-1	-1	1	-1	-1	1	-1
4	1	1	-1	1	-1	-1	1	-1	-1
5	-1	-1	1	1	-1	-1	1	-1	-1
6	1	-1	1	-1	1	-1	-1	1	-1
7	-1	1	1	-1	-1	1	-1	-1	1
8	1	1	1	1	1	1	1	1	1

Fractional Factorial Design

The coded values in the last three columns are calculated by multiplying the values in the columns associated with the individual factors that form the interaction.

For example, the uppermost cell of column D = AB is calculated by multiplying the corresponding cell of column A with the corresponding cell of column B.

This is continued down the column until it is completed. You can see that this column is exactly the same as the column for factor D.

Both of these columns have been shaded. The same approach is used to calculate the values for columns AC (which is the same as E) and BC (which is the same as F).

If we generated columns with relevant low and high values for all possible combinations of the six factors, we would observe a number of columns the same as each other as indicated by the alias structure.

So let's assume we have run the experiment. We have recorded the results of each run in the response column of the table below.

What we need to know is the effect that each factor and interaction has on the response, and which of those effects is significant.

(Note: I have not shown all possible combinations of the six factors in the table for practical reasons.)

Run	A	B	C	D	E	F	D = AB	E = AC	F = BC	Response
1	-1	-1	-1	1	1	1	1	1	1	210
2	1	-1	-1	-1	-1	1	-1	-1	1	150
3	-1	1	-1	-1	1	-1	-1	1	-1	160
4	1	1	-1	1	-1	-1	1	-1	-1	220
5	-1	-1	1	1	-1	-1	1	-1	-1	210
6	1	-1	1	-1	1	-1	-1	1	-1	180
7	-1	1	1	-1	-1	1	-1	-1	1	160
8	1	1	1	1	1	1	1	1	1	180

	A	B	C	D	E	F	D = AB	E = AC	F = BC
Avg (+)	182.5	180	182.5	205	182.5	175	205	182.5	175
Avg (-)	185	187.5	185	162.5	185	192.5	162.5	185	192.5
Effect	**-2.5**	**-7.5**	**-2.5**	**42.5**	**-2.5**	**-17.5**	**42.5**	**-2.5**	**-17.5**

Fractional Factorial Design with Results

The effect for each factor and interaction (shown in the row at the bottom of the table) is the average change in response when the factor or interaction moves from a Low level (-1) to a High level (+1).

That value is calculated using the following equation.

(the avg. response values at the high level) – (the avg. response values at the low level)

For example, the equation to calculate the effect of factor A is shown in the table below.

$$\textbf{Effect} = \frac{(150+220+180+180)}{4} - \frac{(210+160+210+160)}{4}$$

$$= 182.5 - 185$$

$$= -2.5$$

A negative value would indicate that when the factor or interaction moves from a low level to a high level, the response value drops by the amount shown (e.g., an effect of -2.5 means a drop of 2.5 units from low level to high level settings or in other words the high level setting achieves a result 2.5 less than the low level setting).

To identify all effects of all interactions, we would need to develop a table with many more columns than we have shown above.

That is where the value of software packages such as SigmaXL and Minitab is realised.

Using Minitab, similar results are produced and displayed in the Multiple Regression Table.

The following terms are totally confounded with other terms and were removed:
A*B, A*C, A*D, A*E, B*C, B*D, B*E, B*F, C*D, C*E, C*F, D*E, D*F, E*F

Coded Coefficients

Term	Effect	Coef	SE Coef	T-Value	P-Value	VIF
Constant		183.7	*	*	*	
A	-2.500	-1.250	*	*	*	1.00
B	-7.500	-3.750	*	*	*	1.00
C	-2.500	-1.250	*	*	*	1.00
D	42.50	21.25	*	*	*	1.00
E	-2.500	-1.250	*	*	*	1.00
F	-17.500	-8.750	*	*	*	1.00
A*F	-17.500	-8.750	*	*	*	1.00

Model Summary

S	R-sq	R-sq(adj)	R-sq(pred)
*	100.00%	*	*

Figure 267: Multiple Regression Table for DOE - Minitab

Note that interaction terms that are confounded with other terms have been automatically removed and not displayed. Whilst we know that the calculated effects are the same, the software applies the **Hierarchical Ordering Principle** and only identifies the lowest order effects from those that are confounded.

For example we know that D and the interaction of AB mathematically produce the same effect, though we only see the factor D represented on the regression table.

Notice that P-values are not displayed as there are insufficient degrees of freedom left to facilitate an estimate of error (residuals). We are simply trying to estimate too many things with inadequate resources. P-values are only displayed under three circumstances - (a) Replicated experiments, (b) Designs that include Centre Points, and (c) Reduced Models.

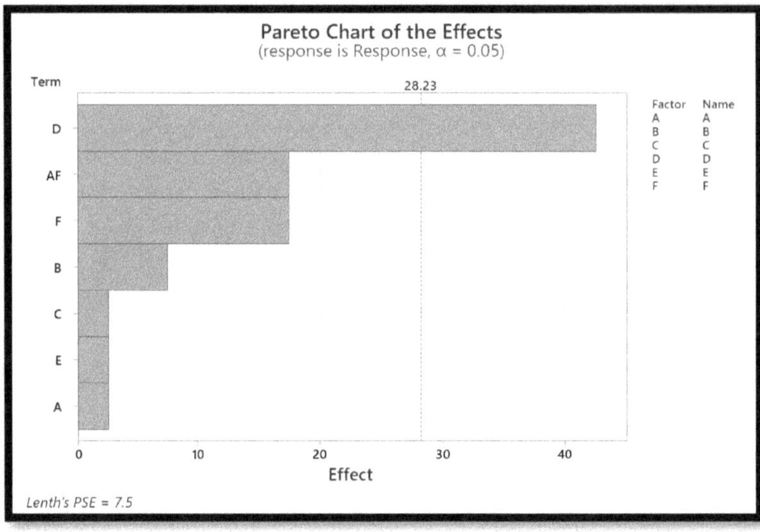

Figure 268: Pareto Chart of Effects – Minitab

To start our analysis we first apply the **Effect Sparsity Principle** by observing the charts to see which critical few effects we should focus our attention on. Both charts indicate that the main factor of significance is D. The main effects plot (below) validates this.

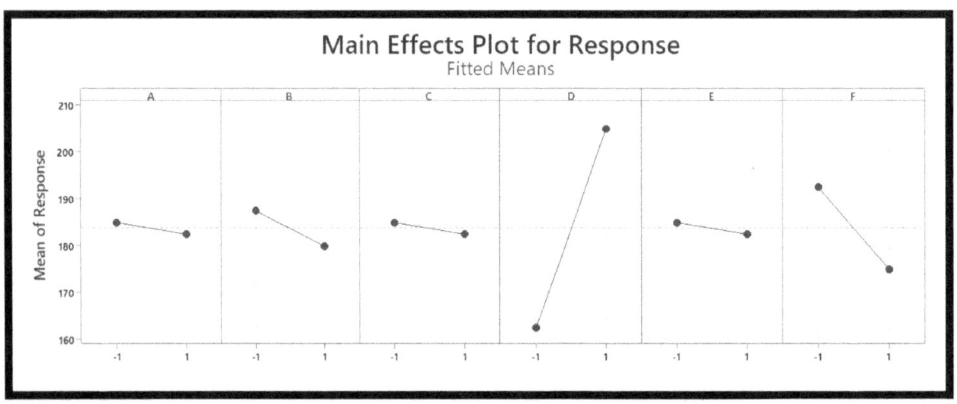

Figure 269: Main Effects Plot - Minitab

We know from our original design that D is aliased with the two-way interaction of A*B. In applying the **Hierarchical Ordering Principle** we can assume that the effect of factor D is probably more significant than the effect of the interaction of A*B, as we know that the lower order effects are more likely to be significant than higher order effects.

Through application of the **Effect Heredity Principle** we can rule out the possibility of the interaction of A*B being significant as neither A nor B are themselves significant.

Therefore our conclusion is that the significant effect is attributed to factor D, now referred to as the main effect.

CAUTION IN USING REGRESSION MODELS FROM DOE

Hopefully you remember our conversation at the end of the Linear Regression section of this book about using regression models to predict?

The key point made was that if you intend using the model you should be extremely cautious of 'extrapolating' it beyond the range of x values used in the analysis. Since we are still using regression models, the same caution applies to designed experiments.

There is also one other consideration with designed experiments. The values of x in a linear regression study are randomly placed between the highest and lowest values, accordingly the *linear* relationship can be confirmed.

With DOE, the values of x are only the high and low values with nothing in between. Thus, the type of relationship between any factor (x) and the response variable (y) could be curved or straight. We have no way of knowing for this experiment without the use of centre points.

What are the implications for you in using the regression model? Let me answer this with a series of diagrams.

Exhibit 1:

Suppose our experiment involved two level settings without any centre points and we obtained response values for these settings as shown in the diagram.

Our simple regression model based on the equation $y = f(x)$ would allow us to insert values of x and determine what the response value y would be.

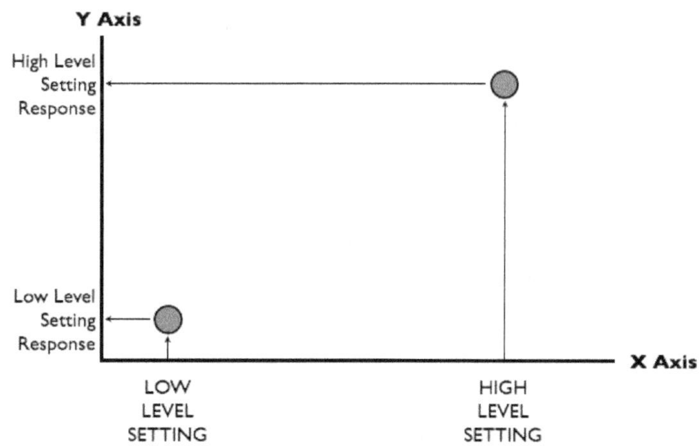

Exhibit 2:

Suppose we assumed a *linear* relationship between the factor (x) and the response (y).

If we were to insert a different factor setting for x into the regression model, we would predict our response as shown in the diagram.

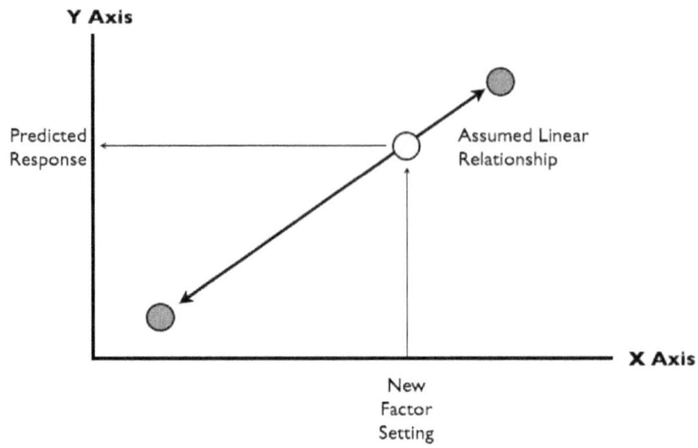

Exhibit 3:

What if our assumption of a linear relationship was incorrect and the relationship actually had curvature in it, what impact would that have on our work?

As the diagram shows, the actual response (y) would be significantly different than the predicted response.

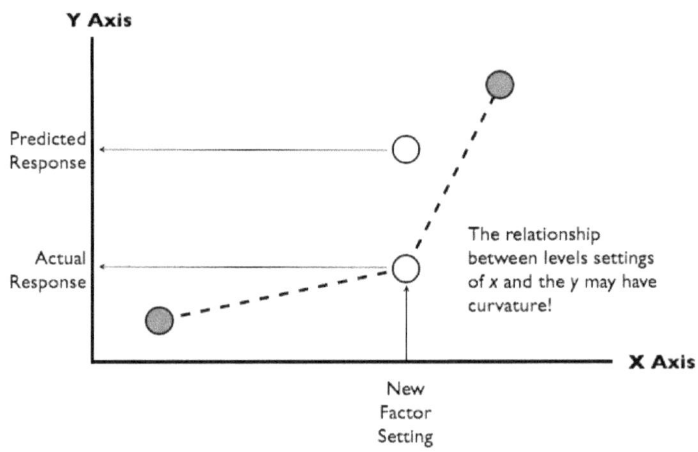

To put this in simple terms, you should not use any values for any of the x's in optimising the response variable, other than the values used in the experiment.

Key Learning Points

1. Designed experiments are used to create a response and be present to observe the results in order to understand cause effect relationships.
2. Screening designs are Resolution III designs.
3. Confounding issues that occur in all 'fractional factorial' designs can be resolved through the application of the principles of:
    a. Effect Sparsity
    b. Effect Heredity
    c. Hierarchical Ordering

4. The model is useful when certain assumptions are met. Residuals must be analysed to ensure these assumptions are not violated.
5. DOE is also used in the improve phase to optimise the performance of a process by developing a regression model.
6. When optimising the response value (the process), only use values for different factor settings that were used in the experiment. Choose your factor settings carefully when you design the experiment.

Recommended Reading

- Levine D., Ramsey P., Smidt R., 1994, *Applied Statistics for Engineers and Scientists*, Prentice Hall,
- Wu C.F., Wu J., Hamanda M., 2000, *Experiments: Planning, Analysis, and Parameter Design Optimisation*, Edition 1, Wiley-Interscience,
- Montgomery, Douglas, 1997, *Design and Analysis of Experiments*, Wiley

CHAPTER 16: ANALYSE PHASE TOOLKIT

ATTRIBUTE CONTROL CHARTS

np Chart	Attribute chart used to plot the number of items in a consistent sized sample or subgroup that are non-conforming (defective).
Centre Line	$n\bar{p} = \dfrac{\text{Total number of non comforming items in all subgroups}}{\text{Number of sub groups}}$
Control Limits	$UCL = n\bar{p} + 3\sqrt{n\bar{p}(1-\bar{p})}$ $LCL = n\bar{p} - 3\sqrt{n\bar{p}(1-\bar{p})}$

p Chart	Attribute chart used to plot the proportion of units that are non-conforming (defective). They can be used with both equal and unequal sample or subgroup sizes
Centre Line	$\bar{p} = \dfrac{\text{Total number of non comforming items in all subgroups}}{\text{Total number of items in all sub groups}}$
Control Limits (Average subgroup size method)	$UCL = \bar{p} + 3\sqrt{\dfrac{\bar{p}(1-\bar{p})}{n}}$ $LCL = \bar{p} - 3\sqrt{\dfrac{\bar{p}(1-\bar{p})}{n}}$

c Chart	Attribute chart used to plot the relevant count of defects when the subgroup size remains constant.
Centre Line	$\bar{c} = \dfrac{\text{Total number of events of interest}}{\text{Number sub groups}}$
Control Limits	$UCL = \bar{c} + 3\sqrt{\bar{c}}$ $LCL = \bar{c} - 3\sqrt{\bar{c}}$

u Chart	Attribute chart used to plot the statistic 'u', which is the ratio of number of defects counted to the size of the subgroup. Used when the size of the subgroup is not consistent.
Centre Line	$\bar{u} = \dfrac{\text{Total number of events of interest}}{\text{Total number of units in all sub groups}}$
Control Limits	$UCL = \bar{u} + 3\sqrt{\dfrac{\bar{u}}{n_i}}$ $\quad LCL = \bar{u} - 3\sqrt{\dfrac{\bar{u}}{n_i}}$

VARIABLES CONTROL CHARTS

Chart	Chart Type	Centre Line	Control Limits
R Chart (Range)	Variables (n < 10)	$\bar{R} = \dfrac{\text{The sum of sub group ranges}}{\text{Total number of sub groups}}$	$UCL = D_4\bar{R}$ $LCL = D_3\bar{R}$
X-bar Chart (Used with R chart)	Variables (n < 10)	$\bar{\bar{X}} = \dfrac{\text{The sum of sub group averages}}{\text{Total number of sub groups}}$	$UCL = \bar{\bar{X}} + A_2\bar{R}$ $LCL = \bar{\bar{X}} - A_2\bar{R}$
S Chart (Standard Deviation)	Variables (n ≥ 10)	$\bar{s} = \dfrac{\text{The sum of sub group standard deviations}}{\text{Total number of sub groups}}$	$UCL = B_4\bar{s}$ $LCL = B_3\bar{s}$
X-bar Chart (Used with S Chart)	Variables (n ≥ 10)	$\bar{\bar{X}} = \dfrac{\text{The sum of sub group averages}}{\text{Total number of sub groups}}$	$UCL = \bar{\bar{X}} + A_3\bar{s}$ $LCL = \bar{\bar{X}} - A_3\bar{s}$
MR Chart (Moving Range)	Variables	$\overline{MR} = \dfrac{\text{The sum of moving averages}}{\text{Total number of moving range values}}$ $(k-1)$	$UCL(MR) = D_4\overline{MR}$ $LCL(MR) = D_3\overline{MR}$
I Chart X Chart (Individuals)	Variables	$\bar{x} = \dfrac{\text{The sum of all values}}{\text{Total number of values}}$	$UCL(X) = \bar{x} + E_2\overline{MR}$ $LCL(X) = \bar{x} - E_2\overline{MR}$

NOTE: The values of respective control chart 'bias control' factors can be obtained from the table shown in appendices.

STATISTICAL ANALYSIS TOOLS

Categorical and Numerical Variables

Purpose	Relevant Concepts	Graphical Tools Used for Visualising Relationships	Statistical Analysis Tools for Validating Inferences (+ Prediction Modelling)
To compare samples [that can be grouped or categorized] for the purposes of identifying whether or not there are differences across 2 or more independent populations.	Differences between the elements within **categorical** variables and their affect on a numerical Y	Pie Chart (categorised Y) Bar Chart (categorised Y) Pareto Chart (categorised Y) Multi Vari Chart Interval Plot Stratified Histograms Stratified Box Plots ANOM Charts Time Series Plots	Chi-Square Proportion Tests *t* Tests / *z* Tests Equal Variance Tests ANOVA / ANOM Median Tests Design of Experiments Logistic Regression (categorised Y)
To identify strength of any relationships between numerical variables.	Correlation between **numerical** variables (Xs and Ys)	Scatter Plot Matrix Plot Contour Plot Surface Plot	Pearson's Correlation Logistic Regression (categorised Y) Linear Regression (prediction models) Design of Experiments (prediction models)

Studying XY Relationships

The type of dependent and independent variables you are working with determines which tool you choose to examine relationships between *x*'s and *y*'s.

The matrices below are a different way of arranging the information presented in the table above.

Visually Displaying Relationships

Dependent Variable / Effect / Response (*Y*)

		Categorical Y	Numerical Y
Independent Variable / Cause / Factor (*X*)	**Categorical X**	Pie Chart, Bar Chart or Column Chart (using counts), Pareto Chart	Stratified Box Plots, Stratified Histograms, ANOM Charts Time Series Plots, Multi-Vari Chart
	Numerical X	Stratified Histograms, Stratified Box Plots	Scatter Plot, Marginal Plot, Matrix Plot, Contour Plot / Surface Plot

Statistically Validating Relationships

		Dependent Variable / Effect / Response (*Y*)	
		Categorical Y	**Numerical Y**
Independent Variable / Cause / Factor (*X*)	**Categorical X**	Chi-Square, Logistic Regression, Proportion Tests	*t* Tests, *z* Tests, Analysis of Variance, Analysis of Means, Equal Variance Tests, Median Tests, Design of Experiments (DOE)
	Numerical X	Logistic Regression	Pearson's Correlation, Linear Regression (for developing prediction models), Design of Experiments (DOE)

HYPOTHESIS TESTING WORKSHEET

What is it?

The hypothesis testing worksheet is a tool designed to ensure that you (a) follow the full Hypothesis Testing process; and (b) capture all relevant information as a part of the study.

Instructions

The tool is self-explanatory and compliments the hypothesis testing process presented earlier.

My **Null Hypothesis**? **H_0:**	My **Alternate Hypothesis**? **H_A:**
What **Significance Level** (α) will I use?	What **Hypothesis Test** will I use?

What **assumptions** must I satisfy for this test?

-
-
-
-

TEST RESULTS

My test **P-value**?

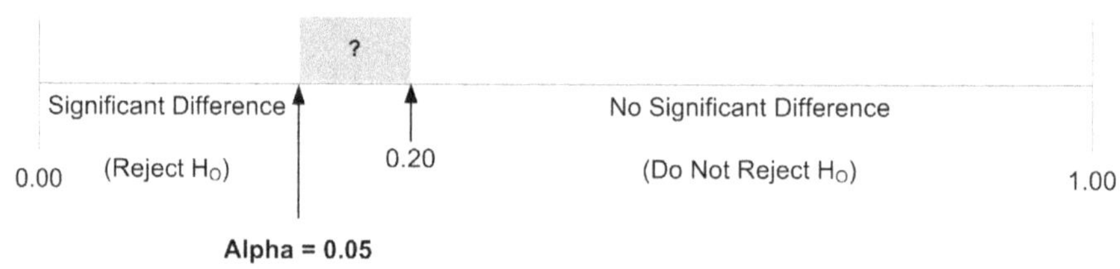

My **observations**:

My **conclusion**:

TAKT TIME CHART

What is it?

A Takt Time Chart emphasises the time taken in each step of a process and how it relates to the rate of production necessary to meet customer demand.

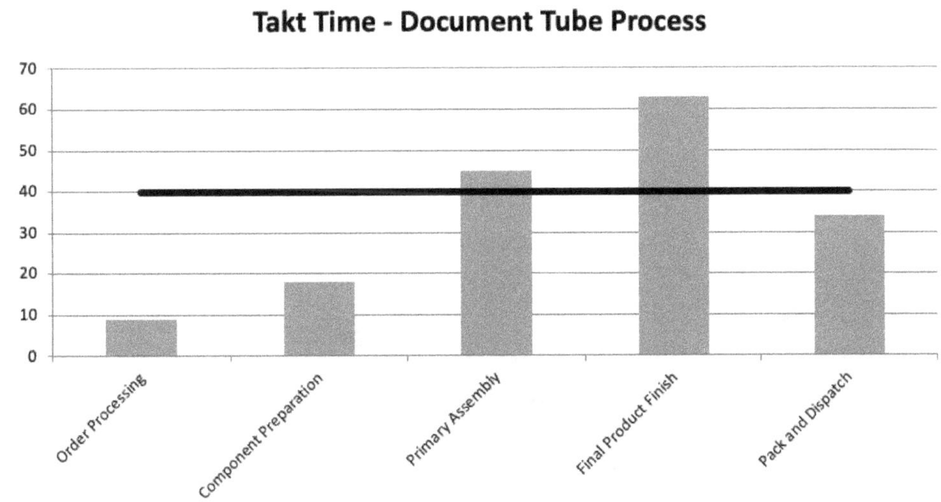

Instructions

Step 1 - Determine how long each step in the process takes to complete. If you have already determined cycle times for each of the process steps you simply use that data.

Step 2 - Plot results in a vertical bar chart as shown above.

Step 3 - Calculate Takt Time (the time required to produce one unit to meet customer supply requirements) as defined by the following equation.

- $$\text{Takt Time} = \frac{\text{Net Operating Time Per Period}}{\text{Customer Demand Per Period}}$$
- Net Operating Time = Total time available, less unproductive time such as lunch, morning tea, afternoon tea etc.

Step 4 - Plot a Takt Time line on the bar chart as shown. Takt time can also be referred to as *lead time.*

Step 5 – Take action to address obvious constraints and time traps. (refer to the improve phase)

SPAGHETTI DIAGRAM

What is it?

Spaghetti diagrams are graphical tools for visually displaying the flow or movement of information, materials, people or products in a process. The visual display makes opportunities to eliminate waste associated with motion more obvious.

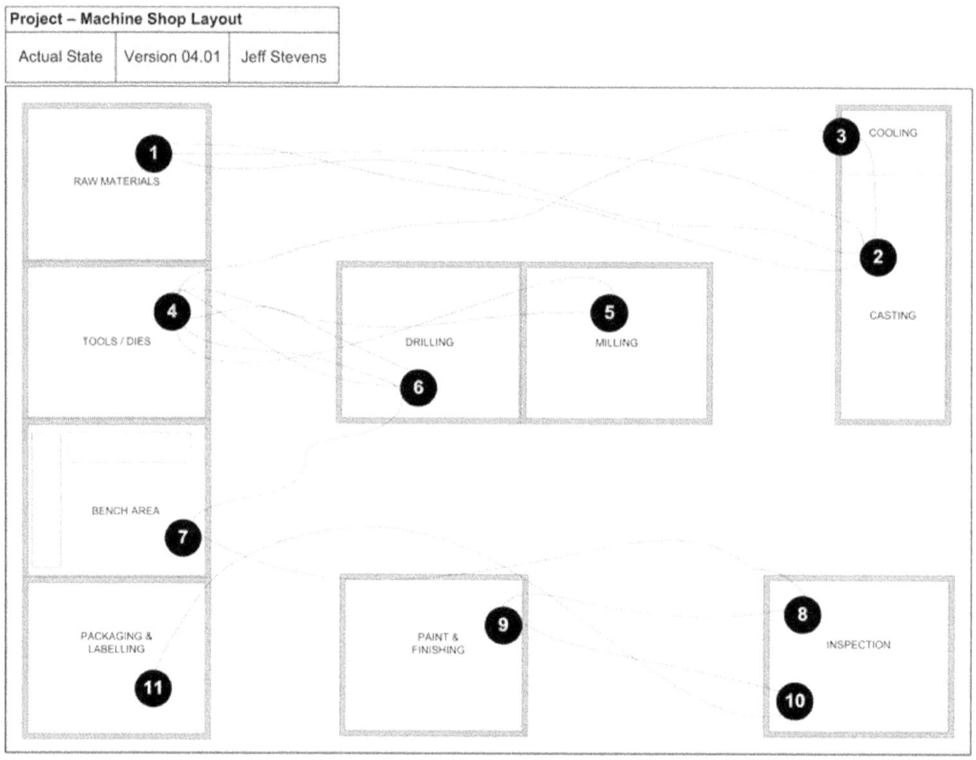

Instructions

Each of the steps in a process is numbered and the sequence is overlaid on the workplace layout by a continuous line that indicates where each of the steps occurs.

Step 1 – Draw a plan of the workplace layout. You could even take a photo of the workplace looking down into it if space and resources permit.

Step 2 – Draw a continuous line to indicate the flow of a person's physical movement (or flow of materials, information or products) from the beginning to the end of the specified process.

Step 3 – Validate the flow pattern with people who actually work in the process.

Step 4 – Evaluate the flow pattern. A pattern of crisscrossing lines like that in the diagram indicates that opportunities exist to improve process flow by

- Modifying the layout of the workplace and arrangement of tools and resources
- Modify the process itself (remove unnecessary steps etc)

CAUSE EFFECT DIAGRAM (FISHBONE)

What is it?

Sometimes referred to as the Ishikawa or Fishbone Diagram, the cause effect diagram is a visual model that helps focus a team's discussion around identification of the potential root cause or causes of a specific condition or problem.

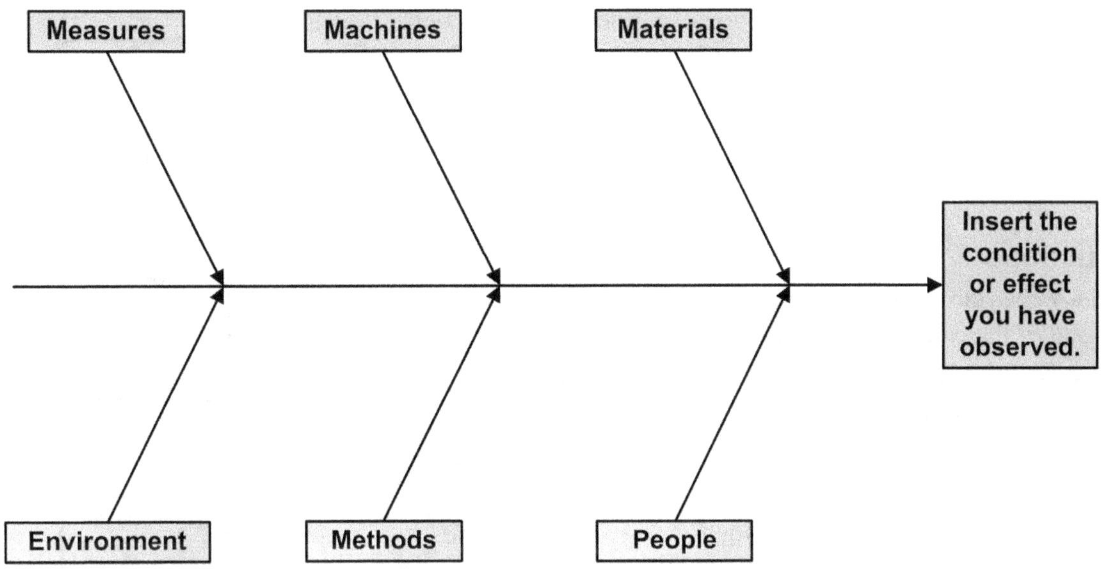

Instructions

Step 1 Preparation - Prepare the diagram.

Step 2 The Problem - Write down your problem or condition (or even a question related to the effect you have observed) and place it at the head of the diagram.

Step 3 Potential Causes - Ask questions of the condition or effect you observe. Keep asking until ideas are generated.

- What causes variation in …
- What caus<u>es</u> this …
- What caus<u>ed</u> this …

Channelling Alternative – You could channel brainstorm by focusing in turn on the specific categories. The question might sound like 'what environmental factor could cause this condition', or 'what might cause this condition within the machines category'.

Step 4 Remove Confirmed Non Causes - Ask 'is there any evidence that would indicate any of these is not a root cause?' If it does then exclude the idea from the list, if it doesn't exist then leave the idea in the list.

Step 5 Reduce the List - Short list to the top 1 or 2 potential causes using multi voting. Again, the people in your team will focus on the most probable causes on the basis of process knowledge and experience; you simply need to ask the right question.

- Which of these causes do you believe are the most significant causes of ……

5 WHAT (AKA 5 WHY'S) CAUSE EFFECT CHAIN

What is it?

The 5 What Cause Effect (CE) Chain is a visual thinking tool that helps the team to identify potential root causes for simple or very well defined problems.

The tool is particularly useful when you experience a simple well defined variation in performance or some simple event based problem.

It is often called the 5 Why's. However, we refer to it as the 5 What's as a reminder to use the correct questioning technique when applying this tool.

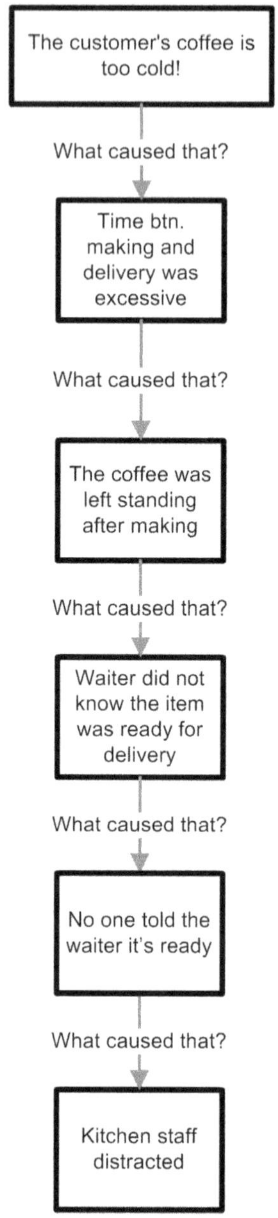

Instructions

Step 1 - Write down your problem or condition and place it at the start point of the cause effect chain.

Step 2 - Ask: 'what causes that' (or what caused that) in reference to the condition or effect you observe.

Step 3 - Continue to ask this question of each subsequent cause until you have asked it no more than 5 times.

Step 4 - Choose the point at which you can interrupt the cause effect chain.

Step 5 – Validate the cause.

CAUSE EFFECT STRUCTURE TREE

What is it?

The cause effect structure tree is a visual tool that helps the team to identify root causes at a much deeper level of analysis using the principles of '5 What Cause Effect Chain'. The tool is particularly useful when you are analysing a focused event or condition. It is often used as a follow up to the 'Cause Effect Diagram'; once more specific causes have been identified.

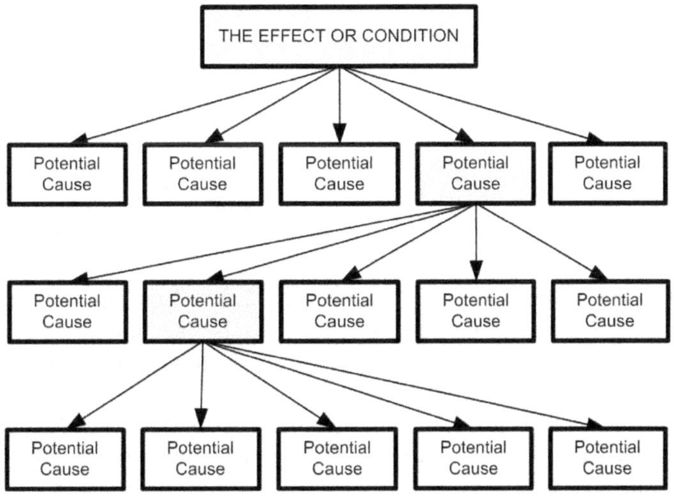

Instructions

The cause effect structure tree is created in seven steps:

Step 1 - Write your problem or condition and place it at the start point of the structure tree.

Step 2 - Ask 'what causes this' (or what caused this) of the condition or effect you observe. Keep asking until ideas are generated.

Step 3 - Capture the first five causes identified – remember that you have participants who are intimately knowledgeable about the process and the first ideas generated are based on that knowledge which is primarily held at the unconscious level of thinking. The right question brings these to the surface first; to push too far in a process, which by the way is not meant to be creative, starts to push the boundaries of rational thinking.

Step 4 - Ask 'is there any evidence that would indicate any of these is not a root cause?' If it does then exclude the idea from the list, if it doesn't exist then leave the idea in the list.

Step 5 - Short list to the top 1 or 2 potential causes using multi voting. Again, the people in your team will focus on the most probable causes on the basis of process knowledge and experience.

Step 6 – You should not have 1 or 2 potential causes. Simply repeat steps 2 to 5 for every potential cause that remains.

Step 7 - Continue to repeat for the new level of potential causes, you should not proceed beyond 5 levels. Stop if you get to a cause that you cannot influence.

Step 8 – Validate the potential cause or causes identified.

CORRELATION AND REGRESSION SUMMARY OF TERMS

Item	Definition	Range of Values	What it means
R	Correlation coefficient	-1 to +1	An indication of the strength of the linear relationship between the response (*y* values) and the predictor or explanatory variable (*x* values). A result close to zero indicates no relationship.
R^2 R-sq	Coefficient of determination	0.00 to 1.00	This indicates the amount of variation in the response (*y* values) that is explained by its relationship with the independent or explanatory variable (*x* values). Multiply by 100 to explain the relationship in percentage terms.
R^2 R-sq (adj)	Coefficient of determination	0.00 to 1.00	A modified R-sq adjusted for the number of terms in the model. When unnecessary terms are included in the model, R-sq can be artificially high.
P-value	The probability that the slope is significantly different than zero	0.00 to 1.00	If P-values are less than 0.05, (a) the constant is significant and (b) the slopes of the fitted lines for each *x* is significant in the regression model.
Residual	The difference between an observed value of Y and the predicted value of Y	No limit	Where common cause variation exists only, residuals (error) will be normally distributed with a mean of zero.
S	Standard deviation of residuals	0 and higher	This gives an indication of how much the typical observed value differs from the predicted value.
Standardised Residual	Equals the residual divided by the standard deviation	–3 to +3 (approx.)	A standardised residual with an absolute value of >3 is an unusual observation that should be investigated. Minitab reports those with values of >2.
Influential Observation	An observation with an X value that has a large influence on the values of coefficients.	No limit	Can be observed as an outlier. A decision is necessary as to whether they should be included in the regression analysis.
VIF	Variance inflation factor	1 and higher	A measure of collinearity between predictor variables. Results above 5 may indicate that there is excessive correlation between predictor variables, hence regression coefficients may be poorly estimated.

Quantification of Degree of Association in Correlation and Regression

Correlation statistics complement your regression work by quantifying the degree of association between variables.

The table below shows the approximate relationship between Pearson Correlation Statistic (r), Coefficient of Determination Value (R-Sq) and the degree of association.

Pearson Correlation Coefficient (R)	R-Square Percentage Value (R-Sq%)	Degree of Association
0.90 ≤ (R) ≤ 1.00	(R-Sq) ≥ 80%	Strong
0.70 ≤ (R) < 0.90	50% ≤ (R-Sq) ≤ 80%	Moderate
(R) < 0.70	(R-Sq) < 50%	Weak

DOE WORKSHEET

This tool is reasonably self-explanatory and includes an example of how it might be used.

DESIGN DETAILS
Experiment Type
Full factorial DOE
No. of Blocks
0
No. of Centre Points
0
No. of Replicates / Runs
2 Replicates / 16 Runs
Resolution
Full resolution

RESPONSE VARIABLES (y)		
Primary Response (y_1)		
Metric:	**LSL**	**USL**
Battery life in minutes	240 min	na
Secondary Response (y_2)		
Metric:	**LSL**	**USL**

FACTORS (x)	
Factor	**Level Settings**
x_1 Battery Type	- Low quality (NC) CP – none + High quality (NMH)
x_2 Connector Type	- Standard CP – none + Gold plated
x_3 Temperature of Room	- Ambient (26-28C) CP + Cold (17-19C)
x_4	- CP +
x_5	- CP +
x_6	- CP +
x_7	- CP +
x_8	- CP +

NOISE VARIABLES & STRATEGY FOR ADDRESSING		
Eliminate	**Randomise**	**Block**
Operator PC Model / Type Automated functions	Day of the week Humidity	

CONCLUSIONS
Battery type is a main effect with an average increase in battery life of 437.5 minutes when there is a change from low quality to high quality battery. The effects of connector type and temperature on battery life are insignificant. There is no evidence of any two way or higher interactions.

MODEL VALIDATION
Residuals versus fits show non-constant variance across the range of fitted values. The observation order shows sequential trends. The model should not be used for prediction without treatment.

Legend: CP = Centre Points, LSL = Lower Specification Limit, USL = Upper Specification Limit

CHAPTER 17: ANALYSE PHASE TOLLGATE & CHECKLISTS

TOLLGATE QUESTIONS

The following questions are the kind that may be asked by your Master Black Belt or Lean Six Sigma Project sponsor during an 'Analyse Phase Tollgate Review' which is indicated as the point between step twelve and step thirteen on our 20-step roadmap.

	Lean	Six Sigma
<u>CHARTER / SCOPE</u> • What revisions need to be made to the charter? • How has the scope of the project changed? • What changes need to be made to the project time line?	✓	✓
<u>Stability ANALYSIS</u> • Did you observe any special cause variation in this process? • How do you propose to treat that variation? • After you treat it, what are your intentions?		✓
<u>Sources of Variation</u> • What key variables have you identified as sources of process variation? • How do you know these are sources of variation? • How did you validate these as sources of variation? • Are you able to eliminate these from the process?		✓
<u>CAUSE & EFFECT ANALYSIS</u> • What major causes of variation (or problem) have you identified? • How did you go about identifying these as major causes? • Who was involved in the process? • How did you validate the cause and effect relationships?		✓

	Lean	Six Sigma
<u>SOURCES OF WASTE</u> • Have you analysed the process from a waste perspective? • How did you do that? • What did your analysis reveal? • Where is the greatest opportunity to remove waste from the process? • How did you validate that? • Have you studied cycle time? • Where is most time consumed in this process? • How did you determine that? • How much time is spent adding value in this process? • How do you know that? • Which steps have you broken down further into sub-process flowcharts? • Why did you choose to break those steps down? • What opportunities exist to reduce the non-value adding or unnecessary time? • How have you validated that?	✓	
<u>Communications</u> • What communications have you undertaken with key stakeholders?	✓	✓
<u>GENERAL</u> • What challenges are you experiencing that I can assist with? • What is your plan from here?	✓	✓

ANALYSE PHASE CHECKLIST

Six Sigma Specific Project

If you have responded appropriately to each of the following statements, then you are ready to move to the 'Improve' phase of your project.		YES	NO	NA
1	Analysed performance data using control charts and are able to state whether the process is or is not in a state of statistical control.			
2	Stratified the data in multiple ways to find the source of variation and the appropriate level at which to analyse for root causes.			
3	Validated the differences between potential sources of variation using statistical methods.			
4	Conducted a root cause analysis and generated relevant root cause hypothesis to explain the effect being observed.			
5	Validated root causes using appropriate evidentiary methods.			
6	Commenced work to implement any 'early wins' identified by the team during the analysis phase.			

Lean Specific Project

If you have responded appropriately to each of the following statements, then you are ready to move to the 'Improve' phase of your project.		YES	NO	NA
1	Conducted an analysis of process performance against Takt Time and have identified any constraints and time traps.			
2	Identified where the greatest opportunity is to improve efficiency against the key project metric.			
3	Visually examined the sub-process flowchart and identified bottlenecks, reworks, inefficient or unnecessary handoffs that may be contributing to the effect being observed.			
4	Commenced work to implement any 'early wins' identified by the team during the analysis phase.			

CHAPTER 18: PROJECT 'IMPROVE' PHASE

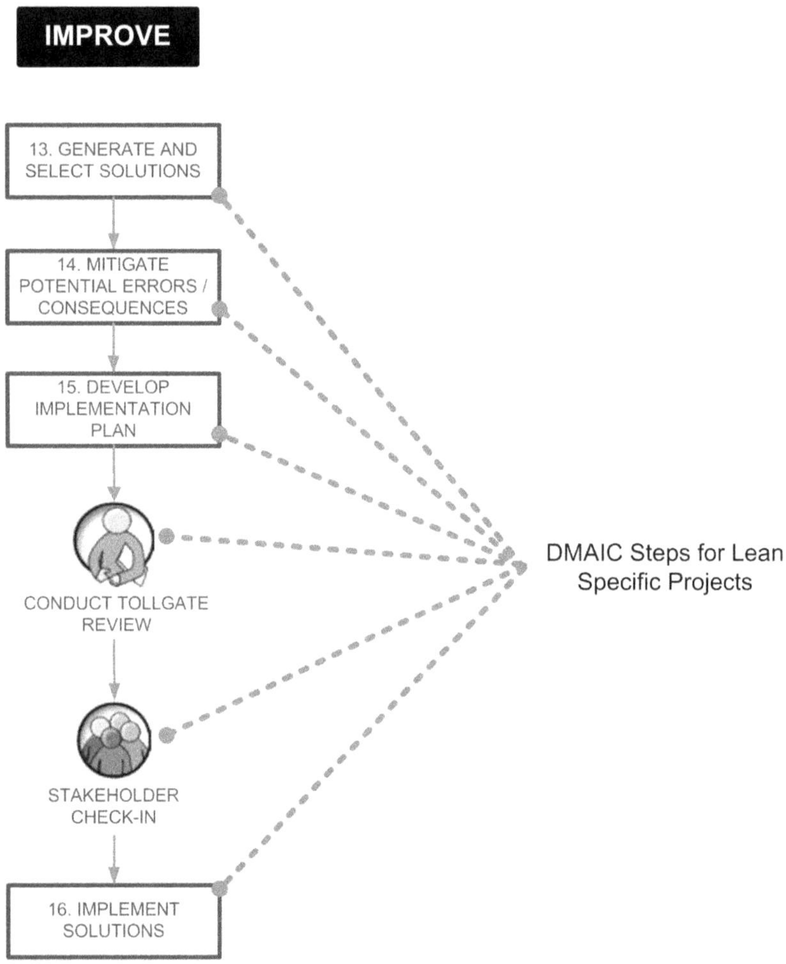

THE IMPROVE PHASE AS A PROCESS

Improve is the fourth phase of the team's work. It is the point where the rubber starts to hit the road. The major causes of variation or major sources of waste have been identified and the team is now in a position to identify ways to treat those causes and sources in ways that ensure improvements will be rapidly delivered and sustained.

The IMPROVE Phase as a Process

The following table represents our view of the 'improve' phase as a process at this point in the project.

INPUTS	PROCESS	OUTPUTS
Six Sigma Specific Project A list of validated causes **Lean Specific Project** Knowledge of what needs to be treated in order to minimise or eliminate waste from the process	**Six Sigma Specific Project** 1. Selection of the improvement strategy 2. Generate potential solutions through a variety of means 3. Select most appropriate solutions 4. Develop an implementation plan 5. Implement solutions through application of project management and change leadership skills **Lean Specific Project** 1. Utilise the most appropriate lean tools to treat identified sources of waste 2. Implement solutions through application of project management and change leadership skills	Solutions are implemented and the new process is operational

Selection of the Improvement Strategy

Before generating solutions, it will serve the team well to think about the type of solutions that would offer the best value to the project work. The type of solution strategy will be determined by how far up the performance curve the process actually is. To choose an improvement strategy when the process is already performing near its potential would probably be a waste of time and effort. On the other hand, to be thinking about redesigning the process at considerable cost and effort when there is plenty of opportunity to extract value from the existing process might also prove a missed opportunity.

Generation of Potential Solution Ideas

Potential solution ideas are generated using tools and processes that open up the idea pipeline. The key in this step is to generate as many ideas as possible and *then* sort them out. Creativity and innovation is a theme that should permeate this phase of work.

Selection of Solutions

The solutions chosen are those that have the greatest impact on the problem at hand. This can occur when the solutions treat the root causes that were validated during the analyse phase of the work. Innovation and creativity are replaced by rational thinking.

Quick Efficiency Improvements with Lean

The lean toolkit provides a range of tools for treating sources of waste and rapidly improving process efficiency.

Planning for Implementation

The planning phase involves determining what needs to be done, who will do it, when will it be done, how will it be done, and how much will it cost to be done. Numerous tools are used in this process to generate the information required of an effective implementation plan, and the skills of project management will come to the fore.

Piloting Solutions

Some solutions may require piloting before they are implemented. Reasons for this might include (a) to test solutions, (b) test the implementation plan or (c) generate buy in through proving the solution to key stakeholders. Piloting is not required for all solutions.

Implementing Solutions

Having done all that work in planning and piloting, the full-scale implementation takes place through the completion of scheduled activities. The Black Belt's project management and change leadership skills come to the fore during the transition to the new and desired state.

COMMON IMPROVE PHASE TOOLS

TECHNICAL TOOLS / PROCESSES	PEOPLE TOOLS / PROCESSES
Six Sigma Specific Project Regression Models Benchmarking, Idea Generation and Selection Tools, FMEA **Lean Specific Project** 5S, Pull Systems, Work Cell Optimisation, Process Balancing, SMED / QCO, Visual Workplace, Total Productivity Maintenance (TPM), Error Proofing (Poka Yoke), FMEA **General Tools** Project Management Tools, Pilot Studies	Facilitation Processes and Tools Meeting Tools (Agenda, Parking Lot, Meeting Feedback) Team Building Processes Stakeholder Engagement Plan Communications Plan Progress Review Meetings (Other tools not covered in this text include Consequence Benefit Analysis, Evidence Planning, Force Field Analysis)

IMPROVEMENT STRATEGIES FOR SIX SIGMA

Solutions strategies chosen by a team will vary from project to project. A team might choose to get the most out of the existing process by giving it a 'tweak'. They might choose to design a new process to replace the old process, and make a radical change. Then again, they might choose to just add new equipment or other resources to the process to ensure that supply is able to meet demand. To select a relevant improvement strategy a Black Belt must first understand the concept of process performance entitlement.

Process Performance Entitlement

The *performance potential* of a process can be referred to as 'process performance entitlement'. Each and every process has a design performance entitlement. A range of factors determines the level, including the type of technology used and the type of process used to produce the intended result. The concept of performance entitlement is better explained in diagrammatic format.

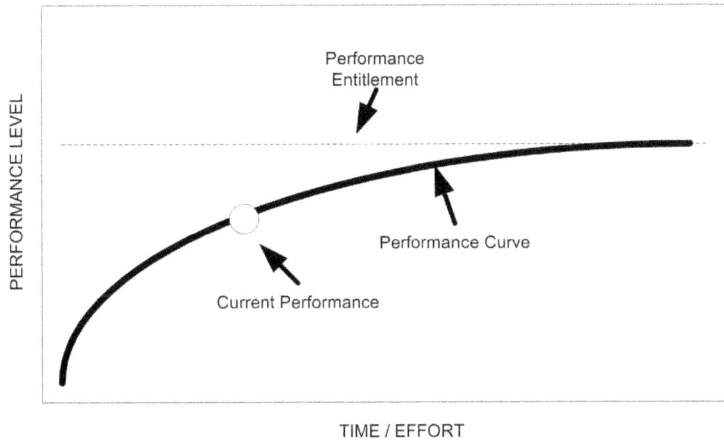

Figure 270: Process Performance Entitlement Concept

<u>Current Entitlement</u>

Let's take the example of an athlete. Over time, the athlete achieves better results based on the degree of improvement in certain inputs and processes that produce the desired outputs. These inputs include quality and quantity of training, attitude, thought processes, diet, and perhaps many others.

Improvements are quite significant earlier on in the process. However, the degree of improvement gets exponentially harder to achieve as the athlete moves up the performance curve.

For example, in golf it is relatively easy to drop 2 strokes when you have a handicap of 36 or 27. It is significantly harder to drop 2 strokes when you are playing off a handicap of 6.

Think about marathon runners. They will make considerable improvements in their times when they first start running. It would be relatively easy to reduce times by 20 minutes over the 42 kilometres. However, when they are near their peak, improvements start to get measured in minutes and seconds. The same principles apply to a work process.

The time and effort gets significantly greater as the performance of the process approaches its designed potential or performance entitlement.

Whilst at the lower portions of the performance curve, it is appropriate to use a process improvement strategy to move up the curve. i.e. To incrementally improve the existing process.

<u>Beyond the Current Entitlement</u>

Let's go back to the example of the athlete again. For the athlete to achieve a result beyond their existing entitlement, it would require a significant change in their genetic structure, biological capability or the process itself to produce large gains in output performance.

The practice of taking performance enhancing drugs is aligned with the concept of exceeding performance entitlement. (Note: This is not to say we support this approach in any way)

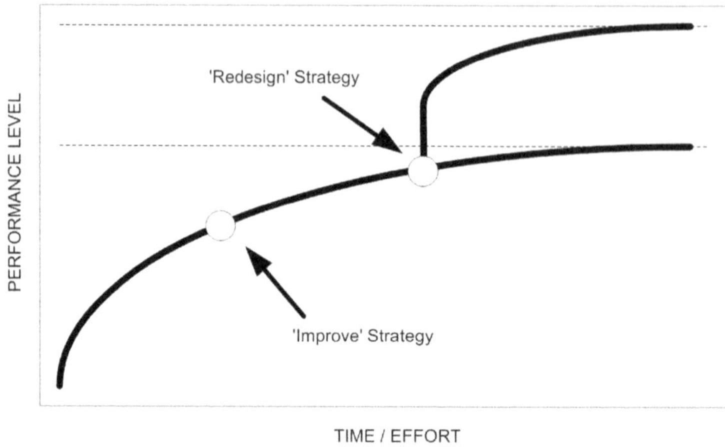

Figure 271: Exceeding Process Entitlement

For any golfer to exceed his or her current potential it would require at least a swing rebuild. Think about the golfers who have incorporated compensations into their game. Suppose a golfer cannot hit the ball straight and always slices severely, so they compensate by aiming off target and having an extremely strong grip. Their current potential would be much less than a golfer with a technically sound swing. It does not mean that they could not beat the other golfer; it just means that the potential of the technically sound golfer is probably greater. To exceed their current potential, they would need to rebuild their swing so that it is more technically sound and the compensations are no longer a part of the swing process.

The same applies to work processes. To take the performance of a process beyond its current entitlement means that the process as it stands must be fundamentally changed to generate a new entitlement.

Performance Improvement Strategies

Depending on (a) the level of performance the Black Belt wishes to generate from the work process and (b) the level of performance the process is currently at, a Black Belt can choose from a number of different strategies for solutions generation.

- **Incremental Improvement** – This is achieved through improving the existing process, just tweaking it if you like. Steps in the existing process may be dropped or added, or adjustments to inputs or the numerous variables that affect the output may be made. The process still remains essentially the same however, and the performance entitlement doesn't really change. In our 'Change Mastery' program, we refer to this type of change as 'Gradual Change'.
- **Resourced Improvement** – Achieved by adding resources to the process. How many golfers have purchased a new set of perimeter weighted irons, a radical new putter, a titanium driver, all for the purpose of increased performance? This is the concept of challenging current performance entitlement through resources, and without changing the process in any way. In the workplace this strategy might involve the replacement of plant or equipment. For example, a company that produced computer chips experienced such growing demand that finally it exceeded the capability of the plant that produced the chips. It was found that the main piece of equipment that performed the soldering work was experiencing a defect rate of approximately 40%. The decision was made to upgrade the machine to one with a much greater capacity and dispose of the older one. With the new machine in place, supply once again exceeded demand, however, no real change was made to the process.

- **Exponential Improvement or Step Changes** – This is the most radical change, and is often described as a 'step change'. By redesigning the process, the intention is to establish a higher level of performance and entitlement. I always recall the story of Phil Mickelson, professional golfer, who took 8 months off to completely rebuild his swing. When he came back to play the PGA Tour, he expected to play at a much higher level than with the old swing. In essence, he was using a new process. In our 'Change Mastery' program, we refer to this type of change as 'Radical Change'.

Using This knowledge

So how does a Black Belt use this knowledge in a practical way?

The choice of which strategy to undertake depends on (a) the type of process being worked on, and (b) the degree of improvement targeted. A process for using this knowledge is as follows:

- Discuss the concept of process performance entitlement with the team
- Identify the current performance level of the process
- Identify the performance goal
- Describe the gap between current and targeted performance levels
- Discuss and select a suitable strategy for bridging the performance gap

Studies have shown that in manufacturing and service industries there appears to be a wall at about the 4.7 sigma level. If process performance is near this level, then it is probable that an exponential change strategy would need to be employed to go beyond.

However, if the process were currently performing at the 2 to 4 sigma level, then an incremental improvement strategy would be beneficial. In other industries such as mining, it may be the case that current entitlement is much lower than in manufacturing.

GENERATE AND SELECT SOLUTIONS (STEP 13)

The solution generation phase is the point that most people want to get to in the first instance. In fact it seems to be the natural tendency for most people to offer solutions right at the start of the project. Just think about the experiences of most people. They undertake years of study to learn how to find answers to problems. They get told by the boss, 'Don't bring me problems, bring me solutions.' They know the process so well that the solutions are obvious – just ask them. Well the moment has finally come. The team now has a list of *validated* root causes, so they are ready to start treating them in creative ways.

How does a team come up with solutions? There are many approaches to choose from, and we will discuss some of the most common including:

- Benchmarking
- Idea generation methods including multiple variants of brainstorming

A GOOD SIX SIGMA SOLUTION

What is a good solution?

To answer this question, we need to think about the process the team has followed to this point in time. They've generated a list of root causes for a specific effect that has been observed. In doing so the discussion has focused the team's work around understanding the cause effect chain that leads to the observed effect.

The most effective solutions are those that interrupt this cause effect chain, and that can occur at any point along the chain. For example, suppose we had the situation where excessive cycle time was being experienced with equipment repairs. A cause effect chain might look like that shown above.

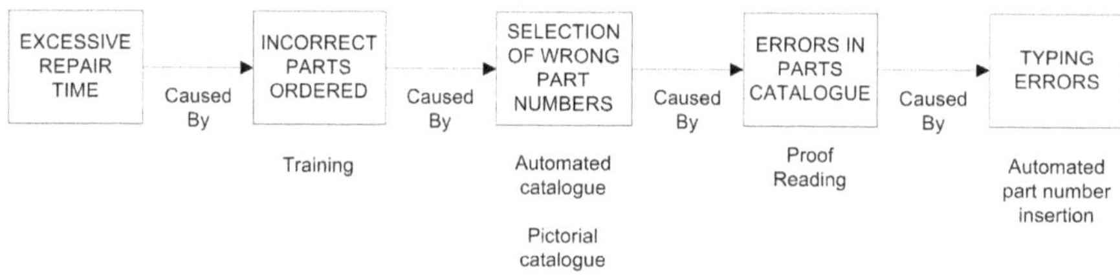

A number of different solutions can be generated that 'potentially' interrupt the chain at varying points. The point in the chain that was finally identified during root cause analysis will therefore determine the type of solutions chosen. To summarise the point, it's important to remember that the most effective solutions are those that treat validated root causes and interrupt the cause effect chain.

Now, we shouldn't lose sight of the fact that not only is the ability of a solution to treat the root cause a factor in determining the best solutions, but also factors linked to the business itself as well as stakeholders.

Factors such as:

- Acceptability
- Fit within constraints
- Needs of the business or customers

These factors will often form the foundation for decision-making criteria.

SOLUTION GENERATION APPROACHES AND TOOLS

There is no single way or best way to generate solutions in process improvement work. There are many ways to approach solution generation as well as an almost unlimited variety of tools to use. You choose an approach based on the context of your work, your capability, your desired outcome, the specific goals your project is charged with and the limitations of the team's capability.

Approach	**Tools**
Get Clues from Other Companies	• Benchmarking
Treat Validated Causes	• Regression Models (Linear Regression, DOE) • Channel Brainstorm • Nominal Group Technique • Solution Thought Mapping

Approach	Tools
Use Creativity and Innovation	• Anti Solution Brainstorm • Word Association • Picture Association • Analogy Association (process)

SHEWHART-DEMING PDCA / PDSA CYCLE

Before we discuss the specific tools here, I want to first give you some information regarding the approach of two highly regarded thinkers in the area of process improvement – Walter Shewhart and Dr. W. Edwards Deming.

During the early 20th century, Walter Shewhart undertook extensive work in the development of a scientific process for understanding the acquisition of knowledge. His model stemmed from the belief that knowledge begins and ends with experimental data, but the data at which it ends is the not the same data at which it began.

Shewhart applied his principles practically when he identified the three steps of quality control in manufacturing.

1. Specification
2. Production
3. Inspection (judgment of quality)

Shewhart noted that specifications could not be set without some form of inspection, and this information was not available until some production had taken place.

Shewhart also observed that the sequence corresponded to the process of generating a hypothesis, undertaking experimentation, and testing the hypothesis. These three steps together formed a dynamic process for the acquisition of knowledge.

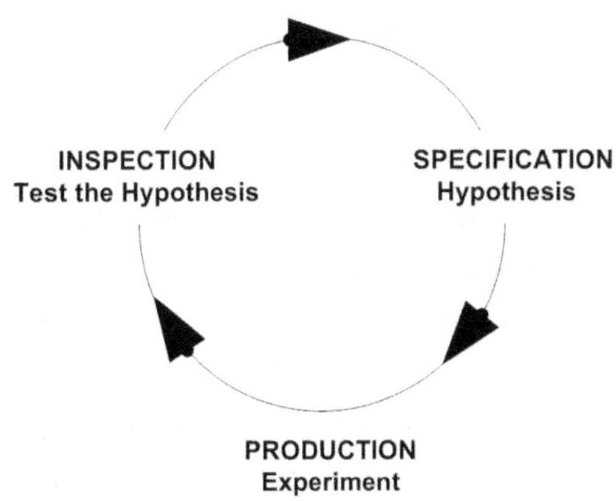

The model was revised by Shewhart and Deming in order for it to be applied to process improvement work.

The revised model was originally called the PDCA cycle, but later changed by Deming to the Shewhart-Deming PDSA cycle. (Plan-Do-Study-Act).

The PDCA cycle is logical and provides a simple four-step sequence for learning and improvement that are applied later in this text as the framework for Benchmarking and Pilot Studies.

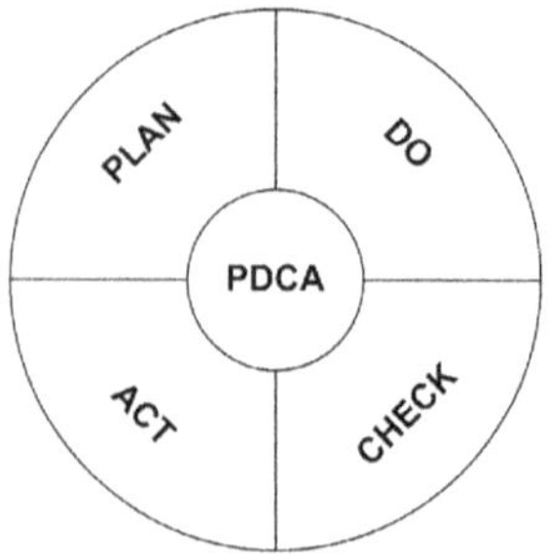

PLAN: A plan is devised for the purpose of undertaking a test, experiment, study or change for the purpose of improvement.

DO: The plan is executed.

CHECK (STUDY): Results of actions taken are checked or studied to identify the key learnings.

ACT: Action is taken to continue with the work, do it differently, or abandon it.

BENCHMARKING

Do you know who is responsible for inventing the 'windows' concept that we know so well today? How about the mouse you use with your computers. Xerox invented them. Now that may be a surprise to many of you, because we know that Apple Computers brought them to prominence. Where did they get the idea? Well surprisingly enough, they got it from Xerox, that's where. Some of the best products in the world today came about because the makers took a look at what other companies were doing and adapted those ideas to their own needs.

One of the factors that contributed to General Electric's enormous success during the 80's and 90's under the guidance of the then CEO, Jack Welch, was the drive to eliminate the 'not invented here' syndrome that often prevents creativity and growth. Looking to see what was happening outside of GE, in effect Benchmarking was a strategy actively driven by the CEO during those years that contributed to enormous growth in the company's value.

What is Benchmarking?

In the words of Robert Camp, "Benchmarking is the search for industry best practices that lead to superior performance." He uses the term 'best practice', though my fear is the term alludes to the belief that the practice is as good as it gets. I prefer the term 'leading practice' in that the practice is only leading at that point in time. There will always be another activity that is leading practice at some time in the future.

Benchmarking is a form of knowledge sharing, and it is most effective when information flows two ways between companies involved. In fact, the American Productivity and Quality Centre (APQC) defines benchmarking as: ".....the process of identifying, sharing and using knowledge and best practices."

Benchmarking – an everyday practice

People benchmark almost every day, albeit unconsciously. Have you ever watched someone using a software program on a PC, for example MS Word, and you observe that person use a command or do something that you have never seen before? You know how to get to that same point only it is the long way of doing it. What do you do? You usually ask them how they did that, and then you add that command or activity to your portfolio of PC skills. That's benchmarking; observing leading practice and then adapting it to your particular needs.

Benchmarking occurs in many other arenas. Football teams go and watch other football teams play to see what plays they have incorporated into their game. Golfers receiving lessons are often video taped and then shown how their swing compares to a top-level golfer with a similar physical make up.

I attended a Lean Six Sigma Conference in Melbourne, Australia back in 2002, where I met with a large number of Consultants and representatives from the business improvement groups within a number of major Australian corporations. I asked every person I came into contact with about the value they got from the seminar, and almost all said it was seeing what everyone else was doing. These professionals realised that if they did not stay in contact with leading practice, they were going to be left behind in a highly competitive world.

As I said, benchmarking is an everyday practice. We do it quite naturally and even unconsciously. In the following pages I want to provide you with a brief look at how to undertake benchmarking in a formal way for your business improvement project work.

How can benchmarking drive improvements

Two significant benefits can be gained by benchmarking:

- Technical – technological breakthroughs, enhanced processes and optimised inputs can all be observed through benchmarking.
- Cultural – benchmarking can break down resistance to change by providing examples of better practice, busting assumptions that improvement cannot be achieved, and stimulating different levels of thinking. Creating a culture of continual improvement and drive towards outstanding performance. Shifting the corporate mindset from one of complacency to one with a strong sense of urgency to improve.

Types of benchmarking

There are three types of benchmarking to consider:

Internal

Internal benchmarking occurs when an organisation benchmarks within the bounds of its own organisation. For a single company, this may occur between functional work areas or departments. For a multi-national or multi-business company, this may occur between business units.

Competitive

Competitive benchmarking occurs when an organisation benchmarks within the industry in which it competes. It might benchmark competitors, suppliers, customers, or anyone involved in the industry or companion industry.

For example, a Shared Business Service operating within a global company based in Australia leads a 'benchmarking consortium' to which a number of direct competitors and companion industry businesses participate. They share knowledge of leading results and practices associated with the management of human resources and financial administration.

Functional

Functional benchmarking occurs when an organisation benchmarks outside its own industry. It might benchmark the leaders of these industries, or leading companies that have similar functions, or companies just known for their success.

Some astounding breakthroughs have been generated through functional benchmarking. One manganese producer in South Africa was plagued with problems in dealing with the 'fines' produced in their plant. A Six Sigma team conducted a benchmark study of a chocolate producer, knowing that the chocolate production process produced 'fines' as well. Their study revealed a number of leading practices that were adopted into the manganese production process.

One coal mine in the Australian state of New South Wales, undertook a project to reduce downtime associated with their conveying system. The project team undertook a benchmark study of a major airline, a company known for its reliability in moving vast volumes of passenger luggage. A number of leading practices were incorporated in the solution package at the end of the project.

Sources of Benchmarking Information

Benchmarking is not just the process of visiting another organisation to see what they are doing. Benchmarking data is available from a wide range of sources. In fact, these sources should be the first port of call for business improvement project teams.

Some common sources include:

- **Publications** – monthly magazines, newsletters, newspapers, journals, periodicals etc
- **On Line Media** – company web sites, information sharing web sites, own company intranet
- **Affiliations** –affiliations bring together professionals with some common theme. Themes can be industry specific such as mining or technology, or non-industry specific such as Australian Institute of Management.
- **Consulting Firms** – having worked with a broad range of clients, possibly spanning multiple industries, consulting firms usually have a broad range of experience.
- **Seminars** – seminars are held frequently around the country covering a myriad of topics. Seminars also offer the opportunity to connect with people that have similar work interests and perhaps another source of benchmark data.

How To Benchmark

There are four steps in conducting a benchmarking activity:

1. **PLAN** the benchmark study
2. **DO** the benchmark study
3. **CHECK** the benchmark study
4. **ACT** on the benchmark study

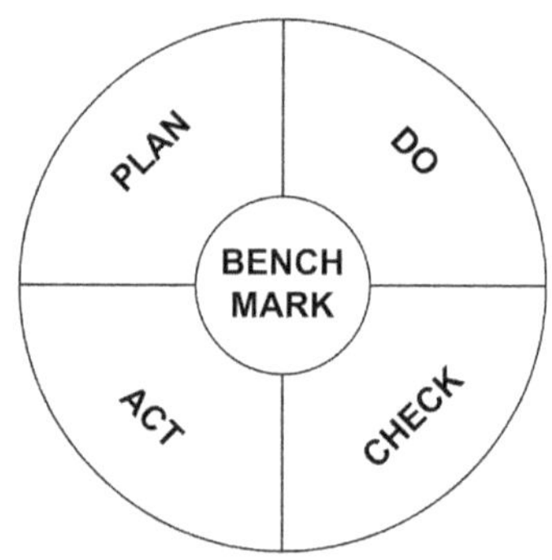

Figure 272: The Four Step Benchmark Process

'PLAN' the Benchmarking Study

Before any planning starts, the team must first decide the process they want to undertake a benchmarking study for. Knowing what is going to be benchmarked, the team can then commence the planning phase. The planning phase of benchmarking answers the following questions:

- **What performance output is going to be benchmarked?** The output should be one that is important to the customer, hence have an impact on the success of the business. By answering this question, the team's work is focused in the right direction from the start.
- **Who to benchmark?** Potential candidates are identified, and screening questions are formulated. Screening questions should be formulated in such a way that high performers who are prepared to participate in information sharing are able to be separated from those that are either not at the

performance levels you desire, or who have a 'closed shop' approach to business practices.

- **What to benchmark?** The team identifies what it is that they are looking for and the questions they want answered about practices that contribute to the results being achieved. The purpose is to identify 'leading practice'.
- **How to benchmark?** There are many approaches that can be undertaken for benchmarking. Four of the most common are indicated in the table below.

APPROACH	REQUIREMENTS	ADVANTAGES	DISADVANTAGES
Face to Face	Point of contact Detailed company research	Richness of communication Visual data is obtainable On the spot clarification	Usually higher cost – particularly where companies are geographically dispersed Longer cycle time
Telephone	Point of contact Well planned discussion guide	Short cycle time Minimal cost On the spot clarification	Limited information
Electronic Media	Common software Easy to complete forms	Short cycle time Multiple sources can be benchmarked Minimal cost	Limited information without immediate clarification
Online (Web Site / Intranet)	Access to company information	Short cycle time Minimal cost	Information is usually limited to results only, and not the underlying practice that led to those results No clarification

'DO' the Benchmarking Study

The team's ultimate goal in undertaking benchmarking is to improve the performance level of the project process. With that in mind, the team should be benchmarking companies that are achieving high levels of performance. It makes no sense to benchmark any old company regardless of their performance. Performance is what you see at the end of the process. This performance (y) is a function of many variables (x's), and in fact within these variables will be the leading practices that you want to identify.

When starting the process of identifying who should be a company that you benchmark, your screening questions should include those that help you determine who has the level of performance worthy of finding out about.

One thing to remember is this, even though a company is achieving the desired level of performance, their practices may not be accessible or transferable. Some discussion needs to take place to discuss whether or not these factors will be limiting factors on the value of benchmarking a particular company.

Once organisations are screened, the benchmarking focus shifts to identifying the practices that contribute to the results being achieved. Planned questions are asked with a view to identifying 'leading practice' that is accessible and transferable.

To summarise, there are two steps in the 'Do' phase:

- Screen for high performers (the outputs or outcomes)
- Identify practices that contribute to performance (the process)

'CHECK' the Benchmarking Study

The key activities in this phase are to identify practices that enable or hinder leading performance. The team presents a final report that details findings and insights, and a list of leading practices. After a period of discussion, an initial action plan to adapt relevant practices is developed by the team.

I always discuss the concept of sharing information with students in Six Sigma seminars. When I say sharing, I mean two-way sharing of information.

My experience has been that many people are not entirely comfortable with this. Let me offer this view. If I have an idea and I share this with you and you share one idea with me, how many ideas do we now have each? Obviously two each. If I share this same idea with another person and they share one idea with me, how many ideas do we all have now? I have three while you have two each. If I share my idea with a third person and they share one idea with me, how many ideas do we now have?

What pattern do you see emerging here?

It seems that in simplistic terms, the more widely I share with people who are prepared to share two ways, the further ahead I get in terms of ideas. Whilst this is just a hypothetical scenario, my experience has been that this is how it can work in reality. The more you give, the more you will get. The wider you share, the more you will grow in comparison to those who do not share information. Knowledge is not power, the ability to access and share knowledge is power.

'ACT' on the Benchmarking Study

The team should not just 'clone' or 'copy' identified practices. Leading practices that have been identified should be *adapted* to the project process, with the goal of taking performance beyond that of competitors.

Always remember two things when benchmarking:

- If you only ever copy practices from other organisations, you will always be a follower
- Today's leading practice is tomorrows legacy system

Leading practices from multiple organisations may be combined. For example, Motorola combined leading practice from multiple ideas into their 'bandit' pager to produce a product that was virtually defect free.

Before adapting practices, it may prove useful to assess the potential consequence of adapting these practices into your organisation. In the absence of a formal methodology, this assessment can simply take the form of asking the following questions of the new practice;

- If we adapted this practice, what could be negatively impacted?
- What could the impact result in?
- How severe would this impact be?
- What is the likelihood of this occurring?
- What can we do to either reduce the likelihood of this occurring, or manage the impact?

Matching Performance with Maturity and Sophistication

'Not all leading practices can be adopted by every organisation.'

Think about the scenario where a person with an older 2000 model laptop computer installs Windows Vista Professional and Microsoft Office 2008. The performance of that software would be less than optimal, and in fact it would probably not perform as well as the old Windows XP and MS Office 2000 program. The sophistication of the PC does not support the level of sophistication that exists in the software. It functions best when installed in a PC with an appropriate level of sophistication.

This concept has relevance when we talk about adapting leading practices. Highly mature and sophisticated organisations may not have practices that can be adapted by a less sophisticated organisation. For example, a company that is extremely progressive and works in an industry where technology is extremely modern and sophisticated (technology based industries) may demonstrate leading practices in information processing that cannot be effectively employed in a less sophisticated industry (for example mining). This can also present challenges when adopting leading practices and advanced technologies in less industrially mature countries.

Key Learning Points

- Benchmarking is the search for leading practice.
- Leading practice today is the legacy system of tomorrow.
- If an organisation only ever changes on the basis of benchmarked practices, they may only ever be a follower.
- Do not clone leading practice; the key to success is adapting practices to suit the maturity and sophistication of the organisation with the goal of exceeding competitor performance.

THE CONCEPT OF CREATIVITY

The Concept of Creativity

Creativity and innovation, these are such wonderful topics. They are components of life that can be very rewarding, something for the dreamers. However, it is something that does not seem to come easily to some people. Why is that? Have you ever struggled to get people to come up with 'out of the box' ideas? To be able to deal with this you need to understand the reason why this is often difficult for some people. The reason can be simply explained by the way in which people's thinking matures over time.

- When we are born, our thought processes are instinctive. As a baby, when someone touches the centre of our hand, we automatically close the hand.
- As youths, we are extremely creative. We have imaginary friends and think in ways that adults often don't understand. We describe things in ways that rational people would not think of and we have an insatiable curiosity about the world and our environment.
- As we get experienced in the ways of the world, our thinking becomes intuitive during the period of 15 to 25 years.
- And by the time we reach around 25 years of age we become rational in our thinking.

We can represent this process diagrammatically in the form shown below.

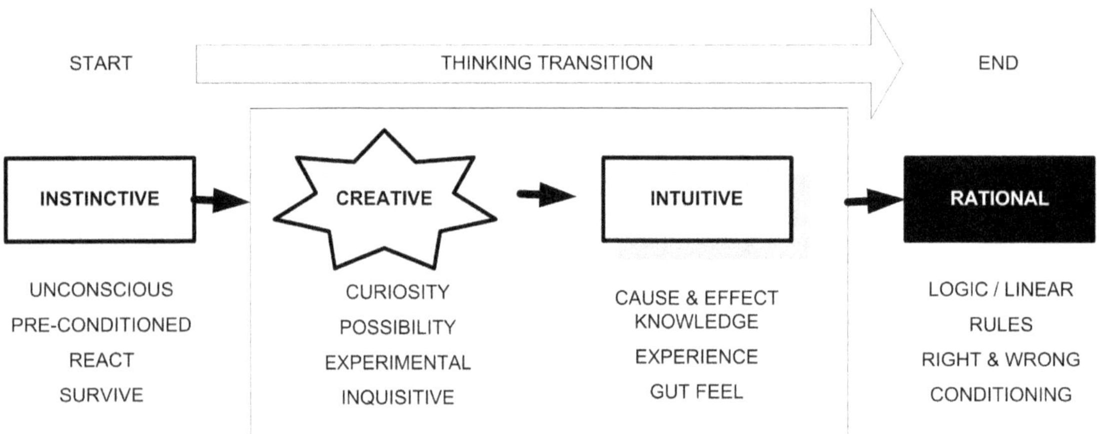

Figure 273: Thinking Maturity Model

Tony Buzan (2003)[36] tells a wonderful story that demonstrates two concepts: how our thinking changes over time and how we tend to think in a confined dimension created by experience and rational thinking. A group of researchers were conducting IQ testing of children. The test involved participants selecting the correct answers to questions from multiple choice lists. One question involved selecting the 'odd one out' from four different images. The choices were an image of the *sun,* an image of the *moon,* an image of the *earth* and the final image was of a *lemon.* A ten-year old boy who undertook the test immediately chose one of the images.

[36] Buzan, Tony. *'Brain Child'*, Thorsons, London (2003), pp. 60-61

Which one do you suppose he chose?

The boy chose the *earth* as the odd one out.

So upon completion of the test, this boy's IQ level was marked down as with many of the other questions; he had failed to identify the *obvious* answer. Many of his answers were so bizarre that the testers wondered whether or not the boy suffered from mental retardation of some kind.

They brought the boy back to the clinic as a follow up and analysed his answers one by one to find out the thinking behind the answers. When asked why he chose the *earth* instead of the *lemon* with regard to the specific question mentioned, in amazement at their lack of perception he stated "because it's the only blue one."

His creative thinking process was in a dimension beyond the logical thinking of the testers. As they analysed his other answers, they found that his intellectual process was far more complex and creative than the relatively uncreative thinking of the testers.

<u>Our Education System</u>

This change in thinking is an evolutionary process, not revolutionary. The interesting thing is that our education system supports and promotes the concept of rational thinking. Formal education often prescribes thinking boundaries and analytical rules. As we gain experience, we develop specialised knowledge and condition rigid processes for how we think and approach certain situations. Individuals lose the ability to take mental detours, to innovate or improvise, to mentally experiment. It is our goal – to be rational thinkers, and probably for good reason too.

Without the ability to create routine stable patterns for dealing with a world that is itself routine and stable, we would have difficulty functioning each day. Rational thinking is exactly what we need most of the time. But when we need to be creative, that type of thinking does not work.

When we leave school we are trained to provide the 'right' answers to the technical aspects of any problem in our field of expertise.

I do not recall having ever been taught in school to be creative or to facilitate creative thinking in a team of people to help them come up with a solution.

'Think about this for a minute – we start school with a box of multi coloured crayons and finish school with one blue pen! How interesting!'

So when we ask people to be creative, in general we are fighting the effects of time and environmental conditioning. That is not to say that all people find it difficult to be creative during adulthood.

I have noticed a common quality among people I have met in my lifetime whom I consider creative, and that is the quality of youthful exuberance. When they are in a creative frame of mind, they do not take life too seriously; they are able to laugh at themselves, they often play practical jokes and pranks, and more often than not, they have an abundance of energy and enthusiasm. The conceptual blocks developed over time tend to disappear when these people are around.

If you get the opportunity, try to get these types of people on your team for at least the solution generation stage of the project.

Now knowing that not all people can spontaneously bounce from rational to creative thinking, the idea creation tools in this book are designed to help create an environment where creativity can occur.

<u>What Is Creativity?</u>

The following is an extract from Edward de Bono's Serious Creativity (1996)[37].

'At the simplest level, 'creative' means bringing into being something that was not there before. In a sense, 'creating a mess' is an example of creativity. The mess was not here before and has been brought into being.'

In the context of a business improvement project, creativity is the generation of lots of new ideas without inhibition, and combining ideas in different and often irrational ways. It requires the ability to not be bound by beliefs, limitations or constraints, or our natural tendency for 'vertical thinking'.

De Bono (1995) prefers to use the term 'lateral thinking'. He differentiates between lateral thinking and vertical thinking in this way. Vertical thinking is the process of building on a known position. Each step taken depends on where you are at a particular moment. He describes this as building up from a base or digging the same hole deeper. Some idea generating tools (e.g. brain writing, brain mapping) have a tendency towards vertical thinking. Lateral thinking on the other hand is a sideways move. It involves trying new concepts, entirely new perceptions; new points of entry. Lateral thinking is associated with exploration, with possibility and what might be. Analogy based idea generation tools are examples of ways to intervene the vertical way of thinking and push the thinking process sideways.

<u>A New Organisational Approach</u>

The old approach to creativity in organisations was that only a few people were considered to be creative. Only those involved in the strategic areas of the business, engineers, outsiders in the form of consultants were creative or allowed to be creative. In existing times, change occurs much faster than it has ever before and the old approach can't produce results fast enough. So now the new way emerges. The new way is to encourage everyone to be creative with breakthrough ideas. Creativity must be cultivated more widely than the traditional approach, and more people must be involved if results are to be produced fast enough in our ever-changing world.

Creative Environments

The environment can have a significant impact on the ability of team members to be creative. Over time, each of us builds 'associations' with certain parts of the organisation. Do you find it much better to get away from the office to some foreign environment if you want to write a report, memo or letter? Do you find it difficult to put pen to paper in your office? I recently attended a presentation on innovation by John Cleese of Monty Python fame. In reference to the book 'Hair Brain, Tortoise Mind' he talks about creating a tortoise enclosure; a place where you have the time and mental space to just slow down and let thoughts flow.

Taking my cue from J.K. Rowling who created most of the Harry Potter books in a café, I spend many hours in cafes and holiday resorts thinking, creating and planning in respect of our business and various products we offer. In fact, this book was mostly written on planes, in cafes and at various resorts around the world.

---

[37] de Bono, Edward. *'Serious Creativity'*, Harper Collins, London (1996), p. 3

Think about this for a moment. Each of us builds associations throughout our lives. We each have associations with specific parts of our workplace that are either positive or negative. For example, if every meeting we have in the main meeting room is an emotional challenge that leaves us feeling bad about attending, we will associate negative emotions with that meeting room. Just like Pavlov's dog started salivating each time the bell was rung, the negative association we have with that room will be unconsciously conditioned and creativity becomes a challenge in that particular environment.

Suggestions

How do you create an environment suitable for creativity? Let me offer some suggestions.

- Get out of the office environment where emotional associations have been formed
- Eliminate distractions such as phones and email
- Allocate time
- Use bright colours in your environment (yellow is a favourite)
- Use music (find out about the 'Mozart Effect)
- Involve creative people who can act as a stimulus to wider creativity
- Formally establish a low risk environment, one free from criticism – use ground rules
- Perform work in an environment that is aesthetically pleasing; i.e. outdoors, around the pool
- Encourage building upon ideas
- Undertake a creative, out of the box thinking activity prior to work on the project content to set the tone
- Have lots of fun and laughs

Facilitating Creativity

To facilitate creativity, make use of the tools that interrupt logical thinking patterns, be an explorer yourself, respect others, actively listen, and avoid those killer phrases and words such as 'but'.

Creativity tools offered in this and other books help by:

- Breaking or interrupting patterns of thinking
- Enhancing traditional brainstorming methods
- Creating links between seemingly unrelated ideas
- Breaking down ideas to look at their parts and principles

Idea Incubation

One thing that facilitators very soon learn is that not everybody thinks in the same way. It's common for trainers to find that the same people keep answering questions while an individual or particular group of people tends not to answer. One reason for this is linked to the time it takes individual people to process certain information in their minds. When asked for ideas to solve problems, it's not uncommon for some individuals to generate lots of ideas while other individuals tend not to produce the same volume, if any at all.

Think about this for a moment. Ideas are produced as an output to a mental process. The process starts with some form of stimulus such as a question or statement. The stimulus incubates in the mind until an idea is presented, and then the idea is externalised in some way.

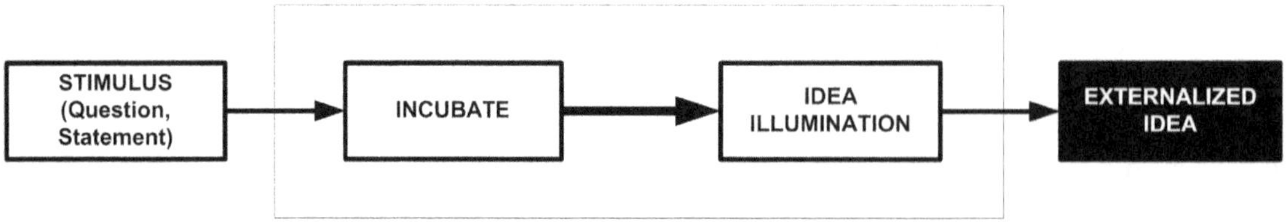

Figure 274: Idea Incubation Model

Each person incubates ideas at their own rate. Some people produce ideas in an extremely short time, while others produce their ideas over a longer period of time. In effect, those people have a longer incubation period. The time and way we incubate ideas is affected by thinking preferences, experience, assumptions or artificial constraints, perception of the problem or question at hand and even the environment in which the thinking takes place.

Now the impact for Black Belts is this: unless people are given time to allow this incubation to occur, many ideas will be missed. With this thought in mind, let me offer some suggestions:

- **Defer decisions** until after participants have been allowed to incubate ideas overnight.
- **Take a break** between idea generation and decision-making, allow for additional ideas after the break. (Refer to 'I' time in Chapter 5 – Project Leadership)

To illustrate the way in which creativity in problem solving is affected by various factors, try the following activities. Some suggested answers are provided at appendices.

Nine Dots

Your task is to draw four straight lines that pass through all nine dots without lifting your pencil off the paper.

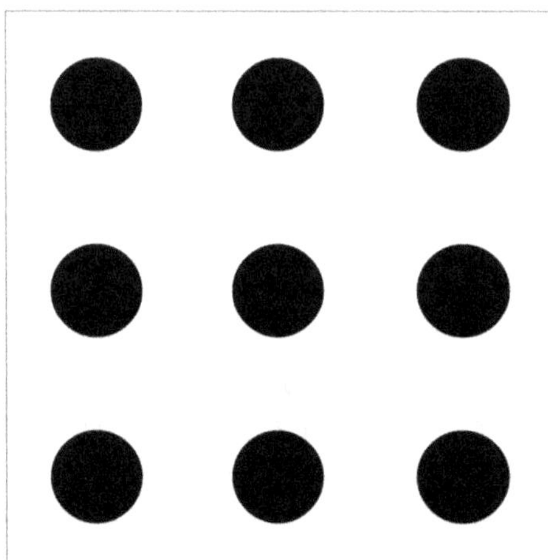

Figure 275: Nine Dots Activity

If the task seems impossible, try removing the constraints or assumptions you have placed around the figure. When you complete it with four lines, try completing the same tasks with only three lines.

Join the Boxes Activity

Your task is to join each of the pairs of boxes with single unbroken lines. The rules for doing this are:

- The lines cannot go outside the perimeter of the box.
- The lines cannot intersect.
- Only pairs of lettered boxes must be joined.

The end result will show 3 lines joining the 3 pairs of lettered boxes (i.e., A with A, B with B and C with C).

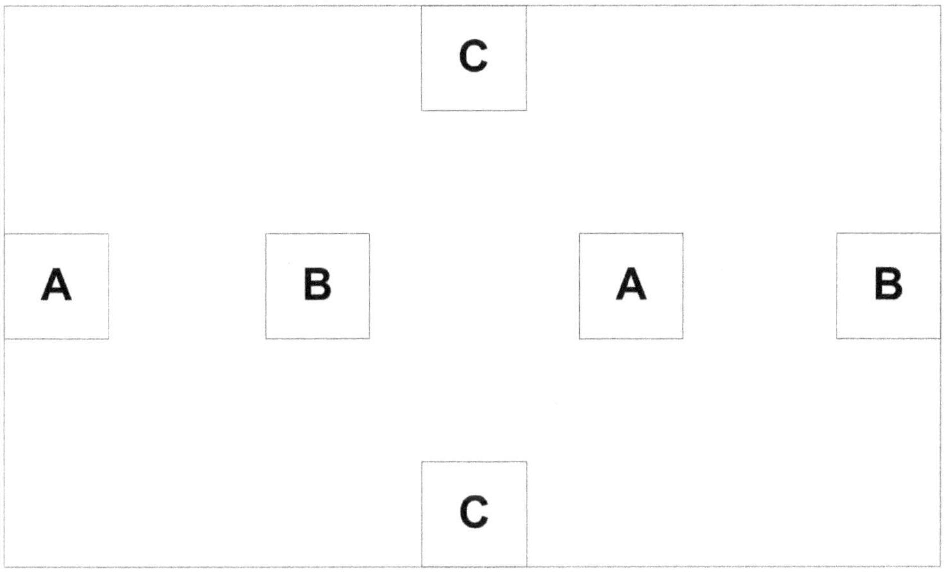

Figure 276: Join the Boxes

There are no tricks to doing this. If you're having problems coming up with an answer, change the way you think about the lines. Identify the assumptions you have made and change them if they are self imposed. This activity tends to be easier for visually oriented people.

Roman Numerals

The Roman numeral 9 is represented by the symbol below. By adding a single line, change it to represent the numeral 6.

Figure 277: Roman Numeral 9

Once again, if you have trouble solving this, challenge your own assumptions, challenge the way you think about lines, or even challenge the way you think about the desired outcome.

Related Numbers

What is the relationship between the numbers shown in the sequence below?

854917

Trouble solving this one, then change the way you're thinking about the numbers themselves.

Rebus Puzzles

Rebus puzzles are pictorial representations of common phrases or terms. For example, Symphon represents the phrase 'unfinished symphony'. See if you can solve the following.

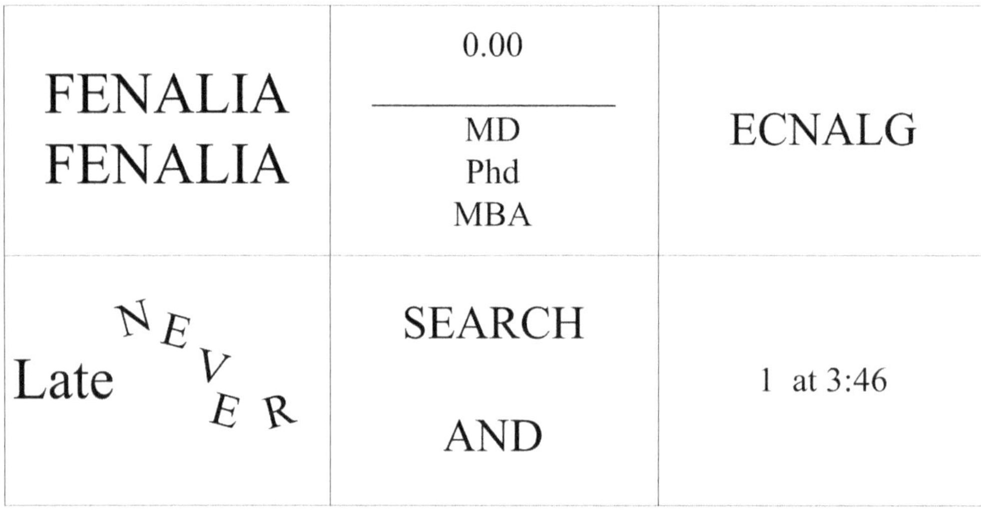

If you are having trouble solving these, change the way you view the representation. Don't just try to read the words, think about other elements such as position, size, special relationships or even how the representation can be observed in another way.

THE 'GOOD IDEAS' PROCESS

Core to business improvement project leadership is the ability to facilitate the generation and selection of ideas. There are countless approaches to this aspect of facilitation. However, one common theme emerges. That is the requirement to open up to many ideas before narrowing down on the most relevant.

The 'GOOD' Ideas Process for Achieving Agreement

In running seminars I work with many teams comprised of people from a diverse range of industries. One of the tasks we undertake during seminars delivered in-house to companies is to choose a restaurant to go to for a group dinner. Each time we do this the conversation follows a consistent process.

In the first instance, the groups generate a large number of ideas of possible locations. They then begin to drop off a few of these on the basis of availability, tastes and preferences. Finally a decision is made on a single restaurant, usually on the basis of some form of voting.

The process followed is something we intuitively do when commencing from a large number of choices to finally choosing one of the options.

1. State the desired outcome
2. Ask the question
3. Generate a list of choices
4. Start organising these by removing those with no chance of being selected
5. Decide on one of the options

The challenge for us as facilitators is to utilise a sequence like this in a deliberate manner. Having a formal process is the foundation for achieving consistent results in the most effective and efficient manner. We will be challenged when we realise that some people prefer specific elements of this process. For example, some people prefer to just get to the decision without procrastinating, while others love the step associated with idea generation and creativity.

By understanding these differences, you will be in a better position to deal with individual engagement and emotions during the process.

The process shown below is based on this sequence of steps. There are many more tools than the ones shown that can be added to the portfolio, however the focus is on those tools that are likely to be used more often.

I have called the process I use to identify and make decisions about ideas, the 'GOOD Ideas' process. I liken it to a funnelling process where a large number of ideas are collected, regardless of their relevance, and then they are passed through a series of sieves that progressively get more selective. The end result is a logical group of ideas that are relevant to the question being asked.

The GOOD Ideas process consists of five steps. The first two steps are used repetitively throughout the process. The steps are:

1. Define your **Desired Outcome**. The answer to the question – "What exactly do you want to achieve?" - should be made clear up front. In fact, I encourage team leaders to write this up on the white board or flip-chart so that it can be used as a continual source of reference.
2. Ask **GOOD** questions. Have you ever heard of the GIGO principle? (Garbage In, Garbage Out) This step of the GOOD ideas process is founded on a principle that I will refer to as GOGI. If you ask a poorly phrased question of people (garbage out), then you will not get the quality of response that you desire (garbage in). Always remember one thing – 'Ask and thou shall receive'. So in the context of our work here, a well-phrased question will initiate thought processes, discussion and therefore input that is relevant to the desired outcome you are targeting. Focused thought and discussion is the result. A poorly phrased question increases the risk of the ideas not being relevant and the discussion going off track. In the art and science of facilitation this is the art component.
3. **OPEN** the discussion to all possible ideas. This is the step during which ideas are not analysed, but rather collected regardless of their relevance. It is often the case that an idea that some may think are not relevant, could trigger thoughts about an idea that is relevant, and may not have been generated if the first idea was not captured. Our focus here is on quantity not quality.
4. **ORGANISE** ideas into a manageable number of probable ideas. Our focus now changes from the quantity approach to the quality approach. The goal is to drop off those ideas that probably do not provide the best answer to the question asked.
5. **DECIDE** which ideas are relevant. At this point, we make a decision about which ideas we will run with, and this comes from having an understanding of which ideas are more likely to be relevant.

In summary, the process follows these steps.

- Clearly define what your desired outcome is up front.
- Focus thoughts and discussion by asking good questions
- Generate as many ideas as possible without analysing any – this is where the aspect of creativity is promoted
- Drop those ideas that are least likely to be relevant – this creates a short list of ideas that now should be analysed for relevance
- Select those ideas that are most likely to be relevant – this takes the list of ideas down to those that have met certain criteria that set a foundation for success

Linking GOOD Ideas Process with Tools

The table below demonstrates the link between the GOOD ideas process and associated tools.

ELEMENT	GOAL
DESIRED OUTCOME	To Create Focus on the End Point Be explicit on what your desired outcome of the discussion is.
GOOD QUESTIONS	To Generate Appropriate Thought Patterns Ask a well-phrased question that is linked to the outcome you want to achieve.
OPEN	Open Up to Many Ideas Think up lots of new and innovate ideas Borrow ideas from other seemingly unrelated subjects
ORGANISE	Organise Ideas Rearrange for understanding Reduce the size of the list
DECIDE	Decide Which Ideas Are More Likely to Result in Success Eliminate those that cannot progress Choose between non-mutually exclusive ideas Choose between mutually exclusive ideas

STATING DESIRED OUTCOMES

Knowing what it is that you want is a driving force for aligned discussion and actions. Defining the outcome at the beginning of the process forces the facilitator to think about how the discussion will be managed.

It also provides a source of continual reference to keep the discussion on track, particularly if the desired outcome is written and clearly visible to all.

GOOD QUESTIONS TO FOCUS THOUGHTS AND DISCUSSION

If there is one thing that a Black Belt must master, it is the ability to ask good questions. Good questioning focuses thoughts and discussion. Remember the concept of Garbage Out, Garbage In that I mentioned earlier. There is nothing more frustrating than to struggle with getting input from a group of people. If you want to focus the group effectively, you need to identify good questions to ask.

Useful Planning Questions

To identify the questions you need to ask, consider the following questions to focus your own mind.

- What input do I need from the group?
    - I want them to identify the potential causes of the problem
    - I want them to identify potential solutions that will treat the causes?
    - I want them to provide ideas for ....
- What do they need to know for them to give that input?
    - They need to know the extent of the problem.
    - They need to know the root causes of the problem.
    - They need to know the focal point of the discussion.
- What would be a poor question to ask that would lead to poor input?
    - (A question with no reference to the point of focus) What are some causes? What could we do?
- What question should I ask that will focus their thoughts around the input I need to get from them?
    - What might be causes of .... ?
    - What would be potential solutions that would overcome / solve / treat this cause?
    - What would be some ideas that would .... ?

OPEN UP TO NEW IDEAS

Two very important points to remember when entering the process of idea generation:

- Avoid discussing limitations: These will have a tendency to impose barriers to creative thinking.
- Do not discuss ideas as they come up: Capture everything as it is worded by the source.

Tools for Generating Ideas

Some of the most commonly used idea generation tools are those that either help team members think of new and unusual ideas, or borrow ideas or principles from other seemingly unrelated ideas.

Thinking up a lot of ideas – some new, some unusual	Borrowing ideas or principles from other seemingly unrelated fields
• Popcorn Brainstorming • Nominal Group Technique • Anti Solution Brainstorm • Channel Brainstorm • Brain Writing • Solution Thought Mapping	• Analogy Association • Picture Association • Word Association

Tools for Generating Ideas

An interesting observation is that most of these tools are variants of the process of brainstorming. The most common of these tools are detailed in the 'Improve' phase toolbox.

<u>A Tip for Black Belts - Interrupting Patterns of Thinking</u>

One thing all facilitators must remember is this.

'The pattern of thinking that gets a team to a specific stuck point in the process will not get them out of it.'

For example, say a team is struggling to generate the answers to some specific problem (this could be anything such as scoping issues, problem statement defining etc). To break through that point there needs to be a change in the pattern of thinking. An interruption in thought pattern can be achieved in numerous ways through changing the point of focus. Different approaches that are effective in interrupting patterns of thinking include these:

- Change the approach you are using
- Ask a question that has absolutely nothing to do with the subject at hand (confusion is useful in shifting thinking away from a stuck point)
- Take a break
- Move to something else and then come back later
- Introduce an analogy to the discussion (such as 'if you were in space and you had to reduce the ……')

What we have introduced you to in this chapter are tools and techniques for interrupting or breaking regular thought patterns. For that reason I like to refer to these as 'pattern intervention' tools or techniques.

ORGANISE IDEAS

Tools for Organising Ideas

The purpose of this step is to organise ideas and commence the process of eliminating ideas from the final list.

Reducing the size of the list	Rearranging Ideas
• Removing Duplicates from the List • Multi Voting	• Affinity Grouping

Tools for Organising Ideas

These tools are described in detail in the 'Improve' phase toolbox.

Packaging Raw Solution Ideas for Decision Making

Having generated a number of ideas, the team needs to package these ideas into solution statements before making any decisions. The way ewe do that is quite simple.

- **Consolidate Similar Ideas** – Where a large number of ideas are generated, similar ideas can be combined into one solution idea using the affinity grouping process.
- **Name / Describe the Solution** - You do this by simply stating what the proposed solution is in a way that people understand what it involves.
- **Link Solutions to the Problem (Cause) Being Treated** – This can be achieved by asking whether or not the solution treats identified root causes. The team can then make educated guesses as to what impact the solution ideas would have on the problem or the root causes. Any idea that does not treat root causes in some way will probably not have a link to the desired outcomes of the project in any case.
- **State How the Solution Treats the Cause** – Write up a short description of how the solutions actually impact the identified problem or root causes.

The examples shown below are of three different solutions statements that comprise three parts:

- Solution description
- Cause being treated
- How the solution contributes to solving the problem

Solution Description	What problem (cause) are you treating with this solution?	How does it resolve that problem (treat the cause)?
Remove the need for Forman approval.	The excess number of steps / handoffs in the process.	By reducing the number of steps in the process, it reduces the cycle time to complete the work.
Replace all bearings with sealed type bearings	Accelerated wear due to contamination of the grease within the bearings	The seal prevents the influx of dirt and material into the bearing resulting in a longer life cycle

Solution Description	What problem (cause) are you treating with this solution?	How does it resolve that problem (treat the cause)?
Build a mechanism that shakes the wagons as they unload	Material getting caught in the wagons and not being dropped when unloading	Vibration of the wagon will lessen contents while tipping and accelerate the dump rate

Packaging Raw Solutions for Decision Making

DECIDE ON FINAL SOLUTIONS

What does the term 'decide' mean? To decide means to cut off from [all other alternatives].

How you decide will have an impact on the commitment of those who are going to do the work, hence there is a need for the team to decide 'how to decide'. The level of commitment expected of the team must be reflected in the degree of involvement of the team in the decision making process. The diagram below shows some approaches and the correlation between expected buy in and level of involvement.

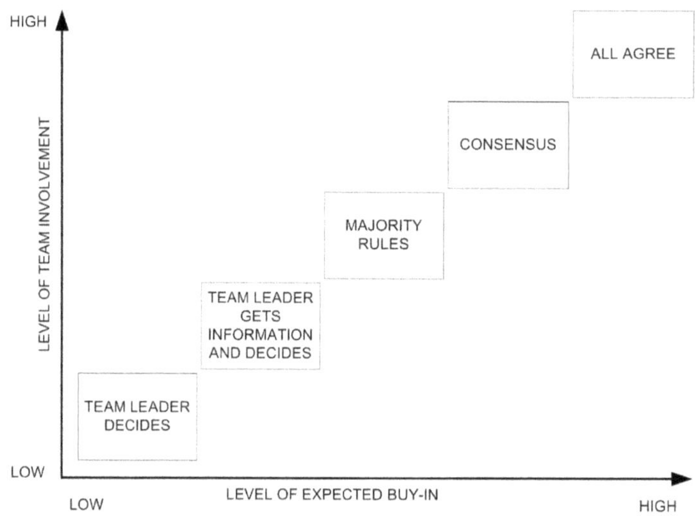

Figure 278: Team Involvement versus Level of Buy In

The factors that most commonly affect the choice of decision-making style include those proposed by Victor Vroom and Phillip Yetton[38] in their 'leader participation model'.

- **Quality Requirement** - The importance associated with the technical quality of the solution.
- **Leader Information** – The sufficiency of information held by the team leader to make a high-quality decision.
- **Commitment Requirement** – The importance of team commitment to the decision.
- **Problem Structure** – How well the problem is structured.
- **Commitment Probability** – The probability of the team being committed to the decision if the leader

[38] Robbins, S.P., Waters-Marsh, T., Cacioppe, R., Millett, B. (1994), *'Organisational Behaviour – Concepts, Controversies and Applications'*, Prentice hall, Sydney, pp. 491-492

were to make the decision.

- **Goal Congruence** – The degree to which the team shares the goals associated with the project.
- **Team Conflict** – The degree of conflict within the team over proposed solutions.
- **Team Information** – The sufficiency of information held by the team to make a high-quality decision.

> Tip for Black Belts
> Always consider this when choosing approaches to idea generation and selection: The greater the level of involvement in solution generation and selection by the team, the greater their level of commitment to making those solutions work.

DECISION APPROACHES AND TOOLS

There is no single way or best way to choose which solution or solutions you will implement in process improvement work. To make sound decisions, all we need remember are two simple points:

- Decision-making is a process of logic, not a creative process.
- Solutions are ultimately chosen by comparison against one another in some form.

Logic Based Comparison Tools

Approach	Tools
Criteria Comparison	Absolute Criteria Screening Weighted Criteria Rating
Paired Comparison	Paired Ranking
Consequence / Success Comparison	Potential Failure Analysis Potential Consequence Analysis
Financial Payoff Comparison	Net Present Value (NPV) Internal Rate of Return (IRR) Return on Investment (ROI) Payback Period
Non-Financial Payoff Comparison	Payoff Analysis (Impact versus Effort)

How do we choose which tools to use? The metaphor of a 'sieving' process might best describe the approach.

Sieving for the Best Ideas

Our work in making decisions about which ideas to carry forward can be liked to a process of passing ideas through a series of sieves, each layer progressively getting finer and finer so only the real gems pop out at the end. The desired outcome is to very quickly drop ideas that cannot possibly progress, then analyse those ideas that can progress in more detail so we choose the solution or solutions that will give us the greatest improvement.

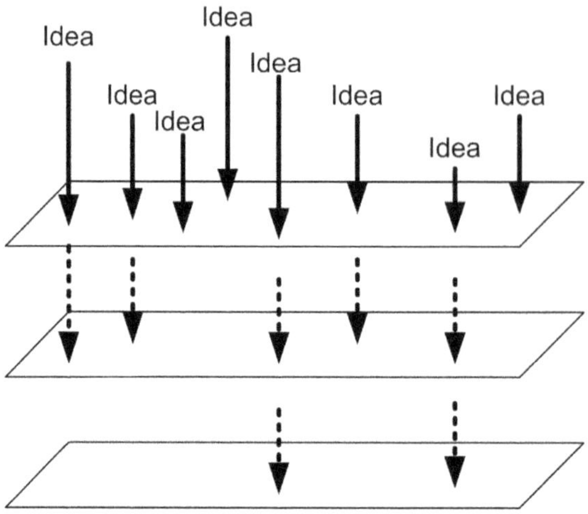

Figure 279: Sieving for Best Ideas

Logic in the Process of Selecting Ideas

In choosing tools to use you must be familiar with the terms 'mutually exclusive' and 'non-mutually exclusive'.

MUTUALLY EXCLUSIVE: If you were shopping to buy a refrigerator for your home, you would have to narrow your choice down to one item. As you would only be buying one refrigerator, it would be a situation of this one OR that one. Your choices in this situation are referred to as 'mutually exclusive' as you can only have one.

NON-MUTUALLY EXCLUSIVE: However, if you were shopping for flowers for your garden, you might narrow your choices down to a range of flowers with the intention of buying a whole carload. It would be a situation of this one AND that one. Your choices in this situation are referred to as 'non-mutually exclusive' as you can have many of them.

With those terms in mind, let's take a look at the decision-making tools and the sequence in which they might be applied.

Eliminate Ideas That Cannot Progress	**Choose Between Groups of Non-mutually Exclusive Ideas .... OR**	**Choose Between Groups of Mutually Exclusive Ideas**
Absolute Criteria Screening	Payoff Analysis Potential Failure Analysis Potential Consequence Analysis	Paired Ranking Weighted Criteria Rating Financial Models

Tools for Selecting Ideas

These tools may be combined in a sequence of decisions. For example, a team may use the Payoff Analysis to select a final short list which is then prioritised using Weighted Criteria Rating. These approaches are detailed in the 'Improve' phase toolbox.

Benefits of Using Decision Making Processes

What are the benefits of using processes and tools to make the decision about which ideas to take forward? Think about this for a moment, you are a part of a team that contributes a large number of ideas to solve a problem. The decision as to which ideas are taken forward is retained by the team leader or given to a small number of people to make. To what degree would you be aligned with that decision, supposing for a moment that not one of your ideas was selected? In many cases I am sure that you would not be happy with the choices with thoughts running through your mind of a lack of fairness in the decision making process. It is unlikely in such circumstances that you would leave the meeting and support the decision.

The benefits of using tools to make the decision include:

- Team members see and participate in the decision making process so are confident in its fairness
- The emotional connection with ideas is more likely to be severed and a higher degree of team commitment can be expected
- Ideas chosen are more likely to solve the problem
- Ideas chosen are more likely to be accepted on the first occasion as they will fit within the constraints and limitations of the business
- Ideas chosen are more likely to satisfy criteria important to the customer and the business itself

<u>Tip for Black Belts</u>

- Tools do not make decisions, the team does.
- Just because a particular process produces a specific idea as that which best fits the criteria, doesn't mean you have to implement that solutions.
- Always ask 'does this make sense to us to implement this or these solutions?'

FINANCIAL MODELS IN DECISION MAKING

The selection of solutions may well have a significant impact on the ability of work processes to contribute to the achievement of strategic business objectives. Numeric models are also used to make such decisions, the most common being financial models. Financial models for decision making include:

- Payback Period
- Return on Investment (ROI)
- Net Present Value (NPV)
- Internal Rate of Return (IRR)

Business leaders favour these types of models for they talk the language of organisational value. The limitation of these types of models is that they are based on cash-flow forecasts.

Payback Period

Payback period is the time taken to gain a return equal to the original financial investment. The period of time associated with the payback is usually expressed in years and months, and is calculated by dividing the original financial investment by the annual net after-tax cash inflow.

This equation is illustrated in the following example.

$$\text{Payback} = \frac{\text{Original Financial Investment}}{\text{Annual net after-tax cash inflow}}$$

$$= \frac{\$50{,}000}{\$15{,}000}$$

$$= 3.3 \text{ years}$$

Table 52: Payback Calculations

This approach can be used to compare solutions that are mutually exclusive. Consider the example where the team identifies two solutions to reduce the number of defects produced by their process. Both solutions have the same initial cost ($50,000). However, their cash flows perform differently over the four-year period under analysis.

The table below can be used to compare cash flows and subsequent payback periods.

Year	Solution A Cash Flow	Solution B Cash Flow
0	(50,000)	(50,000)
1	15,000	30,000
2	20,000	25,000
3	25,000	20,000
4	30,000	15,000
Payback Period	3 Years	2 Years

Solution B recovers the original outlay sooner than Solution A. Where the decision is to choose solutions on the basis of shortest payback period, Solution B would be chosen.

This approach has both advantages and disadvantages.

Advantages	Disadvantages
• Simple to use • Reduces financial risk • Uncertainty of future cash flows is reduced • Faster payback has a favourable short-term effect on earnings per share • The payback period is a selection criteria that business leaders are familiar with	• The time value of money is not considered • The payback period does not take into consideration the total context of the project and long-term returns • The results are based on projected cash flow, all other financials are ignored • Whilst the duration of financial risk is reduced, risk exposure is not quantified

Return on Investment (ROI)

Another popular method for investment appraisal that does look at the whole project is return on investment (ROI). ROI is simply the average annual profit divided by the number of years the investment will run, converted into a percentage.

$$\text{Average Annual Profit} = \frac{\text{(Total Inflows)} - \text{(Total Outlay)}}{\text{Number of Years of Investment}}$$

$$\text{ROI} = \frac{\text{Average Annual Profit}}{\text{Original Investment}} \times 100$$

Table 53: Return On Investment Calculations

Using our initial example, the projected return on investment for each solution is as shown below.

Year	Solution A Cash Flow	Solution B Cash Flow
0	(50,000)	(50,000)
1	15,000	30,000
2	20,000	25,000
3	25,000	20,000
4	30,000	15,000
Total Inflows	$90,000	$90,000

$$\text{Annual Profit} = \frac{90{,}000 - 50{,}000}{4 \text{ years}} = \$10{,}000 \text{ per year (both solutions)}$$

$$\text{ROI} = \frac{10{,}000}{50{,}000} \times 100 = \mathbf{20\%}$$

Like other methods, return on investment has its advantages and disadvantages.

Advantages	Disadvantages
• Simple to use • Considers cash flow over the whole project • The result is expressed as a percentage return on investment, a parameter that is readily understood by business leaders	• The time value of money is not considered – profit is averaged out over a period of years so solutions with high initial cash flow may be ranked equally with solutions that have low initial cash flow but high profits later

To address the shortcomings of ROI and Payback with respect to the time value of money, a discounted cash flow technique must be used. This is particularly desirable in an environment of high interest rates and inflation.

Discounted Cash Flow

Discounted cash flow methods take into account the value of money over time. For example, whilst $1,000 today will have the monetary value at the same time next year, it will not have the same worth or buying power. We value $1,000 much more than $1,000 in the future. There are two basic methods for modelling this effect: (a) Net Present Value (NPV) and (b) Internal Rate of Return (IRR).

Whilst these methods take into account the value of money over time, they are based on forecasted cash flows and an accurate prediction of interest rates.

Net Present Value (NPV)

To understand NPV we must first understand the concept of compound interest. By investing $1,000 at 10 percent, it will be worth $1,100 in one year, and after two years it will have a compounded value of $1,210. NPV in effect, is the reverse of compounded interest.

If you were offered $1,210 in two years time, and inflation and interest rates equated to 10 percent, it would be worth $1,000 today (present value) if we work backwards. The net present value (NPV) is calculated when we combine cash flow over a number of years in this way.

When calculating NPV, the initial effect of cash flow discounting is assumed to act at the end of the first year (or beginning of the second year), therefore all first year cash flows are at present value.

The key equations for calculating NPV are:

Projected Cash Flow =	Income – expenditure
Present Value =	Cash flow x discount factor
Discount factor =	$1/(1+i)^n$
Where:	i = forecast interest rate
	n = number of years from start date

Table 54: Net Present Value (NPV) Calculations

The discount factor is derived from the reciprocal of the compound interest formula and can be read from a table of discounting factors. Using the table, it is not necessary to undertake the entire calculation.

Table of Discounting Factors

Years	1	2	3	4	5
10%	0.9091	0.8264	0.7513	0.683	0.6209
11%	0.9009	0.8116	0.7312	0.6587	0.5935
12%	0.8929	0.7972	0.7118	0.6355	0.5674
13%	0.885	0.7831	0.693	0.6133	0.5428
14%	0.8772	0.7695	0.675	0.5921	0.5194
15%	0.8696	0.7561	0.6575	0.5718	0.4972
16%	0.8621	0.7432	0.6407	0.5523	0.4761
17%	0.8547	0.7305	0.6244	0.5337	0.4561
18%	0.8475	0.7182	0.6086	0.5158	0.4371
19%	0.8403	0.7062	0.5934	0.4987	0.419
20%	0.8333	0.6944	0.5787	0.4823	0.4019

Table of Discounting Factors

The NPV helps make a decision about which of the solutions to choose on the basis of the value of each in today's terms. The solution with the highest NPV should be chosen.

Consider our two example solutions with a discounting factor of 10 percent

Year	Solution A Cash Flow	Discount Factor (10%)	Present Value
0	(50,000)	1	(50,000)
1	15,000	0.9091	13,636
2	20,000	0.8264	16,528
3	25,000	0.7513	18,782
4	30,000	0.683	20,490
		TOTAL NPV	$19,436

Year	Solution B Cash Flow	Discount Factor (10%)	Present Value
0	(50,000)	1	(50,000)
1	30,000	0.9091	27,273
2	25,000	0.8264	20,660
3	20,000	0.7513	15,026
4	15,000	0.683	10,245
		TOTAL NPV	$23,204

Using NPV, the team would select Solution B with an NPV of $23,204 over Solution A with an NPV of $19,436. When a negative value for NPV is calculated, the solution should be automatically rejected because the project would lose money.

It's important to point out that we've applied discount factors as though these figures were relevant at the 'beginning of the year'. If they were 'end of year' figures, discount factors would be applied earlier and final figures would be different (refer to NPV and IRR functions in MS Excel shown on following pages).

Like all other methods, NPV has its advantages and disadvantages.

Advantages	Disadvantages
• The time value of money is considered • Direct comparisons are able to be made on the basis of today's value • The whole project is considered • Sensitivity analysis can be undertaken through changing discount rates	• The accuracy is determined by the accuracy of predicted discount rates and cash flows • Non financial data is not included • A fixed discount rate is used for the duration of the analysis, when varying discount rates may be more realistic

Calculating NPV With MS Excel

MS Excel offers a Net Present Value (NPV) function for making these calculations.

However, note that all figures are treated as 'end of year' figures, thus discounts are applied earlier than in the table on the previous page.

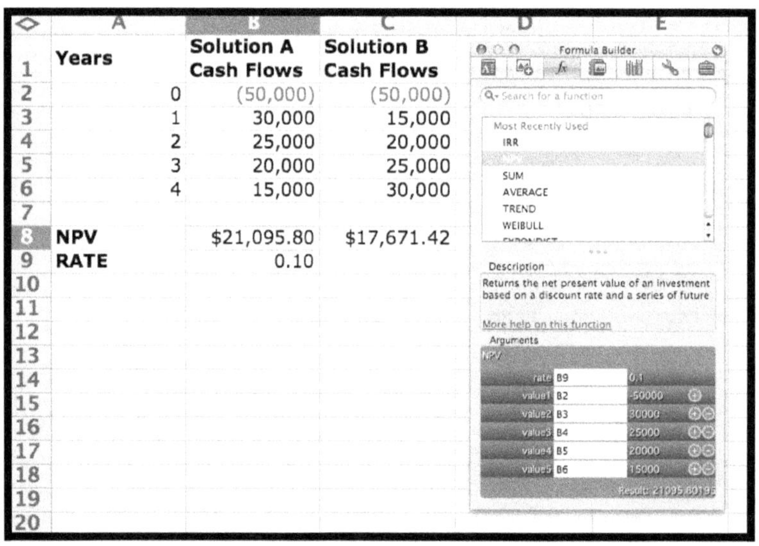

Figure 280: NPV Function with MS Excel

Internal Rate of Return (IRR)

In simple terms, the IRR of a solution is the discount factor when the NPV is equal to zero. This can be calculated by either a trial and error approach or by plotting NPV against IRR.

Calculating IRR With MS Excel

MS Excel provides a function for calculating IRR.

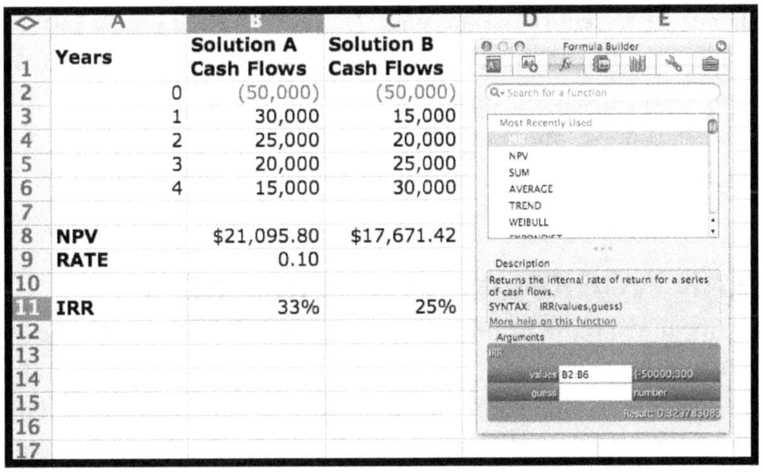

	A		B	C
1	Years		Solution A Cash Flows	Solution B Cash Flows
2		0	(50,000)	(50,000)
3		1	30,000	15,000
4		2	25,000	20,000
5		3	20,000	25,000
6		4	15,000	30,000
7				
8	NPV		$21,095.80	$17,671.42
9	RATE		0.10	
10				
11	IRR		33%	25%

Figure 281: IRR Function with MS Excel

An Internal Rate of Return calculation shows Solution A has an IRR of 33 percent while Solution B has an IRR of 25 percent.

QUICK EFFICIENCY IMPROVEMENTS WITH LEAN (STEP 13)

To this point I've discussed a variety of tools for generating solution ideas. These have mostly been discussed in the context of cause and effect analysis within a Six Sigma project framework. Lean differs from Six Sigma in that most of the solution tools are very specific in the outcome they pursue and most are applied to the source of waste you've identified in your process.

For example, when you identify a time trap in your process using the Takt Time Chart, you are most likely to undertake Process Balancing to rectify the problem. If you identified excess movement in your Spaghetti Diagram, you might find Work Cell Optimisation is most appropriate for reducing that movement.

Over the following pages I will discuss a range of Lean tools that you can use to rapidly create process improvements and minimise, if not eliminate waste.

One of the first steps a team might undertake in reducing waste is to implement 5S, or as we will explain it here, 6S.

CREATING A LEAN WORKPLACE WITH 5S AND 6S

5S and 6S are both used for the purpose of producing and maintaining a clear, safe, organised workplace as a foundation for maximum performance.

In our explanation here we are including Safety in addition to the normal elements of the 5S model. We are doing this because many users of the tool work in small businesses where they don't have formal safety programs like the larger corporations. So it makes sense to add it in.

If 5S is more relevant to your situation, simply drop that S from the model.

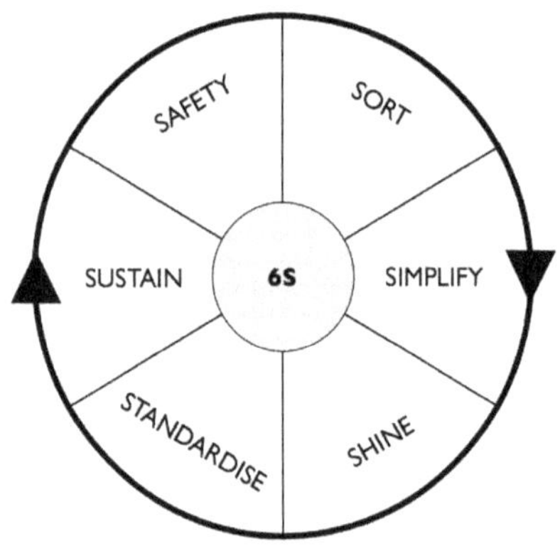

Figure 282: 6S Elements

Six Elements of 6S

Implementing 6S involves continually improving in the six specific areas or focal points:

- **Safety:** Making the respective area a safe place to occupy and work.
- **Sort:** Removing anything that is not needed from the workplace - only the bare essentials are kept.
- **Simplify:** Sometimes referred to as 'set in order', simplification occurs when needed items are arranged, labelled or identified in such a way that anyone can find information or materials with little effort.

- **Shine:** Cleaning the workplace so that it is free of dirt, grime, dust, spills or anything that contributes to it being a dirty or unhealthy workplace.
- **Standardise:** Making sure daily tasks are standardised so they can be performed in a consistent manner by anyone.
- **Sustain:** Generating a system where 6S can become a discipline and part of the way peak performance is maintained in the workplace. This usually involves ongoing evaluation and measuring against the 6S elements, recognising achievements and reporting progress. Possibly the most important factor in sustainability is the engagement and involvement of all employees.

Implementing 6S

Implementation of 6S is one of the first steps to take in improving business in a manufacturing or production environment. Early implementation may be less critical in office or service environments, though all areas will benefit, particularly if safety is given high priority on the business agenda.

Implementation simply involves following the six-step sequence described below.

Safety

Make the respective area a safe place to occupy and work. Focus might be given to:

- Removing hazards
- Marking or identifying potential hazards that cannot be removed
- Having safe work instructions available for reference
- Marking or identifying safe-ways or clear-ways
- Having relevant Personal Protective Equipment available for use

Sort

Remove anything that is not needed from the workplace. Only the bare essentials are kept. Unnecessary items might include:

- Old reference manuals or equipment handbooks
- Files not needed / outdated files
- Non working / broken tools or equipment
- Signs, posters or notices that are no longer relevant
- Cleaning materials
- Unnecessary items that have accumulated

Simplify

Sometimes referred to as 'set in order', simplification occurs when needed items are arranged, labelled or identified in such a way that anyone can find information or materials with little effort. Simplification might involve any or all of these activities.

- Labelling tools or equipment
- Labelling file and material storage locations
- Marking boundaries of specific work areas
- Erecting signs

Shine

Clean the workplace so that it is free of dirt, grime, dust, spills or anything that contributes to it being a dirty or unhealthy workplace. Specific areas of focus include these:

- Health and Safety – eliminating anything that might pose a risk to safety or health.
- Cleanliness – removing dust, dirt, grime, stains, smudges or anything that contributes to an unclean workplace.
- Waste – removing waste, or scrap materials or shredding files no longer required.

Standardise

The goal is to standardise daily tasks so they can be performed consistently by anyone. The following actions should be considered in the process of standardisation.

- Determining how tasks should be done for maximum efficiency.
- Documenting processes in the form of 'standard operating procedures' so that they are readily accessible for others who might have to perform any of the tasks.
- Standardising the 6S system by defining who does what and documenting guidelines for sorting, simplifying, shining and sustaining.

Sustain

Generate a system where 6S can become a discipline and part of the way peak performance is maintained in the workplace. This usually involves ongoing evaluation and measuring against the 6S elements, recognising achievements and reporting progress. Possibly the most important factor in sustainability is the engagement and involvement of all employees.

Evaluating 6S Performance

Evaluating 6S performance is simply a process of analysing how well each area is performing against each of the six elements. The chart shown below provides an example of the results of a 6S evaluation where a maximum score of 20 points can be achieved for each element using specific assessment criteria. The evaluation worksheet that produces this chart is shown on the following page.

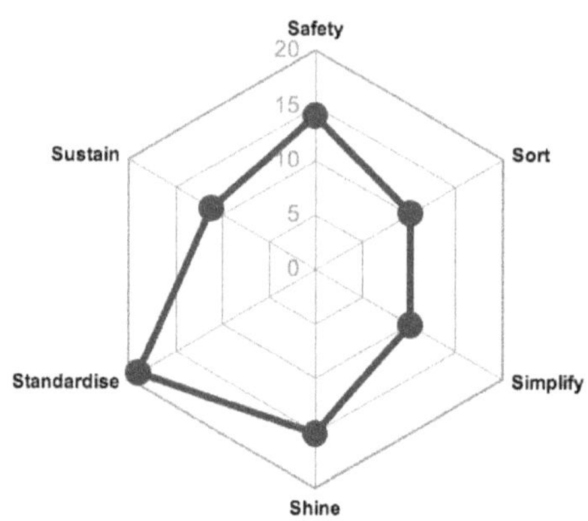

Figure 283: 6S Evaluation Chart

6S Evaluation Worksheet Example

Here is an example of what a 6S evaluation might look like. Each organisation should design its own evaluation template according to their specific business requirements.

6S Evaluation Worksheet

Date: ____________________

Evaluator: ____________________ Workplace: ____________________

Legend: 5 = Outstanding 4 = Very good 3 = Good 2 = Acceptable 1 = Rectify later 0 = Rectify immediately

1 SAFETY	GOING HOME EVERYDAY WITHOUT INJURY		0	1	2	3	4	5
1.1	There are no safety hazards present (water, oil, chemical, machinery etc)	➲	1					
1.2	Hazardous areas are marked and dilineated	➲					1	
1.3	Lock and tag procedures are being complied with	➲				1		
1.4	Where PPE is required, instructions are displayed on clean and visible signs	➲						1
1.5	Safety equipment is serviceable (includes fire equipment and PPE)	➲			1			
		SCORE	0	0	2	3	4	5

2 SORT	ELIMINATE THE CLUTTER AND IF NOT NEEDED, GET RID OF IT		0	1	2	3	4	5
2.1	Unnecessary items are not on desks or in office space	➲		1				
2.2	Bins do not contain scrap	➲				1		
2.3	Outdated / unneeded notices are not on walls, notice boards or on display	➲				1		
2.4	Excess inventory, supplies, parts or materials are not in the area	➲		1				
2.5	Unserviceable equipment is removed for disposal or maintenance, not left lying around	➲			1			
		SCORE	0	2	2	6	0	0

3 SIMPLIFY	A PLACE FOR EVERYTHING, EVERYTHING IN ITS PLACE		0	1	2	3	4	5
3.1	Correct location for items are clearly marked and / or labelled	➲			1			
3.2	Employees in the work area know where to find equipment and materials	➲		1				
3.3	Equipment locations are marked appropriately	➲			1			
3.4	Items are put away immediately after use	➲			1			
3.5	Height and quantity limits are clearly marked where relevant	➲				1		
		SCORE	0	1	6	3	0	0

4 SHINE	A CLEAN WORKPLACE FOR EVERYBODY TO ENJOY		0	1	2	3	4	5
4.1	Waste materials have been removed	➲				1		
4.2	Files are shredded and displosed	➲				1		
4.3	Floors are swept and clean	➲			1			
4.4	Windows are clean	➲			1			
4.5	Dust has been removed	➲						1
		SCORE	0	0	4	6	0	5

5 STANDARDISE	MIINIMISING VARIATION		0	1	2	3	4	5
5.1	Standard tasks are documented	➲					1	
5.2	Standard Operating Procedures are visible and accessible	➲		1				1
5.3	Checklists for cleaning and maintenance jobs exist and are readily accessible	➲			1			
5.4	All staff are trained in standard operating procedures	➲				1		
5.5	Items for performance of standard jobs can be accessed within 30 seconds	➲					1	
		SCORE	0	1	2	3	8	5

6 SUSTAIN	CREATING A DISCIPLINED CULTURE		0	1	2	3	4	5
6.1	Evaluation is conducted regularly according to a schedule	➲						1
6.2	Workers in the area have been trained in 6S	➲		1				
6.3	6S checklists and standards are available and up to date	➲				1		
6.4	Personal belongings are stored correctly in a designated location	➲		1				
6.4	A daily 6S audit has been conducted this week	➲		1				
		SCORE	0	3	0	3	0	5

Element	SAFETY	SORT	SIMPLIFY	SHINE	STD	SUSTAIN
Score	14	10	10	15	19	11

Figure 284: 6S Evaluation Template

PROCESS BALANCING

Process Balancing is essential for a company to **meet customer demand** without the unnecessary **build up of inventory and work in progress through inefficient production**. Take the following as an example. The rate at which a process must produce units to meet customer demand is 1 every 7 minutes.

The Takt Time Chart shows that additional time is contributed to the process by two of the steps (5 and 8). Production rate in this situation cannot be any better than the longest process step (which is 11 minutes for step 5). So in this case customer demand cannot possibly be met.

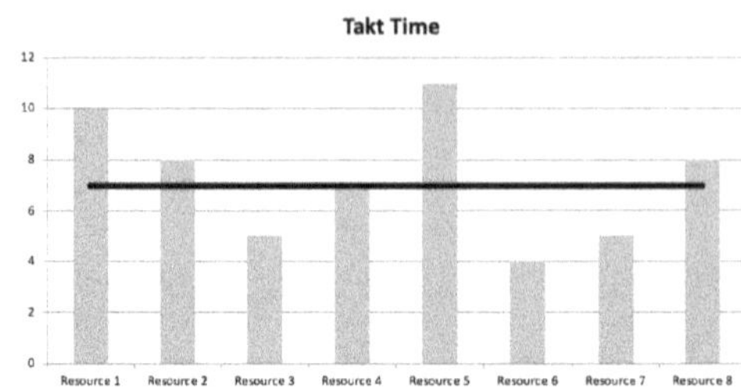

What's also interesting is the fact that there are steps in this process where excess capacity exists. For example steps 1, 2 and 3 can produce faster than Takt Rate and create waste through the build up of excess inventory (work in progress).

A **perfectly balanced process** would be one where:

1. No steps take *longer than* Takt Time to complete; and
2. No steps take *less than* Takt Time to complete.

In the **Balanced Process** all steps can be completed in the same time as Takt time. Therefore customer demand can be met without a build up of inventory or work in progress.

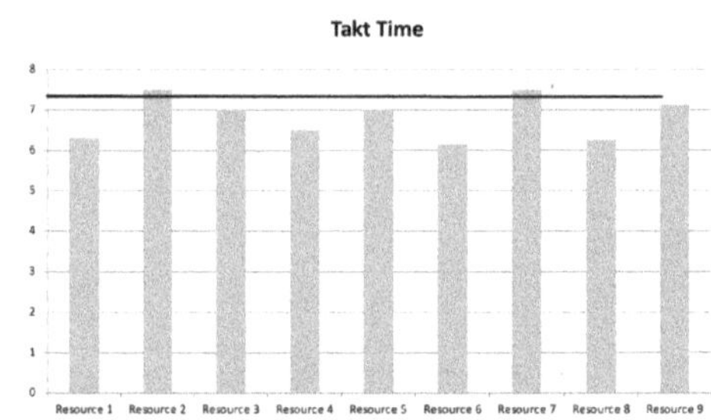

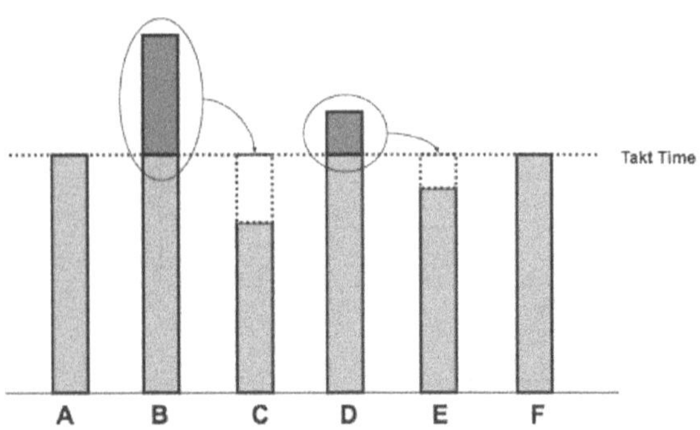

<u>The Theory</u>

The theory is quite simple; take excess time from one process step and either:

- Eliminate it altogether, or
- Transfer it to a step where there is excess capacity.

The Practical Nature of Process Balancing

In theory this is quite simple, in practice it takes thought, planning and a shift in thinking to balance a process effectively.

Principles for Process Balancing Design

Balancing your process is not just simply a matter of rearranging work. The function of a process is affected by many factors. Accordingly you should consider applying these principles in pursuing a balanced process.

- Stabilise lead time before any improvement work (remove special cause variation)
- Minimise Takt time variation
- Maximise the efficiency of resources
- Maximise the utilisation of space
- Minimise the number of process steps
- Minimise the need for process re-balancing as changes in demand are experienced

Balancing a process may require *increasing time* in certain steps and *reducing time* in others.

Methods for Reducing Time

When the time to complete a process step exceeds the production rate, time must be reduced to enable the process to meet customer demand.

- Remove or minimise non-value adding time / work (refer to time value analysis)
- Balance labour across process steps (more labour focus on this step)
- Minimise movement or motion (refer to spaghetti diagrams)
- Standardise improved methods of working (training, reinforcement, documentation etc)
- Optimise material, part and tool accessibility (work cell design etc)

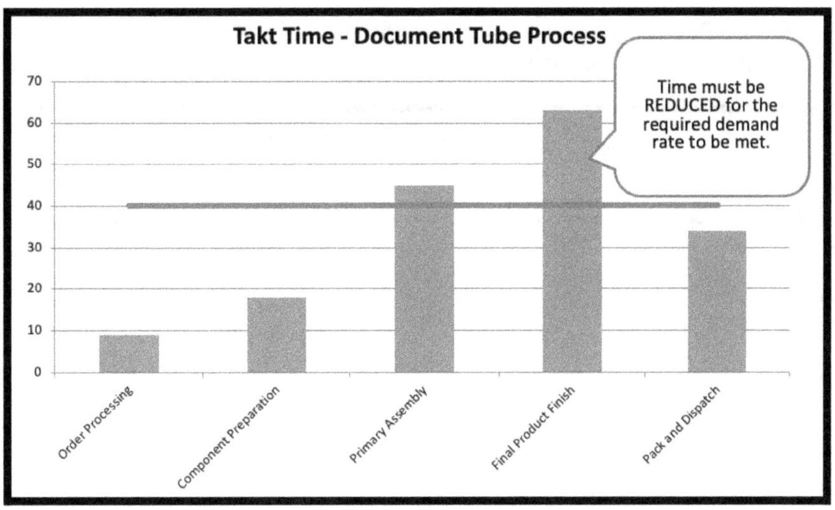

Methods for Increasing Time

When the time to complete a process step is less than production rate, time must be increased to enable the process to meet customer demand without creating a build up in WIP or inventory.

- Multi task employees (increase workload of some employees)
- Consolidate or group process steps – reduce labour requirements

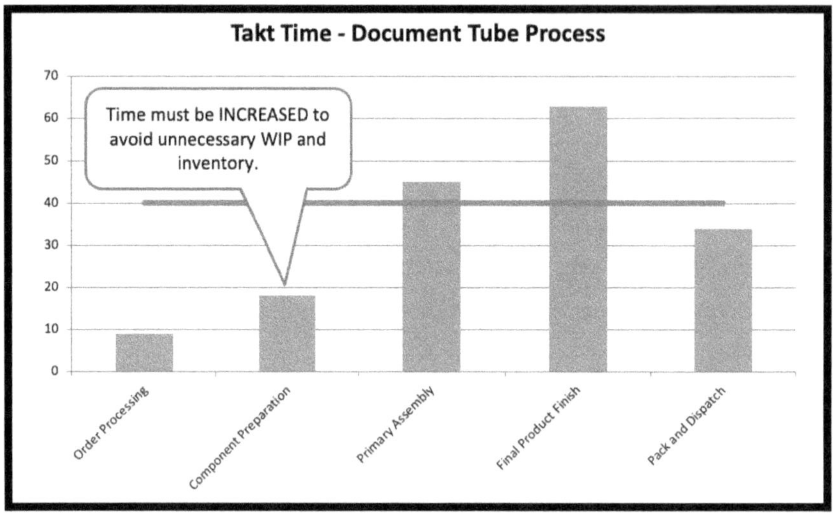

Case Study – Document Tube Factory

Taking into consideration methods for reducing time when it is excessive and increasing time when capacity is excessive, our team has now designed a process where the lead time of 40 minutes can be consistently met.

Customers will obviously appreciate the fact that units are delivered on time, and business leaders will appreciate the massive reduction in inventory.

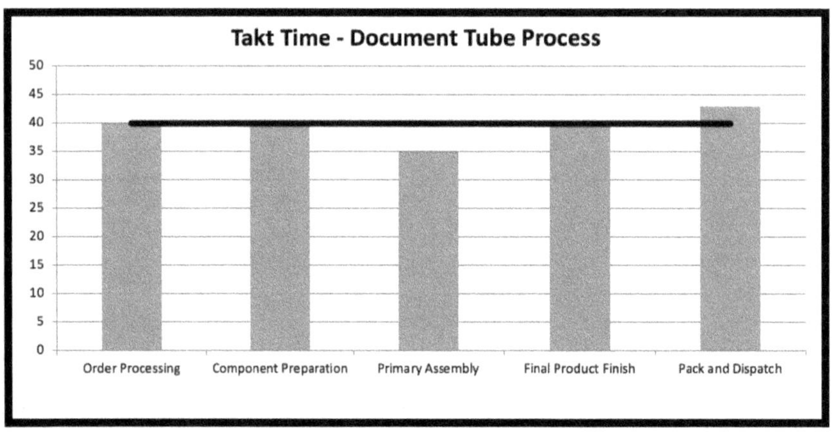

Figure 285: Balanced Process for Document Tube Process

GENERIC PULL SYSTEMS

A Generic Pull System creates a situation where there is a limit or cap on work in progress (WIP) or things in progress (TIP) so that lead time for a product or service is consistent and predictable.

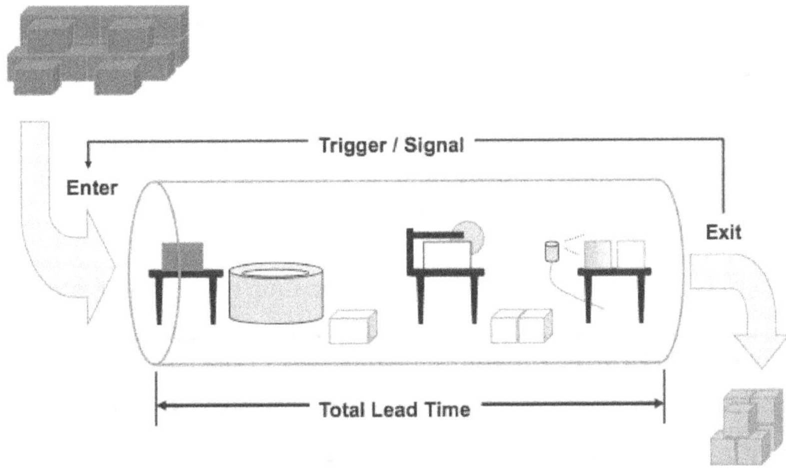

If we take a simplistic macro view of a manufacturing process, we might describe it in this way.

- Materials enter the process
- These materials are transformed as they pass through the process
- Completed products exit the process and are then passed on to end user customers

Products are either pushed through the process based on volume expectations or they are pulled through the process based on customer needs and the status of the process.

Let's explore the difference between pull and push in this context.

A Push System Versus A Pull System

A PUSH System is one which:

- Schedules the release of work based on customer demand
- Controls throughput and observes work in progress (WIP)
- Is inherently a make-to-order system driven by orders or forecasts, not system status

By contrast, a PULL System is one which:

- Authorises the release of work based on system status and what has been consumed
- Controls work in progress (WIP) and observes throughput
- Is inherently a make-to-stock system driven by production authorisation signals which are the result of voids in the process

In reality, most systems have aspects of both push and pull.

Benefits of a Pull System

With respect to process and business efficiency, pull systems are by far more appropriate. The benefits of a pull system include:

- Reduced manufacturing costs (releases of work are choked off before the system is overloaded)

- Reduced lead-time variability
- Improved quality
- Maintained flexibility

A generic pull system is essential in situations where lead-time is a vital component in satisfying customers and non-value adding work contributes a significant amount to overall processing time and costs.

Case Study – Document Tube Factory

Setting It Up

The first step in creating the pull system for document tube manufacture is to determine the maximum level of work in progress (WIP Max). Using a five-step calculation process shown in the table below, we find that WIP Max is equal to 20 units. (Refer to notes on PCE)

NOTE: It is vitally important that you use the correct denomination throughout the calculation.

(a) Calculate current Total Lead Time Total LT = WIP ÷ Avg. Completion Rate	Total LT = 48 units ÷ 8 per day = 6 days (6 days = 54 hours = 3,240 minutes)
(b) Calculate current Process Cycle Efficiency (PCE) PCE = Value Added Time ÷ Total LT	PCE = 131 minutes ÷ 3,240 minutes = 0.0404
(c) Determine your target level of PCE Fabrication Processes should achieve PCE in the range of 0.10 to 0.25.	Target PCE = 0.10
(d) Calculate your target lead-time Target LT = Value Added Time ÷ Target PCE	Target LT = 131 minutes ÷ 0.10 = 1,310 minutes (= 21 hours 50 minutes = 2.43 days)
(e) Calculate WIP Max WIP Max = Target LT x Completion Rate	WIP Max = 2.43 days x 8 per day = 19.44 (rounded up to 20 units)

Creating the Pull System

The second phase is to initiate a system for releasing work into the process.

(a) The actual WIP for this process was found to be 48 units.

(b) The team agreed that the guidelines for releasing work would be:

If WIP ≥ 20 units (WIP Max), work would not be released

If WIP < 20 units (WIP Max), sufficient work was going to be released to allow the process to reach 20 units in the system

(c) If there were going to be customer impacts from the non-release of work, the team also agreed to implement the following strategies:

Increase capacity so that WIP is lowered (can be temporary)

Process work on a first in, first out (FIFO) process; or alternatively

Process High Priority Orders before Low Priority Orders

SINGLE MINUTE EXCHANGE OF DIE (S.M.E.D.)

Developed by Shigeo Shingo between the late 1940s and 1960s, Single Minute Exchange of Die, or SMED as it is often referred to, is one of the many lean production methods for reducing waste in a manufacturing process.

The aim of applying SMED methodology is to systematically reduce the time lost in production due to machine set-ups. Actual time lost can be anything from days to hours.

Often referred to as **Quick Changeover**, SMED is a concept that says *all changeovers* (and even startups) can and should take less than 10 minutes, hence the term Single Minute. SMED has application to almost every production situation.

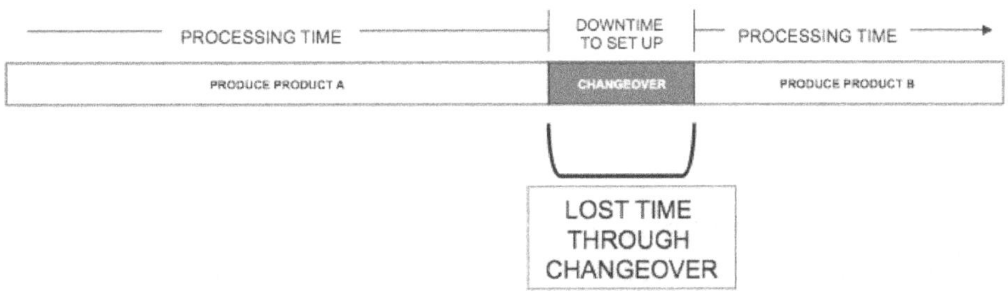

Did you know that at Toyota, set-ups were reduced from 3-hours (in 1945) to less than 3-minutes (in 1971)?

Changeover and Industry Application

Changeover Time is the elapsed time between finishing the last part of the previous batch, and finishing the first one of the next batch at full production speed. If you are required to run the first few at a slower than normal rate, or make minor adjustments to get the quality right, then that counts as part of the changeover time.

Changeover Time is also referred to in other ways across different industries.

- Aircraft-on-Ground time (Aviation industry)
- Clean-down time (food industry)
- Die change time (moulding, stamping or extruding)
- Make-ready time (print industry)
- Process purge time (chemical & pharmaceutical industry)
- Tool Change time

Strategies for Reducing Changeover Time

Shigeo Shingo (1989)[39] identifies eight techniques that should be considered when pursuing SMED. These are included in the three major strategies discussed here.

1. Separate Internal From External Tasks

Internal Tasks: Set up tasks that must be performed when the process is stopped. For example, you can't change the chuck on a lathe while it's still running.

[39] A study of the Toyota Production System, Shigeo Shingo, Productivity Press, 1989, p 47

External Tasks: Set up tasks that can be performed while the previous batch's production is still running or once the next batch is underway. Basically these tasks are about getting ready for the changeover and then tidying up afterwards. For example, getting tools to remove a die or heating a die before installation takes place.

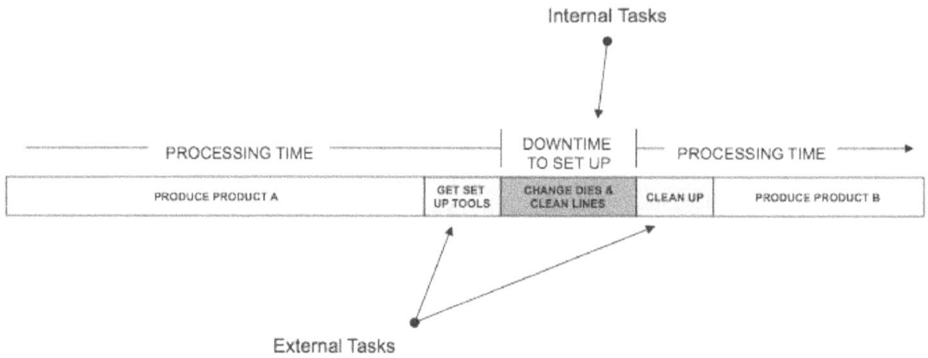

2: Convert Internal Tasks Into External Tasks.

An external task occurs while production continues, so it makes sense that any internal tasks converted will result in saved time. This may require the establishment of parallel operations in some cases.

3: Streamline All Changeover Tasks.

- Simplify work
- Standardise function, not shape
- Eliminate or reduce movement – redesign workplace so tools etc are within arms reach
- Eliminate or reduce time associated with fixings – as Shigeo Shingo observed, it's only the last turn of a bolt that tightens it - the rest is just movement
- Use functional clamps or eliminate fasteners altogether
- Eliminate or reduce internal adjustments
- Establish parallel operations
- Use intermediate jigs
- Mechanise

Formula 1 Racing Example

In a Formula 1 racing pit stop we can observe many examples of these techniques in action.

- During changeover, there is little movement as everything is at hand
- A great deal of set up occurs as a parallel operation while the car is still racing
- Refuelling is simply a matter of plugging in the hose without having to remove any fuel cap and unplugging the refuelling mechanism after the tank is full
- Jacking up the car is as simple as plugging in a pneumatic hose
- A single nut is used to hold the wheel on and torque of the nut is set by the pneumatic wrench used to remove and re-attach the nut

Achieving The Goal of SMED Through Replication

Work with SMED is not undertaken once and then the team has done their job. Single minute exchange of die may not be achieved in the first iteration, thus multiple iterations are necessary. For each iteration of the process, a 40 to 50 percent improvement in set-up times should be targeted and expected; accordingly several iterations may be necessary to break the ten-minute barrier.

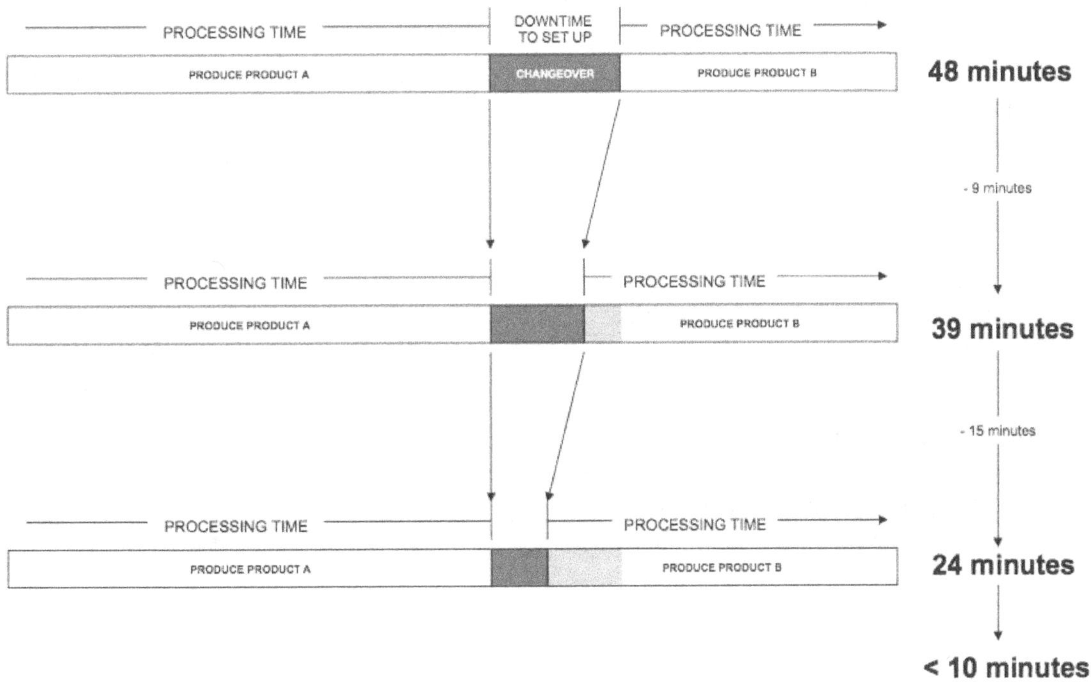

Figure 286: Achieving the Goal of SMED Through Replication

WORK CELL OPTIMISATION

WCO is simply the optimisation of the design and arrangement of work cells with an intent to maximise efficiency, minimise time and eliminate mistakes.

A work-cell is simply a logical arrangement or grouping of resources (machines, tools and personnel) in a manufacturing environment, which produces a family of like products. Each cell has a leader whose role is to manage work-flow with the goal of improving the quality, speed and cost of the process. Workcells are structured on the principles of Lean Manufacturing described by Womack, Jones and Roos (1991)[40].

WCO should be used when you have inefficiency in workflow, in other words too much movement associated with people and materials.

BEFORE

Taking a look at our example spaghetti diagram we see far too much movement occurring through a poorly designed workplace.

Through a simple redesign, movement can be significantly reduced. In this case work stations have been arranged almost in a U shape layout in a sequence that follows the process of manufacture.

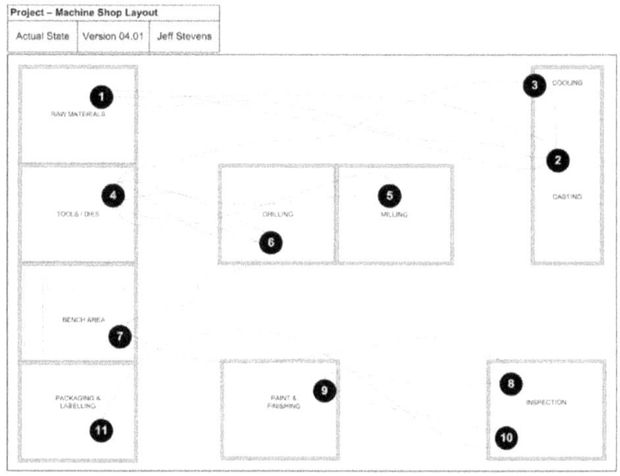

AFTER

The end result is far greater efficiency of work and reduced production time.

While this presents the entire process and floor plan for a workshop, the concept can be applied at a specific work station or work cell level.

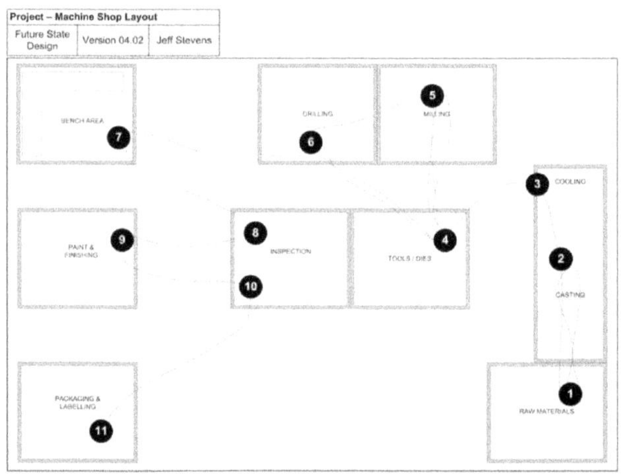

[40] Womack, J P., Jones, D T., Roos, D., *'The Machine That Changed the World'*, Harper Business (1991)

TOTAL PRODUCTIVE MAINTENANCE (TPM)

Think of productive equipment as you would your car or mobile phone or any piece of equipment in your home - they are productive for you when they are ready to go when you need them and they work when you use them. TPM is clearly about machinery and maintenance, yet its focus is on more than just breakdown maintenance.

For TPM to function effectively, machinery must (a) Be available for use when you need them, and (b) Be shut down in such a fashion as to be ready the next time you need them.

TPM is a Maintenance Initiative

TPM is a proactive methodology that primarily has three goals.

(a) Prevent any kind of waste associated with plant or machinery before it occurs,

(b) Significantly increase production, and

(c) Positively impact employee morale and job satisfaction.

TPM achieves this through bringing maintenance into focus as a vitally important part of the business. It's no longer regarded as a non-value adding or non-profit activity. Down time for maintenance is scheduled into the operational day, and in some cases as an integral part of the manufacturing process.

If machine uptime is not predictable, and if process capability is not sustained, a process cannot produce at the rate required to meet customer demand. Thus, the ultimate goal is to maximize productivity through holding emergency and unscheduled maintenance to a minimum.

This is achieved through the implementation of 8 TPM Pillars.

The 8 Pillars of TPM

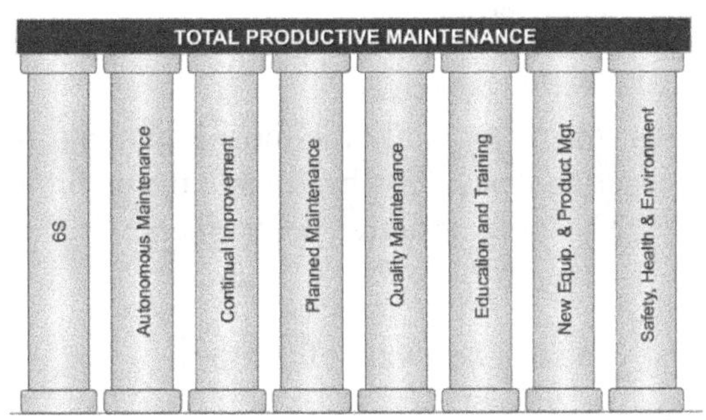

Figure 287: Eight Pillars of TPM

Pillar 1: 6S

TPM starts with 6S (or 5S in most cases) to organise the workplace. Maximum productivity cannot be achieved effectively in a disorganised workplace.

Pillar 2: Autonomous Maintenance (Jishu Hozen)

The operator is the key player in autonomous maintenance. This pillar is geared towards freeing up skilled maintenance people to spend time on more value adding activities by developing the capability of all operators to take care of small maintenance tasks.

Pillar 3: Continual Improvement (Kobetsu Kaizen)

The focus of Kaizen is the elimination of waste through making small improvements on a continual basis with the involvement of all operators. The principle is that a large number of small improvements are more effective overall than a small number of big improvements.

Pillar 4: Planned Maintenance

The desired outcome is to have properly functioning machines and equipment that produce defect free products. Maintenance itself can be broken down into four categories:

- Preventive Maintenance
- Breakdown Maintenance
- Corrective Maintenance
- Maintenance Prevention

Pillar 5: Quality Maintenance (Hinshitsu Hozen)

This pillar could also be referred to as 'maintenance for quality'. The desired outcome is to achieve defect free production through a focus on treating defect causes attributed to plant or machinery.

Pillar 6: Education and Training

This pillar focuses on developing the skill of all operators in the areas of maintenance, problem solving, cause and effect analysis, variation reduction etc. This means providing operators with skills from various methodologies such as Lean, Six Sigma and any Systematic Problem Solving approaches.

Pillar 7: New Equipment & Product Management

The desired outcome of this pillar is to reduce waste that occurs during the installation of a new machine or the commencement of production of a new product.

Pillar 8: Safety, Health and the Environment

While presented as the eighth pillar, this is probably the most important. In our approach, it is included in 6S. The focus of this pillar is on ensuring that safety, health and the environment are never compromised by the operation of plant or machinery. This pillar is active in all others.

TPM Metrics

The metrics of interest in TPM that you must be aware of are these:

- Overall Equipment Effectiveness (OEE)
- Mean Time Between Failures (MTBF)
- Mean Time To Recovery (MTTR)

Metric 1 - Overall Equipment Effectiveness (OEE)

OEE is a measure of how well a plant or manufacturing equipment is running by contrast to the ideal plant. TPM targets should include an OEE of 90 percent as a minimum.

OEE incorporates a number of metrics including Availability, Performance Rate and Quality Rate.

In that regard OEE takes a more holistic view of losses having an impact on equipment performance – not having it available when needed, not running at the ideal rate and not producing a quality output first pass.

Typical losses include:

Availability
- Time to set-up / start-up
- Unscheduled downtime / breakdowns

Performance Rate
- Reduction in speed
- Minor unrecorded stoppages

Quality Rate
- Rejected units
- Reworked units

Overall Equipment Effectiveness is calculated by the following equation:

OEE(%) = Availability (A%) x Performance (P%) x Quality (Q%)

Where:

- Availability (A%) = actual time available / time planned to be available
- Performance (P%) = units produced / theoretical production rate
- Quality (Q%) = good units / total units produced

Some companies have simplified OEE by reducing the equation to:

OEE = Actual Output ÷ Theoretical Maximum Output

Metric 2 - Mean Time Between Failures (MTBF)

MTBF is the average time between failures of a system. Any calculations of MTBF assume that a system is fixed or repaired after each failure, and then returned to service immediately after failure. The average time between failing and being returned to service can also be referred to as Mean Down Time (MDT).

One common misconception about the MTBF is that it specifies the average time when the likelihood of failure occurring equals the likelihood of not having a failure occur (i.e., 0.50). This is only true for certain symmetric distributions. In many cases, such as with Exponential or Poisson probability distributions, which are both asymmetric, this is not the case. For example, the probability that an item will fail after MTBF has arrived is approximately 0.63 for an exponential failure distribution.

For typical distributions with some variance, MTBF only represents an aggregate statistic. It is not suitable for predicting specific time to failure due to the level of uncertainty arising from the variability in the time-to-failure distribution. (to understand more precise methods of prediction, refer to the section on probability distributions presented earlier in this text)

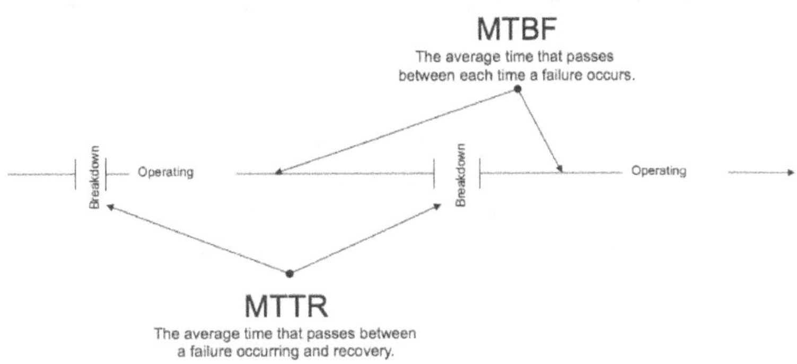

Metric 3 - Mean Time to Recovery (MTTR)

MTTR is simply the average time for a machine, plant or device to recover from a non-terminal failure.

MITIGATING OR ELIMINATING CONSEQUENCES / FAILURES (STEP 14)

ANTICIPATING CONSEQUENCES OF NEW SOLUTIONS

Every single thing we do, every action we take, every solution we implement is one link in an infinitely long cause and effect chain. There will be benefits, there will also be potential for the creation of new problems. When we implement a solution we set a new cause in motion. That is why we must anticipate and plan for any outcomes that are not desirable. As I mentioned in my 2005 publication, *Systematic Problem Solving for Managers*, work of this nature might be referred to as *predictive cause effect analysis*.

All solutions bring consequences, as well as solving a problem they can also introduce problems. Think about some of these solutions that have solved problems in the world.

- Plastic bags
- Motor vehicles
- Mobile phones
- Guns
- Plastics
- Tyres
- Concrete
- Hypodermic needles
- Computer screens
- Email

Every single one of these has also created problems. Problems like how to dispose of plastic bags, tyres and computer screens, how to deal with increasing pollution, how to stop people using email as their primary communication medium and so on.

In recognising that solutions can bring other problems, it's important that we anticipate these potential problems before they occur.

Just because a solution presents another problem, does that mean we do not use the solution? If we do use a solution, do we take action to deal with every potential problem it creates? The answer in both cases is no. This is where we have to make decisions on the basis of what potential these problems have to occur and how severe the consequences of their occurrence would be.

The more likely they are to occur and the more severe the consequence, the greater argument for doing something about it. That could involve planning some action to minimise the secondary problem, or even not using the solution.

Potential Consequence Analysis

Since *'Systematic Problem Solving for Managers'* addresses predictive cause and effect analysis at length, I've decided to simply show you the tool we presented in that text and encourage you to obtain a copy if you would like to study and know more about this topic as well as problem solving methodologies. Predictive cause effect analysis (or potential consequence analysis) is undertaken by asking and answering five simple questions:

- *What problems might this solution create?*
- *How likely are those problems to occur?*
- *If they did occur, how severe would be the result?*
- *For which of these must we plan?*
- *What will we do to address these potential problems?*

The process is accompanied by a simple tool used for documenting the answers from this series of questions.

The example below drawn from my publication, *'Systematic Problem Solving for Managers'*, is a potential consequence analysis for a simple solution called plastic bags.

Many of you will notice its similarity with the process of risk analysis.

What problems might this solution create?	Likelihood	Severity	Risk Rating	Action Plan
People put them over their head and suffer injury.	3 (could)	4 (major)	12	1. Place air / drainage holes in the bottom of all bags
Bags clog eco systems through incorrect disposal.	3 (could)	5 (significant)	15	1. Charge people for bags 2. Limit the life of bags by making out of plastic that degrades quickly in sunlight 3. (other actions)
Bags cause harm to marine life through disposal into water systems.	3 (could)	5 (significant)	15	

A process I will discuss at length is related to one of the most useful and adaptable processes I have ever used - Failure Mode and Effect Analysis.

ANTICIPATING AND ADDRESSING FAILURES WITH FMEA

All of the cause and effect material we have covered has concentrated on identifying the cause of a specific outcome or effect. We have started at a single effect and worked backwards. This is an extremely effective way to find causes of variation or causes of an event. However, it is not the only way to approach process improvement.

There will be occasions when the problems you are confronted with can be better solved by studying the process in more detail, and determining what can or does go wrong within each of the steps of that process.

During the late 1990s I had the opportunity to run a major community hospital in a remote part of a developing country. When I took over the leadership role of the hospital, it was experiencing a range of problems from both a business viewpoint and a customer perspective. One of the most obvious problems that resulted in a stream of complaints was associated with outpatient customer service.

The hospital was treating more than 13,000 outpatients per month, many of them working for the company that provided the facilities and most of the funds to run the hospital. With such a large workload it was no surprise that most of the complaints related to how long it took to see and treat outpatients. We referred to this time as 'outpatient cycle time'.

The initial approach in treating this problem was to study the cause of excessive outpatient cycle time, using traditional cause and effect analysis tools. The process was quite effective in helping determine solutions to obvious causes. However, it took us only part of the way to making a big impact.

The second approach, that ultimately proved invaluable, was to break down the outpatient treatment process into its individual steps. These steps were then studied to determine how they contributed to excess cycle time.

By studying the potential failures in each of the steps, a more complete action plan was developed to address a wide range of causes along the entire process chain.

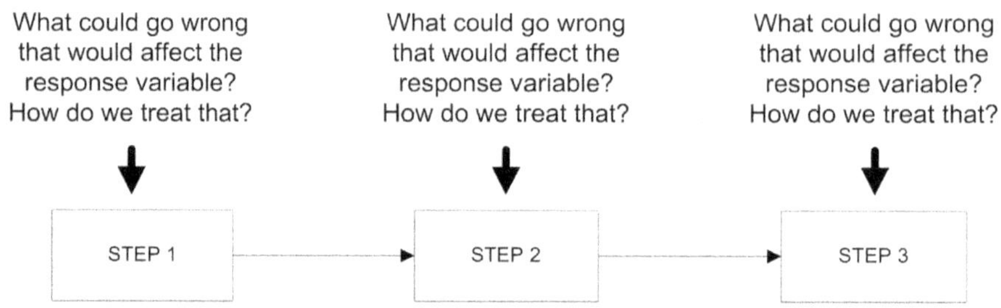

This approach is known throughout the process improvement world as Failure Mode and Effect Analysis, or FMEA for short. In my experience, it is one of the most useful, yet often overlooked, methods for improving process performance.

Failure Mode and Effect Analysis (FMEA)

Failure Mode and Effect Analysis (FMEA) is just a fancy way of saying 'analysing what can go wrong with the process and the effect of that going wrong'. I guess we could simplify it even further and use the words cause and effect analysis.

It is a process that can be used for studying what can go wrong within a process, or with a service or product, and identifying the causes. It does take cause and effect analysis to another level by identifying solutions to any problems identified.

The desired outcome of the process is to develop an action plan to address the causes of problems.

FMEA has been around for many years. In fact the United States Military developed FMEA with some of their documentation dated as early as 1949. Their initial FMEA approach was primarily used as a reliability evaluation technique for determining the effect of system and equipment failures. These failures were classified according to their impact on personnel safety, equipment safety or mission success.

How does FMEA work?

Let's be very clear about one thing; FMEA *is not a tool*, it is a process.

Because the process is supported with a tool, like many other quality improvement processes, there is often a misconception that the work is all about the tool. It is important to recognise that like most other tools used in planning and making improvements, the FMEA tool provides a foundation for framing a series of questions and focusing the associated discussion.

The questions that are asked focus users on key elements that contribute to the desired outcome – to create an action plan for addressing potential causes of things that can go wrong. The key to success is the series of questions and the sequence in which they are asked.

Undertaking FMEA is a repetitive process in that a sequence is followed as many times as is required to study all steps of a process or elements of a product or service.

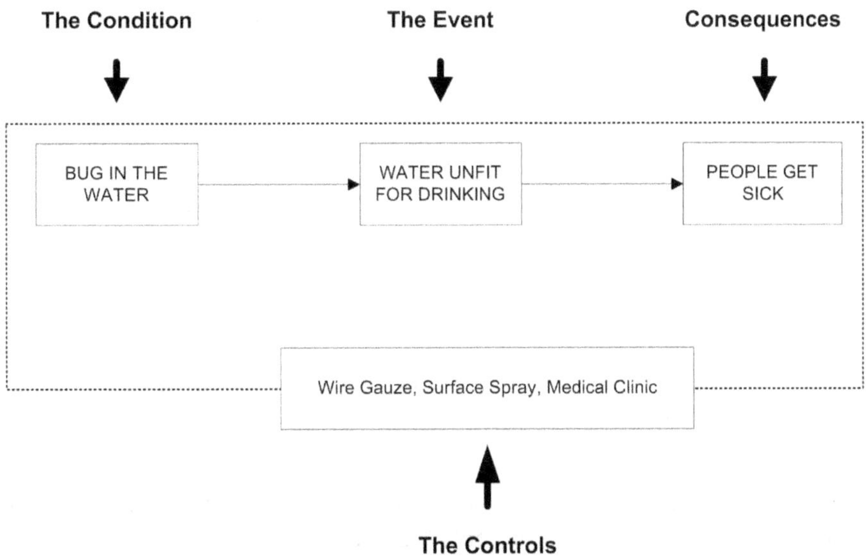

Figure 289: FMEA Framework

When undertaking a *process* FMEA, each step of that process is assessed for potential failure modes. A failure mode is an event (e.g. water unfit for drinking) that has potential consequences (people get sick), and is caused by some condition or action (a bug in the water). The system has controls in place (wire gauze, surface spray, a medical clinic) to help prevent the event occurring or mitigate the impact if it does occur.

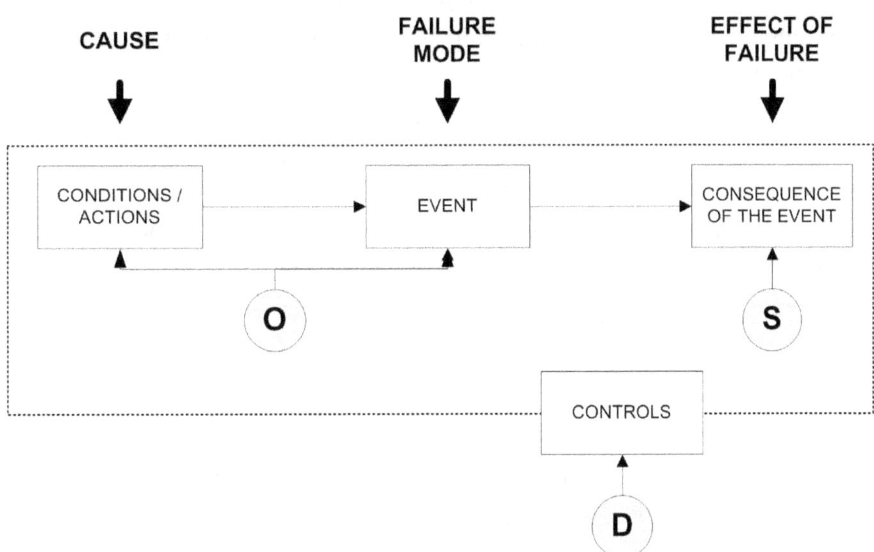

Figure 290: Analysis and Rating Framework

In order to quantify the risks, each failure mode is rated against three dimensions:

- **Severity** (S) – A rating for how severe the consequence of the failure would be.
- **Occurrence** (O) – A rating for the likelihood of the potential failure mode occurring as a result of a particular cause, within the existing level of control. Failure modes are usually caused by conditions (a specific environmental state such as wet road) or actions (something someone does or does not do, such as select the wrong part number).
- **Control** (C) – A rating for the adequacy of existing controls for proactively or reactively dealing with the potential failure mode.

NOTE: Numerous textbooks refer to 'detection' instead of 'control'. I have found that the detection approach tends to be focused on a reactive control environment, hence my decision to study the 'control' environment from both a reactive and proactive perspective.

Simply Ask the Right Questions

To conduct an FMEA with the desired outcome of ensuring there is 'minimal variation in cake taste', I would simply document the process and then ask a series of questions about each of the steps in the process.

The questions I would ask are these.

- *'What is the process step we are concerned with?'* (If we were to study the process of baking a cake, we might choose the step of mixing ingredients together.)
- *'What can go wrong?'* (We could put in too much sugar – this is the event or what we refer to as the failure mode.)
- *'If this failure mode occurred, what could be the consequences?'* (It might taste too sweet for most people, not everyone likes the cake – this is the consequence of the event or failure mode occurring.)
- 'How severe would those consequences be in the context of our analysis?' (This would be significant as a consequence.)
- *'What condition or action could cause this failure to occur?'* (Not measuring the amount of sugar – this is the condition or action that contributed to the event occurring.)
- 'What is the likelihood of this failure occurring as a result of this condition or action?' (It could happen in most circumstances.)
- 'What controls do we currently have in place to prevent the failure mode from occurring or detect the failure if it does occur?' (We have a recipe and we do taste testing when the cake is made – this is the control framework.)
- *'How would you rate the effectiveness of those controls?'* (Controls are predominantly reactive in that we find the problem after it has occurred.)

The questions are repeated until all steps in the process have been analysed. Finishing the FMEA simply involves developing an action plan for treating those failure modes that we believe contribute most to problems with the particular response variable under consideration.

FMEA Terminology

Before an FMEA can be undertaken, it is necessary to understand a number of terms. Many of these terms have already been used in the example previously discussed.

Potential Failure Mode

A potential failure mode simply describes what can go wrong for a particular step of the process. Let me give you a couple of examples. In the process of refuelling a vehicle at a self-service petrol station, a potential failure mode for the step of 'fill the tank with petrol', would be 'the nozzle falls out of the filler opening'. In the process of changing a flat tyre on a vehicle, a potential failure mode for the step of 'remove the wheel' would be 'the vehicle rolls off the jack'. These failure modes describe the event that would occur without describing the impact of that event occurring.

Potential Effects

In traditional approaches to FMEA, an effect is defined as an adverse consequence confined to something that the customer might experience. For example, if the nozzle falls out of the filler opening in the 'fill the tank with petrol' step, the potential effect might be that it slides down the side of the vehicle and scratches the paint.

The term customer is not limited to the end user. Many processes you work with in your workplace are part of a sequence of processes, and the customer is the process next in the sequence.

Severity

Severity is an assessment of how serious the 'Potential Effect' of the failure mode is in the context of your analysis. The context is based on the overall concept you are working to improve. For example, if we are working on minimising variation in cake taste for the customer, that becomes the context for our severity ratings. If we were studying safety, then impact on safety would form the context for our severity ratings.

Potential Causes

Potential causes in this context are the likely conditions or actions that result in the failure modes occurring. For example, the cause of 'the nozzle falling out of the filler opening' might be that 'the operator let go of the filler nozzle' – an action. The cause might also be that 'the serrations along the lower edge of the nozzle are worn and no longer hold onto the edge of the filler opening' – a condition.

As we now know, potential causes can usually be found within the categories of People, Machinery, Methods, Measurement, the Environment or Materials.

Occurrence

The term occurrence is simply a reference to how likely a particular failure mode will happen as a result of the specific conditions or actions (the causes).

Controls

Controls are mechanisms for proactively and / or reactively dealing with things that can go wrong. For example, protective clothing is a control for reducing the consequences of a failure occurring that could injure a person. In FMEA, controls are anything that either contributes to the prevention or detection of a failure mode, the mitigation of the impact of a failure mode occurring, or warning that a failure mode is about to occur.

Risk Priority Number

The risk priority number (RPN) is used to help prioritise the failure modes identified in the FMEA. The RPN is the mathematical product of the Severity Rating x Occurrence Rating x Control Rating or S x O x C.

The FMEA Process

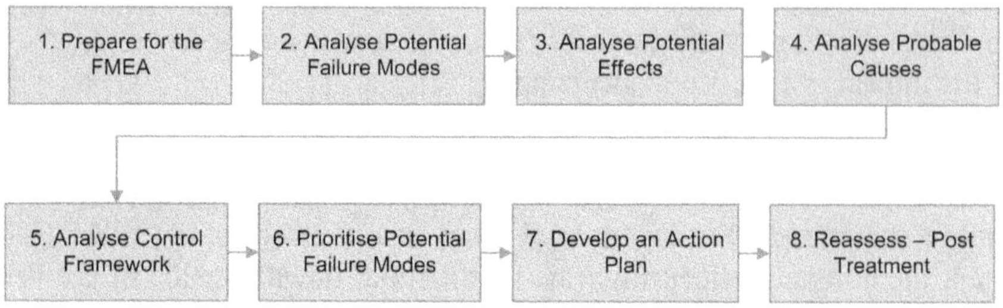

Figure 291: FMEA Process

FMEA is completed in 8 steps. The process is supported by a worksheet that allows the user to capture information as it's generated.

As you will see, the worksheet is laid out according to the sequence followed.

The step in the FMEA process relevant for each column is indicated in the table shown below.

Process Step	Failure Mode	Potential Effect	S	Potential Cause	O	Current Controls	C	RPN	Action	Who	When	S	O	C	RPN
2	2	3	3	4	4	5	5	6	7	7	7	8	8	8	8

Figure 292:FMEA Worksheet

Case Study – The Coffee Shop

To help understand the FMEA process, it will be useful to see how it works with a simple example.

Let's take the process for making a 'milk based' cup of coffee.

The process having been mapped by the team in the define phase looks like this.

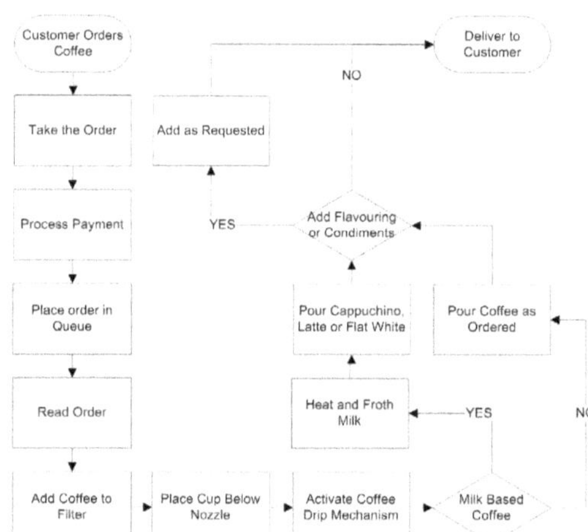

Step 1 – Prepare for the FMEA

The first step in FMEA is the preparation phase of the work, sometimes referred to as 'establishing the context'. Completing this work involves three tasks.

(1) Identify the process that is going to be analysed - This involves naming it and documenting it as a diagram or flowchart.

(2) Ensure the purpose of the FMEA is clearly understood - Most process improvement text books that I have read refer to FMEA in a manufacturing context and study failure modes with only the customer in mind. The fact is that FMEA can be used in many work contexts, not just for impact on customer satisfaction. In addition to minimising the impact of process or product defects on an organisation's customers, FMEA can also be used for studying ways to:

- reduce safety risk
- minimise impact to production
- optimise product quality

(3) Define the criteria against which the assessment of severity, likelihood of occurrence and adequacy of controls will be evaluated -

An example rating scale is shown below.

Severity Ratings (S)		**Occurrence Ratings (O)**		**Control Ratings (C)**	
5	Product unfit for use and cannot be repaired	5	Almost Certain – expected to occur under most conditions.	5	No Controls – will not anticipate or detect a deviation or failure.
4	Product unfit for use but can be repaired	4	Likely – likely to occur under many conditions.	4	Partially Reactive – will identify a deviation or failure but will not impact on the consequences of it occurring.
3	Defect is obvious, can continue to be used for a limited time before failure will occur	3	Could Happen – could occur under some conditions.	3	Reactive Only – will mitigate the impact of a deviation or failure after it has occurred.
2	Defect is obvious but can continued to be used without repair	2	Unlikely – not likely to occur under most conditions.	2	Proactive Only – will reduce the likelihood of a deviation or failure occurring.
1	Defect is not obvious	1	Rare – may occur only under exceptional circumstances.	1	Combination Proactive and Reactive – will prevent or provide early warning of a deviation of failure, and mitigate any impact.

Example Rating Scales – Process or Product FMEA

On more than one occasion I've seen facilitators fail to give this step the attention it needs. The end result – they have to back track to work on building common understanding on allocation of ratings to each part of the study. Time spent in this phase is vital if you are going to set yourself up for success in minimising errors in any process.

Example Rating Scales:

Criteria are usually associated with some form of rating scale, usually 1 to 5 or 1 to 10. Whilst many of the textbooks I have read refer to 1 to 10 scales, I have a preference for a 1 to 5 scale for one reason – it simplifies the process of allocating ratings. The purpose of FMEA is not to come up with a comprehensive rating for each failure mode, but rather to prioritise failure modes. With that in mind, I choose to keep it as simple as possible so the work gets completed expediently.

The rating scales shown in the previous table are examples of qualitative terms and associated ratings that can be used for a simple process or product FMEA.

More specific quantitative terms for occurrence ratings based on data or process history can be used if so desired. I recommend that you keep the FMEA as simple as possible and use more comprehensive rating scales only where they add value to your work.

Step 2 – Identify What Can Go Wrong (Failure Modes)

Failure modes in this context are really risks. The risks in this case are associated with all of the ways that the steps in a process could fail to perform its desired function. For example: When receiving input over a phone from a customer, an automated transfer mechanism may not be able to understand the number quoted by the customer, or background noise is too severe to be able to distinguish the customer's voice.

To identify potential failure modes, ask the following questions:

- FEATURE OR STEP – *'What is the process step or product feature that concerns us?'* The steps in the process must be documented in advance in preparation for your FMEA work. In this very simple example let's just focus on two of the steps.
- FAILURE MODE IDENTIFICATION – *'What could go wrong that would impact the variable of interest?'* This is a description of the event that can occur without indicating how severe it would be if it occurred. Multiple failure modes can be identified for a single process step – limit what you capture to those failure modes that are realistic.

The answers to these questions are captured in the FMEA worksheet.

Failure Mode & Effect Analysis									**Action Plan**						
Feature or Process Step	**Failure Mode**	**Potential Effect**	**S**	**Potential Cause**	**O**	**Current Controls**	**C**	**RPN**	**Action**	**Who**	**When**	**S**	**O**	**C**	**RPN**
Froth the Milk	Insufficient or excess frothing							0							
Pour the Coffee	Wrong coffee poured							0							

Step 3 – Analyse Potential Effects

If any of the potential failure modes occur, they will usually create an effect, or in other words, a consequence. Ask the following question to help you describe in a few words what the impact of that failure would be.

- POTENTIAL EFFECTS – *'If this failure mode occurred, what could be the consequences (or potential effects)?'*
- Identify those consequences that can occur as a result of the failure mode. Whilst it may be possible to identify multiple effects for a failure mode, by focusing your work around the worst-case scenario

you will avoid unnecessary complexity in your work.

- SEVERITY – *'How severe would those consequences be in the context of our analysis?'*
- Allocate a rating (S) according to the answers you give and how best they fit with the rating scale you created in step 1. The severity should be rated with the context of the analysis in mind. For example, a high severity rating in the context of customer satisfaction (the product being unfit for use) would probably equate to a low severity rating in the context of safety (no injuries).

The answers to these questions are captured in the FMEA worksheet.

Failure Mode & Effect Analysis									Action Plan						
Feature or Process Step	Failure Mode	Potential Effect	S	Potential Cause	O	Current Controls	C	RPN	Action	Who	When	S	O	C	RPN
Froth the Milk	Insufficient or excess frothing	too cold or too hot, burnt milk, lost customer	4					0							
Pour the Coffee	Wrong coffee poured	incorrect order delivered, lost customer	5					0							

Step 4 – Identify the Probable Causes of These Failure Modes

At this point in the process, we try and identify what it is that would probably cause these failures to occur. These failure modes and their consequences do not just happen of their own volition. They are usually caused by something else, and identifying these potential causes serves us in two ways. First, we will be in a better position to identify ways to treat the potential failure and second, we can improve our understanding of the likelihood of the failure occurring on the basis of this cause. These questions will help you complete this step.

- POTENTIAL CAUSES – *'What conditions or actions could cause this failure to occur?'*
- List the potential causes. Cause and effect analysis methods can be used to study causes of failure modes. The most useful approach I have found is to do a simple analysis using a cause-effect structure tree as presented in Chapter 15. This process reduces the number of potential causes to those most likely. In the absence of such an approach, it is not uncommon to find yourself identifying a lengthy list of potential causes, including those that may not be relevant.
- OCCURRENCE – *'What is the likelihood of this failure occurring as a result of these conditions or actions?'* or *'How often do you think this failure would occur as a result of these conditions or actions?'*
- Allocate a rating (O) according to the answer you give to these questions and how they fit within your occurrence rating scale.

The answers to these questions are captured in the FMEA worksheet.

Failure Mode & Effect Analysis									Action Plan						
Feature or Process Step	Failure Mode	Potential Effect	S	Potential Cause	O	Current Controls	C	RPN	Action	Who	When	S	O	C	RPN
Froth the Milk	Insufficient or excess frothing	too cold or too hot, burnt milk, lost customer	4	inexperience, unaware of temperature, distracted	4			0							
Pour the Coffee	Wrong coffee poured	incorrect order delivered, lost customer	5	incorrect or illegible order	3			0							

Step 5 – Analyse the Level of Control That Is Currently in Place

It is highly likely that some form of control that is intended to prevent the failure occurring, or in some way help manage the event if it does occur is currently in place. Controls can be just about anything. For example a 'recipe' is a form of control designed to prevent a cake baking process going off track. Training is a form of control, as is an inspection at the end of a production line. Controls can be of two types; proactive if they address the potential failure before it occurs, or reactive if they detect and manage the failure in some way only after it has occurred. The following questions will help you analyse controls currently in place.

- CURRENT CONTROLS – *'What controls do we have in place to prevent the failure mode from occurring or deal with the failure if it does occur?'*
- List all of the controls in place that either help to make sure a failure does not occur, or helps detect a failure or mitigate the impact of a failure after it occurs.
- CONTROL – *'How would you rate the effectiveness of those controls?'*
- Allocate a rating (C) according to the answer you give to these questions and how they fit within your controls rating scale.

The answers to these questions are captured in the FMEA worksheet.

Failure Mode & Effect Analysis									Action Plan						
Feature or Process Step	Failure Mode	Potential Effect	S	Potential Cause	O	Current Controls	C	RPN	Action	Who	When	S	O	C	RPN
Froth the Milk	Insufficient or excess frothing	too cold or too hot, burnt milk, lost customer	4	inexperience, unaware of temperature, distracted	4	customer feedback, return policy	4								
Pour the Coffee	Wrong coffee poured	incorrect order delivered, lost customer	5	incorrect or illegible order	3	customer feedback, return policy	4								

Step 6 – Prioritise Potential Failures

The last step of the analysis phase is the prioritisation of the failure modes that you've identified. You prioritise to ensure you address the largest risks first and direct your energies to the areas most needed.

To prioritise you simply calculate a risk value for each failure mode and then sort from largest to smallest. The value you give each failure mode is called a Risk Priority Number (RPN). This value is the product of the Severity Rating multiplied by the Occurrence Rating multiplied by the Control Rating. The equation is:

RPN = S x O x C

These values are captured in the FMEA worksheet.

Failure Mode & Effect Analysis									Action Plan						
Feature or Process Step	**Failure Mode**	**Potential Effect**	**S**	**Potential Cause**	**O**	**Current Controls**	**C**	**RPN**	**Action**	**Who**	**When**	**S**	**O**	**C**	**RPN**
Froth the Milk	Insufficient or excess frothing	too cold or too hot, burnt milk, lost customer	4	inexperience, unaware of temperature, distracted	4	customer feedback, return policy	4	**64**							
Pour the Coffee	Wrong coffee poured	incorrect order delivered, lost customer	5	incorrect or illegible order	3	customer feedback, return policy	4	**60**							

Prioritisation Option 1 - The Pareto Principle

When RPN values are plotted on a Pareto chart, failure modes can be viewed in order from largest RPN to smallest RPN.

A Black Belt would start at the highest end and work down the list in order of RPN, treating causes. This is not to suggest that all failure modes have to be treated, only that they should be treated in order of size of the risk as indicated by the RPN.

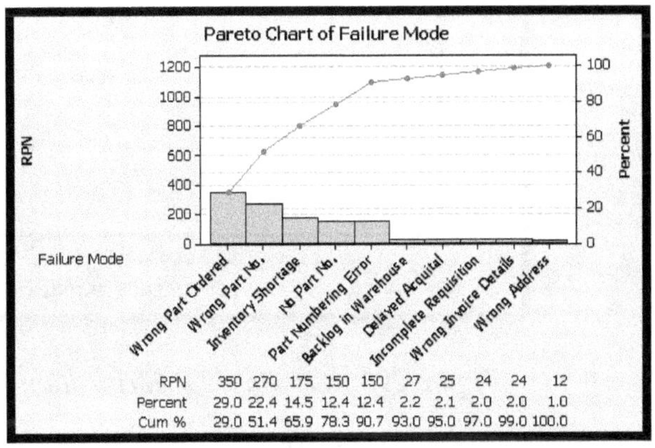

In the example shown, the team might choose to treat the top 5 failure modes.

Prioritisation Option Two – Levels of Risk

The following diagram, which presents another way of approaching this issue, may be of assistance. It allows us to look at prioritisation through the frame of three levels of risk.

Significant (Critical) Risks – As these risks are those that are critical in respect of their impact on the customer, a control plan must be in place to address each of these.

Major Risks – Although less critical than significant risks in respect to severity rating, these risks on average have a higher likelihood of occurring, thus the need to develop a control plan to address each of these.

Minor to Moderate Risks – The remainder of risks can be sorted with the top 20 percent of these (according to rating) being addressed in control plans.

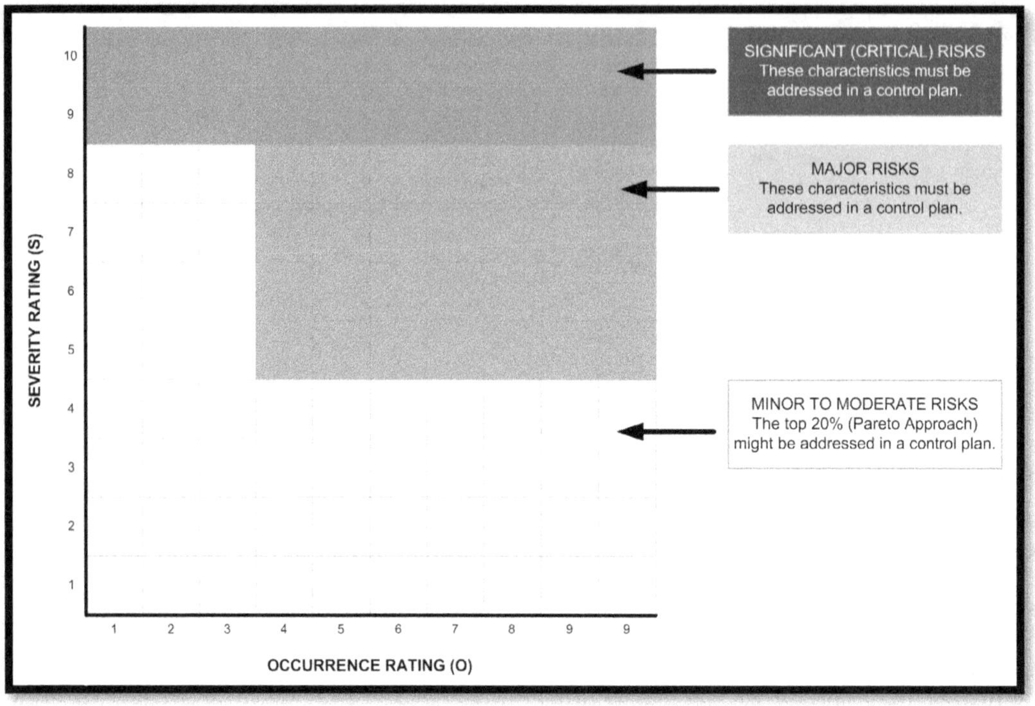

Figure 293: Risk Based Prioritisation Across Dimensions of Severity & Occurrence

<u>Step 7 – Develop an Action Plan</u>

The analysis phase is now complete. You know the potential failure modes for the process, their potential consequences and likely causes. You also know which failure modes pose the greatest risk. The challenging question to answer is always – 'Which of these failure modes do we treat?' Do we treat all of them or do we just treat a few? This is where the RPN values do their job. The most common approach is to start at the highest value and work down the list in order of largest to smallest, developing an action plan as you go for treating causes of failure modes. This is not to suggest that all failure modes have to be treated, only that they should be treated in order of size of the risk as indicated by the RPN.

<u>What actions should be considered?</u>

The actions to take are usually those that fall within one of the following strategies. These strategies are arranged in order from the most effective to least effective.

Concentrate on Likelihood:

- **Prevent the failure mode occurring** – eliminating or changing a step within the process might achieve this, or you could take some other proactive action that results in impossibility of the failure mode occurring. For example, installing metal bars over windows would make it virtually impossible to fall out of a window inadvertently.
- **Reduce the likelihood of the failure mode occurring** – any action that results in the reduced probability that the failure mode will occur falls in this category. For example, by having drop down lists on an electronic form results in the reduced likelihood of an error occurring when completing the form.

Manage the Consequences:

- **Minimise the consequences of the event occurring** – Any action that results in the impact of any failure mode being reduced falls into the category of 'impact minimisation'. One of the most common examples of this type of action in industry today is the wearing of personal protective clothing. Whilst this has no influence over preventing a failure mode occurring, it helps reduce the consequences of the occurrence. For example, an employee wearing eye protection will suffer far less damage, if any, in the event of being struck with a flying object. However, the wearing of glasses does not prevent the object being flung in the first place.

- **Transfer the risk** - one of the most common strategies in this regard is the strategy of taking out insurance. When the failure mode occurs, the insurance company accepts the consequences.

Implement Detection or Early Warning:

- **Increase the ability to detect a defect produced by the process** – the introduction of quality control mechanisms create a system whereby defects are intercepted before they impact the customer.
- **Provide early warning that the failure mode will occur** – processes or devices that give warning that a failure mode could occur or is about to occur can either facilitate intercepting the failure mode so that customers are not impacted, or prevent the failure mode occurring in the first place. The installation of gauges or alarms on some systems provides the basis for monitoring and early warning.

Reduce Uncertainty:

- **Reassess the risks** – Where there is some doubt about the assessment, it is a legitimate strategy to reassess risks. In this case it is not unusual to involve other personnel in the assessment to give another view. However, I do not recommend that this be captured as an action on the FMEA worksheet.

The actions you choose are captured in the FMEA worksheet. Who is responsible and when, are also captured as a part of the action plan.

Failure Mode & Effect Analysis									Action Plan						
Feature or Process Step	**Failure Mode**	**Potential Effect**	**S**	**Potential Cause**	**O**	**Current Controls**	**C**	**RPN**	**Action**	**Who**	**When**	**S**	**O**	**C**	**RPN**
Froth the Milk	Insufficient or excess frothing	too cold or too hot, burnt milk, lost customer	4	inexperience, unaware of temperature, distracted	4	customer feedback, return policy	4	**64**	include temp gauge in the process	GL	5/01/09				
Pour the Coffee	Wrong coffee poured	incorrect order delivered, lost customer	5	incorrect or illegible order	3	customer feedback, return policy	4	**60**	printed orders from till, money back policy	MK	1/02/09				

Step 8 – Assess the Effectiveness of Planned Actions

Once actions for addressing failure modes have been identified, it is good practice to reassess risks on the assumption that the treatment actions had been undertaken. In essence this is a reality check to see that your RPN values are reduced if the actions are taken.

Unless the failure mode is eliminated, the severity rating usually remains the same. The most common changes occur in the ratings associated with occurrence and controls.

The completed FMEA worksheet will look something like this.

Failure Mode & Effect Analysis									Action Plan						
Feature or Process Step	**Failure Mode**	**Potential Effect**	**S**	**Potential Cause**	**O**	**Current Controls**	**C**	**RPN**	**Action**	**Who**	**When**	**S**	**O**	**C**	**RPN**
Froth the Milk	Insufficient or excess frothing	too cold or too hot, burnt milk, lost customer	4	inexperience, unaware of temperature, distracted	4	customer feedback, return policy	4	**64**	include temp gauge in the process	GL	5/01/09	4	3	2	**24**
Pour the Coffee	Wrong coffee poured	incorrect order delivered, lost customer	5	incorrect or illegible order	3	customer feedback, return policy	4	**60**	printed orders from till, money back policy	MK	1/02/09	3	2	2	**12**

Other Context Applications for FMEA

As I indicated earlier, FMEA can be used in a variety of contexts. For example, it can be used to study potential failure modes that affect safety, service quality, product quality or even production. The only change required is to determine relevant severity ratings for the relevant context of your analysis. For example, if we wanted to study failure modes associated with safety in a process, severity ratings would need to be adjusted to reflect different levels of safety impact severity.

Some examples of severity ratings for each of these contexts are shown in the table below.

Product Quality		**Production Process**		**Customer Satisfaction**		**Safety Impact**	
5	Product unfit for use and cannot be repaired	5	Production is stopped (> 24 hours)	5	Generate bad publicity, negative impact on market position	5	Avoidable fatality
4	Product unfit for use but can be repaired	4	Lengthy delay (> 8 hours, < 24 hours)	4	Lose customer to competitor	4	Permanent disabling injuries
3	Defect is obvious, can continue to be used for a limited time before failure will occur	3	Partial malfunction, moderate delay (> 1 hour, < 8 hours)	3	Moderate dissatisfaction that may be passed on by word of mouth	3	Non permanent disabling injuries
2	Defect is obvious but can continue to be used without repair	2	Minor delay (< 1 hour)	2	Minor dissatisfaction that can be resolved	2	Hospitalisation necessary but no lasting effects
1	Defect is not obvious	1	No delay to process	1	Customer not affected	1	First aid required only

Example Severity Ratings for Different Contexts

Alternative Rating Scales

The following rating scales are common examples of qualitative terms and associated ratings that can be used for FMEA. These are most commonly used in manufacturing environments.

Severity	Occurrence (Time / Probability)	Detection
10. Injure a customer or employee	10. More than once every 2 days / > 30%	10. Defect caused by failure is not detectable
9. Be illegal	9. Once every 3 – 4 days / < 30%	9. Occasional units are checked for defects
8. Render the product or service unfit for use	8. Once per week / < 5%	8. Units are systematically sampled and inspected
7. Cause extreme customer dissatisfaction	7. Once per month / < 1%	7. All units are manually inspected
6. Cause a partial malfunction	6. Once every 3 months / < .03%	6. Manual inspection with mistake proofing modifications
5. Cause a loss of performance that is likely to result in a complaint	5. Once every 6 months / < 1 per 10,000	5. Process is monitored and manually inspected
4. Cause a minor performance loss	4. Once per year / < 6 per 100,000	4. SPC is used with an immediate reaction to out of control conditions
3. Cause a minor nuisance with no loss of performance	3. Once every 1 – 3 years / < 6 per million	3. SPC as above with 100% inspection surrounding out of control conditions
2. Go unnoticed with a minor affect on performance	2. Once every 3 – 6 years / < 1 per 10 million	2. All units are automatically inspected
1. Go unnoticed and not affect performance in any way	1. Once every 6 - 100 years / < 2 per billion	1. Defect is obvious and can be kept from affecting the customer

FMEA Application Tips

Rational Thinking - FMEA is not a creativity session. It requires rational thinking with knowledge of the process, product or service.

Group Size - To undertake FMEA in a large group may prove quite challenging. A small group of content knowledgeable people is often more effective with respect to identifying failure modes and undertaking the respective analysis in the most efficient way possible. I recommend that Black Belts undertake the FMEA with a group of 2 or 3, and then provide a briefing session for the remainder of the team to validate the work.

Validate with Customers - It may prove useful to validate your work with customers, particularly in light of the fact that an FMEA is about understanding and treating potential negative customer impacts.

MISTAKE PROOFING & MISTAKE PREVENTION

Defects and errors in processing cost businesses millions, if not billions of dollars in waste, lost time and lost customers each year. It's pure waste that in many ways we have come to consider as acceptable. Try telling your staff that you want zero defects and you are likely to get comments like – 'It can't be done' or in Australia they might respond with 'You've got to be joking mate'.

For some reason in our culture (western) we're conditioned to believe defect free or mistake free is not possible, yet this is not a belief held in some other cultures that achieve some remarkable results in processing. They know that technology and engineering today is so advanced we just need to take advantage of it and mistake free is possible.

Proofing and Prevention Terms

The two terms we must be familiar with are *mistake proofing* and *mistake prevention.*

Mistake Proofing is the process of making it impossible for a mistake to be passed on to the next step in the process. The mistake is still made; it just gets picked up before it gets passed on.

By contrast, **Mistake Prevention** is the process of making it impossible for a mistake to be made in a process. The error or mistake does not get made in the first place.

Here are some examples of each of these approaches.

Mistake Proofing	Mistake Prevention
• Pre-delivery inspections • Software programming that sends you back to the previous step if you insert PO Box address in an order form when only a residential address for delivery is acceptable • System in a manufacturing process that automatically separates and rejects defective units from those that are functional	• Drop list of choices on an online form that must be chosen before moving on • Set pin layouts for wiring connections • Automatic power off when a photo copier door is opened • Electronic checklist fixed into a process • Shut down idle control for a piece of heavy machinery

While many ideas are implemented with a view to mistake prevention, often they can still result in a mistake occurring due to human interaction with the process.

For example:

- Colour coded wires – can still join wrong wires together
- Colour coded ski runs – can still have a beginner take on the most difficult ski run
- Automatic change calculation on a cash register – can still give incorrect change

Approach to Mistake Proofing & Mistake Prevention

When undertaking mistake proofing and mistake prevention, I recommend a simple strategy to keep in mind.

1. Seek to *prevent mistakes* from occurring in the first instance.
2. Seek to *mistake proof* when you are unable to prevent mistakes from being made.

SOLUTION IMPLEMENTATION PLANNING (STEP 14)

Having made a decision as to which solutions will be implemented, the team is now ready to start the process of implementation. This is the part of the sequence where change starts to take place and the tools and skills of 'change leadership' and 'project management' come into greater focus. A simple schedule bar chart (Gantt Chart) may suffice in getting the team to the point of identifying solutions. However, a schedule bar chart alone will not be enough for this phase of project work.

PROJECT MANAGEMENT

The tools and skills of project management are integral to successfully implementing solutions. In this chapter we will briefly discuss some of the key concepts of project management that are relevant to your work as a Six Sigma Black Belt.

History of Project Management

Project management is often associated with the construction of the great Pyramids of Egypt and the Great Wall of China, however, little documentation exists to indicate the methods used for managing such complex projects. Project management techniques and skills can only be inferred. I'm sure you've seen the documentaries hypothesising about the way in which the pyramids were built. Modern day project management has a strong association with schedule bar charts developed by Henry Gantt in the early 1900's. The history of the bar chart can be traced back to World War 1 when Gantt used the bar chart as a visual aid for managing his shipbuilding projects. In acknowledgement of his contribution, schedule bar charts are often referred to as Gantt charts.

The 1950's and 1960's era of work in aerospace and military projects saw the development of many of the distinctive project management tools and techniques used today. For example, program evaluation and review technique (PERT) and work breakdown structures (WBS) were developed in these industries. Critical path method (CPM) and network diagrams were contributions from the construction industry during this period also.

Many of the tools developed during these periods have withstood the test of time, and we will refer to a number of them as we work through the 'improve' phase of DMAIC.

Defining Project Management

To understand project management, we should first understand what a project is. The Project Management Institute's (PMI) guide to the 'Project Management Body of Knowledge' (PMBOK) defines a **project** as: *'..... a temporary endeavour undertaken to create a unique product or service. Temporary means that every project has a definite end. Unique means that the product or service is different in some distinguishing way from all similar products or services.'*

Project management is defined by James Lewis (2002)[41] as: *'..... facilitating the planning, scheduling, and controlling of all activities that must be done to achieve project objectives.'*

Before we discuss some of the key elements of planning, scheduling and controlling the implementation of project solutions, there are some principles that a Black Belt must remember:

- Project management is not just scheduling – in the absence of the other ingredients of project management, a project schedule will help a Black Belt document their failure with great precision.

[41] Lewis, J.P., (2002), *'Fundamentals of Project Management'*, AMACOM, New York, p. 4

- The people who are to do the work must help plan it – it is a mistake to plan the project for the team. The role of a project manager is to enable the team to get the work completed, not do it for them.

Project Constraints

A project usually operates under four constraints.

- **Cost** - Project costs, downstream maintenance costs, budget limitations, exchange rates.
- **Performance / Quality** - The level of performance or quality expected at the end of the project.
- **Time** - Project duration, activity duration, timing of reviews and approvals.
- **Scope** - The extent of work to be completed during the project and the extent of participation by internal resources.

According to Lewis (2002), one of the most common causes of project failure is when the project sponsor or project sponsor dictates all four of these constraints. In other words they make demands for the project manager to complete the project by a certain deadline, within budget, at a given scope while achieving specific performance levels. Such a dictation leaves no room to move for the team, and the likelihood that they will accept any responsibility for not staying within constraints, or even commit to these limitations, is low.

Anyone who has ever worked with geometry will know that if they are given values for the three sides of a triangle, they can calculate the area, or if they know the area and the lengths of two sides, they can calculate the length of the remaining side. The same principle applies to these four constraints that are represented in the triangle diagram. The sponsor can dictate any three of these constraints, however the team should determine the value of the fourth. This ensures the commitment of all parties involved to the success of the project.

Project Management Body of Knowledge

The Project Management Institute has identified nine general areas of knowledge that a Project Manager needs in order to be effective. These are:

1. **Project Integration Management** – Ensuring that the project is properly planned executed and controlled, including the exercise of formal project change control.
2. **Project Scope Management** – Includes developing a scope statement that defines project boundaries, subdividing work into components with defined deliverables, verifying that the planned scope was achieved and developing scope change procedures.
3. **Project Time Management** – Developing practical schedules, and controlling work to see that the schedule is met.
4. **Project Cost Management** – Estimating project costs, budgeting and tracking costs to keep the project within budget.

5. **Project Quality Management** – Includes both quality assurance and quality control. Assurance refers to the activities of planning to meet quality requirements, and control refers to the activities of monitoring results to ensure conformance with requirements.
6. **Project HR Management** – Identifying HR requirements of the project, defining roles and responsibilities and reporting arrangements and acquiring and managing these resources.
7. **Project Communications Management** – Planning, executing and controlling the acquisition and dissemination of all information relevant to stakeholders such as status, milestones and events.
8. **Project Risk Management** – Identifying, analysing and responding to project risks. This includes minimising the probability and consequence of negative events, and maximising the probability and consequence of positive events.
9. **Project Procurement Management** – Determining what must be procured, calling for bids or quotations, selecting suppliers, administering and closing contracts.

As the intent of this book is not to be a complete text for project management, these nine elements are only briefly covered. A complete document is available from the Project Management Institute web site: www.pmi.org .

Implementation Project Life Cycle

Lean Six Sigma projects are usually completed in five phases

1. Conceptualisation
2. Definition
3. Planning
4. Execution
5. Closeout

The implementation life cycle consists of the *last four phases*.

	|---------------------- SOLUTION IMPLEMENTATION ---------------------|			
1. CONCEPT	**2. DEFINE**	**3. PLAN**	**4. EXECUTE**	**5. CLOSE OUT**
1.1 Solutions are selected for treating validated (a) causes of variation, or (b) sources of waste.	2.1 The solution implementation project mission is stated 2.2 Specific implementation project objectives are defined	3.1 Technical work is planned 3.2 Change leadership work is planned 3.3 Work is scheduled 3.4 Plan to manage implementation project risks is developed	4.1 Work schedules are actioned 4.2 Progress is monitored and reviewed 4.3 Necessary corrective action is taken	5.1 Final work is reviewed 5.2 Lesson learnt are identified and documented 5.3 Key learnings are shared 5.4 Achievements are celebrated and recognised

Figure 294: Lean Six Sigma Solution Implementation Project

1. Solution Phase – The concept phase of a Lean Six Sigma project consists of the sequence of steps that produce solutions for treating identified root causes of variation. This includes the relevant steps in the define, measure, analyse and improve phases.

2. Definition Phase – In this phase, the project is defined by determining (a) the project vision and mission, (b) project objectives or desired outcomes, (c) expectations of the sponsor / stakeholders with respect to time, cost, and performance.

3. Planning Phase – During this phase, the team determines what must be done, who will do it, how it will be done, when it must be done by, how much it will cost and what is needed to complete it. Various tools and techniques support this phase.

4. Execution Phase – In the execution phase, scheduled actions are undertaken according to the plan. We often find that the team works hard in creating an implementation plan, but the plan is not followed. Why plan if it isn't going to be used is the logical question? Plans are developed for the purpose of helping achieve the desired outcome. Progress against the plan is monitored throughout this phase. Where deviations are discovered, action is taken to get the plan back on track or alternatively modify the plan.

5. Closeout Phase – Once the plan has been completed, it is important to review work taken to identify what can be learnt and taken on board to make the next round of work much more effective and efficient.

Ingredients of the Implementation Project Plan

Planning is a fundamental of project management and an absolute imperative. Without an effective plan, the probability that implementation will be successful is virtually zero.

Project team leaders often make a fundamental mistake during the planning phase of their implementation project. Their focus is directed towards getting the solution or change implemented. However, the standard approach often lacks the necessary focus on sustainability of those solutions. By sustainability I mean that the new way of working is continued over time and not just when first introduced. To effectively undertake planning for implementation, a Black Belt must remember one thing. The old way of working, thinking and focusing all contribute to achievement of the same old results. Not only does the Black Belt need to change the way people work to get the desired results, they must also change their way of thinking and what they focus on. With that in mind, the ingredients of an implementation plan listed below incorporate both the technical requirements of implementation and elements that contribute to ensuring focus and thinking is aligned towards the desired result. Some of the most common ingredients of an effective implementation plan include:

- Project vision, mission and objectives
- Work Breakdown Structure (WBS)
- Project Scheduling
- Responsibility Allocation
- Stakeholder Engagement
- Communications
- Project Risk Management
- Project Financials (Cost Schedules and Cash Flow Breakdown)

DEFINING THE IMPROVEMENT PROJECT

The easiest way to explain this aspect of the project is to show an example.

Mission: **Objectives:**

To effectively and efficiently implement project solutions.	Implement to the following standards by 27th of November, 2008. • Within budget • To the desired level of performance • Scope fulfilled

One thing you should take notice of is the project objectives. They address all four constraints of a project in some way – time, cost, scope and performance.

These will become important to you a little later as most project risks relate to these four factors.

WORK PLANNING AND ACTIVITY SCHEDULING

The only tool available for scheduling projects until about 1958 was the schedule bar chart. Schedule bar charts, commonly referred to as Gantt Charts, are simple to construct and remain one of the most popular tools for communicating to team members what they need to do by when.

Additional tools now exist in the form of Work Breakdown Structures, Network diagrams, PERT and CPM. These are discussed in more detail on the following pages.

Relationship Between Planning and Scheduling Tools

Before we get into the detail of this section, I want you to understand how the various tools relate to the process and end product of work planning and activity scheduling.

The diagram below shows a simple schedule bar chart (Gantt Chart) with a table of data above it that contains the necessary input for creating the final schedule of work and any associated charts.

ACTIVITY	PREDECESSOR	DURATION	EARLY START	EARLY FINISH	LATE START	LATE FINISH
A		2	0	2	0	2
B		4	0	4	4	8
C	A	2	2	4	2	4
D	B	4	4	8	8	12
E	C	5	4	9	7	12
F	C	8	4	12	4	12

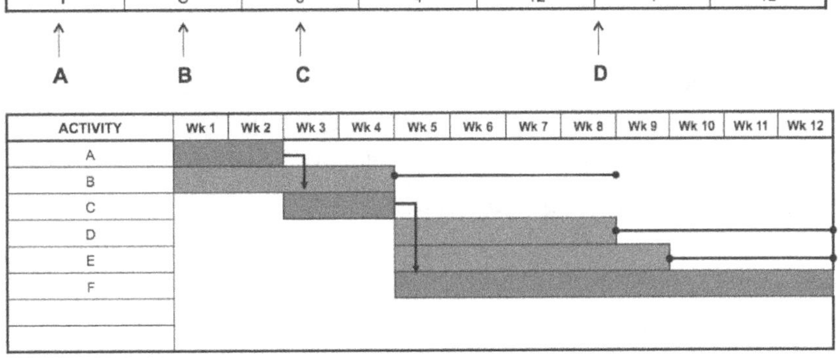

The various project management tools discussed over the following pages relate to this diagram in the following ways.

- **Activities** (column A) are determined with Work Breakdown Structure (WBS)
- **Predecessors** for activities (column B) are determined with Network Diagrams
- Task **duration** (column C) is determined with Program Evaluation & Review Technique (PERT)
- Information for determining **critical path** is identified with Critical Path Method (CPM)

If you have no real knowledge of the tools mentioned here at this point, my hope is that you would come back to this page.

Work Breakdown Structure (WBS)

A significant challenge for Black Belts leading implementation projects is the process of determining what needs to be done, how long it will take and what it will cost to do these things. Projects often fail due to inaccurate estimates, and a significant source of stress and criticism is the failure to meet deadlines or major milestones.

One of the most useful tools for helping a Black Belt accomplish these things is the Work Breakdown Structure (WBS). The WBS is built around a simple idea, tasks can continually be subdivided into smaller tasks until a level is reached where no further subdivision can take place. At that point, estimates of duration and cost are usually easier to perform than at the macro levels. As well as simplification, estimates are usually more accurate at this level.

As an example, consider the task of cleaning the house.

A work breakdown structure might look like the example below.

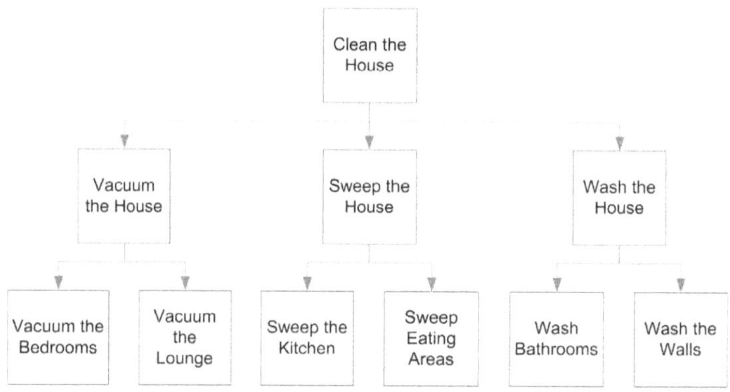

Figure 295: Work Breakdown Structure Example

It's often a challenge for a facilitator to manage inputs considering the different ways that individuals think. Some individuals are able to think at a high level working their way down the structure, while others only think in micro detail and offer numerous points at the first level. One way of managing this is to ask questions that force people to think at a higher level (less detail). For example:

- *What is the desired outcome (the highest level)?*
- *What would be the three big things (the next lower level) if done that would result in this being achieved (the higher level)?*

This second question can be repeated for each item to break each down into the next lower level.

Horizontal Format

A work breakdown structure can also be presented using horizontal boxes as shown below.

Figure 296: Work Breakdown Structure - Horizontal Format

Indented Text Format

Whilst boxes are an excellent way to visually present the work breakdown structure, in the absence of relevant software the development of these may be quite time consuming. Indented text provides the same information as the boxes.

1. **Clean the House Project**
   - 1.1. Wash
     - 1.1.1. Walls
     - 1.1.2. Bathrooms
   - 1.2. Sweep
     - 1.2.1. Eating areas
     - 1.2.2. Kitchen
   - 1.3. Vacuum
     - 1.3.1. Lounge
     - 1.3.2. Bedrooms

How Many Levels

One challenge the project manager has to deal with is determining how many levels to break work down into. These tips might prove useful as a guide in making such a determination:

- A typical WBS has 3 to 6 levels of work – according to Lewis (2002), twenty levels is considered to be the upper limit
- Stop the breakdown when (a) you get to the point where you can estimate time and cost to the desired level of accuracy, or (b) the work will take as long as the smallest unit of time you want to measure; e.g. if you want to estimate to the nearest day, stop when the steps take 1 day to perform
- A work breakdown structure is prepared prior to developing a schedule of tasks
- The WBS does not show the sequence in which work is performed

- The people who will do the work, should participate in the development of the work breakdown structure

Tips for Dealing With Excess Detail

If people give too much detail in a breakdown level (from macro level to very detailed level in one bound), ask them to break the component down into a specific number of pieces. I.e., *'In three steps, describe what has to be done to commission the plant?'* This question forces them to 'chunk' their ideas up to a higher level. *Then* each of these can be broken down further.

Once the WBS is completed, the team is able to schedule specific activities and allocate responsibilities.

Network Diagrams

Arrow diagrams or Network diagrams are created to show the interdependencies and sequence of tasks within the schedule. The **Activity-on-Node** (AON) diagram shown depicts work as a box or node. The arrows show the sequence of work. We can see from the diagram that tasks A and B are performed concurrently, and task D is done after A is completed, etc.

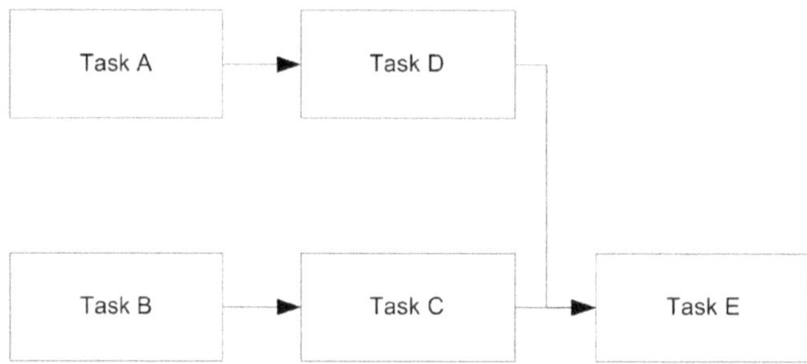

Figure 297: Activity on Node Network Diagram

The diagram below refers to an alternative form of network diagram - **Activity-on-Arrow** (AOA). The arrows represent the tasks and the circles represent events. The events are binary events; meaning they have either occurred or they have not. In project management terminology, event does not have the same meaning as say a sporting type event. The event in this case refers to when something has just started or just finished. This form of network diagram is unlikely to be used in Lean Six Sigma project work.

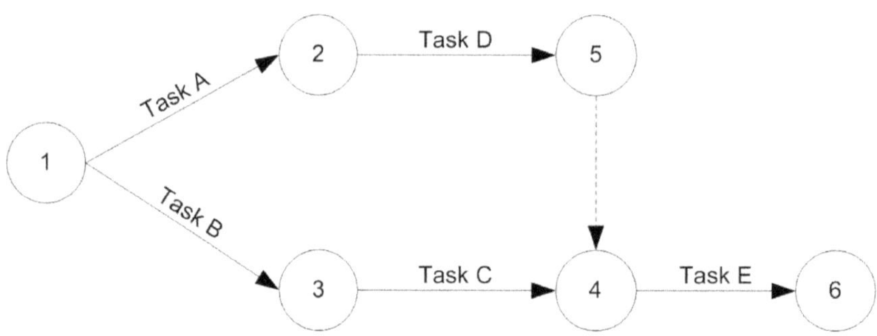

Figure 298: Activity on Arrow Network Diagram

Program Evaluation & Review Technique (PERT)

PERT was developed by the US Navy and the Booze, Allen and Hamilton Consulting Group. Its original purpose was to manage project risk associated with the Polaris Submarine Project during the late 1950's.

When to Use PERT

The main difference between PERT and CPM (critical path method) is that PERT uses probability whilst CPM does not. Thus, PERT is referred to as a 'probabilistic' method in that it is used when you do not know exactly how long the tasks will take, only that they will *probably* take a certain time frame to complete.

By contrast, CPM is referred to as a 'deterministic' method in that it assumes a task will take as long as you have determined.

PERT is used to calculate an expected time for each task. These are then used as input to the application of CPM.

Project Manager Situation	Project Manager's Course of Action
1. You know exactly how long each task will take to complete.	Identify task duration as you create your sequence of tasks in CPM
2. You do not know exactly how long each task will take to complete, you can only estimate.	Use PERT to identify 'expected times' for each tasks Use 'expected times' as input to CPM

Calculating Expected Time and Variance

With PERT it is possible to calculate the probability an activity will be completed within a certain time frame. In the absence of solid historical data, managers are often uncertain as to the times different activities will take. For this reason, the developers of PERT employed a three-dimensional probabilistic model based on three time estimates for each activity.

These estimates are:

- **o = optimistic time:** the time an activity will take if everything goes as well as possible. The possibility of this should be small, perhaps one in a hundred.
- **m = most likely time:** the most realistic time estimate for the activity based on knowledge at hand.
- **p = pessimistic time:** the time an activity would take assuming extremely unfavourable conditions. Like optimistic time, the possibility of this should be small.

The expected time (t) for completing any tasks is estimated using a simple equation that takes the estimates o, m and p into consideration.

PERT assumes these time estimates follow the beta probability distribution as it has been found to be appropriate in determining expected time frame and variance for activity completion times.

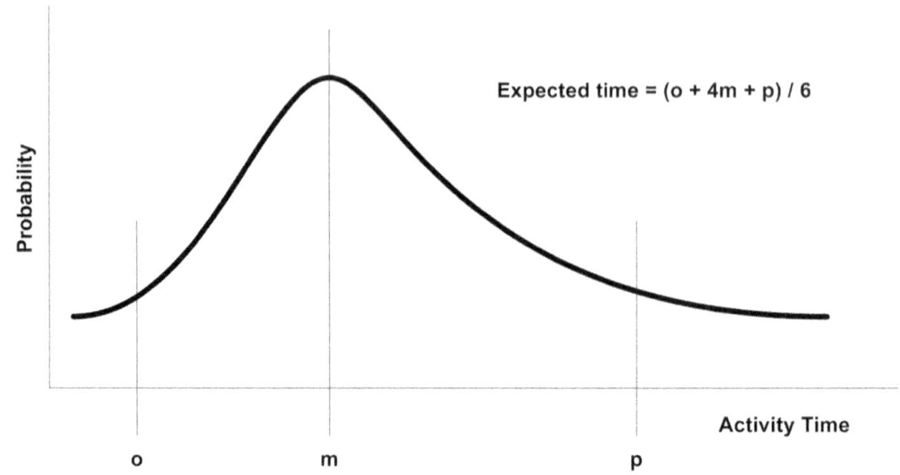

Figure 299: Beta Probability Distribution for PERT

The following table provides an example of how you might layout expected time and variance calculations. Refer to the case study in this chapter for a full example of the use of PERT.

Activity	Optimistic (o)	Most Likely (m)	Pessimistic (p)	Expected $t = \frac{o + 4m + p}{6}$	Variance $\left(\frac{p - o}{6}\right)^2$
Task A	1	2	3	2	0.111
Task B	2	3	10	4	1.777

<u>Expected Time Versus Variance</u>

So what do the numbers mean? The diagram below visually depicts the beta probability distributions associated with Tasks A and B in the table above. Obviously with greater variance, there is greater risk associated with completing the work on time.

As you now know PERT helps you identify expected time values for each detailed task in an implementation plan where there is uncertainty about time. These are used as input to CPM.

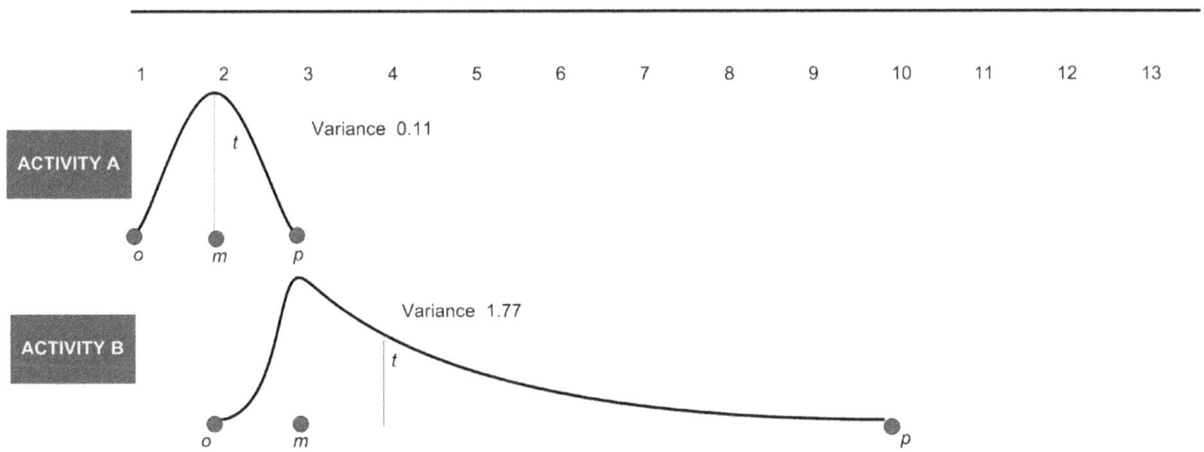

Figure 300: Beta Probability Distributions for Individual Tasks

Critical Path Method (CPM)

Remington Rand Univac developed the critical path method (CPM) during the late 1950's.

Critical Path calculations are undertaken by software these days, however unless you know how the work is done then you may not fully comprehend the meanings of the terms used in CPM.

CPM answers the following questions for the project manager:

- *How long will the project take?*
- *What activities have room to move (slack)?*
- *What activities have no room to move and are critical to completing the project on time?*

CPM Notations

The following notations are an integral part of CPM.

- **Early Start** – The earliest date by which an activity can start, assuming all predecessors have been completed.
- **Early Finish** – The earliest date by which an activity can finish, assuming all predecessors have been completed.
- **Late Start** – The latest date by which an activity can start to ensure the planned completion date is met.
- **Late Finish** - The latest date by which an activity can finish to ensure the planned completion date is met.
- **Activity Box** – The activity box captures the values associated with the times listed above, as well as the duration of respective activities and slack time. The activity box we will use in this text is consistent with that produced in Microsoft Visio software.

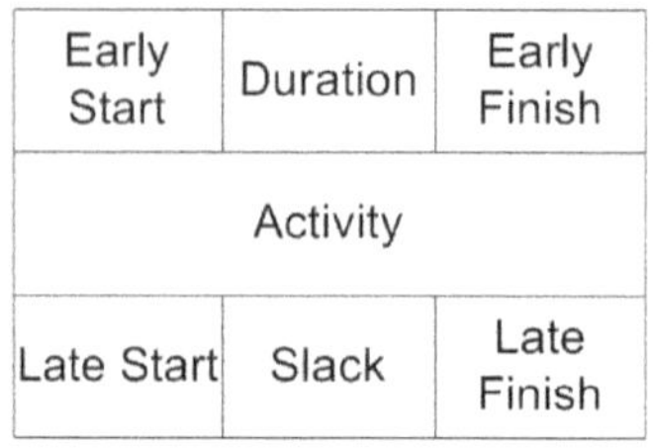

Figure 301: CPM Activity Box

Critical Path Method

Calculating critical path is a process involving the completion of three steps.

1. Create a Network Diagram

The first step in determining critical path is to create a network diagram of relevant activities in their sequence. The activities, if not known, can be determined using WBS.

For demonstration purposes, suppose we had a simple project with the following schedule data.

Activity	Duration	Predecessor
A	1	
B	3	A
C	2	A
D	4	B
E	3	C
F	2	D, E

If you had 'expected times' using PERT, those figures are used for your duration column. A network diagram using Activity-on-Node would now look like this.

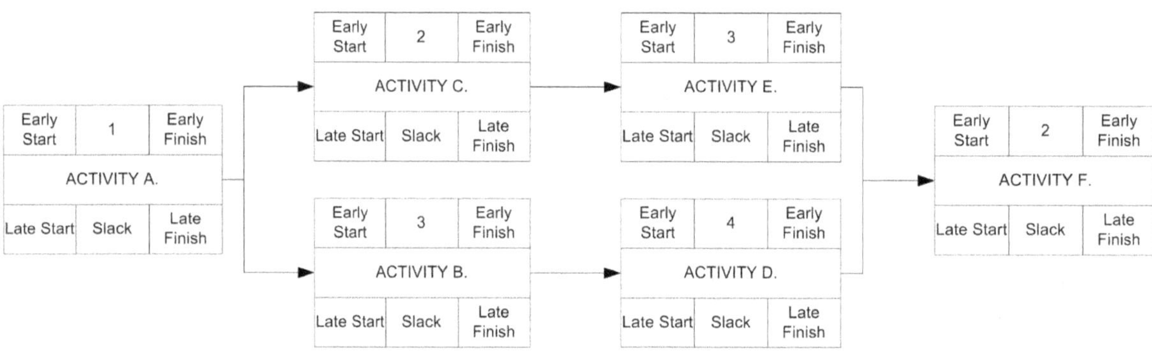

Figure 302: Network Diagram with Task Duration

The network diagram provides us with a visual representation of the process. However, we're unable to determine which of the paths through the process is critical without more information. To determine that, we need to complete the next two steps.

2. Determine ES & EF Using Forward Pass Computations

The term **forward pass** is used to define the task of estimating ES and EF during CPM activities. As the first activity in the sequence, its Early Start is at the start of week 1 so it is given a value of 0. With an expected duration of 1 week, its Early Finish is computed by adding the duration to the Early Start time to get 0 + 1 = week 1. These values are then inserted in the Early Start and Early Finish quadrants of the respective activity box.

Activity B has a duration of 3 weeks. The earliest it can start is when activity A is completed. So activity A's Early Finish time becomes activity B's Early Start time, in this case week 1. Activity B's Early Finish time is computed by adding the duration to the Early Start time to get 1 + 3 = week 4. These values are inserted in the Early Start and Early Finish quadrants of the respective activity box.

This activity is continued until the forward pass is completed for all activities, and the network diagram looks like that below. A point to remember, in this approach the Early Finish time for one task, is the Early Start time for the following activity.

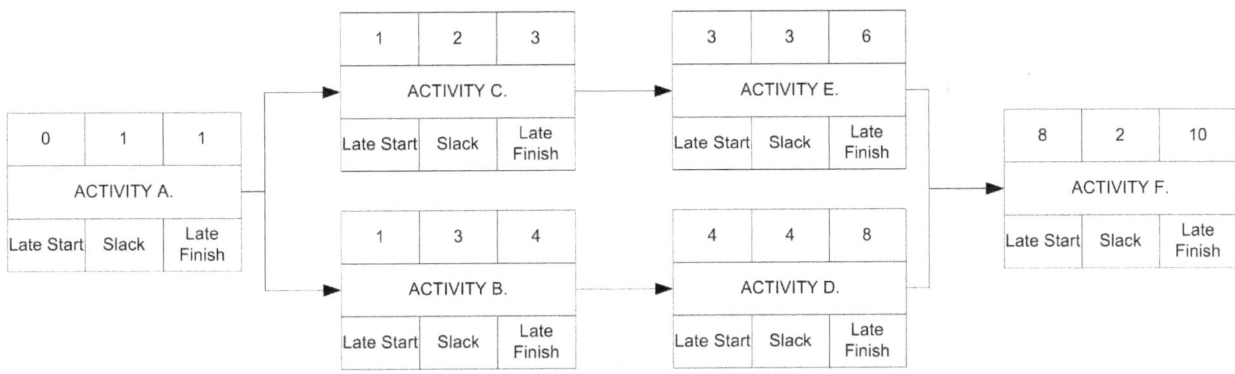

Figure 303: Forward Pass Computation – Early Start and Early Finish

The completed network diagram shows that the project will take 10 weeks to complete at the earliest. This work completes the forward pass computations to determine the earliest finish times for each activity, and the project overall. The rule to remember when undertaking forward pass computations is:

When multiple activities precede another activity, the earliest time that activity can be started is the **larger** of the earliest finish times of the activities preceding it.

3. Determine LS & LF Using Backward Pass Computations

A backward pass is made through the network to compute the Late Start and Late Finish times for each activity. We don't want the project to end any later than its earliest completion date, so at this time we will accept that this project will have a Late Finish time of week 10.

The last activity in the network is activity F with a duration of 2 weeks. To complete the project in 10 weeks, the latest it can finish is week 10, therefore its Late Start is equal to this value less the duration, 10 – 2 = week 8. These values are inserted in the Late Start and Late Finish quadrants of the respective activity box.

Activity E can finish as late as the earliest start data for activity F without affecting the duration of the project. So its Late Finish is equal to activity F's Late Start value which is week 8. Activity E's Late Start is computed by subtracting the duration of the activity from the Late Finish value to get 8 – 3 = week 5. You may have noticed that the Early Finish and Late Finish for this activity are different. In fact it seems that this activity can start anytime from week 3 to week 5 without affecting the duration of the project. This difference in early and late times is referred to as 'slack' or 'float', depending on the text. The values for Late Start, Late Finish and Slack can now be inserted in the relevant quadrants of the respective activity box.

This activity is continued until the backward pass is completed for all activities, and the network diagram looks like that below.

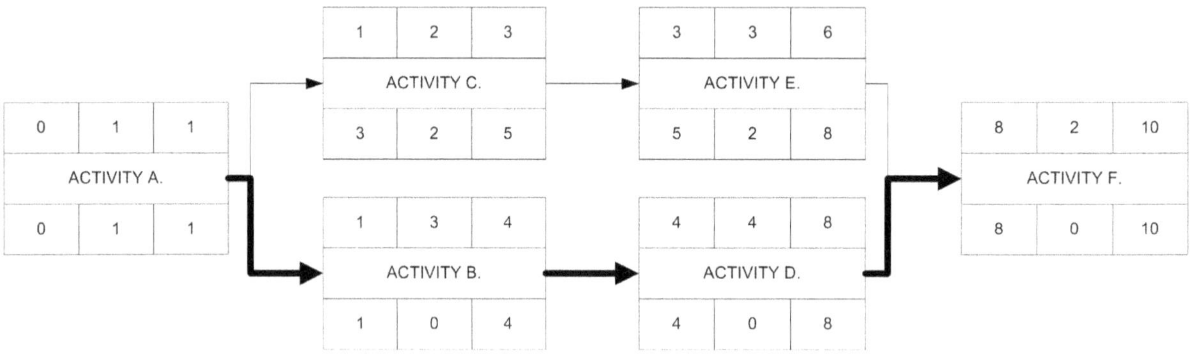

Figure 304: Backward Pass Computation – Late Start and Late Finish

The rule to remember when undertaking backward pass computations is this - When multiple activities follow one another, the latest time an activity can be finished is the **smaller** of the latest start times of the activities after it.

Having completed the CPM network diagram for our example, I have highlighted the path that flows through those activities where the ES / EF and LS/ LF values are the same. There is no slack or float on this path.

By definition, any activity without any slack is referred to as **critical**, and the path through the network without any float is called the **critical path**. If any work falls behind schedule on this path, the time frame for the project will slip accordingly.

For example, if activity B takes one week longer, then the project will take eleven weeks.

Activities with slack or float should not be ignored. Whilst they have less chance of delaying the project, any slippage beyond the stated Late Finish time will cause it to become critical.

Schedule Bar Charts

A schedule bar chart documents the schedule of activities in a visual representation across time. The user is able to see:

- How long the project takes
- How long each step takes
- The critical path
- The division of labour when responsibilities are allocated

These types of charts can be traced back to World War 1 when Henry Gantt used the bar chart as a visual aid in managing shipbuilding projects.

The following is a schedule bar chart in its simplest form.

The top is a calendar with a time scale in days and the activities in the schedule are listed in the column on the left. The horizontal bars represent the scheduling of each task from start to finish.

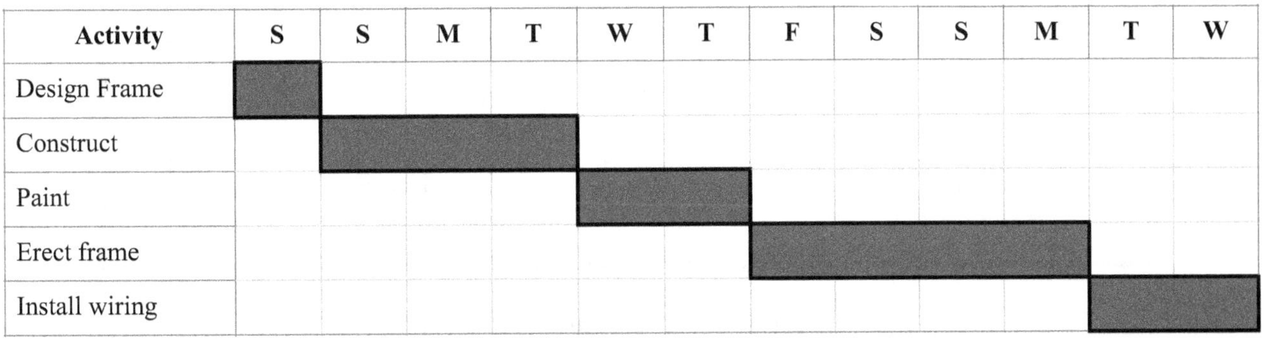

Figure 305: Schedule Bar Chart

A table of data like that shown below will help in the preparation of the schedule bar chart.

ACTIVITY	DURATION	PREDECESSOR
1. Design frame	1 day	
2. Construct	3 days	1
3. Paint	2 days	2
4. Erect frame	4 days	3
5. Install wiring	2 days	4

Table of Schedule Bar Chart Data

Whilst not absolutely necessary for simple projects, this tool becomes important when the project activities are large and complex. The tool has stood the test of time and is widely used in project management. A survey conducted by Microsoft Project users found that the bar chart was the preferred tool for planning and controlling projects by 80 percent of managers.

One drawback of the bar chart in its original form is that it did not show the interdependencies of work, so it was difficult to tell how slippage of one task affected the rest of the work. During the late 1950's and early 1960's two methods were developed to help overcome this work – PERT and CPM.

MICROSOFT PROJECT

With access to MS Project or similar project management software, construction of Gantt Charts and identification of Critical Paths can be performed with little effort on your part.

	Task Name	Leveling Delay	Duration	Start	Finish	Predecessors	Resources
1	A. Construct Internal Components	0 edays	2 days	Mon 5/01/09	Tue 6/01/09		T Grey
2	B. Modify the Roof and Floor	0 edays	4 days	Mon 5/01/09	Thu 8/01/09		F Michaels
3	C. Construct the Collection Stack	0 edays	2 days	Wed 7/01/09	Thu 8/01/09	1	C Nixon
4	D. Pour Slab and Install Fittings	0 edays	4 days	Fri 9/01/09	Wed 14/01/09	2	T Grey
5	E. Construct High Temp. Burner	0 edays	3 days	Fri 9/01/09	Tue 13/01/09	3	C Nixon
6	F. Install Control System	0 edays	4 days	Fri 9/01/09	Wed 14/01/09	3	G Wallace
7	G. Install Device	0 edays	6 days	Thu 15/01/09	Thu 22/01/09	4,5	T Grey
8	H. Inspect Work & Test Operation	0 edays	2 days	Fri 23/01/09	Mon 26/01/09	6,7	V Lyons

Figure 306: Gantt Chart Data Table

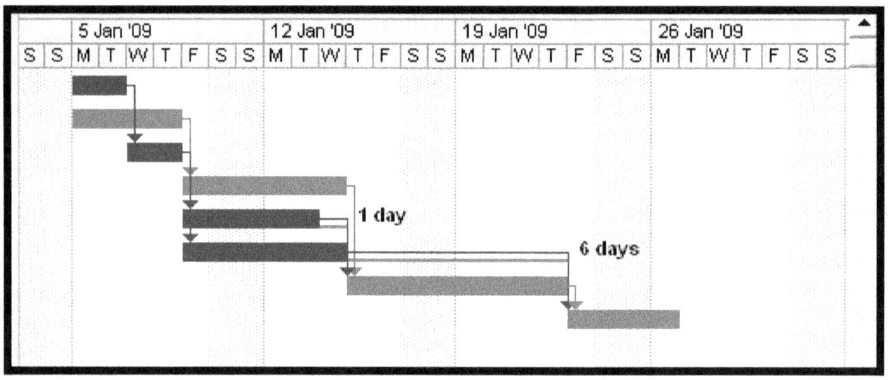

Figure 307: Gantt Chart Showing Critical Path

What many users of MS Project are not aware of is the PERT function. PERT tools can be accessed through the 'View > Toolbars' menu. Notice the term 'expected duration' is used instead of the term 'most likely duration'. Duration in this case refers to the calculated value based on the PERT equation.

	Task Name	Duration	Optimistic Dur.	Expected Dur.	Pessimistic Dur.
1	A. Construct Internal Components	2 days	1 day	2 days	3 days
2	B. Modify the Roof and Floor	4 days	2 days	3 days	10 days
3	C. Construct the Collection Stack	2 days	1 day	2 days	3 days
4	D. Pour Slab and Install Fittings	4 days	2 days	4 days	6 days
5	E. Construct High Temp. Burner	3 days	1 day	2 days	9 days
6	F. Install Control System	4 days	1 day	4 days	7 days
7	G. Install Device	6 days	3 days	5 days	13 days
8	H. Inspect Work & Test Operation	2 days	1 day	2 days	3 days

Figure 308: Input Form for PERT Calculation

PROJECT RISK MANAGEMENT

I remember getting a battery-operated train as a Christmas present when I was a child. When the ON button was activated, the train would self propel around the lounge room bumping into everything in its path. The front wheels were arranged in such a way that when it bumped into an immovable obstruction, it would simply make a whole lot of noise, back away and take another path until it bumped into some other obstruction. Its life simply consisted of bumping into obstacles and changing direction until eventually it ran out of energy. Unless a Black Belt undertakes some form of risk management for their implementation project, they risk operating much like this train did. When you meet obstructions you will have to change direction and if this continues to happen you'll be forced to abandon your original plan and shift into an ad hoc project management approach.

A Black Belt must not ignore the fact that there will be uncertainty in the implementation of their solutions. Risk and uncertainty go hand in hand, and for even simple projects it must be managed.

The purpose of this section is to provide an overview of project risk and opportunity management. Risk is experienced when you are exposed to the consequences of uncertainty. In the absence of uncertainty, there is no risk, as you would know with 100 percent confidence what would occur.

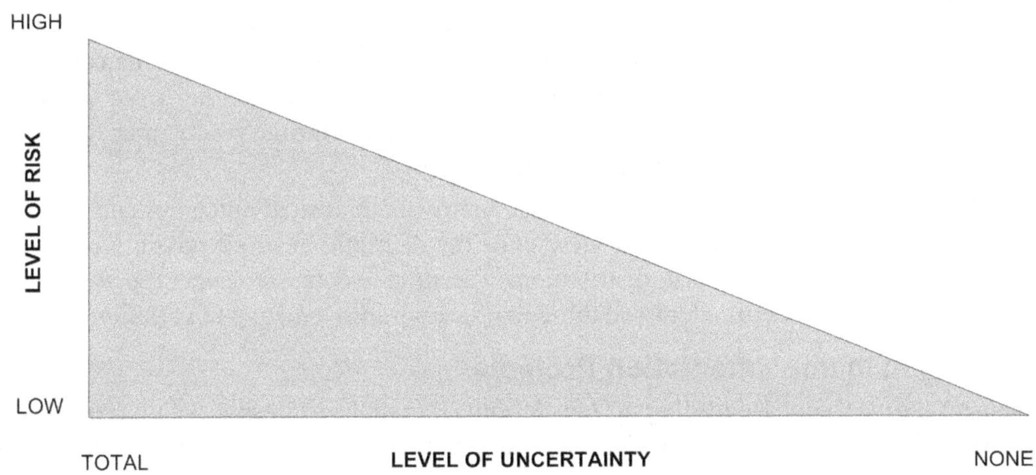

Figure 309: Risk versus Uncertainty

Some key terms used in this section are:

- **Risk** – When quantified, risk is a measure of the amount of uncertainty that exists in a project.
- **Uncertainty** – Uncertainty is defined by Heerkens (2002)[42] as *"an absence of information, knowledge, or understanding regarding the outcome of an action, decision or event."* Uncertainty and information are inextricably linked.

[42] Heerkens, G.R., (2002), *'Project Management'*, McGraw-Hill, New York, p. 142

<table>
<tr><th colspan="5">Total Risk -------------------------------- Moderate Risk ------------------------------------ No Risk</th></tr>
<tr><td>No Information</td><td></td><td>Partial Information</td><td></td><td>Complete Information</td></tr>
<tr><td>Total Uncertainty</td><td></td><td>Partial Uncertainty</td><td></td><td>Total Certainty</td></tr>
</table>

Figure 310: Relationship Between Risk, Information and Uncertainty

Dimensions of Risk

Traditionally, we view risk as something associated with what can go wrong that will hurt us. Something bad even. However, that is not the complete picture of risk. Risk has multiple dimensions:

- **Hazard** – The traditional focus of risk management is on managing the downside associated with the consequences of an adverse event such as loss, fraud, damage and any other negative form of risk. Hazard risk is addressed through compliance and contingency planning (insurance, instructions, audits, response plans etc).
- **Opportunity** – Usually an investment or financial focus is required to take action required to maximise the upside within the constraints of the organisation's environment. A view from this dimension is implicit in the concept that risk and return have a strong relationship. A lot of the work that goes into deploying Lean Six Sigma in a business is for the purpose of managing opportunity based risk, that is putting in place a strategy for capturing and benefiting from opportunities that would otherwise go unrealised. Opportunity risk is addressed through value management (hedging, futures, scenario planning, proactive improvement etc).
- **Variation** – Risk associated with the difference between anticipated outcomes and actual outcomes. Whilst more academic in nature, this view is of the distribution of all possible outcomes and the uncertainty associated with that distribution. Variation exists somewhere between hazard and opportunity. Variation risk is addressed through process improvement and variation management.

Risk Management in Implementation Projects

Risk management during the phase leading up to solution generation, addresses both hazard-based risk and opportunity-based risk. For example, strategies such as operating agreements are put in place to reduce the likelihood of conflict between parties that could have a negative impact on the project. On the other hand, the work of the team leader in facilitating the process largely addresses the risk of missing opportunities to generate the best solutions. Both sides of the equation are addressed, albeit unconsciously on many occasions.

By contrast, risk management during the implementation phase largely addresses hazard-based risk. The purpose of risk management during this phase is to maximise the probability that implementation project objectives will be achieved.

When thought out carefully, these objectives are usually linked to the constraints of the implementation project i.e. time, cost, performance/quality and scope, therefore anything that can adversely affect any of these should be addressed. By minimising these impacts, the project should be completed on time, within budget, according to scope and achieve the level of performance expected by stakeholders.

Common Sources of Uncertainty

Some of the most common sources of uncertainty or risk for a Lean or Six Sigma project include these:

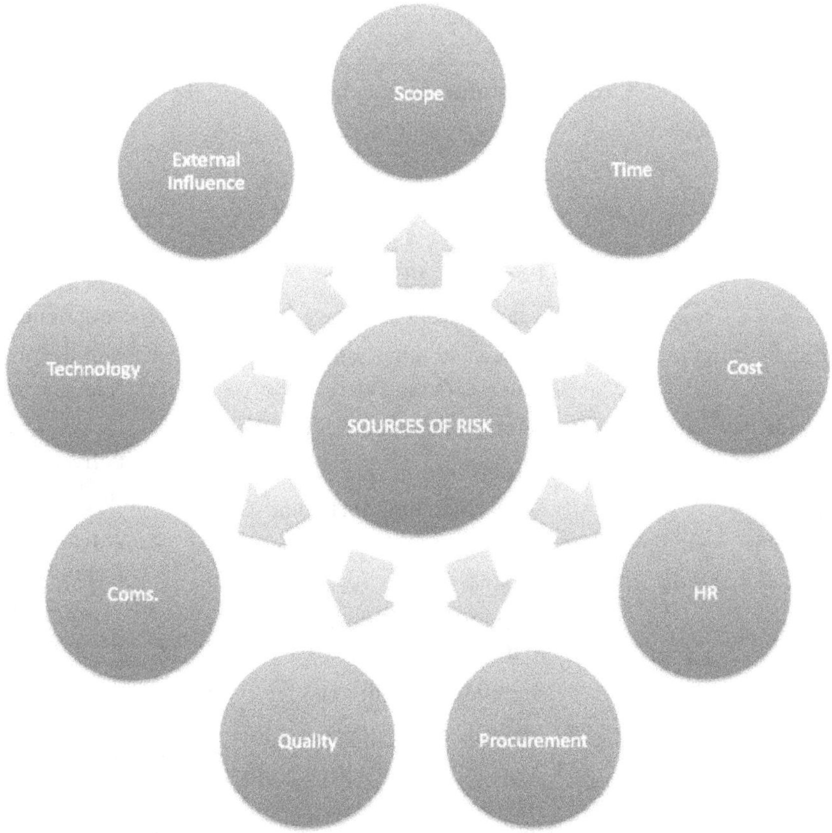

Figure 311: Sources of Uncertainty (Risk) for Projects

1. **Scope** – Feasibility, extent of work, customer driven scope changes, design errors.
2. **Time** – Schedules, critical path, duration, launch data, timings for reviews and approvals.
3. **Cost** – Budget, cash flow, downstream maintenance costs, inflation, exchange rates.
4. **Technology** – Scalability, design, organisational or industry suitability, upgradeability.
5. **Human Resources** – Availability, skills matching, commitment.
6. **Procurement** – Lead times, availability, supplier reliability, quality.
7. **Performance / Quality** – Requirements, standards.
8. **Communications** – Information flow, feedback.
9. **External Influences** – Laws, regulations, environment.

Common Problems Experienced During Projects

The purpose of risk management is ultimately to minimise or eliminate the effect of things that can hurt the success of the project. Some of the most common problems that can arise during a Six Sigma solution implementation project are detailed in the following table.

Scope	**Human Resources**	**Performance / Quality**
• Scope creep through influence of sponsor, sponsor or customer • Scope underestimation • Changing project objectives **Time** • Underestimation of project duration • Unrealistic completion date • Late approvals • Impacts on time by management reviews • Delayed tasks that impact the critical path **Cost** • Underestimation of project costs • Currency rate changes • Cash flow incorrectly forecast	• Called away to focus on other work • Misaligned priorities, not committed to project goals • Poor skills fit • Team members change • Leave and other scheduled issues affecting attendance • Interpersonal conflict • Ethical issues • Issues affecting health and safety **Procurement** • Cannot source relevant materials • Supplier reliability lacking • Material quality unacceptable • Availability and deliverability issues • Lead times are underestimated • Price changes	• Low quality work • Changing customer expectations **Communications** • Unclear lines of communication • Fail to communicate to relevant stakeholders • Conflicting messages being delivered **Technology** • Advancements or changes in technology • Incompatibility with existing technology • Need to upgrade existing hardware **External Influences** • Government intervention • Poor weather • Crisis or natural disaster • Changing technology

Common Problems for Six Sigma Projects

Lean Six Sigma project team leaders experience many of these problems throughout a project (not just at the implementation stage), particularly those concerned with time, scope and human resources. Problems such as these are the basis for project risk, and the level of risk is proportionate to the level of uncertainty about their occurrence.

Benefits of Risk Management

While we recognise that risk management works towards ensuring project objectives are met, there are a number of other benefits.

1. Ensuring that there are no unpleasant surprises by anticipating what might happen. The benefits are:	Reduced time wastage Improved response to deviations Reduce 'shock' levels when something happens
2. Maximising the probability of successful implementation of solutions through having contingency plans to deal with anticipated deviations from the planned path. The benefits are:	Improved knowledge Improved decision making Reduced variation Increase the probability of completing (a) on time, (b) within budget, (c) to the expected performance level, and (d) to the defined scope
3. Maximising project credibility through awareness that risks are being managed. The benefits are:	Increased stakeholder confidence Demonstrated and documented due diligence Improved communications

How to Undertake an Implementation Project Risk Analysis

Risk management in a project comprises five steps that meet the standards of risk management in Australia (AS:4360.2004).

Step 1 – Establish the Context

Step 2 – Identify Risks

Step 3 – Assess Risks

Step 4 – Treat Risks

Step 5 – Monitor Risks

Step 1. Establish the Context

The setting of the context for the risk study includes:

- The development of criteria for rating risks during the assessment phase, and
- Identifying project objectives.

Some common terms used to rate likelihood and severity are shown below:

Likelihood Rating (L) **	Severity Rating (S)
1 – Rare	1 – Insignificant / No Real Impact
2 – Unlikely to occur	2 – Minor Impact
3 – Could happen in most circumstances	3 – Moderate Impact
4 – Likely to occur in most circumstances	4 – Major Impact
5 – Almost certain to occur	5 – Catastrophic Impact
** Likelihood could be based on occurrence frequency, i.e., rare = never happened, unlikely = occurred once in past 5 years etc	

Objectives are documented in the 'Project Risk Worksheet' to ensure that (a) the team does not lose sight of the purpose of this work, and (b) focus is sustained throughout the process.

Project:	**Date Issued:**	**Page:**	1 of 1
	Date Revised:	**Revision No:**	**File No:**

Project Objectives:	- On time - To expected level of performance	- Within Budget - According to scope

What Can Happen	**Existing Controls**	**L**	**Potential Effect**	**S**	**RR**	**Action**	**Who**	**When**	**L**	**S**	**RR**

Figure 312: Project Risk Management Planning Worksheet

Step 2. Identify Risks

Having established the risk assessment context, the next step is to identify the risks that could prevent the team from achieving the objectives of the project. This step is the most important, and often most difficult in the process. Any risk left unidentified, will not be addressed and therefore the team will not have a contingency to deal with the risk if it arises.

The discussion sequence for identifying risks consists of one step repeated until all risks are identified.

Step 2.1 - Brainstorm potential risks by asking; *'What can happen that might prevent the achievement of objectives?'* You could refer back to the 9 sources of uncertainty previously mentioned in answering this question.

Risks for the project are those events that if they occur, work towards preventing project objectives being achieved. These are documented in the 'Project Risk Worksheet'.

Project Objectives:	- On time - To expected level of performance	- Within Budget - According to scope

What Can Happen	**Existing Controls**	**L**	**Potential Effect**	**S**	**RR**	**Action**	**Who**	**When**	**L**	**S**	**RR**
Monsoon Rains cause flooding											
Team given other work beyond project work											
Times are underestimated											

Step 3. Assess Risks

Having identified risks for the project, the next step is to assess these risks. Assessing risks requires that each risk be evaluated on (a) how severe the consequences would be if the event occurs, and (b) the likelihood of the event occurring in the first place given certain controls are in place already. These rating values are then multiplied together to give a Risk Rating that becomes the basis for prioritisation. The purpose of this step is to identify the areas of risk that require addressing, and bearing in mind we have limited resources, a risk priority will help determine which risks to address first.

The sequence for assessing risks consists of five steps that are repeated for each identified risk.

Step 3.1 – Identify the controls that are currently in place to manage the respective risks.

Step 3.2 – Rate the likelihood (L) of the event occurring in the existing control environment, using a 1 – 5 scale similar to this one.

- Rare (1)
- Unlikely (2)
- Could Happen (3)
- Likely (4)
- Almost Certain (5)

Step 3.3 – Determine and document the potential effect the risk event would have on the achievement of respective objectives, should it occur.

Step 3.4 – Rate the severity (S) of that effect using a 1 – 5 scale similar to this one.

- Insignificant (1)
- Minor (2)
- Moderate (3)
- Major (4)
- Catastrophic (5)

Step 3.5 – Determine the risk rating (RR) by multiplying the severity rating by the likelihood rating. Risk ratings range from 1 to 25.

Results are recorded in the project risk worksheet.

Project Objectives:	- On time - To expected level of performance					- Within Budget - According to scope					
What Can Happen	**Existing Controls**	**L**	**Potential Effect**	**S**	**RR**	**Action**	**Who**	**When**	**L**	**S**	**RR**
Monsoon Rains cause flooding	Weather forecasts	3	Work delays, costs to repair	4	**12**						
Team given other work beyond project work	Project leadership at the sponsor level	4	Reduced staff, work takes longer to complete, costs for contract staff	4	**16**						
Times are underestimated	PERT, Weekly project review	3	Work takes longer	2	**6**						

Project risks can be displayed in a matrix format for visual display. One of the most common formats is the five by five matrix shown below, adapted from Australian Standards for Risk Management (AS:4360.2004).

This matrix plots the likelihood or probability of an event occurring against the impact or consequences of it occurring. Risks are categorised as Low, Moderate, High or Extreme.

The ratings correspond to risk ratings identified in the worksheet above.

HAZARD RISK PROFILE

LIKELIHOOD	Insignificant (1)	Minor (2)	Moderate (3)	Major (4)	Catastrophic (5)
Almost Certain (5)	5	10	15	20	25
Likely (4)	4	8	12	16	20
Could Happen (3)	3	6	9	12	15
Unlikely (2)	2	4	6	8	10
Rare (1)	1	2	3	4	5

CONSEQUENCE RATING

Adapted from AS/NZ 4360:2004

LOW RISK | MODERATE RISK | HIGH RISK | EXTREME RISK

Rating Hazard Based Risk

A similar approach can be taken with risks based on opportunity. The main change is to the terminology used to rate the opportunity and the likelihood of it being realised.

OPPORTUNITY RISK PROFILE

LIKELIHOOD	Insignificant (1)	Minor (2)	Moderate (3)	Major (4)	Significant (5)
Easy (5)	5	10	15	20	25
Moderately Easy (4)	4	8	12	16	20
Moderate (3)	3	6	9	12	15
Moderately Hard (2)	2	4	6	8	10
Hard (1)	1	2	3	4	5

OPPORTUNITY RATING

Adapted from AS/NZ 4360:2004

SMALL OPPORTUNITY | MODERATE OPPORTUNITY | SIGNIFICANT OPPORTUNITY | OUTSTANDING OPPORTUNITY

Rating Opportunity Based Risk

Step 4. Treat Risks

Having identified and assessed project risks, the next step is to identify a risk response plan that defines ways to address adverse risks and maximise opportunities before they occur.

Step 4.1 – Identify actions to treat risks. The range of actions considered can be selected from these strategies.

- **Eliminate the risk** – Look into methods of eliminating the risk in the first instance. If the risk can be eliminated altogether, this is the ultimate outcome.
- **Reduce the likelihood of the risk event occurring** – This strategy acknowledges that the event can still occur so it is not eliminated altogether. However, if the likelihood of it occurring can be reduced, then this is the next best measure. This strategy may involve piloting solutions before they are rolled out, or building agreement around the provision of resources in advance.
- **Early Warning** – Early warning mechanisms offer the opportunity for the project leader to know that the event is going to occur, and provide time to put a contingency plan in action to either eliminate or mitigate the risks. An operating agreement with suppliers of staff that they will provide 48 hours notice of their withdrawal is an example of an early warning strategy.
- **Mitigate the risk** – Mitigating the risk means preparing a contingency plan to minimise the effect of the risk should the event occur. Mitigation strategies might include having contingencies for additional staff, or a plan to do alternate work should an activity that is a predecessor to other activities be delayed.
- **Transfer the risk** – By transferring the risk, the potential consequences will be felt by someone else. Common ways of transferring risk include contracting and insurance.
- **Accept the risks** – The decision to accept risk is a legitimate strategy, and one that is exercised many times a day. The choice to accept risk will be driven by the risk propensity of the team involved.

Responses may be a combination of any or all of these strategies as they are not mutually exclusive. It would be wise to try and treat risks using strategies in the order in which they appear above.

<u>Questions To Work Through</u>

Accordingly the series of questions you might now begin to ask are these.

- *'What could we do that would eliminate this risk altogether?'*
- *'How could we reduce the likelihood of this event occurring?'*
- *'What could we do or put in place that would warn us of the events occurrence before it actually happens?'*
- *'What could we do to minimize its effect should this actually happen?'*
- *'How could we transfer this risk to somewhere or someone else?'*
- *'Are we prepared to accept this risk?'*

Step 4.2 – Reassess risks post-treatment. At the point that an action plan has been identified, the team should reassess the risks assuming that these actions have been taken. The purpose is to develop an understanding of the degree of impact that actions will have on the risk profile of the project.

The results of this work are included in the final six columns of the 'Project Risk Worksheet' as shown in the example that follows.

The risk management plan must convert into an action plan for it to be effective. Defining what must be done, who is responsible for doing it and when it needs to be completed by ensures that the risk management plan is activated. These details become inputs into the implementation plan.

Project Objectives:	- On time - To expected level of performance					- Within Budget - According to scope					
What Can Happen	**Existing Controls**	**L**	**Potential Effect**	**S**	**RR**	**Action**	**Who**	**When**	**L**	**S**	**RR**
Monsoon Rains cause flooding	Weather forecasts	3	Work delays, costs to repair	4	**12**	Take out insurance	Finance Rep.	21.7.02	3	3	**9**
Team given other work beyond project work	Project leadership at the sponsor level	4	Reduced staff, work takes longer to complete, costs for contract staff	4	**16**	Establish operating agreements	Team Leader	21.7.02	2	4	**8**
Times are underestimated	PERT, Weekly project review	3	Work takes longer	2	**6**	Weekly review	Team Leader	Ongoing	3	2	**6**

Step 5. Monitor Risks

Risk monitoring is simply the process of reviewing project risks and management plans over time. Risk management is not a static activity that is done once and then forgotten. Risk management is continuous in response to changing circumstances in which the implementation of solutions takes place.

Key Learning Points

- All projects have uncertainty, thus, all projects are exposed to risk.
- Project risk management consists of 5 steps: (a) establish the context, (b) identify the risks, (c) assess the risks, (d) treat the risks, and (e) monitor the risks.
- Multiple strategies can be employed in response to risks, the optimum strategy is to eliminate the risk altogether
- Risk management strategies must convert into an action plan that defines what has to be done, who is responsible and when it must be completed by.

THE CULTURAL ELEMENTS OF CHANGE

The success of change should be determined by whether or not the change actually takes place in the organisation and whether or not it is sustained over the long term. Think for a moment about a change in your personal or working life that was unsuccessful. A change that was not made fully and the old way persisted, or when made, did not last over time and ultimately the old way once again persisted. What were the key elements that contributed to that change being unsuccessful?

Looking for the Clues

Now think for a moment about a change in your personal or working life that was successful, a change that took place and was sustained over time. The old way no longer existed. What were the key elements that contributed to that change being successful?

I have asked these questions many times of seminar participants and over a number of years I recorded the top 5 responses to each question in a business context. The most common responses I get are these.

Unsuccessful Change	**Successful Change**
Did not know why the change was necessary	Those affected were on board
Didn't really know what the desired outcome was	Leaders were committed to the change
No buy-in by those affected	Change took place quickly
There was no plan	Knew why the change was important
Poor communication	Widespread communication of the change

What do you notice about these elements? Well for a start you may have noticed that not one of them is about the quality of the technical aspects of the change. Every element deals with issues associated with the people side of the equation – the emotional or soft side of doing something different.

Making Change Fail

Let's take a view of change from another angle. If I asked you how you would make change fail, what would you say? This is another question I have asked many participants in my seminars and the responses I get usually look something like these.

- Don't tell anyone about it
- Don't explain the reason why the change is necessary
- Don't plan the change
- Do not involve the people affected
- Implement it when there are a lot of other change initiatives taking place
- Role model conflicting behaviours

Once again, almost all of these actions are focused on the 'people' side of the change equation.

Now where do we traditionally focus our attention? I think it's fair to say that our focus is usually on the technical elements of change. Our goal is to make the technical aspects of the change as good as possible, according to our own perception. The education system supports this.

Think for a moment about what you learnt at school or at university. You learnt how to develop the perfect solution to the problem, how to design and engineer the best structure possible, how to create a software program that was so good you did not need any other program to access or share information, how to design a process that ensured everyone did the same thing to perfection every time. Not much use to you when no one wants to use or work with these technical ideas.

So when we roll out these changes and find that they do not work as anticipated and everyone is resisting the idea, where do we go then? Most of the time we go back and improve the technical aspects of the idea and roll it out again, much to the frustration of those who have no intention of supporting the change you propose. In fact, this approach often results in a higher level of resistance the second time around.

Two Sides to the Equation

So what's my point? The key lesson here is that there are two sides to the equation – the operational or technical elements of the change and the emotional or commitment elements of the change.

'The effectiveness (E) of any change will always be a function of the quality (Q) of the technical side of the strategy or solution, and the level of commitment (C) of stakeholders to making the transition to the desired new state:

Thus E = Q x C.'

One part of the equation without the other is not a recipe for success. However, the most significant contributing factor in successful or unsuccessful change is that associated with motivation or what we should refer to as emotional commitment.

Someone once said to me we need acceptance by stakeholders. My view is this, we might accept something but that never means we are actually committed to it. Someone might accept that we have to have speed limits on the highway, but if they consciously drive at 120 kph when the signs display a 100 kph limit, they were never really committed now were they?

At this point in time we've only discussed tools and ingredients of the plan associated with the technical aspects of the implementation. We have not touched on any subjects that deal with the 'emotional side' of implementation other than mention a communication plan.

Over the next few pages I will introduce you to a number of tools that will assist you in your solution implementation efforts. This is only an introduction by the way, and by no means a complete set of ingredients for managing this side of any change.

ENGAGING STAKEHOLDERS

The pivotal element in ensuring any change is successful, is commitment and coalition from the key stakeholders. A stakeholder is any person who is impacted by the change, or who can impact the change. *Key stakeholders* are those critical to the success of the change. Many good ideas have failed in organisations due to the right people not being committed to the idea, for whatever reason.

Why People Resist

To be able to engage people during a time of change requires that we understand why it is people resist change. Each and every day of our lives we are all engaged in routine activities as well as change activities. Most of us routinely get up each day and consistently employ a process for getting ready for work. Most people drive to work along the same route each day and park their vehicle in the same area. We start work using the same process each day and do our job the way *we* know it should be done. Another comfortable day is what we want to achieve. All of these are routine processes that we know well and do over and over many times.

Now we also engage in change many times throughout the day. We change our clothes in the morning and at night as a minimum, we shower or bath to change state from dirty to clean, most men shave each morning to change their appearance while women put on makeup to change theirs. Each week we change our situation from one of empty pantries to full pantries by going grocery shopping.

These types of changes are successfully undertaken from an emotional sense for a number of reasons. First of all we are comfortable with these changes.

Why is that?

Well, all of us have a need for certainty in our lives. We need to be certain that we will wake up in the morning, we will have food on the table, we will get to work alive. We like to be certain we can actually do the change required. When uncertainty creeps into our life, particularly when it is unwanted uncertainty, we experience negative emotions. For those activities previously listed, we experience a feeling of certainty about the outcome, about the benefits we will gain, about our ability to make the change successfully. In fact, we are so certain of some activities that we don't even think about it. We can even do other things at the same time.

When people resist change, it is mostly because they fear the uncertainty it brings to their lives. People feel certain they know how to do their current job successfully, it is good for them and the organisation, their job is secure, they will be liked in their current peer group, they have a future for their family, and many other personal outcomes. By forcing change *on them*, resistance may come from those who experience uncertainty about the new state. (This uncertainty might be about their job security, their future, the future of the organisation, the impact of the change on their family and routines and that the new state is actually good for them and the organisation.)

Many people have uncertainties about their ability to learn to do the work the new way. All of these uncertainties introduce fear, fear that they will fail, that they will lose their job, that the change will hurt their family, that they will lose their peer group and no longer fit in or be liked. Whether these fears are real or only perceived, they must be addressed before their commitment will be forthcoming.

Overcoming Resistance

The steps in establishing commitment and coalition from key stakeholders are quite simple, yet often not undertaken effectively. The process involves:

- Evaluating stakeholder commitment; and
- Preparing a stakeholder engagement plan.

Evaluating Stakeholder Commitment

The first step to engage a stakeholder audience is to understand where they are positioned with respect to the proposed change. Stakeholder commitment evaluation is undertaken in two simple steps.

- Identify the key stakeholders
- Identify their level of commitment to the change, as perceived by you, and the gap that exists between where they are and where they need to be for the change to successfully occur.

The outcome of this process is a worksheet that helps the team to visually determine where they should focus their attention. One way to determine the level of commitment is to think about stakeholders according to the behavioural descriptors listed below.

- **Take Action to Prevent (Saboteurs)** – They speak out against the change and take action to prevent it occurring. These are the people who can sabotage the change efforts. Where they have influence over others, they mustn't be ignored.

- **Speak Out Against (Prophets of Doom)** – These people speak out against the change, however, do not take any action to prevent it occurring. Their conversation focuses on the downside associated with the proposed change.
- **Neutral (Fence Sitters)** – These people are non-committal either way, they show no real concern as to whether or not the change takes place. Whilst they say nothing against the proposed change, they do or say nothing to help.
- **Speak Up in Support (Marketers)** – These are the people who are openly supportive of the change, however, they do not take any action to help make it happen. As we know, actions speak louder than words, so when these people are business leaders, words may not be enough.
- **Take Action to Make Happen (Change Agents)** – These people are your sponsors of change. They are highly supportive of the change and take action to help make it happen. Where these people are the leaders of the business, stakeholders are more likely to get on board.

The following table shows an example of a completed analysis. From the worksheet we can see that of the stakeholders listed, two are totally on board with the idea, two are neutral, and one is totally against the solution (indicated by the ✖). The symbol ✔ indicates the level of commitment required.

	COMMITMENT LEVEL				
STAKEHOLDERS	**Take Action to Prevent Happening**	**Talk Negatively**	**Neutral**	**Talk Positively**	**Take Action to Make Happen**
Mary the Manager					✖✔
Oscar the Operator			✖	✔	
Steve the Safety Superintendent					✖✔
Fred the Plant Foreman	✖			✔	
Terry the transport supervisor			✖✔		

Figure 313: Stakeholder Commitment Evaluation Worksheet

One thing I need to caution you about when using this approach is that the evaluation is based on the perception of those involved. There is the possibility that your perceptions about a stakeholder are completely wrong, and you've gone too far up the inference ladder. On numerous occasions I have seen two people evaluate the same stakeholder individually, and end up with completely different results.

I recommend these actions as a way of managing this risk.

- Discuss commitment at the behavioural level – what has been observed or what you think might be observed.
- Validate your evaluation by either (a) asking someone who knows the stakeholder, or (b) asking the stakeholder directly.

The second major step in the sequence is to prepare an engagement strategy for shifting people to the desired level of commitment.

The Keys To Effective Stakeholder Engagement

The principles behind the development of engagement strategies are simply these.

If the team can achieve the following, the greater the likelihood the stakeholder will support the change:

- **Connect the current problem to some pain** that a stakeholder recognises and feels, create some desire for change to take place.
- **Alleviate the specific concerns** (fears or uncertainties) that a stakeholder has with respect to the proposed change, or alternatively change their perception.
- **Anticipate the potential negative impacts** of the project and ensure these are either (a) treated, or (b) known and framed in a way that is most positive.
- **Satisfy *any* interests** the stakeholder may have – this may be linked to changing perceptions associated with concerns
- **Anticipate the potential positive impacts** of the change to the stakeholder personally or the organisation, and ensure these are brought to the attention of the stakeholder.
- **Present the evidence in a form** that is preferred by, and matches the evidence strategies of the stakeholder.

Stakeholder Engagement Planning

A sample engagement plan is shown below.

<table>
<tr><td colspan="2">Stakeholder: Fred the Foreman</td><td colspan="2">Level of Commitment Reqd: Take Action to Make Change Happen</td></tr>
<tr><td>1. Interests / Values:
Fishing, motorbike riding,
Safety of staff, being recognised for what they achieve.</td><td>2. The Problem:
Downtime is causing them to miss their daily production targets,
Boss pressure to explain,
Weekly pressure to make up shortfalls.</td><td colspan="2">3. Concerns or Objections:
Does not have the skill to use or manage new technology, too old to learn,
How much time this might take,
Not all shifts will be on board with this.</td></tr>
<tr><td>4. Potential Negative Impacts:
Some union pushback,
A couple of weeks teething problems.</td><td>5. Potential Benefits:
Hit production targets more frequently,
Less pressure from bosses,
They achieve more.</td><td colspan="2">6. Evidence Strategy:
Data showing current problem - percentage of days below target,
Union leader commentary on performance and bonus impact,
Letter from CEO about future issues and drive for meeting targets now.</td></tr>
<tr><td colspan="2">Action Plan:</td><td>Who:</td><td>By When:</td></tr>
<tr><td colspan="2">Assemble the data of under performance, create the presentation</td><td>John</td><td>19.7.2023</td></tr>
<tr><td colspan="2">Discuss the plan with the union leadership group and its impact on employee bonuses, organise for them to present to Fred and his team</td><td>John</td><td>20.7.2023</td></tr>
<tr><td colspan="2">Meet with the CEO, discuss the plan, obtain written details about future issues and reasons for the drive now</td><td>Mike</td><td>21.7.02</td></tr>
<tr><td colspan="2">Conduct a presentation for all stakeholders</td><td>Mike</td><td>25.7.2023</td></tr>
</table>

Figure 314: Stakeholder Engagement Plan

More details on how to undertake stakeholder commitment evaluation and engagement planning are shown in the 'Improve Toolkit'.

Confidentiality

For obvious reasons, this work must be completed with an agreement on confidentiality. Imagine for a moment that this work was left laying around for Fred the Foreman to read. I have observed this occurrence on more than one occasion, and the respective Black Belts learned the lesson of confidentiality the hard way. The effect on respective stakeholders was not conducive to generating engagement.

Key Learning Points

- Work must remain confidential.
- Work must result in a clear set of actions with defined accountabilities.
- Stakeholder commitment evaluation must be undertaken before any change is initiated – resistance is natural so anticipate it and work with it.
- Validate your assessment of the level of commitment of stakeholders

COMMUNICATION PLANNING

Communication is an extremely important element of change. I've heard it said that *you can never over communicate in a time of change*. Communications can take many forms, not all of them effective, particularly during times of change. It's not uncommon to see email used by change leaders as a means to influence change. How effective would that be in influencing an individual who is not committed to the change? The most effective way to influence change when resistance exists is in a face-to-face scenario.

Communication Plan

A communication plan can take many forms, the following is an example of one format we use.

<table>
<tr><th colspan="5">Communication Plan</th></tr>
<tr><td colspan="2" rowspan="2">Project:
PC DEPLOYMENT</td><td>Date Issued:</td><td>Page:</td><td>1 of 1</td></tr>
<tr><td>Date Revised:</td><td>Revision No:</td><td>File No:</td></tr>
<tr><th>Audience</th><th>Content</th><th>Timing</th><th>Medium</th><th>Responsibility</th></tr>
<tr><td>PC Technicians</td><td>Project overview including problem worked on
Process used to generate and validate solutions
Solutions for reducing deployment cycle time for PC's
Implementation plan overview</td><td>By 31 August 2001</td><td>Presentation</td><td>Project communication team</td></tr>
<tr><td>Management Team
Workforce</td><td>Implementation status</td><td>Fortnightly after 31.8.01</td><td>Six Sigma Newsletter</td><td>Project team leader</td></tr>
</table>

Figure 315: Communication Plan

When creating a communication plan the team must answer these questions.

- *'Who must we communicate to?'* (the audience)
- *'What do they need to know?'* (the content)
- *'When and how often do they need to know it?'* (timing)
- *'How can it be communicated so that we can be sure the communication and intended meaning is received?'* (medium)
- *'Who is responsible for the communication?'* (who takes action)

Communication Principles

Some key communication principles for a Black Belt to consider when thinking about communication are these"

- Communication should be planned with a clear purpose
- A consistent message must come through in all communications
- Multiple mediums should be used
- The timing and purpose of communication must be considered when determining how to communicate

FORCE FIELD ANALYSIS

It is the job of the Black Belt to monitor progress throughout the solution implementation period. It is not unusual for a change to lose momentum, particularly when the focus of the organisation and its people is constantly changing.

Whilst there are many forces helping to drive the change, there will always be forces that are a hindrance. It is a mistake to assume that the momentum for change will sustain itself and these hindering forces will not have any impact on the project. A wise Black Belt recognises it takes energy to keep the project moving forward, and in order to achieve that they must continually monitor the pulse of change.

A tool that helps monitor that pulse is 'Force Field Analysis'. Force field analysis is an idea borrowed from a specific mechanical engineering discipline referred to as *free-body diagrams*. Mechanical engineers use free-body diagrams to identify the forces acting on a body, the purpose of which is to ascertain those forces that lead to a state of equilibrium.

The same principles are applied in Force Field Analysis where the status quo is the state of equilibrium. By undertaking Force Field Analysis a team is able to understand the forces that enable the desired state of motion towards a particular outcome, and those forces that are holding the system back or prevent the desired state of motion towards the desired outcome.

Terminology

Two terms you must be familiar with are 'enabling force' and 'restraining force'. Let me explain these in this way. An **Enabler** is an *existing* force that is helping the change to occur. These can be forces that are drawing people towards the desired state, or forces that are driving people away from the current state. A **Restrainer** on the other hand is an *existing* force that is hindering or preventing the change from occurring.

When choosing a course of action, the strategies available to you are these.

- Build on or strengthen the enablers,
- Overcome or weaken the restrainers, and
- A combination of building on the enablers and weakening restrainers

Force Field Analysis

The following is an example of a completed 'Force Field Analysis' completed by a deployment team during the third year of implementation of a Lean Six Sigma initiative.

Enabling Forces	Restraining Forces
• GM's recognition of the value of Lean Six Sigma • The recognised need to be competitive with respect to product quality • The focus of senior managers on margins ($) • Business improvement infrastructure • Delivery of Lean and Six Sigma basics training across the workforce • Financial returns being achieved by other companies using Lean or Six Sigma	• Conflict between project work and regular job KPI's for part time Black Belts • Varying levels of commitment by different members of the executive team • Focus on other strategic initiatives • Lack of understanding of the operating system that is needed to support Lean Six Sigma project work at the leader level
Action Plan: • Prepare job descriptions for Black Belts and sign off by GM • (other actions)	

Figure 316: Force Field Analysis

PILOTING SOLUTIONS AND IMPLEMENTATION PLANS

There will be occasions when it is prudent to test your proposed solutions before a full-scale implementation takes place. On those occasions, a 'pilot' might be relevant. So what is a pilot? A pilot is essentially a miniaturised version of the implementation of your solution, tested under conditions that resemble those in which the full-scale implementation would take place. Informal piloting concepts affect our every day lives.

Piloting – A Common Occurrence

Think about activities in your kitchen for example. Have you ever made pancakes? Have you ever used a small amount of the mixture to make one small pancake to start with and then taste test it? Why do you do that? Well for one, you get an opportunity to find out if the work (making pancakes) is going to be successful when you implement it fully (let everyone eat pancakes). This provides an opportunity to go back to the planned work (the pancake mixture in this case) and improving it before full implementation. This is the concept of piloting.

I recently watched a documentary on Formula 1 racing with a focus on the development of the racecars. It was particularly interesting to see the engineers conducting 'pilot' studies on specific parts of the racecar in isolation to other parts. For example, they would run the engine under full race conditions in a lab. The engine was mounted in a device that allowed it to be accelerated and decelerated for the duration of a Formula 1 race, under loads and conditions and for as long as would be experienced in an actual race. Knowledge about how the engine will perform and how maximum performance can be extracted from the engine is a foundation for being that little bit better than the competitor, and in the world of Formula 1 racing every hundredth of a second counts.

The purpose of a pilot study is to understand or learn what does work and what doesn't work, and how the solution can be improved so that we minimise the risk of solution or implementation failure.

Pilot Study Strategies

A number of different strategies can be employed in a pilot study.

Computer Simulation

Where process or product variables are relatively predictable, computer simulation allows complex models to be quickly programmed. These have proven popular in engineering and design. Many studies are conducted on new designs for Formula 1 race cars using computer simulation.

Limit the Time

In limiting the time, only a small number of process cycles with the new solution will be studied. 'Resistors' may approach a study with a defined end point with a much more open mind than a longer-term study.

Limit the Scope

Some solutions can be tested in only a portion of the organisation. For example, where new software is being installed in an organisation, it is first trialled with a small section or group of people before roll out to the rest of the organisation.

Scaled Modeling

Where people have difficulty 'seeing' the solution in action, it sometimes lends itself to the creation of a scaled model. For example, motor vehicle manufacturers actually make clay models of their new cars before making any decision about its future. When trying to sell a new design for the office to the executive team, a CEO might present a miniature model to support the discussion. Where your solution involves the shifting or rearranging of plant or equipment, the solution may be more easily sold if stakeholders can see it.

Real Life Simulation

This approach requires the creating of a 'real life' experiment that replicates the environment and conditions under which the solution would have to operate. The outputs may or may not be sold to customers, depending on the circumstances. In both cases the process and its outputs can be evaluated to understand what full scale implementation would operate like. Ok Tedi Copper Mine in Papua New Guinea tested an idea for increasing gold recoveries by running a small pilot project in the actual plant during 2000. The technology proved successful so they were able to go into full-scale production with a high degree of confidence.

Partial Solution

Sometimes the entire solution may not be able to be tested. However, it may be possible to run independent pilot studies on specific components of the solution.

What is an Effective Pilot Study?

An effective pilot study is one where the results of the study are the same as those you would get under a full-scale implementation.

Imagine for a moment that a test pilot took a new plane on a test flight. He found that the plane flew well and was able to recommend that development should take place. Now when the planes rolled off the assembly line, suppose for a moment that the first two crashed under normal flying conditions. The pilot study did not reveal the flaw with the plane design hence the pilot was unsuccessful. Had the test pilot crashed the plane during its test flight revealing the flaws that existed that would have been an effective 'pilot study' in the context of knowing what would happen during full-scale implementation. It was the 'test flight' that would have been unsuccessful.

An Ineffective Pilot Study

An example of what can occur is provided by an organisation that implemented a high-risk technology project in northern Australia during the 1990's. The technology was tested at an operation in Venezuela using local input samples and operating under the conditions acceptable in local culture. The pilot study showed that the technology was successful, and as a result the full-scale implementation of a billion-dollar operation took place in Australia. The pilot study turned out to be less than successful - it showed a result that was not a true representation of what would occur in a full-scale operation using that technology. The environment and conditions under which the pilot was conducted did not represent what they would be at the actual site.

What value does a pilot offer?

A pilot study provides you with the opportunity to:

- Discover opportunities for improvement before full-scale production
- Minimise the risk of failure
- Increase support / buy-in
- Test and improve the implementation plan

When would you consider conducting a pilot?

Pilot studies are not conducted on every occasion. Many changes occur without ever being piloted. However, there are occasions when a pilot study might prove useful:

- When there are significant costs associated with implementation
- When reversing the change would be difficult or impossible
- When there are significant technical risks with the solution
- When the workforce needs to be convinced to overcome resistance

Factors for a Successful project

I often ask Black Belt training participants to prepare a list of all the things they would do or not do to make a pilot study fail. Some of the most common ideas on these lists include:

- Do not duplicate the real environment in which the actual work will take place
- Do not communicate the purpose of the work
- Only test some variables and make assumptions about the remainder
- Do not define any measures
- Run the pilot in too short a time frame
- Do not record any results or activities for later reference
- Don't define the scope of the study
- Change study participants before the study is completed

There are many ways to reduce the probability of a pilot study being successful, and the sad thing is that these types of actions (or lack thereof) continue to affect pilot studies in many industries. To maximise the probability of successful piloting, some key factors must be considered.

- The pilot must be conducted under conditions that represent the environment in which the implementation will take place. BHP Billiton is the major shareholder of the Ekati diamond mine in the north west territories of Alaska. The mine operates in an environment of extreme cold with fluctuations in time frames for sunlight and dark similar to the north and south poles. A pilot was conducted at that location that showed successful results. Learnings were incorporated in the full-scale implementation, and the mining operation proved enormously successful.

- A debrief must be factored into the process with an honest post-mortem of results not biased by personal connection
- The site of the pilot study must have the leader and employees as willing participants
- The pilot study must be well planned
- Specific measures must be identified

Conducting the Pilot Study

As with Benchmarking activities, a pilot study can be undertaken in four simple steps.

1. **PLAN** the pilot study
2. **DO** the pilot study
3. **CHECK** the results from the pilot study
4. **ACT** on the results of the pilot study

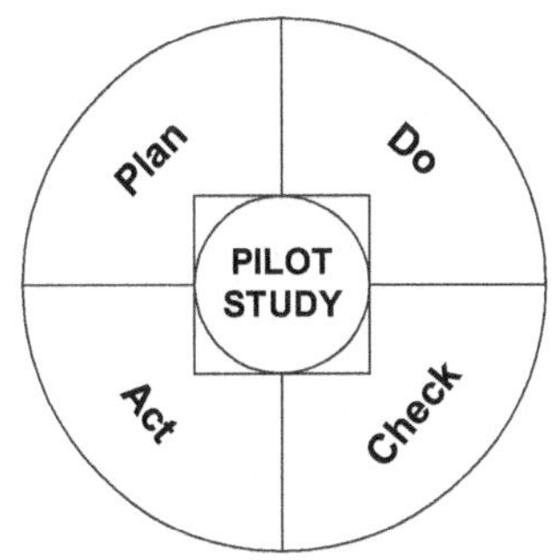

Figure 317: Four Step Piloting Process

'PLAN' the Pilot Study

The planning phase of a pilot study is one of the most important. A well-planned study will provide the required information in the most efficient manner. To complete the pilot plan, a number of key tasks must be addressed.

- **Define the scope of the pilot study** – The scope of the pilot study provides answers to the following questions.
    - *How large / complex will the pilot be?*
    - *Where will the study be conducted?* A location should be chosen that provides a good representation of the environment where the actual full-scale implementation would take place. Both technical and cultural factors must be considered when choosing the location. **Technical** – skills, capability, control of variables. **Cultural** – tolerance for change, quality of relationships, adaptability.
    - *Who will be involved in the study?* The people involved in the study must be willing participants, and where relevant the leader of that site must be supportive.
    - *How long will the study be conducted?* The time frame should be sufficient for multiple cycles to occur. A study of only one cycle may not provide sufficient representative information.

- **Assign roles and responsibilities** – Make sure competencies are matched with responsibilities.
- **Define the sequence of events** – As with any project, a schedule of events and activities will ensure that the pilot study can be managed well. Common activities in a pilot study include:
    - Site briefing
    - Pilot construction (where relevant)
    - Training of participants
    - Collection of data
    - Pilot reviews (weekly / monthly etc.)
    - Pilot closure
    - Final study report
- **Specify measures of success** – The levels or standards of performance targeted must be specified. The measures associated with these standards will form the basis for ongoing monitoring of the study.
- **Plan to manage risks** – A pilot study does not come without risk. A risk study and associated risk management plan will ensure that controls are put in place to eliminate or mitigate risks that may eventuate during the course of the study. These questions might assist.
    - *What can go wrong?*
    - *What would cause that to happen?*
    - *How likely is that to happen?*
    - *What can we do to prevent this from happening?*
    - *What contingency plan should we have in case this happens anyway?*
    - *What will trigger us to use that contingency plan?*

'DO' the Pilot Study

Doing the pilot study quite simply involves executing the action plan. During the execution phase, remember to do the following.

- Measure and track results
- Log all activities
- Record environmental conditions where relevant
- Meet regularly to review results

'CHECK' the Pilot Study

At the completion of the study, the results are formally documented and studied. Some key questions should be asked during this phase.

- What were the actual results?
- What was the difference between the actual results and the expected results?
- Where were they different – What were the root causes that created the difference?
- What can be done to treat root causes?

When comparing results with baseline results, remember you must use statistical analysis tools if you are working with samples. For example, if you wanted to compare the average results from a sample to a targeted value, you must use hypothesis testing tools to be able to confidently make an inference about the overall performance of the process.

'ACT' on the Pilot Study

The actions taken after a pilot study depend entirely on the results of the study. The suggestions below assume one thing – the study is a true representation of what would occur in a full-scale implementation.

- The results were less than expected – The team could either (a) treat root causes and continue with the study using the improved process, or (b) shut down the pilot study and shelve the project.
- The results were as expected – The team should take key learnings away and revise the implementation plan.

Key Learning Points

- A successful pilot is one that provides a representation of what the full scale implementation would be like, regardless of whether the performance of the process, product or service is good or bad.
- Plan thoroughly and make sure the scope is defined up front
- Plan to manage risks
- Appoint a project leader who will be 100% committed and remain with the pilot until completed
- Involve people who are committed to doing the pilot properly
- Validate the data that is collected – make sure it is useful and not misleading
- Be honest about results of the pilot

'A key role of the Project Leader during the pilot study is to be visible and available. This can be a significant challenge as there will invariably be many issues to contend with. However, it is critical that these issues are dealt with in a timely manner during the study.'

Harry Sinko

PRE-IMPLEMENTATION STAKEHOLDER CHECK-IN

Before any implementation takes place, a Black Belt must check-in with key stakeholders. A useful way to prepare for this meeting is to put yourself in the shoes of the project sponsor. You then ask yourself *'What questions would I ask a Black Belt if I were project sponsor during this meeting?'*

This may guide you along a useful path in your preparation. Some of the questions you might be required to answer during this meeting include:

<u>Benchmarking</u>

- What benchmarking did you undertake?
- What was the basis for choosing these places for your benchmarking?
- How was the benchmarking study undertaken?
- What were the results?
- How did these results impact your process improvement work?

<u>Solutions</u>

- What are your proposed solutions?
- How did you identify these?
- How did you make your final choice of solutions?
- How many ideas did you have to choose from?
- Who was involved in the process?
- How are these solutions linked to validated root causes?

<u>Process Changes</u>

- What does the new process look like?
- What principles did you apply in redesigning it?
- Who was involved?
- What benefits will this new process offer?

<u>Economic Factors</u>

- How do you know this project still has a valid business case?
- What benefits do you anticipate from the project?
- How do you intend tracking and reporting benefits once implementation is completed?

<u>Implementation Plan</u>

- What is your implementation plan?
- Who was involved in the planning?
- Who is responsible for what activities in this implementation?
- What risks have you identified?
- How have you planned to deal with these risks?
- What contingencies have you planned?
- What triggers have you identified for stopping implementation?
- What resources do you need to get this implemented?

- How do you plan to conduct handover to the process owner?

Piloting

- Have you conducted a pilot?
- Where did you conduct the pilot?
- How did you choose this location?
- How long did the pilot study take?
- What were the measures of success for the pilot?
- How did you review the pilot at its completion?
- What did you learn from the pilot?
- How did the pilot affect your solutions or implementation plan?

Solution Impacts on the Organisation

- How will the implementation of these solutions affect other parts of the business?
- How do you plan to deal with that?

Emotional Elements of Change

- What is your plan to deal with the emotional aspects of the proposed changes?
- What work have you undertaken to identify levels of stakeholder commitment?
- How do you propose to engage the commitment of those that may exhibit resistance?
- What systems and structures require changing to support the proposed solutions?

Monitoring

- How do you plan to monitor progress from a change perspective?
- How do you plan to monitor the performance of the process post implementation?
- What benefits do you expect to see from the project?
- How do you propose to track these benefits?

Use this list to prepare for your pre-implementation stakeholder check-in.

CHAPTER 19: IMPROVE PHASE TOOLKIT

TOOLS FOR GENERATING SOLUTIONS – BRAINSTORMING

What is it?

Brainstorming is a process for generating ideas that was developed in 1941 by A.F. Osborne. The 'popcorn' method involves ideas coming from the group in no particular order.

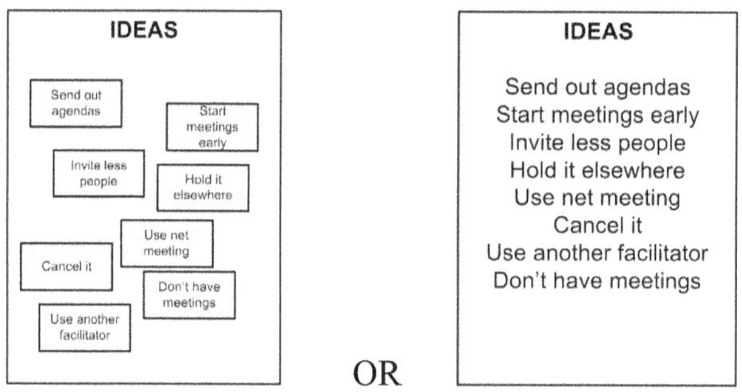

Figure 318: Standard (Popcorn) Brainstorming

The purpose of Brainstorming is to generate a large number of ideas in a short period of time, in such a way as to promote creativity, and to do so free of criticism. It is usually used when the group is highly interactive and ideas are likely to be free flowing from all participants.

Instructions

Step 1 – Identify the appropriate group of people to involve in the brainstorming session.

Step 2 – State the desired outcome of the session. (e.g.: to identify 3 – 5 ideas for …..)

Step 3 – Describe the approach you will use (brainstorming) and the rules associated with the approach.

Step 4 – Ask a specific question to stimulate thought processes. Ensure that the question is clearly understood.

Step 5 – Capture all ideas as they are generated (in writing or with post it notes).

The Rules of Brainstorming

- Capture ideas as they are generated – use the words of the author when you are writing the ideas on a flip-chart.
- Avoid any discussion of ideas during the session – discussion will immediately channel team member thoughts away from the goal of idea generation.
- Do not criticise ideas. Criticism creates an environment where ideas are held back and creativity will not be achieved.

- Listen to all team members' ideas, look for connections or ideas that can be built upon.
- Encourage a low risk creative environment. Do not censor ideas.
- When using Post It Notes, have team members state their idea verbally as they write it down.

NOMINAL GROUP TECHNIQUE

What is it?

Nominal group technique is an extension of the brainstorming method. However, the idea generation component is performed in silence. Its purpose is to generate ideas in a systematic but independent fashion.

It is usually used when normal popcorn brainstorm methods are not suitable for the team in question. NGT is useful for ensuring involvement by all team members when there are either dominant or overly submissive members of a team.

Instructions

This method restricts discussion or interpersonal communication during the process, hence the term 'nominal'. Group members are all physically present but they operate independently.

Step 1 – Each member of the group independently writes his or her ideas down.

Step 2 – This silent period is followed by each member presenting one idea to the group.

Step 3 - Each member takes his or her turn, going around the group, presenting a single idea until all ideas have been presented and recorded.

ANTI SOLUTION BRAINSTORM

What is it?

Anti solution is another variant of the brainstorming method. However, the idea generation component starts a pattern of thinking from another angle. Its purpose is to generate ideas in a way that capitalises on our ability to identify how to make things fail.

It is usually used as an alternative to normal brainstorming to stimulate different thought and discussion patterns.

Instructions

Step 1 – Identify the appropriate group of people to involve in the brainstorming session.

Step 2 – State the desired outcome of the session. (e.g.: to identify 3 – 5 ideas for …..)

Step 3 – Describe the approach you will use (brainstorming) and the rules associated with the approach.

Step 4 – Ask for ideas as to how the team could do the reverse of the goal of the project, for example, when the goal is to identify a solution for minimising cycle time, ask for ideas to make cycle time longer.

Step 5 – Identify the underlying principle of the ideas generated and then generate ideas for solving the problem using those principles.

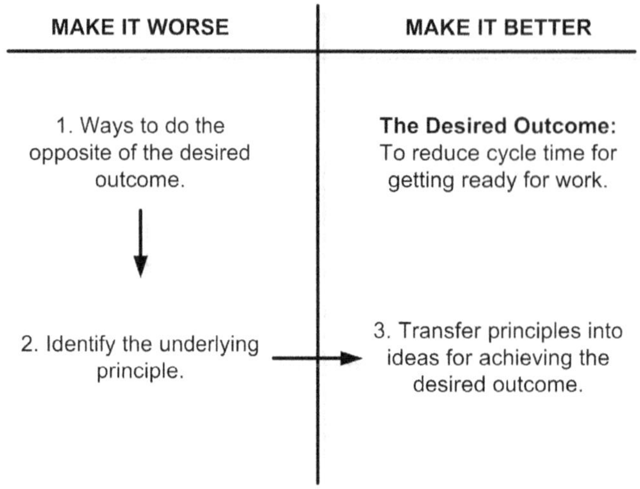

Figure 319: Anti Solution Process

CHANNEL BRAINSTORM

What is it?

Channel brainstorming is yet another variant of the brainstorming method. Its purpose is to generate ideas according to specific categories or segments.

It is usually used as an alternative to normal brainstorming to focus thought patterns in specific subject areas. It is particularly useful when dealing with large groups of people and the facilitator needs to keep the entire group active, yet not be overwhelmed by numbers.

Instructions

Step 1 – Identify the categories into which ideas will be generated.

Step 2 – Have teams work on one category at a time, generating as many ideas as they can within a designated time frame.

Step 3 – Rotate teams to the next category and repeat step 2. Continue to do so until all teams have visited all categories.

Category / Theme 1	Category / Theme 2	Category / Theme 3

Figure 320: Channel Brainstorming

SOLUTION THOUGHT MAPPING

What is it?

Based on the concept of Mind Maps (created by Tony Buzan) Solution Thought Mapping (or ST Mapping) is simply a tool for organising thinking and stimulating ideas. Thought mapping is a wonderful way to unleash the power of imagination and association.

Though ST Maps can be created in many ways, they do have some common elements.

- They all have a natural structure that radiates from a central theme.
- They apply a brain friendly set of rules that incorporate lines, symbols, words and images.
- They all make use of visually stimulating elements (eg: colour, lines, pathways, drawings).

The Benefits of ST Mapping

- It encourages problem solving by generating thoughts around new pathways that radiate out from preceding thoughts.
- It encourages creativity by forcing participants away from only using the structured side of their brain, to the right brain creative thinking side.
- It is enjoyable to look at and easy to remember.

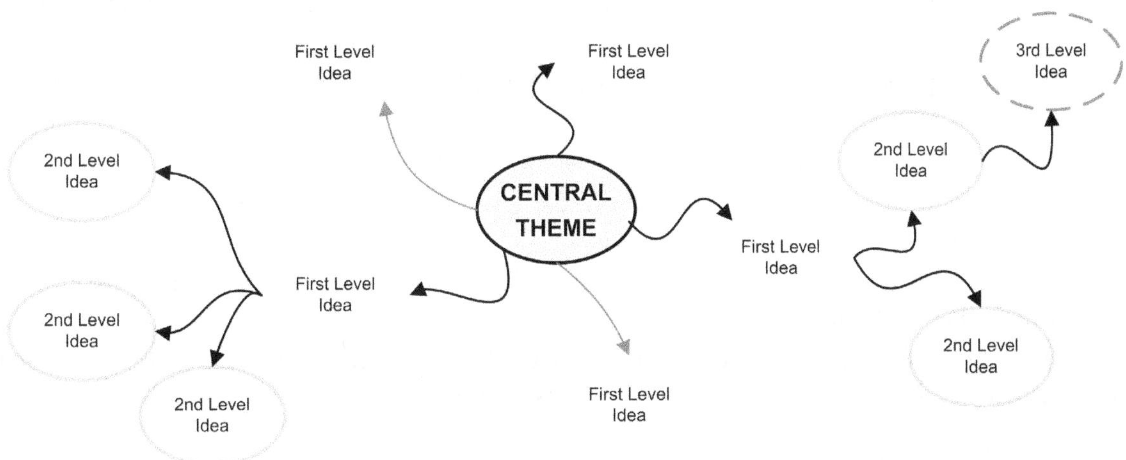

Figure 321: Solution Thought Map Format

Instructions (Traditional Scribed Approach)

A traditional approach for facilitating the creation of a ST Maps involves a single scribe capturing information as it is generated.

Step 1 – With a blank sheet in landscape form, draw the central theme in the centre of the sheet (using colours) and label it. In the context of our work here, the central theme might represent the problem or opportunity you are working on in your project.

Step 2 – Write down the validated causes as the first level ideas. Draw branches coming out from around the central theme to connect with these items.

Step 3 – For each cause ask: *'How can we treat this cause in order to make improvements with the primary metric?'*

Step 4 – Write down ideas directly on the map and encompass these with randomly shaped and coloured boundaries.

Step 5 – Once again, connect the ideas to the one at the level above it using curved lines. Continue until a map comprising multiple levels of thinking is created.

Every idea on the tentacles of the map is a potential solution or part of a potential solution, and can be considered when you start to organise ideas.

Step 6 – Using the map and its web of associations as the reference, generate a short list of potential solution statements to the side. These can comprise ideas from multiple layers into single solution ideas.

Instructions (Team Post It Note Approach)

The use of Post-it Notes in creating ST maps involves all participants writing their own ideas and placing them on the map as they come up. Key steps in doing it this way are:

Step 1 – With a blank sheet in landscape form, draw the central theme in the centre of the sheet (using colours) and label it. In the context of our work here, the central theme might represent the problem or opportunity you are working on in your project.

Step 2 – Write down the validated causes as the first level ideas. Draw branches coming out from around the central theme to visually make the connection with these items.

Step 3 – For each cause ask: *'How can we treat this cause in order to make improvements with the primary metric?'*

Step 4 – Have participants write their ideas on Post It Notes (using colour and shapes) and place them on the map.

Step 5 – As they do this, have them call out the idea so that others hear the idea.

Step 6 – Once again, connect the ideas to the one at the level above it using curved lines. Continue until a map comprising multiple levels of thinking is created.

Every idea on the tentacles of the map is a potential solution or part of a potential solution, and can be considered when you start to organise ideas.

Step 7 – Using the map and its web of associations as the reference, generate a short list of potential solution statements to the side. These can comprise ideas from multiple layers into single solution ideas.

Rules for ST Mapping

The following rules ensure that the thought mapping process engages the creativity part of the brain of participants and draws upon the connections that exist and those that are created in our neural networks during the process.

- Use an image (or big words in a coloured shape) for the central theme as images help stimulate imagination.
- Use colours throughout. Colours add vibrancy to the map and contribute to the level of creative energy.
- Make all branches curved as opposed to straight lines. Straight lines are boring to the brain, whilst curved lines are attractive and more appealing to the eye.
- Use 1 or 2 key words per idea. Phrases and sentences have a tendency to dampen the effect that single words provide in triggering ideas and thought patterns.

Example Solution Thought Map

The following example is taken from the work of a team of Lean Six Sigma practitioners attempting to minimise the cycle time for firing mini catapults during a training course.

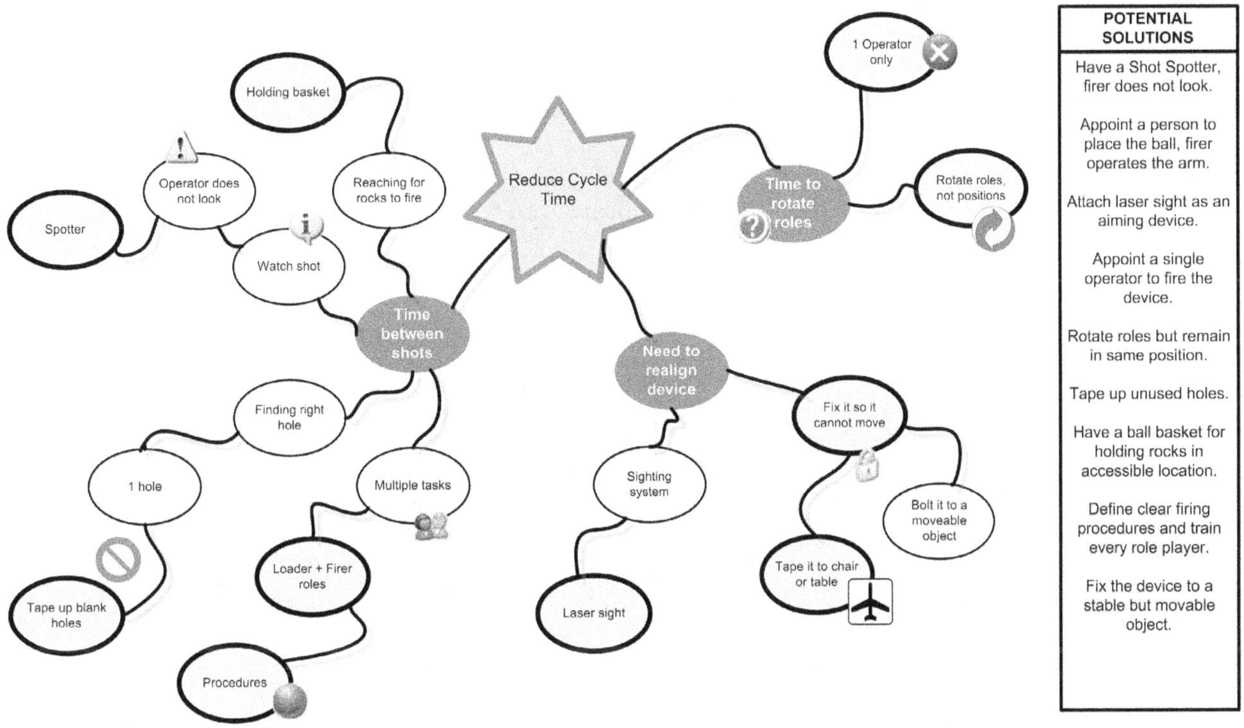

Figure 322: Solution Thought Mapping Example

ANALOGY ASSOCIATION (PROCESS ANALOGY)

What is it?

Analogy Association is a process where some analogy is used to help prompt thinking beyond vertical thinking patterns. When it comes to processes, the following shows examples of where one process can be used as an idea generating analogy for another process.

CAR WASH ...	**is an analogy for ...**	reducing CLEANING cycle time
RACING CAR PIT STOP ...	**is an analogy for ...**	minimising time to SERVICE A HAUL TRUCK
CONVEYING PASSENGER LUGGAGE ...	**is an analogy for ....**	improving conveyor layout in a MANUFACTURING PLANT
ORDERING GOODS ONLINE ...	**is an analogy for ....**	reducing the error rate in ORDERING AND SUPPLYING PARTS from a warehouse

Instructions

Step 1 – Identify an appropriate analogy.

Step 2 – Brainstorm ideas from the analogy that fit the context of your improvement goal. (E.g. minimise cycle time)

Step 3 – Transfer ideas to create solutions to the problem.

TOOLS FOR ORGANISING IDEAS - REMOVING DUPLICATES

What is it?

The removal of duplicates is simply that – taking duplicates and removing them from the list of ideas.

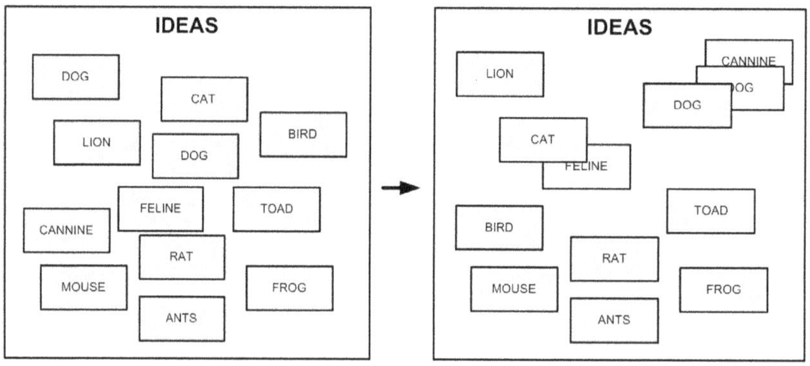

Figure 323: Removing Duplicates

The purpose of removing duplicates is to identify ideas that have exactly the same meaning or are identical words. By removing duplicates we are able to reduce the list and eliminate time wasting on multiple ideas that are exactly the same.

This approach is usually the first tool used when the organising phase commences. Some idea generation tools and approaches often do not produce duplicates. However, the opportunity to identify duplicates should be considered, regardless of the approach.

Instructions

Step 1 – Have the group identify ideas that they believe are the same. These can be of two types – (a) ideas that are identical words, or (b) ideas that have identical meaning.

Step 2 – Where the ideas may be those with identical meaning, ask the authors of the ideas to confirm meaning.

Step 3 – Only those ideas with identical words or identical meanings are removed so that only one remains.

Example

From the list of ideas shown, we can see that the dog words are **exactly the same words**, therefore they are considered to be duplicates. We can see that the words dog and canine have **exactly the same meaning**, although they are not the same words, thus they are classified as duplicates. The words mouse and rat have different meanings, therefore although they are similar, they are not considered to be duplicates. The authors in this case intended cat and feline to have the same meaning.

MULTI VOTING

What is it?

Multi voting is used to reduce the list of ideas to a manageable number of ideas. By using multi voting, the content expertise of the team will drive them towards choosing those ideas that are more likely to be the best ideas for achieving the desired outcome.

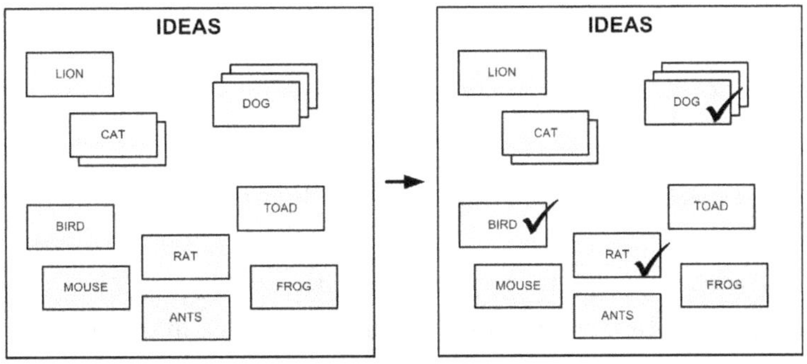

Figure 324: Multi Voting

It is usually used when the team has a good knowledge of the content being discussed. In the absence of that knowledge, the choices made are less likely to be the most appropriate for achieving the desired outcome.

Instructions

Step 1 - Count the total number of ideas - (n)

Step 2 - Divide the total number of ideas by 3 - (n/3)

Step 3 - From the list of ideas, each person chooses n/3 ideas to place a tick against as their preferred choices

Step 4 - Identify the top n/3 ideas according to the number of ticks beside each idea

WEIGHTED MULTI VOTING

Notice that each person is instructed to place one tick against one idea. Where each person is able to cast their ticks anyway they like, including multiple ticks per idea, this introduces weighting to the result – hence the name Weighted Multi Voting.

Before undertaking this weighted approach, always consider the risk of bias that weighting can introduce.

ADVOCACY

What is it?

Advocacy is an opportunity for someone to advocate for an idea.

Advocacy is usually undertaken at the end of the 'organise' phase after the shortened list is identified through the use of other tools.

The purpose of advocacy is to provide the opportunity for any team member to advocate for an idea that they feel strongly about, but was not included in the short list. This prevents the situation where a team member's contribution is affected by feelings of exclusion.

Instructions

Step 1 - Ask 'Does anyone wish to advocate for any idea that they feel strongly about, but we have not chosen in the shortened list?

Step 2 - Any team member may advocate for any idea they feel should be included.

Step 3 - Consensus is sought about including or not including the idea in the shortened list.

Tip for Facilitators

Much can be gained by including the idea. More importantly, think about how a team member might be impacted by not including the idea. The decision-making tools used later in the process ultimately determine the relevance of the idea in any case.

AFFINITY GROUPING

Think for a moment about how you organise your kitchen. In most cases you put your food in one cupboard or set of cupboards, pots and pans in another area and cutlery and utensils somewhere else. You group these items into natural categories based on similarities between each individual item. Take a look in your food cupboard. Do you locate condiments in one area, cereals in another, and packet mixes in yet another? Most people do. In fact, we do this in many facets of our lives including how we organise our toolbox, tackle box, wardrobe and bathroom cupboards. Why do we do that? Generally we are far more capable of working with all of these individual items when we have them 'chunked' into logical categories.

This is the principle of the process known as 'affinity grouping' (also called Affinity Diagram, Affinity Storyboarding or simply Storyboarding).

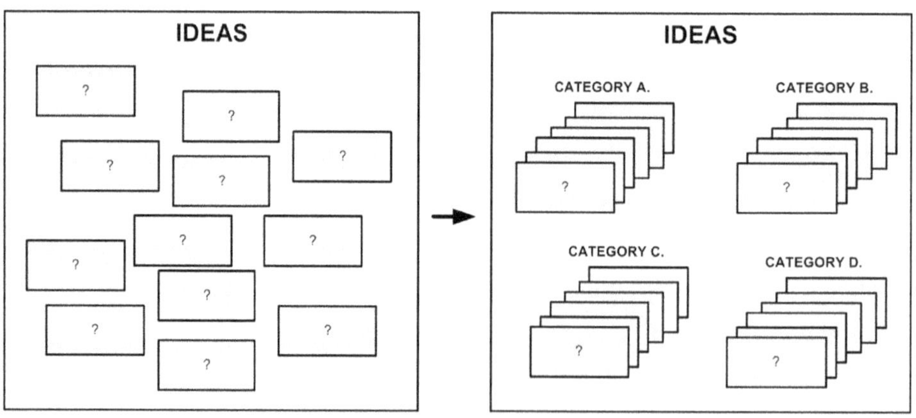

Figure 325: Affinity Grouping

The purpose of Affinity Grouping is to group 'like ideas' into logical categories. People are able to more easily understand the ideas when they are grouped into logical 'chunks' at the higher level.

This approach is useful when a team has a large number of ideas to sort through.

Instructions

Step 1 – Similar ideas are grouped together by the team.

Step 2 – Each category is given a name or heading.

Notes for Facilitators

It is interesting to note that you can give the same set of ideas to different teams, and in most cases they will come up with a different set of categories. People all have different maps of the world, therefore they view things in individual ways. There is no right or wrong, just differences. Think about a list of possible holiday locations from around the world. These could be categorised in many different ways – by culture, by existing season, by hemisphere, and so on. The categories are not important. What is important is that the teams own these categories rather than the facilitator.

TOOLS FOR CHOOSING SOLUTIONS - ABSOLUTE CRITERIA SCREENING

What is it?

This process is referred to as *Absolute Criteria Screening*. It's used for evaluating each solution idea against absolute criteria. To understand how this works, recognise that absolute criteria are 'must haves' as opposed to 'nice to haves'. Where an idea does not meet any of the absolute criteria then it does not progress any further.

Potential Solution	Criterion A	Criterion B	Criterion C	Criterion D	Criterion E	
Idea A	✓	✓	✓	✓	✓	PASS
Idea B	✓	✓	✗			
Idea C	✗					
Idea D	✓	✓	✓	✓	✓	PASS

This process is used when constraints or limitations are imposed on the project team. For example, financial, legislative or organisational constraints might be absolutes against which each idea must be considered.

Instructions

Step 1 – Identify the criteria against which each idea is to be evaluated. These are often determined up front as 'project constraints'.

Step 2 – Evaluate each idea, one at a time, against criteria until it does not meet a criteria, or it meets all criteria.

Step 3 – Drop those ideas that do not meet all criteria from the list.

Absolute Criteria

By absolute we mean criteria are 'must haves' - any suggestion that does not meet all criteria is dropped from the list. Where do we get these constraints? Who determines these? They can be sourced from:

- Legislation,
- Company policies,
- Managers / Supervisors, and
- Customers.

Examples of absolute criteria are:

- Solution investment must payback within x days.
- Solutions must not breach legal requirements associated with ....
- Solutions must comply with our policy of .....
- The idea must be able to be implemented within x days.

There are occasions where absolute criteria can be re-negotiated at the point of origin. For example, where a financial constraint is imposed this value might be re-negotiated.

PAYOFF ANALYSIS

What is it

Payoff analysis is a process used to differentiate between ideas on the basis of how easy they are to implement and how much positive impact they have on the desired outcome. These two dimensions contribute to a determination about 'payoff' and form the Payoff Matrix shown.

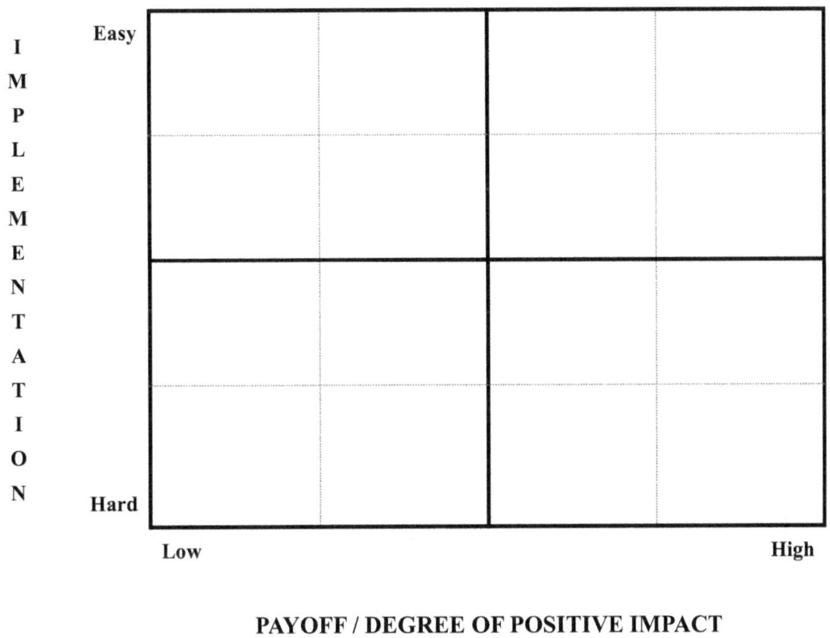

Payoff analysis is used when you have a large number of ideas and wish to reduce the list on the basis of how well they fit certain criteria. It can be used in deciding which ideas to implement when they are not mutually exclusive (can do multiple ideas at one time). For mutually exclusive ideas (can only do one or the other) this tool reduces the list. However, another tool may be required to choose the top idea.

Instructions

Step 1 – Establish agreement on the meaning of terms used as criteria. All team members must understand what 'ease of implementation' and 'degree of positive impact' actually means to them.

Step 2 – Evaluate each idea against both criteria. Ask 'How easy is this to implement?', 'How much positive impact will this idea have on the problem?

Step 3 – Plot the idea at the agreed location on the matrix.

Step 4 – Focus on ideas that are (a) easy to implement, and (b) have a high positive impact on the problem.

POTENTIAL FAILURE ANALYSIS

What is it?

Potential failure analysis is a process used to differentiate between ideas on the basis of how likely solutions are to fail and how much negative impact any such failure would have on the customer. The discussion of ideas against these two dimensions contributes to the team being able to make a determination about 'risk', and these form the dimensions of the Potential Failure Matrix shown.

LIKELY TO FAIL	1 (Nil)	2 (Minor)	3 (Moderate)	5 (Major)	10 (Significant)
10 (Highly Likely)	10	20	30	50	100
5 (Probable)	5	10	15	25	50
3 (Could)	3	6	9	15	30
2 (Unlikely)	2	4	6	10	20
1 (Never)	1	2	3	5	10

Impact Of Failure On The Customer

The potential failure analysis is used when you have a large number of ideas and wish to reduce the list on the basis of risk. As with the payoff analysis, it can be used in deciding which ideas to implement when they are not mutually exclusive (can do multiple ideas at one time). For mutually exclusive ideas (can only do one or the other), this tool reduces the list. However, another tool may be required to choose the top idea.

This tool may be more appropriate in situations where new machinery, equipment or technologies are going to solve the problem. A focus on failure is not my preferred option in other cases.

Instructions

Step 1 – Establish agreement on the rating scale used for each criterion [the ratings scales and descriptors shown in the matrix are examples only]. All team members must understand what 'impact of failure on the customer' and 'likelihood of failure' actually means to them, and how to rate each idea according to the rating scales.

Step 2 – Evaluate each idea against both criteria. Ask 'What could cause this solution to fail, and how likely is that to occur?' and 'If it did fail, how much impact would that have on the customer?'

Step 3 – Plot the idea at the agreed location on the matrix and allocate a potential failure risk rating (the product of ratings).

Step 4 – Prioritise ideas from lowest to highest according to the risk rating given to each. Low values, hence low risk given priority over high values.

Rating Scales

Whilst the most common rating scales used are 1 to 5, the rating scales shown use a scale that jumps from 5 to 10 for the highest value. With this scale, weighting is given to the higher end of each dimension of the matrix so that higher risk solutions drop off, and the probability of getting lower risk solutions is much higher.

WEIGHTED CRITERIA SCREENING

What is it?

Weighted Criteria is used to prioritise ideas on the basis of how well they fit weighted criteria important to the quality of the proposed solutions.

Criteria (Weighting)	Criterion 1 (5)		Criterion 2 (3)		Criterion 3 (2)		Criterion 4 (4)		
Potential Solution	Rate	**Weighted**	Rate	**Weighted**	Rate	**Weighted**	Rate	**Weighted**	**TOTAL**
Idea 1	5	**25**	4	**12**	3	**6**	4	**16**	**59**

Can be used when you have a large number of ideas that you wish to sort into a priority list.

Instructions

Step 1 – Identify the criteria against which each idea can be evaluated.

Step 2 – Allocate weightings to each of the criteria.

Step 3 – Evaluate ideas against criteria.

Step 4 – Calculate the weighted score for each idea and prioritise the list accordingly.

1. Identifying Criteria

Teams often find it difficult to determine the criteria against which to evaluate each of the ideas. This often stems from the fact that you are attempting to create a scenario that is essentially an unknown concept for which the team has no reference point. One of the simplest ways to move the team beyond this point is to start from a known concept. Let me give you an example of what I mean. Most of us have bought a car at one time or another, so if we can link the concept of evaluating options against criteria in this particular scenario, the team are likely to learn the concept quickly.

I started the discussion with one particular group I worked with at a business in Western Australia by asking them if they have ever bought a car. Whenever I ask this question the response is usually the same with a unanimous “yes” (except when I work in some of the less developed countries). I then ask them how they decided which car to buy in circumstances where they had to choose between a number of different options. The most useful of the ideas put forward are captured on the board. Responses are usually along the lines of:

- ‘I bought the fastest car’
- ‘I wanted the one with the best fuel economy’
- ‘I picked the car that would stick to the road and handle better’
- ‘I chose the one with the best level of safety for my family’

The answers given provide clues to the ‘qualities’ that are desired of the cars purchased, the basis for comparing each of the options against the other. The better the vehicle demonstrates these qualities, the more likely they are to buy that vehicle. So after explaining the concept of qualities, my next action is to do a short demonstration of the tool to buy a car. To generate the list of criteria to insert into the tool, I simply ask – ‘What qualities would we like to have in the car we buy?’ The answers given are usually along these lines:

- Comfort
- Safety
- Power
- Economy
- Resale Value

These qualities (or attributes) become the criteria against which each of the options can be rated. When choosing between solutions in a project context, I simply modify the question to – ‘What qualities would we like to have in our solutions?’ The most common answers include these:

- Impact on the problem
- Ease of implementation
- Speed with which the solution can be implemented
- User friendliness
- Maintainability
- Sustainability
- Upgradeability
- Expected working life

2. Allocating Weightings

There are multiple approaches shown in various reference books. The approach shown is only one approach that has worked well for me.

Step 2.1 – Choose the criterion that is most important – allocate maximum weighting of 5. Only one idea will have the maximum weighting of five.

Step 2.2 - Sort the remainder of criteria and allocate ratings of 1 to 4.

3. Evaluating Ideas Against Criteria and Each Other

Whilst each idea is being evaluated against specific criteria, it is helpful to compare ideas against one another. Again, there are multiple approaches to this work. The approach shown is one that has worked well for me.

Step 3.1 - Choose the best-fit idea for the first criterion and allocate highest rating of 5. Only one idea will be given the highest rating.

Step 3.2 - Evaluate the remaining ideas against each other allocating ratings from 1 to 4. Remember, this was meant to be a comparative method for separating ideas from one another.

Step 3.3 – Repeat for each criterion until all ratings are made.

Step 3.4 – Calculate the weighted rating for each idea versus criteria across the matrix.

Notes:

By only giving one criterion the highest weighting, and one idea the highest rating for each criterion, there is less chance of ideas having the same total weighted value at the end of the process.

A rating scale based on specific measured values for some or all criterion can be established to assist in separating ideas, however, this may make Step 3.1 redundant.

PAIRED RANKING

What is it?

Paired Ranking is a process used to differentiate between ideas on the basis of comparing each combination of 2 solution ideas and finding the idea that tends to be the best one more often than the others. The process is supported with the use of a Paired Ranking Matrix.

	SOLUTION	A	B	C	D	E	F	G	H	I	J	K	L	SCORE
A	Walk	-	A	A	D	E	F							2
B	Fly		-	C	D	E	F							0
C	Train			-	D	E	F							1
D	Scooter				-	E	F							3
E	Jog					-	E							5
F	Roller Skate						-							4
G								-						
H									-					
I										-				
J											-			
K												-		
L													-	
Preferred Solution		Jog												
Second Preference		Roller Skate												

Paired ranking is used when you have a moderate number of ideas. As with the payoff analysis and potential failure analysis, it can be used for deciding which ideas to implement when they are not mutually exclusive (can do multiple ideas at one time). For mutually exclusive ideas (can only do one or the other), this tool reduces the list. However, another tool may be required to choose the top idea.

Instructions

Step 1 – Place your list of solutions in the left side column and reference by a letter (A, B etc).

NOTE: If you have more than 12 ideas, either reduce the list using another tool (e.g., payoff analysis) or create a larger matrix.

Step 2 – Starting with idea A, move across the table and evaluate the first idea against every other idea. Ask 'Of these two ideas, which one will have the greatest positive impact on the problem?'

Step 3 – Continue for each of the ideas in the left column.

Step 4 – Count how many times each idea is preferred (the total number of times the letter appears in the matrix) and indicate in the score column.

Step 5 – Identify the preferred solutions.

LEAN IMPROVEMENT TOOLS – LEAN IMPROVEMENT STRATEGIES

A multitude of choices exist for how to actually make processes far more efficient. Some of the most common strategies are:

Parallel Processing	Parallel processing means to perform tasks concurrently (at the same time). Steps performed at the same time are performed in parallel, hence the name. Parallel processing reduces the overall cycle time of a process. The risk of parallel processing is that changes or decisions made that affect one of the paths is not communicated to the other path. The problem is realised when the two paths converge.
Straight Line Processing	Straight line processing is quite simply the arranging of steps in a single line sequence. This type of process is easiest to manage. The disadvantage of linear processing is that cycle time is greater than parallel processing.
Minimise the Number of Process Steps	As a process increases in complexity [number of steps], so increases the risk of things going wrong and cycle time being extended. The less steps in a process, the greater the ability to eliminate defects and minimise variation. Through simplification of the process, less people and less non-value adding activities are involved.
Reduce Non-Value Adding Time	Non-value adding time identified during process analysis can be reduced by either (a) eliminating non-value adding steps from the process, or alternatively (b) reducing the time taken to complete the non-value adding step.
Manage Time Traps & Constraints	Most processes experience points where capacity causes a slowdown in the process. The process flow in this case is only as good as the capacity of the time trap. When managing time traps, always consider the entire process and the effect on downstream steps in the process when the process flow is widened at an upstream point. Increasing process flow does not always require the addition of people or equipment.
Front End Decisions	The deferring of decisions to a downstream point in a process can result in work being completed on incorrect assumptions. Upstream decisions reduce the probability of unnecessary work, rework and rushed work.
Eliminate Handoffs	Studies have shown that the elimination of a handoff can reduce cycle time by up to 10 percent. Unnecessary handoffs should be removed from the process in order to simplify it and reduce cycle time.
Standardise Handoff Requirements	When handoffs are necessary between functions, the more efficiently these are performed the greater the ability to eliminate defects, control variation and minimise cycle time.

These strategies will be useful starting point for a team's discussion on methods for reducing cycle time, defects and variation in a process.

PROCESS BALANCING

What is it?

Process balancing is a process used to help a company to more effectively **meet customer demand** without the unnecessary **build up of inventory and work in progress through inefficient production**. The primary goal is to balance throughput so that the rate of production matches the rate of customer requirement. Process balancing is used in conjunction with other Lean improvement tools.

Instructions

Step 1 – Create a Takt Time Chart and identify where process constraints exist.

In the example shown, C is the time trap as it defines the rate of production.

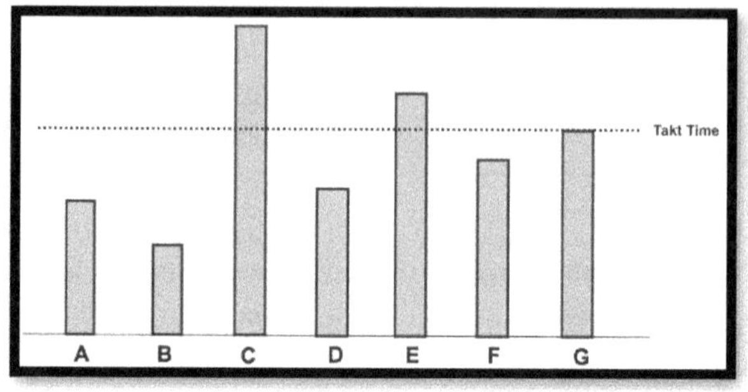

Step 2 – Take action to reduce excess time where the process is constrained.

- Eliminate it altogether (remove non-value adding time, minimise movement, optimise work cell design and resource accessibility), or
- Transfer it to a step where there is excess capacity (balance labour across steps).

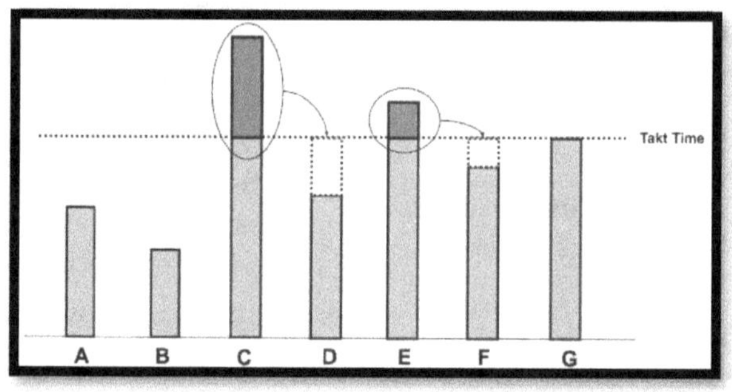

Step 3 – Take action to reduce excess capacity.

- Consolidate parallel process steps into a linear sequence (reduce labour requirements),
- Multi-task employees.

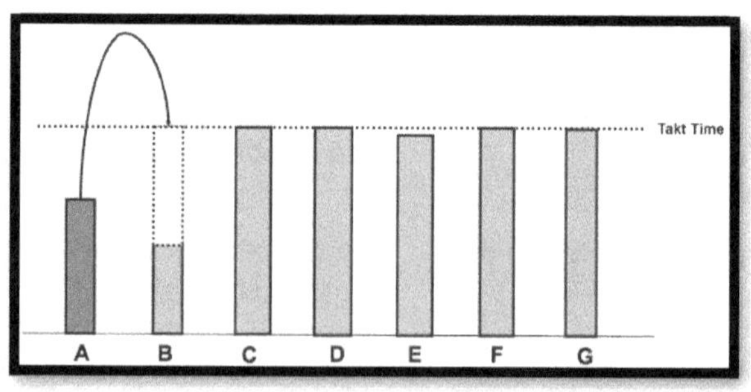

Step 4 – Document the new process and train operators as required.

PULL SYSTEMS

What is it?

A Generic Pull System is a framework for limiting or capping work in progress (WIP) or things in progress (TIP) so that lead time for a product or service is consistent and predictable.

Instructions

Step 1 – Determine Your Maximum Level of Work in Progress (WIP Max)

A worked example is shown in the right side column for reference purposes.

(a) Calculate current Total Lead Time Total LT = WIP ÷ Avg. Completion Rate	Total LT = 18 units ÷ 2 per day = 9 days (9 days @ 10 hours = 90 hours)
(b) Calculate current Process Cycle Efficiency (PCE) PCE = Value Added Time ÷ Total LT	PCE = 16 hours ÷ 90 hours = 0.17
(c) Determine your target level of PCE (Industry application lower end and world class values are shown opposite)	Machining Processes: 0.01 to 0.20 Fabrication Processes: 0.10 to 0.25 Continuous Flow Manufacturing Processes: 0.05 to 0.30 Service Processes: 0.10 to 0.50
(d) Calculate your target lead-time Target LT = Value Added Time ÷ Target PCE	Target LT = 16 hours ÷ 0.20 = 80 hours (80 hours = 8 days)
(e) Calculate WIP Max WIP Max = Target LT x Completion Rate	WIP Max = 8 x 2 = 16 units

Step 2 – Initiate a System for Releasing Work into the Process

(a) Calculate Actual WIP

(b) Determine Work Release

  If WIP ≥ WIP Max, do not release work

  If WIP < WIP Max, release sufficient work to reach WIP Max

(c) Manage Customer Impacts from Non-release of Work

  Increase capacity so that WIP is lowered (can be temporary)

  Process work on a first in, first out (FIFO) process; or alternatively

  Process High Priority Orders before Low Priority Orders

(d) Implement Procedures for Maintaining the Pull System

SINGLE MINUTE EXCHANGE OF DIE (SMED) / QUICK CHANGEOVER

What is it?

SMED is a process for systematically reducing the time lost in production due to machine set-ups or changeovers.

We also refer to this as sick changeover or QCO.

Instructions

Step 1. OBSERVE the current process for changeover and document the steps using the SMED Worksheet.

Step 2. Separate the INTERNAL and EXTERNAL activities and record actual time taken.

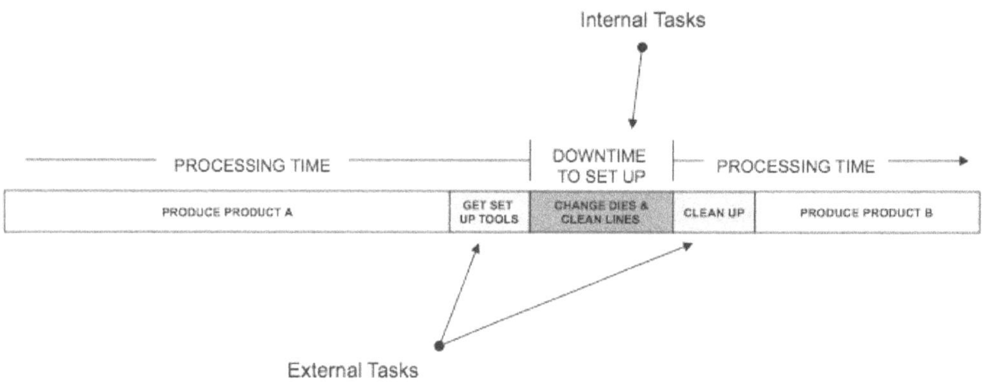

Step 3. CONVERT (where possible) Internal Tasks into External Tasks.

Step 4. STREAMLINE the remaining Internal Tasks.

- Simplify work
- Standardise function, not shape
- Eliminate or reduce movement – redesign workplace so tools etc are within arms reach
- Eliminate or reduce time associated with fixings – as Shigeo Shingo observed, it's only the last turn of a bolt that tightens it - the rest is just movement
- Use functional clamps or eliminate fasteners altogether
- Eliminate or reduce internal adjustments
- Establish parallel operations
- Use intermediate jigs
- Mechanise

Step 5. STREAMLINE External Tasks.

Step 6. DOCUMENT the new procedure, and any actions that are yet to be completed.

Step 7. REPEAT steps 1 to 6 - For each iteration of the process, a 40 to 50 percent improvement in set-up times should be targeted and expected, accordingly several iterations may be necessary to break the ten minute barrier.

SMED / QCO WORKSHEET

The process described on the previous page is supported with this simple to use SMED / QCO Worksheet.

Name of Changeover Process		Current Changeover Time			Targeted Changeover Time		
No.	Task / Activity	Actual Time		Planned Improvement	Target Time		Necessary Actions
		Internal	External		Internal	External	

WORK CELL OPTIMISATION

What is it?

WCO is simply the optimisation of the design and arrangement of work cells with an intent to maximise efficiency, minimise time and eliminate mistakes.

It should be used when you have inefficiency in workflow, in other words too much movement associated with people and materials.

Instructions

Step 1 - Stabilise lead time through the process

Step 2 - Ensure consistent supply of parts and materials

Step 3 - Ensure the process is capable of meeting customer demand and customer quality requirements

Step 4 – Design work cell layout so movement / motion is reduced to a minimum.

The following diagrams represent common work cell designs to choose from.

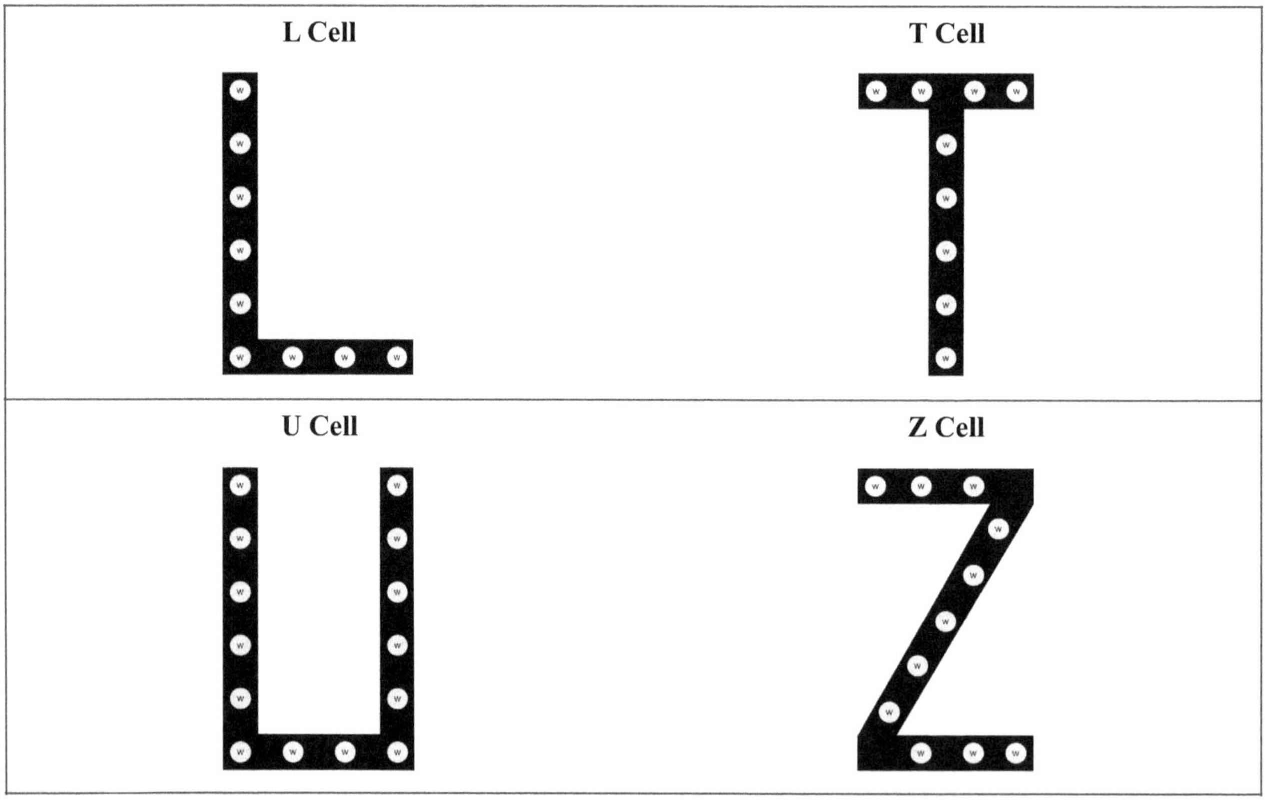

Step 5 – Create the work cell

TOTAL PRODUCTIVE MAINTENANCE

What is it?

TPM is a proactive methodology that primarily seeks to (a) prevent any kind of waste associated with plant or machinery before it occurs, (b) significantly increase production, and (c) positively impact employee morale and job satisfaction.

TPM achieves this through bringing maintenance into focus as a vitally important part of the business.

Instructions

Step 1 – Evaluate Current Conditions so that you understand the current state of performance with respect to:

- Availability
- Utilisation
- Productivity
- Maintenance and repair costs

Step 2 – Return Equipment to a Reliable Condition by -

- Cleaning it internally and externally (including degreasing and changing of filters)
- Lubricating all joints and moving parts
- Tagging or making note of required repairs
- Repairing equipment

Step 3 – Eliminate Breakdowns

- Review repairs that have been made
- Identify and treat factors that contribute to failures
- Improve access to relevant parts of machinery to assist with inspection, lubrication etc

Step 4 – Establish a TPM Database by documenting

- Repair tasks undertaken frequently
- What is repaired
- When repairs are performed
- Who performs the repairs

Step 5 – Prevent Defects from Occurring

- Train operators in predictive maintenance techniques
- Train operators in problem solving techniques
- Establish visual controls
- Implement 6S housekeeping process / system
- Review failures and take action to prevent or predict

Step 6 – Track Performance / TPM Data

- Mean Time Between Failures (MTBF)
- Mean Time To Repair (MTTR)

MISTAKE PROOFING & MISTAKE PREVENTION

What is it?

Mistake Proofing is the process of making it impossible for a mistake to be passed on to the next step in the process. The mistake is still made, but it gets corrected before it is passed on.

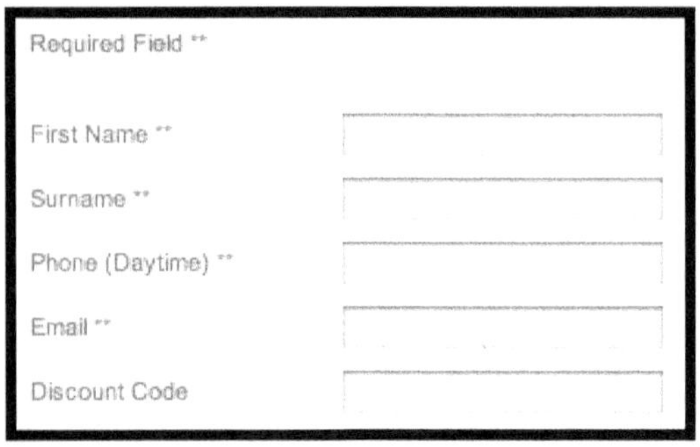
Required Field **
First Name **
Surname **
Phone (Daytime) **
Email **
Discount Code

Online transactions provide many examples of mistake proofing. In the example shown, a person registering for one of our events must insert certain details (see required fields).

If they fail to do so, the registration will not proceed and the applicant is shown which details must be included before it will be accepted.

The mistake is made, but it is not passed on.

By contrast, **Mistake Prevention** is the process of making it impossible for a mistake to be made in a process. The error or mistake does not get made in the first place.

Instructions

Step 1 - Define the mistake or defect.

Step 2 - Identify the impact it has on customers. Ask: *'How does this defect impact the customer?'*

Step 3 - Identify where the mistake or defect is discovered. Ask: *'Where in the process is the defect actually first discovered?'*

Step 4 - Identify where the mistake or defect is created. Ask: *'Where in the process is the defect actually created?'*

Step 5 - Undertake cause effect analysis to identify the potential cause or causes of the defect or mistake. Use any of the cause effect analysis tools previously discussed. (i.e. Cause Effect Diagram, Cause Effect Structure Tree, Five What Cause Effect Chain etc)

Step 6 - Validate hypothesised causes.

Step 7 - Identify and select ways to treat validated causes in this order.

- **Mistake Prevention** – Action that makes it impossible for the mistake to occur in the first place.

  Ask: *'What might prevent this mistake from occurring in the first place?'*
- **Mistake Proofing** - Action that makes it impossible for a defect to be passed on in the process.

  Ask: *'What could potentially stop this defect being passed on to the next step in the process if it occurs?'*

Step 8 - Develop and validate solutions.

Using FMEA for Mistake Proofing

Failure Mode & Effect Analysis (FMEA) should be considered as a mistake proofing process. Simple adaptation of the questions you ask will ensure your focus remains on prevention and proofing processes against defects or mistakes.

FAILURE MODE & EFFECT ANALYSIS (FMEA)

What is it?

Failure Mode and Effect Analysis (FMEA) is a process for analysing risks associated with a process, service or product. Its fundamental purpose is to recommend and take actions that reduce identified risks. The focus of the analysis is on customer impact and production.

The worksheet for undertaking Potential FMEA is laid out as shown below.

<table>
<tr><td colspan="6" rowspan="2">Process / Product / Service:</td><td colspan="4">Date Issued:</td><td>Page:</td><td colspan="5">1 of 1</td></tr>
<tr><td colspan="4">Date Revised:</td><td colspan="2">Revision No:</td><td colspan="4">File No:</td></tr>
<tr><td>Feature or Process Step</td><td>Failure Mode</td><td>Potential Effect</td><td>S</td><td>Potential Cause</td><td>O</td><td>Current Controls</td><td>C</td><td>RPN</td><td>Action</td><td>Who</td><td>When</td><td>S</td><td>O</td><td>C</td><td>RPN</td></tr>
<tr><td></td><td></td><td></td><td></td><td></td><td></td><td></td><td></td><td></td><td></td><td></td><td></td><td></td><td></td><td></td><td></td></tr>
</table>

Instructions

Step 1 - Prepare for the FMEA

- Identify the Process – *'What process are we studying?'* Name the process and document the steps.
- Determine the Purpose of the Study – State the purpose as to increase customer satisfaction, reduce safety risk or minimise impact to production. The purpose must be stated to ensure the correct context is applied throughout the analysis.
- Define Assessment Criteria – Determine the ratings for severity, likelihood of occurrence and adequacy of controls before any analysis.

Step 2 - Analyse Potential Failure Modes

- Identify The Feature Or Step – *'What is the process step (or product feature) that concerns us?'*
- Identify Potential Failure Modes – *'What could go wrong?'* This is a description of an event that can occur without indicating how severe it would be.

Step 3 - Analyse Potential Effects

- Identify Potential Effects – *'If this failure mode occurred, what could be the consequences (or potential effects)?'*
- Rate The Severity – *'How severe would those consequences be in the context of our analysis?'* Allocate a rating (S) according to the answers you give and how best they fit with the rating scale you created in step 1.

Step 4 - Analyse Probable Causes

- Identify Potential Causes – *'What conditions or actions could cause this failure to occur?'* List the potential cause/s. Cause and effect analysis tools such as Cause Effect Structure Trees can be used to study causes of failure modes.
- Rate The Likelihood Of Occurrence – *'What is the likelihood of this failure occurring as a result of these conditions or actions?'* or *'How often do you think this failure would occur as a result of these conditions or actions?'* Allocate a rating (O) according to the answer you give to these questions.

Step 5 - Analyse the Control Framework

- Identify Existing Controls – *'What controls do we have in place to prevent the failure mode from occurring or to detect the failure if it does occur?'* Controls can be proactive – they prevent the failure occurring, or reactive – they detect the failure only after it has occurred.
- Rate The Effectiveness Of Controls – *'How would you rate the effectiveness of those controls?'* Allocate a rating (C) according to the answers you give to the question.
- Complete For All Elements - Repeat steps 2 to 5 until all process steps or elements of the study have been analysed.

Step 6 - Prioritise Potential Failure Modes

- Calculate RPN - The risk priority number is calculated by multiplying Severity Rating x Occurrence Rating x Control Rating.
- (RPN = S x O x C)
- Prioritise Failure Modes – Sort failure modes from highest RPN to lowest RPN.

Step 7 - Develop an Action Plan

- Select Actions – Select actions to treat failure modes that reduce the likelihood of occurrence, mitigate consequences and / or detect failures before or after they occur.

Step 8 - Reassess Failure Modes – Post Treatment

- Recalculate RPN Values – Assume that action plans have been completed, and with that assumption in mind, reassess failure modes by calculating a post treatment RPN value for each.

SCHEDULE BAR CHART

What is it?

The schedule bar chart is used to visually display the sequence of activities that must be undertaken to complete a project.

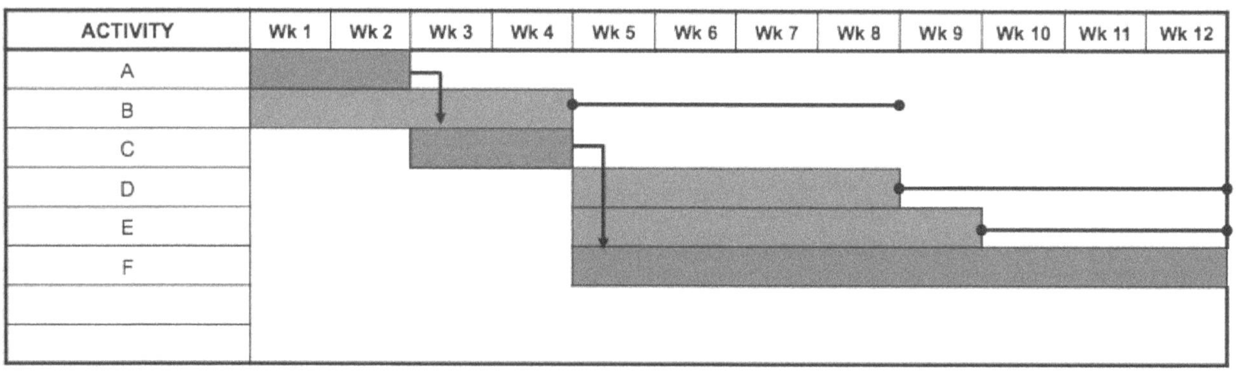

Instructions

Step 1 – Identify all of the tasks that need to be completed. These can be identified with the **Work Breakdown Structure (WBS)** process.

Step 2 – Create a **Network Diagram** so that the sequence of tasks is defined.

Step 3 – Identify the duration of each task and their respective start and finish dates. Where uncertainty about task time frame exists, use **Program Evaluation Review Technique (PERT)** to define expected task time.

Step 4 – Identify early and late start and finish times for each task as well as the project's **Critical Path**.

Step 5 – Visually display the duration of each task using a horizontal bar that corresponds to the relevant dates on a calendar across the top row of the chart. Using arrows and colours, indicate the following.

- Predecessors
- Critical Path

Each of the various tools mentioned here are explained over the following pages using the same project data.

WORK BREAKDOWN STRUCTURE

What is it?

WBS is a simple process for breaking down a project into a comprehensive list of detailed actions that must be taken to achieve the desired outcome. Its purpose is *'to sub-divide the scope of work into manageable work packages which can be estimated, planned and assigned for completion.'*

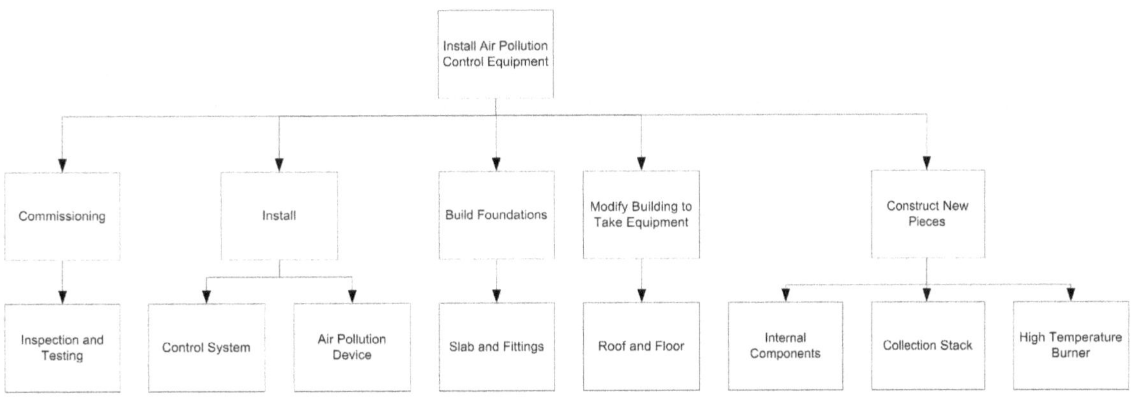

Instructions

Step 1 – Define the end result of the finished project

Step 2 – Starting at the macro level, sequentially break the project down into lower levels of detailed work until the stated task provides sufficient clarity and can be allocated for effective completion

NETWORK DIAGRAM

What is it?

A process for identifying the interdependencies and sequence of tasks within a project schedule.

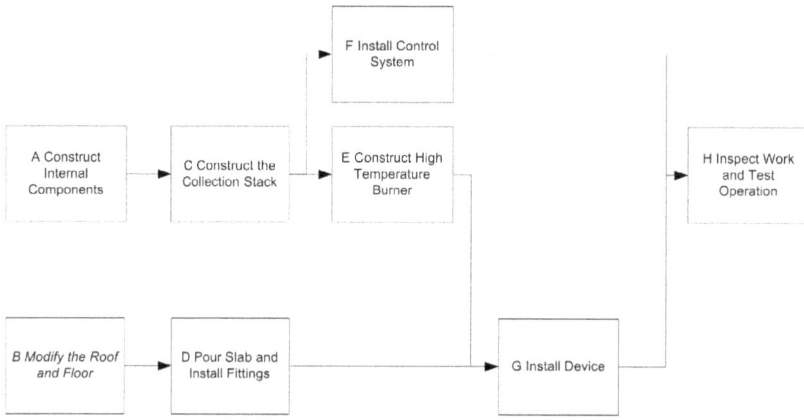

Instructions

Step 1 – Identify the tasks (WBS)

Step 2 – Visually layout the tasks in their sequence

Step 3 – Indicate sequence (and predecessors) with lines that show the direction of work flow

PERT WORKSHEET

What is it?

Activity	Predecessor	Optimistic (o)	Most Likely (m)	Pessimistic (p)	Expected $t = \frac{o + 4m + p}{6}$	Variance $\left(\frac{p-o}{6}\right)^2$
A. Construct Internal Components		1	2	3	2	0.11
B. Modify the Roof and Floor		2	3	10	4	1.77
C. Construct the Collection Stack	A	1	2	3	2	0.11
D. Pour Slab and Install Fittings	B	2	4	6	4	0.44
E. Construct High Temp Burner	C	1	2	9	3	1.77
F. Install Control System	C	1	4	7	4	1.00
G. Install Device	D, E	3	5	13	6	2.75
H. Inspect Work & Test Operation	F, G	1	2	3	2	0.11

The PERT worksheet is a table that helps calculate expected task times and variances based on estimates of (a) optimistic time, (b) pessimistic time and (c) most likely time.

The tool is used primarily to identify expected time frames for completion of each activity when there is risk of variation in the duration of activities. The results of the PERT are often used as inputs into Critical Path studies or activity scheduling with bar charts.

Instructions

Step 1 – Identify **optimistic time** for each activity, the time an activity will take if everything goes as well as possible. The possibility of this should be small, perhaps one in a hundred.

Step 2 – Identify **most likely time**, the most realistic time estimate for the activity based on knowledge at hand.

Step 3 – Identify **pessimistic time**, the time an activity would take assuming extremely unfavourable conditions. Like optimistic time, the possibility of this should be small.

Step 4 – Calculate **expected time** using the equation provided.

Step 5 – Calculate **activity variance** using the equation provided.

CRITICAL PATH METHOD

What is it?

Critical Path Method (CPM) is used to answer the following questions for a project manager:

- *How long will the project take?*
- *What activities have room to move (slack)?*
- *What activities have no room to move and are critical to completing the project on time?*

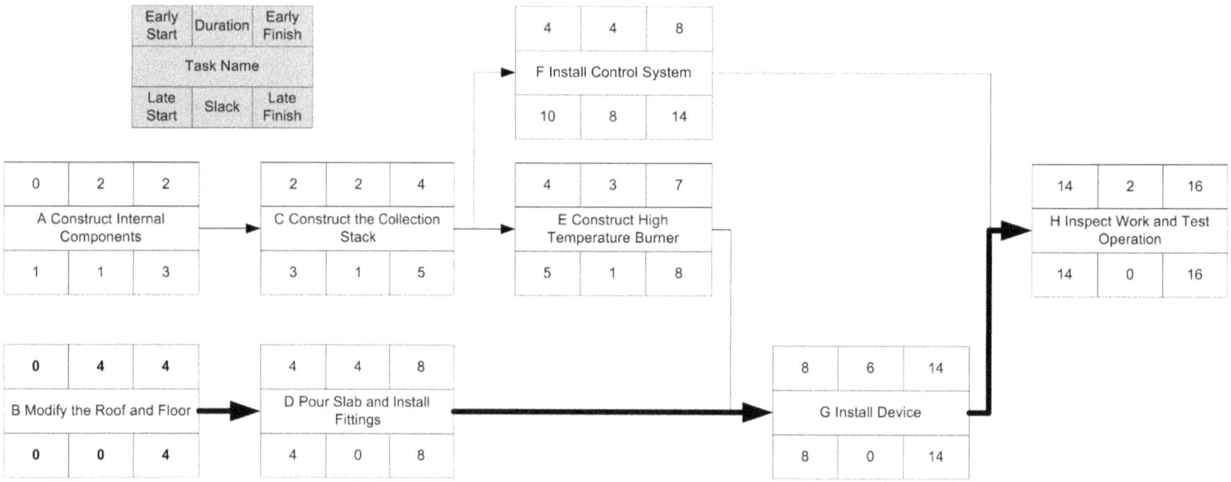

Instructions

Step 1 – Create a diagram of activities in their relevant sequence (network diagram).

Step 2 – Calculate Early Start (ES) and Early Finish (EF) times by 'forward pass' computation.

Step 3 – Calculate Late Start (LS) and Late Finish (LF) times by 'backward pass' computation.

RESPONSIBILITY MATRIX

What is it?

The responsibility matrix is a table in which activities associated with a project are recorded alongside their predecessors and linked to relevant project participants.

Its purpose is to provide relevant information to assist with managing the project.

- Who does what
- How long tasks will take
- When tasks must start
- When tasks must be completed by

Project: Air Pollution Control			Date Issued:				Page:	1 of 1			
			Date Revised:				Revision No:		File No: RC1.1		
			PROJECT PARTICIPANTS							**TIMINGS**	
ACTIVITIES	**DUR**	**IP**	**Tom**	**Vicki**	**Fiona**	**Con**	**Geoff**			**Start**	**End**
A. Construct Internal Components	2	-	**R**	A						05/01	06/01
B. Modify the Roof and Floor	4	-			**R**					05/01	08/01
C. Construct the Collection Stack	2	**A**	S	I	I	**R**	I			07/01	08/01
D. Pour Slab and Install Fittings	4	**B**	R			I				09/01	14/01
E. Construct High Temp Burner	3	**C**	S			**R**	I			09/01	13/01
F. Install Control System	4	**C**		I			**R**			09/01	14/01
G. Install Device	6	**D, E**	**R**	I						15/01	22/01
H. Inspect Work & Test Operation	2	**F, G**		**R**						23/01	26/01

LEGEND:
DUR – Duration **IP** – Immediate Predecessor
R – Responsible **A** – Approve **D** – Decide **S** – Support **I** – Inform Blank – Not Involved

It is usually prepared after the sequence of tasks is identified using either a network diagram or schedule bar chart.

Note: There are many ways to document who does what in a project, this is but one approach to consider.

STAKEHOLDER COMMITMENT EVALUATION

What is it?

The Stakeholder Commitment Evaluation process is used to determine the level of commitment of key stakeholders. The worksheet helps define (a) where key stakeholders sit with respect to their commitment for the intended change, and (b) the gap to where they must be as a **minimum** for the change to be achievable and sustainable.

It is generally used before undertaking any change, usually during the planning phase.

It should also be used at regular intervals during the transition to the new state to ensure the 'pulse' of commitment is being monitored.

	COMMITMENT LEVEL				
STAKEHOLDERS	**Take Action to Prevent Happening**	**Talk Negatively**	**Neutral**	**Talk Positively**	**Take Action to Make Happen**
Mary the Manager					✖ ✔
Oscar the Operator			✖	✔	
Steve the Safety Superintendent					✖ ✔
Fred the Plant Foreman	✖			✔	
Terry the Transport Supervisor			✖ ✔		

Instructions

STEP 1 Identify key stakeholders (anyone affected by the change, or who can effect the change) Ask: *'Who are the key stakeholders associated with the change?'*

STEP 2 Identify where each currently sits, or where they are likely to sit with respect to their commitment to the change proposed Ask: *'What is the current (or probable) level of commitment of the stakeholder?'*

STEP 3 Identify where each needs to be as a minimum to make the change stick over time. Ask: *'Where does the stakeholder need to be as a minimum to make this change successful?'*

Rating Commitment Levels

- **Take Action to Prevent (Saboteurs)** – speaks out against the change and takes action to prevent it occurring.
- **Speak Out Against (Prophets of Doom)** – speaks out against the change however does not take any action to prevent it occurring.
- **Neutral (Fence Sitters)** – is non-committal either way, shows no real concern whether or not the change takes place, says nothing against nor in support of the change.
- **Speak Up for the Change (Marketers)** – is openly supportive of the change, however does not take any action to help make it happen.
- **Take Action to Make Happen (Change Agents)** – is highly supportive of the change and takes action to help make it happen.

STAKEHOLDER ENGAGEMENT PLAN

What is it?

A Stakeholder Engagement Plan is used to develop a course of action for engaging stakeholders.

Engagement can be generated through the application of strategies that alleviate concerns about the proposed change, reframing any potential negative impacts, highlighting the potential benefits for the stakeholder and satisfying their broad interests.

The process is used when a gap has been identified between where a key stakeholder must be for the change to be successful and where they currently sit.

<table>
<tr><td colspan="2">Stakeholder: ?</td><td colspan="2">Level of Commitment Reqd: ?</td></tr>
<tr><td>1. Interests / Values:
?</td><td>2. The Problem:
?</td><td colspan="2">3. Concerns or Objections:
?</td></tr>
<tr><td>4. Potential Negative Impacts:
?</td><td>5. Potential Benefits:
?</td><td colspan="2">6. Evidence Strategy:
?</td></tr>
<tr><td colspan="2">Action Plan:</td><td>Who:</td><td>By When:</td></tr>
<tr><td colspan="2"></td><td></td><td></td></tr>
</table>

Instructions

STEP 1 Determine who the stakeholders or stakeholder groups are who need to be engaged.

STEP 2 Identify the level of commitment you require from them for the change to be successful. (eg; neutral, talk positively or take action)

- This becomes the target, and a reference point for determining whether or not the proposed strategies will be adequate.

STEP 3 Identify the broad interests / values of the stakeholder.

- ASK: '*What are they interested in / what is important to them?*'
- These are the influence levers that the team can tap to engage the stakeholder. They don't necessarily have to be linked to the project.

STEP 4 Identify the problem this change is solving in terms of how it affects stakeholders.

- ASK: '*What problem are you fixing that hurts them?*'

STEP 5 Identify the specific concerns or objections of the stakeholder.

- ASK: '*What concerns or objections might stakeholders have about the proposed change?*'
- These concerns, whether real or perceived, must be addressed in some way.

STEP 6 Identify the potential negative impacts to the stakeholder of the proposed change.

- ASK: '*How can this proposed change actually hurt or inconvenience the stakeholder?*'

STEP 7 Identify the potential benefits of the change for the stakeholder.

- ASK '*What are the potential benefits for the stakeholder when this change is completed?*'
- These benefits help answer the question, 'What's in it for me?', and can be used to change the way in which a stakeholder views the proposed change.

STEP 8 Determine suitable strategies to engage the stakeholder.

- ASK: '*How can we PROVE to them that not changing is a pain for them?*'
- ASK: '*How can we REFRAME the way in which the stakeholder views potential impacts, or reduce the potential negative effects, or change the way they perceive the impact or effects?*'
- ASK: '*How can we ALLEVIATE the concerns that the stakeholder has of the proposed change?*'
- ASK: '*How can we LINK the proposed change to any broad interests that the stakeholder has, satisfy their interests or at least make some connection?*'
- ASK: '*How can we INCREASE or highlight the benefits of the proposed change, make them aware of the benefits?*'

STEP 9 Validate Strategies. Refer back to the desired level of commitment and

- ASK: '*Are these strategies likely to engage the stakeholder to the level of commitment desired?*'
- If not, continue the discussion around engagement strategies.

STEP 10 Develop your action plan.

- Strategies must be converted into action, with responsibility and completion dates specified and agreed to.

COMMUNICATIONS PLAN

What is it?

The communications plan is a worksheet for defining and documenting the key elements associated with an effective communication strategy. The worksheet is used during the planning phase for any change, usually at the beginning of any major Lean Six Sigma project and during the work associated with solution implementation planning.

<table>
<tr><th colspan="6">Communication Plan</th></tr>
<tr><td colspan="2" rowspan="2">Project:</td><td colspan="2">Date Issued:</td><td>Page:</td><td>1 of 1</td></tr>
<tr><td colspan="2">Date Revised:</td><td>Revision No:</td><td>File No:</td></tr>
<tr><th>Audience</th><th colspan="2">Content</th><th>Timing</th><th>Medium</th><th>Responsibility</th></tr>
<tr><td></td><td colspan="2"></td><td></td><td></td><td></td></tr>
<tr><td></td><td colspan="2"></td><td></td><td></td><td></td></tr>
</table>

Instructions

STEP 1 Determine who the audience is by asking *'Who needs to be informed for this change to be successful?'* Document in the 'Audience' column of the worksheet.

STEP 2 Determine what the purpose is for communicating to each audience group by asking *'What is our purpose for communicating with this audience?'*

STEP 3 Determine what information each needs to know about the proposed change for the purpose to be achieved. Document in the 'Content' column of the worksheet.

STEP 4 Decide when and how often do they need to receive information. Document in the 'Timing' column of the worksheet.

STEP 5 Determine the medium most appropriate for ensuring effective communication. Choices are numerous and might include (a) newsletter, (b) tool box talks, (c) shift change over briefings, (d) radio talk back, (e) face-to-face discussion, (f) formal presentation, or even (g) phone call. Document in the 'Medium' column of the worksheet.

STEP 6 Determine who is responsible for taking action and document in the 'Responsibility' column of the worksheet.

FORCE FIELD ANALYSIS

What is it?

This process is called Force Field Analysis. Its purpose is to identify forces working for and against the change, and determine actions a team might take to change the balance of these forces so that momentum is towards successful implementation of the proposed change.

Enabling Forces	**Restraining Forces**
(Any existing force that is helping the change to occur. These can be forces that people are drawing people towards the desired state, or forces that are driving people away from the current state)	(Any existing force that is hindering or preventing the change from occurring)
Action Plan:	

Instructions:

STEP 1 Identify enabling forces. Ask: *'What are the existing forces that are driving this change, or helping this change to occur?'*

STEP 2 Identify restraining forces. Ask: *'What are the existing forces that are hindering or preventing this change from occurring?'*

STEP 3 (optional) Indicate the relative strength of each of these forces. You can use arrows or numbers. You might also use multi voting to choose the most significant forces on each side.

STEP 4 Develop actions to build on enablers and / or overcome the restrainers. You can also use other tools to identify causes (root cause analysis) or overcome resistance (engagement plans) or to choose actions (payoff matrix etc).

Key Strategies

When choosing a course of action, the strategies available to you are:

- Build on enablers
- Overcome restrainers
- A combination – Build on enablers and overcome restrainers

PROJECT RISK MANAGEMENT

What is it?

Project risk management is the process of managing the occurrence of any situation that might prevent a team from achieving project objectives.

Instructions

Using the following format, implementation project risk management is a 5-step process.

Project:	**Date Issued:**	**Page:**	1 of 1
	Date Revised:	**Revision No:**	**File No:**

Project Objectives:	- On time - To expected level of performance	- Within Budget - According to scope

What Can Happen	**Existing Controls**	**L**	**Potential Effect**	**S**	**RR**	**Action**	**Who**	**When**	**L**	**S**	**RR**

STEP 1 Establish the Context

- Define criteria for rating risks during the assessment phase, and
- Identify project objectives.

Likelihood Rating (L) **	**Severity Rating (S)**
1 – Rare	1 – Insignificant / No Real Impact
2 – Unlikely to occur	2 – Minor Impact
3 – Could happen in most circumstances	3 – Moderate Impact
4 – Likely to occur in most circumstances	4 – Major Impact
5 – Almost certain to occur	5 – Catastrophic Impact
** Likelihood could also be rated on frequency of occurrence, i.e., rare = has never happened, unlikely to occur = occurred once in past 5 years etc	

STEP 2 Identify Risks

- Brainstorm potential risks by asking; *'What can happen that might prevent the achievement of objectives?'* You could refer back to the sources of uncertainty discussed in the previous chapter to help answer this question.

STEP 3 Assess Risks

- Identify the controls that are currently in place to manage the respective risks.
- Rate the likelihood (L) of the event occurring in the existing control environment, using a 1 – 5 scale similar to this one.
- Determine and document the potential effect the risk event would have on the achievement of

respective objectives, should it occur.

- Rate the severity (S) of that effect using a 1 – 5 scale similar to this one.
- Determine the risk rating (RR) by multiplying the severity rating by the likelihood rating. With a 1 to 5 scale risk ratings will range from 1 to a maximum of 25.

STEP 4 Treat Risks

- Identify actions to treat risks based on a number of strategy choices.
    - Eliminate the Risk: *'What could we do that would eliminate this risk altogether?'*
    - Reduce Likelihood of Occurrence: *'How could we reduce the likelihood of this event occurring?'*
    - Early Warning: *'What could we do or put in place that would warn us of the events occurrence before it actually happens?'*
    - Mitigate the Risk: *'What could we do to minimise its effect should this actually happen?'*
    - Transfer Risk: *'How could we transfer this risk to somewhere or someone else?'*
    - Accept the Risk: *'Are we prepared to accept this risk?'*
- Reassess risks post-treatment.

STEP 5 Monitor Risks

- Review project risks and management plans over time.

PILOT STUDY CHECKLIST

PHASE	ACTIVITIES	COMPLETED
PLAN	The scope of the study is defined and describes: Size of the study Where it will be conducted Who will be involved How long the study will be conducted	☐
	Roles and responsibilities for the pilot study are defined and have been communicated to relevant participants.	☐
	The schedule of events is documented and includes: Site briefing Pilot construction (where relevant) Training for participants Collection of data Pilot reviews Pilot closure Final study report and presentation	☐
	Measures of success are defined and a monitoring plan is prepared.	☐
	Study risks have been identified and contingencies prepared to deal with unacceptable risks.	☐
DO	Results are being tracked and recorded	☐
	Activities are being logged	☐
	Environmental conditions (where relevant) are also being logged	☐
	Regular reviews are being conducted with all key participants.	☐
CHECK	Actual results are summarised.	☐
	Any difference between actual and expected results are documented and the root causes of the gap have been studied.	☐
	A plan to treat validated root causes has been prepared.	☐
ACT	Root causes of variation between actual and expected results have been treated.	☐
	The implementation plan has been revised to incorporate relevant learnings.	☐
	The results of the pilot study have been communicated to key stakeholders.	☐

CHAPTER 20: IMPROVE PHASE TOLLGATE & CHECKLISTS

TOLLGATE QUESTIONS

The following questions are the kind that may be asked by your Master Black Belt or Lean Six Sigma Project sponsor during a 'Improve Phase Tollgate Review' which is indicated as the point between steps fifteen and sixteen on our 20-step roadmap.

	Lean	Six Sigma
<u>CHARTER / SCOPE</u> • What revisions need to be made to the charter? • How has the scope of the project changed? • What changes need to be made to the project time line?	✓	✓
<u>BENCHMARKING</u> • Did you undertake any benchmarking studies? • What were they? • What was the basis for choosing these places for your benchmarking? • How was the benchmarking study undertaken? • What were the results? • How did these results impact your process improvement work?		✓
<u>SOLUTION IDENTIFICATION</u> • What are your proposed solutions or changes? • What process did you use to identify these? • How did you make your final choice of solutions? • Who was involved in the process? • How do you know these solutions will make a difference? • How are these solutions linked to validated causes or key factors?	✓	✓
<u>PROCESS IMPROVEMENT</u> • Do you intend changing the process (steps) itself? • What does the new process look like? • What principles did you apply in redesigning it? • Who was involved in the process? • How do you know this new process will result in an improved outcome? • What benefits will this new process offer?	✓	✓

	Lean	Six Sigma
PILOTING • Did you pilot any of these solutions? • Where did you do that pilot? • How did you choose that location? • How long did the pilot study take? • How did you go about measuring the success of the pilot? • What did you learn from the pilot?		✓
SOLUTION IMPLEMENTATION • What is your plan for implementing these solutions? • Who was involved in the planning process? • What risks have you identified? • How have you planned to deal with these risks? • How will the implementation of these solutions affect other parts of the business?	✓	✓
CHANGE STRATEGY • What work have you undertaken to identify stakeholder commitment? • What is your plan for getting buy-in from key stakeholders? • How do you propose to engage those that may exhibit resistance? • What systems or structures require changing to support the proposed solutions or the new level of performance expected? • How do you know that your solutions will be sustainable over the long term?	✓	✓
MONITORING / TRACKING BENEFITS • How do you plan to monitor the performance of the process post implementation? • Given what you know now, what benefits do you expect to see from the project? • How do you propose to track these benefits?	✓	✓
GENERAL • What challenges are you experiencing that I can assist with? • What is your plan from here?	✓	✓

'IMPROVE' PHASE CHECKLIST

Six Sigma Specific Project

If you have responded appropriately to each of the following statements, then you are ready to move to the 'Control' phase of your project.		YES	NO	NA
1	A benchmarking study of relevant organisations or work sites has been undertaken and adaptable ideas have been identified.			
2	A wide range of potential solutions were identified with the involvement of key process participants / operators.			
3	Final solutions that treat validated causes of variation have been chosen by the team using a systematic decision making process.			
4	Unintended consequences of implementing proposed solutions have been identified and a plan created for dealing with these.			
5	A risk management plan has been put in place to deal with risks that affect the achievement of implementation project objectives.			
6	Have conducted a pilot study to identify what would occur under conditions of full-scale implementation.			
7	Evaluated results of the pilot study and confirmed that project goals can be achieved.			
8	Have modified the implementation plan as a result of the learnings from the pilot study.			
9	A training plan for aligning skills to the requirements of the solution has been prepared.			
10	Have developed a communications plan to support implementation.			
11	Anticipated levels of commitment to proposed solutions have been analysed and stakeholder engagement plans have been developed.			
12	A change response plan for managing the change has been developed and is comprised of: • Key indicators of success • Off track warning signs • Details of actions to take when off track signs are observed			
13	A plan to align relevant performance systems and structures to solutions and the new level of performance has been developed.			
14	Solutions and the implementation plan have been validated with the process owner, project sponsor and relevant key stakeholders.			
15	Project storyboard has been updated.			

Lean Specific Project

If you have responded appropriately to each of the following statements, then you are ready to move to the 'Control' phase of your project.		YES	NO	NA
1	Solutions for treating sources of waste were identified with the involvement of key process participants / operators.			
2	Unintended consequences of implementing proposed solutions have been identified and a plan created for dealing with these.			
3	A risk management plan has been put in place to deal with risks that affect the achievement of implementation project objectives.			
4	A training plan for aligning skills to the requirements of the solution has been prepared.			
5	Have developed a communications plan to support implementation.			
6	Anticipated levels of commitment to proposed solutions have been analysed and stakeholder engagement plans have been developed.			
7	A change response plan for managing the change has been developed and is comprised of: • Key indicators of success • Off track warning signs • Details of actions to take when off track signs are observed			
8	A plan to align relevant performance systems and structures to solutions and the new level of performance has been developed.			
9	Solutions and the implementation plan have been validated with the process owner, project sponsor and relevant key stakeholders.			
10	Project storyboard has been updated.			

CHAPTER 21: PROJECT 'CONTROL' PHASE

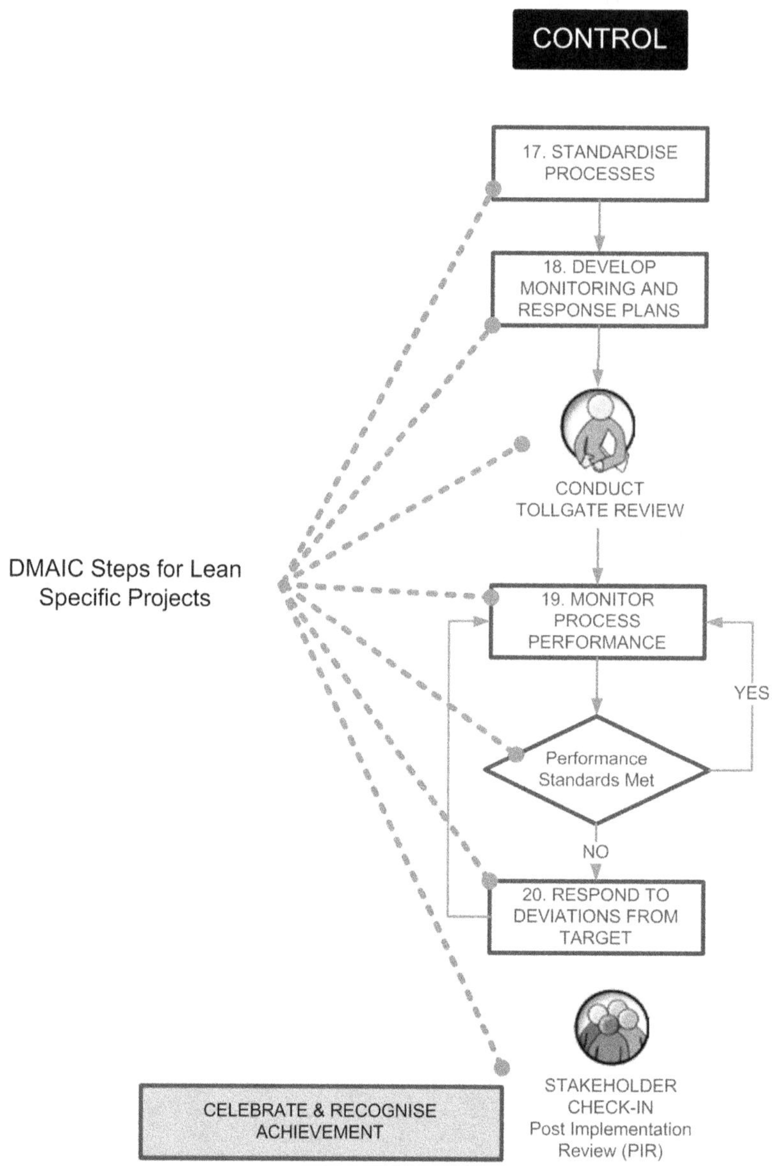

Have you ever tried to write with your weak hand? If I asked you to write with that hand for a full week, how long do you think you would sustain it?

The bottom line is this, doing something different is not that challenging to sustain for a short while, even if it's difficult to do. However, over the long term the natural tendency is to return to the old way of doing things. Old ways are very hard to break.

THE CONTROL PHASE AS A PROCESS

Control is the fifth phase of the team's work. The purpose of the control phase is to make sure the new way of working is sustained over time. This phase of DMAIC is complemented by the tools and skills taught in Change Leadership training courses. Our focus here is on the technical aspects of DMAIC.

The CONTROL Phase as a Process

The following table represents our view of the 'control' phase as a process at this point in the project.

INPUTS	PROCESS	OUTPUTS
Solutions are implemented and the new process is operational	1. Standardise Processes 2. Monitor Process Performance 3. Respond to performance deviations 4. Close the project and celebrate achievements	A self sustaining system of performing work A monitoring plan that is a foundation for continual process improvement planning

Standardisation of the Process

Now that the new way is effectively in place, the Black Belt must ensure that everyone knows how the work is to be done and it is done the same way across the organisation. Standardisation reduces the possibility of variation.

Monitoring of Process Performance

The activities of monitoring are inextricably linked to the activities of responding during the control phase.

Responding to Performance Deviations

Responding to performance deviations is simply the process of taking action when an out of control or out of specification situation arises.

COMMON CONTROL PHASE TOOLS

TECHNICAL TOOLS / PROCESSES	PEOPLE TOOLS / PROCESSES
Standard Operating Procedures Critical-to-Quality Tree Diagram SIPOC Cause Effect Tree Diagram CE Matrix Process Performance Monitoring Plan Statistical Process Control Plan Control Charts Visual Process Controls, Performance Dashboards	Facilitation Processes and Tools Meeting Tools (Agenda, Parking Lot, Meeting Feedback) Systems and Structures Alignment Plan

STANDARDISE PROCESSES (STEP 16)

Standardisation of processes is achieved when the new process is thoroughly documented, disseminated and participants are trained in the application of the new process.

DOCUMENT THE PROCESS

Have you ever given a set of written instructions to someone to guide them to some place that they have never seen before? Did they get there? Did you leave something out, or did they interpret your instructions in some way that was not intended? Without good directions, that person risks not getting to the intended destination. Such is the case with documenting processes.

Documentation of the new process is an important task that the Black Belt must complete before closing the project. Here are some useful tips to help you in your documentation work.

- **Use Pictures** – Have you ever installed a Hewlett Packard printer? The most recent package I purchased came with a large fold out card made up of pictorial instructions. I was impressed by the simplicity of it all. Pictures, videos, flowcharts, diagrams are powerful ways to get the message across as intended. Remember this, the majority of people in the world predominantly process information through visual representation. Where written instructions are necessary, they should be accompanied by visual aids.
- **Avoid Technical Jargon** – Avoid jargon, abbreviations and technical talk unless the person reading the material is fluent in this language.
- **Brevity** – Keep it as brief as possible. Make use of bullet points and minimal conversational pieces. Many items of electrical equipment today come with detailed instruction manuals and summary booklets or cards. If you have ever received one, which one did you read? I'll bet it was the summary card or booklet. People are exposed to so much written information today that they are more likely to read a brief document rather than some thick journal.
- **Create with user input and contribution** – If you want people to use it, get them to help create it. Not only will the contents be more user friendly, the users will learn about the contents in the process.
- **Test before roll out** – Test any documentation by having someone follow the instructions, preferably someone who does not know the process. If they are able to undertake the task, this will confirm the usefulness of the document. This is a form of piloting.

- **Contingencies** – Anticipate problems and include tips or instructions for users, much like the troubleshooting guides you see in computer instruction manuals.

Remember this, the more effective you are in documenting the process, the higher the probability of long-term success. Prepare your documentation through the eyes of the user.

PLAN FOR TRAINING

The introduction of a new process necessitates the need to train those who work with the process. Unless people are trained in how the new process is used, variation will be inherent in the system and the sustainability of the new process will be challenged. To plan training, a number of key elements must be considered by the team.

- Who is going to be trained?
- What training will they undertake? This will be driven by the gap between current skill level and desired skill level. The answer to this question will come from answering the following three questions.

  Q. What is their current level of skill?

  Q. What is the required level of skill?

  Q. What must be taught to get them to the required level of skill?
- How, when and where will they be trained?

Project:		**Date Issued:**		**Page:**	of
		Date Revised:		**Revision No:**	**File No:**
Participants	**Subject Matter**	**Method of Delivery**	**Timing**	**Location**	**Responsibility**

Figure 326: Training Plan Worksheet

Methods of Training

A multitude of approaches are available to deliver training. Some of these include:

- Web based online training
- Self teaching through problem based learning
- On the job training
- Mentoring or buddy systems
- Face to face in the classroom
- Video teaching
- Stage plays and role plays
- One on one
- Observation and modelling
- Reading

All trainers should remember two key points:

- Just because training is delivered, it doesn't automatically mean that learning takes place
- Learning can occur even when training is not being delivered

MONITOR PROCESS PERFORMANCE (STEP 17)

DEVELOPING A MONITORING PLAN

One method of identifying the real cause variables (x's) that should be monitored is to prioritise them according to how important they are or how much impact they have across the range of efficiency and effectiveness measures.

This approach is particularly useful when (a) customers of a process have a range of requirements spanning both the product or service, and the process itself, and (b) project work has been focused on improving performance with respect to some business requirement.

Four Simple Steps

- **STEP 1** Identify the important y's for your project. These can be the variables identified through documenting the high level process and key requirements in SIPOC format. This would include customer and business requirements.
- **STEP 2** Identify the input and process variables that have a cause effect relationship with the project's primary metric (main y) and the other important y's chosen (secondary metrics). These can be the variables identified during the 'analyse' phase of the project, or additional work can be undertaken using tools that help identify cause effect relationships. (CE Diagram, XY Worksheet or CE Tree Diagram)
- **STEP 3** Choose relevant x's that have the most impact on the y's chosen for your monitoring plan. (CE Matrix)
- **STEP 4** Create a monitoring plan and display results in a relevant graphical way. (Monitoring Plan and a variety of charts and graphs)

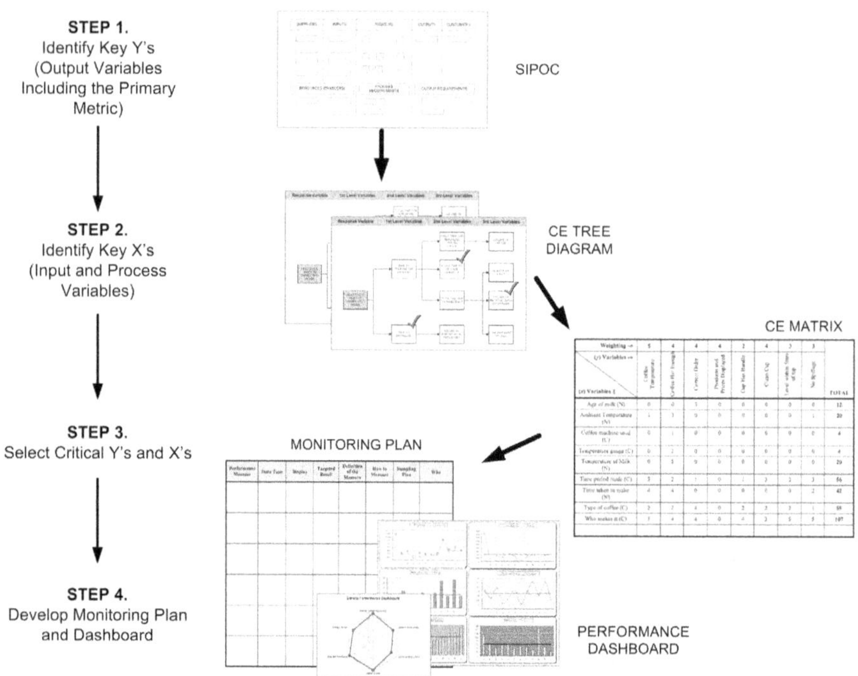

Figure 327: Sequence and Tools for Developing Monitoring Plans

DOCUMENT THE PROCESS WITH SIPOC

All of the work completed at this point can now be summarised into a model that shows the relationship of all key elements associated with the process including:

This model is most commonly referred to as a SIPOC, which is the acronym for Suppliers, Inputs, Process, Outputs and Customers.

SIPOC Format

The SIPOC is comprised of eight elements laid out in the following format.

<table>
<tr><th>Suppliers</th><th>Inputs</th><th>Process</th><th>Outputs</th><th>Customers</th></tr>
<tr><td>(who supplies the inputs)</td><td>(the inputs required to be able to produce the outputs of the process)</td><td>(a high level macro process map)</td><td>(the tangible products or services provided to the customer)</td><td>(the recipient/s of the outputs defined)</td></tr>
<tr><th colspan="2">Input Requirements</th><th>Business Requirements</th><th colspan="2">Customer Requirements</th></tr>
<tr><td colspan="2">(the requirements that must be met by suppliers for relevant inputs)</td><td>(the requirements the business related to specific business needs)</td><td colspan="2">(the requirements the customer has of the outputs provided - must be met to prevent a 'defect' being experienced)</td></tr>
</table>

Figure 328: SIPOC Format

Sequence For Documenting Processes in SIPOC Form

The SIPOC is created in the following sequence:

- **STEP 1** **P**rocess boundaries are established and the high level process is mapped. (Process Flowcharts)
- **STEP 2** **O**utputs are defined – by identifying outputs first, the team can then have a discussion around who is the real customer of those outputs. Outputs are the tangible products or services provided by the process.
- **STEP 3** **C**ustomers are identified – the people who receive your tangible products or services.
- **STEP 4** **I**nputs to the process are listed – now that you know the process and its outputs, you are able to identify the inputs you need to create the outputs. Inputs include materials that are consumed or transformed and information or data. Whilst also inputs, fixed resources enable the transformation of inputs to take place and are grouped separately as 'resources'.
- **STEP 5** **S**uppliers of these inputs are identified – having identified the inputs, the identification of suppliers is quite easy.
- **STEP 6** **R**equirements of the CUSTOMER are specified with respect to the output (product or service) and the process itself. (Customer Comments Translation, CTQ Tree Diagram)
- **STEP 7** **R**equirements of the BUSINESS are specified.
- **STEP 8** **R**equirements related to your INPUTS are specified.

The documentation of these key elements in a SIPOC sets you up to identify your key output variables (y's) for your performance monitoring plan.

PROCESS MAPPING

To map the process you will use flowcharts. Flowcharts are graphical representations of the sequence of steps in a process.

What is the purpose of flowcharting? By graphically representing the steps in a process, a team will be able to:

- Clarify the steps and sequence of events
- Generate common understanding within a team of operators
- Identify improvement opportunities such as complexities, delays, reworks, bottlenecks and waste
- Make problems in the process more obvious
- Reveal to the team how the process *really* works

Process Mapping - First or Last Step

One thing worth considering is that this is the step where time can vary considerably, if only due to differences in opinions on what the process actually looks like. Individuals will have a different view of the process based on their level of interaction with it. I have found it useful to sometimes save this, the most challenging work until all of the other work in completing the SIPOC is finalised. If you intend capturing a detailed flowchart, it may serve you at this point to only bound the process by identifying the start and end points, complete all other aspects of the SIPOC and then return and finish the process flowchart.

Processes Within Processes

Before we discuss the different types of flowcharts, it is important that we explain the concept of **processes within processes**.

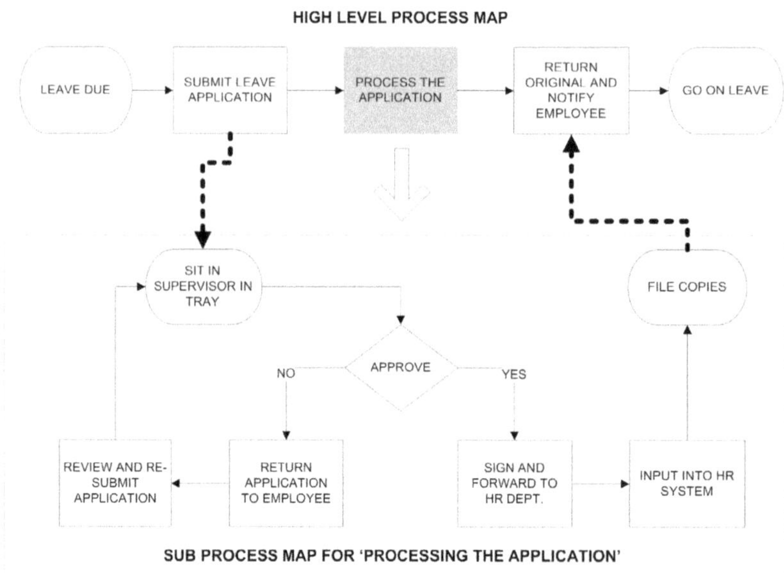

Figure 329: Processes within Processes

If we take a look at the process in the diagram above, we see that at the highest level the entire leave application process for this company can be mapped in 5 steps.

This is possible when we map the higher level groupings of all the little steps that occur in this process. These groupings can then be broken down into sub-processes as shown in the diagram. The 'process application' step can be broken down further into 7 steps that occur between 'submitting the leave application' and 'returning the original to the employee'.

The process could be broken down even further if required. For example, we could take the step of 'input into the HR system' and break it down into a sequence of more detailed steps.

Tip for Dealing With Excessive Detail

The level that people interact with a process will determine how high a level they think of the process in terms of steps. For example, if I asked the CEO of Boeing how many steps in creating a Boeing 747 aircraft, he might tell me 7 steps. That is the level of his interaction. If I asked the engineer who assembles the components of the fuselage how many steps are there in creating a Boeing 747, he would probably tell me thousands because that is his level of interaction.

This often poses challenges for teams when trying to map at the highest level. The Black Belt will ask for the steps in the process at the highest level and often get the micro steps from the team.

So rather than try and force them to think at a higher level, the most useful tool to use is the Affinity Storyboard. Let the team throw forth the steps at their thinking level, and then if it is micro in nature, ask them to group them into logical categories and give those categories a process step name.

You will be surprised how easy it is to get back to the high level.

Flowchart Types

There are many different types of flowcharts, the most common include:

- High Level Flowchart
- Detailed Activity Flowchart
- Cross Functional Flowchart
- Work Flowcharts

At this point we will only discuss the high level flowchart and activity flowchart.

High Level Flowchart

The high level flowchart is a representation of the steps in a process at the macro level.

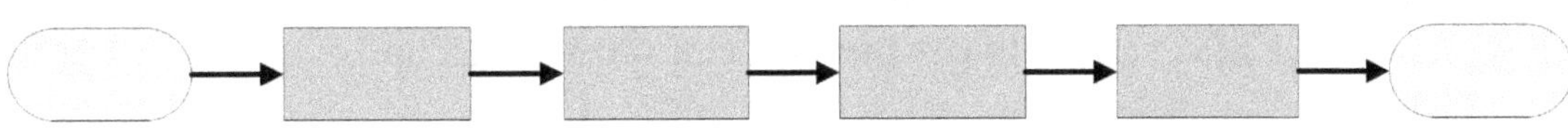

Figure 330: High Level Flowchart

High-level flowcharting identifies the macro steps so that you and your team can view and understand the sequence of events that occur in the process you are working on. The SIPOC was never really intended to be a tool for communicating 'standard operating procedures' to operators. However, if it serves you to do that, then go ahead and use a more detailed process flowcharting approach. My preference is to use the high level flowchart at this point in a project.

Just in case your preference is to document the process at a more detailed activity level, let's also review the activity flowchart.

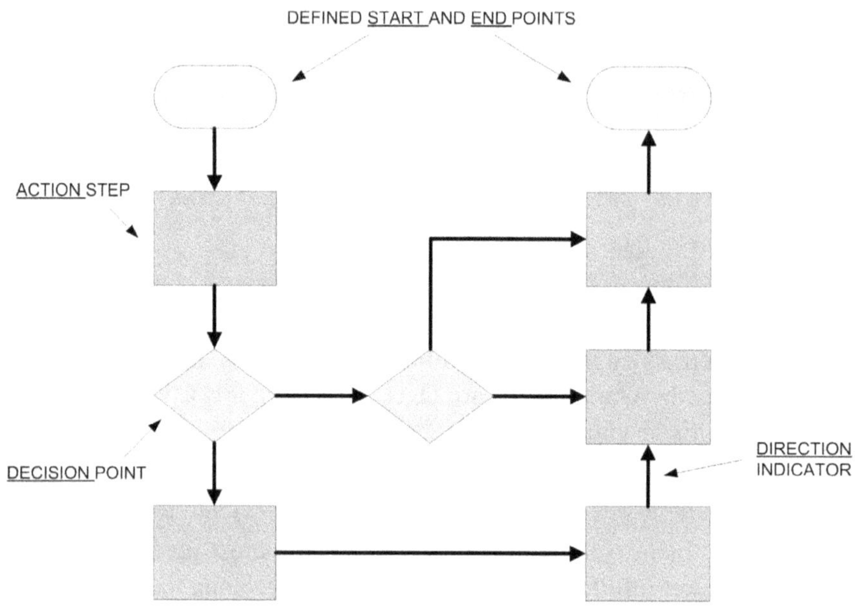

Figure 331: Activity Flowchart

Activity Flowchart

An **activity flowchart** on the other hand (shown on the previous page) presents process information at a more detailed activity based level. It may well comprise the sub-steps from one or more of the steps in the high level flowchart.

Methods of Facilitation

The high level flowchart is created by documenting the 5 to 10 step high level (macro) process you have been working on. You can approach this as a facilitator in a number of different ways, depending very much on the process being mapped and the thought processes of the group. I have found that the closer to the work the team members are, the more detailed the team tends to be in terms of the steps they describe in the process.

- **Sequential** – The facilitator asks the group to identify the first step in the sequence, then the next step and so on until all steps are identified. This is useful when the group is able to think at the macro process level.
- **Brainstormed Steps** – The facilitator asks the group to identify all of the steps as they come to mind, these steps are then arranged in chronological order.
- **Storyboarding** – The steps are brainstormed, these are then grouped into categories, the categories are given titles [as action steps], and then arranged chronologically. These titles form the steps at the macro level. This is particularly useful when the group generates a large number of micro level steps.

It is obvious that there are many more steps within each of the steps shown, however there is no need to identify any more than the 5 to 10 steps at this point in time. These individual macro level steps can be broken down further into sub-processes as required later when we understand more about where to focus our efforts.

Processes That People Do Not Follow All Of The Time

Problems often occur when people do not follow the designated process. So what is happening in the process? Quite simply, a decision making step has been introduced by those using the process.

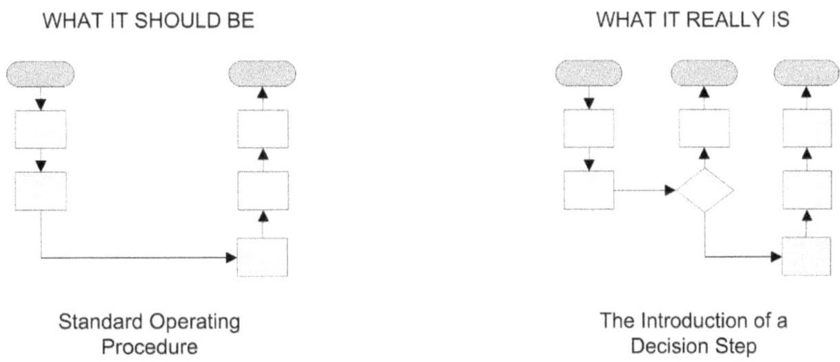

Figure 332: Unplanned Decision Steps in Processes

I worked with a mining business in Western Australia where staff were on most occasions, failing to forward the first part of a safety incident report to relevant supervisors. Whilst the desired process was clear in the requirement, users had introduced a decision making step – 'do I forward part 1 of the form'. If the answer was yes, the form was forwarded, if the answer was no, then the form was not forwarded.

When mapping a process where multiple courses of action are taking place, you will need to have a discussion around where the additional decision making steps have been introduced.

Processes That Include Waiting Time Or Queueing Time

Process mapping on the first pass may miss waiting or queueing steps. This becomes obvious when you start to undertake value analysis in the process analysis stage.

Options – identify another step, include the time frame in the original step – benefits of identifying a separate step is that you can focus on eliminating the step or making it as efficient as possible.

Four Levels Of Process

There are four levels of process which are described in the following table.

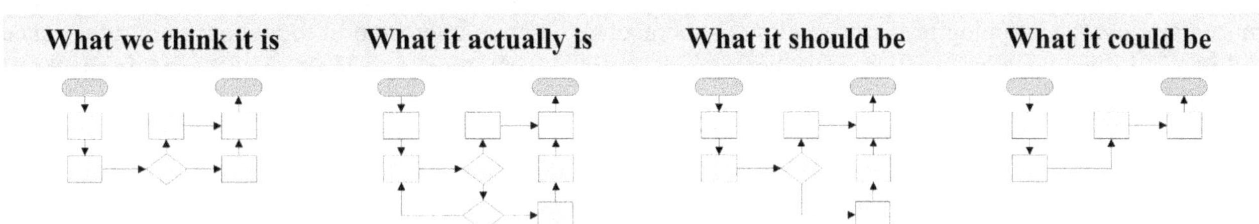

This is our first pass process map developed by the team	This is the 'as is' process map refined through (a) validation with the people who work in or with the process, or (b) by actually following the steps in the process itself	This is the new process created during the 'improve' phase of our project	This is a process developed through the use of 'Process Design' tools

Table 63: Four Levels of Process

A common mistake teams tend to make is to map a process as they think it 'should be'. It is essential that the team identifies the **'As Is'** process, hence the need to validate after the initial mapping session.

THE CUSTOMER AS THE CENTRAL THEME

As I've said many times, Lean Six Sigma is a strategy for continually improving work processes. Thus, process documentation is a fundamental skill for all teams working on Lean Six Sigma projects. Now a process is simply a series or sequence of steps that takes inputs and turns them into outputs.

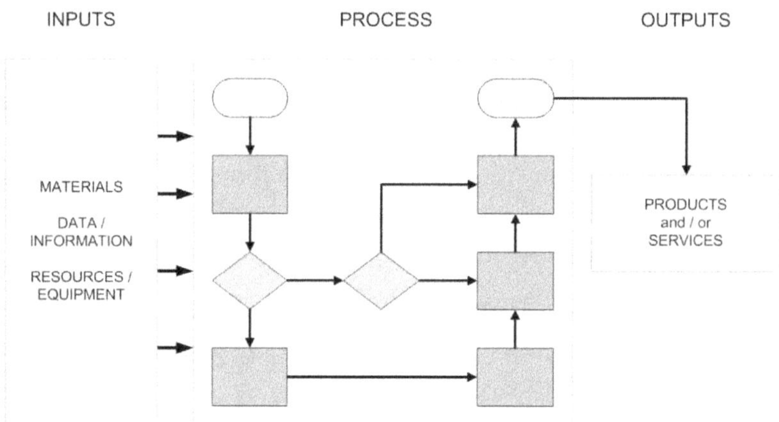

Figure 333: Basic Process Components

Processes are all around us in our everyday working and personal lives, and we participate in many ways at (a) the input level, (b) the process itself and (c) at the output level. Documenting the process at this time is more than just the mapping of the process steps themselves. We are interested in the whole spectrum, hence the need to document information regarding inputs, outputs, customers and their specific requirements of outputs produced.

Identifying The Customer

'Six sigma quality is built around the customer. Everything starts and ends with ..... customers. They define quality and set expectations. They rightfully expect performance, reliability, competitive prices, on time delivery, service and clear and accurate transaction processing.'

Dr. Mikel Harry

Total quality management is focused on the requirements of the customer. On the personal front, people only go back to restaurants that fully satisfy them and they shop regularly at stores that meet their needs. They fly on airlines that provide friendly, efficient service.

A good friend of mine always says: "Businesses exist to create value for customers, the consequence of doing that well is financial profit." Whilst some might debate those words, the principle of adding value to customers is a key one. Assuming there is a market, if *you* add more value than your competitor you will be financially rewarded.

Radisson Resort Led by Example

It has been my pleasure over the long period between 2000 and 2012 to have hosted seminars at the Radisson Resort on the Gold Coast in Queensland, Australia. The service at this venue was always outstanding. Both General Managers of the hotel during this period, Xerxes and Gerard, who became close friends, were continually focused on adding value to the customer. Resort staff lived by their motto – 'Yes We Can'. As a result the resort had proven a very popular conference location.

I not only continued to use the facility for seminars, but promoted the venue to my acquaintances and friends and planned to use the facility for the delivery of additional services offered by our company. Their focus on adding value to the customer has already resulted in long-term financial benefits for them and a strong relationship with us.

Customer Retention

Most organisations give the bulk of their focus to acquiring new customers, and very little on retaining existing customers. Studies[43] have shown that existing customers are worth as much as 5 times more than new customers, and the costs of retaining a current customer is only 25 percent of the cost of acquiring a new customer.

Lowenstein[44] says that the life cycle of a customer can be defined in 5 stages:

1. **Acquisition** – converting a prospect or potential customer to a customer, usually high cost
2. **Retention** – keeping the existing customer, about 25 percent of the cost of acquiring a new customer
3. **Attrition** – as dissatisfaction creeps in, customer enthusiasm for the company's products or services fade
4. **Defection** – loss of the customer
5. **Reacquisition** – once again acquiring the customer but at a much higher cost

According to Simmerman (1993)[45], by retaining 5% more of their existing customers, a company can increase profits by 100 percent.

Types of Customers

There are two main types of customers – internal and external. External customers can be further subdivided into Primary, Secondary and Intermediate Customers. The relationship that a company develops with either of these basic types determines the company's ability to be effective in delivering customer satisfaction.

---

[43] Industrial Engineering, (February 1995), *"Emphasize Customer Retention over Customer Acquisition"*, Industrial Engineering

[44] Lowenstein, M.W. (1995), *Customer Retention: An integrated Process for Keeping Your Best Customers*, Milwaukee: ASQ Quality Press

[45] Simmerman, S.J. (November, 1993), *"Achieving Service Quality Improvements"*, Quality Progress

Internal Customers

Kaoru Ishikawa (1985)[46] coined the phrase 'the next operation as customer' in order to remove the barriers that existed between departments.

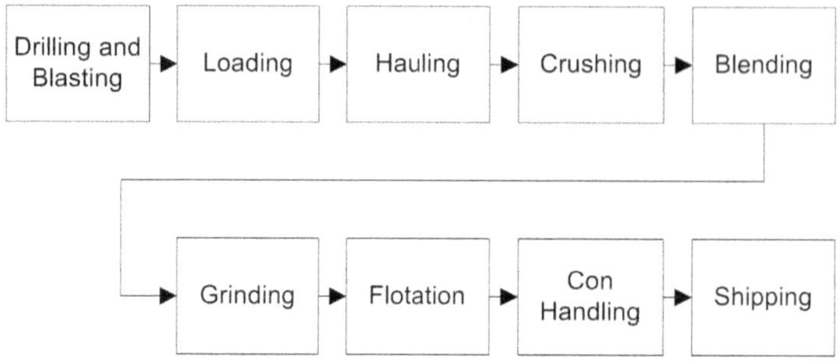

Figure 334: Primary Value Chain for a Copper Mine

When we view the value chain of an organisation, we see that it comprises a series of processes. Each process provides outputs to their internal customers – the next process in line. The outputs of one process are effectively the inputs of the next in line process. Each of these processes also receives inputs from other suppliers.

The value chain example shows the series of processes involved in transforming ore into metal concentrate at a copper mine. Each process step produces outputs that are the inputs to the next process in the sequence. Thus, the next process step is the internal customer of the upstream process step.

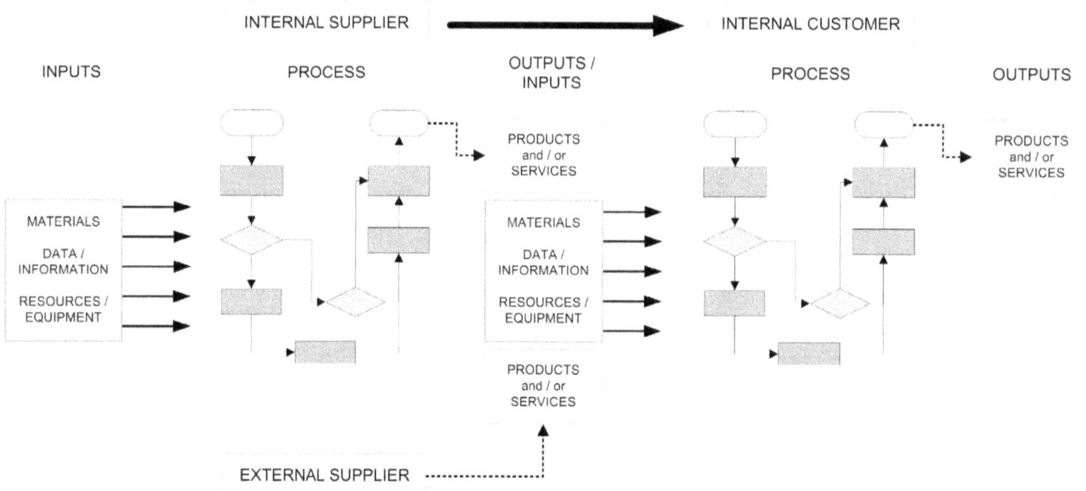

Figure 335: Internal Suppliers and Internal Customers

An internal customer has the same range of emotions as a personal customer when disappointed, cheated or short-changed. Where an internal customer pays for the service provided by an internal supplier, their

46 Ishikawa, K. (1985). *What is Total Quality Control, The Japanese Way*, Englewood Cliffs, NJ: Prentice hall.

response to poor service is often similar to that of an external customer – business is taken to a supplier who can meet their service and product requirements.

It is not uncommon to forget about our internal customers, possibly due to the fact that in most situations, no transaction (sales) takes place upon receipt of our outputs. If we treated all of our internal customers as paying customers, the focus might be more appropriate. Always remember, an internal customer today might well be a supplier tomorrow and what goes around comes around.

External Customers

External customers include three types:

- Primary customers
- Secondary customers
- Intermediate customers

Primary Customers

The primary customer is ultimately the recipient of the tangible goods or services that the process produces. Primary customers can also be called 'end users'. For example:

- A woman who goes into a motor vehicle dealer's showroom and buys a new vehicle is a primary customer – as she is paying for the product she has the right to place requirements on the quality of the vehicle and the service offered.

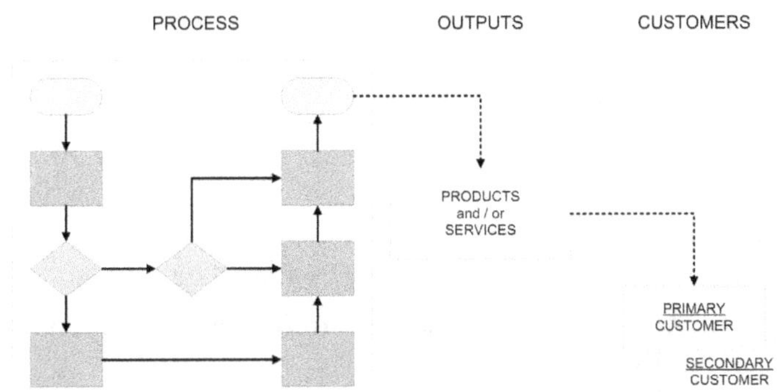

Figure 336: Process with Primary and Secondary Customers

Secondary Customers

Secondary customers are those who benefit indirectly via the primary customer's acquisition of a product or service. They are not the recipient of products or services in the first instance, however they are impacted by the purchase of the product or service. For example:

- The husband and children are secondary customers to the mother buying a new car.

Intermediate Customers

According to Geddes (1993)[47], intermediate customers purchase the product or service from the supplier, and then resell, repackage, assemble, or modify the product or service for sale to primary customers.

[47] Geddes, L. (1993), *Through the Customer's Eyes*, New York: AMACOM

Whilst providing additional sales opportunities for a business, the intermediate customers will also have requirements in addition to the Primary customers of the product or service. The concept of 'customers' customers' is relevant here, and is mentioned later in this chapter.

Examples of intermediate customers include:

- Retailers
- Wholesalers
- Distributors
- Manufacturers' representatives
- Transport companies

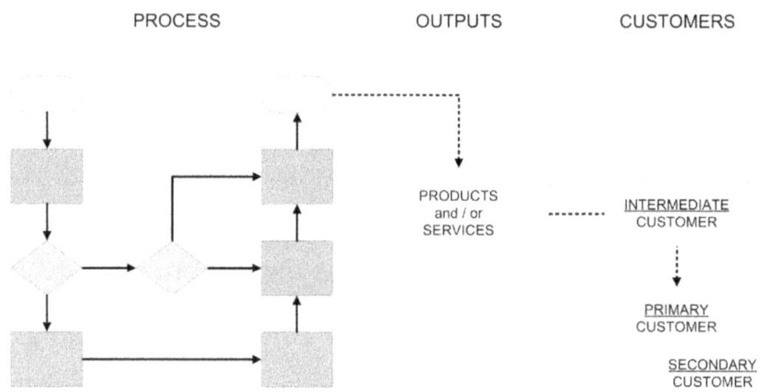

Figure 337: Process with Intermediate Customers

<u>The Business as a Customer</u>

The business itself is a beneficiary of the process. Whilst it does not receive the goods or services as a user, it does benefit from sales and the resulting profit generated by the process.

In this case, I like to refer to the business as a **tertiary customer**. Now as a tertiary customer, the business will have requirements of the process associated with:

- Costs
- Sales
- Margins / profits
- Return on investment / payback etc

Often a process improvement project will be selected on the basis of business requirements. For example, a process may be selected for a focus on cost reduction. In this scenario, the focus of the project team will be on meeting new business requirements without compromising customer requirements.

DEFINING CUSTOMER REQUIREMENTS

Customers' requirements drive the process. Requirements are the measures against which you can determine whether or not your process is ultimately satisfying the needs of its customers. A process that cannot satisfy customers' needs has no value to anyone, including the business itself.

So what is a requirement? In the context of Lean Six Sigma, a requirement can be defined this way:

Requirement: (*n*): *the specific and measurable characteristic that determines whether or not the customers' needs have been met*

Our work around identifying customers' requirements is for the purpose of answering two simple questions.

- *What requirements does the customer have of the output?* (the quality of the product or service)
- *What requirements does the customer have of the process?* (the quality of the customers interaction with the process)

It is useful to remember these two questions, as they might prove useful when interacting with customers, and when discussing customers' requirements with your project team.

Types Of Customer Requirements

Output requirements can be of two types.

- **Product Quality Requirements** refer to the qualities or features that customers expect of the end product.
- **Service Quality Requirements** refer to the qualities or features that customers expect of a service provided. These requirements may refer to efficiency characteristics such as cycle time.

Moments of Truth

Jan Carlzon, the former CEO of the Scandinavian airline company SAS, coined the phrase **'Moments of Truth'**. He learnt that customers focus on their interactions with a company's employees. Where these interactions did not meet their expectations, their loyalty was negatively impacted. These interactions usually occur during a step in some process and they are essentially a 'moment of truth' for the process in the eyes of the customer as the customer has expectations of the process as well as the process outputs. It is at these points that a customer can form an opinion about your company, either positive or negative.

Carlzon believed that his business was really made up of the points in time when the 10 million customers of SAS interacted with the company's employees. Interestingly enough, this equated to some 50 million 'moments of truth' for SAS airlines every year.

How do you identify and use the idea of moments of truth? One suggested approach is:

- To imagine yourself moving through the process as a customer
- Describe what you are doing and where you interact with the process
- Identify what could happen to cause the customer to form an opinion either good or bad about your company, and finally
- Identify what you can do in the short term and long term to delight the customer

These types of activities are integral to meeting customers' unstated expectations of the characteristics of an interaction with a process.

Business Requirements Versus Customer Requirements

The business itself will also have requirements of the product or process. These often remain unstated, however when a project is initiated by the business for the purpose of reducing risk or cost, these requirements will need to be clarified. These requirements will be quite different from the internal or external customer, and the following table provides examples to help show that difference.

Business	Customer
• Risk (safety, health, environment, production, financial etc) • Cost Per Unit (margins) • Cycle Time (to market, resolution etc) • HR Issues (morale)	• Value (value for money) • Product quality • Service quality • Cycle time (delivery, response etc)

The Process for Defining Customers' Requirements

Defining customer requirements involves four simple steps.

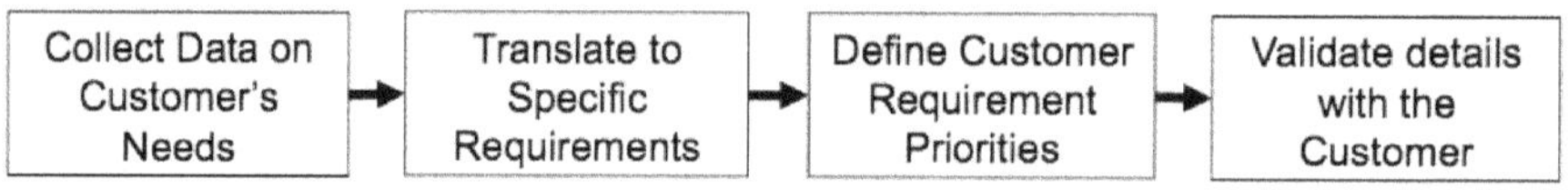

Figure 338: Four Steps to Defining Customers' Requirements

1. Collect Data on Customer Needs - A variety of approaches [both proactive and reactive] can be undertaken, including translation of customer comments, customer observation, being a customer, customer interaction and market research. Should data exist in respect of the requirements of customers, this should be analysed in the first instance for relevance. This data may exist *within* your organisation, or *externally* to your organisation. Always remember, customers' requirements are constantly changing in most cases as we continue to improve the products and services we offer. The output of this step is a list of customers' comments and / or needs.

2. Translate Needs to Specific Requirements - Comments are translated to identify the underlying needs. Needs are analysed further until requirements are defined. All three characteristics [specific, measurable and relevant] need to be included for the requirements to be effective measures against which to assess process performance.

3. Define Customer Requirement Priorities - Customers often have multiple needs that the product, service or process must satisfy. However, in acknowledging that not all can be fully satisfied, and not all needs are of equal importance, it is essential that those most important to the customer are the focus of your attention.

4. Validate Requirements - All requirements and any prioritisation work you do, **must** be validated with customers. An erroneous requirement may drive the focus of your work in the wrong direction. Alterations and additional specifics identified during the step should be included in the final list of prioritised requirement statements.

Collecting Data on Customer Needs

Any work previously done in respect of defining customer requirements will need to be reviewed. It makes no sense to undertake data collection when data already exists, unless that data is no longer valid. Customers' requirements can, and do change, therefore a mistake would be to only use existing data without validating its relevance.

Approaches

This step in the process can be quite difficult to get right. A number of different approaches can be undertaken to identify customers' requirements. I will discuss the following in this book.

- Customer Complaints
- Customer Comments
- Customer Observations
- Be a Customer
- Customer Interaction (Surveys, Interviews, Focus Groups)
- Market Research

Customers' Complaints

Complaints made by customers are a useful way to identify which of their requirements are not being met. Do you remember the last time you had an experience where your requirements were not met and you were unhappy with some product or service. Did you complain to the provider of the product or service? Research in the United States has shown that less than 1 in 10 customers actually complain.

Customers' Comments

Comments made by customers can provide an opportunity to identify the issues they are concerned with in respect to a product or service. These comments can be good or bad, complaints or compliments. Both types are useful, however the compliments are often overlooked. There is one drawback on relying on customer complaints to identify their requirements. As I said earlier, only a low proportion of dissatisfied customers ever complain. The complaints may not be representative of the needs or expectations of the majority of customers. In any case, customers are more likely to tell their friends and acquaintances, the result being that your organisation suffers credibility or reputation damage that you are never going to be conscious of until it is too late.

If we translate these comments into underlying needs [in the eyes of the customer], we will then be able to identify specific requirements that define how these needs are met.

Customer Observation

Another approach that can provide tremendous data on customer requirements is to observe customers as they use the products or services you offer. By seeing how they use the outputs, you may be able to identify what is and is not important to the customer.

This should not be confused with the concept of **'process observation'**. More than one of the major banks in Australia details observers to watch staff serving customers. The purpose of this is not to determine customer requirements, but rather to undertake assessment of staff in the performance of work. This is more about checking that customers' service requirements are being met, and that opportunities to sell additional products are being created.

Be a Customer

Observing the process through the customers' eyes or participating in the use of the service or product as an end user provides a different perspective and helps define requirements on the basis of experience.

At least one of the major airlines around today sends staff on international trips to experience the service currently being provided, and to identify the things that cause the customer the most grief. The concept of 'e-tickets' for airline travellers was developed by an airline using this approach.

Customer Interaction

Customer interaction is the most common method of identifying customer requirements.

This approach has one major drawback. Customers are often not able to define their requirements, as sometimes they just do not know what their requirements really are. One thing is certain however, when they are not met they become obvious to the customer.

I recall stories told to me about certain fast food chains that undertook surveys and/or focus groups to identify customer requirements with a view to improving existing and/or adding new products to their menus. Customers involved said they wanted pizza that was low fat and burgers with lean meat and healthy ingredients. The companies involved produced products that met these requirements, however they failed to sell. Now why do you suppose that was the case? These firms found out the hard way about **'positive response bias'**. This involves the customer making statements that make themselves or you feel good. They are positive statements, but do not necessarily represent that which the customer really wants. Those facilitating the identification of customer requirements through customer interaction should be aware of this bias.

There are a number of different approaches that can be taken, including:

Interview

A one on one conversation with a customer to establish the answers to specific, pre-prepared questions that help identify and validate what is important to them in respect to the process and its outputs.

Survey

A set of written questions is sent to customers so that they can answer using either their own words or standardised answers from a multiple choice scale. I have no doubt that we've all received calls from survey service providers – use of a specific product etc.

A University of Michigan statistician (Likert) showed that a scale of 1 to 5 is far more effective than a larger scale. When given choices from large scales (1 to 10), participants rarely use the whole range, instead tending to use the extremities of the scale (1 to 3, or 8 to 10). This scale is known as the Likert Scale, named after the statistician who developed it and is commonly used in the surveying of customers.

Focus Group

A group of customers are brought together to focus on answering some specific questions that will help define their requirements.

Market Research

Researching the types of requirements being met by other organisations' products or services may provide useful data on what customers want. Where those organisations experience a large market share, benchmarking will be a sound practice in identifying leading practice.

At least one hotel receives market research information about the types of conferences being requested, from what countries, etc.

Pros and Cons

A summary of the most common approaches and their advantages and disadvantages is shown in the following table.

Approach	Description	Advantages	Disadvantages
Survey	A set of specific questions answered by the customer using various forms of media	Face to face interaction Speed of data collection Inexpensive when conducted electronically	Limited response rates Lacks clarification Limited to fixed questions – inflexible Expensive and time consuming when conducted manually May not be representative – only very happy or very unhappy customers participate Generates post survey expectations
Interviews	One on one conversation to establish answers to specific questions.	Specific information – clarification Direct answers / accuracy Not influenced by group think	Time and cost Topic specific Idea restrictive Generates post interview expectations
Be a Customer	Observe or experience the product or service through the eyes of the customer.	Experience the actual service level Data is quickly available	Small sample size Provides challenges for employee role players to remain objective The role player already understands the jargon and requirements of the business
Observe the Customer	Observe customers to see how they use the product or service.	Low cost Non invasive	No clarification of observations Time consuming Observers may make assumptions
Customer Complaints	Comments passed on by customers when they are dissatisfied with your product or service.	Low cost Serious concerns can be captured	A totally reactive approach May not be representative of the majority of customers Focus is on the negative
Customer Comments	Comments passed on by customers, including complimentary comments	Low cost Serious concerns can be captured Both positive and negative comments are useful	A totally reactive approach May not be representative of the majority of customers

Approach	Description	Advantages	Disadvantages
Focus Group	A group of customers are brought together to focus on answering specific questions.	Different views can be gleaned from a cross section of customers Open format that encourages ideas Involves customers in an interactive way	May result in group think Time and cost May not be quantitative in a way useful for statistical analysis (requires thought and planning)
Market Research	Researching the broader market, both with own customers and with customers of competitors	Broader sample group Accurate data from a wider sample group Flexible targeting – specific or diverse	Expensive Time consuming Inflexibility when conducted by a service provider

Thinking About Customers' Customers

A concept that is not often thought about, but one that can add significant value to an organisation is the idea of focusing on the requirements of the customers' customers, or what could be referred to as 'Indirect Customers'.

Let's take the example of a producer of Liquid Crystal Displays (LCD). This type of customer is referred to in some reference materials as an 'Intermediary Customer'. Their 'Direct Customers' in this case are producers of equipment that have LCD's. These direct customers will have requirements around the product and the process that are relevant to the creation of their products, such as weight, dimensions, type of fittings, cycle time for delivery etc. The customers of these producers however, who are the indirect customers of the LCD producer, will have requirements in respect of the LCD's that differ to the equipment producers'. These requirements might include clarity, definition, colour etc.

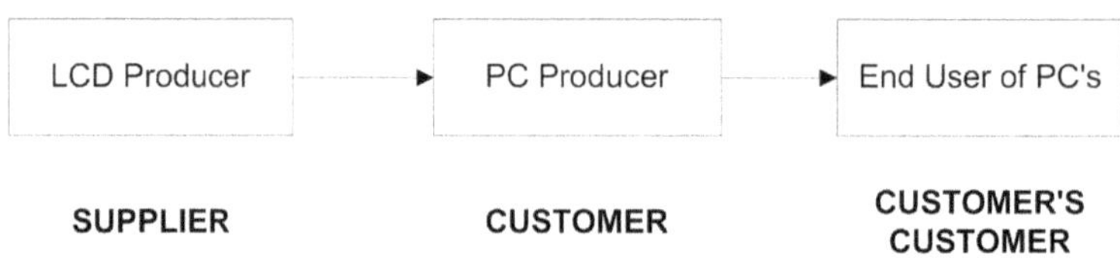

Figure 339: LCD Producer's Customer Chain

An LCD producer who is able to better meet the requirements of these indirect customers, whilst meeting the requirements of the direct customer, is more likely to sell their product. There is also a value add for the direct customer in that the final customers are more likely to buy their product over others.

The same set of tools can be used to determine the requirements of customers' customers, however the source of that data may change according to circumstances. Where the direct customer is not able to specify the requirements of the indirect customer, then it would be necessary for the producer to either find out from their indirect customer, or work with the direct customer in obtaining this information.

Translating Needs Into Requirements

Needs Versus Requirements

Before we go on, let's take a moment to look at the difference between a need and a requirement.

Needs, while indicating necessity, are usually quite broad in their form.

Need (*n*): *circumstances in which something is desired (I need time to myself), or that require some course of action (I need you to build this); a thing that is wanted (the customer needs to be safe)*

By contrast, a requirement is a much more specific element associated with the verb require.

Require (*v*): *specify as compulsory (the level of compliance required by law); (require something of) regarding an action, ability, or quality as due from (someone) by virtue of their position (the specific quality required of the company as a supplier)*

Customer Requirement: (*n*): *the specific and measurable characteristic that determines whether or not the customers' needs have been met*

Here are some examples that help demonstrate the difference and the relationship between customer needs and customer requirements as we might view it through the eyes of the customer.

CUSTOMER NEEDS	CUSTOMER REQUIREMENTS
I need: The correct length part	**My need will be met if:** The part is in the range of 25.5 mm to 26.5 mm in length
The task to be completed in a reasonable time frame	The task is completed within 20 minutes of commencement
Nothing higher than an acceptable level of impurities	The product has an impurity level of less than 0.25 percent
A moisture content that allows consistent flow	Moisture content is not less than 15 percent and not greater than 20 percent
Simple documentation	The documentation does not exceed the maximum length of 1 double sided page

Figure 340: Customer Needs Versus Customer Requirements

Extracting Needs and Requirements With Good Questions

The key to identifying needs and requirements is to ask good quality questions. These are probably the most useful questions I have found for this work when talking to customers.

- *'What is it that you need?'*
- *'What would it take to meet that need?'* OR *'How would I know when I have met your need?'*

Crafting Requirement Statements

The final thing we need to really understand about requirements is the characteristics of a well-worded requirement. Crafted well, a requirement will exhibit four characteristics.

- **Specific** – referring to one characteristic or feature only, multiple characteristics or features dilute the ability to effectively measure the requirement.

- **Measurable** – phrased in measurable and / or observable terms, when a requirement is in this format it is easy to determine whether or not the requirement has or has not been met. Ultimately it will be 'sensory rich' in that you can use one of the senses to measure.
- **Yes or No Evaluation** – the answer to the question: "Did we meet this requirement?" is either yes we did, or no we did not.
- **Relevant** – linked to a specific product, service feature or moment of truth relevant to the process, a requirement that is not linked is not meaningful in measuring the performance of the process.

These questions may assist in assessing the wording of your customers' requirements.

- *'Will we be able to test whether or not the requirement has been met?'*
- *'Is this requirement easy to understand?'*
- *'Is this requirement a reflection of what the customer really needs of our product or service?'*

Critical to Quality Tree Diagram

If a product or service meets or exceeds a customer's requirements, then a specific need or needs is being satisfied. There is a clear relationship between needs and requirements. For example, my need for timely transport to the airport is satisfied if I am picked up at the agreed time and delivered to the airport no later than 45 minutes prior to boarding. My need for safe transport is satisfied if we have no safety incidents en-route to the airport. My need for comfortable transport is satisfied if the temperature is between 20 and 24 degrees Celsius in the motor vehicle.

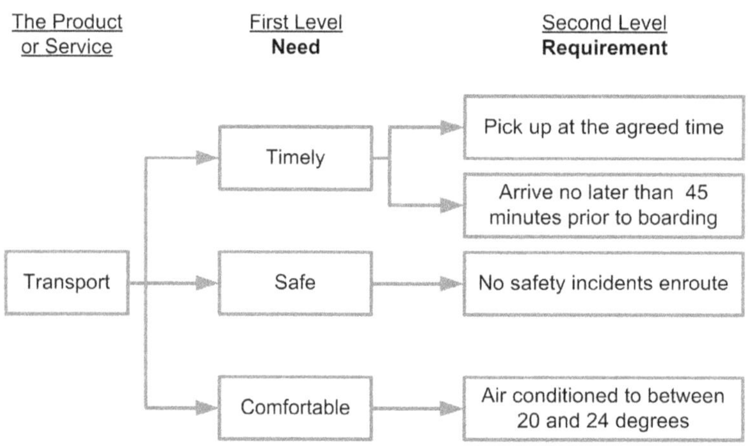

Figure 341: CTQ Tree Diagram

A useful way to get to specific requirements and measures is to use a CTQ Tree Diagram. Much like a tree chart, the approach progressively gets more detailed as you move left to right, and is based on the known relationships that exist between the product or service, the needs that the customer has of the product or service, and the specific requirements that if met would ensure that the customers' needs were satisfied.

Case Study – the Coffee Shop

The first step was to identify needs and respective requirements associated with the product, (cup of coffee) and the coffee making process itself.

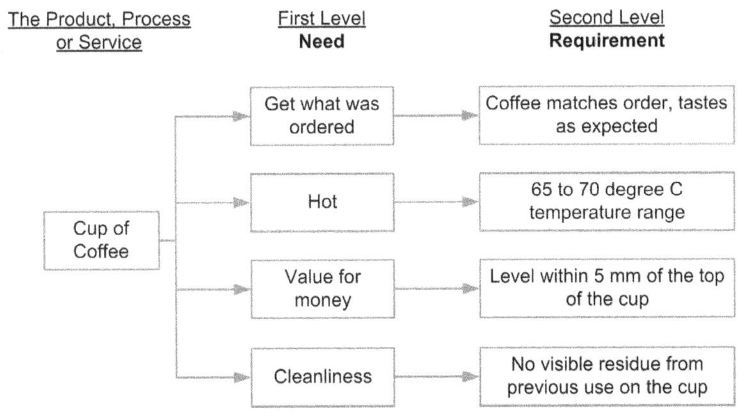

Figure 342: Case Study - Product Requirements

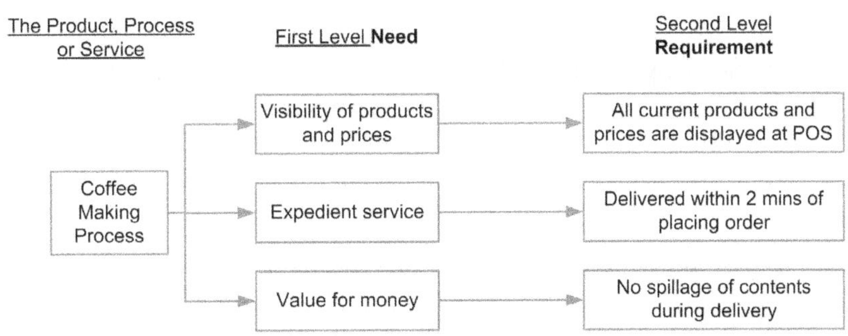

Figure 343: Case Study - Process Requirements

Translating Customer Comments Into Requirements

Often customers will make comments about a product or service. Both good and bad comments provide clues as to what the customer really wants. I had the fortunate experience of working with a processing plant that received ore from another functional area of the company. The recoveries of saleable product from the ore they received were extremely inconsistent. The variation in their performance was something that they found very frustrating. However, when I asked the process owners what they required to get the best out of the material they received, they could not tell me.

During our discussion I asked them about the best month they had ever experienced. In answer to a specific question about what they liked about the material they received, a comment made was: "we loved the consistency in the grade of the material". Now this comment provided a clue to their true requirements – (a) to receive consistent grade material, and (b) to be notified 24 hours ahead of time of the grade of the material coming.

Below are some more examples of how comments can be translated into specific requirements using a tool called a 'Customer Comments Worksheet'.

Comments	Needs Being / Not Being Met	Specific Requirement
"I always have to wait in line too long"	Reasonable Queueing Time	Queue for no longer than 5 minutes
"These things never last long"	Reasonable Product Life cycle	A life cycle of no less than 6 months
"When I leave the writing on the white board for longer than an hour, it won't erase fully, leaving smudge marks"	Ability to erase	100% same day erasure without residue
"I hate it when I have to run to catch a connection"	On time exit from the plane	To exit from the plane no later than 15 minutes after the scheduled arrival time
"I usually hang up when I keep getting redirected."	Number of reconnections to desired service point	No more than 2 connections to get to inquiry destination

Customer Comment Worksheet

You may notice that the underlying need is often worded in such a way as to describe an attribute of the process or outputs. Some of the most **common underlying needs** are usually linked to the following characteristics:

- Cycle time / Speed
- Availability
- Access
- Usability
- Quality
- Accuracy
- Completeness
- Efficiency
- Understandability
- Maintainability

Some **common mistakes** that you need to avoid during this work are:

- When determining underlying needs, end up identifying causes of problems
- When determining the specific requirement, end up identifying solutions

Always remember that this is **not** a root cause analysis, nor is it a mechanism for identifying solutions to treat root causes.

The following questions are useful in determining inputs to each of the columns.

- **Comments -** What is the customer saying about the process or outputs? (can be both good or bad comments) There may be some need to probe for deeper meaning so that the comment is better understood. For example, if the customer at a restaurant said, "This meal sucks", you would need to delve deeper so that the comment makes some sense. The customer's comment may well mean that they did not get the meal at a suitable temperature.
- **Underlying Needs -** What is the underlying need of the customer? OR What is the need of the customer that is not / is being met? In the case of our restaurant customer, the need that is not being met is the need for a hot meal.

- **Requirements** - What are the specific requirements of the customer that if met, would ensure satisfaction of their needs? Our restaurant customer might be satisfied if the meal is delivered within 2 minutes of it being cooked, as this would ensure that the meal was hot.

Instructions for using the Customer Comments Worksheet are detailed in the Control Toolkit in the next chapter.

Case Study – the Coffee Shop

The second step taken was to analyse the comments of the customer. The most relevant are reflected in the worksheet.

Comments	Needs Being / Not Being Met	Specific Requirement
"I wish the coffee was hotter"	Hot Coffee	Hot enough that it can not be drunk without sipping
"I love the way the swirl of colour occurs in the latte"	Aesthetically pleasing	Coffee and milk layers visible at delivery (for latte)
"I cannot drink the latte when you give it to me in a cup with no handle"	Ability to hold the cup of coffee with ease	Coffee delivered in a cup with a handle

Case Study - Customer Comments

Some of the comments are relevant to the output of the process, while some are relevant to the process itself. Needs and requirements are now transferred from here to our requirements tables.

Prioritising Customer Requirements

Why Prioritise?

Customers often have multiple needs that the output or process must ideally satisfy. However, it is often not possible to satisfy all of these. Take the case of software developers for example. Customers have multiple needs that they would like satisfied in respect of software products, however, not all needs are going to be able to be satisfied fully. For example, a software developer may have to consider the needs of the customer with respect to usability of the software, its capability, reliability, ease of installation, ability to upgrade, and even the quality of documentation that accompanies the software. What is quite simple to install and use may not have the capability of more complex software.

In recognising that not all needs may be fully satisfied, it is essential that those most important to the customer are the focus of our attention.

How To Prioritise

There are a two different methods we use for prioritising.

- Numbered Prioritisation
- Kano Analysis

Numbered Prioritisation

Prioritisation is often determined by the needs of the customer. For example, prioritisation based on needs is an approach taken by some software developing companies. One of the reasons they take this approach is due to the fact that they produce many different products, however customers essentially have similar 'needs' in respect of software. In the example shown below, customers' software associated needs have been prioritised according to a numbered scale.

Priority	Need
1	**Usability** – how user friendly is the software
2	**Capability** – the capability of the software relevant to the designed functionality
3	**Reliability** – how reliable the software is with respect to continuous use without crashing
4	**Install-ability** – how easy the software is to install
5	**Upgrade-ability** – the ease with which the software can be upgraded
6	**Instructions** – the quality of the instructions / help system that accompanies the software

Numbered Prioritisation Example

As with all prioritisation, three things must be considered:

- Prioritisation must be validated with customers
- Customer priorities may change over time
- Additional needs, thus requirements may be introduced later

Case Study - the Coffee Shop

In the coffee shop example, the customers' needs have been prioritised on the basis of the order in which they wanted needs met.

Priority	Needs	Requirements
1	To get what was ordered	Coffee matches order – tastes as expected
2	Cleanliness	No visible residue from previous use on the cup
3	Hot	65 to 70 degree (Celsius) temperature range
4	Value for money	Level within 5mm of top of cup No spillage of contents during delivery
5	Expedient service	Delivered within 2 minutes of placing order
6	Visibility of products and prices	All current products and prices are displayed at point of sale
7	To be able to hold the hot cup of coffee with ease	Coffee delivered in a cup with a handle
8	Aesthetically pleasing	Coffee and milk layers visible at delivery (for latte)

Case Study - Customer Priorities by Numbers

Numbered prioritisation has its place, though it is not my preferred method. The principles of Kano Analysis provide a more effective method for prioritisation in this case.

Kano Analysis

Dr Noriaki Kano, who was a key participant in the Japanese quality movement, is well known for his 'Kano Model'. It is a useful model when undertaking work with Quality Function Deployment, process design and any research and development of products or services.

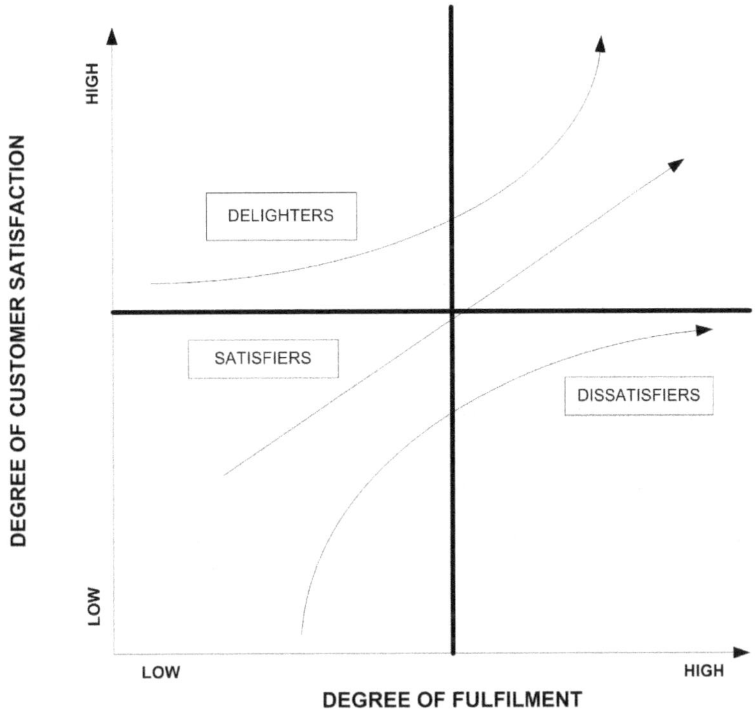

Figure 344: Kano Model

Dr Kano recognised that customer requirements could be divided into three categories.

- **Dissatisfiers** – These are the requirements that Dr Kano says "must be" met, and are sometimes called the 'basic requirements'. Customers may not notice if they are met, however, they will not buy the product or service if they are not met. For example, having hot water in your motel room is a basic requirement. It is not something that you necessarily notice. However, if it does not work then you would most likely be extremely dissatisfied.

  Any requirement that causes the customer to be totally *dissatisfied* when it is not met, and *neutral* when met falls into this category.

- **Satisfiers** – These requirements are sometimes called 'variable or performance requirements', the better your performance in meeting these, the better your customer satisfaction. Dr Kano refers to these as the "more is better" requirements. For example, the service given to me at the Radisson Resort on the Gold Coast in Australia is friendlier and more efficient than at other conference venues I have used. On the basis of that, I am more satisfied by the service offered at that venue than others.

  If your 'basic requirements' are being met, then many of the requirements you identify in your Six Sigma project work will fall within this category.

  When a customer's level of satisfaction or dissatisfaction is determined by how well the requirement is met, this requirement falls into this category.

- **Delighters** - These are sometimes called 'latent requirements'. These are features or characteristics of a product or service that the customer does not express. They go beyond the expectations of the customer, and are often not known by the customer. For example, I bought an LG television and it had a feature called a 'natural algorithm eye' that adjusted the screen's contrast according to the ambient light. I was absolutely delighted with the feature, however, I had no requirements of this in the first instance.

  Any requirement that causes the customer to be *delighted* when it is met, and *neutral* when it is not met falls into this category.

Kano Analysis requires continued work as the requirements of customers change over time. What was once a delighter may ultimately become a 'basic requirement'. I would now only buy a television that has an automatic contrast adjustment for ambient light, yet it is something that I never knew about a short time ago.

You may remember a time when a radio or a car air conditioner was a delighter to a car buyer. It has now become standard fitting in most vehicles, and I would dare to say that most people would not buy a car without these being installed. What was once a delighter is now a basic requirement.

Even if you had recently done a Kano Analysis, you might need to do it again.

This approach can be taken by simply prioritising needs on the basis of their fit within each of the categories described by Dr. Kano.

The following table provides a guide for prioritising using an alphabetical rating.

Category	Description	Rating
Must be met / Must haves	Requirements that must be met – critical to quality	**A**
Should be met / Should haves	Requirements that should be met, the more the better	**B**
Nice to meet / Nice to haves	Requirements that are nice to meet however have virtually no impact on customer satisfaction	**C**

Guide for Prioritisation Using Principles of the Kano Model

Case Study - the Coffee Shop

So let's take a second look at the coffee shop example. In the previous activity, customers' needs were prioritised in the numbered order in which they wanted needs met. Now let's prioritise using the Kano approach.

Priority	Needs	Requirements
A	To get what was ordered	Coffee matches order – tastes as expected
A	Hot	65 to 70 degree (Celsius) temperature range
A	Visibility of products and prices	All current products and prices are displayed at point of sale
A	To be able to hold the hot cup of coffee with ease	Coffee delivered in a cup with a handle
A	Cleanliness	No visible residue from previous use on the cup
B	Value for money	Level within 5mm of top of cup No spillage of contents during delivery
B	Expedient service	Delivered within 2 minutes of placing order
C	Aesthetically pleasing	Coffee and milk layers visible at delivery (for latte)

Case Study - Customer Priorities Using The Kano Model

Prioritising Requirements Directly

There may be occasions when prioritisation of requirements themselves may be more appropriate. One case may be where multiple requirements contribute to the satisfaction of a single need. For example, if I have a need for high performance in a motor vehicle, my requirements might be specific to acceleration, braking, and top speed.

CASE STUDY – THE COFFEE SHOP

<table>
<tr><th>Suppliers</th><th>Inputs</th><th colspan="2">Process</th><th>Outputs</th><th>Customers</th></tr>
<tr>
<td>Council
Parmalat via Coles
Ambrosia Coffee
Various via Coles
Ambrosia Coffee

Customer
Ambrosia Coffee
Us

Latavia
Us
Us
Us
Us</td>
<td>Materials
Water
Milk
Coffee Beans
Condiments
Foam cups
Data / Info
Customer order
Recipe
Menu
Resources
Coffee machine
Staff
Ceramic cups
Utensils
Temperature probe</td>
<td colspan="2">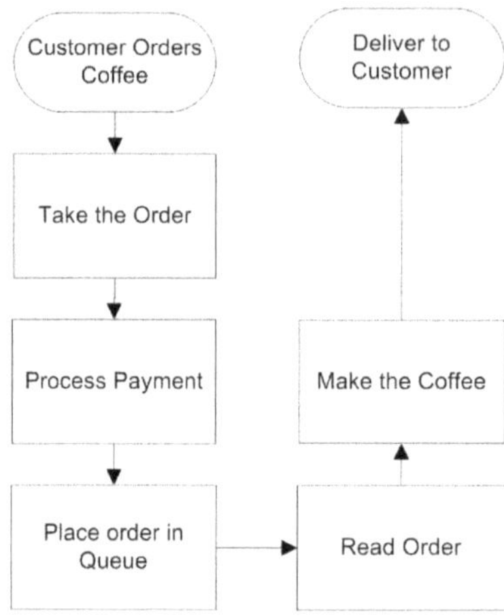
</td>
<td>Cup of Coffee (milk based latte, flat white, cappuccino etc)</td>
<td>Coffee Connoisseurs</td>
</tr>
<tr><th colspan="2">Input Requirements</th><th colspan="2">Business Requirements</th><th colspan="2">Customer Requirements</th></tr>
<tr>
<td colspan="2">• Mill produced within last 24 hours
• Bags of Coffee – sealed and within 'use by period'
• Foam Cups – no holes and 3 standard sizes (S R L)
• Customer order is legible
• Cup warming facilities with machine</td>
<td colspan="2">• Zero discards
• Zero spillage
• Zero breakages
• Zero injuries to staff or customers</td>
<td colspan="2">• A. Coffee matches order, tastes as expected
• A. 65-70 degree (Celsius) temperature range
• A. All products and prices visible at point of sale
• A. Delivered in cup with handle
• A. No visible residue from previous use (clean)
• B. Level within 5mm of top
• B. No spillage during delivery
• B. Delivered within 2 minutes
• C. Coffee / milk layers visible</td>
</tr>
</table>

Figure 345: SIPOC Example

IDENTIFYING AND SELECTING MEASURES

Measurement Principles

When determining what to measure at this point in your project, remember these principles.

What You Measure You Will Get

Measures will drive behaviour, so consider carefully what behaviours will result from the measures you choose. This is an all too common problem in organisations structured on the basis of functions. Let me give you an example. A mining company built around underground coal mining, has a number of core functions. Two of these are 'Development' and the 'Longwall'. In simple terms, development refers to the work associated with preparing the piece of ore body for the 'Longwall' to come along and extract the coal. The development involves extracting coal from channels along each side of the ore body in advance of the 'Longwall'. The 'Longwall' is exactly that, it is a wall of hydraulic ceiling supports that move slowly forward as a cutting device travels back and forth extracting coal.

Large volumes of gas are released when coal mining, and when these gases exceed certain limits, the extraction work conducted by the 'Longwall' has to cease for safety reasons, resulting in delays to production. To release this gas, the development crew moving ahead of the 'Longwall' must drill holes into the ore body in such a way that as much gas as possible is released from the ore body before the 'Longwall' reaches it. That task requires a scientific approach to where the holes are drilled. So if you think about this from a process perspective, the 'Longwall' is the customer of the development crew. So if we measured performance of the development crew on the basis of 'metres drilled per day', what behaviours do you think that would drive? Would this measure drive the development crew towards minimising the amount of gas in the ore body? In this particular scenario the crew would drill as many metres per day as they could, regardless of location. They are not driven towards any consideration about minimising gas in the ore body for the 'Longwall'. The measure of 'metres per day' will not drive the behaviours necessary for minimising delays. If the crew was measured on the basis of 'Longwall' delays or gas levels, their behaviour might be quite different.

Measuring Activity Does Not Guarantee Results

Many a business has initiated measures, with good intention I might mention, that ultimately add little or no value to the desired outcome. Often these measures are related to activities and not results. Let me give you an example.

A mid size company located in Western Australia had a strong and commendable focus on health safety and environment. In an effort to reach their target of 'Zero Harm', they introduced a measure that was linked to performance remuneration. The measure was the number of Safe Act Observation Reports submitted. Each member of the organisation was required to complete and submit two Safe Act Observation Reports per week.

I had the opportunity to work with a group who were trying to reduce the number of errors in the submitted reports, and it was interesting to find out that these reports apparently had no impact on the number of safety incidents that were occurring across the business, or so that was the perception. What was happening was this: Many staff members, knowing that they had to make up numbers, would complete the handwritten reports at their desk each week without actually going out into the workplace and doing the observation and survey required of the report. The measure drove a numbers mentality and the desired outcome was never achieved.

I spent a number of years as a police officer, and about 3 of those years in traffic enforcement. I was always asked about traffic infringement notice quotas that I had to meet, and the good news is that there was never any quota. Imagine for a moment if that *was* how the performance of Traffic Police was measured.

This measuring of activity would probably have little impact on the road toll.

Measure What You Want to Manage

What do we measure at this point in time for a Lean Six Sigma project?

The words of Deming *'What gets measured gets done'* have application here. To manage the outputs of a process (the effects or y's), you need to manage input and process variables (the causes or x's). To be able to *manage* these you need to *measure* them.

A Balanced View of Performance Measures

As we know, business processes primarily drive business results. Yet how often do we only focus on measuring performance outputs? These are only lag indicators in that they give an indication of what has already occurred. A more useful approach to take is that of a 'balanced scorecard'.

Monitoring a combination of input, process and output measures allow you to understand cause and effect relationships and even take action to prevent a downstream drop in performance. With a balanced approach, the team will be able to monitor 'lead' indicators (upstream measures that give an indication of what performance will be like in the future) as well as 'lag' indicators.

The Balanced Scorecard

It is worth noting the Balanced Scorecard approach first discussed by Drs. Robert Kaplan and David Norton in a 1992 Harvard Business Review article titled *'The Balanced Scorecard - Measures that Drive Performance'*. This article sparked interest in the concept and resulted in the publishing of a 1996 bestseller, *'The Balanced Scorecard: Translating Strategy into Action'*. Whilst there may be nothing new about using key measurements to monitor performance of an organisation, Kaplan and Norton have recommended the scope be broadened to force managers and leaders of an organisation to view their business from different perspectives.

The four perspectives that a performance measurement system should cover are; (a) the financial perspective, (b) the customer perspective, (c) the business process perspective, and (d) the learning and growth perspective.

Kaplan and Norton suggest generic measures for each of these areas, including:

- **Finances** – return on capital invested, cash flow, revenue, profit, turnover per employee, return on assets,
- **Customers** – market share, delivery performance,
- **Business Process** – cycle times, inventory turns, cost, quality,
- **Learning and Growth** - percentage revenue from new services, number of employee suggestions, improvements

Balancing Measures for Your Project

When choosing measures for your monitoring plan consider these points.

- Changes to the process as a result of your project work can affect other variables not yet considered.
- Changes to these other variables can impact your customers and the business itself and we must make sure that this impact is not adverse.

Step 1 – Identify Key Response Variables

To identify your key project response variables, consider these four questions in generating ideas. You might find it useful to refer to the SIPOC in this process.

Four Questions

- Q1. *What is the primary metric for this project?*
- Q2. *What other metrics would help us understand how well the customers' critical-to-quality requirements of the end product are being met?*
- Q3. *What other metrics would help us understand how well the customers' critical-to-quality requirements of the service or process itself are being met?*
- Q4. *What other metrics would help us understand how well the business's requirements of the process are being met?*

Case Study – the Coffee Shop

Referring to our Coffee Shop SIPOC, the following list of potential response measures of relevance to this project might be created.

Q1. *What is the primary metric for this project?*	Coffee Temperature
Q2. *What other metrics would help us understand how well the customers' critical-to-quality requirements of the end product are being met?*	Order Accuracy
Q3. *What other metrics would help us understand how well the customers' critical-to-quality requirements of the service or process itself are being met?*	Cycle Time for Delivery
Q4. *What other metrics would help us understand how well the business's requirements of the process are being met?*	Yield Rate (Proportion of Defect Free Products)

From this list you should only choose those that are most important to your project. In this case we've only identified four measures so the decision of what to measure is relatively easy to make.

Step 2 - Identify Key Predictor Variables

Key predictor variables (x's) for your performance monitoring plan can be identified in any number of ways. Provided you've assembled the right type of team, it could be as simple as focusing on validated causes from work completed earlier in the project, or even just a brainstorming session.

However, at this point in time why would we want to drop the rigour we've displayed throughout the project just to get to the end quickly? The following tools will help you maintain that rigour when selecting key predictor variables for your monitoring plan.

Cause Effect (CE) Tree Diagram

Tree diagrams are widely used visual thinking aids in the world of process improvement. They allow users to progressively breakdown a main or central concept into smaller elements and are by far my favourite approach for this step of a project. A tree diagram can also be used to understand cause effect relationships, hence the name CE Tree Diagram.

In the example shown, you can see the variable under analysis is 'heat cycle time' for a nickel granulising process. The tree diagram has been used to break it down into those variables that are most significant in creating variation in the response metric. In this case if we vary the elements identified, heat cycle time varies.

The team has chosen three particular variables as those that make sense to include in a performance monitoring plan (identified with a tick).

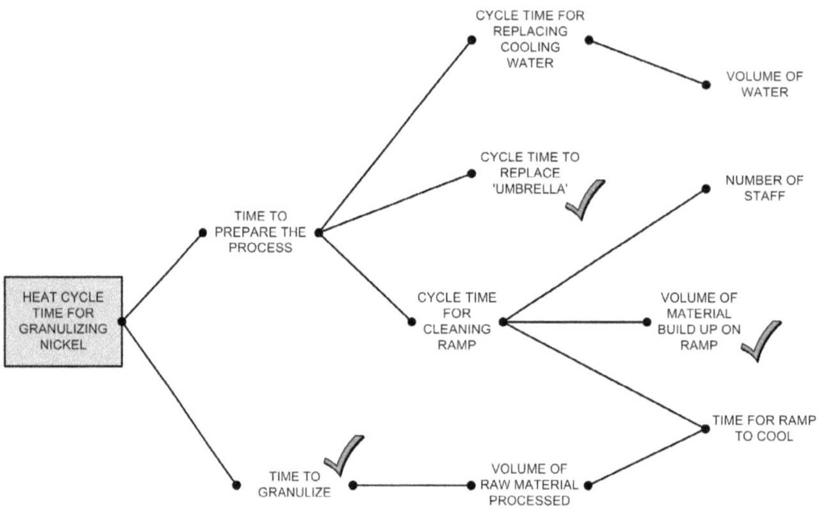

Figure 346: Cause Effect Tree Diagram Example

In the approach described above, CE Tree diagrams are constructed in two major steps.

STEP 1 Identify potential variables by asking the following question repeatedly to as many as three levels of detail.

Ask: *'What 2 or 3 variables are most responsible for creating variation in (insert variable)?'*

Obviously you insert the 'response variable' you are analysing in the space provided. The question is repeated for each new level, stopping at around the third level of detail. The end result is a tree of variables.

STEP 2 Choose no more than 3 variables that should be considered for your project's monitoring plan.

NOTE: You might also choose to create the tree diagram in a more rigid manner similar to the Cause Effect Structure Tree.

My preference is for this more flexible and what could be perceived as a less organised approach.

Case Study – the Coffee Shop

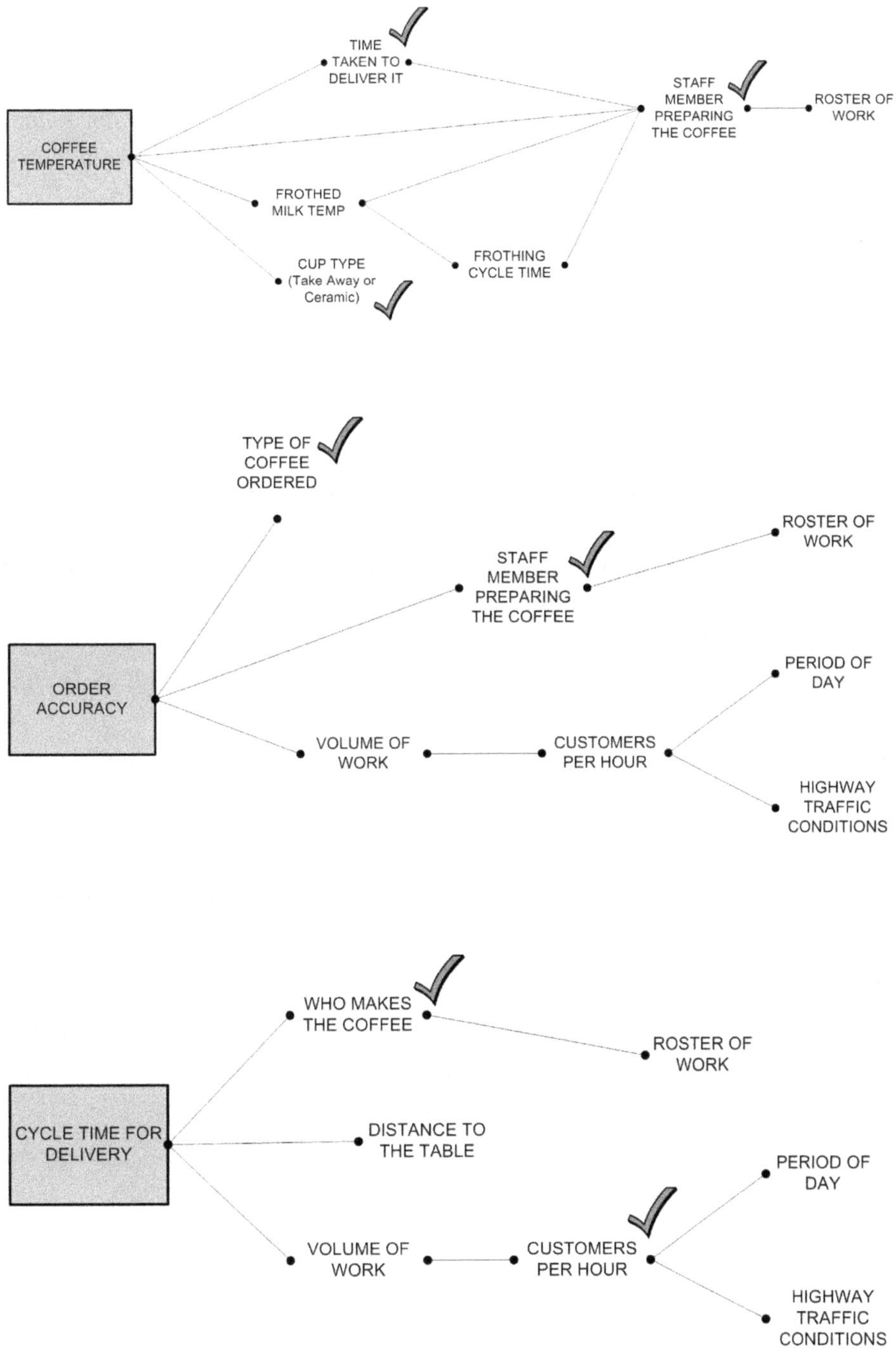

Figure 347: CE Tree Diagrams for Coffee Shop Case Study

XY Worksheet – An Alternative Method

While not my preferred approach, an alternative method you can use to identify key predictor variables is an XY Worksheet. This tool was discussed as a part of the 'data collection planning' process in this text so I will only refer to it here. It is simply a process of asking a sequence of three questions.

- **Q1.** *'What variables (the x's in this case) potentially have an impact on variability in the response variable of interest (y)?'* It helps to look for variables within the six standard categories defined in the Cause Effect Diagram.
    - Materials
    - Machines
    - Measures
    - Methods
    - Environment
    - People
- **Q2.** *'If we recorded values for this variable, what type of data would it generate?'* (It would be either Categorical or Numerical.)
- **Q3.** *'If we vary this x (ask for every x) within its normal operating range, how much effect would it have on variation in the response variable (y)?'* (We rate the effect on a scale of 0 to 5 that is explained in the Measure Phase toolkit in more detail.)

These questions focus the discussion on finding what the team believes to be the most significant *x*'s in *xy* relationship model.

IMPORTANT – Where changes have taken place to certain variables because of solutions you've implemented, only consider the operating range of those variables now that solutions are in place. If the variable has been totally controlled, you should rate its impact on the response variable accordingly. For example, if ambient temperature in our coffee shop case study was a problem and the environment was now totally temperature controlled, the operating range would be so small its impact on the response would now be insignificant.

Set Up For Success

This process works extremely well in identifying key project variables under the following circumstances.

- The team is comprised of people *who work in and have experience with* the process in question.
- The completed *SIPOC is available* as a reference for identifying variables.
- Only make a judgment about effect on *y* based on the *realistic or actual operating range* of the variable in question. Always consider the range post-solution implementation.

Now we know what the key predictor variables might be for our project, we need to reduce the list of variables to only those most important to a monitoring plan.

Step 3 – Choose Measures with the CE Matrix

One method of identifying root cause variables that should be monitored is to prioritise them according to how important they are or how much impact they have across the range of efficiency and effectiveness measures. This approach is particularly useful when (a) customers of a process have a range of requirements spanning both the product or service, and the process itself, and (b) project work has been focused on improving performance with respect to some business requirement.

Three Steps

Choosing final measures with the CE Matrix is completed in three major steps.

STEP 1 Insert the primary metric (primary *y*) and important secondary metrics (secondary *y*'s) that you have chosen to monitor.

STEP 2 Input the key predictor variables that have a significant relationship with the primary metric and selected secondary metrics. (refer to output from CE Tree Diagrams).

STEP 3 Prioritise predictor variables (the *x*'s) according to the degree of impact they have on the range of primary and secondary metrics (*y*'s) and choose those to include in your plan.

Cause Effect (CE) Matrix

A matrix diagram can be used to systematically identify and analyse the existence and strength of the relationship between any two sets of variables. Matrix diagrams can take on many forms, and in this case I will present one variant.

A CE matrix is focused on helping a team understand the relationship between cause variables and key response variables. It does this by showing the degree of influence input or process variables (*x*'s) have on respective efficiency and effectiveness metrics (*y*'s). The purpose of this work is to identify the *x*'s that have the greatest impact on respective *y*'s, according to how important each individual *y* is. Once identified, the team is in a position to determine (a) which of the variables should be monitored, and possibly (b) where opportunities exist for future work on improving process performance even further.

In the example shown in the case study, the team has created a CE Matrix to identify which predictor variables to monitor as a part of the monitoring plan. The variables chosen were those with the greatest impact on important response variables for this project.

Case Study – the Coffee Shop

Weighting ⇒	**5**	**4**	**2**	**3**	
(*y*) Variables ⇒ **(*x*) Variables ⇓**	Coffee Temp.	Order Accuracy	Cycle Time for Delivery	Yield Rate	**TOTAL**
Who Makes the Coffee – the Barista (C)	5	4	3	4	**59**
Customers Per Hour (N)	3	3	5	3	**46**
Time Taken to Deliver (N)	5	1	5	2	**45**
Type of Coffee (C)	2	5	1	1	**35**
Cup Type (C)	5	1	1	1	**34**

Figure 348: Cause Effect Matrix for Coffee Shop

In allocating weightings for response variables across the top and rating each predictor variable in the left column, the team used a 1 to 5 scale similar to that shown in option 1 below. An alternative approach would be to use a rating scale similar to that used in QFD (Quality Function Deployment) as shown in option 2.

Option 1

1 =	Low
2 =	Moderate
3 =	Medium
4 =	Major
5 =	Significant

Option 2

9 =	Strong relationship between x and y
5 =	Moderate relationship between x and y
2 =	Weak relationship between x and y
1 =	No relationship between x and y

CE Matrix Rating Scale Options

The degree of impact each cause variable has on respective y's is always based on the collective experience of team members and available data.

A Pareto Chart might even be created using total scores for each predictor variable to visually display results.

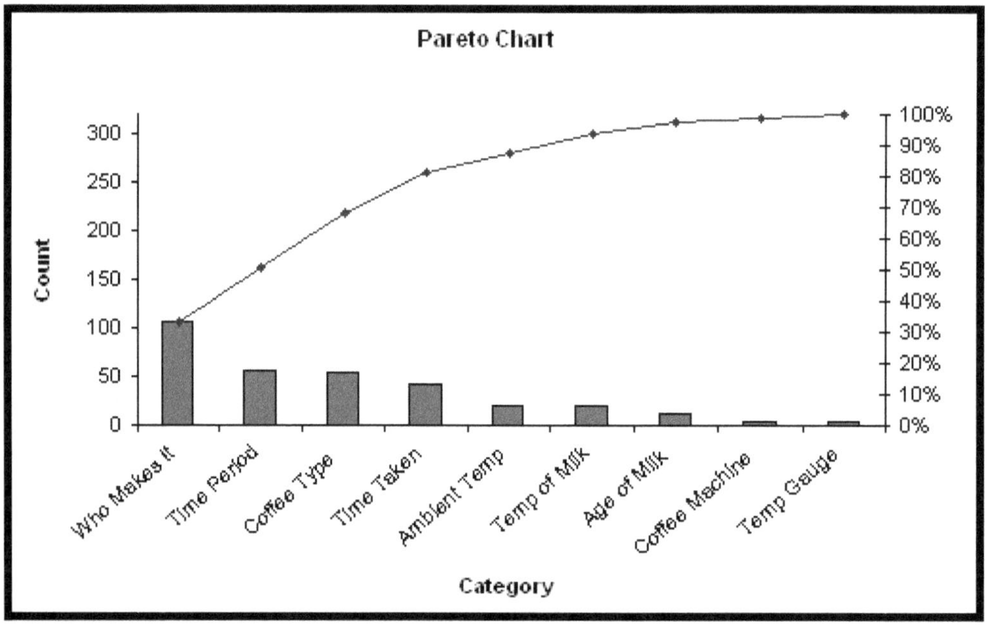

Whilst no Pareto effect will be evident, the chart can be used to arrange variables in descending order to help determine which of the cause variables should be (a) monitored, and (b) considered as potential project targets as a part of the continual improvement program.

PERFORMANCE MONITORING PLAN

Monitoring performance requires effective planning. The method of planning offered is similar to the process undertaken in data collection planning in the measure phase of the project. The framework offered is just one of many approaches that can be undertaken, so it may well be a starting point for you to develop your own framework for a monitoring plan.

Key Questions for Performance Monitoring

Planning performance monitoring is the same as data collection. It requires the team to answer six questions:

- Q1. Ask: *What performance measures will provide a balanced view of process performance with regard to efficiency and effectiveness?*

  The answers to this question can be determined from the work undertaken with CE Tree Diagrams and the CE Matrix. As a guide, a measurement 'Six Pack' may be sufficient to provide a balanced view of performance without drowning stakeholders in irrelevant data.
- Q2. Ask: *What is the targeted level of performance?*
- Q3. Ask: *What is the definition of this measure and how is the measurement undertaken?*
- Q4. Ask: *How big a sample will we collect and what method of sampling will we employ?*
- Q5. Ask: *How can we best display the data?*
- Q6. Ask: *Who will be responsible for ensuring that the measurements are undertaken and charts / performance dashboards are updated?*

Performance Monitoring versus Data Collection

The key thing to remember here is this plan differs from a data collection plan (as used in the 'measure' phase) in a number of ways:

1. The intent is not to collect data purely for the purpose of analysing for source and cause of variation, the intent is to collect data that will be presented in a performance dashboard of some kind.
2. You will need to discuss and translate the variables you have finally chosen in your CE Matrix into a form suitable for presentation, e.g. an important input variable might be 'cup type' but the measure you will display might be 'defect rate by cup type'. To get a feel for how this works, compare the Case Study CE Matrix with the Case Study Monitoring Plan.

Case Study – the Coffee Shop

The data generated from these questions are the inputs for a performance monitoring plan like the one shown below.

Performance Variable	Target Value	What to Measure	How to Measure	Sampling Plan	How to Display	Who
Coffee Temperature (milk based coffee)	65C to 70C (mid range)	The temperate (C°) of cup content prior to delivery	Aim laser temp gauge at centre of content, record temp C° to	10 sequentially every hour	Xbar-R Chart	Wait Staff
Order Accuracy (see Process Yield below)	--	--	--	--	--	--
Average Cycle Time for Delivery	< 2 min.	Time in minutes to produce and deliver to customer	Write time of delivery on docket, calculate gap in minutes and seconds versus order time on docket	10 dockets recorded sequentially every hour	Run Chart of Average Cycle Time by Hour	Wait staff collect dockets Mgr create chart
Process Yield (Defect Free Rate)	100%	Proportion of coffees that meet requirements of customer	Record rejected coffees, subtract reject total from total coffees recorded on POS system and calculate the defect free percentage	Total	Radar Chart of Actual % versus Target %	Wait record defects Mgr update radar chart daily
Defect Free Rate by Coffee Type (latte etc)	100%	Proportion of coffees defect free by type	As above for Coffee Type	Total	As above	As above
Defect Free Rate by Cup Type (foam or ceramic)	100%	Proportion of coffees defect free for each class	As above for Classification (id. on docket as takeaway or eat in)	Total	As above	As above
Defect Free Rate by Barista	100%	Proportion of coffees defect free by Barista	As above for 'Barista who makes it'	Total	Pie charts with % by Barista	As above
Customers Per Hour	na			Total	Run Chart of Customers Per Hour	

Figure 349: Process Performance Monitoring Plan for Coffee Shop Project

CONTROL PROCESS PERFORMANCE (STEP 18)

CHOOSING A METHOD OF CONTROL

There are many different types of processes in the business world today. Different processes require the use of different control mechanisms, primarily determined by the cyclic nature of the process, and the degree of repetition or standardisation of the process.

The following examples will help you understand the different types of processes and the types of controls that are most useful for each.

Low Repetition / Low Frequency Process

Examples include:

- Painting a piece of artwork
- Writing a score of music
- Making a movie
- Shifting a conveyor system in an open cut mine
- Constructing a custom designed building structure

The essence of these processes is that the steps of the process can be significantly different for each cycle and the cyclic frequency is low. It also seems that these processes produce a unique output for each cycle.

The most useful forms of control include (a) progress reviews, and (b) status reports.

High Repetition / Low Frequency Process

Examples might include:

- Flying a plane
- Racing a formula one car
- Conducting a training course

The nature of these processes is that the process steps have a high level of standardisation. However, the cyclic frequency for this process is low. There seems to be a lot of room for variation in each of the steps within the process.

The most useful forms of control include - (a) standard operating procedures, (b) checklists, and (c) agendas or schedules.

Low Repetition / High Frequency Process

These types of processes are often macro processes that over-shadow or are integrated with other work processes. They are not a common process type in Six Sigma work. Examples include:

- Equipment breakdown repairs
- Safe work process (particularly evident in the mining industry)

The nature of these processes is one of low standardisation of the steps, yet the process is cycled frequently.

The most useful forms of control include – (a) Bar charts, (b) Pie charts, (c) Pareto charts, and (d) Risk profiles.

High Repetition / High Frequency Process

These processes are the most common form in Lean Six Sigma project work. Examples of this type include:

- Making standard components in a production line
- Extracting metal from raw materials in the mining industry

The nature of these types of processes is one of highly standardised steps and a high cyclic frequency.

The most useful forms of control include Control Charts.

Control Selection Matrix

The matrix shown is useful for selecting the most useful form of control for each type of process you might encounter.

Process Performance Controls

	Low Frequency	**High Frequency**
Highly Standardised	Standard Operating Procedures, Instructions, Checklists, Agendas, Schedules	Control Charts (e.g., X-Bar R Chart, I-MR Chart)
Low Standardisation	Project Plans, Progress Monitoring, Status Reports	Risk Profiles, Standard Charts (e.g., Pie, Bar, Pareto etc)

Figure 350: Control Selection Matrix

CONTROL FEEDBACK LOOPS

What is meant by the term 'control'? In the context of our Lean Six Sigma project work, it means:

'To ensure that the process, hence its products and services, perform to a specified standard by monitoring performance and responding to deviations from standard.'

Think about work associated with 'financial control' in a department of a company. Financial control involves monitoring expenditure, comparing actual expenditure to planned expenditure, and taking some form of corrective action when over spending occurs.

Now when we talk about 'quality control', we talk about a similar strategy. Quality control involves monitoring quality performance, comparing actual performance to planned performance, and taking corrective action when performance is at an unacceptable level.

Regardless of the type of control being discussed, feedback loops are required.

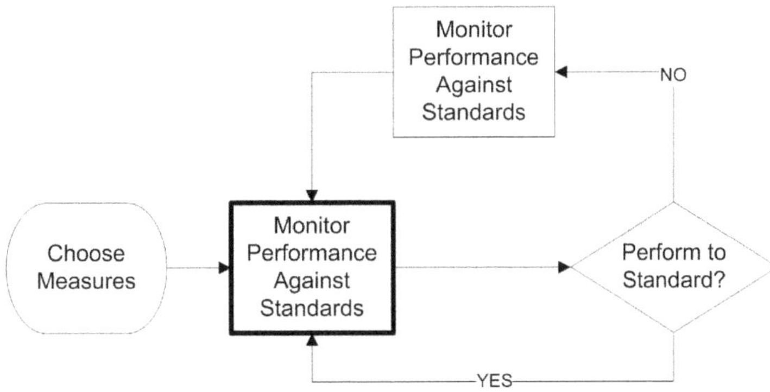

Table 351: Control Feedback Loop

Creating a Control Feedback Loop

The simplest and usually the most effective form of feedback loop for process performance control involves the following steps:

- **STEP 1** Choosing the measures to be used in the control feedback loop. Smart Black Belts will make use of both lag and lead performance indicators as discussed in the next section.
- **STEP 2** Monitoring these measures of performance, and comparing against planned or expected standards or specifications. When performance is to standard or specification, monitoring activities continue to occur.
- **STEP 3** Taking corrective action when performance is not to standard or specification.

Monitoring and corrective action can be either manual or automated. In automated systems, no human intervention is required. For example, thermostats are often employed to maintain temperature within a specified range. Manual control on the other hand, sometimes referred to as 'self control', involves human participation.

The text on the following pages provides some useful tools that address each of these steps for highly repetitive, highly cyclic processes.

VISUAL PROCESS CONTROLS

Visual process controls are simply displays or visual indicators or markers that inform and help operators to:

- Identify abnormal or unsafe conditions
- Perform work safely
- Understand and apply standard methods of operation
- Determine work priorities
- Understand performance targets
- Understand and communicate performance results
- Provide feedback to supervisors and other teams

Possibly the most significant impact of visual process controls is through reducing time wasting by virtually eliminating the need for meetings.

Safety Controls

Normal Conditions

Visual controls can be used to guide behaviour patterns for normal working conditions.

- Danger areas, 'no go' zones
- Areas where personal protective equipment (PPE) must be worn
- Areas of responsibility
- Operating area for machinery or moving plant
- Movement areas
- Collection areas, muster points

Figure 352: Safety Signs

Abnormal Conditions

Visual controls are also used to indicate any abnormal working conditions that operators must be aware of.

- Equipment shutdowns and lockouts
- Damaged equipment
- Dangerous areas due to some unplanned change

Production Controls

Takt Boards

Takt boards are designed to provide information to production teams about:

- Planned work
- Cumulative variance between actual and planned
- Completion rates

An example is shown below.

Production Summary Boards

Summary boards can be used to communicate information relevant to your workplace. Content might include:

- Work in Progress (WIP)
- The economic value of actual WIP
- Takt rate (actual versus desired)
- Production rates (actual versus desired)
- Lead time (actual versus desired)
- Safety performance

		Orders	Takt Rate	Notices
Yesterday (Actual)		14	0.93 p/h	
Today (Planned)		13	1.3 p/h	
Time	**Planned**	**Actual**	**Variance**	**Comments**
06-07	1	1	0	
07-08	1	1	0	
08-09	1	1	0	
09-10	2	1	-1	Wet day, slow drying
10-11	1	1	0	
11-12	1	1	0	
LUNCH				
13-14	2	1	-1	
14-15	1	1	0	
15-16	1	1	0	3 hours overtime
16-17	2	4	0	
TOTAL	**13**	**13**	**0**	Takt Rate = 1 p/h

Figure 353: Takt Board for Production Team

Performance Dashboards

The challenge is now to convert your plan into a dashboard from which you can see a snapshot of process performance. No doubt you are familiar with performance dashboards so let me just quickly discuss a couple of different options.

Performance Six Pack

The following example of a 'performance six pack' displays key numbers in a graphical format for monitoring and managing the performance of a business.

The key variables included in this example are:

- Revenue versus Operating Cost
- Net Cash Flow with Average Cash Flow
- Number of Units Invoiced with Average
- Services Charges with Average
- Debtors with Average
- Creditors with Average

Performance dashboards of this nature can be applied in any situation where the monitoring and management of multiple variables are important in achieving performance goals.

In the example shown figures are updated monthly. Obviously the time span for updating figures depends entirely on the particular needs of the process manager.

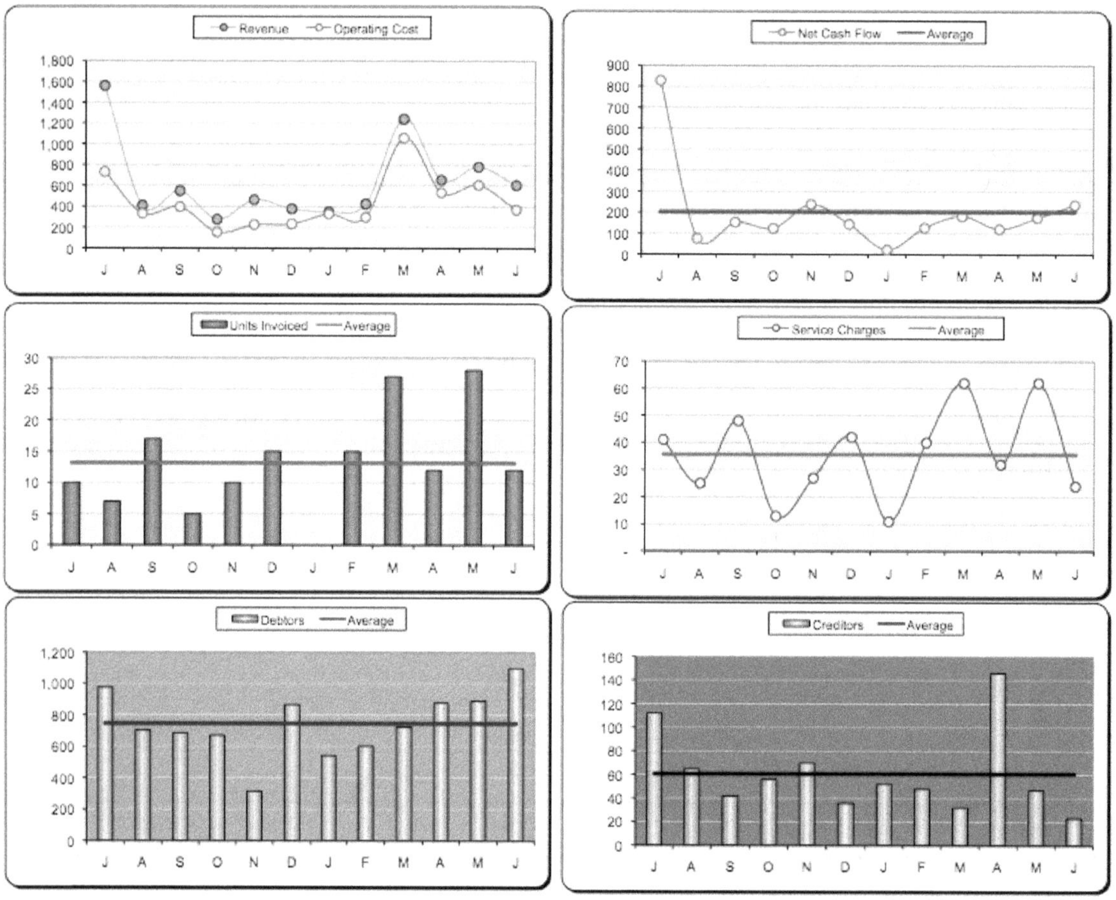

Figure 354: Performance Six Pack

<u>Radar Charts</u>

A **Radar Chart** is a useful way of displaying current performance results against leading practice or targeted performance results. Radar charts are sometimes referred to as 'Arachnoids'.

The outside range of the chart is the targeted or ideal level of performance for each of the labelled measures. The inside lined area indicates the level of performance at the time of measuring. The gap between the outer ring and inner lined area is the opportunity for improvement to reach the targets set.

A Radar Chart serves multiple purposes:

- To consolidate and make strengths and weaknesses visible
- To provide a snapshot of the opportunities to make improvement in process performance
- Display a balanced collection of important performance measures

<u>Case Study – the Coffee Shop</u>

The following example of a 'radar chart' displays key performance figures (as percentages) against a target value for monitoring and managing the performance of baristas in our café.

The key variables included in this example are drawn from the monitoring plan:

- Performance against the 2 minute delivery target (not referred to in the monitoring plan)
- Total defect free rate for all milk based coffees
- Yield for three types of milk based coffees – Latte, Cappuccino and Flat White
- Yield for two classifications of milk based coffees – Eat in or Takeaway

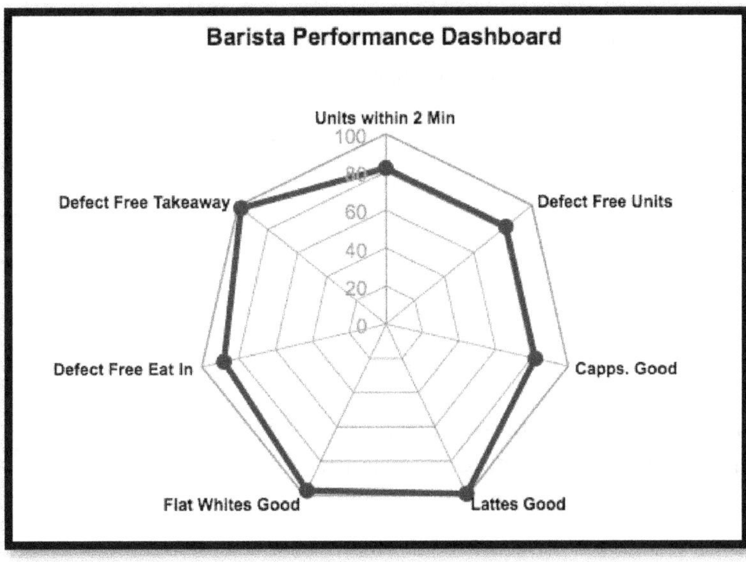

Figure 355: Radar Chart for Barista Performance

Radar charts can be combined with any other form of chart to create a performance dashboard.

Displaying Performance Dashboards

By displaying a dashboard of a 'Balanced' family of measures, a team can effectively monitor and influence progress across a variety of aspects of process performance. Some ways a performance dashboard can be used include these:

- Post regularly in a public place where all relevant process users can view
- Use to report overall performance to project stakeholders on an ongoing basis
- Host on the company intranet and provide links to project stakeholders

STATISTICAL PROCESS CONTROL

All processes have variation, regardless of how well they are performing. As a part of the overall DMAIC approach, particularly for a Six Sigma specific project, a Black Belt must have a good understanding of the concept of statistical process control and be able to apply it in an operational setting.

While statistical process control is discussed in detail in Chapter 5, it may serve us to quickly remind ourselves of the key points about variation.

When a process is *in a state of statistical control* it is said to be a stable process. Only common cause variation is operating on the process – there are no undue influences by any of the sources of variation.

This situation might be visualised like this.

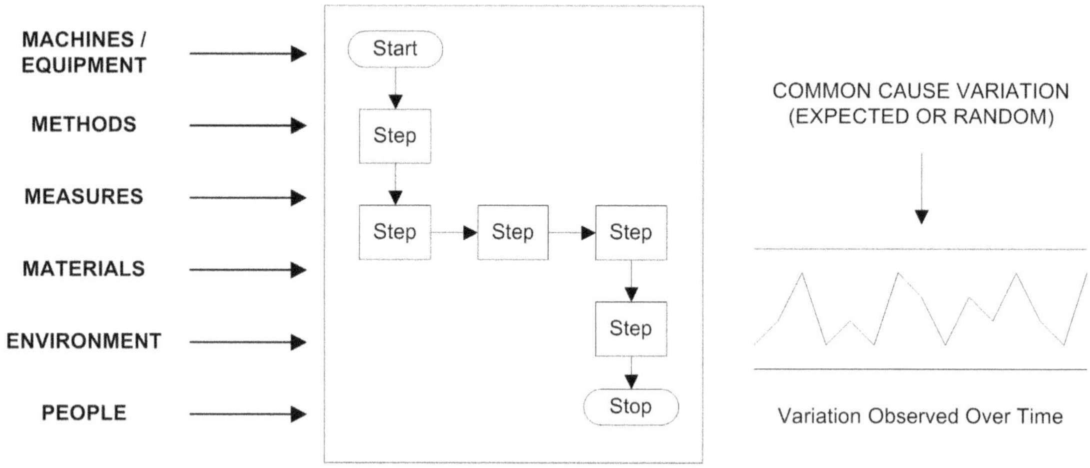

Figure 356: Common Cause Variation

When a process has special cause variation operating on it, it is said to be *'out of statistical control'* – it is affected by the undue influence by one or more of the sources of variation.

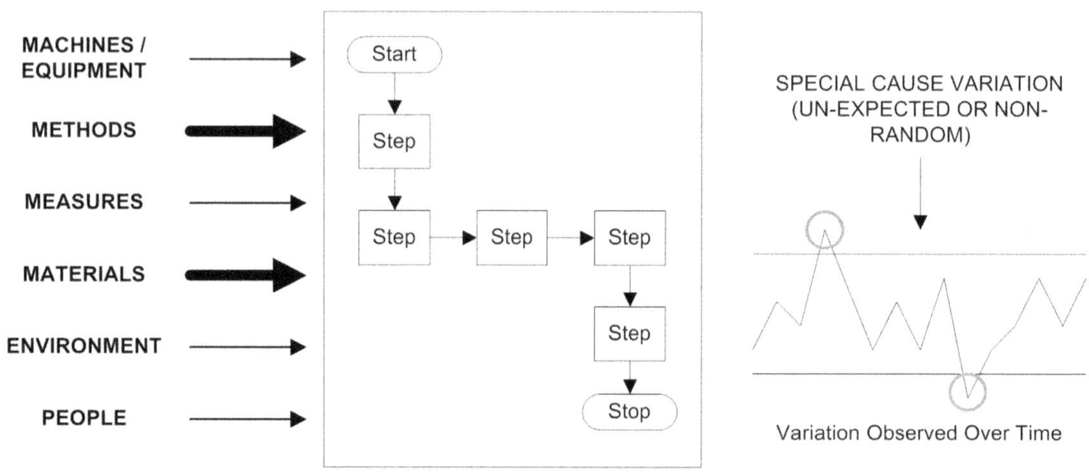

Figure 357: Special Cause Variation

Process Performance Control Planning

Process performance control planning is simply the documentation of relevant process details and instructions in order for operators to monitor and respond to performance deviations.

The planning process described here is comprised of three elements.

Process Control Points

- **Control Points** – The new process flowchart is documented and recorded on the worksheet to provide a visual guide for how the work is performed. A visual representation of the points where performance / quality controls will be placed is also included.

  In the example below the process for making milk based coffees has been prepared as an activity flowchart. The single quality control point is represented by the black numbered circle as indicated. It's at this point (a) temperature is recorded as a control mechanism and (b) any planned corrective action will be triggered.

  While a single value outside a defined range might trigger some corrective action, it may also be the case that data analysed over time using some relevant control chart shows a pattern that triggers some corrective action.

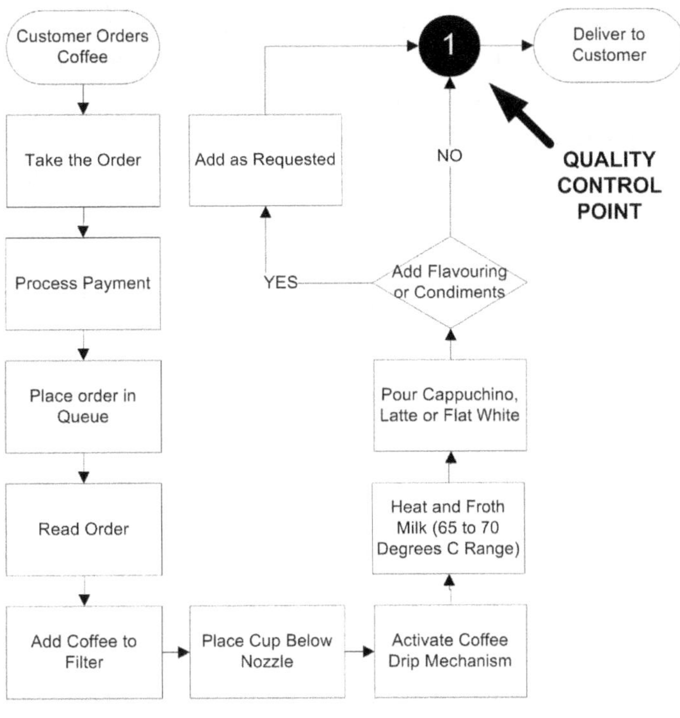

Figure 358: Coffee Process with Quality Control Points

Process Monitoring

The monitoring plan component describes what variables will be collected at each defined control point and how they will be analysed.

Key Performance Variables – KPV's are either key output variables linked to critical-to-quality requirements of the customer, or key input variables linked to causal factors that have a correlation to key output variables. These may be variables associated with the root causes identified during the 'analyse' phase of project work.

Specification Limits – Upper and Lower specification limits are determined by customers and provide criteria for determining the capability of the process.

Target Specification – The specified target is the ideal result for each KPV being monitored.

What, How & Who – The what, how and who elements detail the operational definition of the measure and who is responsible for collecting data.

Sample Size and Frequency – The sampling plan stipulates how many data points will be collected each time a sample is taken and how often this sampling takes place.

Control Chart Type – The type of data being collected will determine the type of control chart used. The most common used are Xbar-R Charts and I-MR Charts. For more information on which control charts to use, refer to Chapter 15 of this text.

(NOTE: If the response plan is totally focused on corrective action when a value is outside specification limits, there is probably no need to even use a control chart, in this case leave this section blank.)

The Response Plan

The purpose of the response plan is to define corrective action to be taken and what will trigger that action.

Trigger – A trigger is an event or result, when observed is cause for action to be taken. This trigger is ultimately a decision rule for activating the response plan and it may be based on:

- The results of a single data point and its relationship with specification limits (e.g. a single value above upper specification limit triggers some action).
- The outcomes of studying a series of data points and their relationship with process behaviour (e.g. a process that is showing a shift pattern even though it may be inside specification limits).

Corrective Action – The corrective action component of the plan describes the course of action to be taken in the event that the trigger is observed, who is responsible for taking that action and who must be notified in the event of action being taken.

Case Study – the Coffee Shop

PROCESS CONTROL POINTS

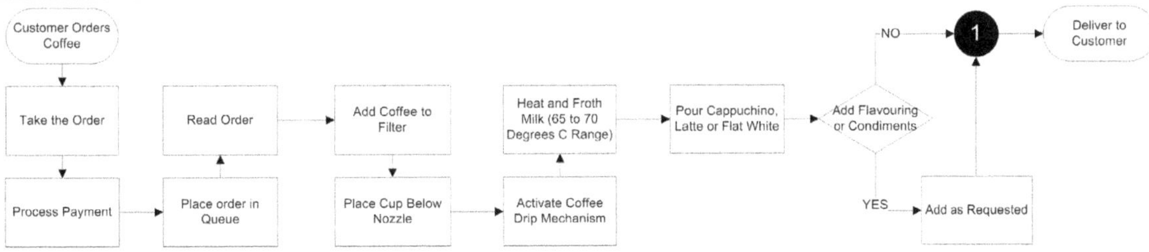

PROCESS MONITORING PLAN		
Key Performance Variables	(Point 1) Coffee Temperature	(Point 1) Cycle Time for Delivery
LSL	65 degrees (Celsius)	Na
USL	70 degrees (Celsius)	2 minutes
Target	Midrange	< 2 minutes
What will be measured	The temperate (C^{o}) of cup content prior to delivery	Time in minutes to produce and deliver product to customer
How will it be measured	Aim laser temp gauge at centre of content, record temp C^{o} to nearest 10th	Write time of delivery on docket, calculate gap in minutes and secs. versus order time on docket
Who will measure it	Wait Staff	Wait Staff
Sample Size and Frequency	10 sequentially every hour	10 sequentially every hour
Control Chart Type	(Not required)	Xbar-S Chart

RESPONSE PLAN		
Trigger:	Temp < $65^{o}C$ or > $70\ ^{o}C$	Evidence of shift or drift > 2min
Action:	Return product to Barista	Discuss trend with staff
Who Takes Action:	Wait Staff	Manager
Notification:	Record defect	na

Figure 359: Process Control Plan

PROJECT CLOSURE

All Lean and Six Sigma projects must finally come to an end. Remember the definition of a project – it does have a defined life. It is my opinion that the end of the project occurs when:

- Tasks associated with the solution implementation plan are completed and solutions are implemented
- The new process is institutionalised
- Performance controls have been implemented
- Performance has been monitored for a period of time to ensure improvements are actually made

Closing the Project

The process for formally closing a project includes:

- Commission plant or equipment where relevant
- Completing the project storyboard
- Preparing for the final project review
- Handover to the process owner
- Reviewing and documenting lessons learned (what worked and what would be done differently next time)
- Sharing key learnings for the betterment of the organisation and employees alike
- Celebration of the completion of the project

A piece of advice that I give all Black Belts is that a project closure should be an event or a point in time that is known or recognisable. People should be able to observe and document project closure and this can be achieved through various means including:

- Formal signing off by the process owner and project sponsor / leader
- A photograph and / or article in the company newsletter
- A formal event or function

Celebration

The final celebration should as a minimum, be a way of acknowledging the work of the team in completing the project, and contributing to the value of the organisation as a whole. The team may choose to extend the celebration beyond a private affair, to include those outside the team who contributed to its success and recognise their support as well. Irrespective, the effect of celebrating should never be underestimated.

CHAPTER 22: THE CONTROL PHASE TOOLKIT

TRAINING PLAN

What is it?

The training plan is a worksheet for defining and documenting the key elements associated with an effective training strategy.

The worksheet is used during the control phase for any Lean Six Sigma project, usually after the new process has been defined and is ready for roll out.

Participants	Subject Matter	Method of Delivery	Timing	Location	Responsibility

Instructions

STEP 1 Determine who the participants are by asking: *'Who needs to be trained for this process to be institutionalised?'* Document in the 'Participant' column of the worksheet.

STEP 2 Determine what the purpose is for communicating to each audience group by asking: *'What is our purpose for communicating with this audience?'*

Step 3 – Determine what the training needs are for these participants for the goal of standardisation to be achieved. These can be identified by asking three simple questions:

- Ask: *'What do they need to be able to do or what do they need to know?'*
- Ask: *'What can they currently do or what do they currently know?'*
- Ask: *'What do they need to learn to fill the skill or knowledge gap?'*

Document in the 'Subject Matter' column of the worksheet.

STEP 4 Decide how the training will be delivered. Document in the 'Method of Delivery' column of the worksheet.

STEP 5 Determine the timing for delivery of training. Document in the 'Timing' column of the worksheet.

STEP 6 Determine where the training will be delivered and document in the 'Location' column of the worksheet.

STEP 7 Determine who is going to be responsible for ensuring that the training takes place. Document in the 'Responsibility' column of the worksheet.

SIPOC

What is it?

This tool is called a SIPOC, which is the acronym for Suppliers, Inputs, Process, Outputs and Customers. In reference materials it is also referred to as a SIPOCR, or SIPOC+R.

The purpose of this tool is to consolidate the high level process and all of the elements associated with it, including inputs, outputs and requirements of customers, the business and the process itself.

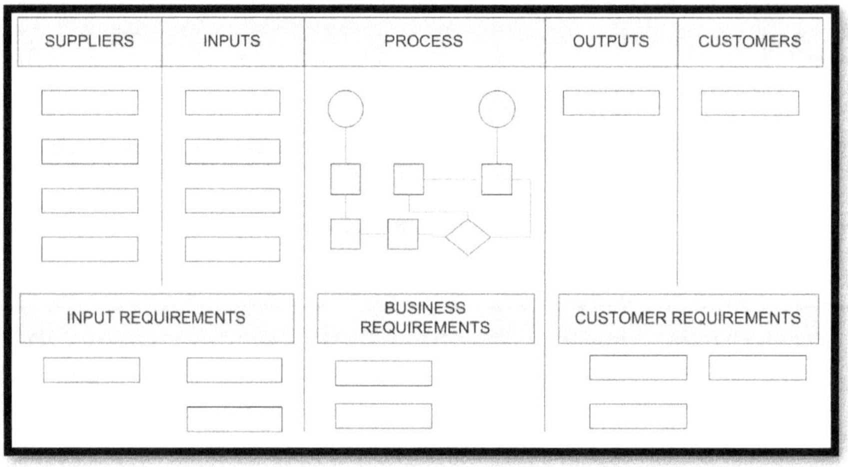

Instructions

STEP 1 Process boundaries are established and the high level process is mapped.

STEP 2 Outputs are defined – by identifying outputs first, the team can then have a discussion around who is the real customer of those outputs. Outputs are the tangible products or services provided by the process.

STEP 3 Customers are identified – the people who receive your tangible products or services.

STEP 4 Inputs to the process are listed – now that you know the process and its outputs, you are able to identify the inputs you need to create the outputs. Inputs include materials that are consumed or transformed and information or data. Whilst also inputs, fixed resources enable the transformation of inputs to take place and are grouped separately as 'resources'.

STEP 5 Suppliers of these inputs are identified – having identified the inputs, the identification of suppliers is quite easy.

STEP 6 Requirements of the CUSTOMER are specified with respect to the output (product or service) and the process itself. (Comments Translation, CTQ Tree Diagram, Prioritisation Worksheet, Kano Analysis)

STEP 7 Requirements of the BUSINESS are specified.

STEP 8 Requirements related to your process INPUTS are specified.

ACTIVITY FLOWCHART

What is it?

An activity flowchart is a visual representation of the sequence of activities that occur in a process between defined start and end points. It incorporates decision points as well as action steps.

Instructions

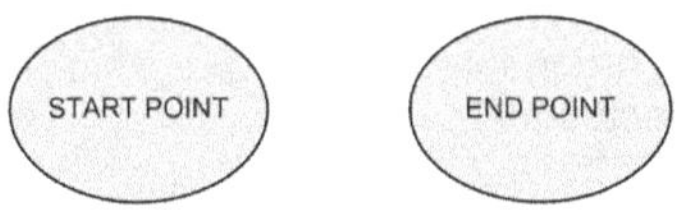

STEP 1 Define the boundaries (start and end points) of the process.

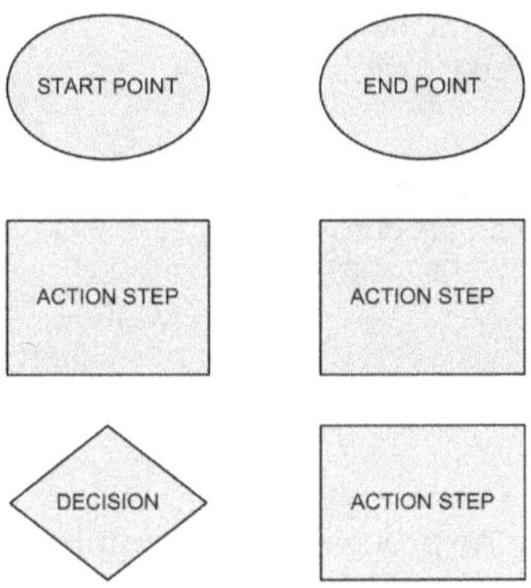

STEP 2 Identify the action and decision steps as they are performed (in chronological order).

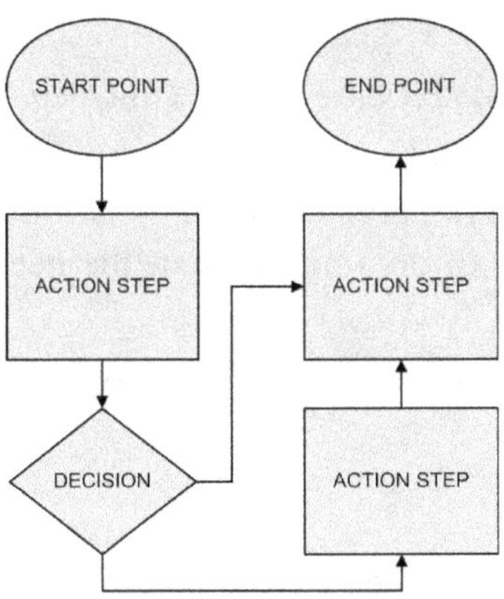

STEP 3 Draw arrows to indicate the path to follow through the process.

STEP 4 Validate the process with those who do the process.

CTQ TREE DIAGRAM

What is it?

The CTQ Tree Diagram is a tool used to help focus conversation and series of questions around identifying the needs of customers and translate these into specific requirements.

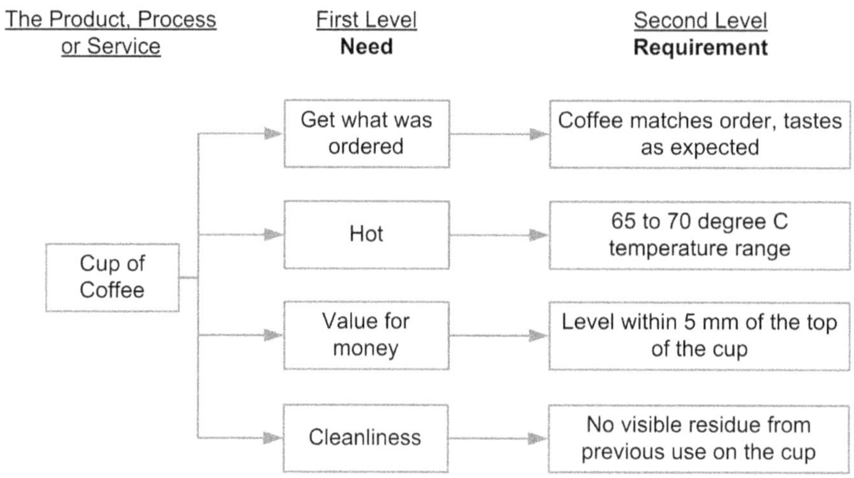

Instructions

STEP 1 Define the tangible product, service or process.

Ask: *'What is the product or service we are concerned with?'*

STEP 2 Identify the need of the customer with respect to the product, service or process. For example the customer may need the service to be completed in a timely fashion. A useful way to identify needs from a customer is to ask the customer to describe the product or service as it would be if it satisfied them. For example, a customer might describe a transport service as safe and comfortable, or a cup of coffee that was hot, freshly brewed, delivered quickly and tastes as expected.

Ask: *'What needs does the customer have with respect to this product, service or process?'* OR *'How would the customer describe the product, service or process in its ideal state?'*

STEP 3 Define the specific requirements that the customer has of the product or service, that if met would satisfy their need. For example, if the service were completed within 2 hours of commencement, the need for timeliness would be met.

Ask: *'What is the specific requirement of the customer, that if met would ensure that their need is satisfied?'*

Tips for Facilitators

- The product, service or process must be stated as a noun.
- Requirements should be (a) specific, (b) measurable, (c) form the basis for a yes we did meet it or no we did not meet it answer, and (d) relevant to the product or service.

CUSTOMER COMMENTS WORKSHEET

What is it?

The 'customer comments worksheet' provides a basis for translating customers' comments into specific requirements.

It is not uncommon for a customer to not know what they really want with respect to a product or service, however comments they make often provide clues to what they really require of a product or service.

Comments (What is the customer saying about the process or its outputs?)	**Need Being or Not Being Met** (What is the underlying need that is / is not being met?)	**Specific Requirement** (What is the specific requirement of the customer, that if met would ensure that their need is satisfied?)
"I always have to wait in line too long"	Reasonable Queueing Time	Queue for no longer than 5 minutes
"These things never last long"	Reasonable Product Life cycle	A life cycle of no less than 6 months

Instructions

STEP 1 Identify comments made by customers, both good and bad.

Ask: *'What is the customer saying about the process or its outputs?'*

STEP 2 Identify the underlying need that the comment refers to. This will be a need that is or is not being met, according to the type of comment. For example, a comment such as "These things never last long" provides a clue to the customers' need for a reasonable product life cycle.

Ask: *'What is the underlying need that is or is not being met?'*

STEP 3 Define the specific requirements that the customer has of the product or service, that if met would satisfy their need. For example, if the product lasts no less than 6 months, the need for a reasonable life cycle would be met.

Ask: *'What is the specific requirement of the customer, that if met would ensure that their need is satisfied?'*

Tips for Facilitators

- Requirements should be (a) specific, (b) measurable, (c) form the basis for a yes we did meet it or no we did not meet it answer, and (d) relevant to the product or service.
- The CTQ Tree Diagram can be used to assist in the discussion process.

CUSTOMER PRIORITIES WORKSHEET

What is it?

Customers often have multiple needs that the output or process must ideally satisfy. However, it is often not possible to satisfy all of these. The Customer Priorities Worksheet helps you to prioritise needs according to how important they are to the customer.

Depending on circumstances, you may find it more appropriate to prioritise requirements directly instead of needs.

Priority	Need	Requirement
A	To get what was ordered	Coffee matches order – tastes as expected
A	Hot	65 to 70 degree (Celsius) temperature range
A	Visibility of products and prices	All current products and prices are displayed at point of sale

Legend

A – Must be met B – Should be met C – Nice to meet

Instructions

Prioritisation can be undertaken using multiple approaches including (a) numbered ranking, or (b) Kano Analysis.

To prioritise using Kano Analysis follow these steps:

STEP 1 List customers' needs and key requirements on the worksheet. (can be drawn from the CTQ Tree Diagram)

STEP 2 Allocate a rating according to whether the requirement is a must have (A) or a should have (B) or a nice to have (C).

STEP 3 Prioritise in descending order.

Tips for Facilitators

- A 'must have' requirement is one that if not met would result in the customer rejecting the product or service. The existence of this is expected and its absence is a cause for dissatisfaction.
- A 'should have' requirement is one that is variable, the better it is met the more the customer is satisfied.
- A 'nice to have' requirement is one that the customer may not really expect, however is a delighter when met.

CAUSE EFFECT (CE) TREE DIAGRAM

What is it?

The Cause Effect Tree Diagram is a visual aid that helps the team to drill down to the most appropriate predictor variables that you might consider for your performance monitoring plan.

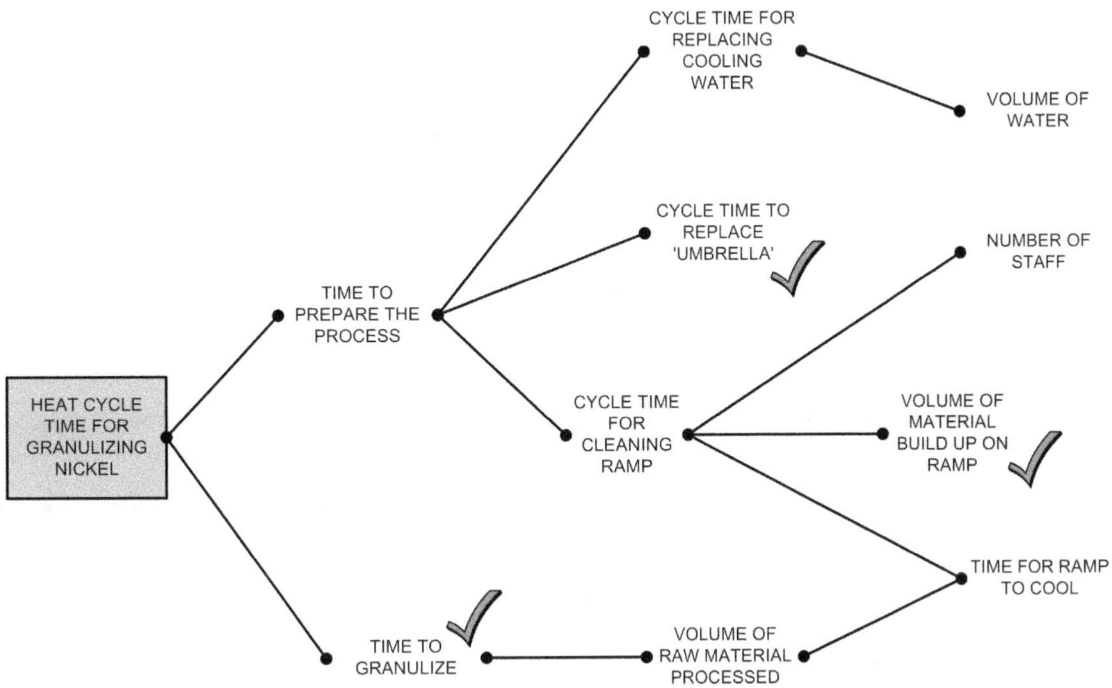

Instructions

STEP 1 Write the 'response variable' at the start point of the structure tree.

STEP 2 Identify variables that are most likely to cause variation in the response by asking the following question repeatedly to as many as three levels of detail.

Ask: *'What 2 or 3 variables are most responsible for creating variation in (insert variable)?'*

Simply insert the 'response variable' in the space provided. Capture the first 2 or 3 variables stated – remember that you have participants who are intimately knowledgeable about the process and the first ideas generated are based on that knowledge which is primarily held at the unconscious level of thinking. The right question brings these to the surface first. To push too far in a process, which by the way is not meant to be creative, starts to push the boundaries of rational thinking.

STEP 3 The question is repeated for each new level, stopping at about the third level of detail. The end result is a tree of variables.

STEP 4 Reduce your list and choose no more than 3 variables that should be considered for your project's monitoring plan using a process such as multi voting. Provided you ask the right questions, the people in your team will focus on the most significant causes because of process knowledge and experience.

CAUSE EFFECT (CE) MATRIX

What is it?

The CE Matrix, also referred to as an XY Diagram, XY Matrix or Prioritisation Matrix, helps a team understand the relationship between cause variables and key response variables. It does this by showing the degree of influence input or process variables (*x*'s) have on variation associated with key response variables (*y*'s). The purpose of the work at this point in time is to identify the *x*'s that have the greatest impact on respective *y*'s, according to how important each individual *y* is, so that a decision can be made about which variables to include in the performance monitoring plan.

Weighting ⇒	**5**	**4**	**3**		
(*y*'s) ⇒ **(*x*'s) ⇓**	**Availability**	**Utilisation**	**Cost Per Unit**		**TOTAL**
Scheduled Maintenance Cycle Time (N)	5	1	5		**44**
Unscheduled downtime (N)	4	1	2		**30**
Time to Repair Breakdowns (N)	4	2	4		**40**

Instructions

STEP 1 Key response variables are listed in the row for *y*'s. It may be appropriate when you have a large number of variables that you reduce the list to only those that are relevant to this project. The primary metric is listed first in the left column, secondary metrics are listed to the right of that.

(NOTE: Where the project is focused on improving some variable of importance to the business that is of no consequence to the primary customer, this variable must be included in this row. Examples might include primary metrics such as process throughput or process yield.)

STEP 2 Identify and list the variables that you know impacts the primary metric in the column for *x*'s. We might refer to these *x*'s as predictor variables.

STEP 3 Repeat steps 1 and 2 for secondary metrics. CE Tree Diagrams or other types of Cause and Effect Diagrams will prove useful in completing this work.

(NOTE: I like to indicate the type of variable, Numerical or Categorical, to help me think about how I might graphically display the variable when chosen.)

STEP 4 Allocate weightings to primary and secondary metrics (*y*'s) on a relevant scale (see rating scale option 1 shown on the following page) according to how important they are to business results. In allocating weightings, consideration must be given to the importance of different effectiveness metrics to customers and the subsequent impact on business results.

The primary metric of the project must be allocated the highest rating (i.e. a rating of 5) with all secondary metrics scaled down below that (i.e. rated on a scale of 1 to 4).

STEP 5 Rate predictor variables (*x*'s) according to the degree of impact they have on each of the respective primary and secondary metrics.

Ask: *'If we were to vary this x across its normal range of variation, how much impact would that have on the y?'* Once again, use a relevant scale to allocate values. (see rating scale options below).

STEP 6 Calculate total scores across the rows for each x by summing the ratings multiplied by their respective weightings.

STEP 7 Sort the *total column* in order of highest value to lowest value. The variables with the highest values are those that are most likely to impact process performance and should be included in the Performance Monitoring Plan.

STEP 8 Select the critical few response and predictor variables you will use in your plan.

Rating Scales – Option 1

In allocating weightings and ratings for each variable, a 1 to 5 scale can be used where:

- 5 = Significant
- 4 = Major
- 3 = Medium
- 2 = Moderate
- 1 = Low

Rating Scales – Option 2

The relationship between x variables and y variables can be quantified in any number of ways. Another way is drawn from Quality Function Deployment (QFD) and that is to use a scale from 0 to 9 where:

- 9 = A strong relationship between x and y
- 3 = A moderate relationship between x and y
- 1 = A weak relationship between x and y
- 0 = No relationship between x and y

This is an example of this approach.

Weighting ⇒	**5**	**4**	**3**		
(y's) ⇒ **(x's) ⇓**	**Coffee Temp**	**Order Accuracy**	**Fill Level**		**TOTAL**
Who Makes the Coffee	9	9	9		**108**
Milk Temperature	9	0	0		**45**
Type of Coffee	1	9	0		**41**

PERFORMANCE MONITORING PLAN

What is it?

The Performance Monitoring Plan (like the data collection plan in the measure phase) is a tool for consolidating multiple measures into a single plan for monitoring the ongoing performance of the process across a balanced family of measures. Measures identified in the CE Matrix become the key inputs to the plan.

Performance Variable	Target Value	What to Measure	How to Measure	Sampling Plan	How to Display	Who
Coffee Temperature (milk based coffee)	65C to 70C (mid range)	The temperate (C^o) of cup content prior to delivery	Aim laser temp gauge at centre of content, record temp C^o to nearest 10th	10 sequentially every hour	Xbar-R Chart	Wait Staff
Process Yield (Defect Free Rate)	100%	Proportion of coffees that meet requirements of customer	Record rejected coffees, subtract reject total from total coffees recorded on POS system and calculate the defect free percentage	Total	Radar Chart of Actual % versus Target %	Wait staff Mgr update radar chart daily

Instructions

Planning data collection requires the team to answer 7 questions with respect to each measure of interest. Each of these questions generates input to the corresponding part of the Performance Monitoring Plan.

Question	Supporting Tools
Q1. Ask: *'What performance measures will provide a balanced view of process performance for this project?'*	SIPOC, CE Tree Diagram, CE Matrix
Q2. Ask: *What is the targeted level of performance?'*	Specification Limits
Q3. Ask: *What is the definition of this measure and how is the measurement undertaken?'*	Operational Definition
Q4. Ask: *How big a sample will we collect and what method of sampling will we employ?'*	Sample Size Equations Sampling Methods
Q5. Ask: *How can we best display the data?'*	Charts / Plots / Dashboards
Q6. Ask: *Who will be responsible for ensuring that the measurements are undertaken and charts / performance dashboards are updated?'*	

PROCESS PERFORMANCE CONTROL PLAN

What is it?

On most occasions for Lean Six Sigma project work, statistical process control will be a suitable method for controlling process performance. The Process Performance Control Plan is a framework for planning the use of statistical process control methods, including the development of appropriate responses for deviations.

PROCESS CONTROL POINTS

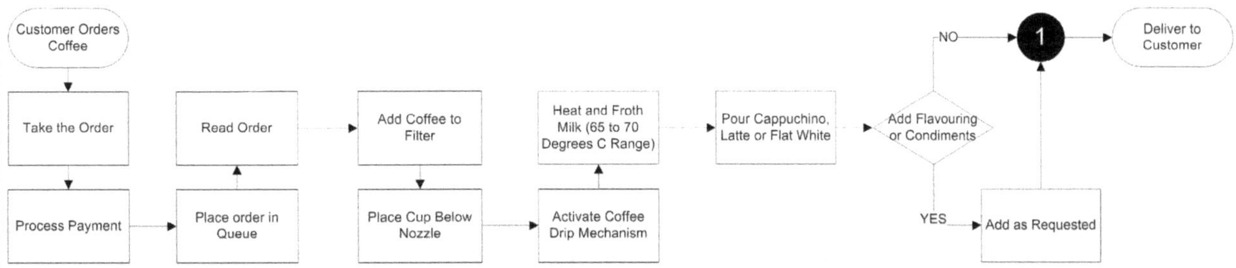

PROCESS MONITORING PLAN

Key Performance Variables	(Point 1) Coffee Temperature	(Point 1) Cycle Time	
LSL	65 degrees (Celsius)	Na	
USL	70 degrees (Celsius)	2 minutes	
Target	Midrange	< 2 minutes	
What will be measured	The temperate (C°) of cup content prior to delivery	Time in minutes to produce and deliver product to customer	
How will it be measured	Aim laser temp gauge at centre of content, record temp C° to nearest 10th	Write time of delivery on docket, calculate gap in minutes and secs. versus order time on docket	
Who will measure it	Wait Staff	Wait Staff	
Sample Size and Frequency	10 every hour	10 every hour	
Control Chart Type	(Not required)	Xbar-S Chart	

RESPONSE PLAN

Trigger:	Temp < 65°C or > 70 °C	Evidence of shift or drift towards > 2min	
Action:	Return product	Discuss with staff	
Who Takes Action:	Wait Staff	Manager	
Notification:	Record defect	na	

Instructions

Process Control Points

STEP 1 Document the new process flowchart and include a visual representation of the points where controls will be applied. Insert in the space provided.

Process Monitoring Plan

STEP 2 Determine the key performance variables (KPVs) for the process. KPV's are usually key output variables linked to critical-to-quality requirements of the customer, or key input variables linked to causal factors that have a correlation to key output variables.

- These may be variables associated with the root causes identified during the 'analyse' phase of project work.

STEP 3 Define and document Upper and Lower specification limits as described by customers.

STEP 4 Specify the targeted level of performance. This is the ideal result for each KPV being monitored.

STEP 5 Operationally define the measure by describing what will be measured and how it will be measured and determine who is responsible for collecting data.

STEP 6 Develop the sampling plan by determining how many data points will be collected each time a sample is taken and how often this sampling will take place.

STEP 7 Using a relevant decision flowchart, determine the type of control chart to be used for monitoring process stability.

- A control chart may not be necessary when the trigger for corrective action is only based on its relationship with specification limits.

Response Plan

STEP 8 Determine what will be a trigger to corrective action. A trigger is an event or result, when observed is cause for action to be taken. This trigger is ultimately a decision rule for activating the response plan and it may be based on:

- The results of a single data point and its relationship with specification limits (e.g. a single value above upper specification limit triggers some action).
- The outcomes of studying a series of data points and their relationship with process behaviour (e.g. a process that is showing a shift pattern even though it may be inside specification limits).

STEP 9 Determine the course of action to be taken in the event that the trigger is observed. Describe who is responsible for taking that action and who must be notified in the event of action being taken.

CHAPTER 23: CONTROL PHASE TOLLGATE & CHECKLISTS

TOLLGATE QUESTIONS

The following questions are the kind that may be asked by your Master Black Belt or Lean Six Sigma Project sponsor during a 'Control Phase Tollgate Review' which is indicated as the point between step eighteen and step nineteen on our 20-step roadmap.

	Lean	Six Sigma
CHARTER / SCOPE • What revisions need to be or have been made to the charter? • How has the scope of the project changed? • What changes need to be made to the project time line?	✓	✓
PROCESS STANDARDISATION • Did your work result in changes to the process of work? • How did you document that new process? • How do you plan to institutionalise that new process?	✓	✓
CUSTOMER IMPACT • How did you go about identifying customers' needs and requirements for this process? • How did you validate those customers' requirements? • How do you know changes in the process will not adversely affect customers?	✓	✓
PROCESS PERFORMANCE MONITORING & CONTROL • How do you intend to monitor process performance? • What specific variables have you included in your monitoring plan? • Why did you choose those variables over others not included? • Which of these are really lead indicators that provide early warning of changes to outcomes? • How will performance results be communicated? • What control mechanisms do you plan to put in place so operators can respond to deviations from the expected level of performance?	✓	✓

	Lean	Six Sigma
BENEFITS • What improvements have you observed to date? • What benefits have been realised and captured? • How are benefits going to be tracked? • How do you intend to ensure that claimed benefits are real?	✓	✓
LEARNINGS • What have you learnt during this experience? • What learnings have you shared? • What learnings should be shared? • How do you intend to make your learnings accessible to other project team leaders? • How have you documented your project work? • How can people access information about your work?	✓	✓
TEAM RECOGNITION • What activities have you undertaken to date to recognise and reward team members for their work? • What have you planned to do to recognise and reward team members for their contribution?	✓	✓

CONTROL PHASE CHECKLIST

Lean and Six Sigma Specific Projects

If you have responded appropriately to each of the following statements, then congratulations – you are ready to apply what you have learnt to another project.		YES	NO	NA
1	The new process has been documented and institutionalised through relevant training.			
2	Measures for monitoring performance of the process have been selected.			
3	A performance monitoring plan that describes how performance will be monitored has been generated.			
4	A statistical process control plan defining corrective action to take when specific triggers are observed has been put into effect.			
5	The closure of the project can be formally recognised as a specific point in time.			
6	The process owner has formally taken responsibility for the future performance of the process.			
7	The project storyboard / poster has been updated.			
8	The contribution of the team in the projects success has been formally celebrated.			
9	The performance of the process has been monitored over time, and the goals of the project have been achieved.			

CHAPTER 24: TERMS AND DEFINITIONS

TERMS AND DEFINITIONS

One of the indicators of culture is the language used by an organisation. A shift to the use of process improvement methodology introduces new terms as a part of its language. The following list provides definitions for commons terms encountered in Six Sigma.

Andon Lights: A visual control device in a production area, not unlike a traffic light system. They are used to alert managers or supervisors to a variety of conditions. They can be used to communicate needs around materials, support or other quality issues.

- Green = all systems are go
- Yellow = parts are low or an employee has a question
- Red = parts are out of stock or equipment repairs are needed

Asymptotic: The curve associated with a distribution is infinite and theoretically extends indefinitely in both directions without touching the axis. Thus the curve is 'asymptotic' to the X-axis.

Autonomation: This is simply automation with a human touch. Refers to semi-automatic processes where the operator and machine work together. Autonomation allows worker-machine separation. For example, autonomation exists where a machine detects problems and automatically shuts down. It is simply the concept of enabling people and processes to autonomously detect and respond to abnormal conditions. Autonomation is also known by the Japanese term *Jidoka*.

Balanced Production: When this is achieved, all operations or functions produce units at the same rate or cycle time. In a balanced system, the function cycle time is less than 'TAKT' time.

Batch Delay: This is the amount of waiting time experienced by an operation or unit of product while other operations or units are completed or processed.

Batch Processing: This refers to the movement of large numbers of identical units through the manufacturing process at the same time.

Binary Variable: A discrete random variable that has only two possible values. For example, defect or non defect, good or bad, sold or not sold etc. Often these events are referred to in terms of success or failure.

Bivariate Data: Paired values obtained by measuring two different characteristics of an observed unit. (Refer to the Simple Linear Regression section of this text)

Black Belt: A person qualified in the skills of Six Sigma – usually a full time role.

Box Plot: A graph that summarises the distribution of a set of data values. The upper and lower ends of the center box represent the 25th and 75th percentiles of the data. Suspected outliers usually appear as *'s.

Sponsor: Someone who takes responsibility for leading a Six Sigma project at the strategic level. Black belts usually report to and work with project sponsors.

Collinearity: In a multiple regression with more than one X variable, collinearity exists when two or more X variables are nearly linearly combinations of each other. Collinearity is also referred to as multicollinearity and ill conditioning.

Contingency Table: When individual values are cross-classified by levels of two different factors, the tabulated counts for all combinations of levels of the two factors are recorded in a contingency table. The following is an example.

Gender	With Mobile Phone	Without Mobile Phone
Male	73	27
Female	85	15

Continuous Flow Manufacturing (CFM): When materials move one piece at a time through the process, at a rate determined by the supply requirement of the customer.

Continuous Numerical Variables: Data generated through measuring characteristics using an infinitely divisible scale, the result depending on the accuracy of the instrument being used to measure. (e.g. time, weight, length, width etc)

Core Processes: The essential activities performed by an organisation in the production and delivery of products or services to its customers. This includes primary functions involved in the production process, and secondary functions that enable or support the production process.

Correlation: A linear association between two variables, usually represented by x and y. Correlation is usually measured by a correlation coefficient with values ranging from -1 to 1, for example Pearson's Correlation Coefficient (R).

Critical To Quality: Attributes of a product or service that are most important to the customer.

Cubic Function: A cubic function is of the form $y = ax^3 + bx^2 + cx + d$ (also see Linear Function and Quadratic Function).

Curvilinear Function: A function whose plotted values follow a continuous but not necessarily straight line. Examples include polynomial, cubic, quadratic, logistic and exponential curves.

Customer: The recipient of the tangible products or services produced by a process.

Customer Value: A characteristic of a product or service for which the customer is prepared to pay.

Cycle Time: The time that passes between the start and completion of a process or process step (e.g. leave processing, software loading etc).

Defect: A failure to meet a customer's requirement.

Defect Elimination: Eliminating the occurrence of defects, in effect doing things right the first time.

Descriptive Statistics: Describing, summarising and displaying the characteristics of data (typically a sample of data from a population). Descriptive statistics encompass both quantitative and graphical techniques.

Design For Six Sigma: Designing a process to meet customers' requirements to a Six Sigma standard (sometimes the acronym DFSS is used).

Discrete Attributes: Data that is generated from categorical variables and is qualitative in the information it provides. These variables yield values that can only be placed into categories or classes. (e.g. pass or fail, teams in the soccer world cup, causes of failure, defective or non-defective are all discrete attributes)

Discrete Numerical Variables: Data generated through counting attributes, the results are whole units that are not divisible. (e.g. number of defects, number of males, number of players, number of complaints)

DMADV: The acronym for the process design / redesign process – Define, Measures, Analyse, Design and Verify.

DMAIC: The acronym for the process improvement process – Define, Measure, Analyse, Improve and Control.

Effectiveness: Doing work that meets the requirements of customers.

Efficiency: Minimising the use of resources (time, labour, money, materials etc).

Error-proofing: This is the process of designing or engineering a potential failure or cause of failure out of a product or process.

Error-proofing Devices: Any mechanical, electrical, pneumatic or hydraulic device that signals the occurrence of an error or prevents an error being made.

Error-proofing Feature: Any digital or virtual feature that signals the occurrence of an error or prevents an error being made.

5S: Five S refers to a method for creating a clean and orderly work environment with a view to exposing waste and errors. Originally developed by Hiroyuki Hirano, the five S's are sort, shine, set in order, standardise and sustain. The Japanese equivalent or the 5S terms are Seiri (organisation), Seiton (tidiness), Seiso (purity), Seiketso (cleanliness) and Shitsuke (discipline).

FIFO (first in, first out): A method used in production to ensure that the oldest items in a batch are the first ones to move forward in the production process.

Flow Manufacturing: The primary goal of flow manufacturing is 'faster response to customer demand'. It is simply a manufacturing methodology focused on pulling items from suppliers through a synchronised manufacturing process to the end product.

Frequency Distribution: A table into which data is arranged into relative numerically ordered classes or categories. Frequency distributions can be created for categorical and numerical data.

Green Belt: This is a person qualified in the skills of Lean Six Sigma at a basic level – usually a part time role.

Ground Rules: Rules established by a team to ensure that behaviours during a meeting contribute to the achievement of desired outcomes. Ground rules are a foundation for creating norms of behaviour for the team.

Handoffs: The handover of responsibility for critical or non-critical tasks to other individuals or functions.

Hetroscedasticity: Exists when data sets come from different populations and do not have the same variance. The opposite of this is referred to as a state of *homoscedasticity*.

Heteroscedasticity: Exists when the standard deviations of a response (dependent) variable, stratified across the different values of an independent categorical variable, are non-constant or vary widely.

Histogram: A graph that displays the frequencies of binned data in such a way that the frequency of values in each bin is represented by the height of the bar. Each bin corresponds to a group of values along a numerical continuum.

Homoscedasticity: Also known as homogeneity of variance, is an assumption of equal or similar variances in different groups being compared. This is an important assumption of some parametric statistical tests because they are sensitive to uneven variances in samples which can result in biased and skewed test results. In the absence of homoscedasticity a state of *heteroscedasticity* exists.

Hoshin Kanri: A strategic planning approach that integrates the practices of leadership with those of management.

Hypothesis: A proposition, idea, theory or other statement adopted as a starting point for discussion, investigation, study etc. The term hypothesis is used to describe an idea or theory associated with statistical differences between populations and root cause analysis.

Input: Materials, resources or information used by the process to create outputs.

Internal Representation System: A reference to the modalities that we use to mentally create, store and re-present information. The way we code information in this regard is either visual (images), auditory (sounds) or kinaesthetic (feelings). The other two senses of taste (gustatory) and smell (olfactory) are usually included in the kinaesthetic modality.

Interval Estimate – Two values that define or bound at some specified probability level, a range of values that will enclose the unknown population parameter.

Inventory: Refers to any part, product or material that is not immediately required and sits for a period of time in a production line, store or stockpile. Inventory includes raw materials, work in progress as well as finished or final products.

Inventory Turns: The number of times inventory is consumed in a specific period of time.

Just-in-Time (JIT): A term used widely in the manufacturing world to refer to a method where downstream operations pull required parts needed from upstream operations at the required time. Lean thinking concepts are required for the successful implementation of a JIT approach to manufacturing.

Kaizen: This is the Japanese term for 'continuous improvement'. A 'Kaizen Event' is any action that results in or is intended to result in improvement to an existing process.

A closer look at the term 'Kaizen' reveals that the real Japanese meaning is 'to take apart and put back together in a better way'. In the context of business, a 'Kaizen Blitz' refers to 'a rapid and overpowering effort to take apart a process, product, system or service and put it back together in a better way'.

Kanban: This refers to a stocking technique using containers, cards or electronic signals to trigger the flow of materials according to actual production or manufacturing needs and not predictions and forecasts. The term comes from the Japanese word for 'signal'.

Kurtosis: A value that describes the relative concentration of values in the centre of the distribution as compared to the tails. In effect, it is a measure of 'peaked-ness'; i.e. the higher the kurtosis value, the more peaked the distribution is.

Lead Time: This is the total time it will take to meet a customer request or demand as defined by the supplier. (see Little's Law for calculation)

Linear Function: A linear function is of the form y = ax + b (also see Cubic Function and Quadratic Function).

Little's Law: Sometimes referred to as the 'law of velocity', this is the equation used to calculate total lead time. It simply involves dividing total work in progress by the average completion rate. Reducing total lead time involves increasing capacity or average completion rate, or reducing work in progress.

Load Balancing: The process of finding a balance between process capacity and process volume requirements.

Load Levelling: The process of adjusting a production schedule so that unexpected changes in customer demand are met.

Mass Production: (See traditional manufacturing)

Meta-Program: Mental patterns that we habitually use to filter information for the purpose of choosing that which we consider to be significant, motivational, inspirational, and ultimately worth keeping and taking notice of.

Minitab®: The name usually used to describe a statistical analysis software package. It is the same name as the company that created the software: Minitab Inc.

Mistake-proofing: Any activities designed to implement change to an operation for the purpose of reducing or eliminating mistakes.

Moments Of Truth: Those moments where the customer interfaces with the process and can form an opinion about your organisation, either good or bad.

Muda: This is the Japanese term for waste. Anything that interrupts the flow of products and services through the value stream and out to the customer is referred to as Muda.

Multiple Regression: A regression model in which the fitted values of the response variable (y) is a function of the values of more than one predictor variable (x). The most common form of multiple regression is multiple linear regression.

Nonlinear Functions: A function that is not linear and cannot be made into a linear function through the transformation of the response variable (y).

Non-Value Added Work: Process steps that add no value (rework, customer does not care about it, does not transform the product or service in any way) to the process or customer.

Non Parametric Tests: Tests that do not make any distribution assumptions, unlike the case of parametric tests which do make such assumptions.

Output: The tangible products or services produced by the process.

One Piece Flow: This is the process of producing one unit at a time, as opposed to batch processing.

Parameter: A numerical measure that describes a characteristic of a population. A parameter is usually represented by a Greek symbol.

Parametric Tests: Statistical testing methods that can only be used when the assumptions associated with underlying distributions are met. For example, a two sample t test can only be used when the distribution of sample means follows a normal distribution.

Pareto Analysis: Analysing data using the principles of the 80/20 rule: 80 percent of the problems are caused by 20 percent of the causes. Usually involves the generation of a Pareto chart, which is simply a bar chart with data arranged from highest to lowest values.

Point Estimate: A single value determined from sample data, used as an estimate of the value of an unknown population parameter.

Point of Use Inventory: Inventory that is positioned at the location where it will be used.

Poka-Yoke: A Poka-Yoke device is one that prevents incorrect or defective parts from being produced or assembled, or provides for the identification of an error. The Japanese meaning of the term Poka-Yoke is 'to avoid (Yokeru) errors (Poka)'.

Primary Metric: The measure of most interest or one primary to the work being undertaken.

Process: The series of steps that converts inputs into outputs.

Process Capability: The maximum performance your process is capable of delivering.

Process Cycle Efficiency: PCE is a measure of overall process health and is calculated as a percentage by dividing value added time by total lead time (refer to Little's Law). A perfectly efficient process would have 100 percent of its time adding value to the customer. A PCE of 25 percent is considered to be world class, although it will vary according to different applications.

Process Delay: The time a lot or batch must wait until it enters the next process.

Process Flowchart: A diagram that visually identifies the flow or sequence of events in a process.

Production Rate: (see Takt Rate)

Production Smoothing: The process of synchronising the production of different products to match customer demand.

Pull System: A pull system is one in which goods are produced on demand from a downstream process. In a production process it is the flow of resources when it is needed.

Push System: A common (and inefficient) approach is for an operation to produce goods and then hand them off to a downstream process, irrespective of their demands. The flow of resources is pushed by upstream operations and excess goods are stored until needed, resulting in excess inventory.

Quadratic Function: A quadratic function is of the form $y = ax^2 + bx + c$ (also see Cubic Function and Linear Function).

Quality Function Deployment: Quality Function Deployment (QFD) is a process used to directly link the voice of the customer to internal processes. QFD is used extensively in design of products and services, and forms an integral part of Design for Six Sigma (DFSS). It can be used for manufacturing, service delivery and technology development.

Residuals: The difference between the observed value of a response variable and the expected value that is fitted under a hypothesised model.

Requirement: The verbal representation of customers' needs or expectations, that are specific, measurable and relevant.

Seamless: The integration of end-to-end processes in the business value chain so that transition from one to the next is neither disruptive nor confusing, but rather smooth and consistent.

Secondary Metric: The measure that contributes to variation in the primary metric. In this context, can be used to indicate independent variables forming part of a data collection plan.

Sigma: The Greek word for variation

Significance Level: The pre-selected level of a statistical test that is the probability of rejecting the null hypothesis when it is in fact true. Also referred to as 'alpha', the most common value used in hypothesis testing is 0.05.

SIPOC: The acronym for suppliers, inputs, process, outputs and customers. Used to refer to the table that documents information associated with these elements as well as customer requirements.

Six Sigma Process: A process that only produces 3.4 defects per million opportunities.

Skewness: Skewness is a measure of asymmetry (lack of symmetry). A distribution with a skewness value of zero is perfectly symmetrical.

SMED: (Single Minute Exchange of Dies) A set of techniques for minimising the time taken to change over and set up for production runs. The goal is to take no longer than a period of time in minutes indicated by single digits. For example 8 minutes 30 seconds to change over dies is less than a double digit time frame in minutes.

Statistic: A numerical measure that describes a characteristic of a sample of data. A statistic is usually represented by a Roman symbol.

Statistics: The science of collecting and studying quantitative data.

Stratification: A term used to refer to the process of slicing and dicing data up into relevant categories or subsamples based on one or more characteristics of a population. For example, data for pizza delivery times can be broken up or stratified into delivery times by driver.

Streamline: To streamline a process is to reduce time spent on non-value adding activities such as travel, inspection, rework, re-handle, transport and the like.

Supplier: One who supplies inputs to the process.

6S: Six S is an extension of the Five S concept. The six S's are safety, sort, shine, set in order, standardise and sustain.

Takt Time: TAKT is the German term for the baton used by an orchestra conductor to regulate the beat or timing at which the musicians play. In the context of manufacturing, it is the pace or rate at which completed products are finished. For example, if your process has a Takt time of 22 minutes, that means you must produce a completed product every 22 minutes to match customer demand. Takt time is calculated to define the speed of the manufacturing line and the cycle times for manufacturing operations. To calculate Takt time you simply divide (a) available work time per day by (b) daily unit demand (or units per day required by the customer).

Takt Rate: While takt time refers to the time period for delivering single units, takt rate refers to units to be delivered per some time period. In the context of continuous production, it is the pace or rate at which units need to be produced within a specified time frame and would be stated as 100,000 tonnes per day for example.

Total Lead Time: (see Lead Time)

Traditional Manufacturing: Known by the term 'mass production', this involves grouping like processes together and then producing large batches of a part. These parts are then held in queue until the next stage of production takes place. This is sometimes referred to as 'batch and queue production'.

Transfer Function: An equation that describes the relationship between the input and the output of a system, subsystem, or equipment in terms of transfer characteristics. In this context, the transfer function most commonly referred to is $y = f(x)$.

VA/NVA Ratio: This is a ratio that is calculated by comparing the amount of value added time to non value added time in a work process.

Value Adding: Steps in a process that add value (done right the first time, transforms the product, the customer cares about it) to the service or product being produced.

Value Enabling: Steps in a process that do not necessarily add value to the service or product being produced, but are necessary for the existence of value adding activities. For example, auditing an internal system may not add value to the product line, however it ensures compliance with legislation that is necessary for continuing the production of products and services.

Value Stream: A value stream is all activities or operations required for the design, ordering, production and delivery of products or services to a customer.

Value Stream Mapping: The process of documenting the flow of information, materials and production required for each product or service offered by a company using simple graphics and icons.

Variation: Inconsistencies in attributes of a product or service.

Visual Control: The placement in plain view of all tools, parts, production indicators and activities for production system performance so that the status and function of the system can be quickly and easily understood. A visual control can be as simple as lines defining the boundaries of a specific work cell.

Waste: Waste is any activity that uses time, resources or space but does not add value to a product or service. Activities associated with any of these categories are essentially waste:

- Defects
- Inventory
- Motion
- Transportation
- Over Production
- Waiting
- Non Value Added Processing

WIP: WIP is work in progress or units partially completed passing through a process, WIP is waste.

WIP Time: The time that a unit will wait for a downstream process to begin work on it.

Work Cell: A work cell comprises a series of machines or processes that perform different operations in a tight sequence to permit single piece flow. Work cells are typically arranged in U, L, T or Z shape to maximise flow and minimise waste.

Workflow: This refers to the steps or motions made by suppliers, employees and distributors to complete work tasks.

Workflow Diagram: A workflow diagram is one that shows equipment layout and the actual movement of materials and people in the production process. It maximises the use of graphics and icons to represent the flow of work.

PART 4: APPENDICES

APPENDIX A - EXPONENTIAL EQUATIONS

Named after an 18th century Swiss mathematician, Euler's number e is used widely in mathematical problems involving natural growth and decay. It is an irrational number like π, and must be approximated.

The value of e is found by taking the expression: $\left(1+\frac{1}{n}\right)^n$, and calculating the result for increasing values of n.

$n = 1$	$\left(1+\frac{1}{n}\right)^n = \left(1+\frac{1}{1}\right)^1 = 2$
$n = 2$	$\left(1+\frac{1}{n}\right)^n = \left(1+\frac{1}{2}\right)^2 = 2.25$
$n = 3$	$\left(1+\frac{1}{n}\right)^n = \left(1+\frac{1}{3}\right)^3 = 2.37037$
$n = 5$	$\left(1+\frac{1}{n}\right)^n = \left(1+\frac{1}{5}\right)^5 = 2.48832$
$n = 10$	$\left(1+\frac{1}{n}\right)^n = \left(1+\frac{1}{10}\right)^{10} = 2.59374$
$n = 100$	$\left(1+\frac{1}{n}\right)^n = \left(1+\frac{1}{100}\right)^{100} = 2.70481$
$n = 1{,}000$	$\left(1+\frac{1}{n}\right)^n = \left(1+\frac{1}{1000}\right)^{1000} = 2.71692$
$n = 10{,}000$	$\left(1+\frac{1}{n}\right)^n = \left(1+\frac{1}{10000}\right)^{10000} = 2.71815$

As n increases in the equation $\left(1+\frac{1}{n}\right)^n$, the result gets closer and closer to 2.718281 or the value of e where:

$$e = \lim_{n\to\infty}\left(1+\frac{1}{n}\right)^n$$

APPENDIX B - TABLE OF VARIABLE CONTROL CHART FACTORS

	X-bar Chart		S Chart		Estimating σ			R Chart		X Chart
Subgroup Size n	A_2	A_3	B_3	B_4	c_4	d_2	d_3	D_3	D_4	E2
2	1.880	2.659	0	3.267	0.7979	1.128	0.853	0	3.267	2.660
3	1.023	1.954	0	2.568	0.8862	1.693	0.888	0	2.575	1.772
4	0.729	1.628	0	2.266	0.9213	2.059	0.880	0	2.282	1.457
5	0.577	1.427	0	2.089	0.9400	2.326	0.864	0	2.114	1.290
6	0.483	1.287	0.030	1.970	0.9515	2.534	0.848	0	2.004	1.184
7	0.419	1.182	0.118	1.882	0.9594	2.704	0.833	0.076	1.924	1.109
8	0.373	1.099	0.185	1.815	0.9650	2.847	0.820	0.136	1.864	1.054
9	0.337	1.032	0.239	1.761	0.9693	2.970	0.808	0.184	1.816	1.010
10	0.308	0.975	0.284	1.716	0.9727	3.078	0.797	0.223	1.777	0.975
11	0.285	0.927	0.321	1.679	0.9754	3.173	0.787	0.256	1.744	0.945
12	0.266	0.886	0.354	1.646	0.9776	3.258	0.778	0.284	1.716	0.921
13	0.249	0.850	0.382	1.618	0.9794	3.336	0.770	0.308	1.692	0.899
14	0.235	0.817	0.406	1.594	0.9810	3.407	0.763	0.329	1.671	0.881
15	0.223	0.789	0.428	1.572	0.9823	3.472	0.756	0.348	1.652	0.864
16	0.212	0.763	0.448	1.552	0.9835	3.532	0.750	0.364	1.636	0.849
17	0.203	0.739	0.466	1.534	0.9845	3.588	0.744	0.379	1.621	0.836
18	0.194	0.718	0.482	1.518	0.9854	3.640	0.739	0.392	1.608	0.824
19	0.187	0.698	0.497	1.503	0.9862	3.689	0.734	0.404	1.596	0.813
20	0.180	0.680	0.510	1.490	0.9869	3.735	0.729	0.414	1.586	0.803
21	0.173	0.663	0.523	1.477	0.9876	3.778	0.724	0.425	1.575	0.794
22	0.167	0.647	0.534	1.466	0.9882	3.819	0.720	0.434	1.566	0.786
23	0.162	0.633	0.545	1.455	0.9887	3.858	0.716	0.443	1.557	0.778
24	0.157	0.619	0.555	1.445	0.9892	3.895	0.712	0.452	1.548	0.770
25	0.153	0.606	0.565	1.435	0.9896	3.931	0.708	0.459	1.541	0.763

APPENDIX C - 'PROCESS SIGMA' CONVERSION TABLE

DPMO	Process Sigma (ST)	Process Sigma (LT)	Yield (LT)	DPMO	Process Sigma (ST)	Process Sigma (LT)	Yield (LT)
3.4	6	4.5	99.99966%	66,800	3	1.5	93.3200%
5	5.9	4.4	99.9995%	80,800	2.9	1.4	91.9200%
8	5.8	4.3	99.9992%	96,800	2.8	1.3	90.3200%
10	5.7	4.2	99.9990%	115,000	2.7	1.2	88.5000%
20	5.6	4.1	99.9980%	135,000	2.6	1.1	86.5000%
30	5.5	4.0	99.9970%	158,000	2.5	1.0	84.2000%
40	5.4	3.9	99.9960%	184,000	2.4	0.9	81.6000%
70	5.3	3.8	99.9930%	212,000	2.3	0.8	78.8000%
100	5.2	3.7	99.9900%	242,000	2.2	0.7	75.8000%
150	5.1	3.6	99.9850%	274,000	2.1	0.6	72.6000%
230	5	3.5	99.9770%	308,000	2	0.5	69.2000%
330	4.9	3.4	99.9670%	344,000	1.9	0.4	65.6000%
480	4.8	3.3	99.9520%	382,000	1.8	0.3	61.8000%
680	4.7	3.2	99.9320%	420,000	1.7	0.2	58.0000%
960	4.6	3.1	99.9040%	460,000	1.6	0.1	54.0000%
1,350	4.5	3.0	99.8650%	500,000	1.5	0.09	50.0000%
1,860	4.4	2.9	99.8140%	540,000	1.4	0.08	46.0000%
2,550	4.3	2.8	99.7450%	570,000	1.3	0.07	43.0000%
3,460	4.2	2.7	99.6540%	610,000	1.2	0.06	39.0000%
4,660	4.1	2.6	99.5340%	650,000	1.1	0.05	35.0000%
6,210	4	2.5	99.3790%	690,000	1	0.04	31.0000%
8,190	3.9	2.4	99.1810%	720,000	0.9	0.03	28.0000%
10,700	3.8	2.3	98.9300%	750,000	0.8	0.02	25.0000%
13,900	3.7	2.2	98.6100%	780,000	0.7	0.01	22.0000%
17,800	3.6	2.1	98.2200%	810,000	0.6		19.0000%
22,700	3.5	2.0	97.7300%	840,000	0.5		16.0000%
28,700	3.4	1.9	97.1300%	860,000	0.4		14.0000%
35,900	3.3	1.8	96.4100%	880,000	0.3		12.0000%
44,600	3.2	1.7	95.5400%	900,000	0.2		10.0000%
54,800	3.1	1.6	94.5200%	920,000	0.1		8.0000%

APPENDIX D - Z_{ST} TO DPMO CONVERSION TABLE

Z (ST)	.00	.01	.02	.03	.04	.05	.06	.07	.08	.09
1.5	500,000	496,000	492,000	488,000	484,000	480,100	476,100	472,100	468,100	464,100
1.6	460,200	456,200	452,200	448,300	444,300	440,400	436,400	432,500	428,600	424,700
1.7	420,700	416,800	412,900	409,000	405,200	401,300	397,400	393,600	389,700	385,900
1.8	382,100	378,300	374,500	370,700	366,900	363,200	359,400	355,700	352,000	348,300
1.9	344,600	340,900	337,200	333,600	330,000	326,400	322,800	319,200	315,600	312,100
2.0	308,500	305,000	301,500	298,100	294,600	291,200	287,700	284,300	281,000	277,600
2.1	274,300	270,900	267,600	264,300	261,100	257,800	254,600	251,400	248,300	245,100
2.2	242,000	238,900	235,800	232,700	229,700	226,600	223,600	220,700	217,700	214,800
2.3	211.900	209,000	206,100	203,300	200,500	197,700	194,900	192,200	189,400	186,700
2.4	184,100	181,400	178,800	176,200	173,600	171,100	168,500	166,000	163,500	161,100
2.5	158,700	156,200	153,900	151,500	149,200	146,900	144,600	142,300	140,100	137,900
2.6	135,700	133,500	131,400	129,200	127,100	125,100	123,000	121,000	119,000	117,000
2.7	115,100	113,100	111,200	109,300	107,500	105,600	103,800	102,000	100,300	98,530
2.8	96,800	95,100	93,420	91,760	90,120	88,510	86,910	85,340	83,790	82,260
2.9	80,760	79,270	77,800	76,360	74,930	73,530	72,140	70,780	69,440	68,110
3.0	66,810	65,520	64,260	63,010	61,780	60,570	59,380	58,210	57,050	55,920
3.1	54,800	53,700	52,620	51,550	50,500	49,470	48,460	47,460	46,480	45,510
3.2	44,570	43,630	42,720	41,820	40,930	40,060	39,200	38,360	37,540	36,730
3.3	35,930	35,150	34,380	33,630	32,880	32,160	31,440	30,740	30,050	29,380
3.4	28,720	28,070	27,430	26,800	26,190	25,590	25,000	24,420	23,850	23,300
3.5	22,750	22,220	21,690	21,180	20,680	20,180	19,700	19,203	18,760	18,310
3.6	17,860	17,430	17,000	16,590	15,180	15,780	15,390	15,000	14,630	14,260
3.7	13,900	13,550	13,210	12,870	12,550	12,220	11,910	11,600	11,300	11,010
3.8	10,720	10,440	10,170	9,903	9,642	9,387	9,137	8,894	8,656	8,424
3.9	8,198	7,976	7,760	7,549	7,344	7,143	6,947	6,756	6,569	6,387
4.0	6,210	6,036	5,868	5,703	5,543	5,386	5,234	5,085	4,940	4,799
4.1	4,661	4,527	4,396	4,269	4,145	4,024	3,907	3,792	3,681	3,572
4.2	3,467	3,364	3,264	3,167	3,072	2,980	2,890	2,803	2,718	2,635
4.3	2,555	2,477	2,401	2,327	2,256	2,186	2,118	2,052	1,988	1,926
4.4	1,866	1,807	1,750	1,695	1,641	1,589	1,538	1,489	1,441	1,395
4.5	1,350	1,306	1,264	1,223	1,183	1,144	1,107	1,070	1,035	1,001
4.6	968	935	904	874	845	816	789	762	736	711

Z (ST)	.00	.01	.02	.03	.04	.05	.06	.07	.08	.09
4.7	687	664	641	619	598	577	557	538	519	501
4.8	484	467	450	434	419	404	390	376	363	350
4.9	337	325	313	302	291	280	270	260	251	242
5.0	233	224	216	208	200	193	186	179	172	166
5.1	159	153	147	142	136	131	126	121	117	112
5.2	108	104	100	96	92	89	85	82	79	75
5.3	72	70	67	64	62	59	57	55	52	50
5.4	48	46	44	43	41	39	38	36	35	33
5.5	32	30	29	28	27	26	25	24	23	22
5.6	21	20.0	19.0	18.0	17.0	17.0	16.0	15.3	14.7	14.0
5.7	13.4	12.9	12.3	11.7	11.3	10.8	10.3	9.9	9.4	9.0
5.8	8.6	8.2	7.9	7.5	7.2	6.9	6.6	6.3	6.0	5.7
5.9	5.4	5.2	5.0	4.8	4.6	4.4	4.2	4.0	3.8	3.6
6.0	3.4	3.3	3.1	3.0	2.9	2.7	2.6	2.5	2.4	2.3

APPENDIX E - Z TABLE FOR NORMAL DISTRIBUTION

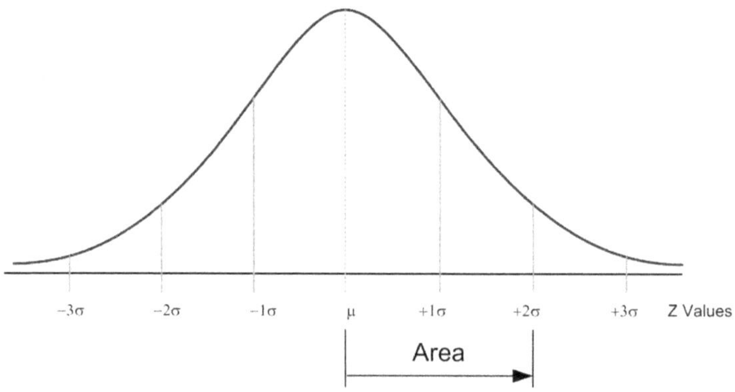

Z Value	.00	.01	.02	.03	.04	.05	.06	.07	.08	.09
0.0	.0000	.0040	.0080	.0120	.0160	.0199	.0239	.0279	.0319	.0359
0.1	.0398	.0438	.0478	.0517	.0557	.0596	.0636	.0675	.0714	.0753
0.2	.0793	.0832	.0871	.0910	.0948	.0987	.1026	.1064	.1103	.1141
0.3	.1179	.1217	.1255	.1293	.1331	.1368	.1406	.1443	.1480	.1517
0.4	.1554	.1591	.1628	.1664	.1700	.1736	.1772	.1808	.1844	.1879
0.5	.1915	.1950	.1985	.2019	.2054	.2088	.2123	.2157	.2190	.2224
0.6	.2257	.2291	.2324	.2357	.2389	.2422	.2454	.2486	.2518	.2549
0.7	.2580	.2612	.2642	.2673	.2704	.2734	.2764	.2794	.2823	.2852
0.8	.2881	.2910	.2939	.2967	.2995	.3023	.3051	.3078	.3106	.3133
0.9	.3159	.3186	.3212	.3238	.3264	.3289	.3315	.3340	.3365	.3389
1.0	.3413	.3438	.3461	.3485	.3508	.3531	.3554	.3577	.3599	.3621
1.1	.3643	.3665	.3686	.3708	.3729	.3749	.3770	.3790	.3810	.3830
1.2	.3849	.3869	.3888	.3907	.3925	.3944	.3962	.3980	.3997	.4015
1.3	.4032	.4049	.4066	.4082	.4099	.4115	.4131	.4147	.4162	.4177
1.4	.4192	.4207	.4222	.4236	.4251	.4265	.4279	.4292	.4306	.4319
1.5	.4332	.4345	.4357	.4370	.4382	.4394	.4406	.4418	.4429	.4441
1.6	.4452	.4463	.4474	.4484	.4495	.4505	.4515	.4525	.4535	.4545
1.7	.4554	.4564	.4573	.4582	.4591	.4599	.4608	.4616	.4625	.4633
1.8	.4641	.4649	.4656	.4664	.4671	.4678	.4686	.4693	.4699	.4706
1.9	.4713	.4719	.4726	.4732	.4738	.4744	.4750	.4756	.4761	.4767
2.0	.4772	.4778	.4783	.4788	.4793	.4798	.4803	.4808	.4812	.4817
2.1	.4821	.4826	.4830	.4834	.4838	.4842	.4846	.4850	.4854	.4857
2.2	.4861	.4864	.4868	.4871	.4875	.4878	.4881	.4884	.4887	.4890

Z Value	.00	.01	.02	.03	.04	.05	.06	.07	.08	.09
2.3	.4893	.4896	.4898	.4901	.4904	.4906	.4909	.4911	.4913	.4916
2.4	.4918	.4920	.4922	.4925	.4927	.4929	.4931	.4932	.4934	.4936
2.5	.4938	.4940	.4941	.4943	.4945	.4946	.4948	.4949	.4951	.4952
2.6	.4953	.4955	.4956	.4957	.4959	.4960	.4961	.4962	.4963	.4964
2.7	.4965	.4966	.4967	.4968	.4969	.4970	.4971	.4972	.4973	.4974
2.8	.4974	.4975	.4976	.4977	.4977	.4978	.4979	.4979	.4980	.4981
2.9	.4981	.4982	.4982	.4983	.4984	.4984	.4985	.4985	.4986	.4986
3.0	.49865	.49869	.49874	.49878	.49882	.49886	.49889	.49893	.49897	.49900
3.1	.49903	.49906	.49910	.49913	.49916	.49918	.49921	.49924	.49926	.49929
3.2	.49931	.49934	.49936	.49938	.49940	.49942.	49944	.49946	.49948	.49950
3.3	.49952	.49953	.49955	.49957	.49958	.49960	.49961	.49962	.49964	.49965
3.4	.49966	.49968	.49969	.49970	.49971	.49972	.49973	.49974	.49975	.49976
3.5	.49977	.49978	.49978	.49979	.49980	.49981	.49981	.49982	.49983	.49983
3.6	.49984	.49985	.49985	.49986	.49986	.49987	.49987	.49988	.49988	.49989
3.7	.49989	.49990	.49990	.49990	.49991	.49991	.49992	.49992	.49992	.49992
3.8	.49993	.49993	.49993	.49994	.49994	.49994	.49994	.49995	.49995	.49995
3.9	.49995	.49995	.49996	.49996	.49996	.49996	.49996	.49996	.49997	.49997

EXAMPLE
Z Value = 1.06

Z Value	.00	.01	.02	.03	.04	.05	.06	.07	.08	.09
0.0	.0000	.0040	.0080	.0120	.0160	.0199	[illegible]	.0279	.0319	.0359
0.1	.0398	.0438	.0478	.0517	.0557	.0596	[illegible]	.0675	.0714	.0753
0.2	.0793	.0832	.0871	.0910	.0948	.0987	[illegible]	.1064	.1103	.1141
0.3	.1179	.1217	.1255	.1293	.1331	.1368	[illegible]	.1443	.1480	.1517
0.4	.1554	.1591	.1628	.1664	.1700	.1736	[illegible]	.1808	.1844	.1879
0.5	.1915	.1950	.1985	.2019	.2054	.2088	[illegible]	.2157	.2190	.2224
0.6	.2257	.2291	.2324	.2357	.2389	.2422	[illegible]	.2486	.2518	.2549
0.7	.2580	.2612	.2642	.2673	.2704	.2734	[illegible]	.2794	.2823	.2852
0.8	.2881	.2910	.2939	.2967	.2995	.3023	[illegible]	.3078	.3106	.3133
0.9	.3159	.3186	.3212	.3238	.3264	.3289	[illegible]	.3340	.3365	.3389
1.0	[illegible]	[illegible]	[illegible]	[illegible]	[illegible]	[illegible]	.3554	.3577	.3599	.3621

Area underneath the normal distribution curve from 0 to 1.06 = 0.3554 or 35.54%

Area underneath the normal distribution curve between -1.06 and 1.06 = 2 x 0.3554 = 0.7108 or 71.08%

APPENDIX F - CRITICAL VALUES FOR T DISTRIBUTION

Degrees of Freedom (df)	$t_{\alpha/2}$ Values				
	t 0.10	t 0.05	t 0.025	t 0.01	t 0.005
1	3.078	6.314	12.706	31.821	63.657
2	1.886	2.920	4.303	6.965	9.925
3	1.638	2.353	3.182	4.541	5.841
4	1.533	2.132	2.776	3.747	4.604
5	1.476	2.015	2.571	3.365	4.032
6	1.440	1.943	2.447	3.143	3.707
7	1.415	1.895	2.365	2.998	3.499
8	1.397	1.860	2.306	2.896	3.355
9	1.383	1.833	2.262	2.821	3.250
10	1.372	1.812	2.228	2.764	3.169
11	1.363	1.796	2.201	2.718	3.106
12	1.356	1.782	2.179	2.681	3.055
13	1.350	1.771	2.160	2.650	3.012
14	1.345	1.761	2.145	2.624	2.977
15	1.341	1.753	2.131	2.602	2.947
16	1.337	1.746	2.120	2.583	2.921
17	1.333	1.740	2.110	2.567	2.898
18	1.330	1.734	2.101	2.552	2.878
19	1.328	1.729	2.093	2.539	2.861
20	1.325	1.725	2.086	2.528	2.845
21	1.323	1.721	2.080	2.518	2.831
22	1.321	1.717	2.074	2.508	2.819
23	1.319	1.714	2.069	2.500	2.807
24	1.318	1.711	2.064	2.492	2.797
25	1.316	1.708	2.060	2.485	2.787
26	1.315	1.706	2.056	2.479	2.779
27	1.314	1.703	2.052	2.473	2.771
28	1.313	1.701	2.048	2.467	2.763
29	1.311	1.699	2.045	2.462	2.756
n >= 30	1.282	1.645	1.960	2.326	2.576

APPENDIX G – ANSWERS TO PROBLEMS

Nine Dots Activity

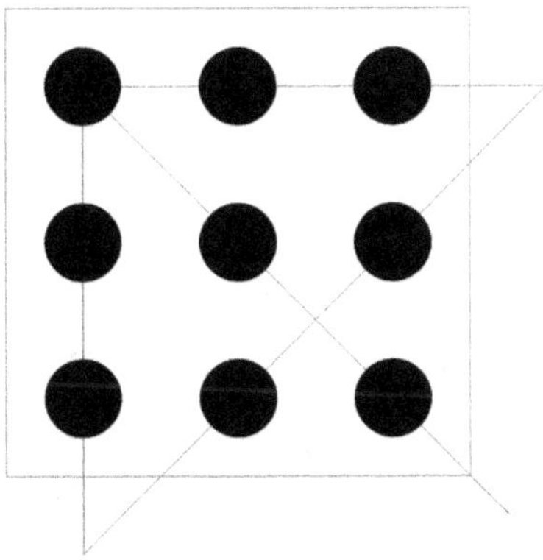

Join the Boxes

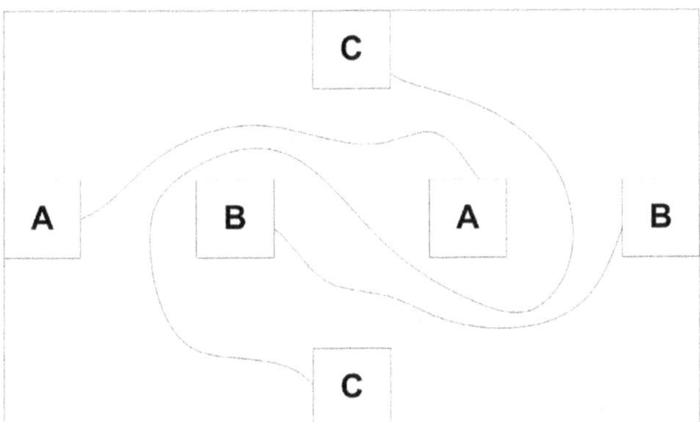

Roman Numerals

SIX

Related Numbers

They're arranged alphabetically.

Rebus Puzzles

Paraphernalia	Three degrees below zero	Backward Glance
Better late than never	Search high and low	One at a time

APPENDIX H – LEAN PROJECTS AND THE 20 STEP DMAIC ROADMAP

The arrows depict the author's view of how a Lean specific project can pass through the 20 step DMAIC roadmap.

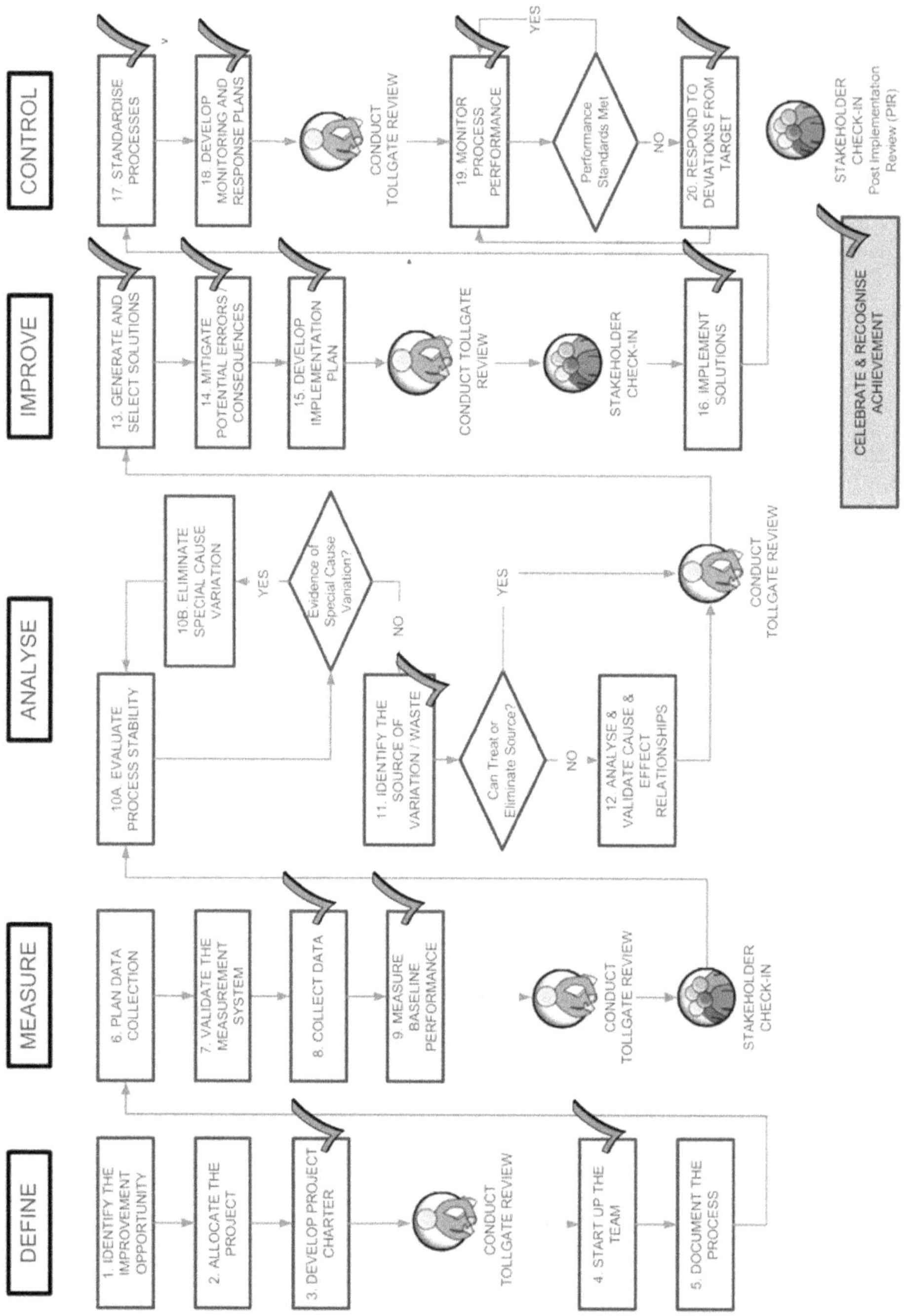

APPENDIX I - ACCELERATED PROJECTS / KAIZEN

(**Note:** This appendix is a blending of two approaches to rapid project completion prepared by Harry Sinko and the author)

The #1 Rule of Improvement Project Time Frames

> *'Where did this thinking about how long a typical [improvement] project should take, come from? I now think that this belief about typical time frame for a project has been developed through experience with more complex types of projects. …… The reality is this – the minimum time frame for project completion depends entirely upon the type of project being undertaken. The only rule that I promote about project duration is this:*
>
> ***A project should take no longer than 12 to 16 weeks to complete.'***

If you can complete a project in one week, why not do it? Stipulating that a project takes three months to complete, as I was told when first trained with Six Sigma, does not make sense to me.

Let me offer you two reasons why I promote a 'maximum time' as the only time frame principle.

1. Business leaders must see results in a reasonable time frame if you want their continued support and involvement.
2. Momentum for continual improvement is more likely to be generated when projects are being completed in a reasonable time and success is frequently experienced.

A Philosophy of Continual and Rapid Improvement

Completing projects in a minimum amount of time provides a number of benefits to key stakeholders and participants associated with an organisation employing Lean Six Sigma methodology. The most obvious benefit is prompt realisation of financial benefits. However, this is only the tip of the iceberg as additional gains can be experienced by organisations, as well as direct benefits for customers and employees.

A significant benefit that accelerated projects can deliver is a more rapid building of a continuous improvement culture within the organisation. This is possible where there are a number of accelerated projects running concurrently with larger more complex projects. However it must be said that all projects have the ability to be accelerated, even the larger type. This may not be immediately obvious to you given the size of this book and the amount of tools contained within it; however this section should help resolve this dichotomy.

Any change in an organisation can be challenging as successful and sustainable change fundamentally means a different way of doing things. Organisations and the people within them building or transitioning to a Continuous Improvement culture are challenged by this reality constantly. Accelerated projects can greatly assist this effort through the presentation of high frequency opportunities for employees to engage in. This engagement not only delivers measurable benefits to the organisation and its customers, it also provides the opportunity to improve the workplace and employee contribution and self worth.

This high frequency opportunity environment introduces quicker learning cycles leading to increased competency and confidence building in project leaders, management and employees. Managed and executed well it also creates a collaborative and 'can-do 'environment where greater levels of responsibility and autonomy flourish.

Building critical mass to transit to and sustain a CI culture within any organisation is largely about two things, motivating employees and demonstrating positive achievement.

It is no secret that employees who are (a) asked to contribute to overcoming challenges, (b) engaged in problem solving and (c) considered as being able to contribute to solutions develop a sense of worth, ownership and pride. They are naturally much more motivated.

Given that, accelerated projects offer high frequency opportunities that lead to high frequency learning cycles (using new tools and techniques) which creates a breeding ground for capability building and confidence development which in turn leads to successful outcomes and achievements.

This is why we strongly support and encourage a strong and healthy diet of accelerated projects in any organisation. In this section we will discuss two variations to accelerated projects. Both approaches utilise the DMAIC framework, albeit an abridged version as is depicted in the flowchart on the following page.

1. The Accelerated Project Approach

The accelerated approach is based on the following six principles:

- **1. LOGIC** - The logic of the DMAIC model is still applied.
- **2. MINIMUM WORK** - The only steps completed and tools used are those necessary for getting optimum solutions and generating buy-in from key stakeholders.
- **3. PRE-WORK** - Data collection and analysis is undertaken before bringing the project team together.
- **4. FOCUSED ANALYSIS** - Analysis [of any kind] is only undertaken to answer specific questions and confirm or negate cause & effect relationships.
- **5. TIME FRAME** - The project is conducted as a series of meetings in a short period of time (i.e. 1 week).
- **6. TEAM** - Team member resources are appropriately allocated, scheduled and made available for the duration of project work. A team leader that plans the entire project before it starts will be able to inform relevant stakeholders of resource requirements in advance.

If you apply these principles, our experience is your Lean or Six Sigma project can take as little as 3-days to produce a solution implementation plan. You may not be able to have solutions implemented in that time frame, but you can certainly walk away with a plan for making the change happen.

Accelerated Project Process With DMAIC

The flowchart on the following page depicts the author's approach to accelerating improvement projects with reference to the DMAIC roadmap.

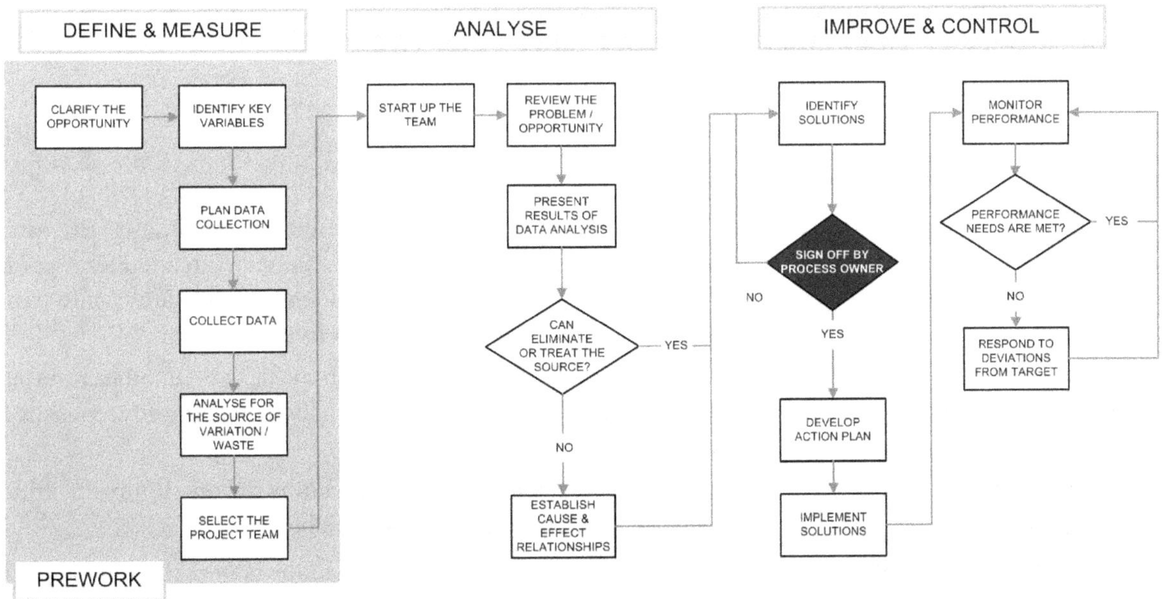

Accelerated Project Process with DMAIC

2. Kaizen

Kaizen is a specific type of structured accelerated project. It was first developed in organisations applying a Lean framework. It also closely follows the DMAIC framework represented in previous diagram.

It is beneficial to think about it as three key stages:

1. Preparation
2. The Kaizen event
3. Follow up

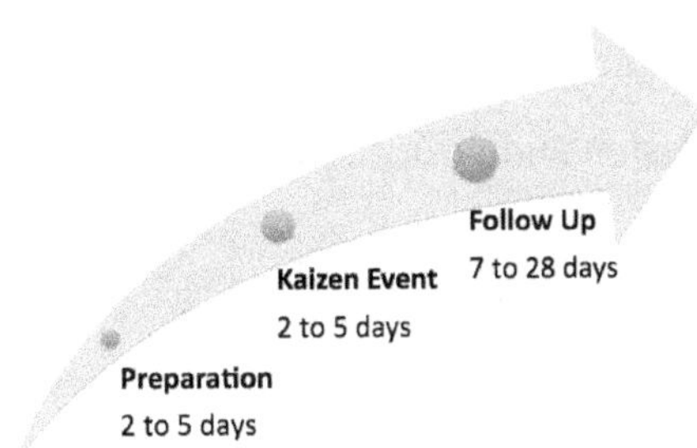

1. Preparation

This first stage is similar to the 'pre-work' phase of the Accelerated Project Process previously described. This stage includes:

- Clarifying the opportunity and establish an agreed project charter
- Identifying the key variables
- Planning data collection and collecting any available historical data

- Selecting and advising the project team
- Securing logistics, i.e. area with appropriate tools, materials and equipment
- Scheduling any support requirements
- Notifying the management team

2. The Kaizen Event

This stage is nominally planned for a consecutive period of days typically between 2 to 5 days. But since there are variations that may have to be planned subject to circumstances, this is only intended as a guide. As an example of our experience, a natural split that often works well is to condense days 1 and 2 into a one day event separated by a period of time and then running days three through to five.

For the purposes of this discussion we will work on the premise that the Kaizen event is planned to run for 5 days. This includes the last two steps of Define & Measure, along with the Analyse and Improve phases in the Accelerated Project Process.

One final point; the Kaizen program should be considered and as such planned as an on-site event. Since there is a large practical component, this allows workplace incursions to take place.

Let's take a look at how a Kaizen Event might be conducted.

Day 1

- Final preparation
- Initial team meeting, introduction and development.
- Review charter and agenda for the week
- Introduce prepared materials and information

Day 2

- Complete Value Stream Mapping (VSM) and collect additional data
- Calculate process performance
- Analyse VSM and prioritise focus areas

Day 3

- Review VSM Analysis and include and further relevant information
- Conduct solution generation session and prioritise solutions
- Plan solution implementation
- Present proposed solutions to process owner
- Implement/refine solutions

Day 4

- Complete solution implementation
- Prepare and conduct appropriate training
- Finalise standard operating procedures
- Establish new process measures
- Calculate and confirm benefits

Day 5

- Prepare final presentation/storyboard
- Complete training and documentation update
- Prepare final state VSM
- Complete Kaizen evaluation
- Document follow up action plan
- Deliver final presentation

The table below represents a typical 5-day event program.

<table>
<tr><td>MON</td><td colspan="2">Finalise Kaizen Event Preparation</td><td rowspan="5">LUNCH</td><td colspan="2">Introduction, agenda review, team development activities, ground rules, team training</td><td>Measure – Introduce, validate, additional data</td></tr>
<tr><td>TUE</td><td>Measure – Collect and prepare additional data</td><td>Analyse – Existing and additional data</td><td colspan="3">Analyse – Establish root cause and prioritise focus area to prepare solutions</td></tr>
<tr><td>WED</td><td colspan="2">Improve – Solution generation, selection and packaging</td><td colspan="2">Solution implementation review meeting</td><td>Improve – Implement improvements, refine design</td></tr>
<tr><td>THU</td><td colspan="2">Improve – Implement refined improvements, conduct training</td><td colspan="3">Control – Finalise SOP documentation, establish new process measures, calculate benefits</td></tr>
<tr><td>FRI</td><td>Prepare final presentation</td><td>Complete training and document final future state VSM</td><td>Complete Kaizen review, outcomes and storyboard</td><td>Establish follow up action plan</td><td>Deliver final presentation</td></tr>
</table>

3. Follow Up

This stage consists of the steps associated with the Control phase of the Accelerated Project Process, which includes performance monitoring, corrective action response plans and training. It should also include any follow up actions identified during the Kaizen week.

Key Learnings

- All projects can be accelerated
- Accelerated projects offer high cycle of learning environments that build confidence and competence
- Accelerated projects deliver many significant benefits to the organisation's stakeholders
- There are a number of variations in executing accelerated projects.

APPENDIX J - BIBLIOGRAPHY

The main references used in the development of this text are listed below.

(2000), *'Users Guide 2: Data Analysis and Quality Tool'*, MINITAB Inc.

Bank, J., (1992), *'The Essence of Total Quality Management'*, Prentice Hall, New Jersey

Brue, G., (2002), *'Six Sigma for Managers'*, McGraw-Hill, New York

Burke, R., (1999), *'Project Management – Planning and Control Techniques'*, 3rd Edition, Wiley & Sons, New York

Buzan, T. (2002), *'How to Mind Map'*, Thorsons, London

Buzan, T. (2003), *'Brain Child'*, Thorsons, London

Carlopio, J., Andrewartha, G., Armstrong, H., (1997), *'Developing Management Skills in Australia'*, Longman, South Melbourne

Chowdhury, S., (2001), *'The Power of Six Sigma'*, Pearson Education Ltd, London

Clark, L. J., (1991), *'The Essentials of Business Statistics 1'*, New Jersey: Research & Education Association

Craig, M., (2000), *'Visual Thinking'*, Continuum, London

Creveling, C.M., Slutsky, J.L., Antis, D. Jnr., (2003), *'Design for Six Sigma: In Technology and Product Development'*, Prentice Hall, New Jersey

Croucher, J.S., (1998), *'Introductory Mathematics & Statistics for Business'*, 3rd Edition, McGraw-Hill, New York

Day, Ronald G., *'Quality Function Deployment – Linking a Company with Its Customers'*, ASQ Quality Press (1993).

De Bono, E., (1995), *'Serious Creativity'*, Harper Collins, London

Eckes, G., (2003), *'Six Sigma for Everyone'*, Wiley & Sons, New Jersey

Fox, A., (2002), *'Fast Track Managing Conflict'*, Spiro Press, London

Goal/QPC, *'The Black Belt Memory Jogger'*, Goal/QPC, NH

Goal/QPC, *'The Black Belt Memory Jogger II'*, Goal/QPC, NH

Goldratt, E.M., Cox, J., (1984), *'The Goal – A Process of Ongoing Improvement'*, 2nd Revised Edition, The North River Press, Great Barrington

Gosling, J., (1995), *'Introductory Statistics'*, Pascal Press, Sydney

Harry, M., Schroeder, R., (2000), *'Six Sigma – The Breakthrough Management Strategy'*, Doubleday, New York

Heerkens, G.R., (2002), *'Project Management'*, McGraw-Hill, New York

Henry, J.E., Hartzler, M., (1998), *'Tools for Virtual Teams – A Team Fitness Companion'*, ASQ Quality Press, Wisconsin

Heizer, J., Render, B., (1999), *'Operations Management'*, 5th Edition, Prentice Hall, New Jersey

Hoerl, R., Snee, R.D., (2002), *'Statistical Thinking – Improving Business Performance'*, Duxbury, Pacific Grove, California

Hosmer, D.W., Lemeshow, S., (2000), *'Applied Logistic Regression'*, 2nd Ed, John Wiley & Sons Inc.

Justice, T., Jamieson, D.W., ((1999), *'The Facilitator's Fieldbook'*, AMACOM, New York

King, B., (1987), *'Better Designs in Half the Time: Implementing QFD in America'*, Methuen, MA

Lee Sye, G.W., (2007), *'Process Alchemy 2nd Edition'*, Soarent, Brisbane, Australia

Lee Sye, G.W., (2005), *'It's Still Not a Problem – Systematic Problem Solving for Business*, Soarent, Brisbane, Australia

Levine, D.M., Ramsey, P.P., Smidt, R.K., (2001), *'Applied Statistics for Engineers and Scientists'*, New Jersey: Prentice-Hall Inc.

Lewis, J.P., (2002), *'Fundamentals of Project Management'*, 2nd Edition, American Management Association, New York

Mehrabian, A. (1971), *'Silent Messages'*, Belmart: Wardsworth

Meredith, G., Williams, B., (1999), *'Managing Finance – Essential Skills for Managers'*, McGraw-Hill, New York

Montgomery, Douglas, (1997), *Design and Analysis of Experiments*, Wiley

Pande, S.P., Neuman, R.P., Cavanagh, R.R., (2002), *'The Six Sigma Way – Team Fieldbook'*, Mcgraw-Hill, New York

Peters, T., Austin, N., (1986), *'A Passion for Excellence: The Leadership Difference'*, Harper Collins

Pyzdek, T., (2003), *'The Six Sigma Handbook'*, McGraw-Hill, New York

Render, B., Stair Jnr, R.M., (2000), *'Quantitative Analysis for Management'*, 7th Edition, Prentice Hall, New Jersey

Rice, W.B.,(1947), *'Control Charts in Factor Management'*, John Wiley, New York

Robbins, S.P., Waters-Marsh, T., Cacioppe, R., Millett, B., (1994), *'Organisational Behaviour – Concepts, Controversies and Applications'*, Prentice Hall, New York

Rossi, E.L., (1980), *'The Collected Papers of Milton H Erickson'*, Irvington, New York

Senge, P., (1993), *'The Fifth Discipline: The Art and Practice Of The Learning Organisation'*, Random House

Senge, P., Kleiner, A., Roberts, C., Ross, R., Smith, B., (1994), *'The Fifth Discipline Fieldbook: Strategies and Tools for Building a Learning Organisation'*, Doubleday, New York

Wu C.F., Wu J., Hamanda M., (2000), *Experiments: Planning, Analysis, and Parameter Design Optimisation*, Edition 1, Wiley-Interscience,

More About The Author

Educator, Performance Coach and Prolific Writer

George Lee Sye was born in 1959, he has found his niche as an author, leadership educator, and business improvement trainer and coach.

George founded Soarent Vision Pty Ltd in 2000 and has continually run that company as Managing Director.

He founded his first Professional Learning Hub in 2016, and then converted this into its 3rd iteration, and what is now the 9 Skills Factory professional development platform.

He is the platform's lead trainer and this is where he delivers the bulk of his business improvement coaching and leadership education to the world.

More information can be found at - www.9skillsfactory.com

Background

As he says, he has been involved in, and passionate about continuous improvement continually since he first started work in 1975. Going on to get his trade as motor mechanic, he demonstrated a strong propensity for problem solving.

He went on to take that skill into a career with the government working in high risk environments and leading specialist tactical operations.

George's fascination with human behaviour started in the mid 1980s. Intent on understanding how to accelerate the process of building connection and rapport with people in his work, he began a journey of discovery that saw him merge the soft skills of influence with the more technical aspects of problem solving and improvement.

Today

Through his seminars, personal coaching, audio and printed books, George has devoted himself to passing on his knowledge and skill for how to become a master of process improvement and change leadership.

What he has learnt through reading, trial and error and an incredible diversity of experiences is now the backdrop of an incredible body of knowledge that makes up his leadership and business improvement training programs.

His success in guiding the professional development of others has come predominantly through his belief that delivering an idea without a way of using it is nothing more than giving people another topic of conversation. Unless the idea converts to some form of action or behavioural change that positively affects a person's life or business, it is a waste of time.

His ability to simplify what are often considered to be complex topics is remarkable. As a result, he has been able to create considerable value for companies with whom he has worked in the area of business improvement, and his popularity as a corporate educator, speaker and personal coach has grown consistently.

George has fingers in a number of pies including his podcast *The George Experiment* which he launched in 2018. He is also an avid motorcycle enthusiast with the ultimate part time job as an on track ride coach with the *California Superbike School.*

Photo of the author at Phillip Island GP Circuit (2022) - courtesy of SD Pics Photography

Since 2002 he has written a multitude of books, most of which are now distributed on Amazon. For more information about George and his work, visit his web sites.

georgeleesye.com / 9skillsfactory.com / georgeleesye.com/books

Testimonials

George Lee Sye has a cognitive and conceptual ability that is by definition 'genius', however sincere humility would see him embarrassed by such a label. It is rare in each of our lifetimes that we have the opportunity to engage with an individual with George's abilities, altruism and (he would be embarrassed again by this) - compassion, for he actually does care about each person he meets. In previous occupations I would have followed George into any high-risk situation and trusted him with my life implicitly.

Dr. John Rolfe - Queensland Police Service

Thank you for teaching the teacher more about life and leadership. Your course has challenged me to change my personal and professional life for the better. The combination of psychology, theory and good practice has had a significant impact and I now know I can make the vision a reality. Thank you too, for being a mentor and more importantly a friend.

Kevin Tutt - Prince Alfred College

Spending time listening to George was like a glass overflowing. He not only gave us insight into improving our business but our personal lives also. We made changes in all areas of our lives immediately and following the steps George outlines continue to do so. George is not only inspirational but REAL, that's what makes him so successful.

Cobby Vines - Betty Beans Cafes

You are an inspiration to both of us and your seminar could not have come at a better time for us. We speak very highly of your seminar and your books to everyone we meet. Many of our friends, both business and personal, have expressed interest in attending one of your seminars and we could sell a book just about every day. We want to have an impact on people's lives the way you have inspired us.

Sharon Stuckey

Just wanted to let you know how much I enjoyed the course - truly life changing! THANK YOU!! I've already used some of the techniques on both my husband and young friend and the changes are rippling out!

Deanne Tindale - Dreamvast (Owner)

Thank you for showing me a way in which I can focus on changing my behaviour, beliefs, conduct and ultimately my life for the better and by doing so, demonstrating to the people around me that one has to change him / herself before changing anything else.

Volker Koepke - Executive Chef Radisson Resorts

OTHER BOOKS BY GEORGE LEE SYE

How To Take Control of Your Brain

The simple, yet profoundly important art of self-communication.

The Problem Solving Brain

George's philosophies and simple methods for approaching the inevitable challenges of life.

Delivering the Perfect Pitch

A profoundly effective strategy for turning any presentation into a persuasive pitch for buy-in.

Selecting Great Improvement Projects

A simple guide to identifying projects for improvement practitioners.

Systematic Problem Solving for Managers

A systematic approach to problem solving in business, a must for every improvement practitioner.

Extraordinary Team Leadership

A guide to the effective leadership of teams who work on projects and business improvement initiatives.

PERFORMANCE EDUCATION AND COACHING SERVICES

Through his training platform - www.9skillsfactory.com - George offers cutting edge capability development for high potential people who seek to master effective business execution, continual and sustainable improvement, and leading value adding and sustainable change.

CONTACT DETAILS

Soarent Publishing
ABN: 896 9941 6331
PO Box 267
Ravenshoe, Queensland
AUSTRALIA
4888
W: www.georgeleesye.com
W: www.9skillsfactory.com